abled. Plaintiffs primarily used the Rehabilitation Act of 1973 (29 U.S.C.A. § 701 et seq.), the earliest law of this type. But the Rehabilitation Act has a limited scope: it applies only to federally funded workplaces and institutions, and says nothing about those that do not receive government money.

With passage of the ADA in 1990, Congress gave broad protection to people with AIDS who work in the private sector. In general, the ADA is designed to increase access for disabled persons, and it also forbids discrimination in hiring or promotion in companies with fifteen or more employees. Specifically, employers may not discriminate if the person in question is otherwise qualified for the job. Moreover, they cannot use tests to screen out disabled persons, and they must provide reasonable accommodation for disabled workers. The ADA, which took effect in 1992, has quickly emerged as the primary means for bringing AIDS-related discrimination lawsuits.

**AIDS and Health Care**  Closely related to work is the issue of health care. In some cases, the two overlap: health insurance, Social Security, and disability benefits for AIDS victims were often hard to obtain during the 1980s. Insurance was particularly difficult because employers feared rising costs and insurance companies did not want to pay claims. To avoid the costs of AIDS, insurance companies used two traditional industry techniques: they attempted to exclude AIDS coverage from general policies, and they placed caps (limits on benefits payments) on AIDS-related coverage.

In January 1995, the settlement in a lawsuit brought by a Philadelphia construction worker with AIDS illustrated that the ADA can be used to fight caps on coverage. In 1992, the joint union-management fund for the Laborers' District Council placed a $10,000 limit on AIDS benefits, in stark contrast to the $100,000 allowed for other catastrophic illnesses. At that time, the fund said the cap on AIDS benefits was designed to curb all health costs. In 1993, the EEOC ruled that it violated the ADA, and, backed by the AIDS Law Project of Philadelphia, the worker sued. Rather than fight an expensive lawsuit, the insurance fund settled.

**AIDS and Education**  Issues in the field of education include the rights of HIV-positive students to attend class and of HIV-positive teachers to teach, the confidentiality of HIV records, and how best to teach young people about AIDS. A few areas have been settled in court: for instance, the right of students to attend classes was of greater concern in the early years of the epidemic, and no longer remains in dispute.

Certain students with AIDS may assert their right to public education under the Education for All Handicapped Children Act of 1975 (EAHCA), but the law is only relevant in cases involving special education programs. More commonly, students' rights are protected by the Rehabilitation Act.

Schools play a major role in the effort to educate the public on AIDS. Several states have mandated AIDS prevention instruction in their schools. But the subject is controversial: it evokes personal, political, and moral reactions to sexuality. During the 1980s, those who often criticized liberal approaches to sex education argued that AIDS materials should not be explicit, encourage sexuality, promote the use of contraceptives, or favorably portray gays and lesbians.

**Civil Litigation**  TORT law has seen an explosion of AIDS-related suits. This area of law is used to discourage individuals from subjecting others to unreasonable risks, and to compensate those who have been injured by unreasonably risky behavior. The greatest number of AIDS-related LIABILITY lawsuits has involved the receipt of HIV-infected blood and blood products. A second group has concerned the sexual transmission of HIV. A third group involves AIDS-related psychic distress. In these cases, plaintiffs have successfully sued and recovered damages for their fear of having contracted HIV.

CROSS-REFERENCES

Disabled Persons; Discrimination; Food and Drug Administration; Gay and Lesbian Rights; Health Care; Patients' Rights; Physicians and Surgeons; Privacy.

← Cross-references at end of article

BIOGRAPHY

*Gloria Allred*

← Biography of contributor to American law

**ALLRED, GLORIA**  Gloria Allred, born July 3, 1941, in Philadelphia, is a flamboyant, widely recognized lawyer, feminist, activist, and radio talk show host. Though her critics dismiss her as a publicity monger and a dilettante, Allred has received praise from others who believe that she is a master at using the power of the news media to draw attention to the day-to-day struggles of ordinary people.

Born Gloria Rachel Bloom, Allred grew up in Philadelphia with her parents, Morris Bloom, a door-to-door salesman, and Stella Davidson Bloom, a homemaker. Her conventional middle-class childhood gave no hint of the outspoken activist to come. Allred graduated with honors from the University of Pennsylvania in 1963 with a bachelor's degree in English. She moved to New York to pursue a master's degree in teaching at New York University. While interested in the CIVIL RIGHTS movement, which was beginning to gain momentum, she earned her master's degree in 19__

Timeline for subject of biography, including general historical events and life events →

GLORIA ALLRED 1941–

[timeline graphic with years 1925, 1950, 1975, 2000]

Philadelphia to teach at a high school with a predominantly black enrollment.

Allred says her interest in the struggle for equal rights arose from personal experiences. While she was in college, she married, gave birth to a daughter, and divorced. Unable to collect CHILD SUPPORT from her former husband, she was forced to return to her parents' home. She also recalls being paid less than a man for what she considered equal work. The reason given was that the man had a family to support, but at the time, Allred was the single mother of an infant.

After moving to California, Allred taught in the turbulent Watts section of Los Angeles and became the first full-time female staff member in United Teachers of Los Angeles, the union representing Los Angeles teachers. The experience stirred her interest in CIVIL RIGHTS and collective bargaining and prompted her to go to law school. She received her law degree, with honors, from Loyola Marymount University, Los Angeles, Law School in 1974. Soon after, she entered a law firm partnership with her classmates Nathan Goldberg and Michael Maroko.

Allred is probably the most flamboyant and well known member of her firm. She has achieved notoriety and name recognition through staged press conferences and demonstrations publicizing and dramatizing the cause she is championing at the time. She also accepts controversial cases that naturally attract media attention. During her years in practice, she has successfully sued Los Angeles County to stop the practice of shackling and chaining pregnant inmates during labor and delivery; put a halt on the city of El Segundo's quizzing job applicants about their sexual histories (*Thorne v. City of El Segundo*, 802 F.2d 1131 [9th Cir. 1986]); represented a client who was turned down for a job as a police officer after a six-hour lie detector exam that included questions about her sex life; and sued a dry cleaning establishment for discrimination because it charged more to launder women's shirts than men's.

Allred relishes confrontation, and her showy tactics have earned her both praise and criticism.

← Internal cross references

"THERE ARE ENOUGH HIGH HURDLES TO CLIMB, AS ONE TRAVELS THROUGH LIFE, WITHOUT HAVING TO SCALE ARTIFICIAL BARRIERS CREATED BY LAW OR SILLY REGULATIONS."

← Quotation from subject of biography

← Full cite for case

Defending what many have called self-promoting publicity stunts, Allred says she tries to use the few moments she is in the spotlight to make her point as forcefully as possible. Her detractors say that she wastes her time and energy on trivial issues that do not advance any worthwhile cause and deflect attention away from serious issues. Yet, she points out, she is often stopped on the street by people who recognize her and want to thank her for taking on the small fights that no one else wants.

Some critics say she is all show and no substance. But Allred has many supporters as well. Among them is Justice Joan Dempsey Klein, of the California Court of Appeal, who credits Allred with moving women's issues forward. Klein also points out that Allred saves her dramatics for outside the courtroom and always observes proper decorum when before the bench. According to Klein, Allred is always well-prepared and, for that reason, is quite successful.

Dressed in her trademark reds and electric blues, her striking black hair set off by deep red lipstick, Allred is a potent combination of scholarship and theatrics. Her keen intelligence and shrewd understanding of the power of the media have made her a contemporary success story in the world of law and politics.

**ARBITER**  [*Latin, One who attends something to view it as a spectator or witness.*] Any person who is given an absolute power to judge and rule on a matter in a dispute.

Definition enclosed in book logos with Latin translation provided →

# WEST'S ENCYCLOPEDIA *of* AMERICAN LAW

# WEST'S ENCYCLOPEDIA *of* AMERICAN LAW

Volume 2

**WEST PUBLISHING COMPANY**

MINNEAPOLIS/SAINT PAUL   NEW YORK   LOS ANGELES   SAN FRANCISCO

This encyclopedia is the result of efforts by numerous individuals and entities from the Twin Cities and around the United States. West Group wishes to thank all who made this publication, its quality and content, a priority in their lives.

In addition to the individuals who worked on *West's Encyclopedia of American Law*, West Group recognizes Harold W. Chase (1922–1982) for his contributions to *The Guide to American Law: Everyone's Legal Encyclopedia.*

COPYRIGHT ©1998 By
   WEST GROUP
   610 Opperman Drive
   P.O. Box 64526
   St. Paul, MN 55164-0526

05 04 03 02 01 00 99 98    8 7 6 5 4 3 2 1 0
Library of Congress Cataloging in
   Publication Data
ISBN: 0-314-20155-6 (Hard)

West's encyclopedia of American law.
     p.    cm.
    Includes bibliographical references and
     indexes.
     ISBN 0-314-20155-6 (hard  :
     alk. paper)
     1. Law—United States—Encyclopedias.
     2. Law—United States—Popular works.
    I. West Publishing Company.
   KF154.W47   1997
   348.73'03 —dc20
   [347.30803]          96-34350
                      CIP

**PRODUCTION CREDITS**
*Cover, interior design, and page layout:* David J.
   Farr, ImageSmythe
*Composition:* Carlisle Communications
*Proofreading:* Maureen Meyer
*Photo research:* Elsa Peterson Ltd.
*Art research:* Nanette E. Bertaut
*Editorial research:* Pat Lewis
*Artwork:* Patricia Isaacs, Parrot Graphics;
   Alice B. Thiede/William A. Thiede,
   Carto-Graphics
*Indexing:* Schroeder Indexing Services

This publication is designed to provide information on the subjects covered. It is sold with the understanding that the publisher is not engaged in rendering legal or other professional advice. If legal advice or other professional assistance is required, the services of a competent professional person should be sought.

## WEST'S COMMITMENT TO THE ENVIRONMENT

In 1906, West Publishing Company began recycling materials left over from the production of books. This began a tradition of efficient and responsible use of resources. Today, 100 percent of our legal bound volumes are printed on acid-free, recycled paper consisting of 50 percent new paper pulp and 50 percent paper that has undergone a de-inking process. We also use vegetable-based inks to print all of our books. West recycles nearly 27,700,000 pounds of scrap paper annually—the equivalent of 229,300 trees. Since the 1960s, West has devised ways to capture and recycle waste inks, solvents, oils, and vapors created in the printing process. We also recycle plastics of all kinds, wood, glass, corrugated cardboard, and batteries, and have eliminated the use of polystyrene book packaging. We at West are proud of the longevity and the scope of our commitment to the environment.

West pocket parts and advance sheets are printed on recyclable paper and can be collected and recycled with newspapers. Staples do not have to be removed. Bound volumes can be recycled after removing the cover.

Production, printing, and binding by West Group.

# B

**BACKDATING** Predating a document or INSTRUMENT prior to the date it was actually drawn. The negotiability of an instrument is not affected by the fact that it is backdated.

**BACK PAY AWARD** A legally enforceable decree ordering an employer to pay to an employee retroactively a designated increase in his or her salary that occurred during a particular period of employment. A decision rendered by a judicial or quasi-judicial body that an employee has a legal right to collect accrued salary that has not been paid out to him or her.

Back pay awards ensue from litigation involving employment DISCRIMINATION and issues regarding labor-management relations. Federal civil rights legislation provides for back pay awards to compensate the victim for economic losses suffered as a result of discrimination.

**BACK TO WORK AGREEMENT** The accord reached between an employer and a union to which his or her employees belong that establishes the terms and conditions governing the return of striking employees to work.

Disputes involving back to work agreements are subject to applicable federal and state laws governing labor-management relations. See also LABOR UNION; STRIKE.

**BACON, SIR FRANCIS** Sir Francis Bacon was an English lawyer and statesman whose philosophical theories and writings influenced the development of scientific and legal thought in Great Britain and the United States.

Bacon was born in 1561, the second son of Sir Nicholas Bacon, the lord keeper of the great seal, and Lady Ann, whose brother-in-law was Baron Burghley (William Cecil), the first minister to Queen Elizabeth I. Bacon, like his father, was educated at Trinity College, Cambridge, where he enrolled at the age of twelve. In 1576 he was admitted to Gray's Inn, one of the four Inns of Court in London, which were institutions established for legal education. He also spent time in France as a member of the English ambassador's staff, before his father's sudden death required him to return to England and resume his legal education so that he could support his family. After completing his studies, Bacon became a BARRISTER in 1582 and then attained the posts of reader (lecturer at the Inn) and bencher (senior member of the Inn).

In 1584, at the age of twenty-three, Bacon was elected to the House of Commons, representing Taunton, Liverpool, the county of Middlesex, Southampton, Ipswich, and the University of Cambridge. In 1594, he argued his first major case, *Chudleigh's Case* (1 Co. Rep. 1136, 76 Eng. Rep. 261 [K.B. 1594]), which

*Employees striking in Rochester, New York, rely on their union, Communications Workers of America, to negotiate a back to work agreement with their employer.*

WAYNE SCARBERRY/PHOTOREPORTERS

involved the interpretation of complex inheritance statutes. He also began writing about science and philosophy and started work on his first major volume, *Temporis Partus Maximus* (The greatest part of time), though the book, along with many of his earliest works, was never published and thus disappeared.

Through his friendship with Robert Devereux, the Earl of Essex, Bacon became acquainted with Queen Elizabeth I and he eventually became her counsel around 1600. As counsel, Bacon later took part in the prosecution of Essex, from whom he had become estranged, for treason, and for these efforts Bacon was knighted in 1603. In 1605, he published his first book, *The Advancement of Learning*, a collection of essays on philosophy that he dedicated to King James I. Later the same year, he married Alice Barnham, the daughter of a wealthy London politician.

Bacon continued to curry the king's favor by assisting James in his plans to unite Scotland with England, and was named to the post of solicitor general in 1607. He also continued to write, publishing in 1609 *The Wisdom of the Ancients*, in which he analyzed the meaning of ancient myths. Seeking promotion to attorney general, Bacon advised the king concerning affairs of state and the relationship between the Crown and Parliament. He successfully engineered the ouster of the chief justice of the common pleas, Sir Edward Coke, a longtime rival who had earlier occupied solicitor and attorney general posts that Bacon had sought. Bacon finally became attorney general in 1613, which enabled him to continue his feud with Coke. He eventually prosecuted Coke for his role in the case of Edmond Peacham, a clergyman charged with treason for advocating rebellion against oppression in an unpublished treatise, leading to Coke's dismissal in 1616. Bacon continued his service to the king and was appointed lord keeper of the great seal in 1617. A year later, he became lord chancellor of England, a post he held until 1621.

Bacon, a man of great intellect and energy, was often torn between his ambitions for higher

"JUDGES MUST BE AWARE OF HARD CONSTRUCTIONS AND STRAINED INFERENCES, FOR THERE IS NO WORSE TORTURE THAN THE TORTURE OF LAWS."

office and his keen interest in science and philosophy. Though he was primarily concerned with his service to the Crown during most of his adult life, he did devote time to the study of philosophy. He was an early proponent of inductive reasoning, the theory that by analyzing observed facts, one can establish general laws or principles about how the world works. This theory is the opposite of deductive reasoning, which holds that one can draw specific conclusions by reasoning from more general premises. Bacon believed inductive reasoning to be more useful because it permitted the development of new theories that could be more generally and widely applied to a variety of situations. The legal systems of many countries, including the United States, were eventually grounded on the application of general laws derived from specific fact situations to govern conduct.

Bacon was likewise a strong believer in empiricism, the belief that experience is the most important source of knowledge. According to Bacon, scientists should try to learn about the world by using information gathered through the senses rather than by using reason or rules set forth by religious or political authority. Empiricism, like inductive reasoning, also influenced the development of later legal philosophies, in this case theories that viewed the law and justice as emerging from social life and experience.

Bacon was a prolific writer throughout his life, authoring a number of works expounding his theories. The *Novum Organum*, his most well known and widely read philosophical work, was published in 1620. The *Instauratio Magna* (Great instauration, from the Latin word *instaurare*, "to renew or begin afresh") was a comprehensive plan in which Bacon attempted to reorganize and redefine the sciences; it also contained his views concerning logic and scientific experimentation. In his philosophical writings, Bacon argued that the mind should be purged of what he termed idols, or tendencies to err. These idols, he maintained, arose from human nature, individual experience, and lan-

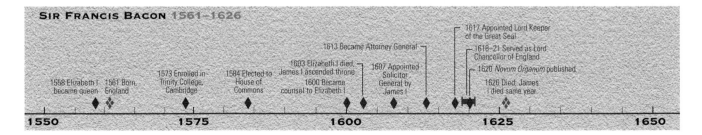

**SIR FRANCIS BACON 1561–1626**

1617 Appointed Lord Keeper of the Great Seal

1613 Became Attorney General

1618–21 Served as Lord Chancellor of England

1603 Elizabeth I died, James I ascended throne

1607 Appointed Solicitor General by James I

1620 *Novum Organum* published

1558 Elizabeth I became queen

1561 Born, England

1573 Enrolled in Trinity College, Cambridge

1584 Elected to House of Commons

1600 Became counsel to Elizabeth I

1626 Died; James I died same year

1550     1575     1600     1625     1650

guage. In addition, Bacon kept an extensive diary, which was discovered after his death. The notebook, known as the *Commentarius Solutus* (Loose commentary), contained his notes about, among other things, his debts, his garden, and his health.

Later in his life, Bacon began to fall out of favor with the Crown. In 1618, the king criticized him for interfering in the marriage of Coke's daughter. In 1621, Bacon was charged with accepting a bribe concerning a grievance committee over which he had presided. Bacon admitted in a full confession that he had received gifts, but denied that they had influenced his judgment. Though he begged for mercy, Bacon found the king unsympathetic to his case and was forced to resign his office. Bacon was sentenced to a stiff fine (which was later suspended), imprisonment in the Tower of London (which actually lasted only four days), exclusion from holding any state office, and prohibition from coming within the vicinity of the Court of King's Bench.

Following his ouster from the court, Bacon returned to his large estate at Gorhambury, in rural England, to devote all of his energies to research and writing. He prepared digests of the laws and wrote a history of Great Britain and its monarchs. He planned to write six separate natural histories, but only two were completed: *Historia Ventorum* (History of the winds), which was published in 1622, and *Historia Vitae et Mortis* (History of life and death), which appeared the following year. He also wrote the *History of Henry VII*, published in 1622. In 1621, he enlarged his volume of *Essays*, which he had first published in 1597, and in 1627, he published *The New Atlantis*. He also corresponded with Italian philosophers and sent his work to them. Over the years, some writers have suggested that Bacon may have been the true author of William Shakespeare's plays, but because no concrete proof has been offered, the theory has been discounted by most scholars.

Sometime around 1623, Bacon, in ill health, was finally granted an audience with the king, but he was not granted a pardon for his offenses. In London, on April 9, 1626, he died of bronchitis he contracted while conducting experiments on the effects of refrigeration on poultry.

See also COKE, SIR EDWARD; INNS OF COURT.

**BAD FAITH**  The FRAUDULENT deception of another person; the intentional or MALICIOUS refusal to perform some duty or contractual obligation.

Bad faith is not the same as prior judgment or NEGLIGENCE. One can make an honest mistake about one's own rights and duties, but when the rights of someone else are intentionally or maliciously infringed upon, such conduct demonstrates bad faith.

The existence of bad faith can minimize or nullify any claims that a person alleges in a lawsuit. PUNITIVE DAMAGES, attorney's fees, or both, may be awarded to a party who must defend himself or herself in an ACTION brought in bad faith.

Bad faith is a term commonly used in the law of CONTRACTS and other commercial dealings, such as COMMERCIAL PAPER, and in SECURED TRANSACTIONS. It is the opposite of GOOD FAITH, the observance of reasonable standards of fair dealings in trade that is required of every merchant.

A government official who selectively enforces a nondiscriminatory law against the members of a particular group or race, thereby violating the CIVIL RIGHTS of those individuals, is acting in bad faith.

**BADGER, GEORGE EDMUND** George Edmund Badger was a lawyer, judge, and politician, and the subject of a U.S. Supreme Court confirmation battle in 1853.

The only son of a lawyer who died prematurely and a daughter of a Revolutionary War leader, Badger was born on April 17, 1795, in New Bern, North Carolina. He was first educated at a local academy and then attended Yale College. Because of poverty, he was forced to leave the college after only two years. He then returned home to North Carolina to study law. In 1814, he served for a short time as a major in a militia called out to repel a threatened British invasion. A year later, he was admitted to the North Carolina bar. He quickly built a reputation as a brilliant and persuasive trial and appel-

**BIOGRAPHY**

LIBRARY OF CONGRESS

*George Edmund Badger*

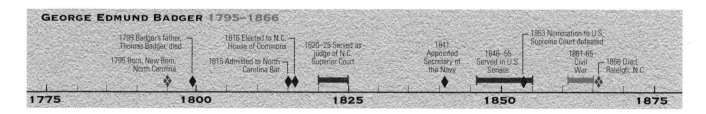

GEORGE EDMUND BADGER 1795–1866

- 1799 Badger's father, Thomas Badger, died
- 1795 Born, New Bern, North Carolina
- 1816 Elected to N.C. House of Commons
- 1815 Admitted to North Carolina Bar
- 1820–25 Served as judge of N.C. Superior Court
- 1841 Appointed Secretary of the Navy
- 1846–55 Served in U.S. Senate
- 1853 Nomination to U.S. Supreme Court defeated
- 1861–65 Civil War
- 1866 Died, Raleigh, N.C.

1775     1800     1825     1850     1875

late lawyer. In 1820, after four years of representing New Bern in the state house of commons, he was elected a judge of the superior court, where he served five years before resigning to practice law in Raleigh.

Initially a strong supporter of Andrew Jackson, Badger became a Whig in the mid-1830s and was appointed secretary of the Navy in 1841 by President William H. Harrison. He served for less than a year in this position and thus had little opportunity to have a lasting effect. However, during his tenure, he did recommend a home squadron to patrol the Caribbean and the Gulf of Mexico. He also authorized the construction of two steam vessels.

In 1846, Badger was elected to the U.S. Senate. As a senator, he strongly opposed the policies of the Polk administration. He also proposed reform of the Supreme Court's docket and advocated salary increases for the justices. In January 1853, President Millard Fillmore, who had lost the 1852 election to Franklin Pierce, nominated Badger for a vacancy on the Court. Badger's nomination was met with widespread criticism from the Democratic papers of the South. Senators from Alabama, Louisiana, and Mississippi opposed his nomination because he resided outside the Fifth Circuit, where the vacancy on the Court arose. Even the Whig press, though it supported the proposed appointment, stated that "as a statesman, [Badger] is of no account, and as a politician detestable."

On previous occasions, the Senate had usually granted quick confirmation to a senator nominated for the Court, with little debate. But it postponed consideration of Badger's nomination until March 1853, so that Pierce could fill the vacancy with his own nominee—effectively defeating Badger's nomination. The same tactic would also be used to defeat later Supreme Court nominees.

Badger served in the Senate until 1855. After his retirement, he continued to practice law and took an active role in politics, helping to organize the Constitutional Union party in 1861. This party was made up of conservative Whigs who had been alienated by the emergence of Abraham Lincoln as the leader of the Republi-

"NOW IT WAS SAID . . . THAT AFTER A LONG PERIOD OF PUBLIC SERVICE GENTLEMEN LEARN TO LOOK RATHER LIGHTLY ON CONSTITUTIONAL RESTRICTIONS."

**BIOGRAPHY**

READING PUBLIC MUSEUM

*George Frederick Baer*

can party during the presidential election of 1860. In its platform, the Constitutional Union party took no stand on the issue of slavery and strongly advocated preservation of the Union. Badger was elected as a Union candidate, but a convention was never held.

Though he was widely known as a nationalist, when the Civil War broke out, Badger was elected to the North Carolina secession convention. At first, he argued against secession, contending that it was unconstitutional. Instead, he offered a declaration of independence, which was rejected. As a result, he reluctantly voted for secession.

Badger continued to practice law in North Carolina until his death in 1866.

See also FILLMORE, MILLARD; SLAVERY.

**BAER, GEORGE FREDERICK** George Frederick Baer was born September 26, 1842, near Lavansville, Pennsylvania. Baer was educated at Franklin and Marshall College, where he received an honorary master of arts degree in 1875 and a doctor of laws degree in 1886.

During the Civil War, Baer fought on the side of the Union at Bull Run, Antietam, Chancellorsville, and Fredericksburg.

He was admitted to the bar in 1864, moved to Reading, Pennsylvania, in 1868, and in 1870 performed the duties of counselor for the Philadelphia and Reading Railroad Company. He became a director of the railroad, acted as legal advisor to magnate J. P. Morgan, and was instrumental in the restructuring of the railroad in 1893. In 1901, he was president of the Philadelphia and Reading Railway Company, the Philadelphia and Reading Coal & Iron Company, and the Central Railroad Company of New Jersey.

When the United Mine Workers went on strike in Pennsylvania in 1902, Baer gained notoriety for his lack of sympathy for the plight of the miners.

Baer died April 26, 1914, in Philadelphia, Pennsylvania.

**BAIL** 📖 The system that governs the status of individuals charged with committing crimes, from the time of their arrest to the time of their trial, and pending appeal, with the major purpose of ensuring their presence at trial. 📖

GEORGE FREDERICK BAER 1842–1914

1842 Born near Lavansville, Pa.

1861–65 U.S. Civil War
1862 Fought in Civil War battles at Antietam and Chancellorsville

1864 Admitted to Pennsylvania bar

1870 Served as counselor for Philadelphia and Reading R.R.

1901 Served as President of P & R Railroad

1902 United Mine Workers strike

1914 Died, Philadelphia, Pa.

1914–18 World War I

1825          1850          1875          1900          1925

In general, an individual accused of a crime must be held in the custody of the court until his or her guilt or innocence is determined. However, the court has the option of releasing the individual before that determination is made, and this option is called bail. Bail is set by the judge during the defendant's first appearance. For many MISDEMEANORS, bail need not be set. For example, the defendant may be released on the issuance of a CITATION such as a ticket for a driving violation, or when booked for a minor misdemeanor at a police station or jail. But for major misdemeanors and FELONIES, the defendant must appear before a judge before bail is determined.

The courts have several methods available for releasing defendants on bail. Which of these methods is used is determined by the judge. One alternative is for the defendant to post a BAIL BOND, or pledge of money. The bond can be signed by a professional SURETY holder, the accused, or the family and friends of the accused. Signing the bail bond is a promise that the defendant will appear in the specified criminal proceeding. The defendant's failure to appear will cause the signers of the bond to pay to the court the amount designated. The amount of bail is generally an arbitrary amount determined in light of the seriousness of the alleged offense.

A defendant can also be released upon her or his own RECOGNIZANCE, which is the defendant's written, uninsured promise to return for trial. Such a release occurs only if the suspect has steady employment, stable family ties, and a history of residence in the community. Willful violation of the terms of a personal recognizance constitutes a CRIME.

Other conditions may also be set regarding the release of the defendant. The Bail Reform Act of 1984 (18 U.S.C.A. §§ 3141–3150) provided for many additional conditions that do not rely upon finances and that reflected current trends to move away from financial requirements for freedom. These conditions came about, in part, owing to concerns regard-

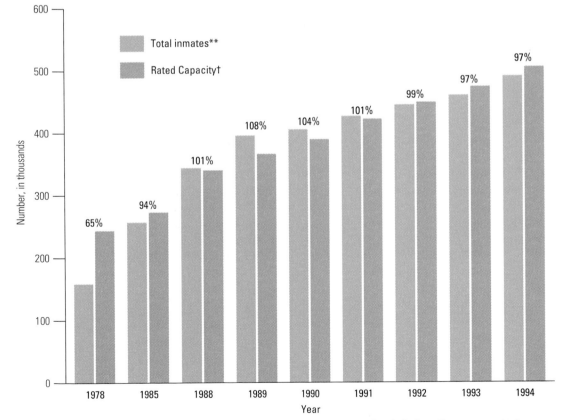

**Jail\* Inmate Population in U.S., 1978 to 1994**

\* A jail is a facility usually operated by a local law enforcement agency that holds persons detained pending adjudication and/or persons committed after adjudication to one year of jail time or less.
\*\* Excludes populations in federal and state prisons and other correctional institutions; institutions exclusively for juveniles; state-operated jails in Alaska, Connecticut, Delaware, Hawaii, Rhode Island, and Vermont; and other facilities that retain persons for fewer than 48 hours.
†These numbers are calculated from total inmates and percent of capacity numbers.

Source: U.S. Bureau of Justice Statistics, *Profile of Jail Inmates, 1978 and 1989; Jail Inmates,* annual; and *1988 Census of Local Jails.*

ing the discriminatory nature of bail toward the poor. The Bail Reform Act allows for conditional releases dependent upon such circumstances as maintaining employment, meeting curfews, and receiving medical or psychiatric treatment.

**Civil Actions** A defendant in a CIVIL ACTION can be arrested to ensure that he or she will appear in court to respond to the plaintiff's claims. Civil arrest prevents a defendant from leaving the jurisdiction to evade the litigation, and from attempting to conceal or dispose of ASSETS in order to keep the plaintiff from collecting on the judgment if the plaintiff prevails. Since civil arrest is a drastic remedy, state laws must be consulted to determine when it may be used. The purpose of bail in a civil action is to ensure the presence of the defendant at trial and to guarantee the payment of a DEBT or the fulfillment of some civil duty, as ordered by the court.

The court sets the amount of bail, which is generally based on the probable amount of damage against the defendant. In some instances, if informed of changed circumstances, the court might increase or reduce bail. Cash, as opposed to a bail bond, may be deposited with the court only where authorized by statute. The purpose of the arrest and the statutory provisions determine whether this deposit may be used to pay the judgment awarded to the plaintiff.

**Criminal Prosecutions** The objective of bail in CRIMINAL ACTIONS is to prevent the imprisonment of the accused prior to trial while ensuring her or his appearance at trial. Constitutional and statutory rights to bail prior to conviction exist for most offenses, but state constitutional provisions and statutes must be consulted to determine the offenses to which bail applies. The Bail Reform Act of 1984 governs bail in federal offenses. It provides the federal magistrate with alternatives to the incarceration of the defendant. If the charge is a noncapital offense (an offense not punishable by death), the defendant may be released on her or his own recognizance. If there is a reasonable likelihood that the defendant will not return for trial, the judge may impose bail. The judge may also release the defendant into the custody of a designated person or organization for supervision. Restricting the residence, extent of travel, and personal associations of the accused are other options.

**Discretion of the Court** A court exercises its discretion with respect to the allowance of bail. In reaching its decision, it evaluates the circumstances of the particular case, including the existence of doubt as to the accused's appearance at trial. Unreasonable delay or postponement in the proceeding, which is not attributable to the accused, usually constitutes a ground for bail—in some JURISDICTIONS, by absolute right; more frequently, at the discretion of the court.

In jurisdictions in which it is neither proscribed nor regarded as an absolute right, the grant of bail pending a motion for a new trial, a review, or an appeal is also discretionary. The grant of bail is then determined in light of the probability of reversal, the nature of the crime, the likelihood of the defendant's escape, and the character of the defendant.

The decision to grant or deny bail is reviewable, but the scope of the review is limited to whether the court abused its discretion in its determination.

The amount of bail set is within the discretion of the court. Once fixed, it should not be modified, except for good cause. An increase cannot be authorized when the ARREST WARRANT specifies the amount of the bail. An application for a change in bail is presented to the court by a MOTION based on an AFFIDAVIT (a voluntary written statement of facts) confirmed by the oath of the person making it. The affidavit must be taken before a person authorized to administer such an oath and must contain the facts justifying the change. The EIGHTH AMENDMENT to the Constitution and the provisions of most state constitutions prohibit excessive bail, meaning bail in an amount greater than that necessary to ensure the defendant's appearance at trial.

The Bail Reform Act of 1984 helped to set guidelines allowing courts to consider the danger a defendant might present if released on bail. This response to the problem of crimes committed by individuals who had been released on bail marked a significant departure from earlier philosophies surrounding bail. Bail laws took on a new importance; not only would they ensure the appearance of the defendant in proceedings, but also they would see to the safety of the community into which the defendant was released.

Pursuant to the 1984 act, if the court deems that the accused may, in fact, pose a threat to the safety of the community, the accused may be held without bail. In 1987, *United States v. Salerno*, 481 U.S. 739, 107 S. Ct. 2095, 95 L. Ed. 2d 697, addressed the constitutionality of holding an individual without bail while awaiting criminal trial. The Supreme Court held that DUE PROCESS was not violated by the detention of individuals without bail.

**Breach and Forfeiture** A breach of the bail bond occurs in both civil and criminal actions when the defendant "jumps bail" or "skips bail"—that is, deliberately fails to return to court on the specified date, thereby forfeiting the amount of the bond. The act of jumping bail is either a misdemeanor or a felony, depending upon statute. The mandatory appearance required in a bail arrangement consists not merely of responding to the charges but also of attendance by the defendant at the trial and sentencing by the court. Appearance by counsel ordinarily does not prevent a breach, although under some statutes, where the offense is a misdemeanor, such an appearance might be sufficient.

Where a bond is breached, the court enters a judgment of FORFEITURE of the bail. In some jurisdictions, the judgment is appealable, but only if the failure to comply with the conditions of the bond was excusable and the state suffered no loss of rights against the defendant.

A final judgment normally cannot be entered on recognizance or bail bond without additional proceedings. Such proceedings are usually of a civil nature and follow the forfeiture of bail. These proceedings can be commenced by a WRIT (a court order) of *scire facias* (a judicial writ requiring the person against whom it is brought to show cause why the party bringing it should not have advantage of such record) or by an independent action.

**BAIL BOND** ⬛ A written promise signed by a defendant or a SURETY (one who promises to act in place of another) to pay an amount fixed by a court should the defendant named in the document fail to appear in court for the designated criminal proceeding at the date and time specified. ⬛

A bail bond is one method used to obtain the release of a defendant awaiting trial upon criminal charges from the custody of law enforcement officials. The defendant, the defendant's family and friends, or a professional bail bond agent (or bail agent) executes a document that promises to forfeit the sum of money determined by the court to be commensurate with the gravity for the alleged offense if the defendant fails to return for the trial date.

Most defendants are financially unable to post their own BAIL, so they seek help from a bail agent, who, for a nonrefundable fee of 10 percent to 20 percent of the amount of the bail, posts bail. A bail agent becomes liable to the court for the full amount of bail if the defendant fails to appear for the court date. Before agreeing to assume the risk of posting bail, the bail agent requires COLLATERAL from the defendant,

such as jewelry, securities, or written guaranties by creditworthy friends or relatives of the defendant. This collateral acts as security to ensure repayment for any losses the bail agent might incur. If the defendant appears to be a "poor risk," and unlikely to return to court for trial, the bail agent will refuse to post bail. A defendant who has a record of steady employment, has resided in the community for a reasonable length of time, and has no prior criminal record is considered to be a good risk.

The bail agent, the defendant, or other interested party posts bail in the form of the bail bond at the court to which the defendant is to return for the proceeding. The court clerk issues a bail ticket or similar document, which is sent to the police to notify them that bail has been met. The defendant will be released from custody when the bail ticket is received by the police. Liability under the bail bond ends when the defendant fulfills the conditions of the bond by appearing in court on the specified date, or if its terms become impossible to execute, such as by the death of the defendant or his or her arrest, detention, or imprisonment on another offense in the same or different jurisdiction.

If a defendant fails to appear for trial on the date specified in the bail bond, the court will issue a warrant for the defendant's arrest for "jumping bail," and the amount of the bond will be forfeited to the court. The bail agent is

*A bail bond agent promises to pay the amount specified by the court if a defendant fails to appear for trial, in exchange for a 10 to 20 percent fee.*

authorized by statute to arrest the defendant and bring him or her back for criminal proceedings.

The state of Kentucky enacted a law making it illegal to post bail for profit, thereby outlawing the occupation of bail bond agent.

A bail bond may be similarly used in cases of civil arrest to prevent a defendant from fleeing a jurisdiction to avoid litigation or fraudulently concealing or disposing of ASSETS in order to become JUDGMENT PROOF (incapable of satisfying an award made against him or her if the plaintiff is successful).

**BAILEE** 📖 One to whom PERSONAL PROPERTY is entrusted for a particular purpose by another, the BAILOR, according to the terms of an express or implied agreement. 📖

**BAILEY, FRANCIS LEE** The career of attorney F. Lee Bailey is a celebrated one. Few criminal defense lawyers have earned as much success or notoriety as the tough-talking former Marine lieutenant, known for winning what have often been considered hopeless cases. Early in his career, Bailey built a reputation for fastidious attention to detail as an investigator who could ferret out the minutiae needed to acquit his clients. His CROSS-EXAMINATION style—long on hard-hitting machismo—earned him comparisons to some of the twentieth century's most noted lawyers. By his midthirties, he had won a string of victories in shocking, nationally publicized cases, including an important U.S. Supreme Court ruling on PRETRIAL PUBLICITY. His books on law became best-sellers, but controversy followed his criticisms of the legal system and his sometimes risky defense strategies. In 1994, he joined the defense team in Orenthal James ("O. J.") Simpson's trial for the murder of Nicole Brown Simpson and her friend Ronald Lyle Goldman.

Bailey might never have become a lawyer if he had not dropped out of college. Born in the Boston suburb of Waltham, Massachusetts, on June 10, 1933, he was the son of an advertising man and a schoolteacher who founded a large nursery school. In his teens, Bailey excelled at Kimball Union Academy, a prep school, and

**BIOGRAPHY**

*F. Lee Bailey*

won a scholarship to attend Harvard in 1950. His goal was to study English. Yet academia could not hold him for long; he wanted adventure. Dropping out of Harvard at the end of his sophomore year, he enrolled in the Navy flight training program and eventually joined the Marines, where he at first flew jet fighters. Soon Bailey had switched gears and was defending accused service members as part of the legal staff at the Cherry Point Marine Corps Air Station in North Carolina. Military life would leave its mark on him. More than forty years later, he would write articles about jets for *Flying* magazine and, while defending Simpson, would say that he had spoken with a witness who was a veteran, as one Marine to another.

The experience of fighting COURTS-MARTIAL convinced Bailey to become a lawyer in civilian life. Leaving the service with the rank of second lieutenant, he entered Boston University Law School, which admitted him on the strength of his considerable military law practice. Once again, his ambition could scarcely be satisfied in books, and the precocious student founded a private detective agency. The firm did fieldwork to help attorneys prepare their cases, and Bailey claimed to devote sixty hours a week to this endeavor alone. It paid off: he handled some two thousand cases, honed his skills as an investigator, and later sold the agency. The long extracurricular hours did not stop him from finishing, in 1960, at the top of his class with the highest grade point average in the school's history.

Bailey next studied the lie detector at the Keeler Polygraph Institute in Chicago, a tool much used in the courtrooms of the era. The skill he acquired there led to his first job, at age twenty-seven, as a polygraph expert hired by the defense in a highly publicized Boston trial, the *Torso Murder* case—so named because prosecutors charged the defendant, George Edgerly, with dismembering his wife and dumping the pieces of her body in the Merrimack River. Edgerly had failed a lie detector test, making the case difficult for the defense. Bailey was hired to help turn the case around. When the lead attorney

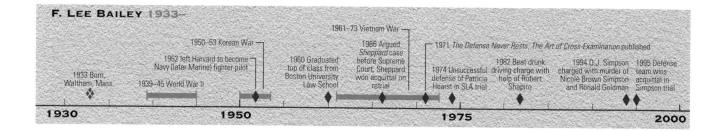

**F. LEE BAILEY 1933–**

1933 Born, Waltham, Mass.

1939–45 World War II

1950–53 Korean War

1952 left Harvard to become Navy (later Marine) fighter pilot

1960 Graduated top of class from Boston University Law School

1961–73 Vietnam War

1966 Argued *Sheppard* case before Supreme Court; Sheppard won acquittal on retrial

1971 *The Defense Never Rests: The Art of Cross-Examination* published

1974 Unsuccessful defense of Patricia Hearst in SLA trial

1982 Beat drunk driving charge with help of Robert Shapiro

1994 O.J. Simpson charged with murder of Nicole Brown Simpson and Ronald Goldman

1995 Defense team wins acquittal in Simpson trial

1930    1950    1975    2000

suffered a heart attack, Bailey took over the case and won an ACQUITTAL for the defendant. His victory in the Edgerly case was the first of several in high profile cases over the next decade. Most notable was Bailey's role in the murder appeal of Dr. SAMUEL H. SHEPPARD, who had been convicted of second-degree murder in the bludgeoning death of his wife, Marilyn Sheppard. In 1966, Bailey helped convince the U.S. Supreme Court that the trial judge had erred in not shielding Sheppard from pretrial publicity, thus denying him a fair trial—establishing an important new standard for defendants' rights (*Sheppard v. Maxwell*, 384 U.S. 333, 86 S. Ct. 1507, 16 L. Ed. 2d 600). He subsequently cleared Sheppard. See also TRIAL.

The *Sheppard* case launched Bailey's career. Not only was he now proven in court, he was also doing well in celebrity. News magazines extolled his skills at cross-examination, with *Life Magazine* saying in 1967 that he was "methodical and relentless, boring in and tunneling under his prey like a determined badger" (*Life* 1967). Frequently, comparisons to the fictional television character Perry Mason cropped up, which Bailey resented; just as often came comparisons to the great criminal defense lawyer CLARENCE DARROW, which he did nothing to discourage. Preparation and analysis were Bailey's most renowned legal skills, yet what brought him public attention was his talent for theatrics. His style was swaggering: he could thunderously tell a courtroom that the charges against his client were "10 pounds of hogwash in a five-pound bag" or declare that he had just won a "thumping acquittal." He viewed litigation as "the true substitute for gladiatorial combat." By the time the ABC television network gave him a slot in 1967 on the program *Good Company*, where he chatted up celebrities, he was himself a household name. His 1971 book, *The Defense Never Rests: The Art of Cross-Examination*, became a best-seller. Several legal, nonfiction, and fiction books followed.

Fame for Bailey was a double-edged sword, bringing both attention and criticism. Often sought out by the news media for his opinions, he used their interviews as soapboxes from which to call for legal reforms. He argued that criminal defense attorneys needed several additional years of training; held that fewer frivolous lawsuits would tie up the courts if the U.S. legal system were to imitate the more rigorous British one; and, on the lecture circuit, even suggested that crime could be prevented by making it illegal for people to carry more than $500 at a time. He also simply liked the limelight: as the equally famous attorney Melvin M.

Belli recalled, he and Bailey once stood at a bar betting each other $5 over who would be recognized first. Not all of Bailey's pronouncements met with praise; his outspokenness was sometimes seen as grandstanding. Ironically, for the attorney who had won *Sheppard*, he was criticized by the Massachusetts Bar Association for saying too much outside of court, and in 1971, the Supreme Court of New Jersey barred him from practicing law there for a year for similar reasons.

In 1974, Bailey faced his Waterloo when he unsuccessfully defended the publishing heiress Patricia Hearst. Hearst had stunned U.S. citizens when, after being KIDNAPPED, she was photographed carrying an automatic weapon in a San Francisco bank heist. On trial for ROBBERY, she claimed to have been brainwashed by her abductors, a terrorist group known as the Symbionese Liberation Army (SLA). In orchestrating her defense, Bailey was widely criticized for the risky strategy of putting her on the witness stand, where she took the FIFTH AMENDMENT forty-two times to avoid answering questions. Years after her conviction, Hearst herself blamed Bailey, arguing in a 1980 appeal that the attorney had been less interested in her defense than in writing a book about the case. The U.S. Ninth Circuit Court of Appeals ruled that "Bailey's potential conflict of interest is virtually admitted," and granted Hearst a new hearing (*U.S. v. Hearst*, 638 F. 2d 1190 [9th Cir. 1980]). See also HEARST, PATTY.

After the Hearst trial, Bailey disappeared from public view for a time. Nevertheless, his reputation as "flamboyant" and a "legend" persisted and he continued to win cases. In 1982, he attracted national attention again when he beat a drunk driving charge with legal representation from his friend, ROBERT L. SHAPIRO. Bailey complained that the police had picked on him because he was famous. Soon he was campaigning publicly against what he saw as police harassment, warning, "The cops have decided to set some fierce public examples of their new hard line, probably to scare drivers into going easy on the booze." He promptly wrote a legal self-help book titled *How to Protect Yourself against Cops in California and Other Strange Places*, purporting to be a guide to avoiding unfair drunk driving convictions.

In 1994, the trial of Simpson returned Bailey to the spotlight when he and Shapiro were hired for the defense team. However, before the trial even began, the old friends engaged in a public feud. Shapiro accused Bailey of trying to destroy his credibility by leaking information to the press, comparing Bailey to a snake and

"THOSE WHO THINK THE INFORMATION BROUGHT OUT AT A CRIMINAL TRIAL IS THE TRUTH, THE WHOLE TRUTH, AND NOTHING BUT THE TRUTH ARE FOOLS."

demanding his removal from the case. In reply, Bailey criticized his colleague's "public outburst." According to *Newsweek*, Simpson admonished the two bickering attorneys, reminding them that his life was at stake. The spat died down, and, in March 1995, Bailey cross-examined a key prosecution witness, police detective Mark Fuhrman.

Surrounded by high expectations, the cross-examination was widely portrayed as a comeback attempt for the sixty-two-year-old Bailey. He rose to the occasion with high expectations of his own, promising to "dismantle" Fuhrman. The defense had branded the detective a racist and alleged that he had planted a key piece of evidence at Simpson's estate: a bloody glove. Bailey's difficult job was to prove that Fuhrman had planted evidence and had once used the pejorative *nigger*; Fuhrman never conceded either point, despite several days of grilling on the stand. Prosecutor MARCIA CLARK attacked Bailey on several points, arguing that he had misrepresented what a Marine sergeant would testify to as to Fuhrman's language in the Marines, and that he was manufacturing evidence with his conjecture that Fuhrman had sneaked the bloody glove to the crime scene in a plastic bag in his sock.

After Bailey's questioning of Fuhrman, several prominent legal analysts argued that he had flopped. He defended his performance, in *Time Magazine*, using a comparison that recalled the earliest praises of his career: "I'm not Perry Mason; nobody is. Other lawyers whom I respect told me that given what I had to work with, it was good. Norman Mailer called me and said it was flawless. So I feel good."

In March 1996 Bailey himself became the subject of criminal prosecution after he and the United States government had a disagreement over who was entitled to millions of dollars of stock formerly held by Claude Duboc, a drug dealer and client of Bailey. The government demanded forfeiture of the stock, but Bailey said a plea bargain he had negotiated with the government on behalf of Duboc allowed Bailey to keep it. When Bailey refused to surrender 2.3 million dollars to the federal district court in Tallahassee, Florida, he was sentenced to six months in jail for contempt.

See also COCHRAN, JOHNNIE; SIMPSON, O. J.

**BAILIFF**    An individual who is entrusted with some authority, care, guardianship, or jurisdiction over designated persons or property. One who acts in a managerial or ministerial capacity or takes care of land, goods, and CHATTELS of another in order to make the best profit for the owner. A minor officer of a court serving primarily as a messenger or usher. A low-level court official or sheriff's deputy whose duty is to preserve and protect orderly conduct in court proceedings.

**BAILMENT**    The temporary placement of control over, or possession of, PERSONAL PROPERTY by one person, the BAILOR, into the hands of another, the BAILEE, for a designated purpose upon which the parties have agreed.

The term *bailment* is derived from the French *bailler*, "to deliver." It is generally considered to be a contractual relationship since the bailor and bailee, either expressly or impliedly, bind themselves to act according to particular terms. The bailee receives only control or possession of the property while the bailor retains the ownership interests in it. During the specific period a bailment exists, the bailee's interest in the property is superior to that of all others, including the bailor, unless the bailee violates some term of the agreement. Once the purpose for which the property has been delivered has been accomplished, the property will be returned to the bailor or otherwise disposed of pursuant to the bailor's directions.

A bailment is not the same as a SALE, which is an intentional transfer of ownership of personal property in exchange for something of value. A bailment involves only a transfer of POSSESSION or custody, not of ownership. A rental or LEASE of personal property might be a bailment, depending upon the agreement of the parties. A bailment is created when a parking garage attendant, the bailee, is given the keys to a motor vehicle by its owner, the bailor. The owner, in addition to renting the space, has transferred possession and control of the vehicle by relinquishing its keys to the attendant. If the keys were not made available and the vehicle was locked, the arrangement would be strictly a rental or lease, since there was no transfer of possession.

A GRATUITOUS loan and the delivery of property for repair or safekeeping are also typical situations in which a bailment is created.

**Categories**    There are three types of bailments: (1) for the benefit of the bailor and bailee; (2) for the sole benefit of the bailor; and (3) for the sole benefit of the bailee.

A bailment for the mutual benefit of the parties is created when there is an exchange of performances between the parties. A bailment for the repair of an item is a bailment for mutual benefit when the bailee receives a fee in exchange for his or her work.

A bailor receives the sole benefit from a bailment when a bailee acts gratuitously—for example, if a restaurant, a bailee, provides an attended coatroom free of charge to its customers, the bailors. By virtue of the terms of the bailment, the bailee agrees to act without any expectation of compensation.

A bailment is created for the sole benefit of the bailee when both parties agree the property temporarily in the bailee's custody is to be used to his or her own advantage without giving anything to the bailor in return. The loan of a book from a library is a bailment for the sole benefit of the bailee.

**Elements** Three elements are generally necessary for the existence of a bailment: delivery, acceptance, and consideration.

Actual possession of or control over property must be delivered to a bailee in order to create a bailment. The DELIVERY of actual possession of an item allows the bailee to accomplish his or her duties toward the property without the interference of others. Control over property is not necessarily the same as physical custody of it but, rather, is a type of constructive delivery. The bailor gives the bailee the means of access to taking custody of it, without its actual delivery. The law construes such action as the equivalent of the physical transfer of the item. The delivery of the keys to a safe-deposit box is constructive delivery of its contents.

A requisite to the creation of a bailment is the express or implied ACCEPTANCE of possession of or control over the property by the bailee. A person cannot unwittingly become a bailee. Because a bailment is a CONTRACT, knowledge and acceptance of its terms are essential to its enforcement.

CONSIDERATION, the exchange of something of value, must be present for a bailment to exist. Unlike the consideration required for most contracts, as long as one party gives up something of value, such action is regarded as good consideration. It is sufficient that the bailor suffer loss of use of the property by relinquishing its control to the bailee; the bailor has given up something of value—the immediate right to control the property.

**Rights and Liabilities** The bailment contract embodying general principles of the law of bailments governs the rights and duties of the bailor and bailee. The duty of CARE that must be exercised by a bailee varies, depending on the type of bailment.

In a bailment for mutual benefit, the bailee must take reasonable care of the bailed property. A bailee who fails to do so may be held liable for any damages incurred from his or her NEGLIGENCE. When a bailor receives the sole benefit from the bailment, the bailee has a lesser duty to care for the property and is financially responsible only if he or she has been grossly negligent or has acted in BAD FAITH in taking care of the property. In contrast, a bailee for whose sole benefit property has been bailed must exercise extraordinary care for the property. The bailee can use the property only in the manner authorized by the terms of the bailment. The bailee is liable for any injuries to

*A library patron's use of library books and materials is a bailment for the sole benefit of the bailee.*

*The rental of a truck is a bailment for the mutual benefit of the parties. The bailment is terminated when the customer returns the truck.*

the property from failure to properly care for or use it.

Once the purpose of the bailment has been completed, the bailee usually must return the property to the bailor, or account for it, depending upon the terms of the contract. If, through no fault of his or her own, the return of the property is delayed or becomes impossible—for example, when it is lost during the course of the bailment—the bailee will not be held liable for nondelivery on demand. In all other situations, however, the bailee will be responsible for the tort of conversion for unjustifiable failure to redeliver the property as well as its unauthorized use.

The provisions of the bailment contract may restrict the LIABILITY of a bailee for negligent care or unauthorized use of the property. Such terms may not, however, absolve the bailee from all liability for the consequences of his or her own FRAUD or negligence. The bailor must have notice of all such limitations on liability. The restrictions will be enforced in any action brought for DAMAGES as long as the contract does not violate the law or public policy. Similarly, a bailee may extend his or her liability to the bailor by contract provision.

**Termination**  A bailment is ended when its purpose has been achieved, when the parties agree that it is terminated, or when the bailed property is destroyed. A bailment created for an indefinite period is terminable at will by either party, as long as the other party receives due notice of the intended termination. Once a bailment ends, the bailee must return the property to the bailor or possibly be liable for CONVERSION.

**BAILOR**  📖 One who places control over or possession of PERSONAL PROPERTY in the hands of another, a BAILEE, for its care, safekeeping, or use, in accordance to the terms of a mutual agreement. 📖

**BAIT AND SWITCH**  📖 A deceptive sales technique that involves advertising a low-priced item to attract customers to a store, then persuading them to buy more expensive goods by failing to have a sufficient supply of the advertised item on hand or by disparaging its quality. 📖

This practice is illegal in many states under their CONSUMER PROTECTION laws.

**BAKER, ELLA JOSEPHINE**  Ella Josephine Baker helped found the U.S. civil rights movement and organize three national civil rights organizations.

Baker was born in Norfolk, Virginia, on December 13, 1903, the second of three children of Georgianna Ross Baker and Blake Baker.

Baker's mother insisted that her children do well in school, because she felt that they needed an education in order to live a full life. Baker was sent to a private boarding school from ninth grade to twelfth grade, after her mother decided that she and her siblings were not receiving high-quality instruction in the public school they had been attending. In 1918, Baker began studying at Shaw University, an all-black school in Raleigh, North Carolina, that offered high school and college-level instruction.

Baker graduated from Shaw University in 1927, ranked first in her class. However, she did not have enough money for further schooling to become either a medical missionary or a social worker, occupations to which she had aspired. Her college degree in hand, she went to New York City.

While living in New York, Baker wrote articles for Harlem newspapers, including the *West Indian Review*. Living and working in Harlem during the mid- to late 1920s, she became a part of the Harlem Renaissance, a period of high artistic achievement and greater awareness of the possibilities for equality, justice, and true freedom. Baker participated in political discussions with many people, all over New York City. She later recalled, "Wherever there was a discussion, I'd go. It didn't matter if it was all men, and maybe I was the only woman . . . it didn't matter."

In the early days of the Great Depression, Baker was working for a Harlem newspaper along with George Samuel Schuyler, who was well known in the black community for his writing and who frequently railed against racial prejudice. In one article, Schuyler proposed that African Americans set up cooperatives to purchase goods in larger quantities, at lower prices than they could get otherwise. The response to this article was so positive that Schuyler decided to set up a cooperative on his own with Baker's help. Baker learned a great deal in this experience, and became an acknowledged expert on consumer affairs, a new idea that she helped introduce to the black community nationwide. In 1935, she was hired by the Works Progress Administration (WPA), a group of programs set up by President Franklin D. Roosevelt's New Deal, to teach people living in Harlem how to purchase the most for the little money they had.

Baker worked for the WPA until 1938, when she left to become an assistant field secretary for the National Association for the Advancement of Colored People (NAACP), the first civil rights organization established in the United States.

At that time the NAACP had fewer members in the South than in any other part of the United States, and most of its members were professionals—doctors, lawyers, and teachers. Baker believed that the organization had to reach the larger population of working people in order to accomplish its tasks. She targeted factory workers, household workers, and construction workers and tried to get them to support the NAACP. By 1941, thanks to Baker and the other NAACP field staffers, the NAACP's southern membership rolls had increased significantly.

In 1942 Baker was promoted to director of branches for the organization. In that position, she helped branch offices organize fund-raising and membership drives and encouraged them to become involved in local affairs to improve the lot of black people in their communities. Through her contact with the branch offices, the organization became aware of court cases they could bring on behalf of blacks who were denied their civil rights, such as access to public institutions of higher education.

**BIOGRAPHY**

*Ella Josephine Baker*

In 1954 Baker was named as president of the New York City branch of the NAACP. In May of that year, the U.S. Supreme Court issued its landmark decision in *Brown v. Board of Education*, 347 U.S. 483, 74 S. Ct. 686, 98 L. Ed. 873. The Court ruled in *Brown* that "separate but equal" schools for blacks and whites were unconstitutional. As a result, school districts in cities across the nation had to make sure they were not violating the law. Based on her experience raising her niece, Jackie, Baker believed that New York City schools were segregated, and she and other community leaders pressured city hall to examine the school system more closely for evidence of illegal segregation. The next year, the mayor of New York City asked Baker to join his newly created Commission on School Integration.

To present the commission's findings to parents of schoolchildren, Baker set up meetings around New York City. When she found that many parents were deeply concerned over the quality of their neighborhood schools, Baker encouraged them to petition the school board to allow their children to attend schools of their own choosing. In response to the petitions, New York developed one of the first open-enrollment plans for public schools. Open enrollment allowed public school students to attend schools outside their own neighborhoods, without requiring them to change their residency or pay extra tuition or transportation costs.

A new chapter in the civil rights movement began when Rosa Parks refused to give up her seat on a Montgomery, Alabama, bus on December 1, 1955. In Montgomery, black passengers could sit only in the back of the bus, behind the first ten rows of seats. Whites could sit in the black section of the bus, but when they did, a black person could not sit next to or in front of a white person. And black people could be forced to give up their seats if a white person had no place to sit.

Parks was an officer of the NAACP's Montgomery branch and had worked with Baker on the NAACP's Leadership Conference, a program designed to help local members develop

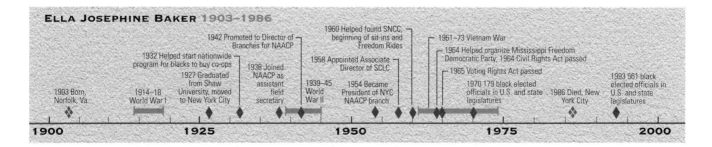

ELLA JOSEPHINE BAKER 1903–1986

1903 Born, Norfolk, Va.

1914–18 World War I

1927 Graduated from Shaw University, moved to New York City

1932 Helped start nationwide program for blacks to buy co-ops

1938 Joined NAACP as assistant field secretary

1939–45 World War II

1942 Promoted to Director of Branches for NAACP

1954 Became President of NYC NAACP branch

1958 Appointed Associate Director of SCLC

1960 Helped found SNCC; beginning of sit-ins and Freedom Rides

1961–73 Vietnam War

1964 Helped organize Mississippi Freedom Democratic Party; 1964 Civil Rights Act passed

1965 Voting Rights Act passed

1970 179 black elected officials in U.S. and state legislatures

1986 Died, New York City

1993 561 black elected officials in U.S. and state legislatures

1900　1925　1950　1975　2000

their leadership skills. In support of Parks, leaders of Montgomery's black community, including Dr. Martin Luther King, Jr., organized a BOYCOTT of the Montgomery bus system. The boycott lasted from December 1, 1955, until December 20, 1956, when blacks in Montgomery heard that the U.S. Supreme Court had ruled on December 17 that Montgomery's bus segregation laws were unconstitutional (*Gayle v. Browder*, 352 U.S. 903, 77 S. Ct. 145, 1 L. Ed. 2d 114 [Nov. 13, 1956], *reh'g denied*, 352 U.S. 950, 77 S. Ct. 323, 1 L. Ed. 2d 245).

After the success of the Montgomery bus boycott, Baker and others eventually convinced King to call a meeting of southern black leaders to plan to extend the battle. The meeting King called was to take place in Atlanta on January 11, 1957. The evening before, several locations in Montgomery were bombed, including homes of white and black supporters of the civil rights movement. King and the Rev. Ralph D. Abernathy, whose home was one of those bombed, left the meeting to investigate the incidents. Baker and an associate stayed in Atlanta to manage the conference with Coretta Scott King and the Rev. Fred L. Shuttlesworth. This meeting was the beginning of the Southern Christian Leadership Conference (SCLC), an umbrella organization for groups fighting for civil rights.

One of the SCLC's first nationwide efforts was the Crusade for Citizenship, a voter registration program. By September 1959, when the organization had not motivated masses of African Americans to register, Baker proposed three changes that she believed would result in a stronger organization. The first suggestion was to create an overarching plan to coordinate the activities of SCLC member groups. The second was to actively develop the leadership skills of people in the member organizations who had demonstrated abilities in that area. The third was to organize black southerners to fight every form of DISCRIMINATION by using mass action and nonviolent resistance.

One method of nonviolent resistance, the sit-in, was used as early as 1942 by a civil rights organization called the Congress of Racial Equality (CORE) to protest racial discrimination. Not until 1960, however, were sit-ins widely used as a form of protest. In February 1960, four black students sat at the lunch counter in a Woolworth's store in Greensboro, North Carolina. They were refused service, because it was a "whites-only" lunch counter, but remained seated until the store closed for the day. News of the incident spread quickly, and area high school and college students joined them in the following days. By the end of March, students had staged sit-ins in many other southern cities. Baker realized that although the sit-ins were generating publicity for the civil rights movement, their influence would be greater if they were better coordinated, so in April 1960 Baker organized a conference for student civil rights activists at Shaw University. Over three hundred students attended the meeting, which was the genesis of the Student Nonviolent Coordinating Committee (SNCC). Among those attending were Marion Barry, future mayor and future city council member of Washington, D.C., and Julian Bond, future Georgia legislator.

Baker resigned from the SCLC and became SNCC's adviser and organized its main office. SNCC developed a unique, separate identity within the civil rights movement because of Baker's style of leadership. Baker believed that everyone in an organization should lead it, so she made sure that everyone in attendance at meetings stated an opinion, and that no other single civil rights leader or organization, including the NAACP and King, directed the activities of the committee. When SNCC nearly split apart over whether to pursue direct action (such as the Montgomery bus boycott and the Greensboro sit-ins) or voter registration, Baker suggested that the organization could do both, setting the stage for the 1961 Freedom Rides.

The Freedom Rides were begun in 1961 as a response to a 1960 ruling, *Boynton v. Virginia*, 364 U.S. 206, 81 S. Ct. 182, 5 L. Ed. 2d 206, in which the Supreme Court decided that interstate buses and trains, and the facilities in the terminals that served them, could not constitutionally remain segregated. The ruling was flagrantly ignored throughout the South. The Freedom Riders, who were both black and white, intended to stop the segregation by traveling together along the routes where segregated facilities were located. The Freedom Rides drew the attention of the Congress, which began debate on a civil rights bill in the summer of 1963. The 1964 Civil Rights Act, as the bill was called, was finally passed on July 2, 1964, guaranteeing African Americans equal protection in the use of hotels, restaurants, and other public establishments; in job opportunities, raises, and promotions; and in the use of public schools (Pub. L. No. 88-352, 78 Stat. 241).

While the Freedom Riders traveled across the South, SNCC also pursued voter registration. In 1963, Baker went to Mississippi to help with the Freedom Vote, a project of CORE and SNCC. The Freedom Vote was a mock election

"STRONG PEOPLE DON'T NEED STRONG LEADERS."

intended to demonstrate that, contrary to the opinions held by many white southerners, blacks were interested in voting. Baker assisted the project by speaking at rallies, setting up polling places, and collecting and counting the ballots on voting day. The Freedom Vote was a big success: more than 80,000 of the 90,000 people who cast ballots that day were black, even though only around 20,000 blacks were registered for real elections. Two years later, in August 1965, the efforts of Baker and thousands of other activists bore fruit when the Voting Rights Act (Pub. L. No. 89-110, 79 Stat. 437) was passed. The Voting Rights Act nearly eliminated one of the last ways that had been used to prevent African Americans from voting—the literacy test—by prohibiting its use in states where fewer than 50 percent of eligible voters were registered.

In 1964 Baker again helped organize a civil rights group. The group was the Mississippi Freedom Democratic Party (MFDP), begun in response to an established political party, the Mississippi Democratic party. The MFDP attempted to represent the state of Mississippi at the 1964 Democratic National Convention in Atlantic City, New Jersey, by claiming that, as an interracial group, it was better able to do so than the all-white Mississippi Democratic party. Hubert H. Humphrey, vice president of the United States, and Walter F. Mondale, Minnesota attorney general, suggested a compromise: two MFDP members could be named as delegates to the convention, but would not be part of Mississippi's delegation. The MFDP refused this offer, but its request was the catalyst for a new rule passed by the national Democratic party, that all state delegations would have to be racially mixed.

After achieving notable successes in the U.S. civil rights movement, Baker continued to serve as SNCC's mentor as the organization became involved in protests against the Vietnam War, and as an advocate for the free speech movement and women's rights. She also worked toward increased civil rights for blacks in other countries, including the former Southern Rhodesia, now Zimbabwe; South Africa; and Puerto Rico.

Baker died in New York City on December 13, 1986, her eighty-third birthday. By that time, some of the organizations she had been involved with no longer existed. SNCC fell apart after dissension developed over black power, or black independence from white America. The MFDP lasted through the 1967 elections, winning offices in local races, but was no longer needed after African Americans were allowed to join the state Democratic party. However, Baker's work lives on in a generation of black U.S. leaders she nurtured and encouraged, who are able to carry on the struggle for civil and human rights worldwide.

### CROSS-REFERENCES

*Brown v. Board of Education of Topeka, Kansas;* Civil Rights Movement; King, Martin Luther, Jr.; National Association for the Advancement of Colored People; Parks, Rosa; School Desegregation; Voting Rights.

**BAKER v. CARR** The ideal of ONE PERSON, ONE VOTE motivated the founders of the United States of America to establish a CENSUS when they drafted the U.S. Constitution in 1787. Although that ideal has not yet been fully realized—because the census still undercounts minorities, among others—the country took a giant step closer to equal representation for every citizen nearly two centuries later, during the era of the civil rights movement. On March 26, 1962, the U.S. Supreme Court ruled in the landmark case of *Baker v. Carr*, 369 U.S. 186, 82 S. Ct. 691, 7 L. Ed. 2d 663 (1962), that state congressional districts of unequal size were unconstitutional. In a ruling that Chief Justice Earl Warren later called the most important of his tenure on the Court, Justice William J. Brennan, Jr., wrote, "A citizen's right to vote free of arbitrary impairment by state action has been judicially recognized as a right secured by the Constitution."

Also significant because it examined the notion of "political questions" and whether courts could address them, the *Baker* case became a springboard for future apportionment lawsuits. In June 1964, the Supreme Court ruled on appeals from fifteen states that had used *Baker* as a PRECEDENT, holding that both houses of a state legislature must be apportioned substantially on the basis of population. Within two years, every state had taken some type of apportionment action. By the late 1960s, congressional districts around the country had been redrawn to meet the Supreme Court's call for equal representation, and after the 1970 census, underrepresented urban areas were finally given an equal voice in Congress.

Every decade since 1790, U.S. citizens have complied with the Constitution and counted themselves. Whereas on its simplest level the census is a means to document historical changes in the U.S. population, it also determines how federal funds, power, political clout, and representation are divided, or apportioned, among the people of the United States. It was the notion of representation, more specifically equal representation, that compelled Charles

## State Legislative Apportionment before *Baker v. Carr*

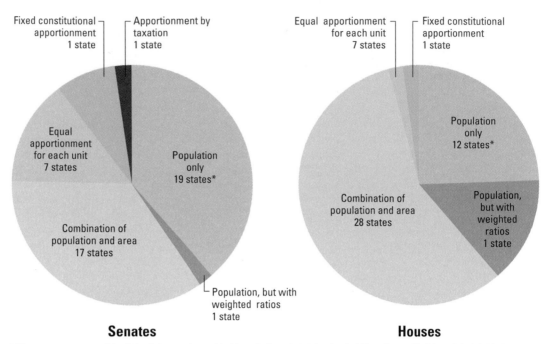

**Senates**

**Houses**

\* Fifty states are represented, but Nebraska has a unicameral legislature (only one legislative chamber). The unicameral legislature is included in the percentage calculation for both houses and senates.

Source: Gordon E. Baker, *State Constitutions: Reapportionment* (New York: National Municipal League, 1960), 5.

W. Baker and other qualified voters in Tennessee to bring a lawsuit against Tennessee's secretary of state Joe C. Carr, on the grounds that the state's 1901 apportionment statute (Acts Tenn. 1901, c. 122) violated the Fourteenth Amendment of the Constitution. The plaintiffs argued that Tennessee's method of unequally apportioning the members of the general assembly among the state's ninety-five counties unconstitutionally deprived people in the state of equal protection of the laws and was obsolete because of a significant growth and population shift since 1900.

The plaintiffs' first round in court brought failure when a three-judge panel of the U.S. District Court for the Middle District of Tennessee dismissed their COMPLAINT on December 21, 1959 (*Baker*, 179 F. Supp. 824). The panel dismissed the complaint on two grounds: (1) that the court lacked JURISDICTION of the subject matter because it was a political question and (2) that the complaint failed to state a CLAIM upon which RELIEF could be granted.

The plaintiffs appealed, and on November 21, 1964, the U.S. Supreme Court ruled that it had probable jurisdiction in the matter. This decision was significant because before the Supreme Court heard the *Baker* case, courts had abstained from addressing apportionment issues

because they were considered political in nature. In the 1946 Supreme Court case *Colegrove v. Green*, 328 U.S. 549, 66 S. Ct. 1198, 90 L. Ed. 1432 (1946), Justice Felix Frankfurter called apportionment a "political thicket" into which the judiciary should not venture. The subsequent ruling in *Baker* changed that interpretation, stating that federal courts possessed jurisdiction of the subject, that the citizens in Tennessee were entitled to relief, and that the federal district court in the state could settle the challenge to the apportionment statute of Tennessee.

In addressing the concern of some of his fellow Supreme Court justices, who warned that the matter before them was a political question and therefore not appropriately dealt with in a court of law, Justice Brennan carefully wrote—and rewrote, ten times—his opinion in the 1962 decision. Stated Brennan, "The mere fact that the suit seeks protection of a political right does not mean it presents a political question. Such an objection is little more than a play upon words." He added that the plaintiffs' complaint did present a JUSTICIABLE constitutional CAUSE OF ACTION and that the Fourteenth Amendment did provide judicial protection to the right asserted. Justices Frankfurter and John Marshall Harlan dissented, saying that Brennan should not inject the Court "into the clash of political forces and political settlements." The Court's 6–2 ruling in favor of the plaintiffs forced state legislatures to reapportion their seats to reflect population shifts before the elections that were to occur in the fall of 1962. It also decreed one person, one vote as part of the United States' constitutional heritage and opened the door to challenging state voting procedures and malapportionment on constitutional grounds.

In his book *Turning Point: A Candidate, a State, and a Nation Come of Age*, former president Jimmy Carter described how revolutionary the *Baker* decision was in the 1960s and how it transformed state politics, especially southern politics. Carter wrote that the Georgia state government, like many others, proposed a number of stalling ploys, fake reapportionment plans, and other ways to avoid the shift in political power that the one-person, one-vote ruling had been designed to cause. "The beneficiaries of the [old] system were the ones now charged with . . . changing it," he said. "At the same time, they would be reducing drastically the relative voting strength of their own constituents. It was understandable that [they] would do everything possible to circumvent or postpone the effect of the court's mandate." Federal judges rejected the bogus plans, however, and by late summer 1962, the state's political process had been thrown wide open. Incumbent politicians were suddenly without districts, and new seats had opened up. In these circumstances, a few weeks before the election, Carter decided to run for the Georgia State Senate.

### CROSS-REFERENCES

Apportionment; Brennan, William J., Jr.; Equal Protection; Failure to State a Claim; Fourteenth Amendment; Frankfurter, Felix; Political Question; *Reynolds v. Sims*; Voting Rights.

## BAKKE AFFIRMATIVE ACTION CASE

See REGENTS OF THE UNIVERSITY OF CALIFORNIA V. BAKKE.

## BALANCE SHEET 
A comprehensive FINANCIAL STATEMENT that is a summarized assessment of a company's accounts specifying its assets and liabilities. A report, usually prepared by independent auditors or accountants, which includes a full and complete statement of all receipts and disbursements of a particular business. A review that shows a general balance or summation of all accounts without showing the particular items that make up the several accounts. 

## BALANCING 
A process sometimes used by the Supreme Court in deciding between the competing interests represented in a case. 

Used most often to decide constitutional cases, balancing is one of two main legal decision-making methods, the other being categorization or STRICT CONSTRUCTION. Balancing involves weighing competing rights against each other and analyzing the relative strengths of many different factors. A balancing decision is dependent upon the circumstances of each individual case. Therefore, the outcome is difficult to predict. On the other hand, categorization is a classification and labeling process. It involves identifying a right and how it was infringed upon, and analogizing these findings to a previously decided case or PRECEDENT. Hence, the outcome is more predictable.

Balancing may take one of two forms. In the first, the Court may measure competing interests against each other and determine which carries the most weight. For example, in *New York v. Ferber*, 458 U.S. 747, 102 S. Ct. 3348, 73 L. Ed. 2d 1113 (1982), the Court upheld a statute criminalizing distribution of child pornography because the evil eliminated by the statute far outweighed any infringement on free speech interests. In the second form of balancing, the Court attempts to "strike a balance" between competing interests. Thus, in *Tennessee v. Garner*, 471 U.S. 1, 105 S. Ct. 1694, 85 L. Ed. 2d 1 (1985), the Court held that a police officer may use DEADLY FORCE to stop a fleeing felon if the officer has PROBABLE CAUSE to believe that the suspect poses a threat of serious physical harm to others. In *Garner*, the Court did not find that one interest clearly outweighed the other. Instead, both the state's interest in law enforcement and the individual's interest in being free from harm were weighed in the analysis and given due recognition.

Balancing was first used by the Court in the late 1930s and early 1940s when the judiciary began to reject the rigid formalism and mechanical jurisprudence characteristic of the nineteenth and early twentieth centuries. Before the balancing era, in *Lochner v. New York*, 198 U.S. 45, 25 S. Ct. 539, 49 L. Ed. 937 (1905), the Court held that a New York statute setting maximum work hours was constitutional because such regulation was within the state's POLICE POWER. In reaching this decision, the Court did not attempt to balance the rights of the individuals against the state's interests, but took a straightforward look at the language of the statute and found it valid. According to this earlier Court, "The purpose of a statute must be determined from the natural and legal effect of the language employed. . . . It seems to us that the real object and purpose [of the statute] were simply to regulate the hours of labor between the master and his employees."

Early proponents of balancing included such prominent Supreme Court justices as Oliver Wendell Holmes, Jr., Louis D. Brandeis, and Harlan F. Stone, all of whom sat on the Court in the early to middle 1900s. Holmes, sometimes called the patron saint of the antiformalist movement, was one of the first to espouse the idea that the law is and should be an evolving product of social experience. He assailed the notion that rigid formulas could be applied to all situations before the Court. "[T]he law is a logical development, like everything else," he wrote. In a similar vein, Brandeis criticized the Court for ignoring contemporary social, political, and economic problems. He said, "[W]hether a measure relating to the public welfare is arbitrary or unreasonable . . . should be based upon a consideration of relevant facts, actual or possible" (*Adams v. Tanner*, 244 U.S. 590, 37 S. Ct. 662, 61 L. Ed. 1336 [1917] [Brandeis, J., dissenting]). In another case, he wrote, "Whether a law enacted in the exercise of the police power is justly subject to the charge of being unreasonable or arbitrary can ordinarily be determined only by a consideration of the contemporary conditions, social, industrial, and political, of the community to be affected thereby. Resort to such facts is necessary, among other things, in order to appreciate the evils sought to be remedied and the possible effects of the remedy proposed" (*Truax v. Corrigan*, 257 U.S. 312, 42 S. Ct. 124, 66 L. Ed. 254 [1921] [Brandeis, J., dissenting]). Similarly, Stone forcefully advocated "consideration of all the facts and circumstances" in a case, including societal conditions that affected the parties, the controversy, and the outcome (*DiSanto v. Pennsylvania*, 273 U.S. 34, 47 S. Ct. 267, 71 L. Ed. 524 [1927] [Stone, J., dissenting]).

The Court uses a balancing approach most often to decide cases where constitutionally protected individual rights conflict with governmental interests. Many of the landmark constitutional cases of the 1960s, 1970s, and 1980s were decided in this manner, including *Roe v. Wade*, 410 U.S. 113, 93 S. Ct. 705, 35 L. Ed. 2d 47 (1973), which legalized ABORTION. In reaching its decision in *Roe*, the Court found that in the first trimester of pregnancy, a woman's right to privacy outweighed the state's interest in protecting health, but in the later stages of pregnancy, the state's interest gradually outweighed the woman's.

Contrary to popular belief, however, the Court has not used balancing as its primary method of deciding constitutional cases. In fact, some of the most important constitutional cases of the twentieth century were decided without any balancing of competing interests: for example, *Brown v. Board of Education*, 347 U.S. 483, 74 S. Ct. 686, 98 L. Ed. 873 (1954) (outlawing segregated public schools); *Gideon v. Wainwright*, 372 U.S. 335, 83 S. Ct. 792, 9 L. Ed. 2d 799 (1963) (guaranteeing indigent defendants appointed counsel in felony cases); and *Griswold v. Connecticut*, 381 U.S. 479, 85 S. Ct. 1678, 14 L. Ed. 2d 510 (1965) (outlawing state laws prohibiting contraceptives).

Balancing has always aroused controversy among legal scholars and judges. Critics contend that it gives too much discretion to judges and amounts to a usurpation of the legislative function. They maintain that it is a vague and arbitrary method of measuring unequal interests against each other and that it results in unpredictable decision making. One vocal critic of balancing is Justice Antonin Scalia. In his dissenting opinion in *Bendix Autolite Corp. v. Midwesco Enterprises*, 486 U.S. 888, 108 S. Ct. 2218, 100 L. Ed. 2d 896 (1988), he characterized the balancing of competing interests as an illusion. "[T]he scale analogy is not really appropriate," he wrote, "since the interests on both sides are incommensurate. It is more like judging whether a particular line is longer than a particular rock is heavy."

Scalia's frontal attack on balancing gained force in the 1990s when he was joined on the Court by other justices who shared his philosophy that the Constitution should be construed strictly and literally. Evidence that Scalia's view was held by others on the Court can be found in the 1995 decision *Vernonia School District 47J v. Acton*, ___U.S. ___, 115 S. Ct. 2386, 132 L. Ed. 2d 564, which held that schools could legally perform random drug tests on student athletes. The decision employed a straightforward analysis of the rationality of the schools' policy to conduct random drug tests and dismissed concerns about infringement of the students' FOURTH AMENDMENT right to be free from unreasonable searches. Writing for the majority, Scalia said, "The most significant element in this case is . . . that the policy was undertaken in furtherance of the government's responsibilities, under a public school system, as guardian and tutor of children entrusted to its care." The Court held that the testing was a type of search that "a reasonable guardian and tutor might undertake."

Three justices disagreed vehemently. Writing for the dissent, Justice Sandra Day O'Connor emphasized her belief that the decision did not give due recognition to the students' constitutional rights and went too far in its broad approval of "intrusive, blanket searches of school children, most of whom are innocent, for evidence of serious wrongdoing." Under the ruling, she said, students no longer enjoyed "the Fourth Amendment's . . . most basic . . . protection: its strong preference for an individualized suspicion requirement."

Justice O'Connor's dissent in *Acton* echoed her strong approval of balancing competing interests and assessing a statute's intrusion on individual rights. O'Connor expressed her belief that balancing is an essential step in the Court's decision-making process, in *Employment Division, Department of Human Resources v. Smith*, 494 U.S. 872, 110 S. Ct. 1595, 108 L. Ed. 2d 876 (1990). The respondents in *Smith* were Native Americans who were fired from their jobs because they ingested peyote as part of a religious ceremony. The Court held that the state could deny them unemployment benefits without violating the Free Exercise Clause of the FIRST AMENDMENT. O'Connor concurred with the result but took issue with the majority's failure to consider the effect the disputed statute had on the free exercise of religion. "To me," O'Connor wrote, "the sounder approach— the approach more consistent with our role as judges to decide each case on its individual merits—is to apply [a] test in each case to determine whether the burden on the specific plaintiffs before us is constitutionally significant and whether the particular . . . interest asserted by the State before us is compelling."

Although its popularity waxes and wanes with the composition of the Supreme Court, balancing remains a widely used albeit controversial judicial tool. It provides the Court with the flexibility to consider all factors affecting a decision.

### CROSS-REFERENCES
Brandeis, Louis D.; Holmes, Oliver Wendell, Jr.; Judicial Review; Jurisprudence; O'Connor, Sandra Day; Scalia, Antonin; Stone, Harlan F.

**BIOGRAPHY**

*Henry Baldwin*

**BALDWIN, HENRY** Henry Baldwin was a prominent Pennsylvania attorney and politician who later became an associate justice of the U.S. Supreme Court, where he served for fourteen years.

Descended from an aristocratic British family dating back to the seventeenth century, Baldwin was born January 14, 1780, in New Haven, Connecticut. He grew up on a farm near New Haven and later moved to the city to attend Yale College. After graduating with honors in 1797, he studied law in Philadelphia with Alexander J. Dallas, a noted attorney. Admitted to the bar a short time later, Baldwin originally planned to establish a practice in Ohio, but instead settled in Pittsburgh. He then established a successful law firm with two other young attorneys. By his midtwenties, Baldwin had established a reputation as a legal scholar, in part because of his thorough and well-researched law BRIEFS. He had also developed an extensive personal law library, which contained a large collection of valuable English case reports and was among the finest and largest in the Northeast. Furthermore, Baldwin and his law partners were known for their political and civic leadership. The three published a newspaper, the *Tree of Liberty*, which supported the Republican party of western Pennsylvania. In addition to his political activities and his law practice, Baldwin found time for business, acting as part-owner of several mills in Pennsylvania and Ohio.

After the death of his first wife, Baldwin married Sally Ellicott, and they established a residence in Crawford County, Pennsylvania. In 1816, Baldwin was elected representative to the U.S. Congress for that area. As a congressman, Baldwin was active in trade issues and was a strong advocate of TARIFF protection. He was also involved in mediating boundary disputes between northern and southern states and their representatives. He was twice reelected to the House. In 1822, he was forced to resign his seat because of illness. He returned home to Pennsylvania, where he once again practiced law and was active in local political affairs.

**HENRY BALDWIN 1780–1844**

1775–83 American Revolution

1780 Born, New Haven, Conn.

1787 Pennsylvania ratified U.S. Constitution

1797 Received LL.D. from Yale University

1816–22 Represented Pennsylvania in U.S. House of Representatives

1829 Appointed to U.S. Supreme Court by Andrew Jackson

1837 *A General View of the Origin and Nature of the Constitution and Government in the United States* published

1844 Died, Philadelphia, Pa.

1775    1800    1825    1850

Baldwin soon became an avid supporter of ANDREW JACKSON and was a trusted adviser to Jackson concerning Pennsylvania politics. After Jackson was elected president in 1828, Baldwin hoped to become secretary of the treasury, but the appointment instead went to Samuel D. Ingham. The following year, after the death of Justice Bushrod Washington, Jackson nominated Baldwin to the U.S. Supreme Court, against the wishes of his vice president, John C. Calhoun, who preferred another candidate. Though Baldwin's protectionist views created some controversy, he was confirmed by the Senate with only two dissenting votes, from southern senators who opposed his policies on tariffs.

On the bench, Baldwin was at first a strong supporter of the liberal views of Chief Justice JOHN MARSHALL but gradually moved toward a more moderate interpretation of the Constitution, favoring neither state sovereignty nor federal supremacy. In 1837, he published a pamphlet, *A General View of the Origin and Nature of the Constitution and Government of the United States,* in which he set forth what he termed his "peculiar views of the Constitution." In this work, he emphasized his position as a moderate on the Court, stating that he tended to take the Constitution "as it is, and to expound it by the accepted rules of interpretation." Baldwin also believed that the Court must be politically sensitive when determining which powers belonged to the federal government and which remained with the states.

One of Baldwin's most influential majority opinions was *United States v. Arredondo,* 31 U.S. 691, 6 Pet. 691, 8 L. Ed. 547 (1832), in which the Court held that public policy prevented the government from violating federal land treaties. With respect to the issue of SLAVERY, however, Baldwin's views were considered to be much more radical than those held by other members of the Court. In *Groves v. Slaughter,* 40 U.S. 449, 15 Pet. 449, 10 L. Ed. 800 (1841), the Court considered the constitutionality of a Mississippi provision that prevented the importation of slaves into the state. The Court ultimately struck down the statute on technical reasons, but Baldwin, in a separate opinion, argued that slaves were property as well as persons and viewed the prohibition as an obstruction of interstate commerce. He was the sole dissenter in *United States v. The Schooner Armistead,* 40 U.S. 518, 15 Pet. 518, 10 L. Ed. 826 (1841), in which the Court held that slaves who had mutinied and taken over the slave ship transporting them from Africa should be set free. Though he did not write an opinion, Baldwin had earlier maintained that the slaves should be returned to the custody of the slave traders.

As was the practice in the Court at the time, Baldwin traveled the CIRCUIT he represented, which included Pennsylvania and New Jersey, to hear cases. He heard important cases involving the construction of a will that made a bequest for charitable purposes and also presided over the trial of John F. Braddel, who in 1840 was accused of robbing the mails.

In his later years, Baldwin was plagued by financial and personal difficulties. He never fully recovered from losing a great deal of money during the depression of 1820. He also suffered from the failure of several speculative businesses, and he had to support some of his adult children when they got into financial trouble. He was eventually forced to sell his renowned personal law library to the Library of Congress to raise money. He also published and sold volumes of the opinions he decided while traveling the circuit.

At the same time, Baldwin's behavior became erratic and he was widely reported to be suffering from mental illness. While on the bench, he was often restless, inattentive, and abusive to litigants and his fellow justices. While on the circuit, he also exhibited bizarre behavior at times, often having coffee and cakes brought to him while he heard cases. Chief Justice ROGER B. TANEY was reported to be so concerned about Baldwin's unpredictable behavior that he advised President Jackson not to take action against the Bank of the United States because Baldwin, as presiding judge over the case in Philadelphia, would be unreliable.

Baldwin's tenure on the Court ended on April 21, 1844, when he died of paralysis at the age of sixty-four. He was deeply in debt at the time of his death, and friends and family took up a collection to pay for his funeral expenses.

**BALDWIN, JOSEPH GLOVER** Joseph Glover Baldwin achieved prominence as a jurist and author despite his lack of formal education.

Baldwin was born in January, 1815, near Winchester, Virginia. After establishing a legal practice in 1836 in DeKalb, Mississippi, he relocated to Alabama and entered the legislature of the state in 1844, serving for five years.

In 1854 Baldwin moved again, this time to San Francisco. He maintained a successful practice and was involved in the formulation of the judicial system of San Francisco. He officially entered the judiciary in 1858, presiding as associate justice of the California Supreme Court until 1862.

"WORDS ARE BUT THE EVIDENCE OF INTENTION; THEIR IMPORT IS THEIR MEANING, TO BE GATHERED FROM THE CONTEXT, AND THEIR CONNECTION WITH THE SUBJECT MATTER."

**BIOGRAPHY**

*Joseph Glover Baldwin*

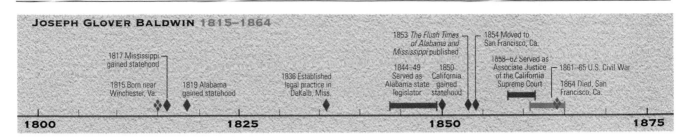

JOSEPH GLOVER BALDWIN 1815–1864

1817 Mississippi
gained statehood

1815 Born near
Winchester, Va.

1819 Alabama
gained statehood

1836 Established
legal practice in
DeKalb, Miss.

1853 The Flush Times
of Alabama and
Mississippi published

1844–49
Served as
Alabama state
legislator

1850
California
gained
statehood

1854 Moved to
San Francisco, Ca.

1858–62 Served as
Associate Justice
of the California
Supreme Court

1861–65 U.S. Civil War

1864 Died, San
Francisco, Ca.

1800        1825        1850        1875

As an author, Baldwin is famous for *The Flush Times of Alabama and Mississippi* (1853) and *Party Leaders* (1855). He died September 30, 1864, in San Francisco, California.

**BALDWIN, ROGER NASH**    Roger Nash Baldwin spent his life crusading for CIVIL RIGHTS and liberties and was one of the principal founders of the American Civil Liberties Union (ACLU).

Baldwin was born January 21, 1884, in Wellesley, Massachusetts, into a comfortably well-to-do Boston Brahmin family. His ancestral roots reached back to what he once referred to as "the inescapable Mayflower." His father, Frank Fenno Baldwin, was a conservative businessman. His mother, Lucy Cushing Nash, instilled in her children a love of art, literature, and music. Baldwin's parents raised their six children with all the privileges and advantages their wealth could provide, but they also emphasized service to others. The family attended the Unitarian Church, where an emphasis on helping others sowed in Baldwin the seeds of a social work career.

Baldwin was an unconventional boy who was not interested in competitive endeavors and shared his mother's interest in literature and art. He was a nonconformist who was influenced by HENRY DAVID THOREAU's philosophy of individualism and self-reliance. Although his parents were conservative, the young Baldwin was introduced to many progressive leaders at the home of his uncle and aunt, William Baldwin and Ruth Standish Bowles Baldwin. His uncle was president of the Long Island Railroad, and he also worked to end prostitution, was director of the National Child Labor Committee, and was a trustee of Tuskegee Institute. His aunt supported the fledgling labor movement and was a founder of the National Urban League, a trustee of Smith College, and a member of the Socialist party. The couple often entertained the social reformers of the day, and Baldwin was influenced by his exposure to their somewhat radical ideas.

Baldwin was educated at Harvard, earning both a bachelor's degree and a master's degree there. In 1906, he left the East and headed for

**BIOGRAPHY**

*Roger Nash Baldwin*

St. Louis to be a social worker. He directed a social settlement house for poor people and taught the first sociology courses offered at Washington University, in St. Louis. He became the chief probation officer of the St. Louis Juvenile Court in 1908. While in that position, he and Bernard Flexner coauthored the first textbook on the juvenile courts. Their book, *Juvenile Courts and Probation*, set out professional standards for juvenile practice and was the standard text in the field until the 1960s. In 1910, Baldwin became the secretary of the St. Louis Civic League, an urban reform agency supporting civic causes.

While working in St. Louis, Baldwin met and became friends with the anarchist EMMA GOLDMAN. His first defense of free speech came in 1912 when he spoke in support of MARGARET SANGER, an early crusader for birth control and reproductive rights, whose lecture was shut down by the police. Through the social work profession he was attracted to the reform movement and the labor movement. He organized the Division on Industrial and Economic Problems at the 1916 meeting of the National Conference of Social Work, and wrote a report calling for cooperative production and distribution systems to replace competitive labor systems.

In 1917, when the United States entered World War I, Baldwin organized the American Union against Militarism (AUAM), which was later replaced by the National Civil Liberties Bureau (NCLB). In its early days, the AUAM was concerned with defending those who refused to be drafted to serve in the war. Baldwin was among the CONSCIENTIOUS OBJECTORS opposed to the draft, and he was sentenced to a year in jail for his refusal to register. In a speech to the court before he was sentenced, he explained that his reason for opposing the draft was his "uncompromising opposition to the principle of conscription of life by the state for any purpose whatever, in time of war or peace."

After his release from prison, Baldwin worked as a common laborer around the Midwest and joined the radical International Workers of the World (IWW) union. He returned to New York in 1920 to help reorganize and

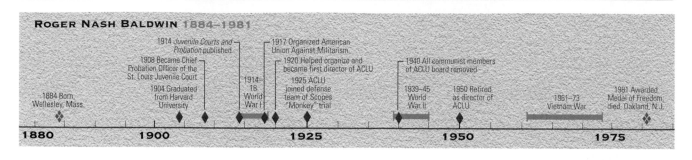

ROGER NASH BALDWIN 1884–1981

1914 *Juvenile Courts and Probation* published.

1908 Became Chief Probation Officer of the St. Louis Juvenile Court.

1917 Organized American Union Against Militarism.

1920 Helped organize and became first director of ACLU

1914–18 World War I

1904 Graduated from Harvard University

1884 Born, Wellesley, Mass.

1925 ACLU joined defense team of Scopes "Monkey" trial

1940 All communist members of ACLU board removed

1939–45 World War II

1950 Retired as director of ACLU

1961–73 Vietnam War

1981 Awarded Medal of Freedom; died, Oakland, N.J.

1880    1900    1925    1950    1975

reconstitute the NCLB with two conservative lawyers, Albert DeSilver and Walter Nelles, who shared his passion for championing the rights of the oppressed. Baldwin agreed to head the new organization, named the American Civil Liberties Union, and carry out its unique mission to impartially defend the civil liberties of all U.S. citizens, regardless of their affiliation or activities. Baldwin was launched in what would be a long and vigorous struggle to create "a society with a minimum of compulsion, a maximum of individual freedom and of voluntary association, and the abolition of exploitation and poverty."

Perhaps it was inevitable that Baldwin would become associated with leftist causes, since the people most in need of free speech protection during the 1920s and 1930s were often political liberals and radicals. He once told an interviewer that during this time he was heavily influenced by the Marxist theory that "the real center in society was the organized underdog in the trade unions," which he believed was true although only part of the whole picture.

Baldwin came to realize that the civil liberties of right-wing groups were just as likely to be infringed as those of left-wingers. Bewildered and frustrated by liberal groups who opposed the ACLU's support of free speech rights for the American Nazi party or the Ku Klux Klan, Baldwin said, "[T]hese people can be just as great tyrants as the other side . . . helping them get freedom didn't help the cause of freedom." Referring to the wide variety of causes the ACLU defended over the years, Baldwin said, "I always felt from the beginning that you had to defend people you disliked and feared as well as those you admired." Although not a member of any party, he supported the causes of Communists, Socialists, and other leftist organizations during the 1920s and 1930s. However, in 1940, when he began to realize that the *Communist* label was being used by totalitarian governments, he wrote a resolution that resulted in the removal of all the Communist members of the ACLU board.

"[OUR GOAL IS] A SOCIETY WITH A MINIMUM OF COMPULSION, A MAXIMUM OF INDIVIDUAL FREEDOM AND OF VOLUNTARY ASSOCIATION, AND THE ABOLITION OF EXPLOITATION AND POVERTY."

Ironically, Baldwin's resolution became the model for government LOYALTY OATHS, which the ACLU later attacked in court.

Although he was a card-carrying *Wobbly*, as members of the IWW were called, Baldwin could not be categorized as liberal or conservative. He was active in the National Audubon Society, the American Political Science Association, and a number of other organizations on both ends of the political spectrum. The only label Baldwin accepted for himself was that of reformer: "I am dead certain that human progress depends on those heretics, rebels and dreamers who have been my kin in spirit and whose 'holy discontent' has challenged established authority and created the expanding visions mankind may yet realize."

During the years of Baldwin's leadership, the ACLU, using volunteer lawyers, was involved in a wide variety of civil liberties cases, especially involving free speech and assembly. One concerned a 1925 Tennessee law forbidding the teaching of evolution in public schools. The ACLU defended a science teacher, John Thomas Scopes, charged with violating the law (*Scopes v. State*, 152 Tenn. 424, 278 S.W. 57 [1925]; 154 Tenn. 105, 289 S.W. 363 [1927]). William Jennings Bryan, a three-time presidential candidate and well-known fundamentalist, helped the state attorney general prosecute the case, and the notorious CLARENCE DARROW, a self-proclaimed atheist, defended Scopes. The trial ended with Scopes being convicted, although the verdict was later overturned because of a judicial error. The trial brought the issue of academic freedom to the public's attention and probably helped stunt the growth of the anti-evolution movement.

The ACLU was involved in the Sacco-Vanzetti murder case, in which it was widely believed that the two defendants, Nicolo Sacco and Bartolomeo Vanzetti, were scapegoated because they were Italian anarchists and draft resisters. Baldwin led the ACLU into the anti-censorship arena in the fight to lift the importation ban on such books as James Joyce's

*Ulysses.* In 1938, the ACLU obtained an INJUNC-TION against Mayor Frank Hague of Jersey City, ordering him to cease antiunion activities. ACLU lawyers defended the free expression and free press rights of the Jehovah's Witnesses, whose anti-Catholic rhetoric and aggressive canvassing tactics came under attack. They successfully argued that Henry Ford had a First Amendment right to express his antiunion views as long as he did not threaten workers. Possibly the most controversial cases accepted by the ACLU were those that challenged the free speech rights of unpopular groups such as the Ku Klux Klan, the German-American Bund, and the American Nazi party.

During World War II, Baldwin and the ACLU opposed the movement of Japanese Americans from their homes on the West Coast to relocation camps. After the war, he helped General Douglas MacArthur set up a civil liberties policy for the occupation forces in Japan. He also consulted on civil liberties issues in the U.S. zone of occupied Germany.

Baldwin, always a nonconformist, lived an ascetic lifestyle, wearing the same ill-fitting suit for years at a time and accepting a subsistence salary from the ACLU. He was married for fifteen years to Madeleine Z. Doty, a reformist lawyer. They divorced in 1934, and in 1936 he married another reformer, Evelyn Preston, whose two sons he adopted. The couple had one child, Helen Baldwin Mannoni.

Baldwin retired as head of the ACLU in 1950, but he never retired from the causes to which he was committed. He continued working until the day he died, August 26, 1981, at age ninety-seven. A few months before his death, President Jimmy Carter awarded him the Medal of Freedom, the United States' highest civilian tribute. Reflecting on that honor, Baldwin expressed the philosophy he had lived by all his life: "Never yield your courage—your courage to live, your courage to fight, to resist, to develop your own lives, to be free." It is clear that Baldwin never yielded his courage, and that he remained to the end a dauntless crusader for freedom and liberty for all U.S. citizens.

**BIOGRAPHY**

CULVER PICTURES

*Simeon Eben Baldwin*

"EDUCATION, IF IT BE REAL, IS ONE OF THE GREAT GIFTS OF LIFE."

**CROSS-REFERENCES**

American Civil Liberties Union; Communism; First Amendment; Freedom of Speech; Japanese-American Evacuation Cases; Sacco (Nicolo) and Vanzetti (Bartolomeo); Scopes, John T.

**BALDWIN, SIMEON EBEN** Simeon Eben Baldwin was born February 5, 1840. He earned a bachelor of arts degree from Yale in 1861, received a master of arts degree in 1864, and then pursued legal studies at Yale and Harvard. Four honorary doctor of laws degrees were bestowed upon him: by Harvard in 1891; Columbia, in 1911; Wesleyan, in 1912; and Yale, in 1916.

Baldwin was admitted to the bar in 1863. In 1869 he returned to Yale to teach at the Yale Law School until 1919, when he became professor emeritus.

In 1893, Baldwin entered the judiciary, presiding as associate justice of the Supreme Court of Errors of Connecticut until 1907 and as chief justice until 1910. From 1910 to 1914, Baldwin was governor of Connecticut.

Baldwin contributed to the formulation of many areas of Connecticut law. He was instrumental in amending the general statutes of Connecticut as well as the system of taxation.

Baldwin wrote numerous publications, including *A Digest of All the Reported Cases of Connecticut* (1871–72); *Modern Political Institutions* (1898); *American Railroad Law* (1904); *The American Judiciary* (1905); *The Relations of Education to Citizenship* (1912); and *The Young Man and the Law* (1919).

He died January 30, 1927, in New Haven, Connecticut.

**BALLINGER, WILLIAM PITT** William Pitt Ballinger achieved prominence as a distinguished Texas lawyer, which earned him the name the "Nestor of the Texas bar."

Ballinger was born in 1825 in Barbourville, Kentucky. From 1840 to 1841 Ballinger attended St. Mary's College, then began to study law on his own. His father was clerk of the courts of Knox County and hired the young Ballinger to work as a deputy clerk and gain more legal background.

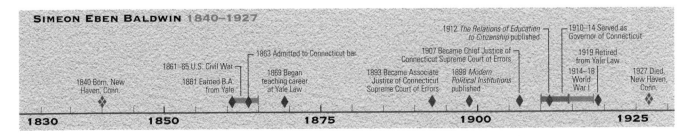

SIMEON EBEN BALDWIN 1840–1927

1840 Born, New Haven, Conn.

1861–65 U.S. Civil War

1861 Earned B.A. from Yale

1863 Admitted to Connecticut bar

1869 Began teaching career at Yale Law

1893 Became Associate Justice of Connecticut Supreme Court of Errors

1898 *Modern Political Institutions* published

1907 Became Chief Justice of Connecticut Supreme Court of Errors

1912 *The Relations of Education to Citizenship* published

1910–14 Served as Governor of Connecticut

1914–18 World War I

1919 Retired from Yale Law

1927 Died, New Haven, Conn.

1830    1850    1875    1900    1925

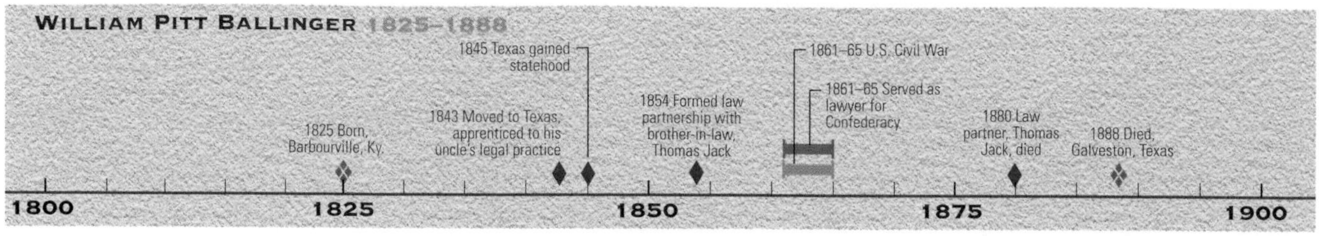

WILLIAM PITT BALLINGER 1825–1888
1825 Born, Barbourville, Ky.
1843 Moved to Texas, apprenticed to his uncle's legal practice
1845 Texas gained statehood
1854 Formed law partnership with brother-in-law, Thomas Jack
1861–65 U.S. Civil War
1861–65 Served as lawyer for Confederacy
1880 Law partner, Thomas Jack, died
1888 Died, Galveston, Texas
1800
1825
1850
1875
1900


**BIOGRAPHY**

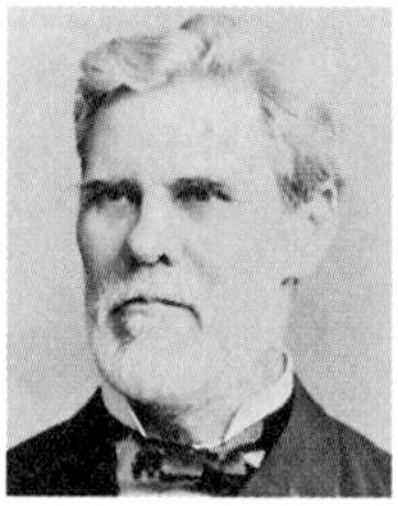

*William Pitt Ballinger*

"THE NATIONAL GOVERNMENT MAY BE REESTABLISHED—THE POLITICAL UNION MAY BE PERPETUATED, BUT IF SO, IT WILL BE BY FORCE."

In 1843 Ballinger moved to Texas and resided with an uncle who was a practitioner. Ballinger acted as his uncle's apprentice before serving a tour of military duty in the Mexican War. After Texas was admitted to the Union in 1845, and Ballinger returned from the war in 1846, he was one of the first to be licensed to practice law in the new state.

Ballinger married into a prominent Texas family in 1850 and in 1854 formed a law firm in Galveston with his new brother-in-law, Thomas M. Jack. Their partnership, which ended in 1880, the year of Jack's death, was highly regarded throughout the South, particularly in cases dealing with land claims.

In 1854 Ballinger sought interstate business for his firm, and traveled to New York, Boston, and Philadelphia. The trip was successful, and the firm began to specialize and earn a reputation in corporate law.

As hostilities increased in the South during the pre-Civil War days, Ballinger proclaimed his support of the Union; he favored slavery, but not secession. When Texas seceded, however, Ballinger supported his state.

Ballinger served the Confederacy as a lawyer as well as a receiver of enemy property. The Sequestration Act provided for the seizure and sale of such property, the proceeds of which were deposited into a special Confederate treasury.

After the war, Ballinger reached the peak of his success as an eminent corporate lawyer and was considered for a seat on the United States Supreme Court. He died January 20, 1888, in Galveston, Texas.

**BALLOON PAYMENT** The final INSTALLMENT of a loan to be paid in an amount that is disproportionately larger than the regular installment.

When a loan is made, repayment of the PRINCIPAL, which is the amount of the loan, plus the INTEREST that is owed on it, is divided into installments due at regular intervals—for example, every month. The earlier installments are usually payment of interest and a minimal amount of principal, while the later installments are primarily principal. When a balloon payment is provided in a loan agreement there are a number of installments for the same small amount prior to the balloon payment.

People with irregular or seasonal sources of income find a balloon payment provision in a loan useful for budgeting their expenses. This is not the case, however, for the average consumer. Frequently, a consumer is persuaded to enter a loan agreement providing a balloon payment that otherwise would be unwise for her or him. The consumer underestimates the full effect that the balloon payment will have on his or her budget by focusing on the small amounts to be repaid during the early stages of the loan. It is not uncommon for a consumer to be unable to pay the balloon payment when it is due. The consumer is presented with a dilemma: either the consumer must return the item bought with the loan to the lender, thereby losing the money paid out in earlier installments, or the consumer can refinance by taking out an additional loan to use its proceeds to pay the balloon payment.

A balloon payment provision in a loan is not illegal per se. Federal and state legislatures have enacted various laws designed to protect consumers from being victimized by such a loan. The Federal Truth in Lending Act (15 U.S.C.A. § 1601 et seq.) requires that a balloon payment—defined as an amount more than twice the size of a regularly scheduled equal installment—must be disclosed to the consumer. The consumer must be informed if refinancing is permitted and, if so, under what conditions. A CREDITOR who fails to disclose such information can be held liable to the consumer for twice the amount of the FINANCE CHARGE, in addition to the costs incurred by the consumer in bringing a lawsuit. He or she can also be prosecuted and subject to a fine of up to $5,000, one year's imprisonment, or both.

Some states restrict the use of balloon payments to loans involving consumers with irregular or seasonal incomes. Those states that have enacted the provisions of the UNIFORM CONSUMER CREDIT CODE do not limit the use of balloon payments, but they give the consumer the right to refinance the amount of such payment without penalty at terms no more than those in the original loan agreement.

A *balloon note* is the name given to a PROMISSORY NOTE in which repayment involves a balloon payment. A *balloon mortgage* is a written instrument that exchanges REAL PROPERTY as security for the repayment of a DEBT, the last installment of which is a balloon payment, frequently all the principal of the debt. MORTGAGES with balloon payment provisions are prohibited in some states.

### CROSS-REFERENCES

Consumer Credit Protection Act; Consumer Protection; Truth-in-Lending Act.

**BANC** [*French, Bench.*] The location where a court customarily or permanently sits.

When a court is sitting in banc (or EN BANC), it means that a meeting or session of all the judges of a court is taking place. The usual purpose of sitting in banc is to hear arguments on DEMURRERS or MOTIONS for a new trial.

**BANKER'S LIEN** An enforceable right of a bank to hold in its possession any money or property belonging to a customer and to apply it to the repayment of any outstanding DEBT owed to the bank, provided that, to the bank's knowledge, such property is not part of a TRUST fund or is not already burdened with other debts.

**BANK FOR INTERNATIONAL SETTLEMENT** The Bank for International Settlement was established under the law of Switzerland. It also has legal capacity pursuant to the MUNICIPAL law of each of its member states, but it lacks international legal capacity. It was denied a specific international personality. The bank is, therefore, solely in the control of its members.

**BANK OF THE UNITED STATES** The American Revolutionary War resulted in the emergence of a new country faced with the task of establishing a fundamental basis for government embodying the principles of freedom for which the colonists had fought. The need for a sound financial system was most urgent, and this was remedied by the creation of the First Bank of the United States in 1791.

ALEXANDER HAMILTON, first U.S. secretary of the treasury, devised the original plan for the bank. It was argued that the Constitution did not empower Congress to institute such a bank, and that the bank was partial to commercial interests as opposed to those of farmers. Congress, nonetheless, endorsed the passage of the bank's CHARTER.

The bank, located in Philadelphia, began with ASSETS of $10 million, one-fifth of this money furnished by the federal government, the remainder provided by outside investors. Its affairs were administered by twenty-five directors. The bank's powers were limited to commercial enterprises, and loans were processed at six percent interest. The first bank performed well, but renewal of its charter in 1811 was thwarted by the argument against its constitutionality and by the opposition of agricultural workers. The First Bank of the United States closed for business in 1811 with a profit.

The need for a second national bank became apparent in 1816, after the War of 1812 catapulted the country into a financial crisis. However, the constitutionality of such a bank was still in dispute. In the case of *McCulloch v. Maryland*, the Supreme Court, in an opinion by Chief Justice John Marshall, held that Congress possessed the authority to create a national bank and that the states lacked the power to tax it (17 U.S. [4 Wheat.] 316, 4 L. Ed. 579 [1819]).

The new bank began on a grander scale, with capital amounting to $35 million. For the first three years it tottered on the verge of disaster under the mismanagement of its chief administrator, William Jones. When Jones left the bank in 1819, Langdon Cheeves assumed his duties, and the bank became sound. By the time Nicholas Biddle became president in 1823, the bank was functioning efficiently, and it remained a reliable system of finance for the next ten years.

In 1832, Biddle requested renewal of the charter, which was due to expire in 1836. The bank again met opposition by those who believed it had become too powerful. President

*Alexander Hamilton, the first U.S. secretary of the treasury, helped to establish the Bank of the United States in Philadelphia in 1791. The bank provided commercial loans.*

CULVER PICTURES

ANDREW JACKSON led the opposition, and the controversy became an issue in his presidential election campaign in 1832 against HENRY CLAY. Clay, an advocate of the bank, had encouraged Biddle to apply for the charter renewal earlier than necessary.

The reelection of Andrew Jackson sounded the death knell for the Second Bank of the United States. He rejected the renewal of the charter and in 1833 deposited federal monies into selected state banks, termed "pet banks." The loss of federal funds greatly crippled the effectiveness of the bank, and it closed in 1836, the year its charter expired.

### CROSS-REFERENCES
Marshall, John; *McCulloch v. Maryland*.

## BANKRUPTCY
A federally authorized procedure by which a DEBTOR—an individual, CORPORATION, or municipality—is relieved of total LIABILITY for its DEBTS by making court-approved arrangements for their partial repayment.

Once considered a shameful last resort, bankruptcy in the United States is emerging as an acceptable method of resolving serious financial troubles. A record one million individuals filed for bankruptcy protection in the United States in the peak year of 1992, and between 1984 and 1994 the number of personal bankruptcy filings doubled. Corporate bankruptcies are commonplace, particularly when corporations are the target of lawsuits, and even local governments seek debt relief through bankruptcy laws.

The goal of modern bankruptcy is to allow the debtor to have a "fresh start," and the CREDITOR to be repaid. Through bankruptcy, debtors LIQUIDATE their ASSETS or restructure their finances to fund their debts. Bankruptcy law provides that individual debtors may keep certain exempt assets, such as a home, a car, and common household goods, thus maintaining a basic standard of living while working to repay creditors. Debtors are then better able to emerge productive members of society, albeit with significantly flawed CREDIT records.

### History of U.S. Bankruptcy Laws
U.S. bankruptcy laws have their roots in English laws dating from the sixteenth century. Early English laws punished debtors seeking to avoid their financial responsibilities, usually by imprisonment. Beginning in the eighteenth century, changing attitudes inspired the development of debt DISCHARGE. Courts began to nullify debts as a reward for the debtor's cooperation in trying to reduce them. The public increasingly viewed debtors with pity, as well as a realization that punishments such as imprisonment often were useless to creditors. Thus, a law at first designed to punish the debtor evolved into a law protecting the debtor while encouraging the resolution of outstanding monetary obligations.

England's eighteenth-century insight did not find its way into the first U.S. bankruptcy statutes; instead, laws based largely on England's earlier punitive bankruptcy statutes governed U.S. colonies. After the signing of the Declaration of Independence, individual states had their own laws addressing disputes between debtors and creditors, and these laws varied widely.

In 1789, the U.S. Constitution granted Congress the power to establish uniformity with a federal bankruptcy law, but more than a decade passed before Congress finally adopted the Bankruptcy Act of 1800. This act, like early bankruptcy laws in England, emphasized creditor RELIEF and did not allow debtors to file for relief voluntarily. Great public dissatisfaction prompted the act's repeal three years after its enactment.

Philosophical debates over whom bankruptcy laws should protect, debtor or creditor, had Congress struggling for the next forty years to pass uniform federal bankruptcy legislation. The passage of the Bankruptcy Act of 1841 offered debtors greater protections and for the first time allowed them the option of voluntarily seeking bankruptcy relief. This act lasted eighteen months. A third bankruptcy act passed in 1867 and was repealed in 1878.

The Bankruptcy Act of 1898 endured, thanks in part to numerous amendments, for eighty years, and became the basis for current bankruptcy laws. The 1898 act established bankruptcy courts and provided for bankruptcy trustees. Congress replaced this act with the Bankruptcy Reform Act of 1978 (11 U.S.C.A. § 101 et seq.), which, along with major amendments passed in 1984, 1986, and 1994, is known as the bankruptcy code.

### Federal versus State Bankruptcy Laws
In general, state laws govern financial obligations such as those involving debts created by CONTRACTS—rental leases, telephone service, and doctor bills, for example. But once a debtor or creditor seeks bankruptcy relief, federal law applies, overriding state law. This is because the U.S. Constitution grants Congress the power to "establish . . . uniform Laws on the subject of Bankruptcies throughout the United States" (U.S. Const. art. I, § 8). Federal bankruptcy power maintains uniformity among the states, encouraging interstate commerce

and promoting the country's economic stability. States retain JURISDICTION over certain debtor-creditor issues that do not conflict with, or are not addressed by, federal bankruptcy law.

**Types of Federal Bankruptcy Proceedings** Federal bankruptcy law provides two distinct forms of relief: LIQUIDATION, and REHABILITATION, also known as REORGANIZATION. The vast majority of bankruptcy filings in the United States involve liquidation, governed by chapter seven of the bankruptcy code. In a chapter seven *liquidation* case, a TRUSTEE collects the debtor's nonexempt assets and converts them into cash. The trustee then distributes the resulting fund to the creditors in order of priority described in the bankruptcy code. Creditors frequently receive only a portion, and sometimes none, of the money owed to them by the bankrupt debtor.

When the debtor is an individual, once the liquidation and distribution are complete, the bankruptcy court may discharge any remaining debt. When the debtor is a corporation, upon liquidation and distribution, the corporation becomes defunct. Remaining corporate debts are not formally discharged, as they are with individuals. Instead, creditors face the impossibility of pursuing debts against a corporation that no longer exists, making formal discharge unnecessary.

*Rehabilitation*, or *reorganization*, of debt is an option courts usually favor because it provides creditors with a better opportunity to recoup what is owed to them. Rehabilitative bankruptcies are governed most often by chapter eleven or chapter thirteen of the bankruptcy code. Chapter eleven typically applies to individuals with excessive or complex debts, or to large commercial entities such as corporations. Chapter thirteen typically applies to individual consumers with smaller debts.

Unlike liquidation, rehabilitation provides the debtor with an opportunity to retain nonexempt assets. In return, the debtor must agree to pay debts in strict accordance with a REORGANIZATION PLAN approved by the bankruptcy court. During this repayment period, creditors are unable to pursue debts beyond the provisions of the reorganization plan. This gives the debtor the chance to restructure affairs in the effort to meet financial obligations.

To be eligible for rehabilitative bankruptcy, the debtor must have sufficient income to make a reorganization plan feasible. If the debtor fails to comply with the reorganization plan, the bankruptcy court may order liquidation. A debtor who successfully completes the reorganization plan is entitled to a discharge of re-

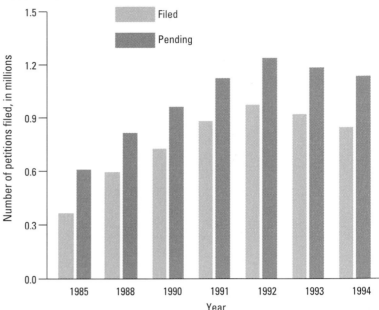

**Bankruptcy Petitions Filed and Pending, 1985 to 1994**

Source: Administrative Office of the U.S. Courts, *Annual Report of the Director.*

maining debts. In keeping with the general preference for bankruptcy rehabilitation rather than liquidation, the goal of this policy is to reward the conscientious debtor who works to help creditors by resolving his or her debts.

Farmers and municipalities may seek reorganization through the bankruptcy code's special chapters. Chapter twelve assists debt-ridden family farmers, who also may be entitled to relief under chapter eleven or chapter thirteen. When a local government seeks bankruptcy protection, it must turn to the debt reorganization provisions of chapter nine.

**Orange County Bankruptcy and Chapter Nine** Seldom used, chapter nine attained notoriety in late 1994 following the bankruptcy of Orange County, California, the largest MUNICIPAL bankruptcy in history. A county of 2.6 million people with one of the highest per capita incomes in the United States, Orange County held an investment fund comprised largely of derivatives based on an incorrect speculation on the direction of interest rates. The problem was made worse because they had borrowed the money they were investing. When interest rates began to climb in 1994, Orange County's LEVERAGED investments drained the investment fund's value, prompting lenders to require additional COLLATERAL. The only way to raise the collateral was to sell the investments at the worst possible time. The result was a $1.7 billion loss. After consulting with finance ex-

# GAMBLING WITH BANKRUPTCY EXEMPTIONS

In bankruptcy cases, individual debtors have the privilege of retaining certain amounts or types of property that otherwise would be subject to liquidation or seizure by creditors to satisfy debts. Laws protecting these forms of property are called exemptions.

Consistent with the goal of allowing the debtor a "fresh start," exemptions in bankruptcy cases help ensure that the debtor, upon emerging from bankruptcy, is not destitute. Exemption statutes generally permit the debtor to keep such things as a home, a car, and personal goods like clothes. Although exemptions inhibit the creditor's ability to collect debts, they relieve the state of the burden of providing the debtor's basic needs.

IN FOCUS

The bankruptcy code provides a list of uniform exemptions, but also allows individual states to *opt out of* (override) these exemptions (11 U.S.C.A. § 522 [1995]). Thus, the types and amounts of property exemptions differ greatly and depend upon the debtor's state of residence.

A debtor residing in a state that has not opted out is entitled to the exemptions described in the bankruptcy code. Examples of code exemptions are the debtor's aggregate interest of up to $15,000 in a home; up to $2,400 in a motor vehicle; up to $8,000 in household furnishings, household goods, clothes, appliances, books, animals, crops, and musical instruments; up to $1,000 in jewelry; up to $1,500 in professional books or tools of the debtor's trade; and certain unmatured life insurance policies owned by the debtor. The debtor also may claim an exemption for

professionally prescribed health aids, such as electric wheel-chairs.

The majority of states have chosen to opt out of the uniform federal exemptions, replacing them with exemptions created by their own legislatures. *Homestead exemptions*, which excuse all or part of the value in the debtor's home, are the most common state-mandated exemptions. These are not uniform across states. For instance: Missouri mimics the federal government by placing a dollar limit on the exemption—but at $8,000, its cap is meager in comparison (Mo. Ann. Stat. § 513.475 [Vernon 1995]). The bordering state of Iowa limits the homestead exemption by acreage rather than dollar amount (Iowa Code Ann. §§ 561.1, 561.2 [West 1994]). Florida allows a homestead exemption without limits (Fla. Const. art. X, § 4(a) (1)). This lack of uniformity raises the question of fairness: bankruptcy laws are federal in nature, yet a debtor in Florida may have a significant financial advantage over a debtor in Missouri, owing to different exemption laws.

Notwithstanding the broad variance among states when it comes to bankruptcy exemptions, critics charge that even the uniform federal system can be grossly unfair. For example, assume two debtors, Arlene and Ben, each have estates valued at $28,000. Arlene, a dentist, has $15,000 of equity in her home. She has $8,000 worth of furniture and household goods. Her car is worth $4,000, and she owns dental tools valued at $1,000.

Ben is an art lover. He owns no car,

no furniture, and no house, having chosen instead to spend his money on paintings and sculptures that are now worth $26,000. His clothes, musical instruments, and other household goods are worth $2,000.

Arlene and Ben have estates of equal value, but when the federal exemption statute is followed, Arlene can claim $27,200 in exemptions, whereas Ben can claim only $16,300: Arlene receives exemptions worth $15,000 for her homestead, $8,000 for her household goods, $2,400 for her car, and $1,000 for her dental tools, and an $800 general exemption for property not covered by other exemptions; Ben may claim an $8,000 exemption for his art and other household goods, as well as a general exemption worth $8,300, which replaces his unused homestead exemption.

Critics suggest that one problem with exemption laws is that legislators must determine the property that will best enable the average debtor to remain self-sufficient following a bankruptcy. Unconventional debtors, such as Ben, frequently are penalized as a result. In addition, laws that place monetary limits on exemptions often do nothing to help the debtor achieve a fresh start. When the value of certain property is worth more than the exemption, it is said to be only partially exempt, and must be completely liquidated. Following liquidation, the debtor receives the value of the exemption in cash from the liquidation proceeds. Thus, in the case of Arlene's $4,000 car, the bankruptcy trustee would sell the car and from the sale proceeds give Arlene $2,400, the amount of the exemption. Arlene could then spend the money on a tropical va-

perts and reviewing alternatives, county officials filed for chapter nine protection on December 6, 1994.

Residents of the affluent county faced immediate repercussions. Close to 10 percent of the fifteen thousand Orange County employees lost their jobs. School budgets were slashed, infrastructure improvements were put on hold, and experts predicted that property values in Or-

ange County would decline. Legal fees involved in a bankruptcy of this complexity are extensive, and officials did not expect Orange County to emerge from bankruptcy for several years.

Critics of current bankruptcy law argue that irresponsible debtors too frequently receive protection at the expense of noncreditors, such as the residents of Orange County. Victims who allege corporate NEGLIGENCE and sue for injuries cation instead of a replacement car, rendering the vehicle exemption law virtually meaningless.

Debtors may also take advantage of exemption laws by transferring assets before filing for bankruptcy protection. For example, Ben could sell nonexempt artwork and, with the proceeds, purchase a small condominium. He could then file for bankruptcy and claim a homestead exemption, increasing by $7,500 his postbankruptcy estate.

Congress actually supports this type of prebankruptcy planning, permitting the debtor "to make full use of the exemptions to which he is entitled under the law" (S. Rep. No. 989, 95th Cong., 2d Sess. [1978]). Still, courts view some prebankruptcy asset transfers as fraudulent, particularly when they involve large dollar amounts and there is evidence of an intent to hinder, delay, or defraud creditors. Upon a finding of fraud, the bankruptcy court may deny discharge of the debtor's debts. But what constitutes a fraudulent transfer is often unclear and seemingly arbitrary.

Two bankruptcy cases from Minnesota exemplify the confusion surrounding fraudulent and nonfraudulent prebankruptcy transfers. The debtors in both cases were doctors who lost money in the same investment and who hired the same attorney to help them with their prebankruptcy planning. The outcomes of the cases differed significantly.

Before filing for bankruptcy, Omar Tveten liquidated most of his nonexempt assets, including his home. With the proceeds, he purchased life insurance and annuities valued at almost $700,000. Both the life insurance and the annuities were considered exempt under Minnesota law; however, the bankruptcy court held that the large amount converted was an indication of fraud and therefore refused to discharge

Tveten's bankruptcy debts (*Norwest Bank Nebraska v. Tveten*, 848 F.2d 871 [8th Cir. 1988]).

Robert J. Johnson also transferred assets before filing for bankruptcy. Johnson converted nonexempt property into property exempt under Minnesota law: he purchased $8,000 in musical instruments, $4,000 in life insurance, and $250,000 in annuities from fraternal organizations, and he retired (paid off) $175,000 of the debt on his $285,000 home. The court focused on Johnson's claim for homestead exemption, and in particular the $175,000 mortgage payment made just before filing for bankruptcy. As the court in *Tveten* demonstrated, an unusually large asset transfer can indicate fraud. But in *Johnson*, the court held that the homestead exemption was valid, stating that the value of an asset transfer to homestead property, unlike the value of an asset transfer to property in another exemption category, is of little relevance because "no exemption is more central to the legitimate aims of state lawmakers than a homestead exemption" (*Panuska v. Johnson*, 880 F.2d 78 [8th Cir. 1989]).

Legal commentators have criticized the *Tveten* and *Johnson* decisions as being arbitrary, and providing no clear lines to assist debtors in prebankruptcy planning. Critics charge that the different outcomes are simply a result of different judges presiding at the initial bankruptcy court level, because the facts of the cases were so similar. Bankruptcy attorneys are frustrated by a lack of uniformity among court decisions that apply similar principles but reach different results, and also a lack of uniformity in exemption laws among states.

Indeed, *forum shopping* (searching out the most advantageous jurisdiction in which to file for bankruptcy) is preva-

lent because of the wide diversity of state exemption laws. *In re Coplan*, 156 B.R. 88 (Bankr. M.D. Fla. 1993), illustrates the problem. The debtors, Lee Coplan and Rebecca Coplan, incurred substantial debt in their home state of Wisconsin before moving to Florida. After residing in Florida for one year and purchasing a house for $228,000, they sought bankruptcy relief and a homestead exemption under Florida law (West's F.S.A. Const. Art. 10, § 4(a)(1)), which allows an exemption for the full value of the homestead. The court found that the Coplans had engaged in a systematic conversion of assets by selling their home in Wisconsin and paying cash for their new home in Florida. This was done, according to the court, solely for the purpose of placing the assets out of the reach of creditors. As a result, the bankruptcy court in Florida allowed a homestead exemption of only $40,000, the extent provided by Wisconsin law (W.S.A. 815.20(1)). Yet other bankruptcy decisions have held that a conversion of nonexempt property to exempt property for the purpose of placing such property out of reach of creditors will not alone deprive the debtor of the exemption (see, e.g., *In re Levine*, 139 B.R. 551 [Bankr. M.D. Fla. 1992]).

Exemption is an integral part of bankruptcy law, but a difficult area to navigate. Courts and legislatures must constantly determine whether exemptions constitute fair and just vehicles by which debtors can achieve a fresh start without getting a head start at the expense of creditors. Unfortunately for attorneys, debtors, creditors, and trustees, the laws regarding exemptions are inconsistent. Attempting to maximize the benefits granted by bankruptcy exemptions can be more of a gamble than a science.

---

from dangerous products also become unwilling creditors when the corporation files for bankruptcy. But negligent or not, corporations battling multiple lawsuits often rely on the traditional rationale supporting bankruptcy: that it offers an opportunity to pay debts that might otherwise go unpaid.

**Dow Corning Corporation and Chapter Eleven** Dow Corning Corporation was a ma-

jor manufacturer of silicone breast implants used in reconstructive and plastic surgeries. In 1991, after receiving thousands of complaints of health problems from women with silicone implants, the U.S. Food and Drug Administration banned the devices from widespread use. Women who had obtained the silicone implants in breast reconstruction or breast enlargement surgeries complained that the implants leaked, causing a variety of adverse conditions such as crippling pain, memory loss, lupus, and connective tissue disease. Dow Corning soon became a defendant in a worldwide product liability CLASS ACTION suit as well as at least nineteen thousand individual lawsuits.

Citing an inability to contribute $2 billion to a $4.2 billion settlement fund and pay for the defense of thousands of individual lawsuits, Dow Corning filed for chapter eleven bankruptcy protection in May 1995. The bankruptcy move halted new lawsuits and enabled the company to consolidate existing claims while preserving business operations. As a result of the filing, Dow Corning stalled its obligation to contribute to the settlement fund.

The Dow Corning strategy was similar to that employed in the mid-1980s by A. H. Robins Company, distributor of the Dalkon Shield intrauterine device for birth control. Like Dow Corning, A. H. Robins faced financial ruin owing to thousands of PRODUCT LIABILITY lawsuits filed at the same time. Also like Dow Corning, A. H. Robins sought relief under chapter eleven of the bankruptcy code, which allowed the company time to formulate a plan to pay the many outstanding claims. A reorganization plan approved by the courts involved the merger of A. H. Robins with American Home Products Corporation, which agreed to establish a $2.5 billion trust fund to pay outstanding product liability claims (*In re A. H. Robins Co.*, 880 F.2d 694 [4th Cir. 1989]).

On May 22, 1995, Dow Corning filed a request to stay all litigation against its parent companies, Dow Chemical Company and Corning Incorporated, so that company lawyers could concentrate on the bankruptcy reorganization. That move further threatened the chance of recovery for the plaintiffs seeking compensation for injury.

**Family Farmers and Chapter Twelve** In 1986, responding to an economic farm crisis in the United States, Congress designed chapter twelve to apply to family farmers whose aggregate debts did not exceed $1.5 million. Congress passed the law to help farmers attain a financial fresh start through reorganization rather than liquidation. Before chapter twelve's existence, family farmers found it difficult to meet the prerequisites of bankruptcy reorganization under chapter eleven or chapter thirteen, often because they were unable to demonstrate sufficient income to make a reorganization plan feasible. Chapter twelve eased some requirements for qualifying farmers.

Congress created chapter twelve as an experiment, and scheduled its automatic repeal for 1993. Determining that additional time was necessary to evaluate the effectiveness of the law, Congress in 1993 voted to extend it until 1998. Should lawmakers decide the law is beneficial, they may grant an additional extension or make chapter twelve a permanent part of the bankruptcy code.

**Federal Bankruptcy Jurisdiction and Procedure** Regardless of the type of bankruptcy and the parties involved, basic key jurisdictional and procedural issues affect every bankruptcy case. Procedural uniformity makes bankruptcies more consistent, predictable, efficient, and fair.

**Judges and Trustees** Pursuant to federal statute, U.S. courts of appeals appoint bankruptcy judges to preside over bankruptcy cases (28 U.S.C.A. § 152 [1995]). Bankruptcy judges make up a unit of the federal district courts called bankruptcy court. Actual jurisdiction over bankruptcy matters lies with the district court judges, who then refer the matters to the bankruptcy court unit and the bankruptcy judges.

A trustee is appointed to conduct an impartial ADMINISTRATION of the bankrupt's nonexempt assets, known as the bankruptcy estate. The trustee represents the bankruptcy estate, which upon the filing of bankruptcy becomes a legal entity separate from the debtor. The trustee may sue or be sued on behalf of the estate. Other trustee powers vary depending on the type of bankruptcy, and can include challenging transfers of estate assets, selling or liquidating assets, objecting to the claims of creditors, and objecting to the discharge of debts. All bankruptcy cases except chapter eleven cases require trustees, who are most commonly private citizens elected by creditors or appointed by the U.S. trustee.

The office of the U.S. trustee, permanently established in 1986, is responsible for overseeing the administration of bankruptcy cases. The U.S. attorney general appoints a U.S. trustee to each bankruptcy region. It is the job of the U.S. trustee in some cases to appoint trustees, and in all cases to ensure that trustees administer bankruptcy estates competently and honestly. U.S. trustees also monitor and report debtor abuse and FRAUD, and oversee certain debtor activity such as the filing of fees and reports.

**Procedures** Today, debtors file the vast majority of bankruptcy cases. A bankruptcy filing by a debtor is known as *voluntary bankruptcy*. The mere filing of a voluntary petition for bankruptcy operates as a judicial order for relief, and allows the debtor immediate protection from creditors without the necessity of a HEARING or other formal adjudication.

Chapter seven and chapter eleven of the bankruptcy code allow creditors the option of filing for relief against the debtor, also known as *involuntary bankruptcy*. The law requires that before a debtor can be subjected to involuntary bankruptcy, there must be a minimum number of creditors or a minimum amount of debt. Further protecting the debtor is the right to file a response, or ANSWER, to the ALLEGATIONS in the creditors' petition for involuntary bankruptcy. Unlike voluntary bankruptcies, which allow relief immediately upon the filing of the petition, involuntary bankruptcies do not provide creditors with relief until the debtor has had an opportunity to respond and the court has determined that relief is appropriate.

When the debtor timely responds to an involuntary bankruptcy filing, the court will grant relief to the creditors and formally place the debtor in bankruptcy only under certain circumstances, such as when the debtor generally is failing to pay debts on time. When, after litigation, the court dismisses an involuntary bankruptcy filing, the court may order the creditors to pay the debtor's attorney fees, COMPENSATORY DAMAGES for loss of property or loss of business, or PUNITIVE DAMAGES. This reduces the likelihood that creditors will file involuntary bankruptcy petitions frivolously or abusively.

One of the most important rights a debtor in bankruptcy receives is called the automatic STAY. The *automatic stay* essentially freezes all debt-collection activity, forcing creditors and other interested parties to wait for the bankruptcy court to resolve the case equitably and evenhandedly. The relief is automatic, taking effect as soon as a party files a bankruptcy petition. In a voluntary chapter seven case, the automatic stay gives the trustee time to collect, and then distribute to creditors, property in the bankruptcy estate. In voluntary chapter eleven and chapter thirteen cases, the automatic stay gives the debtor time to establish a plan of financial reorganization. In involuntary bankruptcy cases, the automatic stay gives the debtor time to respond to the petition. The automatic stay terminates once the bankruptcy court dismisses, discharges, or otherwise terminates the bankruptcy case, but a *party in interest* (a party with a valid claim against the bankruptcy estate) may petition the court for relief from the automatic stay by showing good cause.

The bankruptcy code allows bankruptcy judges to dismiss bankruptcy cases when certain conditions exist. The debtor, the creditor, or another interested party may ask the court to dismiss the case. Petitioners—debtors in a voluntary case, or creditors in an involuntary case—may seek to withdraw their petitions. In some types of bankruptcy cases, a petitioner's right to dismissal is absolute; other types of bankruptcy cases require a hearing and judicial approval before the case is dismissed. Particularly with voluntary bankruptcies, creditors, the court, or the U.S. trustee has the power to terminate bankruptcy cases when the debtor engages in dilatory or uncooperative behavior, or when the debtor substantially abuses the rights granted under bankruptcy laws.

**Recent Developments in Federal Bankruptcy Law** Brought about by a surge in bankruptcy filings and public concern over inequities in the system, the Bankruptcy Reform Act of 1994 is one illustration of Congress's continuing effort to protect the rights of both debtors and creditors. Consistent with Congress's goal of promoting reorganization over liquidation, the legislation made it easier for individual debtors to qualify for chapter thirteen reorganization. Previously, individuals with more than $450,000 in debt were not eligible to file under chapter thirteen, and instead were forced to reorganize under the more complex and expensive chapter eleven or to liquidate under chapter seven. The 1994 amendments allow debtors with up to $1 million in outstanding financial obligations to reorganize under chapter thirteen.

The new law helps creditors by prohibiting the discharge of credit card debts used to pay federal taxes, or those exceeding $1,000 incurred within sixty days before the bankruptcy filing. In this way, the law deters debtors from shopping sprees and other abuses just before filing for bankruptcy. Creditors also benefit from new provisions that set forth additional grounds for obtaining relief from the automatic stay, and require speedier adjudication of requests for relief from the stay.

See also PETITION IN BANKRUPTCY.

**BANKS AND BANKING** Authorized financial institutions and the business in which they engage, which encompasses the receipt of money for deposit, to be payable according to the terms of the account; collection of checks presented for payment; issuance of loans to individuals who meet certain requirements; discount of commercial paper; and other money-related functions.

Banks have existed since the founding of the United States, and their operation has been shaped and refined by major events in U.S. history. Banking was a rocky and fickle enterprise, with periods of economic fortune and peril, between the 1830s and the early twentieth century. In the late nineteenth century, the restrained money policies of the U.S. Department of the TREASURY, namely an unwillingness to issue more bank notes to eastern-based national banks, contributed to a scarcity of cash in many midwestern states. A few states went so far as to charter local banks and authorize them to print their own money. The COLLATERAL or capital that backed these local banks was often of only nominal value. By the 1890s, there was a full-fledged bank panic. Depositors rushed to banks to withdraw their money, only to find in many cases that the banks did not have the money on hand. This experience prompted insurance reforms that developed during the next fifty years. The lack of a regulated money supply led to the passage of the Federal Reserve Act in 1913 (found in scattered sections of 12 U.S.C.A.), creating the FEDERAL RESERVE Bank System.

Even as the banks sometimes suffered, there were stories of economic gain and wealth made through their operation. Industrial enterprises were sweeping the country, and their need for financing was seized upon by men like J. P. Morgan (1837–1913). Morgan made his fortune as a banker and financier of various projects. His House of Morgan was one of the most powerful financial institutions in the world. Morgan's holdings and interests included railroads, coal, steel, and steamships. His

involvement in what we now consider commercial banking and SECURITIES would later raise concern over the appropriateness of mixing these two industries, especially after the stock market crash of 1929 and the ensuing instability in banking. Between 1929 and 1933, thousands of banks failed. By 1933, President FRANKLIN D. ROOSEVELT had temporarily closed all U.S. banks because of a widespread lack of confidence in the institutions. These events played a major role in the Great Depression and in the future reform of banking.

In 1933, Congress held hearings on the commingling of the banking and securities industries. Out of these hearings, a reform act that strictly separated commercial banking from securities banking was created (12 U.S.C.A. §§ 347a, 347b, 412). The act became known as the GLASS-STEAGALL ACT, after the two senators who sponsored it, Carter Glass (D-Va.) and Henry B. Steagall (D-Ala.). The Glass-Steagall Act also created the FEDERAL DEPOSIT INSURANCE CORPORATION (FDIC), which insures money deposited at member banks against loss. Since its passage, Glass-Steagall has been the law of the land, with minor fine-tuning on several occasions.

Despite the Glass-Steagall reforms, periods of instability have continued to reappear in the banking industry. Between 1982 and 1987, about six hundred banks failed in the United

*A bank panic in the late nineteenth century prompted one illustrator to speculate on why deposits were not available to ordinary bank customers.*

States. Over one-third of the closures occurred in Texas. Many of the failed banks closed permanently, with their customers' deposits compensated by the FDIC; others were taken over by the FDIC and reorganized and eventually reopened.

**Categories of Banks**   There are two main categories of banks: federally chartered national banks and state-chartered banks.

A national bank is incorporated and operates under the laws of the United States, subject to the approval and oversight of the comptroller of the currency, an office established as a part of the Department of the Treasury in 1863 by the National Bank Act (12 U.S.C.A. §§ 21, 24, 38, 105, 121, 141 note).

All national banks are required to become members of the Federal Reserve System. The Federal Reserve, established in 1913, is a central bank with twelve regional district banks in the United States. The Federal Reserve creates and implements national fiscal policies affecting nearly every facet of banking. The system assists in the transfer of funds, handles government deposits and DEBT issues, and regulates member banks to achieve uniform commercial procedure. The Federal Reserve regulates the availability and cost of CREDIT, through the buying and selling of securities, mainly government BONDS. It also issues Federal Reserve notes, which account for almost all the paper money in the United States.

A board of governors oversees the work of the Federal Reserve. This board was approved in 1935 and replaced the Federal Reserve Board. The seven-member board of governors is appointed to fourteen-year terms by the president of the United States with Senate approval.

Each district reserve bank has a board of directors with nine members. Three nonbankers and three bankers are elected to each board of directors by the member bank, and three directors are named by the Federal Reserve Board of Governors.

A member bank must keep a reserve (a specific amount of funds) deposited with one of the district reserve banks. The reserve bank then issues Federal Reserve notes to the member bank or credits its account. Both methods provide stability in meeting customers' needs in the member bank.

One major benefit of belonging to the Federal Reserve System is that deposits in member banks are automatically insured by the FDIC. The FDIC protects each account in a member bank for up to $100,000 should the bank become insolvent.

A state-chartered bank is granted authority by the state in which it operates and is under the regulation of an appropriate state agency. Many state-chartered banks also choose to belong to the Federal Reserve System, thus ensuring coverage by the FDIC.

Banks that are not members of the Federal Reserve System can still be protected by the FDIC if they can meet certain requirements and if they submit an application.

The Interstate Banking and Branching Efficiency Act of 1994 (scattered sections of 12 U.S.C.A.) elevated banking from a regional enterprise to a more national pursuit. Previously, a nationally chartered bank had to obtain a CHARTER and set up a separate institution in each state where it wished to do business; the 1994 legislation removed this requirement. Also, throughout the 1980s and the early 1990s, a number of states passed laws that allowed for reciprocal interstate banking. This trend resulted in a patchwork of regional compacts between various states, most heavily concentrated in the New England states.

**Types of Banks**   The term *bank* is generally used to refer to commercial banks; however, it can also be used to refer to savings institutions, savings and loan associations, and building and loan associations.

A commercial bank is authorized to receive demand deposits (payable on order) and time deposits (payable on a specific date), lend money, provide services for FIDUCIARY funds, issue LETTERS OF CREDIT, and accept and pay DRAFTS. A commercial bank not only serves its depositors but also can offer INSTALLMENT loans, commercial long-term loans, and credit cards.

A savings bank does not offer as wide a range of services. Its primary goal is to serve its depositors through providing loans for purposes such as home improvement, MORTGAGES, and education. By law, a savings bank can offer a higher interest rate to its depositors than can a commercial bank.

A SAVINGS AND LOAN ASSOCIATION (S and L) is similar to a savings bank in offering savings accounts. It traditionally restricts the loans it makes to housing-related purposes including mortgages, home improvement, and construction, although, some S and Ls have entered into educational loans for their customers. An S and L can be granted its charter by either a state or the federal government; in the case of a federal charter, the organization is known as a federal savings and loan. Federally chartered S and Ls have their own system that functions in a manner similar to that of the Federal Reserve System, called the Federal Home Loan Banks

*A savings bank provides loans for home improvement, mortgages, and education, and can offer a higher interest rate to depositors than can a commercial bank. Savings banks are one of several types of banks that can be insured by the FDIC.*

that banks must maintain a minimum amount of capital. Banks acquire capital by selling CAPITAL STOCK to shareholders. The money shareholders pay for the capital stock becomes the working capital of the bank. The working capital is put in a trust fund to protect the bank's depositors. In turn, shareholders receive certificates that prove their ownership of STOCK in the bank. The working capital of a bank cannot be diminished. DIVIDENDS to shareholders must be paid only from the profits or surplus of the bank.

Shareholders have their legal relationship with a bank defined by the terms outlined in the CONTRACT to purchase capital stock. With the investment in a bank comes certain rights, such as the right to inspect the bank's books and records and the right to vote at shareholders' meetings. Shareholders may not personally sue a bank, but they can, under appropriate circumstances, bring a STOCKHOLDER'S DERIVATIVE SUIT on behalf of the bank (sue a third party for injury done to the bank when the bank fails to sue on its own). Shareholders also are not usually personally liable for the debts and acts of a bank, because the corporate form limits their LIABILITY. However, if shareholders have consented to or accepted benefits of unauthorized banking practices or illegal acts of the BOARD OF DIRECTORS, they are not immune from liability.

**Bank Officials** The election and term of office of a bank's board of directors are governed by statute or by the charter of the bank. The liabilities and duties of bank officials are prescribed by statute, charter, BYLAWS, customary banking practices, and employment contracts. Directors and bank officers are both responsible for the conduct and honorable management of a bank's affairs, although their duties and liabilities are not the same.

Officers and directors are liable to a bank for losses it incurs as a result of their illegal, fraudulent, or wrongful conduct. Liability is imposed for EMBEZZLEMENT, illegal use of funds or other ASSETS, false representation about the bank's condition made to deceive others, or fraudulent purchases or loans. The failure to exercise reasonable care in the execution of their duties also renders officials liable if such failure brings about bank losses. If such losses result from an error in judgment, liability will not be imposed so long as the officials acted in GOOD FAITH with reasonable skill and care. Officers and directors will not be held liable for the acts of their employees if they exercise caution in hiring qualified personnel and supervise them carefully. CIVIL ACTIONS against bank officials are

System. Like the Federal Reserve System, the Federal Home Loan Banks System provides an insurance program of up to $100,000 for each account; this program is called the Federal Savings and Loan Insurance Corporation (FSLIC). The Federal Home Loan Banks System also provides membership options for state-chartered S and Ls, and an option for just FSLIC coverage for S and Ls that can satisfy certain requirements.

A BUILDING AND LOAN ASSOCIATION is a special type of S and L that restricts its lending to home mortgages.

The distinctions between these financial organizations has become narrower as federal legislation has expanded the range of services that can be offered by each type of institution.

**Bank Financial Structure** Banks are usually incorporated, and like any CORPORATION must be backed by a certain amount of capital (money or other assets). Banking laws specify maintained in the form of stockholders' derivative suits. Criminal statutes determine the liability of officers and directors for illegal acts against their bank.

**Bank Duties** The powers and duties of a bank are determined by the terms of its charter and the legislation under which it was created (either federal or state regulations). A bank can, through its governing board, enact reasonable rules and regulations for the efficient operation of its business.

**Deposits** A deposit is a sum of money placed in an account to be held by a bank for the depositor. A customer can deposit money by cash or by a check or other document that represents cash. Deposits are how banks survive. The deposited money establishes a DEBTOR and CREDITOR relationship between the bank and the depositor. Most often, the bank pays the depositing customer INTEREST for its use of the money until the customer withdraws the funds. The bank has the right to impose rules and regulations managing the deposit, such as restrictions governing the rate of interest the deposited money will earn and guidelines for its withdrawal.

**Collections** A primary function of a bank is to make collections of items such as checks and drafts deposited by customers. The bank acts as an AGENT for the customer. Collection occurs when the DRAWEE bank (the bank ordered by the check to make payment) takes funds from the account of the DRAWER (its customer who has written the check) and presents it to the collecting bank.

**Checks** A CHECK is a written order made by a drawer to her or his bank to pay a designated person or organization (the PAYEE) the amount

*A primary function of a bank is to make collections of items such as checks and drafts deposited by customers.*

specified on the check. Payment pursuant to the check must be made in strict compliance with its terms. The drawer's account must be reduced by the amount specified on the check. A check is a demand instrument, which means it must be paid by the drawee bank on the demand of, or when presented by, the payee or the agent of the payee, the collecting bank.

A payee usually receives payment of a check upon endorsing it and presenting it to a bank in which the payee has an account. The bank can require the payee to present identification to prove a relationship with the bank, before cashing the check. It has no obligation to cash a check for a person who is not a depositor, since it can refuse payment to a stranger. However, it must HONOR (pay) a check if the payee has sufficient funds on deposit with the bank to cover the amount paid if the drawer of the check does not have adequate funds in his or her account to pay it.

A CERTIFIED CHECK is guaranteed by a bank, at the request of its drawer or endorser, to be cashable by the payee or succeeding holder. A bank is not obligated to certify a check, but it usually will do so for a customer who has sufficient funds to pay it, in exchange for a nominal fee. A certified check is considered the same as cash because any bank must honor it when the payee presents it for payment.

A drawer can revoke a check unless it has been certified or has been paid to the payee. The notice of revocation is often called a STOP PAYMENT ORDER. A check is automatically revoked if the drawer dies before it is paid or certified, since the drawer's bank has no authority to complete the transaction under that circumstance. However, if the drawer's bank does not receive notice of the drawer's death, it is not held liable for the payment or certification of that drawer's checks.

Upon request, a bank must return to the drawer all the checks it has paid, so that the drawer can inspect the canceled checks to ensure that no FORGERIES or errors have occurred, in adjusting the balance of her or his checking account. This review of checks is usually completed through the monthly statement. If the drawer finds an error or forgery, it is her or his obligation to notify the bank promptly or to accept full responsibility for whatever loss has been incurred.

***Bank liabilities*** A bank has a DUTY to know a customer's SIGNATURE and therefore is generally liable for charging the customer's account with a forged check. A bank can recover the loss from the forger but not from the person who in good faith and without knowledge of the crime gave something in exchange for the forged check. If the depositor's NEGLIGENCE was a factor in the forgery, the bank can be excused from the liability.

A bank is also responsible for determining the genuineness of the endorsement when a depositor presents a check for payment. A bank is liable if it pays a check that has been materially altered, unless the alteration was due to the drawer's fault or negligence. If a bank pays a check that has a forged endorsement, it is liable for the loss if it is promptly notified by the customer. In both cases, the bank is entitled to recover the amount of its loss from the thief or forger.

A drawee bank that is ordered to pay a check drawn on it is usually not entitled to recover payment it has made on a forged check. If, however, the drawee bank can demonstrate that the collecting bank was negligent in its collection duties, the drawee bank may be able to establish a right of recovery.

A bank can also be liable for the wrongful DISHONOR or refusal to pay of a check that it has certified, since by definition of certification it has agreed to become absolutely liable to the payee or holder of the check.

If a bank has paid a check that has been properly revoked by its drawer, it must reimburse the drawer for the loss.

*Drawer liabilities* A drawer who writes a check for an amount greater than the funds on deposit in his or her checking account is liable to the bank. Such a check, called an OVERDRAFT, sometimes results in a loan from the bank to the drawer's account for the amount by which the account is deficient, depending on the terms of the account. In this case, the drawer must repay the bank the amount lent plus interest. The bank can also decide not to provide the deficient funds and can refuse to pay the check, in which case the check is considered "bounced." The drawer then becomes liable to the bank for a handling fee for the check, as well as remaining liable to the payee or subsequent HOLDER of the check for the amount due. Many times, the holder of a returned, or bounced, check will impose another fee on the drawer.

**Loans and Discounts** A major function of a bank is the issuance of loans to applicants who meet certain qualifications. In a loan transaction, the bank and the debtor execute a PROMISSORY NOTE and a separate agreement in which the terms and conditions of the loan are detailed. The interest charged on the amount lent can differ based on many variables. One variable is a benchmark interest rate established by the Federal Reserve Bank Board of Governors,

also known as the prime rate, at the time the loan is made. Another variable is the length of repayment. The collateral provided to secure the loan, in case the borrower DEFAULTS, can also affect the interest rate. In any case, the interest rate must not exceed that permitted by law. The loan must be repaid according to the terms specified in the loan agreement. In case of default, the agreement determines the procedures to be followed.

Banks also purchase COMMERCIAL PAPERS, which are commercial loans, at a discount from creditors who have entered into long-term contracts with debtors. A creditor sells a commercial paper to a bank for less than its FACE VALUE because it seeks immediate payment. The bank profits from the difference between the discount price it paid and the face value of the bond, which it will receive when the debtor has finished repaying the loan. Types of commercial paper are educational loans and home mortgages.

**Electronic Banking** Many banks are replacing traditional checks and deposit slips with electronic fund transfer (EFT) systems, which utilize sophisticated computer technology to facilitate banking and payment needs. Routine banking by means of EFT is considered safer, easier, and more convenient for customers.

Many types of EFT systems are available, including automated teller machines; pay-by-phone systems; automatic deposits of regularly received checks, such as paychecks; automated payment of recurring bills; point-of-sale transfers or debit cards, where a customer gives a merchant a card and the amount is automatically transferred from the customer's account; and transfer and payment by customers' home computers.

When an EFT service is arranged, the customer receives an EFT card that will activate the system and the bank is legally required to disclose the terms and conditions of the account. These terms and conditions include the customer's liability and the notification process to follow if an EFT card is lost or stolen; the type of transactions in which a customer can take part; the procedure for correction of errors; and the extent of information that can be disclosed to a third party without improper infringement on the customer's PRIVACY. If a bank is planning to change the terms of an account—for example, by imposing a fee for transactions previously conducted free of charge—the customer must receive written notice before the change will be effective.

Banks must send account statements for EFT transactions on a monthly basis. The

*Electronic banking, including the use of automated teller machines, is replacing traditional banking methods in many areas.*

statements must have the amount, date, and type of transaction; the customer's account number; the account's opening and closing balances; charges for the transfers or for continuation of the service; and an address and telephone number for referral of account questions or mistakes.

EFT transactions have become a highly competitive area of banking, with banks offering various bonuses such as no fee for the use of a card when the account holder meets certain provisions such as maintaining a minimum balance. Also, the explosion of personal and home office computing has increased pressure on banks to provide services on-line. Several computer software companies produce technology that can complete many routine banking services, like automatic bill paying, at a customer's home.

Customers who engage in transactions at automated teller machines and in point-of-sale transfers must have access to RECEIPTS that identify the amount, date, and type of transfer; the customer's account number; the identity of the parties to the transaction; and the location of the terminal. No similar requirements exist for pay-by-phone transactions.

Banks have a wide range of options available to notify a customer that a check has been directly deposited into her or his account.

If a customer has arranged for automatic payment of regularly recurring bills, like mortgage or utility bills, the customer has a limited period of time, usually up to three days before the payment is made, in which to order the bank to stop payment. When the amounts of such bills vary, as with utility bills, the bank must notify the customer of the payment date in sufficient time so that there will be enough funds in the account to cover the debt.

If the customer discovers a mistake in an account, the bank must be notified orally or in writing after the erroneous statement is received. The bank must investigate the claim. Often, after several days, the customer's account will be temporarily recredited with the disputed amount. After the investigation is complete, the bank is required to notify the customer in writing if it concludes that no error occurred. It must provide copies of its decision and explain how it reached its findings. Then the customer must return the amount of the error if it was recredited to his or her account.

A customer is liable if an unauthorized transfer is made because an EFT card or other device is stolen, lost, or used without permission. This liability can be limited if the customer notifies the bank within two business days of the discovery of the misdeed; it is extended to $500 if the customer fails to comply with the notice requirement. A customer can assume unlimited liability if she or he fails to report any unauthorized charges to an account within a specified period after receiving the monthly statement.

A customer is entitled to sue a bank for COMPENSATORY DAMAGES caused by the bank's wrongful failure to perform the terms and conditions of an EFT account, such as refusing to pay a charge if the customer's account has more than adequate funds to do so. The customer can also recover a maximum penalty of $1,000, attorneys' fees, and costs in an action based upon violation of this law.

**Interstate Banking and Branching** In late 1994, the 103d Congress authorized significant reforms to interstate banking and branching law. The Interstate Banking Law (Pub. L. No. 103-328), also referred to as the Riegle-Neal Interstate Banking and Branching Efficiency Act of 1994, provided the banking industry with major legislative changes. The Interstate Banking Act was expected to accelerate the trend of bank MERGERS. These mergers are a benefit to the nation's largest banks, which will likely see savings of millions of dollars resulting from streamlining.

See also BANK OF THE UNITED STATES.

**BANKS, DENNIS** Native American activist, organizer, and protest leader Dennis Banks helped found the influential American Indian Movement (AIM). Under his passionate leadership in the late 1960s and early 1970s, AIM championed Native American self-sufficiency, traditions, and values. Its demand for federal recognition of century-old TREATY rights led to violent clashes with authorities, and the Federal Bureau of Investigation (FBI) branded AIM an extremist group. In turn, illegal actions by the FBI led to Banks's ACQUITTAL on charges stemming from his role in AIM's occupation of Wounded Knee, South Dakota, in 1973. While heightening national awareness of Native American issues, Banks faced prosecution several times. He spent nearly a decade as a criminal fugitive, receiving a form of political asylum in California from then governor Jerry Brown before surrendering in 1984 and serving a shortened prison term. Since 1978, Banks has led a Native American spiritual organization in Kentucky called Sacred Run.

Banks was born April 12, 1937, in Leech Lake, Minnesota. His difficult early life began during one of many periods of upheaval in federal policy regarding Native Americans. Like many Anishinabe Ojibwa, or Chippewa, children, he was sent at the age of five to schools operated by the federal Bureau of Indian Affairs (BIA), and he spent part of his

childhood being shuttled between boarding schools in North and South Dakota. The BIA managed such schools in accordance with a landmark change in federal policy known as the Indian Reorganization Act of 1934 (25 U.S.C.A. § 461 et seq.). Under the terms of this so-called new deal for Indians—a plan for tribal government that many traditional Native Americans had resisted—schools were to have been improved over those in previous decades that sought to Christianize or "civilize" their pupils. But the schools still deemphasized Native American culture by forbidding the speaking of the Ojibwa language, Lakota. Thus, like many of his generation, Banks lost his native tongue.

At the age of nineteen, Banks joined the U.S. Air Force and served in Japan. Discharged in the late 1950s, he returned to Minnesota, where he faced the same problems as do young Native American men in the 1990s: alienation from his culture, unemployment, poverty, alcoholism, and crime. "I was heading down a road that was filled with wine, whiskey and booze," Banks later recalled. "Then I landed in prison." In 1966, he was convicted for burglarizing a grocery store and began serving thirty-one months of a three-and-a-half-year sentence in Stillwater State Penitentiary, in Minnesota. In prison, Banks met fellow convict Clyde Bellecourt, also an Ojibwa. The two men and others founded AIM in July 1968 with several goals in mind. They wanted to address the problems that beset their people and find solutions to basic needs such as housing and employment. To help Native Americans live successfully off reservations, they would start so-called survival schools. But fundamentally, they wanted to preserve their vanishing culture. AIM's emblem was an upside-down U.S. flag, what Banks called the international distress signal for people in trouble.

When the first AIM chapter started in Minneapolis in 1968, Banks would often use a police radio to guide him to the scene when officers were arresting Native Americans. Intending to prevent police abuses, he was frequently arrested on charges of interference.

**BIOGRAPHY**

*Dennis Banks*

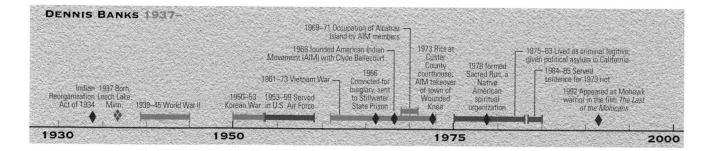

This kind of tough, streetwise advocacy helped spread the movement, making Banks, Bellecourt, and another AIM leader, Russell Means, heroes to many of their generation.

Over the next four years, the movement spread to all fifty states and to Canada. The organization's political message had widespread appeal for Native Americans who felt betrayed by the federal government's Indian Reorganization Act. Not only was this new deal perceived as no deal, but many believed that it opened the way for massive federal land grabs of Indian territory on which valuable minerals were located. Banks and his fellow leaders decided to reclaim former Indian territory, announcing that they would symbolically "retake the country from west to east" like the "wagon train in reverse."

The militancy of their claims was soon demonstrated. In its first act of protest, on November 4, 1969, AIM seized the abandoned federal prison on Alcatraz Island, in San Francisco Bay, California. Two hundred activists claimed the island as free Indian land and demanded that an educational and cultural center be established there. In ironic press statements, they announced the establishment of a Bureau of Caucasian Affairs, and offered to pay the U.S. government $24, in mockery of the 1626 purchase of Manhattan Island from Indians by Dutch settlers. The occupation, which lasted nineteen months, stirred up considerable publicity. The U.S. House of Representatives passed a JOINT RESOLUTION directing President Richard M. Nixon to negotiate with the activists, but his administration's offer to build a park on the island was laughed off. U.S. marshals ultimately arrested the activists remaining on the island in June 1971.

In April 1971, Banks led several AIM members in a week-long takeover of the Fort Snelling Military Base, in St. Paul. Seizing an abandoned building, the group announced that it intended to start an Indian survival school there. Senator Walter F. Mondale agreed to negotiate with Banks, but before he could, a federal Special Weapons and Tactics (SWAT) unit arrested the protesters. Around the United States, other occupations of government property took place as AIM chapters demonstrated against broken treaties. As a white backlash against the protests began, several Indians were beaten or shot. Charges of MANSLAUGHTER brought against white attackers usually ended in acquittal, inflaming the Indian movement. It maintained that little or no help was forthcoming from the BIA or the FBI.

In response, car caravans converged on Washington, D.C., on November 2, 1972, in a protest rally dubbed the Trail of Broken Treaties. AIM presented a twenty-point proposal demanding that the government revamp the BIA, recognize Indian SOVEREIGNTY, restore the power of Indians to negotiate treaties, and create a review board to study treaty violations. A group of four hundred protesters seized the BIA building; clashed with riot squads; and, renaming the facility the Native American Embassy, ransacked files that Banks said contained evidence of federal mistreatment of Indians. Banks told reporters, "We are trying to bring about some meaningful change for the Indian community. If this is the only action that will bring change, then you can count on demonstrations like this 365 days a year." On November 6, the Nixon White House agreed to negotiate. After two days, Banks's followers departed in return for the appointment of a special panel to investigate conditions on Indian reservations. But within a week after the takeover, federal funding was cut off for three of AIM's survival schools.

In early 1973, a turning point occurred in Banks's life and the direction of AIM. On February 6, he led an AIM protest two hundred strong in Custer, South Dakota, after a white man accused of killing an Indian in a barroom brawl was charged with INVOLUNTARY MANSLAUGHTER. Banks met with local officials, but when the slain man's mother, Sarah Bad Heart Bull, tried to enter the courthouse, she and other Native Americans were beaten by the police. A riot ensued, in which AIM members set fire to police cars and the chamber of commerce office. For his role in the Custer incident, Banks was charged with ARSON, BURGLARY, and MALICIOUS damage to a public building, all of which he denied. But his radicalization was complete. "We had reached a point in history where we could not tolerate the abuse any longer," Banks later explained, "where mothers could not tolerate the mistreatment that goes on on the reservations any longer, they could not see another Indian youngster die."

Three weeks later, Banks, Means, and other AIM members took over the town of Wounded Knee on the Pine Ridge Reservation in South Dakota. For Native Americans, the town has a bitter place in history: it is the site where, in 1890, three hundred unarmed Sioux men, women, and children were massacred by the Seventh Cavalry of the U.S. Army. Banks and Means hoped to invoke this symbolism by seizing the town by armed force and issuing new demands. They wanted the federal government to investigate the BIA and to address treaty violations, and they denounced recent tribal

"WHAT WE HAVE DONE, WE DID FOR THE SEVENTH GENERATION TO COME. . . . WE DID NOT DO THESE THINGS FOR OURSELVES . . . [BUT] SO THAT THE SEVENTH GENERATION MAY BE BORN FREE."

elections as corrupt manipulations by white U.S. citizens. As national attention focused on the growing army of some three hundred FBI agents and U.S. MARSHALS, and the armored personnel carriers surrounding the militants' fortifications, gunfire was frequently exchanged. Over seventy-one days, while the government ordered surrender without AMNESTY, the town was held. "We laid down our weapons at Wounded Knee," Banks told the press from within the stronghold, recalling the 1890 massacre. "Those weapons weren't just bows and guns, but also a sense of pride."

The takeover ended on May 9, 1973. Pentagon documents later revealed that the U.S. Army had readied a vast military arsenal to clear out AIM members, including over 170,000 rounds of ammunition, grenade launchers, explosives, gas, helicopters, and jets. In the end, however, casualties were limited: two Native Americans were killed and several wounded; three members of the government forces were wounded, including one agent who was paralyzed. As a condition of surrendering, AIM was once again promised a federal investigation of its demands, but none was forthcoming.

Banks and Means were prosecuted on ten FELONY counts each in a dramatic eight-month trial in St. Paul, during which federal marshals used Mace on courtroom spectators. The defendants alleged that their takeover of Wounded Knee was justified by the government's violations of the 1868 Treaty of Fort Laramie—a pact in which the Sioux Indians had been promised government protection for ending their armed resistance. But the case against Means and Banks foundered on revelations that the FBI had used illegal wiretaps and had changed documents, among other illegalities, in mounting its prosecution. On September 16, 1974, all charges were dismissed.

Although Banks acted as a negotiator during the mid-1970s, settling disputes between Native Americans and authorities, other aspects of his life soon changed for the worse. In July 1975, a South Dakota jury convicted him on charges of RIOT and ASSAULT with a deadly weapon for his role in the 1973 riot at the Custer County Courthouse. The conviction carried a maximum sentence of fifteen years in prison. Before sentencing, Banks heard prison guards say he would not last twenty minutes in the South Dakota State Penitentiary. He fled, only to be arrested by FBI agents on January 23, 1976, in northern California. A massive petition movement supported by the actors Jane Fonda and Marlon Brando appealed to Gover-

nor Brown on Banks's behalf. Brown reduced Banks's bail, refused EXTRADITION requests from South Dakota, and informed authorities there that he was protecting Banks because of sworn statements that Banks's life would be endangered if he were imprisoned. Banks lived freely in California, serving as chancellor of the two-year Indian college Deganawidah-Quetzalcoatl University, until the 1983 inauguration of Republican governor George Deukmejian ended his asylum.

Banks then took sanctuary on the Onondaga Reservation in New York. Because reservations in the state are not under federal JURISDICTION, the FBI chose not to arrest him as long as he remained there.

After nine years of life as a FUGITIVE, Banks gave himself up to state authorities in South Dakota in fall 1984. His request for CLEMENCY was denied, and he was sentenced to three years in prison. After his PAROLE on December 9, 1985, he spent time on the Pine Ridge Reservation, where, through his success at persuading Honeywell and other companies to locate factories there, employment doubled. But his legal troubles continued. Banks had been charged with illegal possession of dynamite stemming from the 1975 arrest of his wife, Kamook Nichols. A lower court dismissed the charges in 1983 on the ground that Banks and three other defendants had been denied their SIXTH AMENDMENT right to a SPEEDY TRIAL, and a second federal court upheld the ruling. But on January 21, 1986, the members of the U.S. Supreme Court, in a 5–4 vote, held that their rights had not been violated, because they were free without BAIL and not under INDICTMENT during the ninety-month delay in their prosecution. Banks pleaded guilty on March 8, 1988, and received five years' PROBATION.

Banks continued to serve as director of Sacred Run, an organization he founded in 1978 to address Native American spiritual concerns. He led "spiritual runs," cross-country treks in the United States, Canada, Europe, and Japan. In 1992, he appeared as a Mohawk warrior in the film *The Last of the Mohicans.* Remaining active in politics, he worked on behalf of the imprisoned Ojibwa Leonard Peltier, convicted in 1977 of the murder of two FBI agents. With AIM no longer a force on reservations, Banks looked back on the accomplishments of his movement: "The awareness of [Indians] by non-Indians has grown and the mood of the country has changed—even though the bureaucracy still controls federal Indian policy."

## BAR ASSOCIATION 📖 An organization of lawyers established to promote professional competence, enforce standards of ethical conduct, and encourage a spirit of public service among members of the legal profession. 📖

The mission of a bar association is frequently described in the words of Roscoe Pound, legal scholar and dean of Harvard Law School from 1916 to 1936: "[T]o promote and maintain the practice of law as a profession, that is, as a learned art pursued in the spirit of a public service—in the spirit of a service of furthering the administration of justice through and according to law."

Bar associations accomplish these objectives by offering continuing education for lawyers in the form of publications and seminars. This education includes instruction on recent developments in the law and in managing a law practice successfully as a business. Bar associations encourage members to offer pro bono legal services (to provide legal services at no cost to members of society who cannot afford them). Bar associations develop guidelines and rules relating to ETHICS and professional responsibility and enforce SANCTIONS for violation of rules governing lawyer conduct. Bar associations also offer ATTORNEYS the opportunity to meet socially to discuss employment prospects and legal theories.

The International Bar Association, based in London, is for lawyers and law firms involved in the practice of international law. In the United States, bar associations exist on the national, state, and local levels. Examples are the AMERICAN BAR ASSOCIATION (ABA) and the FEDERAL BAR ASSOCIATION on the national level, the New Jersey State Bar Association and the Florida Bar Association on the state level, and the New York City Bar Association on the local level. Some law schools have what they call student bar associations for the student body as a whole, and distinct, smaller bar associations for students with a common ethnic background or an interest in a specific area of practice.

In thirty-one states, membership in the state bar association is mandatory for those licensed to practice law. In the remaining nineteen states, membership in the state bar association is voluntary. When lawyers are required to join the bar in order to practice law, the bar is said to be integrated, or unified. Integration is gen-erally accomplished by the enactment of a statute giving the highest court of the state the authority to integrate the bar, or by rule of that court in the exercise of its inherent power. In effect, lawyers are not free to resign from an INTEGRATED BAR, because by doing so, they lose the privilege to practice law.

The modern U.S. bar association traces its beginnings to the midnineteenth century. At that time, the practice of law was largely unregulated. People in need of legal services had no assurance that the lawyers they hired had had even minimum legal training. To address this situation, leaders of the legal profession began to organize self-governing bar associations to establish standards of education and of professional conduct. The first Code of Professional Ethics was formulated by the Alabama State Bar Association in 1887. The American Bar Association (ABA) Canons of Professional Ethics followed, in 1908, and were subsequently adopted in whole or in part throughout the United States. These canons were revised and expanded in 1969, as the Model Code of Professional Ethics, and again in 1983, as the Model Rules of Professional Conduct.

Among the major issues of concern to bar associations in the 1990s are the following:

- A perceived decline in professionalism among lawyers, manifested by a decline in civility and professional courtesy.
- A conflict between lawyers' ethical responsibilities and their business interests. Critics within and outside the legal profession complain that some lawyers seek out clients using unethical methods, and engage in litigation of questionable merit in the pursuit of personal profit rather than in the interests of justice.
- The politicization of bar associations. On some occasions, bar associations have taken positions on hotly contested social and political issues. Critics argue that the conflict within the membership over these issues distracts bar associations from their primary duty of regulating the practice of law.

## BARBOUR, PHILIP PENDLETON Philip Pendleton Barbour, an associate justice of the U.S. Supreme Court, was a strong advocate of STATES' RIGHTS and the STRICT CONSTRUCTION of the Constitution.

The son of a wealthy planter from one of Virginia's oldest families, Barbour was born May 25, 1783, in Orange County, Virginia. He was educated locally and excelled in languages and classical literature. At seventeen, he became an apprentice to an Orange County lawyer. After less than a year clerking and studying law,

Barbour left Virginia for Kentucky, where he practiced law for a short time. In 1801, he returned to Virginia to attend the College of William and Mary, in Williamsburg, where he briefly studied law. A year later, he established a law practice in Orange County, and quickly gained a reputation for his outstanding oratorical abilities in the courtroom. In 1804, he married Frances Johnson, the daughter of a local planter, with whom he had seven children.

Barbour's family was both socially prominent and politically active. His father, Thomas Barbour, was a member of the Virginia House of Burgesses for many years, and his older brother became a Virginia governor, U.S. senator, and secretary of war under President JOHN QUINCY ADAMS, whose administration Barbour would eventually oppose. Encouraged by his father's and brother's successes, in 1812 Barbour ran for and won a seat in the Virginia House of Delegates. Two years later, he won a seat in the U.S. Congress and aligned himself with a group of older Republicans who favored strict construction of the Constitution and a limited federal government. Barbour served as Speaker of the House from 1821 until 1823, when he was defeated by Henry Clay. In 1824, Barbour chose not to run for reelection to Congress, and returned to Virginia to resume his law practice.

During his career as a practicing attorney, Barbour was involved in a number of important cases. He argued the state's position before the U.S. Supreme Court in *Cohen v. Virginia*, 19 U.S. 264, 6 Wheat. 264, 5 L. Ed. 257 (1821), a landmark suit that helped to clarify the role of the federal courts in reviewing state court decisions. In *Cohen* the Court held that the federal judiciary could review cases arising in the state courts that involved constitutional issues. Though Barbour lost the case, his vigorous representation helped to further establish his reputation as a strong defender of the states against what he often saw as the growing encroachment of the federal government.

In 1825, after considering and then declining an offer from Thomas Jefferson to join the law faculty at the University of Virginia, Barbour

*Philip Pendleton Barbour*

"WHAT IS SETTLED BY THE CONSTITUTION CANNOT BE ALTERED BY LAW."

was appointed to the General Court for the Eastern District of Virginia, a state trial court, where he served for almost two years. In 1827, at the urging of his constituents, Barbour ran unopposed for Congress, though he lost the Speaker's race to fellow Virginian Andrew Stevenson. During his second stint in Congress, Barbour was a vocal opponent of President Adams, even though Barbour's brother James Barbour was a member of the Adams cabinet. Barbour objected to the administration's spending policies and to the imposition of a TARIFF in 1828. He also continued his relentless advocacy of states' rights and the narrow construction of the Constitution, introducing an unsuccessful bill in 1829 requiring that five of the seven justices on the U.S. Supreme Court concur in any decision involving a constitutional question.

In the late 1820s, Barbour became a strong supporter of ANDREW JACKSON, who defeated the incumbent Adams in 1828. Barbour was considered for a position in the Jackson cabinet but was not appointed. In 1829, Barbour was chosen president of the Virginia Constitutional Convention, replacing the ailing James Monroe. During the sometimes tumultuous convention, Barbour argued for APPORTIONMENT of representation based on both white population and property ownership, and argued that the latter should be a qualification for the right to vote. Barbour also sided with the conservative slaveholders in the eastern part of the state against citizens in the western part of the state who, opposed to SLAVERY, eventually formed a separate state, West Virginia.

Barbour's unwavering support of Jackson and his policies earned him an appointment as a federal judge for eastern Virginia in 1830. In 1832, he was briefly a candidate for vice president against MARTIN VAN BUREN, even though Van Buren was Jackson's choice in his reelection bid. Barbour soon withdrew his candidacy to preserve party unity, and threw his support to Van Buren.

As early as 1831, Barbour was rumored to be next in line for a seat on the U.S. Supreme Court as soon as Jackson, now in his second term, had an opportunity to make an appoint-

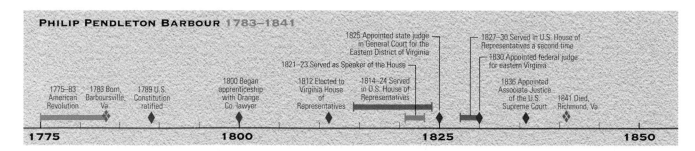

PHILIP PENDLETON BARBOUR 1783–1841

1775–83 American Revolution

1783 Born, Barboursville, Va.

1789 U.S. Constitution ratified

1800 Began apprenticeship with Orange Co. lawyer

1812 Elected to Virginia House of Representatives

1814–24 Served in U.S. House of Representatives

1821–23 Served as Speaker of the House

1825 Appointed state judge in General Court for the Eastern District of Virginia

1827–30 Served in U.S. House of Representatives a second time

1830 Appointed federal judge for eastern Virginia

1836 Appointed Associate Justice of the U.S. Supreme Court

1841 Died, Richmond, Va.

1775    1800    1825    1850

ment. Nationalists, who disagreed with Barbour's states' rights and strict constructionist views, opposed Barbour as a possible candidate for the Court. In 1836 Barbour was nominated to succeed retiring justice Gabriel Duval, at the same time that ROGER B. TANEY was nominated as chief justice and confirmed to succeed JOHN MARSHALL, also retiring. As expected, Barbour's nomination drew criticism, but he was nevertheless confirmed by a vote of 30–11.

Barbour wrote only a dozen opinions for the Court. His most important majority opinion was in *City of New York v. Miln*, 36 U.S. 102, 11 Pet. 102, 9 L. Ed. 648 (1837). At issue in *Miln* was a New York state law requiring captains of vessels arriving at ports to provide harbor authorities with the names, ages, birthplaces, and occupations of arriving passengers. The Court considered whether the law was an unconstitutional invasion of the exclusive federal right to regulate interstate and international trade. The Court ruled that the law was a legitimate exercise of the state's "POLICE POWER" to protect the health and welfare of its citizens. The decision provided the perfect opportunity for Barbour to expound upon his states' rights views. He wrote that the state not only had the right to impose such laws but also the "solemn duty ... to advance the safety, happiness and prosperity of its people, and to provide for the general welfare, by any and every act of legislation, which it may deem to be conducive to these ends." The decision marked a significant departure from the philosophy of the previous Court, headed by Marshall, which had emphasized the importance of federal authority in matters that even indirectly involved interstate and international commerce. Though influential, *Miln* was criticized and limited by subsequent decisions of the Court.

In February 1841, at age fifty-eight, Barbour died suddenly of a heart attack. He thus served only five years on the Court, completing one of the shortest terms in its history.

**BAR EXAMINATION** A written test that an individual must pass before becoming licensed to PRACTICE law as an ATTORNEY.

Bar examinations are regulated by states, and their specific requirements vary from state to state. Generally, they cover numerous legal topics and consist of multiple-choice questions or essay questions, or a combination. Most states administer a standardized multiple-choice test known as the *Multistate Bar Examination* as at least part of the bar examination requirement.

Each state has an interest in protecting its citizens by ensuring the quality and competency of lawyers who receive LICENSES to practice there. In addition to requiring bar candidates to pass a difficult and comprehensive test of substantive legal knowledge, most jurisdictions also require proof of graduation from an ACCREDITED LAW SCHOOL and successful completion of a character background review. With few exceptions, only people who satisfy these strict requirements and are licensed by a state bar may practice law in that state. Critics of this system of attorney licensure argue that its true purpose is to reduce competition between lawyers by regulating the number of lawyers admitted to the bar.

Historically, lawyers have played an active role in determining who, and how many, would join their ranks as members of the bar. This tradition predates the U.S. Constitution by more than six centuries, when English courts governed who would be allowed to practice law. Courts have long relied on the rationale that the integrity and competency of practicing attorneys directly affect the quality of justice dispensed.

The U.S. legal system has adopted this rationale. Before 1828, states allowed practicing attorneys to determine the competency of prospective attorneys. Strict rules developed by lawyers at that time typically required an individual to obtain a college degree and work several years as an attorney's APPRENTICE before being admitted to the practice of law. Because attorneys controlled who would get apprenticeships, the general public perceived the system as catering to the elite.

A decline of elitist attitudes surrounding the election of President Andrew Jackson in 1828 prompted a change in the attorney licensing system. State legislatures divested the authority granted attorneys and reclaimed control of bar admission standards, which became far less stringent and far less exclusive. Apprenticeships remained the most common form of legal study, but by 1860, only nine states required any form of LEGAL EDUCATION for admission to the bar. Written bar examinations, when required, were cursory.

By the late 1800s, a surge in formal law schools spurred a decline in legal apprenticeship programs. A new wave of interest in improving standards of legal education and bar admission prompted the founding of the AMERICAN BAR ASSOCIATION in 1878 and the American Association of Law Schools in 1900. These groups encouraged tougher bar admission standards, including the requirement that all bar candidates complete a written examination used to assess their fitness to practice law. Today, every state offers a bar examination.

Administrative bodies established in each state generally govern the standards and particularities of the bar examination. In keeping with the tradition of attorney self-regulation, these boards usually are made up, at least in part, of licensed attorneys. The boards determine what legal topics will be covered; what types of questions will be asked; what grading methods will be applied; and the locations, dates, and times of examinations. Nearly every state requires, as one component of the examination, the *Multistate Bar Examination.*

The *Multistate Bar Examination* contains two hundred multiple-choice questions covering six legal topics: contracts, constitutional law, criminal law and procedure, evidence, real property, and torts. Examinees have six hours to complete the exam, or 1.8 minutes for each question. This computer-graded test is offered twice a year, usually in July and February. Indiana, Iowa, Louisiana, Washington, and Puerto Rico are the only United States jurisdictions that have not adopted the *Multistate Bar Examination.*

Most states also require bar candidates to complete a test of their knowledge of state laws. Examinees usually take this portion of the exam on the day before or after the *Multistate Bar*

*Examination.* This state-specific examination often contains essay questions or multiple-choice questions, or a combination. It may cover a different range of legal topics than does the *Multistate Bar Examination,* although some topics are duplicated by the two tests.

More than half the states require, in addition, a passing score on the standardized multiple-choice test of legal and professional ETHICS called the *Multistate Professional Responsibility Examination.* Bar applicants normally take this two-hour test several weeks before or after they take the bar examination. The *Multistate Professional Responsibility Examination* tests the applicants' knowledge of the American Bar Association's Model Rules of Professional Conduct. Topics include attorney-client confidentiality, conflicts of interest, and attorney advertising.

In a few states, an attorney may be licensed to practice law without taking the state's bar examination. Wisconsin permits graduates of accredited Wisconsin law schools to become licensed attorneys without taking any bar examination. Other states offer reciprocity, by accepting *Multistate Bar Examination* scores attained in other jurisdictions or by waiving the bar examination requirement for experienced attorneys licensed in other jurisdictions.

Jurisdictions also differ in their approach to legal education requirements. Most states require bar applicants to graduate from law schools accredited by the American Bar Association. Some states, such as California and Georgia, will admit bar candidates who received law degrees from unaccredited law schools under certain circumstances. California, Maine, New York, Vermont, Virginia, Washington, and Wyoming do not require law degrees at all, but alternatively require several years of legal study—also known as reading law—with a licensed attorney. Whatever the legal education requirements, all members of the bar must pass the bar examination.

**BARGAIN** 📖 A RECIPROCAL understanding, CONTRACT, or AGREEMENT of any sort usually pertaining to the loan, sale, or exchange of property between two parties, one of whom wants to dispose of an item that the other wants to obtain. To work out the terms of an agreement; to negotiate in GOOD FAITH for the purpose of entering into an agreement. 📖

A union engages in COLLECTIVE BARGAINING on proposed contract terms.

**BARGAINING AGENT** 📖 A union that possesses the sole authority to act on behalf of all the employees of a particular type in a company. 📖

## Major Collective Bargaining Settlements
Change in Wage and Compensation Rates Negotiated and Number of Workers Affected

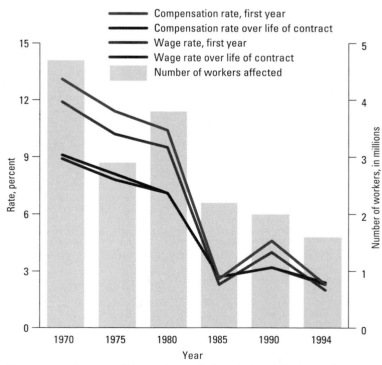

* Data represents private nonfarm industry settlements affecting production and related workers in manufacturing and nonsupervisory workers in nonmanufacturing industries. Wage data cover units with 1,000 workers or more. Compensation data relate to units of 5,000 workers or more. Data relate to contracts negotiated in calendar year.

Source: U.S. Bureau of Labor Statistics, *Compensation and Working Conditions,* monthly.

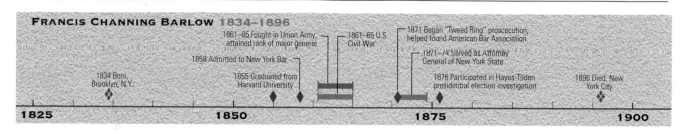

FRANCIS CHANNING BARLOW 1834–1896

1861–65 Fought in Union Army, attained rank of major general
1861–65 U.S. Civil War
1871 Began "Tweed Ring" prosecution; helped found American Bar Association
1858 Admitted to New York Bar
1871–74 Served as Attorney General of New York State
1834 Born, Brooklyn, N.Y.
1855 Graduated from Harvard University
1876 Participated in Hayes-Tilden presidential election investigation
1896 Died, New York City

1825    1850    1875    1900

A bargaining agent is certified by the National Labor Relations Board (NLRB) as the exclusive representative of a certain type of employee. The International Garment Workers Union, for example, might act as the bargaining agent for all seamstresses employed at a particular dress factory. See also LABOR LAW; LABOR UNION.

## BARLOW, FRANCIS CHANNING

Francis Channing Barlow achieved prominence as a lawyer and a soldier. Barlow was born October 19, 1834, in Brooklyn, New York. He graduated from Harvard in 1855, and was admitted to the New York bar in 1858. From 1859 to 1861, and also in 1866, Barlow practiced law.

At the onset of the Civil War in 1861, Barlow joined the Union Army and fought at various battles, including Fair Oaks, Antietam, Chancellorsville, and Spottsylvania. He was wounded at Gettysburg in 1863 but returned to service, and by the end of the war he had earned the rank of major general.

After the Civil War Barlow became secretary of state of New York, serving from 1865 to 1867, and 1869 to 1870. In 1869, he was U.S. marshal for the southern district of New York. He performed the duties of New York attorney general from 1871 to 1873, and was instrumental in the early proceedings concerning the prosecution of the Tweed Ring, a group of corrupt New York politicians. See also TAMMANY HALL.

Barlow returned to his law practice in 1874. In 1876, he participated in the investigation of the controversial Hayes-Tilden presidential election results. He died January 11, 1896, in New York City.

## BARR, WILLIAM PELHAM

William Pelham Barr served as ATTORNEY GENERAL of the United States from 1991 to 1993 under President GEORGE BUSH.

The son of Donald Barr and Mary Ahern Barr, Barr was born May 23, 1950, in New York City, and was schooled there. He completed an undergraduate degree at New York's Columbia University in 1971, and began a two-year master's program in Chinese studies. Armed with his graduate degree, he moved to Washington, D.C., in 1973, and went to work as a staff

**BIOGRAPHY**

*Francis Channing Barlow*

officer with the Central Intelligence Agency (CIA). He was accompanied by his wife, Christine Moynihan, to whom he was married on June 23, 1973.

While working at the CIA, Barr enrolled in the night program at George Washington University Law School. He earned his law degree in 1977, graduating second in his class. After law school, he clerked for one year with the presiding judge of the District of Columbia Circuit Court. He was admitted to the Virginia bar in 1977, and to the District of Columbia bar in 1978. Also in 1978, Barr was offered, and accepted, an associate position at the Washington, D.C., law firm of Shaw, Pittman, Potts, and Trowbridge. There, he concentrated on civil litigation and federal administrative practice.

In 1982, Barr was named to President Ronald Reagan's Domestic Policy Council. During his two years of service, he became well known and respected by the administration and leaders in the Republican party. Barr returned to Shaw, Pittman in 1984, to resume his legal career. He was made a partner of the firm in 1985.

After several years in private practice, Barr reentered public service in 1989, when he was named assistant attorney general by the Bush administration. He took over the Justice Department's Office of Legal Counsel, where his role was to advise the White House, and the attorney general and other administration officials. Historically, the Office of Legal Counsel has been called upon to reassure presidents that their intended actions are within the law.

As assistant attorney general, Barr authored two controversial advisory opinions that allowed President Bush to expand his war on drugs and to apprehend Panamanian drug lord Manuel Noriega. One opinion (13 U.S. Op. Off. Legal Counsel 387) held that U.S. military forces could be assigned to law enforcement operations abroad, and the other (13 U.S. Op. Off. Legal Counsel 195) that the president had authority to order the Federal Bureau of Investigation (FBI) to arrest fugitives overseas without consent of the local government.

Barr was named deputy attorney general in

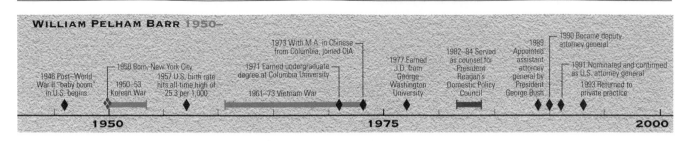

WILLIAM PELHAM BARR 1950–

1946 Post–World War II "baby boom" in U.S. begins

1950 Born, New York City

1950–53 Korean War

1957 U.S. birth rate hits all-time high of 25.3 per 1,000

1961–73 Vietnam War

1971 Earned undergraduate degree at Columbia University

1973 With M.A. in Chinese from Columbia, joined CIA

1977 Earned J.D. from George Washington University

1982–84 Served as counsel for President Reagan's Domestic Policy Council

1989 Appointed assistant attorney general by President George Bush

1990 Became deputy attorney general

1991 Nominated and confirmed as U.S. attorney general

1993 Returned to private practice

1950          1975          2000

1990. He became acting attorney general in June 1991 when RICHARD THORNBURGH resigned to enter the race for a U.S. Senate seat in Pennsylvania. Barr was nominated and confirmed as attorney general in the fall of 1991, becoming, at age forty-one, the youngest person to hold that post since Ramsey Clark, who was appointed in 1967.

After years of unpleasant and adversarial relationships with Attorneys General EDWIN MEESE III and Thornburgh, Congress welcomed Barr's appointment. Members of Congress praised his candor and cooperation, and they supported his decision to launch internal investigations into the Justice Department's handling of the Bank of Credit and Commerce International (BCCI) scandal and the Inslaw computer scandal. BCCI was shut down by bank regulators in 1991 for massive fraud, theft, money laundering, and the financing of arms deals and terrorist activities. Depositors lost billions when the bank's assets were seized. Inslaw, Inc., accused the JUSTICE DEPARTMENT of conspiring to steal its proprietary software after the company's government contract had been revoked.

The American Bar Association was encouraged by Barr's willingness to reconsider a Thornburgh decision that prevented local bar associations from interviewing judicial nominees, and a *National Law Journal* editorial praised the department planned by the new attorney general as less political, more open, and more "inclined toward integrity" than the departments run by his immediate predecessors in the Reagan and Bush administrations (Nov. 25, 1991).

Barr's honeymoon with the Democratic Congress and the nation's legal press did not last. He was soon criticized for his inability to obtain CIA cooperation in the BCCI and Banca Nazionale del Lavoro (BNL) investigations, and for delays in closing down the BCCI. A CIA investigation revealed that an Atlanta, Georgia, branch of the BNL had provided fraudulent loans to Iraq—loans that helped Saddam Hussein to build his military strength. His internal investigation of the theft of an Inslaw-

## BIOGRAPHY

JAMES COLBURN/PHOTOREPORTERS

*William Pelham Barr*

"I DON'T CARE HOW MUCH POLITICAL PRESSURE IS BROUGHT TO BEAR . . . [OR THAT] THE OP-EDS [AND] JOURNALISTS ARE SAYING . . . IT'S NOT FAST ENOUGH FOR THEM. THE STANDARD WILL STAY WHERE IT IS."

developed computer program by government officials was tagged a whitewash. He angered Japanese officials when he announced a change in ANTITRUST policy that allowed the Justice Department to bring cases against Japanese CARTELS that restricted U.S. exports. And he fought popular opinion and strong evidence of improprieties by the Justice Department when he continued to support the DEPORTATION of John Demjanjuk—wrongly accused of being the infamous Nazi death camp guard Ivan the Terrible.

Finally, Barr took the unprecedented step of denying a congressional request for an independent investigation into the events known as Iraqgate. Barr said he and the Justice Department would conduct their own investigation to determine whether anyone in the Bush administration had committed a crime by giving aid to Saddam Hussein prior to the Iraqi invasion of Kuwait and the resulting Persian Gulf War.

Ongoing questions about the administration's knowledge of, and involvement in, Iraqgate contributed to Bush's defeat in the presidential election of 1992, and ended Barr's tenure as the nation's attorney general.

In spite of his bright beginning, Barr was unable to depart significantly from the agendas and operational styles of his predecessors and the presidents they served. According to the *National Law Journal*, "Under Presidents Reagan and Bush and their Attorneys General Ed Meese, Dick Thornburgh and William P. Barr, the nation witnessed the politicization of the [Justice D]epartment beyond anything that has gone before" (Dec. 7, 1992).

In 1993, Barr returned to Shaw, Pittman and resumed the practice of law. At the time, he was a member of the American Bar Association, the Virginia State Bar Association, and the District of Columbia Bar Association.

### CROSS-REFERENCES
Banks and Banking; Computer Crime.

**BARRATRY** 📖 In CRIMINAL LAW, the frequent incitement of lawsuits and quarrels that is a punishable offense. 📖

Barratry is most commonly applied to an ATTORNEY who attempts to bring about a lawsuit that will be profitable to her or him. Barratry is an offense both at COMMON LAW and under some state statutes. The broader common-law crime has been limited by certain statutes. An attorney who is overly officious in instigating or encouraging prosecution of groundless LITIGATION might be guilty of common barratry under a particular statute. The requirement for the crime of barratry is that repeated or persistent acts of litigation are performed by the accused. Barratry is generally a MISDEMEANOR punishable by fine or imprisonment. In the case of an attorney, disbarment is the usual punishment. Since few cases have been prosecuted, barratry is considered by the legal community at large to be an archaic crime. This is particularly true today due to a highly litigious atmosphere.

In maritime law, barratry is the commission of an act by the master or mariners of a vessel for an unlawful or fraudulent purpose that is contrary to the duty owed to the owners, by which act the owners sustain injury.

A form of barratry is misconduct of the master of a ship in taking commodities on board that subject the ship to seizure for SMUGGLING. It is essential in barratry that a criminal act or intent exist on the part of the master or mariners which inures to their own benefit and causes injury to the owners of the ship.

**BARRISTER** In English law, an attorney who has an exclusive right of argument in all the superior courts.

A barrister is a counselor who is learned in law and who has been admitted to plead at the bar. A barrister drafts the PLEADINGS in all cases, with the exception of the simplest ones. Distinguished from an attorney, which is an English lawyer who conducts matters out of court, a barrister engages in the actual argument of cases or the conduct of the trial.

**BARTER** The EXCHANGE of goods or services without the use of money as currency.

Barter is a CONTRACT wherein parties trade goods or commodities for other goods, as opposed to sale or exchange of goods for money. Barter is not applicable to contracts involving land, but solely to contracts relating to goods and services. For example, when a tenant exchanges the performance of various maintenance tasks around a house for free room and board, a barter has taken place.

**BASEBALL** Although certain laws have protected citizens from monopolies on power and money for decades, the legal decisions surrounding "America's favorite pastime" have allowed it to remain exempt from most forms of government intervention. Through the years, major league baseball (MLB) has escaped mea-

sures that would have ended its exclusive control over contracts and copyrights and its all-around MONOPOLY on professional U.S. baseball. Meanwhile, as contracts and team expenditures have come to run well into the millions of dollars, many have come to see baseball as less of a sport than a business—and a business that should be regulated. The United States still reveres baseball, but fans, players, and owners all hope that government decisions will save it from labor strikes and a host of other ills. The government, however, continues to do little other than let baseball remain a special, nationally protected institution.

The professional growth of baseball—and some of its headaches—followed a natural economic progression. Much of the sport's origin is shrouded in myth, but it is thought that it got off to its humble start sometime in the nineteenth century. The first organized contest probably happened on June 19, 1846, between two amateur teams: the New York Nine and the Knickerbockers. In 1869, the Cincinnati Red Stockings, a professional team, paved the way for other franchises to come into existence. In 1871, the National Association of Professional Baseball Players was born. The ensuing days

### Barrister
### Comparison of the increase in the number of barristers licensed for practice at the bar in England and Wales, Northern Ireland, and the United States

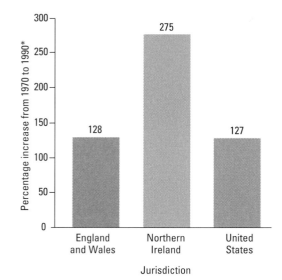

* The numbers for the United States are actually for the statistical year 1991.

Source: England, Wales, Northern Ireland: CSO. U.S. bar membership: 1970, *The 1971 Lawyer Statistical Report,* 1971 (copyright); 1980, *The Lawyer Statistical Report: A Statistical Profile of the U.S. Legal Profession in the 1980s,* 1985 (copyright); 1991, *1991 Lawyer Statistical Report: The U.S. Legal Profession in the 1990s,* 1994 (copyright).

*The 1892 Cleveland
Baseball Club.*

belong to popular remembrance. Abner Doubleday formed the National League in 1876, and
baseball has existed somewhere between game
and profitable enterprise ever since.

From its early days, the courts have failed to
see baseball as posing a threat to the laws of
business. The monumental SHERMAN ANTI-
TRUST ACT of 1890 (15 U.S.C.A. § 1 et seq.)—a
statute prohibiting monopolies—forbids undue
RESTRAINT OF TRADE on commerce between
states. In 1920, an appeals court ruled that the
fact that baseball operates on an interstate level
was part of its unobjectionable nature as a sport
(*National League of Professional Baseball Clubs v.
Federal Baseball Club of Baltimore*, 50 App. D.C.
165, 269 F. 681). It stated, in general reference
to other forms of trade and commerce, that
"the Sherman Anti-Trust Act . . . does not apply, unless the effect of the act complained of on
interstate commerce is direct, not merely indirect or incidental." Baseball, the court found,
did not pose a threat to the economy of the
world of sports.

The *National League* case stemmed from
allegations made by the Federal League's Baltimore Terrapins. In the early 1900s, the struggling Federal League had sought to become a
venture of the major leagues and had competed
with other major league FRANCHISES. But the
National and American Leagues bought out
many of the Federal teams, sometimes player by

player, with offers they could not refuse. The
Terrapins, one of the last surviving vestiges of
the Federal League, sued the National League.
Representatives of the Terrapins argued that
MLB owners had treated the Terrapins with
scorn, offering them only $50,000 in settlement
for damages incurred by the buyouts. In court,
the Terrapins argued that MLB had violated
ANTITRUST LAWS and had participated in mo-
nopolizing ventures.

The case made it all the way to the Supreme
Court (*National League*, 259 U.S. 200, 42 S. Ct.
465, 66 L. Ed. 898 (1922)). In 1922, the Court
made a classic decision. The long-standing verdict of the case, affirmed by Justice OLIVER
WENDELL HOLMES, JR., declared baseball to be,
first and foremost, a sport and not a business. In
Holmes's words, baseball activities were "purely
state affairs." The decision gave baseball the
unique status of being the only official professional sports organization to be exempt from
antimonopoly laws. In effect, the decision protected baseball as a national treasure.

The *National League* decision was reaffirmed
in 1953 with *Toolson v. New York Yankees*, 346
U.S. 356, 74 S. Ct. 78, 98 L. Ed. 64. In a brief
statement, the Court ruled against the plaintiff,
minor league player George Toolson. Toolson's
arguments were based on the complaint that
baseball was a monopoly that offered him unfair
contract deals. The Court said Congress alone

had been given the right to exercise powers that could break up the structure of baseball's professional organization.

The controversial issue in *Toolson* was baseball's reserve clause. This clause stood as the earliest symbol of the sport's underlying business nature. It stated that once a player had accepted a CONTRACT to play for a certain team, the player was bound to serve that team for one year and must enter into a new contract with the same team "for the succeeding season at a salary to be determined by the parties to such contract." It was agreed that if a player violated the reserve clause, the athlete would be guilty of "contract jumping" and would be ineligible to serve in any club of the leagues until formally reinstated.

The reserve clause guaranteed players little more than an income. Players attacked it. In the 1970s, Curtis C. Flood, center fielder for the St. Louis Cardinals, brought charges against Bowie K. Kuhn, acting commissioner of baseball. The issue was a player's free agency, which Flood had requested and Kuhn had denied. Free agency is the freedom to negotiate a contract with any team, basically a release from the reserve clause. Taking his case to the Supreme Court, Flood argued that the reserve clause unfairly prevented him from striking deals with other teams that would pay him more for his services. The Supreme Court decided on June 19, 1972, that it did not have the authority to act (*Flood v. Kuhn*, 407 U.S. 258, 92 S. Ct. 2099,

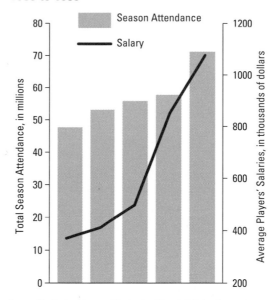

## Attendance at U.S. Major League Baseball Games and Average Players' Salaries, 1985 to 1993

Source: The National League of Professional Baseball Clubs, New York, N.Y., *National League Green Book;* The American League of Professional Baseball Clubs, New York, N.Y., *American League Red Book;* Major League Baseball Players Association, New York, N.Y.

32 L. Ed. 2d 728). Only baseball's acting commissioner could designate free agency.

Player discontent, as a reaction to the decision, set the stage for more free agency bids, and ARBITRATION between players and owners began in 1973. In January 1976, Andy Messer-

*In 1994 a players' strike caused baseball team owners to cancel the remainder of the season. Jacobs Field in Cleveland stood empty for the rest of that summer and fall.*

smith's success in obtaining free agency ushered in a new era of high stakes: players could now dictate certain terms of employment, and hence came the dawn of multimillion-dollar contracts.

Money was also at issue in a case related to another aspect of the game. After more than a century of professional play, in 1986 televised broadcasts of baseball and the COPYRIGHT laws surrounding them came into question. Players felt that the terms of their employment did not include their performances for television audiences. They insisted that the telecasts and the profits being derived from them were being made without their consent. In *Baltimore Orioles v. Major League Baseball Players Ass'n*, 805 F.2d 663 (7th Cir. 1986), major league clubs sought a DECLARATORY JUDGMENT that they possessed an exclusive right to broadcast games. The major league players argued that their performances were not copyrightable works because they lacked sufficient artistic merit. Refusing to cut into the control of MLB over the airwaves, the federal appellate court ruled that the telecasts were indeed copyrightable works and that clubs were entitled to the revenues derived from them.

Throughout these cases, decisions about the economy of baseball have been left to the players and owners. For this reason, baseball has been referred to as an anomaly in relation to the nation's antitrust laws, and its exemption has been called "an aberration confined to baseball" (*Flood*). The push for congressional action to eliminate this exemption reached a fever pitch with the baseball players' STRIKE of 1994–95. The strike left many in baseball, including fans, disenfranchised. Senator Howard M. Metzenbaum, an Ohio Democrat who headed the subcommittee on antitrust laws, led the fight to remove the antitrust exemption from baseball. However, the 234-day strike ended in an agreement between owners and players, in which owners promised to pay "luxury taxes" on clubs with high payrolls. Congress was spared the necessity of acting.

See also SPORTS LAW.

**BASE FEE** 📖 An interest in REAL PROPERTY that has the potential to last forever, provided a specific contingency does not occur. 📖

For example, a grantee might be given an estate in blackacre, "provided the land is not used for illegal purposes."

This type of fee is also known as a *conditional*, *determinable*, or *qualified fee*.

**BASE LINE** 📖 Survey line used in the government survey to establish township lines. Horizontal elevation line used as a centerline in a highway survey. 📖

**BASIS** 📖 The minimum, fundamental constituents, foundation, or support of a thing or a system without which the thing or system would cease to exist. In accounting, the value assigned to an ASSET that is sold or transferred so that it can be determined whether a gain or loss has resulted from the transaction. The amount that property is estimated to be worth at the time it is received for tax purposes. 📖

**BASTARDY ACTION** 📖 An archaic name given to a court proceeding in which the paternity of an illegitimate child is determined in order to impose and enforce support obligations upon the father. 📖

The term *bastardy action* is derived from the early common-law use of the word *bastard* to describe a child born out of wedlock. Modern legislation refers to such proceedings as FILIATION PROCEEDINGS or PATERNITY SUITS because of the derogatory connotation of the term *bastard*.

Although such proceedings are typically CIVIL ACTIONS, a few states have established such actions as criminal proceedings. See also ILLEGITIMACY.

**BATES, DAISY LEE GATSON** Daisy Lee Gatson Bates was a CIVIL RIGHTS activist and newspaper publisher who was a key figure in the integration of public schools in Little Rock, Arkansas, in the late 1950s. When a storm of violent public protest swept Little Rock, Bates orchestrated the strategies that would reverse two hundred years of state-sanctioned segregation.

Bates was born in 1920 in Huttig, in the lumbering region of southeast Arkansas. When she was a baby, her mother was raped and murdered. No one was prosecuted for the crime, but suspicion in the town centered on three white men. After her mother's death, her father fled, leaving Bates with his best friends, Orlee Smith and Susie Smith, who adopted her and raised her as their only child. They were kind and indulgent parents and Bates grew to be a strong-willed and determined child. When she was eight, she learned of the circumstances of her birth and adoption. The painful knowledge of her parents' suffering and the harsh realities of life in the rural south became driving forces in Bates's life.

Although she grew up during difficult economic times, Bates's childhood was relatively comfortable. Her relationship with her adoptive parents was warm and loving, and she was especially close to her father. Nevertheless, Bates's childhood was not easy. Like other black children, she experienced the sting of racial DISCRIMINATION from an early age. She attended a segregated public school, using worn text-

UPI/CORBIS-BETTMANN

*Daisy Lee Gatson Bates*

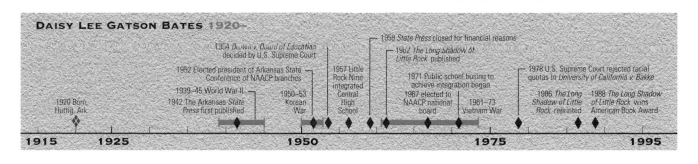

**DAISY LEE GATSON BATES 1920–**

- 1920 Born, Huttig, Ark.
- 1939–45 World War II
- 1942 The Arkansas *State Press* first published
- 1952 Elected president of Arkansas State Conference of NAACP branches
- 1954 *Brown v. Board of Education* decided by U.S. Supreme Court
- 1950–53 Korean War
- 1957 Little Rock Nine integrated Central High School
- 1959 *State Press* closed for financial reasons
- 1962 *The Long Shadow of Little Rock* published
- 1967 elected to NAACP national board
- 1971 Public school busing to achieve integration began
- 1961–73 Vietnam War
- 1978 U.S. Supreme Court rejected racial quotas in *University of California v. Bakke*
- 1986 *The Long Shadow of Little Rock* reprinted
- 1988 *The Long Shadow of Little Rock* wins American Book Award

1915    1925    1950    1975    1995

books handed down from the white children's school. Her school was little more than a room with a potbellied stove that gave so little heat she and her classmates often kept their coats on all day.

In 1941 Orlee Smith became gravely ill. When he knew he was going to die, he called his daughter to his side. He was aware of the anger and hurt she carried because of her mother's death and her father's disappearance, and because of the bigotry that was a part of their everyday life. He counseled her not to let hatred and hostility control her but rather to use her strong feelings as a catalyst to work for change. He said,

> Don't hate white people just because they're white. If you hate, make it count for something. Hate the humiliations we are living under in the South. Hate the discrimination that eats away at the soul of every black man and woman. Hate the insults hurled at us by white scum—then try to do something about it, or your hate won't spell a thing.

Smith's death became a kind of rebirth for Bates. She did not know it then, but his words would strengthen and sustain her resolve during the difficult struggles she was to face.

In 1942 Bates married Lucius Christopher Bates, an insurance agent and friend of her late father's, and settled in Little Rock. Her husband had majored in journalism at Wilberforce College, in Ohio, and the young couple pooled their savings and began publishing the Arkansas *State Press*. While writing and publishing the fledgling paper, Bates also enrolled in business administration and public relations courses at Shorter College, in Rome, Georgia. The *State Press* quickly became the largest and most influential black paper in Arkansas.

With the entry of the United States into World War II, Camp Robinson, near Little Rock, was reopened. The influx of soldiers, many of whom were black men from northern

"WE'VE GOT TO DECIDE IF IT'S GOING TO BE THIS GENERATION OR NEVER."

cities, caused racial tensions to rise in the city. The *State Press* had gained a reputation as an independent "voice of the people" and regularly attacked police brutality, segregation, and inequities in the criminal justice system. When the paper reported a particularly gruesome incident in which a black soldier was killed by a white policeman, many advertisers who were wary of antagonizing their white patrons withdrew their support, and circulation of the paper dropped. However, the Bateses were able to stay afloat and eventually regain their advertisers and rebuild the paper's circulation. Their tenacity paid off in changes in working and living conditions for blacks in Arkansas. For example, as a result of their reporting on police brutality in black neighborhoods, black police officers were hired to patrol those areas.

From their earliest days in Little Rock, Bates and her husband were active in the local branch of the National Association for the Advancement of Colored People (NAACP). In 1952, Bates was elected president of the Arkansas State Conference of NAACP branches. When the Supreme Court handed down its historic decision in *Brown v. Board of Education* (347 U.S. 483, 74 S. Ct. 686, 98 L. Ed. 873 (1954)), in 1954, declaring that segregated schools are "inherently unequal," she and her colleagues began pressing for implementation of the Court's mandate to desegregate the schools "with all deliberate speed" (*Brown v. Board of Education*, 349 U.S. 294 at 301, 75 S. Ct. 753 at 756, 99 L. Ed. 1083 [1955]). Because of her prominent position with the NAACP, Bates found herself a central character in the integration battle that soon erupted in Little Rock.

The Little Rock School Board chose nine black students to be the first to integrate Little Rock Central High School. Planning and coordination of the activities of the group, which came to be known as the Little Rock Nine, fell to Bates. By September 1, 1957, angry crowds had begun milling around Central High to protest and try to prevent the enrollment of the black students. On September 2, the day before school was to open, Governor Orval Faubus dispatched the Arkansas National Guard and ordered it to surround Central. Claiming that he was protecting Little Rock's citizens from possible mob violence, he declared that no black students would be allowed to enter the school and that "blood [would] run in the streets" if any attempted to do so.

NAACP lawyers Wiley Branton and THURGOOD MARSHALL (later a U.S. Supreme Court justice) promptly obtained an INJUNCTION against Faubus's interference, but Faubus refused to withdraw the troops. Bates decided to have the students enter the school in a group. She contacted eight of them and told them to assemble at a designated intersection the morning of September 4 and travel to school together. The ninth student, Elizabeth Eckford, did not receive word of the plan. Unaware of the maelstrom awaiting her, Eckford arrived at Central High alone and was taunted, jeered, and accosted by hundreds of white people as reporters and photographers from around the world observed and recorded the scene. The National Guard did not attempt to help Eckford but instead blocked her entrance to the school. Neither she nor any of the other members of the Little Rock Nine—who arrived later in a group, as arranged—were allowed to pass through the line of Guard members surrounding the school.

The attempt by Bates and the nine students to enter Central set off a series of violent incidents that went on for seventeen days. On September 20, attorneys Branton and Marshall obtained an injunction barring the use of the National Guard to interfere with integration at Central High. By this time, the Bateses' home had become the unofficial center of activity and communication for the integration effort. Reporters from all over the United States came and went, some staying days or weeks.

On September 23 all the Little Rock Nine met at the Bates home to try again to exercise their right to enter Central High. Traveling in two cars they drove to a side entrance of the building, away from the persistent throng, and were escorted into the school by police officers. Again mob violence spread through the city. Later in the day the students were secretly removed from the school through a delivery entrance, and the chief of police declared that Little Rock was under a reign of terror.

The next day the black students remained at home. The mayor and the chief of police appealed to the U.S. Department of Justice for assistance. In response, President DWIGHT D. EISENHOWER federalized the Arkansas National Guard and ordered Secretary of Defense Charles E. Wilson to enforce the integration order. Wilson ordered one thousand paratroopers from the 101st Airborne ("Screaming Eagles") Division of the 327th Infantry Regiment into Little Rock to restore order.

On September 25 the Little Rock Nine assembled again at the Bates home. Under the protection of the paratroopers they were taken to Central High, where they entered under the watchful eyes of hundreds of reporters, photographers, and news camera operators. The paratroopers remained at Central until September 30, when they withdrew to Camp Robinson, twelve miles away. The federalized Arkansas National Guard remained on patrol at Central until the end of the school year. Although it was not necessary to recall the paratroopers, and the number of minority students in Little Rock's formerly white schools steadily increased, violence, hatred, and acrimony continued to plague the city for many years.

Bates endured many attempts to harass and intimidate her, including rocks thrown through her window, gunshots fired at her house, dynamite exploded near her house, and crosses burned on her lawn. In late October 1957 she was arrested under a newly enacted ordinance that required officials of organizations to supply information regarding membership, donors, amounts of contributions, and expenditures. Although she was found guilty under the ordinance, the conviction was later overturned by the Supreme Court on grounds that the ordinance requirement interfered with the members' FREEDOM OF ASSOCIATION (*Bates* et al. *v. City of Little Rock* et. al., 361 U.S. 516, 80 S. Ct. 412, 4 L. Ed. 480 [1960]). In 1959 she and her husband were forced to close the *State Press* for financial reasons.

Through all the harassment Bates remained determined to keep the wheels of the integration movement going forward. After closing the newspaper she traveled throughout the United States working on behalf of the Democratic National Committee and the Johnson administration's antipoverty programs. In 1965 she suffered a stroke and returned to Little Rock, but she continued to be active in the NAACP and in 1967 was elected to its national board. In 1968 she moved to Mitchellville, Arkansas, to organize the Mitchellville Office of Economic Opportunity Self-Help Project. The project was responsible for new water and sewer systems, paved streets, a community center, and a swimming pool.

In 1984 Bates revived the *State Press* and was awarded honorary degrees by the University of Arkansas and Washington University. In 1986 the University of Arkansas Press published a reprint edition of her autobiography, *The Long Shadow of Little Rock*, and in 1988 the book received the American Book Award, the first reprint edition to be given that honor.

In 1987 Bates sold the *State Press* but she remained a consultant for the paper. In spite of failing health, she continued to be active in community organizations.

**CROSS-REFERENCES**

*Brown v. Board of Education of Topeka, Kansas*; Civil Rights Movement; National Association for the Advancement of Colored People; School Desegregation.

**BATES, EDWARD** Edward Bates served as U.S. attorney general in the cabinet of President ABRAHAM LINCOLN from 1861 to 1864.

Bates was born September 4, 1793, in Belmont, Virginia. He left his native Virginia at the age of twenty-one and settled in Missouri, where he concentrated his career efforts.

Bates was admitted to the Missouri bar in 1816 and was attorney general from 1820 to 1822. He was also a member of the Missouri Constitutional Convention in 1820.

In 1822 Bates began the legislative phase of his career as a member of the Missouri House of Representatives. In 1827 he became a representative for Missouri in the U.S. House of Representatives, serving for two years, and then returned to state government as a member of the Missouri Senate, serving from 1830 to 1834. In 1834 he became a member of the Missouri House of Representatives for a second time. Bates was also a U.S. district attorney from 1821 to 1826.

Bates was an unsuccessful presidential nominee at the Republican National Convention of 1860. He died March 25, 1869, in St. Louis, Missouri.

**BIOGRAPHY**

CULVER PICTURES

*Edward Bates*

"LIBERTY CANNOT EXIST EXCEPT UNDER GOVERNMENT OF LAW."

THE BETTMANN ARCHIVE

*Battel, like dueling, is the use of physical force to resolve disputes.*

was tried by God, was the party who was in the right in the dispute.

**BATTERING** See DOMESTIC VIOLENCE.

**BATTERY** At COMMON LAW, an intentional unpermitted act causing harmful or offensive contact with the "person" of another.

Battery is concerned with the right to have one's body left alone by others.

Battery is both a TORT and a CRIME. Its essential element, harmful or offensive contact, is the same in both areas of the law. The main distinction between the two categories lies in the penalty imposed. A defendant sued for a tort is civilly liable to the plaintiff for DAMAGES. The punishment for criminal battery is a fine, imprisonment, or both. Usually battery is prosecuted as a crime only in cases involving serious harm to the victim.

**Elements** The following elements must be proven to establish a case for battery: (1) an act by a defendant; (2) an intent to cause harmful or offensive contact on the part of the defendant; and (3) harmful or offensive contact to the plaintiff.

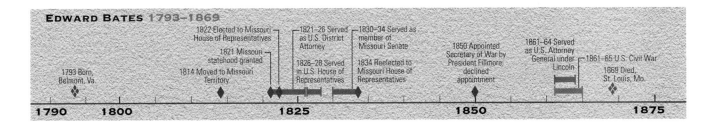

EDWARD BATES 1793-1869

1793 Born, Belmont, Va.

1814 Moved to Missouri Territory

1821 Missouri statehood granted

1822 Elected to Missouri House of Representatives

1821–26 Served as U.S. District Attorney

1826–28 Served in U.S. House of Representatives

1830–34 Served as member of Missouri Senate

1834 Reelected to Missouri House of Representatives

1850 Appointed Secretary of War by President Fillmore; declined appointment

1861–64 Served as U.S. Attorney General under Lincoln

1861–65 U.S. Civil War

1869 Died, St. Louis, Mo.

1790    1800    1825    1850    1875

**BATTEL** Physical combat engaged in by an accuser and accused to resolve their differences, usually involving a serious crime or ownership of land. It was recognized by the English king from the eleventh to seventeenth centuries.

Trial by battel was introduced into England by William the Conqueror. It was based upon the belief that the winner of the battle, which

**The Act** The act must result in one of two forms of contact. Causing any physical harm or INJURY to the victim—such as a cut, a burn, or a bullet wound—could constitute battery, but actual injury is not required. Even though there is no apparent bruise following harmful contact, the defendant can still be guilty of battery; occurrence of a physical illness subsequent to the contact may also be ACTIONABLE. The second type of contact that may constitute battery causes no actual physical harm but is, instead, offensive or insulting to the victim. Examples include spitting in someone's face or offensively touching someone against his or her will.

Touching the person of someone is defined as including not only contacts with the body, but also with anything closely connected with the body, such as clothing or an item carried in the person's hand. For example, a battery may be committed by intentionally knocking a hat off someone's head or knocking a glass out of someone's hand.

**Intent** Although the contact must be intended, there is no requirement that the defendant intend to harm or injure the victim. In tort law, the INTENT must be either SPECIFIC INTENT—the contact was specifically intended—or GENERAL INTENT—the defendant was substantially certain that the act would cause the contact. The intent element is satisfied in criminal law when the act is done with an intent to injure or with CRIMINAL NEGLIGENCE—failure to use care to avoid criminal consequences. The intent for criminal law is also present when the defendant's conduct is unlawful even though it does not amount to criminal negligence.

Intent is not negated if the aim of the contact was a joke. As with all torts, however, consent is a defense. Under certain circumstances consent to a battery is assumed. A person who walks in a crowded area impliedly consents to a degree of contact that is inevitable and reasonable. Consent may also be assumed if the parties had a prior relationship unless the victim gave the defendant a previous warning.

There is no requirement that the plaintiff be aware of a battery at the time it is committed. The gist of the action is the lack of consent to contact. It is no defense that the victim was sleeping or unconscious at the time.

**Harmful or Offensive Conduct** It is not necessary for the defendant's wrongful act to result in direct contact with the victim. It is sufficient if the act sets in motion a force that results in the contact. A defendant who whipped a horse on which a plaintiff was riding, causing the plaintiff to fall and be injured, was found guilty of battery. Provided all other elements of the offense are present, the offense may also be committed by causing the victim to harm himself. A defendant who fails to act when he or she has a duty to do so is guilty—as where a nurse fails to warn a blind patient that he is headed toward an open window, causing him to fall and injure himself.

**Aggravated Battery** When a battery is committed with intent to do serious harm or murder, or when it is done with a dangerous weapon, it is described as aggravated. A weapon is considered dangerous whenever the purpose for using it is to cause death or serious harm. State statutes define aggravated battery in various ways—such as ASSAULT with intent to kill. Under such statutes, assault means both battery and assault. It is punishable as a FELONY in all states.

**Punishment** In a CIVIL ACTION for tortious battery, the penalty is damages. A jury determines the amount to be awarded, which in most cases is based on the harm done to the plaintiff. Even though a plaintiff suffers no actual injury, NOMINAL DAMAGES (a small sum) may still be awarded on the theory that there has been an invasion of a right. Also, a court may award PUNITIVE DAMAGES aimed at punishing the defendant for the wrongful act.

Criminal battery is punishable by a fine, imprisonment, or both. If it is considered aggravated the penalties are greater.

## BAYLOR, ROBERT EMMETT BLEDSOE

Robert Emmett Bledsoe Baylor achieved prominence as a jurist and a Baptist preacher.

Baylor was born May 10, 1793, in Lincoln County, Kentucky. He began his political career in 1819 with service in the Kentucky legislature, moving to the Alabama legislature in 1824. He represented Alabama in the U.S. House of Representatives from 1829 to 1831.

In 1839 Baylor settled in Texas and began a judicial career. He sat on the bench of the Texas district court in 1841, then served a term as associate judge of the Texas Supreme Court from 1841 to 1845. From 1845 to 1861, he rendered decisions as a U.S. district judge. He was also instrumental in the formation of the Texas state constitution.

**BIOGRAPHY**

THE TEXAS COLLECTION, BAYLOR UNIVERSITY

*Robert Emmett Bledsoe Baylor*

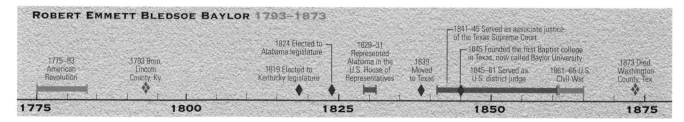

ROBERT EMMETT BLEDSOE BAYLOR 1793–1873

1775–83 American Revolution

1793 Born, Lincoln County, Ky.

1819 Elected to Kentucky legislature

1824 Elected to Alabama legislature

1829–31 Represented Alabama in the U.S. House of Representatives

1839 Moved to Texas

1841–45 Served as associate justice of the Texas Supreme Court

1845 Founded the first Baptist college in Texas, now called Baylor University

1845–61 Served as U.S. district judge

1861–65 U.S. Civil War

1873 Died, Washington County, Tex.

1775    1800    1825    1850    1875

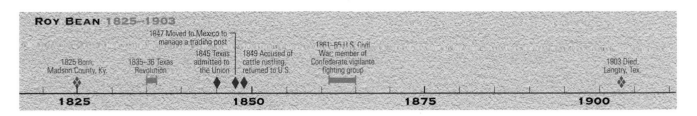

ROY BEAN 1825-1903

1825 Born, Madson County, Ky. | 1835–36 Texas Revolution | 1845 Texas admitted to the Union | 1847 Moved to Mexico to manage a trading post | 1849 Accused of cattle rustling, returned to U.S. | 1861–65 U.S. Civil War; member of Confederate vigilante fighting group | 1903 Died, Langtry, Tex.

1825 · 1850 · 1875 · 1900

As a Baptist preacher, Baylor procured a charter for the first Baptist college in Texas. This college, located at Waco, became Baylor University, named for its founder.

Baylor died December 30, 1873, in Washington County, Texas.

**BEAN, ROY** Roy Bean achieved prominence for his unconventional law enforcement procedures. His methods for enforcing the law were questionable and unorthodox.

Bean was born circa 1825, in Mason County, Kentucky. His career included many undertakings, not always legal. In 1847, he was in charge of a trading post in Mexico. Accused of cattle rustling in 1849, he was forced back to the United States. He was a member of a group of vigilantes who fought for the Confederacy during the Civil War. Bean was a saloonkeeper and a gambler in the postwar years. In 1882 Bean settled in Texas.

He changed the name of the Texas camp where he lived from Vinegaroon to Langtry and established himself as justice of the peace. His saloon was the courthouse where Bean presided as judge, using a law book, a gun, his sense of humor, and practical thinking as his guides to making judicial decisions.

Bean died March 16, 1903, in Langtry.

**BEARD, CHARLES AUSTIN** Few academicians achieve the public recognition and professional respect accorded to historian Charles Austin Beard. His polemic *An Economic Interpretation of the Constitution of the United States* stirred debate among fellow scholars and the U.S. public by contradicting the popular understanding of how and why the United States was founded. A brilliant, original thinker, Beard achieved a unique prominence among twentieth-century historians and political scientists.

**BIOGRAPHY**

*Roy Bean*

"THAT'S MY RULIN'."

**BIOGRAPHY**

*Charles Austin Beard*

Beard was born to well-to-do parents in Knightstown, Indiana, on November 27, 1874. After graduating from Indiana's DePauw University in 1898, he sailed to England to attend the University of Oxford. While at Oxford, he helped establish Ruskin Hall, a college for British working men that represented to Beard the liberation of the English masses from upper-class domination. In Beard's mind, Ruskin Hall was a symbol and precursor of the true political democracy that would be ushered in by the industrial revolution.

In 1900 Beard returned briefly to the United States to marry Mary Ritter. An intellectual in her own right, Mary Ritter Beard became an invaluable critic and collaborator in the more than fifty books produced during Beard's prolific career. After his marriage, Beard resumed his studies in England, then returned permanently to the United States. He earned his doctor's degree from New York City's Columbia University and in 1904 accepted a teaching position in political science at Columbia.

In 1913, Beard published *An Economic Interpretation of the Constitution of the United States.* The book created a mild sensation because it suggested that the United States was not yet a true democracy. Even more disturbing to some U.S. citizens was Beard's argument that the U.S. Constitution was designed primarily to protect the property rights of the wealthy capitalists attending the Constitutional Convention. He insisted that self-interest, not democratic principles, motivated the Founding Fathers. To Beard, the Constitution was a tribute to the power of class, not democracy.

Although several U.S. politicians criticized Beard's unorthodox view of U.S. history, many of his colleagues praised his innovative ap-

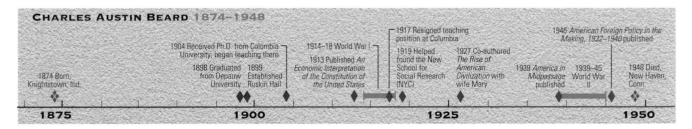

CHARLES AUSTIN BEARD 1874-1948

1874 Born, Knightstown, Ind. | 1898 Graduated from Depauw University | 1899 Established Ruskin Hall | 1904 Received Ph.D. from Columbia University; began teaching there | 1913 Published *An Economic Interpretation of the Constitution of the United States* | 1914–18 World War I | 1917 Resigned teaching position at Columbia | 1919 Helped found the New School for Social Research (NYC) | 1927 Co-authored *The Rise of American Civilization* with wife Mary | 1939 *America in Midpassage* published | 1939–45 World War II | 1946 *American Foreign Policy in the Making, 1932–1940* published | 1948 Died, New Haven, Conn.

1875 · 1900 · 1925 · 1950

proach. They understood how the private economic interests of the colonial ruling class could have had a far-reaching effect on the nascent U.S. government.

In 1917 Beard protested the firing of several Columbia University faculty members by resigning his own position. Beard had been outraged when the university dismissed his colleagues for their refusal to support the United States' involvement in World War I. In 1919 he helped found the New School for Social Research in New York City.

In 1927 Beard produced another remarkable tome, *The Rise of American Civilization*. Coauthored by his wife, it provided an overview of U.S. history with further insights into the government's origins. This sprawling, two-volume set was followed by *America in Midpassage*, in 1939, and *The American Spirit*, in 1942.

During the early 1930s, Beard wrote extensively about the nature of historical knowledge. He was particularly interested in historians' personal biases and the effect of those biases on the presentation of historical facts.

Beard died in 1948, at the age of seventy-three. He is remembered as an accomplished historian who influenced the way U.S. citizens view their own history.

**CROSS-REFERENCES**

Constitution of the United States; Constitution of the United States: Constitutional Convention of 1787; Constitution of the United States *In Focus: Federalists vs. Anti-Federalists*.

**BEARER** One who is the holder or possessor of an instrument that is negotiable—for example, a CHECK, a DRAFT, or a NOTE—and upon which a specific payee is not designated.

A NEGOTIABLE INSTRUMENT that is payable to "bearer" or to "cash" or to "the order of cash," that is, not naming a payee, is a bearer instrument, and is called "bearer" paper.

**BEASLEY, MERCER** Mercer Beasley was an eminent New Jersey jurist.

Beasley was born March 27, 1815, in Philadelphia, Pennsylvania. He was admitted to the bar in 1838, and established a successful legal practice in Trenton, New Jersey, before pursu-

**BIOGRAPHY**

*Mercer Beasley*

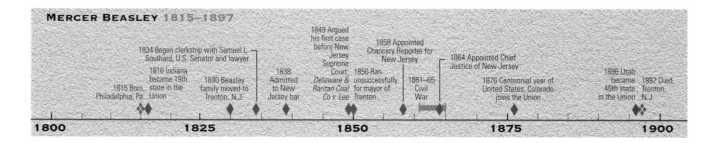

**MERCER BEASLEY 1815–1897**

1815 Born, in Philadelphia, Pa.

1816 Indiana became 19th state in the Union

1830 Beasley family moved to Trenton, N.J.

1834 Began clerkship with Samuel L. Southard, U.S. Senator and lawyer

1838 Admitted to New Jersey bar

1849 Argued his first case before New Jersey Supreme Court

1850 Ran unsuccessfully for mayor of Trenton; *Delaware & Raritan Coal Co v. Lee*

1858 Appointed Chancery Reporter for New Jersey

1861–65 Civil War

1864 Appointed Chief Justice of New Jersey

1876 Centennial year of United States; Colorado joins the Union

1896 Utah became 45th state in the Union

1897 Died, Trenton, N.J.

1800 — 1825 — 1850 — 1875 — 1900

Although Beard was closely associated with the U.S. progressive movement and social reforms, he disagreed with several aspects of Franklin D. Roosevelt's New Deal programs. In 1934 he began an acrimonious, decade-long campaign against Roosevelt's foreign policy. In *American Foreign Policy in the Making, 1932–1940* (1946) and *President Roosevelt and the Coming of War* (1948), Beard maintained that the United States had backed Japan into a corner and had forced the country into a war. His extreme isolationist views damaged his professional reputation to some extent.

**BIOGRAPHY**

*Cesare Bonesano Beccaria*

ing a career in the judicial system.

In 1864 he began service as chief justice of New Jersey and remained on the bench for thirty-three years. He gained prominence for his equitable decisions, particularly those concerning political dissent.

Beasley died February 19, 1897, in Trenton.

**BECCARIA, CESARE BONESANO, MARCHESE DI** Cesare Bonesano Beccaria was an expert in law and economics and put forth new principles in both fields which were widely accepted throughout Europe.

Beccaria was born March 15, 1738. He taught

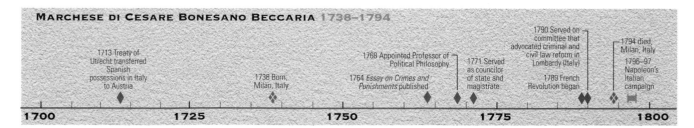

**MARCHESE DI CESARE BONESANO BECCARIA 1738–1794**

1713 Treaty of Utrecht transferred Spanish possessions in Italy to Austria

1738 Born, Milan, Italy

1764 *Essay on Crimes and Punishments* published

1768 Appointed Professor of Political Philosophy

1771 Served as councilor of state and magistrate

1789 French Revolution began

1790 Served on committee that advocated criminal and civil law reform in Lombardy (Italy)

1794 died, Milan, Italy

1796–97 Napoleon's Italian campaign

1700 — 1725 — 1750 — 1775 — 1800

law and economics in Milan. He vehemently opposed CAPITAL PUNISHMENT and cruel treatment of prisoners. His economic theories concerned wages and labor and influenced such eminent economists as Adam Smith and Thomas Robert Malthus.

In 1771 Beccaria served as councilor of state and magistrate; in 1790, he was a member of a committee that advocated reform of criminal and civil law in Lombardy.

Beccaria's ideas were published in 1764 in his *Essay on Crimes and Punishments*. The book was well received throughout Europe and greatly influenced changes in European economic and legal systems.

He died November 8, 1794, in Milan.

**BECKET, SAINT THOMAS** Saint Thomas Becket was CHANCELLOR of England and archbishop of Canterbury during the reign of HENRY II and was martyred following a bitter battle with the monarchy over royal control of church law.

Becket was born around 1118 in London, England, the son of a prosperous London merchant and his wife who were of Norman ancestry. He was first educated at a monastery in Merton, just outside London, and then in London grammar schools. In his late teens, he was sent to Paris for further schooling, including the study of logic, rhetoric, and philosophy. At age twenty-one, after his mother had died and his father had lost his fortune, Becket returned to London and became a city clerk to three sheriffs. Three years later, in about 1143, his father introduced him to Theobald, archbishop of Canterbury. Becket soon joined Theobald's household, becoming a clerk and later a close adviser to the archbishop. In about 1150, Theobald sent Becket to Italy and France to study civil and CANON LAW. Upon his return to Theobald's court in 1152, Becket was able to secure the papal letters that prevented the English king Stephen from crowning his son to be successor to the throne. Becket's intervention permitted Henry II, in 1154, to become the king of England.

In the same year, Theobald appointed Becket archdeacon of Canterbury. Less than

**BIOGRAPHY**

*Saint Thomas Becket*

three months later, on Theobald's recommendation and in gratitude for Becket's role in helping him to gain the throne, Henry II named Becket chancellor of England.

Becket became the king's most trusted adviser and a constant and devoted companion. He was an effective chancellor, leading troops into war, repairing castles, conducting foreign policy, and negotiating a marriage between Prince Henry, son of the king, and the daughter of King Louis VII of France. Becket lived luxuriously, holding extravagant receptions and dressing in splendid clothes. Theobald disapproved of his protégé's lavish lifestyle. To Theobald, it was inappropriate for Becket, who still remained archdeacon while serving as chancellor, to surround himself with worldly things. Becket ignored the concerns of his mentor and even refused to visit Theobald on his deathbed.

After Theobald died in 1161, Henry appointed Becket archbishop of Canterbury in 1162. Becket, aware of the influence he now wielded as a religious leader, promptly abandoned the trappings of his previous life as chancellor. He devoted himself to the study of canon law and to the spiritual obligations of his new role. He also became involved in a series of clashes between the church and the state that put him at odds with King Henry, his closest friend and confidant.

In late 1163 Henry decided to abolish certain privileges enjoyed by the clergy, which exempted them, when they were accused of crimes, from the jurisdiction of the civil courts. Criminous clerks, as they were known, were instead allowed to stand trial before a bishop in the ECCLESIASTICAL (church) COURTS, which usually resulted in much milder punishments. Under Henry's reforms, an accused clerk would be required to appear first in a civil court to answer the charges. If the clerk denied the offense and asked to be heard in an ecclesiastical court, the clerk would then appear before a bishop. If convicted by the ecclesiastical court, the clerk would return to the civil court to face charges as a layperson.

Becket vehemently opposed Henry's mea-

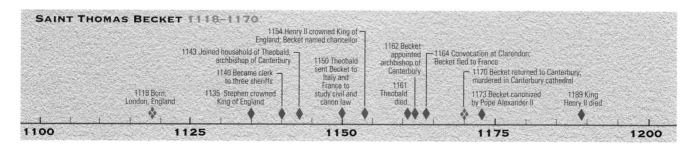

**SAINT THOMAS BECKET 1118–1170**

- 1118 Born, London, England
- 1135 Stephen crowned King of England
- 1140 Became clerk to three sheriffs
- 1143 Joined household of Theobald, archbishop of Canterbury
- 1150 Theobald sent Becket to Italy and France to study civil and canon law
- 1154 Henry II crowned King of England; Becket named chancellor
- 1161 Theobald died
- 1162 Becket appointed archbishop of Canterbury
- 1164 Convocation at Clarendon; Becket fled to France
- 1170 Becket returned to Canterbury; murdered in Canterbury cathedral
- 1173 Becket canonized by Pope Alexander II
- 1189 King Henry II died

| 1100 | 1125 | 1150 | 1175 | 1200 |

sures. He maintained that they subjected the clergy to be punished twice for the same offense: the clergy, he argued, would lose their clerical status in the ecclesiastical courts and would also face secular penalties imposed by the civil courts. However, under intense pressure from the monarchy, Becket eventually relented and agreed verbally to Henry's proposals.

In January 1164 Henry summoned a convocation at Clarendon, where he planned to put his reforms into a document known as the Constitutions of CLARENDON, and to secure Becket's signature. But at the last minute, Becket repudiated his previous verbal agreement to the measures and refused to sign the documents, on the grounds that they violated canon law. Becket's defiance incurred the wrath of the king, who denounced him as a traitor to the throne. Henry then threatened to imprison Becket or at least force him to resign as archbishop. Becket, fearing for his safety, fled to France in late 1164 and remained in exile at Flanders for the next six years. In France, Becket struck back at Henry by excommunicating several of his councilors and threatening to excommunicate the king as well.

In 1169 Henry and Becket attempted a reconciliation, but Henry soon incensed Becket by having Roger, the archbishop of York and a rival of Becket's, crown Prince Henry as his successor. Such coronations were traditionally undertaken by the archbishop of Canterbury. Becket retaliated by suspending Roger and the other bishops who participated in the coronation.

In late 1170 Henry and Becket briefly resolved their differences and Becket returned to Canterbury amid great fanfare. Almost immediately, however, officers of the king demanded that Becket absolve the suspended bishops involved in Prince Henry's coronation. Becket steadfastly refused, maintaining that only the pope had the authority to give absolution.

The king, by now exasperated with Becket, is said to have uttered, in a fit of anger, "Will nobody rid me of this turbulent priest?" Four of his knights took his plea literally and on December 29, 1170, went to Canterbury, where they confronted Becket in the cathedral and again demanded that he absolve the suspended

*"IF IT BE A QUESTION OF TEMPORAL MATTERS, WE SHOULD RATHER FEAR THE LOSS OF SOULS THAN OF TEMPORALITIES."*

**BIOGRAPHY**

*Henry Ward Beecher*

*"IT USUALLY TAKES A HUNDRED YEARS TO MAKE A LAW, AND THEN, AFTER IT HAS DONE ITS WORK, IT USUALLY TAKES A HUNDRED YEARS TO GET RID OF IT."*

bishops. Becket refused. The knights beat him over the head repeatedly with their swords until he died.

Word of Becket's murder spread quickly, and his tomb soon became a shrine visited by thousands of pilgrims. Becket, in his early fifties at the time of his death, was canonized by Pope Alexander II in 1173. Henry II did penance at Canterbury and was absolved of the murder. The four assassins did fourteen years' service in the Holy Land as penance for the crime. A later English king, Henry III, had Becket's remains placed in a more elaborate tomb at Canterbury, which remained a popular place of pilgrimage. The religious journeys to Becket's tomb became the basis for Chaucer's masterpiece *Canterbury Tales*, which was written almost two hundred years after Becket's death.

In 1538 Henry VIII became embroiled in his own struggles with the church and viewed the pilgrimages to Becket's tomb with increasing hostility. As a result, he had the shrine destroyed and reportedly had Becket's bones burned.

**BEECHER, HENRY WARD**  Henry Ward Beecher was one of the most prominent U.S. ministers of the nineteenth century as well as an active participant in various reform movements.

Beecher was born June 24, 1813, in Litchfield, Connecticut. He was the son of preacher Lyman Beecher and the brother of Harriet Beecher Stowe, author of *Uncle Tom's Cabin*. He studied at Amherst College and Lane Theological Seminary and served as a novice minister in Indiana before becoming minister at the Plymouth Congregational Church in Brooklyn, New York, in 1847. A liberal thinker, Beecher was in favor of such principles as women's suffrage, ABOLITION of SLAVERY, and acceptance of the theory of evolution and often lectured on these and other controversial ideas from the pulpit.

Beecher excelled as a speaker and in 1863 he went on a lecture tour throughout England and spoke in support of the Union position in the Civil War.

In 1875, Beecher, regarded as one of the United States' foremost preachers, was involved in a sensational trial that damaged his honor. Journalist Theodore Tilton accused the minis-

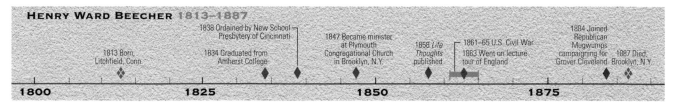

**HENRY WARD BEECHER** 1813–1887

- 1813 Born, Litchfield, Conn.
- 1834 Graduated from Amherst College
- 1838 Ordained by New School Presbytery of Cincinnati
- 1847 Became minister at Plymouth Congregational Church in Brooklyn, N.Y.
- 1858 *Life Thoughts* published
- 1861–65 U.S. Civil War
- 1863 Went on lecture tour of England
- 1884 Joined Republican Mugwumps campaigning for Grover Cleveland
- 1887 Died, Brooklyn, N.Y.

1800 — 1825 — 1850 — 1875

ter of committing ADULTERY with Mrs. Tilton. Beecher was expertly defended by his attorney, William M. Evarts, and, after a lengthy trial, the jury could not agree on a verdict. Beecher's church proclaimed him the victor and officially cleared him of the charges. In spite of the scandal, Beecher continued to be an influential force in the U.S. ministry until his death on March 8, 1887, in Brooklyn.

See also WOMEN'S RIGHTS.

**BELIEF** 📖 Mental reliance on or acceptance of a particular concept, which is arrived at by weighing external EVIDENCE, FACTS, and personal observation and experience. 📖

Belief is essentially a subjective feeling about the validity of an idea or set of facts. It is more than a mere SUSPICION and less than concrete knowledge. Unlike suspicion, which is based primarily on inner personal conviction, belief is founded upon assurance gained by empirical evidence and from other people. Positive knowledge, as contrasted with belief, is the clear perception of existing facts.

Belief has been defined as having faith in an idea or formulating a conclusion as the result of considering information. INFORMATION AND BELIEF is a legal term that is used to describe an ALLEGATION based upon GOOD FAITH rather than firsthand knowledge.

**BELL, DERRICK ALBERT, JR.** Derrick Albert Bell, Jr., was the first tenured black law professor at Harvard Law School, a renegade civil rights scholar and proponent, and a prolific author of civil rights–related works, including the critically acclaimed books *And We Are Not Saved: The Elusive Quest for Racial Justice* (1987) and *Faces at the Bottom of the Well: The Permanence of Racism* (1992).

Bell was born November 6, 1930, in Pittsburgh. The seeds of his views on racial injustice—and his response to racial bigotry and prejudice—were sown in the Depression. When he was five years old, he watched his mother, Ada Bell, demand that the family's landlord fix the rotted stairs behind their apartment. His mother finally told the landlord, who had ig-

nored her requests for months, that she refused to pay the rent unless he fixed the stairs. A few days later, the landlord fixed their steps—and all the other broken steps on their road. Bell's interpretation of the event? "Good things happen when you push." Bell has also said that he carries his father's "dignified suspicion" of whites in hard-time Pittsburgh and his mother's homespun conception of a rights-based economy of self-respecting agitation.

The eldest of four children, Bell earned a bachelor of arts degree from Duquesne University in 1952 and then served in the Korean War. While in the Air Force, Bell made his first discreet push for racial equality: he complained about black soldiers having to sit in the back of the bus whenever they left base. After his military stint, he attended the University of Pittsburgh School of Law, lived at home, and kept the books for his father, Derrick Bell, Sr., who ran a trash-collection business. Bell also worked as the associate editor for the *Pittsburgh Law Review*, a prestigious position for a student to hold at any law school. He competed strenuously in law school and has admitted to being "a little obnoxious" in his attempt to succeed in an otherwise all-white class: in the yearbook, underneath his picture, is written, "Knows everything and wants others to know he knows everything."

After graduating fourth in his class and being admitted to the District of Columbia bar in 1957, Bell applied to a top local law firm, which had asked the law school to send over its best students. "When I walked in, there were all these gasps," he said. "It was like a line of heart attacks down the hall." Bell did not get the job, but he did go on to become one of only three black attorneys at the U.S. Department of Justice, Civil Rights Division. His first professional act of defiance came in 1959, when he quit his job at the Department of Justice in protest after being told to give up his membership in the NATIONAL ASSOCIATION FOR THE ADVANCEMENT OF COLORED PEOPLE (NAACP), which the Justice Department considered a conflict of interest.

**BIOGRAPHY**

*Derrick Albert Bell, Jr.*

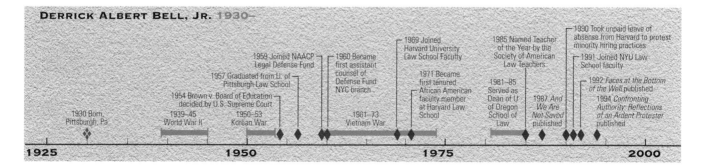

DERRICK ALBERT BELL, JR. 1930–

- 1930 Born, Pittsburgh, Pa
- 1939–45 World War II
- 1950–53 Korean War
- 1954 Brown v. Board of Education decided by U.S. Supreme Court
- 1957 Graduated from U. of Pittsburgh Law School
- 1959 Joined NAACP Legal Defense Fund
- 1960 Became first assistant counsel of Defense Fund NYC branch
- 1961–73 Vietnam War
- 1969 Joined Harvard University Law School Faculty
- 1971 Became first tenured African American faculty member at Harvard Law School
- 1981–85 Served as Dean of U of Oregon School of Law
- 1985 Named Teacher of the Year by the Society of American Law Teachers
- 1987 *And We Are Not Saved* published
- 1990 Took unpaid leave of absence from Harvard to protest minority hiring practices
- 1991 Joined NYU Law School faculty
- 1992 *Faces at the Bottom of the Well* published
- 1994 *Confronting Authority: Reflections of an Ardent Protester* published

1925     1950     1975     2000

Bell subsequently passed the Pennsylvania bar and took a job with the NAACP Legal Defense Fund—which had been established in 1940 by his new boss, THURGOOD MARSHALL, to champion the cause of racial equality. After starting as the executive secretary for the Pittsburgh branch of the Defense Fund, Bell was promoted to first assistant counsel at the New York City branch, where he remained from 1960 to 1966. While working as a civil rights lawyer, he confronted many difficult people and situations—from judges predisposed to ruling against his black clients to segregated public buildings. During this time, Bell spent a night in jail in Mississippi for refusing to leave a train station's "whites-only" waiting room. He oversaw three hundred SCHOOL DESEGREGATION cases and played a central role in getting JAMES MEREDITH, a black student, admitted to the all-white University of Mississippi, despite the resistance of Governor Ross Barnett. "Down South, I learned a lot. . . . It just seems that unless something's pushed, unless you litigate, nothing happens," Bell said.

In 1966 Bell was admitted to the New York bar. From 1966 to 1968, he ran the U.S. Department of Health, Education, and Welfare's Office for Civil Rights. In 1968 he moved to California and became the executive director of the Western Center of Law and Poverty, at the University of Southern California (USC). He passed the California bar in 1969 and taught law as an adjunct professor at USC's law center.

After the 1968 assassination of Dr. MARTIN LUTHER KING, JR., and inner-city riots, Bell received a number of offers to teach law, including one from Harvard. He accepted Harvard's offer and lectured there from 1969 to 1971, after telling the school that he was willing to be the first black there but not the last. In 1971, after challenging Dean Derek Bok to vote on Bell's TENURE as promised, he became the law school's first tenured African American faculty member, a position he kept until December 1980. During his tenure, he wrote four books dealing with race and the law.

Bell left Harvard in January 1981 to become a professor and the dean of the University of Oregon School of Law. He resigned from there in 1985, when the school refused to back his decision to offer tenure to an Asian American woman. The same year, the Society of American Law Teachers named him Teacher of the Year.

Bell spent the next year as a visiting professor at Stanford Law School, where, once again, he found himself mired in controversy—this time for his revisionist teaching of constitu-

tional law. Some Stanford law students, who disliked Bell's interpretation of the Constitution, pressured the faculty into offering supplemental lectures from other professors. Shortly before the first of these additional lectures, Stanford's Black Law Student Association staged a protest, and the administration made a formal apology to Bell.

In 1986 Bell returned to Harvard to teach law. He soon was caught up—yet again—in racial discord. During commencement exercises in May 1987, he staged a four-day round-the-clock sit-in inside his office to protest the denial of tenure to two members of the CRITICAL LEGAL STUDIES movement, a leftist movement that challenges the basic tenets of legal education and scholarship. Also in 1987, Bell's alter ego, Geneva Crenshaw, first came to life in the pages of his book *And We Are Not Saved.* At the fulcrum of this collection of ten allegorical tales was the contention that racism is an immutable, permanent problem in U.S. society; Bell used Socratic dialogues between himself, as narrator, and Crenshaw, a black civil rights lawyer, to measure the "progress" of blacks since *Brown v. Board of Education,* 349 U.S. 294, 75 S. Ct. 753, 99 L. Ed. 1083 (1955). Further, in 1987, Bell spoke out in support of Justice Thurgood Marshall, whose minority report that year had criticized the Constitution and blacks' "token presence" in the bicentennial celebrations: "We need . . . more candor about why the *Constitution* was written the way it was and what still needs to be done to insure individual rights," said Bell.

The following year, Bell wrote *Civil Rights in Two Thousand Four: Where Will We Be?* Also in 1988, he wrote a scathing indictment of Harvard Law's AFFIRMATIVE ACTION performance; his article, published in 1989 by the *Michigan Law Review,* gave a fictional account of how Harvard came to hire more minorities only after the school's black faculty and the university president were killed in a terrorist bombing. Bell was privately criticized for having dared to paint a grisly portrait of the president of Harvard being blown to pieces. Robert C. Clark, a professor at Harvard and a future dean of the school, objected to Bell's many protests, saying, "This is a university, not a lunch counter in the Deep South." "In its own way, this law school is as much in need of reform as the lunch counters of the South, although in a far more subtle way," said Bell. Clark later apologized and spoke of sharing Bell's goal of building a diverse faculty.

Bell's dissension at Harvard came to a head in the spring of 1990, when Professor Regina Austin was denied tenure at the law school. In

"CIVIL RIGHTS CAMPAIGNS AIMED AT CHANGING THE RULES WITHOUT AFFECTING THE UNDERLYING STATUS QUO."

early April, students on fifty law campuses boycotted classes in a call for more minority teachers; later that month, Bell announced that he would step down—and forgo his $100,000 annual salary—until a black or other minority woman was considered for tenure. Of the school's sixty-five full-time professors at the time, five were white women and five were black men.

Bell's position was that qualified black professors were not getting through an obsolete and irrelevant tenure-granting process, despite their qualifications and the valuable perspective they could provide law students. He said the traditional checklist for tenure—Was the candidate at the top of his or her law class? an editor on law review? someone with prestigious clerkships?—must be made more flexible when considering minority professors. "The traditional way of doing legal scholarship doesn't do justice to our experience," said Bell. "But minorities who are trying to blaze new trails in legal academia are meeting opposition and silencing." Comparing Bell to ROSA PARKS—a black woman who refused to sit in the back of the bus in Montgomery, Alabama, in 1955—the Reverend JESSE JACKSON offered in May 1990 to mediate between the school and Bell. Harvard turned down the offer.

Many observers marveled at the public attention attracted by Bell's dramatic move at Harvard—among them, Richard H. Chused, professor of the Georgetown University Law Center, who in 1989 published an empirical study demonstrating the lack of diversity within law school faculties, and Nathaniel R. Jones, judge for the federal Ninth Circuit Court of Appeals and a part-time Harvard Law instructor. Not all of Bell's colleagues agreed with this form of protest, however. Professor Charles Fried, of Harvard Law, called Bell "off his head," and others termed him "counterproductive." Dean Clark continued to assert that Harvard should make appointments based on merits and not because of protests.

Bell's struggle with Harvard may not have been entirely for naught: in September 1992, Dean Clark acknowledged bitter divisions within the school and created a working group of faculty, students, and staff to improve the level of civility and community and to foster discussion of issues that have shaken the institution. And in June 1993, Harvard granted tenure to its seventh black law professor, Charles Ogletree.

**CROSS-REFERENCES**

Civil Rights; Discrimination; Legal Education.

## BIOGRAPHY

*Griffin Boyette Bell*

"IF YOU BELIEVE IN EXALTING THE BILL OF RIGHTS . . . YOU HAVE TO BE FOR THE INDIVIDUAL, EVEN IF IT MEANS BEING AGAINST THE GOVERNMENT."

**BELL, GRIFFIN BOYETTE**  Griffin Boyette Bell served as U.S. attorney general from 1977 to 1979 under President JIMMY CARTER and as a judge on the Court of Appeals for the Fifth Circuit from 1961 to 1976. He is also nationally recognized for his skills as a corporate lawyer.

Bell was born October 31, 1918, in Americus, Georgia, only twelve miles from Plains, Georgia, the boyhood home of Carter. (In fact, Carter and Bell knew each other as children.) Bell served in the U.S. Army during World War II. After the war, he studied at Mercer University Law School, graduating cum laude in 1948. He gained admission to the Georgia bar in 1947.

Bell practiced law in Savannah, Georgia, and Rome, Georgia, from 1947 to 1953, after which he moved to Atlanta to work in the prestigious firm of King and Spalding, where he eventually earned the position of managing partner. Bell also became involved in politics, serving from 1959 to 1961 as chief of staff to Governor S. Ernest Vandiver, of Georgia.

SCHOOL DESEGREGATION was a heated issue at the time. Governor Vandiver vigorously opposed desegregation, inventing the slogan No, Not One to symbolize his goal of keeping Georgia's schools completely segregated. Bell acted as a moderating influence on Vandiver, working behind the scenes to ease tensions with African American leaders. Eventually, Vandiver

**GRIFFIN BOYETTE BELL 1918–**

1914–18 World War I

1918 Born, Americus, Ga.

1941–46 Served in U.S. Army during World War II; rose to rank of Major

1948 Earned LL.B. cum laude from Mercer University Law School

1950–53 Korean War

1954 *Brown v. Board of Education* struck down "separate but equal doctrine," a major victory in the battle for school desegregation

1959 Became chief of staff to Governor Ernest Vandiver of Ga.

1961 Appointed to U.S. Court of Appeals for the Fifth Circuit by President Kennedy; University of Georgia admitted first black students

1961–73 Vietnam War

1965–66 Served as chairman of the Atlanta Committee on Crime and Delinquency

1971 Public school busing to achieve integration began in several states

1977 Appointed U.S. attorney general by President Carter; markedly increased female and minority representation in high-ranking posts and judgeships

1979 Returned to private practice at King and Spalding

1982 *Taking Care of the Law* published

1985–86 Served as President of the American College of Trial Lawyers

1900    1925    1950    1975    2000

and the Georgia legislature agreed to conditional desegregation.

Bell served as cochairman of JOHN F. KENNEDY's Georgia election campaign in 1960. His success at that task won him an appointment as judge to the U.S. Court of Appeals for the Fifth Circuit in 1961, a position he held through 1976. During his fifteen years on the bench, he took part in over 3,000 cases, 141 of them involving school desegregation.

Observers have categorized Bell's judicial decisions as moderate to conservative. He generally supported CIVIL RIGHTS advocates in employment and VOTING RIGHTS cases, but opposed busing as a means to achieve school desegregation. At times, his decisions could have been described as liberal, as when he supported attempts to place more African Americans on JURIES and approved AFFIRMATIVE ACTION hiring for the Mississippi Highway Patrol. His most influential work was the initiation of a reform scheme that improved the efficiency of the court system.

Bell also served as cochairman of the Atlanta Commission on Crime and Delinquency from 1965 to 1966. He resigned from the appeals court in 1976, resumed private practice, and served as legal adviser to Carter during Carter's presidential campaign that year. Following his election as president, Carter named Bell attorney general, a move that disappointed those who had hoped Carter would appoint an African American or a woman to the office. Bell's nomination ran into trouble when it was revealed that he belonged to three clubs that were in effect racially segregated. Bell agreed to quit the clubs, and was nominated to the post of attorney general on January 25, 1977.

Upon taking office, Bell defused some of the opposition to his appointment by naming African Americans to the posts of solicitor general and assistant attorney general. He also appointed women to other key positions in the department and to federal judgeships. Later, Bell proudly pointed out that forty-one women were appointed and confirmed to the federal bench during the Carter administration, producing an eightfold increase in the number of federal judgeships occupied by women. As attorney general, Bell again championed court re-

form and also pushed for greater FEDERAL BUREAU OF INVESTIGATION involvement in pursuing white-collar, narcotics, and ANTITRUST violations.

Bell resigned as attorney general in 1979 and resumed his work in private practice as senior partner at King and Spalding. Bell has been called on frequently by Fortune 500 corporations for advice on difficult legal issues. He led independent investigations of Exxon Corporation's actions following a 1989 oil spill in Prince William Sound, off the coast of Alaska, and, in 1992, Dow Corning Corporation's handling of lawsuits resulting from its silicone breast implants.

Bell served as cochairman of the National Task Force on Violent Crime in 1981 and cochairman of the Committee on Federal Ethics in 1989. He has also served as president of the American College of Trial Lawyers. Bell received an honorary doctor of laws degree from Mercer University in 1967 and the Order of the Coif from Vanderbilt Law School. In 1982, he published a book, *Taking Care of the Law*, that related his experiences as attorney general and set forth his recommendations for legal reform and the reduction of government bureaucracy.

**BELL, JOHN** John Bell was born February 15, 1797, near Nashville, Tennessee. He graduated from Cumberland College in Nashville in 1817 and was admitted to the bar in the same year. He practiced law in Franklin and Nashville, Tennessee, before entering politics.

From 1827 to 1841, Bell served as a congressman for Tennessee in the U.S. House of Representatives. He voiced strong opposition to Andrew Jackson's program for the deposit of federal funds into state banks and to the elimination of the BANK OF THE UNITED STATES.

Bell was secretary of war in 1841 and then U.S. senator for Tennessee for twelve years beginning in 1847.

In 1860 Bell was the unsuccessful presidential candidate of a small party known as the Constitutional Union Party. He favored a cautious policy concerning SLAVERY and opposed the South's SECESSION from the Union until the battle of Fort Sumter signaled the outbreak of the Civil War; he then encouraged Tennessee to join the Confederacy.

**BIOGRAPHY**

CORBIS-BETTMANN

*John Bell*

"IT FOLLOWS THAT POPULARITY IS NOT ALWAYS THE BEST TEST OF MERIT, OR OF GENERAL PROPRIETY."

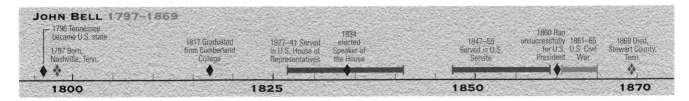

**JOHN BELL 1797–1869**

1796 Tennessee became U.S. state
1797 Born, Nashville, Tenn.
1817 Graduated from Cumberland College
1827–41 Served in U.S. House of Representatives
1834 elected Speaker of the House
1847–59 Served in U.S. Senate
1860 Ran unsuccessfully for U.S. President
1861–65 U.S. Civil War
1869 Died, Stewart County, Tenn.

1800    1825    1850    1870

Bell died September 10, 1869, in Stewart County, Tennessee.

**BELOW** In an inferior, subordinate, or lower place in regard to any entity.

A court below is a lower court through which a case has passed. A case is removed for REVIEW from the court below to the court above, or a higher court. The FORUM where a lawsuit is initially brought is called an INFERIOR COURT, or the court below.

**BENCH** A FORUM of justice comprised of the JUDGE or judges of a court. The seat of the court occupied by the judges.

The bench is used to refer to a group of judges as a collective whole. It is a tribunal or place where justice is administered. To appear before the full bench means to appear before the entire group of judges of the court.

**BENCH TRIAL** A TRIAL conducted before a judge presiding without a JURY.

**BENCH WARRANT** A process that is initiated by the court PRO SE in order to attach or arrest a person. An order that a judge, or group of judges, issues directly to the police with the purpose of directing a person's arrest.

A bench warrant is used for ATTACHMENT or arrest in a case of CONTEMPT, which is the willful disregard or disobedience of an authority such as the court. A bench warrant is also issued when an INDICTMENT, which is a written accusation of a person's guilt for an act or omission, is handed down. A third instance where a bench warrant is issued is to obtain a WITNESS who disobeys a SUBPOENA, which is a command to appear at a specified time and place to present TESTIMONY upon a certain matter.

**BENEFICIAL ASSOCIATION** An incorporated or voluntary nonprofit organization that has been created primarily to protect and aid its members and their dependents.

*Beneficial association* is an all-inclusive term referring to an organization that exists for the mutual assistance of its members or its members' families, relatives, or designated BENEFICIARIES, during times of hardship, such as illness or financial need. The assistance provided by a beneficial association can take the form of life, accident, burial, or health INSURANCE. Beneficial associations may also be called benevolent associations, fraternal societies, fraternal orders, or friendly associations or societies.

**History** Early beneficial associations were similar to the English friendly societies, which first appeared in the 1500s. Working people organized these clubs to provide sickness and death benefits for members. Several fraternal societies established branches in the United States and Canada in the early 1800s.

The Ancient Order of United Workmen, founded in 1868, was the first beneficial association to pay substantial death benefits. Other groups that followed the model of the Ancient

A sample bench warrant for the state of New York

STATE OF NEW YORK
COUNTY OF _____ ss.:
IN THE NAME OF THE PEOPLE OF THE STATE
OF NEW YORK
To: [*Address warrant to any police officer whose geographical area of employment embraces either the place where the offense charged was allegedly committed or the locality of the court by which the warrant is issued or to any uniformed court officer for a court in New York City, Nassau County or Suffolk County that is part of the unified court system for execution in the building wherein such court officer is employed*]

An indictment having been filed on the _____ day of _____, 19____, in the County Court of the State of New York, County of _____, charging _____ with the crime of [*specify crime*], and said _____, being at liberty on his or her own recognizance [*or on bail*] pursuant to an order of this court dated _____, 19____, and this court considering that it is necessary to review such order,

YOU ARE THEREFORE COMMANDED forthwith to arrest the above named _____ and bring him or her before this court for the purpose aforesaid.

Dated at the City of _____, New York, this _____ day of _____, 19____.

[*Signature of Issuing Judge*]
_____
[*Official Title of Subscriber*]

Order of Workmen were soon created. These early associations and societies furnished life insurance to members whose income was so low they could not have otherwise obtained insurance benefits. In addition, many of these associations provided companionship and social activities for their members.

The National Fraternal Congress was formed in 1886 to provide state regulation and uniform legislation for beneficial associations. In 1901, a group of associations and societies formed the Associated Fraternities of America. In 1913, the two groups merged to form the National Fraternal Congress of America.

Beneficial associations include the Police Benevolent Association, Loyal Order of the Moose, Knights of Columbus, Independent Order of Odd Fellows, and Benevolent and Protective Order of Elks. Many of these associations are secret lodges, with passwords, ceremonies, and initiation rites.

**Organization and Incorporation**  The COMMON-LAW right of CONTRACT authorizes the formation of a beneficial association through the voluntary association of its members. Incorporation of a beneficial association may occur either by a specific legislative act or under general statutes that expressly authorize such incorporation. Some states codify laws pertaining to the formation and incorporation of beneficial associations in their nonprofit corporation law; they do so because beneficial associations may not be formed with the purpose of bringing a financial benefit to their founders.

A beneficial association is organized through its charter, constitution, and bylaws.

**Charter**  The CHARTER of a benevolent association is the basis of its legal existence and the source of its power to carry out the objects of its creation. A charter is analogous to ARTICLES OF INCORPORATION and becomes part of the contract of membership when one joins the beneficial association. For beneficial associations that elect to INCORPORATE, the charter will be embodied in the articles of incorporation. Regardless of whether the association is incorporated, the charter incorporates by reference the general laws of the state where the association is formed.

**Constitution and Bylaws**  The CONSTITUTION of a benevolent association defines the fundamental principles that will govern the duties of the association and its officers, and the regulation of its membership. Unless the constitution is expressly embodied in the charter, it is regarded as a code of laws similar in effect to BYLAWS. A constitutional provision will prevail over a provision of a conflicting bylaw because it is viewed as a fundamental rule for the government of the association.

Beneficial associations may adopt bylaws that will determine all questions of discipline, doctrine, and internal policy and will regulate the association's general business activities. The enactment of a bylaw is governed by provisions contained in either the charter or the constitution. Bylaws must be in accordance with the law and PUBLIC POLICY, must be REASONABLE, and must apply to all members uniformly. The constitution and the bylaws form a binding contract between and upon all the organization's members. Finally, bylaws also provide for the DISSOLUTION of a beneficial association.

**Rights, Powers, and Liabilities**  The authority and powers of beneficial associations are subject to the statutes under which the associations are formed and organized. An incorporated association may not enlarge the powers granted to it by the statute under which it was created. Certain powers, such as the power to enter into contractual relations, may be implied when they are essential to the accomplishment of the association's objectives. Contracts are binding upon the association where they have been executed by the appropriate officers of the association. Through its proper committees or officers, a beneficial association may enter into a LEASE.

Generally, a beneficial association has no power to borrow money. However, some states permit proper officers or committees to execute BONDS and MORTGAGES in order to secure building loans.

Ordinarily, beneficial associations can transact business in places other than the state within which they have been organized.

Because beneficial associations are founded on the principle of mutuality, where each member shares all the benefits as well as all the burdens, they do not have CAPITAL STOCK, nor do all associations maintain a fund for paying benefits. If a fund is not maintained, each member promises to contribute an equal share with every other member as the association's need for funds arises.

Unless a statute makes a distinction, courts generally recognize a beneficial association certificate containing insurance features to be the same as any other similar insurance contract. If the certificate INDEMNIFIES a member in case of disability or death, the association will be regarded as a mutual insurance company. However, beneficial associations are not the same as insurance companies. First, beneficial associations do not have as a purpose the goal of indemnifying or securing against loss; rather, they create a TRUST fund with their members' dues, from which they may provide relief to their members. Second, beneficial associations are not created for profit. Third, these associations do not advertise for business but limit their clientele to their members. Finally, whereas an insurance company fixes a beneficiary's rights with the terms of the insurance policy, a beneficial association member's rights to receive benefits depend on both the certificate and the constitution and bylaws of the association.

**Power to Acquire Funds and Property** A beneficial association may acquire and dispose of property in a proper manner and for proper purposes, whether by SALE, DEED, lease, mortgage, or other document. A valid BEQUEST of property for charitable purposes may be made to an association that has been incorporated and authorized by its charter to hold property for such purposes.

The funds of a beneficial association should be spent according to the association's purpose as defined by its charter, articles of incorporation, constitution, or bylaws.

**Benefits** A beneficial association's bylaws and controlling statutes specifically designate which benefits are payable to its members, and the types of benefits provided are restricted to those specified.

Beneficial associations may make payments in two ways. The first is based on the contractual agreement between the association and its members. As with an insurance policy, the members' dues are a contribution to a fund from which specified benefits are paid upon a proper claim. Any disputes arising from this contractual relationship may ultimately be resolved in a court of law.

The second way a beneficial association confers payments is through an act of benevolence. The term *benevolence* means the doing of a kind or helpful action towards another, under no obligation except an ethical one. A beneficial association may appoint a board to review applications for benefits not based on the contractual relationship. This board could, for example, extend additional financial benefits to a disabled member who has exhausted the benefits specified in the bylaws. If such a benefit is given as a matter of benevolence, it may not be claimed as a right, and it is not enforceable in court. Likewise, a beneficial association could donate money to a civic activity as an act of benevolence.

An association may set forth certain CONDITIONS precedent to the receipt of benefits by its members. Such conditions must be met before the right to receive benefits may be enforced.

If a member of a beneficial association DEFAULTS on the payment of dues, the member might lose the right to receive benefits.

In general, one claiming benefits from an association must exhaust all remedies within the organization before seeking judicial relief.

**Liabilities** A beneficial association may not ordinarily be held liable in TORT or contract for unauthorized acts of its members or agents. A voluntary unincorporated beneficial association is considered to be a JOINT enterprise, and no LIABILITY for tort exists between those engaged therein. An unincorporated association, may, however, be held responsible for DAMAGES resulting from the NEGLIGENCE of its employees in work of a noncharitable character.

**BENEFICIAL INTEREST** 📖 Profits or advantages from property derived from the terms of a trust agreement. 📖

A BENEFICIARY of a TRUST has a beneficial interest in the trust property, the LEGAL TITLE of which is held by the TRUSTEE. The beneficiary receives the advantages of ownership of the property which the trustee holds and distributes according to the terms of the trust agreement.

**BENEFICIAL USE** 📖 A right to utilize REAL PROPERTY, including light, air, and access to it, in any lawful manner to gain a PROFIT, advantage, or ENJOYMENT from it. A right to enjoy real or PERSONAL PROPERTY held by a person who has EQUITABLE title to it while LEGAL TITLE is held by another. 📖

A beneficial use involves greater rights than a mere right to POSSESSION of land, since it extends to the light and air over the land and ACCESS to it, which can be infringed by the beneficial use of other property by another owner. If a dispute arises from the conflicting ways in which two adjoining landowners exercise their respective beneficial uses of their property, a court, exercising its discretion, may adjudicate those rights.

A BENEFICIARY of a TRUST has beneficial use of the trust property, the legal title to which is held by the TRUSTEE.

**BENEFICIARY** 📖 An organization or a person for whom a TRUST is created and who thereby receives the benefits of the trust. One who inherits under a WILL. A person entitled to a BENEFICIAL INTEREST or a right to profits, benefit, or advantage from a contract. 📖

**BENEFIT OF CLERGY** 📖 In old England, the privilege of clergy that allowed them to avoid trial by all courts of the civil government. 📖

Originally members of the clergy were exempted from CAPITAL PUNISHMENT upon conviction of particular crimes based on this privilege, but it did not encompass crimes of either high TREASON or MISDEMEANORS.

Benefit of clergy existed to alleviate the severity of criminal laws as applied to the clergy. It was, however, found to promote such extensive abuses that it was ultimately eliminated. Benefit of clergy does not exist in the United States today.

The phrase "without the benefit of clergy" is used colloquially to describe a couple living together outside a legal marriage.

**BENJAMIN, JUDAH PHILIP** Judah Philip Benjamin was attorney general of the Confederate States of America under President Jefferson Davis. Though described by many as a brilliant, self-made man, he was also characterized as the "dark prince of the Confederacy" in Robert W. Service's poem "John Brown's Body."

Benjamin was born August 6, 1811, on St. Croix Island, in the British West Indies. His parents, Philip Benjamin and Rebecca de Mendes Benjamin, were Sephardic Jews who had immigrated to the West Indies from Spain. Hearing that Jews were tolerated and allowed to prosper in the U.S. Carolinas, the family moved to the United States in 1813, settling in Charleston, South Carolina. Young Benjamin attended the Fayetteville Academy, in Fayetteville, North Carolina, and entered Yale in 1825 at the age of fourteen. He was the top student in his class when he was expelled in 1827. He was charged with stealing from a fellow student, but the allegations were never proved. Though Benjamin was not an observant Jew, historians acknowledge that anti-Semitism was probably at the heart of the charges and his dismissal from school.

Following his expulsion, Benjamin moved to New Orleans, where he clerked in a commercial house and studied law until he was admitted to the bar in 1832. (A commercial house of the early 1800s was usually involved in the financial transactions around the movement of goods, i.e., lending, bonding, insuring, fees for trans-

**BIOGRAPHY**

CULVER PICTURES

*Judah Philip Benjamin*

port, rent for storage, and contracts of sales.) While studying, he supplemented his income by giving English lessons to the French Creole aristocracy. One of his pupils, Natalie St. Martin, became his wife in a Roman Catholic ceremony in 1833. Though his wife was extravagant and notoriously promiscuous, Benjamin indulged her. Many of his peers commented that Benjamin's wealth could be attributed more to the demands of his wife than to his personal ambitions. For her, he acquired the Belle Chase sugar plantation and an elegant townhouse on Bourbon Street in New Orleans.

His real estate purchases were made possible by a growing and successful law practice. By 1834 he had secured his place in the local legal community through a joint publishing venture with Thomas Slidell. Their *Digest of the Reported Decisions of the Superior Court of the Late Territory of Orleans and of the Supreme Court of Louisiana* was widely used. Benjamin's national reputation as a lawyer was established by his participation in a case involving the brig *Creole*. His brief—which reviewed the status of SLAVERY under both international law and U.S. domestic law—was printed as a pamphlet and widely circulated. In this more liberal period of his life, he believed and argued that slavery was against the laws of humans and nature. He would later reverse his position.

Benjamin began his political career in 1842 when he was elected as the Whig candidate to the lower house of the Louisiana Legislature. He attended the Louisiana Constitutional Convention from 1844 to 1845. Benjamin's wife was not supportive of his interest in politics, or tolerant of his absences. In 1845, after eleven years of marriage, she moved to Paris. The couple rarely lived together again as husband and wife, but they never divorced—and Benjamin's lifelong devotion to his wife has been well documented.

After his wife's departure, Benjamin retreated to his plantation, from 1845 to 1848, and began to experiment with sugar chemistry and processing. Ultimately, he lost the plantation when a friend defaulted on a note that Benjamin had signed.

**JUDAH PHILIP BENJAMIN 1811–1884**

1811 Born, St. Croix, British West Indies

1813 Family immigrated to Charleston, S.C.

1827 Moved to Louisiana

1842 Elected to Louisiana Legislature

1852 Became first Jewish U.S. Senator

1861 Appointed attorney general of the Confederacy

1861–65 U.S. Civil War

1862–65 Served as secretary of state of the Confederacy

1865 Fled to England to avoid post-war prosecution

1866 Admitted to English bar at Lincoln's Inn

1872 Selected as Queen's Counsel

1883 Retired to France

1884 Died, Paris, France

1800     1825     1850     1875     1895

Despite his business reversals, Benjamin had "great dreams about the future development of American commerce" and found himself with a renewed commitment to political service. He shared a growing belief in the South that foreign commerce would strengthen the region and restore the balance of power lost by the COMPROMISE OF 1850. In 1852 Benjamin ran as a Whig party candidate for one of Louisiana's U.S. Senate seats.

His successful bid for office made him the nation's first Jewish U.S. senator. Also in 1852, Benjamin was nominated to the U.S. Supreme Court by President MILLARD FILLMORE. Preferring to take his seat in the Senate, Benjamin declined Fillmore's offer and thereby missed the opportunity to be the first Jewish Supreme Court justice. Benjamin also turned down an appointment as ambassador to Spain, in 1853. Mindful of the escalating national conflict between North and South, he wanted to stay in the United States. In 1854 he wrote, "[A] gulf ... is already opened between the Northern and Southern Whigs. . . . God knows what awaits us. The future looks full of gloom to me."

In 1856 Benjamin left the Whig party and joined the more conservative southern Democrats. He was reelected to the Senate and continued to serve Louisiana there until the Civil War. Following the election of ABRAHAM LINCOLN in 1860, Benjamin advised SECESSION; he resigned his Senate seat when Louisiana voted to leave the Union.

Benjamin was named attorney general of the Confederate States of America in early 1861. He served as attorney general until November 21, 1861, when he became secretary of war. He inherited a war department that was disorganized and deeply in debt. Throughout 1862, the Confederacy suffered both human resource and equipment shortages, and severe casualties.

A plan by Benjamin to build troop strength by drafting slaves—with the promise of emancipation for service—was prepared and sent to the Confederate congress. Seeing the initiative as a threat to the principle of slavery, the congress failed to pass the measure. Benjamin was eventually charged with inefficiency, and a motion to remove him from his post was drafted.

President Davis, still confident in Benjamin's abilities, stepped in and appointed him secretary of state on March 18, 1862. Benjamin served in that capacity until the fall of the Confederacy, but he never fully regained his popularity with the Southern people. Viewed in a historical context, Benjamin's service and loyalty to the Confederacy are extraordinary and commendable—especially in light of the extreme anti-Semitism and hatred that pervaded the South throughout the war years.

After Robert E. Lee's surrender to Ulysses S. Grant at Appomattox Courthouse on April 9, 1865, U.S. agents targeted Benjamin for capture because it was assumed, falsely, that he knew the location of large sums of money. After a brief stop in North Carolina, Benjamin headed south to Florida. Garbed as a Frenchman and speaking fluent French, he passed himself off as a journalist, Monsieur Bonfals (which translates as Mr. Good Disguise). Because Benjamin was too fat to ride a horse, he traveled by cart in the company of a former Confederate officer from New Orleans who pretended to be his interpreter.

On May 1, 1865, federal agents increased their efforts to locate all Confederate fugitives, and the *New York Times* called for Jefferson Davis, Judah Benjamin, and Confederate secretary of war John C. Breckenridge to die "the most disgraceful death on the gallows." The price on Benjamin's head was $40,000, dead or alive. But by May Benjamin had already made it to Tampa.

With the help of Confederate sympathizers and former Confederate soldiers, Benjamin traveled from Tampa to the Gamble Mansion on Florida's southwest coast. En route, he presented himself as Mr. Howard, a farmer and cattle buyer. With federal troops closing in, he was twice forced to hide in a canebrake near the mansion to avoid capture. Eventually, Benjamin was moved to Sarasota Bay, where he sailed down the coast to Knight's Key with Captain Frederick Tresca, a former blockade runner, and H. A. McLeod, an experienced sailor for hire. The trio reached Knight's Key on July 7, 1865. From there, Benjamin boarded a boat for Bimini, in the Bahamas. After this vessel was shipwrecked, he was rescued and returned to Florida, where he again faced capture by federal agents. Benjamin eventually reached Bimini, and then set sail for England. He arrived in England on August 30, 1865, after almost five months of dangerous and grueling travel.

Without funds, Benjamin made the necessary arrangements to practice law in England. He was admitted to the bar at Lincoln's Inn in 1866, and he was soon a respected member of the British bar. Most of his cases focused on corporate law. He also wrote about matters pertaining to business and corporate law. His *Treatise on the Law and Sale of Personal Property: With Special Reference to the American Decisions and the French Code and Civil Law* was published

"THE NATION WHICH PRESENTS ITSELF WITH AN ORGANIZED GOVERNMENT AND . . . INSTITUTIONS CREATED BY THE FREE WILL OF THE CITIZENS . . . [MAY] DEMAND ITS RIGHT RECOGNITION."

in 1868. Commonly known as *Benjamin on Sales*, the book was a definitive source on commercial matters on both sides of the Atlantic for the next twenty-five years. In 1872, Benjamin was selected Queen's Counsel. He practiced law in England until 1883, when he retired to France. He is credited with making major contributions to the British Empire's dominance of world trade in the last half of the nineteenth century.

Benjamin died May 6, 1884, in Paris. He was buried at the Pere Lachaise Cemetery under a headstone marked Philippe Benjamin.

## BENJAMIN, PARK

Park Benjamin was an eminent patent lawyer and author.

Benjamin was born May 11, 1849. A graduate of the U.S. Naval Academy in 1867, he left the navy in 1869 and earned a bachelor of laws degree from Albany Law School in 1870.

From 1872 to 1878, Benjamin was associate editor of the *Scientific American* and became editor-in-chief of *Appleton's Cyclopedia of Applied Mechanics* in 1892.

Benjamin wrote *The United States Naval Academy* (1900) and numerous essays and naval articles for various periodicals.

He died August 21, 1922, in New York City.

*Park Benjamin*

who believed that all persons are intellectually equal and that differences arise solely from educational opportunities. Helvetius also formulated a theory that good is measured by the degree of self-content experienced by a person, and that self-interest is the compelling force for all action. This latter belief had a profound effect on Bentham, who incorporated the idea in the formulation of the basic principles of Utilitarianism.

In 1789, Bentham gained public attention with publication of his *Introduction to the Principles of Morals and Legislation*, which set forth his fundamental principles. He believed that the greatest happiness for the greatest number is the basis of morality. Happiness and pleasure were the same, and included social, intellectual, and moral as well as physical pleasures. Each pleasure has certain characteristics, including intensity and duration, and Bentham established a scale of measurement to judge the worth of a pleasure or a pain. Each person strives to do what makes him or her happiest. The happiness of an individual and the general welfare are complementary; the achievement of the greatest amount of happiness is the goal of morality.

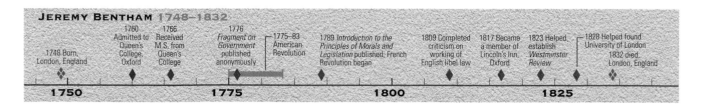

PARK BENJAMIN 1849–1922

1860 Lenoir constructed the first internal combustion engine
1849 Born, New York City
1861–65 U.S. Civil War
1867 Graduated from U.S. Naval Academy
1870 Received bachelor of laws from Albany Law School (NY)
1872–78 Worked as associate editor at *Scientific American*
1879 Edison invented the incandescent light bulb
1888 Eastman introduced the "Kodak" box camera
1892 Became editor-in-chief of *Appleton's Cyclopedia of Applied Mechanics*
1898 *A History of Electricity* is published
1908 Henry Ford introduced the Model T
1914–18 World War I
1922 Died, New York City

1850    1875    1900    1925

## BENTHAM, JEREMY

Jeremy Bentham achieved prominence as a philosopher, a jurist, a reformer, and as the founder of Utilitarianism.

Bentham was born February 15, 1748. He was educated at Oxford and admitted to the bar but decided against the practice of law. Bentham chose to pursue a career in legal, political, and social reform, applying principles of ethical philosophy to these endeavors.

He was greatly influenced by the work of Claude Adrien Helvetius, a French philosopher

*Jeremy Bentham*

Bentham applied his views to reform legislation, feeling that the purpose of the law was to maximize total happiness within the limitations of government. As a result, Bentham achieved great advances in prison reform, criminal law, civil service, and insurance and was active in the compilation of laws into comprehensible text.

Bentham attempted to persuade President JAMES MADISON to adopt a code of laws devised by Bentham with rules and previous cases added as illustrations of the utilization of the legal

JEREMY BENTHAM 1748–1832

1748 Born, London, England
1760 Admitted to Queen's College, Oxford
1766 Received M.S. from Queen's College
1776 *Fragment on Government* published anonymously
1775–83 American Revolution
1789 *Introduction to the Principles of Morals and Legislation* published; French Revolution began
1809 Completed criticism on working of English libel law
1817 Became a member of Lincoln's Inn, Oxford
1823 Helped establish *Westminster Review*
1828 Helped found University of London
1832 died, London, England

1750    1775    1800    1825

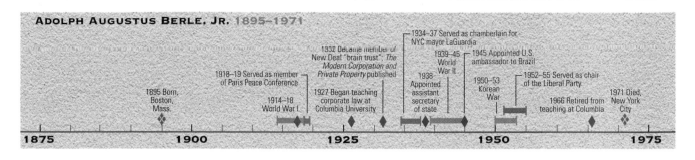

ADOLPH AUGUSTUS BERLE, JR. 1895–1971

1934–37 Served as chamberlain for NYC mayor LaGuardia

1932 Became member of New Deal "brain trust"; *The Modern Corporation and Private Property* published

1939–45 World War II    1945 Appointed U.S. ambassador to Brazil

1938 Appointed assistant secretary of state

1918–19 Served as member of Paris Peace Conference

1950–53 Korean War

1952–55 Served as chair of the Liberal Party

1895 Born, Boston, Mass.

1914–18 World War I

1927 Began teaching corporate law at Columbia University

1966 Retired from teaching at Columbia

1971 Died, New York City

1875    1900    1925    1950    1975

---

theory involved. Madison rejected the idea in 1811, but in the 1830s, a group of American reformers adopted several of Bentham's policies with the objective of formulating a simplified code of law.

Bentham was also instrumental in establishing the University of London. He had many followers, including the eminent British philosopher JOHN STUART MILL.

He died June 6, 1832, in London.

See also UTILITARIANISM.

**BEQUEATH** 📖 To dispose of PERSONAL PROPERTY owned by a DECEDENT at the time of death as a gift under the provisions of the decedent's WILL. 📖

The term *bequeath* applies only to personal property. A TESTATOR, to give REAL PROPERTY to someone in a TESTAMENTARY provision, DEVISES it. *Bequeath* is sometimes used as a synonym for *devise*.

**BEQUEST** 📖 A gift of PERSONAL PROPERTY, such as money, stock, bonds, or jewelry, owned by a DECEDENT at the time of death which is directed by the provisions of the decedent's WILL; a LEGACY. 📖

A bequest is not the same as a DEVISE (a TESTAMENTARY gift of REAL PROPERTY) although the terms are often used interchangeably. When this occurs, a bequest can be a gift of real property if the testator's intention to dispose of real property is clearly demonstrated in the will.

There are different types of bequests. A *charitable bequest* is a gift intended to serve a religious, educational, political, or general social purpose to benefit mankind, aimed at the community or a particular segment of it. Charitable bequests also reduce the ESTATE TAXES that might be owed on the ESTATE left by a decedent.

A *demonstrative bequest* is a gift of money that must be paid from a particular source, such as a designated bank account or the sale of stock in a designated corporation.

A *general bequest* is a gift of money or other property that can be paid or taken from the decedent's general ASSETS and not from a specific fund designated by the terms of the will.

**BIOGRAPHY**

*Adolph Augustus Berle, Jr.*

"ALL POWERS GRANTED TO A CORPORATION . . . WHETHER DERIVED FROM STATUTE OR CHARTER . . . [ARE] EXERCISABLE ONLY FOR THE RATABLE BENEFIT OF ALL THE SHAREHOLDERS AS THEIR INTEREST APPEARS."

**BIOGRAPHY**

*John Macpherson Berrien*

**BERLE, ADOLPH AUGUSTUS, JR.** Adolph Augustus Berle, Jr., was a diplomat, teacher, and writer.

Berle was born January 29, 1895, in Boston, Massachusetts. He was educated at Harvard, receiving a bachelor of arts degree in 1913, a master of arts degree in 1914, and a bachelor of laws degree in 1916, in which year he was also admitted to the bar.

After military duty in World War I, Berle served as a U.S. representative at the Paris Peace Conference during 1918 and 1919. He opposed the conditions of the Versailles Treaty and resigned from the delegation. He returned to the United States and established his legal practice in New York City.

Berle began teaching corporate law at Columbia University in 1927. During the 1930s, he assisted the administration of President FRANKLIN DELANO ROOSEVELT in the formulation of New Deal legislation concerning SECURITIES and banking.

From 1938 to 1944, Berle was assistant secretary of state; in 1945 he was U.S. ambassador to Brazil; and in 1946 he returned to Columbia University to continue his teaching career. He helped establish the Liberal party and acted as its chairman from 1952 to 1955.

One of Berle's several publications was *The Modern Corporation and Private Property* (1932), written with coauthor G. C. Means.

Berle died February 17, 1971, in New York City.

**BERRIEN, JOHN MACPHERSON** John Macpherson Berrien served as U.S. attorney general under President ANDREW JACKSON.

Berrien was born August 23, 1781, in New Jersey. He graduated from Princeton in 1796 and was admitted to the Georgia bar in 1799. He began his judicial career in Georgia as a circuit court judge in 1810 and remained on the bench until 1821.

Berrien sat in the Georgia Senate from 1822 to 1823. From 1824 to 1829, he represented Georgia in the U.S. Senate, as a member of the Democratic party.

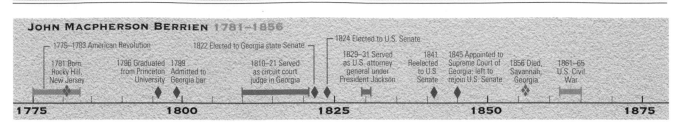

JOHN MACPHERSON BERRIEN 1781–1856

1775–1783 American Revolution

1822 Elected to Georgia state Senate

1824 Elected to U.S. Senate

1781 Born, Rocky Hill, New Jersey

1796 Graduated from Princeton University

1799 Admitted to Georgia bar

1810–21 Served as circuit court judge in Georgia

1829–31 Served as U.S. attorney general under President Jackson

1841 Reelected to U.S. Senate

1845 Appointed to Supreme Court of Georgia; left to rejoin U.S. Senate

1856 Died, Savannah, Georgia

1861–65 U.S. Civil War

1775       1800       1825       1850       1875

He served as U.S. attorney general from 1829 to 1831. He again served as senator from Georgia from 1841 to 1845 and from 1845 to 1852 as a member of the Whig Party.

**BEST EVIDENCE** 📖 An original document or object offered as PROOF of a FACT in a lawsuit as opposed to a photocopy of, or other substitute for, the item or the TESTIMONY of a WITNESS describing it. 📖

Best evidence, also known as PRIMARY EVIDENCE, usually denotes an original writing, which is considered the most reliable proof of its existence and its contents. If it is available to, and obtainable by, a party, it must be offered into EVIDENCE at a trial. Best evidence is distinguishable from SECONDARY EVIDENCE, a reproduction of an original or testimony establishing its existence, which will be ADMISSIBLE as proof only if the best evidence cannot be obtained, and ensuring no fault of the party seeking to present it.

The principle that the best available evidence must be presented as proof in a lawsuit is embodied in the best-evidence rule.

**BESTIALITY** 📖 Sexual relations between a human being and an animal. 📖

At COMMON LAW, bestiality was considered a crime against nature and was punishable by death.

Today, it is prohibited by statutes in most states as a form of SODOMY. The penalty for committing the offense is a fine, imprisonment, or both.

**BEYOND A REASONABLE DOUBT** 📖 The standard that must be met by the prosecution's EVIDENCE in a criminal prosecution: that no other logical explanation can be derived from the facts except that the defendant committed the crime, thereby overcoming the PRESUMPTION that a person is innocent until proven guilty. 📖

The term connotes that evidence establishes a particular point to a moral certainty and it is beyond dispute that any reasonable alternative is possible. It does not mean that no doubt exists as to the accused's guilt, only that no REASONABLE DOUBT is possible from the evidence presented. This standard is distinguishable from the standard of PROOF applied in civil lawsuits: a PREPONDERANCE OF THE EVIDENCE,

"IF THIS POWER IS NOT GRANTED BY THE CONSTITUTION, IT IS VERY CERTAIN, THAT NO SERIES OF USURPATION CAN GIVE IT A LEGITIMATE EXISTENCE IN THAT INSTRUMENT."

*Although the House and Senate are divided into two houses, they occasionally meet in joint session.*

which means that the evidence more likely than not establishes a particular point.

*Beyond a reasonable doubt* is the highest standard of proof that must be met in any trial.

**BIAS** 📖 A predisposition or a preconceived opinion that prevents a person from impartially evaluating facts that have been presented for determination; a PREJUDICE. 📖

A judge who demonstrates bias in a hearing over which he or she presides has a mental attitude toward a party to the litigation that hinders the judge from supervising fairly the course of the trial, thereby depriving the party of the right to a fair trial. A judge may RECUSE himself or herself to avoid the appearance of bias.

If, during the VOIR DIRE, a prospective juror indicates bias toward either party in a lawsuit, the juror can be successfully challenged for cause and denied a seat on the JURY.

**BICAMERAL** 📖 The division of a legislative or judicial body into two components or chambers. 📖

The CONGRESS OF THE UNITED STATES is a bicameral legislature, since it is divided into two houses, the Senate and the House of Representatives.

UPI/CORBIS-BETTMANN

**BICKEL, ALEXANDER MORDECAI** Alexander Mordecai Bickel was a noted legal scholar, law professor, and essayist who wrote extensively about constitutional law issues and

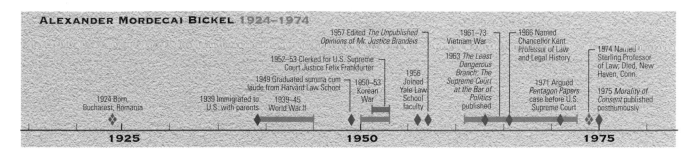

ALEXANDER MORDECAI BICKEL 1924–1974

1957 Edited *The Unpublished Opinions of Mr. Justice Brandeis*

1952–53 Clerked for U.S. Supreme Court Justice Felix Frankfurter

1949 Graduated summa cum laude from Harvard Law School

1950–53 Korean War

1956 Joined Yale Law School faculty

1961–73 Vietnam War

1963 *The Least Dangerous Branch: The Supreme Court at the Bar of Politics* published

1966 Named Chancellor Kent Professor of Law and Legal History

1971 Argued *Pentagon Papers* case before U.S. Supreme Court

1974 Named Sterling Professor of Law; Died, New Haven, Conn.

1975 *Morality of Consent* published posthumously

1924 Born, Bucharest, Romania

1939 Immigrated to U.S. with parents

1939–45 World War II

1925        1950        1975

Bickel was born December 17, 1924, in Bucharest, Romania, and immigrated to the United States with his parents in 1939. He attended the City College of New York, graduating Phi Beta Kappa in 1947, and Harvard Law School, where he served as editor of the *Harvard Law Review* and graduated summa cum laude in 1949.

Following law school, Bickel clerked for Judge Calvert Magruder of the U.S. Court of Appeals in Boston. From 1950 to 1952 he was a State Department law officer in Frankfurt, Germany, and he was a member of the European Defense Community Observer Delegation in Paris. He returned to the United States to become law clerk to Justice FELIX FRANKFURTER during the U.S. Supreme Court's 1952–53 term.

Bickel assisted Justice Frankfurter in the Court's consideration of the landmark desegregation decision in *Brown v. Board of Education*, 349 U.S. 483, 74 S. Ct. 686, 98 L. Ed. 873 (1954). The plaintiffs in *Brown* challenged the assignment of black and white students to separate public schools. The Court held that such racial segregation in public education was unconstitutional. During his clerkship with Frankfurter, Bickel studied the Fourteenth Amendment extensively and concluded that the Constitution did provide that congressional or judicial action could be used to abolish school segregation.

After completing his clerkship with Justice Frankfurter, Bickel joined the faculty of Yale Law School, in 1956. He was named Chancellor Kent Professor of Law and Legal History in 1966, and Sterling Professor of Law in 1974, the year of his death.

Bickel wrote a number of influential books and essays. In addition to longer works, he published more than a hundred articles in newspapers and magazines. He edited *The Unpublished Opinions of Mr. Justice Brandeis*, a volume of eleven BRANDEIS draft opinions concerning the issue of judicial restraint, a major theme in much of Bickel's later writings. In his most influential work, *The Least Dangerous Branch:*

**BIOGRAPHY**

*Alexander Mordecai Bickel*

"[THE JUDICIARY IS] THE LEAST DANGEROUS BRANCH OF OUR GOVERNMENT."

*The Supreme Court at the Bar of Politics* (1963), Bickel argued that courts should make decisions that are grounded in history and in the values found in the Constitution, and should not make decisions that cannot gain public support. He believed that judges should exercise care to avoid deciding constitutional issues if other grounds for a ruling are available, such as grounds for refusing to hear the case or grounds for using doctrines like statutory construction to decide the case.

In *The Supreme Court and the Idea of Progress* (1970), another work advocating judicial restraint, Bickel criticized the activism of the WARREN COURT in tackling social issues. He noted that "history has little tolerance for . . . [the Court's] reasonable judgments that turn out to be wrong." Bickel also argued for judicial restraint in the so-called *Pentagon Papers* case, *New York Times Co. v. United States*, 403 U.S. 713, 91 S. Ct. 2140, 29 L. Ed. 2d 822 (1971), in which he represented the *New York Times* before the Supreme Court. In *Pentagon Papers*, the government sought to prevent the *New York Times* and the *Washington Post* from publishing the contents of a classified study titled *History of U.S. Decision-Making Process on Viet Nam Policy*. Rather than arguing that PRIOR RESTRAINT of the publication of the classified material was unconstitutional, Bickel instead maintained that the government had been unable to rebut the heavy PRESUMPTION against prior restraint and that such restraint was to be found in congressional legislation rather than in assertions of governmental power. The Court ultimately rejected the government's claim that the papers should not be published, and several of the justices adopted Bickel's analysis in their opinions.

A recognized expert on the SUPREME COURT OF THE UNITED STATES, Bickel served as a member of the Study Group on the Caseload of the Supreme Court. In 1973, he authored *The Caseload of the Supreme Court—and What, If Anything, to Do about It*, in which he concluded that the Court's caseload should be reduced. Easing the Court's workload is critical, he argued, to ensure careful deliberation of important issues and to avoid transforming the Court "into a high-speed, high-volume enterprise" that would "mock the idea of justice and mock the substantive reforms of a generation."

See also JUDICIARY.

**BIGAMY** The offense of willfully and knowingly entering into a second MARRIAGE while validly married to another individual.

Bigamy was an offense in the English ECCLESIASTICAL COURTS but was not an offense under

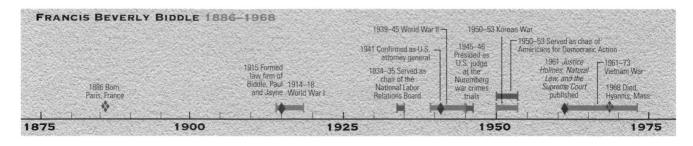

**FRANCIS BEVERLY BIDDLE 1886–1968**

1875 — 1886 Born, Paris, France — 1900 — 1915 Formed law firm of Biddle, Paul and Jayne — 1914–18 World War I — 1925 — 1834–35 Served as chair of the National Labor Relations Board — 1941 Confirmed as U.S. attorney general — 1939–45 World War II — 1945–46 Presided as U.S. judge at the Nuremberg war crimes trials — 1950 — 1950–53 Korean War — 1950–53 Served as chair of Americans for Democratic Action — 1961 *Justice Holmes, Natural Law, and the Supreme Court* published — 1961–73 Vietnam War — 1968 Died, Hyannis, Mass. — 1975

## BIDDLE, FRANCIS BEVERLY

Francis Beverly Biddle achieved prominence as a jurist.

Biddle was born May 9, 1886, in Paris, France. He was a graduate of Harvard, class of 1909, and earned a bachelor of laws degree from his alma mater in 1911. From 1911 to 1912, he was private secretary to OLIVER WENDELL HOLMES, JR., an eminent U.S. Supreme Court justice.

In 1912, Biddle was admitted to the Pennsylvania bar and from 1915 to 1939, practiced with two successful Philadelphia law firms—Biddle, Paul and Jayne, and Barnes, Biddle and Myers—specializing in corporation law.

Biddle served as special assistant U.S. attorney from 1922 to 1926 and as chairman of the National Labor Relations Board from 1934 to 1935. In 1939, he presided for one year as a justice of the U.S. Circuit Court of Appeals.

Biddle was solicitor general of the United States in 1940, and the following year he became U.S. attorney general for a three-year period. From 1945 to 1946, he presided as a U.S. judge at the Nuremberg trials of Nazi war criminals. See also NUREMBERG TRIALS.

He died October 4, 1968, in Hyannis, Massachusetts.

## BIFURCATED TRIAL

One judicial proceeding that is divided into two stages in which different issues are addressed separately by the court.

A common example of a bifurcated TRIAL is one in which the question of LIABILITY in a PERSONAL INJURY case is tried separately from and prior to a trial on the amount of DAMAGES to be awarded if liability is found. A bifurcated trial in such a case is advantageous because if the defendant is not found liable, there is no need to spend the money or time in the presentation of PROOF and WITNESSES on the issue of damages.

In criminal procedure, a bifurcated trial is useful where the issues of SANITY and guilt or guilt and punishment must be decided.

**BIOGRAPHY**

*Francis Beverly Biddle*

"TO BLAME THE PUBLIC IS BUT THE EXCUSE OF THOSE WHO HAVE BEEN UNABLE TO INFLUENCE THE PUBLIC."

COMMON LAW. It was subsequently made a CRIME by statute.

Bigamy is punishable by either a fine or imprisonment, depending on the law of each individual state. In some jurisdictions, bigamy is a ground for DIVORCE. A bigamous marriage is always VOID.

**Elements** The existence of a VALID marriage entered into by the accused party prior to the bigamous marriage is an essential element of the offense. No particular type of ceremony is required, and even a COMMON-LAW MARRIAGE can suffice. The bigamist must be aware that his or her spouse is living at the time of the subsequent marriage.

An INDICTMENT for bigamy is sufficiently supported even by the existence of a *voidable marriage*, one that is valid until annulled. If neither party seeks an ANNULMENT, then the remarriage of either constitutes bigamy.

No bigamy exists where the first marriage was terminated by annulment or divorce prior to the second marriage. A divorce that was fraudulent or defective, however, is not a defense to a charge of bigamy.

Unless otherwise provided by statute, COHABITATION is not a requisite element of the offense. Bigamy is committed by the mere performance of the second marriage.

Ordinarily the law of the area where the bigamous marriage occurred has JURISDICTION in the prosecution of the crime. Some statutes, however, provide that the accused may be convicted in the state where the bigamous cohabitation takes place, even though the marriage occurred elsewhere.

**Defenses** Under certain statutes it is not considered bigamous for an individual to remarry after elapse of a certain designated period during which the former spouse was absent and thought to be dead. Remarriage before the statutory period, however, constitutes bigamy since the first marriage is still regarded as valid.

In some jurisdictions a sincere and reasonable belief that a valid divorce has been granted is a defense to bigamy. In most, however, it is not. Neither erroneous legal advice nor ignorance nor mistake regarding the law is a defense.

A divorce or annulment obtained subsequent to a second bigamous marriage is no defense. The belief that it is not unlawful to have more than one spouse will not prevent prosecution nor will the claim that religious beliefs compelled an individual to remarry. It is no defense that the second spouse was aware of the first marriage or that the first spouse knew of the second marriage.

## BIGELOW, MELVILLE MADISON

Melville Madison Bigelow achieved prominence as an author, legal historian, and a founder of Boston University Law School.

Bigelow was born August 2, 1846, in Eaton Rapids, Michigan. He was educated at the University of Michigan, where he earned a bachelor of arts degree in 1866, a bachelor of laws degree in 1868, and a master of arts degree in 1871. He also received a master of arts degree and a doctor of philosophy degree from Harvard in 1879. Two doctor of laws degrees were bestowed upon him, from Northwestern University in 1896, and the University of Michigan in 1912.

Bigelow taught law at the University of Michigan and the Northwestern University

*Melville Madison Bigelow*

A bilateral contract is distinguishable from a UNILATERAL CONTRACT, a promise made by one party in exchange for the PERFORMANCE of some act by the other party. The party to a unilateral contract whose performance is sought is not obligated to act, but if he or she does, the party that made the promise is bound to comply with the terms of the agreement. In a bilateral contract both parties are bound by their exchange of promises.

Both parties to a bilateral contract make promises. With respect to the promise in issue, the party making the promise is the promisor and the other party is the promisee. The legal detriment incurred by the promisee consists of a different promise by him or her to do something or refrain from doing something that he or she was not previously legally obligated to do or to refrain from doing. This legal detriment constitutes CONSIDERATION, the cause, motive, or benefit that induces one to enter into a contract. Consideration is an essential component of a contract.

MUTUALITY OF OBLIGATION must exist in an enforceable bilateral contract, and this involves the concept of reciprocity. *A* cannot enforce *B*'s promise unless *A*'s promise entails a legal detriment, and *B* can enforce *A*'s promise only if *B*'s promise involves a legal detriment.

If a MINOR enters a bilateral contract with an adult that is unenforceable due to the minor's age, the adult party cannot assert absence of mutuality as a defense if the minor sues to enforce the contract. This principle applies to

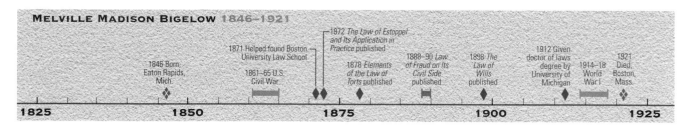

MELVILLE MADISON BIGELOW 1846–1921

1846 Born, Eaton Rapids, Mich.

1861–65 U.S. Civil War

1871 Helped found Boston University Law School

1872 *The Law of Estoppel and Its Application in Practice* published

1878 *Elements of the Law of Torts* published

1888–90 *Law of Fraud on Its Civil Side* published

1898 *The Law of Wills* published

1912 Given doctor of laws degree by University of Michigan

1914–18 World War I

1921 Died, Boston, Mass.

1825    1850    1875    1900    1925

Law School and also held a professorship at Boston University Law School.

Bigelow's *Elements of the Law of Torts* (1878) was used as a basic legal textbook. His numerous other publications included *Law of Fraud on its Civil Side* (1888–1890); *The Law of Estoppel and its Application in Practice* (1872); and *History of Procedure in England from the Norman Conquests: The Norman Period* 1066–1204 (1880).

He died May 4, 1921, in Boston.

## BILATERAL CONTRACT

An agreement formed by an exchange of PROMISES in which the promise of one party is consideration supporting the promise of the other party.

"GOVERNMENT FROM THE TOP IS RIGHT ONLY WHEN IT PROCEEDS FROM BELOW, WITH SUPPORT ALL THE WAY UP."

any situation where the law grants a particular party a privilege to avoid a contract because of his or her status.

## BILL

A DECLARATION in writing. A document listing separate items. An itemized account of charges or costs. In EQUITY practice, the first PLEADING in the ACTION, the paper in which the plaintiff sets out his or her case and demands relief from the defendant.

A BILL OF INDICTMENT is a formal written document accusing someone of having committed a crime. It is presented to a GRAND JURY for its consideration and decision whether to act on it. A BILL OF RIGHTS is a formal declaration that

*Bills are debated in the House of Representatives before they are sent to the president for a signature or veto.*

the people have certain rights and liberties. Rights are often asserted when there is a change in government, and a bill of rights has been included in the federal and many state constitutions in the United States.

A BILL OF PARTICULARS itemizes all of the facts making up a claim asserted in a lawsuit. It is delivered to the opposing party in order to sharpen the issues in dispute. A BILL OF REVIEW lists errors alleged to have been made by a trial court. It is presented to a court that has JURIS-DICTION to correct those errors or reverse the decision.

A bill of costs is a certified, itemized statement of expenses incurred by the successful party in a lawsuit. Courts are generally empowered to order the losing party to reimburse the winning party for some or all of these expenses. A BILL OF SALE is a writing that lists property exchanged in a bargain for money or something else of value.

A bill corresponds to the declaration made by the plaintiff when beginning a COMMON-LAW ACTION. Modern rules of pleading have merged the procedures for handling cases at law and in

equity, and the modern equivalent of both the bill in equity and the declaration at law is the COMPLAINT.

**BILL OF ATTAINDER** ◫ A special legislative enactment that imposes a death sentence without a judicial trial upon a particular person or class of persons suspected of committing serious offenses, such as TREASON or a FELONY. ◫

A bill of attainder is prohibited by Article I, Section 9, Clause 3 of the Constitution because it deprives the person or persons singled out for punishment of the safeguards of a trial by jury.

**BILL OF EXCHANGE** ◫ A three-party NE-GOTIABLE INSTRUMENT in which the first party, the DRAWER, presents an order for the payment of a sum certain on a second party, the DRAWEE, for payment to a third party, the PAYEE, on demand or at a fixed future date. ◫

A bill of exchange is distinguishable from a PROMISSORY NOTE, since it does not contain a promise and the drawer does not expressly pledge to pay it. It is similar to a NOTE, however, since it is payable either on demand or at a specific time.

The terms *bill of exchange* and DRAFT are synonymous; however, the former is generally used in international law, whereas the latter is used in the UNIFORM COMMERCIAL CODE.

**BILL OF INDICTMENT** ◫ A formal written document that is drawn up by a government prosecutor accusing a designated person of having committed a FELONY or MISDEMEANOR and which is presented to a GRAND JURY so that it may take action upon it. ◫

**BILL OF LADING** ◫ A document signed by a CARRIER (a transporter of goods) or the carrier's representative and issued to a consignor (the shipper of goods) that evidences the receipt of goods for shipment to a specified designation and person. ◫

Carriers using all modes of transportation issue bills of lading when they undertake the transportation of cargo. A bill of lading is, in addition to a RECEIPT for the DELIVERY of goods, a CONTRACT for their carriage and a DOCUMENT OF TITLE to them. Its terms describe the FREIGHT for identification purposes; state the name of the consignor and the provisions of the contract for shipment; and direct the cargo to be delivered to the order or ASSIGNS of a particular person, the consignee, at a designated location.

There are two basic types of bills of lading. A straight bill of lading is one in which the goods are consigned to a designated party. An order bill is one in which the goods are consigned to the order of a named party. This distinction is important in determining whether a bill of lading is negotiable (capable of transferring title

Form 31 Uniform

(uniform Domestic Order Bill of Lading, adopted by Carriers in Official, Southern, Western and Illinois Classification Territories, March 15, 1922, as amended August 1, 1938, and June 15, 1941.)

UNIFORM ORDER BILL OF LADING

ORIGINAL

Shipper's No. _____

Agent's No. _____

ST. LOUIS-SAN FRANCISCO RAILWAY COMPANY

RECEIVED, subject to the classifications and tariffs in effect on the date of the issue of this Bill of Lading.

*At* _____ 19 ____ *From* _____

the property described below, in apparent good order, except as noted (contents and condition of contents of packages unknown), marked, consigned, and destined as indicated below, which said company (the word company being understood throughout this contract as meaning any person or corporation in possession of the property under the contract) agrees to carry to its usual place of delivery at said destination, if on its own road or its own water line, otherwise to deliver to another carrier on the route to said destination. It is mutually agreed, as to each carrier of all or any of said property over all or any portion of said route to destination, and as to each party at any time interested in all or any of said property, that every service to be performed hereunder shall be subject to all the conditions not prohibited by law, whether printed or written, herein contained, including the conditions on back hereof, which are hereby agreed to by the shipper and accepted for himself and his assigns.

**The surrender of this original ORDER Bill of Lading properly indorsed shall be required before the delivery of the property. Inspection of property covered by this Bill of Lading will not be permitted unless provided by law or unless permission is indorsed on this Original Bill of Lading or given in writing by the shipper.**

Consigned to ORDER OF _____

Destination _____ State of _____ County of _____

Notify _____

At _____ State of _____ County of _____

Route _____

Delivering Carrier _____ Car Initial _____ Car No. _____

| No. Pkgs. | DESCRIPTION OF ARTICLES, SPECIAL MARKS, AND EXCEPTIONS | *Weight (Subject to Correction) | Class or Rate | Check Col. | |
|---|---|---|---|---|---|
| | | | | | Subject to Section 7 of conditions, if this shipment is to be delivered to the consignee without recourse on the consignor, the consignor shall sign the following statement: |
| | | | | | The carrier shall not make delivery of this shipment without payment of freight and all other lawful charges. |
| | | | | | |
| | | | | | _____ (Signature of Consignor) |
| | | | | | If charges are to be prepaid, write or stamp here, "To be Prepaid." |
| | | | | | |
| | | | | | Received $_____ to apply in prepayment of the charges on the property described hereon. |
| | | | | | |
| | | | | | _____ (Agent or Cashier) |
| | | | | | Per _____ (The signature here acknowledges only the amount prepaid.) |

*If the shipment moves between two ports by a carrier by water, the law requires that the bill of lading shall state whether it is "carrier's or shipper's weight."

NOTE—Where the rate is dependent on value, shippers are required to state specifically in writing the agreed or declared value of the property.

The agreed or declared value of the property is hereby specifically stated by the shipper to be set exceeding ............... per ................

Charges Advanced:

$ _____

_____ Shipper.   _____ Agent.

Per _____   Per _____

Permanent Post-Office Address of Shipper _____ 1

[contract terms omitted]

A sample railway order bill of lading

to the goods covered under it by its delivery or endorsement). If its terms provide that the freight is to be delivered to the BEARER (or possessor) of the bill, to the order of a named party, or, as recognized in overseas trade, to a named person or assigns, a bill, as a document of title, is negotiable. In contrast, a straight bill is not negotiable.

State laws, which often include provisions from the UNIFORM COMMERCIAL CODE, regulate the duties and liabilities imposed by bills of lading covering goods shipped within state boundaries. Federal law, embodied in the Interstate Commerce Act (49 U.S.C. [1976 Ed.] § 1 et seq.) apply to bills of lading covering goods traveling in interstate commerce.

See also CONSIGNMENT; SHIPPING LAW.

**BILL OF PARTICULARS** 📖 A written statement used in both civil and criminal actions that is submitted by a PLAINTIFF or a PROSECUTOR at the request of a DEFENDANT, giving the defendant detailed information concerning the claims or charges made against him or her. 📖

In CIVIL ACTIONS a bill of particulars is a written demand for the specifics of why an ACTION at law was brought. Although usually requested by a defendant, it can be demanded by a plaintiff if the defendant makes a COUNTERCLAIM for a SETOFF or asserts a defense against him or her. A bill can be submitted either voluntarily or pursuant to a court order for compliance with the demand. Its function is to give the party who requests it knowledge of what the opposing party has ALLEGED in order to protect the party requesting the bill from surprise and in order to establish the real issues of the action. It also serves to expedite the orderly progress of judicial proceedings by reducing, if not eliminating, the need for the amendment of ambiguous or vague PLEADINGS. A bill of particu-

A sample bill of particulars

To: _____, attorney for the defendant.

You will please take notice that the following is a bill of particulars in the above-entitled action in which plaintiff seeks to recover damages for personal injuries occasioned by defendant's negligence.

I

The acts complained of in the complaint on file herein were committed on _____, 19__, at approximately __ __.m.

II

The acts above mentioned occurred at _____ [set out place and the manner in which the injury complained of occurred].

III

The plaintiff was seriously injured, and the injuries consisted of the following:_____ [set out each injury complained of, its nature, location, and extent, in so far as the injury has not been specifically set forth in the complaint].

IV

By reason of the above, plaintiff was forced to expend, and did expend, the sum of $_____ for medical attention and hospitalization and drugs, of which the following is an itemized statement: _____.

V

Plaintiff was confined to bed from _____, 19__, until _____, 19__, and after arising from bed, plaintiff was unable to return to _____ [his or her] usual employment or occupation until _____, 19__.

VI

By reason of the above-mentioned injuries, plaintiff has been rendered less capable of performing the duties and labor required in _____ [his or her] usual occupation or calling in the following respects: _____ [set out impediments occasioned by the injuries].

Dated _____, 19__.

[Signature]

lars is neither a pleading nor PROOF of the facts it states, but, rather, an elucidation of a pleading. It is not to be used as a DISCOVERY device to learn the EVIDENCE or strategy to be used at trial by the opposing party.

State codes of CIVIL PROCEDURE impose rules that govern the use of bills of particulars in civil actions brought in state court. In federal courts the Federal Rules of Civil Procedure have replaced the use of a bill of particulars with a MOTION for a more definite statement. If, however, the information sought by such a motion is obtainable by use of discovery mechanisms, the motion will be denied.

In criminal law, a bill of particulars serves the same purpose. It is submitted by the prosecution to the defendant, at the defendant's demand, to provide the facts alleged in the COMPLAINT or the INDICTMENT that related to the commission of the crime. The defendant is given notice of the offenses with which he or she is charged so that a defense may be prepared and the possibility of SURPRISE or DOUBLE JEOPARDY avoided. As in civil procedure, a bill of particulars is not intended to serve as a discovery device.

State codes of CRIMINAL PROCEDURE and the Federal Rules of Criminal Procedure regulate the use of bills of particulars in criminal prosecutions in their respective courts.

**BILL OF REVIEW** In the practice of EQUITY courts, a paper filed with a court after expiration of the time for filing a PETITION for a rehearing in order to request, due to exceptional circumstances, the correction or reversal of a final JUDGMENT or DECREE.

The use of a bill of review is limited to three situations: (1) the correction of a judgment that has incorporated errors found in the record of the case; (2) the reversal of a judgment because of recent discovery of EVIDENCE that is decisive on the issues of the case but that could not have been found in time for the trial; and (3) the setting aside of a judgment based upon proceedings that were tainted by FRAUD, such as perjured testimony.

In states where courts of equity and law have merged, a bill of review has been replaced by a MOTION for relief from a judgment or decree, governed by state rules of CIVIL PROCEDURE. A motion for relief from a judgment or order serves the same function in federal courts as provided by Rule 60 of the Federal Rules of Civil Procedure, which abolished bills of review.

**BILL OF RIGHTS** The first ten AMENDMENTS to the U.S. Constitution, ratified in 1791, which set forth and guarantee certain fundamental rights and privileges of individuals, including freedom of religion, speech, press, and assembly; guarantee of a speedy jury trial in criminal cases; and protection against excessive BAIL and CRUEL AND UNUSUAL PUNISHMENT.

A list of fundamental rights included in each state constitution.

A declaration of individual rights and freedoms, usually issued by a national government.

As a fundamental guarantee of individual liberty, the Bill of Rights forms a vital aspect of U.S. law and government. It establishes a number of legal principles that have had a decisive effect upon U.S. law and society, including the functioning of the criminal justice system, the separation of church and state, and the exercise of FREEDOM OF SPEECH.

The concept of a bill of rights as a statement of basic individual freedoms derives in part from the English Bill of Rights, passed in 1689. This document, which was created after the Glorious Revolution of 1688, established the terms by which William and Mary were accepted as king and queen of England. It forbade the monarchy to suspend laws, raise taxes, or maintain an army without consent of Parliament. It also declared that freedom of speech in Parliament could not be challenged, protected those accused of crimes from "excessive bail" and "cruel and unusual punishments," and provided a number of other privileges and freedoms (1 Will. & Mar., Sess. 2, C. 2).

Nearly a century later, seven of the thirteen states of the newly independent United States of America adopted a bill of rights as part of their state constitutions, and the remaining six included elements of the English Bill of Rights in the bodies of their constitutions. Virginia, the first state to adopt a bill of rights, passed its Declaration of Rights in 1776. Drafted largely by George Mason, Virginia's declaration became a model for later state bills of rights and ultimately for the federal Bill of Rights, and it remains a part of that state's constitution.

At the Constitutional Convention of 1787, the Framers of the U.S. Constitution used the English Bill of Rights and state bills of rights as resources as they sought to define the fundamental principles and institutions of U.S. government. However, they declined to add a bill of rights to the Constitution, on the grounds that the Constitution itself provided adequate protection from intrusive government. Indeed, the Constitution contained some elements of the English Bill of Rights, including Congress's exclusive power to maintain armed forces and, on the federal level, to pass laws and impose

# UNITED STATES BILL OF RIGHTS

*Articles in Addition to, and Amendment of, the Constitution of the United States of America, Proposed by Congress, and Ratified by the Legislatures of the several States Pursuant to the Fifth Article of the Original Constitution*

## Article [I]

Congress shall make no law respecting an establishment of religion, or prohibiting the free exercise thereof; or abridging the freedom of speech, or of the press; or the right of the people peaceably to assemble, and to petition the Government for a redress of grievances.

## Article [II]

A well regulated Militia, being necessary to the security of a free State, the right of the people to keep and bear Arms, shall not be infringed.

## Article [III]

No Soldier shall, in time of peace be quartered in any house, without the consent of the Owner, nor in time of war, but in a manner to be prescribed by law.

## Article [IV]

The right of the people to be secure in their persons, houses, papers, and effects, against unreasonable searches and seizures, shall not be violated, and no Warrants shall issue, but upon probable cause, supported by Oath or affirmation, and particularly describing the place to be searched, and the persons or things to be seized.

## Article [V]

No person shall be held to answer for a capital, or otherwise infamous crime, unless on a presentment or indictment of a Grand jury, except in cases arising in the land or naval forces, or in the Militia, when in actual service in time of War or public danger; nor shall any person be subject for the same offense to be twice put in jeopardy of life or limb; nor shall be compelled in any criminal case to be a witness against himself, nor be deprived of life, liberty, or property, without due process of law; nor shall private property be taken for public use, without just compensation.

## Article [VI]

In all criminal prosecutions, the accused shall enjoy the right to a speedy and public trial, by an impartial jury of the State and district wherein the crime shall have been committed, which district shall have been previously ascertained by law, and to be informed of the nature and cause of the accusation; to be confronted with the witnesses against him; to have compulsory process for obtaining Witnesses in his favor, and to have the Assistance of Counsel for his defense.

## Article [VII]

In Suits at common law, where the value in controversy shall exceed twenty dollars, the right of trial by jury shall be preserved, and no fact tried by a jury, shall be otherwise reexamined in any Court of the United States, than according to the rules of the common law.

## Article [VIII]

Excessive bail shall not be required, nor excessive fines imposed, nor cruel and unusual punishments inflicted.

## Article [IX]

The enumeration in the Constitution, of certain rights, shall not be construed to deny or disparage others retained by the people.

## Article [X]

The powers not delegated to the United States by the Constitution, nor prohibited by it to the States, are reserved to the States respectively, or to the people.

## ENGLISH BILL OF RIGHTS

1 William and Mary, sess. 2, Cap. 2 *Statutes of the Realm*, vol. 6, pp. 142-145

An act declaring the rights and liberties of the subject and settling the succession of the crown.

Whereas the Lords Spiritual and Temporal and Commons assembled at Westminster, lawfully, fully, and freely representing all the states of the people of this realm, did upon the thirteenth day of February in the year of our Lord one thousand six hundred eighty-eight present unto their Majesties, then called and known by the names and style of William and Mary, prince and princess of Orange, being present in their proper persons, a certain declaration in writing made by the said Lords and Commons in the words following, viz:*

Whereas the late King James the Second, by the assistance of divers evil councillors, judges, and ministers employed by him, did endeavor to subvert and extirpate the Protestant religion and the laws and liberties of the kingdom;

By assuming and exercising a power of dispensing with and suspending of laws and the execution of laws without consent of Parliament;

By committing and prosecuting divers worthy prelates for humbly petitioning to be excused from concurring to the said assumed power;

By issuing and causing to be executed a commission under the great seal for erecting a court called the Court of Commissioners for Ecclesiastical Causes;

By levying money for and to the use of the crown by pretense of prerogative for other time and in other manner than the same was granted by Parliament;

By raising and keeping a standing army within this kingdom in time of peace without consent of Parliament and quartering soldiers contrary to law;

By causing several good subjects being Protestants to be disarmed at the same time when papists were both armed and employed contrary to law;

By violating the freedom of election of members to serve in Parliament;

By prosecutions in the Court of King's Bench for matters and causes cognizable only in Parliament and by divers other arbitrary and illegal courses;

And whereas of late years, partial, corrupt, and unqualified persons have been returned and served on juries in trials, and particularly divers jurors in trials for high treason which were not freeholders;

And excessive bail hath been required of persons committed in criminal cases to elude the benefit of the laws made for the liberty of the subjects;

And excessive fines have been imposed;

And illegal and cruel punishments inflicted;

And several grants and promises made of fines and forfeitures before any conviction or judgment against the persons upon whom the same were to be levied;

All which are utterly and directly contrary to the known laws and statutes and freedom of this realm.

And whereas the said late King James the Second having abdicated the government, and the throne being thereby vacant, his Highness the prince of Orange (whom it hath pleased Almighty God to make the glorious instrument of delivering this kingdom from popery and arbitrary power) did, by the advice of the Lords Spiritual and Temporal and divers principal persons of the Commons, cause letters to be written to the Lords Spiritual and Temporal being Protestants and other letters to the several counties, cities, universities, boroughs, and cinque ports for the choosing of such persons to represent them as were of right to be sent to Parliament, to meet and sit at Westminster upon the two and twentieth day of January in this year one thousand six hundred eighty and eight, in order to such an establishment as that their religion, laws, and liberties might not again be in danger of being subverted; upon which letters, elections having been accordingly made.

*Until 1752, the legal year in England began on March 25. Thus, in modern dating, February 13, 1688, would be February 13, 1689.

And thereupon the said Lords Spiritual and Temporal and Commons, pursuant to their respective letters and elections being now assembled in a full and free representative of this nation, taking into their most serious consideration the best means for attaining the ends aforesaid, do in the first place (as their ancestors in like case have usually done) for the vindicating and asserting their ancient rights and liberties, declare

That the pretended power of suspending of laws or the execution of laws by regal authority without consent of Parliament is illegal;

That the pretended power of dispensing with laws or the execution of laws by regal authority, as it hath been assumed and exercised of late, is illegal;

That the commission for erecting the late Court of Commissioners for Ecclesiastical Causes, and all other commissions and courts of like nature, are illegal and pernicious;

That levying money for or to the use of the crown by pretence of prerogative without grant of Parliament, for longer time or in other manner than the same is or shall be granted, is illegal;

That it is the right of the subjects to petition the king, and all commitments and prosecutions for such petitioning are illegal;

That the raising or keeping a standing army within the kingdom in time of peace, unless it be with consent of Parliament, is against law;

That the subjects which are Protestants may have arms for their defense suitable to their conditions and as allowed by law;

That election of members of Parliament ought to be free;

That the freedom of speech and debates or proceedings in Parliament ought not to be impeached or questioned in any court or place out of Parliament;

That excessive bail ought not to be required, nor excessive fines imposed, nor cruel and unusual punishments inflicted;

That jurors ought to be duly impanelled and returned, and jurors which pass upon men in trials for high treason ought to be freeholders;

That all grants and promises of fines and forfeitures of particular persons before conviction are illegal and void;

And that, for redress of all grievances and for the amending, strengthening, and preserving of the laws, Parliaments ought to be held frequently.

And they do claim, demand, and insist upon all and singular the premises as their undoubted rights and liberties, and that no declarations, judgments, doings, or proceedings to the prejudice of the people in any of the said premises ought in any wise to be drawn hereafter into consequence or example. To which demand of their rights, they are particularly encouraged by the declaration of his Highness the prince of Orange, as being the only means for obtaining a full redress and remedy therein. Having therefore an entire confidence that his said Highness the prince of Orange will perfect the deliverance so far advanced by him and will still preserve them from the violation of their rights which they have here asserted and from all other attempts upon their religion, rights, and liberties, the said Lords Spiritual and Temporal and Commons assembled at Westminster do resolve that William and Mary, prince and princess of Orange, be and be declared king and queen of England, France, and Ireland and the dominions thereunto belonging,* to hold the crown and royal dignity of the said kingdom and dominions to them, the said prince and princess, during their lives and the life of the survivor of them; and that the sole and full exercise of the regal power be only in and executed by the said prince of Orange in the names of the said prince and princess during their joint lives, and after their deceases the said crown and royal dignity of the said kingdoms and dominions to be to the heirs of the body of the said princess, and for default of such issue to the Princess Anne of Denmark and the heirs of her body, and for default of such issue to the heirs of the body of the said prince of Orange. And the Lords Spiritual and Temporal and Commons do pray the said prince and princess to accept the

---

*English monarchs styled themselves king or queen of France between 1340 and 1801. The custom began when the English became embroiled in the Hundred Years War with France and King Edward III of England, whose mother was a French princess, claimed the French throne.

same accordingly; and that the oaths hereafter mentioned be taken by all persons of whom the oaths of allegiance and supremacy might be required by law, instead of them; and that the said oaths of allegiance and supremacy be abrogated:

I, A. B., do sincerely promise and swear that I will be faithful and bear true allegiance to their Majesties King William and Queen Mary. So help me God.

I, A. B., do swear that I do from my heart abhor, detest, and abjure as impious and heretical this damnable doctrine and position, that princes excommunicated or deprived by the pope or any authority of the see of Rome may be deposed or murdered by their subjects or any other whatsoever. And I do declare that no foreign prince, person, prelate, state, or potentate hath or ought to have any jurisdiction, power, superiority, preeminence, or authority, ecclesiastical or spiritual, within this realm. So help me God.

Upon which, their said Majesties did accept the crown and royal dignity of the kingdoms of England, France, and Ireland and the dominions thereunto belonging, according to the resolution and desire of the said Lords and Commons contained in the said declaration. And thereupon their Majesties were pleased that the said Lords Spiritual and Temporal and Commons, being the two Houses of Parliament, should continue to sit and, with their Majesties' royal concurrence, make effectual provision for the settlement of the religion, laws, and liberties of this kingdom, so that the same for the future might not be in danger again of being subverted. To which the said Lords Spiritual and Temporal and Commons did agree and proceed to act accordingly.

Now in pursuance of the premises, the said Lords Spiritual and Temporal and Commons in Parliament assembled, for the ratifying, confirming, and establishing the said declaration and the articles, clauses, matters, and things therein contained by the force of a law made in due form by authority of Parliament, do pray that it may be declared and enacted that all and singular the rights and liberties asserted and claimed in the said declaration are the true ancient and indubitable rights and liberties of the people of this kingdom and so shall be esteemed, allowed, adjudged, deemed, and taken to be; and that all and every the particulars aforesaid shall be firmly and strictly holden and observed as they are expressed in the said declaration; and all officers and ministers whatsoever shall serve their Majesties and their successors according to the same in all times to come. And the said Lords Spiritual and Temporal and Commons, seriously considering how it hath pleased Almighty God in his marvelous providence and merciful goodness to this nation to provide and preserve their said Majesties' royal persons most happily to reign over us upon the throne of their ancestors, for which they render unto him from the bottom of their hearts their humblest thanks and praises, do truly, firmly, assuredly, and in the sincerity of their hearts think, and do hereby recognize, acknowledge, and declare that King James the Second having abdicated the government and their Majesties having accepted the crown and royal dignity as aforesaid, their said Majesties did become, were, are, and of right ought to be by the laws of this realm our sovereign liege lord and lady, king and queen of England, France, and Ireland and the dominions thereunto belonging; in and to whose princely persons, the royal state, crown, and dignity of the said realms with all honors, styles, titles, regalities, prerogatives, powers, jurisdictions, and authorities to the same belonging and appertaining are most fully, rightfully, and entirely invested and incorporated, united and annexed.

And for preventing all questions and divisions in this realm by reason of any pretended titles to the crown, and for preserving a certainty in the succession thereof, in and upon which the unity, peace, tranquility, and safety of this nation doth under God wholly consist and depend, the said Lords Spiritual and Temporal and Commons do beseech their Majesties that it may be enacted, established, and declared that the crown and regal government of the said kingdoms and dominions, with all and singular the premises thereunto belonging and appertaining, shall be and continue to their said Majesties and the survivor of them during their lives and the life of the survivor of them; and that the entire, perfect, and full exercise of the regal power and government be only in and executed by his Majesty in the names of both their Majesties during their joint lives; and after their deceases, the said crown and premises shall be and remain to the heirs of the body of her Majesty and, for default of such issue, to her Royal Highness the Princess Anne of Denmark and the heirs of her body and, for default of such issue, to the heirs of the body of his said Majesty. And thereunto the said

Lords Spiritual and Temporal and Commons do in the name of all the people aforesaid most humbly and faithfully submit themselves, their heirs, and posterities forever and do faithfully promise that they will stand to maintain and defend their said Majesties and also the limitation and succession of the crown, herein specified and contained, to the utmost of their powers with their lives and estates against all persons whatsoever that shall attempt any thing to the contrary.

And whereas it hath been found by experience that it is inconsistent with the safety and welfare of this Protestant kingdom to be governed by a popish prince, or by any king or queen marrying a papist, the said Lords Spiritual and Temporal and Commons do further pray that it may be enacted that all and every person and persons that is, are, or shall be reconciled to, or shall hold communion with, the see or church of Rome, or shall profess the popish religion or shall marry a papist, shall be excluded and be forever incapable to inherit, possess, or enjoy the crown and government of this realm and Ireland and the dominions thereunto belonging or any part of the same, or to have, use, or exercise any regal power, authority, or jurisdiction within the same. And in all and every such case or cases, the people of these realms shall be and are hereby absolved of their allegiance. And the said crown and government shall from time to time descend to and be enjoyed by such person or persons being Protestants, as should have inherited and enjoyed the same in case the said person or persons so reconciled, holding communion, or professing or marrying as aforesaid were naturally dead. And that every king and queen of this realm, who at any time hereafter shall come to and succeed in the imperial crown of this kingdom, shall on the first day of the meeting of the first Parliament next after his or her coming to the crown, sitting in his or her throne in the House of Peers, in the presence of the Lords and Commons therein assembled, or at his or her coronation before such person or persons who shall administer the coronation oath to him or her at the time of his or her taking the said oath (which shall first happen), make, subscribe, and audibly repeat the declaration mentioned in the statute made in the thirtieth year of the reign of King Charles the Second entitled *An Act for the more effectual preserving the king's person and government by disabling papists from sitting in either House of Parliament.* But if it shall happen that such king or queen upon his or her succession to the crown of this realm shall be under the age of twelve years, then every such king or queen shall make, subscribe, and audibly repeat the said declaration at his or her coronation, or the first day of the meeting of the first Parliament as aforesaid which shall first happen after such king or queen shall have attained the said age of twelve years. All which their Majesties are contented and pleased shall be declared, enacted, and established by authority of this present Parliament and shall stand, remain, and be the law of this realm forever. And the same are by their said Majesties, by and with the advice and consent of the Lords Spiritual and Temporal and Commons in Parliament assembled and by the authority of the same, declared, enacted, and established accordingly.

And be it further declared and enacted by the authority aforesaid that, from and after this present session of Parliament, no dispensation by non obstante of or to any statute, or any part thereof, shall be allowed but that the same shall be held void and of no effect, except a dispensation be allowed of in such statutes, and except in such cases as shall be specially provided for by one or more bill or bills to be passed during this present session of Parliament.

Provided that no charter or grant or pardon granted before the three and twentieth day of October in the year of our Lord one thousand six hundred eighty-nine shall be anyway impeached or invalidated by this act, but that the same shall be and remain of the same force and effect in law and no other than as if this act had never been made.

taxes. The Constitution also incorporated other specific rights traditional in English law, including that of HABEAS CORPUS, which protects against unlawful imprisonment. However, the Constitution made no mention of other basic rights of constitutional government such as freedom of speech, press, and religion, and the rights of those accused of crimes.

During the Constitution's ratification process, from 1787 to 1789, state ratifying conventions pointed out the lack of such fundamental guarantees in the Constitution and submitted lists of proposed constitutional amendments. The Federalists, who supported ratification of the Constitution, eventually conceded and promised to attach a bill of rights to the document. The leading contributors to the creation of these amendments—which came collectively to be called the Bill of Rights—were Mason, THOMAS JEFFERSON, and JAMES MADISON, with Madison serving as their principal author and sponsor on the floor of the U.S. House during the First Congress.

On September 25, 1789, twelve amendments to the Constitution were submitted to the states by the required two-thirds majority of Congress. Two of the amendments—which dealt with congressional pay and the apportionment, or assignment, of congressional seats to the states—were voted down by the states. The other ten amendments were ratified by December 15, 1791.

Scholars have described the Bill of Rights as protecting three different types of human rights: (1) rights of conscience, including the First Amendment's freedom of speech and religion; (2) rights of those accused of crimes, such as the Eighth Amendment's protection against excessive bail and fines; and (3) rights of property, such as the Fifth Amendment's provision that no one may be deprived of property without DUE PROCESS OF LAW.

One vital issue in the history of the interpretation of the Bill of Rights has concerned its application to the states. In the case of *Barron ex rel. Tiernan v. Mayor of Baltimore*, 32 U.S. (7 Pet.) 243, 8 L. Ed. 672, the Supreme Court ruled that the Bill of Rights applied only to the federal government. However, by the 1920s, the Court, using a principle known as the incorporation doctrine, had begun to apply selected elements of the first ten amendments to the states. According to this doctrine, elements of the Bill of Rights may be applied to the states through the Due Process Clause of the FOURTEENTH AMENDMENT, which holds that no state shall "deprive any person of life, liberty, or property, without due process of law." Thus in 1925 the Supreme Court ruled that the First Amendment protections of freedom of speech applied to the states as well as the federal government (*Gitlow v. New York*, 268 U.S. 652, 45 S. Ct. 625, 69 L. Ed. 1138). Incorporation gave the Supreme Court wide power to strike down state laws that it deemed to be in violation of the Constitution's Bill of Rights.

By the end of the twentieth century, nearly all provisions of the Bill of Rights had been declared binding on the states. Only five provisions of the Bill of Rights had not been applied to the states: (1) the Second Amendment's right to bear arms; (2) the Third Amendment's prohibition against involuntary quartering of troops; (3) the Fifth Amendment's requirement

of GRAND JURY indictment in capital cases; (4) the Seventh Amendment's provision for trial by JURY in civil cases; and (5) the Eighth Amendment's prohibition of excessive bail and fines.

States are free to provide additional protections beyond those offered in the federal Bill of Rights, but they may not reduce CIVIL RIGHTS or liberties to standards lower than those of the federal Constitution.

Other countries have passed bills of rights that differ from those of England and the United States. In 1789 the Constituent Assembly of France passed the Declaration of the Rights of Man, a document that stated the philosophical principles of the French Revolution. Canada adopted the Act for the Recognition and Protection of Human Rights and Fundamental Freedoms in 1960 (8-9 Eliz. II, ch. 44, § 1(c)-(f) (Can.)) and the Charter of Rights and

## Bill of Rights

Ratification by the original 13 states of the Bill of Rights

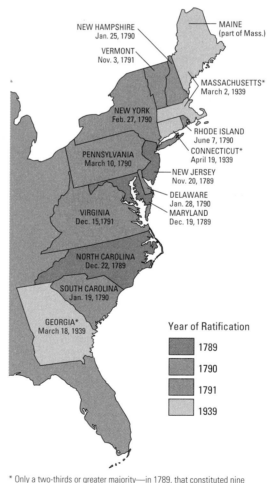

NEW HAMPSHIRE
Jan. 25, 1790

MAINE
(part of Mass.)

VERMONT
Nov. 3, 1791

MASSACHUSETTS*
March 2, 1939

NEW YORK
Feb. 27, 1790

RHODE ISLAND
June 7, 1790

CONNECTICUT*
April 19, 1939

PENNSYLVANIA
March 10, 1790

NEW JERSEY
Nov. 20, 1789

DELAWARE
Jan. 28, 1790

MARYLAND
Dec. 19, 1789

VIRGINIA
Dec. 15, 1791

NORTH CAROLINA
Dec. 22, 1789

SOUTH CAROLINA
Jan. 19, 1790

GEORGIA*
March 18, 1939

Year of Ratification

1789
1790
1791
1939

* Only a two-thirds or greater majority—in 1789, that constituted nine states—was required to ratify the Constitution and its amendments. Virginia's ratification on Dec. 15, 1791, was the last one needed for ratification.

Source: *World Almanac*, 1996 edition.

Freedoms in 1982 (Can. Const. [Constitution Act, 1982] pt. I).

### CROSS-REFERENCES

Eminent Domain; Equal Protection; Freedom of Association; Freedom of the Press; *Gitlow v. New York*; Privilege against Self-Incrimination; Religion; Right to Counsel; Searches and Seizures; Speedy Trial; Virginia Declaration of Rights; individual amendments.

**BILL OF SALE** ◳ In the law of CONTRACTS, a written agreement, previously required to be under SEAL, by which one person transfers to another a right to, or interest in, PERSONAL PROPERTY and GOODS, a legal instrument that conveys TITLE in property from seller to purchaser. ◳

**BILLS AND NOTES** ◳ An archaic term that designated the body of law currently known as the law of COMMERCIAL PAPER, which governs the methods by which commercial transactions are financed and facilitated by the execution and transfer of documents that contain promises to repay DEBTS according to the terms specified in the documents. ◳

**BILLS OF CREDIT** ◳ Non-interest-bearing PROMISSORY NOTES issued by the government and backed by its faith and credit to be paid when

A sample bill of sale

BILL OF SALE—AUTOMOBILE

_____
Our File Number

Know all by these presents:

In consideration of _____ Dollars ($_____) to _____ in hand paid by _____ the receipt of which is hereby acknowledged, _____ _____ do _____ bargain, sell and convey to the said _____
_____

one _____ as is. Factory No. _____ Motor No. _____
   (Make)   (Style)

And do hereby covenant and agree to warrant and defend the sale of said automobile unto the said _____
_____

against any lawful claims and demands of all and every person or persons whatsoever.

(This car is sold as accepted and is not guaranteed.)

Witness _____ hand this _____ day of _____, 19____

Witnesses:                      Signed _____
_____    _____
_____    _____

State of _____ ss.:
County of _____

On this _____ day of _____, 19____, before me personally came _____ _____, to me known, and known to me to be the individual described in and who executed the foregoing instrument, and he or she thereupon duly acknowledged to me that he or she executed the same.

_____
Notary Public.

My Commission Expires _____, 19____

DELIVERY RECEIPT

Received of _____
_____

the above described automobile in satisfactory condition.

Date _____ 19____     _____

presented by their holders, which are in the form of currency and are intended to be circulated and exchanged in the community as money.

The federal government, acting through the Federal Reserve banks, issues bills of credit in the form of dollar bills that are promises to pay the specific denominations indicated on them to the bearer of such paper on demand. Article I, Section 10 of the Constitution, in order to provide a uniform standard of money throughout the United States, prohibits states from issuing their own bills of credit for circulation as currency.

**BINDER** A written document that records the essential provisions of a CONTRACT of INSURANCE and temporarily protects the INSURED until an insurance company has investigated the risks to be covered, or until a formal policy is issued.

A receipt for cash or for a check that is deposited by a prospective buyer with the seller to secure the right to purchase real estate at terms that have been agreed upon by both buyer and seller.

**BINDING AUTHORITY** Source of law that a judge must examine or evaluate in a decision of a case.

STATUTES from the same state where a case is being brought, or higher court decisions, are binding authority for a judge.

According to the Federal SUPREMACY CLAUSE, which is Article VI of the Constitution, all laws made pursuant to the Constitution are to be considered the supreme law of the land. They are entitled to legal superiority over any conflicting state law or constitutional provision.

**BINDING OVER** The requirement imposed by a court or a magistrate upon a person to enter into a RECOGNIZANCE or to post BAIL to ensure that he or she will appear for trial. The transfer of a case from a lower court to a higher court or to a GRAND JURY after PROBABLE CAUSE to believe that the defendant committed the crime has been established.

**BINGHAM, JOHN ARMOR** John Armor Bingham was born January 21, 1815, at Mercer, Pennsylvania. He attended Franklin College

**BIOGRAPHY**

*John Armor Bingham*

"IT IS CLEARLY THE RIGHT OF THE REPUBLIC TO LIVE AND TO DEFEND ITS LIFE . . . [JUST] AS IT IS THE RIGHT OF THE INDIVIDUAL TO LIVE SO LONG AS GOD GIVES HIM LIFE."

**BIOGRAPHY**

*Horace Binney*

"THE BAR IS A LARGE AND DIVERSIFIED BODY. LIKE THE WEB OF OUR LIFE, IT IS A MINGLED YARN, GOOD AND ILL TOGETHER."

and pursued legal studies before establishing a successful legal practice in Cadiz in 1840.

In 1854, Bingham became an Ohio representative to Congress, serving until 1873, with the exception of one session in 1864. In 1864, he became judge advocate and, subsequently, solicitor of the court of claims. After his congressional tenure, he was minister to Japan until 1885.

Bingham gained fame for his participation in three significant historical events. He presided as special judge advocate at the proceedings against the assassins of ABRAHAM LINCOLN; he delivered the closing speech at the IMPEACHMENT trial of President ANDREW JOHNSON; and he was instrumental in shaping the Privileges and Immunities Clause added to the Fourteenth Amendment. In the last-mentioned endeavor Bingham worked with Senators Thaddeus Stevens of Pennsylvania, Jacob Howard of Michigan, and Lyman Trumbull of Illinois. The clause prohibited a state from abridging the PRIVILEGES AND IMMUNITIES guaranteed to a citizen of the United States.

Bingham died March 19, 1900, in Cadiz, Ohio.

**BINNEY, HORACE** Horace Binney was born January 4, 1780. He graduated from Harvard in 1797 and was admitted to the Philadelphia bar in 1800.

In 1806, Binney became a member of the Pennsylvania legislature, serving until 1807. In 1808 he became a director of the first BANK OF THE UNITED STATES, then returned to his political career in 1810 as a member of the Philadelphia Common Council and, from 1816 to 1819, the Philadelphia Select Council.

As a counselor, Binney displayed his legal expertise in cases concerning land titles. He won a famous victory in the Girard Trust Case of 1844, which involved the legality of a charitable legacy left to Philadelphia by philanthropist Stephen Girard. Binney defended the validity of this gift and set a precedent for interpretation of the law in regard to charitable bequests. See also TRUSTS.

Binney was a representative for Pennsylvania in the U.S. House of Representatives from 1833

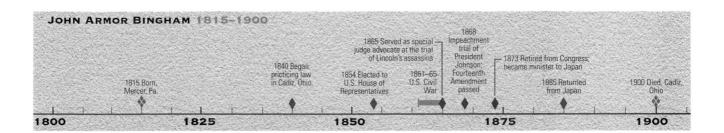

JOHN ARMOR BINGHAM 1815–1900

1815 Born, Mercer, Pa.

1840 Began practicing law in Cadiz, Ohio.

1854 Elected to U.S. House of Representatives

1861–65 U.S. Civil War

1865 Served as special judge advocate at the trial of Lincoln's assassins

1868 Impeachment trial of President Johnson; Fourteenth Amendment passed

1873 Retired from Congress; became minister to Japan

1885 Returned from Japan

1900 Died, Cadiz, Ohio

1800    1825    1850    1875    1900

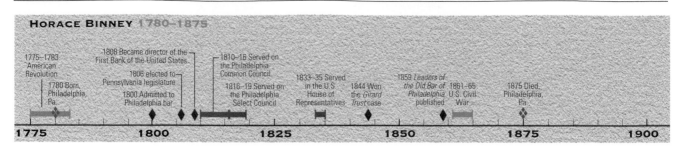

to 1835. He opposed the views of ANDREW JACKSON on the Second Bank of the United States: Binney favored the federal bank, while Jackson preferred the use of state banks for federal deposits.

Binney wrote several biographies and case reports, including *Leaders of the Old Bar of Philadelphia* (1859). He died August 12, 1875, in Philadelphia.

**BIRTH CONTROL** ▨ A measure or measures undertaken to prevent conception. ▨

In the 1800s, temperance unions and anti-vice societies headed efforts to prohibit birth control in the United States. Anthony Comstock, the secretary of the Society for the Suppression of Vice, advocated a highly influential law passed by Congress in 1873. It was titled the Act for the Suppression of Trade in, and Circulation of Obscene Literature and Articles of Immoral Use, but known popularly as the Comstock Act (18 U.S.C.A. § 1416-62 [1964]; 19 U.S.C.A. § 1305 [1964]). The Comstock Act prohibited the use of the mail system to transmit obscene materials or articles addressing or for use in the prevention of conception, including information on birth control methods or birth control devices as well as birth control devices themselves.

Soon after the federal government passed the Comstock Act, over half the states passed similar laws. All but two of the rest of the states already had laws banning the sale, distribution, or advertising of contraceptives. Connecticut had a law that prohibited even the *use* of contraceptives; it was passed with little or no consideration for its enforceability.

Despite popular opposition, birth control had its advocates, including Margaret Sanger. In 1916, Sanger opened the first birth control clinic in the United States, in New York City. For doing so, she and her sister Ethel Byrne, who worked with her, were prosecuted under the state's version of the Comstock law (*People v. Byrne*, 99 Misc. 1, 163 N.Y.S. 682 [1917]; *People v. Sanger*, 179 A.D. 939, 166 N.Y.S. 1107 [1917]). Both were convicted and sentenced to thirty days in a workhouse.

After serving her sentence, Sanger continued to attack the Comstock Act. She established the National Committee for Federal Legislation for Birth Control, headquartered in Washington, D.C., and proposed the "doctor's bill." This bill advocated change in the government's policy toward birth control, by citing the numerous instances in which women had died owing to illegal ABORTIONS and unwanted pregnancies. The bill was defeated, due, in part, to opposition from the Catholic Church and other religious groups.

But when the issue of Sanger's sending birth control devices through the mail to a doctor was pressed in *United States v. One Package*, 13 F. Supp. 334 (S.D.N.Y. 1936), the court ruled that the Comstock Act was not concerned with preventing distribution of items that might save the life or promote the well-being of a doctor's patients. Sanger had sought to challenge the Comstock Act by breaking it and sending contraception in the mail. Her efforts were victorious and the exception was made. The doctor to whom Sanger had sent the device was granted its possession.

Sanger furthered her role in reforming attitudes toward birth control by founding the Planned Parenthood Federation of America in 1942. Planned Parenthood merged previously existing birth control federations and promoted a range of birth control options. In the 1950s, Sanger went on to support the work of Dr. Gregory Pincus, whose research eventually produced the revolutionary birth control pill.

By the 1960s, partly as a result of Sanger's efforts, popular and legal attitudes toward birth control began to change. The case of *Griswold v. Connecticut*, 381 U.S. 479, 85 S. Ct. 1678, 14 L. Ed. 2d 510 (1965), loosened the restrictions of the Comstock Act. When the Planned Parenthood League of Connecticut opened in 1961, its executive director, Estelle Griswold, faced charges of violating Connecticut's ban on the use of contraceptives (Conn. Gen. Stat. Ann. §§ 53-32, 54-196 [1958]).

A divided Supreme Court overturned Griswold's conviction with a groundbreaking opin-

## All Women Age 15–44

**Birth Control**
Contraceptive use by women of childbearing age, 15 to 44 years old, in 1990

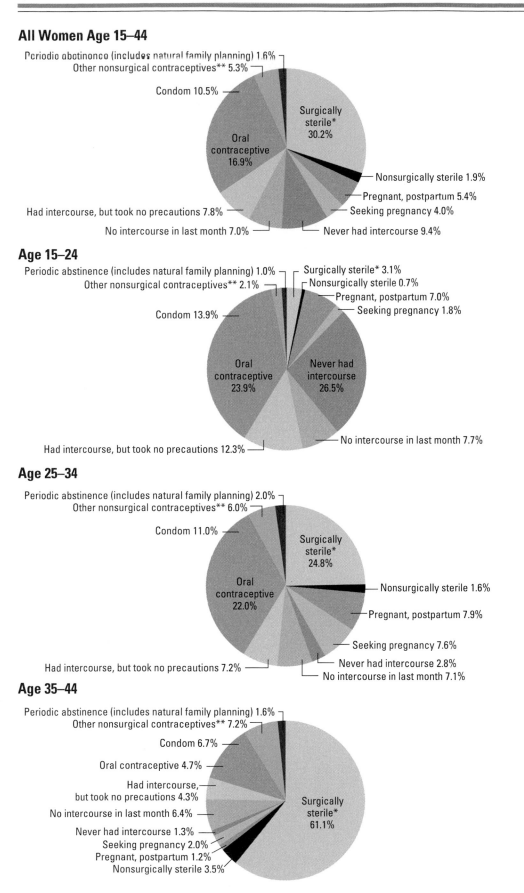

Periodic abstinence (includes natural family planning) 1.6%
Other nonsurgical contraceptives** 5.3%
Condom 10.5%
Oral contraceptive 16.9%
Had intercourse, but took no precautions 7.8%
No intercourse in last month 7.0%
Surgically sterile* 30.2%
Nonsurgically sterile 1.9%
Pregnant, postpartum 5.4%
Seeking pregnancy 4.0%
Never had intercourse 9.4%

## Age 15–24

Periodic abstinence (includes natural family planning) 1.0%
Other nonsurgical contraceptives** 2.1%
Condom 13.9%
Oral contraceptive 23.9%
Had intercourse, but took no precautions 12.3%
Surgically sterile* 3.1%
Nonsurgically sterile 0.7%
Pregnant, postpartum 7.0%
Seeking pregnancy 1.8%
Never had intercourse 26.5%
No intercourse in last month 7.7%

## Age 25–34

Periodic abstinence (includes natural family planning) 2.0%
Other nonsurgical contraceptives** 6.0%
Condom 11.0%
Oral contraceptive 22.0%
Had intercourse, but took no precautions 7.2%
Surgically sterile* 24.8%
Nonsurgically sterile 1.6%
Pregnant, postpartum 7.9%
Seeking pregnancy 7.6%
Never had intercourse 2.8%
No intercourse in last month 7.1%

## Age 35–44

Periodic abstinence (includes natural family planning) 1.6%
Other nonsurgical contraceptives** 7.2%
Condom 6.7%
Oral contraceptive 4.7%
Had intercourse, but took no precautions 4.3%
No intercourse in last month 6.4%
Never had intercourse 1.3%
Seeking pregnancy 2.0%
Pregnant, postpartum 1.2%
Nonsurgically sterile 3.5%
Surgically sterile* 61.1%

\* Includes sterilizations performed on woman for contraceptive or medical reasons, as well as sterilization performed on husband or partner.
** Includes IUD, diaphragm, douching, withdrawal, sponges, suppositories, and other methods.

Source: U.S. National Center for Health Statistics, *Advance Data from Vital and Health Statistics,* No. 182.

*In 1991 New York City schools began making condoms available to students such as these seventeen-year-olds.*

ion that established a constitutional right to marital privacy. The Court threw out the underlying Connecticut statute, which prohibited both using contraception, and assisting or counseling others in its use. The majority opinion, authored by Justice WILLIAM O. DOUGLAS, looked briefly at a series of prior cases in which the Court had found rights not specifically enumerated in the Constitution—for example, the right of FREEDOM OF ASSOCIATION, which the Court has said is protected by the FIRST AMENDMENT, even though that phrase is not used there (for example, *NAACP v. Alabama*, 357 U.S. 449, 78 S. Ct. 1163, 2 L. Ed. 2d 1488 [1958]). Douglas concluded that various guarantees contained in the Bill of Rights' Amendments One, Three, Four, Five, Nine, and Fourteen, taken together, create "zones of privacy," which include a right of marital privacy. The Connecticut statute, which could allow police officers to search a marital bedroom for evidence of contraception, was held unconstitutional; the government did not have a right to make such intrusions into the marital relationship.

The other branches of the government followed the Court's lead. President LYNDON B. JOHNSON endorsed public funding for family planning services in 1966, and the federal government began to subsidize birth control ser-

vices for low-income families. In 1970 President RICHARD M. NIXON signed the Family Planning Services and Population Research Act (42 U.S.C.A. § 201 et seq.). This act supported activities related to population research and family planning.

More and more, the Comstock Act came to be seen as part of a former era, until, in 1971, the essential components of it were repealed. But this repeal was not necessarily followed by all the states. In the 1972 case of *Eisenstad v. Baird*, 405 U.S. 438, 92 S. Ct. 1029, 31 L. Ed. 2d 349, the Court struck down a Massachusetts law still on the books that allowed distribution of contraceptives to married couples only. The Court held that the Massachusetts law denied single persons EQUAL PROTECTION, in violation of the FOURTEENTH AMENDMENT.

In the 1977 case of *Carey v. Population Services International*, 431 U.S. 678, 97 S. Ct. 2010, 52 L. Ed. 2d 675, the Supreme Court continued to expand constitutional protections in the area of birth control. The Court imposed a strict standard of review for a New York law that it labeled "defective." The law had prohibited anyone but PHYSICIANS from distributing contraceptives to MINORS under sixteen years of age. The law had also prohibited anyone but licensed PHARMACISTS from distributing contra-

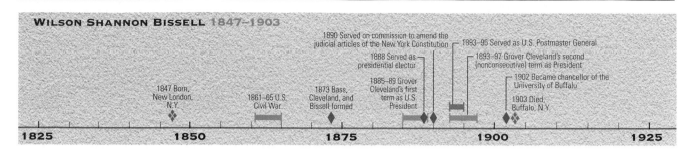

**WILSON SHANNON BISSELL 1847–1903**

1890 Served on commission to amend the
judicial articles of the New York Constitution

1893–95 Served as U.S. Postmaster General

1888 Served as
presidential elector

1893–97 Grover Cleveland's second
(nonconsecutive) term as President

1902 Became chancellor of the
University of Buffalo

1847 Born,
New London,
N.Y.

1861–65 U.S.
Civil War

1873 Bass,
Cleveland, and
Bissell formed

1885–89 Grover
Cleveland's first
term as U.S.
President

1903 Died,
Buffalo, N.Y.

1825    1850    1875    1900    1925

---

ceptives to persons over sixteen. *Carey* allowed makers of contraceptives more freedom to distribute and sell them to teens.

Although these early decisions of the Supreme Court opened up the sale and distribution of birth control to the general public, they did not address the issue of school distribution of condoms to high school students. In an effort to decrease the spread of AIDS among New York City's teenagers, the New York Board of Education, in February 1991, directed high schools to make condoms available to students who requested them. AIDS awareness classes were also required. Some of the students' parents objected. They claimed that the availability of condoms violated the New York Public Health Law, section 2504; condom distribution, the parents said, constituted a health service to minor children without parental consent. Parents also argued that condom distribution violated their free exercise of religion.

On December 30, 1993, New York's Supreme Court, Appellate Division, issued a ruling in favor of the parents, prohibiting distribution of condoms to unemancipated minor students without prior consent. The court held that the condom distribution program lacked statutory or COMMON-LAW authority, and that it violated the parents' DUE PROCESS rights under the Fourteenth Amendment and the New York Constitution (*Alfonso v. Fernandez*, 195 A.D.2d 46, 606 N.Y.S.2d 259, 88 Ed. Law Rep. 747).

Similar cases were brought throughout the United States. The school boards of San Francisco, Seattle, and Los Angeles all disagreed with the New York court, and authorized the distribution of condoms to students. As a general rule, however, court decisions established that although parents have no control over public school curriculum, they may reserve the right to withdraw their children from classes on birth control and AIDS prevention.

### CROSS-REFERENCES

Druggist; Family Law; *Griswold v. Connecticut*; Marriage; Parent and Child; Privacy; Reproduction; Sanger, Margaret; Schools and School Districts.

**BIOGRAPHY**

*Wilson Shannon Bissell*

**BIOGRAPHY**

LIBRARY OF CONGRESS

*Hugo Lafayette Black*

**BISSELL, WILSON SHANNON**  Wilson Shannon Bissell was born December 31, 1847, in New London, New York. He graduated from Yale in 1869 and received a doctor of laws degree in 1893. In 1872 he established a legal practice with Lyman K. Bass and in 1873 GROVER CLEVELAND joined the firm, forming Bass, Cleveland and Bissell.

In 1888 Bissell acted as a presidential elector and in 1890, served on a commission to amend the judicial articles of the New York Constitution.

Grover Cleveland, as president of the United States in 1893, selected his former law partner to serve as U.S. postmaster general, which post Bissell held until 1895.

Extending his career to the field of education, Bissell became chancellor of the University of Buffalo in 1902. He died October 6, 1903, in Buffalo.

**BLACK, HUGO LAFAYETTE**  Hugo LaFayette Black was an associate justice on the U.S. Supreme Court for nearly thirty-four years, serving one of the longest and most influential terms in the history of the Court.

Black was born February 27, 1886, in Harlan, Alabama, the eighth child of a storekeeper and farmer. He was raised in rural Alabama and attended local schools. At the age of seventeen, Black entered Birmingham Medical College. He decided that he was more suited to the study of law, however, and left the college after one year to attend the University of Alabama Law School, where he received his bachelor of laws degree in 1906. In the same year, Black was admitted to the Alabama bar. He practiced briefly in Ashland, Alabama, near his childhood home. He then moved to Birmingham, where he quickly developed a successful practice in tort, labor, and contract law. In 1911, he was appointed a judge on the Birmingham Police Court, but he resigned eighteen months later to return to private practice. In 1914, Black was elected county prosecutor for Jefferson County, Alabama, and gained local prominence for his investigation of brutal police tactics used to

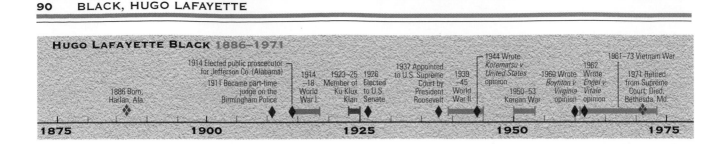

question suspects at the county jail. In 1917 Black resigned his position as prosecutor and enlisted in the Army. He remained in the United States and served as a captain of the artillery for a year. Then he resumed his private practice in Birmingham, where he frequently represented local workers in personal injury suits and served as an attorney for the local chapter of the United Mine Workers. In 1921 he married Josephine Foster, with whom he had three children.

In 1923 Black joined the Birmingham chapter of the Ku Klux Klan (KKK). He remained a member for two years. He commented later that, at the time, he believed joining the group could further his political and professional career.

In 1926, Black, a Democrat, won a seat in the U.S. Senate, overcoming four other Democrats in the race. Black served in the Senate for nearly ten years and gained prominence as a tenacious and sometimes relentless investigator into the activities of Washington, D.C., lobbyists for public utilities. He was also a member of the Senate Judiciary Committee and a staunch supporter of President FRANKLIN D. ROOSEVELT's New Deal legislation. A longtime supporter of organized labor, Black helped secure passage of the Fair Labor Standards Act of 1938 (29 U.S.C.A. § 201 et seq.), which established a minimum wage and a forty-hour workweek for enterprises in interstate commerce.

In August 1937, Black became Roosevelt's first appointee to the U.S. Supreme Court, nominated to replace retiring justice Willis Van Devanter. Initially, Black's nomination was met with some opposition. Some critics cited his relative lack of judicial experience; others expressed concern about his "judicial temperament," given the aggressive and even abrasive manner that he was said to display when interrogating witnesses while a senator. Black was nevertheless confirmed in October 1937, by a vote of 63–16. Shortly afterward came confirmation of rumors that had been circulating throughout Washington, D.C., about Black's KKK ties in the mid-1920s. The controversy

died quickly after Black spoke about the matter in a radio address. He admitted that he had once been a member but maintained that he had resigned many years earlier and had disavowed any further association with the organization.

Throughout his long career on the Court, Black wrote a number of landmark decisions concerning CIVIL RIGHTS, free speech, and other important constitutional issues. In *Chambers v. Florida*, 309 U.S. 227, 60 S. Ct. 472, 84 L. Ed. 716 (1940), he wrote the majority opinion overturning the death sentences of several blacks who had been coerced, through many hours of police interrogation, into confessing to murder. The *Chambers* decision, which came early in Black's tenure on the Court and was the first major civil rights decision he wrote, did much to alleviate the fears of civil libertarians about his earlier KKK involvement. In another civil rights case, *Boynton v. Virginia*, 364 U.S. 454, 81 S. Ct. 182, 5 L. Ed. 2d 206 (1960), Black wrote the majority opinion holding that racial segregation in facilities for travelers violated the Interstate Commerce Act (49 U.S.C.A. § 501 et seq.).

Black had represented many labor organizations while a practicing attorney, and he continued his strong pro-labor stance throughout his career on the Court. In *National Labor Relations Board v. Waterman Steamship Corp.*, 309 U.S. 206, 60 S. Ct. 493, 84 L. Ed. 704 (1940), which involved a dispute over unfair labor practices, Black wrote for the majority that the court of appeals could not substitute its judgment for that of the National Labor Relations Board. In his dissent in *United Public Workers v. Mitchell*, 330 U.S. 75, 67 S. Ct. 556, 91 L. Ed. 754 (1947), he opposed restrictions that prohibited federal government workers from participating in political campaigns. In *Youngstown Sheet & Tube Co. v. Sawyer*, 343 U.S. 579, 72 S. Ct. 863, 96 L. Ed. 1153 (1952), the Court, with Black writing the majority opinion, held that President HARRY S. TRUMAN did not have the authority to seize most of the United States' steel mills to avert a threatened STRIKE.

Black strongly believed that the Due Process Clause of the FOURTEENTH AMENDMENT to the Constitution—which provides that "[n]o State shall make or enforce any law which shall abridge the privileges or immunities of citizens of the United States"—means that the first eight amendments of the Bill of Rights must be applied to the states as well as to the federal government. Eventually, a majority of the Court agreed with him. In *Gideon v. Wainwright*, 372 U.S. 335, 83 S. Ct. 792, 9 L. Ed. 2d 799 (1963), Black wrote for the majority that states must provide defense counsel to indigent defendants accused of a FELONY, at any "critical stage" of the criminal proceedings. In *Pointer v. Texas*, 380 U.S. 400, 85 S. Ct. 1065, 13 L. Ed. 2d 923 (1965), in another majority opinion, Black wrote that the SIXTH AMENDMENT right of an accused to confront WITNESSES extends to defendants in state cases.

Black always carried a copy of the Constitution in his pocket. He was a staunch defender of the FIRST AMENDMENT and vehemently opposed any restrictions on the FREEDOM OF SPEECH. He dissented in *Dennis v. United States*, 341 U.S. 494, 71 S. Ct. 857, 95 L. Ed. 1137 (1951), which upheld a federal statute making it a crime to advocate the overthrow of the government by force. Black rejected the Court's reliance on the "clear-and-present-danger" test, in which the Court considered whether such a serious danger existed that the restriction of speech was justified. Black wrote, "There is hope . . . that in calmer times, when present pressures, passions and fears subside, this or some other Court will restore the First Amendment liberties to the high preferred place where they belong in society." He joined Justice WILLIAM O. DOUGLAS's dissent in the OBSCENITY case *Roth v. United States*, 354 U.S. 476, 77 S. Ct. 1304, 1 L. Ed. 2d 1498 (1957), in which Douglas maintained that even "prurient" material was entitled to absolute First Amendment protection. In the First Amendment case *Engel v. Vitale*, 370 U.S. 421, 82 S. Ct. 1261, 8 L. Ed. 2d 601 (1962), he wrote the majority opinion holding that voluntary prayers sponsored by public schools are unconstitutional. He stated, "It is neither sacrilegious nor antireligious to say that each separate government in this country should stay out of the business of . . . sanctioning . . . prayers and leave that purely religious function to the people themselves and to those the people choose to look to for religious guidance." One of Black's last opinions before leaving the Court was for the *Pentagon Papers* case, *New York Times Co. v. United States*, 403 U.S. 713, 91 S. Ct. 2140, 29 L. Ed. 2d 822 (1971), in which he concurred in the Court's holding that the government could not prevent publication of a classified study on the Vietnam War.

Black departed from his liberal views in *Korematsu v. United States*, 323 U.S. 214, 65 S. Ct. 193, 89 L. Ed. 194 (1944), a widely criticized decision, for which he wrote the majority opinion upholding the internment of Japanese Americans during World War II. Despite the condemnation of *Korematsu* in the years following the war, Black stood by the decision, maintaining that it was justified by the climate of fear that existed at the time. In addition, his strict construction of the Constitution led him to write other opinions that sometimes seem inconsistent with his liberal views. He dissented in *Griswold v. Connecticut*, 381 U.S. 469, 85 S. Ct. 1678, 14 L. Ed. 2d 510 (1965), in which the Court struck down, on privacy grounds, a state law that prohibited the sale of contraceptives. Black maintained that no right of privacy could be found to emanate "from one or more constitutional provisions."

While on the Court, Black was known for being sometimes antagonistic toward other justices with whom he disagreed. The Court's tradition of keeping private its inner workings and the nature of the personal relationships between the justices was broken when Black became engaged in an unusually public feud with Justice ROBERT H. JACKSON in 1946. The dispute began when Jackson, in a letter to the Senate and House Judiciary Committees, accused Black of a CONFLICT OF INTEREST for participating in two labor decisions that were argued by a former law partner of Black's. Jackson failed to mention that Black and the attorney had dissolved their partnership nineteen years earlier and had hardly seen each other since. Black, in turn, publicly criticized Jackson's leave of absence from the Court from 1945 to 1946 to serve as the U.S. prosecutor at the NUREMBERG TRIALS, calling those proceedings a "high grade lynching party." Jackson was in line for the chief justice seat, which had been vacated in 1946, and he blamed Black when the appointment went to FRED M. VINSON, selected by President Truman to restore peace among the members of the Court. Following Vinson's appointment, Black and Jackson were outwardly cordial to each other, though Jackson was reported to have remained resentful, believing that Black's actions had denied him the post of chief justice.

Healthy and vigorous well into his later life, Black was an avid tennis player who often

"THE LAYMAN'S CONSTITUTIONAL VIEW IS THAT WHAT HE LIKES IS CONSTITUTIONAL AND THAT WHICH HE DOESN'T LIKE IS UNCONSTITUTIONAL."

shared the court with his law clerks. On September 17, 1971, Black resigned from the Court at the age of eighty-five. He died just eight days later after suffering a massive stroke.

### CROSS-REFERENCES

*Dennis v. United States; Engel v. Vitale;* Freedom of the Press; *Gideon v. Wainwright; Griswold v. Connecticut;* Incorporation Doctrine; Japanese-American Evacuation Cases; *Korematsu v. United States; New York Times v. United States;* Right to Counsel; *Roth v. United States;* School Prayer; *Youngstown Sheet and Tube Co. v. Sawyer.*

## BLACK, JEREMIAH SULLIVAN

Jeremiah Sullivan Black was a prominent lawyer, judge, and U.S. attorney general, and also an unsuccessful nominee for the U.S. Supreme Court.

Black was born January 10, 1810, in Stony Creek, Pennsylvania. He was raised in rural Pennsylvania and was largely self-educated through his own reading and study of Shakespeare, the Bible, and other works of literature. He originally planned a career in medicine, but his father arranged for him to study law with Chauncey Forward, a prominent local attorney and politician. After three years with Forward, Black was admitted to the Pennsylvania bar, in late 1830. Forward then left his practice to take a seat in the U.S. Congress and turned over his clients to Black, enabling Black to develop a lucrative law practice of his own. Black married Forward's daughter in 1836, and they had two children.

Black soon became active in Democratic politics and was appointed deputy attorney general for his county. In 1842 he was appointed judge of the district court, and nine years later, he was elected to the state supreme court. He won reelection to the state high court in 1854, and served as chief justice for three years. While an appellate judge, Black was best known for his opinions defining and construing the meaning of corporate charters.

A longtime supporter of President JAMES BUCHANAN, Black was appointed U.S. attorney general by Buchanan in 1857. While attorney general, Black gained recognition for launching a vigorous prosecution of fraudulent land schemes in California. The investigation,

"JUSTICE TRAVELS WITH A LEADEN HEEL, BUT STRIKES WITH AN IRON HAND."

headed by EDWIN M. STANTON, Black's eventual successor, resulted in the U.S. Supreme Court's reversing many district court cases involving land fraud. Black also enforced federal laws concerning the slave trade and the return of fugitive slaves. In addition, Black helped establish the Buchanan administration's position on secession, urging the president to maintain a strong Unionist stance.

In a shuffle of cabinet offices in December 1860, Black served for a short time as secretary of state. During his brief tenure, South Carolina became the first state to secede from the Union, and Black was a key adviser to Buchanan in handling the crisis.

In January 1861, with only a few weeks left in his own term as president, Buchanan named Black to a seat on the U.S. Supreme Court that had been vacant for eight months. Republican senators, anxious to give the incoming president, ABRAHAM LINCOLN, his first appointment to the Court, opposed Black. Furthermore, although Black was a strong supporter of the Union, he was not an abolitionist. As a result, his nomination was harshly criticized by the Northern antislavery press and by Democrat Stephen A. Douglas, who had just lost the election to Lincoln. Also, Southern senators who might have supported Black were resigning from the Senate to join the Confederacy. Had Buchanan acted earlier to fill the seat, Black could have been easily confirmed. Instead, he was rejected 26–25.

Deeply disappointed at his narrow defeat, Black returned to his home in York, Pennsylvania. He then suffered a number of personal setbacks, including the loss of his life savings, which he had entrusted to a relative for investment, and a rapid decline in health. In late 1861, Black's health gradually started to improve and he resumed practicing law. In December of that year, he was appointed reporter of decisions for the U.S. Supreme Court, a position created by Congress in 1816. As reporter, Black was primarily responsible for editing, publishing, and distributing the Court's opinions. The reporter was paid a modest yearly salary and usually earned additional in-

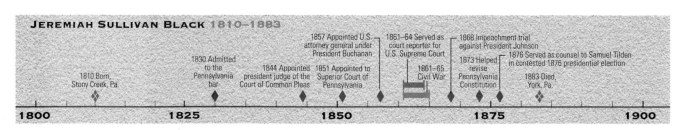

JEREMIAH SULLIVAN BLACK 1810–1883

1800 — 1825 — 1850 — 1875 — 1900

1810 Born, Stony Creek, Pa.

1830 Admitted to the Pennsylvania bar

1844 Appointed president judge of the Court of Common Pleas

1851 Appointed to Superior Court of Pennsylvania

1857 Appointed U.S. attorney general under President Buchanan

1861–64 Served as court reporter for U.S. Supreme Court

1861–65 Civil War

1868 Impeachment trial against President Johnson

1873 Helped revise Pennsylvania Constitution

1876 Served as counsel to Samuel Tilden in contested 1876 presidential election

1883 Died, York, Pa.

come selling copies of the bound volume in which an important case appeared or printing and selling a significant opinion separately in a pamphlet. In those days, the volumes produced by a particular reporter usually bore the reporter's name on the spine. Black served as reporter for three years and produced *Black's Reports,* two volumes of opinions that earned him high praise.

In 1864, Black left the Court and returned to private practice in Pennsylvania. He handled several important cases before the U.S. Supreme Court, including *Ex parte Milligan,* 71 U.S. (4 Wall.) 2, 18 L. Ed. 281 (1866). In *Milligan,* the Court held that the president lacked the power to authorize military tribunals to try civilians when they could be tried in civil courts. See also MILLIGAN, EX PARTE. Black also remained involved in the continuing litigation over California land titles, and earned high fees for his services.

Black was a close friend of President ANDREW JOHNSON, who assumed the presidency after Lincoln was assassinated. Black was initially engaged to represent Johnson in his IMPEACHMENT trial but withdrew after disagreements with Johnson's other lawyers arose. He also served as counsel to SAMUEL J. TILDEN, an unsuccessful Democratic presidential candidate, in an investigation of the disputed results of the 1876 presidential election.

Black continued to practice law and remain active in civic affairs until 1883, when he died at the age of seventy-three.

**BLACKACRE** A fictitious designation that legal writers use to describe a piece of land.

The term *Blackacre* is often used in comparison with *Whiteacre* in order to distinguish one parcel of land from another.

**BLACKFORD, ISAAC N.** Isaac N. Blackford achieved prominence as a jurist.

Blackford was born November 6, 1786, in Bound Brook, New Jersey. A graduate of Princeton, Blackford served as clerk and recorder of Washington County, Indiana, in 1813. The following year he became a district court judge.

Blackford participated in state politics as a county delegate to the Indiana legislature, serving as speaker in 1816.

In 1817 Blackford returned to the judiciary and sat as a justice of the Indiana Supreme Court until 1852. He subsequently sat as a U.S. Court of Claims judge from 1855 to 1859.

Blackford died December 31, 1859, in Washington, D.C.

**BLACK LETTER LAW** A term used to describe basic principles of law that are accepted by a majority of judges in most states.

The term probably derives from the practice of publishers of encyclopedias and legal treatises to highlight principles of law by printing them in boldface type.

**BLACKLIST** A list of individuals or organizations designated for special DISCRIMINATION or BOYCOTT; also to put a person or organization on such a list.

Blacklists have been used for centuries as a means to identify and discriminate against undesirable individuals or organizations. A blacklist might consist, for example, of a list of names developed by a company that refuses to hire individuals who have been identified as union organizers; a country that seeks to boycott trade with other countries for political reasons; a LABOR UNION that identifies firms with which it will not work; or a government that wishes to specify who will not be allowed entry into the country.

Many types of blacklists are legal. For example, a store may maintain a list of individuals who have not paid their bills and deny them CREDIT privileges. Similarly, credit reports can effectively function as blacklists by identifying individuals who are poor credit risks.

Because the purpose of blacklists is to exclude and discriminate, they can also result in unfair and illegal discrimination. In some cases, blacklists have done great damage to people's lives, locking them out of employment in their chosen careers or denying them access to influential organizations. For example, if a labor union makes a blacklist of workers who refuse to become members or conform to its rules, it has committed an unfair labor practice in violation of federal laws. Blacklists may also necessitate disclosure laws. State and federal fair credit reporting acts, for example, require that access to information in a credit report must be given,

**BIOGRAPHY**

*Isaac N. Blackford*

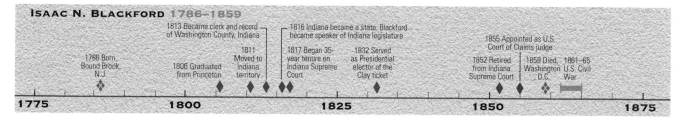

ISAAC N. BLACKFORD 1786–1859

1786 Born, Bound Brook, N.J.

1806 Graduated from Princeton

1811 Moved to Indiana territory

1813 Became clerk and record of Washington County, Indiana

1816 Indiana became a state; Blackford became speaker of Indiana legislature

1817 Began 35-year tenure on Indiana Supreme Court

1832 Served as Presidential elector of the Clay ticket

1852 Retired from Indiana Supreme Court

1855 Appointed as U.S. Court of Claims judge

1859 Died, Washington, D.C.

1861–65 U.S. Civil War

1775    1800    1825    1850    1875

upon request, to the person to whom the information applies.

The most famous instance of blacklisting in U.S. history occurred in the entertainment industry during the 1940s and 1950s. Motion picture companies, radio and television broadcasters, and other firms in that industry developed blacklists of individuals accused of being Communist sympathizers. Those firms then denied employment to those who were named on the blacklists.

Blacklisting in Hollywood came about largely through the work of the House Un-American Activities Committee (HUAC), which was formed to investigate the activities of Communist, fascist, or other supposedly subversive and "un-American" political groups. Though the committee purported to be concerned with all types of potential subversion, after World War II ended in 1945 and relations with the Soviet Union subsequently deteriorated, it focused largely on COMMUNISM as a threat to the internal stability of the United States. In highly publicized hearings in 1947, 1951–52, and 1953–55 the committee sought to ferret out Communist sympathizers, conspiracies, and propaganda in the entertainment industry.

The HUAC hearings produced lists of individuals who either had been identified by witnesses as Communists or had refused to answer questions in appearances before the committee on the grounds of the FIRST AMENDMENT, which protects free speech and free association, or the FIFTH AMENDMENT, which protects against SELF-INCRIMINATION. Entertainment industry companies, fearing that they would be perceived by the public as pro-Communist if they employed people named in the hearings, then used these lists as blacklists. They refused to hire hundreds of actors, writers, and other entertainment professionals named in the HUAC hearings. Many promising careers were thus ended and much potentially edifying art was lost.

Some of the first victims of Hollywood blacklisting were known as the Hollywood Ten. In the October 1947 HUAC Hearings Regarding Communist Infiltration of the Motion Picture Industry, ten Hollywood screenwriters and directors—Alvah Bessie, Herbert Biberman, Lester Cole, Edward Dmytryk, Ring Lardner, Jr., John Howard Lawson, Albert Maltz, Samuel Ornitz, Adrian Scott, and Dalton Trumbo—appeared under SUBPOENA, or court order, before the committee. Each of them refused to answer questions regarding affiliation with the Communist party on the grounds that such questions violated their First Amendment right to privacy, or a right to remain silent, regarding their political beliefs or affiliations. The courts rejected this argument, found the Hollywood Ten guilty of CONTEMPT of Congress, and gave them prison sentences lasting from six months to one year.

Nine of the ten were blacklisted in the film industry. (Ironically, the man conducting the 1947 HUAC hearings, Representative J. Parnell Thomas (R-N.J.), joined Lardner in federal prison in 1950 after Thomas was convicted of stealing government funds.)

Subpoenaed witnesses in these hearings faced a dilemma: on the one hand, they could invoke constitutional protection such as the Fifth Amendment, thereby implying current or former membership in the Communist party, putting themselves on the blacklist, and ending their chances of ever working in the entertainment industry again; on the other hand, they could "name names," or identify their friends as Communists, thereby betraying those close to them. In many cases, people were blacklisted for past political affiliations that they had abandoned. During the anti-Communist hysteria that gripped the nation in the 1950s, Congress's investigations into the Hollywood film industry went unchecked and the resulting blacklists destroyed numerous promising careers.

### CROSS-REFERENCES

Communism *In Focus: House Un-American Activities Committee*; Entertainment Law; Freedom of Association; Freedom of Speech.

**BLACKMAIL** ◨ The CRIME involving a threat for purposes of compelling a person to do an act against his or her will, or for purposes of taking the person's money or property. ◨

The term *blackmail* originally denoted a payment made by English persons residing along the border of Scotland to influential Scottish chieftains in exchange for protection from thieves and marauders.

In blackmail the threat might consist of physical injury to the threatened person or to someone loved by that person, or injury to a person's reputation. In some cases the victim is told that an illegal act he or she had previously committed will be exposed if the victim fails to comply with the demand.

Although blackmail is generally synonymous with EXTORTION, some states distinguish the offenses by requiring that the former be in writing.

Blackmail is punishable by a fine, imprisonment, or both.

See also THREATS.

**BLACK MONDAY** See STOCK MARKET.

**BLACKMUN, HARRY ANDREW** Harry Andrew Blackmun, associate justice of the U.S. Supreme Court from 1970 to 1994, stepped into a political maelstrom when he authored the much-lauded, much-reviled 1973 opinion *Roe v. Wade*, 410 U.S. 113, 93 S. Ct. 705, 35 L. Ed. 2d 147. *Roe* guaranteed access to safe, legal abortions for women in the first trimester of pregnancy. Depending on one's viewpoint, Blackmun was either a public hero or a Supreme Court villain, for authoring the opinion upholding a woman's right to privacy in the matter of abortion.

An unassuming and highly intelligent man, Blackmun seemed an unlikely symbol for an explosive social and political issue. Born November 12, 1908, in Nashville, Illinois, he spent his childhood in St. Paul, Minnesota, where his father ran a hardware and grocery store. Blackmun was an outstanding student and received a scholarship to Harvard University, where he graduated summa cum laude with a mathematics degree in 1929. He went on to earn a law degree from Harvard Law School in 1932.

Blackmun's first job out of law school was a federal clerkship for Judge John B. Sanborn, of the U.S. Court of Appeals for the Eighth Circuit. After his clerkship, Blackmun spent the next sixteen years practicing law in Minneapolis as a tax and trust specialist at a large, prestigious firm. In 1941, Blackmun and Dorothy E. Clark married; they later raised three children.

Blackmun also taught at the St. Paul College of Law (later renamed the William Mitchell College of Law) and at the University of Minnesota Law School. In 1950, he became head counsel at the Mayo Clinic, in Rochester, Minnesota, a position he particularly enjoyed because of a lifelong interest in medicine.

In 1959 President DWIGHT D. EISENHOWER appointed Blackmun to the U.S. Court of Appeals for the Eighth Circuit to replace his former boss, Judge Sanborn. While on the appeals court, Blackmun was a diligent and fair-minded judge, with a conservative outlook. A significant portion of his decisions involved tax issues.

**BIOGRAPHY**

*Harry Andrew Blackmun*

"ABORTION RAISES MORAL AND SPIRITUAL QUESTIONS OVER WHICH HONORABLE PERSONS CAN DISAGREE SINCERELY AND PROFOUNDLY. BUT THOSE DISAGREEMENTS . . . DO NOT NOW RELIEVE US OF OUR DUTY TO APPLY THE CONSTITUTION FAITHFULLY."

Blackmun sat on the Eighth Circuit until 1970 when President RICHARD M. NIXON appointed him to the U.S. Supreme Court. Blackmun was Nixon's third choice for the Supreme Court seat formerly held by Associate Justice Abe Fortas. Earlier, Nixon had nominated Clement F. Haynsworth, Jr., and G. Harrold Carswell, two candidates with unconvincing qualifications. After the Senate refused to confirm either Haynsworth or Carswell, Nixon turned to Blackmun as a candidate with sterling legal credentials and a fine personal reputation. Unlike the rancorous Senate proceedings for the two failed candidates, Blackmun's confirmation hearing was quick and congenial. He was approved unanimously by the Senate on May 12, 1970.

When Blackmun joined the Supreme Court, he teamed up with his boyhood friend WARREN E. BURGER, who was chief justice. Years before, Blackmun had been best man at Burger's wedding. The two St. Paul natives were immediately dubbed the Minnesota Twins.

Blackmun entered the Court with the reputation of being a hardworking, irreproachable, and conservative jurist. During his quarter century on the Supreme Court, his reputation changed in one significant way: although he continued to be seen as hardworking and irreproachable, he was perceived less and less as a conservative.

Court observers noted that Blackmun's voting record indicated a swing to the political left. His support for civil liberties in the areas of commercial speech and the rights of aliens, as well as his acceptance of a broadened judicial role, resulted in an alliance with liberal justices THURGOOD MARSHALL and WILLIAM J. BRENNAN, JR.

Blackmun insisted that he was merely taking a central ground on the issues before the Court. Nevertheless, in 1991, he acknowledged the change in public perception, saying, "having been appointed by a Republican president and being accused now of being a flaming liberal, the Republicans think I'm a traitor and the

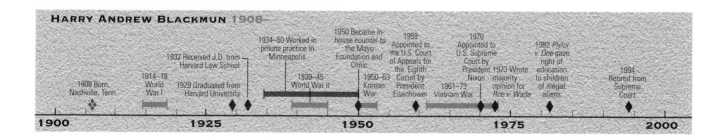

HARRY ANDREW BLACKMUN 1908–

1900 · 1925 · 1950 · 1975 · 2000

1908 Born, Nashville, Tenn.

1914–18 World War I

1929 Graduated from Harvard University

1932 Received J.D. from Harvard Law School

1934–50 Worked in private practice in Minneapolis

1939–45 World War II

1950 Became in-house counsel to the Mayo Foundation and Clinic

1950–53 Korean War

1959 Appointed to the U.S. Court of Appeals for the Eighth Circuit by President Eisenhower

1961–73 Vietnam War

1970 Appointed to U.S. Supreme Court by President Nixon

1973 Wrote majority opinion for *Roe v. Wade*

1982 *Plyler v. Doe* gave right of education to children of illegal aliens

1994 Retired from Supreme Court

Democrats don't trust me. And so I twist in the wind, I hope, beholden to no one, and that's just exactly where I want to be."

*Roe* is Blackmun's most famous contribution as a Supreme Court justice. Writing for the seven-member majority, Blackmun ruled that women could obtain abortions without interference from the state as a matter of right under the FOURTEENTH AMENDMENT to the U.S. Constitution. The case came about as a challenge to a Texas law (Vernon's Ann. Tex. P.C. arts. 1191-1194, 1196) that made abortion illegal unless performed to save the life of the mother. The law was challenged by a pregnant woman as a violation of her right to privacy.

Blackmun held that the privacy rights of the pregnant woman outweighed the state's interest. His knowledge of medical issues is evident in the case. Blackmun based his ruling on a three-part division of pregnancy: the first trimester, when a woman can obtain an abortion and the state has no interest; the second trimester, when the state has an interest in the licensing of the performing physician; and the last trimester, when the fetus is considered viable, or capable of living outside the mother's womb, and the state's interest reaches a level where the state may restrict access to abortion. Although Blackmun earned praise for this ruling, he also became the target of protests and death threats.

In another indication of his more liberal leanings, Blackmun publicly denounced CAPITAL PUNISHMENT in 1994. He declared that he would no longer support the death penalty in cases before the Supreme Court, reversing his earlier hard-line support for criminal penalties.

Blackmun announced his retirement from the Court in April 1994.

**CROSS-REFERENCES**

Abortion; Privacy; *Roe v. Wade.*

**BLACK PANTHER PARTY** No group better dramatized the anger that fueled the 1960s black power movement than the Black Panther Party for Self-Defense (BPP). For five tumultuous years, the Panthers brought a fierce cry for justice and equality to the streets of the largest U.S. cities. Its members flashed across TV screens in black berets and leather coats, shotguns and law books in hand, confronting the police or storming the California Legislature. Political demands issued from the party's newspaper; loudspeakers boomed at rallies for jailed Panther leaders. Behind the scenes, the FEDERAL BUREAU OF INVESTIGATION (FBI) spent millions of dollars in a secret counterintelligence program aimed at destroying the group. By the time a 1976 congressional report revealed the extent of the FBI's efforts, it was too late. Shoot-outs with police officers, conflicts with other groups, murder, prison sentences, and internal dissent had destroyed the Black Panthers. The details surrounding the 1969 shooting deaths of two party leaders by Chicago police remain unclear. The other party leaders split in 1972 and one of them, Bobby Seale, ran for mayor of Oakland in 1973, losing in a runoff. By 1975 the last of the group, a splinter faction under Eldridge Cleaver, had disappeared.

Before the advent of the Panthers, the mid-1960s saw gradual progress in the struggle for civil rights. This progress was too slow for many African Americans. Traditional civil rights groups such as MARTIN LUTHER KING, JR.'s Southern Christian Leadership Conference (SCLC) were focusing their efforts on ending segregation in the South, but conditions in urban areas were reaching a boiling point. Younger activists increasingly turned away from these older groups and toward leaders such as Stokely Carmichael, whose Student Nonviolent Coordinating Committee (SNCC) demanded not merely integration but economic and social liberation for African Americans. Black power was Carmichael's message, and in Mississippi, he had organized an all-black political party that took as its symbol a snarling black panther. The ethos of black power spread quickly to urban areas in the North, East, and West, where integration alone had not soothed the problems of racism, poverty, and violence.

Police violence against African Americans was a common complaint in impoverished Oakland, California. By 1966, two young men had had enough. One was HUEY P. NEWTON, age twenty-three, a first-year law student. With his friend BOBBY SEALE, age thirty, Newton founded the BPP, with the intent of monitoring police officers when they made arrests. This bold tactic—already being employed in Minneapolis by the nascent American Indian Movement (AIM)—was entirely legal. Also legal under California state law was the practice of carrying a loaded weapon, as long as it was visible. But legal or not, the sight of Newton and Seale bearing shotguns as they rushed to the scene of an arrest had enormous shock value. To police officers and citizens alike, this represented a huge change from the previously nonviolent demonstrations of civil rights activists. Although they did not use the guns and maintained the legally required eight to ten feet from officers, the Panthers inspired fear. They also quickly won respect from neighbors who saw them as standing up to the predominantly white police force. The law books they carried—and from which they read criminal suspects

their rights—appeared to many in the community to give the Panthers a kind of legitimacy.

Attracting new members through their high visibility, the Panthers sprang to national attention in 1967. Antagonism toward the party by law enforcement officials had prompted California lawmakers to consider GUN CONTROL. In May 1967, legislators met in Sacramento, the state capital, to discuss a bill that would criminalize the carrying of loaded weapons within city limits. To Seale and Newton, chairman and minister of defense of the BPP, respectively, the proposed law was unjust. Governor RONALD REAGAN was on the lawn of the state legislature as thirty armed Black Panthers arrived and entered the building. TV cameras followed the group's progress to the legislative chambers, where they were stopped by police officers, Seale shouting, "Is this the way the racist government works—[you] won't let a man exercise his constitutional rights?" He then read a prepared statement:

> The Black Panther Party calls upon American people in general and black people in particular to take full note of the racist California legislature which is now considering legislation aimed at keeping the black people disarmed and powerless, at the very same time that racist police agencies throughout the country are intensifying the terror, brutality, murder and repression of black people.

The Panthers kept their guns, left the building, and were subsequently disarmed by the police.

No sooner had the demonstration ended than the national media denounced the Panthers as antiwhite radicals. For many white U.S. citizens, the Panthers symbolized terror. The party denied being antiwhite, but a new political focus now superseded its original goal of self-defense. In a ten-point program, the Panthers called for full employment, better housing and education, and juries composed of African Americans. It denounced the war in Vietnam and the military draft. Some of its demands went further. Point 3 said the group wanted an end to the robbing of the black community by the whites. Another point called for the release

*Armed members of the Black Panther party entered the California state capitol to protest a bill restricting the carrying of arms in public.*

of all African American men from prison. The group's major political objective was self-determination. It demanded United Nations–supervised elections in the black community, which it dubbed the black colony, for blacks only, so that "black colonials" could determine their own national destiny.

To advance its cause, the party published the *Black Panther* newspaper. Its articles, cartoons, and imagery reflected a hardening stance. The police were caricatured as pigs—introducing a term of condemnation that would enter the national vernacular—and a recurring image was that of a Black Panther holding a gun to the head of a pig in a police uniform. However extreme such rhetoric may sound in the 1990s, it galvanized young African Americans coming of age in the Vietnam era. BPP chapters sprang up nationwide, and by 1968 as many as five thousand members worked from BPP offices in twenty-five major U.S. cities. Prominent activists, including Stokely Carmichael and Eldridge Cleaver, joined the party. Cleaver had achieved national prominence for his 1967 essay collection *Soul on Ice*. As the BPP's minister of information, he had a voice that struck exactly the tone the Panthers wanted, a blend of determination, outrage, and threat. "These racist Gestapo pigs," Cleaver told reporters, "have to stop brutalizing our community or we are going to take up arms and we are going to drive them out."

On another front, the Panthers proceeded with charitable services to African American communities, called Serve the People programs. They organized health clinics and schools. Holding food drives, they rounded up groceries and distributed them for free. Morning breakfast programs for African American children served food and spirituals, as kids sang "Black Is Beautiful." White liberals supported the Panthers, writing supportive articles in intellectual journals such as the *New York Review of Books;* writing books that showed admiration for their style, like Norman Mailer's *The White Negro;* and inviting them to fashionable fundraising parties, as did composer and conductor Leonard Bernstein. But this support was far from unanimous; the author Thomas C. Wolfe coined the phrase *radical chic* to satirize it.

The successes achieved by the Panthers in Oakland and beyond were soon overshadowed by violence as tense confrontations between the police and Panther members erupted in gunfire. In October 1967, after a gun battle left one officer wounded and another dead, Newton was arrested. "Free Huey!" became a cry at protests across the United States while Newton remained in jail. From his cell, he told national TV audiences that the plight of African Americans was similar to that of the Vietnamese. "The police occupy our community," he said, "as a foreign troop occupies territory." Convicted of murder, he remained in prison until August 1970. An appeals court later threw out the conviction.

The violence continued, as the police began raiding BPP offices. In 1968, a confrontation in West Oakland left three officers and two Panther members wounded. A seventeen-year-old Panther was killed. Seale announced on television that black people should organize so that they could retaliate against racist police brutality and attacks.

In 1969, Seale too was in court. The police had arrested him at an antiwar demonstration outside the 1968 Democratic National Convention in Chicago. He was charged with rioting. During the trial of Seale and other demonstrators—dubbed the CHICAGO EIGHT—federal district court judge Julius J. Hoffman ordered the vociferous Seale handcuffed to a chair and gagged, a move that inspired such public revulsion that a MISTRIAL was declared.

Over the next three years, Panther members came to trial in several cities. In 1971, for example, twenty-one Panther members were tried in New York on charges of conspiring to commit murder and arson. They all were acquitted.

The Panthers affected the highest circles of federal law enforcement. J. EDGAR HOOVER, director of the FBI, considered them a black nationalist hate group. In November 1968, he ordered FBI field agents to begin destabilizing the group by exploiting dissension within its ranks. This end was to be achieved through the FBI's Counterintelligence Program (COINTELPRO), a surveillance and misinformation program widely used in the late 1960s against civil rights, black power, and various leftist groups. The FBI infiltrated the Panther membership with informants, wiretapped telephones, mailed fake letters to leaders, and spread innuendo both inside and outside the party. Documentation of the counterintelligence campaign would emerge in a report issued in 1976 by the U.S. Senate Select Committee to Study Government Operations, titled *The FBI's Covert Program to Destroy the Black Panther Party.* The report revealed that the FBI had gone to great lengths, some of them illegal, to pit the Panthers against themselves and other groups.

The destabilization worked. The FBI managed to exacerbate a bloody feud between the Panthers and another California-based group, United Slaves (US). It poured resources into

*In 1968 two Oakland police officers fired shots into the headquarters of the Black Panther party, destroying the front window. There were no injuries and the officers were dismissed from the force.*

making leaders suspicious of each other, notably aggravating a rift between Newton and Cleaver. Perhaps its most egregious involvement came during a 1969 operation against Fred Hampton, the Chicago-based chairman of the Illinois BPP. In late 1967, the FBI launched a disinformation campaign against the nineteen-year-old, and his file in the FBI's Racial Matters Squad soon swelled to over four thousand pages. When Hampton fell under suspicion in the murder of two Chicago police officers, an FBI informant provided authorities with a detailed floor plan of his apartment. On December 4, 1969, police officers raided the apartment. Hampton and another Panther member were killed; four others were wounded. The Panthers alleged that the incident was an ASSASSINATION. Several official and private inquiries were conducted, including one led by Roy Wilkins, executive director of the NAACP, and RAMSEY CLARK, former U.S. attorney general. Lawsuits brought against the FBI by the victims' survivors dragged through the courts until 1983, when the federal government agreed to pay them a $1.85 million settlement. U.S. district court judge John F. Grady imposed sanctions on the FBI for having covered up facts in the case. For the Illinois Panther chapter, however, the raid in 1969 had signaled the beginning of the end.

In disarray in 1972, the Panthers soon collapsed. Its leadership feuded, police and FBI harassment took a heavy toll, and the black power movement had nearly expired. Charged with murder, Cleaver had fled to Cuba and Algeria, where he continued to urge African Americans on to revolution. Cleaver maintained his Black Panther faction in exile until 1975. Seale and Newton preferred nonviolent solutions. After the Panthers disbanded, Seale ran for mayor of Oakland in 1973, winning a third of the vote. He later became a public speaker and a community liaison on behalf of Temple University's African American studies program. Newton earned a doctor's degree from the University of California, Santa Cruz, but his legal problems continued. In March 1987, he was convicted for being a felon in possession of a firearm—despite the overturning of his original murder conviction—and sentenced to three years' imprisonment. In 1989, he was again in prison, serving time for a PAROLE violation for possessing cocaine. He died in August 1989, after being shot during a drug deal in the neighborhood where he began the Panthers.

The legacy of Newton and Seale's party is debatable. Its alliance with international revolutionary leaders—Mao Tse-tung, Fidel Castro, and Ho Chi Minh, to name a few—cost it credibility in the eyes of mainstream U.S. citizens. An organization devoted originally to the aim of self-defense for beleaguered urban African Americans, it nose-dived into violence and terror. For this reason, the BPP is customarily dismissed as an extremist, self-destructive exponent of the black power movement. But this transformation owed something to the harassment of the Panthers by law enforcement agencies. In turn, the calculated federal and local campaigns against the Panthers initiated the group's most tangible effect on U.S. law: highlighting FBI counterintelligence against U.S. citizens was a noteworthy gain. In the years following the death of FBI director Hoover, pressure for reforms dismantled the apparatus he single-handedly used against his political enemies.

Drawing attention to the issue of urban police brutality was another major Panther contribution, one that grew as a concern in subsequent years. In addition, the group's focus on the questionable number of African American men fighting the U.S. war in Vietnam inspired black intellectuals to criticize the role of race in the U.S. military. Moreover, in the party's passionate ten-point program were the seeds of ideas that eventually took root in the U.S. legal system: by the 1990s, juries increasingly reflected the racial composition of the communities in which defendants lived. As the history of the civil rights movement demonstrates, such change came slowly, begrudgingly, and often at great personal cost to the men and women who fought for it.

#### CROSS-REFERENCES

Civil Rights Movement; Cleaver, Eldridge; Terrorism; Vietnam War.

### BLACKSTONE, SIR WILLIAM    The

groundwork for U.S. jurisprudence lies in a four-volume eighteenth-century publication by British legal commentator Sir William Blackstone. Blackstone's *Commentaries on the Laws of England* provided a systematic analysis of English COMMON LAW. Published between 1765 and 1769, the TREATISE was an exhaustive compilation of Blackstone's Oxford University lectures on law. *Commentaries* was unprecedented in scope and purpose, and profoundly influenced

*Sir William Blackstone*

"IT IS BETTER THAT TEN GUILTY PERSONS ESCAPE THAN ONE INNOCENT SUFFER."

the development of common law and LEGAL EDUCATION in England and the United States.

Born July 10, 1723, Blackstone was the son of Mary Blackstone and Charles Blackstone, of London. Blackstone's father, a silk merchant, died before Blackstone was born; his mother died while he was a young boy. Raised by an older brother and tutored by an uncle, Blackstone attended Charterhouse and Pembroke College, at Oxford University, where his education included a thorough exposure to mathematics and logic. Blackstone entered All Souls College, Oxford, in 1743, and became a fellow in 1744.

In preparation for a law practice, Blackstone received a CIVIL LAW degree in 1745, and became a BARRISTER in 1746. In 1750, he became a doctor of civil law. One year later, he was selected as an assessor (judge) of Chancellor's Court.

In 1755, after three years of a lusterless law practice, Blackstone decided to devote all of his time to teaching law at Oxford. His first book, published in 1757, was titled *An Analysis of the Laws of England*. In 1758, Blackstone was named Oxford's Vinerian Professor of English Law, receiving the first chair of common law ever established at the university. Blackstone's lectures were well received, providing students with a comprehensive introduction to the laws of England.

The success of his lectures enhanced Blackstone's career. In 1761 he became a bencher (supervisor and lecturer) at Oxford's Middle Temple. The same year, he was elected to Parliament, where he served for seven years—although, according to most historians, he was not an especially ambitious or effective politician. Also in 1761, Blackstone married Sarah Clitherow, with whom he had nine children.

In 1765, Blackstone published the first of his four volumes of *Commentaries*. The treatise discussed the cases, rules, and legal principles outlined in his popular Oxford lectures. Each volume concentrated on a particular area of law—personal rights, property rights, torts, or criminal law. As Blackstone analyzed the laws,

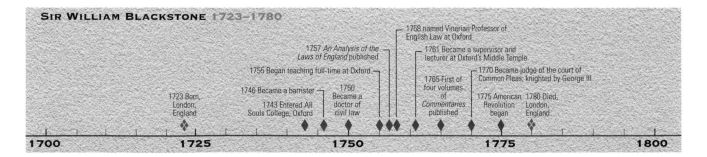

**SIR WILLIAM BLACKSTONE 1723–1780**

1758 named Vinerian Professor of English Law at Oxford

1757 *An Analysis of the Laws of England* published

1761 Became a supervisor and lecturer at Oxford's Middle Temple

1755 Began teaching full-time at Oxford

1770 Became judge of the court of Common Pleas; knighted by George III

1746 Became a barrister

1723 Born, London, England

1750 Became a doctor of civil law

1765 First of four volumes of *Commentaries* published

1743 Entered All Souls College, Oxford

1775 American Revolution began

1780 Died, London, England

1700    1725    1750    1775    1800

he also revealed their relationship to a higher power. Throughout his *Commentaries*, Blackstone wove the concept of "NATURAL LAW," or God's laws imposed on humankind.

Some critics maintain that Blackstone's view of British law was misleading because a logical, cohesive legal system simply did not exist at the time he was writing. Also, they argue that although Blackstone's writing style was graceful, he sometimes treated legal terms loosely. Yet even his harshest critics concede that Blackstone's effort to synthesize English law was indeed impressive, as was the effect of his treatise in his country and beyond.

Blackstone's *Commentaries* was particularly influential in the United States as the new nation sought to establish its own laws and legal system. Although Blackstone is no longer cited by practicing attorneys—his importance in the United States decreased dramatically during the twentieth century—he remains a revered figure in U.S. law. Over thirty editions of *Commentaries* have been printed in the United States and England.

In 1770, Blackstone became judge of the Court of Common Pleas and was knighted. He died on February 14, 1780, at age fifty-seven.

See also BLACKSTONE'S COMMENTARIES.

**BLACKSTONE'S COMMENTARIES** 📖 A series of lectures delivered by the English jurist Sir WILLIAM BLACKSTONE at Oxford in 1753 and published as *Commentaries on the Laws of England* in four volumes between 1765 and 1769, which systematized and clarified the amorphous body of English law. 📖

The *Commentaries* are the first attempt to state the entire corpus of the COMMON LAW. They were acclaimed internationally and their PRECEPTS were applied to the study and practice of law in England and the United States. They exerted a tremendous influence on the American bar, both because of their intrinsic value and because they were the only TREATISES readily available during that period of U.S. history. The *Commentaries* were the primary reference tools for lawyers and judges until the nineteenth century because the APPELLATE COURTS in America did not regularly submit their opinions for publication in bound volumes. Although there were court reporters, their records of decisions were incomplete and sporadic; and few attorneys could afford a comprehensive library.

Since the common law of England was incorporated into the legal systems of the colonies, Blackstone's summaries rendered the legal system accessible to the entire educated class of the colonies. Dissatisfaction with the common-law restrictions on freedom of speech and the press was an important aspect of the burgeoning resentment of English rule; and the knowledge and intellectual stimulation provided by Blackstone thereby played a role in causing the American Revolution. Blackstone's books, which were periodically updated by American editors, constituted a major source of law for approximately fifty years after the American Revolution.

The *Commentaries* are viewed as the most comprehensive summary of the entire body of English law ever compiled by a single author. Their clarity, sophistication, and formality have caused them to be highly regarded. While studying to be a lawyer, Abraham Lincoln reportedly read Blackstone by candlelight.

Blackstone did have detractors, however, most notably THOMAS JEFFERSON and JEREMY BENTHAM, the English Utilitarian philosopher. Jefferson believed that Blackstone and his followers were "Tories" and that he was a negative influence on America in the sense that more attention needed to be devoted to "whiggism" or "republicanism." Bentham criticized Blackstone for his perception that English law needed no improvement and for his imprecise analysis of the historical and social factors underlying systems of justice.

Although the *Commentaries* might seem antiquated by current standards, Blackstone's work represented a tremendous advance in the study of law and played a significant role in the development of the American legal system.

**BLAIR, JOHN, JR.** John Blair, Jr., was among the original members of the U.S. Supreme Court. Nominated by President GEORGE WASHINGTON, Blair began his term as an associate justice shortly after the Court's establishment on February 2, 1790. Considered a fair-minded, incorruptible jurist, he remained on the bench for six years.

Blair was born in 1732 into a wealthy, well-established Virginia family. His parents were John Blair, Sr., a public official with important political connections, and Mary Munro (or Monro) Blair, whose father was a rector in Virginia's St. John's Parish. In 1754, Blair graduated from the College of William and Mary (founded by his great-uncle), and he then studied law at Oxford's Middle Temple, in London.

In 1756 Blair returned to Virginia with his Scottish wife, Jean Balfour, and began a successful law practice in Williamsburg. He served in the House of Burgesses as a representative of William and Mary from 1766 to 1770. (The House of Burgesses was a colonial assembly of elected officials and the governor.) He served as clerk of the governor's council from 1770 to

**BIOGRAPHY**

*John Blair, Jr.*

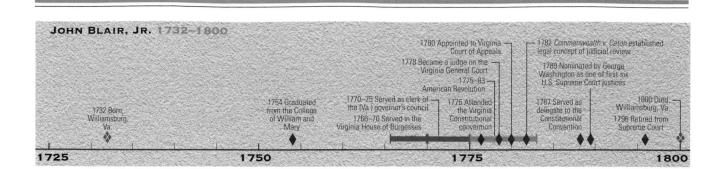

1780 Appointed to Virginia Court of Appeals
1778 Became a judge on the Virginia General Court
1775–83 American Revolution
1782 *Commonwealth v. Caton* established legal concept of judicial review
1789 Nominated by George Washington as one of first six U.S. Supreme Court justices
1732 Born, Williamsburg, Va.
1754 Graduated from the College of William and Mary
1770–75 Served as clerk of the [Va.] governor's council
1766–70 Served in the Virginia House of Burgesses
1776 Attended the Virginia Constitutional convention
1787 Served as delegate to the Constitutional Convention
1800 Died, Williamsburg, Va.
1796 Retired from Supreme Court

1725    1750    1775    1800

1775. Blair attended the Virginia Constitutional Convention and the Virginia Privy Council in 1776. (The Privy Council was an advisory group to the English monarchy.)

Before his ascension to the U.S. Supreme Court, Blair performed judicial duties for various state courts. He became a judge on the newly established Virginia General Court in 1778. In 1780, he became chancellor of the high court of chancery and was appointed to Virginia's first court of appeals.

In the 1782 chancery case *Commonwealth v. Caton*, 8 Va. (4 Call) 5, Blair concluded that courts were entitled to review state legislation and to invalidate any laws found unconstitutional. The legal concept of JUDICIAL REVIEW—whereby the courts examine legislative acts and determine their constitutionality—was later embraced fully by the U.S. Supreme Court, in the landmark case *Marbury v. Madison*, 5 U.S. 137, 2 L. Ed. 60 (1803).

In 1787 Blair served as a delegate to the Constitutional Convention in Philadelphia. Soon afterward he was appointed to the Virginia Court of Appeals. Blair received his greatest judicial honor when President Washington nominated him, along with five other men, to the first High Court on September 24, 1789. (At the time, only six justices sat on the Supreme Court. By 1869 the number had risen to nine.) Blair was confirmed by the U.S. Senate on September 26, 1789.

As an associate justice, Blair took part in *Chisholm v. Georgia*, 2 U.S. 419, 1 L. Ed. 440 (1793), the Supreme Court's first major opinion. The issue before the Court was state SOVEREIGNTY and whether a citizen of one state could sue another state in FEDERAL COURT over a disputed claim. The Supreme Court ruled that under Article III, Section 2, of the U.S. Constitution, a citizen of one state could indeed sue another state in federal court.

Many states decried the outcome of *Chisholm*, fearing lawsuits that would lead to economic disaster. Four years after the decision was handed down, Congress ratified the ELEVENTH AMENDMENT to the U.S. Constitution, which prohibited citizens of one state from suing another state without the consent of the defendant state. The amendment in effect overturned *Chisholm*.

Until the 1860s, U.S. Supreme Court justices sat on a CIRCUIT COURT as well as the High Court. In *Hayburn's Case*, 2 U.S. 408, 1 L. Ed. 436 (1792), Blair broke new ground as a federal appeals judge by ruling that a congressional act ordering circuit judges to serve as pension commissioners was unconstitutional. Blair noted that the supervision of a federal pension plan was not a judicial duty. He ruled that the designation of circuit judges as administrators violated the SEPARATION-OF-POWERS doctrine.

Blair retired from the High Court on January 27, 1796, citing the stress of serving on both the Supreme Court and the circuit court, which in Blair's case stretched from New Jersey to Virginia. He died in his native Williamsburg at age sixty-eight, in 1800.

**BLANK** 📖 Lacking something essential to fulfillment or completeness; unrestricted or open. A space left empty for the insertion of one or more words or marks in a written document that will effectuate its meaning or make it legally operative. A printed legal FORM in which the standard or necessary words are printed in their proper order with spaces left open, to be filled with names, dates, figures, and additional clauses. 📖

A blank check is one that is unrestricted as to the amount to be paid.

**BLANK ENDORSEMENT** 📖 The writing of the name of a person who holds a NEGOTIABLE INSTRUMENT on the back of the document without specifically designating to whom the paper is to be paid, which transfers the rights that the signer had in the instrument to the person who presents it for payment. 📖

When a person endorses a paycheck, for example, with just a SIGNATURE, such as "John Jones," the bank is authorized to pay the check to anyone who presents it for payment, since there is no specification or restriction as to

"BEING CALLED UPON FOR AN ACCOUNT OF WHAT MONEY I MAY HAVE IN HAND BELONGING TO HIS MAJESTY, I HAVE ONLY TO SAY THAT I HAVE NOT ANY."

whom the check can be paid. A negotiable instrument that has a blank endorsement is called bearer paper.

**BLASPHEMY** The MALICIOUS or WANTON reproach of God, either written or oral. In English law, the offense of speaking disparaging words about God, Jesus Christ, the Bible, or the Book of Common Prayer with the intent to undermine religious beliefs and promote contempt and hatred for the church as well as general immorality. In U.S. law, any maliciously intended written or oral accusation made against God or religion with the purpose of dishonoring the divine majesty and alienating mankind from the love and reverence of God.

Blasphemy is a COMMON-LAW offense and also an offense by statute in certain jurisdictions. It must be uttered in the presence of another person or persons or published in order to be an offense. Mere use of PROFANITY is not considered blasphemy.

Blasphemy statutes are rarely, if ever, enforced today.

**BLATCHFORD, SAMUEL** Samuel Blatchford was an astute and conscientious jurist who served on the U.S. Supreme Court from 1882 to 1893. He was known primarily for his maritime and patent expertise and for his remarkable productivity. During his eleven-year tenure on the High Court he wrote 430 opinions and two dissents. His most noteworthy opinions, *Chicago, Milwaukee & St. Paul Railway Co. v. Minnesota*, 134 U.S. 418, 10 S. Ct. 462, 33 L. Ed. 970 (1890), and *Budd v. People of New York*, 143 U.S. 517, 12 S. Ct. 468, 36 L. Ed. 247 (1892), were roundly criticized for their apparently contradictory conclusions about DUE PROCESS under the FOURTEENTH AMENDMENT of the U.S. Constitution.

Blatchford was born in New York City on March 9, 1820, the son of Richard Blatchford, a lawyer, and Julia Ann Mumford. He attended Columbia College (renamed Columbia University), and graduated with honors at age seventeen in 1837. Blatchford served as a trustee of Columbia from 1867 to 1893.

After graduation Blatchford became the pri-

"THE IMPORTANCE OF A LEARNED, [AND] HIGH-TONED BAR, TO THE PROPER DISCHARGE OF THE FUNCTIONS OF THE BENCH, CANNOT BE TOO HIGHLY ESTIMATED. THE STREAM CAN NEVER RISE HIGHER THAN THE FOUNTAIN."

**BIOGRAPHY**

*Samuel Blatchford*

vate secretary of Governor William H. Seward of New York, a family friend. Blatchford studied law, was admitted to the New York bar in 1842, and practiced for three years with his father in Manhattan. Blatchford then joined Seward's law firm in Auburn, New York. He married Caroline Appleton in 1844.

In 1854 Blatchford started his own law firm and he eventually became a respected authority on international, maritime, and patent law. Because of his extensive knowledge of patent law he was asked by lawmakers to help write key federal statutes governing patent infringement.

Blatchford made a significant contribution to the legal profession by organizing a reporting system for federal case law. During much of the nineteenth century federal opinions were not compiled or readily accessible to practicing lawyers. In 1852 Blatchford collected and published federal court admiralty decisions in *Blatchford's Circuit Court Reports*, a series that grew to twenty-four volumes. He also produced *Blatchford's and Howland's Reports*, a volume of admiralty cases from the District Court for the Southern District of New York, and *Blatchford's Prize Cases*, a collection of cases from circuit and district courts. His case reporting is credited with improving legal research.

Although Blatchford turned down an opportunity to sit on the New York Supreme Court in 1855, he eventually accepted another court appointment and rose through the ranks of the judiciary. In 1867 he was appointed by President ANDREW JOHNSON as district judge of the Southern District of New York. Nine years later President RUTHERFORD B. HAYES named him circuit judge for the second judicial circuit.

Blatchford reached the pinnacle of his career in 1882, when President CHESTER A. ARTHUR nominated him to the U.S. Supreme Court. Blatchford was Arthur's third choice for the seat vacated by Ward Hunt. Although the U.S. Senate had already confirmed New York politician ROSCOE CONKLING, Arthur's first choice, Conkling declined to serve. Arthur's second choice, Senator George F. Edmunds, of Vermont, also turned down the honor. Known as a

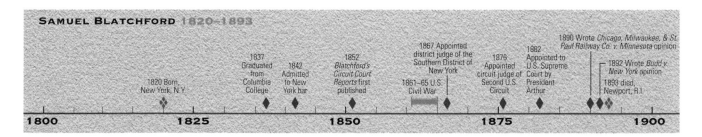

**SAMUEL BLATCHFORD 1820–1893**

1820 Born, New York, N.Y.

1837 Graduated from Columbia College

1842 Admitted to New York bar

1852 *Blatchford's Circuit Court Reports* first published

1861–65 U.S. Civil War

1867 Appointed district judge of the Southern District of New York

1876 Appointed circuit judge of Second U.S. Circuit

1882 Appointed to U.S. Supreme Court by President Arthur

1890 Wrote *Chicago, Milwaukee, & St. Paul Railway Co. v. Minnesota* opinion

1892 Wrote *Budd v. New York* opinion

1893 died, Newport, R.I.

1800    1825    1850    1875    1900

hardworking and capable lawyer and judge, Blatchford accepted the nomination and was easily confirmed.

In 1890, Blatchford wrote *Chicago, Milwaukee*, an opinion that shielded business from public regulation. The Court ruled that the reasonableness of railroad rates could not be decided by an independent commission established by the Minnesota Legislature. The state law establishing the commission was ruled unconstitutional because it did not allow for court review and therefore violated the railway's right to due process. Two years later, in *Budd*, Blatchford changed course and the Court held that the state legislature could determine business rates affecting the public interest. The inconsistency between the two cases produced widespread criticism.

Blatchford wrote one significant civil liberties opinion, *Counselman v. Hitchcock*, 142 U.S. 547, 12 S. Ct. 195, 35 L. Ed. 1110 (1892), a case that strengthened the constitutional right against SELF-INCRIMINATION. Blatchford held that under the FIFTH AMENDMENT of the U.S. Constitution, a WITNESS could not be ordered to testify unless the state promised never to use the information against her or him.

Blatchford died in 1893 in Newport, Rhode Island, at age seventy-three.

**BLOCK**   A segment of a town or city surrounded by streets and avenues on at least three sides and usually occupied by buildings, though it may be composed solely of vacant lots. The section of a city enclosed by streets that is described by a map which indicates how a portion of land will be subdivided.  

**BLOCKADE** See NEUTRALITY.

**BLOCKBUSTING**   The practice of illegally frightening homeowners by telling them that people who are members of a particular race, religion, or national origin are moving into their neighborhood and that they should expect a decline in the value of their property. The purpose of this scheme is to get the homeowners to sell out at a deflated price.  

An unscrupulous real estate agent will subsequently sell the vacated homes to minority group members at an inflated price, thereby obtaining a large profit. Fair access to housing is defeated by blockbusting.

**BLOOD FEUD**   Avenging the wrongful death of a person's kin by killing the murderer or by receiving compensation from the murderer's possessions.  

During the Middle Ages all European nations had similar customs concerning the murder of their inhabitants. The closest next of kin

*The Hatfield-McCoy feud went on for about thirty-five years following the Civil War, which had put the two families on opposite sides. Numerous brutal murders forced the state of Kentucky to take action against the Hatfields in a trial in the 1880s. Here "Devil Anse," head of the Hatfields, poses with his sons.*

to a person who had wrongfully died at the hands of another had the primary duty to retaliate against the killer. This obligation was subject to certain laws and customs concerning the type of permissible vengeance, the amount of compensation that could be exacted, the location at which the compensation was to be made, and the circumstances in which compensation was not required. For example, a blood feud was not sanctioned if the person killed was a convicted thief or if the person who did the killing did so to defend his lord or a close female family member. The idea of the imprisonment of a person who had committed a homicide was unknown during this period of history.

There is dispute over whether the blood feud was legal under Teutonic or Anglo-Saxon law. During the ninth-century reign of Alfred, a feud could lawfully commence only after an attempt was made to exact the price of a life. The price, called *weregild*, also applied when other atrocious personal offenses were committed and was paid partly to the monarch for the loss of a subject, partly to the lord for the loss of a vassal, and partly to the next of kin of the injured person. In Anglo-Saxon law, the amount of compensation, called *angylde*, was fixed at law and varied with the status of the person killed.

The Catholic Church exerted much influence to have a death avenged through the payment of compensation, not further violence, but the blood feud continued throughout England until after the Norman Conquest (1066).

**BLOTTER**   A written record of arrests and other occurrences maintained by the police. The report kept by the police when a suspect is booked, which involves the written recording of facts about the person's arrest and the charges against him or her.  

**BLUE BOOK**   A publication that establishes the correct form of case CITATIONS or of references to a legal authority showing where information can be found. A volume that explains the organization of a state government and provides the names of state officials. 📖

**BLUE RIBBON JURY** 📖 A group of highly qualified persons selected by a court on the request of either party to a lawsuit to decide complex and specialized disputes. 📖

A blue ribbon jury is also known as a special JURY. From the earliest period of COMMON LAW, such juries were used to try cases beyond the understanding of the average person so that justice could be administered as fairly as possible. A number of states still provide for blue ribbon juries by statute. It is not an absolute right in all jurisdictions, however, but rather a matter wherein the court can exercise its discretion.

The use of a blue ribbon jury does not violate the constitutional guarantees of trial by a fair and impartial jury or EQUAL PROTECTION of laws if the process by which its jurors are selected is neither arbitrary nor invidiously discriminatory. See also DUE PROCESS OF LAW.

**BLUE SKY LAW** 📖 A popular name for state statutes providing for the regulation and supervision of SECURITIES offerings and sales, to protect citizen-investors from investing in fraudulent companies. Most blue sky laws require the registration of new issues of securities with a state agency that reviews selling documents for accuracy and completeness. Blue sky laws also often regulate securities brokers and salespeople. 📖

Almost all states have adopted blue sky laws, regulating the sale of securities—investments in BONDS, MUTUAL FUNDS, limited PARTNERSHIPS, and so forth. These laws acquired their name as early as 1917, when the Supreme Court issued a decision on "speculative schemes which have no more basis than so many feet of 'blue sky' " (*Hall v. Geiger–Jones Co.*, 242 U.S. 539, 37 S. Ct. 217, 61 L. Ed. 480).

Blue sky laws place requirements on CORPORATIONS and securities dealerships that offer investments for sale to the public in a particular state. These laws are in many cases adopted from the Uniform Securities Act, and are usually enforced primarily by the state's attorney general's office. The federal SECURITIES AND EXCHANGE COMMISSION (SEC) enforces federal laws that concern foreign and interstate transactions.

State blue sky laws require corporations to register securities before selling them so that regulators can check their marketing information for accuracy. National on-line computer networks that became widely available in the mid-1990s posed new problems for states trying to enforce these requirements. Texas, Ohio, and New Jersey were among states that by 1995 had begun prosecuting some of the thousands of dealers who were offering unregistered investment opportunities to small investors on computer bulletin boards.

State laws usually require corporations to file financial information, and can deny corporations the privilege of doing business if their profile or history is risky. State investigators can determine whether a corporation's financial structure allows it to sell certain securities.

The laws also spell out the qualifications of BROKERS, dealers, salespeople, investment advisers, and others who work in the securities business. They require dealers to identify the type of investments they are planning to sell and where.

Among the activities blue sky laws seek to prevent are hard-sell tactics. Telephone "stock-peddling" techniques that are high-pressure and misleading can result in the suspension of a broker's license. A 1992 survey by Louis Harris and Associates indicated that more than one-third of all U.S. citizens had received a phone call about investing, and five percent had made a purchase. Many states now require that brokerages and corporations selling on the public market also provide a printed PROSPECTUS that describes the risks of investing.

What happens when blue sky laws do not work? States often provide an avenue for victims of illegally sold securities to try to recover their money, sometimes in addition to criminal prosecution. Investors can charge MISREPRESENTATION or lack of suitability and can demand restitution from the broker in ARBITRATION. CLASS ACTION suits can also be filed against a fraudulent brokerage or corporation. See also SECURITIES; STOCK.

**BOARD OF DIRECTORS** 📖 A group of people comprising the governing body of a CORPORATION. 📖

The shareholders of a corporation hold an election to choose people who have been nominated to direct or manage the corporation as a board. In the past nearly all states required that at least three directors run a corporation. The laws have changed, however, since many corporations have only one or two shareholders and therefore require only one or two directors to serve on the board.

Directors are elected at the first annual meeting of shareholders and at each successive annual meeting for one-year terms, unless they are divided into classes. In a corporation that divides its directors into classes, called a classified board, conditions are often imposed concerning the minimum size of the board, the minimum number of directors to be elected annually, and the maximum number of classes or maximum terms. The purpose of a classified board, which is expressly permitted by most statutes, is to make TAKEOVER attempts more difficult by staggering the terms of the directors.

Removal of a director during the course of his or her term may occur for cause by shareholders or by the board itself if there is a provision in the BYLAWS or ARTICLES OF INCORPORATION that confers such power upon them. The removal of a director for cause is reviewable by a court. Many jurisdictions have put into effect statutes that concern the removal of directors with or without cause.

The functions of directors involve a FIDUCIARY duty to the corporation. Directors are in control of others' property and their powers are derived primarily from statute.

Directors are responsible for determining and executing corporate policy. For example, they make decisions regarding supervision of the entire enterprise and regarding products and services.

Liabilities of directors extend to both their individual and joint actions. A director who commits a TORT against his or her corporation can be held personally liable.

Directors are bound by certain duties such as the duty to act within the scope of their authority and to exercise due care in the performance of their corporate tasks.

**BODY** 📖 The principal part of anything as distinguished from its subordinate parts, as in the main part of an instrument. An individual, an organization, or an entity given legal recognition, such as a corporation or "body corporate." A compilation of laws known as a "body of laws." 📖

**BODY EXECUTION** 📖 An arrest; a seizure of a defendant. 📖

A SHERIFF or other public officer can be ordered by a court to arrest a defendant and the officer executes the order by taking the body of the defendant into custody. The order itself may be called a CAPIAS, or *capias ad satisfaciendum* (Latin for "that you take him in order to satisfy it").

## BOGGS, CORINNE CLAIBORNE

Corinne Claiborne ("Lindy") Boggs was a Democratic representative from New Orleans, the first woman from Louisiana elected to the U.S. Congress. During her seventeen years in Congress her warmth, grace, and boundless energy made her a popular and effective politician.

Boggs was born March 13, 1916, on Brunswick Plantation, Louisiana, to wealth and privilege. Her father owned a successful sugar plantation. She received her bachelor's degree in 1935 from Sophie Newcomb College at Tulane University and taught history in Romeville, Louisiana. Her 1938 marriage to Hale Boggs marked the beginning of an enduring and formidable political dynasty.

Boggs and her husband first went to Washington in 1940 when he was a first-year representative from New Orleans. Then only twenty-four and twenty-six years old, respectively, the young couple devoted themselves to the Democratic party. Boggs's husband lost his bid for reelection in 1942, but regained his seat in 1946, beginning a string of twenty-two consecutive victories by him or Boggs. During the years that her husband was in Congress, Boggs, in addition to raising their three children, worked as his campaign manager, did community work in New Orleans, organized social events, and devised an innovative bill-tracking system for her husband at a time when no such system existed. When her husband was killed in an airplane crash in 1972 Boggs ran in the special election to fill his seat. She won easily, becoming Louisiana's first woman—and one of only fourteen women—in Congress.

Although Boggs took her seat in 1973 as a first-year representative, her three decades as a

**BIOGRAPHY**

*Lindy Boggs*

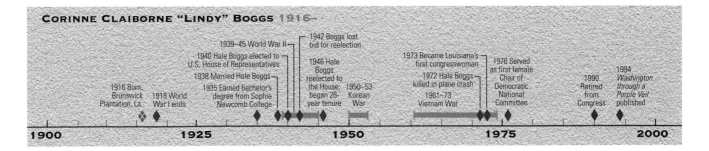

CORINNE CLAIBORNE "LINDY" BOGGS 1916–

- 1916 Born, Brunswick Plantation, La.
- 1918 World War I ends
- 1935 Earned bachelor's degree from Sophie Newcomb College
- 1938 Married Hale Boggs
- 1939–45 World War II
- 1940 Hale Boggs elected to U.S. House of Representatives
- 1942 Boggs lost bid for reelection
- 1946 Hale Boggs reelected to the House; began 26-year tenure
- 1950–53 Korean War
- 1961–73 Vietnam War
- 1972 Hale Boggs killed in plane crash
- 1973 Became Louisiana's first congresswoman
- 1976 Served as first female Chair of Democratic National Committee
- 1990 Retired from Congress
- 1994 *Washington through a Purple Veil* published

1900    1925    1950    1975    2000

congressional wife had given her the types of contacts enjoyed only by senior members. The friendships and alliances she had developed with prominent Democrats helped her gain an appointment to the House Appropriations Committee. There she used her influence to deliver many important appropriations to her home district, including money for colleges, hospitals, housing projects, a $10 million energy research center at the University of New Orleans, and numerous navigational and hurricane protection projects. Boggs employed a savvy combination of southern charm and persistence to achieve her many successes. But Moon Landrieu, a former New Orleans mayor and former Department of Housing and Urban Development secretary, believes that it is a mistake to think Boggs was successful simply because she has a kind and winning personality. "When she [is] committed to a position and makes up her mind, you are talking about a very formidable will," he said.

Boggs built a reputation as a compassionate, even-tempered lawmaker who quietly worked long hours in the nitty-gritty behind-the-scenes operation of the Appropriations Committee. It is said that she never had a bad word to say about anybody, and even when pressed to criticize potential opponents, she simply said, "I've never known anybody who came to me who I didn't think would probably do a good job if they were elected."

Boggs's other "firsts" included being the first woman to chair the Democratic National Convention, in 1976, and the first female regent of the Smithsonian Institution. At the time of her retirement, she was the only white congressperson representing a district where most of the voters were African American, defying the conventional wisdom that voters prefer candidates of their own race.

In addition to her work on the Appropriations Committee, Boggs served on the Banking, Currency, and Housing Committee, where she worked to pass legislation aimed at solving the housing problems of elderly people and members of other low- and middle-income groups. A strong supporter of equal opportunities for women, she helped pass legislation that guarantees equal access to CREDIT and prohibits discrimination on the basis of sex in the granting of small-business loans.

During her many years in Washington, D.C., Boggs acted as an unofficial hostess for the Democratic party, presiding over parties and receptions attended by most of the Democrats in the nation's capital. Unfailingly gracious, thoughtful, and charming, she is well liked by all who know her. According to a former colleague, Senator J. Bennett Johnston (D-La.), she "changed the very fabric, the feel, the texture of politics in Washington and in Louisiana." Johnston says that, even during acrimonious debates, when Boggs enters the room, "the mood will change. And by the time she leaves the room, she has usually left with what she came to get."

The tragedy of her husband's death motivated Boggs to run for Congress and another personal tragedy was the catalyst for her retirement. In 1990 she announced she would not run for reelection, citing among other reasons her desire to spend more time with her eldest daughter, Barbara Sigmund, the mayor of Princeton, New Jersey, who was terminally ill. "This chapter in my service to the public is ending," she said. In looking back on her career, Boggs expressed pride in having played a "small role in opening doors for blacks and women," in helping to fund Head Start, and in securing money for businesses owned by minorities and women. She stressed that leaving public office would not mean the end of her career. "I will continue to actively participate in community activities here and in Washington," she said. Her announcement prompted a flood of warm and affectionate tributes from colleagues who recalled her "unparalleled intelligence, grace, courage and charm." Senator Bennett saluted her for her integrity and for her ability to raise the level of debate whenever she entered a room. Her younger daughter, Corinne ("Cokie") Roberts, a journalist and congressional reporter for public radio and ABC News, simply noted, "She makes us all behave."

Since leaving the House, Boggs has lectured at Tulane University and the University of New Orleans and established the Hale and Lindy Boggs Center for Legislative Affairs, at Georgetown University Law School. In January 1991 she attended the dedication of the Lindy Claiborne Boggs Room, a reading room for congresswomen at the U.S. Capitol. Boggs, the "grande dame of Louisiana politics," is noted for her compassion, her devotion to equal opportunity, and her charming personality. She has dedicated her life to public service, and the people of New Orleans have been immeasurably enriched by her commitment.

**BOILERPLATE** A description of uniform language used normally in legal documents that has a definite, unvarying meaning in the same context that denotes that the words have not

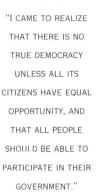

"I CAME TO REALIZE THAT THERE IS NO TRUE DEMOCRACY UNLESS ALL ITS CITIZENS HAVE EQUAL OPPORTUNITY, AND THAT ALL PEOPLE SHOULD BE ABLE TO PARTICIPATE IN THEIR GOVERNMENT."

been individually fashioned to address the legal issue presented.

**BOLIN, JANE MATILDA** Jane Matilda Bolin was the first black woman judge in the United States.

Bolin was born April 11, 1908, in Poughkeepsie, New York, to Gaius C. Bolin and Matilda Emery Bolin. Her father, who was born to a Native American mother and a black father, was the first black to graduate from Williams College. He went on to become a lawyer and practiced law in Poughkeepsie for over fifty years. Bolin's mother was born in England and immigrated to the United States with her parents.

Bolin was raised in a comfortable middle-class family. She attended public elementary and secondary schools. After graduation from high school she entered Wellesley College and soon was named a Wellesley Scholar, one of the top twenty women in her class. She received her bachelor of arts degree, with honors, in 1928.

Shortly after her graduation from college Bolin announced her intention to attend Yale Law School. Her father was at first opposed to the idea because he felt that the law was a profession unsuited to women. He let his daughter know he would prefer she pursue teaching but she was determined to become a lawyer. She graduated from Yale Law School in 1931, the first African American woman to do so.

Bolin was admitted to the New York bar in 1932 and began her legal career with her father and brother's law firm in Poughkeepsie. In 1933 she married Ralph E. Mizelle, also an attorney, and they settled in New York City.

Bolin's judicial career commenced just a few years after she and her husband began practicing law together. On April 7, 1937, she was named assistant corporate counsel in New York City's law department. She served two years in that position before being summoned, to her complete surprise, to the office of Mayor Fiorello La Guardia. On July 22, 1939, La Guardia appointed her justice of the Domestic Relations Court of the City of New York (later called the family court), making her the first

"I'D RATHER SEE IF I CAN HELP A CHILD THAN SETTLE AN ARGUMENT BETWEEN ADULTS OVER MONEY."

black woman judge in the United States. She presided over family court cases for four consecutive ten-year terms, until she reached the mandatory retirement age of seventy.

In her many years on the bench Bolin saw the full spectrum of domestic cases: serious crimes, including homicides, committed by juveniles; nonpayment of family support; spouse battering; child neglect; lack of supervision for children; adoption; and paternity. Upon her retirement in 1978 she noted that during her years as a judge, she had viewed a steady increase in violent behavior among young people. "We always had homicides," she said, "but not in the numbers we have today. I've never seen anything like this, the extent of this violence, never." Asked if she could suggest solutions to the problem, Bolin responded that the answers were very complex and that she could not accept the "easy answers" psychiatrists and social workers were handing out, "saying it's because of the wars . . . or the violent programs on television . . ."

From the beginning of her career Bolin was determined to fight racial prejudice in any way she could. She worked to bring about changes in the way probation officers were assigned to cases in family court. When she became a judge black probation officers were assigned exclusively to cases involving black families; through Bolin's efforts, probation officers were eventually assigned without regard to race or religion. She also instituted a requirement that private social service agencies receiving public funds accept children without regard to ethnic background. "They used to put a big N or PR on the front of every [file], to indicate if the family was black or Puerto Rican," she recalled, because the agencies were segregated.

Bolin has been described as a militant, but quiet, fighter for justice. She earned a reputation as a courageous, no-nonsense, hard worker who never shirked an assignment. In addition to being a committed professional, Bolin served on the boards of a number of organizations: the New York Urban League, the NAACP and its New York chapter, the Harlem Tuberculosis Committee, the legislative committee of the

**JANE MATILDA BOLIN 1908–**

1908 Born, Poughkeepsie, N.Y. | 1914–18 World War I | 1928 Received B.A. from Wellesley College | 1931 Became first black woman graduate of Yale Law School | 1937 Appointed assistant corporation counsel of New York City | 1939 Became first black woman judge in U.S. when Mayor La Guardia appointed her to the New York City Domestic Relations Court | 1939–45 World War II | 1950–53 Korean War | 1959–75 Vietnam War | 1967 Thurgood Marshall became first black U.S. Supreme Court justice | 1978 Retired at then-mandatory age of 70; became member of New York State Regents Review Committee

1900 · 1925 · 1950 · 1975 · 2000

United Neighborhood Houses, the Wiltwick School for Boys, the Dalton School, and the Harlem Lawyers' Association. She was a member of the Committee on Children of New York City, the Scholarship Service and Fund for Negro Students, and the Committee against Discrimination in Housing.

Bolin and her first husband had one child, Yorke Bolin Mizelle, who was born in 1941 and became a New York businessman. Asked how she combined motherhood, community activities, and a high-pressure career, Bolin said, "I didn't get all the sleep I needed, and I didn't get to travel as much as I would have liked, because I felt my first obligation was to my child." Bolin's first husband died in 1943. In 1950, she married Walter P. Offutt, Jr., a minister, who died in 1974. She had one grandchild.

In recognition of her many accomplishments and contributions to the field of family law, Bolin has received many awards, including honorary doctor of laws degrees from Morgan State University, Western College for Women, Tuskegee University, Hampton University, and Williams College. However, asked to recount her most memorable experience, she did not speak of her many achievements. Rather, she told the story of a child who was in trouble and whose mother asked Bolin to send the child to the same institution where she had spent some time. When Bolin said she preferred to help the mother keep her child at home, the woman told her the institution had helped her, and she wanted the same help for her child. In her typically compassionate and empathetic manner, Bolin listened to the mother's reasoning and complied with her wishes.

After her retirement, Bolin worked as a family law consultant and did volunteer tutoring in math and reading with public school children. Her dignity, compassion, and unquestioned fairness are remembered by all who appeared in her court.

**BONA FIDE** 📖 [*Latin, In good faith.*] Honest; genuine; actual; authentic; acting without the intention of defrauding. 📖

A bona fide purchaser is one who purchases property for a valuable CONSIDERATION that is inducement for entering into a CONTRACT and without suspicion of being defrauded or deceived by the seller. He or she has no notice of any defects of the TITLE. A bona fide purchaser pays in GOOD FAITH full value for the property and, without any FRAUD, goes into possession.

**BONDS** 📖 Written documents by which a government, corporation, or individual—the OBLIGOR—promises to perform a certain act, usually the payment of a definite sum of money, to another—the OBLIGEE—on a certain date. 📖

In most cases, a bond is issued by a public or private entity to an investor who, by purchasing the bond, loans the issuer money. Governments and CORPORATIONS issue bonds to investors to raise capital. Each bond has a *par value*, or FACE VALUE, and is issued at a fixed or variable interest rate; however, bonds can often be purchased for less or more than their par value. This means that the YIELD, or total return on a bond, varies based on the price the investor pays for the bond and the bond's interest rate. Generally, the more secure a bond is, or the stronger the assurance that the bond will be paid in full upon maturity, the less the bond will yield to the investor. Bonds that are not very secure investments tend to have higher returns. Junk bonds, for example, are high-risk, high-yield bonds. Except for the high-risk variety, bonds tend to be relatively solid, predictable investments, with prices that vary less than those of STOCKS on the stock market. As a result, litigation because of unpaid bond agreements has rarely proved necessary.

The most common type of bond is the *simple bond*. This bond is sold with a fixed interest rate and then redeemed at a set time. Several varieties of simple bonds exist. Municipal governments issue simple bonds to pay for public projects—schools, highways, stadiums, and so forth. The U.S. Treasury issues simple bonds to cover federal activities. Foreign governments issue simple bonds known as Yankee bonds, to U.S. investors. And corporations issue simple bonds to raise capital for modernization, expansion, and operating expenses.

*Conditional bonds* do not involve capital loans. Most of these bonds are obtained from persons or corporations that promise to pay, should they become liable. The payment is usually a nonrefundable fee or a percentage of the face value of the bond. A BAIL BOND is a common type of conditional bond. With a bail bond, the person who posts the bond promises to pay the court a particular sum if the accused person fails to return to court for further proceedings on the date specified. Once a bond payer satisfies the terms of a conditional bond, the liability is discharged. If the bond goes into DEFAULT (i.e., the obligations specified are not met) the amount becomes immediately due. Parties can also mutually decide to cancel a conditional bond.

The emergence of simple government and corporate bonds into the modern marketplace began with the economic boom of the 1920s. Immediately after World War I, the U.S.

## Bonds
Corporate and foreign bond holdings in the U.S., 1980 to 1994

### 1980 total holdings (in billions of dollars), $508

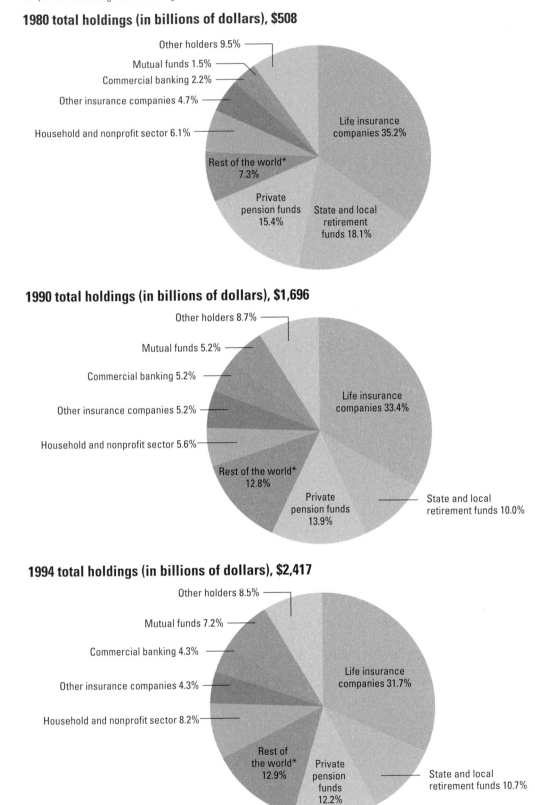

Other holders 9.5%
Mutual funds 1.5%
Commercial banking 2.2%
Other insurance companies 4.7%
Household and nonprofit sector 6.1%
Rest of the world* 7.3%
Private pension funds 15.4%
Life insurance companies 35.2%
State and local retirement funds 18.1%

### 1990 total holdings (in billions of dollars), $1,696

Other holders 8.7%
Mutual funds 5.2%
Commercial banking 5.2%
Other insurance companies 5.2%
Household and nonprofit sector 5.6%
Rest of the world* 12.8%
Private pension funds 13.9%
Life insurance companies 33.4%
State and local retirement funds 10.0%

### 1994 total holdings (in billions of dollars), $2,417

Other holders 8.5%
Mutual funds 7.2%
Commercial banking 4.3%
Other insurance companies 4.3%
Household and nonprofit sector 8.2%
Rest of the world* 12.9%
Private pension funds 12.2%
Life insurance companies 31.7%
State and local retirement funds 10.7%

*Holdings of U.S. issues by foreign residents.

Source: Board of Governors of the Federal Reserve System, *Flow of Funds Accounts*, March 1995 quarterly diskettes.

# Michael R. Milken: Genius, Villain, or Scapegoat?

Few business personalities have attracted as much attention—both negative and positive—as bond market financier Michael R. Milken. After earning an estimated $1.1 billion in the 1980s as the head of Drexel Burnham Lambert's securities branch, Milken fell from grace in the press and in the eyes of many investors. In 1990 the Securities Exchange Commission charged Milken with securities fraud. In U.S. district court, Milken was fined $600 million and sentenced to ten years behind bars. Some of Milken's associates believed that he had been made a scapegoat; Milken's prosecution, they argued, was little more than an attempt to pass judgment on the 1980s, sometimes cast as the decade of greed.

Milken had formerly been heralded by *The Wall Street Journal* as one of the century's most important financial thinkers. In the 1970s, after finishing studies at the University of Pennsylvania's Wharton Business School, Milken was early in anticipating the boom of the junk bond market. He used his understanding of trends in investment activity, along with innovative approaches, to capitalize on what he called high-reward bonds. The junk bond boom led to both Milken's ascent and his incrimination. Milken's correct assessment of the junk bond boom paid off for him. While working for the powerful Drexel Burnham Lambert firm, his profits made him a billionaire. But how he made those profits also led to his downfall. The government held evidence implicating Milken in manipulation of stocks, insider trading, and bribery of investment managers.

With fines and damages in civil lawsuits totaling $1 billion, Milken became one of several newsmaking white-collar criminals of the 1980s. After his sentencing, *The Wall Street Journal* retracted its praise of the man, saying that "evidence now suggests that Mr. Milken's theory was wrong—and that he was far from the genius he seemed to be about junk bonds." (*National Review* 31 August 1992). Milken's theory held that the high yields of junk bonds would draw investors to purchase many of them and that defaults on these securities would be few. The intense corporate competition of the 1980s waned, however, and in later years, investors moved away from junk bonds in search of other investment opportunities. Ironically, following his release from prison, after serving only two years of his sentence, Milken was invited to lecture on ethics in business at the University of California, Los Angeles. The one-time billionaire was left with $300 million from his days as the king of junk bonds. To critics, Milken is an icon of the money-mad 1980s, a financial wizard driven by the promise of vast wealth to push the limits of securities law.

economy rewarded investors who were eager to see expansions in industrial growth. For most of the 1920s, until just before the Great Depression, interest rates remained low. The bond market became sophisticated enough to raise funds for the U.S. Treasury, domestic corporations, and foreign borrowers. It also proved useful during World War II, when the federal government depended on the sale of war bonds to finance its military efforts.

In the 1980s a different kind of boom in the U.S. economy sent the bond market in a more problematic direction. Even though high-yielding bonds tend to be less reliable investments than low-yielding ones, rapidly increasing business activity in the 1980s led to large-scale buying of these high-risk investments. Corporations successfully bought out the stock of other corporations by raising money through the sale of millions of dollars of junk bonds. (Junk bonds have been given low ratings when measured by standard investment criteria— hence the pejorative name.)

Troubles soon arose from the shaky foundation of the junk bond market. One of the country's leading figures in fostering junk bond investments, Michael R. Milken, faced government charges that he manipulated bond prices, traded on inside information, and bribed investment managers. Milken's image was further complicated by his working with the convicted stock baron Ivan F. Boesky. In April 1990, in *Securities & Exchange Commission v. Milken*, 1990 WL 455346, Fed. Sec. L. Rep. p. 95, 200 (S.D.N.Y. 1990), Milken pleaded guilty to six felonies, including CONSPIRACY, securities fraud, and aiding and abetting the filing of a false document with the SECURITIES AND EXCHANGE COMMISSION. At the time of the initial settlement, Milken agreed to pay $600 million in fines and reparations. In November 1990, federal judge Kimba M. Wood sentenced Milken to ten years in jail. Milken served only two years of his sentence.

Problems have also arisen with bonds issued by governments. For instance, when California's Orange County issued $169 million in municipal bonds in June 1994, future taxes and other general revenues were expected to pay for the interest and principal of the bonds. But on December 6, 1994, the county filed Chapter Nine petitions in BANKRUPTCY court. The county could not pay bond bearers, since the money set aside for them had been depleted. By 1995, losses in the Orange County investment pools approached $1.7 billion. Representatives of the county found themselves in court, being sued by the company representing investors. In *In re County of Orange*, 179 B.R. 185, 26 Bankr. Ct. Dec. 1050 (Bankr. C. D. Cal., 1995), the bankruptcy court denied bondholders' claims to county revenues derived after the Chapter Nine filing. The interests of bondholders were seriously injured.

Nevertheless, bonds continue as popular investments. Junk bonds especially have regained favor as a means for earning considerable returns. The relatively high interest rates of junk bonds have entailed risks for buyers, but Wall Street analysts have argued that the rewards of this return outweigh the dangers. Indeed, the bond market in general has even thrived in times of crisis.

See also SECURITIES.

**BOOKING** 📖 The procedure by which law enforcement officials record facts about the arrest of and charges against a suspect such as the crime for which the arrest was made, together with information concerning the identification of the suspect and other pertinent facts. 📖

This information is written down on the police BLOTTER in the police station. The process of booking may also include photographing and fingerprinting.

**BOOKKEEPING** 📖 The process of systematically and methodically recording the financial accounts and transactions of an entity. 📖

Double-entry bookkeeping is an ACCOUNTING system that requires that for every financial transaction there must be a DEBIT and a CREDIT. When merchandise is sold for cost, there is a debit to cash and a credit to sales.

**BOOK VALUE** 📖 The current value of an asset. The book value of an asset at any time is its cost minus its accumulated depreciation. (Depreciation reflects the decrease in the useful life of an asset due to use of the asset.) Companies use book value to determine the point at which they have recovered the cost of an asset.

The net asset value of a company's securities. This is calculated by subtracting from the company's total assets the following items: intangible assets (such as goodwill), current liabilities, and long-term liabilities and equity issues. This figure, divided by the total number of bonds or of shares of stock, is the book value per bond or per share of stock. 📖

The calculation of book value is important in determining the value of a company that is being liquidated. For example, if a corporation has 100,000 shares of stock issued and outstanding and its assets total $5 million and its intangible assets and all liabilities total $1.6 million, its net asset value is $3.4 million and its book value per share is $34.

**BORDEN, LIZZIE** The trial of Lizzie Borden shows the effect that public opinion can have on the life of an accused person, regardless of the outcome of a fair trial.

Lizzie Borden was born July 19, 1860. She was a plain, outspoken woman who lived with her father, stepmother, and sister in a house on Second Street in Fall River, a small industrial city located in southeastern Massachusetts.

According to local rumors, the Borden family was not noted for its harmonious relationships. Andrew Borden was a quiet, unpleasant man who had two daughters, Lizzie and Emma, by a previous marriage, and who had married his present wife in 1865. Neither Lizzie nor Emma favored the union and animosity existed among the three Borden women.

On August 4, 1892, the residents of Fall River were shocked and frightened by the brutal ax murders of Andrew Borden and his wife. The killings were committed at the Borden home in daylight. Emma Borden was out of town, but Lizzie discovered her father's body on the couch in the living room; she immedi-

*The public condemned Lizzie Borden as an ax murderer even though a jury found her not guilty.*

ately sent a servant, Bridget, for help. Upon their return, Bridget and a neighbor found the body of Lizzie's stepmother in an upstairs bedroom.

The town was in an uproar and the newspapers seized the opportunity to sensationalize an already lurid story. Lizzie became the prime suspect, and throughout Fall River, speculation spread about her actions on that fatal day, suggesting that Lizzie attacked her stepmother and afterward carefully cleaned the ax and changed her clothes. She then did her normal housework until her father returned from town to take a nap on the couch. While he slept, Lizzie killed him, and again cleaned the ax and her clothing. Chemical tests did not provide any substantial evidence because the alleged murder weapon, the ax, was cleaned so thoroughly.

The story of the murders was embellished with continued fragmented reports of Lizzie's behavior. One source claimed that Lizzie was devoid of any emotion when the corpses were found; another witnessed Lizzie in the act of burning a dress shortly after the murders were committed; still another stated that the suspect had attempted to purchase poison as recently as one day before the killings. The condemning public showed Lizzie no mercy, and some unknown rhymer composed a grotesque verse relating the events. The rhyme, still familiar today, reads:

Lizzie Borden took an ax
And gave her mother forty whacks;
When she saw what she had done
She gave her father forty-one.

An INQUEST was held five days after the discovery of the murders, and Lizzie was subsequently arrested. The trial began in New Bedford, Massachusetts, in June 1893, and lasted thirteen days. Those days were filled with contradictory accounts of the crime, but the main point of contention concerned Lizzie's assertion that she was in the barn at the time the murders were committed, between 11:00 A.M. and 11:15 A.M. An ice cream vendor corrobo-

rated Lizzie's story by testifying that he had seen the defendant leaving the barn at the aforementioned time. The defense attorney argued brilliantly on his client's behalf—the EVIDENCE was mostly circumstantial—and the jury found Lizzie Borden not guilty of the murder of her parents.

Lizzie Borden was acquitted by the jury but not by the public. After her death on June 1, 1927, in Fall River, she was still not exonerated in the public mind; she is famous only in connection with the bloody events of August 4, 1892.

**BORK, ROBERT HERON**  Robert Heron Bork, conservative legal scholar, author, and former federal appellate judge, was one of President RONALD REAGAN's most controversial nominees for the U.S. Supreme Court.

When Bork was nominated to the Supreme Court in July 1987 his opponents ridiculed him as an archconservative who wanted to take away the rights and freedoms enjoyed by the political mainstream. They may have been surprised to learn that Bork began his career at the other end of the political spectrum. Born March 1, 1927, in Pittsburgh, Bork spent his high school and college years as a socialist. He attended the University of Chicago, where he received his bachelor's degree in 1948. In 1952, as a University of Chicago law student, Bork was a New Deal liberal supporting Adlai Stevenson for president. Eventually, his political philosophy changed to embrace free-market libertarianism: the law and economics program at the University of Chicago, a bastion of free enterprise research and laissez-faire economic theory, convinced Bork that government should not intervene in the economy.

Bork received his law degree in 1953. After serving two hitches in the U.S. Marine Corps he practiced for a large law firm in Chicago, where he specialized in antitrust law. In 1962, Bork accepted a position teaching antitrust and constitutional law at Yale University. At Yale, he developed his doctrine of "original intent and judicial restraint," which stated that courts can protect only the rights that are guaranteed in

BIOGRAPHY

*Robert Heron Bork*

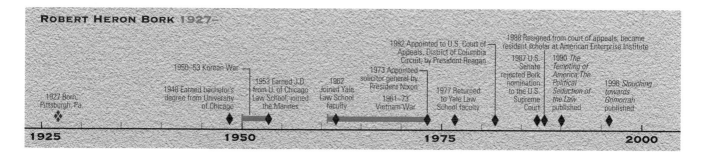

the Constitution; all other rights are subject to limitation by Congress and the legislatures. In deciding which rights are to be afforded constitutional protection, courts must be guided by the ORIGINAL INTENT of the Constitution's Framers. For example, the FOURTEENTH AMENDMENT was intended to grant EQUAL PROTECTION under the laws to black citizens; therefore, Bork argued, it cannot be used to approve or mandate AFFIRMATIVE ACTION for women.

President RICHARD M. NIXON appointed Bork solicitor general in 1973. Later that year, by order of Nixon and at the request of the attorney general, who had resigned in protest against the order, Bork fired Special Prosecutor Archibald Cox at a crucial stage of the Watergate investigation. Those events came to be known as the Saturday Night Massacre. In 1977 Bork returned to Yale and in 1981 he left Yale for private practice in Washington, D.C. The following year President Reagan appointed him to the U.S. Court of Appeals, District of Columbia Circuit. On July 1, 1987, Bork was nominated to the Supreme Court to replace retiring associate justice Lewis F. Powell, Jr.

Over the years, Bork criticized many Supreme Court decisions. In a 1963 article in *The New Republic*, Bork attacked the proposed Public Accommodations Act—which became title II of the Civil Rights Act of 1964 (78 Stat. 2441, 42 U.S.C.A. § 2000a)—as an infringement of the right of free association. Eight years later, in an article in the *Indiana Law Journal*, Bork summarized his view of the Constitution and pointed out Court decisions that, in his opinion, were unconstitutional. He declared that the Constitution provided no unwritten protections, and therefore guaranteed no right to privacy, contrary to what the Court had established in *Griswold v. Connecticut*, 381 U.S. 479, 85 S. Ct. 1678, 14 L. Ed. 2d 510 (1965). Privacy, Bork said, was a free-floating right not derived in a principled fashion from the Constitution. If no right of privacy existed in *Griswold*, then, according to Bork, the landmark ABORTION case *Roe v. Wade* (410 U.S. 113, 93 S. Ct. 705, 35 L. Ed. 2d 147 [1973]) was wrongly decided.

Similarly unprincipled, said Bork, were the decisions of the WARREN COURT that affected voting practices and established the principle of "ONE PERSON, ONE VOTE." Bork also said POLL TAXES (devices often used to keep poor blacks from voting in the South) were not necessarily unconstitutional. In addition, according to Bork, the FIRST AMENDMENT should protect only political speech. When he was solicitor general, Bork criticized *Shelley v. Kraemer*, 334 U.S. 1,

68 S. Ct. 836, 92 L. Ed. 1161 (1948), a landmark civil rights decision that outlawed the enforcement of RESTRICTIVE COVENANTS in the courts. Finally, Bork publicly expressed his belief that it would be healthy to reintroduce religion into the public schools.

In the summer of 1987 the United States witnessed the most contentious Supreme Court confirmation battle in the two-hundred-year history of the Constitution. The battle over Bork's confirmation turned into a fight-to-the-finish for ideological control of the Court, and in a very real sense for the Constitution itself. Bork was a prolific legal scholar who had left a vast "paper trail" for his opponents to pore over in the search for ammunition to block his appointment to the Court. While leaders of the political right such as the Reverend Jerry L. Falwell and Pat Robertson praised Bork as a savior for a "morally misguided" Court, a coalition of prominent civil rights and other organizations, including the National Association for the Advancement of Colored People, Common Cause, People for the American Way, the National Organization for Women, the National Abortion Rights Action League, and the American Civil Liberties Union, came together quickly to fight the nomination. LOBBYING efforts on both sides of the struggle were very aggressive. Clearly, both liberals and conservatives saw the Bork nomination as the culmination of all previous showdowns between the left and the right throughout the Reagan administration. Liberals were particularly determined to stop the nomination. Despite evidence to the contrary, the White House continued to insist that Bork was a moderate conservative like Justice Powell and a model practitioner of judicial restraint.

Bork's confirmation hearing before the Senate Judiciary Committee in September 1987 seemed to hurt his appointment more than any criticisms since the announcement of his nomination. His testimony further stirred his critics to label Bork as much further to the right on the political and legal spectrum than many Americans. In addition, during the hearings, Bork revised or backed down from some of his previous positions, which seemed to indicate that he was willing to change his mind in order to gain the nomination. Commentators believe that this helped convince many undecided senators to vote against him. On October 6 the Senate Judiciary Committee rejected Bork's nomination by a vote of 9–5. In a vote by the full Senate on October 23, Bork's nomination to the Supreme Court was rejected by a margin of 58 to 42.

"[LAW IS] VULNERABLE TO THE WINDS OF INTELLECTUAL OR MORAL FASHION, WHICH IT THEN VALIDATES AS THE COMMANDS OF OUR MOST BASIC CONCEPT."

Critics of original intent saw Bork's rejection as a victory for the perception of the Constitution as a "living" instrument, to be adapted to human needs by a judiciary with sufficient discretion to decide what public values are important enough to protect from majority rule. Bork's supporters called him a victim of liberal attacks.

Bork resigned from the court of appeals in February 1988 and became a resident scholar at the conservative think tank, the American Enterprise Institute. He continued to write and comment on U.S. law and society.

### CROSS-REFERENCES

Chicago School; *Griswold v. Connecticut*; Privacy; *Roe v. Wade*; Supreme Court of the United States; Watergate.

**BOSONE, REVA BECK** Reva Beck Bosone was Utah's first woman judge and the first woman elected to the House of Representatives from that state.

Bosone was born April 1, 1895, in American Fork, Utah, the only daughter among the four children of Christian M. Beck and Zilpha Chipman Beck. Her father was of Danish extraction, and her mother was a descendant of the 1847 Mormon pioneers and of the Mayflower pilgrims. After attending elementary and high schools in American Fork, Bosone went to Westminster Junior College, in Salt Lake City, and in 1919 received her bachelor of arts degree from the University of California at Berkeley. From 1920 to 1927 she taught high school in Utah and was the head of the Department of Public Speaking, Debating, and Dramatic Arts in Ogden, Utah.

Inspired by her mother's admonition that a country is no better than its laws, Bosone decided that the best way to serve all the people was to become a lawmaker. Bosone read law at the University of Utah and earned her doctor of laws degree in 1930. While she was studying law Bosone married Joseph P. Bosone, a lawyer, on October 8, 1929, and gave birth to her only child, Zilpha Teresa Bosone, on September 1, 1930.

**BIOGRAPHY**

SPECIAL COLLECTIONS, UNIVERSITY OF UTAH LIBRARY

*Reva Beck Bosone*

After she received her law degree Bosone moved with her husband and daughter to the mining region of Carbon County, Utah, where the couple opened a law firm. Bosone practiced law there until she became a candidate for the state legislature in 1933. After conducting a door-to-door campaign with her two-year-old daughter in her arms, she was elected to the Utah House of Representatives from Carbon County. She returned to the House in the next session, after being elected from Salt Lake County in 1935. She distinguished herself by being elected majority floor leader and by becoming the first woman member of the influential Sifting (Rules) Committee, as well as its chairman. She played an integral role in the passage of a minimum wage–and–hour law for women and children and of the Utah child labor constitutional amendment. Her efforts in these areas earned her commendations from FRANCES PERKINS, labor reformer and U.S. secretary of labor, and from Eleanor Roosevelt, wife of President Franklin D. Roosevelt.

After leaving the Utah Legislature in 1936 Bosone returned to private practice for a short time before being elected a Salt Lake City judge in police and traffic court. In her judicial position, to which she was reelected until 1948, she instituted what were then extraordinary traffic fines: $300 for drunken driving and $200 for reckless driving. During her tenure on the bench traffic cases more than tripled but only three appeals from her judgments were sustained.

Bosone and her husband were divorced in 1940. In 1948 Bosone left the judiciary to become a legislator again, this time as a U.S. representative from the Second Congressional District of Utah, the first woman U.S. representative from that state. At the time, she summarized her philosophy about the role of a legislator:

> The biggest need . . . is for people . . . who will do what they believe is right and not worry about the political consequences to themselves.

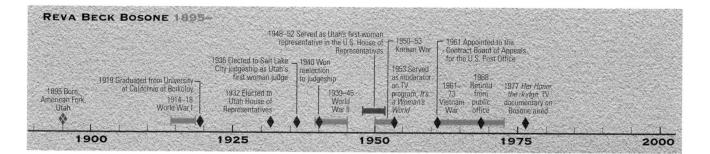

REVA BECK BOSONE 1895–

1895 Born, American Fork, Utah

1914–18 World War I

1919 Graduated from University of California at Berkeley

1932 Elected to Utah House of Representatives

1936 Elected to Salt Lake City judgeship as Utah's first woman judge

1940 Won reelection to judgeship

1939–45 World War II

1948–52 Served as Utah's first woman representative in the U.S. House of Representatives

1950–53 Korean War

1953 Served as moderator on TV program, *It's a Woman's World*

1961 Appointed to the Contract Board of Appeals for the U.S. Post Office

1961–73 Vietnam War

1968 Retired from public office

1977 *Her Honor, the Judge,* TV documentary on Bosone aired

1900    1925    1950    1975    2000

While serving in the House, Bosone was the first woman appointed to the Interior Committee. After her reelection in 1950, she was a member of the House Select Committee on Current Pornographic Materials. She also pushed for legislation to remove Native Americans from government guardianship and sponsored water and soil conservation initiatives for the West.

Bosone ran for reelection in 1952 and in 1954 but was defeated both times. After her loss in 1954 she returned to private law practice until 1958, when she became legal counsel for the Subcommittee of Safety and Compensation of the House Committee on Education. Three years later Postmaster General J. Edward Day appointed her a judicial officer and chairwoman of the Contract Board of Appeals for the U.S. Post Office Department. In this position, which she held until her retirement in 1968, Bosone was authorized to make final decisions for the department in obscenity cases and fraud cases.

Throughout her professional life Bosone had a special interest in the problems of alcoholism and juvenile delinquency. In 1947–48 she was director of the Utah State Board for Education on Alcoholism. Her work in these areas resulted in her being elected to Utah's Hall of Fame in 1943. During World War II, she was an active member of the United War Fund Committee of Utah and of the Veterans Central Welfare Committee.

Bosone was a pioneer in the use of television as a communication medium. In 1953 she moderated a program called *It's a Woman's World*, which received the Zenith Television Award for excellence in local programming. Her long and distinguished career was highlighted in a 1977 television documentary, *Her Honor, the Judge*.

Bosone has received numerous recognitions and awards for her contributions to the worlds of law and politics. In 1965 her name was on the list of possible nominees for the U.S. Supreme Court. The University of California at Berkeley conferred on her the Distinguished Service in Government Award in 1970 and Westminster College awarded her an honorary doctor of humanities degree in 1973. Also in 1973 she received an award for her efforts to raise the status of women in Utah. And in 1977 she received an honorary doctorate from the University of Utah.

## BOSTON MASSACRE SOLDIERS   The Boston Massacre, March 5, 1770, was an event that exemplified the growing tension between the American colonies and England which would subsequently result in the outbreak of the Revolutionary War.

"IF A LEGISLATOR . . . IS A WEAKLING WHO SUCCUMBS TO THE LUSH CROONING OF CERTAIN LOBBYISTS, BLAME THE CONSTITUENCY, WHICH SHOULD HAVE BEEN MORE INTERESTED IN SENDING A QUALIFIED CANDIDATE."

In 1767 the English Parliament had levied an import tax on tea, glass, paper, and lead. The duties were labeled the TOWNSHEND ACTS—part of a series of unpopular taxes directed at the colonists without their representation. The colonists retaliated with attacks on English representatives and officials, and troops were dispatched to America to restore order. The agitation between the colonists and the English soldiers increased, reaching a climax on the evening of March 5.

An apprentice antagonized an English soldier on guard duty and the soldier cuffed the boy on the ear with his firearm. The incident drew a gathering of hostile colonists, and the guard, alarmed at the size of the mob, called for help. The chief officer of the unit, Captain Thomas Preston, arrived with seven men. In an instant several shots were fired into the crowd of colonists: three men were killed at once; two more died later.

The city of Boston braced itself for more violence; Lieutenant Governor Thomas Hutchinson calmed the crowd by promising the incarceration of the guilty soldiers to be followed by a trial for murder.

Political leader Samuel Adams was influential in building a public case against the soldiers through his bombastic speeches and newspaper articles. He published a pamphlet that related the events of the violent evening as told by eyewitnesses; all the reports were decidedly in support of the colonists. The pamphlet, however, was not distributed in Boston, due to the belief that it might interfere with the fairness of the trial.

The trial became a controversial issue with political aspects. In addition to the murder charge, the legal action intensified the struggle between the King's men, who desired a verdict in their favor to counteract the tactics of Samuel Adams, and the colonists, who wanted the trial to be an example to Parliament against further use of the militia to restrain their freedom.

Lieutenant Governor Hutchinson believed that an immediate court hearing would be detrimental and unfair to the King's men; he advocated a series of postponements and the trial finally began in the fall of 1770. ROBERT TREAT PAINE served as prosecutor, and JOHN ADAMS (cousin to Samuel Adams) and Josiah Quincy were the defense counselors.

The trial progressed and arguments were presented for both sides. The defense was determined to prove that the soldiers were acting in self-defense. The prosecution attempted to show that the soldiers were guilty of malice with intent to kill.

Captain Preston was tried separately (there is evidence that the jury was packed in his favor). He was acquitted and he hastily left Boston.

Eight soldiers were next brought to trial and six were acquitted. The remaining two soldiers were found guilty of manslaughter (as opposed to murder). The method of punishment was branding on the thumb. The two soldiers, Matthew Killroy and Hugh Montgomery, received their penalty and were discharged from the military.

The irony of the Boston tragedy is that it need never have occurred. Shortly before the night of the bloodshed Parliament had decided to repeal the Townshend Acts that had so greatly agitated the colonists. Word of this decision did not reach Boston until later.

The acts were revoked later in 1770, after the Boston Massacre; one tax remained, however, and that was a minimal tax on tea. This tea tax would later precipitate the Boston Tea Party.

**BOTTOMRY** 📖 A CONTRACT, in maritime law, by which money is borrowed for a specified term by the owner of a ship for its use, equipment, or repair for which the ship is pledged as COLLATERAL. If the ship is lost in the specified voyage or during the limited time, the lender will lose his or her money according to the provisions of the contract. A contract by which a ship or its freight is pledged as security for a loan, which is to be repaid only in the event that the ship survives a specific risk, voyage, or period. 📖

A bottomry bond is the instrument that embodies the contract or agreement of bottomry.

**BOUDINOT, ELIAS** The first lawyer admitted to practice before the U.S. Supreme Court was New Jersey patriot Elias Boudinot. A good friend of President George Washington's, Boudinot was a prominent public official who strongly supported the American Revolution. Boudinot held several key positions in the Continental Congress and signed the 1783 peace treaty with England after the United States' victory in the War of Independence. After the war he aligned himself with Federalists John Adams and Alexander Hamilton. Like them,

"... THERE ARE NO EXPRESS WORDS; AND THIS IS THE CASE WITH MOST OF THE POWERS EXERCISED BY CONGRESS."

**BIOGRAPHY**

SEELEY G. MUDD MANUSCRIPT LIBRARY/PRINCETON UNIVERSITY

*Elias Boudinot*

Boudinot supported a strong, centralized national government and distrusted many of the principles of participatory democracy.

Born May 2, 1740, in Philadelphia, Boudinot studied law and was admitted to the New Jersey bar in 1760. By 1770 he had risen to the prestigious level of SERJEANT at law. Although Boudinot began his career as a political conservative, he eventually supported the colonies' efforts to break away from English domination. He joined the Revolutionary party after the U.S. War of Independence erupted and served as deputy of New Jersey's provincial assembly.

Boudinot was a representative to the Continental Congress from 1777 to 1784. He was president of the Congress from 1782 to 1784 and was named secretary of foreign affairs. He became commissary general of prisoners in 1777 and donated a large sum of his own money to help improve prison conditions. In 1787 Boudinot played a key role in obtaining New Jersey's ratification of the new U.S. Constitution.

In 1789 Boudinot became a member of the House of Representatives from New Jersey, holding office during the first three sessions of Congress. Once the U.S. Supreme Court was officially established, Boudinot became the first lawyer admitted to practice before it, on February 5, 1790. He also served as a trustee of Princeton University and was director of the U.S. Mint in Philadelphia from 1795 to 1805.

In the later years of his life, Boudinot's interests turned from politics to evangelical theology. Founder and president of the American Bible Association, Boudinot proposed a universal acceptance of religion as a cure for society's ills.

Boudinot died in New Jersey on October 24, 1821, at age eighty-one.

**BOUNDARIES** 📖 Natural or artificial separations or divisions between adjoining properties to show their limits. 📖

Boundaries are used to establish private and public ownership by determining the exact location of the points at which one piece of land is distinguishable from another. They are also used to mark the functional and jurisdictional

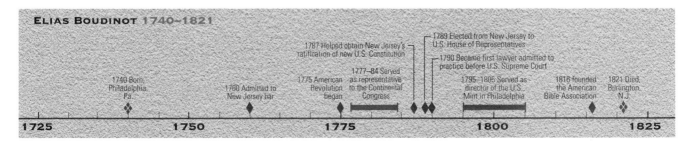

ELIAS BOUDINOT 1740–1821

1740 Born, Philadelphia, Pa.

1760 Admitted to New Jersey bar

1775 American Revolution began

1777–84 Served as representative to the Continental Congress

1787 Helped obtain New Jersey's ratification of new U.S. Constitution

1789 Elected from New Jersey to U.S. House of Representatives

1790 Became first lawyer admitted to practice before U.S. Supreme Court

1795–1805 Served as director of the U.S. Mint in Philadelphia

1816 Founded the American Bible Association

1821 Died, Burlington, N.J.

1725    1750    1775    1800    1825

limits of political subdivisions. For example, in the United States, boundaries are used to define villages, towns, cities, counties, and states.

The setting of boundaries is a characteristic of the modern era of history during which centralized states emerged that required both protection against attacks and definition of their populations. Historically, natural objects such as rivers and mountains served this purpose. Accurate determination of boundaries requires surveying and cartography, which were not widely utilized until the early nineteenth century. But even in the late twentieth century, with scientific information methods available, mapmakers occasionally are forced to turn to ancient landmarks and memories when attempting to set boundaries. For example, for centuries the borders within the Arabian peninsula had been loosely defined by tribes' grazing patterns. Following Saddam Hussein's invasion of Kuwait and subsequent defeat in 1991, United Nations mapmakers attempted to determine the exact border between Iraq and Kuwait. The United Nations enlisted the help of British border expert Julian Walker, who sought out elderly guides who could describe the loca-

tions of landmarks referred to in earlier records and provide a starting place for demarcation of the border.

Boundary disputes can last for centuries, undermining efforts to end long-standing animosities. In May 1994, at the signing of the historic self-rule accord for Palestinians in the Israeli-occupied West Bank and Gaza Strip, the chairman of the Palestinian Liberation Organization, Yasir Arafat, suddenly refused to sign six maps appended to the agreement. After much discussion with his advisers, Arafat added an Arabic disclaimer to the maps which made the point that the boundaries of the ancient West Bank town of Jericho were still in dispute, and signed the accord.

Several types of maritime boundaries exist, such as the territorial sea, which is a belt of coastal waters—controlled by the adjacent state and subject to rights such as those of foreign ships to passage—whose boundary is a line measured three miles from the low-water mark along the shore; contiguous zones, which extend beyond the territorial sea to a maximum of twelve miles, within which the controlling state may act to prevent or punish violations of its

*Within the boundaries of an exclusive economic zone, a nation has the right to drill for oil, explore, and manage marine life.*

THE TELEGRAPH COLOUR LIBRARY/FPG

regulations; and a two-hundred-mile exclusive economic zone, subject to a nation's rights of exploration, exploitation, conservation, and management of marine life, which was authorized by the Third United Nations Conference on the Law of the Sea.

Marine boundaries provide fertile ground for international conflict. In June 1990, the United States and the Soviet Union signed an agreement resolving a sixteen-hundred-mile-long maritime boundary dispute that began in 1977. The area at issue, some twenty-one thousand square nautical miles, contained valuable fishing grounds and possible oil and gas fields. The conflict had its origins in 1867, when czarist Russia sold Alaska to the United States. It was not until more than one hundred years later, while establishing their respective two-hundred-mile fisheries zones off the coasts of Alaska and Siberia in the Bering Sea, Chukchi Sea, and Arctic Ocean, that the two countries realized they had each set a different boundary for Alaska.

Even marine boundaries that have been widely accepted for years can be suddenly ignored. For example, in March 1995, Canada seized a Spanish trawler fishing for halibut in international waters just beyond Canada's two-hundred-mile boundary. Foreign Affairs Minister Andre Ouellet, of Canada, claimed that a catastrophic decline in fishing stock in recent years gave Canada moral authority to extend its jurisdiction beyond the internationally recognized two-hundred-mile maritime limit.

Boundaries in INLAND WATERS, such as the Canadian-U.S. boundary through the Great Lakes, follow a median line equidistant from the opposite shores. Boundaries in navigable rivers are set at the middle of the *thalweg*, which is the deepest or most navigable channel, as distinguished from the geographic center or a line midway between the banks (*United States v. Louisiana*, 470 U.S. 93, 105 S. Ct. 1074, 84 L. Ed. 2d 73 [1985]). As the thalweg shifts owing to the accumulation of sediment in the river, the geographic boundary also shifts. The ISLAND exception to the rule of thalweg provides that if there is a divided river flow around an island, a boundary once established on one side of the island remains there, even if the main downstream navigation channel shifts to the island's other side (*Louisiana v. Mississippi*, __U.S.__, 116 S. Ct. 290, 133 L. Ed. 2d 265 [1995]).

Some observers believe that the traditional role of boundaries as buffer regions protecting the national security of nations began to change in the 1950s. Lawrence Herzog, professor of Mexican-American studies at San Diego State University, described the evolution of large-scale cities along the borders of nations, which he called transfrontier metropolises, that share ecological resources such as water and environmental problems such as sewage control and air pollution. Traditionally, divergent laws and customs in boundary areas have discouraged economic development by interfering with the movement of labor and commodities across borders. But with the emergence of two important world regions—Western Europe and the United States–Mexico border zone—economic development in cities along borders has become intertwined.

According to Herzog, such border urbanization has generated legal and political concerns not previously addressed by international law. The emerging need for transborder cooperation in the areas of transportation, land use, and environmental regulation requires the development of new planning and policy guidelines that address the changing role of boundaries.

### CROSS-REFERENCES

Fish and Fishing; International Waterways; Territorial Waters.

**BOUNTY** A subsidy paid to a category of persons who have performed a public service.

Bounty is the proper term to be applied when the services of several persons are sought, and each person who fulfills the offer is entitled to the promised compensation, as in the case of the killing of destructive wild animals. In contrast, a REWARD compensates a single service to be performed only once, such as in the capture of a fugitive, and, therefore, will be earned solely by the person who succeeds in this regard.

Under federal law, no bounty may be paid to induce any person to enlist in the ARMED SERVICES. A clothing allowance or enlistment bonus authorized by law does not, however, constitute a bounty.

**BOYCOTT** A lawful concerted attempt by a group of people to express displeasure with, or obtain concessions from, a particular person or company by refusing to do business with them. An unlawful attempt that is prohibited by the SHERMAN ANTI-TRUST ACT (15 U.S.C.A. § 1 et seq.), to adversely affect a company through threat, coercion, or intimidation of its employees, or to prevent others from doing business with said company. A practice utilized in labor disputes whereby an organized group of employees bands together and refrains from dealing with an employer, the legality of which is determined by applicable provisions of statutes governing labor-management relations. See also LABOR LAW.

A classic example of this is a consumer boycott whereby a group of customers refuses to purchase a particular product in order to indicate their dissatisfaction with excessive prices or the offensive actions of a particular manufacturer or producer.

**BOYLE, JOHN** John Boyle was born October 28, 1774, near Tazewell in Botetourt County, Virginia. He was admitted to the Kentucky bar in 1797 and established a legal practice in Lancaster, Kentucky, before entering government service.

In 1800 Boyle participated in the Kentucky House of Representatives. He served in the U.S. House of Representatives as a member from Kentucky from 1803 to 1809 and participated in the IMPEACHMENT hearings of Justice SAMUEL CHASE, who was accused but found not guilty of prejudice in certain rulings.

ana from 1810 to 1814, and in Baltimore from 1814 to 1817.

After serving as deputy attorney general and district judge in Louisiana, Brackenridge was a member of the Maryland legislature from 1814 to 1817 and from 1819 to 1821. He was a strong supporter of the South American nations, and in 1817 was sent to South America as part of a commission to study the political conditions of the area. Subsequently, he relocated to Florida where he worked for Governor Andrew Jackson from 1821 to 1832, serving as secretary and judge of the Florida Territory.

As an author, Brackenridge wrote many publications, including *Views of Louisiana* (1814); *History of the Late War* (1816); *Voyage to South America* (1819); *Letters to the Public*, (1832); and *History of the Western Insurrection in Western Pennsylvania* (1859).

**BIOGRAPHY**

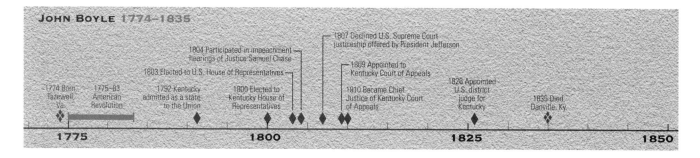

**JOHN BOYLE 1774–1835**

1807 Declined U.S. Supreme Court justiceship offered by President Jefferson

1804 Participated in impeachment hearings of Justice Samuel Chase

1803 Elected to U.S. House of Representatives

1809 Appointed to Kentucky Court of Appeals

1774 Born Tazewell, Va.

1775–83 American Revolution

1792 Kentucky admitted as a state to the Union

1800 Elected to Kentucky House of Representatives

1810 Became Chief Justice of Kentucky Court of Appeals

1826 Appointed U.S. district judge for Kentucky

1835 Died, Danville, Ky.

1775    1800    1825    1850

Boyle presided over the Kentucky Court of Appeals from 1809 to 1810, acting as chief justice from 1810 to 1826. In that same year he became U.S. district judge for Kentucky and remained in that position until his death January 28, 1835, near Danville, Kentucky.

**BRACKENRIDGE, HENRY MARIE** Henry Marie Brackenridge was an eminent lawyer, statesman, and author.

Brackenridge was born May 11, 1786. His legal education was varied, including the study of law in Pittsburgh, Pennsylvania, admiralty law in Baltimore, Maryland, and Spanish law in New Orleans, Louisiana. He was admitted to the Pennsylvania bar in 1806 and practiced law in Pennsylvania as well as Missouri and Louisi-

**BIOGRAPHY**

*Henry Marie Brackenridge*

Brackenridge died January 18, 1871, in Pittsburgh.

**BRACKET** 📖 The category of the percentage of INCOME TAX found on the tax tables set by the Internal Revenue Code, within which a taxpayer falls based upon his or her TAXABLE INCOME. 📖

**BRACTON, HENRY DE** Henry de Bracton was a medieval jurist and priest whose masterful TREATISE on COMMON LAW and procedure provided a framework for the early English legal system.

Bracton's famous *De legibus et consuetudinibus Angliae* (On the laws and customs of England) was a systematic explanation of English law for judges and practitioners during the reign of

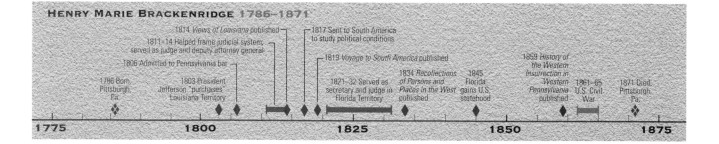

**HENRY MARIE BRACKENRIDGE 1786–1871**

1814 *Views of Louisiana* published

1811–14 Helped frame judicial system; served as judge and deputy attorney general

1806 Admitted to Pennsylvania bar

1817 Sent to South America to study political conditions

1819 *Voyage to South America* published

1859 *History of the Western Insurrection in Western Pennsylvania* published

1786 Born, Pittsburgh, Pa.

1803 President Jefferson "purchases" Louisiana Territory

1821–32 Served as secretary and judge in Florida Territory

1834 *Recollections of Persons and Places in the West* published

1845 Florida gains U.S. statehood

1861–65 U.S. Civil War

1871 Died, Pittsburgh, Pa.

1775    1800    1825    1850    1875

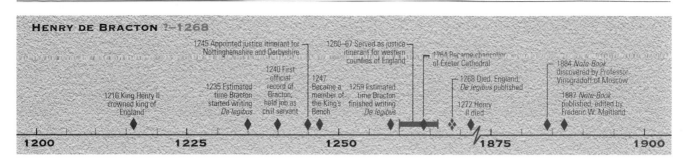

**HENRY DE BRACTON ?–1268**

1245 Appointed justice itinerant for Nottinghamshire and Derbyshire

1260–67 Served as justice itinerant for western counties of England

1264 Became chancellor of Exeter Cathedral

1884 Note-Book discovered by Professor Vinogradoff of Moscow

1240 First official record of Bracton, held job as civil servant

1247 Became a member of the King's Bench

1259 Estimated time Bracton finished writing De legibus

1268 Died, England; De legibus published

1887 Note-Book published, edited by Frederic W. Maitland

1216 King Henry III crowned king of England

1235 Estimated time Bracton started writing De legibus

1272 Henry II died

1200    1225    1250    1875    1900

---

King Henry III. *De legibus* and another of Bracton's works, *Note-Book*, helped shape the system of CASE LAW and PLEADINGS that began during the monarchy of King HENRY II. Although reliance on Bracton's works declined as English statutory law grew, historians consider *De legibus* the high point of medieval legal scholarship.

Bracton's exact date of birth early in the thirteenth century is unknown. His family, whose name sometimes appears as Bratton or Bretton, owned land near Devon, England. Richard, Earl of Cornwall, the brother of King Henry III, and William de Raleigh, a prominent common-law judge, were important benefactors who helped advance Bracton's legal career.

By 1240 Bracton had the job of civil servant, a relatively lucrative position during the Middle Ages. In 1245 he was appointed to the judiciary. In 1247 he became a member of the KING'S BENCH, where he served for ten years. After 1257 he held several assignments, including that of chancellor of Exeter Cathedral. During the Middle Ages it was not unusual for a priest to serve also as a judge.

*De legibus* first appeared after Bracton's death in 1268. Although the original manuscript is lost, approximately three hundred reedited and hand copied manuscripts circulated during the thirteenth and fourteenth centuries. Intended as a guide to English law and procedure, *De legibus* combines aspects of ROMAN and CANON LAW. Bracton was influenced by the *Institutes* of JUSTINIAN I and by medieval textbooks of Axo, Tancred, and Raymond of Penafort. His treatise

**BIOGRAPHY**

**BIOGRAPHY**

includes a section of basic principles and a section of WRITS and commentary. It emphasizes the development and application of case law as written by judges grappling with medieval legal questions.

Bracton's *Note-Book* is a compendium of two thousand judicial opinions. Some historians believe that other medieval jurists contributed to the work, which was discovered in 1884. *Note-Book* was edited by FREDERIC W. MAITLAND and published in 1887.

**BRADFORD, WILLIAM**    William Bradford, born November 4, 1729, in Plympton, Massachusetts, was a student of both law and medicine. After practicing medicine in Warren, Rhode Island, Bradford was admitted to the bar in 1767 and established his legal practice in Bristol, Rhode Island.

From 1764 to 1765 Bradford was a member of the Rhode Island House of Representatives, and served as speaker. He continued his career in that state, serving on the Rhode Island Committee of Correspondence in 1773, and acting as deputy governor of Rhode Island from 1775 to 1778.

Bradford was elected senator from Rhode Island in 1793, serving in the U.S. Senate until 1797, and acting as president pro tem in that same year.

He died July 6, 1808, in Bristol.

**BRADFORD, WILLIAM**    William Bradford was born September 14, 1755, in Philadelphia. He graduated from Princeton University with a bachelor of arts degree in 1772 and a master of arts degree in 1775.

Before beginning his legal career Bradford

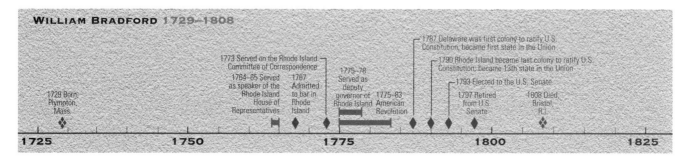

**WILLIAM BRADFORD 1729–1808**

1787 Delaware was first colony to ratify U.S. Constitution; became first state in the Union

1773 Served on the Rhode Island Committee of Correspondence

1790 Rhode Island became last colony to ratify U.S. Constitution; became 13th state in the Union

1764–65 Served as speaker of the Rhode Island House of Representatives

1767 Admitted to bar in Rhode Island

1775–78 Served as deputy governor of Rhode Island

1775–83 American Revolution

1793 Elected to the U.S. Senate

1797 Retired from U.S. Senate

1729 Born, Plympton, Mass.

1808 Died, Bristol, R.I.

1725    1750    1775    1800    1825

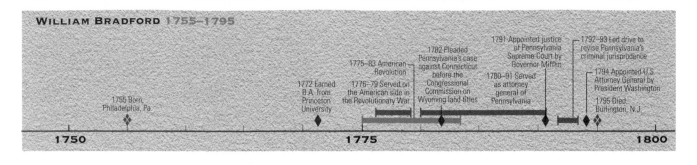

WILLIAM BRADFORD 1755–1795

1755 Born, Philadelphia, Pa.

1772 Earned B.A. from Princeton University

1775–83 American Revolution

1776–79 Served on the American side in the Revolutionary War

1782 Pleaded Pennsylvania's case against Connecticut before the Congressional Commission on Wyoming land titles

1780–91 Served as attorney general of Pennsylvania

1791 Appointed justice of Pennsylvania Supreme Court by Governor Mifflin

1792–93 Led drive to revise Pennsylvania's criminal jurisprudence

1794 Appointed U.S. Attorney General by President Washington

1795 Died, Burlington, N.J.

1750    1775    1800

served in the Revolutionary War from 1776 to 1779, fought in numerous battles, including Valley Forge, and emerged with the rank of colonel in the Continental army. After his tour of duty, he was admitted to the Pennsylvania bar and established a legal practice in Yorktown, Pennsylvania.

Bradford served as Pennsylvania attorney general for an eleven-year period, from 1780 to 1791. He entered the judiciary in the latter year and presided as judge of the Pennsylvania Supreme Court for three years.

In 1794 Bradford was selected by President GEORGE WASHINGTON to serve as U.S. Attorney General for one year, the second man to hold this post. He died August 23, 1795, and was buried in Burlington, New Jersey.

**BRADLEY, JOSEPH P.** Joseph P. Bradley was appointed to the U.S. Supreme Court in 1870 in a successful move by President ULYSSES S. GRANT to *pack the court*, or fill vacancies on the bench with jurists who support the president's actions. Grant nominated Bradley and fellow Republican WILLIAM STRONG with the almost public understanding that they would save the invalidated Legal Tender Act (12 Stat. 345, 532, 709). As expected, Bradley and Strong voted to uphold the constitutionality of the act. Bradley went on to serve as an associate justice for twenty-two years and, as was the custom, as a traveling circuit judge for the Fifth (Southern) Circuit.

The eldest of eleven children, Bradley was born March 14, 1813, in Berne, New York, and raised on a farm. He relied on his intelligence, ambition, and strong work ethic to make a name for himself in the legal profession. An

**BIOGRAPHY**

*William Bradford*

**BIOGRAPHY**

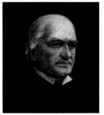

*Joseph P. Bradley*

1836 graduate of New Jersey's Rutgers College, Bradley was a self-taught lawyer who was admitted to the New Jersey bar in 1839. In 1859 he received an honorary law degree from Lafayette College, in Easton, Pennsylvania.

Bradley's marriage to Mary Hornblower helped open doors in the legal community. His wife's father, William Hornblower, was chief justice of the New Jersey Supreme Court. Bradley built a successful law practice with a large business clientele that included the troubled Camden and Amboy Railroad. His expertise was in patent and commercial law.

Bradley's appointment to the Supreme Court on February 7, 1870 came shortly after the Court ruled that the Legal Tender Act was unconstitutional. In 1862 Congress had used the act to issue treasury notes as a substitute for gold in its efforts to pay off Civil War debts. Upon reviewing the legislation, the Supreme Court invalidated the issuance of the paper money (*Hepburn v. Griswold* [8 Wall.], 75 U.S. 603, 19 L. Ed. 513 [1869]).

Court observers predicted that Grant's new appointees would agree to reverse *Hepburn* because of their long-standing ties to commercial interests. They were right: Bradley and Strong did vote to overturn, thereby upholding the legality of the notes (the *Second Legal Tender* case, or *Knox v. Lee*, 79 U.S. [12 Wall.] 457, 20 L. Ed. 287 [1870]).

Bradley's Supreme Court and circuit court opinions often fail the test of time. Although his contemporaries praised him for his keen intellect and legal acumen, many of his decisions are by today's standards patently offensive in outcome and reasoning.

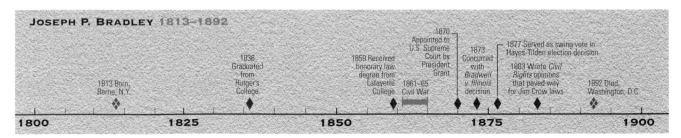

JOSEPH P. BRADLEY 1813–1892

1813 Born, Berne, N.Y.

1836 Graduated from Rutger's College

1859 Received honorary law degree from Lafayette College

1861–65 Civil War

1870 Appointed to U.S. Supreme Court by President Grant

1873 Concurred with *Bradwell v. Illinois* decision

1877 Served as swing-vote in Hayes-Tilden election decision

1883 Wrote *Civil Rights* opinions that paved way for Jim Crow laws

1892 Died, Washington, D.C.

1800    1825    1850    1875    1900

Bradley wrote the majority opinion in the infamous *Civil Rights* cases, 109 U.S. 3, 3 S. Ct. 18, 27 L. Ed. 835 (1883), which declared the CIVIL RIGHTS ACT of 1875 (18 Stat. 336) unconstitutional. The Civil Rights Act was established to ensure the equal treatment of African Americans in public facilities and accommodations. In effect, that decision sanctioned racial segregation and paved the way for discriminatory JIM CROW LAWS.

According to the Court, civil rights legislation could not prevent DISCRIMINATION by private individuals. Although the THIRTEENTH AMENDMENT of the U.S. Constitution outlawed SLAVERY, and the FOURTEENTH AMENDMENT barred racial discrimination by states, according to the Court discrimination by private citizens was allowable. Bradley argued that prejudice was not amenable to legislation. If private business owners refused to serve or accommodate African Americans, Congress could not force them to do so. In this view, purely private conduct was not covered by the post–Civil War constitutional amendments.

In a famous dissent, Associate Justice JOHN MARSHALL HARLAN pointed out that because the restaurants, inns, theaters, and hotels owned by private citizens are actually quite public, discrimination against African Americans in these places should not be tolerated. Harlan's dissent was later used to bolster support for the Civil Rights Act of 1964 (42 U.S.C.A. § 2000 et seq.).

In *Bradwell v. Illinois*, 83 U.S. (16 Wall.) 130, 21 L. Ed. 442 (1872), Bradley concurred in the decision to reject MYRA BRADWELL's bid to practice law in Illinois. Bradwell had studied law with her husband and passed the Illinois bar examination. However, Illinois denied her admission to the bar because she was female. Bradwell appealed her case to the U.S. Supreme Court, claiming that the Fourteenth Amendment to the U.S. Constitution protected her right to practice in her chosen profession. The Supreme Court ruled otherwise. Bradley wrote in concurring DICTA that God had created woman to be wife and mother, not lawyer.

In the *Slaughter-House* cases, 83 U.S. (16

> "THE STUDY OF LAW [IS] A SUBJECT OF LIVING INTEREST AND IMPORTANCE, INDEPENDENT OF ITS ATTRACTIONS AS A PROFESSIONAL CALLING."

**BIOGRAPHY**

*Myra Colby Bradwell*

Wall.) 36, 21 L. Ed. 394 (1873), Bradley's dissent foretold the Court's changing philosophy on due process for businesses. In this case, Louisiana butchers objected to a state law that allowed only one company to slaughter cattle in New Orleans. The Court sided with the state, but Bradley's dissent was later used to argue for the protection of commercial enterprises from state government intrusion.

Bradley was chosen in 1877 to sit on the Hayes-Tilden Electoral Commission to determine the results of the presidential election between Republican candidate RUTHERFORD B. HAYES and his Democratic opponent, SAMUEL J. TILDEN. Bradley was the swing vote; he replaced Justice David Davis, a political independent who could not fulfill his term on the electoral commission. Bradley voted for Hayes, his fellow Republican.

Bradley died in Washington, D.C., on January 22, 1892, at the age of seventy-nine.

See also CIVIL RIGHTS CASES; SLAUGHTER-HOUSE CASES.

## BRADWELL, MYRA COLBY

Myra Bradwell was a legal editor and an early leader in the struggle for WOMEN'S RIGHTS, especially in the legal profession.

Bradwell was born February 12, 1831, in Manchester, Vermont. After an early childhood in Portage, New York, she moved with her family to Illinois and attended the ladies seminary in Elgin, where she subsequently became a teacher. In 1852 she married James B. Bradwell, an Englishman who had immigrated to the United States and studied law in Memphis, Tennessee. The Bradwells established a private school in Memphis but moved to Chicago in 1854. There James Bradwell opened a law office and eventually became a judge of the Cook County Court.

After the move to Chicago Bradwell began to study law with her husband with the intention of becoming his assistant; she later decided to establish a practice of her own. In 1868 she founded the *Chicago Legal News*, a weekly legal newspaper. With Bradwell serving as both editor and business manager, the *News* quickly

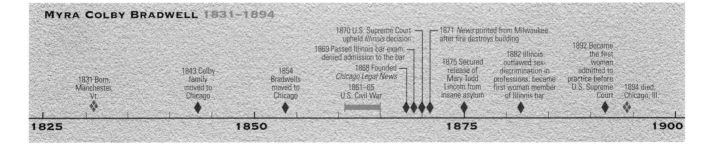

**MYRA COLBY BRADWELL 1831–1894**

- 1831 Born, Manchester, Vt.
- 1843 Colby family moved to Chicago
- 1854 Bradwells moved to Chicago
- 1861–65 U.S. Civil War
- 1868 Founded *Chicago Legal News*
- 1869 Passed Illinois bar exam; denied admission to the bar
- 1870 U.S. Supreme Court upheld *Illinois* decision
- 1871 *News* printed from Milwaukee after fire destroys building
- 1875 Secured release of Mary Todd Lincoln from insane asylum
- 1882 Illinois outlawed sex-discrimination in professions; became first woman member of Illinois bar
- 1892 Became the first woman admitted to practice before U.S. Supreme Court
- 1894 died, Chicago, Ill.

1825     1850     1875     1900

became a success. It was chartered by the Illinois legislature, which also passed legislation establishing the paper as a valid place for the publication of legal notices and allowing state laws and opinions published in the paper to be offered as evidence in court. Under her editorial leadership, the *News* called for the regulation of corporations, the enactment of zoning ordinances, and the establishment of professional standards for the legal profession. The *News* building was destroyed in the Chicago fire of 1871 but Bradwell quickly arranged to have the paper printed in Milwaukee, Wisconsin, and published the next issue on schedule.

In 1869, after passing the state bar examination, Bradwell applied to the Illinois Supreme Court for admission to the bar. The court rejected her application on the ground that as a married woman she "would be bound neither by her express contracts nor by those implied contracts which it is the policy of the law to create between attorney and client." She reapplied, but the court rejected her again, this time because she was a woman, regardless of her marital status. The court said that if it were to admit women to the bar, it would be exercising its authority in a manner "never contemplated" by the state legislature when it granted that authority (*In re Bradwell*, 55 Ill. 535 [1870]). She appealed to the U.S. Supreme Court, which upheld the Illinois decision, saying that it could not interfere with each state's right to regulate the granting of licenses within its borders (*Bradwell v. People*, 16 Wall [83 U.S.] 130, 21 L. Ed. 442 [1872]).

In 1882, however, the Illinois legislature passed a law guaranteeing all persons, regardless of sex, the right to select a profession as they wished. Although Bradwell never reapplied for admission to the bar, the Illinois Supreme Court informed her that her original application had been accepted. As a result, she became the first woman member of the Illinois State Bar Association; she was also the first woman member of the Illinois Press Association. On March 28, 1892, she was admitted to practice before the U.S. Supreme Court.

> "ONE THING WE CLAIM—THAT WOMAN HAS THE RIGHT TO THINK AND ACT AS AN INDIVIDUAL—BELIEVING IF THE GREAT FATHER HAD INTENDED IT TO BE OTHERWISE, HE WOULD HAVE PLACED EVE IN A CAGE AND GIVEN ADAM THE KEY."

**BIOGRAPHY**

*Louis Dembitz Brandeis*

In addition to her efforts to win admission to the bar, Bradwell played a role in the broader women's rights movement. She was active in the Illinois Woman Suffrage Association and helped form the American Woman Suffrage Association. She was also influential in the passage of laws by the Illinois legislature that gave married women the right to keep wages they earned and protected the rights of widows.

During the latter years of her life, Bradwell was one of a number of Chicago citizens who worked to secure the World's Fair for their city. When the fair was held in 1893 she chaired the committee on law reform of its auxiliary congress.

Bradwell died February 14, 1894, in Chicago, Illinois.

**BRANDEIS, LOUIS DEMBITZ** Louis Dembitz Brandeis's lifelong commitment to public service and social reform earned him the epithet the People's Lawyer. His twenty-three years on the Supreme Court were characterized by a deep respect for civil liberties and by an abiding distrust of centralized power in the hands of business and government.

Brandeis was famous for his prodigious intellect and his well-crafted, detailed dissents. He was a man of principle who enhanced the image of the legal profession by living up to his belief that lawyers should possess "the moral courage in the face of financial loss and personal ill-will to stand for right and justice."

Brandeis was born November 13, 1856, in Louisville, Kentucky, the youngest of four children of Adolph Brandeis and Fredericka Dembitz Brandeis. His parents were refined and well-to-do immigrants who left Prague, then part of Bohemia, in 1849. A brilliant student, Brandeis excelled in the public schools in Louisville. He also attended the Annen-Realschule, in Dresden, Germany, during his family's 1873–75 pilgrimage to Europe.

Although Brandeis did not have a college degree, he was admitted into Harvard Law School and graduated at the top of his class in 1877. Brandeis had an obvious passion for law and he considered the years at Harvard among the happiest in his life. His ties to the university

**LOUIS DEMBITZ BRANDEIS 1856–1941**

| | | | | | 1914 *Other People's Money—and How the Bankers Use It* published | 1916 Became first Jewish American on U.S. Supreme Court—appointed by President Wilson | | 1941 Died, Washington, D.C. | 1948 Brandeis University named in his honor |
| 1856 Born, Louisville, Ky. | 1861–65 U.S. Civil War | 1877 Graduated top of class from Harvard Law School | 1886 Helped found the *Harvard Law Review* | 1890 Co-wrote *The Right to Privacy* with Samuel D. Warren | 1908 *Muller v. Oregon* established the use of the "Brandeis brief" | 1914–18 World War I | 1928 Wrote dissent for *Olmstead v. United States* | 1939 Retired from Supreme Court | 1939–45 World War II |

| 1850 | 1875 | 1900 | 1925 | 1950 |

were strengthened further in 1886 when he became one of the founders of the influential *Harvard Law Review.* Brandeis and Samuel D. Warren wrote a legendary article, "The Right to Privacy," in the December 1890 issue of the *Review.* It previewed Brandeis's Supreme Court opinions asserting privacy as a constitutionally guaranteed right.

After a year of graduate work Brandeis moved to St. Louis in 1878 to begin a law practice. He soon missed the intellectual stimulation of the East Coast and moved back to Boston, where he began a successful law practice with Warren. Their large firm had an impressive clientele and made Brandeis wealthy, although money held little interest for him. As he established himself professionally, Brandeis socialized with Boston's intellectual elite. In 1891, he married Alice Goldmark, a distant cousin, with whom he had two daughters.

Brandeis zealously embraced the ideals of the Progressive movement of the early twentieth century. He proved his dedication to social reform by serving as unpaid counsel in several public interest cases. Brandeis was one of the first U.S. lawyers to offer *pro bono services* (free legal services for people unable to afford an attorney). Along with a passionate belief in the virtue of volunteer legal work, Brandeis had a sense of fairness that compelled him to compensate his firm for any time spent in public service.

Brandeis worked without a fee to fight monopolistic streetcar FRANCHISES in Boston and to improve the questionable practices of life insurance companies. One of his most satisfying achievements was the creation of a savings bank plan that enabled people to obtain life insurance at reasonable rates. Brandeis also argued for the constitutionality of maximum hour and minimum wage laws.

In 1914, Brandeis published *Other People's Money—and How the Bankers Use It,* a denunciation of TRUSTS and investment banking. The book helped inspire important ANTITRUST legislation and earned the antipathy of many U.S. bankers and businesspeople.

Brandeis also created a new style of legal writing, appropriately called the Brandeis BRIEF. With his sister-in-law Josephine Goldmark, of the National Consumer's League, Brandeis produced the first legal brief to include copious supporting data. For *Muller v. State of Oregon,* 208 U.S. 412, 28 S. Ct. 324, 52 L. Ed. 551 (1908), Brandeis wrote more than one hundred pages in favor of an Oregon state law mandating a maximum ten-hour workday for women. Later, when asked for an appropriate title for the seminal *Muller* brief, Brandeis replied, *What Any Fool Knows.* In the document, he described the deleterious physical and mental effects on women of extended periods of manual labor. He included references to sociology, psychology, history, politics, employment statistics, and economics; this method of amassing data from several different disciplines to persuade the court became popular with other lawyers. The legal principles of the case were discussed in about two pages.

In 1916 Brandeis was appointed by President WOODROW WILSON to fill the associate justice seat vacated by Joseph R. Lamar. Brandeis thus became the first Jewish American to be nominated for the High Court. His Senate confirmation hearing was a bitter, drawn-out affair because of business's fierce opposition to him and his progressive politics. Anti-Semitism was also an element in the extended, four-month proceedings. Despite virulent criticism from insurance and banking officials, Brandeis was confirmed by the Senate, 47–22.

As a Supreme Court justice, Brandeis is remembered for his eloquent dissents, often joined by colleague OLIVER WENDELL HOLMES, JR. Brandeis's dissents frequently signaled how the Court would rule in future cases. For example, his 1928 dissent in *Olmstead v. United States,* 277 U.S. 438, 48 S. Ct. 564, 72 L. Ed. 944, anticipated the reasoning and outcome of a Supreme Court case heard years later.

In *Olmstead,* Brandeis objected to the nearly unrestricted use of government wiretaps. Although the *Olmstead* majority approved state wiretapping unless a physical TRESPASS was involved, Brandeis considered wholesale eavesdropping unconstitutional. In his view it violated the Fourth Amendment, prohibiting unreasonable government searches, and the FIFTH AMENDMENT, forbidding the deprivation of liberty without due process. Brandeis argued that the right to be left alone was guaranteed by the Constitution.

Almost forty years later, his views on privacy were adopted in *Katz v. United States,* 389 U.S. 347, 88 S. Ct. 507, 19 L. Ed. 2d 576 (1967). In *Katz,* relying heavily on Brandeis's reasoning, the Court overturned *Olmstead,* ruling that government wiretaps were permissible only if they met procedural requirements of the Fourth Amendment.

Despite his own clear convictions, Brandeis refused to declare a law unconstitutional simply because he disagreed with it. Particularly in economic matters, Brandeis exercised judicial restraint by deferring to Congress and its legislative power.

"EXPERIENCE SHOULD TEACH US TO BE MOST ON OUR GUARD TO PROTECT LIBERTY WHEN THE GOVERNMENT'S PURPOSES ARE BENEFICIENT."

Brandeis was an ardent defender of civil liberties. Throughout his career, he strongly urged the Court to use the FOURTEENTH AMENDMENT to apply the Bill of Rights to the states. In particular, Brandeis declared that laws abridging free speech and assembly must be challenged if no emergency exists to justify them. Unless speech causes clear and imminent danger, it is unreservedly protected.

Although Brandeis was a nonobservant Jew, he was a respected leader of the American Zionist movement. From 1914 to 1921, Brandeis gave his name and public support to the movement to create a Jewish state in Palestine. In his later years Brandeis advised President FRANKLIN D. ROOSEVELT on the establishment of a Jewish homeland and the BOYCOTT of German products.

Brandeis retired from the Court on February 13, 1939. He died at age eighty-four, on October 5, 1941.

Brandeis was honored in 1948 when a new institution of higher learning was named after him. Brandeis University is a private, Jewish-sponsored, coeducational college in Waltham, Massachusetts. The nonsectarian school offers both undergraduate and graduate degrees.

### CROSS-REFERENCES

Electronic Surveillance; *Olmstead v. United States*; Privacy; Wire Tapping.

## BREACH OF MARRIAGE PROMISE 📖 A COMMON-LAW right of action for breaking a commitment to enter into matrimony. 📖

The RIGHT OF ACTION for breach of a marriage promise has been abolished in a majority of states.

**Agreement to Marry** An agreement to marry is different from all other contractual relations. The reason for this is that both its object and the relationship created between the parties are completely different from those of any other CONTRACT. In order to recover for breach of promise, the plaintiff must establish that the two parties had a VALID existing contract to marry. This can be accomplished by a showing that both parties had a clear intent for the agreement to be binding.

If the parties to a contract to marry are incapable of creating a valid agreement due to a legal DISABILITY, a lawsuit for breach of marriage promise cannot be sustained. Generally, a valid defense to such an action is the INFANCY of the promisor at the time of the agreement. The infancy of the promisee, however, is not a valid defense. Statutes provide the ages of infancy.

An individual who is incapable of making a contract due to INCOMPETENCE will not be held liable for breach of promise. Similarly, a promise to marry someone who is already married is INVALID, provided the promisee knew this fact. Where the plaintiff was unaware that the promisor was already married, however, he or she may recover. Upon the legal termination of the MARRIAGE by DIVORCE, ANNULMENT, or death of the former spouse, a defendant who breaches a promise to marry the plaintiff may be held liable.

A breach of contract action cannot be maintained where a marriage would be unlawful due to INCEST.

**Offer and Acceptance** Fundamental elements to the creation of a marriage contract are an OFFER and ACCEPTANCE. It is not necessary that the offer be in formal language. The key requirement is that both parties comprehend that there was a clearly intended offer of marriage. A statement of the intention to marry to a third person, absent any other indicated intent, is not enough.

An acceptance of an offer to marry must be given within a reasonable period of time. Such acceptance need not be formal but may be implied from the promisee's behavior.

For a marriage contract to be enforceable, there must be a showing that there has been a MEETING OF THE MINDS of the individuals to the agreement. A promise to marry induced by DURESS is invalid. Similarly, a promise to marry made by fraudulent inducement—or fraudulent concealment of facts that would prevent the making of the agreement if revealed or disclosed—will render the promise invalid and relieve the innocent party from all liability.

A promise to marry must be based upon legal CONSIDERATION. Generally, one individual's promise is adequate consideration for the promise of the other party. A promise to marry must not be based solely upon illegal or immoral consideration, such as sexual relations between the parties. A promise based upon legal consideration will not, however, be vitiated merely because unlawful sexual intercourse took place between the parties either prior to or following the promise.

If a promise to marry is CONDITIONAL, LIABILITY for its breach will arise only following the performance or occurrence of the agreed condition.

A contract to marry may be manifested by many promises made at different times; however, there is only a single contract, and only a single breach can take place.

A contract to marry can be rescinded either by mutual consent of the parties, or in instances of FRAUD or duress. The consent to postpone a marriage alone does not constitute a release of the obligation to perform it.

**Breach** Unless there is a legally justifiable reason, an unwillingness to perform one's promise to marry creates a breach of promise to marry. Mere postponement of the wedding does not constitute a breach unless it is done arbitrarily and for no good reason. In such case, the postponement can be regarded as equivalent to a refusal to comply with the marital promise.

**Defenses** Defenses exist other than the invalidity or termination of the marriage contract and lack of capacity.

The invalidity of the plaintiff's divorce from a former spouse may be used as a defense only if the issue of the divorce is raised on the ground that there was a lack of JURISDICTION on the part of the court to permit the divorce. If the plaintiff had an invalid divorce, the defendant cannot be held liable for breach of the marriage promise because the plaintiff was still lawfully wed to his or her former spouse and, therefore, could not validly contract a marriage with the defendant.

A valid defense to a breach of marriage promise is the plaintiff's refusal to marry the defendant. The defendant cannot later defend himself or herself on the basis of the fact that he or she subsequently offered to marry the plaintiff. The engagement of the plaintiff to another individual at the time of entering into a contract with the defendant is not a defense. Similarly, the marriage of the plaintiff to another party subsequent to the defendant's breach does not excuse the defendant of liability for a breach. Unattractive personality traits, or offensive conduct, such as DRUNKENNESS, cannot be used as a defense. Where the objectionable behavior amounts to a FELONY, however, it can be used as a defense against the plaintiff in a breach of marriage promise action.

Generally, a defendant will successfully defeat an action by alleging physical incapacity or disease that makes it either unsafe or improper to enter into marriage. If a defendant has knowledge of the disability when he or she promises to marry the plaintiff there is no defense. A disability on the part of the defendant that would not interfere with the marital relationship is insufficient to relieve a defendant of his promise.

**Damages** The nature and form of an action for breach of marriage promise is contractual. Recoverable DAMAGES include COMPENSATORY DAMAGES for injury to the feelings and health of the plaintiff as well as to his or her reputation. A plaintiff may also recover damages for any financial loss resulting from the breach, comparable to the recovery in a breach of any other contract action, in addition to compensation for loss of advantages that would have stemmed from a marital relationship with the defendant.

*A lawyer examines documents relating to a breach of marriage promise contention in an etching done from a painting by W. Denby Sadler.*

**BREACH OF THE PEACE** A comprehensive term encompassing acts or conduct that seriously endanger or disturb public peace and order.

A breach of the peace was a COMMON-LAW offense, but is presently governed by statute in many states. It is frequently defined as consti-

### Breach of the Peace

Persons arrested for disorderly conduct, by sex and age, in 1993

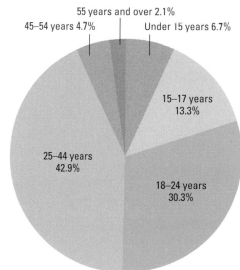

55 years and over 2.1%
45–54 years 4.7%
Under 15 years 6.7%
15–17 years 13.3%
18–24 years 30.3%
25–44 years 42.9%

Arrests (not charges) reported for "disorderly conduct" totalled 607,000 in 1993.

Source: U.S. Federal Bureau of Investigation, *Crime in the United States*, annual.

tuting a form of DISORDERLY CONDUCT. Examples include using abusive or OBSCENE language in a public place, resisting a lawful arrest, and trespassing or damaging property when accompanied by violence.

Statutes commonly require that conduct constituting a breach of the peace must be clearly a type of misbehavior resulting in public unrest or disturbance. As an example, a prostitute who solicited men walking by on a public street from her window was found guilty of breaching the peace, but a man who raised his voice to a police officer while the officer was issuing a ticket to him was not guilty of the same offense.

A breach of the peace is synonymous with a DISTURBANCE OF THE PEACE. Jurisdictions that do not have a specific statutory provision for the offense may punish it as a form of disorderly conduct. The usual penalty imposed is either a fine, imprisonment, or both.

**BREAKING** 📖 To use physical force to separate or damage a solid object. 📖

When used in criminal statutes as an element of BURGLARY or HOUSEBREAKING, to forcibly remove any part of a house that protects it from unauthorized entry such as locks, latches, windows, or doors, to gain access to the house with the intent to commit a crime; to use force or violence in escaping from a house after a FELONY has been committed or attempted therein.

The slightest physical force—for example, lifting a latch, releasing a bolt, or opening an unlocked door or window—is enough to constitute breaking.

**BREESE, SIDNEY** Sidney Breese was born July 15, 1800, in Whitesboro, New York. He graduated from Union College in Schenectady, New York, in 1818. Breese was admitted to the Illinois bar in 1820 and concentrated his career efforts in that state.

In 1821, Breese was appointed postmaster of Kaskasia, Illinois. From 1822 to 1826, he served as prosecuting attorney for the Illinois Circuit Court, and from 1827 to 1829, he performed the duties of federal district attorney. In 1831, he published *Breese's Reports*, a compilation of the decisions of the Illinois Supreme Court from 1820 to 1831.

"WITH NATIONS, MIGHT IS TOO COMMONLY REGARDED AS RIGHT."

**BIOGRAPHY**

LIBRARY OF CONGRESS

*Sidney Breese*

In 1832, Breese fought in the Black Hawk War, which was a conflict between the white settlers of Illinois and the Sac and Fox Indians. After the war Breese resumed his legal career.

In 1835 Breese was selected as a judge for the Illinois Circuit Court and he remained on the bench until 1841. From 1841 to 1842, he served as justice of the Supreme Court of Illinois.

Breese's career continued to be varied during the latter part of his life. He was elected to the United States Senate in 1843, and represented Illinois until 1849. During his senatorial term, from 1845 to 1849, he also acted as administrator of the Smithsonian Institution. In 1850, he became a member of the House of Representatives of Illinois. In 1857, he was again selected to act as justice of the Supreme Court of Illinois. He served on the bench until 1878, becoming chief justice of this court in 1873. In 1873, Breese was responsible for the noteworthy court decision in the so-called GRANGER Cases, specifically the case of *Munn v. Illinois*, 69 Ill. 80, by deciding in favor of STATES' RIGHTS in the regulation of grain elevators.

As an author, Breese gained prominence with the publication in 1869 of *Origin and History of the Pacific Railroad*.

He died June 27, 1878, in Pinckneyville, Illinois.

**BRENNAN, WILLIAM JOSEPH, JR.** William Joseph Brennan, Jr., was the first Roman Catholic appointed to the Supreme Court and served as associate justice of the Court from 1956 to 1990. His unshakable belief in the Constitution as the guardian of individual rights and liberties garnered both respect and criticism.

Brennan was born April 25, 1906, in Newark, New Jersey. He was the second of eight children of William Joseph Brennan and Agnes McDermott Brennan, Irish immigrants who settled in Newark in the 1890s. His father worked as a coal shoveler in a brewery and, according to Brennan, was the most influential person in Brennan's life. He was also a labor leader and municipal reformer who imbued Brennan with a profound social conscience and an affinity for activism.

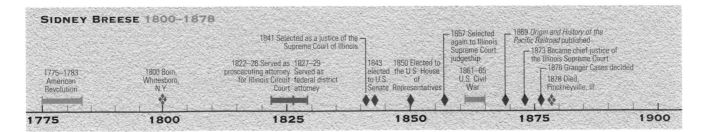

**SIDNEY BREESE 1800–1878**

| 1775–1783 American Revolution | 1800 Born, Whitesboro, N.Y. | 1822–26 Served as prosecuting attorney for Illinois Circuit Court | 1827–29 Served as federal district attorney | 1841 Selected as a justice of the Supreme Court of Illinois | 1843 elected to U.S. Senate | 1850 Elected to the U.S. House of Representatives | 1857 Selected again to Illinois Supreme Court judgeship | 1861–65 U.S. Civil War | 1869 *Origin and History of the Pacific Railroad* published | 1873 Became chief justice of the Illinois Supreme Court | 1876 Granger Cases decided | 1878 Died, Pinckneyville, Ill. |

| 1775 | 1800 | 1825 | 1850 | 1875 | 1900 |

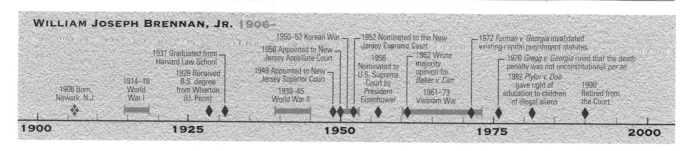

**WILLIAM JOSEPH BRENNAN, JR.** 1906-

- 1906 Born, Newark, N.J.
- 1914-18 World War I
- 1928 Received B.S. degree from Wharton (U. Penn)
- 1931 Graduated from Harvard Law School
- 1939-45 World War II
- 1949 Appointed to New Jersey Superior Court
- 1950 Appointed to New Jersey Appellate Court
- 1950-53 Korean War
- 1952 Nominated to the New Jersey Supreme Court
- 1956 Nominated to U.S. Supreme Court by President Eisenhower
- 1961-73 Vietnam War
- 1962 Wrote majority opinion for *Baker v. Carr*
- 1972 *Furman v. Georgia* invalidated existing capital punishment statutes
- 1976 *Gregg v. Georgia* ruled that the death penalty was not unconstitutional *per se*
- 1982 *Plyler v. Doe* gave right of education to children of illegal aliens
- 1990 Retired from the Court

1900     1925     1950     1975     2000

Brennan received his early education in Newark public schools, and attended the Wharton School of Finance and Commerce, at the University of Pennsylvania, where he received his bachelor of science degree, cum laude, in 1928. He earned a scholarship to Harvard University Law School, where he studied under FELIX FRANKFURTER, who would later be his colleague on the Supreme Court. Brennan graduated near the top of his class in 1931.

He began his legal career in 1932 with the Newark law firm of Pitney, Hardin, and Skinner. The firm later added Brennan as a partner and became Pitney, Hardin, Ward, and Brennan. He specialized in labor law and showed a unique talent for successfully negotiating employer-employee disputes. During World War II, Brennan served in the Army and eventually became the labor branch chief, Civilian Personnel Division of Army Ordnance. He rose to the rank of colonel and was awarded the Legion of Merit for services to the Army and Army Air Forces procurement programs.

After his Army service, Brennan returned to private practice, counseling large manufacturing corporations on labor matters. In 1949, he was tapped by New Jersey's Republican governor to serve on the state's superior court. Assigned to the appellate division, he distinguished himself by implementing reforms that relieved congestion in the court calendar. He was appointed to the New Jersey Supreme Court, and took his seat on March 24, 1952. While there, he helped institute a pretrial conference system that shortened and simplified trials and encouraged settlements, resulting in fewer and speedier trials.

Brennan had served only four years on the New Jersey Supreme Court when, to the surprise of everyone, including Brennan, President DWIGHT D. EISENHOWER nominated him to serve on the U.S. Supreme Court. Eisenhower, a Republican, would later regard his appointment of the liberal Democrat as one of his worst mistakes, along with his earlier appointment of Chief Justice EARL WARREN. Together, Brennan and Warren led the Court into an unprecedented era of judicial activism that was anathema to conservatives like Eisenhower.

**BIOGRAPHY**

*William Joseph Brennan, Jr.*

Brennan quickly established himself as a staunch supporter of the rights and liberties guaranteed by the Constitution. He insisted that the Bill of Rights applies to all U.S. citizens, whether of the lowest or the highest stature. Brennan invited controversy with his view that the Constitution's guarantees must be constantly evolving.

Said Brennan, "The genius of the Constitution rests not in any static meaning it might have had in a world that is dead and gone, but in the adaptability of its great principles to cope with current problems."

Brennan's broad interpretation of the Constitution puts him at odds with more conservative members of the Court who construe the Constitution as narrowly as possible and attempt to ascertain the ORIGINAL INTENT of the drafters. The conservatives believe that if a right or freedom is not clearly conferred by the Constitution or by judicial PRECEDENT, it is not the job of the Court to try to find it there. They place the burden on the individual to show that the right or protection sought exists. Conversely, Brennan and like-minded liberals approach a case by asking whether anything in the Bill of Rights explicitly prevents the Court from finding that the right or protection exists, and they look to the government to prove that the right does not exist. Ironically, when a case involves the use of government power, the opposing groups tend to adopt each other's philosophy: conservatives ask whether anything in the law prevents the exercise of the power, and liberals like Brennan ask whether the power is explicitly allowed by the Constitution or some other statute.

In spite of his single-minded determination to read the Constitution as broadly as possible, Brennan often acted as a mediator between the liberal and conservative wings of the Court. A warm and charming man who is universally well liked, he used his formidable intellectual and technical skills in tandem with his innate diplomacy to build coalitions on some of the most divisive issues of the time. "You cannot dislike this man on a personal level, no matter how destructive he's been to the values you hold dear," declared Charles J. Cooper, assistant attorney general under President Ronald Reagan and an ideological archenemy of Brennan. Brennan is respected by friends and adversaries alike. In fact, although he is a lifelong Democrat, his appointments to the judiciary were recommended by conservative Republicans.

It is impossible to overstate the effect Brennan had on the law of the land from 1960 to 1990. He was the architect of pivotal decisions that shaped U.S. life during those years, including *Eisenstadt v. Baird*, 405 U.S. 438, 92 S. Ct. 1029, 31 L. Ed. 2d 349, a 1972 decision that struck down a law prohibiting the distribution of contraceptives to unmarried women. Brennan recognized a constitutional "right to privacy" protecting "the decision whether to bear or beget a child." His reasoning in *Eisenstadt* became the foundation for *Roe v. Wade*, 410 U.S. 113, 93 S. Ct. 705, 35 L. Ed. 2d 147, the 1973 decision that removed many barriers to legal ABORTIONS.

Early in his career Brennan wrote the majority opinion in *Baker v. Carr*, 369 U.S. 186, 82 S. Ct. 691, 7 L. Ed. 2d 663 (1962), which allowed federal courts to hear challenges to legislative APPORTIONMENT and paved the way for later Supreme Court cases establishing the concept of "ONE PERSON, ONE VOTE." In *New York Times v. Sullivan*, 376 U.S. 254, 84 S. Ct. 710, 11 L. Ed. 2d 686 (1964), Brennan wrote that the FIRST AMENDMENT protects the press from LIBEL suits brought by public officials, unless actual malice is proved. He extended the FIFTH AMENDMENT right against SELF-INCRIMINATION to prohibit mandatory registration of Communist party members, in *Albertson v. Subversive Activities Control Board* (382 U.S. 70, 86 S. Ct. 194, 15 L. Ed. 2d 165 [1965]). He found that the Constitution prohibits unequal treatment based on race, age, or gender, in a number of decisions, including *In re Winship* (establishing use of the "REASONABLE DOUBT" standard for juveniles); *Frontiero v. Richardson* (extending constitutional scrutiny to gender-based classifications); and *Craig v. Boren* (declaring that gender-based classifications are unconstitutional unless they are substantially related to the achievement of an important government objective) (*In re Winship*, 397 U.S. 358, 90 S. Ct. 1068, 25 L. Ed. 2d 368 [1970]; *Frontiero v. Richardson*, 411 U.S. 677, 93 S. Ct. 1764, 36 L. Ed. 2d 583 [1973]; and *Craig v. Boren*, 429 U.S. 190, 97 S. Ct. 451, 50 L. Ed. 2d 397 [1976]).

Brennan is a strong believer in AFFIRMATIVE ACTION to remedy past DISCRIMINATION, and he wrote numerous opinions on the subject. In *United States v. Weber Aircraft Corp.*, 465 U.S. 792, 104 S. Ct. 1488, 79 L. Ed. 2d 814 (1984),

"LAW CANNOT STAND APART FROM THE SOCIAL CHANGES AROUND IT."

the Court held that it is lawful for employers to adopt voluntary affirmative action programs that are race conscious. Brennan wrote the opinion that upheld limited preferential treatment on the job for women and minorities, in *Johnson v. Transportation Agency of Santa Clara County*, 480 U.S. 616, 107 S. Ct. 1442, 94 L. Ed. 2d 615 (1987), and found in *United States v. Paradise*, 480 U.S. 149, 107 S. Ct. 1053, 94 L. Ed. 2d 203 (1987), that a one-black-for-one-white promotions quota did not violate the Constitution. Finally, in one of his last opinions on affirmative action, Brennan wrote that the Constitution permits preferential treatment of minorities in the awarding of FCC broadcast licenses (*Metro Broadcasting v. FCC*, 497 U.S. 547, 110 S. Ct. 2997, 111 L. Ed. 2d 445 [1990]).

Brennan is an adamant defender of free expression even for the most reprehensible words or acts. In *Texas v. Johnson* (491 U.S. 397, 109 S. Ct. 2533, 105 L. Ed. 2d 342 [1989]) and in *United States v. Eichman* (496 U.S. 310, 110 S. Ct. 2404, 110 L. Ed. 2d 287 [1990]), he wrote opinions invalidating statutes that banned FLAG desecration, on the grounds that they violated the First Amendment. Although recognizing the "special place reserved for the flag in this Nation," he stated, "we do not consecrate the flag by punishing its desecration, for in doing so we dilute the freedom that this cherished emblem represents" (*Johnson*).

He is also an ardent defender of the rights of children, declaring that we must teach young people "that our Constitution is a living reality, not parchment preserved under glass." He was appalled by cases in which the Court seemed to hold that the Bill of Rights does not apply to schoolchildren, and wrote in one dissent that the majority's decision had given school officials the license to act as "thought police" and taught the students "to discount important principles of our government as mere platitudes" (*Hazelwood School Dist. v. Kuhlmeier*, 484 U.S. 260, 285, 290, 108 S. Ct. 562, 577, 580, 98 L. Ed. 2d 592 [1988]).

Brennan earned the highest praise as well as the harshest criticism from his opinions in cases involving the rights of the accused. He steadfastly opposed the use of CAPITAL PUNISHMENT, labeling it state-sanctioned killing, and in one of his final decisions on the Court, he voted against an execution by the state of Virginia. Taking human life, he has said, "is God's work, not man's." When that statement was dismissed as mere sentimentality, he replied, "The most vile murder does not, in my view, release the state from constitutional restraints on the destruction of human dignity. . . . The fatal constitutional infirmity of capital punishment is that it treats members of the human race as nonhuman, as objects to be toyed with and discarded." Brennan's critics point out that his opposition to the death penalty does not seem in harmony with his support of women's right to abortion, which some consider "state-sanctioned killing."

Brennan passionately defends the protections afforded by the Fourth Amendment's prohibition of unreasonable SEARCHES AND SEIZURES. His interpretation of the amendment helped establish the EXCLUSIONARY RULE, which holds that any evidence obtained illegally is tainted and cannot be used against the accused. During the 1980s, the Supreme Court recognized a growing number of exceptions to the rule, prompting Brennan to redouble his efforts to bolster its strength. His advocacy of the rights of criminal defendants brought him sharp criticism, particularly from the media, which often portrayed him as a libertarian who supported the rights of criminals while ignoring those of victims. In a radio interview in 1987, Brennan became uncharacteristically agitated when asked, "Why do you let some of those creeps go? They do such bad things, and on a technicality, you let them go." Brennan replied sharply,

> You and the media ought to be ashamed of yourself to call the provisions and the guarantees of the Bill of Rights technicalities. They're not. We are what we are *because* we have those guarantees, and this Court exists to see that they are faithfully enforced. These guarantees have to be sustained—even though the immediate result is to help out some very unpleasant person. They're there to protect all of us.

Citing advancing age and health concerns, Brennan retired from the Court in July 1990, after thirty-four years as an associate justice. He was replaced by Associate Justice David H. Souter. Although he eventually slowed his pace considerably, he continued to be sought as a speaker and used every opportunity to carry on his campaign for individual rights and liberties.

**BIOGRAPHY**

*David Josiah Brewer*

"YOU CANNOT DISASSOCIATE THE CHARACTER OF THE NATION AND THAT OF ITS CITIZENS."

**CROSS-REFERENCES**
*Baker v. Carr*; Freedom of Speech; Freedom of the Press; Judicial Review; Warren Court

**BREWER, DAVID JOSIAH** David Josiah Brewer was an associate justice of the Supreme Court from 1890 to 1910. A defender of personal liberty and property rights, he also supported STATES' RIGHTS and was opposed to centralization of power in the federal government.

Brewer was born June 20, 1837, in Smyrna, Asia Minor (now Turkey). His father, Josiah Brewer, was a Yale graduate who worked in Turkey as a missionary. His mother, Emilia Field, was the sister of Supreme Court justice STEPHEN J. FIELD, with whom Brewer eventually served. After returning to the United States from their missionary work, the Brewers settled in Wethersfield, Connecticut. Brewer attended Wesleyan University for two years before transferring to Yale, where he graduated with honors in 1856. He studied law for a year with an uncle and then enrolled in Albany Law School. He received his law degree in 1858 and was admitted to the New York bar the same year.

Brewer decided to stake his future on the frontier West. He settled in Leavenworth, Kansas, and almost immediately began his long judicial career. He was appointed commissioner of the U.S. Circuit Court for the District of Kansas in 1861 and was elected judge of the probate and criminal courts of Leavenworth County in 1862. Brewer served as a judge of the first judicial district of Kansas from 1865 to 1869. He briefly left the judiciary in 1869 to become Leavenworth's city attorney, but returned in 1870 when, at the age of thirty-three, he was elected to the Kansas Supreme Court. He sat on the Kansas bench until 1884 when President CHESTER ARTHUR named him to the federal circuit court for the eighth circuit. Five years later, President WILLIAM H. HARRISON appointed him to the U.S. Supreme Court, where he remained until his death.

As a Supreme Court justice, Brewer was known for his ardent support of individual rights against the tyranny of the majority. "Here there is no monarch threatening trespass

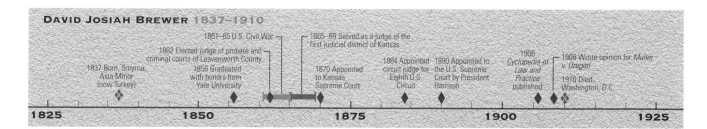

DAVID JOSIAH BREWER 1837–1910

1837 Born, Smyrna, Asia Minor (now Turkey)

1856 Graduated with honors from Yale University

1861–65 U.S. Civil War

1862 Elected judge of probate and criminal courts of Leavenworth County

1865–69 Served as a judge of the first judicial district of Kansas

1870 Appointed to Kansas Supreme Court

1884 Appointed circuit judge for the Eighth U.S. Circuit

1890 Appointed to the U.S. Supreme Court by President Harrison

1906 *Cyclopedia of Law and Practice* published

1908 Wrote opinion for *Muller v. Oregon*

1910 Died, Washington, D.C.

1825　1850　1875　1900　1925

upon an individual," he once said. "The danger is from the multitude—the majority with whom lies the power." Brewer had great compassion for the marginalized members of U.S. society. In 1908, he wrote the opinion for a unanimous Court in *Muller v. Oregon*, 208 U.S. 412, 28 S. Ct. 324, 52 L. Ed. 551, upholding a statute that established maximum work hours for women toiling in laundries. Although he had in 1905 voted to invalidate a similar statute that applied to bakers, in *Lochner v. New York* (198 U.S. 45, 25 S. Ct. 539, 49 L. Ed. 937 [1905]), Brewer was convinced that the particular statute at issue in *Muller* did not unnecessarily limit an individual's contract liberty.

Brewer also wrote strong dissents in several cases limiting the rights of Chinese and Japanese immigrants (see *Fong v. United States*, 149 U.S. 698, 13 S. Ct. 1016, 37 L. Ed. 905 [1893]; *United States v. Sing Tuck*, 194 U.S. 161, 24 S. Ct. 621, 48 L. Ed. 917 [1904]; *United States v. Ju Toy*, 198 U.S. 253, 25 S. Ct. 644, 49 L. Ed. 1040 [1905]; the *Japanese Immigrant* case, 189 U.S. 86, 23 S. Ct. 611, 47 L. Ed. 721 [1903]). His dissent in *Fong*, in which the Court found that the power of Congress to deport ALIENS was inherent in national sovereignty, included this sarcastic indictment of what he considered Congress's arbitrary denial of plaintiffs' rights: "In view of this enactment of the highest legislative body of the foremost Christian nation, may not the thoughtful Chinese disciple of Confucius ask, Why do they send missionaries here?"

Brewer was, in most cases, a moderate conservative. He spoke out against racial DISFRANCHISEMENT in *Giles v. Harris*, 189 U.S. 475, 23 S. Ct. 639, 47 L. Ed. 909 (1903). However, reflecting his belief in states' rights, he held that a state had the right to prohibit integration in an institution it had created (*Berea College v. Kentucky*, 211 U.S. 45, 29 S. Ct. 33, 53 L. Ed. 81 [1908]) and that the federal government lacked power to prosecute a case of racially motivated harassment (*Hodges v. United States*, 203 U.S. 1, 27 S. Ct. 6, 51 L. Ed. 65 [1906]). A lifelong

advocate of international peace, Brewer served as president of a congressional commission investigating a border dispute between Venezuela and British Guyana, and later served on the tribunal that ended the controversy. Brewer advocated women's suffrage and restrictions on immigration. He was a vigorous anti-imperialist who believed that the Philippines should be given independence with guaranteed neutrality.

Brewer was an unusually outgoing justice who lectured frequently and wrote several books, including *The Pew to the Pulpit*, *The Twentieth Century from Another Viewpoint*, *American Citizenship*, and *The United States: A Christian Nation*. He felt strongly that judges have a moral obligation to use their lofty position to lead rather than simply observe. "It is one thing," he once said, "to fail of reaching your ideal. It is an entirely different thing to deliberately turn your back on it."

Brewer died in Washington, D.C., on March 28, 1910.

See also LOCHNER V. NEW YORK.

**BREYER, STEPHEN GERALD** As an Associate Justice of the U.S. Supreme Court, Stephen Breyer is regarded as a judicial moderate. The author, former law professor, and Senate counsel locates his approach to the law in a deep pragmatism: he distrusts broad legal theory, endorses judicial restraint, and wants his legal opinions to be clear enough for a high school student to read. His reputation for forging consensus earned him a nomination to the U.S. Court of Appeals for the First Circuit in 1980, on which he later served as chief of the court from 1990 to 1994. During the 1980s he also helped shape a far-reaching and controversial revision of criminal sentencing guidelines. In April 1994 President BILL CLINTON nominated Breyer to replace the outgoing Supreme Court Associate Justice HARRY A. BLACKMUN, and his appointment was confirmed in July 1994.

Breyer was born on August 15, 1938, in San Francisco. His attorney father and politically active mother set him on a course for achieve-

**BIOGRAPHY**

U.S. SUPREME COURT

*Stephen Gerald Breyer*

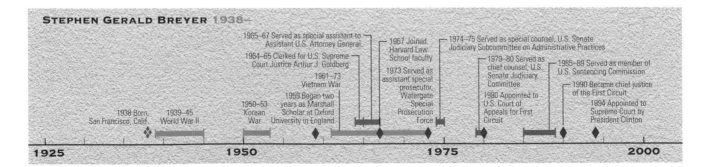

STEPHEN GERALD BREYER 1938–

1938 Born, San Francisco, Calif.

1939–45 World War II

1950–53 Korean War

1959 Began two years as Marshall Scholar at Oxford University in England

1961–73 Vietnam War

1964–65 Clerked for U.S. Supreme Court Justice Arthur J. Goldberg

1965–67 Served as special assistant to Assistant U.S. Attorney General

1967 Joined Harvard Law School faculty

1973 Served as assistant special prosecutor, Watergate Special Prosecution Force

1974–75 Served as special counsel, U.S. Senate Judiciary Subcommittee on Administrative Practices

1979–80 Served as chief counsel, U.S. Senate Judiciary Committee

1980 Appointed to U.S. Court of Appeals for First Circuit

1985–89 Served as member of U.S. Sentencing Commission

1990 Became chief justice of the First Circuit

1994 Appointed to Supreme Court by President Clinton

1925    1950    1975    2000

ment. He earned an A.B. from Stanford University in 1959, followed by a B.A. in philosophy and economics at Oxford University in England. He added a law degree from Harvard Law School in 1964, graduating magna cum laude. Breyer clerked for Supreme Court Justice Arthur J. Goldberg III from 1965 to 1967 and helped write the justice's opinion in the landmark right-to-privacy case, *Griswold v. Connecticut*, 381 U.S. 479, 85 S. Ct. 1678, 14 L. Ed. 2d 510 (1965).

In 1967 Breyer embarked on dual careers in academia and government. He taught courses in antitrust, administrative law, and economic regulation at his alma mater, Harvard Law School. In the same year he was appointed to the office of the Assistant U.S. Attorney General. He gained further prominence in 1974 by serving on the Watergate Special Prosecution Force, which pursued the possibility of impeaching President Richard M. Nixon. As a senior aide to Senator Edward M. Kennedy (D-Mass.) in the 1970s and chief counsel to the Senate Judiciary Committee from 1979 to 1980, Breyer crafted deregulation of the airline and trucking industries while also working on prison reform, judicial confirmations, and fair housing law. He became known for an empirical approach to law, one less swayed by ideology than by careful balancing of facts.

By 1980 Breyer was well-respected by liberals, moderates, and conservatives. Although he had been an aide to the liberal Senator Kennedy, he was adept at promoting agreement between such political opposites as Kennedy and Senator Orrin G. Hatch (R-Utah). This record served Breyer well when President Jimmy Carter nominated him to the U.S. Court of Appeals for the First Circuit. After Carter lost the 1980 election to Ronald Reagan, the Republicans, as is common in an incoming administration, scrapped all but one of Carter's pending judicial appointments. Breyer's appointment was allowed to go through.

Breyer's record on the Court of Appeals was generally moderate. In a 1983 environmental regulatory case, he blocked the Department of the Interior from auctioning oil drilling rights in the North Atlantic without giving ample consideration to alternative proposals (*Commonwealth of Massachusetts v. Watt*, 716 F.2d 946 [1st Cir. 1983]). In the area of ABORTION, he voted to uphold a Massachusetts parental notification law (*Planned Parenthood of Massachusetts v. Bellotti*, 868 F.2d 459 [1st Cir. 1983]). But he joined the majority on the First Circuit in striking down the Bush administration's ban on abortion counseling at family planning clinics

funded by the federal government (*Commonwealth of Massachusetts v. Secretary of Health and Human Services*, 899 F.2d 53 [1st Cir. 1990]).

Appointed to the U.S. Sentencing Commission in 1985, Breyer undertook the job of revising criminal sentencing guidelines. Against strong opposition he persuaded the other seven judges on the panel to base the guidelines on national averages. The changes, which took effect in 1987, have proven controversial. Critics charge that they have too tightly bound judges and produced inequitable results for minority defendants. In response, Breyer has argued that the guidelines have built-in flexibility that allows judges to influence the Sentencing Commission in future revisions.

President Clinton sought Breyer twice for appointment to the Supreme Court. Although close to choosing him in 1993, Clinton instead selected Ruth Bader Ginsburg after Breyer became the target of criticism for late payments on Social Security taxes for a part-time housekeeper. When a second vacancy on the Court opened in 1994, Clinton returned to Breyer. The president compared his intellectual vigor to that of Judge Learned Hand, the renowned appellate judge of the 1920s and 1930s. Minor opposition met the nomination. Critics questioned whether Breyer's 1993 book *Breaking the Vicious Circle: Toward Effective Risk Regulation* went too far in attacking government regulation; others raised doubts about his investment judgment in losing money in the early 1990s in the Lloyd's of London scandal, Britain's largest insurance disaster ever. At the same time, however, he received praise for his past achievements and for a strong commitment to First Amendment rights. The Senate easily confirmed his appointment on July 29, 1994, by a vote of 87–9.

After two years on the Court, Breyer had aligned himself with the Court's moderates. He dissented when the majority struck down a 1990 federal law prohibiting the carrying of handguns outside schools, arguing that protecting schools should fall under Congress's power to regulate interstate commerce (*U.S. v. Lopez*, 115 S. Ct. 1624, 131 L. Ed. 2d 626 [1995]). He also dissented from the Court's ruling in *Tribe of Florida v. Florida* (116 S. Ct. 1114, 134 L. Ed. 2d 252 [1996]), which struck down the 1988 Indian Gaming Regulatory Act for violating STATES' RIGHTS. In a major victory for GAY AND LESBIAN RIGHTS, Breyer joined the majority in overturning Colorado's Amendment 2, which would have removed all legal protection for homosexuals against discrimination (*Romer v. Evans*, 116 S. Ct. 1620, 134 L. Ed. 2d 855

"AS AN APPELLATE JUDGE, I SET . . . A GOAL OF TRYING TO WRITE MY OPINIONS SO THAT A HIGH SCHOOL STUDENT . . . [CAN] UNDERSTAND THE LAW, AS REVEALED IN THAT OPINION—BOTH IN TERMS OF BASIC FAIRNESS AND IN TERMS OF HELPING PEOPLE LEAD DECENT, PRODUCTIVE LIVES."

[1996]). And in a significant First Amendment decision, Breyer wrote the plurality opinion declaring that the government may not require cable TV operators to segregate and block leased access channels that feature offensive or indecent programming (*Denver Area Consortium v. Federal Communications Commission*, 116 S. Ct. 2374 [1996]).

**BRIBERY** 📖 The offering, giving, receiving, or soliciting of something of value for the purpose of influencing the action of an official in the discharge of his or her public or legal duties. 📖

The expectation of a particular voluntary action in return is what makes the difference between a bribe and a private demonstration of goodwill. To offer or provide payment in order to persuade someone with a responsibility to betray that responsibility is known as seeking UNDUE INFLUENCE over that person's actions. When someone with power seeks payment in exchange for certain actions, that person is said to be *peddling influence*. Regardless of who initiates the deal, either party to an act of bribery can be found guilty of the crime independently of the other.

A bribe can consist of immediate cash or of personal favors, a promise of later payment, or anything else the recipient views as valuable. When the U.S. military threatened to cancel a Texas relocation company's contracts to move families to and from military bases, the company allegedly gave four representatives in Congress an all-expenses-paid weekend in Las Vegas in January 1989 and $2,500 in speaking fees. The former president of the company was indicted by a federal GRAND JURY in 1994 on bribery charges for both gifts.

No written agreement is necessary to prove the crime of bribery, but usually a prosecutor must show corrupt INTENT. Bribery charges may involve public officials or private individuals. In the world of professional sports, for example, one boxer might offer another a payoff to "throw" (deliberately lose) an important fight. In the corporate arena, a company could bribe employees of a rival company for recruitment services or other actions at odds with their employer's interests. Even when public officials are involved, a bribe does not need to be harmful to the PUBLIC INTEREST in order to be illegal.

When a public official accepts a bribe, he or she creates a CONFLICT OF INTEREST. That is, the official cannot accommodate the interests of another party without compromising the responsibilities of her or his position.

There is not always consensus over what counts as a bribe. For instance, in many states and at the federal level, certain GIFTS and campaign contributions are not considered bribes and do not draw prosecution unless they can be linked to evidence of undue influence. In this regard, negative public perception of private contributions to elected officials as payola has caused most states to establish legislative ethics committees to review the public-private relationships of house and senate members. Furthermore, both houses of the U.S. Congress passed legislation in 1994 restricting gifts to no more than $20 in value.

It is common for both the recipient and the provider of a bribe to be accused, although bribery is not a joint offense—that is, one person's guilt does not affect the other's. Such was the case when a popular Massachusetts state senator allegedly accepted monthly payments from an investment broker in exchange for trying to persuade state officials to send state pension business to the broker. The legislator and the broker were both indicted on MISDEMEANOR charges in early 1995.

U.S. companies that engage in international bribery can become targets of investigation at home. In January 1995, a former sales director of Lockheed Corporation pleaded guilty to violating the federal Foreign Corrupt Practices Act. Allen R. Love told a U.S. district court that he had paid and helped to cover up a bribe to an Egyptian politician for arranging Egypt's 1989 purchase of three Lockheed transport planes.

Congress adopted the Foreign Corrupt Practices Act in 1977 to outlaw payments that are intended to win contracts from foreign officials. Ironically, the law's passage was triggered by testimony from a former vice president of the same Lockheed Corporation at a U.S. congressional hearing in 1976. In that case, the company's vice president admitted to bribing the prime minister of Japan with more than $1.9 million in the early 1970s, so that Japan would buy Lockheed's TriStar wide-body jets.

The severity of bribery can reach the FELONY level, punishable by a fine or imprisonment, or both. However, charges are sometimes reduced in exchange for helping to convict ACCOMPLICES. For instance, in June 1994, Love pleaded innocent to felony charges of bribery and CONSPIRACY. Later, he pleaded guilty to one misdemeanor count of "indirectly" conspiring, as part of a plea agreement in which he agreed to TESTIFY against the corporation itself, which was also a defendant.

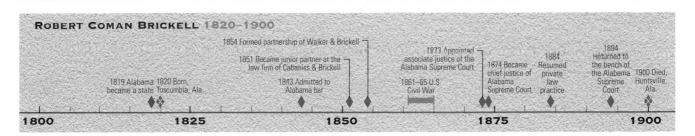

ROBERT COMAN BRICKELL 1820–1900

1854 Formed partnership of Walker & Brickell

1851 Became junior partner at the
law firm of Cabaniss & Brickell

1873 Appointed
associate justice of the
Alabama Supreme Court

1874 Became
chief justice of
Alabama
Supreme Court

1884
Resumed
private
law
practice

1894
Returned to
the bench of
the Alabama
Supreme
Court

1819 Alabama 1820 Born,
became a state Tuscumbia, Ala.

1843 Admitted to
Alabama bar

1861–65 U.S.
Civil War

1900 Died,
Huntsville,
Ala.

1800          1825          1850          1875          1900

## BRICKELL, ROBERT COMAN

Robert Coman Brickell was born April 4, 1824, in Tuscumbia, Alabama. He was admitted to the bar in 1843, began his law practice in Huntsville, Alabama, in 1851, and soon became a respected name in the legal system of that state. He gained a reputation as a supporter of STATES' RIGHTS and believed in SECESSION from the Union prior to the onset of the Civil War.

In 1873, Brickell served as associate justice of the Supreme Court of Alabama. He was selected to act as chief justice of the Alabama Supreme Court in 1874, an appointment he again accepted in 1880. He held this office until 1884.

*Robert Coman
Brickell*

Brickell resumed his law practice in Alabama in 1884 but in 1894 returned to the bench of the Alabama Supreme Court. He died November 20, 1900, in Huntsville.

## BRIDGES

Structures constructed over obstructions to HIGHWAYS or waterways, such as CANALS or rivers, in order to provide continuous and convenient passages for purposes of transportation.

A bridge includes the necessary abutments and approaches that make it accessible. A public bridge that spans obstructions to a public highway is built on land owned by the state government for public use, while a private bridge is built on private property for the use of particular individuals who own it.

## Ten Longest Bridges in the World

As measured by length of span between two center support towers; length does not include approach spans.

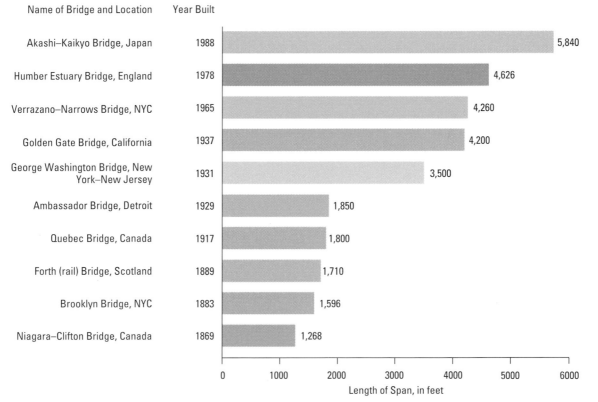

| Name of Bridge and Location | Year Built | Length of Span, in feet |
|---|---|---|
| Akashi–Kaikyo Bridge, Japan | 1988 | 5,840 |
| Humber Estuary Bridge, England | 1978 | 4,626 |
| Verrazano–Narrows Bridge, NYC | 1965 | 4,260 |
| Golden Gate Bridge, California | 1937 | 4,200 |
| George Washington Bridge, New York–New Jersey | 1931 | 3,500 |
| Ambassador Bridge, Detroit | 1929 | 1,850 |
| Quebec Bridge, Canada | 1917 | 1,800 |
| Forth (rail) Bridge, Scotland | 1889 | 1,710 |
| Brooklyn Bridge, NYC | 1883 | 1,596 |
| Niagara–Clifton Bridge, Canada | 1869 | 1,268 |

Source: *Guiness Book of World Records*, 1996 edition.

The construction of public bridges is a function of the state government by virtue of statute and is limited only by contractual or constitutional provisions. A state may exercise its power directly or delegate it to governmental agencies, such as a state highway commission. Cities and municipalities may erect bridges within their borders if authorized to do so by the state legislature. If a bridge is to be built within the borders of a state, the state has control of the project; but if the bridge connects two states, both states share involvement in the venture but must yield to the power of the federal government to supervise matters that have an effect on interstate commerce.

The state determines the location of a bridge subject to public safety and convenience considerations. It may grant a FRANCHISE—special privilege—to erect the bridge to a private bridge company that is chartered to build and maintain bridges. Such a corporation is considered a BUSINESS AFFECTED WITH A PUBLIC INTEREST. A state agency may be organized to receive a franchise to construct a bridge.

The money needed to finance the construction of a bridge is usually raised by appropriations designed for the project—the sale of BONDS pursuant to statute, special assessments, or taxation. The legislature decides whether construction expenses will be borne by the entire state or apportioned among its various subdivisions. It may create special taxing districts to finance the project as long as the district receives a proportional benefit from the bridge. State taxes cannot be used to defray the expense of purely local bridge obligations.

A reasonable TOLL may be charged for using the bridge when authorized by statute. The revenue collected can be used for governmental purposes as well as for the operating and maintenance expenses of the bridge.

The duty to maintain and repair bridges rests with the government agency or private company charged with their operation and maintenance. Statutes frequently require warning signs on guardrails and bridge approaches to caution drivers against known dangers. Civil or criminal LIABILITY may be imposed for DAMAGES resulting from the failure to maintain a bridge properly. No liability exists, however, for any damages incurred by an adjoining landowner from NEGLIGENCE or other wrongful conduct in the construction or maintenance of a bridge by a municipality or government agency unless provided by statute. A private company may be liable, however, if the law in the jurisdiction so provides.

**BRIEF** ◻ A summary of the important points of a longer document. An ABSTRACT of a published judicial opinion prepared by a law student as part of an assignment in the CASE METHOD study of law. A written document drawn up by an attorney for a PARTY in a lawsuit or by a party himself or herself appearing PRO SE that concisely states the (1) issues of a lawsuit; (2) facts that bring the parties to court; (3) relevant laws that can affect the subject of the dispute; and (4) arguments that explain how the law applies to the particular facts so that the case will be decided in the party's favor. ◻

A brief may also contain a synopsis of the EVIDENCE and name the WITNESSES to be presented during the TRIAL. Copies of briefs must be submitted to the court where the case will be heard and to the opposing party.

An appellate brief is a writing that must be filed with an APPELLATE COURT so that it may evaluate whether the decision of the lower court should be reversed because of some error or impropriety that occurred during the trial. A statement of the issues presented for review, a summary of how pertinent laws affect the facts, and a statement of the relief being requested are essential elements of an appellate brief. The APPELLEE's brief will argue that the lower court acted properly in its judgment and request its AFFIRMANCE, while the APPELLANT's brief will attempt to convince the court to REVERSE or VACATE the lower court's judgment because it acted improperly.

See *Milestones in the Law* section.

**BRIGGS, HERBERT W.** Herbert W. Briggs was a prominent figure in the field of INTERNATIONAL LAW where he made important contributions as a scholar and educator and served on the United Nations International Law Commission.

Born in Wilmington, Delaware, in 1900, Briggs was one of a small group of American international lawyers in the twentieth century who did not hold a law degree. He received an A.B. from West Virginia University in Morgantown, West Virginia, in 1921 and a Ph.D. from Johns Hopkins University in Baltimore, Maryland, in 1925. Over the next four years, he studied international law in Brussels, Belgium, and at the Hague Academy of International Law; served as a research associate at the Foreign Policy Association; and taught at Oberlin College in Oberlin, Ohio, and Johns Hopkins. In 1929, he joined the faculty at Cornell University in Ithaca, New York, where he remained until his retirement in 1969. At Cornell, Briggs taught international law, international organiza-

**BIOGRAPHY**

*Herbert W. Briggs*

HERBERT W. BRIGGS 1900–1990

| | | | | | |
|---|---|---|---|---|---|
| 1900 Born, Wilmington, Del. | 1914–18 World War I | 1921 Received A.B. from West Virginia University | 1945 United Nations founded | 1955–67 Served as editor-in-chief of *American Journal of International Law* | 1962–66 Served as member of United Nations International Law Commission |

1938 *The Law of Nations: Cases, Documents and Notes* published

1939–45 World War II

1950–53 Korean War

1968 Named to U.S. delegation to Vienna conference on the Law of Treaties

1969 Retired; became professor emeritus of international law

1959–75 Vietnam War

1990 Died, Ithaca, N.Y.

1900        1925        1950        1975        2000

tion, and international politics as a member of both the Department of Government and the law faculty.

Briggs had a distinguished career as a scholar and editor. His best-known work was *The Law of Nations: Cases, Documents and Notes* (first published in 1938), which became a standard text in international law courses throughout the country. In addition, he was the author of *The Doctrine of Continuous Voyage* (1926), *The International Law Commission* (1965), two sets of lectures at the Hague Academy, and more than eighty articles on international law topics. Throughout most of his career, Briggs was closely associated with the *American Journal of International Law*, serving on the journal's board of editors from 1939 until his death and as editor in chief from 1955 to 1962. He was president of the American Society of International Law in 1959 and 1960.

In addition to his work as an educator and scholar, Briggs also had an active career as an international lawyer. From 1962 to 1966, he was a member of the United Nations International Law Commission. In 1968, he was named to the U.S. delegation to the Vienna Conference on the Law of Treaties. In addition, he served as counsel for Honduras, Spain, and Libya in four cases before the International Court of Justice. He also served as counsel for Canada and Chile in international arbitral proceedings. In 1975, he was one of five persons appointed by the governments of Great Britain and France to serve as a court of arbitration to delimit a portion of the continental shelf in the English Channel. Commenting on Brigg's career, Judge Stephen M. Schwebel of the International Court of Justice said that in all these activities "he was very much the advocate and architect of a more effective international law."

Briggs died January 6, 1990, in Ithaca.

**BRING SUIT** To initiate legal proceedings; to start an ACTION for judicial RELIEF.

Under federal and most state law, a suit is commenced upon the filing of the first paper, which is the COMPLAINT, with the court. STAT-

"THE OPINION THAT 'POLITICAL' TREATIES SHOULD NOT BE SUBJECT TO RIGID JUDICIAL ANALYSIS RESTS UPON MISCONCEPTION AND IS BELIED BY PRACTICE."

UTES OF LIMITATIONS set forth time boundaries within which an action must be brought.

**BROADCASTING** In 1898 Guglielmo Marconi, a twenty-four-year-old Italian, began the world's first commercial radio service. For citizens of the United States, radio—and later television—not only introduced an abundance of entertainment and information, it also raised many legal questions surrounding its implementation and regulation. In radio's earliest days, stations all broadcast at the same frequency; this posed problems because although some stations agreed to share their time, others attempted to broadcast stronger signals over those of their competitors. Problems continued even when stations began to broadcast on separate frequencies. Because broadcasting requires use of the airwaves for the transmission of its signals, and because the airwaves can carry only a limited number of signals, it soon became apparent that some form of regulation was necessary. In 1927, the Radio Act (47 U.S.C.A § 81 et seq.) became law and the Federal Radio Commission (FRC) was created to police the broadcasting industry. Two important tenets of broadcasting were introduced by the law. The first was that stations must broadcast "in the public interest, convenience, or necessity." The second was that the people, not the radio stations, owned the airwaves. In its efforts to see that the airwaves were used in the appropriate manner, government regulation faced obstacles as it attempted to ensure suitable government-funded programming, appropriate programming for children, and equal access to broadcasting for minorities. Additional challenges were created by changing technology as cable television went underground and satellite television took to outer space.

**The History of Radio** In its infancy, broadcasting was much less controversial. Experimental radio broadcasting began in 1910 when Lee De Forest produced a program from the Metropolitan Opera House in New York City. Other experimental radio stations were started at the University of Wisconsin in Madi-

*Carl Menzer was the radio announcer for this 1926 football game in Iowa City. From the mid-1920s to 1950 radio was a major source of entertainment.*

son in 1915 and another in Wilkinsburg, a suburban of Pittsburgh, in 1916.

Detroit radio station WWJ is considered the first commercial radio station in the United States. It began broadcasting on August 20, 1920. Pittsburgh station KDKA grew out of the Wilkinsburg experimental station. Its broadcast of the 1920 presidential election results on November 2, 1920, is generally considered to be the beginning of professional broadcasting. Although fewer than one thousand receivers were tuned in, the excitement of the event created great publicity.

Stations soon started appearing in all parts of the United States. By the end of 1924, 583 radio stations were transmitting and more than 3 million receivers were tuned in. These stations transmitted radio signals using amplitude modulation, the abbreviation of the term becoming the general category AM radio. AM broadcasts can be received at great distances because the radio transmissions bounce off the atmosphere and reach beyond the curve of the earth. However, AM signals are affected by static, thus reducing sound fidelity.

Radio established itself as a national medium with the creation of the first radio network in 1926. In that year the National Broadcasting Company (NBC), led by David Sarnoff, head of its parent company, Radio Corporation of America, presented its first national broadcast. Radio stations around the country entered into

contracts with NBC that allowed them to receive an audio feed through a telephone line, which was then broadcast by the station's radio transmitter. Apart from creating a national radio audience, NBC also introduced the financial cornerstone of commercial radio: networks and local stations would support themselves by selling advertising time. The success of NBC led to the creation of the Columbia Broadcasting System (CBS), led by William Paley.

The success of radio produced problems as well. There was competition for frequencies and increased transmission power. The strongest AM stations have a power of fifty thousand watts. At this strength, a station can be heard at night up to one thousand miles away. The least powerful AM stations operate at 250 watts, which usually limits their range to one or two towns. Unregulated growth of the radio industry led in 1934 to the passage of the Communications Act (40 U.S.C.A. § 791). This act created the Federal Communications Commission (FCC), replacing the FRC. The FCC began regulating broadcasting content. In the 1930s it banned the advertisement of hard liquor and lotteries over the air.

The period from 1925 to 1950 has been called the "Golden Age of Radio." During this period radio was a major source of family entertainment. Every night families would gather around the radio and listen to news, music, comedies, and adventure dramas. Serialized stories aimed mainly at women, dubbed "soap operas," became popular. They were called soap operas because they were initially sponsored by soap companies. President Franklin Roosevelt became the first president to understand the power of radio. He regularly conducted "fireside chats" over the radio between 1933 and 1945. These informal talks helped Roosevelt gain support for his policies.

The importance of radio as a national medium was reinforced during World War II. Edward R. Murrow became a national figure when he broadcast from London during the early years of the war. Following the United States's entrance into the war in December 1941, millions of Americans turned to the radio every day to hear the latest war news.

The popularity of radio continued into the late 1940s until the beginning of television signaled radio's rapid demise as the major source of home entertainment. The popularity of television was so great and so sudden that the FCC had to put a temporary freeze on the granting of licenses, as the number of available broadcast channels was limited. As soon as the freeze was lifted, radio began to lose advertisers to the new medium. Network radio was all but dead by the early 1950s because all of its greatest stars had moved their programs to television. NBC and CBS quickly shifted their focus to the creation of television networks.

Faced with this sudden change, AM radio developed new formats. Music stations began to specialize in top forty popular music, country music, and rhythm and blues music. By the 1990s, talk radio had become a popular and profitable format, making national celebrities of political commentator Rush Limbaugh and "shock jocks" Howard Stern and Don Imus. Stern and Imus received the shock jock designation by their raunchy and outrageous behavior on the air.

Radio broadcasting experienced new growth in the 1960s and 1970s with the licensing of many FM radio stations. FM stations transmit radio signals by frequency modulation, hence the term FM. FM waves do not travel as far as AM waves, but FM waves are not affected by static as much as AM waves. In addition, FM signals produce a much truer reproduction of sound. Since the late 1960s FM stations have had the ability of broadcasting in stereo. This development was a factor in the growth of the popularity of FM stations. Music from records and compact disks can be transmitted in high fidelity.

Despite the dominance of television, radio continues to play a major role in broadcasting.

More than ten thousand radio stations were broadcasting in the United States in 1995.

The FCC continues to serve numerous roles in the radio broadcasting industry. It processes license applications, assigns frequencies and call signs, conducts hearings, enforces regulations, licenses radio operators, and carries out the provisions of the Communications Act.

The U.S. Supreme Court has upheld the FCC's right to police the airwaves for obscene material. In *Federal Communications Commission v. Pacifica Foundation*, 438 U.S. 726, 98 S. Ct. 3026, L. Ed. 2d 1073 (1978), a New York radio station owned by the Pacifica Foundation broadcast comedian George Carlin's monologue on the "seven dirty words you can't say on the radio." When a listener complained to the FCC that he had heard the monologue in his car while his young son was present, the FCC investigated. Although it imposed no formal sanction, the FCC indicated that the complaint would be placed in the station's license file. If any subsequent complaints were received, the commission stated that it would then decide whether any sanctions would be applied. One potential sanction was the loss of the station's license, when it came up for renewal in three years.

Justice John Paul Stevens, writing for the majority, noted that the "broadcast media have established a uniquely pervasive presence in the

CHRISTOPHER SMITH/IMPACT VISUALS

*Howard Stern has been criticized for his outrageous behavior on the air, but his and other AM talk radio programs are very popular.*

lives of all Americans." Offensive material over the airwaves "confronts the citizen, not only in public, but also in the privacy of the home, where individuals right to be left alone plainly outweighs the First Amendment rights of an intruder." In addition, broadcasting is "uniquely accessible to children, even those too young to read." Thus, the Court ruled that the FCC had the constitutional right to take the action it did.

In 1987 the FCC demonstrated its continuing interest in preventing the radio broadcast of indecent or obscene language when it threatened not to renew the licenses of several radio stations in New York and California that were engaged in "shock radio." The talk programs, including one by Howard Stern, were intentionally controversial and given to large doses of profanity and sexual innuendo. Although the FCC's threats made headlines, there was little talk of challenging the agency's regulations.

The FCC had a hand in the growth of political talk radio shows such as Rush Limbaugh's when it repealed the "fairness doctrine" in 1987. Since 1934, the FCC had required broadcasters to devote a reasonable proportion of their air time to discussion of important public issues. Until 1987, the FCC had interpreted this doctrine to require broadcasters engaged in editorials in which specific persons were criticized to provide notice to the persons involved and air time for rebuttal.

The Supreme Court upheld the fairness doctrine as a reasonable balance between the public interest in hearing various points of view and the broadcaster's interests in free expression. *Red Lion Broadcasting Co. v. Federal Communications Commission*, 395 U.S. 367, 89 S. Ct. 1794,

23 L. Ed. 2d 371 (1969). Nevertheless, the doctrine remained controversial until its repeal. Freed from this doctrine, radio show hosts such as Limbaugh were free to criticize public figures without having to give the person air time to respond.

**The History of Television** In 1928, GE displayed the first presentation on a television, but it was quite some time before the invention became a practical reality. The 1930s brought an excitement to those conducting experiments on the new technology. They predicted that television would be as much a part of the life of the United States as radio had become.

In 1939, the National Broadcasting Company (NBC) brought television to the world during the New York World's Fair, and on February 1, 1940, it conducted the first official network television broadcast in the United States. In 1941, the FCC officially authorized commercial television, transferred television sound from AM to FM, and increased the resolution standards for broadcasts. By 1948, thirty-six television stations were broadcasting and over 1 million television sets were receiving. So many applications for new stations were coming in to the FCC that a freeze on requests was instituted. In 1952, the freeze was lifted and seventy ultrahigh-frequency (UHF) channels were added to those already available. By 1953, nearly four hundred stations were providing coverage to nearly 90 percent of the United States; no medium in history could compare to television in its record-breaking implementation.

**The Future of Radio and Television** As the popularity of television and radio continues to grow, controversy and concern continue to develop surrounding their implementation and worth. Issues range from government regulation to suitable ethical content. The future of the broadcast industry is in the hands of the courts and the government as they seek to determine the best possible means of making the broadcast media serve the needs of the society that has grown to depend on them.

**Cable Television** Communications technology advanced again when cable television joined traditional broadcast radio and television. Cable television, or community antenna television (CATV), provides a means for otherwise inaccessible areas to receive broadcast signals that are in some way impeded. The FCC claimed authority over the regulation of cable television in 1966. The claim of this authority was challenged, but in 1968, it was upheld by the Supreme Court (*United States v. Southwestern Cable Co.*, 392 U.S. 157, 88 S. Ct. 1994, 20 L. Ed. 2d 1001).

*This 1948 view of the NBC control booth shows the beginnings of national television.*

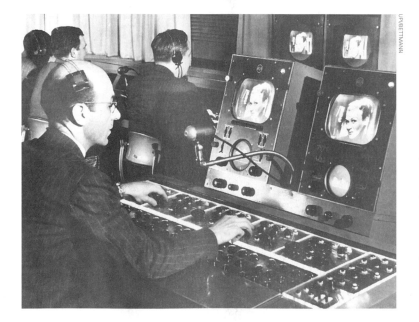

Dealing with cable television has proved to be controversial. The standards that were originally established in the Communications Act apply to broadcast television; cable television is not broadcast across the airwaves—it is transmitted through coaxial cable that may be able to carry over two hundred channels. Because of this, some argue that cable television should be treated more like print media such as newspapers and magazines, than like broadcast television. Since cable operators select the channels that they carry, they argue that they should be treated as "electronic publishers."

Such distinctions are significant because the U.S. Supreme Court has held that the FIRST AMENDMENT will tolerate more government regulation of the broadcast media than of the print media because the physical capacity of the airwaves is limited and cannot accommodate all the existing demand (*FCC v. National Citizens Committee for Broadcasting*, 436 U.S. 775, 98 S. Ct. 2096, 56 L. Ed. 2d 697 [1978]). In other words, without regulation, the competing voices on the airwaves would drown each other out.

In one form or another, government regulation is involved in two issues concerning cable television. One issue is whether cities may limit access to all or part of their territory to a single cable supplier. Many cities have granted what are essentially MONOPOLY franchises, and this practice has been challenged by cable suppliers who argue that disallowing them a FRANCHISE interferes with their free speech rights.

The cable franchise system that exists for cable operators was approved by Congress in 1984 in the Cable Communications Policy Act (15 U.S.C.A. § 21; 18 U.S.C.A. § 2511; 46 U.S.C.A. §§ 484–487; 47 U.S.C.A. § 35 et seq.). This act attempted to balance the interests of cable operators, which wanted less regulation, with the PUBLIC-POLICY concerns of the cities, which wanted guarantees that poorer neighborhoods would be wired for cable and that educational and government programming would not be neglected.

Under 47 U.S.C.A. §§ 541–543, a franchising authority—usually a city or county—may award one or more franchises within its jurisdiction; in practice, most have chosen one. Franchising authorities are authorized to require cable operators to reserve channel space for public, educational, and government use. Operators may also be required to make space available for LEASE for commercial use by persons not affiliated with the operator.

This system of franchising has been attacked from both sides. Some operators have become upset when their applications for franchises were denied in areas where other operators had established franchises. The public has also been concerned over the monopolistic nature of cable operators. Arguments often revolve around the issue of cable rates; competition for cable operators, it is argued, would also lead to competitive pricing of services. Despite this, very few franchising authorities choose to offer more than a single cable operator to an area's residents.

The second issue surrounding the regulation of cable television is whether the FCC's "must-carry" rules, which require a cable operator to carry all local television stations, violate the First Amendment. The must-carry rules were instituted in an effort to ensure that cable television would not undermine the financial viability of free community-oriented television by attracting so many viewers away from local broadcast television stations that the advertising revenues of those stations would plummet. In 1984, a federal appeals court held that the must-carry rules violated the First Amendment (*Quincy Cable TV v. FCC*, 768 F. 2d 1434 [D.C. Cir. 1985]). The Supreme Court denied review of the case, and the FCC eliminated the must-carry rules.

The must-carry rules were problematic for one main reason: although most cable operators have the ability to carry many hundreds of channels, some can carry only a dozen. Requiring the latter to carry all local stations severely limited their ability to attract subscribers. Operators also argued that being forced to carry all local broadcasts caused cable systems to become saturated and deprived cable programmers of opportunities to sell their services.

**Satellite Broadcasting** The new technology of direct-broadcast satellite television is replacing transmission over the airwaves with transmission by satellite signals beamed to the home from space. Like cable television, despite its separation from conventional airwave broadcasting, the new technology has generated legal controversy.

To maintain constant, direct contact between itself and the recipients of its signals, a satellite must hold a geostationary orbit directly above the earth's equator at an altitude of 22,300 miles. (A geostationary orbit is an orbit that keeps the satellite's position fixed with respect to the earth.) The controversy surrounding satellite broadcasting comes not from any limit on the number of signals it can send but instead from the physical limitation of these geostationary orbits.

The world saw its first geostationary satellite launched by the United States in 1963; as of

*Satellite dishes are a common sight as the broadcast of programming changes from transmission over the airwaves to transmission of satellite signals beamed to the earth from space.*

1992, the United States had thirty geostationary satellites orbiting the earth. By the mid-1980s, the United States and other developed countries were quickly filling the equatorial orbit with satellites. Many developing countries feared that by the time they had developed the technology to put up their own satellites, the zone of geostationary orbit in space would be filled and they would be forced to buy broadcast time from countries owning satellites that were already in orbit. In 1985, the International Telecommunication Union (ITU), an agency of the United Nations, established new procedures that would represent the interests of these developing countries.

The ITU originally established a first-come, first-served policy regarding the assignment of geostationary orbits. The World Administrative Radio Conference of 1985 upheld the continuation of this policy, but also voted to guarantee at least one geostationary orbit to each country that was a member of the ITU. The decisions of the 1985 conference were finalized by another session in 1988. Although these decisions supported the interests of the United States in part—it could continue filling geostationary orbits—they caused concern for the FCC. The satellite technology of the United States would not, after all, be allowed to grow unchecked. Orbits that the United States had once assumed would be its to use were reallocated to other countries. The decisions of the World Administrative Radio Conferences of the 1980s gave the FCC even greater cause for regulating the

broadcast industry within the United States and for being more selective about who is granted geostationary orbits and a piece of a broadcast industry that by the year 2000 is expected to bring in more than $10 billion annually.

**Public Broadcasting** Besides investigating developing technologies, the government and the FCC find themselves revisiting issues that have received attention from Congress, the broadcasting industry, and the public. One such issue is public television.

The Corporation for Public Broadcasting (CPB) was established in 1967 as the official, nongovernment allocator of federal money to public television and radio stations across the United States. In 1992, less than thirty years after its creation, the corporation became a political issue for conservatives who objected to the content and perceived philosophy of public programming and to its partial reliance on U.S. tax dollars.

The attacks began after the House of Representatives approved a bill in December 1991 that would increase spending for the corporation from $825 million to $1.1 billion in a three-year period (H.R. Res. 2977, 102d Congress, 1st Sess. [1991]). (The bill was also passed by the Senate and signed into law in August 1992.) Political conservatives claimed that public broadcasting had a liberal bias, a bloated budget, and offensive programming. Complaints ranged from protests about two frank Public Broadcasting Service (PBS) specials on homosexuality, *Tongues Untied* and *The Lost Lan-*

*guage of the Cranes*, to a claim that the Children's Television Network program *Sesame Street* was educationally ineffective and no better than network cartoons.

Public broadcasting claimed that without federal funding through the CPB, its more than one thousand television and radio stations would cease to exist. Most experts agree that this is not true. Only 14 percent of the operating costs for public broadcasting is supplied by the federal government; the remainder comes from corporations, member donations, and other sources. In 1995, the CPB allocated $285.6 million to public broadcasting, and since 1968, Congress has budgeted more than $4 billion to that concern. Yet, if these funds were cut off, public broadcasting, although wounded, probably would survive. Polls showed that most people like public television and want it to continue, but as opposition gathers in Congress and the Senate, it appears that if public broadcasting is to continue, it may have to do so without federal funding.

**Children** There are other concerns surrounding children and television than whether Big Bird can make it without federal support. Radio and television reach no audience more impressionable than a country's youth, and many controversies surround the exposure of children to sex and violence on television.

Another perennial issue of concern for parents and others is the amount of exposure children have to television; time spent in front of the television might be better spent exercising the body and the mind. It is frequently argued that not enough educational programming is available to children. Since the inception of broadcast programming, education has always been considered an important aspect of it. The Children's Television Act (47 U.S.C.A. § 303a et seq.) was enacted in 1990 in an effort to put more educational programming on television. The response of broadcasters has been sluggish, prompting a harsh hearing before Congress in 1993. Despite this legislation, some maintain that next to nothing has been done to remedy the quality of children's television, which House Telecommunications Subcommittee chairman Edward J. Markey (D-Mass.) referred to as "the video equivalent of a Twinkie."

Also, the FCC debates whether children's programs based on toys are program-length commercials. And controversy abounds over Channel One television and Star Broadcasting radio, which are broadcast into classrooms across the United States, mixing "educational" programming with corporate commercials. Critics argue that even when educational programming finds its way into the lives of children, it is corrupted by commercialism that does more to encourage children to buy shoes and soft drinks than it does to educate them on current affairs.

**Minorities** As of 1978, only one percent of all radio and television stations in the United States were run by minorities. In an attempt to diversify broadcasting, the FCC adopted rules that year giving preferential treatment to minorities regarding applications for new station licenses and in taking over failed stations (47 U.S.C.A. § 309). During the Reagan administration, this reform was nearly killed, but Congress saved it. Again, during the Bush administration, an attempt to stop the FCC was launched, this time when the Justice Department asked the Supreme Court to rule against the FCC's new guidelines. The effort to block reform met its final failure in 1990, when the Supreme Court ruled 5–4 to uphold the constitutionality of race-based licensing. The Court held that such AFFIRMATIVE ACTION is allowable in the broadcasting market if its purpose is to "serve important governmental objectives" (*Metro Broadcasting, Inc. v. F.C.C.*, 497 U.S. 547, 110 S. Ct. 2997, 111 L. Ed. 2d 445). Still, in 1990, fewer than five percent of all radio and television licenses were held by minorities.

## Broadcasting

Use of broadcast media, 1970 to 1994

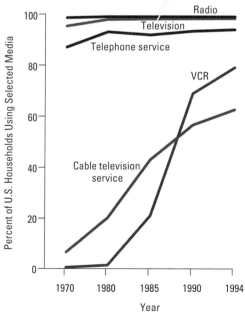

Source: U.S. Bureau of the Census, *Census of Housing* (telephone service); Radio Advertising Bureau, *Radio Facts,* annual (radio); Television Bureau of Advertising, Inc., *Trends in Television,* annual (television, cable television service, and VCRs).

Equal opportunity employment has also become a very important consideration in the process of renewing broadcasting licenses. The NATIONAL ASSOCIATION FOR THE ADVANCEMENT OF COLORED PEOPLE (NAACP) reviews all applications closely to ensure that radio and television stations have provided an opportunity for the employment of minority groups. If any party, such as the NAACP, calls into question the practices of a station, a petition to deny can be filed. If the station cannot provide proof of compliance with equal opportunity standards, it can be denied renewal of its license.

**Current Legislation** In February 1996, President Clinton signed into law the Telecommunications Act of 1996 (Pub. L. No. 104-104), which made a number of major changes to laws governing the telecommunications industry. Among these were deregulatory measures, including provisions allowing local phone companies, long-distance companies, and cable companies to compete over the same services. Another provision requires television manufacturers to include circuitry that would allow parents to screen out programming they did not wish their children to view, such as programs featuring violence. Provisions in this act and other legislation prohibiting the transmission of "indecent" material have met major setbacks in the courts. The courts have been receptive to arguments that the provisions violate the First Amendment.

### CROSS-REFERENCES

Cable Television; Censorship; Courtroom Television Network; Fairness Doctrine; Federal Communications Commission; Freedom of Speech; Mass Communications Law; Telecommunications; Television.

**BROADHEAD, JAMES OVERTON** James Overton Broadhead was born May 29, 1819, in Charlottesville, Virginia. He attended the University of Virginia from 1835 to 1836, studied law in St. Louis, Missouri, and received his license and established his law practice in Bowling Green, Missouri, in 1842.

In 1845, Broadhead began his political career as a member of the Missouri Constitutional

"IF EVERY . . .
AMERICAN CITIZEN
WOULD PERFORM THE
DUTIES OF A CITIZEN
. . . THERE WOULD BE
NO OCCASION OF
INVOKING THE STRONG
ARM OF ARBITRARY
POWER TO PROTECT A
PERSON OR HIS
PROPERTY."

**BIOGRAPHY**

LIBRARY OF CONGRESS

*James Overton
Broadhead*

Convention. In the following year he participated in the Missouri House of Representatives, and in 1850 became a member of the Missouri Senate, serving until 1853.

Broadhead returned to the practice of law, becoming a partner in a St. Louis firm in 1859.

During the pre-Civil War era, Broadhead participated in activities that opposed the Southern cause. He was instrumental in the formation of the Committee of Safety, which restricted the influence of pro-Southern factions in St. Louis, and in 1861 was a member of the Missouri Constitutional Convention, which declared the loyalty of Missouri to the Union.

In 1875, Broadhead attended the Missouri State Constitutional Convention, and in 1876, he gained prominence as government counsel for the Whiskey Ring cases, which involved bribery and dishonesty in the collection of exorbitant liquor taxes.

From 1883 to 1885, Broadhead represented Missouri in the United States House of Representatives, and was a member of the Judiciary Committee. During his later years, he served abroad, acting first as special commissioner to France in 1885, and later as minister to Switzerland for a two-year period.

Broadhead died August 7, 1898, in St. Louis.

**BROKER** An individual or firm employed by others to plan and organize sales or negotiate CONTRACTS for a commission.

A broker's function is to arrange contracts for property in which he or she has no personal interest, POSSESSION, or concern. The broker is an intermediary or negotiator in the contracting of any type of bargain, acting as an AGENT for parties who wish to buy or sell STOCKS, BONDS, real or personal property, COMMODITIES, or services. Rules applicable to AGENCY are generally relevant to most transactions involving brokers. The client is considered the PRINCIPAL and the broker acts as the client's agent. An agent's powers generally extend beyond those of a broker. A distinguishing feature between an agent and a broker is that a broker acts as a middleperson. When a broker arranges a sale, he or she is an agent of both parties.

In order to determine whether or not an

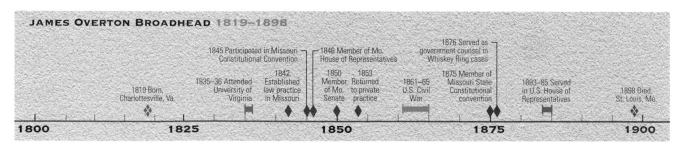

JAMES OVERTON BROADHEAD 1819-1898

1845 Participated in Missouri Constitutional Convention

1846 Member of Mo. House of Representatives

1876 Served as government counsel in Whiskey Ring cases

1819 Born, Charlottesville, Va.

1835-36 Attended University of Virginia

1842 Established law practice in Missouri

1850 Member of Mo. Senate

1853 Returned to private practice

1861-65 U.S. Civil War

1875 Member of Missouri State Constitutional convention

1883-85 Served in U.S. House of Representatives

1898 Died, St. Louis, Mo.

1800    1825    1850    1875    1900

individual is acting as a broker in a transaction, the type of services that are performed must be examined.

**Types of Brokers** There are several kinds of brokers, each of whom deals in different types of transactions.

A bill and note broker negotiates the buying and selling of BILLS OF EXCHANGE and PROMISSORY NOTES.

A commercial or merchandise broker is an individual who works with buyers and sellers by negotiating between them in the buying and selling of goods, without having personal custody of the property. He or she offers services on a commission basis to manufacturers as a sales representative for their product. Such a broker has no control or possession of the product that is sent directly to the buyer; he or she merely acts as a middleperson in all transactions.

An INSURANCE broker acts as an intermediary between the INSURER and the INSURED and is distinguishable from an insurance agent. While an insurance agent is employed by, and represents, a particular insurance company, an insurance broker is a representative of the insured only. An insurance agent is bound by company rules and responsibilities, whereas an insurance broker's only duty is to aid a client. He or she owes no obligation to any company.

Real estate brokers or agents are hired to transact the buying and selling, lease, or rental of REAL PROPERTY on a commission basis. They can also be involved with the purchase and sale of lands, and the acquisition of MORTGAGES for

*Stockbrokers today rely on computer and satellite technology to keep track of the markets but good communication with their clients is still most important.*

others. They may also counsel and advise people who wish to buy or sell real estate.

Stockbrokers buy and sell shares in CORPORATIONS and deal in corporation stock and in other securities. A stockbroker's functions are generally broader than those of other brokers. As more than a mere negotiator, he or she makes a purchase in his or her own name, and ordinarily pays the purchase price. A stockbroker is often responsible for the possession of the SECURITIES with which he or she deals. Conversely, an ordinary broker neither has TITLE to, nor possession of, property that is being purchased or sold. As stockbrokers serve in a greater capacity, their responsibilities also extend beyond those of ordinary brokers.

**Regulation and Conduct of Business** The business or occupation of a broker may be regulated by the state under its POLICE POWER. A municipal corporation has the power to regulate brokers who function within its boundaries if authority to do so is granted by the state.

In order for a broker to engage in business, he or she is generally required to acquire a LICENSE and pay a fee. Brokers who conduct business without a license can be fined by state licensing authorities. Some states make it illegal for any person other than a licensed broker to be paid for services concerning real estate transactions.

Laws exist that impose a license tax on brokers. Within the meaning of such laws, any individual who regularly works as a middleperson or negotiates business transactions for the benefit of others is ordinarily considered a broker. It has been held by a federal court that a statute requiring brokers to obtain a license was only applicable to those people regularly employed as brokers. An individual only casually involved in brokerage through the arrangement

*In the early twentieth century stockbrokers kept track of stock prices by reading the tickertape. Note that even in 1904 this broker had three phones on his desk.*

## Brokers

Employment statistics for the broker-related industries of finance, insurance, and real estate

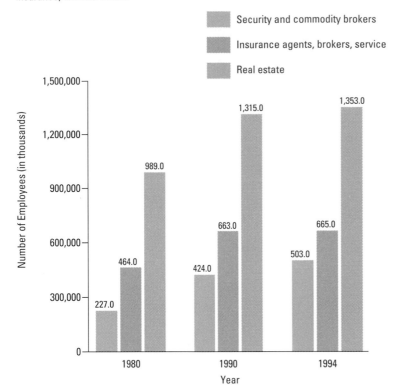

Security and commodity brokers

Insurance agents, brokers, service

Real estate

Source: U.S. Bureau of Labor Statistics, Bulletin 2445, and *Employment and Earnings,* monthly.

of only a few sales would not be considered to be engaged in the business of brokerage.

**Revocation of License** The state's concerns regarding brokers extend beyond initial licensing to the establishment of conditions for the maintenance of a license. The state may provide for the REVOCATION or suspension of brokers' licenses for reasonable grounds.

The power to revoke a license may be vested in a specially designated commission that exists primarily to hear complaints about the fraudulent practices of brokers. Such proceedings are ordinarily informal, and technical court rules generally are not observed.

During a HEARING, the commission is presented with evidence relating to the broker's conduct and must consider whether such conduct warrants denial of the privilege to engage freely in business.

Grounds for revocation of a license are generally based upon FRAUD, dishonesty, incompetence, or BAD FAITH in dealing with the public. A real estate broker's license may be revoked or suspended because of MISREPRESENTATION used to effect a purchase or sale. Generally, the conduct of a broker in negotiating a real estate transaction on behalf of his or her principal is subject

to strict fraud and DECEIT standards, equal to those imposed on his or her principal. It has been held by some courts that the failure of a broker to disclose material facts within his or her knowledge will create LIABILITY. Within the meaning of fraud is the pretense of knowledge on the part of the broker while executing a real estate transaction where no knowledge actually exists—for example, while selling a house a broker states that there are no concealed defects in the house, although he or she does not actually know whether such defects exist or not.

A real estate broker's license may be suspended or revoked if duties are performed unlawfully. In addition, a broker's license can be revoked or suspended if a broker is guilty of racial DISCRIMINATION in the selling and leasing of property. See also CIVIL RIGHTS.

Stockbrokers may be liable for various unethical activities, such as CHURNING, which is the unnecessary trading of stocks to gain additional commissions. A consumer protection organization, the Securities Investor Protection Corporation (SIPC), has been established by Congress to aid customers of securities concerns that go out of business.

**Bonds** State regulations usually require that brokers, especially those engaged in the real estate business, deliver a bond to insure faithful performance of their duties. The liability of the SURETY guaranteeing such a bond extends only to transactions that arise during the normal course of the broker's business and that are intended to be included in the bond.

**Commissions** A broker is ordinarily compensated for services by the payment of a commission, based upon a portion of the value of the property in a particular transaction.

Generally, a commission is earned when negotiations by buyer and seller are completed, and an agreement is reached. It is customary for a broker to deduct and reserve the amount of commission from funds obtained by him or her for a client. The ordinary basis for the calculation of a percentage commission is the total sale price of whatever is sold.

In order for a broker to be entitled to a commission, a sale must be completed for which the broker has been employed.

The broker's right to a commission is not dependent upon the finalization of the transaction unless otherwise agreed upon by the broker and by his or her client.

The compensation of a broker is based upon procurement of a client who is willing and able to purchase. The specific terms of the transaction must be satisfactory to the broker's client. Of paramount importance is the prospective

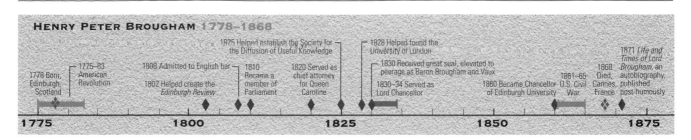

**HENRY PETER BROUGHAM 1778–1868**

1778 Born, Edinburgh, Scotland

1775–83 American Revolution

1808 Admitted to English bar

1802 Helped create the *Edinburgh Review*

1810 Became a member of Parliament

1820 Served as chief attorney for Queen Caroline

1825 Helped establish the Society for the Diffusion of Useful Knowledge

1828 Helped found the University of London

1830 Received great seal, elevated to peerage as Baron Brougham and Vaux

1830–34 Served as Lord Chancellor

1860 Became Chancellor of Edinburgh University

1861–65 U.S. Civil War

1868 Died, Cannes, France

1871 *Life and Times of Lord Brougham*, an autobiography, published posthumously

1775     1800     1825     1850     1875

buyer's ability to provide the required funds at the suitable time. A broker who has properly performed his or her duties should not be denied a commission due to a failure by the parties to consummate the deal.

In the absence of any agreement to be employed by a client, a broker is not to be compensated for voluntary services. Similarly, compensation is not due a broker when a sale is made by an owner after the broker-client relationship has been terminated. A common type of termination is the expiration of a real estate LISTING. This rule against the payment of a commission is absolute—regardless of whether or not the sale is made to an individual whom the broker initially produced—provided the broker was given ample opportunity to complete the transaction and failed to do so. Once a broker has earned his or her commission, a client may not terminate the relationship and complete the transaction himself or herself in order to avoid paying the broker.

Any fraudulent misrepresentations or evidence of bad faith on the part of the broker will defeat his or her right to a commission. Mere NEGLIGENCE in the execution of duties, in the absence of bad faith, does not automatically defeat a broker's right to compensation.

**BROOKINGS INSTITUTION** Founded in 1927, the Brookings Institution is a nonpartisan organization dedicated to research, education, and publication in the fields of economics, foreign policy, and government. It states as its principal purposes: "to aid in the development of sound public policies and to promote public understanding of issues of national importance."

Brookings maintains a 55,000-volume library. It is organized into the following divisions: Advanced Study, Economic Studies, Foreign Policy Studies, Governmental Studies (which includes some legal studies), Foreign Policy Studies, Governmental Studies, Publications, and a Social Science Computation Center.

The institution publishes the *Brookings Bulletin* (quarterly), the *Brookings Papers on Economic Activity* (twice a year), and an *Annual Report*. It also publishes its extensive research in books and reprints.

**BIOGRAPHY**

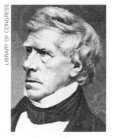

*Henry Peter Brougham*

"ALTHOUGH THE PEOPLE MUST BE THE SOURCE OF THEIR OWN IMPROVEMENT, THEY MAY BE AIDED IN THEIR EFFORTS TO INSTRUCT THEMSELVES."

**BIOGRAPHY**

*Addison Brown*

**BROUGHAM, HENRY PETER** Henry Peter Brougham, also known as Baron Brougham and Vaux, achieved prominence as a lawyer and statesman.

Brougham was born September 18, 1778, in Edinburgh, Scotland. In 1802, Brougham was instrumental in the creation of the publication the *Edinburgh Review*. He subsequently relocated to London and was admitted to the English bar in 1808. He became a member of Parliament in 1810, where he voiced his opposition to slavery and trade restrictions.

Brougham gained fame in 1820 as chief attorney for Queen Caroline, also known as Caroline of Brunswick. Caroline had married George, Prince of Wales, in 1795, and after giving birth to a daughter, they separated, and Caroline lived alone. In 1806, she was accused of giving birth to an illegitimate child, but was found innocent by an inquiry commission. George became king in 1820, and Caroline demanded her place as his queen. Caroline was sued for divorce on grounds of adultery, and the case was taken to the House of Lords; Brougham served as her attorney, and the charges were eventually dropped.

A leader in the field of educational reform, Brougham participated in the establishment of the Society for the Diffusion of Useful Knowledge in 1825, and of the University of London in 1828.

From 1830 to 1834, Brougham served as Lord Chancellor and drafted numerous legal reforms and helped to institute the central criminal court. He died May 7, 1868, in Cannes, France.

**BROWN, ADDISON** Addison Brown gained prominence as a jurist, botanist, and author.

He was born February 21, 1830, in West Newbury, Massachusetts. In 1855, Brown was admitted to the New York bar. From 1881 to 1901, he performed the duties of district judge for the Southern District of New York.

A respected name in the field of botany, Brown acted as one of the founders of the New York Botanical Garden in 1891.

From 1896 to 1898, Brown co-authored three volumes of botanical research with Nathaniel L. Britton. The series was titled *Illustrated Flora of*

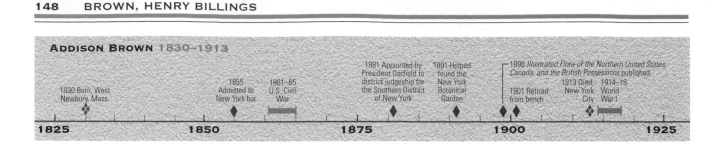

ADDISON BROWN 1830–1913

1830 Born, West Newbury, Mass.

1855 Admitted to New York bar

1861–65 U.S. Civil War

1881 Appointed by President Garfield to district judgeship for the Southern District of New York

1891 Helped found the New York Botanical Garden

1898 Illustrated Flora of the Northern United States, Canada, and the British Possessions published

1901 Retired from bench

1913 Died, New York City

1914–18 World War I

1825    1850    1875    1900    1925

*the Northern United States, Canada and the British Possessions.*

Brown died April 9, 1913, in New York City.

## BROWN, HENRY BILLINGS

Henry Billings Brown was an associate justice of the Supreme Court from 1890 to 1906.

Born to a wealthy family on March 2, 1836, at South Lee, Massachusetts, Brown attended private schools as a child. His father, a prosperous merchant and manufacturer, saw to it that Brown attended Yale University, where he graduated in 1856. After graduation, Brown traveled in Europe for a year, then returned to study law at Yale and Harvard. In 1859 he moved to Detroit and in 1860 he was admitted to the Wayne County bar in Michigan.

Brown was appointed deputy U.S. marshal in 1861. Detroit at that time was a bustling Great Lakes port, and he became involved in the many commercial and maritime legal disputes that arose. Two years later, he was named assistant U.S. attorney for the Eastern District of Michigan. He held this post until May 1868 when he was appointed to fill a short-term vacancy on the Wayne County Circuit Court.

Recognized as the leading authority on ADMIRALTY LAW and maritime law, Brown lectured on the subjects at the University of Michigan Law School, and compiled and published *Brown's Admiralty Reports*. In 1890 President BENJAMIN H. HARRISON appointed him to the U.S. Supreme Court. As a Court member, Brown gained a reputation as a moderate but was a staunch defender of property rights. He was reluctant to extend constitutional protection in criminal procedure and civil liberties disputes, and concurred with the majority in *Lochner v. New York*, 198 U.S. 45, 25 S. Ct. 539, 49 L. Ed. 937 (1905), which struck down a statute calling

### BIOGRAPHY

*Henry Billings Brown*

"THE UNDERLYING FALLACY OF THE PLAINTIFF'S ARGUMENT [RESTS] IN THE ASSUMPTION THAT THE ENFORCED SEPARATION OF THE TWO RACES STAMPS THE COLORED RACE WITH A BADGE OF INFERIORITY."

for maximum work hours for bakers. *Lochner* was consistent with Brown's unwillingness to allow governmental interference with contractual freedom. See also LABOR LAW.

Brown also concurred in the so-called *Insular* cases, which held that residents of U.S. TERRITORIES such as Puerto Rico are not entitled to constitutional protections. However, he departed somewhat from his usual strict adherence to judicial precedence when he voted to uphold the federal INCOME TAX in *Pollock v. Farmers' Loan & Trust Co.*, 158 U.S. 601, 15 S. Ct. 912, 39 L. Ed. 1108 (1895).

Brown is perhaps best remembered as the author of the Court's opinion in *Plessy v. Ferguson*, 163 U.S. 537, 16 S. Ct. 1138, 41 L. Ed. 256, the 1896 decision upholding state-mandated racial segregation in railway cars as long as the accommodations were equal. The "SEPARATE-BUT-EQUAL" doctrine pronounced in *Plessy* became the constitutional foundation for JIM CROW LAWS and racial DISCRIMINATION, particularly in the South. Later opinion condemned the *Plessy* decision, and indeed Brown has often been criticized for his role in it; however, the decision must be viewed in the historical context in which it was written. Also, the language in *Plessy*, requiring equality of treatment, later became the basis of legal challenges to segregation laws.

Failing eyesight forced Brown to retire from the bench in 1906. He died in 1913.

### CROSS-REFERENCES

*Brown v. Board of Education;* Equal Protection; *Plessy v. Ferguson.*

## BROWN, JOSEPH EMERSON

Joseph Emerson Brown was born April 15, 1821, in Pickens District, South Carolina. He was a graduate

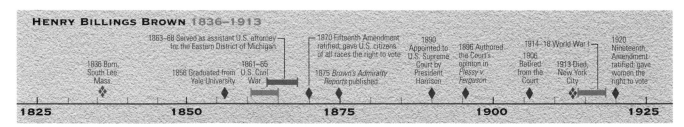

HENRY BILLINGS BROWN 1836–1913

1836 Born, South Lee, Mass.

1863–68 Served as assistant U.S. attorney for the Eastern District of Michigan

1856 Graduated from Yale University

1861–65 U.S. Civil War

1870 Fifteenth Amendment ratified; gave U.S. citizens of all races the right to vote

1875 *Brown's Admiralty Reports* published

1890 Appointed to U.S. Supreme Court by President Harrison

1896 Authored the Court's opinion in *Plessy v. Ferguson*

1914–18 World War I

1906 Retired from the Court

1913 Died, New York City

1920 Nineteenth Amendment ratified; gave women the right to vote

1825    1850    1875    1900    1925

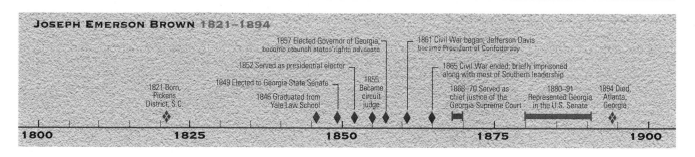

JOSEPH EMERSON BROWN 1821-1894

1821 Born, Pickens District, S.C.

1846 Graduated from Yale Law School

1849 Elected to Georgia State Senate

1852 Served as presidential elector

1855 Became circuit judge

1857 Elected Governor of Georgia; became staunch states' rights advocate

1861 Civil War began; Jefferson Davis became President of Confederacy

1865 Civil War ended; briefly imprisoned along with most of Southern leadership

1868–70 Served as chief justice of the Georgia Supreme Court

1880–91 Represented Georgia in the U.S. Senate

1894 Died, Atlanta, Georgia

1800    1825    1850    1875    1900

of the Yale Law School class of 1846, and was admitted to the Georgia bar.

In 1849 Brown entered politics and served in the Georgia Senate. In 1852 he was a presidential elector and in 1855 he served as a circuit judge.

Brown became governor of Georgia in 1857 and, for the next eight years, voiced his opposition to Jefferson Davis, president of the Confederacy, concerning involuntary service in the armed services and the elimination of the writ of HABEAS CORPUS. He was a strong supporter of STATES' RIGHTS and often spoke out against the authority of a centralized government. In 1865 he was imprisoned but was released by President Andrew Johnson shortly afterwards.

From 1868 to 1870 Brown again served in the judiciary, presiding as chief justice of the Georgia Supreme Court.

Brown entered federal government service in 1880, representing Georgia in the U.S. Senate for an eleven-year period, retiring in 1891. He died November 30, 1894, in Atlanta.

**BROWN, RONALD HARMON** The career of Ronald Harmon Brown is a portrait of a consummate Washington, D.C., insider. As an African American attorney, Brown broke several color barriers during his rapid rise in politics from the 1970s to the early 1990s. He first entered the public eye as a CIVIL RIGHTS leader for the National Urban League. Soon his reputation for persuasiveness and ingenuity led to a variety of assignments: political strategist to Senator Edward M. Kennedy (D-Mass.) and

**BIOGRAPHY**

*Joseph Emerson Brown*

**BIOGRAPHY**

*Ronald Harmon Brown*

JESSE JACKSON, chief counsel of the U.S. Senate Judiciary Committee, and lobbyist for foreign governments. In the 1980s, Brown became the first black chairman of the Democratic National Committee (DNC). He steered the Democratic party toward a more centrist position, thus helping prepare the way for President BILL CLINTON's election in 1992. Clinton picked him to head the Department of COMMERCE. Although Brown had some notable successes in reviving the lifeless bureaucracy, allegations of corruption damaged his tenure.

Born on August 1, 1941, in Washington, D.C., Brown was raised in the company of successful role models. His parents, William Brown and Gloria Brown-Carter, were both graduates of Howard University, and they moved the family to Harlem, where William managed the Hotel Theresa. Brown grew up in the hotel, surrounded by famous black entertainers and celebrities: it was a stopover for them after playing Harlem's Apollo Theater. As a young man, he attended Middlebury College, where he was the school's first black fraternity pledge. He married Alma Arrington in 1962, and then served in the Army from 1963 to 1967, attaining the rank of captain. Leaving the service, he joined the National Urban League as a welfare caseworker. Brown did not toil in the trenches for long. His skill at negotiation stood out, and, after adding a law degree from St. John's University, he became the organization's Washington, D.C., vice president and assumed the role of spokesman.

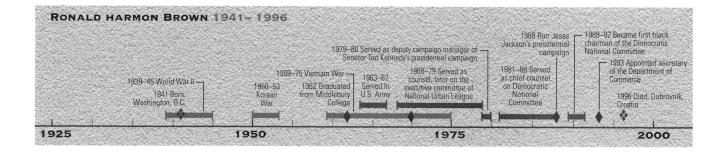

RONALD HARMON BROWN 1941–1996

1939–45 World War II

1941 Born, Washington, D.C.

1950–53 Korean War

1959–75 Vietnam War

1962 Graduated from Middlebury College

1963–67 Served in U.S. Army

1968–79 Served as counsel, later on the executive committee of National Urban League

1979–80 Served as deputy campaign manager of Senator Ted Kennedy's presidential campaign

1981–88 Served as chief counsel on Democratic National Committee

1988 Ran Jesse Jackson's presidential campaign

1989–92 Became first black chairman of the Democratic National Committee

1993 Appointed secretary of the Department of Commerce

1996 Died, Dubrovnik, Croatia

1925    1950    1975    2000

The give-and-take of politics suited Brown. "What I love most," he said, "is changing minds." In 1979 Brown's association with the Democratic party got a boost when Senator Kennedy named Brown his deputy campaign manager in an unsuccessful run at the presidency. The job marked the beginning of a stellar ascent through party politics. Kennedy chose Brown as chief counsel of the Senate Judiciary Committee—and that position led to a stint as chief counsel of the DNC, the party's steering council. By the mid-1980s, Brown was an insider, well-known and highly regarded in the nation's capital.

Politics offers alluring choices to its best-connected practitioners, liberal and conservative, and Brown's next career move was perfectly in step with the ethos of Washington, D.C. Brown became a lobbyist. He joined the Washington, D.C., firm of Patton, Boggs, and Blow, known for its high-profile clients. The attorney had no shortage of these: the businesses he represented included the financial giant American Express and twenty-one different Japanese electronics firms. Yet what gained him notoriety was his representation of foreign nations. He worked for the interests of Zaire, Guatemala, and Haiti, and the last two affiliations, in particular, hurt him. While he lobbied on behalf of Haitian strongman Jean-Claude ("Baby Doc") Duvalier, Haitian citizens suffered political repression and saw their national treasury pillaged. Guatemalans were tortured and murdered. Later, when Brown prepared to assume the high position of secretary of commerce, critics would be quick to recall that he had supported dictators.

Democrats wanted Brown back, and he left LOBBYING to become chairman of the DNC. The job demanded much: Democrats, after all, had failed to capture the White House since 1976. He had to unify a party that had lost three consecutive presidential ELECTIONS, seen massive defections of its traditional voters, and suffered from an identity crisis that split its moderate and left-wing members. He also had to soothe fears that he was too closely allied with one of the party's most liberal leaders, Jesse Jackson. "My chairmanship won't be about race," he told critics. "It will be about the races we win over the next four years." As it happened, Brown was everything the ailing party hoped for. He helped orchestrate a shift to the center in the Democrats' national agenda—abandoning traditional bullishness on TAXATION and WELFARE, for instance, and asserting a pro-business outlook—which paved the way for the centrist candidacy of Clinton. And as a party boss, he was decisive. Once Clinton emerged as the

front-runner, Brown curtailed the primary process; he even secured Jackson's endorsement. "This party was ready," Mickey Kantor, Clinton's campaign manager, said after the election, "and it was because of Ron Brown . . . the best chairman we've ever had."

As a reward, Clinton nominated Brown for the cabinet role of secretary of the Department of Commerce. Originally conceived as a regulatory agency, Commerce had seen better days; by the 1990s, both liberal and conservative critics considered it to be an ineffective bureaucracy tied up in red tape. Despite his credentials and the reform-minded talk of the Clinton administration, Brown's nomination faced some fears and objections. Business worried about his being too tough on it with new regulations. Some critics, such as the Center for Public Integrity, worried about the opposite. This nonpartisan watchdog group argued that Brown was too well connected to avoid potential CONFLICTS OF INTEREST: he would have to regulate industries and foreign countries that he had once represented, seemingly in contradiction to Clinton's promise to clamp down on the selling of influence by political appointees. The group's December 1992 report, *The Torturer's Lobby*, hammered Brown for representing repressive governments. Brown called the Center's charges an attempt at implying "guilt by association." The Senate confirmed him with little difficulty.

As commerce secretary, Brown won praise for breathing new life into the department. He revived its export programs, winning lucrative multibillion-dollar contracts for U.S. aircraft and telecommunications firms. He also presided over a $900 million annual budget for promoting high technology in small and medium-sized business, nearly double the amount spent during the administration of George Bush. The *New Republic* called him "the most formidable Commerce secretary since Herbert Hoover" (1 May 1995). Business fears about his being too liberal proved to be wrong; he was utterly pro-business, even to the point of attracting criticism for helping McDonnell Douglas Corporation secure contracts to build aircraft in China. The liberal Committee for Economic Organizing complained that he was "promoting companies, not jobs."

But scandals nearly sank Brown. In 1993, during Brown's first year as secretary of commerce, a Vietnamese businessman alleged that Brown had accepted a $700,000 bribe from the government of Vietnam to remove a long-standing trade EMBARGO. Brown denied the charge; the Federal Bureau of Investigation

"WE'RE COMPETING EVERYWHERE FOR CONTRACTS BECAUSE THAT MEANS JOBS AND A STRONG ECONOMY, AND WE INTEND TO WIN."

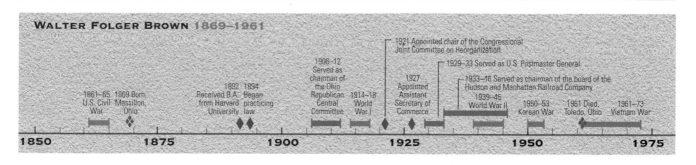

**WALTER FOLGER BROWN** 1869–1961

- 1921 Appointed chair of the Congressional Joint Committee on Reorganization
- 1906–12 Served as chairman of the Ohio Republican Central Committee
- 1929–33 Served as U.S. Postmaster General
- 1927 Appointed Assistant Secretary of Commerce
- 1933–16 Served as chairman of the board of the Hudson and Manhattan Railroad Company
- 1861–65 U.S. Civil War
- 1869 Born, Massillon, Ohio
- 1892 Received B.A. from Harvard University
- 1894 Began practicing law
- 1914–18 World War I
- 1939–45 World War II
- 1950–53 Korean War
- 1961 Died, Toledo, Ohio
- 1961–73 Vietnam War

1850 | 1875 | 1900 | 1925 | 1950 | 1975

conducted a year-long probe, and he was ultimately cleared. By late 1994, rumors spread in the press that he would resign to run Clinton's reelection campaign. In February 1995, new allegations emerged. U.S. attorney general Janet Reno opened another criminal probe into Brown's personal finances. This time, congressional Republicans accused him of violating disclosure requirements and evading taxes. Brown again denied any violation of law, but Republican critics began calling for his dismissal—as well as the elimination of the Department of Commerce itself, which they called irrelevant and outdated. In May 1995, fourteen Republican senators told Attorney General Reno that fairness required that the probe be conducted outside of the Clinton administration. Reno agreed; she requested the appointment of an independent counsel to examine Brown's finances. Particularly troubling was one odd-looking business deal: Brown had earned nearly $500,000 from selling his interest in a firm in which he had never invested.

Brown won high regard for his work in the law. He was the recipient of two American Jurisprudence awards for outstanding achievement in jurisprudence and for outstanding scholastic achievement in poverty law. He served as a trustee of Middlebury College, and as a board member of both the United Negro College Fund and the University of the District of Columbia. He was a fellow of the Institute of Politics, at the John F. Kennedy School of Government, at Harvard University.

On April 3, 1996, Brown was killed in a plane crash near the city of Dubrovnik, Croatia, with thirty-two other Commerce Department officials and U.S. business executives. They had planned to explore investment opportunities for the reconstruction of Croatia and Bosnia-Herzegovina.

**BROWN, WALTER FOLGER** Walter Folger Brown was born May 31, 1869, in Massillon, Ohio. He received a bachelor of arts degree from Harvard University in 1892 and attended Harvard Law School from 1893 to 1894.

**BIOGRAPHY**

*Walter Folger Brown*

Brown practiced law from 1894 to 1927 and entered politics in 1921, serving for three years as chairman of the Congressional Joint Committee on Reorganization. In 1927 he became assistant secretary of commerce, and two years later performed the duties of U.S. postmaster general, acting in this capacity until 1933.

Brown's interests and activities in business were numerous and included service as president and chairman of the board of the Hudson and Manhattan Railroad Company.

Brown died January 26, 1961, in Toledo, Ohio.

## BROWN v. BOARD OF EDUCATION OF TOPEKA, KANSAS

The 1954 landmark decision by the Supreme Court, *Brown v. Board of Education of Topeka, Kansas*, 347 U.S. 483, 47 S. Ct. 686, 98 L. Ed. 873, that held that racial segregation in public education is unconstitutional.

*Brown v. Board of Education* was the most significant of a series of judicial decisions overturning segregation laws—laws that segregate, or separate, whites and blacks. Reversing its 1896 decision in *Plessy v. Ferguson*, 163 U.S. 537, 16 S. Ct. 1138, 41 L. Ed. 256, which established the "SEPARATE-BUT-EQUAL" doctrine that found racial segregation to be constitutional, the Court unanimously decided in *Brown* that laws separating children by race in different schools violated the Equal Protection Clause of the FOURTEENTH AMENDMENT, which provides that "[n]o state shall . . . deny to any person . . . the equal protection of the laws." In making its decision, the Court declared that "separate educational facilities are inherently unequal." Moreover, the Court found that segregated schools promote in African American children a harmful and irreparable sense of inferiority that damages not only their lives but the welfare of U.S. society as a whole.

The principle expressed in *Brown* was used in later decisions of the Supreme Court and lower federal courts to reverse segregation in other fields as well. By the end of the 1960s, laws that had required racial segregation in buses, trains,

APWIDE WORLD PHOTOS

*Linda Brown Smith, shown here at a 1979 ceremony observing the twenty-fifth anniversary of the Supreme Court's school desegregation decision, was the plaintiff in* Brown v. Board of Education of Topeka, Kansas.

bathrooms, and other public places had been overturned, as had many other laws that obstructed the rights of African Americans. *Brown* thus served as a milestone in the struggle for African Americans to gain equal civil rights in U.S. society. It also symbolized the judicial activism of the Supreme Court under Chief Justice Earl Warren, who would go on to lead the Court until 1969 in a remarkable era of change with regard to civil rights.

*Brown* was actually the culmination of a decades-long struggle by both African Americans and sympathetic whites against segregation and other discriminatory laws. Though it is a given today that persons of all races should enjoy equality under the law in the United States, that has not been the case for most of the country's history. Even after the Civil War had ended and the Thirteenth and Fourteenth Amendments had outlawed SLAVERY and guaranteed the civil rights of "all persons born or naturalized in the United States" (U.S. Const. amend. XIV), southern states and localities established the racially discriminatory JIM CROW LAWS—also known as the Black Codes—to keep African Americans from enjoying legal equality with whites. The term *Jim Crow* derives from a popular minstrel song of the nineteenth century. These laws made it difficult or impossible for African Americans to vote, made it illegal for them to use the same public facilities as whites, restricted their travel, forbade interracial marriage, and otherwise attempted to keep them in a state of dependence and inferiority with regard to whites. Most of these laws were

passed after the Reconstruction period following the Civil War, when the military occupation of the South had ended and the radical wing of the Republican party, which under President ABRAHAM LINCOLN had been instrumental in dismantling slavery, had declined in power. By the mid-1870s, southern whites were again in political control of their region, and many quickly sought to return blacks to a position of legal inferiority through passage of discriminatory laws.

In 1896 the legal standing of the Jim Crow laws was strengthened when, in *Plessy v. Ferguson*, the Supreme Court upheld the constitutionality of a Louisiana statute requiring blacks and whites to occupy separate railway cars. The law in question, according to the Court, was not a violation of the Equal Protection Clause of the Fourteenth Amendment as long as the facilities provided for each race were separate but equal. Moreover, the Court voiced its disagreement with attempts to challenge segregation laws and with the ideas critics of segregation used to support those challenges. For example, in its opinion, the Court considered it a "fallacy" that "the enforced separation of the two races stamps the colored race with a badge of inferiority," and it scoffed at the notion that "social prejudices may be overcome by legislation." Ironically, the Court reinforced its decision to uphold the legality of segregation on rail cars by noting the existence of laws "requiring separate schools for colored children." The *Plessy* decision and its separate-but-equal doctrine were later used to uphold segregation in public schools and other public facilities.

African Americans and others who sympathized with their cause were bitterly disappointed by the *Plessy* decision. Over a decade later, in 1909, blacks and whites joined together to form the National Association for the Advancement of Colored People (NAACP), which would eventually coordinate a successful legal challenge to the *Plessy* ruling. The NAACP brought together people of all races in an effort to improve the situation of people of color. Although the NAACP achieved some victories in the fight against Jim Crow laws in the first two decades of its existence, it was not until 1935 that the organization began actively to mount a campaign against segregation in schools. It did so under legal counsels CHARLES HOUSTON and WILLIAM H. HASTIE, and a young assistant, Thurgood Marshall, who would go on to become a member of the Supreme Court from 1967 to 1991.

By 1939, Marshall had become head of the NAACP's legal branch, the NAACP Legal Defense Fund, and by the early 1950s, he and his

*The* Brown *decision was the first of many that dismantled racial segregation in services offered to African Americans (far left) and in public places, such as bus stations (left).*

organization had argued and secured significant legal victories before the Supreme Court that helped set the stage for *Brown*. In *Sweatt v. Painter*, 339 U.S. 629, 70 S. Ct. 848, 94 L. Ed. 1114 (1950), the Court sided with the NAACP Legal Defense Fund when it ruled that a separate law school for blacks in Texas could not provide an education equal to that available to whites at the more established University of Texas Law School. And in another case brought by Marshall's organization, *McLaurin v. Oklahoma State Regents*, 339 U.S. 637, 70 S. Ct. 851, 94 L. Ed. 1149 (1950), the Court ruled that separate library and lecture hall seats for a single black graduate student were a violation of the Fourteenth Amendment. However, neither case addressed the separate-but-equal doctrine of *Plessy*.

In 1952 Marshall and the NAACP Legal Defense Fund brought two more significant cases to the Supreme Court: *Bolling v. Sharpe*, 347 U.S. 497, 74 S. Ct. 693, 98 L. Ed. 884 (1954), which dealt with racial segregation of schools in the District of Columbia, and *Brown*, which was actually a consolidation of four CLASS ACTION suits (suits brought to court on behalf of a group of people) from federal district courts in Delaware, Kansas, South Carolina, and Virginia. The NAACP Legal Defense Fund brought the cases to court on behalf of African American children who were refused admission to schools attended by white children as a result of laws allowing or requiring racial segregation in schools. The plaintiff named in the case, Oliver Brown, had a daughter, Linda Brown, who had been denied admission to an all-white elementary school in Topeka, Kansas, because she was black. In all but the Delaware case, a three-judge federal district court had decided against the African American children and in favor of the school districts, citing as PRECEDENT

the *Plessy* separate-but-equal doctrine. In the Delaware case, the state supreme court also upheld this doctrine, but ordered that black children be sent to superior white schools until schools provided for blacks could be improved to an equal condition.

*Brown* was argued before the Court in 1952 and reargued in 1953. Marshall, in making his statement before the Court, argued that the statutes in question in this case were equivalent to the Black Codes. He pointed out the contradictions in allowing blacks and whites to vote in the same places and attend the same colleges and universities, but not allowing black and white children to attend the same elementary schools. He also maintained that a decision in favor of segregation would effectively be a decision to keep African Americans as near as possible to their former state of slavery. According to Marshall, such a decision would be equivalent to saying that "Negroes are inferior to all other human beings."

JOHN W. DAVIS, who was legal counsel for the state of South Carolina, argued in his closing remarks that the state had honored *Plessy*'s separate-but-equal doctrine through large investments in schools for black students. He claimed that the state had the intention of creating a condition of equality for children of all races and that "the happiness, the progress and the welfare of these children is best promoted in segregated schools." He also maintained that it was not within the JURISDICTION of the U.S. Supreme Court to decide how the state of South Carolina conducted its school system. He told the Court:

Your Honors do not sit, and cannot sit as a glorified Board of Education for the State of South Carolina or any other state. . . .
. . . Neither this Court nor any other

# Oliver Brown and the NAACP

**A**s the man whose name appeared in the title of perhaps the most influential U.S. Supreme Court decision ever, *Brown v. Board of Education,* 347 U.S. 483, 74 S. Ct. 686, 98 L. Ed. 873 (1954), Oliver Brown was an unlikely hero for the civil rights movement. The African American welder, war veteran, and assistant pastor was a quiet, upstanding citizen of Topeka, Kansas, who had never been known to publicly oppose discrimination against his race. However, he took a decisive stand against racial discrimination when he joined one dozen other African American parents in filing suit for the right of their children to attend the elementary schools of Topeka alongside white children.

Brown's participation in the lawsuit was encouraged by the National Association for the Advancement of Colored People (NAACP), which provided necessary legal expertise and organization for the case. Long familiar with the practice of school segregation in Topeka and many other school districts, NAACP lawyers approached Brown and other parents in the summer of 1950 to see if they would join them in a case that challenged that practice.

It was precisely Oliver Brown's modest qualities that made the NAACP choose him as a plaintiff. His reputation for integrity could help mute criticism in a controversial case that stirred up angry emotions in both the white and black communities of Topeka. The city's white majority was largely content to remain with a school system that maintained eighteen all-white elementary schools and four all-black elementary schools. African Americans, meanwhile, feared the case would cause the white community to attack what few civil rights they already possessed. Others could not become involved in such a controversy without the fear of losing their jobs with white employers. For that reason, very few African Americans in Topeka actually belonged to the NAACP.

Like many other African American parents, Brown was upset that his daughter had to travel a long distance to an all-black school when an all-white school was located much nearer their home. He also could not help but notice that the all-white schools were in better repair than the all-black schools. Brown agreed to join in the NAACP's case, and in September 1950, he tried unsuccessfully to register one of his three daughters, Linda Brown, in an all-white school only seven blocks from their house. When the case first came to the U.S. District Court for Kansas in June 1951, Brown testified that his daughter had to travel twenty-one blocks to an all-black school, part of the way through a dangerous railroad switching yard.

In the end, African Americans did not seek to end the system of segregation in public schools merely to have their children travel fewer miles to class or sit in nicer buildings. At stake were much more important issues that affected their status in U.S. society. As expressed by NAACP attorneys in later testimony before the Supreme Court, African Americans had come to see segregated schools as inherently unequal. These schools relegated African Americans to an inferior class, instilled feelings of insecurity, diminished their opportunities, and retarded their mental development. The victory eventually achieved in *Brown* would go a long way toward eliminating those harmful effects of segregation and guaranteeing African Americans their full constitutional rights.

---

court . . . can sit in the chairs of the legislature of South Carolina and mold its educational system, and if it is found to be in its present form unacceptable, the State of South Carolina must devise the alternative.

When the Court handed down its opinion, which was written by Chief Justice Warren on May 14, 1954, it held that segregating children by race violated the Equal Protection Clause of the Fourteenth Amendment, regardless of the equality of the physical facilities and other elements of the schools. The Court based its decision in part on contemporary psychological and sociological studies that demonstrated the harmful effects of segregation on children. In particular, the Court's opinion argued that segregation promotes a sense of inferiority in African American children: "To separate [children] from others of similar age and qualifications solely because of their race generates a feeling of inferiority as to their status in the community that may affect their hearts and minds in a way unlikely ever to be undone." Such a sense of inferiority, the Court maintained, impairs the motivation of African American children to learn and deprives them of benefits they would otherwise receive in a racially integrated school. The Court also supported its decision by stating that education had become an even more important element in U.S. life than it had been when the *Plessy* decision was made in 1896:

Today, education is perhaps the most important function of the state and local governments. . . . It is required in the performance of our most basic public responsibilities. . . . It is the very foundation of good citizenship. Today it is a principal instrument in awakening the child to cultural values, in preparing him for later professional training, and in helping him to adjust normally to his environment. In these days, it is doubtful that any child may reasonably be expected to succeed in life if he is denied the opportunity of an education. Such an opportunity, where the state has undertaken to provide it, is a right which must be made available to all on equal terms.

On the same day that the Court handed down its decision in *Brown*, it decided the related case of *Bolling*. Applying the same principles that it had used in *Brown*, the Court ruled in *Bolling* that racial segregation of schoolchildren in the District of Columbia was unconstitutional.

In the following year, the Supreme Court on reargument made another decision in *Brown* that was designed to establish the methodology by which to enforce desegregation of public schools. *Brown II*, 349 U.S. 294, 75 S. Ct. 753, 99 L. Ed. 1083 (1955), as it has come to be called, determined that school authorities had the principal responsibility for evaluating and solving local educational problems, including those resulting from segregation. The Court decided to REMAND (send back) the individual cases in *Brown* to lower courts in order that those courts might better assess the efforts of school authorities to desegregate the public schools and thereby provide to African American children their equal protection under the laws as promised by the Fourteenth Amendment. The lower courts were directed to take into account any problems concerning school administration, facilities, transportation, and personnel, and to consider any revision of local laws necessary to resolve the problems and achieve desegregation.

*Brown v. Board of Education* dealt only with government-mandated or government-authorized segregation. It did not apply to racial segregation or discrimination related to restaurants, theaters, employment, country clubs, or other parts of the private sector. However, *Brown* fostered changes in the legal and moral outlook of the country that greatly aided future efforts to end racial discrimination as related to employment, housing, and places of public accommodation, and thus greatly affected U.S. race relations.

Despite the promise of *Brown*, desegregation of U.S. schools proceeded slowly. In the years immediately following the decision, many southern school districts resisted or delayed implementation of its desegregation requirements, thereby forcing the Supreme Court and other lower courts to oversee and supervise school administrative functions in many localities. As time went on and southern schools became more integrated, the Court shifted its focus to school districts all over the country, particularly those in cities. In the second half of the twentieth century, many African Americans moved from rural to urban areas, often in the northern states. School districts in many of those urban areas became separated into suburban white districts and urban black districts. In response to this challenge, courts imposed busing requirements during the 1970s: in the interest of creating more racially balanced schools, children were bused to different schools that were sometimes far from their home neighborhoods. In many cities, busing became highly controversial.

By the late 1980s, legal battles surrounding the legacy of the *Brown* decision changed when some school districts began to request that they be released from the court supervision of their operations that had been required by *Brown*. Accordingly, the Supreme Court began to focus on the issue of when a court order to desegregate a school district should be dissolved and autonomy returned to the local school officials and community. In *Board of Education v. Dowell*, 498 U.S. 237, 111 S. Ct. 630, 112 L. Ed. 2d 715 (1991), which dealt with a court-imposed de-

*The* Bolling *decision was handed down on the same day as the* Brown *decision. The plaintiff in* Bolling *was Spottswood Thomas Bolling, a fifteen-year-old Washington, D.C. high-school student.*

segregation plan in Oklahoma City, the Court ruled that a court-ordered desegregation decree may be dissolved when a school district shows that it has taken all "practicable" steps to end a state-imposed dual school system and demonstrates that it is unlikely to revert to its former ways. The ability to dissolve a court-ordered desegregation plan, the Court's opinion stated, would enable a school district that had attempted to achieve the goal of desegregation to avoid "judicial tutelage for the indefinite future."

Justice Marshall, now near the end of his career on the Court, dissented from the majority opinion in *Dowell*. He argued that, given the long history of segregation, it was too early to leave the Oklahoma City school district to its own devices. Though he agreed that perpetual federal judicial supervision of local schools had never been envisioned by the Court, he feared that the Court's decision in this case would simply perpetuate an already unsatisfactory standard of integration in the Oklahoma City school district and in other school districts.

In another case, *Freeman v. Pitts*, 503 U.S. 467, 112 S. Ct. 1430, 118 L. Ed. 2d 108 (1992), the Supreme Court held that district courts may relinquish supervision and control of school districts in incremental stages, before full compliance has been achieved in every facet of school operations. The Court also ruled that once a school district corrects any racial imbalance that violates the Equal Protection Clause of the Fourteenth Amendment, the district has no obligation to remedy a later imbalance caused by population shifts.

As these cases indicate, the issue of desegregation of public schools remains a vital public issue even several decades after the Supreme Court's decision in *Brown*. As a means of both training and socialization, education is still a necessity for U.S. society as a whole and for any individual in particular, and it will undoubtedly remain so in the future. Guided by *Brown*, the U.S. judicial system has decisively concluded that the constitutional provision of equal protection under the laws guarantees that children be entitled to an equal, not a separate, public education.

## CROSS-REFERENCES

Civil Rights; Discrimination; Equal Protection; Marshall, Thurgood; National Association for the Advancement of Colored People; *Plessy v. Ferguson*; Republican Party; School Desegregation; Warren, Earl; Warren Court.

**BIOGRAPHY**

UNITED STATES COURT OF APPEALS

*James Robert Browning*

THE NINTH CIRCUIT IS "THE ONLY COURT IN WHICH, WITHIN OUR BOUNDARIES, IS REPRESENTED ALL THE POINTS OF VIEW, BASICALLY ALL THE PROBLEMS, SOCIAL AND ECONOMIC, OF THE WHOLE NATION. THAT KIND OF COURT CAN MAKE A VERY POSITIVE CONTRIBUTION TO THE DEVELOPMENT OF THE FEDERAL LAW AT THE NATIONAL LEVEL."

**BROWNING, JAMES ROBERT** James Robert Browning, a federal judge, is credited with holding the U.S. Court of Appeals for the Ninth Circuit together at a time when there was enormous pressure to split the nation's largest and busiest CIRCUIT into smaller, more manageable units.

Browning's innovations in JUDICIAL ADMINISTRATION demonstrated that the FEDERAL COURTS, despite ever-increasing caseloads, could continue to provide speedy and effective justice. During his tenure, the Ninth Circuit court, which oversees justice in nine western states and two Pacific territories, grew from a nine-judge panel, to a twenty-eight-judge tribunal that managed more than fifty-five hundred APPEALS a year in the late 1980s.

Browning was born in Great Falls, Montana, on October 1, 1918. He grew up in and attended the public schools of Belt, Montana, a small town east of Great Falls, where his father was a blacksmith and, later, owner of the town's Ford dealership. Browning completed his undergraduate work at the University of Montana and entered that university's law school in 1938, becoming editor in chief of the law review and graduating with honors in 1941. After graduation, he joined the Antitrust Division of the Department of Justice in Washington, D.C.

Two years later, he was inducted as a private into the U.S. Army Infantry. He served in military intelligence in the Pacific theater for three years, attaining the rank of first lieutenant and winning a Bronze Star.

Following World War II, Browning returned to the Justice Department's Antitrust Division, first in Washington, D.C., and then in Seattle, Washington. In 1948, at the age of thirty, he was named chief of the Northwest Regional Office of the division. Before long, he was called back to Washington, D.C., and named assistant chief, General Litigation Section, Antitrust Division. By 1951, he had joined the

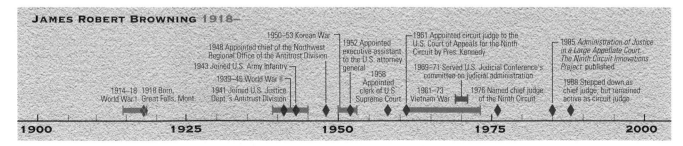

JAMES ROBERT BROWNING 1918–

1914–18 World War I  ◆  1918 Born, Great Falls, Mont.

1939–45 World War II  ◆  1941 Joined U.S. Justice Dept.'s Antitrust Division

1943 Joined U.S. Army Infantry  ◆  1948 Appointed chief of the Northwest Regional Office of the Antitrust Division

1950–53 Korean War  ◆  1952 Appointed executive assistant to the U.S. attorney general

1958 Appointed clerk of U.S. Supreme Court

1961–73 Vietnam War

1961 Appointed circuit judge to the U.S. Court of Appeals for the Ninth Circuit by Pres. Kennedy

1969–71 Served U.S. Judicial Conference's committee on judicial administration

1976 Named chief judge of the Ninth Circuit

1985 *Administration of Justice in a Large Appellate Court: The Ninth Circuit Innovations Project* published

1988 Stepped down as chief judge, but remained active as circuit judge

1900    1925    1950    1975    2000

Civil Division as first assistant. In 1952, he was named executive assistant to the attorney general of the United States. Later that year, he organized the Executive Office of U.S. Attorneys and became its first chief.

Browning left the Department of Justice in 1953 to enter private practice. For the next five years, he was a partner at Perlman, Lyons, and Browning, in Washington, D.C. In 1958, he was named clerk of the U.S. Supreme Court. From this position, he was appointed as a circuit judge to the U.S. Court of Appeals for the Ninth Circuit, by President JOHN F. KENNEDY, on September 18, 1961.

As a circuit judge, Browning became involved with the JUDICIAL CONFERENCE OF THE UNITED STATES and started exploring the field of judicial administration. (The Judicial Conference is the principal machinery through which the federal courts operate and is responsible for establishing the standards and shaping the policies that govern the federal judiciary.)

In the mid-1970s, there was no guarantee of speedy disposition of litigation in the federal courts. The COURTS OF APPEALS, in particular, faced widespread crises because the volume of appeals far exceeded the capacity of the courts to decide them. The Ninth Circuit court was no exception, and, because of its enormous backlog of cases, was the subject of much discussion among scholars, Congress, and the judiciary. Studies to examine the problems of the Ninth Circuit usually presented one of two conclusions: reduce the size of the circuit, or add more judges to the court. There was strong opposition to dividing the circuit, but there was equally strong opinion that adding more judges would make the circuit even more unmanageable.

Browning was named chief judge of the Ninth Circuit on July 1, 1976, and found himself in a position to experiment with his ideas on judicial administration. As the new chief judge, Browning was instrumental in convincing Congress to give the judges of the Ninth Circuit an opportunity to demonstrate that a large circuit with a large court of appeals could perform effectively.

Under Browning's leadership, that challenge was met with remarkable success. Foremost among the innovations initiated by Browning and his colleagues were new methods of case processing and control—including the installation of the first completely computerized DOCKETING (scheduling) system in a federal appellate court. Browning's innovations were later chronicled in a study published by the FEDERAL JUDICIAL CENTER (*Administration of Justice in a Large Appellate Court—The Ninth Circuit Innovations Project* [1985]). The court also created an executive committee to facilitate administrative decision making, assigned similar cases to the same three-judge panel, resolved panel conflicts with a "mini" EN BANC court of eleven judges (rather than with all twenty-eight judges assigned to the circuit), and created a BANKRUPTCY panel to hear bankruptcy appeals exclusively. These modifications and more, from decentralized staffing to fundamental changes in the way the court deliberates, turned the Ninth Circuit into a model for other courts around the country. In addition to speeding justice, Browning's innovations also improved the Ninth Circuit's judicial record over time. In 1984, the Supreme Court reversed twenty-seven of twenty-eight decisions from the Ninth Circuit. By 1987, the circuit's reversal rate was down to 47 percent—and was the third lowest in the country.

On June 15, 1988, after a dozen years as chief judge, Browning stepped down, but not to retire. He remains an active circuit judge handling a full caseload. He also is the administrative chief judge of the Middle Administrative Unit (the Northern and Eastern Districts of California, Arizona, Nevada, Hawaii, Guam, and the Northern Mariana Islands) of the U.S. Court of Appeals.

**BROWNING, ORVILLE HICKMAN** Orville Hickman Browning was born February 10, 1806, in Harrison County, Kentucky. He was educated at Augusta College and admitted to the Kentucky bar in 1831. In that same year, he relocated to Illinois and established his legal practice.

In 1836 Browning served as a member of the Illinois Senate, and in 1842 participated in the

**BIOGRAPHY**

LIBRARY OF CONGRESS

*Orville Hickman Browning*

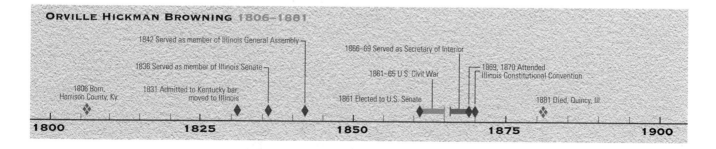

ORVILLE HICKMAN BROWNING 1806–1881

1842 Served as member of Illinois General Assembly

1866–69 Served as Secretary of Interior

1836 Served as member of Illinois Senate

1861–65 U.S. Civil War

1869, 1870 Attended Illinois Constitutional Convention

1806 Born, Harrison County, Ky.

1831 Admitted to Kentucky bar; moved to Illinois

1861 Elected to U.S. Senate

1881 Died, Quincy, Ill.

1800    1825    1850    1875    1900

Illinois General Assembly. He entered the United States Senate in 1861, replacing Stephen A. Douglas as senator from Illinois, and remained at this post until 1862. He gained a reputation for his adversity to several policies of ABRAHAM LINCOLN, including the emancipation of slaves.

From 1866 to 1869 Browning served as U.S. secretary of the interior and also acted as attorney general for a short period in 1868. He attended the Illinois Constitutional Convention during 1869 and 1870.

As a lawyer, Browning specialized in cases involving the Midwestern railroad system.

Browning died August 10, 1881, in Quincy, Illinois.

## BRYAN, WILLIAM JENNINGS

William Jennings Bryan was a prominent figure in U.S. politics during the late nineteenth and early twentieth centuries, and is perhaps best known for his role as assistant to the prosecution in the famous Scopes Monkey Trial of 1925.

Bryan was born March 19, 1860, in Salem, Illinois. His was a devoutly religious family that prayed together three times a day and stressed strict adherence to a literal interpretation of the Bible. His parents, Silas Lilliard Bryan and Mariah Elizabeth Jennings Bryan, were firm believers in education. His mother schooled Bryan and his siblings in their home until they were old enough to be sent away to school. Bryan was an obedient and well disciplined child who was also idealistic. His favorite subject was math because of its orderly reason and logic. He showed early interest in politics and public speaking, and at the age of twelve delivered a campaign speech for his father, who ran unsuccessfully for Congress. It was the beginning of a distinguished career as an orator for Bryan.

In 1875, Bryan was sent to live in Jacksonville, Illinois, to attend the Whipple Academy and Illinois College. During college, he participated in debate and declamation and excelled at long jumping. He graduated from college in 1881 and went on to Union College of Law, in Chicago. In 1883 he returned to Jacksonville and on July 4 opened a law practice. He mar-

**BIOGRAPHY**

BRYAN COLLEGE

*William Jennings Bryan*

ried his sweetheart of five years, Mary Elizabeth Baird, on October 1, 1884. Bryan's young wife proved to be an intellectual match for her husband. After the couple settled in Jacksonville, she took classes at Illinois College, a practice unheard of for a married woman at the time. She later studied law under Bryan's instruction, and was admitted to the bar in Nebraska in 1888.

Bryan had always yearned to go west, to test himself against the frontier. In 1887, he and his wife moved to Lincoln, Nebraska, where he entered a law partnership with a friend. The Bryans became active in civic affairs, and started separate discussion groups for men and women where the subject was often politics. Bryan also began lecturing on religious topics. In 1890, he succumbed to his interest in politics and entered his first campaign for public office. He was the Democratic candidate for Congress from a staunchly Republican district in Nebraska, but he won the election by a comfortable margin and was reelected in 1892. He made a bid for the Senate in 1894 but was defeated. He then turned to journalism and became editor in chief of the *Omaha World-Herald*. By this time, he had developed a reputation as a compelling speaker and was in demand for the popular Chautauqua lecture circuit. (The Chautauqua movement combined education with entertainment, often offered outdoors or in a tent; it took its name from the Chautauqua Lake region in New York, where it originated.)

During his campaign for the Senate, Bryan took up the free silver cause, a political movement that advocated the free coinage of silver. Free silver advocates, mainly indebted farmers in the West and South, wanted the government to issue more money, backed by silver, to ease the debts they were unable to repay because of declining farm prices. The money interests in the East favored sound money and the gold standard. These opposing forces clashed in the 1896 presidential campaign. Bryan emerged as the nominee of four parties: the Democratic, Populist, Silver Republican, and National Silver parties. At the Democratic National Conven-

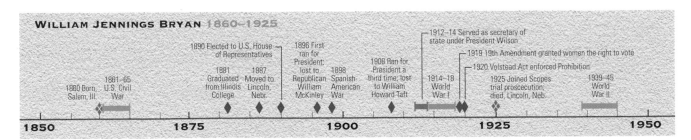

**WILLIAM JENNINGS BRYAN 1860–1925**

| 1850 | 1875 | 1900 | 1925 | 1950 |

1860 Born, Salem, Ill.

1861–65 U.S. Civil War

1881 Graduated from Illinois College

1887 Moved to Lincoln, Nebr.

1890 Elected to U.S. House of Representatives

1896 First ran for President; lost to Republican William McKinley

1898 Spanish-American War

1908 Ran for President a third time; lost to William Howard Taft

1912–14 Served as secretary of state under President Wilson

1914–18 World War I

1919 19th Amendment granted women the right to vote

1920 Volstead Act enforced Prohibition

1925 Joined Scopes trial prosecution; died, Lincoln, Neb.

1939–45 World War II

tion in Chicago, he made his famous "Cross of Gold" speech, in which he cast himself as a champion of the common person against the forces of the powerful and privileged. He passionately declared that those he referred to as the idle holders of money in Wall Street were responsible for the United States' financial woes.

Bryan campaigned tirelessly, traveling over eighteen thousand miles to deliver his electrifying speeches. In the end, he lost to WILLIAM MCKINLEY by less than five percent of the popular vote. But the foundation had been laid for his lifelong themes: the people versus the power of wealth, the workers versus the powerful money holders, the farmers versus the industrial interests. These themes echoed throughout his later attempts to win the presidency.

After serving as a colonel in a noncombat position during the Spanish-American War, Bryan ran for president again in 1900, this time on an anti-expansion theme that was rejected by voters. By 1904, he was falling out of favor with Democrats. He waged a long and exhausting fight to be nominated for president that year, but in the end was content that he had at least influenced the party platform enough so that it included nothing he found objectionable. Then the party nominated Alton B. Parker, who promptly announced that he was in favor of a gold standard. Parker lost the election to THEODORE ROOSEVELT. Bryan was bruised by the party's renunciation of his free silver position, but he rebounded and was nominated for president a third time, in 1908. He ran a strong campaign but lost to WILLIAM HOWARD TAFT.

After the 1908 election, Bryan realized he would never be president. Neverthess, he continued to influence Democratic party policies, and in 1912 he supported WOODROW WILSON's candidacy for president. After Wilson was elected, he selected Bryan as his secretary of state, a position Bryan resigned after two years when his pacifist ideas conflicted with Wilson's policies on U.S. involvement in World War I. After Bryan left the cabinet, his political influence declined rapidly.

During his later years Bryan continued his work in the newspaper business and was a popular lecturer on the Chautauqua circuit. He helped gain passage of the EIGHTEENTH AMENDMENT, which ushered in PROHIBITION, and helped the suffragette movement win the vote for women with passage of the NINETEENTH AMENDMENT.

During the last few years of his life, Bryan wrote numerous articles on religious topics. He felt that World War I was at least partly caused by a pervasive "godlessness" sweeping the world. To Bryan, this godlessness was nowhere more clearly reflected than in Darwin's theory of the evolution of the species. Bryan traveled around the United States preaching a literal interpretation of the Bible and campaigning for laws that banned the teaching of evolution. One such law, passed in Tennessee, prohibited teachers in state-supported schools and universities from teaching any theory of the origin of human life other than the creation story contained in the Bible. In 1925, a science teacher named John Thomas Scopes violated the law and was brought to trial. Hoping for publicity, the state asked Bryan to join the prosecution. He agreed, and found himself facing CLARENCE DARROW, a famous defense attorney who was a self-proclaimed atheist, an opponent of capital punishment, and a defender of unpopular causes. The trial quickly took on the air of a circus, with reporters and photographers from all over the world and the first live radio coverage of such an event broadcast by WGN in Chicago. The media cast the proceeding as a contest between science and the Bible. The defense tried to frame the issue as tolerance for new ideas. Ultimately, however, the prosecution persuaded the judge to confine the case to a question of the state's right to control public education.

Sensing that he was losing control of the trial, Darrow decided to try to unravel the state's case by calling Bryan as a witness. He intended to lead Bryan away from the prosecution's carefully framed issue into a defense of fundamental biblical interpretation. Bryan, whose trial experience had been limited, and who was feeling tired and ill, fell into Darrow's trap and was ridiculed and humiliated by the flamboyant attorney's searing and skillful questions. After Bryan's testimony, the trial was abruptly ended, depriving Bryan of the opportunity to answer Darrow's stinging offense. Nevertheless, the jury deliberated a mere eight minutes before returning a guilty verdict.

The Scopes trial was a victory for Bryan and his supporters, but he had been devastated by Darrow. He stayed in Tennessee to finalize and print the speech he had planned to use in closing argument before the court. Five days after the trial ended, on July 26, 1925, while still in Tennessee, Bryan died in his sleep. As a train bearing his body passed through the countryside on its way to Washington, D.C., thousands of the "common people" Bryan had championed gathered to pay their respects. The nation's capital was in official mourning as

"THE HUMBLEST CITIZEN OF ALL THE LAND, WHEN CLAD IN THE ARMOR OF A RIGHTEOUS CAUSE, IS STRONGER THAN ALL THE HOSTS OF ERROR."

Bryan lay in state. At his request, he was buried with full military honors at Arlington National Cemetery, an ironic footnote to the life of a fervent pacifist.

Although Bryan never won the country's top office, he exerted a strong influence during his long career in public service. Many of the reforms he advocated were eventually adopted, such as income tax, prohibition, women's suffrage, public disclosure of newspaper ownership, and the election of Senators by popular rather than electoral vote. Although he is most often associated with the Scopes trial, his diligent devotion to the causes in which he believed is his most significant legacy.

See also SCOPES, JOHN T.

**BRYAN TREATIES** Beginning in 1913, U.S. Secretary of State WILLIAM JENNINGS BRYAN negotiated a number of bilateral TREATIES for the "Advancement of Peace." The basic aim of these bilateral treaties was to prevent war by interjecting a CONCILIATION process into a dispute between parties to the treaty. Each signatory nominated two members, one a national and one a foreign citizen, to a permanent commission. These four would then choose a fifth member who could not be a national of either state. The commission would review the underlying facts to the dispute and issue a report on the controversy within one year. Until the report was issued the parties agreed to refrain from resorting to hostilities. It was hoped that this process and the inherent delay in issuing a report would lessen tension and preclude resort to armed force to settle the dispute, although each was free to do so after the report was issued. Eventually forty-eight of these treaties were concluded, but few disputes were ever submitted to any of the commissions.

**BRYANT, WILLIAM BENSON** William Benson Bryant is a federal judge whose decisions influenced the outcomes of several famous legal battles of the 1970s.

Bryant was born September 18, 1911, in Wetumpka, Alabama. He moved to Washington, D.C., with his family when he was a child and attended District of Columbia public

"I DO NOT BELIEVE THAT TESTING VIRTUE IS A FUNCTION OF LAW ENFORCEMENT . . . IF, AFTER AN ILLEGAL OFFER IS MADE, THE SUBJECT REJECTS IT . . . THE GOVERNMENT CANNOT PRESS ON."

**BIOGRAPHY**

*William Benson Bryant*

schools. He graduated from Howard University with a bachelor of arts degree in 1932, and went on to earn his bachelor of laws degree from Howard University Law School in 1936. After law school, Bryant worked for the Works Progress Administration and later for the Bureau of Intelligence at the Office of War Information. He joined the Army in 1943, and attained the rank of lieutenant colonel before his discharge in 1947.

Bryant started a law practice in Washington, D.C., in 1948. He left private practice to become an assistant in the office of the U.S. attorney for the District of Columbia from 1951 to 1954. After resigning that post, he joined the law firm of Houston, Bryant, and Gardner, in Washington, D.C., where he worked from 1954 to 1965. Bryant became a law professor at Howard University in 1965, the same year President LYNDON B. JOHNSON appointed him to the federal bench. With his appointment, Bryant became the first African American to serve as a judge at the federal district court level.

During his tenure on the bench, Bryant has presided over several high-profile trials. In May 1972, he overturned the election of W. A. ("Tony") Boyle as president of the United Mine Workers (*Hodgson v. United Mine Workers of America*, 344 F. Supp. 17 [D.D.C.]). Boyle's election was challenged by supporters of his opponent, Joseph A. Yablonski, who had been found murdered along with his wife and daughter three weeks after he lost the 1969 election to Boyle. Bryant found sufficient evidence of wrongdoing by Boyle and his supporters to nullify the election. He ordered the union to hold another election, to be conducted under court supervision. Boyle was subsequently defeated by Arnold Miller, a Yablonski supporter, and in 1974 was convicted of murder for having ordered Yablonski's killing.

Bryant also made several key decisions regarding participants in the scandals that devastated the administration of President RICHARD M. NIXON. In April 1974, he sentenced Herbert L. Porter, a former aide in Nixon's reelection

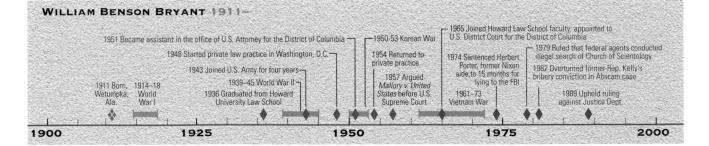

**WILLIAM BENSON BRYANT** 1911–

- 1951 Became assistant in the office of U.S. Attorney for the District of Columbia
- 1948 Started private law practice in Washington, D.C.
- 1943 Joined U.S. Army for four years
- 1911 Born, Wetumpka, Ala.
- 1914–18 World War I
- 1939–45 World War II
- 1936 Graduated from Howard University Law School
- 1950–53 Korean War
- 1954 Returned to private practice
- 1957 Argued *Mallory v. United States* before U.S. Supreme Court
- 1965 Joined Howard Law School faculty; appointed to U.S. District Court for the District of Columbia
- 1974 Sentenced Herbert Porter, former Nixon aide, to 15 months for lying to the FBI
- 1961–73 Vietnam War
- 1979 Ruled that federal agents conducted illegal search of Church of Scientology
- 1982 Overturned former Rep. Kelly's bribery conviction in Abscam case
- 1989 Upheld ruling against Justice Dept.

1900    1925    1950    1975    2000

campaign, to fifteen months in prison for lying to the Federal Bureau of Investigation during its investigation of the Watergate break-in and subsequent cover-up. In November 1974, he ordered White House counsel Philip W. Bucher to produce audiotapes of Oval Office meetings that took place May 1–5, 1971. The order was part of a CLASS ACTION suit brought against the U.S. government on behalf of eight hundred antiwar protesters. The plaintiffs alleged that government officials violated their civil liberties and suspended due process when they ordered the arrest of nearly twelve thousand protesters who marched on the White House on May 1. Most of the arrests in the so-called Mayday Rally were later found to be unlawful.

Bryant is said to be a fair, compassionate, and humble man who treats all people, from law clerks to defendants, as equals. He is also committed to eliminating social injustice; as a defense attorney, he argued and won the Supreme Court case of *Mallory v. United States*, 354 U.S. 449, 77 S. Ct. 1356 (1957). Following *Mallory* police could no longer use CONFESSIONS of criminal defendants secured during long and unnecessary delays between arrest and arraignment. Throughout his career, Bryant has worked to uphold the principle that everyone is entitled to a day in court. After a long and distinguished career on the federal bench, he attained the rank of senior judge in 1981.

**BRYCE, JAMES** James Bryce, also known as the Viscount Bryce of Dechmont, was born May 10, 1838, in Belfast, Ireland. He attended Glasgow and Heidelberg Universities and received a bachelor of arts degree from Oxford University in 1862.

After his admission to the bar in 1867, Bryce practiced law for the next fifteen years. He accepted a professorship at Oxford in 1870, where he taught CIVIL LAW until 1893.

Bryce entered Parliament in 1880 and remained a member until 1907. During this time, he also performed diplomatic duties—serving as undersecretary of foreign affairs in 1886 and chief secretary for Ireland from 1905 to 1906.

**BIOGRAPHY**

*James Buchanan*

**BIOGRAPHY**

COURTESY OF ORIEL COLLEGE, OXFORD

*James Bryce*

From 1907 to 1913, he acted as ambassador to the United States.

In 1913, Bryce participated at the HAGUE TRIBUNAL, the international court of arbitration established in the Netherlands. After World War I, he was active in the formation of the LEAGUE OF NATIONS.

Bryce gained fame for his numerous publications, including *The Holy Roman Empire: The American Commonwealth*, which was published in 1888 and was an important work concerning American government; and *Modern Democracies*, published in 1921.

He died January 22, 1922, in Sidmouth, Devonshire, England.

**BUCHANAN, JAMES** James Buchanan achieved prominence as a statesman and as the fifteenth president of the United States.

Buchanan was born April 23, 1791, near Mercersburg, Pennsylvania. A graduate of Dickinson College in 1809, Buchanan was admitted to the Pennsylvania bar in 1812 before serving a tour of duty in the militia during the War of 1812. After the war, he entered politics and joined the Pennsylvania House of Representatives in 1814.

In 1821 Buchanan began his career in federal politics, representing Pennsylvania in the U.S. House of Representatives until 1831. Later that year, he extended his interests to the field of foreign service and performed the duties of U.S. minister to Russia for a two-year period. He returned to Congress in 1834 and represented Pennsylvania in the U.S. Senate for the next eleven years. From 1845 to 1849, he served as U.S. secretary of state and reentered foreign service in 1853 as U.S. minister to Great Britain until 1856.

Buchanan became unpopular in 1854 with his involvement in the creation of the Ostend Manifesto, which provided for the purchase by the United States of Cuba from Spain; if Spain refused to sell, the manifesto gave the United States the right to seize the country forcibly. Cuba would then become a slave state, which was viewed favorably by Southerners, but which met with vehement opposition by abolitionists.

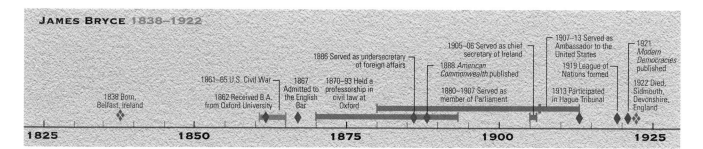

**JAMES BRYCE 1838–1922**

1838 Born, Belfast, Ireland

1861–65 U.S. Civil War

1862 Received B.A. from Oxford University

1867 Admitted to the English Bar

1870–93 Held a professorship in civil law at Oxford

1886 Served as undersecretary of foreign affairs

1880–1907 Served as member of Parliament

1888 *American Commonwealth* published

1905–06 Served as chief secretary of Ireland

1907–13 Served as Ambassador to the United States

1913 Participated in Hague Tribunal

1919 League of Nations formed

1921 *Modern Democracies* published

1922 Died, Sidmouth, Devonshire, England

1825        1850        1875        1900        1925

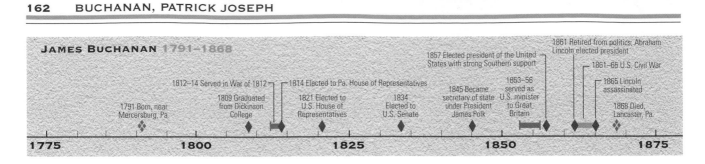

JAMES BUCHANAN 1791–1868

1791 Born, near Mercersburg, Pa.

1809 Graduated from Dickinson College

1812–14 Served in War of 1812

1814 Elected to Pa. House of Representatives

1821 Elected to U.S. House of Representatives

1834 Elected to U.S. Senate

1845 Became secretary of state under President James Polk

1853–56 served as U.S. minister to Great Britain

1857 Elected president of the United States with strong Southern support

1861 Retired from politics; Abraham Lincoln elected president

1861–65 U.S. Civil War

1865 Lincoln assassinated

1868 Died, Lancaster, Pa.

1775    1800    1825    1850    1875

The manifesto was eventually rejected by the U.S. Department of State.

As a presidential candidate in 1857, Buchanan adopted a moderate attitude toward SLAVERY and worked to establish a balance between the proslavery forces and the abolitionists. He believed that slavery was immoral, but that the Constitution provided for the protection of the practice in areas where it already existed. New states, he believed, should have the right to choose whether to be free or slave.

He won great support from the South, and after his election in 1857, Buchanan unsuccessfully attempted to reconcile the strife between the warring factions. He again advocated the acquisition of Cuba and favored the admission of Kansas as a slave state, which earned him disfavor with the northern free states. The strife between North and South continued, and Buchanan was unable to prevent the SECESSION of South Carolina that led to the outbreak of the Civil War. He opposed secession but believed that he did not possess the power to compel states to remain faithful to the Union. When ABRAHAM LINCOLN succeeded Buchanan as president in 1861 the country was ready for civil war. Buchanan retired to Pennsylvania where he died June 1, 1868, in Lancaster.

**BUCHANAN, PATRICK JOSEPH** Political commentator, White House appointee, and presidential candidate Patrick Joseph Buchanan is a leader of far-right conservatism. From modest beginnings as a journalist in the early 1960s, Buchanan became an influential voice in the Republican party. He served in a public relations capacity under three presidents—RICHARD M. NIXON, GERALD R. FORD, and RONALD REAGAN—before running for president himself in 1992. His hard-line positions on ABORTION, immigration, and foreign aid, as well as his battle cry for waging a "cultural war" in the United States, failed to wrest the nomination from GEORGE BUSH. Buchanan tried for the Republican nomination again in 1996, this time losing to Bob Dole. Often the subject of controversy for his writings and speeches, Buchanan is the founder of a political organization called the American Cause, whose slogan is America First.

Born November 2, 1938, in the nation's

"WHAT IS RIGHT AND WHAT IS PRACTICABLE ARE TWO DIFFERENT THINGS."

BIOGRAPHY

*Patrick Joseph Buchanan*

capital, Buchanan was the third of nine children of William Baldwin Buchanan and Catherine E. Crum Buchanan. He grew up under the resolute influences of Catholicism and conservatism, both the hallmarks of his father, a certified public accountant. Buchanan's brilliance at the Jesuit Gonzaga College High School earned him the honor of class valedictorian and a scholarship to Georgetown University. In his senior year of college, the English and philosophy major was already developing the sharp, confrontational style that would mark his professional life. He broke his hand scuffling with police officers over a traffic incident and was suspended from Georgetown for a year. He nonetheless finished third in his class in 1961. He received a master's degree in journalism from Columbia University in 1962.

Like other conservative politicians of his generation, notably Senator JESSE HELMS (R-N.C.) and President Reagan, Buchanan began with a career in the media, which led into politics. He spent three years writing conservative editorials for the *St. Louis Globe-Democrat* before being introduced to Nixon at a dinner party. The politician soon hired the twenty-eight-year-old as an assistant in his law firm. Buchanan wrote speeches for Nixon's 1968 presidential campaign, worked as his press secretary, urged him to choose Spiro T. Agnew as a running mate, and, after the election, became his special assistant. This last position involved reporting on what the news media said about the administration. It was an increasingly thankless job. Buchanan believed that bad news about the Vietnam War, youth protest, and the Watergate scandal was the work of a biased liberal media. He fought back, and is widely thought to have written Vice President Agnew's famous antipress speech in 1969 attacking the "small and unelected elite" whose opinions were critical of the president.

Buchanan escaped the taint that brought down Nixon, in part because he refused to help Nixon aides in their so-called dirty tricks campaign. Buchanan declined to smear Daniel Ellsberg—the former defense analyst who leaked the classified documents known as the Pentagon Papers to the *New York Times*, and whose

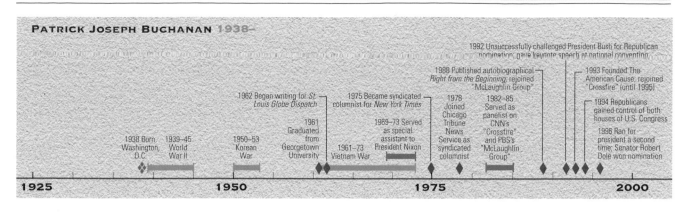

PATRICK JOSEPH BUCHANAN 1938–

1938 Born, Washington, D.C.

1939–45 World War II

1950–53 Korean War

1961 Graduated from Georgetown University

1962 Began writing for *St. Louis Globe Dispatch*

1961–73 Vietnam War

1969–73 Served as special assistant to President Nixon

1975 Became syndicated columnist for *New York Times*

1978 Joined Chicago Tribune News Service as syndicated columnist

1982–85 Served as panelist on CNN's "Crossfire" and PBS's "McLaughlin Group"

1988 Published autobiographical *Right from the Beginning*; rejoined "McLaughlin Group"

1992 Unsuccessfully challenged President Bush for Republican nomination; gave keynote speech at national convention

1993 Founded The American Cause; rejoined "Crossfire" (until 1995)

1994 Republicans gained control of both houses of U.S. Congress

1996 Ran for president a second time; Senator Robert Dole won nomination

1925          1950          1975          2000

psychiatrist's office Nixon aides broke into, helping set in motion the Watergate scandal. In fact, Buchanan later strongly defended the president and denounced the conspirators at U.S. Senate hearings. This testimony saved his career: he was seen as loyal and, more important, as evidently knowing little about the vast extent of the administration's illegalities. Unlike other Nixon insiders, he did not need to rehabilitate his reputation after Nixon left office. He remained in the White House under President Ford until 1975. See also WATERGATE.

Between 1975 and 1985, Buchanan established a national reputation. He wrote a syndicated column that criticized liberals, gays, feminists, and particularly the administration of President JAMES (JIMMY) CARTER. He also made forays into radio and television BROADCASTING, founding what would later become the political debate program *Crossfire* on the Cable News Network (CNN). He rarely pulled punches; liberals and even some conservatives regarded him as a reactionary, but he won an audience with his appeals to traditional values. Although he was earning a reported annual income of $400,000 for his writing and work in radio and television, Buchanan jumped at the offer to serve as director of communications during the second term of President Reagan. The job was a conservative activist's dream: besides shaping Reagan's public image, Buchanan had constant access to the president's ear. Buchanan reportedly used this access to spur Reagan on to taking tougher positions—such as vetoing a farm bailout bill and lavishly praising the anti-Sandinista Contra rebels fighting in Nicaragua as "the moral equal of our Founding Fathers."

Presidential aspirations drew Buchanan into the 1992 race. He was even better known than in the 1980s as the result of his nightly appearances on CNN's *Crossfire*, where he sparred with his liberal colleague Michael E. Kinsley. President Bush's popularity among Republicans was waning, especially in light of a sluggish

"IF WE CAN SEND AN ARMY HALFWAY AROUND THE WORLD TO DEFEND THE BORDERS OF KUWAIT, CAN'T WE DEFEND THE NATIONAL BORDERS OF THE UNITED STATES OF AMERICA?"

economy. Moreover, Buchanan offered a clearly tougher platform than Bush, whom he considered a tepid moderate. "It seemed to me that if we're going to stand for anything," he told the *Washington Times*, "conservative leaders had to at least raise the banner and say, 'This is not conservatism.'" Buchanan's campaign combined populism, nationalism, and social conservatism: he advocated limits on immigration, restrictions on trade, and isolationism in foreign policy, while opposing abortion rights, gay and lesbian rights, and federal arts funding. As he always had in his role as a pundit, the candidate provoked. He ran TV ads featuring gay dancers, and he toured the South criticizing the Voting Rights Act (42 U.S.C.A. § 1971 et. seq. [1965]) and reassuring southerners that hanging the Confederate flag from public buildings was acceptable free expression.

Buchanan's critics also did not pull their punches. Liberals accused him of xenophobia, racism, and homophobia. Conservatives sometimes came to his defense, but not always. Michael Lind, editor of the conservative journal the *National Interest*, wrote that Buchanan represented "conservatism's ugly face." Charges of anti-Semitism followed Buchanan's use of the phrase "Israel and its amen corner" in attacking U.S. intervention in the Persian Gulf War, and among those critical of him was the prominent conservative author and Catholic William F. Buckley, Jr. Buchanan denied the charges: he said he was being tarred for supporting John Demjanjuk, who was accused, then later cleared, of being the Nazi war criminal Ivan the Terrible.

Small flaps attended the Buchanan campaign regularly—one day he was announcing that English immigrants would assimilate better than Zulus, and the next calling for beggars to be removed from the streets. The most severe criticism came in August 1992 after his speech at the GOP national convention. First he knocked the Democratic party's convention as a gathering of "cross-dressers." Then he called for a "cultural war" in which U.S. citizens, like the National Guard putting down the Los Angeles riots, "must take back our cities, and take back our culture, and take back our country." Typical of the liberal response was an editorial in the *New Republic* criticizing Buchanan for advocating "militarized race war" (*Washington Times* 19 July 1993). Mario M. Cuomo, former governor of New York, confronted him on the CBS program *Face the Nation*, asking, "What do you mean by 'culture'? That's a word they used in Nazi Germany." William J. Bennett, former secretary of education, accused him of "flirting with fascism." Buchanan defended himself, blaming secular humanism, Hollywood, the National Endowment for the Arts, and public schools for creating an "adversary culture" contrary to traditional values.

Despite Bush's winning the nomination handily, Buchanan's influence did not wane. Two years later, the themes of his candidacy found expression in the Contract with America's insistence on a constitutional amendment allowing school prayer and in a call for a crackdown on immigration. Moreover, in 1995, his "cultural war" message could be heard from nearly every Republican presidential candidate, especially Bob Dole. Meanwhile, Buchanan announced a second run for the White House campaigning on the same strong conservative positions he had advanced in his campaign in 1992. Though he stayed in the race until the end, Buchanan lost the Republican nomination for president to Dole by a large margin. See also ELECTIONS.

**BUGGERY** The criminal offense of anal or oral copulation by penetration of the male organ into the anus or mouth of another person of either sex or copulation between members of either sex with an animal.

Buggery is historically referred to as a "crime against nature." It is an offense under both COMMON LAW and statutes. Although prosecution for buggery is rare, the punishment upon conviction can be a fine, imprisonment, or both. The term is often used interchangeably with SODOMY.

## BUILDING AND LOAN ASSOCIATION

An organization that exists to accumulate a fund, composed of subscriptions and savings of its members, to help facilitate the purchase or construction of REAL ESTATE by such members by lending them the necessary funds. See also SAVINGS AND LOAN ASSOCIATION.

## BUILDING LINE

A line that a MUNICIPAL CORPORATION establishes, beyond which no building may extend to ensure that its streets will appear uniform.

A building line is also known as the "set back" requirement.

## BUILDING OFFICIALS AND CODE ADMINISTRATORS INTERNATIONAL

The Building Officials and Code Administrators International (BOCA) is an association of professionals employed in the establishment and enforcement of building codes, which are the rules and regulations that govern the design and construction of buildings. BOCA encourages cities and states to adopt uniform building codes, and promotes competence and professionalism in the enforcement of those codes.

The organization was established in 1915 by building officials from nine states and Canada. Their purpose was to provide a forum for the exchange of knowledge and ideas about building safety and construction regulation. In 1950, BOCA published the *BOCA Basic Building Code*. This was the organization's first model code. Within one year, the BOCA code had been adopted by fifty cities.

BOCA currently publishes a series of books called the *BOCA National Codes*, which contain detailed standards for all aspects of building construction. The section on stairways, for example, precisely describes the acceptable height, depth, and width of steps, and the proper placement and configuration of handrails necessary to ensure safety and ease of use. Separate volumes cover general construction, mechanical systems, plumbing, fire prevention, energy conservation, and other areas.

The codes published by BOCA do not in themselves have the force of law. They can be enforced only when they have been adopted by cities, states, or other government bodies with the authority to issue or withhold building permits. A city or state is free to adopt the BOCA codes in whole or in part.

BOCA's codes have been adopted by many states and cities in the eastern and midwestern United States. Other professional associations perform a similar function in other parts of the country, and publish their own building codes: the International Conference of Building Officials serves western states and publishes the *Uniform Building Code*, and the Southern Building Code Congress serves southern states and publishes the *Standard Building Code*. The three regional organizations are working together toward creating a single model code for the United States.

The publication of the codes is BOCA's most important function. The organization also publishes manuals, textbooks, and periodicals for its members. In addition, BOCA continually develops its model code to keep it up-to-date. It conducts regular training and education programs for its members and provides consultation services for local governments. BOCA disseminates information on the quality and acceptability of building materials and systems as well as on new construction techniques.

BOCA's membership consists largely of cities, towns, and government agencies. These "government members" are represented by individual officials who administer rules and regulations on construction, fire safety, property maintenance, development, and land use. A typical official of this kind is a building inspector with duties to examine building plans and make on-site inspections during construction. Contractors, manufacturers, and people in the architectural and engineering professions may also be members of BOCA.

BOCA is funded by the annual dues of its members and through the sale of its publications. It is based in Country Club Hills, Illinois, a suburb of Chicago.

**BULK TRANSFER** ▥ A sale of all or most of the materials, supplies, merchandise, or other INVENTORY of a business at one time that is not normally done in the ordinary course of the seller's business. ▥

Bulk transfers, commonly called bulk sales, have, in the past, been governed by individual state laws, generally called Bulk Sales Acts, which imposed certain requirements on such transfers. These acts were aimed at preventing a seller from secretly selling his or her business and absconding with the proceeds in order to avoid the repayment of any outstanding DEBTS. These laws have been superseded in most states by Article 6 of the UNIFORM COMMERCIAL CODE (UCC), which shares the same purpose but establishes uniform requirements to simplify commercial transactions. A prospective buyer of a business must obtain a list of the CREDITORS of the seller and notify them in advance of the sale so they can take steps to protect themselves against the seller's possible DEFAULT on his or her debts. Failure of a bulk transfer to comply with the UCC neither makes the transfer void nor destroys the creditors' rights to repayment. Depending upon the jurisdiction, the buyer may become personally liable to the seller's creditors up to the value of the assets purchased or the property sold may be levied upon by the creditors for the outstanding debts.

A bulk transfer is not the same as a SECURED TRANSACTION.

**BULLETIN** ▥ A printing of public notices and announcements that discloses the progress of matters affecting the general public and which usually includes provisions for public comment.

A summarized report of a newsworthy item for immediate release to the public. The official publication of an association, business, or institution. ▥

**BURDEN OF GOING FORWARD** ▥ The onus on a PARTY to a case to refute or to explain. ▥

The burden of going forward, also called the burden of producing evidence, burden of production, or the burden of proceeding, requires a party in a lawsuit to refute or explain each item of EVIDENCE introduced as the trial progresses that damages or discredits his or her position in the action. Suppose a person is charged with the possession of stolen goods. After the prosecution has introduced evidence of the defendant's possession of such goods, the defense bears the burden of refuting or explaining the evidence. If the evidence appears unfavorable for the prosecution, it has the burden of going forward to produce more evidence to bolster its claim that the defendant committed the crime. A failure to produce more evidence may result in the judge's dismissing the charges against the defendant. If the prosecution produces such evidence, it shifts the burden of production back to the defendant who must then refute the additional evidence.

In a CIVIL ACTION, the burden of going forward also shifts during the proceeding. The burden of producing evidence shifts to the defendant after the plaintiff rests its case, but it may shift even before that time. In a WRONGFUL DEATH claim, for example, the plaintiff may at a certain point in the trial file a motion asking for a ruling (sometimes a motion for a SUMMARY JUDGMENT or a motion for a DIRECTED VERDICT) in her or his favor by maintaining that she or he has presented sufficient evidence to show that the defendant's actions resulted in the victim's death. The burden then shifts to the defendant

*Architects must follow the recommendations of BOCA when designing a building to be constructed in a municipality that has adopted BOCA's codes.*

MICHAEL NEWMAN/PHOTOEDIT

to produce additional evidence to refute the plaintiff's claim; otherwise, the judge may grant the plaintiff's motion, thus concluding the case in the plaintiff's favor.

**BURDEN OF PERSUASION** ▥ The onus on the party with the burden of PROOF to convince the trier of fact of all elements of his or her case. In a criminal case the burden of the government to produce EVIDENCE of all the necessary elements of the crime BEYOND A REASONABLE DOUBT. ▥

The burden of persuasion is the affirmative duty of a party to establish his or her right to judicial RELIEF by convincing the trier of fact, the judge or the jury, that the facts asserted are true and support the ALLEGATIONS. Whereas the burden of going forward shifts from the prosecution to the defense in a criminal case, or from the plaintiff to the defendant in a civil case, as evidence is presented and disproved, the burden of persuasion remains with the plaintiff or the prosecution until the case is concluded. The phrase *burden of persuasion* is often used interchangeably with the phrase *burden of proof*.

The burden of proof varies depending on whether the proceeding is criminal or civil. In a criminal case, the burden of proof required of the state or government will be satisfied by evidence that demonstrates "beyond a reasonable doubt" that the defendant has committed the crime. Proof beyond a reasonable doubt does not require that the proof be so clear that no possibility of error can exist; no criminal prosecution would ever prevail if that were the standard. On the other hand, REASONABLE DOUBT will be found to exist (and the defendant found not guilty) if the evidence produced only demonstrates that it is slightly more probable that the defendant committed the crime than that she or he did not. The reasonable doubt standard has been defined to mean that the evidence must be so conclusive and complete that all reasonable doubts are removed.

In a civil matter, a plaintiff is required to establish his or her case by "a PREPONDERANCE OF THE EVIDENCE." A preponderance of the evidence is a body of evidence that is of greater weight or is more convincing than the evidence offered in opposition—evidence that as a whole shows that the facts asserted by the plaintiff and sought to be proved are more probable than not.

Another burden of proof applied in some matters is that the evidence must be "CLEAR AND CONVINCING." This standard of proof falls somewhere between the civil preponderance-of-the-evidence standard and the criminal beyond-a-reasonable-doubt standard. Clear and convincing evidence requires the trier of fact to have a "firm belief" that the facts have been established. The clear-and-convincing standard, though not used nearly as often as the other two standards, has been applied to some civil cases, including suits seeking the reformation of a contract. In addition, the Supreme Court of the United States has held that the clear-and-convincing standard is the constitutionally required burden of proof in a civil commitment proceeding (*Addington v. Texas*, 441 U.S. 418, 99 S. Ct. 1804, 60 L. Ed. 2d 323 [1979]).

**BURDEN OF PLEADING** The pleading burden concerns what a party must put in his or her PLEADING when a legal proceeding is first instituted. In a criminal proceeding, this initial pleading is an INDICTMENT or INFORMATION, which alleges that a crime was committed. In a MURDER case, for instance, the prosecutor must plead that the defendant killed the victim. The prosecution thus has the burden of pleading on the issue of whether the defendant killed the victim. On other issues in the case, the burden of pleading may shift to the defendant. For example, if the defendant claims that she or he is insane and thus not responsible for the crime, the defendant has the burden of pleading insanity.

In a civil matter, the initial pleading is a COMPLAINT, which initiates a lawsuit. For instance, in a NEGLIGENCE action, the plaintiff has the burden of pleading that the defendant was negligent and that the plaintiff has been injured or damaged by the actions of the defendant. Likewise, in a CONTRACT claim, the plaintiff must allege that a contract existed and that the defendant breached the contract. Failure to meet the pleading burden can result in dismissal of the claim.

**BUREAUCRACY** ▥ A system of ADMINISTRATION wherein there is a specialization of functions, objective qualifications for office, action according to the adherence to fixed rules, and a hierarchy of authority and delegated power. ▥

Organizations such as the armed forces or ADMINISTRATIVE AGENCIES are common examples of bureaucracies.

**BURGER, WARREN EARL** Warren Earl Burger was a self-made man who rose from modest origins to become the fifteenth CHIEF JUSTICE of the United States.

Burger was born September 17, 1907, in St. Paul, the fourth of seven children of Charles Burger and Katharine Schnittger Burger. His father worked as a railroad cargo inspector and traveling salesman, and the family lived simply on his limited income. Burger began delivering newspapers at the age of nine to help with

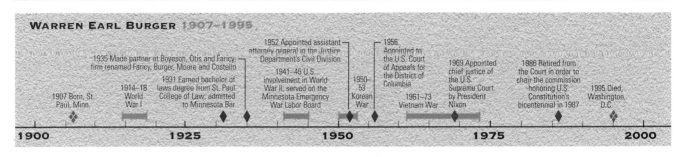

1907 Born, St. Paul, Minn.

1914–18 World War I

1931 Earned bachelor of laws degree from St. Paul College of Law; admitted to Minnesota Bar

1935 Made partner at Boyesen, Otis and Faricy; firm renamed Faricy, Burger, Moore and Costello

1941–45 U.S. involvement in World War II; served on the Minnesota Emergency War Labor Board

1952 Appointed assistant attorney general in the Justice Department's Civil Division

1950–53 Korean War

1956 Appointed to the U.S. Court of Appeals for the District of Columbia

1961–73 Vietnam War

1969 Appointed chief justice of the U.S. Supreme Court by President Nixon

1986 Retired from the Court in order to chair the commission honoring U.S. Constitution's bicentennial in 1987

1995 Died, Washington, D.C.

1900    1925    1950    1975    2000

family finances. At Johnson High School in St. Paul, he participated in music, sports, student government, and the student newspaper. Princeton University offered him a partial scholarship, but because of his family's limited resources, he was unable to accept it. Instead, he took extension courses through the University of Minnesota from 1925 to 1927 and then attended night classes at St. Paul College of Law (now William Mitchell College of Law). Throughout college and law school, Burger supported himself by working as an insurance agent. He earned his bachelor of laws degree, magna cum laude, in 1931.

Burger was admitted to the Minnesota bar in 1931, then entered private practice in St. Paul with Boyesen, Otis, and Faricy. He became a partner in 1935, and the firm was renamed Faricy, Burger, Moore, and Costello. Burger concentrated his practice in corporate, real estate, and probate law. At the same time, he became involved in politics, and in 1934 he helped organize the Minnesota Young Republicans.

Burger was rejected for military service in World War II because of a spinal injury, and instead served on the Minnesota Emergency War Labor Board. After the war he returned to his law practice and became more active in politics. He had played an important part in Harold E. Stassen's successful campaigns for governor of Minnesota in 1938, 1940, and 1942, and acted as floor manager for Stassen's presidential bids at the 1948 and 1952 Republican conventions. These activities brought him to the attention of prominent Republicans. In 1952 he was named assistant attorney general in charge of the Justice Department's Civil Division, which handled all civil cases except antitrust and land litigation.

Burger's career as a jurist began when he was appointed to the U.S. Court of Appeals for the District of Columbia Circuit in 1956. He quickly established his credentials as a law-and-order judge, leading the conservative faction of the court to numerous decisions that favored police officers and prosecutors and curbed the rights of criminal defendants.

### BIOGRAPHY

*Warren Earl Burger*

Burger served on the D.C. circuit court until 1969 when President RICHARD M. NIXON appointed him chief justice of the Supreme Court. In choosing Burger to replace EARL WARREN, Nixon was fulfilling a campaign promise to restrain the Court, which was, according to him, favoring the criminals in U.S. society. Burger's flawless ethical record was a major consideration in his nomination, and his opposition to judicial activism and the expansion of civil rights and liberties made him all that Nixon could have hoped for: a law-and-order judge whose character was beyond reproach. Nixon saw Burger as the conservative antidote to the activist liberalism of the WARREN COURT.

However, the swift and certain counterrevolution that Nixon and others expected from the Burger Court never materialized. Although the Court diluted some earlier liberal decisions, particularly in the area of CRIMINAL PROCEDURE, it stopped far short of overruling them. And although the Burger Court was far less sympathetic to the rights of criminal defendants than the Warren Court had been, it established no clear pattern of repudiating the earlier doctrines. In some areas, such as AFFIRMATIVE ACTION and desegregation, the Burger Court continued in the direction set by the Warren Court, and Burger often cast the swing vote that tipped the balance in favor of the liberals' position. The Burger Court's decision in *Roe v. Wade* (410 U.S. 113, 93 S. Ct. 705, 35 L. Ed. 2d 147 [1973]) established a constitutional right to privacy and made ABORTION legal. Yet Burger refused to support a movement to give gender classifications the same level of scrutiny used for racial DISCRIMINATION. When viewed as a whole, the record shows that Burger was an enigmatic and unpredictable justice, but that he generally stayed the course set by his predecessor. In fact, the Burger Court never directly overruled any major doctrine of the Warren years.

Burger was satisfied with his reputation as a centrist. "It's always been somewhat comforting to know," he once told an interviewer, "that I have been castigated by so-called liberals for being too conservative and castigated by so-called conservatives for being too liberal. Pretty safe position to be in." In the end, the Burger Court reflected its time and place—an era of turbulence and uncertainty, conflict and change, and a country anxious about its future. It was a "contentious Court for a contentious society," and Burger was a pragmatist who strove to reconcile the nation's divisive discord through moderate, narrowly drawn judgments.

Burger left his personal imprint on several important areas of the law. His 1973 opinion in *Miller v. California* (413 U.S. 15, 93 S. Ct. 2607, 37 L. Ed. 2d 419 [1973]) established the use of "contemporary community standards" in determining whether material is obscene. He authored key decisions interpreting the free speech and free press guarantees of the FIRST AMENDMENT, including *Nebraska Press Ass'n v. Stuart*, 427 U.S. 539, 96 S. Ct. 2791, 49 L. Ed. 2d 683 (1976), a 1976 decision prohibiting prepublication restraints to protect criminal defendants from negative PRETRIAL PUBLICITY. Writing for the majority, Burger declared that "prior restraints on speech and publication are the most serious and least tolerable infringement on First Amendment rights." Burger also delivered the opinion invalidating the legislative VETO (*I.N.S. v. Chadha*, 462 U.S. 919, 103 S. Ct. 2764, 77 L. Ed. 2d 317 [1983]), thus preventing Congress from blocking presidential action without passing a law.

Burger's most famous criminal opinion was *United States v. Nixon*, 418 U.S. 683, 94 S. Ct. 3090, 41 L. Ed. 2d 1039 (1974), in which he ordered the embattled president, then deeply enmeshed in the Watergate scandal, to release to Special Prosecutor LEON JAWORSKI the tape recordings that implicated the president in the Watergate cover-up. Nixon's resignation was a direct result of Burger's ruling, and through that decision Burger demonstrated his unwavering belief that all U.S. citizens, including the president who had given him his job, are governed by the same laws.

One of Burger's goals as chief justice was to modernize and streamline the courts to make them more accessible and functional, and he worked tirelessly toward that end. Burger originated the idea of employing professional court administrators, implemented continuing education for judges, and improved coordination between federal and state courts. In addition, he was noted for his outspoken criticism of ill-prepared litigators who use the courts for what he called on-the-job training.

Burger retired from the bench in 1986 to chair the commission honoring the two hundredth anniversary of the signing of the Constitution, which occurred on his eightieth birth-

"FREEDOM OF SPEECH CARRIES WITH IT SOME FREEDOM TO LISTEN."

day, September 17, 1987. He ended his last day on the bench without fanfare, simply announcing that the Court had completed its term and would recess until the first Monday in October. Asked about his future plans, he said, "I have a lot of other things I want to do. . . . I never had any ambition to be a judge. I loved practicing law. If tradition didn't prohibit it, I'd love to go back to practicing law." Upon his retirement, one of his law clerks commented that Burger's most important legacy may be that "he kept most of society's problems truly in balance" (*Washington Post* 22 June 1986). He remained true to the ideals and values he cherished while keeping the Court from veering sharply in any direction. In so doing, he modified the decisions of the Warren Court without unduly straining the social fabric of the nation.

Although sometimes depicted as aloof and unfriendly, particularly toward the media, Burger was admired and respected by those who worked closely with him. He may have been uncomfortable with the shifting values and moral principles sweeping the nation during his tenure, but he did his best to overcome his discomfort and to guide the Court toward decisions that were the least destructive to the country. With his pure white hair, his upright carriage, and his sedate demeanor, he was a dignified presence and a voice of reason, pragmatism, and moderation during a tumultuous time in the nation's history. Burger died in Washington, D.C., on June 25, 1995.

### CROSS-REFERENCES

Freedom of Speech; Freedom of the Press; Obscenity; *Roe v. Wade*; Watergate.

## BURGLARY

The criminal offense of breaking and entering a building illegally for the purpose of committing a crime therein.

Burglary, at COMMON LAW, was the trespassory breaking and entering of the dwelling of another at night with an intent to commit a FELONY therein. It is an offense against possession and habitation. The common-law elements of the offense have been modified in most jurisdictions by statutes that tend to make the crime less restrictive.

### Elements

**Trespass**    The TRESPASS element of the offense signifies that it must occur without the consent of the victim. If the thief gains entry by misrepresenting his or her identity, the element of trespass is satisfied, as there is no consent to entry.

**Breaking**    BREAKING consists of creating an opening for entry into the building. It can be accomplished by removing an object that is blocking an entry or by blasting open a wall. The use of FORCE is not required. The breaking element is satisfied if access is obtained by opening a closed door or window, regardless of whether these are locked.

At common law, entering through a pre-existing opening did not constitute breaking. If one gained access through an open door or window, burglary was not committed. The same rule applied when a door or window was partially open even though it was necessary to open it further in order to ENTER. The rationale underlying this rule was that one who failed to secure his or her dwelling was not entitled to the protection of the law. A majority of states no longer follow this rule, and consider breaking to be the slightest application of force to gain entry through a partially accessible opening.

When entry is gained by a MISREPRESENTATION of identity or by any other trick, it is called CONSTRUCTIVE breaking, which satisfies the breaking requirement of burglary. On the other hand, if a person, such as a servant, has authority to enter, there is no breaking unless he or she breaks into and enters an unauthorized area.

Under the common law, the breaking had to occur immediately before the time of entry. Most JURISDICTIONS that retain the breaking element are in agreement; in others, the breaking can occur during a reasonable time before the entry. Some jurisdictions have completely eliminated the element of breaking from the statutory definition of burglary, while others require it for one degree of burglary and not another.

**Entry**  In the course of a burglary, ENTRY is the act that follows the breaking. Literally, it occurs when there is physical intrusion into another's dwelling or building by any part of the intruder's body. A momentary intrusion will suffice. When a thief kicks open a window to gain access to a dwelling, the momentary insertion of the foot constitutes an entry.

When an instrument is used to gain access to a dwelling, the intrusion of the instrument is not an entry unless it is used to accomplish the intended felony. If the instrument is used to take something from inside the building, there is an entry sufficient for burglary.

An entry may be constructive. In other words, it is not always required that the thief enter the dwelling. If he or she directs another person not legally capable of committing the offense, such as a child, to enter, then the entry is imputed to the thief.

In jurisdictions where breaking is an element of burglary, there must be causation between

the breaking and entry. Although the acts may occur at separate times depending upon statute, the entry must follow from the breaking. Where a hole is drilled into a wall on one day and entry occurs a few days later, there is a causal link between the breaking and entry.

**Dwelling**  At common law, the entry had to be into the dwelling of another to constitute the offense. A dwelling was defined as a house or mansion where one normally sleeps, although it was not necessary that it be occupied at the time of entry. Structures and premises immediately surrounding the dwelling, such as an outhouse or a yard, were also protected since they were considered part of the dwelling.

A dwelling had to be a place of human habitation and occupancy. A storehouse protected by a nightwatchman was not a dwelling even if he occasionally slept in it. If, however, it was within the immediate surroundings of a dwelling, it would be treated as a dwelling for purposes of burglary.

Today, most jurisdictions have expanded the common-law requirement that the offense take place in a dwelling. There is no jurisdiction that retains this requirement for all degrees of burglary. Under modern statutes, the offense can

*Although the use of force is not required for the offense, the destruction of this door in order to enter the building constitutes* breaking, *an element of burglary.*

## Burglary

Persons arrested for burglary, by sex and age, in 1993

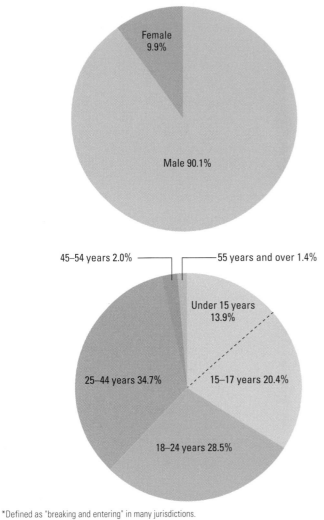

Female 9.9%

Male 90.1%

45–54 years 2.0% — 55 years and over 1.4%

Under 15 years 13.9%

25–44 years 34.7%

15–17 years 20.4%

18–24 years 28.5%

*Defined as "breaking and entering" in many jurisdictions.

Source: U.S.Federal Bureau of Investigation, *Crime in the United States*, annual.

occur in any enclosed structure, regardless of whether it is used for habitation.

**Nighttime** The requirement that the breaking and entering occur at night was an essential element of the offense at common law. Sunrise and sunset were not the means of determining night and day. The proper test was whether the countenance of a human could be discerned by natural light.

Many jurisdictions no longer require that the offense occur at night. Some states have retained it for higher degrees of the offense, but do not require it for all degrees. Under statutes retaining the nighttime element, it is defined as occurring thirty minutes before sunrise or thirty minutes after sunset. It is not necessary that all acts be done on the same night. If the breaking and entering is done one night and the felony is committed a few nights later, the offense is committed.

**Intent** Under the common law, an intent to commit a felony at the time of breaking and entering into the dwelling was an essential element of burglary. Since LARCENY was a felony at common law, an INTENT to commit a larceny would suffice. Statutes vary from one jurisdiction to another. An intent to commit a felony is no longer required for all grades of the offense. In some states an intent to commit any crime will suffice. Many states have retained the felony requirement for higher grades of the offense.

Absent this intent element, a breaking and entry might be a trespass, but not be a burglary.

If a defense to the underlying crime or felony is sufficiently established, there can be no conviction for burglary. For example, if a person charged with burglary is accused of larceny and has a sufficient defense to the larceny charge, then there is no burglary.

**Degrees** Some jurisdictions have a statutory scheme under which the offense is divided into DEGREES. These types of statutes frequently impose heavier penalties when the offense involves the use of force or weapons. Under one such statute, burglary in the third degree is committed by a person knowingly entering or remaining unlawfully in a building with an intent to commit a crime therein. When the same offense is committed with explosives or deadly weapons, or when it results in physical injury to a person who is not a participant in the crime, it is burglary in the first degree, for which there is a greater penalty.

Burglary is a unique type of ATTEMPT crime in that it is generally held not to merge into a completed offense that was intended when the breaking and entry occurred. If a person succeeds in committing the intended crime, he or she is subject to punishment for both the burglary and the intended crime.

Imprisonment is the usual punishment. Under statutes in many states, the severity of the sentence is determined by the degree of the burglary.

**BURKE, EDMUND** Edmund Burke was an orator, philosophical writer, political theorist, and member of Parliament who helped shape political thought in England and the United States during the late eighteenth and early nineteenth centuries.

Burke was born January 12, 1729, in Dublin, Ireland, to a Protestant father and a Roman Catholic mother. His father, a prosperous Dub-

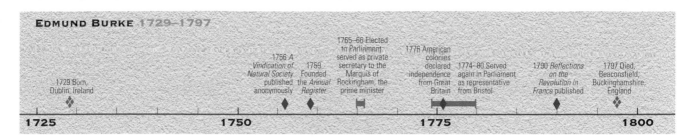

EDMUND BURKE 1729–1797

1729 Born,
Dublin, Ireland

1756 A
Vindication of
Natural Society
published
anonymously

1759
Founded
the Annual
Register

1765–66 Elected
to Parliament;
served as private
secretary to the
Marquis of
Rockingham, the
prime minister

1776 American
colonies
declared
independence
from Great
Britain

1774–80 Served
again in Parliament
as representative
from Bristol

1790 Reflections
on the
Revolution in
France published

1797 Died,
Beaconsfield,
Buckinghamshire,
England

1725        1750        1775        1800

lin attorney, was cold and authoritarian, and the two did not enjoy a close relationship. After graduating from Trinity College, Dublin, in 1750, Burke traveled to England to study law in accord with his father's wishes. However, he did not progress in his legal studies, and he eventually abandoned the law in favor of a literary career.

In 1756 Burke published two philosophical treatises, *A Vindication of Natural Society* and *A Philosophical Enquiry into the Origin of Our Ideas of the Sublime and Beautiful*. These and other works launched Burke's career as a critic of social and political issues. Burke became a member of the literary circle headed by Samuel Johnson, the English author, scholar, and critic. In 1759, Burke founded the *Annual Register*, a yearly survey of world affairs to which he contributed until 1788.

Realizing that the literary life would not pay enough to support a family, Burke entered politics. In 1765, he was appointed private secretary to the Marquis of Rockingham, England's prime minister and a member of the Whig party, marking the beginning of a lifelong alliance between Burke and Rockingham and the Whigs. Burke was also elected to Parliament in 1765. In 1766, Rockingham lost the premiership. Burke was offered employment with the new administration, but chose to remain with the Whig opposition. "I believe in any body of men in England I should have been in the minority," he said. "I have always been in the minority."

Burke believed strongly in opposition politics. Having a party that acts as a watchdog for the incumbent party is the best way, he felt, to avoid corruption and abuse of power. As a member of the opposition, Burke could do what he did best: criticize the government for what he considered unjust or unwise policies. He disagreed with England's policies in North America and urged the government to abolish the tea duty imposed on the colonies. "All government—indeed every human benefit and enjoyment, every virtue and every prudent act—is founded on compromise and barter," he said in 1775, in his *Speech on Conciliation with*

## BIOGRAPHY

*Edmund Burke*

"ALL GOVERNMENT—INDEED, EVERY HUMAN BENEFIT AND ENJOYMENT, EVERY VIRTUE AND EVERY PRUDENT ACT—IS FOUNDED ON COMPROMISE AND BARTER."

*America*. However, despite his dissatisfaction with English policy, he did not support the American revolutionaries. Although he believed that the British had been overly harsh and tyrannical, he also believed in the legislative superiority of the British Parliament over the colonies. In August, 1776, he expressed his despair over the conflict between England and its North American colonies: "I do not know how to wish success to those whose victory is to separate us from a large and noble part of our empire," he wrote. "Still less do I wish success to injustice, oppression, and absurdity. . . . No good can come of any event in this war to any virtuous interest."

Burke vociferously criticized the British government's policies in Ireland as well, and decried the poverty and persecution of Catholics there. Yet, although his sympathies were clearly with the oppressed and powerless in Ireland, he again opposed revolution and urged moderation on both sides. "I believe there are very few cases which will justify a revolt against the established government of a country, let its constitution be what it will, " he said.

Burke's support for established order, even where it meant support for inequalities, was most evident in his harsh criticism of the French Revolution. "[T]he age of chivalry is gone," he wrote in *Reflections on the Revolution in France*. "That of sophisters, economists and calculators has succeeded; and the glory of Europe is gone forever." According to Burke, the French revolutionaries' only purpose was to destroy all traditional authority and property rights. The result, he predicted, would be ANARCHY and the emergence of an autocratic ruler whose reign would be worse than any the revolutionaries had seen before. Burke's prediction proved accurate: the revolution in France led to the Reign of Terror and the regime of Napoleon.

In his condemnation of the French Revolution, Burke presaged American thought on the importance of private property to the preservation of societal harmony. Stephen B. Presser, associate dean and professor at Northwestern University School of Law, wrote that

Burke's attacks on the French, and his spirited defense of private property as a guarantee of order, stability, and prosperity have echoed through the arguments of American judges and statesmen.

Burke's strongest criticism of British policy came in the 1780s when he instigated IMPEACHMENT proceedings against Warren Hastings, governor-general of India. Burke attacked the British East India Company as unjust and oppressive in its treatment of the Indian people. In his *Speech on Opening the Articles of Impeachment of Warren Hastings* (1788), Burke asserted his belief that the exercise of arbitrary political power is never justified. "My Lords ... the King has no arbitrary power to give him [Hastings], your Lordships have not, nor the commons, nor the whole Legislature. We have no arbitrary power to give, because arbitrary power is a thing, which neither any man can hold nor any man can give." Burke's view that political power is held in trust for the benefit of the people is reflected in the basic tenets of U.S. democracy and is at the core of the United States' republican form of government.

Burke has been claimed as a champion of both liberals and conservatives. His denunciation of oppression in India, Ireland, and North America and his staunch opposition to the exercise of arbitrary power endeared him to libertarians and proponents of individual rights. However, his strong faith in established political, religious, and social institutions, and his fear of reform beyond limitations on sovereign power, reverberate in contemporary conservatism. Likewise, his support for CIVIL RIGHTS was tempered with a strong belief in the necessity of individual responsibility. In 1791, he wrote, in *A Letter to a Member of the National Assembly,*

> Men are qualified for civil liberty in exact proportion to their disposition to put moral chains upon their own appetites; in proportion as their love to justice is above their rapacity; in proportion as their soundness and sobriety of understanding is above their vanity and presumption; in proportion as they are more disposed to listen to the counsels of the wise and good, in preference to the flattery of knaves.

Burke was firmly opposed to the substitution of government assistance for individual initiative. In *Thoughts and Details on Scarcity* (1795), he cautioned against "attempts to feed the people out of the hands of the magistrates." He seemed to predict the modern quagmire of WELFARE dependency when he wrote, "and having looked to government for bread, on the very first scarcity they will turn and bite the hand that fed them. To avoid that evil, government will redouble the causes of it; and then it will become inveterate and incurable."

The last few years of Burke's life were marred by the death of his only son, Richard Burke, in 1794. With his wife, Jane Nugent Burke, whom he had married in 1757, Burke had established the harmonious family life he had never known as a child. The premature loss of his son, and the concomitant demise of Burke's dreams and plans for the young man's future, left Burke disconsolate. Although he continued his activities in politics, particularly in the formation of the Irish government, his personal life was clouded with disappointment and bitterness. Burke died three years after his son, on July 9, 1797; yet two hundred years after his death, his philosophies continued to resonate on both sides of the Atlantic.

**BIOGRAPHY**

LIBRARY OF CONGRESS

*Jean Jacques Burlamaqui*

# BURLAMAQUI, JEAN JACQUES

Jean Jacques Burlamaqui achieved prominence as a Swiss jurist and legal author.

Burlamaqui was born July 24, 1694. As an educator, Burlamaqui taught legal studies at Geneva; however, his fame is based primarily on his two publications relating to the law: *Principes du droit naturel*, translated as "Principles of natural law," in 1747; and *Principes au droit politique*, or "Principles of political law," in 1751. He believed in NATURAL LAW and its relationship to God, human intellect, and innate moral responses, and he viewed natural law as the foundation of domestic and INTERNATIONAL LAW.

Burlamaqui died April 3, 1748, in Geneva, Switzerland.

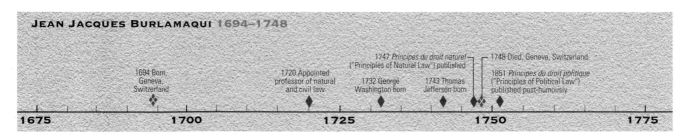

**JEAN JACQUES BURLAMAQUI 1694–1748**

1694 Born, Geneva, Switzerland

1720 Appointed professor of natural and civil law

1732 George Washington born

1747 *Principes du droit naturel* ("Principles of Natural Law") published

1743 Thomas Jefferson born

1748 Died, Geneva, Switzerland

1851 *Principes du droit politique* ("Principles of Political Law") published posthumously

1675    1700    1725    1750    1775

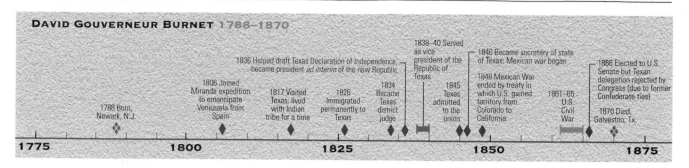

**DAVID GOUVERNEUR BURNET** 1788–1870

1838–40 Served as vice president of the Republic of Texas

1846 Became secretary of state of Texas; Mexican war began

1836 Helped draft Texas Declaration of Independence; became president *ad interim* of the new Republic

1866 Elected to U.S. Senate but Texan delegation rejected by Congress (due to former Confederate ties)

1806 Joined Miranda expedition to emancipate Venezuela from Spain

1848 Mexican War ended by treaty in which U.S. gained territory from Colorado to California

1817 Visited Texas; lived with Indian tribe for a time

1826 Immigrated permanently to Texas

1834 Became Texas district judge

1845 Texas admitted to the union

1861–65 U.S. Civil War

1788 Born, Newark, N.J.

1870 Died, Galveston, Tx.

1775　1800　1825　1850　1875

## BURNET, DAVID GOUVERNEUR

David Gouverneur Burnet centered his career efforts in Texas.

Burnet was born April 4, 1788, in Newark, New Jersey. Before entering politics, Burnet served under Francisco de Miranda in 1806 in an endeavor to liberate Venezuela from Spain. He also studied law and pursued careers in business and speculation.

Burnet relocated to Texas and presided as a Texas district judge in 1834. In 1836 he participated at the Washington-on-the-Brazos Convention, where he drafted the Texas Declaration of Independence; in 1836 he served as the president *ad interim* of the Republic of Texas. He subsequently resigned, but returned to perform the duties of vice president. From 1846 to 1847 he acted as the secretary of state of Texas, the first person to hold such a position in the newly formed state.

Burnet died December 5, 1870, in Galveston, Texas.

## BURR, AARON

Aaron Burr was a soldier, lawyer, and politician and the third VICE PRESIDENT of the United States.

Burr was born February 6, 1756, in Newark, New Jersey. His family traced its ancestry to the Pilgrims and through hundreds of years of English gentry with many members who were prominent in government and politics. Both his parents died when he was young and he and his sister were raised in comfortable circumstances by their maternal uncle. Burr was a bright, charming, handsome, and witty boy who was

**BIOGRAPHY**

STATE PRESERVATION BOARD, AUSTIN, TX

*David Gouverneur Burnet*

**BIOGRAPHY**

LIBRARY OF CONGRESS

*Aaron Burr*

gifted intellectually but decidedly mischievous and difficult to control. From earliest childhood he showed ambition, determination, and leadership.

Burr entered the College of New Jersey (now Princeton University) as a sophomore in 1769 at the age of thirteen and graduated summa cum laude three years later. He then enrolled in LITCHFIELD (Connecticut) LAW SCHOOL, which was run by his brother-in-law and former tutor Tapping Reeve. However, the Revolutionary War and his desire to be a part of it interrupted his studies.

Burr rose swiftly through the ranks of the revolutionary army, displaying daring, energy, courage, and imagination. His small stature and pampered upbringing belied an internal strength that surprised many who knew him. Accompanying Colonel Benedict Arnold's troops in their expedition to Quebec, he endured cold, hunger, and illness. He was made an officer in the Continental Army and soon served with General GEORGE WASHINGTON.

Burr resigned his Army commission in 1779. He resumed the study of law in 1780 and was admitted to the bar in 1782. Later in 1782 he married Theodosia Prevost, a widow ten years his senior, and the following year their only child, a daughter also named Theodosia, was born.

In 1789 Burr was appointed attorney general of the state of New York and in 1791 he was elected a U.S. senator, defeating General Philip Schuyler, the father-in-law of ALEXANDER

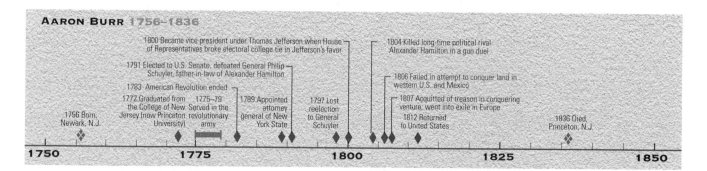

**AARON BURR** 1756–1836

1800 Became vice president under Thomas Jefferson when House of Representatives broke electoral college tie in Jefferson's favor

1804 Killed long-time political rival Alexander Hamilton in a gun duel

1791 Elected to U.S. Senate, defeated General Philip Schuyler, father-in-law of Alexander Hamilton

1783 American Revolution ended

1806 Failed in attempt to conquer land in western U.S. and Mexico

1772 Graduated from the College of New Jersey (now Princeton University)

1775–79 Served in the revolutionary army

1789 Appointed attorney general of New York State

1797 Lost reelection to General Schuyler

1807 Acquitted of treason in conquering venture; went into exile in Europe

1812 Returned to United States

1756 Born, Newark, N.J.

1836 Died, Princeton, N.J.

1750　1775　1800　1825　1850

HAMILTON. This was the beginning of a bitter rivalry with Hamilton that would come to a ruinous conclusion years later.

Burr served in the Senate for six years. In 1797, the voters turned against him and elected his former antagonist, General Schuyler. Burr attributed his loss to Hamilton's assiduous efforts to undermine his support and reputation.

After losing his Senate seat, Burr served a short time in the New York assembly, before entering the presidential race of 1800. He and his opponent, THOMAS JEFFERSON, received the same number of votes in the ELECTORAL COLLEGE, and the election went to the House of Representatives for resolution. Burr and his supporters were unabashedly ambitious in their zeal to win the office. Burr's nemesis Hamilton stepped into the fray, announcing his support for Jefferson and criticizing Burr. Finally, through clever manipulation of the voting process, Hamilton secured the presidency for Jefferson and Burr automatically became vice president. As a result of this peculiar election Congress passed the TWELFTH AMENDMENT, which mandated separate balloting for president and vice president.

Burr's ruthless and opportunistic ambition caused many of his colleagues to shun him both professionally and socially. President Jefferson held him at arm's length, and others in the administration treated him like an outsider. Burr blamed his failure to secure the top office largely on Hamilton and he brooded over perceived injustices. Having lost his beloved wife in 1794, Burr was left with only his daughter, whom he idolized. He devoted as much time and energy as possible to her education and her grooming. However, the young lady was moving into adulthood and a life of her own. In 1801, against her father's wishes, she married Joseph Alston, of South Carolina, and moved to the Palmetto State, leaving Burr alone in Washington, D.C.

Toward the end of his term as vice president, Burr ran for governor of New York but was defeated. During the campaign Hamilton again expressed his distrust of Burr and made other disparaging comments about him. Feeling that his honor had been impugned, Burr challenged Hamilton to a DUEL. Although Hamilton tried to defuse the conflict, Burr was determined to force a confrontation. The two men met at 7:00 A.M. on July 7, 1804. Burr was an excellent marksman, and he killed Hamilton with the first shot. In an ensuing public outcry, Burr was indicted for MURDER. He escaped to his daughter's home in South Carolina until the furor died down and eventually returned to Washington, D.C., to complete his term as vice president.

Burr came to realize that his aspirations to the presidency had been destroyed. His political career in ruins, he left Washington, D.C., and traveled west to explore frontier territory. He also concocted an elaborate CONSPIRACY that was to be his final political undoing. Though complete details of the scheme have never been fully discovered, Burr apparently intended to lead the western states in an insurrection against the federal government. After the states seceded, he planned to install himself as the head of a newly created republic. He then intended to conquer Texas and Mexico. In October 1806 President Jefferson issued a proclamation denouncing Burr's venture. On January 14, 1807, Burr was arrested in Mississippi on a charge of TREASON. He escaped, but was later apprehended in Alabama. Burr's trial began in May 1807, and lasted six months. He was eventually acquitted but his political life was over.

Burr spent the next several years in exile in Europe, where he endured poverty, humiliation, and degradation. In 1812, he quietly returned to the United States, slipping into Boston wearing a disguise and using an assumed name. After a time he resumed a somewhat normal life and opened a law office in New York. Burr's prospects seemed to be brightening when he was dealt two crushing personal blows. First, he learned that his only grandchild, Aaron Burr Alston, had died before Burr returned to the United States. A few months later his beloved daughter perished in a shipwreck while traveling from South Carolina to New York to visit Burr.

Burr was devastated by these losses. A wave of sympathy tempered public opinion toward him, but he was still shunned by those in prominence. He continued his law practice, enjoyed a small circle of supportive friends, and even remarried, though the union was short-lived and unhappy. He quietly and unobtrusively engaged in numerous altruistic and philanthropic ventures, including providing for the education of young men and women of limited resources and adopting an orphan who lived with him until late adolescence.

During the last few years of his life, Burr suffered a series of strokes. At first, he rebounded completely, but each successive episode left him weaker. He died September 14, 1836, and was buried beside his parents and grandfather in Princeton, New Jersey.

"LAW IS WHATEVER IS BOLDLY ASSERTED AND PLAUSIBLY MAINTAINED."

**BURTON, HAROLD HITZ**    Harold Hitz Burton served as a Supreme Court justice during the years the Court outlawed segregation.

Burton was born June 22, 1888, in Jamaica Plain, Massachusetts. He attended Bowdoin College, where he was elected Phi Beta Kappa, and graduated summa cum laude in 1909. He then entered Harvard Law School where he received his bachelor of laws degree in 1912. He married Selma Florence Smith and the couple set out to take advantage of opportunity in the burgeoning Midwest. They settled in Cleveland where Burton established a successful law practice.

Burton served in the infantry in France during World War I. He rose to the rank of captain and was awarded the Purple Heart. In 1923 he began teaching law at Western Reserve University (now Case Western Reserve University) and he remained on the faculty there until 1925.

Burton's political career began to take shape when he was elected to the Ohio legislature in 1929. He also acted as chief legal official of Cleveland from 1929 to 1932. In 1935 he was elected mayor of Cleveland and he was returned to office twice. By 1940 Burton's name and reputation for integrity were well established and he easily won election to the U.S. Senate. He became known in Washington, D.C., as a moderate conservative who advocated U.S. membership in the newly formed United Nations.

When a vacancy occurred on the Supreme Court in 1944, President HARRY S. TRUMAN, a Democrat, was under pressure to name a Republican to fill the slot. Truman did the politically expedient thing: he named Burton, a moderate Republican whom he admired and who would likely be replaced in the Senate by a Democrat. Burton was a popular choice. He was confirmed within a day of his nomination with no testimony heard by the Senate Judiciary Committee and unanimous approval by the full Senate.

Burton was a hardworking, conscientious, dispassionate, and open-minded justice. His

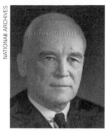

**BIOGRAPHY**

*Harold Hitz Burton*

"THE CONSTITUTION WAS BUILT FOR ROUGH AS WELL AS SMOOTH ROADS."

moderate conservatism was a unifying influence on a highly fractious court. He was noted for his ability to bridge conflicting factions with narrowly written opinions that settled an issue without taking a philosophical stand. He generally supported STATES' RIGHTS against interference by the federal government, except where his sensitivity to human suffering was aroused. In 1947 he wrote a vigorous dissent from the Court's decision to allow Louisiana to execute a prisoner after several previous attempts to execute him had failed. The Court held that the state's continued efforts to execute the man did not constitute "CRUEL AND UNUSUAL" PUNISHMENT. Burton wrote, "It is unthinkable that any state legislature in modern times would enact a statute expressly authorizing CAPITAL PUNISHMENT by repeated applications of an electric current separated by intervals of days or hours until finally death shall result" (*Louisiana ex rel. Francis v. Resweber*, 329 U.S. 459, 67 S. Ct. 374, 91 L. Ed. 422 [1947]).

Burton's decisions in ANTITRUST and labor disputes tended to favor CORPORATIONS and management over unions. He was generally opposed to extending individual rights beyond the letter of the Constitution, but he digressed from that stance in matters of racial segregation and DISCRIMINATION. A decision he authored in 1950 struck down the practice of confining black passengers in railway dining cars to a separate area. "The curtains, partitions and signs [used to mark that area]," he wrote, "emphasize the artificiality of a difference in treatment which serves only to call attention to racial classifications of passengers holding identical tickets and using the same public dining facility" (*Henderson v. U.S.*, 339 U.S. 816, 70 S. Ct. 843, 94 L. Ed. 1302 [1950]). Burton was also a member of the 1954 Court that unanimously declared that segregation in public schools is unconstitutional (*Brown v. Board of Education*, 347 U.S. 483, 74 S. Ct. 686, 98 L. Ed. 873).

Burton was compelled to retire in 1958 because of deteriorating health due to Parkinson's

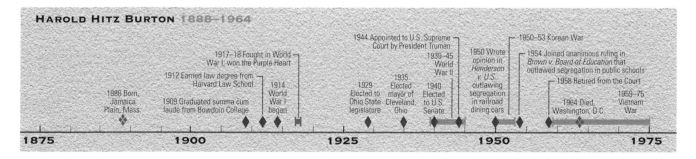

HAROLD HITZ BURTON 1888–1964

1888 Born, Jamaica Plain, Mass.
1909 Graduated summa cum laude from Bowdoin College
1912 Earned law degree from Harvard Law School
1914 World War I began
1917–18 Fought in World War I; won the Purple Heart
1929 Elected to Ohio State legislature
1935 Elected mayor of Cleveland, Ohio
1940 Elected to U.S. Senate
1939–45 World War II
1944 Appointed to U.S. Supreme Court by President Truman
1950 Wrote opinion in *Henderson v. U.S.*, outlawing segregation in railroad dining cars
1950–53 Korean War
1954 Joined unanimous ruling in *Brown v. Board of Education* that outlawed segregation in public schools
1958 Retired from the Court
1964 Died, Washington, D.C.
1959–75 Vietnam War

1875    1900    1925    1950    1975

disease. He died October 28, 1964, in Washington, D.C.

See also BROWN V. BOARD OF EDUCATION OF TOPEKA, KANSAS; WARREN COURT.

## BUSH, GEORGE HERBERT WALKER

George Herbert Walker Bush capped a full and distinguished political career with his election in 1988 as president of the United States. Bush became the forty-first chief executive after serving for eight years as the nation's VICE PRESIDENT under RONALD REAGAN. The most memorable events of his one-term presidency were the Desert Shield and Desert Storm Operations in the Persian Gulf in 1991.

Although Bush was enormously popular in the aftermath of the Persian Gulf War, his standing with the U.S. public plummeted as domestic problems and a sour economy took their toll. In 1992, Bush lost the presidential election to Democratic challenger BILL CLINTON, the governor of Arkansas. Clinton's campaign offered a promise of change and a "new covenant" between citizens and government.

Born June 12, 1924, in Milton, Massachusetts, Bush was the son of Prescott Sheldon Bush, an international banker and U.S. senator from Connecticut, and Dorothy Walker Bush, the daughter of a wealthy St. Louis businessman. Both parents had a tremendous influence on Bush, who was unpretentious and hardworking despite his privileged background.

As a young boy, Bush attended Greenwich Country Day School, in Greenwich, Connecticut, and Phillips Academy, an elite prep school in Andover, Massachusetts. At Andover, Bush excelled academically and athletically. Nicknamed Poppy after his grandfather Walker, Bush was a popular student, serving as class president and captain of the basketball and soccer teams.

When World War II broke out, Bush was determined to see military action. On June 12, 1942, shortly after graduation from Andover, he enlisted in the U.S. Navy. At the age of twenty, he became the youngest commissioned pilot in Navy history. Bush was stationed in the Pacific

*George Herbert Walker Bush*

"A FREE ECONOMY DEMANDS ENGAGEMENT IN THE ECONOMIC MAINSTREAM. ISOLATION AND PROTECTIONISM DOOM [THEIR] PRACTITIONERS TO DEGRADATION AND WANT."

theater and flew dozens of dangerous missions. On September 2, 1944, while Bush was assigned to the USS *Jacinto*, his plane was shot down near a Japanese island. Bush bailed out of the aircraft and was rescued at sea; his crewmen did not survive.

Bush returned to the United States after his tour of duty and entered Yale University, in New Haven, Connecticut. Not surprisingly, Bush had an outstanding college career. He played varsity baseball, was inducted into the Skull and Crossbones secret society, and in 1948 graduated Phi Beta Kappa with a degree in economics.

Before entering Yale in 1945, Bush married Barbara Pierce, the daughter of the publisher of *McCall's* and *Redbook*. Their first child was born during Bush's senior year of college. The couple eventually had six children, including a daughter who died of leukemia in 1953.

After graduating from Yale, Bush and his young family headed for Texas, determined to make their fortune in the oil business. In 1951, Bush started Bush-Overby Oil Development Company, and in 1954, he created Zapata Offshore Company, which designed and built offshore drilling platforms.

Bush's success in the oil business kindled his political ambitions. In 1964, Bush entered the race for U.S. senator from Texas, but lost to Democrat Ralph Yarborough. Two years later, Bush made it to Washington, D.C., as a member of the U.S. House of Representatives from the Seventh District of Texas. Reelected to the House in 1968, Bush was a member of the influential House Ways and Means Committee. In 1970, he again ran for the Texas Senate seat, this time losing to Democrat Lloyd Bentsen.

Despite his defeat Bush's career in public service was far from over. During the 1970s he held a wide range of appointive posts and built up an impressive résumé. From 1971 to 1973 Bush served as the U.S. ambassador to the United Nations. In 1974 he was the chair of the Republican National Committee. In 1974–75 Bush traveled to the People's Republic of China

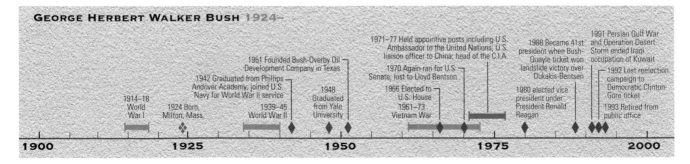

as the U.S. liaison officer. And from 1976 to 1977 Bush was the head of the Central Intelligence Agency.

Confident in his experience and abilities, Bush announced his intention to run for president. From 1977 to 1980 he actively campaigned for the Republican nomination. Although he lost the 1980 GOP nod to Reagan, the conservative governor of California, Bush was chosen by Reagan as his vice presidential candidate. The Reagan-Bush ticket reached the White House easily in 1980, defeating incumbent president JIMMY CARTER and vice president Walter F. Mondale.

Bush was a late convert to Reagan's conservatism. As a U.S. representative in the 1960s Bush had been a political moderate, voting in favor of open housing, the abolishment of the military draft, and the vote for eighteen-year-olds. As vice president under Reagan, Bush became more conservative.

Bush was a loyal vice president and basked in the reflected glory of Reagan, a popular president. When Reagan and Bush ran again in 1984, they won in a landslide victory against Democratic candidate Mondale and his running mate, GERALDINE FERRARO.

In 1988 the Republican party rewarded Bush for his loyal service as vice president. Despite an early defeat in the Iowa caucuses, Bush won the GOP nomination for president. To the surprise of many, Bush chose Dan Quayle, a relatively unknown and inexperienced senator from Indiana, as his running mate. The choice puzzled many political experts who felt that Quayle's credentials were meager.

Bush and Quayle ran against Governor Michael Dukakis of Massachusetts and Bush's old nemesis from Texas, Senator Bentsen. During the campaign Bush resorted to some tactics that seemed out of keeping with his congenial personality. One Bush TV commercial focused on Willie Horton, an African American felon who committed additional crimes upon his release from prison in Massachusetts. Suggesting that Dukakis was soft on crime, the ad capitalized on racial fears and prejudice. Also, despite the soaring deficit, Bush promised to give U.S. citizens a financial break, in the campaign pledge Read My Lips: No New Taxes. After the election Bush's pledge came back to haunt him: once in office, he agreed to tax increases to combat a $140 billion budget deficit.

Bush and Quayle captured the vote in forty states to win the 1988 ELECTION. At his inauguration Bush made an appeal for a "kinder, gentler nation" and shared his vision of volunteers, like "a thousand points of light," helping to solve problems.

The height of Bush's popularity came during Operation Desert Storm, a six-week display of technological warfare against Sadam Hussein in Kuwait and Iraq. When it became clear that the multinational operation had failed to change anything permanently in the Middle East, Bush's popularity decreased.

In 1992 Bush and Quayle squared off against Democratic challengers Clinton and Albert Gore, Jr., a senator from Tennessee. The GOP incumbents won their party's endorsement after a bruising primary fight with conservative columnist PATRICK BUCHANAN. Independent candidate H. Ross Perot, a Texas multimillionaire businessman, also threw his hat into the ring, to further muddle the election scene. Despite Clinton's liabilities—rumors of infidelity, avoidance of the draft, and a "slick" image—Bush was unable to defeat him.

Commentators often argue over the reasons one politician wins or loses, but many agree that a sluggish economy and Bush's broken promise of no new taxes hurt his chances for reelection. Clinton and Gore, a generation younger than Bush, won the election with a promise of change and new beginnings.

After his defeat at the polls Bush and his wife returned to Texas, vowing to spend more time with their children and grandchildren. They divide their time between Texas and Kennebunkport, Maine.

**CROSS-REFERENCES**

Federal Budget; President; United Nations.

## BUSINESS AFFECTED WITH A PUBLIC INTEREST

A commercial venture or an occupation that has become subject to governmental REGULATION by virtue of its offering essential services or products to the community at large.

A business affected with a PUBLIC INTEREST is subject to regulation by the POLICE POWER of the state to protect and to promote the general welfare of the community which it serves. Such a designation does not arise from the fact that the business is large, or that the public receives a benefit or enjoyment from its operation. The enterprise, as a result of its integral participation in the life of the community or by the PRIVILEGE it has been granted by the state to serve the needs of the public, is regulated more strictly by the state than other businesses.

What constitutes a business affected with a public interest varies from state to state. Three classes of businesses have been traditionally regarded as affected with a public interest: (1) those carried on pursuant to a public grant or privilege imposing a duty of making available essential services demanded by the public, such as COMMON CARRIERS and PUBLIC UTILITIES; (2) occupations considered from the earliest times in COMMON LAW to be exceptional, such as the operation of inns or cabs; and (3) businesses that although not public at their inception have become such by devoting their activities to a public use, such as INSURANCE companies and BANKS.

A business affected with a public interest remains the property of its owner, but the community is considered to have such a stake in its operation that it becomes subject to public regulation to the extent of that interest. See also REGULATE.

**BUSINESS CLOSINGS** After advocating such measures for fifteen years, proponents of mandatory plant closing notification secured federal legislation in August 1988 with the Worker Adjustment and Retraining Notification Act, 100 P.L. 379. The measures were initially part of the Omnibus Trade and Competitiveness Act of 1988, P.L. 100-418, 102 Stat. 1159, which President RONALD REAGAN had VE-TOED. After failing to garner the two-thirds majority required for an override, Congress chose to make the plant closing notification provisions into a separate act. In July, the Senate approved the plant closing legislation by a vote of 72 to 23, and the House of Representatives passed it by a vote of 286 to 136. On August 2, 1988, perhaps sensing the popularity of the bill, President Reagan announced his intent to permit the bill to become law without his signature. The bill became automatically effective at midnight, August 3, 1988.

The law requires employers with one hundred or more employees to provide their workers with sixty days' layoff notice when fifty or more workers at a single site will lose their jobs and when affected workers will constitute at least one-third of that site's work force. If 500 or more employees are laid off, however, such notice is required regardless of the percentage of site workers involved. Companies failing to provide the requisite warning face penalties of compensating each dismissed employee for wages and fringe benefits for every day the notice should have been given. Additionally, a $500 payment per day, up to a maximum of $30,000, must be made to local communities when the act's provisions have not been met.

Analogous requirements exist in thirty-eight other countries and in five states. At least twenty other states have proposed such legislation. According to the federal government's General Accounting Office (GAO) survey, prior to this legislation, the national median length of advance notice for the closing of large establishments was seven days. White collar and union blue collar workers averaged as much as fourteen days' TERMINATION notice while non-union

*Employers must notify workers sixty days in advance before laying off fifty or more workers or one-third of the work force at a given site. If 500 or more workers will lose their jobs, notice must be given.*

blue collar workers only received two days' notice. Since 1981 more than five million Americans have lost their jobs because plants were shut down or their positions were eliminated.

Along lines similar to President Reagan's reservations, National Association of Manufacturers president Alexander B. Trowbridge maintained that the legislation "damages the flexibility essential to run a successful business." Moreover, Trowbridge noted that advance notice was not always possible as financially troubled businesses may not be able to predict their status with the precision that the legislation required. To salvage their troubled businesses, these companies might find themselves in the midst of difficult DEBT financing, merging with another company, selling off ASSETS, or bidding on a major CONTRACT, all of which could be hampered by the new law's requirements. He claimed that the required closing notices would discourage customers and jeopardize CREDIT arrangements. A report compiled by the Congressional Office of Technology Assessment titled "Plant Closing: Advance Notice and Rapid Response" (DTA-ITE-321) found contentions such as Trowbridge's to be highly exaggerated because financial emergencies are rarely a factor in plant closings.

Other critics of the legislation cited an R. Nathan Associates study which claimed that the total annual costs for notification would run as high as $1.8 billion, due to lost profits, penalties, and additional administrative costs. The Nathan study found further that about 460,000 lost jobs would be triggered by unnecessary closings as a direct result of the act.

The GAO, however, seriously questioned the Nathan report on the basis of what it claimed was inadequate and flawed analysis and methodology. The Department of Labor also stated in 1986 that "many of the fears regarding advance notification have not been realized in practice." The National Science Foundation claimed to have found proof that, in most labor groups, advance notice significantly shortens joblessness, which in turn translates into better earnings for displaced workers and substantial savings in unemployment insurance. LABOR UNIONS, such as the AFL-CIO, uniformly acclaimed the Worker Adjustment and Retraining Notification Act, 29 U.S.C.A. § 2101 et seq., claiming that when advance notice is combined with severance pay, it improves morale and actually increases worker productivity.

**CROSS-REFERENCES**

Corporations; Employment Law; Labor Law; Unemployment Compensation.

**BUSINESS JUDGMENT RULE** 📖 A legal principle that makes officers, directors, managers, and other AGENTS of a CORPORATION immune from LIABILITY to the corporation for loss incurred in corporate transactions that are within their authority and power to make when sufficient EVIDENCE demonstrates that the transactions were made in GOOD FAITH. 📖

The directors and officers of a corporation are responsible for managing and directing the business and affairs of the corporation. They often face difficult questions concerning whether to acquire other businesses, sell ASSETS, expand into other areas of business, or issue STOCKS and DIVIDENDS. They may also face potential hostile TAKEOVERS by other businesses. To help directors and officers meet these challenges without fear of liability, courts have given substantial deference to the decisions the directors and officers must make. Under the business judgment rule, the officers and directors of a corporation are immune from liability to the corporation for losses incurred in corporate transactions within their authority, so long as the transactions are made in good faith and with reasonable skill and prudence.

The rule originated in *Otis & Co. v. Pennsylvania R. Co.*, 61 F. Supp. 905 (D.C. Pa. 1945). In *Otis*, a shareholder's DERIVATIVE ACTION alleged that corporate directors failed to obtain the best price available in the sale of SECURITIES by dealing with only one investment house and by generally neglecting to "shop around" for the best possible price, resulting in a loss of nearly half a million dollars. The federal district court ruled that although the directors chose the wrong course of action, they acted in good faith and therefore were not liable to the shareholders. The court reasoned that "mistakes or errors in the exercise of honest business judgment do not subject the officers and directors to liability for negligence in the discharge of their appointed duties."

More recently, the business judgment rule has been applied to directors' actions when corporations are faced with a hostile takeover. In *Unocal Corp. v. Mesa Petroleum Co.*, 493 A.2d 946 (Del. Super. 1985), the Delaware Supreme Court upheld the defensive actions taken by a BOARD OF DIRECTORS during a takeover struggle with a minority shareholder. In this case Mesa Petroleum Company made an offer that would have made it the majority shareholder in Unocal Corporation. Under the offer shareholders who sold their Unocal stock would receive $54 a share until Mesa acquired the 37 percent it sought, and then would receive highly speculative Mesa securities instead of cash for any stock sold beyond that 37 percent. To counteract the takeover bid Unocal's directors announced that if Mesa obtained 51 percent of its shares, Unocal would purchase the remaining 49 percent for an exchange of DEBT securities (securities reflected as debt on the books of the corporation) with an aggregate PAR (or face) value of $72 a share, but the offer would not be extended to the 51 percent of stock held by Mesa. Mesa filed suit, alleging that the directors had violated their FIDUCIARY duty by excluding Mesa from the exchange. The court concluded that the directors' actions were protected by the business judgment rule. The court recognized that in responding to hostile takeover bids the directors of a corporation can face a conflict between their own interests and the interests of the corporation and its shareholders. The court stated that the Unocal directors had reasonable grounds to believe that a danger to the corporation existed because of Mesa's actions, and that the defensive actions they took were REASONABLE in relation to the threat they "rationally and reasonably" believed the offer posed.

Despite the seemingly broad scope of the business judgment rule, corporate directors have not always been able to rely upon it as a way to escape liability for their actions. In *Smith v. Van Gorkom*, 488 A.2d 858 (Del. 1985), the Supreme Court of Delaware held that the directors of a corporation failed to exercise informed business judgment and instead acted in a grossly negligent manner by agreeing to sell the company for only $55 a share. The court looked to evidence indicating that the directors reached their decision to sell at that price after hearing only a twenty-minute oral presentation concerning the sale. The court also noted that the directors had received no documentation indicating that the sale price was adequate and had not requested a study to help them determine whether the price was fair. Although the directors were not accused of acting in BAD FAITH, the court stated that the directors' fiduciary duty toward their shareholders required more than merely an absence of bad faith. The directors, according to the court, had an affirmative duty to protect the shareholders by obtaining and reviewing information necessary to help the directors make sound business decisions. By failing to inform themselves they were therefore liable to the shareholders for their bad business decision.

Even when a corporation faces a hostile takeover, the business judgment rule may not insulate its directors from liability. In *Revlon v. MacAndrews & Forbes Holdings*, 506 A.2d 173 (Del. 1985), the company attempting a takeover sought a preliminary INJUNCTION to prevent the corporation that was the target of the takeover from granting a lockup option, which gives a friendly third party the right to purchase part of the target company to help thwart a takeover. The Delaware Supreme Court held that the directors failed to fulfill their duty to preserve the company by not maximizing the sale value of the company for the benefit of its shareholders. According to the court, by instituting the lockup option and halting the bidding, the directors allowed "considerations other than the maximization of shareholder profits to affect their judgment" and thus acted to the detriment of the shareholders. Once the directors determined to sell the corporation, the court held, their role changed from that of "defenders of the corporate bastion to auctioneers charged with getting the best price for the stockholders at the sale of the company." As a result, the court held that the directors were not entitled to the protection of the business judgment rule.

Courts have further held that the business judgment rule will cover the actions of directors only where the directors are disinterested and independent with respect to the action that is at issue. A director is independent when she or he is "in a position to base [her or his] decision on the merits of the issue rather being governed by extraneous considerations or influences"; conversely, a director is considered to be interested if she or he appears to be on both sides of a transaction or expects to derive personal financial benefit from it, as opposed to a benefit to be realized by the corporation or all shareholders generally (*Aronson v. Lewis*, 473 A.2d 805 [Del. 1984]). Thus, if one director stands to receive a substantial financial benefit from the issuance of stock nonetheless designed to counteract a takeover threat, the business judgment rule may not apply to the board of directors' actions. Such ALLEGATIONS of bias, lack of independence, or disinterest must be supported by TANGIBLE evidence.

See also IMMUNITY; NEGLIGENCE.

**BUSINESS RECORD EXCEPTION** 📖 A rule of EVIDENCE that allows routine entries made customarily in financial records, or business logs or files kept in the regular course of business, to be introduced as proof in a lawsuit when the person who made such notations is not available to testify. 📖

This rule, also called the business entry rule, is an exception to the HEARSAY rule. Business records are considered to have a greater degree of reliability and trustworthiness than personal records because of the regular and systematic way in which they are kept and the reliance that a business places on them.

State and federal rules of evidence specify what records qualify for this exception to the hearsay rule.

**BUSINESS ROUNDTABLE** The Business Roundtable is an association of business executives who examine public issues that affect the economy and who develop positions that seek to reflect sound economic and social principles. Established in 1972, the Roundtable was founded in the belief that business executives should take an increased role in the continuing debates about public policy.

The Roundtable believes that the basic interests of business closely parallel the interests of the American people, who are directly involved in the economy as consumers, employees, investors, and suppliers. Thus, business leaders have responsibilities which relate to many factors that affect economic well-being—including jobs, products, services, and return on investment.

As the Roundtable sees it, one of its principal strengths

is the extent of participation by the chief executive officers of the member firms. Working in task forces on specific issues, they direct research, supervise preparation of position papers, recommend policy, and speak out on the issues. In this process, the Roundtable draws on the staffs of member companies for talent and expertise. In addition to the task force, there are a number of standing committees composed mostly of executives at the vice-presidential level.

There are task forces on these topics: accounting principles, antitrust, corporate constituencies, corporate responsibility, economic organization, energy users, environmental responsibility, environmental government regulation, inflation, international trade, national health, taxation, and welfare.

Activities of the task force and committees are reviewed by the Roundtable Policy Committee. Position papers approved by that committee are circulated to members and to the government and are made available for use in the public discussion of issues.

In an effort to ensure a broad base of information for the decision-making process, membership of the Roundtable is diversified. Member selection reflects the goal of having representation varied by business category and by geographic location. Thus, the members—a number of chief executive officers of companies in all fields—can present a cross section of thinking on national issues.

The Roundtable is selective in the issues it studies. A principal criterion is the impact the problem will have on the social and economic well-being of the nation. The Roundtable works only on issues where its members' business experience can make a significant contribution. It has a continuing liaison with other organizations dealing with national problems.

**BUSINESS TRUST** 📖 An unincorporated business organization created by a legal document, a DECLARATION OF TRUST, and used in place of a CORPORATION or PARTNERSHIP for the transaction of various kinds of business with limited LIABILITY. 📖

The use of a business trust, also called a MASSACHUSETTS TRUST or a COMMON-LAW TRUST, originated years ago to circumvent restrictions imposed upon corporate acquisition and development of REAL ESTATE while achieving the limited liability aspect of a corporation. A business trust differs from a corporation in that it does not receive a CHARTER from the state giving it legal recognition; it derives its status from the voluntary action of the individuals who form it. Its use has been expanded to include the purchase of SECURITIES and COMMODITIES.

A business trust is similar to a traditional TRUST in that its TRUSTEES are given LEGAL TITLE to the trust property to administer it for the advantage of its BENEFICIARIES who hold EQUITABLE title to it. A written declaration of trust specifying the terms of the trust, its duration, the powers and duties of the trustees, and the interests of the beneficiaries is essential for the creation of a business trust. The beneficiaries receive certificates of BENEFICIAL INTEREST as evidence of their interest in the trust, which is freely transferable.

In some states, a business trust is subject to the laws of trusts while, in others, the laws of corporations or partnerships govern its existence. The laws of each state in which a business trust is involved in transactions must be consulted to ensure that the trust is treated as an entity whose members have limited liability. If the laws of a particular state consider a business trust to be a partnership, the beneficiaries may be fully liable for any JUDGMENTS rendered against it. The trustees of a business trust are liable to third parties who deal with the trust unless there is a contract provision to the contrary, since they hold legal title to the trust property and may sue and be sued in ACTIONS involving the trust. They may, however, seek INDEMNITY from the trust property and possibly from the beneficiaries.

The property of a business trust is managed and controlled by trustees who have a FIDUCIARY duty to the beneficiaries to act in their best interests. In many states, the participation of the beneficiaries in the management of the property destroys their limited liability, and the arrangement will usually be treated as a partnership.

Profits and losses resulting from the use and investment of the trust property are shared proportionally by the beneficiaries according to their interests in the trusts.

A business trust is considered a corporation for purposes of federal INCOME TAX and similarly under various state income tax laws.

**"BUT FOR" RULE** 📖 In the law of NEGLIGENCE, a principle that provides that the DEFENDANT's conduct is not the cause of an injury to the PLAINTIFF, unless that injury would not have occurred except for ("but for") the defendant's conduct. 📖

In order to be liable in negligence, the defendant's conduct must constitute the PROXIMATE CAUSE, or direct cause, of the plaintiff's injury. The concept of proximate cause encompasses both legal cause and factual cause, and the "but for" rule pertains to the latter. It is also referred to as the SINE QUA NON rule, which means "without which not," or an indispensable requirement or condition. The "but for" rule is a rule of exclusion, in that the defendant's conduct is not a CAUSE of the event, if the event would have occurred without it.

The "but for" rule explains most cases when limited solely to the issue of causation, but it does not resolve one type of situation: if two causes concur to bring about an event, and either one of them, operating independently, would have been sufficient to cause the identical result, some other test is required. This situation arises, for example, when the defendant sets a fire that unites with a fire from some other source, and the combined fires burn the plaintiff's property, although either fire alone would have been sufficient to do so. In such cases, each cause has actually played so significant a role in achieving the result that responsibility must attach to it. Neither may be relieved from that responsibility on the basis that identical harm would have occurred without it, or no liability at all would ensue.

In order to rectify the frequently problematic application of the "but for" rule, some JURISDICTIONS have applied a broader rule, which

provides that the defendant's conduct is a cause of the event if it was a MATERIAL element and a SUBSTANTIAL factor in bringing about the event. The JURY ascertains whether such conduct constitutes a substantial factor, unless the issue is so unambiguous that it is appropriate for judicial determination. The prevailing view is that "substantial factor" is a phrase sufficiently comprehensible to the layperson to supply an adequate guide in INSTRUCTIONS to the jury, and that it is neither possible nor beneficial to simplify it.

In addition to resolving the aforementioned case, the substantial factor test resolves two other types of situations that have proved troublesome, where a similar, but not identical, result would have followed the defendant's act or where one defendant has made an obvious but insignificant contribution to the result. The application of the two rules can achieve the same result in some instances, since, except as indicated, no case has been encountered where the defendant's act could be deemed a substantial factor when the event would have transpired without it. In addition, cases seldom arise where the defendant's conduct would not be such a substantial factor yet was so indispensable a cause that the result would not have ensued without it.

If the defendant's conduct was a substantial factor in causing the plaintiff's injury, he or she will not be absolved from liability simply because other causes have contributed to the result, since such causes are always present. However, a defendant is not necessarily relieved of liability because the negligence of another person is also a contributing cause, and that person, too, is to be held liable for the harm inflicted. The principle of JOINT TORTFEASORS is based primarily upon recognition of the fact that each of two or more causes may be charged with a single result.

**BUTLER, BENJAMIN FRANKLIN**   Benjamin Franklin Butler was born December 14, 1795, in Kinderhook Landing, New York. He was admitted to the New York bar in 1817, and established a legal practice with Martin Van Buren in Albany, New York. From 1821 to 1824 Butler performed the duties of district attorney for Albany County.

**BIOGRAPHY**

LIBRARY OF CONGRESS

*Benjamin Franklin Butler*

---

**BENJAMIN FRANKLIN BUTLER 1795–1858**

1838 Appointed U.S. district attorney in New York; helped organize CUNY Law School

1833 Appointed U.S. attorney general by President Jackson

1836 Martin Van Buren elected president

1845 Reappointed to U.S. district attorney post by President Polk

1821–24 Served as district attorney of Albany County

1827 Elected to New York State Legislature

1841 Returned to private practice

1795 Born, Kinderhook Landing, N.Y.

1817 Established legal practice with Martin Van Buren in Albany

1848 Retired from public service

1858 Died, Paris, France

1861–65 U.S. Civil War

1775        1800        1825        1850        1875

Butler entered politics in 1827, serving in the New York State Legislature for six years. He subsequently acted as U.S. attorney general from 1833 to 1838; during this time he also fulfilled the duties of secretary of war from 1836 to 1837.

In 1838, Butler returned to New York and served as U.S. district attorney from 1838 to 1841 and from 1845 to 1848.

Butler died November 8, 1858, in Paris, France.

## BUTLER, BENJAMIN FRANKLIN

Benjamin Franklin Butler achieved prominence as a politician and military officer.

Butler was born November 5, 1818, in Deerfield, New Hampshire. After graduating in 1838 from Waterbury College, now known as Colby College, Butler was admitted to the Massachusetts bar in 1840. Elected to the Massachusetts House of Representatives in 1853 and the Massachusetts Senate in 1859, he also served a tour of military duty during the Civil War.

At the outbreak of the war, Butler entered the Massachusetts militia as a brigadier general. He participated in the capture of Baltimore, Maryland, in 1861 and led forces against New Orleans, Louisiana, in 1862. After the conquest of New Orleans, Butler became military governor of that city, but his administration was charged with severity, corruption, and graft. After six months, Butler was reassigned to the Eastern Virginia-North Carolina area and commanded the Army of the James in 1863.

Butler acted as administrator for the return of prisoners in 1864, and was assigned to New York to enforce order during the election held in that same year.

After the war, Butler served in the federal government, representing Massachusetts in the U.S. House of Representatives from 1867 to 1875, and from 1877 to 1879. He returned to Massachusetts in 1882 to perform the duties of governor and in 1884 was an unsuccessful nominee for the U.S. presidency, representing two independent parties—the Anti-Monopoly party and the Greenback party.

Butler died January 11, 1893, in Washington, D.C.

**BIOGRAPHY**

*Charles Henry Butler*

"CITIZENS OF THIS COUNTRY ARE ESSENTIALLY LOYAL; BUT THEY ARE MORE LOYAL TO PRINCIPLES THAN THEY ARE TO MEN."

**BIOGRAPHY**

*Benjamin Franklin Butler*

"NEVER HOLD OFFICE. HOLD YOURSELF ABOVE IT [BECAUSE] AN OFFICER IS A SERVANT."

## BUTLER, CHARLES HENRY

Charles Henry Butler served as the Supreme Court reporter of decisions from 1902 to 1916.

Butler was born June 18, 1859, in New York City. He was the son of William Allen Butler, a lawyer, and the grandson of BENJAMIN F. BUTLER, U.S. attorney general during the administration of MARTIN VAN BUREN. Butler attended Princeton University but left school before graduating. He then studied law in his father's New York office for several years, and often accompanied his father to Washington, D.C., when the elder Butler appeared before the U.S. Supreme Court to argue cases. Butler was admitted to the New York state bar in 1882 and subsequently practiced law in New York City. In 1898, he served as the legal expert for the Fairbanks-Herschell Commission, which was convened to adjust the boundary of Alaska and Canada.

In December 1902, Butler left the practice of law to accept an appointment as REPORTER of decisions for the U.S. Supreme Court, a position created by Congress in 1816. In the early days of the Court, the reporter had been primarily responsible for editing, publishing, and distributing the Court's opinions; beginning in 1874, however, Congress provided money for the government to publish the Court's opinions, and thus by the time Butler became reporter, his role was limited to editorial tasks.

While reporter, Butler edited and published volumes 187 to 241 of the *United States Reports*, the official publication of the opinions of the U.S. Supreme Court. During his tenure with the Court, he also was a delegate to the Hague Peace Conference in 1907. He later authored *A Century at the Bar of the Supreme Court of the United States* (1942), a sometimes lighthearted account of the Court's inner workings and his experiences as reporter. In the book, published two years after his death, Butler described his dealings with the justices as "delightful and congenial." He wrote that the work was "very interesting. It was not difficult and did not take all of my time. The salary ... afforded me a comfortable income." Butler also described in some detail the various rules and customs of the Court, including the writ of CERTIORARI and the

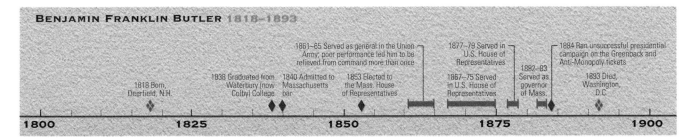

**BENJAMIN FRANKLIN BUTLER 1818–1893**

- 1818 Born, Deerfield, N.H.
- 1838 Graduated from Waterbury (now Colby) College
- 1840 Admitted to Massachusetts bar
- 1853 Elected to the Mass. House of Representatives
- 1861–65 Served as general in the Union Army; poor performance led him to be relieved from command more than once
- 1867–75 Served in U.S. House of Representatives
- 1877–79 Served in U.S. House of Representatives
- 1882–83 Served as governor of Mass.
- 1884 Ran unsuccessful presidential campaign on the Greenback and Anti-Monopoly tickets
- 1893 Died, Washington, D.C.

1800  1825  1850  1875  1900

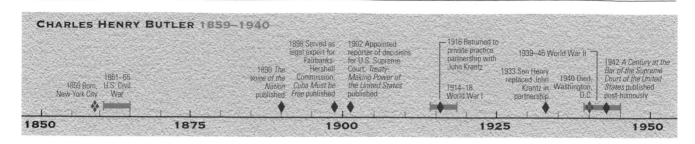

CHARLES HENRY BUTLER 1859–1940

1859 Born, New York City

1861–65 U.S. Civil War

1890 *The Voice of the Nation* published

1898 Served as legal expert for Fairbanks-Hershell Commission; *Cuba Must be Free* published

1902 Appointed reporter of decisions for U.S. Supreme Court; *Treaty-Making Power of the United States* published

1914–18 World War I

1916 Returned to private practice partnership with John Krantz

1933 Son Henry replaced John Krantz in partnership

1939–45 World War II

1940 Died, Washington, D.C.

1942 *A Century at the Bar of the Supreme Court of the United States* published post-humously

1850 · 1875 · 1900 · 1925 · 1950

social etiquette of the Court, and shared anecdotes about lawyers who had argued before the Court. With respect to the reporter's position, Butler discussed the process of preparing HEADNOTES, the paragraphs that appear at the beginning of OPINIONS to summarize the major points of law contained in the opinions. During Butler's tenure, the Court made clear that headnotes were not to be construed as part of the opinions and were instead only the expressions of the reporter about the holdings of the Court.

Butler eventually found his position to be "somewhat monotonous" and noted that "[t]here was nothing constructive about it so far as my part was concerned." In addition, Butler was frustrated by the anonymity of the post and by frequent misunderstandings about his role and duties; he wrote that he was once introduced as the "Head Stenographer of the United States Supreme Court." As a result, Butler resigned from the Court in October 1916, to return to private practice in Washington, D.C. He also wrote extensively about international law, including several works on U.S. relations with Spain and Cuba. He died in 1940, at the age of eighty-one.

See also LAW REPORTS.

## BUTLER, PIERCE

Pierce Butler served as associate justice of the Supreme Court from 1923 to 1939. Known for his conservative views, Butler advocated a *laissez-faire* (French for "let [people] do [as they choose])" philosophy that sought to minimize government interference in the economy. In the 1930s, when FRANKLIN D. ROOSEVELT's New Deal policies sought to increase the power of government in U.S. life, Butler voted against the constitutionality of every New Deal measure that came

**BIOGRAPHY**

*Pierce Butler*

before the Court. By the end of his tenure, Butler was one of the few conservatives on an increasingly liberal Supreme Court, and he became distraught by changes in the Court's interpretation of the Constitution. "This is not government by law, but by caprice," he wrote in a 1939 dissent. "Whimseys may displace deliberate action by chosen representatives and become rules of conduct. To us the outcome seems wholly incompatible with the system under which we are supposed to live" (*United States v. Rock Royal Co-op*, 307 U.S. 533, 59 S. Ct. 993, 83 L. Ed. 1446). Butler dissented in several Supreme Court decisions that overturned laws discriminating against African Americans, and he rarely supported the rights of those with dissenting or radical opinions in society. He did, however, argue consistently for the rights of those accused of crimes.

Those who knew him commented on Butler's stubbornness and occasional bullying, traits that often made his relations with others on the Court less than amicable. Once, after persuading all on the Court but Justice OLIVER WENDELL HOLMES, JR., of the rightness of his opinion on a particular matter, Butler said to Holmes, "I am glad we have finally arrived at a just decision." "Hell is paved with *just* decisions," Holmes responded. Commenting on Butler's conservatism, Holmes characterized Butler as a "monolith" with "no seams the frost can get through." Butler resolutely stuck to his conservative principles even in the depths of the Depression. Something of those views is found in remarks he made in 1916: "Too much paternalism, too much wet-nursing by the state, is destructive of individual initiative and development. An Athlete should not be fed on pre-

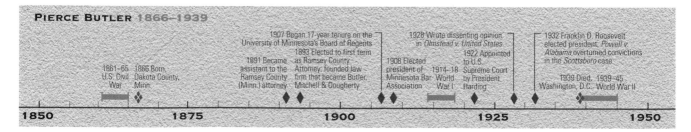

PIERCE BUTLER 1866–1939

1861–65 U.S. Civil War

1866 Born, Dakota County, Minn.

1891 Became assistant to the Ramsey County (Minn.) attorney

1893 Elected to first term as Ramsey County Attorney; founded law firm that became Butler, Mitchell & Dougherty

1907 Began 17-year tenure on the University of Minnesota's Board of Regents

1908 Elected president of Minnesota Bar Association

1914–18 World War I

1922 Appointed to U.S. Supreme Court by President Harding

1928 Wrote dissenting opinion in *Olmstead v. United States*

1932 Franklin D. Roosevelt elected president; *Powell v. Alabama* overturned convictions in the *Scottsboro* case

1939 Died, Washington, D.C.

1939–45 World War II

1850 · 1875 · 1900 · 1925 · 1950

digested food nor should the citizens of tomorrow be so trained that they will expect sustenance from the public 'pap.' "

Many of Butler's later views were shaped by his frontier childhood. Butler was born on St. Patrick's Day, March 17, 1866, in a log cabin in Dakota County, Minnesota. His parents had emigrated from County Wicklow, Ireland, to escape the potato famine of 1848, and eventually established their farm only a few miles from Carleton College, in Northfield, Minnesota, where Butler was admitted in 1883. To help pay his college expenses, he worked in a local dairy. He graduated from Carleton in 1887 with both a bachelor of arts degree and a bachelor of science degree.

After college, Butler moved to St. Paul and studied law at the firm of Pinch and Twohy. He passed the Minnesota bar in 1888 and established a law practice with an associate, Stan Donnelly. In 1891, Butler became assistant to the county attorney for Ramsey County, and in 1893 and 1895 he was elected, as a Democrat, to the office of county attorney, the only elective public office he ever held. While in office, he secured more criminal convictions than any county attorney had done before. Butler ran for the state senate in 1906 but was narrowly defeated. In 1908, he was elected president of the Minnesota State Bar Association. In St. Paul, Butler also met his future wife, Annie Cronin, whom he married in 1891. The couple had eight children.

In 1893, Butler helped establish a St. Paul law firm that evolved into Butler, Mitchell, and Doherty, one of the most successful corporate law firms of its time in what was then called the Northwest. The firm had several railroads as its major clients, including those of James J. Hill, one of the great rail barons. During his career, Butler earned a reputation as the foremost railroad lawyer in the Northwest. His work in railroad litigation eventually brought him to national attention, and allowed him to become friendly with President WILLIAM HOWARD TAFT, who served on the Supreme Court as chief justice from 1921 to 1930 and was later instrumental in securing Butler's nomination to the Court.

On November 23, 1922, President WARREN G. HARDING nominated Butler to succeed retiring justice William R. Day on the Supreme Court. Although Butler was a Democrat, the Republican Harding approved of his laissez-faire economic philosophy and conservative social views. Harding also believed that it would be politically astute to nominate the Roman Catholic Butler to the Court. The last Roman Catholic to serve on the Court had been replaced by Taft in 1921.

Butler's nomination caused a great outcry in liberal circles, particularly from Senators GEORGE W. NORRIS and Robert M. La Follette, and senator-elect Henrik Shipstead, of Minnesota. They pointed to Butler's ties to big business during his legal career, claiming that these would bias his decisions on the bench. They also objected to Butler's actions as a regent of the University of Minnesota, a position he held from 1907 to 1924. Butler, they argued, had used his influence to have several faculty members dismissed. Despite the objections of La Follette and others, the Senate Judiciary Committee unanimously confirmed Butler's nomination on December 13, 1922. On January 2, 1923, the Senate appointed Butler to the Court by a vote of 61–8.

While serving on the Court, Butler fulfilled predictions that he would become a pillar of conservatism. Butler often voted with three other conservatives, Justices James C. McReynolds, George Sutherland, and Willis Van Devanter, himself a former railroad lawyer. Because they consistently voted as a conservative bloc, observers nicknamed this group the Four Horsemen.

Butler's conservatism manifested itself particularly in his emphasis on limiting the power of government. For example, he voted whenever possible against state and federal taxes. In *Coolidge v. Long*, 282 U.S. 582, 51 S. Ct. 306, 75 L. Ed. 562 (1931), writing the Court's opinion, Butler argued that a state inheritance tax was unconstitutional because it violated the Due Process Clause of the FOURTEENTH AMENDMENT, which proclaims that the state shall not deprive a person of liberty without DUE PROCESS OF LAW.

Butler also consistently argued against the rights of government to regulate prices, particularly through his narrow interpretation of the phrase "BUSINESS AFFECTED WITH A PUBLIC INTEREST." At the time, it was common for governments, when they sought to regulate prices charged by businesses, to argue that certain industries had more of the public interest involved in their affairs than others; businesses that were affected with a public interest could therefore be regulated by the government. In *Wolff Packing Co. v. Court of Industrial Relations*, 262 U.S. 522, 43 S. Ct. 630, 67 L. Ed. 1103 (1923), Butler voted with the Court in deciding that the packing industry was not affected with a public interest and therefore could not be made subject to price-control

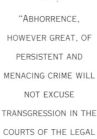

"ABHORRENCE, HOWEVER GREAT, OF PERSISTENT AND MENACING CRIME WILL NOT EXCUSE TRANSGRESSION IN THE COURTS OF THE LEGAL RIGHTS OF THE WORST OFFENDERS."

legislation. Butler and the Court made the same decision with regard to employment agencies in *Ribnik v. McBride*, 277 U.S. 350, 48 S. Ct. 545, 72 L. Ed. 913 (1928). In both *Wolff* and *Ribnik*, the Court found that the laws under consideration violated the Due Process Clause of the Fourteenth Amendment. In *Nebbia v. New York*, 291 U.S. 502, 54 S. Ct. 505, 78 L. Ed. 940 (1934), when an increasingly liberal Court decided to do without the phrase "affected with a public interest" in making its decision and ruled that the state may regulate milk prices, Butler, along with the rest of the Four Horsemen, dissented. This was just one of many dissents Butler and his conservative colleagues would make during the 1930s.

Butler's opinions in the area of civil liberties are less easy to categorize. He argued persuasively for the rights of those accused of crimes, arguing in one opinion, "Abhorrence, however great, of persistent and menacing crime will not excuse transgression in the courts of the legal rights of the worst offenders." He opposed national prohibition and criticized federal agents several times for violating the FOURTH AMENDMENT in their SEARCHES AND SEIZURES. In a case involving WIRE TAPPING by Prohibition agents, *Olmstead v. United States*, 277 U.S. 438, 48 S. Ct. 564, 72 L. Ed. 944 (1928), Butler found himself in the unusual company of the more liberal justices Louis D. Brandeis, Harlan F. Stone, and Holmes. In his dissenting opinion, Butler argued that during the transmission of messages, the exclusive use of any wire belonged to the persons served by it. Law enforcement wiretapping therefore constituted an illegal search for evidence. In *Aldridge v. United States*, 283 U.S. 308, 51 S. Ct. 470, 75 L. Ed. 1054 (1931), Butler voted with the majority in holding that an African American being tried for the murder of a white man was entitled to have the prospective jurors asked whether they had a racial prejudice that would prevent a fair trial. Butler also supported the rights of disabled persons, casting a lone dissenting vote, without opinion, in *Buck v. Bell*, 274 U.S. 200, 47 S. Ct. 584, 71 L. Ed. 1000 (1927), which upheld a 1924 Virginia law allowing for the sterilization of mentally handicapped individuals.

When it came to the civil liberties and FREEDOM OF SPEECH of those in society with radical or dissenting opinions, Butler was less understanding. Ironically, Butler's dissenting opinions in many of these matters undermined the rights for dissent in the larger society. In his dissent against the majority opinion in *Stromberg v. California*, 283 U.S. 359, 51 S. Ct. 532, 75 L. Ed. 1117 (1931), Butler considered lawful the conviction of a young woman found guilty of displaying a red flag in public. The California law under consideration, Cal. Penal Code § 403a, made it a felony to display a red flag as "an emblem of opposition to organized government" or "an invitation . . . to anarchistic action." In *United States v. Schwimmer*, 279 U.S. 644, 49 S. Ct. 448, 73 L. Ed. 889 (1929), Butler wrote the opinion for a majority of six upholding the denial of citizenship to the sixty-year-old Rosika Schwimmer. In her petition for citizenship, Schwimmer had specifically stated that she would refuse to take up arms for the state in any possible circumstances. Writing the Court's opinion, Butler interpreted her statement as opposition to the entire Constitution and therefore the laws of the country: "Taken as a whole it shows that her objection to military service rests on reasons other than mere inability because of her sex and age personally to bear arms . . . [S]he may be opposed to the use of military force as contemplated by our Constitution and laws." Butler dissented from the Court's decision again in *Hague v. Committee of Industrial Organizations*, 307 U.S. 496, 59 S. Ct. 954, 83 L. Ed. 1423 (1939), where he argued for the legality of a city ordinance regulating labor meetings in city parks.

In civil rights and racial issues, Butler resisted changes in established interpretations of the Constitution. In the 1930s, when the Court became more liberal and more actively sought to strike down state laws—particularly racially discriminatory laws—it considered unconstitutional, Butler argued that the Court had overstepped its bounds and that state legislatures were the best judges of what was best for their citizens. In the 1932 decision *Powell v. Alabama*, 287 U.S. 45, 53 S. Ct. 55, 77 L. Ed. 158, the High Court dealt with the *Scottsboro* case, involving African American men who had been convicted in 1931 in Scottsboro, Alabama, of raping two white women. The Court held that the accused men had been deprived of the right of counsel and had therefore been denied due process as guaranteed by the Fourteenth Amendment. Butler's dissenting opinion argued that no denial of due process had occurred and that the Court's decision was an unwarranted "extension of federal authority in a field hitherto occupied exclusively by the several states." In a 1938 case involving an African American denied access to law school by the state of Missouri, Butler's dissenting opinion argued for the constitutionality of the state's action (*Missouri ex rel. Gaines v. Canada*, 305 U.S. 337, 59 S. Ct. 232, 83 L. Ed. 208).

Butler also dissented in several decisions in the 1930s in which the Court struck down JIM CROW LAWS that kept African Americans from voting. In *Breedlove v. Suttles*, 302 U.S. 277, 58 S. Ct. 205, 82 L. Ed. 252 (1937), Butler argued that a POLL TAX (a tax charged to voters at the time they cast their votes) did not violate the Fourteenth Amendment, and in *Lane v. Wilson*, 307 U.S. 268, 59 S. Ct. 872, 83 L. Ed. 1281 (1939), Butler disagreed with the majority's decision to strike down an Oklahoma law that made it difficult for African Americans to register to vote.

Butler and his conservative colleagues also opposed Franklin D. Roosevelt's New Deal social welfare legislation. In his last three terms in office, Butler dissented in seventy-three cases—constituting more than half of the total dissents in his seventeen-year career on the Supreme Court. He dissented in *Helvering v. Davis*, 301 U.S. 619, 57 S. Ct. 904, 81 L. Ed. 1307 (1937), in which the Court upheld the government's right to tax employers and employees to create PENSIONS through the Social Security Act of 1935, 42 U.S.C.A. § 401 et seq. "The Constitution," Butler wrote in his dissent, "grants to the United States no power to pay unemployed persons or to require the states to enact laws . . . for that purpose." Butler wrote the Court's opinion in *Morehead v. New York ex rel. Tipaldo*, 299 U.S. 619, 57 S. Ct. 4, 81 L. Ed. 156 (1936), which supported an earlier decision to strike down a minimum wage law for women.

Butler died of a bladder ailment on November 16, 1939, in Washington, D.C., at age seventy-three. During his tenure, he wrote 323 majority opinions, forty-four dissenting opinions, and three concurring opinions. Butler clung to his dated ideals, even in a world that was fast finding fault with them. As one observer wrote after Butler's death, "he did not change as the frontiers changed; and perhaps this quality of steadfast resistance to a different world was what Justice Holmes had in mind when he spoke of him as a 'monolith.' "

See also OLMSTEAD V. UNITED STATES; POWELL V. ALABAMA.

**BYLAWS** The rules and regulations enacted by an association or a CORPORATION to provide a framework for its operation and management.

Bylaws may specify the qualifications, rights, and liabilities of membership, and the powers, duties, and grounds for the dissolution of an organization.

Sample bylaws

ARTICLE ONE
OFFICES

The principal office of the corporation shall be located at _____ [*address*],_____ [*city*], _____ County, _____ [*state*]. The board of directors shall have the power and authority to establish and maintain branch or subordinate offices at any other locations _____ [within the same city or within the same state or *as the case may be*].

ARTICLE TWO
STOCKHOLDERS

Section 1. *Annual Meeting.* The annual meeting of the stockholders shall be held on the _____ [*ordinal number*] day in the month of _____ in each year, beginning with the year _____, at _____ [*time*], for the purpose of electing directors and for the transaction of such other business as may come before the meeting. If the day fixed for the annual meeting shall be a legal holiday in the State of _____, such meeting shall be held on the next succeeding business day. If the election of directors is not held on the day designated herein for any annual meeting of the shareholders, or at any adjournment thereof, the board of directors shall cause the election to be held at a special meeting of the stockholders as soon thereafter as is convenient.

Section 2. *Special Meetings.* Special meetings of the stockholders, for any purpose or purposes, unless otherwise prescribed by statute, may be called by the president or by the board of directors, and shall be called by the president at the request of the holders of not less than _____ [*number*] of all the outstanding shares of the corporation entitled to vote at the meeting.

Section 3. *Place of Meeting.* The board of directors may designate any place within _____ [*if desired, add:* or without] the State of _____, as the place of meeting for any annual meeting or for any special meeting called by the board of directors. A waiver of notice signed by all stockholders entitled to vote at a meeting may designate any place, either within or without the State of _____, as the place for the holding of such meeting. If no designation is made, or if a special meeting is otherwise called, the place of meeting shall be the principal office of the corporation in the City of _____, _____ [*state*].

Section 4. *Notice of Meeting.* Written or printed notice stating the place, day, and hour of the meeting and, in case of a special meeting, the purpose or purposes for which the meeting is called, shall be delivered not less than _____ nor more than _____ days before the date of the meeting, either personally or by mail, by or at the direction of the president, or the secretary, or the officer or persons calling the meeting, to each shareholder of record entitled to vote at such meeting. If mailed, such notice shall be deemed to be delivered when deposited in the United States mail, addressed to the shareholder at his address as it appears on the stock transfer books of the corporation, with postage thereon prepaid. _____ [*If appropriate, add:* Notice of each meeting shall also be mailed to holders of stock not entitled to vote, as herein provided, but lack of such notice shall not affect the legality of any meeting otherwise properly called and noticed.]

Section 5. *Closing Transfer Books or Fixing Record Date.* For the purpose of determining stockholders entitled to notice of, or to vote at, any meeting of stockholders or any adjournment thereof, or stockholders entitled to receive payment of any dividend, or to make a determination of shareholders for any other proper purpose, the board of directors of the corporation may provide that the stock transfer books shall be closed for a stated period, but not to exceed _____ days. If the stock transfer books shall be closed for the purpose of determining stockholders entitled to notice of, or to vote at, a meeting of stockholders, such books shall be closed for at least _____ days immediately preceding such meeting. In lieu of closing the stock transfer books, the board of directors may fix in advance a date as the record date for any such determination of stockholders, such date in any event to be not more than _____ days, and in case of a meeting of stockholders, not less than_____ days prior to the date on which the particular action requiring such determination of stockholders is to be taken.

If the stock transfer books are not closed and no record date is fixed for the determination of stockholders entitled to notice of, or to vote at, a meeting of stockholders, or of stockholders entitled to receive payment of a dividend, the date that notice of the meeting is mailed or the date on which the resolution of the board of directors declaring such dividend is adopted, as the case may be, shall be the record date for such determination of stockholders. When a determination of stockholders entitled to vote at any meeting of stockholders has been made as provided in this section, such determination shall apply to any adjournment thereof except where the determination has been made through the closing of the stock transfer books and the stated period of closing has expired.

Section 6. *Quorum.* A majority of the outstanding shares of the corporation entitled to vote, represented in person or by proxy, shall constitute a quorum at a meeting of stockholders. If less than a majority of such outstanding shares are represented at a meeting, a majority of the shares so represented may adjourn the meeting from time to time without further notice. At such adjourned meeting at which a quorum is present or represented, any business may be transacted that might have been transacted at the meeting as originally notified. The stockholders present at a duly organized meeting may continue to transact business until adjournment, notwithstanding the withdrawal of enough stockholders to leave less than a quorum.

Section 7. *Proxies.* At all meetings of stockholders, a stockholder may vote by proxy executed in writing by the stockholder or by his duly authorized attorney in fact. Such proxy shall be filed with the secretary of the corporation before or at the time of the meeting. No proxy shall be valid after _____ months from the date of its execution unless otherwise provided in the proxy.

Section 8. *Voting of Shares.* Subject to the provisions of any applicable law _____ [*if desired, add:* or any provision of the _____ (articles *or* certificate) of incorporation or of these bylaws concerning cumulative voting], each outstanding share entitled to vote shall be entitled to one vote on each matter submitted to a vote at a meeting of stockholders.

## ARTICLE THREE
## BOARD OF DIRECTORS

Section 1. *General Powers.* The business and affairs of the corporation shall be managed by its board of directors.

Section 2. *Number, Tenure, and Qualifications.* The number of directors of the corporation shall be _____. Directors shall be elected at the annual meeting of stockholders, and the term of office of each director shall be until the next annual meeting of stockholders and the election and qualification of his or her successor. Directors need not be residents of the State of _____, _____ [but shall be stockholders of the corporation *or* and need not be stockholders of the corporation].

Section 3. *Regular Meetings.* A regular meeting of the board of directors shall be held without notice other than this bylaw immediately after and at the same place as the annual meeting of stockholders. The board of directors may provide, by resolution, the time and place for holding additional regular meetings without other notice than such resolution. Additional regular meetings shall be held at the principal office of the corporation in the absence of any designation in the resolution.

Section 4. *Special Meetings.* Special meetings of the board of directors may be called by or at the request of the president or any _____ [two] directors, and shall be held at the principal office of the corporation or at such other place as the directors may determine.

Section 5. *Notice.* Notice of any special meeting shall be given at least _____ [48 hours *or as the case may be*] before the time fixed for the meeting, by written notice delivered personally or mailed to each director at his or her business address, or by telegram. If mailed, such notice shall be deemed to be delivered when deposited in the United States mail so addressed, with postage thereon prepaid, not less than _____ days prior to the commencement of the above-stated notice period. If notice is given by telegram, such notice shall be deemed to be delivered when the telegram is delivered to the telegraph company. Any director may waive notice of any meeting. The attendance of a director at a meeting shall constitute a waiver of notice of such meeting, except where a director attends a meeting for the express purpose of objecting to the transaction of any business because the meeting is not lawfully called or convened. Neither the business to be transacted at, nor the purpose of, any regular or special meeting of the board of directors need be specified in the notice or waiver of notice of such meeting.

Section 6. *Quorum.* A majority of the number of directors fixed by these bylaws shall constitute a quorum for the transaction of business at any meeting of the board of directors, but if less than such majority is present at a meeting, a majority of the directors present may adjourn the meeting from time to time without further notice.

Section 7. *Board Decisions.* The act of the majority of the directors present at a meeting at which a quorum is present shall be the act of the board of directors _____ [except that vote of not less than _____ *(fraction)* of all the members of the board shall be required for the amendment of or addition to these bylaws *or as the case may be*.]

Section 8. *Vacancies.* Any vacancy occurring in the board of directors may be filled by the affirmative vote of a majority of the remaining directors though less than a quorum of the board of directors. A director elected to fill a vacancy shall be elected for the unexpired term of his or her predecessor in office. Any directorship to be filled by reason of an increase in the number of directors shall be filled by election at an annual meeting or at a special meeting of stockholders called for that purpose.

Section 9. *Compensation.* By resolution of the board of directors, the directors may be paid their expenses, if any, of attendance at each meeting of the board of directors, and may be paid a fixed sum for attendance at each meeting of the board of directors or a stated salary as director. No such payment shall preclude any director from serving the corporation in any other capacity and receiving compensation therefor.

Section 10. *Presumption of Assent.* A director of the corporation who is present at a meeting of the board of directors at which action on any corporate matter is taken shall be presumed to have assented to the action taken unless his or her dissent shall be entered in the minutes of the meeting or unless he or she shall file his or her written dissent to such action with the person acting as the secretary of the meeting before the adjournment thereof or shall forward such dissent by registered mail to the secretary of the corporation immediately after the adjournment of the meeting. Such right to dissent shall not apply to a director who voted in favor of such action.

## ARTICLE FOUR
## OFFICERS

Section 1. *Number.* The officers of the corporation shall be a president, one or more vice-presidents (the number thereof to be determined by the board of directors), a secretary, and a treasurer, each of whom shall be elected by the board of directors. Such other officers and assistant officers as may be deemed necessary may be elected or appointed by the board of directors. Any two or more offices may be held by the same person, except the offices of _____ [president and secretary *or as the case may be*].

Section 2. *Election and Term of Office.* The officers of the corporation to be elected by the board of directors shall be elected annually at the first meeting of the board of directors held after each annual meeting of the stockholders. If the election of officers is not held at such meeting, such election shall be held as soon thereafter as is convenient. Each officer shall hold office until his or her successor has been duly elected and qualifies or until his or her death or until he or she resigns or is removed in the manner hereinafter provided.

Section 3. *Removal.* Any officer or agent elected or appointed by the board of directors may be removed by the board of directors whenever in its judgment the best interests of the corporation would be served thereby, but such removal shall be without prejudice to the contract rights, if any, of the person so removed.

Section 4. *Vacancies.* A vacancy in any office because of death, resignation, removal, disqualification or otherwise, may be filled by the board of directors for the unexpired portion of the term.

Section 5. *Powers and duties.* The powers and duties of the several officers shall be as provided from time to time by resolution or other directive of the board of directors. In the absence of such provisions, the respective officers shall have the powers and shall discharge the duties customarily and usually held and performed by like officers of corporations similar in organization and business purposes to this corporation.

Section 6. *Salaries.* The salaries of the officers shall be fixed from time to time by the board of directors, and no officer shall be prevented from receiving such salary by reason of the fact that he or she is also a director of the corporation.

## ARTICLE FIVE
## CONTRACTS, LOANS, CHECKS, AND DEPOSITS

Section 1. *Contracts.* The board of directors may authorize any officer or officers, agent or agents, to enter into any contract or execute and deliver any instrument in the name of and on behalf of the corporation, and such authority may be general or confined to specific instances.

Section 2. *Loans.* No loans shall be contracted on behalf of the corporation and no evidences of indebtedness shall be issued in its name unless authorized by a resolution of the board of directors. Such authority may be general or confined to specific instances.

Section 3. *Checks, Drafts, or Orders.* All checks, drafts, or other orders for the payment of money, notes, or other evidences of indebtedness issued in the name of the corporation shall be signed by such officer or officers, agent or agents of the corporation and in such manner as shall from time to time be determined by resolution of the board of directors.

Section 4. *Deposits.* All funds of the corporation not otherwise employed shall be deposited from time to time to the credit of the corporation in such banks, trust companies, or other depositaries as the board of directors may select.

## ARTICLE SIX
## CERTIFICATES FOR SHARES; TRANSFERS

Section 1. *Certificates for Shares.* Certificates representing shares of the corporation shall be in such form as shall be determined by the board of directors. Such certificates shall be signed by the president or a vice-president and by the secretary or an assistant secretary. All certificates for shares shall be consecutively numbered or otherwise identified. The name and address of the person to whom the shares represented thereby are issued, with the number of shares and date of issue, shall be entered on the stock transfer books of the corporation. All certificates surrendered to the corporation for transfer shall be canceled and no new certificate shall be issued until the former certificate for a like number of shares shall have been surrendered and canceled, except that in case of a lost, destroyed, or mutilated certificate a new one may be issued therefor on such terms and indemnity to the corporation as the board of directors may prescribe.

Section 2. *Transfer of Shares.* Transfer of shares of the corporation shall be made in the manner specified in the _____ [Uniform Commercial Code *or as the case may be*]. The corporation shall maintain stock transfer books, and any transfer shall be registered thereon only on request and surrender of the stock certificate representing the transferred shares, duly endorsed. The corporation shall have the absolute right to recognize as the owner of any shares of stock issued by it, the person or persons in whose name the certificate representing such shares stands according to the books of the corporation for all proper corporate purposes, including the voting of the shares represented by the certificate at a regular or special meeting of stockholders, and the issuance and payment of dividends on such shares.

## ARTICLE SEVEN
## FISCAL YEAR

The fiscal year of the corporation shall _____ [be the calendar year *or* begin on the _____ (*ordinal number*) day of _____ (*month*) of each year and end at midnight on the _____ (*ordinal number*) day of _____ (*month*) of the following year *or as the case may be*].

## ARTICLE EIGHT
## DIVIDENDS

The board of directors may from time to time declare, and the corporation may pay, dividends on its outstanding shares in the manner and on the terms and conditions provided by law and its _____ [articles *or* certificate] of incorporation.

## ARTICLE NINE
## SEAL

The board of directors shall provide a corporate seal, which shall be circular in form and shall have inscribed thereon the name of the corporation and the state of incorporation and the words "Corporate Seal." The seal shall be stamped or affixed to such documents as may be prescribed by law or custom or by the board of directors.

## ARTICLE TEN
## WAIVER OF NOTICE

Whenever any notice is required to be given to any stockholder or director of the corporation under the provisions of these bylaws or under the provisions of the _____ [articles *or* certificate] of incorporation or under the provisions of law, a waiver thereof in writing, signed by the person or persons entitled to such notice, whether before or after the time stated therein, shall be deemed equivalent to the giving of such notice.

## ARTICLE ELEVEN
## AMENDMENTS

These bylaws may be altered, amended, or repealed and new bylaws may be adopted by the board of directors at any regular or special meeting of the board; provided, however, that the number of directors shall not be increased or decreased nor shall the provisions of Article Two, concerning the stockholders, be substantially altered _____ [*add other limitations as desired*], without the prior approval of the stockholders at a regular or special meeting of the stockholders, or by written consent. _____ [*If appropriate, add:* Changes in and additions to the bylaws by the board of directors shall be reported to the stockholders at their next regular meeting and shall be subject to the approval or disapproval of the stockholders at such meeting. If no action is then taken by the stockholders on a change in or addition to the bylaws, such change or addition shall be deemed to be fully approved and ratified by the stockholders.]

**BYRNES, JAMES FRANCIS** James Francis Byrnes was a self-taught lawyer who was briefly an associate justice of the U.S. Supreme Court during the 1940s and who also served as secretary of state, the governor of South Carolina, a U.S. senator, and an influential member of President FRANKLIN D. ROOSEVELT's cabinet.

Byrnes was born May 2, 1879, in Charleston, South Carolina. Economic circumstances forced him to quit parochial school at the age of fourteen and go to work as a clerk in a Charleston law firm for $2 a week to help support his family. He learned shorthand and eventually obtained a job in Aiken, South Carolina, as the official court reporter for the Second Judicial Circuit, a state court. He studied law in his spare time and was admitted to the South Carolina bar in 1903. He then purchased a newspaper in Aiken, the *Journal and Review*, and served as its editor for five years. Active in the Democratic party, Byrnes was elected district attorney for the Second Judicial Circuit in 1908, and two years later won a seat in the U.S. House of Representatives, where he served for fifteen years. Following an unsuccessful bid for the U.S. Senate, he returned to South Carolina in 1925 to practice law in Spartanburg. In 1930, he again ran for the Senate, and this time he won election.

Initially, Byrnes was a strong advocate of Franklin D. Roosevelt's New Deal legislation and served as Roosevelt's legislative adviser, thus playing a crucial role in securing support in the Senate for Roosevelt's policies. Byrnes also helped the president successfully manage the furor surrounding the chief executive's "court-packing" plan, a bill proposed by Roosevelt to expand the Supreme Court so that he could nominate justices who would uphold New Deal legislation. Roosevelt heeded Byrnes's advice not to seek a vote on the bill after several 1937 decisions indicated that the Court would be more inclined than its members previously had been to hold Roosevelt's programs to be constitutional. Later in his second Senate term, Byrnes joined the Democratic opposition to pro-union New Deal legislation. Nevertheless,

"POVERTY AND IMMORALITY ARE NOT SYNONYMOUS."

he remained close to Roosevelt and helped secure the repeal of the Neutrality Act of 1935, 49 Stat. 1081, and the passage of the Lend-Lease Act of 1941, 22 U.S.C.A. § 411 et seq.

In June 1941, Roosevelt nominated Byrnes to fill the seat on the U.S. Supreme Court vacated by the resignation of Associate Justice James C. McReynolds. Byrnes won confirmation easily, but would serve on the Court for little more than a year, completing the shortest tenure in the history of the Court.

Byrnes wrote only sixteen majority opinions, including *Edwards v. California*, 314 U.S. 160, 62 S. Ct. 164, 86 L. Ed. 119 (1941), in which the Court struck down a California law that made bringing indigents into the state a crime. In his opinion, Byrnes argued that the law posed an unacceptable burden upon interstate commerce. He also wrote the majority opinion in *Taylor v. Georgia*, 315 U.S. 25, 62 S. Ct. 415, 86 L. Ed. 615 (1942), where the Court held that a state penal law that required workers receiving advances to remain at their jobs until the advances were paid back violated the THIRTEENTH AMENDMENT prohibition against INVOLUNTARY SERVITUDE.

Despite these significant contributions, Byrnes was not happy on the Court. He wanted to be more actively involved in the country's war effort. In October 1942, after only sixteen months on the Court, Byrnes resigned his seat. He left the Court at the request of President Roosevelt to become director of the newly created Office of Economic Stabilization, established to help prevent wartime inflation. Less than a year later, Byrnes became head of the Office of War Mobilization, an agency created to manage the production of war and civilian goods. The range of authority and influence Byrnes wielded in both posts led Roosevelt to refer to him publicly as "assistant president."

In Roosevelt's 1944 campaign for a fourth term, Byrnes was considered for the vice presidential nomination when opposition to Henry A. Wallace, the current vice president, surfaced. But Byrnes's pro-management views proved to be unacceptable to labor leaders, and the

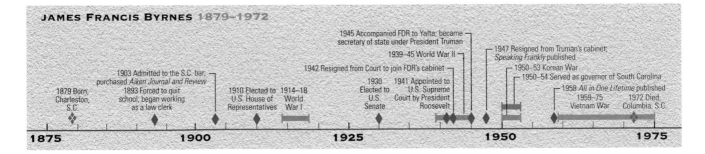

**JAMES FRANCIS BYRNES 1879–1972**

1875 — 1900 — 1925 — 1950 — 1975

- 1879 Born, Charleston, S.C.
- 1893 Forced to quit school; began working as a law clerk
- 1903 Admitted to the S.C. bar; purchased *Aiken Journal and Review*
- 1910 Elected to U.S. House of Representatives
- 1914–18 World War I
- 1930 Elected to U.S. Senate
- 1941 Appointed to U.S. Supreme Court by President Roosevelt
- 1942 Resigned from Court to join FDR's cabinet
- 1939–45 World War II
- 1945 Accompanied FDR to Yalta; became secretary of state under President Truman
- 1947 Resigned from Truman's cabinet; *Speaking Frankly* published
- 1950–53 Korean War
- 1950–54 Served as governor of South Carolina
- 1958 *All in One Lifetime* published
- 1959–75 Vietnam War
- 1972 Died, Columbia, S.C.

nomination instead went to HARRY S. TRUMAN. Byrnes nevertheless remained a close adviser to Roosevelt, accompanying him in 1945 to the YALTA AGREEMENT with Joseph Stalin and Winston Churchill.

Byrnes continued to play a major role in government after Roosevelt's death, when President Truman, a longtime friend, appointed Byrnes secretary of state. Byrnes's service in the state department was controversial. He took criticism for his recommendation that the atomic bomb be used to end the war with Japan. As secretary of state, Byrnes was the chief representative for the United States in a number of high-level international conferences held following the war, including the Potsdam Conference. In negotiations with the Soviet Union, Byrnes favored a settlement that greatly weakened Russia's control over Eastern Europe and increased the United States' monopoly on atomic weapons. He also argued for the reunification of Germany. The Soviets strongly resisted both proposals, and the failure of these negotiations helped to launch the cold war.

Byrnes resigned from the cabinet in 1947 after a disagreement with Truman over his Fair Deal programs, which Byrnes saw as socialistic. After leaving the Truman administration, Byrnes practiced law in Washington, D.C., for several years. In 1947, he published *Speaking Frankly*, an account of his experiences with postwar diplomacy, which became a best-seller.

Byrnes returned to politics in 1950 when he was elected governor of South Carolina. He served for one term, during which he compiled a somewhat mixed record with respect to civil rights. His administration suppressed the activities of the Ku Klux Klan in the state, but Byrnes was a vocal opponent of SCHOOL DESEGREGATION.

After leaving office in 1955, Byrnes retired to Columbia, South Carolina, where he died in 1972. Byrnes remains the only U.S. citizen in the twentieth century to have served in prominent roles in all three branches of the government—legislative, judicial, and executive. His autobiography, which was published in 1958, is titled *All in One Lifetime*.

**CABINET** 📖 The counsel or group of advisers of a king or other chief executive of a government. A group of individuals who advise the PRESIDENT of the United States. 📖

The president's cabinet was created by custom and tradition and was instituted by the first president. The heads of each of the executive departments of the government, including the secretary of state, the secretary of the treasury, the secretary of defense, the attorney general, the secretary of the interior, the secretary of agriculture, the secretary of commerce, the secretary of labor, the secretary of health and human services, the secretary of education, the secretary of housing and urban development, and the secretary of transportation, comprise the cabinet. See also EXECUTIVE BRANCH.

**CABLE TELEVISION** The cable TV industry exploded from modest beginnings in the 1950s into a service that by 1993 reached 61.5 percent of all the U.S. households that had television. Cable was initially a response to a need for improved transmission in areas where signals were weak or nonexistent. By the 1960s, consumers began to demand not only better reception but also more signals. This demand fueled the exponential growth of the industry. In 1993, more than 11,385 cable systems serviced 57,211,600 homes in the United States. The industry has faced many legal issues, including programming and rate regulation, lack of competition, and customer service complaints.

The most contentious issue in cable television arises from Federal Communications Commission (FCC) regulations that require cable operators to allot up to one-third of their channels to local broadcast stations. Known as must-carry rules, these were first enacted in the 1960s in an effort to protect the interests of local broadcasters. In 1985 and 1987, the Court of Appeals for the District of Columbia Circuit held that must-carry rules, as promulgated at the time, violated the FIRST AMENDMENT (see *Quincy Cable TV v. FCC*, 768 F.2d 1434 [1985], *cert. denied*, 476 U.S. 1169, 106 S. Ct. 2889, 90 L. Ed. 2d 977 [1986]; *Century Communications Corp. v. FCC*, 835 F.2d 292 [1987], *cert. denied sub nom. Office of Communication of the United Church of Christ v. FCC*, 486 U.S. 1032, 108 S. Ct. 2014, 129 L. Ed. 2d 497 [1988]).

Congress addressed the must-carry issue in the Cable Television Consumer Protection and Competition Act of 1992 (47 U.S.C.A. § 325 et seq.). The 1992 Cable Act, passed over President George Bush's veto, required cable systems to carry most local broadcast channels and prohibited cable operators from charging local broadcasters to carry their signal. These requirements were challenged on First Amendment grounds in *Turner Broadcasting System v. FCC*, 512 U.S. 622, 114 S. Ct. 2445, 129 L. Ed. 2d 497 (1994). Turner Broadcasting asked the Court to apply a STRICT SCRUTINY test, similar to the one used to evaluate the constitutionality of restrictions on printed material, to determine whether the FCC's regulations infringed the industry's FREEDOM OF SPEECH. The FCC urged the Court to apply the same relaxed standard it had applied to broadcast media in *Red Lion Broadcasting v. FCC*, 395 U.S. 367, 89 S. Ct. 1794, 23 L. Ed. 2d 371 (1969). The Court took

*By 1993 cable television reached more than sixty percent of all the U.S. households that had television.*

a middle ground on cable communications. Noting that cable television is neither strictly a broadcast medium nor a print medium, the Court held that the relaxed scrutiny test adopted in *Red Lion* was inappropriate, but declined to adopt the strict scrutiny protection given to print publications. The Court held that any regulations that are content neutral—in other words, that do not dictate the content of programming and that have an incidental burden on free speech—will be judged by an "intermediate level of scrutiny." Any regulations found to be content based—in other words, that attempt to restrict programming based on its content—will receive the strict scrutiny applied to print media.

The regulation of the rates charged by cable companies is another area of contention between the industry and the government. Before 1984, local franchising authorities regulated the rates charged by franchisees. The 1984 Cable Communications Policy Act (46 U.S.C.A. §§ 484-487, 47 U.S.C.A. § 35, 152 et seq.), which was designed to promote competition and allow competitive market forces to determine rates, deregulated rates for almost all franchisees. Although industry representatives had argued that competition would keep rates reasonable, after deregulation, average monthly cable rates increased far faster than the rate of inflation, in some cases as much as three times faster. During the same period, the average cable subscriber received only six additional

channels, and competition from other operators was almost nonexistent. In 1991, only fifty-three of the more than ninety-six hundred cable systems in the United States had a direct competitor in their service area.

The 1992 Cable Act provided a regulatory structure for basic and expanded programming, but exempted individually sold premium channels, such as HBO and the Disney Channel, and pay-per-view programming. The 1992 act authorized local governments to regulate programming, equipment, and service rates charged by companies in areas where there is no competition. Basic rates could be regulated but only under prescribed circumstances that indicate a lack of competition in the area. According to figures gathered in 1994, the new regulations led to average rate reductions of more than eight percent.

When Congress deregulated the cable industry with the 1984 Cable Act, its primary intent was to promote competition. The 1984 act sought to balance the government's dual goals of providing cable access to all areas and deregulating rates. The industry had argued that competitive market forces would produce competition and stabilize rates. However, competition did not occur in the ensuing years, and cable operators continued to enjoy a MONOPOLY in virtually all service areas. Before 1992, exclusive cable FRANCHISES were granted to the bidders who promised the widest access and most balanced programming. The government felt that this was the best way to ensure that cable's new and expensive technology was available to people in poor and rural areas as well as more

### Cable Television

Number of Subscribers and Monthly Basic Rates, 1970–94

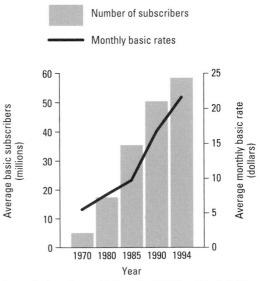

Source: *The Kagan Census of Cable and Pay TV*, 1991; and *The Cable TV Investor*, June 1995.

affluent areas. As a result, bidders who promised more than they delivered were protected from competition. The 1992 Cable Act eliminated many of the barriers to competition that existed before. Most important, it abolished the exclusive franchise agreement, which had been a powerful monopolistic tool.

Although the 1992 act did much to encourage competition, it did not address the 1984 act's ban on ownership of cable companies by local telephone utilities. This ban was challenged in *Chesapeake & Potomac Telephone Co. v. United States*, 42 F.3d 181 (1994), in which the Fourth Circuit Court of Appeals held that it violated the telephone companies' First Amendment right to free speech. The ban was removed by the Telecommunications Act of 1996 (110 Stat. 56), which President Clinton signed in February 1996.

Complaints about poor customer service have plagued the industry and grew in proportion to the phenomenal increase in subscribership during the 1970s and 1980s. A 1991 study conducted by *Consumer Reports* found that customer satisfaction with cable providers was the lowest it had been in sixteen years. Common complaints include the inability of customers to reach company representatives, missed or botched installation and service calls, service outages, and billing problems. The 1992 Cable Act directed the FCC to establish minimum customer service standards for the cable industry. The 1992 act authorized local governments to establish stronger customer service standards than those established by the FCC, and to do so unilaterally, without the consent of the cable operator.

**CROSS-REFERENCES**

Broadcasting; Federal Communications Commission; Telecommunications; Television.

**CAHN, EDMOND**   Edmond Cahn was the author of numerous publications including *The Sense of Injustice* (1949), *The Moral Decision* (1955), and *The Edmond Cahn Reader* (1966).

Cahn was born January 17, 1906, in New Orleans, Louisiana. He received a bachelor of arts degree in 1925 and a doctor of jurisprudence degree in 1927 from Tulane University.

"IN EVERY MATURE SOCIETY, THERE IS CONSIDERABLE OVERLAP BETWEEN LEGAL QUESTIONS AND MORAL QUESTIONS."

**BIOGRAPHY**

*Edmond Cahn*

TULANE UNIVERSITY

He also received a doctor of laws degree from the Jewish Theological Seminary of America in 1962.

After his admission to the Louisiana bar in 1927 and the New York bar in 1928, Cahn established a law firm in New York City and practiced law from 1927 to 1950. He extended his career interests to the field of education and taught at New York University in 1945, accepting a professorship of law in 1948. In 1958 and 1962 he lectured on the philosophy of law at the Hebrew University in Jerusalem and on ethics at the Jewish Theological Seminary of America in 1961.

From 1948 to 1951 he was the director of the Conference on Social Meaning of Legal Concepts. He was awarded the Phillips Prize in Jurisprudence by the American Philosophical Society in 1955.

Cahn died August 9, 1964, in New York City.

**CALENDAR**   A list of cases that are awaiting trial or other settlement, often called a trial list or DOCKET.

A *special calendar* is an all-inclusive listing of cases awaiting trial; it contains dates for trial, names of counsel, and the estimated time required for trial. It is maintained by a trial judge in some states and by a court clerk in others.

*Calendar call* is a court session during which the cases that await trial are called in order to determine the current status of each case and to assign a trial date.

**CALHOUN, JOHN CALDWELL**   John Caldwell Calhoun achieved prominence as a U.S. vice president, Southern politician, and a staunch defender of STATES' RIGHTS.

Calhoun was born March 18, 1782, in Abbeville County, South Carolina. After graduating from Yale University in 1804 and LITCHFIELD LAW SCHOOL in 1806, Calhoun was admitted to the South Carolina bar in 1807 and established a successful legal practice there.

In 1808, Calhoun entered politics, beginning as a member of the South Carolina legislature. Three years later, he began his career in federal government, representing South Carolina in the House of Representatives until 1817. During his tenure, he performed the duties of

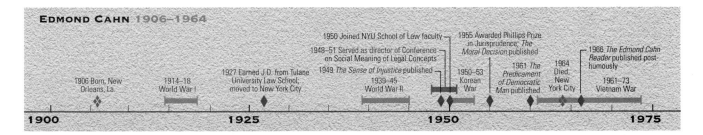

EDMOND CAHN 1906–1964

1906 Born, New Orleans, La.

1914–18 World War I

1927 Earned J.D. from Tulane University Law School; moved to New York City

1948–51 Served as director of Conference on Social Meaning of Legal Concepts

1949 *The Sense of Injustice* published

1939–45 World War II

1950 Joined NYU School of Law faculty

1950–53 Korean War

1955 Awarded Phillips Prize in Jurisprudence; *The Moral Decision* published

1961 *The Predicament of Democratic Man* published

1964 Died, New York City

1966 *The Edmond Cahn Reader* published posthumously

1961–73 Vietnam War

1900        1925        1950        1975

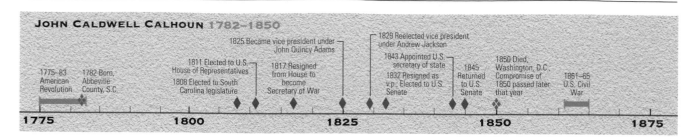

JOHN CALDWELL CALHOUN 1782–1850

1775–83 American Revolution

1782 Born, Abbeville County, S.C.

1808 Elected to South Carolina legislature

1811 Elected to U.S. House of Representatives

1817 Resigned from House to become Secretary of War

1825 Became vice president under John Quincy Adams

1829 Reelected vice president under Andrew Jackson

1843 Appointed U.S. secretary of state

1832 Resigned as v.p.; Elected to U.S. Senate

1845 Returned to U.S. Senate

1850 Died, Washington, D.C.; Compromise of 1850 passed later that year

1861–65 U.S. Civil War

1775    1800    1825    1850    1875

acting chairman of the Committee on Foreign Affairs and in 1811 was a member of the War Hawks, a group that advocated war with England in 1812.

Calhoun resigned from the House in 1817 and assumed the duties of secretary of war for the next eight years. In 1825, he began his first term as vice president of the United States, serving under President JOHN QUINCY ADAMS for four years. He remained in this office during the presidency of ANDREW JACKSON, but relinquished his post in 1832 after a disagreement with Jackson concerning states' rights. The dispute between Jackson and Calhoun resulted in the Nullification Controversy of 1832 and 1833. Calhoun was a proponent of the right of a state to declare a federal law null and void if the state deemed such a law unconstitutional. His attitude was a result of the passage of protective TARIFFS that Calhoun believed favored the interests of the North over those of the South. Calhoun expressed his beliefs in his work, *South Carolina Exposition*, in which he discussed his views of SOVEREIGNTY of the states. He believed that a state had the right to secede from the Union in order to keep the powers of the federal government in check. The Nullification Controversy finally ended with a compromise, and Calhoun emerged as the foremost speaker for the South during that era.

Calhoun represented South Carolina in the U.S. Senate from 1832 to 1843, and again from 1845 to 1850. He continued his campaign for states' rights, supported SLAVERY, and introduced a policy of "concurrent majorities," wherein every area of the United States would participate equally in the exercise of federal power. During the period between his two senatorial terms, Calhoun served as U.S. secretary of state from 1843 to 1845. Calhoun died March 31, 1850, in Washington, D.C.

As an author, Calhoun wrote many publications, including *Disquisition on Government* and *Discourse on the Constitution and Government of the United States*. A compilation of his works from 1851 to 1855 was published posthumously by R. K. Crallé in a six-volume set.

**BIOGRAPHY**

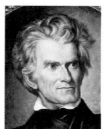

*John Caldwell Calhoun*

"THE RIGHT OF SUFFRAGE IS THE INDISPENSABLE AND PRIMARY PRINCIPLE IN THE FOUNDATION OF A CONSTITUTIONAL GOVERNMENT."

**CALL** 📖 To convoke or summon by public announcement; to request the appearance and participation of several people—such as a call of a jury to serve, a roll call, a call of public election, or a call of names of the members of a legislative body.

In CONTRACT law, the demand for the payment of money according to the contract terms, usually by formal notice.

As applied to CORPORATION law, the demand of the BOARD OF DIRECTORS that subscribers pay an installment or portion of the amount that is still owed on shares that they have agreed to buy. A *call price* is the price paid by a corporation for the redemption of its own securities.

In SECURITIES, a contract that gives a person the right to demand payment of a certain specified number of shares of STOCK at a stated price or upon a fixed date. 📖

**CALVO CLAUSE** 📖 A provision in an agreement between a private individual and a foreign state that says, in effect, that "ALIENS are not entitled to rights and privileges not accorded to nationals, and that, therefore, they may seek redress for grievances only before local authorities." 📖

Under the Calvo Clause, a claimant waives the right to apply to his or her government or to another forum for protection if a claim is denied by local authorities.

**CALVO DOCTRINE** 📖 The principle set forth by an Argentine jurist, Carlos Calvo, that a government has no duty to compensate ALIENS for losses or injuries that they incur as a result of domestic disturbances or a civil war, in cases where the state is not at fault, and, therefore, no justification exists for foreign nations to intervene to secure the settlements of the claims made by their citizens due to such losses or injuries. 📖

**CAMERA** 📖 A chamber, room, or apartment in old English law. A judge's chamber. Treasury, chest, or coffer. 📖

To be IN CAMERA is to be in private or in chambers.

**CAMERAS IN COURT** Cameras and courtrooms have long had an uneasy relationship.

Blaming cameras for disrupting TRIALS, the AMERICAN BAR ASSOCIATION (ABA) led the drive for their removal in the mid-1930s. The effort succeeded: all but two state courts banned them and Congress prohibited them from all federal trials. But the television era ushered in new problems and courts eventually were forced to grapple with the constitutional question of whether TV cameras are injurious to a defendant's right to a fair trial. In 1965, the U.S. Supreme Court appeared to say they are, in *Estes v. Texas*, 381 U.S. 532, 85 S. Ct. 1628, 14 L. Ed. 2d 543, overturning a conviction because cameras had denied a defendant his DUE PROCESS rights. But the Court changed its mind in the 1981 case of *Chandler v. Florida*, 449 U.S. 560, 101 S. Ct. 802, 66 L. Ed. 2d 740. Reacting to the permissiveness of *Chandler*, many states passed legislation allowing televised trials. And from 1991 to 1994 some FEDERAL COURTS conducted an experiment with cameras.

Photographers lost their place in court in the early 1930s thanks to a highly sensational trial, and it would take four decades for them to regain it. In 1934, nearly seven hundred reporters and photographers descended on the New Jersey town where Bruno Hauptmann was on trial for kidnapping and murdering the baby of famous aviator Charles A. Lindbergh and author Anne Morrow Lindbergh. The trial judge allowed still photography, but was unprepared for the barrage of flashbulbs and the presence of a newsreel camera that was smuggled inside the court. Decrying the media circus that resulted, the ABA in 1937 called for prohibiting photography in its Canons of Professional and Judicial Ethics. At the same time the U.S. Congress amended the Federal Rules of Criminal Procedure to ban cameras and any form of broadcasting from federal courts. All but two states— Texas and Colorado—gradually adopted the ABA ban. Later, Texas permitted television cameras and it was a Texas criminal case that led to the next stage of development in this area of U.S. law.

In 1965, the U.S. Supreme Court took up the constitutional issue in *Estes*. This case involved a claim by a convicted swindler that the televising of his heavily publicized trial had deprived him of his right to due process under the FOURTEENTH AMENDMENT. The counterargument advanced by the state of Texas is still the one most pro-camera supporters make today: cameras neither caused distractions nor prejudiced the trial and in fact served the public's right to know in a manner both educational and likely to promote respect for the courts. The

Supreme Court sided with the defendant. Emphasizing the obtrusive technology used in the courtroom, from fat cables to the red light on cameras, the Court decided that the trial had not been fair and overturned the conviction. Yet, to many observers, *Estes* appeared to stop short of announcing that all photographic or broadcast coverage of criminal trials is inherently a denial of due process; it focused narrowly on the particulars in Billie Sol Estes's case. More important, observers noted, the decision looked to the future. "When the advances in these arts permit reporting by . . . television without their present hazards to a fair trial," Justice TOM C. CLARK wrote for the majority in *Estes*, "we will have another case."

Developments in the 1970s changed the picture. Technology had improved, making TV cameras far less disruptive, and the electronic media was demanding the same access to trials enjoyed by the print media. The ABA became much more tentative about its hard-line position. Its Committee on Fair Trial–Free Press recommended that the ABA revise its standards. Encouraged to experiment, a number of states tried short-term pilot programs as a first step toward changing their laws. Then, in 1978, the Conference of State Chief Justices voted 44–1 to approve a resolution allowing the highest court of each state to set its own guidelines for radio, TV, and other photographic coverage. By 1980, nineteen states permitted coverage of trial and appellate courts, three permitted coverage of trial courts only, six permitted coverage of APPELLATE courts only, and twelve others were considering the issue.

*The sensational 1934 trial of Bruno Hauptmann (center) for the kidnapping and murder of the son of Charles Lindbergh and Anne Morrow Lindbergh created such a disruption in the courtroom that in 1937 cameras were banned from nearly all courtrooms.*

# Judge Wapner and *The People's Court*

**B**efore televised trials became commonplace, there was *The People's Court*. This highly popular syndicated TV program ran from 1981 through 1993 and featured retired judge Joseph A. Wapner, of the California Superior Court. Millions of viewers tuned in daily to watch Wapner hear actual cases from small-claims court. The parties agreed to submit to his judgment of their sometimes petty, and often quite funny, disputes, which included claims for fender benders, complaints about plumbing jobs, and even a plaintiff who sued when a liquor store that had sold him a flat can of beer refused to give him a fresh one. The groundbreaking *People's Court* probably did more than any other program before it to open the way for the reality programming tide that swept civil and criminal trials onto television. It also popularized understanding of at least one kind of courtroom process, that of small claims.

The genius of *The People's Court* was its verisimilitude. The program operated by the rules of California's small-claims courts: no lawyers were allowed, aggrieved parties represented themselves, and the damage limit was $1,500. To find participants for the show, Ralph Edwards Productions combed court dockets for cases that were essentially matters of principle. It invited the parties to appear on the program, and they generally said yes. Then, as in real life, each party told its side of the story to the judge, whose decision was final. The show's twelve-year run featured more than five thousand cases.

The affably grumpy, no-nonsense Wapner certainly knew his profession. The former president of the California Judges Association had earned degrees in philosophy and the law from the University of Southern California in the late 1940s, had practiced law for a decade, and had tried civil and criminal cases for twenty years before retiring from the bench in 1979. His TV rulings were commonsensical, swift, and just. The victim of a bum can of beer, for instance, was awarded eighty cents. In another case, one man in a romantic love triangle had bitten off the ear of another rather than give up the woman in question; Wapner awarded the one-eared man $1,500 for pain and suffering. As part of the show's terms, the production company paid all awards, and the aggrieved parties merely agreed to call it a day after the judge passed sentence.

The effect of *The People's Court* has often been debated. The show may have encouraged litigiousness, according to such critics as noted attorney Alan M. Dershowitz, and Judge Abner J. Mikva, of the U.S. Circuit Court of Appeals for the District of Columbia. It is undoubtedly true that the use of small-claims courts increased in the 1980s after the show began airing. Others found in Wapner a traditional model of fairness: in a 1989 essay in the *University of Chicago Law Review,* Justice Antonin Scalia, of the U.S. Supreme Court, saw Wapner as a descendant of Solomon and Louis IX of France. Wapner himself saw the program as educational.

To the public, which made *The People's Court* the fifth-highest-rated syndicated show in the mid-1980s, Wapner became the best-known judge in the United States. A 1989 *Washington Post* poll found that fewer than 10 percent of respondents knew the name of Justice William H. Rehnquist, of the U.S. Supreme Court, but more than half could identify Wapner. Wapner published the book *A View from the Bench* in 1987. After the show's cancellation in 1992, he served as president of the Board of Directors of the Brandeis-Bardin Institute, a Jewish cultural organization in California.

See also Small Claims.

---

The U.S. Supreme Court provided the decisive push with its ruling in *Chandler* in 1981. *Chandler* revisited the *Estes* decision of sixteen years earlier and on quite similar terms: in Florida, two men convicted of burglary claimed that televising their trial over their objections was a denial of due process. At the time Florida was following a pilot program for televising and permitting still photography at state trials under canon 3A(7) of the Florida Code of Judicial Conduct. The parties in *Chandler* read *Estes* differently: the APPELLANTS argued that *Estes* meant that the televising of criminal trials is inherently a denial of due process, whereas the state claimed that *Estes* did not establish any such constitutional rule. Seeking to clarify the earlier ruling, which had comprised no less than six opinions, the Supreme Court agreed with Florida. It held that states could provide access to the electronic media regardless of whether defendants wanted it. Moreover, the burden of showing how cameras have a prejudicial effect on a given trial would fall on the defendant. Chief Justice WARREN E. BURGER's majority opinion cautioned, "Dangers lurk in this, as in most experiments, but unless we were to conclude that television coverage under all conditions is prohibited by the Constitution, the states must be free to experiment."

The freedom to experiment brought cameras firmly into state courts. The ABA abandoned its prohibitive stance and more states began con-

# "RAISE YOUR RIGHT HAND AND TRY TO LOOK NATURAL": THE COURTROOM CAMERA DEBATE

Is allowing television cameras in courtrooms a good idea? U.S. law never tires of debating the question. Widely banned after the sensational 1934 Bruno Hauptmann kidnapping and murder trial, the camera's acceptability has gone in and out of fashion for decades. The courts, the media, lawyers, and scholars have often heralded the camera as if it were democracy's own eye—or railed at it as a leering Peeping Tom. Cameras enlighten the public, supporters say. Cameras corrupt the trial process and yield bad journalism, opponents counter. Only since the mid-1970s has the pro-camera lobby been ascendant. With forty-seven states leaving the decision to permit cameras up to judges, and a cable television network, Court TV, broadcasting nearly as fast as courts can be called to session, televised trials were routine affairs in 1995. But despite complaints, federal trials remained off-limits. And controversy over the media's treatment of the O. J. Simpson murder trial brought new calls for pulling the plug altogether.

In 1934, Hauptmann was tried for kidnapping and murdering the young son of aviator Charles A. Lindbergh and author Anne Morrow Lindbergh. The trial excited the nation, obsessed the news media, and created a circus atmosphere of "expert" commentators, tabloid interviews, souvenir hawkers, and courtroom grandstanding. In 1995, the trial of Simpson, who was accused and ultimately acquitted of the murders of his former wife Nicole Brown Simpson and her friend Ronald Lyle Goldman, caused similar excitement, obsession, and atmospherics. Of course, the camera's role in each case was quite different. One hundred and forty-five journalists crammed into the *Hauptmann* courtroom; and flashbulbs popped and a smuggled newsreel camera turned, all in violation of the trial

IN FOCUS

judge's orders. Afterward, critics deplored the media's behavior. Sixty-one years later, a single television camera was permitted to follow the *Simpson* trial. Critics decried the media "circus," "frenzy," "orgy," and so forth. In both instances, it was said that cameras had skewed the proceedings and given a distorted view of the justice system. Some said the media got Hauptmann convicted; some believe the media got Simpson off.

On the simplest level, then, the debate is about the press. Critics believe journalists are only barely capable of behaving themselves in court. After the *Hauptmann* experience, the American Bar Association (ABA) reacted furiously. It swiftly passed judicial canon 35 of its Canons of Professional and Judicial Ethics:

> Proceedings in court should be conducted with fitting dignity and decorum. The taking of photographs in the courtroom, during sessions of the court or recesses between sessions, and the broadcasting of court proceedings are calculated to detract from the essential dignity of the proceedings, degrade the court and create misconceptions with respect thereto in the mind of the public and should not be permitted.

This 1937 rule influenced the majority of states to ban still cameras, and was amended in 1952 to include TV cameras. Although the ABA has long since changed its views, distrust of the media's intentions survives today in state rules governing courtroom proceedings. These guidelines strictly dictate how many cameras are allowed (usually, one), what they may do (remain stationary), whom they may film (never jurors and sometimes not witnesses), who may operate them (one person), what that

operator may wear (appropriate dress), and when she or he may leave the courtroom (only during recess). It is hardly accidental that the guidelines resemble a teacher's orders to a class.

While generally accepting limits as necessary to the proper administration of justice, supporters of courtroom journalism chafe at the idea that cameras get in the way. In the *Simpson* trial, for example, when Judge Lance Ito threatened to have the camera removed, Floyd Abrams, a noted First Amendment attorney, entered a plea to have it remain: the camera, Abrams said, was "absolutely, positively, 100 percent not guilty." Not surprisingly, this is also the view of Court TV. In its 1995 report called *Facts and Opinions about Cameras in the Courtrooms*, the network noted approvingly that states require shielding witnesses, children, and others from the camera. Exactly, respond opponents. "The first thing to note about such options is that their very existence affirms the adverse effects of cameras on witnesses," wrote Professor Rory K. Little, of the Hastings College of the Law.

This aspect of the debate—the effect on a witness of being filmed—is very contentious. Few people are perfectly comfortable on television; even actors and reporters are prone to stage fright. But trials themselves can be tense events. One view is Court TV's, which attributes nervousness to publicity and speaking in front of a group: "There is no evidence that it is related to the camera, or that [witnesses] would be less nervous in the presence of the judge, jury, defendant and three dozen furiously-scribbling reporters." The network backs up its claim with state court research. But even if the majority of states are satisfied, not every observer is. In 1993, the Washington, D.C., Public Defender Service noted that a substantial percentage of witnesses feel uncomfortable on camera, and the district's U.S. attorney's office has ex-

## "RAISE YOUR RIGHT HAND AND TRY TO LOOK NATURAL": THE COURTROOM CAMERA DEBATE (CONTINUED)

pressed fears about cameras' chilling witness cooperation and even endangering witnesses. The media and tourists may hound witnesses who have appeared on television, and so may others with frightening motives. After Pablo Fenjves testified in the *Simpson* case about noises made by Nicole Brown Simpson's dog, he told *Time* magazine that he received death threats.

Lawyers and judges can also be affected by the camera. Critics say the temptation to grandstand is overwhelming—lawyers will show off, aware that their reputation can be bolstered by flights of impressive speech. Supporters respond that lawyers had big egos long before cameras were there to record them. Yet, can judges keep order, let alone resist the temptation themselves? This is an old question in the debate, and even drew comment by the U.S. Supreme Court in *Estes v. Texas* (381 U.S. 532, 85 S. Ct. 1628, 14 L. Ed. 2d 543 [1965]). In his concurring opinion in that case, Chief Justice Earl Warren looked scathingly on a Texas trial judge who said that he had sworn to uphold the state constitution—not the federal Constitution. (Of course, state judges must uphold both.) "One is entitled to wonder," Warren wrote, "if such a statement would be made in a court of justice by any state trial judge except as an appeal calculated to gain the favor of his viewing audience." And, in 1995, much commentary in the *Simpson* case asked whether Judge Ito had succumbed to the allure of the camera when he allowed prosecutors and defense attorneys to bicker endlessly. No, said supporters: cameras can actually be a corrective for these problems. As attorney Abrams put it, "A single, silent courtroom camera serves as an antidote to such behavior by truthfully showing the public how attorneys and judges actually behave."

The effect on juries concerns critics in a special way. Since juries are not televised, there would seem to be little reason to worry about what they will do in the jury box. Not so. It is what they

may do afterward—especially in high-profile cases—and how that may affect their performance in the box that bothers critics. "[W]orst of all," wrote attorney, author, and camera-opponent Wendy Kaminer, "juries will play to the prospect of appearing on talk shows when the trial is over . . . we can't expect jurors not to be corrupted by publicity." Book deals present another problem. There is the real possibility that people will try to get on juries simply to turn a buck; in fact, one person was dismissed from the *Simpson* jury for allegedly taking notes for this very reason. Thus, opponents argue, cameras can jeopardize the quality of justice: not only can they result in bad juries, but the dismissal of jurors can threaten to sink an entire trial, as it did in the *Simpson* case. Against this argument, supporters can say little except words of regret about human nature. "Maybe we should, at long last, learn a lesson from Snow White's stepmother," Abrams advised. "Our mirrors are not our problem."

Given its length, notoriety, and multiple problems, the *Simpson* case produced a backlash against televising trials. Afterward, some judges barred cameras, and others put new restrictions on them. Vowing that "nothing like the O. J. Simpson case is going to happen in my courtroom," Judge Lawrence Antolini of the California Superior Court limited filming to five minutes a day. Critics mocked supporters' claims that cameras help educate the public. As attorney Kaminer quipped in the *ABA Journal*, "People who claim they watch the *Simpson* case to educate themselves remind me of people who say they buy Playboy for the articles." Court TV took much of the blame for its choice of what to broadcast—not only the *Simpson* case, but the previous trials of Lorena Bobbitt for the castration of her husband and of brothers Erik Menendez and Lyle Menendez for the murder of their parents. One of the network's sharpest scourges, attorney Alan M. Dershowitz, proposed an alternative: a

nonprofit channel to be modeled on the cable network C-Span that would broadcast trials of a more illuminating nature. News programs were criticized, too, for carrying too little footage during a brief experiment in broadcasting federal trials; the Federal Judicial Center determined that the average length of coverage in a newscast was only seventeen seconds.

In the wake of the backlash, supporters backpedaled as quickly as possible. "The obsession with this particular television trial [Simpson's] should not lead to a rejection of televised trials," the *New York Times* declared in an editorial (June 11, 1995). *USA Today* editorialized, "As aberrant as the *Simpson* case is, it has become a civics lesson in the rights against search and seizure, the role of judges and the duties of jurors" (May 5, 1995). Trotting out statistics that showed that its viewers come away with greater understanding and respect for the courts, Court TV argued that "in-court camera coverage is, by definition, as dignified as the process and arguably more 'tasteful' than out-of-court tabloid coverage." And when confronted with the charge that cameras had dragged out the length of the *Simpson* trial, supporters pointed to earlier trials that had lasted much longer without cameras.

The future of cameras in courtrooms is up for grabs. Eager to expand its business, Court TV invites its viewers to help it lobby states for greater access. The network and other supporters especially want the Federal Judicial Conference to reopen federal trials to cameras. Critics shudder at the thought, and after *Simpson*, many proponents concede that this is unlikely. Also unlikely is that camera opponents will get their way in state courtrooms, unless the effect of *Simpson* is so great that it can undo fifty years of legal reforms. The camera fought a long battle to become a fixture in court, and it will be quite difficult to send the camera away.

ducting experiments of their own. By 1995, forty-seven states permitted some form of televising of state trials. But in 1994, the federal court system chose otherwise. The federal JUDICIAL CONFERENCE OF THE UNITED STATES authorized a three-year experiment in 1991 that permitted camera coverage of federal civil trials. Most judges who participated in the experiment, which involved six trial court districts and two appellate districts, viewed the experience favorably; in fact, a report prepared by the Judicial Conference recommended extending camera coverage to all federal district and appellate courts. But in 1994, the conference voted to end the experiment without explanation. Many advocates of televising federal trials blamed this decision on the excessive publicity from the 1994 pretrial hearings in the case of O. J. Simpson, a popular sports and entertainment personality who was accused and later acquitted of murdering his former wife Nicole Brown Simpson and her friend Ronald Lyle Goldman.

See also COURTROOM TELEVISION NETWORK; FREEDOM OF THE PRESS; LINDBERGH KIDNAPPING.

## CAMPBELL, BEN NIGHTHORSE  In 1992
Ben Nighthorse Campbell, a rancher, teacher, judo champion, and jewelry designer became the first American Indian to serve in the U.S. Senate in more than sixty years.

Campbell was born April 13, 1933, in Auburn, California. He is the son of Albert Valdez Campbell, who was part Northern Cheyenne Indian, and Mary Vierra, a Portuguese immigrant. His mother was a patient and occasional employee at a tuberculosis sanitorium when she met his father, who also worked there. They were married in 1929 and had two children, Campbell and his sister, Alberta Campbell, who died at the age of forty-four, an apparent suicide.

Campbell's father was an alcoholic who frequently disappeared, leaving Campbell's mother to support and care for the children. Campbell and his sister spent time in orphanages and foster homes when their mother was too sick to work and provide for them. Eventu-

ally, his father was able to work and the family opened a small grocery store, which prospered later when a freeway was built with an exit ramp at the location of the store.

When Campbell entered high school he had little sense of enthusiasm or direction concerning his education. In 1950 he dropped out and joined the Air Force. He served in the Korean War and was discharged from the service with the rank of airman, second class. He passed the high school equivalency test to receive his general equivalency diploma and in 1957 graduated from San Jose State University with a bachelor's degree in physical education and fine arts.

When he was a teenager Campbell became interested in judo and it became a driving force in his life. "Judo teaches you to persevere, to never give up," he said. "That skill is transferable to business, to school, to politics." Campbell continued to develop his judo skill while he was in the service and, after completing college, he moved to Tokyo, where he lived for four years, studying at Meiji University and perfecting his abilities. In 1963, he won a gold medal at the Pan-American Games, and in 1964, he was captain of the U.S. Olympic Judo Team at the Tokyo Olympic Games.

Campbell's interest in judo has continued throughout his life. After the 1964 Olympics he returned to California to teach high school physical education. During the summers he conducted judo camps for children. He also pioneered judo instruction in physical education programs at California high schools. During this period he met Linda Price—they were married in 1966 and had two children, Shanan, also known as Sweet Medicine Woman, and Colin, whose Indian name is Takes Arrows.

Eventually, Campbell left his job as a physical education teacher and set up an industrial arts program at an alternative high school for troubled students. He also developed a jewelry-making class for adult Indian students. His interest in his Native American heritage began to emerge. When Campbell was growing up, his father hesitated to talk about his ancestry because of his fear that the family would be subjected to discrimination. But Campbell per-

**BIOGRAPHY**

U.S. SENATE PHOTO

*Ben Nighthorse Campbell*

**BEN NIGHTHORSE CAMPBELL 1933–**

1933 Born, Auburn, Calif.

1939–45 World War II

1950 Dropped out of high school; joined U.S. Air Force

1950–53 Korean War

1957 Earned B.A. from San Jose State

1963 Won gold medal at Pan-American Games

1964 Served as captain of U.S. Olympic Judo Team at Tokyo Olympic Games

1961–73 Vietnam War

1977 Moved to ranch in Ignacio, Colo.

1980 Enrolled as official member of Black Horse family and Northern Cheyenne tribe

1982 Elected to Colo. legislature

1986 Elected to U.S. House of Representatives

1992 Elected to U.S. Senate; first Native American senator since 1929

1995 Switched his political affiliation from Democrat to Republican

1925    1950    1975    2000

sisted, and his father finally gave him information that led him to relatives on the Northern Cheyenne reservation in Montana. There, in 1980, he was officially enrolled as a member of the Black Horse family and of the Northern Cheyenne tribe.

Campbell entered the world of politics by chance. He attended a Colorado Democratic party meeting in May 1982 hoping to see a friend whom he thought might be there. Party officials were trying to find someone willing to run for state representative from Campbell's district, against a Republican who was considered a certain winner. No one but Campbell was willing to take on the challenge. To everyone's great surprise, he not only won but carried 57 percent of the vote, including 15 percent of the crossover vote from the Republican side.

Campbell was a Democrat whose blend of fiscal conservatism and social liberalism made him an enigma. During his two terms in the Colorado legislature he was instrumental in the passage of landmark legislation to settle disputes over Indian WATER RIGHTS. Early in his political career, he learned that his positions angered extremists on both ends of the political spectrum. He has little tolerance for single-issue zealots. "I learned early on that the more extreme their position or ideology, the less they have in common with the majority of the electorate," he said. "[They] reduce everything in America to a single issue. They do not judge a legislator on total performance, on what that representative is doing for everybody. They are concerned only with what a legislator does for them on that one single issue."

In 1986, Campbell decided to run for the U.S. House of Representatives from Colorado's third district. Since Indians constitute only two percent of the population of the district, Campbell and his campaign manager decided to downplay his Indian heritage. However, his Native American background along with his diverse credentials—high school dropout, Korean war veteran, small-business owner, Olympic athlete, artist, truck driver, teacher, rancher, and state legislator—was a potent and irresistibly novel combination for both voters and the media. Ordinary people could identify with him as "one of them." The result was a 52–48 percent win for Campbell, making him one of only six challengers nationwide to unseat an incumbent in 1986. On January 6, 1987, he stood proudly between Joseph P. Kennedy II, son of the late Robert F. Kennedy, and John Lewis, son of a black Georgia sharecropper, to be sworn in and take his seat in the One Hundredth Congress.

During his three terms as a U.S. representative, Campbell acted as a spokesman for all Indians, not just those he represented from Colorado. He cosponsored legislation to establish the Museum of the American Indian at the Smithsonian Institution. He also fought to have the Custer National Battlefield Monument renamed the Little Big Horn National Battlefield Monument. The Montana monument, which honors the 1876 battle between General George Armstrong Custer's Seventh Cavalry and a group of Sioux, Cheyenne, and Arapaho Indians camped on the banks of the Little Big Horn River, memorialized and glorified the two hundred soldiers, including General Custer, who perished there. Until 1991 only a wooden marker commemorated the loss of Indian lives. In 1991, largely through Campbell's efforts, Congress changed the monument's name and authorized a more prominent memorial to the Indians who fought and died there.

Toward the end of his third term as a U.S. representative, Campbell expected to retire from politics. However, in April 1992, when Senator Timothy E. Wirth (D-Colo.) unexpectedly announced he would not run for reelection, Campbell decided to run for Wirth's seat. It turned out to be an uphill struggle. Campbell at one point had a ten-point lead over his Republican opponent, but it began to slip. He became discouraged and turned to Indian friends for advice. Their prescription was unorthodox: they prayed for him and performed rituals on his behalf, and advised him to paint his body with red war paint and carry an eagle feather at all times. Campbell did not question their wisdom; he did as they advised, and almost immediately his ratings in the polls improved. Campbell won the election by nearly 10 percent and returned to Washington to become the first Native American senator in over sixty years.

During his first term in the Senate, Campbell was appointed to five key committees: Energy and Natural Resources; Banking, Housing and Urban Affairs; Democratic Policy; Veterans Affairs; and Indian Affairs.

In March 1995, barely two years into his Senate term, Campbell surprised and angered the Democratic party by announcing that he was switching affiliation and aligning himself with the Republicans. The Democratic party responded by calling Campbell a turncoat and Benedict Campbell, and demanding the return of $255,000 in donated funds used to help elect him to the Senate. Campbell replied that his record of voting with the Democratic leadership on most issues should be repayment for the party's support.

See also NATIVE AMERICAN LAW.

"MY GRANDFATHER TOLD ME THAT AT THE LITTLE BIG HORN CUSTER DROPPED THE FLAG AND THE CHEYENNES PICKED IT UP . . . NOW THE FLAG UNITES ALL OF US IN THIS GREAT COUNTRY."

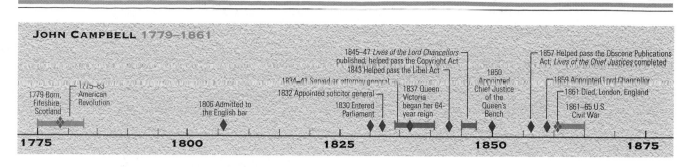

JOHN CAMPBELL 1779–1861

1845–47 *Lives of the Lord Chancellors* published; helped pass the Copyright Act
1843 Helped pass the Libel Act
1834–41 Served as attorney general
1832 Appointed solicitor general
1830 Entered Parliament
1779 Born, Fifeshire, Scotland
1775–83 American Revolution
1806 Admitted to the English bar
1837 Queen Victoria began her 64-year reign
1850 Appointed Chief Justice of the Queen's Bench
1857 Helped pass the Obscene Publications Act; *Lives of the Chief Justices* completed
1859 Appointed Lord Chancellor
1861 Died, London, England
1861–65 U.S. Civil War

1775    1800    1825    1850    1875

## CAMPBELL, JOHN

John Campbell, also known as First Baron Campbell, was born September 15, 1779, in Scotland. He was admitted to the bar in 1806 and pursued a career in British law and politics.

In 1830, Campbell entered Parliament and advocated legal reforms in real property and local government. Two years later he served as solicitor general, and from 1834 to 1841, he was attorney general. In 1850 he performed the duties of Chief Justice of the Queen's Bench and in 1859 became Lord Chancellor.

Campbell is credited with the passage of three important pieces of legislation: the Libel Act, in 1843; the Copyright Act, in 1846; and the Obscene Publications Act, in 1857.

As an author, Campbell is famous for *Lives of the Lord Chancellors*, published from 1845 to 1847, and for *Lives of the Chief Justices*, published from 1849 to 1857.

Campbell died June 23, 1861, in London, England.

## CAMPBELL, JOHN ARCHIBALD

John Archibald Campbell was a politician, a statesman, and an associate justice on the U.S. Supreme Court during the turbulent years preceding the outbreak of the Civil War.

Born June 24, 1811, in Washington, Georgia, the son of a prominent landowner and lawyer, Campbell was a child of exceptional intellectual ability. He entered Franklin College (now the University of Georgia) at the age of eleven and graduated at fourteen with high honors. He then entered West Point but he withdrew after three years to return home and support his family following the death of his father. He also studied law privately and in 1828, at the age of eighteen, he was admitted to

**BIOGRAPHY**

**BIOGRAPHY**

*John Archibald Campbell*

the Georgia bar by a special act of the Georgia legislature. He then moved to Alabama, married, and practiced law, first in Montgomery and then in Mobile.

Widely known for his skilled arguments and his extensive knowledge of the law, Campbell quickly became a leading lawyer in Alabama. He turned down two appointments to the state supreme court, the first one offered to him when he was only twenty-four. An active Democrat, Campbell also found time for politics and, in 1836, he was elected to the first of two terms in the Alabama state legislature. He was a delegate to the Nashville Convention of 1850 which was convened to protect southern rights against what was viewed as the growing encroachment of the North, especially with respect to SLAVERY. Campbell, known for his moderate views, prepared many of the resolutions adopted by the convention, which were conciliatory in nature and designed to avoid inflaming passions on the slavery issue.

Campbell was nominated to the U.S. Supreme Court in March 1853 by President FRANKLIN PIERCE, the new Democratic president, after the Senate had previously refused to act on three candidates offered by the lame-duck president MILLARD FILLMORE. The sitting justices of the Court had taken the unprecedented step of sending a delegation to the president to request that Campbell be nominated to the Court. Campbell, only forty-one at the time, was confirmed unanimously.

Campbell was, for the most part, a vigorous STATES' RIGHTS advocate while on the Court. In his dissent in *Dodge v. Woolsey*, 59 U.S. 331, 18 How. 331, 15 L. Ed. 401 (1855), for example, he argued against the Court's extension of

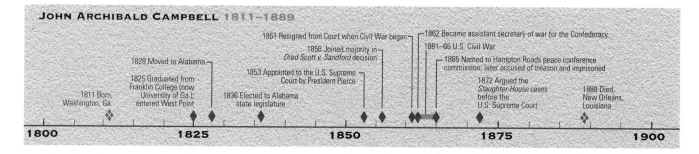

JOHN ARCHIBALD CAMPBELL 1811–1889

1861 Resigned from Court when Civil War began
1856 Joined majority in *Dred Scott v. Sandford* decision
1828 Moved to Alabama
1825 Graduated from Franklin College (now University of Ga.); entered West Point
1853 Appointed to the U.S. Supreme Court by President Pierce
1811 Born, Washington, Ga.
1836 Elected to Alabama state legislature
1862 Became assistant secretary of war for the Confederacy
1861–65 U.S. Civil War
1865 Named to Hampton Roads peace conference commission; later accused of treason and imprisoned
1872 Argued the *Slaughter-House* cases before the U.S. Supreme Court
1889 Died, New Orleans, Louisiana

1800    1825    1850    1875    1900

federal jurisdiction over state-chartered CORPO-RATIONS. Campbell believed that state legislatures should regulate such matters. However, Campbell displayed somewhat more moderate views with respect to slavery. He opposed SECESSION and argued that slavery would eventually disappear on its own and be replaced by free labor if the South were left undisturbed. Upon his appointment to the Court, he freed all his own slaves and then hired only free blacks as servants. But Campbell was nevertheless widely criticized for his views, especially by northern abolitionists, when he joined the majority of the Court in the controversial *Dred Scott* decision. In *Dred Scott v. Sandford*, 60 U.S. 393, 19 How. 393, 15 L. Ed. 691 (U.S. Mo. Dec. Term 1856), the Court held that blacks were not citizens of the United States, with the right to sue in federal court. In his concurring opinion, Campbell contended that the federal government had no choice but to recognize as property whatever the laws of the individual states determined to be property, including slaves. See also DRED SCOTT V. SANDFORD.

In 1861, Campbell served as an unofficial mediator between the federal government and southern commissioners seeking a resolution to the conflict over secession and slavery. Secretary of State William H. Seward, acting through Campbell but without the authority of the president, promised that Fort Sumter, South Carolina, then occupied by federal troops, would be evacuated. When it was instead reinforced, Campbell was accused of treachery by the southern commissioners.

When the Civil War later broke out and Alabama seceded from the union, Campbell remained loyal to his home state and resigned from the Court in April 1861. After returning to the South, he was appointed assistant secretary of war for the Confederacy. When the Confederacy collapsed in 1865, he was named to the commission at the Hampton Roads peace conference, which was convened to help bring about peace between the North and South. The commission failed to reach any agreement. Campbell again attempted to intervene to bring about peace, this time through a private meeting with President ABRAHAM LINCOLN, which resulted in an order allowing the Virginia legislature to convene to consider Lincoln's terms for reconstruction. Within a few days the South surrendered and Lincoln withdrew his approval of the meeting, claiming that Campbell had misconstrued the terms of the plan. After Lincoln's assassination Campbell was accused of TREASON and imprisoned for several months.

Virtually all Campbell's property and belongings in Alabama were destroyed during the war and after his release from prison he faced the prospect of starting over. He decided to settle in New Orleans, where he soon established another successful law practice along with a nationally renowned private law library. He appeared before the U.S. Supreme Court in a number of significant cases, including the *Slaughter-House* cases, 83 U.S. 36, 16 Wall. 36, 21 L. Ed. 394 (1872). In the SLAUGHTER-HOUSE CASES, the Court considered the legality of a statute that granted a corporation chartered by the state of Louisiana the exclusive right to maintain within New Orleans all butcher shops, slaughter pens, stockyards, and stables. Campbell, though previously known for favoring the rights of states, argued that the law created a MONOPOLY in violation of the recently adopted Fourteenth and Fifteenth Amendments of the Constitution. The Court, in construing the FOURTEENTH AMENDMENT for the first time in its history, narrowly rejected Campbell's argument in a 5–4 decision that would be reversed twenty years later.

Campbell continued to practice law for another quarter century before withdrawing to a reclusive retirement in New Orleans. He died in 1889 at the age of seventy-seven.

**CAMPBELL, WILLIAM J.**    When he was named to the federal bench at age thirty-five in 1940, William J. Campbell was the youngest judge ever appointed; at the time of his death, he was the longest-tenured federal judge in the United States, with almost fifty years of service to his credit.

Campbell was born in Chicago on March 19, 1905. The son of a Scottish wool merchant, he grew up in a middle-class neighborhood on the

"THE SUPREME COURT IS A VENERABLE TRIBUNAL THAT DESERVES WELL OF THE COUNTRY. IT OUGHT NOT . . . BE AFFECTED BY REVOLUTIONARY POLITICS AND I SHALL TAKE CARE THAT THROUGH ME THIS SHALL NOT BE DONE."

**BIOGRAPHY**

*William J. Campbell*

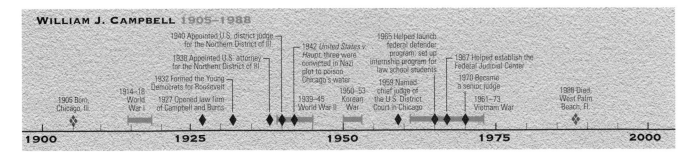

WILLIAM J. CAMPBELL 1905–1988

1905 Born, Chicago, Ill.

1914–18 World War I

1927 Opened law firm of Campbell and Burns

1932 Formed the Young Democrats for Roosevelt

1938 Appointed U.S. attorney for the Northern District of Ill.

1940 Appointed U.S. district judge for the Northern District of Ill.

1939–45 World War II

1942 *United States v. Haupt,* three were convicted in Nazi plot to poison Chicago's water

1950–53 Korean War

1959 Named chief judge of the U.S. District Court in Chicago

1965 Helped launch federal defender program; set up internship program for law school students

1961–73 Vietnam War

1967 Helped establish the Federal Judicial Center

1970 Became a senior judge

1988 Died, West Palm Beach, Fl.

1900    1925    1950    1975    2000

city's west side. There, he attended St. Rita High School and St. Rita College. After graduation, he worked as an insurance claims adjuster while enrolled in a night program at Chicago's Loyola University law school. Campbell earned his doctor of jurisprudence degree in 1926 and was admitted to the Illinois bar in 1927. He returned to Loyola in 1928 to complete a master of laws degree.

Shortly after passing the bar in 1927, Campbell partnered with a longtime friend to open the law firm of Campbell and Burns. The new firm's first major client, the Roman Catholic Archdiocese of Chicago, would have a profound influence on Campbell's professional and personal life, introducing him to the world of Chicago Democratic politics and to his wife.

With the help of church leaders and prominent Chicago Catholics, Campbell formed the Young Democrats for Roosevelt in 1932, when FRANKLIN D. ROOSEVELT was governor of New York and a presidential hopeful. The powerful Chicago Democratic political machine shunned Roosevelt and used its power to thwart Roosevelt's efforts to secure permits for his campaign events. Undaunted, Campbell put a bishop in front of a Catholic Youth Organization band and had them march through the streets of Chicago in an "illegal parade" that brought considerable attention to the candidate. Years later, Campbell said, "Naturally, when all those Irish policemen saw the bishop, they weren't about to do anything but say hello and salute."

After Roosevelt's election, Campbell continued to be an outsider in Chicago Democratic politics, but he had clearly earned Roosevelt's attention and admiration. In 1935 Campbell was named Illinois administrator for the president's National Youth Administration.

In 1938 Campbell was named U.S. attorney for the Northern District of Illinois. Appointed by Roosevelt to fight the Chicago Democratic political machine, Campbell made the most of the job. As a young federal PROSECUTOR, he crossed paths with many of the city's more colorful citizens, including notorious gangster AL CAPONE, and he continually challenged the city's political leaders and their system of influence.

Two years later, in an effort to appease those leaders during an election year, Roosevelt removed Campbell as prosecutor—and appointed him to a federal judgeship. "I got kicked upstairs," Campbell said. "[Roosevelt] needed the machine for the election." Campbell was appointed U.S. district judge for the Northern District of Illinois on October 10, 1940, and he began his long judicial career on October 22.

As a prosecutor, Campbell had been part of the team that convicted Capone of TAX EVASION; in his early years as a judge, he supervised Capone's parole. "I insisted that . . . he never set foot in Cook County [Illinois], and he agreed to it," said Campbell. "I also insisted that he pay every last nickel in taxes he owed the government." Capone protested by paying his millions of dollars in back taxes in pennies. Though a Chicago bank actually counted and verified the amount in a day, Campbell initially threatened to do the job himself, one penny at a time—and to make Capone sit in jail until he had finished.

Only two years into his federal judgeship, Campbell conducted one of the few TREASON trials ever held in the United States (*United States v. Haupt*, 47 F. Supp. 832 [N.D. Ill. 1942], *opinion supplemented by* 47 F. Supp. 836 [N.D. Ill. 1942]). He sentenced three men to death after they had been convicted in a Nazi plot to poison Chicago's water supply. "We had to blaze a trail" in that case, he said, because there were no statutes governing such matters. Campbell said the only guidelines available were in the U.S. Constitution. Though an appellate court later overturned the death sentences (*United States v. Haupt*, 136 F.2d 661 [7th Cir. 1943]), Campbell often called the case a highlight of his career.

Campbell was named chief judge of the U.S. District Court in Chicago on April 6, 1959. In his years on the federal bench, he earned a reputation as an innovative, courageous, and practical jurist. Fellow U.S. district judge James C. Paine said Campbell was "the kind of judge each of us would like to be."

When asked to hear politically charged Illinois reapportionment cases in the late 1950s, Campbell called a historic joint session between the federal court and the Illinois Supreme Court to resolve the issues. (Reapportionment is the realignment or change in legislative districts brought about by changes in population and mandated by the constitutional requirement of equality of representation.) Even though the state legislature had been unwilling or unable to act, Campbell's unique team was able to reapportion Illinois's state and federal legislative districts to the satisfaction of most parties.

In the early 1960s, Campbell summoned a group of private attorneys to a luncheon. There, he pointed out the financial benefit they were realizing from U.S. bankruptcy court case assignments. He asked the group to return the favor by contributing money so that the city might provide lawyers for indigent defendants. They did. "A word from the chief judge went a

"THE CRIME OF TREASON IS THE ONLY CRIME DEFINED BY THE CONSTITUTION. . . . THE REASON FOR THIS, NO DOUBT, WAS THAT ITS AUTHORS AND ADOPTERS CONSIDERED TREASON THE HIGHEST OF ALL CRIMES."

long way," said Hubert Will, another federal district judge in Chicago. Campbell also had a knack for appropriating money for the federal judiciary. Owing in large part to his efforts, the budget for the judiciary between 1960 and 1970 increased from $51 million to $117 million.

Chicago's federal defender program resulting from Campbell's luncheon and gentle arm-twisting was launched in 1965 and became a model for the nation long before such programs were mandated and funded by Congress. Also in 1965, Campbell set up an internship program for law school students. A novel idea in 1965, it is now commonplace.

Campbell was equally committed to the continuing professional education of judges and supporting personnel. He was a force in the establishment of the FEDERAL JUDICIAL CENTER, which is the federal courts' agency for research and continuing education. It was established by statute in 1967 as a separate organization within the federal judicial system (28 U.S.C.A. 620-629). Through the Federal Judicial Center, Campbell participated in hundreds of seminars and workshops in all parts of the United States in order to give new district judges, magistrates, bankruptcy judges, clerks of court, probation officers, and other judicial personnel the benefit of his wisdom and experience.

Campbell served as First District judge representative of the Seventh Circuit on the JUDICIAL CONFERENCE OF THE UNITED STATES (1958–1962); member of the Committee on Pretrial and Protracted Case Procedures (1941–1960); and chairman of the Judicial Conference Committee on the Budget (1960–1970). He was the author of numerous publications, including the first manual on protracted case procedures. Among the many honors accorded him were degrees from Loyola University (doctor of laws, 1955), Lincoln College (doctor of laws, 1960), Duquesne College (doctor of letters, 1965), and Barat College (doctor of canon law, 1966).

Twice during Campbell's first thirty years as a federal judge, he turned down an offer to sit on an APPELLATE COURT as well as an offer to return to a lucrative private law practice. The appellate court was, for him, too far removed from the daily hustle of trial court.

When Supreme Court justice FELIX FRANKFURTER died in 1965, many thought Campbell was certain to be appointed to the High Court by President LYNDON B. JOHNSON. But Johnson chose ABE FORTAS, who resigned under pressure four years later. When asked about the missed opportunity many years later, Campbell said, "Although I knew Johnson intimately and personally, he was bigoted enough not to want two Catholics on the Supreme Court." Justice WILLIAM J. BRENNAN, JR., was the one Catholic already on the Court.

Campbell spent little time lamenting the lost Supreme Court nomination. Late in 1965, he decided to take on Chicago syndicate kingpin Sam Giancana. When Giancana was asked to testify before a Chicago GRAND JURY, he invoked his Fifth Amendment right to remain silent. Campbell did something never done before: he gave Giancana IMMUNITY from prosecution and ordered him to testify. After Giancana refused, he spent the next year in jail on contempt charges.

In spite of his toughness on organized crime and career criminals, Campbell showed compassion for men who refused to fight in the nation's wars. When handing out sentences for draft cases during World War II and the Vietnam War, he often ordered the defendants to perform community service. He did not see draft evaders as criminals and refused to treat them as such.

Campbell became a senior judge on March 19, 1970, his sixty-fifth birthday. Though he was eligible to retire with full pay for the rest of his life, he could not accept the thought of leaving the workforce. As a senior judge, he heard cases first in Chicago, and then in the Southern District of Florida, following a move to West Palm Beach in the mid-1970s. In his last years, he devoted his time to writing opinions for the Chicago-based U.S. Seventh Circuit Court of Appeals. He traveled to Chicago from West Palm Beach twice a year to sit on cases there.

Campbell, who was seen pushing a wheelchair full of legal briefs and court opinions into his chambers well into his eighty-second year, died on October 19, 1988, in West Palm Beach, at the age of eighty-three.

## CANADA AND THE UNITED STATES

The United States and Canada share a unique legal relationship. U.S. law looks northward with a mixture of optimism and cooperation, viewing Canada as an integral part of U.S. economic and environmental policy. The two nations' mutual, largely unguarded five-thousand-mile border does much to explain why: they are each other's largest trading partners, amassing $218 billion in trade in 1992; cross-border travel is easy; and they work together on common concerns about the quality of water and air. However, the relationship has not always been so cooperative. Although environmental treaties date to 1902, economic pacts have taken nearly a century to come to fruition. Traditionally, both countries warily put protec-

*Canada and the United States are each other's largest trading partners. With the passage of NAFTA in 1993, goods and materials cross the border with few restrictions.*

tionism ahead of mutual interest, and they have retaliated in kind against TARIFFS, DUTIES, and other barriers to free trade. Only in 1988 did the two enter into the U.S.-Canada Free Trade Agreement (FTA) (Pub. L. No. 100-449, 102 Stat. 1851), a groundbreaking pact designed to eliminate these barriers. It paved the way for the historic NORTH AMERICAN FREE TRADE AGREEMENT (NAFTA) in 1993.

Early relations between the two countries were rocky. In the mid–nineteenth century, trade foundered on stubborn protectionist policies; each country feared the economic success of the other at its own expense. The 1854 Elgin-Marcy Reciprocity Treaty (10 Stat. 1089) was intended to open up trade on natural resources but it barely lasted a decade. Its failure prompted Canada to spend fruitless years trying to loosen U.S. trade restrictions before formulating, in 1879, a national policy of high tariffs by which it hoped to force the United States back to the negotiating table. But the table remained empty for nearly a century. The only trade agreement between the two nations was the GENERAL AGREEMENT ON TARIFFS AND TRADE (GATT), a one-hundred-nation agreement first promulgated in 1947. The generality of the GATT accords did little to address the specific issues facing these two trading partners and it caused Canada, in particular, frustration. But U.S. prosperity throughout the mid–twentieth century meant it could afford to ignore Canadian overtures.

The two were more willing to negotiate on environmental concerns. The landmark agreement in this area is the Boundary Waters Treaty of 1909. It established the International Joint Commission (IJC) to deal with the issues of water resource management, a set of concerns referred to as transboundary issues because of the two nations' common border. Made up of technical specialists from various federal, state, and provincial governments of the United States and Canada, the IJC has authority to approve joint projects and to investigate complaints. Since the 1970s its duties have expanded as the result of the Great Lakes Water Quality Agreements which established goals for restoring the damaged ecosystem of the Great Lakes. Contemporary concerns facing the IJC include water levels, pollution, acid rain, and climate changes, with a growing emphasis on the use and maintenance of river systems. Critics generally agree that the success and innovation of this commission represent a model for international cooperation.

Despite progressive solutions to environmental problems, it took the United States and Canada until the late 1980s to forge better economic ties. The slow progress toward open trade was due to mutual suspicions, greed, and a long history of retaliatory actions. This hindrance stood in stark contrast to the countries' cultural similarities and cooperation in other areas. They had been allies in both world wars and both remained key members of the NORTH

ATLANTIC TREATY ORGANIZATION (NATO). But war is an unusual experience; military allies can still be less than friends in trade. Then, the last half of the twentieth century unexpectedly changed everything—domestic industrial decline, brought on by a rise in international competition, toppled the United States from a position of preeminence and made Canada more important to its plans for long-range prosperity. Canada underwent a great change in its historically isolationist outlook as it too suffered economically. The 1984 election of a conservative Canadian government led by Prime Minister Brian Mulroney was a watershed event. Mulroney's victory was based on promises of opening U.S. markets to Canadian business. Both sides wanted to remove the barriers of high tariffs, antidumping fees, and countervailing duties (forms of protectionism that limited the expansion of each nation's markets) in order to create new jobs and wealth.

On January 2, 1988, negotiations between the administrations of President RONALD REAGAN and Prime Minister Mulroney resulted in the signing of the FTA. In succeeding where previous generations had failed or not even tried, Reagan declared that the FTA would remove an "invisible barrier of economic suspicion and fear." The pact had five broad goals: (1) eliminate barriers to trade in goods and services, (2) improve fair competition, (3) liberalize investment conditions, (4) establish procedures for a joint administration of the agreement, and (5) lay the foundation for future cooperation. The FTA also relaxed U.S. immigration rules for Canadians, allowing freer travel across the border for businesspersons.

On the administrative level it created a temporary body for resolving disputes, the binational Extraordinary Challenge Committee, which was given a seven-year commission to hear appeals. Not surprisingly, this issue had been the most troublesome during the negotiations preceding the FTA; it proved slightly problematic in practice, too, with the United States generally losing its complaints. Nonetheless, the FTA was seen as a boon for U.S. business as a whole, removing Canadian restrictions that had long been a sore point, and emphasizing the resolution of disputes outside of courtrooms.

The FTA's success laid the groundwork for an even more ambitious trade agreement between the United States, Canada, and Mexico. This was the much-anticipated NAFTA, enacted in 1993. NAFTA's changes were to be phased in over fifteen years, and its purpose is to liberalize trade between the three countries in hopes of emulating the economic cooperation long enjoyed by European nations. In practice, its broad aims have proved highly controversial.

Through the many years spent working out its bugs, the U.S.-Canadian legal relationship has taken great strides away from its early guardedness. Environmental rather than economic cooperation proved easier at first, but the changing forces of international competition ultimately forced the two border nations to the bargaining table. Today, trade is almost unfettered, and the countries are probably destined to remain each other's most important trading partners, relying on each other to provide materials, goods, and services. Future willingness to deal will hinge on many variables, not the least of which is the success or failure of NAFTA in an increasingly competitive world.

**CANALS** ▯ Artificial channels for the conveyance of water, used for navigation, transportation, drainage, or irrigation of land. ▯

As a general rule, states supervise the construction and operation of canals by private canal companies. The site of the canal is selected by the state. State law determines the manner of acquiring property used for construction or maintenance of canals. CONDEMNATION or APPROPRIATION and contract or grant are the usual methods of acquisition. Additional methods include ACCRETION—the gradual accumulation of land by natural causes—and DEDICATION—the gift of land to the government by its owner for public use.

The state has authority to supervise the construction of bridges over public canals. A

*The Panama Canal connects the Atlantic and Pacific oceans. It was completed in 1914 and belongs to the government of the United States.*

city may build bridges over canals within its limits, but it cannot interfere with one constructed and managed by the state on its own property.

State law can confer the power to charge TOLLS for use of a canal. Rates can be neither discriminatory nor in excess of the amount authorized by law.

## CANCELLATION OF AN INSTRUMENT

An EQUITABLE remedy by which a court relieves both parties to a legal document of their obligations under it due to fraud, duress, or other grounds.

*Cancellation* is a term often used interchangeably with RESCISSION, but whereas only a document can be canceled, any AGREEMENT—whether oral or written—can be rescinded. Cancellation is distinguishable from REFORMATION, which is an action by a court to enforce a document after its terms have been reframed in accordance with the intent of the parties, in that cancellation abrogates the duties of the parties under the instrument.

Any instrument by which two or more parties agree to exchange designated performances, such as a CONTRACT, DEED, LEASE, insurance policy, COMMERCIAL PAPER, or a MORTGAGE, may be canceled if the circumstances of the case warrant it.

The judicial remedy of the cancellation of an instrument is granted by a court in its sound discretion exercising its EQUITY powers to do justice. If it is apparent that no injustice will result from restoring both parties to the positions they had prior to the execution of the instrument, an instrument may be set aside.

If the party seeking the cancellation has an adequate remedy at law, for example, and can recover DAMAGES that will give complete relief, cancellation will be denied. It is available, however, if the defendant is JUDGMENT-PROOF, or financially unable to pay damages awarded against him or her. Statutes, too, may provide this equitable remedy as CONCURRENT relief, in addition to damages, in particular cases. The UNIFORM COMMERCIAL CODE permits merchants in SALES transactions to seek the cancellation of a contract, in addition to an award of damages in a breach of contract suit.

A plaintiff is entitled to have an instrument canceled only if he or she has acted equitably in dealings with the defendant. The principles of equity apply to any case in which this equitable remedy is sought.

**Grounds** The cancellation of an instrument must be based upon appropriate grounds, the gist of which makes the enforcement of the instrument inequitable. Such grounds must be

proven by a PREPONDERANCE OF THE EVIDENCE presented in the CIVIL ACTION. A term of a document may provide for its cancellation, and courts will usually act accordingly when the facts warrant it. The setting aside of an instrument that appears to record the agreement of the parties to it is considered a significant intervention by a court, which will not be done for a trivial reason or merely because of a change of mind by one party. The primary grounds for cancellation involve the validity of the instrument itself and the agreement that it embodies.

**Duress** An instrument that was obtained by DURESS, the use of threats or physical harm to compel one party to enter an agreement that he or she would not have made otherwise, can be canceled at the request of the victimized party. If duress was present at the time the contract was entered, the agreement of the parties is a SHAM, as the victim was forced to act against his or her will. It would be inequitable for a court to enforce such an agreement.

**Fraud** An instrument may be set aside if it was induced by FRAUD—an intentional deception of another—to gain an advantage over him or her. To justify cancellation, it must be clearly established that the representations made to the victim were untrue and of such a MATERIAL nature that without them the victim would not have agreed to the transaction. In addition, it must be shown that such statements were made intentionally to defraud the victim and that the statements were relied upon by him or her in the decision to enter the agreement. Fraud vitiates an agreement, which makes it unjust to enforce a document embodying its terms.

If, however, a material MISREPRESENTATION is made innocently by one party, the victim is still

*An instrument may be cancelled if one of the parties was intoxicated at the time of executing the document.*

entitled to have the instrument set aside, as it does not reflect the mutual assent of the parties.

**Mental Incapacity** If an agreement has been made by one party who, at the time of its execution, was mentally incapable of understanding the nature of the transaction, it may be canceled at the request of the victim or the victim's legal representative. This is particularly true when the other party has taken advantage of the victim's incompetence in drawing the terms of the agreement.

Courts frequently cancel an instrument entered by a person so intoxicated at the time of executing the document that he or she does not comprehend its legal ramifications. Cancellation is justified particularly when the INTOXICATION is brought about by the other party in order to deceive the victim about the nature of their agreement.

**Mistake** When the parties have both made a mutual MISTAKE OF FACT concerning the agreement entered, an instrument may be canceled, since there is no real agreement between them. If a unilateral mistake exists, that is, a mistake by one party, a court may set aside the document and restore the parties to their position prior to its execution. In order to justify cancellation, a mistake must be material and involve a significant part of the agreement without which the contract would not have been entered into. If the mistake is the result of the carelessness of one or both parties, a court may deny a request for cancellation.

**Undue Influence** UNDUE INFLUENCE, which is the unfair use of pressure on the will of another to gain an advantage over him or her, is a ground for the cancellation of an instrument because one party's will is so overcome by pressure that the person is effectively deprived of freedom of choice. Undue influence is usually established where there is a confidential relationship between the parties and one of them has a greater bargaining power or influence on the other.

**Forgery or Alteration** The cancellation of an instrument is justified when it has been forged.

If an instrument has been materially altered without the consent or knowledge of the party against whom the change is effective, the instrument may be set aside.

**Preclusion of Relief** A person seeking the equitable relief of the cancellation of an instrument might be precluded from it by WAIVER or ESTOPPEL. The right to such relief may be waived or relinquished by a plaintiff's conduct, such as by failing to pursue a remedy within a reasonable time from the execution of the document, a form of LACHES. The doctrine of EQUITABLE ESTOPPEL—by which a person is precluded by conduct from asserting his or her rights because another has relied on that conduct and will be injured if the relief is not precluded—may also operate in a case in which cancellation of an instrument is sought.

The RATIFICATION of a document by a party prevents its subsequent ABROGATION. If a party knowingly affirms or ratifies an instrument—whether by stating so, or by using the property received under it—he or she is precluded from having it set aside.

**CANON LAW** 📖 Any church's or religion's laws, rules, and regulations; more commonly, the written policies that guide the administration and religious ceremonies of the Roman Catholic Church. 📖

Since the fourth century, the Roman Catholic Church has been developing regulations that have had some influence on secular (non-church-related) legal procedures. These regulations are called canons and are codified in the Code of Canon Law (in Latin, *Codex juris canonici*).

The law of England, which inspired much of the law formed in the United States, was a mixture of canon law and COMMON LAW (principles and rules of action embodied in CASE LAW rather than legislative enactments). Canon law and English common law borrowed heavily from each other throughout medieval times and together formed the basis for many of the legal procedures used in the United States. For example, canon law's influence is still visible in the concepts of the GRAND JURY, PRESENTMENT (a description of a criminal offense that is based on the jury's own knowledge), and some characteristics of U.S. MARRIAGE law.

Canon law has its origins in ancient church writings, decisions made by the general councils of local bishops, and rulings issued by the pope. These ideas were organized in the mid–twelfth century by an Italian law teacher, Gratian. He sorted the collection into religious law, penal law, sacramental law, and other categories. Along with a set of decisions by the pope called Decretals of Gregory IX, Gratian's work formed the main body of canon law for nearly eight hundred years. In 1917, Pope Benedict XV recodified (revised) the canons. Pope John Paul II reissued the Code of Canon Law in 1983—authorizing increased participation of laity in the church, recognizing the needs of disabled people, and making other changes. A related text, the Code of Canons of the Eastern Churches, was reissued by the Holy See (the seat of papal government) in 1990.

In the Middle Ages, canon law was used in ECCLESIASTICAL (church) COURTS to decide many types of cases that in modern times are decided by civil courts, including criminal offenses. This was because most English Christians did not make a great distinction between secular and spiritual offenses. Crimes that were tried by the church included ADULTERY, BLASPHEMY, slander, heresy (opposition to official religious views), money lending, and gambling. From the late fourteenth to the early sixteenth centuries church courts also heard many breach-of-faith cases concerning CONTRACTS, as well as INHERITANCE and marriage-related cases.

Criminal trial procedures in medieval church courts were the source of some features that found their way into common law. Although witnesses were considered the best source of proof of a crime under canon law, suspected offenders could also be tried because of public fame (suspicion in the community that they had committed a crime). An INQUEST made up of twelve men—a forerunner of royal courts' grand juries—said under OATH whether public suspicion existed. If none did, then a judge had no authority to proceed. After establishing public fame, the court's next step was canonical purgation, in which the accused person swore an oath that she or he was innocent. Proof of innocence was accomplished by compurgation, in which several oath helpers would swear that they believed the oath was true. People who objected to the purgation of an accused person had the chance to prove their accusation of guilt.

The use of canon law in governmental decisions is not well documented. In the early fifteenth century, commissions of the English Parliament made use of canonical procedures and canon law experts to decide issues involving laws of war, diplomacy, and other questions. For example, Parliament's justification for deposing King Richard II seems to have been based on papal bulls (decrees).

In modern times, the creation, interpretation, and use of the canons closely resemble those of secular law. The Episcopal Conference of Local Bishops and the National Conference of Catholic Bishops are voting bodies that set policy for the church. When policy has been codified, it is used by judges in Catholic tribunals in determining whether certain practices or requests are acceptable according to the canons. (Catholic tribunals make up the Church's own court system, which interprets canonical policy to resolve questions of church practice.) Case law (previous rulings) is published in *Roman Replies* and has precedential value. Judges may also request assistance from the Canon Law Society of America, a research organization, in interpreting the canons.

Catholics who appear before a tribunal may consult canon lawyers, who are not usually secular lawyers. A canon lawyer typically completes at least two years' worth of course work in the canons. North American canon lawyers receive their degree in canon law from one of two institutions: the Catholic University of America, in Washington, D.C., or St. Paul University, in Ottawa, Ontario, Canada.

By the end of the twentieth century secular law had eclipsed canon law in most aspects of public life. Interbody disagreements within the church are now often handled administratively rather than by a tribunal, but within the confines of canon law. However, the tribunal is still the only place where Catholics can secure a marriage ANNULMENT, and each diocese must maintain a tribunal for this purpose. Divorced Catholics who have been denied an annulment can appeal as far as the Sacred Roman Rota, whose international membership is selected by the pope.

In the 1990s, some dioceses—notably the Archdiocese of Denver—have sought to reduce involvement by civil courts in church disputes by creating dispute resolution mechanisms and other internal mechanisms that make use of the written policies of canon law.

## CANON LAW SOCIETY OF AMERICA

The Canon Law Society of America is a nonprofit research association of canon lawyers that helps the Roman Catholic Church to address contemporary issues and internal conflicts within the framework of the church's system of CANON LAW. The society drafts opinions on topics at the request of bishops and other persons within the church.

Canon law is the set of rules a church or religion establishes for itself in order to make administrative and ecclesiastical (religious) decisions. The Roman Catholic Church has an elaborate body of canon law that has been evolving since the fourth century and which has played a historical role in the development of public law.

The Canon Law Society of America helps Catholic decision makers, especially bishops and tribunal judges, to evaluate and set policy. The church's tribunal courts were the model for secular court systems and operate similarly. Tribunal judges decide cases such as marriage ANNULMENTS based on the facts of each case. When a tribunal judge wants more information before ruling on an unusual or difficult case the judge may request research or an advisory opinion from the Canon Law Society.

The society's written opinions are advisory only and carry no authority in the church. However, the society's position has influenced the church's stand on such controversial topics as whether females may serve as altar attendants (now they may). Other issues addressed by the society in the 1990s include questions about the scope of ordained ministers' duties, the role of lay ministers, and how Mass should be celebrated.

Another activity of the society is to promote the use of codes of canon law issued by the Vatican (the seat of Roman Catholic administration) in 1983 and 1990.

Periodicals produced by the society include the *Canon Law Digest; Proceedings*, which recaps the society's annual meeting; and *Roman Replies and CLSA Advisory Opinions*, which tracks tribunal case law. The society also has published studies on marriage annulment, confidentiality, and due process for persons in the church, a procedural handbook for the clergy, and other materials.

Established in 1939 and based at the Catholic University of America, in Washington, D.C., the society is supported by annual membership dues. In 1995, it consisted of 1,550 members internationally. Membership is open to non-Catholics. Institutions and interested individuals may join as associate members.

**CANONS OF CONSTRUCTION** 📖 The system of basic rules and MAXIMS applied by a court to aid in its interpretation of a written document, such as a statute or contract. 📖

In the case of a STATUTE, certain canons of construction can help a court ascertain what the drafters of the statute—usually Congress or a state legislature—meant by the language used in the law. When a dispute involves a CONTRACT, a court will apply other canons of interpretation, or CONSTRUCTION, to help determine what the parties to the AGREEMENT intended at the time they made the contract.

**Statutory Construction** When considering a statute, a court will apply rules of construction only when the language contained in the statute is ambiguous. Under the "PLAIN-MEANING" RULE, if the intention of the LEGISLATURE is "so apparent from the face of the statute that there can be no question as to its meaning, there is no need for the court to apply canons of construction" (*Overseas Education Ass'n v. Federal Labor Relations Authority*, 876 F.2d 960 [D.C. Cir. 1989]). Thus, before even considering what canons to apply, the court must first determine whether the statute in question is ambiguous. Courts have generally held that a statute is ambiguous when reasonably well-informed persons could understand the language in either of two or more senses (*State ex rel. Neelen v. Lucas*, 24 Wis. 2d 262, 128 N.W.2d 425 [1964]).

If a statute is found to be ambiguous, the court then applies a variety of canons, or rules, to help it determine the meaning of the statute. Issues of statutory construction are generally decided by the judge and not by the jury. In interpreting statutes, a judge tries to ascertain the intent of the legislature in enacting the law. By looking to legislative intent, the court attempts to carry out the will of the lawmaking branch of the government. This philosophy has its origins in the English common law first established over four hundred years ago. As the legal philosopher Sir EDWARD COKE wrote in 1584, "[T]he office of all judges is always to make such construction as shall suppress the mischief, advance the remedy, and to suppress subtle invention and evasions for continuance of the mischief . . . according to the true intent of the makers of the act" (*Heydon's Case*, 3 Co. Rep. 7a, 76 Eng. Rep. 637 [King's Bench 1584]). In more contemporary terms, courts consider the history and nature of the subject matter of the statute; the end to be attained by the law; the "mischief," or wrong, sought to be remedied; and the purpose to be accomplished by the law (*Crowder v. First Federal Savings & Loan Ass'n of Dallas*, 567 S.W.2d 550, Tex. App. 1978). In determining legislative intent courts usually turn to a variety of sources: the language of the statute itself; the LEGISLATIVE HISTORY of prior enactments on a similar subject; the proceedings surrounding the passage of the law, including debates and committee reports; and, if they are available, interpretations of the law by administrative officials.

To aid in the interpretation of an ambiguous law, a court may also look to more "intrinsic" rules not related to the activities preceding the passage of the statute. These rules are applied to help the court analyze the internal structure of the text and the conventional meanings of the terms used in the law. In addition, intrinsic rules may be used when the court has little or no existing legislative history, such as that provided by committee reports or records of other proceedings, to draw on in interpreting the statute.

Some of these canons of construction are expressed in well-known Latin phrases or maxims. Under *ejusdem generis* (of the same kind, class, or nature), when general words follow specific words in a statute where several items have been enumerated, the general words are construed to embrace only objects similar in nature to the objects enumerated by the preceding specific words of the statute. *Ejusdem generis* saves the legislature from having to spell out in advance every contingency to which the statute could apply. For example, in a statute granting a department of conservation the authority to sell "~~gravel, sand, earth or other material,~~" a court held that "other material" could only be interpreted to include materials of the same general type and did not include commercial timber (*Sierra Club v. Kenney*, 88 Ill. 2d 110, 57 Ill. Dec. 851, 429 N.E.2d 1214 [1981]). In the opposite situation, where specific words follow general ones, *ejusdem generis* is also applied; again, the general term embraces only things that are similar to those specifically enumerated.

Another maxim of statutory construction is *expressio unius est exclusio alterius.* Roughly translated, this phrase means that whatever is omitted is understood to be excluded. Thus, if a statute provides for a specific sanction for noncompliance with the statute, other sanctions are excluded and cannot be applied (*Sprague v. State*, 590 P.2d 410 [Alaska 1979]). The maxim is based on the rationale that if the legislature had intended to accommodate a particular remedy or allowance, it would have done so expressly; if the legislature did not provide for such an allowance or event, it should be assumed that it meant not to. The maxim has wide application and has been used by courts to interpret constitutions, treaties, wills, and contracts as well as statutes. Nevertheless, *expressio unius est exclusio alterius* does have its limitations. Courts have held that the maxim should be disregarded where an expanded interpretation of a statute will lead to beneficial results or will serve the purpose for which the statute was enacted.

**Contract Construction** Judges face different challenges when interpreting the terms of a contract. As a result, different canons exist to aid a court in resolving a dispute between the parties to a contract.

As in statutory construction, in a contract dispute the court gives contract terms their plain and ordinary meaning, interpreting them as ordinary, average, or REASONABLE persons would understand them (*Rains v. Becton, Dickinson & Co.*, 246 Neb. 746, 523 N.W.2d 506 [Neb. 1994]). If the language of the contract is clear and unambiguous, there is no room for further interpretation and the court will enforce the contract as written. By doing so, the court gives effect to the parties' intentions in making the contract and avoids adding its own interpretation to the agreement.

If the contract contains ambiguous terms, however, they are strictly construed against the party who drafted the contract. This rule of STRICT CONSTRUCTION is often applied in contracts containing *exculpatory clauses*, or provisions that attempt to insulate a party, usually the party who drafted the contract, from liability.

Thus, when a clause in a contract between a health club and a member, in which the member waived her right to bring legal action for injuries she suffered at the health club, was held to be ambiguous, it was construed strictly against the health club and it was found to be invalid (*Nimis v. St. Paul Turners*, 521 N.W.2d 54 [Minn. App. 1994]).

A court may look to other canons of construction or interpretation if it determines that the terms of a contract are ambiguous. In business situations, the court may consider the COURSE OF DEALING or COURSE OF PERFORMANCE, that is, the pattern of conduct observed in previous transactions between the parties. Such evidence can help the court determine the intent of the parties at the time they entered the contract and provides additional terms that, though they are not expressly contained in the agreement, the court can use to interpret the contract. Thus, where one party to the contract alleges that the other breached the contract by failing to make payment in the proper manner, and the contract contains no express provisions concerning payment, the court can consider how the parties handled the issue of payment in previous transactions to resolve the issue (*AROK Construction Co. v. Indian Construction Services*, 174 Ariz. 291, 848 P.2d 870 [Ariz. App. 1993]).

A court can also look to usage of trade to aid its interpretation of an ambiguous agreement. A *usage of trade* is a commercial practice or industry custom "having such regularity of observance in a place, vocation, or trade as to justify an expectation that it will be observed with respect to a particular agreement" (Restatement [Second] of Contracts § 222 [1981]). As a result, if a contract is unclear about how shipment of a specific type of goods is to be handled, the court can consider evidence of general industry practice in the area to help determine what the parties intended with respect to shipment.

See also TRADE USAGE.

**CANONS OF ETHICS** 📖 Rules that govern the practice of law. 📖

The canons of ETHICS have been replaced by the code of PROFESSIONAL RESPONSIBILITY which sets forth the standards of professional conduct prescribed for lawyers in their professional dealings.

**CANONS OF JUDICIAL ETHICS** See CODE OF JUDICIAL CONDUCT.

**CAPACITY** 📖 The ability, capability, or fitness to do something; a legal right, power, or competency to perform some act. An ability to comprehend both the nature and consequences of one's acts. 📖

Capacity relates to soundness of mind and to an intelligent understanding and perception of one's actions. It is the power either to create or to enter into a legal relation under the same conditions or circumstances as a person of sound mind or normal intelligence would have the power to create or to enter.

A person of normal intelligence and sound mind has the capacity to dispose of his or her property by WILL as he or she sees fit.

A *capacity defense* is used in both criminal and civil actions to describe a lack of fundamental ability to be accountable for one's action that nullifies the element of INTENT when intent is essential to the action, thereby relieving a person of responsibility for it.

An individual under DURESS lacks the capacity to CONTRACT; a child under the age of seven accused of committing a crime lacks criminal capacity.

**CAPIAS** [*Latin, That you take.*] The name for several different kinds of WRITS, or court orders, all of which require an officer to take the defendant into CUSTODY.

For example, a *capias ad audiendum judicium* is a writ that orders the defendant brought back before the court after an appearance in which the person has been found guilty of a MISDE-MEANOR. A *capias ad satisfaciendum* orders the sheriff to take the defendant into custody until a judgment is paid or a discharge is granted on the ground that the defendant is an insolvent debtor. This is a BODY EXECUTION.

**CAPITAL ASSET** Property held by a tax-payer, such as houses, cars, STOCKS, BONDS, and jewelry, or a building owned by a CORPORATION to furnish facilities for its employees.

Excluded from capital assets are certain items stated in the INTERNAL REVENUE CODE, for example (1) trade or business property subject to DEPRECIATION allowance under the tax laws; (2) REAL PROPERTY used in trade or business; (3) certain categories of copyrighted materials and literary property; and (4) accounts or notes receivable acquired in the ordinary course of business.

The determination of what constitutes a capital asset is essential to the tax treatment of the profits from the sale of property as capital gains, which are taxed at a lower rate than ordinary income.

**CAPITALIZE** To regard the cost of an improvement or other purchase as a CAPITAL ASSET for purposes of determining INCOME TAX liability. To calculate the NET WORTH upon which an investment is based. To issue company STOCKS or BONDS to finance an investment.

The owner of a business may capitalize the expense of renovating a factory to maximize his or her after-tax profits, since such expenses may be used to decrease the pretax profits, thereby reducing the amount of profits subject to taxation.

An individual may compute the net worth of shares of stock, in order to treat them as capital assets for income tax purposes. Such treatment often results in more favorable rates of taxation on the profits made when assets are sold because they are considered capital gains.

**CAPITAL PUNISHMENT** The lawful infliction of death as a punishment; the death penalty.

Capital punishment continues to be used in the United States despite controversy over its merits and over its effectiveness as a deterrent to serious crime. A sentence of death may be carried out by one of five lawful means: electrocution, hanging, lethal injection, gas chamber, and firing squad. As of 1995, thirty-eight states employed capital punishment as a sentence; twelve states—Alaska, Hawaii, Iowa, Maine, Massachusetts, Michigan, Minnesota, North Dakota, Rhode Island, Vermont, West Virginia, and Wisconsin—and the District of Columbia did not.

The first known infliction of the death penalty in the American colonies occurred in Jamestown Colony in 1608. During the period of the Revolutionary War, capital punishment apparently was widely accepted—162 documented executions took place in the eighteenth century. At the end of the war eleven colonies wrote new constitutions, and, although nine of them did not allow CRUEL AND UNUSUAL PUNISH-MENT, all authorized capital punishment. In 1790 the First Congress enacted legislation that implemented capital punishment for the crimes of ROBBERY, RAPE, MURDER, and FORGERY of public

*This couple's home is a capital asset unless they use it solely for business.*

MICHAEL NEWMAN/PHOTOEDIT

securities. The nineteenth century saw a dramatic increase in the use of capital punishment with 1,391 documented executions. The death penalty continued as an acceptable practice in the United States for some time.

In 1967 a national moratorium was placed on capital punishment while the Supreme Court considered its constitutionality. In 1972 it appeared that the Court had put an end to the death penalty in the case of *Furman v. Georgia*, 408 U.S. 238, 92 S. Ct. 2726, 33 L. Ed 2d 346, declaring certain capital punishment laws to be unconstitutionally cruel and unusual because juries were applying them arbitrarily and capriciously. It appeared that *Furman* would mark the passing into history of capital punishment in this country.

By 1976, Georgia, Florida, and Texas had drafted new death penalty laws and this time, the Supreme Court upheld them. Of the nine Supreme Court justices, only two, WILLIAM J. BRENNAN, JR., and THURGOOD MARSHALL, persisted in the belief that capital punishment is unconstitutional PER SE. Capital punishment had survived and so had the controversies surrounding it.

Though the Supreme Court has held that the Constitution permits the use of capital punishment, decisions on this issue have divided the Court and done little to convince opponents of the death penalty's fairness. Critics have argued that the death penalty is a cruel and unusual punishment, that it is applied in a racially discriminatory manner, that it lacks a deterrent effect, and that it is just plain wrong.

**Cruel and Unusual Punishment** The EIGHTH AMENDMENT of the U.S. Constitution prohibits the government from inflicting "cruel and unusual punishments." The controversy over the constitutionality of the death penalty lies in the ambiguity of the phrase "cruel and unusual." The first meeting of Congress addressed the phrase for only a few minutes. Congressman William Smith of South Carolina foreshadowed the controversy to come when he stated that the wording of the Eighth Amendment was "too indefinite."

Whereas some argue that the phrase "cruel and unusual" refers to the type of punishment inflicted (such punishments as the severing of limbs would almost certainly be considered cruel and unusual), others feel that the phrase refers to the degree and duration of the punishment. The Supreme Court has rejected both interpretations, leaving the death penalty a legal means of punishing certain criminals.

The FIFTH AMENDMENT seems to supply a clearer basis for assuming the constitutionality of the death penalty. This amendment states

### Capital Punishment

Prisoners Executed under Civil Authority* in the U.S., 1930 to 1993

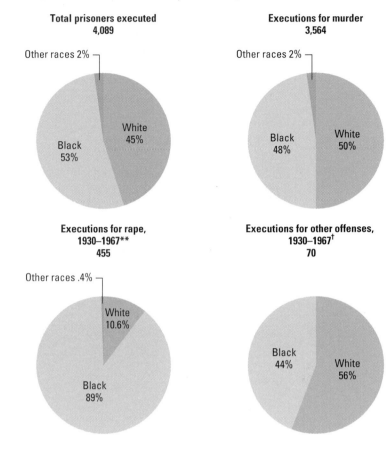

**Total prisoners executed**
**4,089**

Other races 2%
White 45%
Black 53%

**Executions for murder**
**3,564**

Other races 2%
White 50%
Black 48%

**Executions for rape,**
**1930–1967****
**455**

Other races .4%
White 10.6%
Black 89%

**Executions for other offenses,**
**1930–1967†**
**70**

Black 44%
White 56%

*Excludes executions by military authorities. The U.S. Army and Air Force carried out 160 executions in the given time period. The Navy carried out no executions during this period.

**There were no executions for rape from 1968 to 1993.

†"Other offenses" (and their execution numbers) include: armed robbery (25), kidnapping (20), burglary (11), espionage (8), and aggravated assault (6). The espionage executions included 6 in 1942 and 2 in 1953—the Rosenburgs. There were no executions for "other offenses" from 1968 to 1993.

Source: U.S. Law Enforcement Assistance Administration, through 1978; U.S. Bureau of Justice Statistics, *Correctional Populations in the United States*, annual (1978 and thereafter).

that no one shall be "deprived of life, liberty, or property, without due process of law. From this language one can conclude that with DUE PROCESS OF LAW, capital punishment may be imposed.

In *Furman*, the justices who found the death penalty to be unconstitutional pointed to the language of the Eighth Amendment as the basis of their decision. Chief Justice WARREN E. BURGER, who filed a dissenting opinion, relied heavily upon the language of the Fifth Amendment to support his argument that the death penalty was constitutional.

**Racial Bias** In 1983, Professor David C. Baldus, of the University of Iowa College of Law, published a study on the capital punishment system in the state of Georgia. The figures he assembled showed that between 1973

# THE COSTS OF CAPITAL PUNISHMENT

In 1989, the state of Florida executed forty-two-year-old Ted Bundy. Bundy confessed to 28 murders in four states. During his nine years on death row, he survived three stays of execution. Before he was put to death in the electric chair, Bundy cost taxpayers more than $5 million.

In a country where some 70 percent of the population favors the death penalty, many people may feel that Bundy got what he deserved. A further question, however, is whether U.S. taxpayers got their money's worth. When a single sentence of death can cost millions of dollars to carry out, does it make economic sense to retain the death penalty?

At first glance, the costs involved in the execution of an inmate appear simple and minuscule. The state of Florida pays $150 to the executioner, $20 for the last meal, $150 for a new suit for the inmate's burial, and $525 for the undertaker's services and a cof-

IN FOCUS

fin. In Florida, the cost of an execution is less than $1,000.

The actual execution of an inmate is quick and simple; the capital punishment system is far more complex. To resolve issues of unconstitutionality that the Supreme Court found in *Furman v. Georgia*, 408 U.S. 238, 92 S. Ct. 2726, 33 L. Ed. 2d 346 (1972), states found it necessary to introduce a complex appeals process that would guarantee the rights of death row inmates. Capital trials are much more expensive to carry out than are their noncapital counterparts because of the price at stake, the life of the accused. Evidence gathering is also more expensive: evidence must be collected not only to determine the guilt or innocence of the accused but also to support or contradict a sentence of death. All sentences of death face a mandatory review by the state supreme court, at an additional cost of at least $70,000. If a case advances fur-

ther in the state or federal appeals process, the costs are likely to jump to $275,000 or more for each appeal.

Appeals of a death sentence guarantee great expense to the taxpayer, as the state pays both to defend and to prosecute death row inmates. Public defenders in such appeals openly admit that their goal is delay, and prosecutors and state attorneys slow the process by fighting access to public records and allowing death row defendants to sweat out their cases until the last minute.

Abolitionists believe that the existing system cannot be repaired and must be abandoned. The alternative sentence, life imprisonment without parole, achieves the same result as capital punishment, they argue. Like the death penalty, a life sentence permanently removes the convict from the community against which he or she committed crimes. And it is far less expensive.

According to a 1990 study, the total cost to build a maximum-security prison cell is $63,000, which breaks down to

and 1979, killers whose victims were white were eleven times more likely to be sentenced to death than were killers whose victims were black.

Baldus's study was used by death row inmate Warren McClesky in an appeal that came before the Supreme Court (*McClesky v. Kemp*, 481 U.S. 279, 107 S. Ct. 1756, 95 L. Ed. 2d 262). Though the Supreme Court accepted the validity of the study, it found the statistics "insufficient to demonstrate unconstitutional DISCRIMINATION" or "to show irrationality, arbitrariness, and capriciousness."

Other studies have yielded equally staggering numbers regarding the statistical differences between the system's treatment of blacks and whites. For example, between 1976 and 1995, a total of 245 convicts were executed; 84 percent of their victims were white, though fewer than 50 percent of all murder victims are white. Many critics argue that statistics demonstrating racial bias in the administration of capital punishment prove that the death penalty, even if constitutional in concept, is unconstitutional as applied in the United States—violating at least

the Equal Protection Clause of the FOURTEENTH AMENDMENT.

Justice LEWIS F. POWELL, JR., who voted with the majority in *McClesky* to deny a racial bias challenge to the capital punishment system, later informed a biographer that he had since come to regret his vote.

**Deterrent Effect** Since the turn of the twentieth century, many studies have been conducted on the deterrent effect of capital punishment. More often than not, the results have proved inconclusive; no hard evidence exists to verify the theory that the threat of such a harsh punishment will sway criminals from their actions. In fact, some statistics indicate that the opposite is true; in some instances, states employing capital punishment have a higher incidence of HOMICIDE than neighboring states that do not employ the death penalty.

The Supreme Court justices in the *Furman* case, both concurring and dissenting, often referred to studies that showed no conclusive correspondence between capital punishment and the frequency with which capital crimes were committed. A later accounting revealed approximately $5,000 a year in principal and interest. The annual cost to maintain an inmate in this cell is approximately $20,000 a year. Together, these costs mean an annual expenditure of $25,000 to incarcerate an inmate. Based on a sentence term of forty to forty-five years, one inmate would cost the taxpayer only slightly more than $1 million—less than a third of what it would take to see the inmate through execution. A twenty-five-year-old woman convicted of first-degree murder would need to serve a life term to the age of 145 before the costs of incarcerating her would surpass those of executing her.

Not only are the costs of execution excessive but so too are the time delays. It is not unusual for an individual to wait on death row for more than ten years. In the 1995 case *Lackey v. Texas,* __U.S. __, 115 S. Ct. 1421, 131 L. Ed. 2d 304, Clarence Allen Lackey, who had been on death row for seventeen years, claimed that such a duration constituted cruel and unusual punishment. Although his motion was denied, Justices John Paul Stevens and Stephen Breyer admitted that the concern was not without warrant.

Opponents of capital punishment point out that abandoning the death penalty would make available many millions of dollars—as well as thousands of hours—that the courts could reallocate to other aspects of the criminal justice system. The amount of money necessary to execute a single inmate might be used to put several criminals behind bars for the remainder of their lives.

Supporters of capital punishment agree with detractors on one issue: that the death row appeals process is far too complex and expensive. However, whereas opponents of the death penalty use this as a reason to reform sentencing, supporters use it as a reason to reform the system of appeals. Supporters argue that thorough reform of the appeals process would free up as much money as abolishing the death penalty; expenses could be cut while capital punishment is retained.

Immediately following the execution of Bundy, Chief Justice William H. Rehnquist called for changes in the procedure for appealing death sentences. Noting that the Supreme Court had turned down three emergency appeals by Bundy in the hours just prior to his execution, the chief justice said, "Surely it would be a bold person to say that this system could not be improved."

In a 1995 interview, President Bill Clinton, a staunch supporter of capital punishment, called the appeals process ridiculous and in need of reform. Clinton, like other supporters of the death penalty, saw appeals reform as paramount if capital punishment is to be efficiently and effectively carried out.

Supporters also argue that too many rights are provided to death row inmates. The appeals process is too kind to convicts, they argue, and ignores the pain that persists in the aftermath of the criminals' actions. Family members of victims of capital crimes are expected to wait years, while perpetrators abuse the system to forestall execution of the sentence imposed.

In addition to the president, the nation's highest court sides with those who support capital punishment. Under the leadership of Chief Justice Rehnquist, the Supreme Court has moved to limit the number of appeals a death row inmate may file, arguing that endless appeals serve only to undermine the ability of the state to carry out its constitutionally sanctioned punishment.

that during the moratorium on capital punishment, from 1967 to 1976, the national homicide rate nearly doubled. Since then, depending on the study conducted, evidence has been presented to show that capital punishment has no deterrent effect; that the implementation of the death penalty is directly related to a decrease in capital crime; and that the implementation of the death penalty is directly related to an increase in capital crime.

Though some opponents of the death penalty are quick to argue that capital punishment has no deterrent effect, many supporters feel that the purpose of capital punishment is retribution, not deterrence. Many individuals, especially those with close ties to the victim, are more often concerned that the convicted criminal pay for the crime than that other persons be deterred through punishment of the perpetrator.

**Morality and Emotion** Emotions may have played a part in the *Furman* decision. Burger, in his dissent, warned that the Supreme Court's "constitutional inquiry . . . must be divorced from personal feelings as to the morality and efficacy of the death penalty." Justice HARRY A. BLACKMUN, who joined Burger in his dissent, later renounced his belief in the death penalty for reasons that another justice saw as partly personal.

In 1994, in *Callins v. Collins,* 510 U.S. 1141, 114 S. Ct. 1127, 127 L. Ed. 2d 435, Blackmun wrote a dissenting opinion in which he condemned the practice of capital punishment in the United States. Blackmun argued that "no combination of procedural rules or substantive regulations ever [could] save the death penalty from its inherent constitutional deficiencies"— "arbitrariness, discrimination, caprice, and mistake." Justice ANTONIN SCALIA criticized Blackmun's position, writing that Blackmun had based his dissent on intellectual, moral, and personal reasons, rather than on the authority of the Constitution.

**Other Issues** Other controversial aspects of capital punishment disturb the public. Between 1976, when the moratorium on capital punishment was lifted, and 1995,

- More than fifty mentally ill or mentally impaired individuals were put to death

- Nine juveniles were executed
- The cost of executing a death row inmate was three to six times as much as incarcerating him or her for life without parole

Despite the controversy, the constitutionality of capital punishment has been upheld and continues to be an acceptable practice in thirty-eight states, where nearly three thousand inmates waited on death row in 1995.

See also SENTENCE; WITHERSPOON V. ILLINOIS.

## CAPITAL STOCK
📖 All shares constituting ownership of a business, including COMMON STOCK and PREFERRED STOCK. The amount of shares that a corporate charter requires to be subscribed and paid, or secured to be paid, by shareholders. The amount of STOCK that a CORPORATION may issue; the amount actually contributed, subscribed, or secured to be paid on. The LIABILITY of the corporation to its shareholders after creditors' claims have been settled. The valuation of the corporation as a business enterprise. 📖

Capital stock is distinguishable from the property and ASSETS of the corporation. The property of a corporation fluctuates and may be greater or less than the original capital invested, but the capital stock remains intact and unaffected by the vicissitudes of business.

Undivided profits, or surplus, are not part of the capital stock, although they are included in the general capital or assets of the corporation.

The capital stock of a corporation serves only corporate purposes. It functions as security for the CREDITORS of the corporation who have relied on its existence, since it cannot be diverted or withdrawn to the detriment of corporate creditors. Capital stock is sometimes regarded as a trust fund.

## CAPITATION TAX
📖 An assessment levied by the government upon a person at a fixed rate regardless of income or worth. 📖

Since it is a tax upon the individual, and not upon merchandise, a capitation tax is frequently labeled a *head tax*. A POLL TAX is a capitation tax.

## CAPONE, ALPHONSE
Al Capone was a gangster leader who controlled much of Chicago from 1920 to 1931. Chicago in the 1920s vas a city of vice, corruption, and gangland llings, and synonymous with the evildoings of t  era is the name of Al Capone.

apone was born January 17, 1899, in Na,   Italy. His family emigrated from Napl  aly, to New York and Capone was raised in     Brooklyn slums. During his early years in New  ork he made strong gangland contacts and in     he became a member of the John Torrio gan  Torrio, originally from New York, relocated his  eration to Chicago, with Capone at his side.

*Federal and state authorities were never able to prosecute Al Capone for election fraud, gambling, murder, or the illegal transport of liquor. But in 1931 he was convicted of income tax evasion and sent to prison, which ended his career.*

The passage of the VOLSTEAD ACT in 1919 (41 Stat. 305), which prohibited the manufacture, sale, or transportation of liquor, ushered in an era of big business for gangsters. Capone and Torrio were no exception; they operated and organized speakeasies, secret nightclubs that sold the banned liquor. Capone began to gain more power and by the time Torrio retired in 1925, Capone's control had extended to gambling, brothels, and politics. He was responsible for the gangland murders of his rivals and for forcibly controlling election results in certain precincts of Chicago; through these maneuvers, he increased his power and received protection and political favors.

Capone was at the peak of his power in 1931, when he was arrested—ironically—for INCOME TAX evasion. The INTERNAL REVENUE SERVICE succeeded where other authorities had failed: uncovering concrete evidence against Capone for tax evasion. It investigated Capone's earnings and discovered that—despite his huge income, which was judged to be approximately $105 million in 1927—Capone had never filed an income tax return. In October 1931 Capone was tried in a federal court and found guilty. He was required to pay a penalty of $50,000 and to serve eleven years in jail.

An appeal was pursued and Capone spent his first days of captivity in Chicago's Cook County Jail. There he was still awarded the privileges of an underworld king. Warden David Moneypenny allowed him to visit with his gangland associates, including Salvatore "Lucky" Luciano. Capone had requested and was given an isolated place—the death chamber of the Cook County Jail—to meet and conduct business with fellow mobsters.

The appeal was denied, and Capone was sent to a federal jail in Atlanta, Georgia. There he performed the duties of a shoemaker until 1934, at which time he was transferred to Alcatraz in California.

At Alcatraz Capone was not treated with the respect and fear to which he was accustomed. He spent his days as a laundry worker and was harassed by inmates who took pleasure in persecuting the once powerful mob king. Capone's mental capacities dwindled due to an untreated attack of syphilis and in 1939 he was released to the care of his wife and brother. He died January 25, 1947, in Miami Beach, Florida.

**CAPTION** 📖 The standardized heading of a legal instrument, such as a MOTION or a COMPLAINT, which sets forth the names of the PARTIES in controversy, the name of the court, the DOCKET number, and the name of the ACTION. 📖

## CARDOZO, ALBERT

Perhaps the best remembered contribution Albert Cardozo made to U.S. law was in the person of his son, respected scholar and influential Supreme Court Justice Benjamin Cardozo. Like his son, Cardozo was also an attorney and judge, but unlike him, he was moved by strong political and family loyalties that would ultimately prove his undoing.

Cardozo was born in Philadelphia, Pennsylvania, in 1828. His family then moved to New York, where he was educated and became a member of the bar in 1849. Cardozo began his legal career with a reputation for hard work and skillful advocacy and prospered. His marriage in 1854 to Rebecca Nathan, a member of a prominent New York family, gave him important connections.

Sometime in the 1850s, Cardozo established ties with Democratic politics. By the end of the decade, he was a member of the Tammany Society (or Tammany Hall), the hub for Democratic political activity in New York during that era. Through the joint support of Tammany Hall and an otherwise competing Democratic faction, Mozart Hall, Cardozo was elected to the Court of Common Pleas in 1863, taking the bench in 1864.

As a sitting judge with ties to Tammany Hall—an organization that would later be exposed as corrupt—Cardozo often faced strong political pressure. He was criticized for taking the Democrats' side in a case concerning limits on alcohol sales but strong political support kept his reputation intact. In the fall of 1867 he was elected to fill a vacant seat on the New York Supreme Court.

The power and exposure of the state's highest court brought an end to Cardozo's judicial career. By 1872 he was the subject of impeachment hearings, charged with abuse of judicial power and nepotism in awarding receiverships. Though scholars have questioned the strength of the former charge, Cardozo's nepotism was well documented. He frequently referred his relatives and friends. In the face of certain impeachment, Cardozo retired from the bench and returned to private practice. He died November 8, 1885, in New York City.

## CARDOZO, BENJAMIN NATHAN

Benjamin Nathan Cardozo was a New York state court judge, an associate justice on the U.S. Supreme Court, and an influential legal scholar.

Cardozo was born May 24, 1870, in New York City, the youngest son in a family of six children. His parents were descendants of Portuguese and Spanish Jews who had settled in New York before the Revolutionary War. His father, ALBERT CARDOZO, was a trial court judge who was forced to resign his seat because of allegations, which were never proved, of improper conduct involving the then corrupt New York City government. Cardozo was tutored during his early life by well known clergyman and teacher Horatio Alger and entered Columbia College at the age of fifteen. He earned a bachelor's degree in 1889 and a master's degree in 1890, then enrolled at Columbia Law School. He was granted admission to the New York state bar in 1891 without having received his law degree.

After completing his legal training and passing the bar examination, Cardozo began practicing appellate law with his brother. He soon became a prominent practitioner in his own right in the fields of corporate and commercial law. He often acted as consultant to other law firms, writing appeal briefs for other lawyers and appearing frequently before the New York Court of Appeals, the state's highest court. His extensive appellate experience led him to write his first book, *Jurisdiction of the Court of Appeals of the State of New York*, published in 1903. In addition, judges often appointed him to act as referee in complicated matters of commercial law, one of his areas of specialty.

In 1913, after twenty-three years in private practice, Cardozo was nominated and elected as a judge on the New York Supreme Court, the state's trial-level bench. Only six weeks later, he was designated to serve temporarily as an associate judge on the Court of Appeals. He remained a temporary judge of the Court of Appeals until 1917, when he was appointed to fill a vacant and permanent seat, and in 1926 he was elected chief judge.

During his tenure on the Court of Appeals,

**BIOGRAPHY**

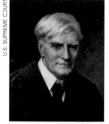

*Benjamin Nathan Cardozo*

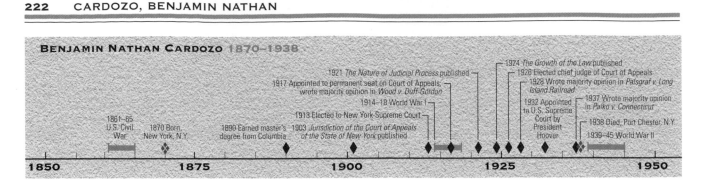

BENJAMIN NATHAN CARDOZO 1870–1938

1924 *The Growth of the Law* published
1926 Elected chief judge of Court of Appeals
1921 *The Nature of Judicial Process* published
1928 Wrote majority opinion in *Palsgraf v. Long Island Railroad*
1917 Appointed to permanent seat on Court of Appeals; wrote majority opinion in *Wood v. Duff-Gordon*
1914–18 World War I
1932 Appointed to U.S. Supreme Court by President Hoover
1937 Wrote majority opinion in *Palko v. Connecticut*
1913 Elected to New York Supreme Court
1861–65 U.S. Civil War
1870 Born, New York, N.Y.
1890 Earned master's degree from Columbia
1903 *Jurisdiction of the Court of Appeals of the State of New York* published
1938 Died, Port Chester, N.Y.
1939–45 World War II

1850    1875    1900    1925    1950

Cardozo made his mark as an influential and celebrated jurist and moved the New York court to the forefront of the nation's state courts. With respect to TORT law, the court under Cardozo greatly expanded the protection offered to individuals injured by the NEGLIGENCE of others. In *MacPherson v. Buick Motor Co.*, 217 N.Y. 382, 111 N.E. 1050 (1916), perhaps Cardozo's most influential tort opinion, the court held Buick liable for the negligent construction of a defective wheel that injured a purchaser who had bought the car not from Buick but from an automobile dealer. Cardozo's decision to look beyond the contractual relationship between the buyer and seller to the manufacturer for redress helped lay the groundwork for the development of PRODUCT LIABILITY, now a common feature of the law, which allows for recovery for injuries even if the consumer had no contractual relationship with the manufacturer. But Cardozo was also willing to impose some commonsense limits on tort LIABILITY. In the classic decision *Palsgraf v. Long Island Railroad*, 248 N.Y. 339, 162 N.E. 99 (1928), he authored the majority opinion establishing that a person can be held negligent only for a harm or injury that is foreseeable and not for every injury that follows from the negligence. As Cardozo put it, "[T]he orbit of the danger as disclosed to the eye of reasonable vigilance would be the orbit of duty."

Cardozo's influence was also strongly felt in the law of CONTRACTS. He wrote the majority opinion in *Wood v. Duff-Gordon*, 222 N.Y. 88, 118 N.E. 214 (1917), perhaps his best known and most widely quoted decision concerning the implied elements of a contract. In *Wood* and his other contract law decisions, Cardozo made clear his views that, whenever possible, courts should attempt to instill fairness in an ambiguous contract by analyzing and interpreting its implicit terms to cover situations that the parties may not have provided for explicitly.

In 1932, when ninety-year-old Oliver Wendell Holmes, Jr., announced his retirement from the U.S. Supreme Court, politicians, law-

"THE GREAT TIDES AND CURRENTS WHICH ENGULF THE REST OF MEN DO NOT TURN ASIDE IN THEIR COURSE AND PASS THE JUDGES BY."

yers, and legal scholars publicly campaigned for Cardozo to succeed him. President HERBERT HOOVER, though impressed with Cardozo's credentials and intellect, was initially lukewarm about nominating him to the Court. Two other New Yorkers, Chief Justice Charles E. Hughes and Justice Harlan F. Stone, were already on the Court and others in Hoover's administration were concerned about appointing a second Jewish justice to serve in addition to Justice Louis D. Brandeis. After Stone offered his resignation (which was not accepted) to make room for Cardozo, Hoover was eventually persuaded to ignore the politics of geography and anti-Semitism and named Cardozo to the Court. On February 24, 1932, Cardozo was confirmed unanimously by a voice vote of the Senate, though he was said to be reluctant to leave his family and friends in New York and move to Washington, D.C., to accept the seat.

Though he served on the Court for only six years, Cardozo authored a number of significant decisions. He authored the majority opinion in the civil rights case *Nixon v. Condon*, 286 U.S. 73, 52 S. Ct. 484, 76 L. Ed. 984 (1932). *Condon* held that a resolution by a state party executive committee, under purported authority of a Texas statute (Vernon's Ann. Civ. St. Tex. art. 3107), which excluded blacks from primary elections, violated the Equal Protection Clause of the FOURTEENTH AMENDMENT. Cardozo, for the most part, supported President FRANKLIN D. ROOSEVELT's New Deal legislation, writing the majority opinions in *Helvering v. Davis*, 301 U.S. 619, 57 S. Ct. 904, 81 L. Ed. 307 (1937), and *Steward Machine Co. v. Davis*, 301 U.S. 548, 57 S. Ct. 883, 81 L. Ed. 1279 (1937), which upheld the constitutionality of the unemployment compensation (Social Security Act § 901–910, 42 U.S.C.A. § 1101–1110) and old-age benefits programs (Social Security Act § 201 et seq., 42 U.S.C.A. § 401 et seq.) of the Social Security Act of 1935. Cardozo also authored a number of significant criminal law decisions while on the Court, including *Palko v. Connecticut*, 302 U.S. 319, 58 S. Ct. 149, 82 L.

Ed. 288 (1937). In *Palko*, the Court held that the Due Process Clause of the Fourteenth Amendment of the Constitution did not require that the Double Jeopardy Clause contained in the FIFTH AMENDMENT be applied to the states. Cardozo favored a "SELECTIVE INCORPORATION" approach to the Fourteenth Amendment, writing that only select protections of the first eight amendments that "represented the very essence of a scheme of ordered liberty, . . . principles of justice so rooted in the traditions and conscience of our people as to be ranked fundamental," should be imposed upon the states. *Palko* represented the beginning of the Supreme Court's long struggle to formulate a test for applying the Due Process Clause of the Fourteenth Amendment as a limit on states' powers.

Cardozo, though remembered for his majority opinions, was not afraid to disagree with the majority and wrote some equally significant and stirring dissents while on the Court. In *Carter v. Carter Coal Co.*, 298 U.S. 238, 56 S. Ct. 855, 80 L. Ed. 1160 (1936), one of many cases arising out of constitutional challenges to Roosevelt's New Deal legislation, the Court in a 6–3 vote struck down the 1935 Bituminous Coal Conservation Act (15 U.S.C.A. §§ 801–827), which authorized fixed prices to help stabilize the coal industry. Cardozo maintained that the law was constitutional and necessary to combat the economic problems created by the Great Depression. He wrote that "[a]fter making every allowance for differen[ces] of opinion as to the most efficient cure, the student of the subject is confronted with the indisputable truth that there are ills to be corrected, and ills that had a direct relation to the maintenance of commerce among the states. . . . An evil existing, and also the power to correct it, the lawmakers were at liberty to use their own discretion in the selection of the means."

Cardozo's body of legal scholarship is not limited to the many important judicial opinions he authored as a state court judge and U.S. Supreme Court justice. He also wrote a number of books which have become classics of legal thought and judicial philosophy. His lectures on the decision-making process that he delivered at Yale Law School and Columbia University early in his career were published in 1921 as a group of essays in *The Nature of the Judicial Process*, which is still widely used as a textbook for first-year law students. He also wrote *The Growth of the Law* (1924), *The Paradox of Legal Science* (1928), and *Law and Literature* (1931). In all his books, Cardozo sought to define the difficult issues faced by a judge in deciding

cases, as well as his beliefs about how the entire legal system could function most effectively.

Cardozo, who never married and remained close to his family throughout his life, was a shy and reclusive man described in one book about the history of the Court as "the hermit philosopher." He remained on the Supreme Court until 1938 when he died of heart trouble at the age of sixty-eight. He is buried in the Cardozo family plot in the cemetery of Shearith Israel congregation at Cypress Hills, Long Island.

### CROSS-REFERENCES

*MacPherson v. Buick Motor Co.; Palsgraf v. Long Island Railroad.*

**CARE** ◫ Watchful attention; custody; diligence; concern; caution; as opposed to NEGLIGENCE or carelessness. ◫

In the law of negligence, the standard of REASONABLE conduct determines the amount of care to be exercised in a situation. The care taken must be proportional to the apparent risk. As danger increases, commensurate caution must be observed.

*Slight care* is the care persons of ordinary prudence generally exercise in regard to their personal affairs of minimal importance.

*Reasonable care*, also known as ordinary care, is the degree of care, diligence, or precaution that may fairly, ordinarily, and properly be expected or required in consideration of the nature of the action, the subject matter, and the surrounding circumstances.

*Great care* is the degree of care that persons of ordinary prudence usually exercise with respect to their personal affairs of great importance.

Another type of care is that which a FIDUCIARY—a person having a duty, created by his or her undertaking, to act primarily for another's benefit—exercises in regard to valuable possessions entrusted to him or her by another.

**CAR-JACKING** ◫ The criminal taking of a motor vehicle from its driver by force, violence, or intimidation. ◫

Car-jacking incidents emerged in increasing numbers in the 1980s and 1990s, after their initial appearance in Detroit. Because the crime is often reported as an auto theft, armed robbery, ASSAULT AND BATTERY, or HOMICIDE, statistics on it are not accurate. According to the Federal Bureau of Investigation (FBI), 19,000 car-jackings were reported in 1991 and 21,000 in the first ten months of 1992. The FBI believes that these figures represent only about one-third of the car-jackings that actually occur in the United States each year. According to the United Press International (UPI), car-jacking attempts in the United States averaged 35,000 a year between 1987 and 1992. This figure includes successful as well as attempted but unsuccessful car-jackings. Lending support to the contention that car-jacking is a violent crime, the UPI's statistics show that guns were used in 59 percent of all car-jackings.

In the early 1990s, car-jackers began targeting older people, women, and tourists—groups of conspicuous vulnerability. The makes and models of the cars targeted for car-jacking vary from city to city—and it is not only the expensive, top-of-the-line cars that are taken but also older and less pricey automobiles. This may be because car-jackings are more crimes of opportunity than of PREMEDITATION. Car-jackers simply wait for an unaware driver, an open window, or an unlocked door.

Car-jacking was formally introduced to Congress during its spring 1992 session by Representative Charles E. Schumer (D-N.Y.). Over the next several months, a new law involving the crime was discussed and developed into the Anti–Car Theft Act of 1992 (18 U.S.C.A. § 2119). The focus was not entirely on car-jacking, but rather on car theft, which had become the number one property crime in the United States, with AUTOMOBILES constituting more than 50 percent of the property U.S. citizens lost to theft.

In the fall of 1992, Pamela Basu and her twenty-two-month-old daughter were car-jacked in Maryland. Basu was forced from her car by two men and, in a struggle to keep her daughter from being hurt, became caught in the seat belt outside the car. She was dragged almost two miles before she was freed from the seat belt; her daughter, still in her car seat, was thrown from the vehicle a short time later. Basu died of massive internal injuries; her daughter was physically unharmed. The publicity surrounding this crime helped fuel the movement that led to the passage of a provision in the Anti–Car Theft Act of 1992 that made car-jacking a federal offense.

President GEORGE BUSH signed the act into law on October 25, 1992. The statute's provision regarding car-jacking was as follows:

> Whoever, possessing a firearm, as defined in section 921 of this title, takes a motor vehicle that has been transported, shipped or received in interstate or foreign commerce from the person or presence of another by force and violence or by intimidation, or attempts to do so, shall—1) be fined under this title or imprisoned not more than 15 years, or both. 2) If serious bodily injury . . . results, be fined under this title or be imprisoned not more than 25 years, or both, and 3) if death results, be fined under this title or imprisoned for any number of years up to life, or both.

Within a few months of its passage, the federal car-jacking statute was challenged under the DOUBLE JEOPARDY Clause of the U.S. Constitution. According to the FIFTH AMENDMENT, no person shall "be subject for the same offence to be twice put in jeopardy of life or limb," meaning that no one can be tried twice for the same crime. After the car-jacking statute was passed, people who used a firearm during the commission of a car-jacking were not only subject to punishment under that statute but also faced mandatory punishment under 18 U.S.C.A. § 924(c), which outlaws the use or carrying of a firearm in relation to a violent crime. The issue came to a head in *United States v. Singleton*, 16 F.3d 1419 (5th Cir. 1994), when the presiding judge ruled that both the firearm portion of the car-jacking statute and the gun statute proscribed the same conduct, and Congress had not shown that it would impose cumulative punishment under these two statutes. Therefore, the gun count in the car-jacking statute violated the Double Jeopardy Clause.

Within several months of *Singleton*, amendments to the car-jacking portion of the Anti–Car Theft Statute were debated in the House of Representatives and Senate. The result was a

### Car-Jacking

U.S. Households Touched by Motor Vehicle Theft in 1992*

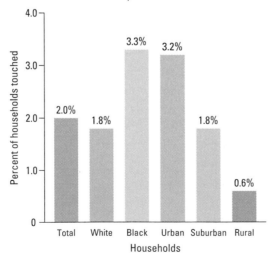

* Number of crimes reported: 1,947,000

Source: U.S. Bureau of Justice Statistics, *Crime and the Nation's Households*, 1992.

provision in the Violent Crime Control and Law Enforcement Act of 1994, 42 U.S.C.A. et seq., Pub. L. No. 104-126, which was signed by President BILL CLINTON. The provision made two significant amendments to 18 U.S.C.A. § 2119. The first was that a death sentence can be handed down in cases where a car-jacking victim is killed. The second was that "possessing a firearm, as defined under section 921 of this title" was deleted and replaced with "with the intent to cause death or serious bodily harm." This removed the double jeopardy problem identified in *Singleton*.

Although car-jacking has been made a federal crime, several states also have legislation on the subject. One is Florida, which has a big tourist industry. In the late 1980s and early 1990s, an increasing number of tourists, most of them foreign, were victims of car-jackings in Florida. Because tourists in well-marked rental cars were common car-jacking victims, Florida passed legislation in 1993 (F.S.A. § 320.0601) that outlawed company logos and license plates that made rental and leased cars obvious. Florida's legislators felt that tourists warranted this extra protection for three main reasons. First, tourists are, more often than not, unfamiliar with the area and are more likely to become lost or end up in a high-crime area. Second, tourists often carry more cash than natives, which makes them prime robbery targets. And finally, fewer tourists are likely to return and testify in court about a crime. By granting tourists the right to drive unmarked rental cars, Florida made them less vulnerable to the crime of car-jacking.

## CARMICHAEL, STOKELY

African American activist, leader, and militant Stokely Carmichael is known for the galvanizing cry Black Power! which helped transform the later years of the CIVIL RIGHTS MOVEMENT. The raised fist that accompanied that slogan was a rallying point for many young African Americans in the late 1960s. Carmichael's forceful presence and organizing skill were compelling reasons to join. In 1966 he was elected chairman of the Student Nonviolent Coordinating Committee

**BIOGRAPHY**

*Stokely Carmichael*

(SNCC), a civil rights organization popularly called Snick. Leaving Atlanta-based SNCC in 1967 with a more radical vision, Carmichael became prime minister of the Oakland-based BLACK PANTHER PARTY for Self-Defense (BPP), perhaps the most militant of 1960s African American groups. Members of Congress denounced him for allegedly seditious speeches, other politicians and civic leaders blamed him for causing riots, and the FEDERAL BUREAU OF INVESTIGATION (FBI) matched this fervor with counterintelligence activities. Bitterly severing his ties with the black power movement in 1969, Carmichael announced that he would work on behalf of Pan-Africanism, a socialist vision of a united Africa. He moved to Guinea, West Africa, and has lived there since.

Carmichael was born in Port of Spain, Trinidad, on June 29, 1941. Two years later, he was placed in a private school, as his father, mother, and two sisters immigrated to the United States. At this school, he earned the nickname Little Man for his quick intelligence and precocious awareness, traits that had him urging his aunt to vote when he was turned away from polling booths at the age of seven. He received a British education at the Tranquillity Boys School, a segregated institution, from the age of ten to eleven, before nearly dying of pneumonia. As an adult, he would recall the Tranquillity School experience with bitterness for "drugging" him with white European views, but at any rate, it was brief. His parents brought him and three sisters to live with them in Harlem in June 1952.

In Harlem, he found conditions disappointingly different from those in Trinidad, where the black majority had found access to positions in elective government and professional employment. His mother, Mabel Carmichael, worked as a maid. His father, Adolphus Carmichael, who had been successful enough as a skilled carpenter to build a large house in Port of Spain, struggled at driving a cab to make ends meet but remained optimistic about the United States. For this dream, Carmichael later said, his father paid a high price, working

STOKELY CARMICHAEL 1941–

1967 *Black Power: Politics of Liberation in America* published — 1968 Expelled by SNCC; became prime minister of Black Panthers

1966 Elected Chairman of SNCC; coined "Black Power" phrase; — 1969 Organized branch of All-African People's Revolutionary Party in Black Panther party organized by Bobby Seale and others — Washington, D.C.; left for self-imposed exile in Guinea, West Africa

1952 Emigrated to U.S. — 1961 Joined Freedom Rides — 1971 *Stokely Speaks; Black Power to Pan-Africanism* published

1939–45 World War II — 1950–53 Korean War — 1960 Entered Howard University; helped found SNCC — 1961–73 Vietnam War — 1978 Changed his name to Kwame Ture

1941 Born, Port of Spain, Trinidad

1925     1950     1975     2000

himself to death and dying the same way he began, poor and black.

By junior high school, Carmichael's disillusionment revolved around a life of marijuana, alcohol, theft, and a street gang of which he was the only nonwhite member. However, when he entered the respected Bronx High School of Science, his scholastic interests blossomed, and he began to read widely in politics and history. Social opportunities began to appear for him, too. Yet he could not later dispel a sense of alienation and anger. "I made the scene in Park Avenue apartments," he recalled in a 1967 interview. "I was the good little nigger and everybody was nice to me. Now that I realize how phony they all were, how I hate myself for it."

Social and political change were in the air as Carmichael was finishing high school. The civil rights movement was in full swing and a new generation of young African Americans began holding lunch counter sit-ins in segregated cafés and restaurants in the South. At first skeptical about these "publicity hounds," Carmichael changed his mind when he saw televised images of white students pouring sugar and ketchup on the heads of the peaceful protesters. By mid-1960 he was in Virginia taking part in a sit-in organized by the Congress of Racial Equality (CORE), a civil rights group founded nearly two decades earlier. Beaten up during his first demonstration, Carmichael was undeterred. He attended more sit-ins and pickets, notably against the F. W. Woolworth Company in New York, as such demonstrations spread widely across the country, resulting in integrated businesses in several states.

Several scholarship offers awaited Carmichael, including one from Harvard. His decision to reject them in favor of attending Howard University in Washington, D.C., marked a turning point in his life. In 1961, CORE sponsored trips by young activists to the South. Known as the Freedom Rides, these journeys were intended to fight segregation. As a freshman, Carmichael went along. He escaped the violent mob beatings that many of the activists suffered while white police officers watched and did nothing, but he and several other CORE activists were arrested in Mississippi, jailed for fifty-three days, zapped with cattle prods, and forced to sleep on hard cell floors. Such treatment was not the worst inflicted on the Freedom Riders: three were murdered. Released finally, he returned to the university and changed his major from medicine to philosophy, in which he took a bachelor's degree upon graduation in 1964.

Leaving Howard, Carmichael became an organizer with SNCC. Founded during his final

year in high school, the group had emerged from meetings organized by Ella J. Baker, the associate executive director of the Southern Christian Leadership Conference (SCLC)—the civil rights organization of which MARTIN LUTHER KING, JR., was president. SNCC contained the seeds of a major change in direction for the civil rights movement. As it grew in the early 1960s, SNCC attracted young volunteers who were impatient with the progress of older organizations such as CORE and the SCLC. It sent black and white young people from predominantly northern, middle-class backgrounds into rural areas of the Deep South, their goal being to educate illiterate farmers, increase voter registration, and set up health clinics. A field organizer for a SNCC task force in Lowndes County, Mississippi, Carmichael brought about noteworthy successes: the number of registered black voters increased from seventy to twenty-six hundred, a dramatic rise for a county in which African Americans outnumbered whites but had no share in political power.

In 1966 Carmichael was elected chairman of SNCC. The group's goal was evolving from integration to liberation. In Mississippi, he had organized a political party called the Lowndes County Freedom Organization. Its symbol, a black panther leaping with a snarl, would become nationally recognized in the years to follow. So would the words Black Power! that Carmichael shouted to black share croppers as he and other participants in the James Meredith Freedom March passed them in June 1966. The cross-state march was a project launched by MEREDITH, who had been the first African American to attend Mississippi University, intended to prove that black citizens could enjoy their rights in the state without fear. Such fear was well placed. On the second day, shotgun blasts badly wounded Meredith. As another march took place and more violence followed, Black Power! became the marchers' chant.

In Carmichael's view, black power meant several things: political power, economic power, and legal power. It was both local and international in scope. "We want control of the institutions of the communities where we live, and we want control of the land, and we want to stop the exploitation of non-white people around the world," he said. This control would be achieved by any means necessary, he promised, drawing on the famous words of the activist Malcolm X. SNCC members carried guns for self-defense, a practice defended by Carmichael this way: "We are not [Martin Luther] King or SCLC. They don't do the kind of work we do nor do they live in the same areas we live in." In contrast to the harmonious message of King, Carmichael's rhetoric stirred fear and antagonism in many members of the mass media, who quickly accused him of reverse racism. *Time Magazine* dubbed him a black powermonger. As riots tore through major U.S. cities in the summers of 1966 and 1967, Carmichael was condemned for making inflammatory speeches that his critics said sparked them.

Within SNCC, more than rhetoric was changing. As the organization began to speak of oppressors and the oppressed, it also took practical steps that distanced it from older civil rights groups. Carmichael had SNCC pull out of the White House Conference on Civil Rights, a move that brought condemnation from the SCLC, the NATIONAL ASSOCIATION FOR THE ADVANCEMENT OF COLORED PEOPLE, and the Urban League; CORE, however, was moving in the same direction. Support for SNCC began to dry up. Older black activists deserted the organization; white supporters withdrew funding. In late 1966 SNCC purged all white members from its ranks.

Law enforcement agencies turned their sights on the increasingly militant group. Fights between the group's members and police officers broke out in several cities. In August 1966 a raid by eighty Philadelphia police officers on a SNCC office resulted in several arrests and charges that dynamite was stored there. As a result, the city's mayor and chief of police tried to bar Carmichael from speaking in Philadelphia. He was soon arrested and convicted in Atlanta of inciting a riot. Federal authorities also became concerned. The FBI had begun surveillance of SNCC in 1960; now it stepped up the supervision. In the summer of 1967, COINTELPRO, the FBI's Counterintelligence Program, officially added SNCC to its list of revolutionary groups to monitor, infiltrate, and, if possible, discredit.

Stepping down from the SNCC chairmanship, Carmichael gave lectures on college campuses and traveled worldwide. To an international audience that viewed him as a revolutionary leader, he gave speeches in Europe, Africa, and North Vietnam. In a talk given in London in July 1967 he so enraged British political leaders that he was barred from entering more than thirty countries in the British Commonwealth. Harsh criticism in the U.S. press followed an appearance in Havana where he said, "We are preparing groups of urban guerrillas for our defense in the cities. . . . It is going to be a fight to the death." President Fidel Castro of Cuba offered Carmichael political asylum, which he declined. Upon Carmichael's return to the United States on December 12, 1967, U.S. marshals seized his passport. Lawmakers in Congress denounced him for TREASON and SEDITION, and, as a result, considered legislation favoring bans on travel by U.S. citizens to countries deemed enemies of the United States.

Overseas, Carmichael had espoused his view of Pan-Africanism. This political movement favored uniting African countries under a common socialist leadership. SNCC expelled Carmichael in August 1968, disagreeing with his political turn, but by this time he had already joined the BPP. Organized to prevent police brutality toward African Americans, the Black Panthers had adopted the symbol Carmichael popularized in Lowndes County, a leaping, snarling black panther. The BPP's members carried guns, demanded equality and justice, and occasionally exchanged gunfire with police officers, leading to the conviction of one of its founders, Huey P. Newton. As honorary prime minister of the BPP, Carmichael organized over two dozen chapters across the country. Black power's growing appeal—and, in the eyes of many white U.S. citizens, its danger—seemed to reach a symbolic height at the 1968 Olympics. There, two medal-winning members of the U.S. Olympic Team raised their fists in expression of their solidarity with the movement, a protest that ended in U.S. officials stripping them of their medals.

Events during this period increased Carmichael's sense of alienation from the United States. He alleged that the FBI harassed him and his wife, Miriam Makeba, a South African–born singer, by following them wherever they went. Carmichael and Makeba felt that Makeba lost singing jobs and recording contracts because of Carmichael's notoriety. When the Black Panthers allied themselves with white radicals he broke with the organization. "The history of Africans living in the U.S. has shown that any premature alliance with white radicals has led to complete subversion of the blacks by the whites," he said in July 1969. He called upon all Africans "as one cohesive force to wage an unrelenting armed struggle against the white Western empire for the liberation of our people." His departure sounded a death knell for the Black Power movement; by the early 1970s it had all but vanished.

In 1969 Carmichael prepared to leave for self-imposed exile in Africa. Before going, he organized a branch of the All-African People's Revolutionary Party (AAPRP) in Washington, D.C., a Pan-Africanist group established the previous year in Guinea, West Africa. After settling in Africa, he briefly returned to the United States in March 1970, and appeared before a congressional subcommittee on national security matters. Questioned about revolutionary groups in the United States, he pleaded the FIFTH AMENDMENT throughout the hearing. Back in Guinea, he worked for the AAPRP, taught at the university in Conakry, and, in 1978, changed his name to Kwame Ture, partly in honor of Sékou Touré, former president of Guinea, who was his friend and benefactor. Following the death of President Touré and the rise of the military government in Guinea, he was jailed several times for unknown reasons.

Carmichael has traveled and spoken widely since the 1980s. In 1982, the British Commonwealth briefly lifted its ban on his crossing its borders, but it quickly renewed the prohibition after he made a 1983 visit to Britain advocating international black solidarity and the overthrow of capitalism. British officials claimed that he urged black lawyers to throw bombs. Later, he paid several visits to the United States. In 1989, looking back on the accomplishments of the civil rights and black power movements, he expressed skepticism. Citing the 304 African

*Matthew Hale Carpenter*

that the hymen be ruptured or the vagina entered. See also ADULTERY; RAPE.

**CAROLENE PRODUCTS FOOTNOTE**
See FOOTNOTE FOUR.

**CARPENTER, MATTHEW HALE** Matthew Hale Carpenter was born December 22, 1824, in Moretown, Vermont. He attended the U.S. Military Academy from 1843 to 1845 and was admitted to the Vermont bar in 1847. His real name was Decatur Merritt Hammond Carpenter and although he was educated in Vermont, he established his public career in Wisconsin.

In 1861 Carpenter served as judge advocate general. He participated in the U.S. Senate, serving as senator from Wisconsin during the years 1869 to 1875 and 1879 to 1881.

His legal skills were displayed in his representation of Secretary of War William W. Belknap at the latter's IMPEACHMENT trial. In 1877 Carpenter acted as legal counsel to Democratic presidential candidate SAMUEL TILDEN during an inquiry held by the electoral commission concerning the contested election results. Tilden lost to RUTHERFORD B. HAYES by one electoral vote.

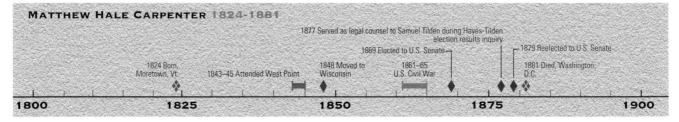

MATTHEW HALE CARPENTER 1824-1881

1877 Served as legal counsel to Samuel Tilden during Hayes-Tilden election results inquiry
1869 Elected to U.S. Senate
1879 Reelected to U.S. Senate
1824 Born, Moretown, Vt.
1843–45 Attended West Point
1848 Moved to Wisconsin
1861–65 U.S. Civil War
1881 Died, Washington, D.C.

1800  1825  1850  1875  1900

American mayors then in office in the United States, he dismissed them as impotent to effect real change. "All of them singularly and in block are powerless inside the racist political structure of the U.S.A.," he said. "These African mayors represent the biggest cities . . . yet the conditions of the masses of our people are worse today in these very cities than before the advent of African mayors."

Carmichael and Makeba divorced in 1978 and he later remarried. He received an honorary doctor of law degree from Shaw University, in North Carolina, and has authored two books, *Black Power: Politics of Liberation in America* (1967) and *Stokely Speaks: Black Power to Pan-Africanism* (1971).

**CARNAL KNOWLEDGE** 📖 Copulation; the act of a man having sexual relations with a woman. 📖

Penetration is an essential element of sexual intercourse, and there is carnal knowledge if even the slightest penetration of the female by the male organ takes place. It is not required

Carpenter died February 24, 1881, in Washington, D.C.

**CARPETBAG JUDGES** During the mid-1800s, judges were elected, and IMPEACHMENT proceedings were at that time an increasingly popular method for their removal. After the Civil War and the Reconstruction period, many judges—both black and white—served the judiciary in the South. A large number of these judges were known as "carpetbag" judges, because they were Northerners who had relocated to the South for personal gains, carrying all their possessions in a carpetbag. They were reputed to be dishonest and incompetent.

Threatened with impeachment, many of these judges left the bench. Not all the charges against the carpetbag judges were accurate, however, and a good number were not any worse than the judges who lived in the area. Several earned prominence, such as Moses Walker—a transient from Ohio—who contributed to the prestige of the Texas Supreme Court. Albion W. Tourgee, another carpetbagger, wrote several books on his years in the South. His most popular book was *A Fool's Errand*, published in 1879. Tourgee was highly regarded for his presentation of liberal opinions concerning interrelationships between blacks and whites.

**CARRIERS** Individuals or businesses that are employed to deliver people or property to an agreed destination.

The two main types of carriers are COMMON CARRIERS and private carriers. A *common carrier*, such as a railroad, airline, or business that offers public transportation, customarily transports property and individuals from one location to another, thus offering its services for the hire of the general population. A *private carrier* is employed by special agreement only and reserves the right to accept or reject employment as a carrier. Private carriers include chartered cargo planes, ships, and buses and are generally not subject to the same regulatory restrictions as common carriers.

Common carriers engaged in interstate transportation are regulated on the federal level pursuant to the COMMERCE CLAUSE of the U.S. Constitution, which provides that "[t]he Congress shall have Power . . . [t]o regulate Commerce . . . among the several States" (art. I, § 8, cl. 3). The government, through the Interstate Commerce Act (49 U.S.C.A. § 10101 et seq.), traditionally regulated charges for interstate transportation by common carriers. Beginning in the late 1970s and early 1980s, however, deregulation of the trucking industry reduced government involvement in establishing rates. Unless a statute states otherwise, a common carrier has broad authority to fix transportation rates so long as the rates are REASONABLE. In determining whether a rate is reasonable, a number of elements are considered. The most essential is the cost of transportation to the carrier, and others include the character and value of the items to be shipped; their weight, bulk, and ability to be handled; and the mileage to be covered. Though common carriers have a great deal of freedom to set interstate rates, they must follow procedures set forth by the INTERSTATE COMMERCE COMMISSION, including filing rates with the commission and publishing them.

A state possesses the authority to monitor and control the management and functions of common carriers operating within its borders and may set the prices charged by carriers doing business within the state. Most state laws require common carriers to file rate schedules with a state regulatory commission.

A common carrier is obligated to provide the necessary facilities to transport the volume of goods expected and to exercise the reasonable care needed to transport the goods safely. In the case of perishable goods, such as frozen or fresh foods, the common carrier must provide refrigerated or ventilated cars to ensure their safe transportation. Likewise, when transporting livestock, a common carrier is required to provide adequate ventilation, bedding, and partitions. The common carrier may be liable for loss or injury to the livestock resulting from defects in the cars it uses to transport the animals.

The carrier must follow any specific shipping directives provided by the shipper and if any instructions are ambiguous, the carrier must hold the goods until the shipper provides clarification. The shipper can select the route and manner by which the goods can be transported, but if no route is specified, the carrier is free to choose any convenient route that does not result in delay to the shipper.

Subject to some exceptions, a common carrier is absolutely liable for loss or damage to the goods it receives for shipment. A common carrier is not liable for loss or injury to goods brought about by an ACT OF GOD, an event such as an unforeseeable flood that could be neither caused nor prevented through the exercise of proper CARE on the part of the carrier. A carrier could, however, be liable for an act of God if it is guilty of NEGLIGENCE after the discovery of an ACCIDENT. For example, a fire started by lightning would ordinarily be considered an act of God, but if the carrier discovered it early and did nothing to abate it, the carrier could still be liable for failing to exercise due DILIGENCE.

In addition, a common carrier is not liable for a loss of goods when the loss is caused by the destruction or APPROPRIATION of the goods by the military forces of a "public enemy" at war with the domestic government. However, merely a declaration of MARTIAL LAW will not relieve the common carrier of LIABILITY, and groups who are not functioning as military forces against the government are not considered public enemies. Thus, a common carrier remains liable for a loss of goods resulting from the acts of a mob, rioters, and strikers, even if the carrier was not negligent and took all possible precautions to prevent the loss.

A carrier will not be held liable for injuries to goods that occur as a result of the shipper's negligence or misconduct. Furthermore, when the nature or value of the goods to be shipped is fraudulently concealed or misrepresented by

# Carriers

Volume of Domestic Intercity Freight and Passenger Traffic, by Type of Transport, 1970 to 1993

Freight traffic is shown in billion ton-miles; passenger traffic is shown in billion passenger-miles. A ton-mile is the movement of one ton of freight for the distance of one mile. A passenger-mile is the movement of one passenger for the distance of one mile. Includes both public and private traffic, revenue and non-revenue.

## Freight traffic

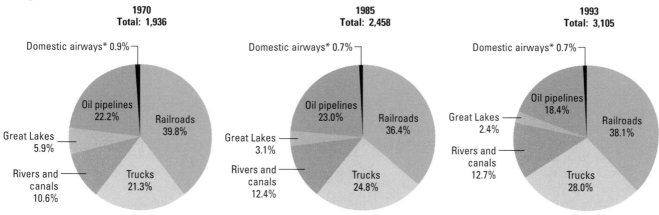

**1970**
**Total: 1,936**

Domestic airways* 0.9%
Oil pipelines 22.2%
Railroads 39.8%
Great Lakes 5.9%
Rivers and canals 10.6%
Trucks 21.3%

**1985**
**Total: 2,458**

Domestic airways* 0.7%
Oil pipelines 23.0%
Railroads 36.4%
Great Lakes 3.1%
Rivers and canals 12.4%
Trucks 24.8%

**1993**
**Total: 3,105**

Domestic airways* 0.7%
Oil pipelines 18.4%
Great Lakes 2.4%
Railroads 38.1%
Rivers and canals 12.7%
Trucks 28.0%

*Revenue service only. Includes express mail and excess baggage.

## Passenger traffic

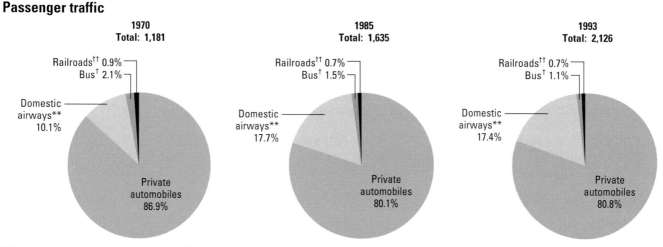

**1970**
**Total: 1,181**

Railroads†† 0.9%
Bus† 2.1%
Domestic airways** 10.1%
Private automobiles 86.9%

**1985**
**Total: 1,635**

Railroads†† 0.7%
Bus† 1.5%
Domestic airways** 17.7%
Private automobiles 80.1%

**1993**
**Total: 2,126**

Railroads†† 0.7%
Bus† 1.1%
Domestic airways** 17.4%
Private automobiles 80.8%

**Includes general aviation (mostly private business) flying.

†Excludes school and urban transit buses.

††Includes intercity (Amtrak) and rail commuter service.

Source: Eno Transportation Foundation, Inc., Lansdowne, Virginia, *Transportation in America*, annual.

the shipper, whether to obtain a lower shipping rate or for any other purpose, the carrier is not liable for any losses incurred. FRAUD can be established by the shipper's silence regarding the value of the goods or by untruthful statements made by the shipper. If the shipper failed to notify the carrier about the nature of the contents of a particular shipment, the carrier is ordinarily exempt from liability if a loss occurs, even if the loss is due to negligence on the part of the carrier.

A common carrier can restrict its liability for damages by clear and unambiguous terms contained in its CONTRACT with the shipper. Questions concerning the validity of such agreements are resolved by state law when shipments within a state are involved and federal law is applied to contractual disputes concerning interstate shipments. A contractual provision releasing the carrier from liability must not contravene PUBLIC POLICY and a carrier that departs from the usual method or route for shipment may not rely upon any limitations on liability contained in the contract.

Some common carriers, like public buses and taxis, transport people from one place to another. A common carrier of passengers, also known as a *public carrier*, transports for hire all persons (within certain limitations) as a regular business and represents itself as being engaged in such a business. A public carrier can deny carriage to people who refuse to comply with its reasonable regulations, who are likely to present danger to other passengers, or who in some way interfere with the safe carriage of passengers.

Common carriers of passengers are subject to extensive regulation by state and federal governments. Many states, for example, require by law that common carriers be inspected annually in order to protect people from the hazards of riding in vehicles that are poorly maintained. A common carrier that transports passengers may also make its own rules and regulations provided they are reasonable and will protect the interests of both the carrier and the passengers.

A carrier of passengers is liable for injuries suffered by passengers as a result of its negligence, but is not an insurer of its passengers' safety. Instead, a common carrier is required to act with the utmost care, skill, and diligence to protect the safety of its passengers as may be mandated by the type of transportation provided and the risk of danger inherent in it. Conversely, a private carrier of passengers must act with only reasonable care and diligence unless the contract for carriage provides otherwise, though some jurisdictions hold a private carrier to the same duty as that applied to common carriers.

Determining whether a carrier is a common carrier, and thus subject to a higher standard of care, has been the subject of some litigation in recent years. For example, a California federal district court held in early 1995 that Disneyland, as the operator of an amusement park ride, qualified as a common carrier and thus should be held to a duty of utmost care and diligence for the safety of its passengers even though the chief purpose of the ride was to entertain and not transport travelers (*Neubauer v. Disneyland*, 875 F. Supp. 672 [C.D. Cal. 1995]). As a result, Disneyland was held liable for injuries the plaintiffs suffered when their boat on an amusement ride was rammed from behind by another boat. The court looked to the broad definition of a common carrier contained in state law and held that any narrowing

of the term *carrier* should take place in the legislature and not in the court.

Some courts have considered whether the age of the passenger affects the duty owed by a common carrier. The Iowa Supreme Court, for example, in 1995 considered whether a school bus owed an additional duty to a child injured as he was struck by a car after safely alighting the bus (*Burton ex rel. Hawkeye Bank of Des Moines v. Des Moines Metropolitan Transit*, 530 N.W.2d 696 [Iowa]). The court declined to extend the duty owed by drivers of school buses to ensure the safety of children alighting the vehicles, holding that the bus company had no duty beyond that owed by a common carrier to protect child passengers from dangers that may reasonably and naturally be anticipated. According to the court, once a passenger alights safely, the passenger (even when he or she is a child) is better able to guard against the danger of moving vehicles; thus, public policy did not support extending a carrier's duty of care to include ensuring that the passenger safely crosses the street.

Unless the carrier is negligent, it is not responsible to a passenger for injuries due to natural causes and due to causes beyond the carrier's control. A common carrier of passengers cannot ordinarily release itself from liability for injuries to a passenger caused by either willful, wrongful conduct or negligence on the part of the carrier. In some jurisdictions, though, a carrier can limit its liability for negligence in exchange for providing a reduced fare or free pass. However, such limitations on liability may be invalid if the reduced fare is not made optional and if passengers are not permitted to buy tickets that provide that the carrier's liability is not limited.

Like common carriers that transport goods, carriers of passengers have also been subject to deregulation by the federal government. The Airline Deregulation Act of 1978 (49 U.S.C.A. § 334, 1301 et seq.) gave airlines almost complete discretion over rates, routes, and services offered. Prior to passage of the act, the Civil Aeronautics Board, a federal agency, exercised exclusive control over pricing in the airline industry.

More recent federal legislation has also affected the responsibilities of carriers to their employees and passengers. In 1990 Congress enacted the Americans with Disabilities Act (ADA) (42 U.S.C.A. § 12201 et seq.), which prohibits employment DISCRIMINATION against a qualified individual with a disability. The ADA further prohibits a carrier covered by the act from discriminating against a qualified individual with a disability because of that disability in regard to job application procedures, hiring, advancement, discharge, compensation, training, and other terms and conditions of employment. The ADA then sets forth in some detail the procedures that the carrier must follow in screening, interviewing, and hiring employees to ensure that individuals with disabilities are not subject to discrimination. In particular, the ADA requires that a carrier provide "reasonable accommodation" for the physical or mental limitations of a qualified applicant or employee with a disability unless the carrier can show that the accommodation would impose an "undue hardship" on business. According to the EQUAL EMPLOYMENT OPPORTUNITY COMMISSION, a reasonable accommodation is a modification or adjustment to a job, practice, or work environment that makes it possible for an individual with a disability to enjoy an equal employment opportunity. An undue hardship has been defined as an action that is unduly costly, extensive, substantial, or disruptive or that would fundamentally alter the nature or operation of the carrier's business.

The ADA has also affected the scope of a carrier's responsibility to its passengers. Under the ADA, carriers of passengers such as buses and rail systems must ensure that their facilities are readily accessible to and usable by individuals with disabilities by providing lifts, ramps, or other mechanisms. Airlines, which are not specifically covered by the ADA, are prohibited from discriminating against disabled individuals under the Air Carrier Access Act (ACAA), 49 U.S.C.A. § 1301 note, 1374, 1374 note, which was enacted in 1986. The ACAA provides that "[n]o air carrier may discriminate against any . . . handicapped individual, by reason of such handicap, in the provision of air transportation" (42 U.S.C.A. § 1374). Like the ADA, it further provides that air carriers must make "reasonable accommodations" for disabled individuals traveling by air.

**CROSS-REFERENCES**

Airlines; Disabled Persons; Railroads; Shipping Law.

**CARRIER'S LIEN** 📖 The right of an individual or organization that publicly advertises itself for hire for the transportation of goods to keep possession of the cargo it has delivered to a destination until the person who is liable to pay the freight charges plus any other expenses incurred by its shipment has done so. 📖

Not all CARRIERS are automatically entitled to have a LIEN for nonpayment of freight charges. A private carrier, one that does not offer its services to the public but transports goods pursuant to a special agreement, does not have a lien on property shipped unless provided by statute or under the terms of the carriage contract.

When a carrier retains goods under a lien it must exercise reasonable care to protect the cargo. It will be liable for any damage to such property that might have been avoided if ordinary precautions had been taken. Damages resulting solely from the detention of the property are the responsibility of the person who has failed to pay the freight charges; he or she must absorb that loss.

**CARRINGTON, EDWARD CODRINGTON** Edward Codrington Carrington was born April 10, 1872, in Washington, D.C. He was admitted to the Maryland bar in 1894 and established his legal practice in Baltimore, specializing in corporation law.

A supporter of the Progressive faction of the Republican party, Carrington served as campaign manager in Maryland for THEODORE ROOSEVELT in the primary election of 1912 while a member of the Republican National Convention. During the same year, he advocated a Progressive National Convention and acted as a delegate to this convention. Carrington also served on the Progressive National Committee and headed the Progressive State Committee of Maryland.

Carrington initiated proceedings in Maryland to combine the Progressives once again with the Republicans, and in 1914 he was nominated by the Republicans for a seat in the U.S. Senate, but was defeated. He spent the remainder of his life as a participant in business activities, which included his service as presi-

**BIOGRAPHY**

*Edward Codrington Carrington*

EDWARD CODRINGTON CARRINGTON 1872–1938

| 1861–65 U.S. Civil War | 1872 Born, Washington, D.C. | 1894 Admitted to the Maryland bar | 1912 Served as Teddy Roosevelt's presidential campaign manager in Maryland | 1914 Nominated as Republican candidate for U.S. Senate from Maryland; defeated in election | 1914–18 World War I | 1929 As president of Hudson River Navigation Corp., fought attempts by New York State to take over public utilities | 1931 Ran unsuccessful campaign for Manhattan Borough President | 1938 Died, Baltimore, Md. | 1939–45 World War II |

1850　1875　1900　1925　1950

dent of the Hudson River Navigation Corporation.

On December 30, 1938, Carrington died in Baltimore.

**CARRINGTON REPORT**  A report delineating proposed changes in LEGAL EDUCATION submitted by Professor Paul D. Carrington of the University of Michigan School of Law, chairman of the Curriculum Study Project Committee of the Association of American Law Schools (AALS), to the AALS on September 7, 1971.

The Carrington Report represented the combined efforts of a committee of legal scholars, but Professor Carrington, due to his role as chairperson, was instrumental in compiling the report. It aroused some controversy among legal educators and commentators at the time of its publication because of the extensiveness of its proposed changes in legal education, particularly in terms of revisions of law school curricula.

The Carrington Report challenges the traditional requirements for a law degree: four years of undergraduate study and three years of law school. The report indicates that the contents and length of the traditional program inhibit the prompt, competent, and efficient delivery of necessary legal services to society.

**CARRY-BACK**  The name given to the method provided under federal tax law that allows a taxpayer to apply net operating losses incurred during one year to the recomputation of INCOME TAX owed to the government for three preceding taxable years.

**CARRYING CHARGES**  Payments made to satisfy expenses incurred as a result of ownership of property, such as land taxes and mortgage payments. Disbursements paid to creditors, in addition to INTEREST, for extending CREDIT.

CONSUMER PROTECTION laws require full disclosure of all carrying charges.

**CARRY-OVER**  The designation of the process by which net operating loss for one year may be applied, as provided by federal tax law, to each of several taxable years following the taxable year of such loss.

**CARSWELL, GEORGE HARROLD**
Through an unexpected appointment, G. Harrold Carswell secured nomination on January 19, 1970, to serve on the U.S. Supreme Court. The appointment by President RICHARD M. NIXON came a mere six months after Carswell was named to the federal appeals court. During highly politicized Senate confirmation hearings, the Republican nominee faced skepticism and concern over his qualifications for the Supreme Court. In the end, Carswell was unable to overcome the opposition to his appointment. On April 8, 1970, he became the second Nixon-appointed candidate to be rejected for the U.S. Supreme Court by the U.S. Senate.

Carswell was born December 22, 1919, to a prominent family in Irwinton, Georgia. After graduating from Duke University in 1941 and from Mercer Law School in 1948, Carswell became a trial attorney in private practice. In 1953, he was appointed by President DWIGHT D. EISENHOWER as U.S. attorney for northern Florida. Carswell held that post until 1958 when he was appointed by Eisenhower to the U.S. District Court for the Northern District of Florida. At age thirty-eight, he was the nation's youngest federal judge. In 1969 Carswell was appointed by Nixon to the U.S. Court of Appeals for the Fifth Circuit.

Carswell's ascent to the U.S. Supreme Court came on the heels of Nixon's ill-fated nomination of CLEMENT F. HAYNESWORTH, JR., of South Carolina. Nixon had nominated Haynesworth

BIOGRAPHY

*G. Harrold Carswell*

*The Carrington Report challenges traditional legal training. It is named for Professor Paul D. Carrington of the University of Michigan School of Law.*

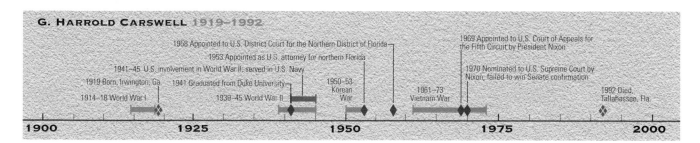

G. HARROLD CARSWELL 1919–1992

1958 Appointed to U.S. District Court for the Northern District of Florida

1953 Appointed as U.S. attorney for northern Florida

1969 Appointed to U.S. Court of Appeals for the Fifth Circuit by President Nixon

1941–45 U.S. involvement in World War II; served in U.S. Navy

1919 Born, Irwinton, Ga.    1941 Graduated from Duke University

1970 Nominated to U.S. Supreme Court by Nixon; failed to win Senate confirmation

1914–18 World War I    1939–45 World War II    1950–53 Korean War    1961–73 Vietnam War    1992 Died, Tallahassee, Fla.

1900    1925    1950    1975    2000

to fill the associate justice seat vacated by ABE FORTAS, who had resigned from the High Court in 1969 under a cloud of ethical violations. Haynesworth, a conservative southerner and a judge on the U.S. Court of Appeals for the Fourth Circuit, had failed to win Senate confirmation by ten votes.

By most standards Carswell was a jurist of marginal talents. In addition, evidence of racist conduct during the 1940s and 1950s brought Carswell's fitness for the bench into serious question. His critics noted that as a lower-court judge Carswell had demonstrated a marked bias against African Americans. In addition, Carswell had made white supremacist comments during a 1948 campaign speech and had attempted as a U.S. attorney to prevent the integration of a public golf course. Although Carswell renounced the bigotry of his past, the damage to his reputation was irreparable.

Carswell also suffered a reputation as a legal lightweight. His opponents noted that a dismal 58 percent of Carswell's judicial decisions had been overruled by higher courts. In a vote of no confidence, the Ripon Society, a Republican group, rated Carswell's performance as a federal judge well below the average level of competence.

Carswell performed poorly during the Senate Judiciary Committee hearings, reinforcing the assertion of his critics that he was an inept nominee. His confirmation chances were further weakened by a much-quoted observation offered in his support by Republican senator Roman Hruska, of Nebraska. The Midwestern politician argued that even if Carswell was mediocre, there were lots of mediocre judges, lawyers, and citizens who were entitled to some representation. Hruska went on to note that not all Supreme Court judges could be Brandeises, Frankfurters, and Cardozos.

A slim majority of senators refused to support a jurist who failed to meet high standards. On April 8, 1970, the Senate voted 51–48 to reject Carswell's nomination. Despite Nixon's dogged insistence that Carswell was a qualified candidate, thirteen Republican senators voted against his confirmation.

Nixon defended his unsuccessful nominee. Refusing to admit his candidate's shortcomings, the president claimed that Carswell was opposed by the Senate because he was a conservative southerner and a believer in the "strict construction," or literal interpretation, of the U.S. Constitution. Nixon's third nominee, HARRY A. BLACKMUN, of Minnesota, met with Senate approval and was confirmed without major incident.

"I AM A SOUTHERNER BY ANCESTRY, BIRTH, TRAINING, INCLINATION, BELIEF, AND PRACTICE."

**BIOGRAPHY**

*James Coolidge Carter*

Shortly after his defeat Carswell resigned from the federal appeals court and announced his candidacy for U.S. senator from Florida. Carswell's senatorial bid did not succeed and he returned to private law practice in Tallahassee. Carswell died in 1992.

**CARTEL**    A combination of producers of any product joined together to control its production, sale, and price, so as to obtain a MONOPOLY and restrict competition in any particular industry or commodity. Cartels exist primarily in Europe, being illegal in the United States by ANTITRUST LAWS. Also, an association by agreement of companies or sections of companies having common interests, designed to prevent extreme or unfair competition and allocate markets, and to promote the interchange of knowledge resulting from scientific and technical research, exchange of patent rights, and standardization of products.

In war, an agreement between two hostile powers for the delivery of prisoners or deserters, or authorizing certain nonhostile intercourse between each other that would otherwise be prevented by the state of war, for example, agreements between enemies for intercommunication by post, telegraph, telephone, or railway.

Although illegal in the United States, foreign cartels influence prices within the United States on imported and smuggled goods that they control. The United States has sued the De Beers diamond cartel several times, and works to stop the flow of illegal narcotics, whose production and distribution are largely controlled by drug cartels.

**CARTER, JAMES COOLIDGE** James Coolidge Carter was a lawyer and leading legal scholar and philosopher of the late nineteenth century.

Born into a poor family on October 14, 1827, in Lancaster, Massachusetts, Carter attended Derby Academy in Hingham, Massachusetts. In 1846 he entered Harvard College. An outstanding student, he graduated fourth in his class in 1850. He then moved to New York City to work as a private tutor and to study law. He returned to Cambridge a year later and enrolled in what was then known as the Dane Law School at Harvard, graduating in 1853. Carter was then admitted to the New York state bar and clerked briefly before founding the firm of Scudder and Carter. He remained associated with the firm for the next fifty-two years.

Carter quickly emerged as a highly skilled and sought-after lawyer. He also became a prominent leader of the New York bar, helping to form the Association of the Bar of the City of

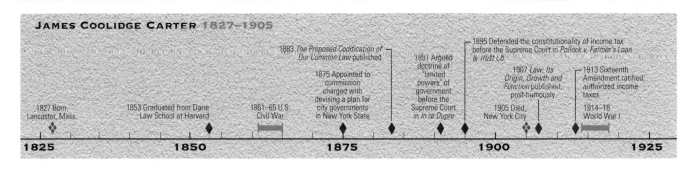

**JAMES COOLIDGE CARTER 1827–1905**

1883 *The Proposed Codification of Our Common Law* published

1875 Appointed to commission charged with devising a plan for city governments in New York State

1891 Argued doctrine of "limited powers" of government before the Supreme Court in *In re Dupre*

1895 Defended the constitutionality of income tax before the Supreme Court in *Pollock v. Farmer's Loan & Trust Co.*

1907 *Law: Its Origin, Growth and Function* published; posthumously

1913 Sixteenth Amendment ratified; authorized income taxes

1827 Born, Lancaster, Mass.

1853 Graduated from Dane Law School at Harvard

1861–65 U.S. Civil War

1905 Died, New York City

1914–18 World War I

1825  1850  1875  1900  1925

New York and serving as the association's president for five terms. He had a strong interest in municipal reform and in 1875 he was appointed by the governor to a commission charged with devising a plan of government for the cities of New York State. He also helped found the National Municipal League and was its president for nine years. Later in his career Carter achieved national prominence as president of the American Bar Association from 1894 to 1895 and for his appearance as counsel for the United States before the Bering Sea Fur-Seal Tribunal of Arbitration in 1893. Carter's opening argument before the tribunal in Paris reportedly lasted seven days.

In addition to his involvement in municipal affairs, Carter devoted his energies to organizing opposition to a proposed civil code for the state of New York. Carter had long been an opponent of the code of procedure, which had been part of the law since 1846, calling it an embarrassment to the practicing bar. In 1883, he authored *The Proposed Codification of Our Common Law,* a widely distributed pamphlet outlining his views, which was influential in the code's eventual defeat in the state legislature. Carter believed that any scheme to reduce the law to statutes was fundamentally unsound and simply could not be carried out. Even if it could be accomplished, he argued, CODIFICATION was undesirable because "[l]aw is not a command or body of commands, but consists of rules springing from the social standard of justice or from the habits and customs from which that standard has itself been derived." He went on to write and speak extensively on the issue of codification throughout his life and his lectures were published after his death as *Law: Its Origin, Growth, and Function* (1907).

Carter strongly believed in restraints on legislative powers and he applied his legal philosophy to important cases he argued before the U.S. Supreme Court. In *In re Dupre,* 143 U.S. 110, 12 S. Ct. 374, 36 L. Ed. 93 (1891), Carter argued that Congress lacked the authority to

"THE FUNCTION OF LAW [IS] THE MARKING OUT OF THE LARGEST AREA WITHIN WHICH EACH INDIVIDUAL COULD MOVE FREELY AND ACT WITHOUT INVADING THE LIKE FREEDOM IN EVERY OTHER—THAT IS, TO INSURE THE LARGEST POSSIBLE FREEDOM."

prohibit as criminal the use of the mails for the circulation of lottery tickets. According to Carter, the federal government could use the powers granted to it by the Constitution for only limited purposes, and to exceed such limits through the law in question usurped the powers reserved to the states under the TENTH AMENDMENT. Carter's doctrine of "limited powers" would be used by other lawyers and scholars to restrict congressional control over interstate commerce and taxes.

Carter again argued for a limited government role in *Smyth v. Ames,* 169 U.S. 466, 18 S. Ct. 418, 42 L. Ed. 819 (1898), in which the U.S. Supreme Court considered whether Nebraska could force its RAILROADS to lower their shipping rates in an attempt to ease economic conditions for farmers. Carter, one of several prominent lawyers representing the railroads, maintained that the shipping charges should be determined not by the state but by "laissez-faire" economics and free competition, which would prevent the imposition of high rates. The Court struck down the law at issue as unconstitutional, but also set guidelines for rate regulation by the states so that future court challenges could be avoided.

Carter created somewhat of a stir among his fellow legal scholars when, in what initially appeared to be a drastic departure from his usual views, he joined a team of other prominent lawyers to defend the constitutionality of an INCOME TAX before the U.S. Supreme Court in *Pollock v. Farmers' Loan & Trust Co.,* 158 U.S. 601, 15 S. Ct. 912, 39 L. Ed. 1108 (1895). Carter argued that the legislature's action in passing the tax must be given due weight and should not be subject to review by a judicial tribunal. Just as government should play a limited role, he contended, the courts' role should be likewise restricted. He argued that the courts should refrain from engaging in "judicial lawmaking" and said, "nothing could be more unwise and dangerous—nothing more foreign to the spirit of the Constitution—than an attempt to baffle and defeat a popular determination by a judgment in a lawsuit ... the only path to safety is to accept the voice of the majority as final." The Supreme Court went on to strike down the general income tax enacted by Congress and held that taxes on income derived from REAL ESTATE and PERSONAL PROPERTY constituted DIRECT TAXES and thus must be apportioned among the states according to population. The decision was effectively negated by the adoption and ratification in 1913 of the SIXTEENTH AMENDMENT, which exempted income taxes from the Constitution's apportionment requirement, but *Pollock* was nevertheless long remembered because of the fervor with which it was argued by Carter and the other attorneys involved.

After his retirement from the practice of law, Carter devoted his time to writing and studying and remained a popular lecturer until his death in 1905 at the age of seventy-eight.

See also POLLOCK V. FARMERS' LOAN & TRUST CO.

## CARTER, JAMES EARL, JR.

As the thirty-ninth president of the United States, Jimmy Carter represented a historical change in national politics. He was the first modern president to be elected from the Deep South. Following a successful career in Georgia—where he was a peanut farmer, state senator, and then governor—Carter entered the White House in January 1977 as a political outsider at a time of distrust in elected officials. His Baptist upbringing guided him in his vision of the office as a post to be used for the nation's moral leadership. However, his presidency was one of only limited success in both its domestic and international endeavors, and voters rejected him for a second term in 1980 by electing RONALD REAGAN in a landslide that marked a new era of Republican control of the executive branch. After leaving Washington, D.C., Carter began a revitalized public life as a prominent human rights activist and diplomat, addressing problems of war, famine, and repression around the globe.

The small farming town of Plains, Georgia, was Carter's birthplace on October 1, 1924.

**BIOGRAPHY**

*Jimmy Carter*

James Earl Carter, Sr., a veteran of World War I, farmed cotton and had a general store. He was conservative, strict, and a firm believer in his son, whom he nicknamed Hot, for Hotshot—because, Carter said, "Daddy never assumed I would fail at anything." Lillian Gordy Carter was a registered nurse. As devout Baptists, the parents expected much from Carter and their three other children. Religion meant steadfastness and a call to charity, as Carter's mother demonstrated by caring for patients without charge. Archery, their community, was predominantly African American. The young Carter worked and played with his black neighbors and, like them, lived without household plumbing or electricity. The experience, along with the virtues of hard work, frugality, and aspiration taught by his parents, shaped the politician he later became. After graduating at the top of his high school class, Carter paid for college with money he had earned and invested by selling peanuts as a boy.

Carter's ambition was naval service. Preparing to enter the U.S. Naval Academy at Annapolis, Maryland, he studied mathematics at Georgia Southwestern College and then the Georgia Institute of Technology. In 1943 he entered Annapolis; he graduated in the top tenth of his class with a bachelor of sciences degree. Soon he married a long-time acquaintance, Rosalynn Smith, and began in earnest to pursue his career in the Navy. He worked as an instructor, saw battleship and submarine duty, and ultimately qualified as a sub commander. He served as senior officer aboard the *Sea Wolf,* the Navy's second atomic submarine. He left the Navy in 1953 after attaining the rank of lieutenant.

The decision to walk away from a promising career came when Carter faced a personal crossroads. His father had died, leaving a powerful legacy: the one-time cotton farmer had become a successful warehouse operator, peanut seed seller, and, finally, member of the Georgia House of Representatives. Carter now followed his father's example in business and politics. In his first year as a peanut farmer, he

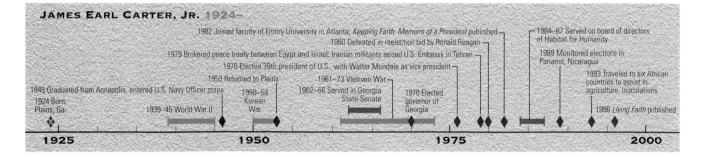

**JAMES EARL CARTER, JR.** 1924–

1982 Joined faculty of Emory University in Atlanta; *Keeping Faith: Memoirs of a President* published
1980 Defeated in reelection bid by Ronald Reagan
1979 Brokered peace treaty between Egypt and Israel; Iranian militants seized U.S. Embassy in Tehran
1978 Elected 39th president of U.S. with Walter Mondale as vice president
1953 Returned to Plains
1961–73 Vietnam War
1946 Graduated from Annapolis, entered U.S. Navy Officer corps
1924 Born, Plains, Ga.
1950–53 Korean War
1962–66 Served in Georgia State Senate
1970 Elected governor of Georgia
1939–45 World War II
1984–87 Served on board of directors of Habitat for Humanity
1989 Monitored elections in Panama, Nicaragua
1993 Traveled to six African countries to assist in agriculture, inoculations
1996 *Living Faith* published

1925          1950          1975          2000

scratched out an income of $200, yet soon the business flourished. Success in political life took longer. Carter quickly became active in civic affairs. He opposed segregation, scorned the local White Citizen's Council, and tried to integrate his church. In the 1950s South such views spelled trouble. When he ran for the Democratic nomination for the state senate in 1962 his opponents stuffed ballot boxes to defeat him. Only after a long legal fight did a court invalidate the nomination because of FRAUD and turn it over to Carter. He won the ELECTION.

State politics established Carter nationally. In two terms as a state senator, from 1962 to 1966, his political philosophy was traditionally liberal yet also bore the mark of a technocrat: he advocated CIVIL RIGHTS, WELFARE, and open government, while insisting on careful budgeting to ensure fiscal responsibility. In 1966 his first run for the governor's office failed but he won the election in 1971. Representing broad political and social changes shaping the region, Carter's governorship helped shake Georgia out of its segregationist past; he appointed African Americans to state government and fostered biracial cooperation through citizens groups. As an administrator he specialized in micromanagement, ordering frequent, strict review of all publicly funded programs. By 1974 Carter was rising within the national Democratic party. His exposure grew as he served as chairman of its campaign committee, and, fulfilling an ambition that began with his election as governor, announced his candidacy for president.

Carter's campaign message was integrity. The United States had just suffered through Vietnam and the Watergate scandal, producing widespread cynicism concerning elected officials. Carter's opponent, GERALD R. FORD, had pardoned Nixon, the man behind Watergate. Carter positioned himself as an honest, openly religious man beyond the political intrigues of Washington. The peanut-farmer-turned-governor seemed to promise a new voice in government and a new set of ideals. At the start of the campaign voters responded eagerly: Carter and his running mate, Walter F. Mondale, led the incumbent, GERALD R. FORD, and his running mate, Bob Dole, by 30 percentage points. But by election day the race was a dead heat. Carter won by the smallest margin since the first World War—57 ELECTORAL COLLEGE votes. The new president walked along Pennsylvania Avenue in his inaugural parade, making a symbolic gesture that would be repeated in the thoroughly populist trappings of the Carter White House—fireside chats and radio call-in

shows, simple furnishings, and fewer limousines. "We must adjust to changing times," he said in his inaugural speech, "and still hold to unchanging principles."

Carter's domestic policies for the United States were those of Georgia writ large. He promoted civil rights, welfare, tax reform, and budgetary control. Almost immediately, however, two major domestic concerns began to dictate his agenda. One was the nation's energy supply. In the late 1970s a severe energy crisis produced the worst fuel shortage in U.S. history coupled with rising international prices for oil. Congress cooperated with Carter's remedies by approving fuel conservation policies, deregulating natural gas prices, and passing a windfall tax on oil company profits. He did not get everything he wanted: a federal court blocked his attempt to decontrol domestic oil prices and Congress denied him authority for gasoline rationing. The second major problem was the economy, which worsened over the course of his term. His efforts to fight inflation—especially controls on consumer credit—produced a recession. Voters grew disgruntled. His approval rating fell and a July 1979 speech in which he blamed the nation's problems on a spiritual "malaise" was disastrous: afterward, a New York Times poll showed that for the first time ever, U.S. citizens, who traditionally had responded 2–1 that they were optimistic about the future, now said nearly 2–1 that they were pessimistic.

Foreign policy gave Carter triumphs and failures. He made HUMAN RIGHTS a top priority in the relationships between the United States and foreign nations, directing Secretary of State Cyrus R. Vance to set a new standard: social and economic rights were to be as important as political and civil rights. Liberals praised the policy; conservatives attacked it as muddled and inconsistently applied. Critics were divided over a controversial treaty with Panama to relinquish control of the Panama Canal by the year 2000, a move the U.S. Senate barely approved. Carter's indisputable triumph was a peace treaty he secured between long-time enemies Israel and Egypt. But he took much of the blame for a seizure of the U.S. Embassy in Tehran by Iranian militants in November 1979. A military rescue mission in 1980 failed and the fifty-two U.S. HOSTAGES were released only after Carter left office.

Further weakening the presidency were scandals within the administration. Andrew Young, his ambassador to the United Nations, resigned amid revelations that he had secretly met members of the Palestine Liberation Or-

"AMERICA DID NOT INVENT HUMAN RIGHTS. IN A VERY REAL SENSE . . . HUMAN RIGHTS INVENTED AMERICA."

ganization, in violation of U.S. policy. Bert Lance, director of the Office of Management and Budget, also resigned in disgrace; he was charged with unethical conduct in his former banking career. And Carter's brother, Billy Carter, caused the president embarrassment. Often seen as a comical figure who had cashed in on Carter's fame by lending his name to a drink called Billy Beer, Billy was revealed to have conducted business with Libya, an enemy nation. A Senate subcommittee report on the incident blamed Carter for not reining in his brother.

By late 1980 Carter had the lowest approval rating of any U.S. president in modern history. Even after an extensive cabinet shake-up, his administration was in disarray. Critics lambasted his policies and, particularly, his methods: he was considered to be too mired in details to execute bold decisions. Editorial cartoonists frequently lampooned him as either a country bumpkin or a hapless, childlike figure, echoing the prevailing sentiment that Carter was incapable of running the country. To make matters worse the Democratic party effectively deserted him. Senator Edward M. Kennedy (D-Mass.) nearly captured the party's presidential nomination and his supporters gained control of the party's platform over Carter's objections. Republicans sensed a bloodbath, and they got it in Ronald Reagan's landslide victory.

Typical of the post-Carter-era assessments was that of historian Burton I. Kaufman, whose 1993 book, *The Presidency of James Earl Carter* scathingly judged Carter as "lacking in leadership, ineffective in dealing with Congress, incapable of defending America's honor abroad, and uncertain about its purpose, priorities and sense of direction." Carter's defenders have largely chosen to blame his 1980 loss on intractable national problems that he did not create as well as on the overwhelming popularity of his opponent. "He didn't have the charisma of a Reagan," THOMAS P. "TIP" O'NEILL, JR., former Democratic Speaker of the House, observed. "He couldn't pull it off." Some inside observers saw Carter's presidency as less a failure than a poor match of his abilities. The author Hendrik

Hertzberg, a former Carter speechwriter, argued, "He was, and is, more of a moral leader than a political leader."

Although Carter's return to Georgia after his 1980 defeat might have been ignominious, it proved otherwise. After his departure from Washington, Carter immersed himself in scholarly and humanitarian pursuits. His work as a professor at Emory University in Atlanta and his prodigious literary output—a memoir and five other books ranging from politics to poetry—were intellectual achievements enough. But he also personally built housing for the poor in the United States and abroad through the nonprofit group Habitat for Humanity. "This is the kind of thing I enjoy doing. The alternative is to loaf around the house and spend my time playing golf or fishing," he told a Canadian newsweekly. He remained a force in world affairs. Human rights were his focal point in this rare second act in public life. His accomplishments in the 1980s and first half of the 1990s seemed the work of a tireless and selfless man: he monitored elections in Central America; negotiated further peace in the Middle East; supervised inoculation programs for children in Africa and elsewhere; and traveled on diplomatic missions to North Korea, Bosnia, and Haiti.

**CROSS-REFERENCES**

Diplomatic Agents; Diplomatic Immunity; Terrorism.

**BIOGRAPHY**

© MICHAEL GLUCK

*Robert Lee Carter*

**CARTER, ROBERT LEE** Robert Lee Carter is a federal district court judge who, as counsel for the NATIONAL ASSOCIATION FOR THE ADVANCEMENT OF COLORED PEOPLE (NAACP), played a pivotal role in the SCHOOL DESEGREGATION cases of the 1950s. Carter argued *Brown v. Board of Education*, 347 U.S. 483, 74 S. Ct. 686, 98 L. Ed. 873 (1954), before the U.S. Supreme Court.

Carter was born March 11, 1917, in Florida. As a child he moved to New Jersey, where he attended public schools in Newark and East Orange. He received his bachelor of arts degree from Lincoln University, in Pennsylvania, in 1937, then went on to earn a bachelor of laws degree from Howard University Law School, graduating magna cum laude in 1940. He also

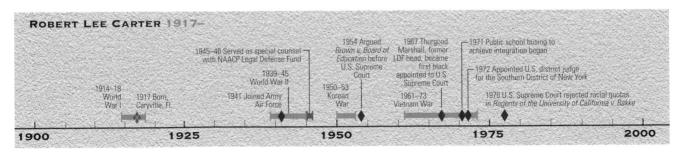

ROBERT LEE CARTER 1917–

1945–46 Served as special counsel with NAACP Legal Defense Fund

1954 Argued *Brown v. Board of Education* before U.S. Supreme Court

1967 Thurgood Marshall, former LDF head, became first black appointed to U.S. Supreme Court

1971 Public school busing to achieve integration began

1939–45 World War II

1972 Appointed U.S. district judge for the Southern District of New York

1914–18 World War I

1917 Born, Caryville, Fl.

1941 Joined Army Air Force

1950–53 Korean War

1961–73 Vietnam War

1978 U.S. Supreme Court rejected racial quotas in *Regents of the University of California v. Bakke*

1900    1925    1950    1975    2000

earned a master of laws degree from Columbia University in 1941.

With World War II heating up, Carter entered the Army Air Force where he encountered racism and segregation. During his time in the Army he pressed charges against two white soldiers who had harassed him with racial slurs. He also refused to live off base as black soldiers were required to do. Because of his outspoken defiance of segregation he was transferred to a different base. Later he successfully defended a black soldier charged with raping a white woman. In retaliation for his participation in the case he was given an administrative discharge, which is neither honorable nor dishonorable and leaves the recipient open to being drafted. He enlisted the help of his mentor and former law professor, WILLIAM H. HASTIE, who would later become the first African American to sit as a lifetime federal judge outside the Virgin Islands. Hastie represented Carter in a petition before the discharge review board, which finally granted Carter an honorable discharge. When Carter left the Army, he had achieved the rank of second lieutenant.

After leaving military service, Carter became assistant special counsel with the NAACP Legal Defense Fund (LDF), a position he held from 1945 to 1946. In 1948 he became director of veterans' affairs for American Veterans (of World War II) AMVETS, where he served until 1949.

In 1950 Carter returned to the NAACP and joined the fight for CIVIL RIGHTS. In 1951 he brought an innovative challenge to the "SEPARATE-BUT-EQUAL" doctrine when he summoned social scientist Kenneth B. Clark as a witness for the plaintiffs in *Briggs v. Elliott* (98 F. Supp. 529 [E.D.S.C. 1951]). Clark testified that his research with black children indicated that their self-image and self-esteem were damaged by any system that separated them from their white peers, whether the system was equal or not. At the time, this was highly unorthodox EVIDENCE to present at trial. Although the court ruled against the plaintiffs in *Briggs*, Clark's testimony had set the stage for the arguments that would be presented in *Brown* and the other school desegregation cases. *Briggs* was later appealed with several other cases, including

"THE BROWN DECISION WAS HISTORIC, NOT BECAUSE OF WHAT IT HAS ACCOMPLISHED IN THE FIELD OF EDUCATION, BUT BECAUSE OF THE TRANSFORMATION IT HAS MADE IN THE WHOLE COMPLEX OF RACE RELATIONS IN THIS COUNTRY."

**BIOGRAPHY**

*Thomas Henry Carter*

*Brown*, which Carter argued and won. His victory in *Brown* established him as a preeminent civil rights attorney and he went on to participate in the appeals of scores of other cases.

Carter continued as an assistant special counsel with the NAACP until becoming general counsel in 1956. He would remain with the NAACP for thirteen more years before leaving to enter private practice. During his years of practice Carter argued twenty-two cases before the Supreme Court, winning all but one.

In 1972 President RICHARD M. NIXON appointed Carter to be a U.S. district judge for the Southern District of New York. During his long and distinguished career, Carter has received numerous awards and recognitions. He was named a Columbia University Urban Fellow (1968–69) and has served as an adjunct professor at New York University Law School (1965–70), Yale University (1975–77), and the University of Michigan Law School (1977). He holds honorary degrees from Lincoln University, in Pennsylvania, Northeastern University, and the College of the Holy Cross.

**CROSS-REFERENCES**

*Brown v. Board of Education of Topeka, Kansas*; Discrimination; Marshall, Thurgood; Warren Court.

**CARTER, THOMAS HENRY** Thomas Henry Carter, born October 30, 1854, in Scioto County, Ohio, concentrated his career efforts in Montana. He pursued legal studies and relocated to Helena in 1882 where he established a successful law practice.

In 1889 Montana was admitted as a state to the United States, and Carter became its first representative to participate in Congress. In this capacity he favored less stringent laws concerning homesteaders. In 1890 he became commissioner of the general land office and was able to put his views into effect, to the advantage of the Western settlers. In 1892 he was the presiding officer of the Republican National Committee and directed the unsuccessful reelection campaign of President BENJAMIN HARRISON.

Carter entered a new phase of his career in 1895 when he became a U.S. senator. He represented Montana until 1901 and again from 1905 to 1911. During his tenure he supported

THOMAS HENRY CARTER 1854–1911

1854 Born, Scioto County, Ohio

1861–65 U.S. Civil War

1882 Moved to Helena, Montana; established law practice

1889 Montana admitted to U.S. statehood

1890 Appointed commissioner of the general land office by President Harrison

1895–1901 Served first term in U.S. Senate

1905 Reelected to second term in U.S. Senate

1910 Glacier National Park established

1911 Died, Helena, Montana

1914–18 World War I

1850        1875        1900        1925

various policies, including bimetallism—the use of both gold and silver as the foundation of the currency system; civil service legislation; a protective TARIFF on raw materials—such as wool, lumber, and lead; and a postal savings system. He also worked extensively in the field of conservation and was instrumental in the establishment of Glacier National Park.

Carter died September 17, 1911, in Helena.

**CASE** 📖 A general term for any ACTION, CAUSE OF ACTION, lawsuit, or controversy. All the EVIDENCE and TESTIMONY compiled and organized by one party in a lawsuit to prove that party's version of the controversy at a trial in court. 📖

**CASE, ACTION ON THE** 📖 One of the old common-law FORMS OF ACTION that provided a remedy for the invasion of personal or property interests. 📖

Action on the case is also called trespass on the case because it developed from the COMMON-LAW action of TRESPASS during the fifteenth century in England. Often it is simply called case.

Case differs from trespass in that it redresses more indirect injuries than the willful invasion of the plaintiff's property contemplated by trespass. It was designed to supplement the action of trespass. For example, a person struck by a log thrown over a fence could maintain an action in trespass against the thrower. If, instead, the wrongdoer tossed the log into the street and the plaintiff was hurt by stumbling over it, the plaintiff could maintain an action on the case rather than in trespass.

In pleading an action on the case the plaintiff sets forth the circumstances of the entire case. In pleading an action on the case the COMPLAINT differed from the forms used in pleading other actions because other actions generally had highly stylized and rigid forms that had to be followed word for word. The plaintiff in the action on the case alleged facts to show that (1) the defendant had some sort of duty; (2) the defendant had violated that duty; and (3) the result was harm to the plaintiff or the plaintiff's property. Over the years, this action developed into a remedy for a wide variety of wrongs that were not redressed by the other forms of action. For example, a plaintiff could sue a defendant who maintained a NUISANCE in the neighborhood; who violated an EASEMENT or a RIGHT OF WAY; or who committed LIBEL, slander, MALICIOUS PROSECUTION, FRAUD, or DECEIT. Most importantly, the action on the case came into common use as the legal method for compensating victims of NEGLIGENCE. It thus became one of the most widely used forms of action in the common-law system and gave birth to the modern law of TORTS.

When EJECTMENT was still considered a modern improvement on trespass in England, it had already been abandoned in New England because of its complicated technical requirements. One of the reasons for the American experience is that law books were scarce in the colonies and many judges were laymen. The most rigid applications of technical formalities came during the first half of the nineteenth century after lawyers gained influence in the legal system.

Soon dissatisfaction with the technicalities of the forms began to peak. CODE PLEADING was then introduced to replace the prior forms of action. An attempt was made to reduce the number of WRITS to some basic few that would be adequate for all the different requirements of modern litigation. Attention was shifted from the form to the elements of a cause of action. Courts asked only whether the plaintiff had stated a claim on which relief could be granted. The objective was to decide whether the plaintiff was entitled to a remedy with as little procedural red tape as possible. When code pleading fell short of this goal the modern law of CIVIL PROCEDURE developed the theory that there should be only one form of action, the CIVIL ACTION.

The old forms of action exist today only as names for procedures based on them and as the foundation of much of the SUBSTANTIVE LAW. In Pennsylvania, for example, the word *trespass* is used for tort actions, and *assumpsit* for lawsuits based upon contracts.

**CASE AGREED ON** 📖 An ACTION in which the parties submit a formal written enumeration of facts that they both accept as correct and complete so that a judge can render a decision based upon conclusions of law that can be drawn from the stated facts. 📖

The parties must agree on all material facts upon which their rights are to be determined. They do not, however, agree upon the legal effects of those facts; therefore, the action presents a JUSTICIABLE controversy, which makes it a matter for judicial determination. The need for a JURY trial is obviated because there are no QUESTIONS OF FACT presented for resolution.

A case agreed on is also known as an AMICABLE ACTION, a CASE STATED, or a FRIENDLY SUIT.

**CASEBOOK** 📖 A printed compilation of judicial decisions illustrating the application of particular principles of a specific field of law, such as TORTS, that is used in LEGAL EDUCATION to teach students under the CASE METHOD system. 📖

**CASE LAW** 📖 Legal principles enunciated and embodied in judicial decisions that are derived from the application of particular areas of law to the facts of individual cases.

As opposed to STATUTES—legislative acts that proscribe certain conduct by demanding or prohibiting something or that declare the legality of particular acts—case law is a dynamic and constantly developing body of law. Each case contains a portion wherein the facts of the controversy are set forth as well as the HOLDING and DICTA—an explanation of how the judge arrived at a particular conclusion. In addition, a case might contain concurring and dissenting OPINIONS of other judges.

Since the U.S. legal system has a COMMON-LAW system, higher court decisions are binding on lower courts in cases with similar facts that raise similar issues. The concept of PRECEDENT, or STARE DECISIS, means to follow or adhere to previously decided cases in judging the case at bar. It means that appellate case law should be considered as binding upon lower courts.

**CASEMENT, SIR ROGER DAVID** Sir Roger David Casement pursued an illustrious career in the British Foreign Service. His achievements were overshadowed by his campaign for Irish nationalism, which eventually led to his trial and execution.

Casement was born September 1, 1864, in Dublin, Ireland. From 1892 to 1904 and from 1906 to 1911, Casement made several noteworthy contributions to the field of British consular service. His investigation of the brutal working conditions of the Congolese on rubber plantations owned by Belgium led to drastic reforms in Africa. He subsequently performed a similar service for workers on British rubber plantations in South America. In 1911 he was knighted for his humanitarian efforts and in 1912 he resigned from foreign service due to illnesses contracted during his work in foreign countries.

Casement returned to Ireland and became interested in the movement for Irish freedom from British rule. He journeyed to Germany and the United States seeking support for an Irish insurrection. In April 1916 Casement received a pledge of aid from Germany but it

**BIOGRAPHY**

*Sir Roger David Casement*

"LOYALTY IS A SENTIMENT, NOT A LAW."

proved inadequate. He returned to Ireland hoping to curtail the planned Easter Rebellion, but British authorities apprehended him upon his arrival.

Accused of TREASON, Casement was put on trial. To add to the sensationalism of the proceedings and the case against him, several of Casement's diaries were publicly distributed. These diaries contained accounts of practices considered to be homosexual in nature. Casement was not given the opportunity to confirm or deny the validity of the diaries and the genuineness of the papers is still in question today.

The evidence against Casement was sufficient for a conviction and he was sentenced to be executed. Originally a Protestant, Casement converted to Roman Catholicism shortly before his death. On August 3, 1916, he was hanged in Pentonville Jail in London, England.

**CASE METHOD**  A system of instruction or study of law focused upon the analysis of court OPINIONS rather than lectures and textbooks; the predominant method of teaching in U.S. law schools today.

CHRISTOPHER COLUMBUS LANGDELL, a law professor, often receives credit for inventing the case method although historians have found evidence that others were teaching by this method before him. Regardless, Langdell by all accounts popularized the case method.

Langdell viewed the law as a science and believed that it should be studied as a science. Law, he said,

> consists of certain principles or doctrines. To have such a mastery of these as to be able to apply them with constant facility and certainty to the ever-tangled skein of human affairs, is what constitutes a true lawyer; and hence to acquire that mastery should be the business of every earnest student of law.

Each doctrine, Langdell said, arrived at its present state by slow degrees, growing and extending through centuries. Langdell's beliefs differed from those of his law professor col-

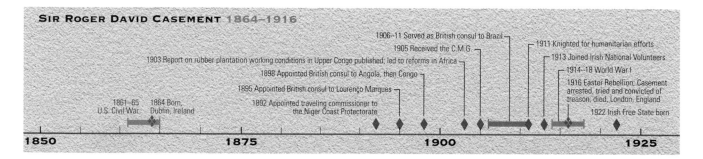

SIR ROGER DAVID CASEMENT 1864–1916

1906–11 Served as British consul to Brazil
1905 Received the C.M.G.
1911 Knighted for humanitarian efforts
1903 Report on rubber plantation working conditions in Upper Congo published; led to reforms in Africa
1913 Joined Irish National Volunteers
1898 Appointed British consul to Angola, then Congo
1914–18 World War I
1895 Appointed British consul to Lourenço Marques
1916 Easter Rebellion; Casement arrested, tried and convicted of treason, died, London, England
1861–65 U.S. Civil War
1864 Born, Dublin, Ireland
1892 Appointed traveling commissioner to the Niger Coast Protectorate
1922 Irish Free State born

1850    1875    1900    1925

CORBIS-BETTMANN

*The case method aroused controversy at Harvard Law School in the late nineteenth century. The class of 1864, shown here, may have included some of the first lawyers trained this way.*

leagues. Throughout the 1800s, the prevalent approach for teaching law school classes was the lecture method. Although professors and textbooks interpreted the meaning of various court decisions, they did not offer a significant opportunity for students to do so on their own. The case method, on the other hand, forced students to read, analyze, and interpret cases themselves. It was Langdell's opinion that law students would be better educated if they were asked to reach their own conclusions about the meaning of judicial decisions.

Langdell's ideas were, at first, overwhelmingly rejected by students, other law professors, and attorneys alike. These critics viewed the case method as chaotic compared with organized lectures. They believed that instead of soliciting law students' opinions regarding cases, professors should simply state their own interpretations. Law students, afraid that they were not learning from Langdell's method, dropped out of his class, leaving him with only a few pupils. Enrollment in the Harvard Law School decreased dramatically because of concern over Langdell's case method and alumni called for his dismissal.

But the president of Harvard University, Charles W. Eliot, supported Langdell and his case method. This backing allowed Langdell to withstand the criticism long enough to prove the case method's success: Langdell's students were becoming capable, skilled attorneys. In 1870 Langdell became law school dean. As time passed he replaced his critics on the Harvard faculty with professors who believed in his system of teaching and the case method soon became the dominant teaching method at Harvard. Other U.S. law schools took note. By the early 1900s, most had adopted the case method,

and it has remained the primary method of legal instruction throughout the twentieth century.

The case method is usually coupled with a type of classroom teaching called the Socratic method. Through the Socratic method students orally respond to an often difficult series of questions designed to help them gain further insight into the meaning of the law. Students learn the skill of critical analysis this way: they learn to discern relevant from irrelevant FACTS; they learn to distinguish between seemingly similar facts and ISSUES; and they learn to analogize between dissimilar facts and issues.

The case method offers certain benefits. For one, cases are usually interesting. They involve real parties with real problems and therefore tend to stimulate students more than do textbooks with only hypothetical problems.

The case method also helps students develop the ability to read and analyze cases, which is a crucial skill for attorneys. Students learn to reduce cases to four basic components: the *facts* of the controversy; the legal *issue* that the court decides; the *holding*, or legal resolution, that the court reaches; and the *reasoning* that the court uses to explain its decision. Students, especially in their first year of legal study, often outline these components in written case BRIEFS, to which they can refer during classes and while they prepare for exams.

Another advantage of the case method is that it teaches, by example, the system of legal precedence. By reading cases, students learn how and why judges adhere, or do not adhere, to law developed in previous cases. Students also learn how judges have the discretion to create law by construing statutes or constitutions.

The case method continues to have critics. One criticism focuses on law school examinations. Typically, law students are tested only once in each class. They face enormous pressure to perform well on this examination since their single score on it usually constitutes their entire grade for the class. It is difficult to test analysis skills, so often these examinations test the students' ability to spot legal issues and apply legal rules. Therefore, although professors try to teach case analysis skills, students tend to focus on simply learning RULES OF LAW in the hope of getting good grades. This diminishes the case method's intended result.

The case method may be unpopular with law students owing to the amount of reading it requires. It is not uncommon for law professors to assign twenty to thirty pages of reading, containing excerpts from four or five cases, each night for each class. Some law professors have argued that pupils learn to analyze cases within the first few months of law school, and that thereafter the case method becomes ineffective because students lose enthusiasm and interest in reading cases.

Another complaint concerns the role of CASE-BOOKS. Casebooks commonly contain cases or case excerpts as well as some explanatory text. They are most often compiled by law professors, who arrange the cases to show legal development or illustrate the meaning of legal principles. These casebooks provide only a small sample of cases, the vast majority of them appellate-level decisions. Thus, law students usually receive little or no exposure to decisions of TRIAL courts. Some commentators suggest that students therefore miss critical elements of a lawyer's initial role: discovering and shaping facts and determining legal strategies to present to the court at the trial level.

Frequently, students do not see legal conflicts in their undeveloped form until they graduate and begin practicing law. Law schools increasingly are trying to remedy that problem by offering instruction in basic lawyering skills. For example, classes in trial advocacy allow students to conduct mock jury trials. Other courses teach client-counseling skills, document-drafting skills, and oral argument skills. The idea is not to abandon the case method entirely but to balance it with other teaching methods.

### CROSS-REFERENCES

Case Law; Court Opinion; Legal Education; Precedent.

## CASE OR CONTROVERSY 📖 A term used

in Article III, Section 2, of the Constitution to describe the structure by which actual, conflicting claims of individuals must be brought before a FEDERAL COURT for resolution if the court is to exercise its JURISDICTION to consider the questions and provide relief. 📖

A case or controversy, also referred to as a JUSTICIABLE controversy, must consist of an actual dispute between parties over their legal rights that remain in conflict at the time the

case is presented and must be a proper matter for judicial determination. A dispute between parties that is MOOT is not a case or controversy because it no longer involves an actual conflict.

## CASE STATED 📖 An ACTION that is brought

upon the agreement of the parties who submit a statement of undisputed facts to the court but who take adversary positions as to the legal ramifications of the facts, thereby requiring a judge to decide the QUESTION OF LAW presented. 📖

A case stated is also called an AMICABLE ACTION, a CASE AGREED ON, or a FRIENDLY SUIT.

## CASEY, WILLIAM JOSEPH    William Jo-

seph Casey was a lawyer with a long and distinguished career in business and public service who later became the controversial director of the CENTRAL INTELLIGENCE AGENCY (CIA) during the Reagan administration.

Casey was born March 13, 1913, in Elmhurst, New York. He received his bachelor's degree from Fordham University in 1934, did graduate work at the Catholic University of America, and then entered St. John's University Law School, graduating with a bachelor of laws degree in 1937. Following his admission to the New York state bar he moved to Washington, D.C., to work for the Research Institute of America, a private organization involved in analyzing economic and political data concerning the New Deal.

During World War II Casey served with Army Intelligence and the Office of Strategic Services (OSS) and, from London, directed the activities of OSS spies. After the war Casey returned to Washington, D.C., and served for two years as special counsel to the Small Business Committee of the U.S. Senate. He remained interested in international relations as a result of his wartime activities, however, and in 1948 he returned to Europe to become associate general counsel for the MARSHALL PLAN. Following his war-related service, he started practicing law and became a partner in a large New York law firm. He also began teaching at New York University, where he lectured on tax law from 1948 to 1962, and taught periodically at the Practicing Law Institute. While practic-

*William Joseph
Casey*

**WILLIAM JOSEPH CASEY 1913-1987**

1913 Born Elmhurst, N.Y.

1914-18 World War I

1941-46 Supervised spy missions for the Office of Strategic Services

1939-45 World War II

1948-62 Lectured on tax law at New York University

1950-53 Korean War

1961-73 Vietnam War

1971-73 Served as chair of the Securities and Exchange Commission

1973-74 Served as undersecretary of state for economic affairs

1980 Ran Ronald Reagan's presidential campaign

1981 Appointed director of the CIA by President Reagan

1984 Congress voted to prohibit aid to the anti-communist Nicaraguan "contra" rebels

1986 Iran-Contra Affair hearings began

1987 Resigned his post at CIA; died, New York City

1900    1925    1950    1975    2000

ing and teaching, he wrote a number of highly successful books on taxes, real estate, and investments, including *Tax Shelter Investments* (1952) and *Accounting Desk Book* (1956), and a book on U.S. history titled *Where and How the War Was Won: An Armchair Guide to the American Revolution* (1976). The profits from his books, in addition to his income from his law practice and his investments, helped to make him a multimillionaire.

In the 1960s, Casey moved from business to politics, running in 1966 for a seat in the U.S. House of Representatives. Though he lost the primary to a more conservative Republican opponent, Casey remained active in the Republican party, writing and conducting research for RICHARD M. NIXON's 1968 presidential campaign. In 1969 he helped the new president set up the Citizens Committee for Peace with Security, which was organized to back Nixon's policy on antimissile weapons, and served on the advisory council of the Arms Control and Disarmament Agency.

In 1971 Nixon appointed Casey chairman of the SECURITIES AND EXCHANGE COMMISSION (SEC), where he quickly became known as a tough administrator who favored strict regulation of stockbrokers. Casey also became unpopular with his fellow SECURITIES lawyers when he named them as defendants in connection with their clients' alleged FRAUDS. While head of the SEC, he persuaded Congress to increase the agency's budget by $1.5 million, which he used to hire more lawyers, accountants, and other specialists to improve the agency's efficiency. In 1974, Casey moved from the SEC to the State Department, where he served as undersecretary of state for economic affairs for two years. He then became president and chairman of the EXPORT-IMPORT BANK, an independent government agency charged with facilitating the export of U.S. goods and services. In 1976 he left government to return to private law practice in New York and Washington, D.C., though he did return to accept an appointment to President GERALD R. FORD's Foreign Intelligence Advisory Board.

In 1981 Casey embarked on what was to be the final and most controversial chapter of his career when President RONALD REAGAN appointed him director of the CIA. The nomination was criticized by some members of Congress as blatantly political because Casey had run Reagan's 1980 presidential campaign. Nevertheless, Casey eventually won congressional approval and became the first director of the agency to be given cabinet-level rank.

"AFFINITIES BETWEEN THE PROFESSION OF LAW AND INTELLIGENCE-GATHERING [INCLUDE] CONFRONTING THE PARADOX OF BEING AT THE SAME TIME SEEKERS OF TRUTH AND PARTISANS IN A CAUSE."

Known for his hard-driving and sometimes confrontational management style, Casey won early praise for improving the CIA's analytical work. But he also drew heavy criticism for the agency's political activity outside the United States when the CIA stepped up its support for anti-Communist organizations in developing countries. Under Casey the agency engaged in intelligence operations in Central America, where it mined Nicaraguan harbors and provided textbooks for the Nicaraguan contras (the rebels fighting the Marxist government of Nicaragua) on how to use violence against civilian officials.

Congress, angered by reports of the operations, voted in 1984 to make aid to the contras illegal. When a diversion of funds to the contras from arms sales to Iran came to light—in a scandal that became known as the IRAN-CONTRA Affair—Casey denied that he had any knowledge or involvement of such sales. Critics charged that as CIA director, Casey should have known about the affair, and suspected that Casey had played a larger role than he acknowledged. In addition, members of Congress criticized Casey for allowing CIA staff members wide latitude to circumvent the prohibition against giving aid to the contras.

Casey was to testify before a Senate panel about the CIA's role in the sale of arms to Iran in December 1986 but became ill and was hospitalized the day before he was to appear. He then underwent surgery for removal of a malignant brain tumor and it was also reported that he was suffering from prostate cancer. In February 1987, after several weeks in the hospital, Casey resigned his post at the CIA. Later that spring congressional hearings on the Iran-Contra Affair commenced. The first witness, retired Air Force major general Richard V. Secord, testified that Casey was involved in providing arms to the Nicaraguan rebels after Congress had outlawed such activity. However, the nature and extent of any involvement by Casey remained unclear. On May 7, 1987, Casey died of pneumonia.

Casey's death left many unanswered questions about the Iran-Contra Affair. However, both Republicans and Democrats praised Casey for his patriotism, intellect, and commitment to public service.

**CASH BASIS** 📖 A method of ACCOUNTING that considers only money actually received as income and only money actually paid out as expense. 📖

For INCOME TAX purposes, TAXABLE INCOME is computed under cash basis accounting as the difference between income received and expenses paid out within the tax year.

Cash basis accounting is not the same as ACCRUAL BASIS accounting.

**CASH SURRENDER VALUE** The amount of money that an INSURANCE company pays an insured upon cancellation of a life insurance policy before death and which is a specific figure assigned to the policy at that particular time, reduced by a charge for administrative expenses.

The cash surrender value of an insurance policy is not based upon its actual value, but upon its reserve value—the face amount of the contract discounted at a specific rate of interest according to the insured's life expectancy. Not all life insurance policies have cash surrender values; the terms of the policy must so provide.

**CASUAL** Irregular, occasional, or accidental; happening without being planned or foreseen.

The term is used to describe an event that is unanticipated or unusual. A *casual sale* is one that is not customary, or done in the usual course of business—such as a jeweler occasionally selling vacuum cleaners.

Casual employment is irregular, periodic, or seasonal employment, such as someone selling ice cream only during the summer. WORKERS' COMPENSATION laws in many states do not apply to casual employment.

**CASUAL EJECTOR** A fictitious and nominal defendant in an action of EJECTMENT.

Ejectment was one of the old common-law FORMS OF ACTION. It could be used to oust an intruder on the plaintiff's land, such as a holdover tenant. It could also be used when there was no intruder, but the owner wished to remove any doubt about his or her right to the land without waiting for someone to sue him or her. In such a case, the strict form of procedure required that the plaintiff name a defendant even when none actually existed. The action was brought against a fictitious person called the casual ejector. The name JOHN DOE was used often for this nonexistent defendant.

**CASUALTY** A serious or fatal ACCIDENT. A person or thing injured, lost, or destroyed. A disastrous occurrence due to sudden, unexpected, or unusual cause. Accident; misfortune or mishap; that which comes by chance or without design. A loss from such an event or cause, as by fire, shipwreck, lightning, etc.

An *inevitable casualty* is one that occurs through no fault of anyone. It happens totally without design, as in the case of an accident resulting from an ACT OF GOD, such as a house struck by lightning or flooded by a storm.

A *casualty loss* is a tax deduction that can be taken for an accident that is incurred in a trade or business, in a transaction entered into for profit, or for the complete or partial loss or destruction of property owned by the taxpayer. It arises from certain specific events such as a fire, an auto accident, or a flood. Casualty losses are computed subject to special rules and are treated as itemized deductions.

Many people purchase *casualty insurance* so that they will be protected or covered in the event of specific misfortune or accident. It is a type of INSURANCE that covers losses resulting from injuries to people.

**CASUS BELLI** [*Latin, Cause of war.*] A term used in INTERNATIONAL LAW to describe an event or occurrence giving rise to or justifying war.

See also WAR.

**CATEGORICAL** That which is unqualified or unconditional.

A *categorical imperative* is a rule, command, or moral obligation that is absolutely and universally binding.

Categorical is also used to describe programs limited to or designed for certain classes of people. Categorical assistance plans are social WELFARE programs extending benefits to members of a particular group, such as Aid to the Elderly, Aid to the Blind, or Aid to Families with Dependent Children.

BIOGRAPHY

**CATON, JOHN DEAN** John Dean Caton was born March 19, 1812, in Monroe, New York. He was admitted to the Illinois bar in 1835. He achieved success in various fields of public service and received an honorary doctor of laws degree from Hamilton College in 1866.

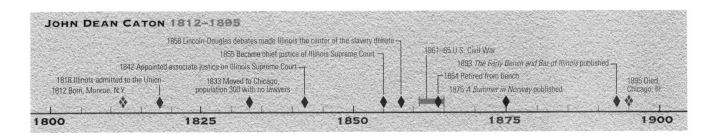

JOHN DEAN CATON 1812–1895

1858 Lincoln-Douglas debates made Illinois the center of the slavery debate
1855 Became chief justice of Illinois Supreme Court
1842 Appointed associate justice on Illinois Supreme Court
1818 Illinois admitted to the Union
1812 Born, Monroe, N.Y.
1833 Moved to Chicago, population 300 with no lawyers
1861–65 U.S. Civil War
1893 *The Early Bench and Bar of Illinois* published
1864 Retired from bench
1875 *A Summer in Norway* published
1895 Died, Chicago, Ill.

1800    1825    1850    1875    1900

In 1834 the first political convention was held in Illinois and Caton participated as its secretary as well as a member. He served on the Illinois Supreme Court, beginning as an associate justice from 1842 to 1864, and acting as chief justice in 1855 and again from 1857 to 1864.

In addition to his legal and political careers, Caton served as president of the Illinois and Mississippi Telegraphic Company from 1852 to 1867, performed the duties of justice of the peace in Ottawa, and gained recognition as an author. His most famous works are *A Summer in Norway*, written in 1875, and *The Antelope and Deer of America*, published in 1877. Caton also contributed numerous articles on nature to the Ottawa Academy of Science.

Caton died July 30, 1895, in Chicago, Illinois.

**CATRON, JOHN**   John Catron served as an associate justice of the U.S. Supreme Court from 1836 to 1865. During his career on the Court Catron was a staunch defender of STATES' RIGHTS and the institution of SLAVERY. He participated in the landmark decisions upholding the power of state governments to regulate local aspects of interstate commerce and, in *Dred Scott v. Sandford*, 60 U.S. (19 How.) 393, 15 L. Ed. 691 (1856), he voted with the Court in deciding that an ex-slave had no rights as a CITIZEN. Despite personal Southern affiliations and his own support of slavery, he backed the Union in the Civil War. A close friend of Andrew Jackson's as early as the War of 1812 and a fellow resident of Nashville, Catron was a true Jacksonian in his outlook. His judicial career and opinions—from a suspicion of large corporations to a fervent support of states' rights—bear all the marks of Jacksonian democracy.

Catron was probably born in Pennsylvania in 1786, a descendant of poor German immigrants. His father, Peter Catron, worked with horses in Pennsylvania and Virginia, and moved to Kentucky in 1804, hoping to establish his own horse farm. Catron grew up with little formal education. He supported himself and his

"THE LAW IS A GREAT AND GROWING SCIENCE, WHICH MUST ENLARGE AND EXPAND WITH THE ADVANCEMENT OF SOCIETY."

**BIOGRAPHY**

*John Catron*

family by herding cattle and grooming horses but he found time to read the classics as well. Around 1812 Catron moved to Sparta, in Tennessee's Cumberland Mountains region. At about the same time he married Matilda Childress; the couple had no children.

Catron read law briefly in Sparta and then joined the Second Tennessee Regiment, a group of local volunteers who sought to avenge the massacre of Fort Mims by the Creek Indians. This unit eventually joined General ANDREW JACKSON's army in Alabama and fought in the War of 1812. Catron became friendly with Jackson, who had passed the bar and served as a judge, and the two corresponded frequently in subsequent years.

After the war Catron returned to the Cumberland Mountains and resumed his legal studies. He was admitted to the Tennessee bar in 1815 and worked both as an attorney in a general legal practice and as a prosecutor in a circuit court. In 1818, Jackson suggested that Catron move to Nashville, then a growing frontier town, where Jackson himself lived and had a plantation. Catron took his advice and developed a lucrative practice in Nashville, with much of his work involving land titles, a busy area of the law on the rapidly growing frontier. By 1824 he was elected to the bench of Tennessee's highest court, the Court of Errors and Appeals. In 1831, the Tennessee legislature created the office of chief justice of the Supreme Court of Errors and Appeals and elected Catron to serve in it. He held the position until 1834.

As a judge, Catron worked principally to resolve the morass of conflicting land claims then before the courts, but he dealt with other issues as well. In separate 1829 rulings Catron denounced both gambling and DUELING, calling the latter no more than "honorable homicide." "The law knows it as a wicked and willful murder, and it is our duty to treat it as such," wrote Catron in his decision for *Smith v. State*, 9 Tenn. 228. "We are placed here firmly and fearlessly to execute the laws of the land, not visionary codes of honor, framed to subserve

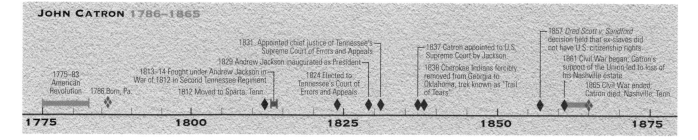

JOHN CATRON 1786–1865

1775–83 American Revolution   1786 Born, Pa.

1813–14 Fought under Andrew Jackson in War of 1812 in Second Tennessee Regiment
1812 Moved to Sparta, Tenn.

1831 Appointed chief justice of Tennessee's Supreme Court of Errors and Appeals
1829 Andrew Jackson inaugurated as President
1824 Elected to Tennessee's Court of Errors and Appeals

1837 Catron appointed to U.S. Supreme Court by Jackson
1838 Cherokee Indians forcibly removed from Georgia to Oklahoma, trek known as "Trail of Tears"

1857 *Dred Scott v. Sandford* decision held that ex-slaves did not have U.S. citizenship rights
1861 Civil War began; Catron's support of the Union led to loss of his Nashville estate
1865 Civil War ended; Catron died, Nashville, Tenn.

1775        1800        1825        1850        1875

the purposes of destruction." In an 1834 case, *Fisher's Negroes v. Dabbs*, 14 Tenn. 119, Catron ruled on the issue of freeing slaves. Slave owners would often grant manumission, or freedom, to their slaves through their wills. Catron argued that the state must approve such contracts before they can be valid, because, he wrote, "free negroes are a very dangerous and most objectionable population where slaves are numerous." Nor would it do to send freed slaves to states where slavery was not practiced, according to Catron. Whether in a slaveholding or nonslaveholding society, the freed African American is "a degraded outcast, and his fancied freedom a delusion." Slaves could only be freed, Catron wrote, if they were sent to the African nation of Liberia.

American Indian affairs, particularly relating to the Cherokee nation, were another pressing issue during Catron's tenure on the Tennessee high court. In 1833, the state legislature, following the earlier example of Georgia's general assembly, passed laws giving itself JURISDICTION over Cherokee land within its boundaries. In *State v. Foreman*, 16 Tenn. 256, it was charged that these laws were unconstitutional. Catron upheld the state laws in a long opinion notable for its brutal attitude toward the Indians. "It was more just," Catron wrote, "that the country should be peopled by Europeans, than continue the haunts of savage beasts, and of men yet more fierce and savage." The Indians were, in his mind, "mere wandering tribes of savages" who "deserve to be exterminated as savage and pernicious beasts." Furthermore, it was simply by right of power that whites could exert their dominance: "Our claim is based on the right to coerce obedience. The claim may be denounced by the moralist. We answer, it is the law of the land. Without its assertion and vigorous execution, this continent never could have been inhabited by our ancestors." The issue resurfaced a few years later during MARTIN VAN BUREN'S presidency when the Cherokee were forced to give up their land and make a long march on what was called the Trail of Tears to land west of the Mississippi.

In 1836 Catron directed Van Buren's presidential campaign in Tennessee. Van Buren won the election, succeeding fellow Democrat Jackson. On his last day in office, March 3, 1837, Jackson appointed two new members—Catron and John McKinley—to the U.S. Supreme Court as required by the Judiciary Act of 1837, which increased the size of the Court from seven to nine members. Catron was confirmed five days later and at age fifty-one became a

sitting justice with ROGER B. TANEY serving as chief justice.

Catron was a strong advocate of states' rights during his tenure on the Court. In the *Thurlow v. Com. of Mass.* cases, 46 U.S. (5 How.) 504, 12 L. Ed. 256 (1847), Catron wrote two opinions upholding the rights of states to regulate the importation of liquor from other states and countries. The cases touched on interpretation of the COMMERCE CLAUSE, the part of the Constitution—Article I, Section 8, Clause 3—that gives the federal government power "[t]o regulate Commerce with foreign Nations, and among the several States, and with the Indian Tribes." Catron argued that the federal government does not have exclusive power to regulate interstate commerce and that where it does not act to regulate commerce the states are free to do so. The state laws in question had encroached on no laws passed by Congress and were therefore valid. According to Catron, "the police power was not touched by the Constitution, but left to the States as the Constitution found it." Catron and the Court ruled similarly in *Cooley v. Board of Wardens*, 53 U.S. (12 How.) 299, 13 L. Ed. 996 (1851), again upholding the ability of states to regulate local aspects of interstate commerce.

Catron dissented from the Court's opinion in several cases involving the states' ability to regulate CORPORATIONS. In one case in which the Court had ruled in favor of a large corporation, Catron expressed concern regarding "the unparalleled increase of corporations throughout the Union . . . ; the ease with which charters containing exclusive privileges and exemptions are obtained; the vast amount of property, power, and exclusive benefits, prejudicial to other classes of society that are vested in and held by these numerous bodies of associated wealth" (*Ohio Life Insurance & Trust Co. v. Debolt*, 57 U.S. [16 How.] 416, 14 L. Ed. 997 [1853]).

Catron played an important role in the famous *Dred Scott* case (*Dred Scott v. Sandford*, 60 U.S. [19 How.] 393, 15 L. Ed. 691 [1857]), which concerned the highly controversial issue of slavery in the territories. Dred Scott was a slave from Missouri whose owner took him into Illinois, where slavery had been outlawed, and the Louisiana Territory, where it had been forbidden as well by the MISSOURI COMPROMISE, the 1820 agreement that attempted to resolve the dispute as to whether new states would be admitted to the Union as free or slave states. When Scott returned to Missouri, he brought suit against his owner, saying that he was free

"POLITICAL SOVEREIGNTY, IN ITS TRUE SENSE, EXISTS ONLY WITH THE PEOPLE. . . . AND IS [THE] POLITICAL AXIOM UPON WHICH THE AMERICAN GOVERNMENT [HAS] BEEN BASED."

because he had resided in free territory. In its decision, the Court, with Catron writing a concurring opinion, held that a slave could not become a citizen under the U.S. Constitution. Scott, the Court argued, was not a citizen and therefore could not sue in federal courts. Chief Justice Taney went further and declared the Missouri Compromise unconstitutional, denying the authority of Congress to exclude slavery from the territories. This was only the second time the Supreme Court had found an act of Congress unconstitutional, the first having been the 1803 decision *Marbury v. Madison* (5 U.S. 137, 1 Cranch 137, 2 L. Ed. 60 [1803]). Many viewed *Dred Scott* as a pro-slavery ruling from a Supreme Court dominated by a Southern majority. The ruling may very well have hastened the coming of the Civil War.

In his concurring opinion Catron emphasized that Congress could not abridge the property rights of slave-owning citizens in the Louisiana Territory by outlawing slavery. He also argued that the Missouri Compromise violated the constitutional guarantee of equal PRIVILEGES AND IMMUNITIES to citizens of all states, a guarantee that was, Catron wrote, a "leading feature of the constitution—a feature on which the Union depends, and which secures to the respective States and their citizens an entire equality of rights" (60 U.S. 393 at 529). Three of the seven concurring justices argued that an African American descended from slaves had no rights as a U.S. citizen and no standing in court. Catron was one of four justices who did not address this last question of whether a freed slave was a citizen or not.

Despite his Southern leanings and the subsequent loss of his estate, Catron supported the Union during the Civil War. As hostilities began to mount and war neared in March 1861, Catron returned to Nashville to try to keep the border states of his judicial circuit—Tennessee, Kentucky, and Missouri—in the Union. Of these, only Tennessee would eventually join the Confederacy. After an angry mob confronted him when he tried to hold federal court in Nashville he was forced to leave for Washington, D.C., accompanied by a military escort, leaving behind an estate worth more than $100,000. During the war Catron continued to support the Union by broadly interpreting the federal government's war powers. In one case he wrote an opinion refusing to release a prisoner if evidence showed that he was a Confederate sympathizer. After 1862 Catron also worked hard to keep order in the states forming his new circuit: Tennessee, Arkansas, Louisiana, Texas, and Kentucky. He stayed in close touch with President ABRAHAM LINCOLN and worked hard to keep the federal judiciary effective during the war.

On May 30, 1865, not long after the South surrendered, Catron died in his adopted city of Nashville, one of the last embodiments of Jacksonian democracy to leave the national scene.

### CROSS-REFERENCES

*Dred Scott v. Sandford;* Judicial Review; Native American Law.

**CAUSA MORTIS** [*Latin, In contemplation of approaching death.*] A phrase sometimes used in reference to a deathbed GIFT, or a gift *causa mortis,* since the giving of the gift is made in expectation of approaching death. A gift causa mortis is distinguishable from a gift INTER VIVOS, which is a gift made during the donor's (the giver's) lifetime.

The DONOR of the gift of PERSONAL PROPERTY must expect to die imminently from a particular ailment or event. This has important consequences in terms of the donor's ability to revoke the gift.

For example, an elderly man is suffering from pneumonia and believes he is going to die as a result of the sickness. He tells his grandson that if he dies, he will give the grandson his pocket watch. If the man recovers and wants to retain his watch, he will be able to do so, because a gift *causa mortis* is effective only if made in CONTEMPLATION OF DEATH due to a known condition and the donor actually dies as a result of that condition.

A gift *causa mortis* is taxed under federal ESTATE TAX law in the same way as a gift bequeathed by a WILL.

**CAUSE** Each separate antecedent of an event. Something that precedes and brings about an effect or a result. A reason for an action or condition. A ground of a legal ACTION. An agent that brings something about. That which in some manner is accountable for a condition that brings about an effect or that produces a cause for the resultant action or state.

A suit, litigation, or action. Any question, civil or criminal, litigated or contested before a court of justice.

If an individual is fired from a job at the bank for EMBEZZLEMENT, he or she is fired *for cause*—as distinguished from decisions or actions considered to be ARBITRARY or capricious.

In CRIMINAL PROCEDURE law, PROBABLE CAUSE is the reasonable basis for the belief that someone has committed a particular crime. Before someone may be arrested or searched by a police officer without a warrant, probable cause must exist. This requirement is imposed to protect people from unreasonable or unrestricted invasions or intrusions by the government. See also SEARCHES AND SEIZURES.

In the law of TORTS, the concept of causality is essential to a person's ability to successfully bring an action for injury against another person. The injured party must establish that the other person brought about the alleged harm. A defendant's LIABILITY is CONTINGENT upon the connection between his or her conduct and the injury to the plaintiff. The plaintiff must prove that his or her injury would not have occurred BUT FOR the defendant's NEGLIGENCE or intentional conduct.

The *actual cause* is the event directly responsible for an injury. If one person shoves another, thereby knocking the other person out an open window and he or she breaks a leg as a result of the fall, the shove is the actual cause of the injury. The IMMEDIATE CAUSE of the injury in this case would be the fall, since it is the cause that came right before the injury, with no intermediate causes. In some cases the actual cause and the immediate cause of an injury may be the same.

*Concurrent causes* are events occurring simultaneously to produce a given result. They are contemporaneous but either event alone would bring about the effect that occurs. If one person stabs another person who is simultaneously being shot by a third person, either act alone could cause the person's injury.

An INTERVENING CAUSE is one that interrupts the normal flow of events between the wrong and the injury. It comes between an expected sequence of occurrences to produce an unanticipated result. If someone driving under the influence of alcohol grazes a telephone pole that is rotted and thus knocks it down, the condition of the pole would be the intervening cause of its collapse. This is important in determining the liability of the intoxicated driver. If the telephone company knew or should have known about the unsafe condition of the pole and negligently failed to replace it, the telephone company would be responsible for the harm caused by the falling pole. Depending upon how hard the driver hit the pole, the driver may be held contributorily negligent, or partially liable, for the accident that took place.

An *intervening efficient cause* is one that totally supersedes the original wrongful act or omission. For example, an intoxicated cabdriver is transporting a person in a cab with faulty brakes. An accident occurs, which is a direct result of the intoxication rather than the faulty brakes. The injury resulting to the passenger is

attributable to the driver's condition. The intervening efficient cause thereby broke the causal connection between the original wrong of the faulty brakes and the injury.

The PROXIMATE CAUSE of an injury is the act or omission of an act without which the harm would not have occurred. This is a concept in the law of torts and involves the question of whether or not a defendant's conduct is so significant as to make him or her liable for a resulting injury. For example, a woman throws a lighted match into a wastepaper basket which starts a fire that burns down a building. The wind carries the flames to the building next door. Her act of throwing the match would be the proximate cause of the fire and the resulting damage; however, she may not be held fully liable for all resulting consequences.

An *unforeseeable cause* is one that unexpectedly and unpredictably results from the proximate cause. The degree of injury sustained is unanticipated or far removed from the negligent or intentional conduct that took place. For example, if a customer in a supermarket irritates a clerk and the clerk pushes the customer out of the way, which results in prolonged bleeding because the person is a hemophiliac, the bleeding is an unforeseeable consequence of the clerk's action. Even if the clerk intentionally pushed the customer, the resulting injury is clearly far removed from the conduct.

A *remote cause* is one that is removed or separate from the proximate cause of an injury. If the injuries suffered by a person admitted to a hospital after being hit by a truck are aggravated by MALPRACTICE, the malpractice is a remote cause of injury to that person. The fact that the cause of an injury is remote does not relieve a defendant of liability for the act or

*If one of these two trains had faulty brakes that prevented the driver from stopping sooner, the bad brakes may have been an intervening cause, but not the actual cause of the crash.*

omission, but there may be an apportionment of liability between the defendants.

**CAUSE OF ACTION** The fact or combination of facts that gives a person the right to seek judicial REDRESS or RELIEF against another. Also, the legal theory forming the basis of a lawsuit.

The cause of action is the heart of the COMPLAINT, which is the PLEADING that initiates a lawsuit. Without an adequately stated cause of action the plaintiff's case can be dismissed at the outset. It is not sufficient merely to state that certain events occurred that entitle the plaintiff to relief. All the elements of each cause of action must be detailed in the complaint. The claims must be supported by the FACTS, the law, and a conclusion that flows from the application of the law to those facts.

The cause of action is often stated in the form of a syllogism, a form of deductive reasoning that begins with a major premise (the applicable RULE OF LAW), proceeds to a minor premise (the facts that gave rise to the CLAIM), and ends with a conclusion. In a cause of action for BATTERY, the rule of law is that any intentional, unpermitted act that causes a harmful or offensive touching of another is a battery. This is the major premise and is stated first. Supporting facts, constituting the minor premise, appear after the rule of law. For example, a statement of facts for a case of battery might be "The plaintiff, while walking through ABC Store on the afternoon of March 11, 1998, was tackled by the defendant, a security guard for the store, who knocked the plaintiff to the floor and held her there by kneeling on her back and holding her arms behind her, while screaming in her ear to open her shopping bag. These actions caused the plaintiff to suffer injuries to her head, chest, shoulders, neck, and back." The cause of action

*A cause of action against this protester might include his blocking entry to a clinic. A cause of action against the police officers might include injury to the protester as he was moved.*

AP/WIDE WORLD PHOTOS

concludes with a statement that the defendant is responsible for the plaintiff's injuries and that the plaintiff is entitled to compensation from the defendant.

The facts or circumstances that entitle a person to seek judicial relief may create more than one cause of action. For example, in the preceding example, the plaintiff might assert claims for assault, battery, intentional infliction of emotional distress, and violation of civil rights. She might also bring claims for negligent hiring (if the guard had a history of violent behavior which the store failed to discover) or negligent supervision. (When damages are caused by an employee it is common to sue both the employee and the employer.) All these causes of action arise from the same set of facts and circumstances but are supported by different rules of law and constitute separate claims for relief.

A cause of action can arise from an act, a failure to perform a legal obligation, a breach of duty, or a violation or invasion of a right. The importance of the act, failure, breach, or violation lies in its legal effect or characterization and in how the facts and circumstances, considered as a whole, relate to applicable law. A set of facts may have no legal effect in one situation, whereas the same or similar facts may have significant legal implications in another situation. For example, tackling a shoplifting suspect who is brandishing a gun is a legitimate action by a security guard and probably would not support a claim for relief if the suspect were injured in the fracas. On the other hand, tackling a shopper who merely acts in a suspicious manner while carrying a shopping bag is a questionable exercise of a guard's duty and may well give rise to JUSTICIABLE causes of action.

**CAVEAT** [Latin, *Let him beware.*] A warning; ADMONITION. A formal notice or warning given by an interested party to a court, judge, or ministerial officer in opposition to certain acts within his or her power and jurisdiction.

Originally, a *caveat* was a document that could be served on either a judge or a public official to give him or her notice that he or she should discontinue a certain proceeding until an opposing party was given an opportunity to be heard.

Used in the past by someone objecting to the appointment of an executor or administrator of an estate or to the granting of a patent for an invention, the term *caveat* is rarely used by modern attorneys.

**CAVEAT EMPTOR** [Latin, *Let the buyer beware.*] A warning that notifies a buyer that the goods he or she is buying are "AS IS," or subject to all defects.

When a sale is subject to this warning the purchaser assumes the risk that the product might be either defective or unsuitable to his or her needs.

This rule is not designed to shield sellers who engage in FRAUD or BAD FAITH dealing by making false or misleading representations about the quality or condition of a particular product. It merely summarizes the concept that a purchaser must examine, judge, and test a product considered for purchase himself or herself.

The modern trend in laws protecting consumers, however, has minimized the importance of this rule. Although the buyer is still required to make a reasonable inspection of goods upon purchase, increased responsibilities have been placed upon the seller, and the doctrine of *caveat venditor* (Latin for "let the seller beware") has become more prevalent. Generally, there is a legal presumption that a seller makes certain warranties unless the buyer and the seller agree otherwise. One such WARRANTY is the implied warranty of merchantability. If a person buys soap, for example, there is an implied warranty that it will clean; if a person buys skis, there is an implied warranty that they will be safe to use on the slopes.

A seller who is in the business of regularly selling a particular type of goods has still greater responsibilities in dealing with an average customer. A person purchasing antiques from an antique dealer, or jewelry from a jeweler, is justified in his or her reliance on the expertise of the seller.

If both the buyer and the seller are negotiating from equal bargaining positions, however, the doctrine of *caveat emptor* would apply.

See also CONSUMER PROTECTION; SALES.

## CEASE AND DESIST ORDER
An order issued by an administrative agency or a court proscribing a person or a business entity from continuing a particular course of conduct.

The force and effect of a cease and desist order are similar to those of an INJUNCTION issued by a court.

## CEDE
To yield up; to assign; to grant; to surrender; to withdraw. Generally used to designate the transfer of territory from one government to another.

## CELEBRATION OF MARRIAGE
A colloquial phrase that refers to the solemnization or formalization of a MARRIAGE.

In a number of states there must be a celebration of a marriage through some type of official government ceremony before a marriage will be legally recognized.

Some statutes provide that every JUSTICE OF THE PEACE of a particular state, every minister, and every religious society be empowered to solemnize marriage. The type of celebration required varies according to state law and religious custom.

## CELIA, A SLAVE
Celia, a slave, was probably born in Missouri in 1836. No documentation of her birth date, birthplace, or parentage exists. Her recorded history begins in the summer of 1850 when she was purchased by Robert Newsom, of Fulton Township, Calloway County, Missouri; at the time of the transaction she was about fourteen years old. Celia's recorded history ends five and a half years later when she was tried and hanged for the MURDER of her owner; she was nineteen years old and the mother of at least two children at the time of her death. Her final resting place and the fate of her children are unknown.

The circumstances of Celia's short life—and the events that led to her hanging—illustrate the realities of slave life in the South and the personal choices the institution of SLAVERY forced upon slaves and slaveholders. The course and outcome of Celia's TRIAL were influenced by individuals and a court system that were trying to reconcile the personal consequences of slavery with existing moral codes, politics, and economics—at a time when nationwide struggles over the same issues were increasingly heated and often violent.

By 1850, when knowledge of Celia begins, Missouri had already been at the center of the national slavery debate for more than a quarter of a century. The U.S. Congress had confronted the dilemma presented by the existence of slavery in a free society in 1819 when Missouri petitioned for statehood. Angry and emotional debates considered whether a territory should be asked to abandon slavery as a condition of statehood. Congress preempted the debate by passing the MISSOURI COMPROMISE, under which it preserved the nation's balance by admitting Maine as a free state in 1820 and Missouri as a slave state in 1821. The Missouri Compromise also drew a line between North and South by limiting the expansion of slavery in the Louisiana Territory to areas south of Missouri.

During this volatile time, Newsom left Virginia and brought his wife and children to the Missouri Territory. In the fall of 1822, with statehood granted and slavery assured for his new home, Newsom settled in southern Calloway County. Hard work and slave labor made him a prosperous farmer—and Calloway County went on to become a large slave-holding county.

Because many core issues of the slave debate were unresolved by the Missouri Compromise, leaders on both sides of the issue knew that it was only a matter of time before the nation's expansion would force another confrontation. That confrontation came in 1850 when Congress found itself waging a battle over the expansion of slavery in territories gained as a result of the Mexican War. Northern politicians wanted to stop the expansion of slavery and assure the admission of California to the Union as a free state. Their Southern counterparts did not want slavery prohibited in territories for which Southern soldiers had fought and died. Missouri, with roughly equal numbers of citizens supporting each side of the issue, was as deeply divided as the nation.

The residents of agriculture-based, slave-holding Calloway County—including Newsom—probably favored the pro-slavery rhetoric and politics described in the papers of the day. The 1850 census for Calloway County, which shows that Newsom owned five male slaves, supports this assumption, as does Newsom's decision to purchase Celia even while the controversy over slavery was escalating to its ultimate conclusion—civil war.

In all likelihood, however, Newsom did not purchase Celia as a political statement. His reasons for buying Celia were much more personal. Newsom's wife had died in 1849. Following her death, his household comprised a widowed daughter named Virginia Waynescot; her children, James Coffee Waynescot, Amelia Waynescot, and Thomas Waynescot; and an unmarried daughter, Mary Newsom. Two sons, Harry Newsom and David Newsom, were married and living nearby.

When Newsom went to purchase Celia, outward appearances suggested that he was looking for a domestic servant to assist his daughters with cooking and household work. Subsequent trial testimony and transcripts indicate otherwise. At any rate, in the spring of 1850 Newsom traveled by wagon to Audrain County, a day's ride to the north of his home, to buy his new slave. On the return trip, Newsom raped the young girl and established the true nature of her future role in the Newsom household.

Over the next four years Celia's life revolved around her role as Newsom's conjugal partner. He provided her with a brick cabin near the main house and other material possessions indicating both her status and his affection for her. He visited her often and he was most likely the father of her first two children.

The kind of relationship Newsom had with Celia was fairly widespread in the South but seldom acknowledged or publicly condoned. Given the daily rhythms and routines of rural life in 1850 Missouri, Newsom's adult daughters were most likely aware of their father's intimate relationship with Celia; because of their economic dependence on their father they also likely did not make an issue of his relationship with the slave. Though not much is known about the details of Celia's interaction with members of the Newsom household, one author concluded from court documents that she must have been a disturbing presence on the Newsom farm.

By 1854, Celia had tired of Newsom's attentions and begun a forbidden relationship with a Newsom slave named George. Sometime in early 1855 George started staying in Celia's cabin when Newsom was not there. Within months, Celia was pregnant and uncertain of the child's father. George, believing the child to be his, pressured Celia to end her physical relationship with their owner. Newsom, believing the child to be his, and unaware of Celia's intimate friendship with George, saw no reason to change the established pattern of their relationship.

Caught in the middle, Celia was forced to make a choice that would eventually cost her her life. At some point in June of 1855, Celia made an attempt to satisfy George's demands and to stop Newsom's sexual advances by appealing to Newsom's daughters. She threatened to hurt Newsom if he did not stop forcing his attentions on her while she was ill (court documents indicate that the early stages of Celia's third pregnancy were difficult, causing her to be sick much of the time). It is not known if his daughters spoke to Newsom on Celia's behalf but it is clear that Newsom's sexual demands on her did not stop. On Saturday, June 23, Celia

*Slaves such as Celia often lived in tiny houses like this one near Savannah, Georgia.*

CORBIS-BETTMANN

confronted her master directly, asking him to leave her alone. He ignored her request and told her he would visit her cabin that evening.

Newsom went to Celia's cabin later that evening and was never seen again. When he did not appear for breakfast on Sunday morning his children and neighbors began to search for him and to question the slaves. A statement from Celia's lover, George, led the family to suspect her involvement in Newsom's disappearance. George told the search party that they were not likely to find anything unless they searched near Celia's cabin.

Celia initially denied any involvement in Newsom's disappearance. But worn down by questioning, she finally confessed to his murder. She admitted that Newsom had come to her cabin the night before. She described how she struck him twice with a large stick to stop his advances. Realizing she had killed him, she decided to burn his body in the fireplace to cover her crime. She buried the bones that did not burn under the hearth and she enlisted the help of Newsom's own grandson, James Coffee Waynescot, to carry the ashes out of the cabin on Sunday morning. A buckle and buttons retrieved from the ashes and bone fragments found under the hearth confirmed her story.

On Monday, June 25, *State v. Celia, a Slave*, Celia File No. 4496, began. Two local justices, D. M. Whyte and Isaac P. Howe, and a jury of six men—George Thomas, Daniel Robinson, John Wells, Simpson Hyton, George Brown, and John Carrington—considered an AFFIDAVIT filed by David Newsom accusing Celia of murder. They found PROBABLE CAUSE to charge her with murder and she was arrested and taken to the Fulton County jail. An October trial date was set and Judge William Augustus Hall was named to preside.

Newspaper accounts of the murder at the Newsom farm fueled local fears by reporting that the crime was committed without sufficient cause (no mention was made of Celia's intimate relationship with the victim or her reasons for attacking him). These fears, along with Celia's physical condition and the belief that her two children were in the cabin at the time of the murder, led the community to believe that Celia did not commit the crime on her own.

Acts of violence by slaves and the possibility of CONSPIRACY and organized slave rebellion were very much on the minds of Calloway County residents in the spring of 1855. A free-slave conflict in neighboring Kansas Territory had moved from debate to bloodshed. Passage of the KANSAS-NEBRASKA ACT, which called for "popular sovereignty" in the territo-ries, along with a threatened repeal of the Missouri Compromise, made Kansas Territory a national battleground. Northern activists channeled antislavery settlers into the territory hoping they would eventually vote against slav-ery. Slaves themselves were encouraged to com-mit violent acts as a means of asserting their rights and winning their freedom. Missouri residents poured across the Kansas-Missouri border to antagonize Northern settlers, support pro-slavery residents, and keep the slaves in submission.

With supporters on both sides of the slavery issue watching the proceedings, Judge Hall was under pressure to see that Celia received cred-ible representation at her trial. On August 16 he appointed John Jameson and his associates to defend her. Jameson was a popular citizen in Fulton Township. He was a slave owner but he was not personally involved in the ongoing slavery debates. He had practiced law in the community for three decades and had repre-sented Missouri for three terms in the U.S. Congress. With political savvy and a reputation as an excellent trial lawyer, Jameson was accept-able to those on both sides of the conflict.

On October 9 Celia entered the Calloway County Courthouse for trial. After dealing with numerous preliminary and procedural matters, including JURY selection, Celia's attorneys en-tered a plea of not guilty to the charge of murdering Newsom. Like the inquest jury, Ce-lia's trial jury was made up of male residents of the county: all were married and had children, all but one were farmers, about half were slave owners, and none were as prosperous as New-som. Though certainly not Celia's peers, they were as good a jury as could be expected for the time.

The next day testimony began. The prosecu-tion stressed the facts of the case and reminded the jury that Celia had confessed to the murder.

The defense focused on Celia's sexual ex-ploitation and the motive for her actions. Jame-son argued that Celia was entitled, by law, to use DEADLY FORCE to protect herself from RAPE, regardless of her previous sexual relationship with the victim. His argument was unconven-tional and bold because it was based on a Missouri statute that had been created to pro-tect white women; in most of the South sexual assault on a slave was considered TRESPASS, and owners could not be accused of trespass on their own property.

After concluding their arguments, both sides were allowed to propose jury instructions for Judge Hall's consideration. Jameson requested several instructions that would have allowed

Celia to be ACQUITTED if the jury found from the evidence that she had killed Newsom in an effort to prevent his sexual advances. The prosecution objected to Jameson's instructions and Hall ultimately refused to deliver them to the jury. Denied any grounds for acquitting her, the jury found Celia guilty of murder.

On October 11 Celia's attorneys filed a MOTION to set aside the jury VERDICT and grant a new trial. Judge Hall's prejudicial rulings and his refusal to issue critical jury instructions were cited as grounds for the motion. On October 13 Hall denied the defense motion and Celia was sentenced to death by hanging on November 16. This execution date may have been set to allow for delivery of Celia's expected child; under Missouri law a pregnant woman could not be executed. Court records indicate she delivered a stillborn baby while in custody.

After the sentencing, Judge Hall was asked to issue a STAY of execution while Celia's case was appealed to the Missouri Supreme Court. He refused. Though no record of the appeals document exists, Jameson probably included many of the same arguments and issues outlined in his motion for a new trial. By early November the Missouri Supreme Court had not considered the APPEAL. When it looked as though Celia would be executed before her appeal was heard, her supporters took drastic measures. On the night of November 11 she was helped to "escape" from jail. She was not returned to custody until after her original execution date had passed. Upon her return a new execution date of December 21 was set.

On December 6 Jameson wrote a letter to Judge Abiel Leonard asking the Missouri Supreme Court to issue a stay of execution until the case could be heard. On December 14 the court ruled that it found no probable cause for an appeal. Accordingly, the stay of execution was refused. Celia's fate was sealed by the same court that had earlier exhibited its pro-slavery leanings in the famous *Dred Scott* decision, in which a majority of the court ruled that a slave remained a slave—even if he traveled and lived in free territory (*Dred Scott v. Sandford*, 60 U.S. (19 How.) 393, 15 L. Ed. 691 [1857]).

The Missouri Supreme Court's ruling in Celia's case was filed in the circuit court of Calloway County on December 18. On the afternoon of Friday, December 21, Celia was hanged for the murder of Newsom. In a final statement, she repeated her story: she had acted alone, she had struck Newsom to stop his advances, and she had not intended to kill him. Unable, or unwilling, to challenge the underlying beliefs and behaviors that allowed slavery to exist, Missouri's pre–Civil War supreme court failed to extend the protection of an existing law to a slave.

**CEMETERIES** 📖 Areas that are set aside by public authority or private persons for the burial of the dead. 📖

A *public cemetery* is open for use by the community at large while a *private cemetery* is used only by a small segment of a community or by a family.

A cemetery includes not only the actual grave sites but also surrounding areas such as avenues, walks, and grounds.

Cemeteries are not governed by laws that apply to real property or corporations due to their inherently different nature. Most states have established laws that specifically apply to cemeteries.

**Establishment and Regulation** The establishment of a cemetery involves the process of formally designating a tract of land for use for the burial of the dead. It must be set apart, marked, and distinguished from adjoining ground as a graveyard.

The state, in the exercise of its POLICE POWER, has the right to regulate the creation of cemeteries by providing for their establishment and discontinuance as well as to monitor their use. Private interests in the place of burial are subject to the control of public authorities, which have the right to require the disinterment of bodies if deemed necessary.

Burial sites may not be absolutely prohibited by legislative action inasmuch as they are considered indispensable and directly related to the public health. Provisions in corporate CHARTERS cannot prevent the exercise of police powers with regard to which lands may be used for burial purposes, since burial in certain places might create a public NUISANCE.

**Regulation by Municipal Corporations** Subject to express legislative authority, and by virtue of its general police powers, a municipality may reasonably regulate places of burial within its borders. The key requirement is that a municipality may not act arbitrarily with regard to the regulations it adopts.

The power of a municipality to regulate cemeteries is an ongoing one that may be exercised as required by considerations of public health and welfare. Regulations may prohibit such things as future burials in existing cemeteries, the enlargement of existing cemeteries, or the establishment of new ones.

A municipality may own and maintain a cemetery when it is expressly authorized to do so. General control may be exercised over a cemetery that a municipality owns, but control

*TOM MCCARTHY/PHOTOEDIT*

*This cemetery adjoins a residential area. A state or local government may not prohibit use of the cemetery simply because it is close to houses.*

may not be exercised arbitrarily, capriciously, or unreasonably.

**Corporations and Associations** A cemetery corporation, as defined expressly by statute, is any CORPORATION formed for the burial of the dead in a receptacle or vault. Such a corporation may or may not be organized for pecuniary profit and may or may not be organized under the general corporate law.

The members of a cemetery corporation are those people who own plots according to express statutory provisions. They cannot make a profit out of the sales of lots if the corporation is not for profit. Nor can they make a gift of their plot to another independent corporation.

If statute permits, cemetery corporations may issue STOCK and pay DIVIDENDS to stockholders. Stockholders may enact BYLAWS.

Some statutes provide that a cemetery may give land shares, which are certificates entitling the holder to receive a portion of the profit from the subsequent sales of plots, in exchange for payment for the land purchased. This type of certificate is not a stock certificate, but is in the nature of a nonnegotiable promise to pay money.

**Location** The establishment of cemeteries may be prohibited by state or local legislative bodies, but only under certain circumstances. The interment of DEAD BODIES is necessary and proper and therefore the prohibition of the establishment of a cemetery must be based on the potential danger to human life or health. State and municipal bodies are not permitted to prohibit burial for such reasons as the value of adjoining land being lessened or because a cemetery might be a source of annoyance to inhabitants of the surrounding community.

Under some statutory provisions a cemetery cannot be established within a certain distance of a private residence, store, or other place of business without the owner's consent. Similarly, certain statutes provide that, prior to the establishment of a cemetery, consent must be obtained from the county or municipal authorities within whose limits the cemetery will be located.

**Title and Rights of Owners of Plots, Grounds, or Graves** The purchaser of a plot in a cemetery is generally regarded as obtaining only a limited PROPERTY RIGHT. He or she acquires a PRIVILEGE, EASEMENT, or LICENSE to make burials in the purchased plot, exclusive of all other people, provided that the land remains a cemetery.

The plot owner's interest is a property right entitled to protection from invasion and the TITLE is a legal estate. The owner's rights are subject to the police power of the state as well as the rules of the cemetery and any restrictions made in the CONTRACT of sale.

A cemetery corporation may cancel the contract of sale of a plot where regulations of the corporation that are part of the contract are violated by the sale due to a MISTAKE of fact. A purchaser may, in turn, RESCIND the contract where substantial MISREPRESENTATIONS have been made by the corporation.

Plot holders cannot be prevented by cemetery owners from erecting markers, entering the grounds, or interring family members in the plots they own. If a plot owner dies INTESTATE, the rights to the plot pass to the HEIRS in the same manner that PERSONAL PROPERTY passes in the absence of a will. A gravestone or marker is the personal property of whoever places it near a grave and its ownership is passed to this person's heirs.

ABANDONMENT is the only way in which the use of land as a cemetery may cease. It takes place either by removal of all the interred bodies or by NEGLECT to such a degree that the property is no longer identifiable as a cemetery. The removal of bodies may be ordered by public authorities when necessitated by the public health. The owner of a cemetery may opt to discontinue the sale of plots as initially planned, but permission to do so from government officials might be a prerequisite.

**Duties as to Care and Maintenance**
The owner of a plot has the duty to care for and maintain the plot either personally or through an AGENT. A cemetery's TRUSTEES may supervise plots to prevent them from disintegrating to the point of unsightliness.

If a statute so requires, a cemetery association must care for its plots. If a charter imposes a duty upon the association to keep the grounds in repair, this obligation does not encompass plots sold to individuals.

A cemetery association has the duty to maintain the premises in a reasonably safe condition. This includes the proper maintenance of portions of the cemetery used for travel or occupation by attendants of burials.

Uniform and reasonable rules and regulations may be made for the care and management of lots by the proprietors of a cemetery. Such rules must be equal in their operation. An unreasonable rule would be to prohibit the owner of a lot from hiring his own caretaker; however, a rule requiring that such work be done by competent persons would be reasonable.

**Right of Burial** Everyone is entitled to a decent burial in a suitable place. The right to be interred in a particular cemetery is an easement, license, or privilege. An element of this right is the privilege to be buried according to the usual custom in the community and pursuant to the rules and regulations set forth by the proprietor of the cemetery. When an individual does not purchase a plot subject to any restrictions on burial, the proprietors have no subsequent power to limit such right unreasonably.

An individual who obtains the right to be buried in a cemetery subject to the control of a religious organization takes the plot subject to the organization's rules. This may limit the burial right to its members or to those in communion with such organizations. The church has exclusive JURISDICTION over the question of whether or not a person is in communion with a religious organization and thereby entitled to burial in its cemetery.

**Interference with Owner's Rights** A CAUSE OF ACTION may be based upon the interference with the rights of a plot owner. An unlawful and unwarranted interference with an individual's exercise of the right of burial in a cemetery lot is a TORT. An infringement of the rights of a plot owner may be prevented by an INJUNCTION if an injury is threatened.

Either criminal or civil LIABILITY, or both, exist for TRESPASS or other types of injuries to a cemetery or to individual burial plots.

If a burial ground or plot is wrongfully invaded or desecrated, an action of trespass may be brought against the wrongdoer.

VANDALISM and destruction of tombstones are criminal offenses. The person who erects a tombstone may maintain an action for injury to it. After that person's death, his or her heirs may prosecute such an action.

Generally, the measure of DAMAGES for trespass is the cost of restoration. Since there is a strong PUBLIC POLICY against injury to gravesites due to the indignity of the act, PUNITIVE DAMAGES—intended to deter future acts of desecration—may be awarded.

**CENSORSHIP**  The suppression or proscription of speech or writing that is deemed OBSCENE, indecent, or unduly controversial.

When a government agency prohibits such speech or writing, the party being censored frequently raises the FIRST AMENDMENT rights of freedom of speech and press.

The term *censorship* derives from the official duties of the Roman censor who, beginning in 443 B.C., conducted the census by counting, assessing, and evaluating the populace. Originally neutral in tone, the term has come to mean the suppression of ideas or images by the government or others with authority.

Throughout history, societies practiced various forms of censorship in the belief that the community, as represented by the government, was responsible for molding the individual. For example, the ancient Greek philosopher Plato advocated various degrees of censorship in *The Republic;* the content of important texts and the dissemination of knowledge were tightly controlled in ancient Chinese society as is much information in modern China; and for centuries the Roman Catholic Church's *Index Librorum Prohibitorum* proscribed much literature as contrary to the church's teachings.

The English-speaking world began wrestling with issues of censorship in the seventeenth century. In his *Areopagitica* (1644) John Milton argued in favor of the right to publish, free from government restraint. In the United States the First Amendment to the Constitution (1787) guaranteed FREEDOM OF SPEECH and FREEDOM OF THE PRESS.

The history and culture of the United States emphasize individual rights and demonstrate a wariness of governmental attempts to censor. Censorship in this country tests the First Amendment rights of individuals to communicate freely against the government's interests in curbing certain communications that it perceives as harmful to itself or the public.

**Abortion** In some cases, the government can constitutionally censor the speech of those who receive federal funding. For example, the Supreme Court ruled in *Rust v. Sullivan*, 500 U.S. 173, 111 S. Ct. 1759, 114 L. Ed. 2d 233 (1991), that, without restricting First Amendment rights, the government can ban ABORTION counseling in federally funded health clinics.

**Prisoners' Mail** If the government's interest is penological it also has broader rights to censor speech. Prisoners' outgoing mail can be censored in order to thwart escape plans, shield the recipients from obscene or menacing letters, or circumvent inaccurate or adverse reports about prison conditions. Under the Supreme Court ruling in *Procunier v. Martinez*, 416 U.S. 396, 94 S. Ct. 1800, 40 L. Ed. 2d 224 (1974), prison administrators can censor prisoners' personal correspondence only if it is necessary to maintain security, order, or rehabilitation efforts. Such censorship can be neither random nor excessively troublesome.

**Entertainment** Perhaps the most visible form of censorship is that affecting the entertainment industry. Theater and film, as types of public entertainment, affect the common interest and can hence be subjected to certain types of governmental regulation. But attempts to regulate or censor often risk obstructing the free speech rights of playwrights, screenwriters, filmmakers, performers, and distributors.

The U.S. Supreme Court has ruled that it is lawful to censor obscene entertainment to safeguard children from PORNOGRAPHY and to protect adults from unknowingly or involuntarily viewing indecent materials (*Ginsberg v. New*

*York*, 390 U.S. 629, 88 S. Ct. 1274, 20 L. Ed. 2d 195 [1968]). Although Supreme Court interpretation permits individuals to view OBSCENITY in the privacy of their homes (*Stanley v. Georgia*, 394 U.S. 557, 89 S. Ct. 1243, 22 L. Ed. 2d 542 [1969]), theaters and movie houses are public places and therefore subject to regulation (*Paris Adult Theatre I v. Slaton*, 413 U.S. 49, 93 S. Ct. 2628, 37 L. Ed. 2d 446 [1973]). The difficulty with such censorship is in trying to determine what is "obscene."

In *Miller v. California*, 413 U.S. 15, 93 S. Ct. 2607, 37 L. Ed. 2d 419 (1973), the Supreme Court concluded that a work is obscene and can be regulated if it appeals to a viewer's prurient interest; portrays sexual conduct in a patently offensive way; and lacks serious literary, artistic, political, or scientific value. The Court further ruled that interpretations of this definition may vary across the United States and that communities may apply their own local standards to determine obscenity.

To avoid government censorship, the Motion Picture Association of America (MPAA) regulates itself through a voluntary rating system. The system does not have statutory authority but is used to help the industry conform with statutes designed to protect children. Recognizing a 1968 Supreme Court decision that favored limited censorship for MINORS (*Ginsberg v. New York*, 390 U.S. 629, 88 S. Ct. 1274, 20 L. Ed. 2d 195), the MPAA has devised a rating system based on the viewer's age. A G rating signals subject matter suitable for general audiences; PG stands for Parental Guidance Suggested; PG-13 strongly advises guidance for children under age thirteen because of possibly inappropriate material; R requires accompaniment by an adult for children under age seventeen, or eighteen in some states; and NC-17 or X prohibit anyone under age seventeen, or eighteen in some states, from entering the theater.

Radio and television have also met with governmental pressure to control the content of their broadcasts. Spurred on by the belief that violence on television adversely affects children's behavior and attitudes, Congress has attempted several times to encourage the media to adopt voluntary guidelines in the hope that less violence on television will lead to a less violent society. Although none of Congress's acts have been deemed outright censorship, government intrusion into BROADCASTING to discourage certain types of speech has not been welcomed by all. The various pieces of legislation raise questions about media self-censorship and the role of the FEDERAL COMMUNICATIONS COMMISSION (FCC) in regulating freedom of expression.

In response to congressional pressure the National Association of Broadcasters adopted the Family Viewing Policy in 1974 to limit the first hour of prime-time programming to material suitable for families. The policy was found unconstitutional in 1976 (*Writers Guild of America, West, Inc. v. F.C.C.*, 423 F. Supp. 1064 [C.D. Cal., 1976]).

Congress addressed the content of children's television with the Children's Television Act of 1990 (47 U.S.C.A. §§ 303a–303b [Supp. III 1991]), which limits the amount of advertising on children's television and compels broadcasters to air educational programs. Failure to comply with the act could jeopardize renewal of a station's LICENSE. Critics point out that the act has not improved children's programming because of its vague standards and the FCC's disinclination to enforce it.

The Television Violence Act (47 U.S.C.A. § 303c [Supp. III 1991]), proposed in 1986 by Senator Paul Simon (D-Ill.), was signed into law by President George Bush in December 1990. This act, which expired in 1993, was intended to prompt the networks, cable industry, and independent stations to decrease the amount of violence shown on television. Although it did not constitute direct government regulation, the act was criticized as a governmental attempt to impose its values on society by discouraging, if not suppressing, unpopular ideas.

The Telecommunications Act of 1996, 110 Stat. 56, requires television manufacturers to create a chip, known as the V-chip, which will allow parents to block out violent programs. The chip is to operate in conjuction with a rating system implemented by TV broadcasters that rates programs for violent and sexual content.

Radio broadcasts have also come under scrutiny. In *FCC v. Pacifica Foundation*, 438 U.S. 726, 98 S. Ct. 3026, 57 L. Ed. 2d 1073 (1978), the Supreme Court ruled that a daytime broadcast of George Carlin's "Seven Dirty Words" monologue violated the prohibition of indecency in 18 U.S.C.A. § 1464 (1948) and was therefore subject to regulation. To many, this ruling gave the FCC further authority to censor speech and dictate values.

**Music** Just as the entertainment industry has faced regulation or censorship for allegedly violent, obscene, or indecent material, so has the recording industry. Claiming that some popular music erodes morals by encouraging violence, drug abuse, and sexual promiscuity, the Parents' Music Resource Center, founded in 1985 by Tipper Gore, the wife of the future vice president, Albert Gore, Jr., successfully lobbied the music industry to place warning labels on records that may feature lyrics inappropriate for children.

Concerned about the rising rate of violent crime against law enforcement officers, the assistant director of public affairs for the Federal Bureau of Investigation (FBI) sent a letter in August 1989 to Priority Records to protest a rap group's lyrics. N.W.A., a Los Angeles–based rap group, recorded on its album *Straight Outta Compton* the song "Fuck tha Police," which violently protested police brutality. Although the letter from the FBI was a protest, not an attempt at regulation, many in the music industry interpreted it as an example of indirect censorship through intimidation.

Perhaps the most famous legal proceedings to censor music involved the rap group 2 Live Crew. In early 1990, a Florida circuit judge banned all sales of the group's album *As Nasty As They Wanna Be* on the grounds that the lyrics of several of its songs, including "Me So Horny," violated community standards for obscenity. The group brought suit to have the ban lifted in *Skyywalker Records v. Navarro*, 742 F. Supp. 638 (S.D. Fla. 1990), but the judge upheld the obscenity ruling. A black record store owner was arrested for continuing to sell the album and two members of 2 Live Crew were arrested on obscenity charges after a performance. The band members were acquitted of all charges in October 1990 but the debate continues between those demanding free expression in music and those seeking to censor allegedly obscene material.

**Art** For almost as long as artists have been creating art, governments have both supported and censored artists' work. Ancient Athens, the Roman Empire, and the medieval Catholic Church financed many projects, whereas totalitarian regimes, for example, banned many works and repressed artists. The U.S. Congress was reluctant to fund art that might subsequently be construed as national art, or as government-approved art until 1960s activism encouraged it to do so. In 1965 the NATIONAL FOUNDATION ON THE ARTS AND THE HUMANITIES was established to foster excellence in the arts by providing stipends to deserving artists.

Controversy over the role of government support of the arts arose in the late 1980s with two artists who received NEA funding. In 1988 the photographer Andres Serrano received harsh condemnation for his photograph titled *Piss Christ* which depicted a plastic crucifix floating in a jar of Serrano's urine. Numerous senators sent letters of protest to the NEA, insisting that the agency cease underwriting vulgar art. A second furor arose in 1989 over the work of another photographer, Robert Mapplethorpe, who received NEA support for his work, which depicted flowers, nude children, and homosexuality and sadomasochism.

Senator JESSE HELMS (R-N.C.) argued the most vociferously against the NEA's choices and introduced legislation to ban funding of "obscene or indecent art" (1989 H.R. 2788 [codified at 20 U.S.C.A. § 953 et seq. (1989)]). The Helms Amendment, adopted in October 1989, gave the NEA great power and latitude to define obscenity and quash alternative artistic visions. To enforce the new amendment, the NEA established an "obscenity pledge," which required artists to promise they would not use government money to create works of an obscene nature. The art world strongly resisted this measure: many museum directors resigned in protest and several well-known artists returned their NEA grants.

Two important cases tested the power of the NEA to censor artistic production. In *Bella Lewitsky Dance Foundation v. Frohnmayer*, 754 F. Supp. 774 (C.D. Cal. 1991), a dance company refused to sign the obscenity pledge and sued on the ground that the pledge was unconstitutional. A California district court agreed that the pledge violated the First Amendment right to free speech and that its vagueness denied the dance company DUE PROCESS under the FIFTH AMENDMENT.

In *New School v. Frohnmayer*, No. 90-3510 (S.D.N.Y. 1990), the New School for Social Research, in New York City, turned down a grant, claiming that the obscenity pledge acted as PRIOR RESTRAINT and therefore breached the school's First Amendment rights. Before the constitutionality of the prior restraint argument was decided the NEA released the school from its obligation to sign the pledge.

The NEA abolished the obscenity pledge in November 1990, but in its place instituted a "decency clause" (1990 Amendments, Pub. L. No. 101-512, § 103(b), 104 Stat. 1963 [codified at 20 U.S.C.A. § 954(d)(1990)]), which required award recipients to ensure that their works met certain standards of decency. Failure to comply with this demand could mean suspension of grant payments.

Again the art world protested. In *Finley v.*

*Demonstrators at 1990 NEA hearings protest the power of the NEA to define and refuse to fund "obscene" art.*

*NEA*, 795 F. Supp. 1457 (C.D. Cal. 1992), artists known as the NEA Four—Karen Finley, John Fleck, Holly Hughes, and Tim Miller—sued the NEA over the decency clause. A California district court agreed with the artists. The *Finley* court held that the decency clause, like the obscenity pledge, was unconstitutional because its vagueness denied the artists the due process guaranteed by the Fifth Amendment and because its too-general restriction suppressed speech.

**Books** U.S. parents send their children to public schools to receive an education and to learn the fundamental values on which their democratic society is based. Conflict ensues when parents believe that certain schoolbooks contain material that is objectionable on political, moral, or religious grounds and should be banned in order to protect their children from exposure to allegedly harmful ideas. In some instances school boards have responded by physically removing books from school library shelves. In one 1982 study that polled 860 school librarians, 34 percent reported parental or community protests to books. In general, advocates of book banning maintain that censorship is warranted to redress social ills, whereas critics believe that freedom of speech is more important and useful to society than is imposing values through censorship.

Book banning as a way to remedy social problems was first tested by the Supreme Court in *Board of Education v. Pico*, 457 U.S. 853, 102 S. Ct. 2799, 73 L. Ed. 2d 435 (1982). In *Pico* parents objected to nine books in the high school library, most of which were subsequently removed by the school board. The nine books were *Slaughterhouse Five*, by Kurt Vonnegut, Jr.;

## Censorship

**List of book titles frequently banned from public educational institutions**

*Go Ask Alice*, Anonymous (1971)
*Manchild in the Promised Land*, Claude Brown (1965)
*Soul on Ice*, Eldridge Cleaver (1968)
*Catch-22*, Joseph Heller (1955)
''The Lottery,'' Shirley Jackson (1948)
*To Kill a Mockingbird*, Harper Lee (1960)
*Naked Ape*, Desmond Morris (1967)
*The Learning Tree*, Gordon Parks (1963)
*The Bell Jar*, Sylvia Plath (1963)
*Catcher in the Rye*, J. D. Salinger (1951)
*The Grapes of Wrath*, John Steinbeck (1939)
*Of Mice and Men*, John Steinbeck (1937)
*Down These Mean Streets*, Piri Thomas (1967)
*Cat's Cradle*, Kurt Vonnegut, Jr. (1963)
*God Bless You, Mr. Rosewater*, Kurt Vonnegut, Jr. (1964)
*Slaughterhouse Five*, Kurt Vonnegut, Jr. (1969)
*Black Boy*, Richard Wright (1945)

Source: *Banned!: Book Censorship in the Schools*, by Donald J. Rogers, 1988.

*Naked Ape*, by Desmond Morris; *Down These Mean Streets*, by Piri Thomas; *Best Short Stories of Negro Writers*, edited by Langston Hughes; *Laughing Boy*, by Oliver LaFarge; *Black Boy*, by Richard Wright; *A Hero Ain't Nothin' But a Sandwich*, by Alice Childress; *Soul on Ice*, by Eldridge Cleaver; and *Go Ask Alice*, by an anonymous author.

*Pico* debated the authority of local school boards to censor material in the interest of protecting students. The case reached the Supreme Court because lower courts were unable to devise standards for testing the constitutionality of book removal. The Supreme Court ruled that it is unconstitutional for public school boards to abridge students' First Amendment rights by banning books. Although school boards have the power to determine which books should sit on library shelves, they do not have the authority to censor.

Books published by commercial presses for sale to the general public sometimes meet with harsh condemnation and subsequent action that could be tantamount to censorship. In November 1990, Simon and Schuster canceled its contract with author Bret E. Ellis to publish his novel *American Psycho*, citing the work's graphic violence and sexual brutality. The National Writers Union decried the cancellation as contrary to free speech and artistic expression and as censorship. The publishing house defended its editorial judgment by claiming it did not want to put its imprint on a book of questionable taste and value. Vintage Books, a division of Random House, soon acquired the novel, and published it in March 1991.

**Students' Speech** Students' free speech rights sometimes clash with schools' interest in maintaining control of public education. Students' First Amendment liberties were affirmed by the landmark *Tinker v. Des Moines Independent Community School District*, 393 U.S. 503, 89 S. Ct. 733, 21 L. Ed. 2d 731 (1969), which ruled that public school students could not be penalized for wearing symbols, such as black armbands, to protest the Vietnam War.

Two subsequent cases dealing with issues of censorship in school newspapers pointed to a more restrictive judicial view of students' right to free expression. In *Hazelwood School District v. Kuhlmeier*, 484 U.S. 260, 108 S. Ct. 562, 98 L. Ed. 2d 592 (1988), the Supreme Court ruled in favor of a Hazelwood, Missouri, school principal who removed several articles from a student newspaper. The articles dealt with teen pregnancy and a student's feelings about her parents' divorce. The court in *Hazelwood* held that a school newspaper is not a public forum, and thus granted school officials the right to determine what type of student speech is appropriate and to regulate such speech.

Three years later, the ruling in *Planned Parenthood v. Clark County School District*, 941 F.2d 817 (9th Cir. 1991), was based on *Hazelwood*. In *Planned Parenthood*, a public high school newspaper solicited advertisements from local businesses, including Planned Parenthood. The principal refused to allow Planned Parenthood to place an advertisement in school publications and Planned Parenthood sued the school district. The Ninth Circuit Court of Appeals upheld a district court decision that a public high school publication is not a public forum and that the school could therefore accept or reject advertisements. Both *Hazelwood* and *Planned Parenthood* concluded that because public high schools are nonpublic forums, school districts can apply a limited degree of censorship.

Hundreds of public universities in the United States have speech codes to regulate students' choice of words. Speech can be constitutionally curtailed in some circumstances. For example, public COLLEGES AND UNIVERSITIES can forbid threats of violence, prohibit obscene language and conduct (although it is extremely difficult to define or prove obscenity), and punish students for using defamatory speech against each other, all without violating the First Amendment. Numerous cases have successfully contested free speech limitations on campus, suggesting that a majority of these codes are unconstitutional.

In *Doe v. University of Michigan*, 721 F. Supp. 852 (E.D. Mich. 1989), a biopsychology student maintained that the university's speech code prevented him from freely discussing controversial ideas about biologically based differences between the sexes and races. A district court ruled that the university's code proscribed too great a range of speech and therefore was an unconstitutional infringement on the plaintiff's First Amendment rights. The court also held that the overbroad nature of the code denied his due process rights.

A University of Wisconsin student was accused of violating the university's speech codes by yelling rude comments at a woman. In *U.W.M. Post, Inc. v. Board of Regents*, 774 F. Supp. 1163 (E.D. Wis. 1991), the university's speech code was also struck down as overbroad. Two years later school officials punished fraternity brothers at George Mason University for dressing in drag and staging an "ugly woman contest." In *Iota X Chapter v. George Mason University*, 993 F.2d 386 (1993), the Fourth Circuit found that the university had violated the First Amendment because it did not sanction the fraternity merely for its conduct, but rather for the message conveyed by the "ugly woman contest," which ran counter to the views the university sought to foster.

**Internet** Computer-mediated communication grows explosively every year and in some ways outpaces and obviates current legal principles. The prevailing concept of law applies to real-world events and transactions, and, as those in the legal field are realizing, may unravel when exercised in cyberspace. As more and more people transmit widely divergent messages on the electronic highway, issues of free speech and censorship become increasingly complicated and regulations difficult to enforce.

The first case of criminal prosecution of electronic communication involved the distribution of pornography over an electronic bulletin board system (BBS). In *United States v. Thomas*, No. CR-94-20019-G (W.D. Tenn. 1994), Robert Thomas and Carleen Thomas were found guilty of disseminating obscene materials by interstate telephone lines and computer. From their home in California, the Thomases ran an adults-only private BBS from which subscribers could download computer graphics files and order sexually explicit photographs and videotapes while on-line. To gather evidence against the couple, a Memphis postal inspector, under an assumed name, downloaded to his computer many of the pornographic electronic files and ordered tapes.

The Thomases were charged with, among other things, transporting obscene materials across state lines. The couple attempted to transfer their case to the Northern District of California, so that their materials would be measured against that community's standards of obscenity, rather than the obscenity standards of the Western District of Tennessee. The district judge denied their request, noting that in obscenity prosecutions the trial can be held

*Many galleries and museums canceled exhibits of Robert Mapplethorpe's art in 1989, when the NEA was criticized for having funded what some legislators called "obscene" art.*

either in the district from which the material was sent or where it was received.

The "virtual" nature of cyberspace poses a number of problems for courts and legislatures on the issue of obscenity. Among the most difficult of these is the issue of community standards. Because the Internet brings together people from all over the United States and all over the world, it defies identification with any particular community. Other difficulties are the criminal element of knowledge and the issue of dissemination. Persons may post and receive information on Internet bulletin boards without the knowledge of those who maintain the BBS, making it difficult to determine whether the BBS operators "knowingly disseminated" obscene materials.

In 1996 Congress passed the Communications Decency Act of 1996, which punished disseminating "indecent" material over the Internet. A U.S. district court struck down the act as a violation of the First Amendment. The ruling did not affect obscene material and child pornography, as those materials were already illegal.

As the Internet continues to grow as a medium of world communication, the conflict between censorship and free speech rights will continue.

### CROSS-REFERENCES

Art Law; Entertainment Law; Movie Ratings; Schools and School Districts.

**CENSUS** ▢ An official count of the population of a particular area, such as a district, state, or nation. ▢

The U.S. Constitution requires that a census of the entire population, CITIZENS and noncitizens alike, be made every ten years (art. I, § 2, cl. 3). The FOURTEENTH AMENDMENT to the Constitution directs that the census will be used to determine the number of members of the U.S. HOUSE OF REPRESENTATIVES from each state. The census is conducted by the U.S. Census Bureau, an agency established in 1899 within the U.S. Department of Commerce. The data gathered by the U.S. Census Bureau are used by the states to draw boundaries for congressional and state legislative districts, and by local governments to establish districts for other representative bodies such as county legislatures, city councils, and boards of supervisors.

Census data are also used to allocate federal and state funding and services. By the mid-1990s, more than $50 billion in federal aid for education, housing, and health programs to states and cities was distributed annually based on census numbers. In addition, census information is used in academic research and is sought by product manufacturers and marketers who want to know the demographics of potential consumers.

The first U.S. census took place in 1790 when some six hundred U.S. marshals went door-to-door counting approximately 3.9 million people. The 1790 census consisted of fewer than ten questions, which for each household included the name of the head of the family, the number of free white males over and under sixteen years of age, the number of free white females, the number of all other free persons, and the number of slaves.

The 1890 census counted 63 million U.S. citizens and reflected a dramatic increase in immigration, urbanization, and industrialization. That census showed that for the first time fewer than half of all U.S. workers were employed on farms. The 1890 census included questions regarding military service during the Civil War, number of years in the United States, naturalization status, reading and writing ability, and mental and physical disabilities.

By 1980 the Census Bureau conceded that the decennial censuses were undercounting portions of the population, usually low-income and minority groups in the inner cities. In follow-up surveys after the 1980 census the bureau determined that it had missed some 3.2 million persons, or 1.4 percent of the population. For example, a 1986 post-census survey of East Los Angeles estimated that the 1980 census missed about 10 percent of the Latino community, seven percent of the Asian community, and nine percent of the black community. Census officials determined that overall, nearly six percent of the black and Hispanic populations were uncounted and less than one percent of the white population.

By May 1987, the Census Bureau had determined that the 1990 census could be adjusted for undercounting by using a technique called a post-enumeration survey (PES). The PES would allow the census to be checked for accuracy by sending census takers back to a given number of households that would be representative of the entire U.S. population and comparing the information gathered with the initial head count. If discrepancies arose, the bureau could make corrections and project them to neighborhoods with similar demographic characteristics. But in October 1987, officials from the U.S. Department of Commerce (DOC), which oversees the Census Bureau, had decided against making any statistical adjustment to the 1990 census. As a result, in 1988, New York, Los Angeles, and several other cities, as well as a number of states and organizations, brought suit in federal district court. They claimed that the secretary's decision not to adjust the 1990 census violated their right to EQUAL PROTECTION under the FIFTH AMENDMENT to the Constitution and asked the court to ENJOIN the census. They also argued that the COMMERCE DEPARTMENT's actions were politically motivated by a

## Census

Resident Population of United States, by Race and Region

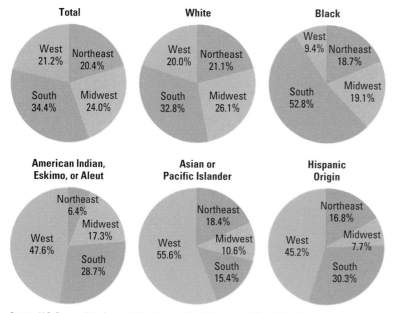

Source: U.S. Bureau of the Census, *1990 Census of Population, General Population Characteristics, United States.*

Republican administration that realized that the undercounted population is historically Democratic. The defendants moved to dismiss the COMPLAINT, contending that the secretary's decision was not subject to judicial review. In *City of New York v. United States Department of Commerce*, 713 F. Supp. 48 (E.D.N.Y. 1989), the district court denied the motion to dismiss, holding that the plaintiffs had STANDING (the legal right) to challenge the census on constitutional grounds and that the court could review the secretary's decision.

Following the district court's decision the parties entered into a STIPULATION in July 1989 by which plaintiffs would withdraw their motion to enjoin the census and the DOC would reconsider its 1987 decision not to adjust the 1990 census. The agreement required the DOC to conduct a PES of not fewer than 150,000 households as part of the 1990 census in order to produce corrected counts usable for congressional and legislative reapportionment and redistricting. The agreement also required the DOC to develop guidelines under which the secretary would assess any proposed adjustment. In March 1990 the DOC issued final guidelines. The plaintiffs challenged them in court on the grounds that they were impermissibly vague and were biased against any adjustment to the 1990 census. In *City of New York*, 739 F. Supp. 761 (E.D.N.Y. 1990), the district court held that the guidelines satisfied the defendants' obligations under the 1989 stipulation. The Census Bureau then began the 1990 census.

The 1990 census employed more than 425,000 workers who gathered information on an estimated 250 million people in 106 million households. For the first time, the Census Bureau combined technology with traditional door knocking, using coast-to-coast computerized maps of all 7.5 million census tracts in the United States. The bureau predicted that these maps would reduce the number of errors caused by census workers' reliance on outdated state and local maps. The census cost some $2.6 billion—65 percent more than the 1980 census—making it the most expensive count ever conducted.

In March 1990, the bureau mailed or hand delivered more than 106 million questionnaires, one to every household in the country. Most households received a short form consisting of fourteen questions covering personal characteristics and housing. One in six U.S. households received a long form with forty-five additional questions on topics such as utilities, tax, mortgage, and rent payments; place of birth; ethnic

*Most households received the short form of the 1990 census questionnaire and returned it by mail.*

origin; and work habits. From March to June 1990 census workers continued the data collection. The bureau set aside March 20, 1990, as "homeless night." On that night, census takers, many hired from among the homeless population or those who worked with them, visited shelters and low-cost motels from 6:00 P.M. to midnight; counted homeless people on the streets from 2:00 A.M. to 4:00 A.M.; and from 4:00 A.M. to 6:30 A.M. stood outside abandoned buildings, counting those who emerged.

The homeless count caused a great deal of controversy. The 1990 census reported 228,600 HOMELESS PERSONS in the United States, compared with earlier estimates of 500,000 to 3 million. Advocates for homeless people argued that the Census Bureau had surveyed only a third of the country's cities and counties and had visited only a limited number of locations. The bureau acknowledged that its workers had avoided actually going into hideaways such as abandoned buildings and dumpsters because of safety concerns and admitted that many winter shelters had closed by the time the census was taken in late March. The bureau maintained that its homeless survey was not intended to produce a definitive count of the homeless population.

In October 1990 the Census Bureau issued estimated U.S. population figures of approximately 254 million, based on a tracking of birth, death, and immigration records. In December the bureau released a final U.S. population tally of some 249 million, based on the actual mailed census questionnaires and house-to-house interviews. The discrepancy between the two sets of numbers indicated that the 1990 census missed some 5 million U.S. residents.

By December 31, 1990, the bureau reported to the president population figures for each

*Census workers went to shelters in an attempt to count homeless people in the 1990 census.*

state as well as the number of seats in the U.S. House of Representatives that each state would receive. Between January and March 1991, states with early deadlines for redrawing legislative districts received totals of all persons of voting age, broken down by race. By April 1, 1991, most other states received the voting age and race data. Between April 1991 and 1993 the Census Bureau released statistics compiled from the long forms, including information on income, marital status, disabilities, types of housing, and education.

In April 1991, the bureau announced the results of its PES. Estimates drawn from the PES revealed that the census had resulted in a national undercount of 2.1 percent, or approximately 5.3 million persons out of a total population of approximately 255 million, the largest undercounting in the history of the census. For example, in one south central Los Angeles neighborhood, officials determined that census takers had underreported the number of occupants in 38 percent of fifty-eight hundred households. As expected, the undercount was greater for members of racial and ethnic minorities. Hispanics were undercounted by 5.2 percent, Native Americans by 5.0 percent, African Americans by 4.8 percent, and Asian Pacific Islanders by 3.1 percent. The PES-calculated undercount for non–African Americans was 1.7 percent and for non-Hispanic whites, 1.2 percent. Among major cities with high undercounts were Los Angeles (5.1 percent), Houston (5 percent), Washington, D.C. (5 percent), Dallas (4.8 percent), Miami (4.6 percent), Detroit (3.5 percent), and New York (3 percent).

Among the reasons given for the low counts were that certain segments of the population did not believe the Census Bureau's promise that information is confidential and will not be shared with other government agencies such as the Immigration and Naturalization Service, the local housing authority, or the police; did not have addresses and thus were missed because the 1990 census was conducted primarily by mail; lived in urban high-crime areas where census takers were afraid to go door-to-door; were illegal immigrants; feared the government in general; or lacked proficiency in English.

According to the bureau, if the adjusted count were adopted, Arizona and California would each gain a seat in the House of Representatives and Wisconsin and Pennsylvania would each lose one seat. These discrepancies led state officials to renew their plea for an adjustment of the census using the PES.

In July 1991 Secretary of Commerce Robert A. Mosbacher announced his decision not to adjust the 1990 census to account for the missing 5 million people. Mosbacher said that although he was troubled by the undercount of minorities, his decision supported the integrity of the census and that the resulting disadvantage to minorities should not be remedied in the official census. He also expressed concern that adjustment might not improve distribution of representatives among the states and that uncertainty as to the methods of adjustment and assumptions behind them might cause even more dispute about the accuracy of the census.

The plaintiffs in *City of New York* attacked the secretary's decision, contending that it was tainted by partisan political influence and violated the Constitution, the Administrative Procedure Act of 1946, and the 1989 stipulation agreed to by both parties in the case. After a thirteen-day BENCH (non-jury) TRIAL, the district court concluded that it could not overturn the secretary's decision (*City of New York*, 822 F. Supp. 906 [E.D.N.Y. 1993]). On appeal, the court of appeals concluded that, given the admittedly greater accuracy of the adjusted count, the secretary's decision was not entitled to be upheld without a showing by the secretary that the refusal to adjust the census was essential to the achievement of a legitimate government objective (*City of New York*, 34 F.3d 1114 [2d Cir. 1994]). On appeal, the Supreme Court reversed the decision of the Second Circuit, holding that the secretary's decision not to adjust the census was within the government's discretion (__ U.S. __, 134 L. Ed. 2d 167, 116 S. Ct. 1091 [1996]).

By October 1991, at least five state legislatures had filed requests under the FREEDOM OF INFORMATION ACT (FOIA) (5 U.S.C.A. § 552 et seq.) to see the adjusted census figures in order to decide which set of numbers should be used to redraw state political boundaries. Secretary Mosbacher refused to make the adjusted numbers public, claiming they were flawed and their release could disrupt the redistricting process. In *Assembly of California v. United States Department of Commerce*, 797 F. Supp. 1554 (E.D. Cal. 1992), California state officials brought an action under the FOIA to enjoin the U.S. Department of Commerce from withholding computer tapes containing statistically adjusted census data for California. The DOC claimed that the information was protected from disclosure under an exemption to the FOIA. But the district court said the exemption did not apply to the census data and ordered the DOC to release the tapes. The court of appeals affirmed the district court's order to release the tapes (*Assembly of California*, 968 F.2d 916 [9th Cir. 1992]).

In a similar case the U.S. Court of Appeals for the Eleventh Circuit reached the opposite result. In *Florida House of Representatives v. United States Department of Commerce*, 961 F.2d 941 (11th Cir. 1992), the Florida House of Representatives brought an FOIA action to compel the Department of Commerce to release all the adjusted census data for Florida. The district court granted SUMMARY JUDGMENT for Florida and the Department of Commerce appealed (*Florida House of Representatives*, No. TCA 91-40387-WS [N.D. Fla. 1992]). The Eleventh Circuit reversed, finding that the census data were exempted from disclosure under the FOIA. The U.S. Supreme Court declined to review the case (*Florida House of Representatives*, 506 U.S. 969, 113 S. Ct. 446, 121 L. Ed. 2d 363 [1992]).

In light of the controversy over the 1990 census, government officials and demographers have debated how best to conduct the census in the year 2000 and later. Many demographers argue that the U.S. population has become too mobile and too uncooperative to allow reliance on mail-in-surveys and door-to-door interviews. An increase in the number of non-English speakers, undocumented immigrants, and homeless persons has made census taking more difficult and residents will become more diverse and less tolerant of government intrusion in the future. The American Statistical Association has urged the government to use scientific sampling surveys to estimate the population that has been the most difficult to count.

In preparation for the 2000 census the bureau conducted a test census in the spring of 1995 at three sites—Paterson, New Jersey; Oakland, California; and six parishes in north-

western Louisiana. The sites were selected because of their ethnic diversity and their large number of multidwelling housing units. In Paterson the bureau experimented with a multimedia kiosk, which allowed residents to answer census questions by touching a screen. In Oakland all identified households were sent a census form and blank forms were also made available at libraries, post offices, and the state department of motor vehicles. The bureau also experimented with using statistical samples from random surveys to estimate total population.

In the summer of 1995, Congress cut the budget of the Census Bureau by millions of dollars in its program to reduce federal expenditures. Bureau officials said the cuts would inhibit the bureau's ability to test new census techniques and technology that they hoped would increase the accuracy of the year 2000 census. Continuing public pressure and lawsuits over census figures could lead to new methods or new funding.

See also APPORTIONMENT.

## CENTER FOR CONSTITUTIONAL RIGHTS
The Center for Constitutional Rights (CRR) is a nonprofit legal and educational organization dedicated to advancing and protecting the rights guaranteed by the U.S. Constitution and the Declaration of Human Rights. Since its formation in 1966 by attorneys working for civil rights demonstrators in the South, the CCR has been a forceful advocate of CIVIL RIGHTS for all people. The New York City–based organization seeks to halt what it describes as a steady erosion of civil liberties in the United States and elsewhere. The group addresses such areas as international HUMAN RIGHTS, government misconduct, sexual politics, indigenous peoples' rights, nuclear and environmental hazards, WOMEN'S RIGHTS, civil rights,

*Critics of the homeless count in the 1990 census claim that census workers did not go far enough in searching out the homeless population.*

*William Kunstler was a cofounder of the Center for Constitutional Rights, which has taken on cases for disadvantaged and sometimes controversial clients.*

FREEDOM OF THE PRESS, racism, ELECTRONIC SURVEILLANCE, criminal trials, AFFIRMATIVE ACTION, and abuse of the GRAND JURY process.

Cofounded by attorneys WILLIAM M. KUNSTLER and Morton Stavis and others in the heady days of 1960s social activism, the left-leaning CCR describes itself as "committed to the creative use of law as a positive force for social change." The CCR has consistently generated legal and political controversy. The group had African American civil rights leader MARTIN LUTHER KING, JR., as one of its first clients and since then it has continued to take on cases for disadvantaged and oppressed people. It has won favorable decisions for such diverse figures as antinuclear leaders in the Micronesian republic of Belau; American Indian protesters at Wounded Knee, South Dakota; and a film company that sought to distribute U.S.-made documentaries in foreign countries without U.S. government interference.

Much of the center's work has involved international causes and foreign clients. In the early 1970s the CCR sued the U.S. government to discover answers regarding U.S. citizens missing in Chile and U.S. involvement in the support of Chilean leader Salvador Allende. The group has broken ground in the battle to establish the right to sue foreign governments or individuals in U.S. courts. In 1986 the CCR represented the government of President Corazon Aquino, of the Philippines, in its fight to recover millions of dollars in assets taken by former dictator Ferdinand Marcos. In another case, *Filartiga v. Pena-Irala*, 630 F.2d 876 (2d Cir. 1980), the organization won a settlement of $10.4 million for a Paraguayan boy who brought the suit against an exiled dictator of Paraguay who had ordered the boy's torture. In the early and mid-1990s, the CCR also included among its causes the support of United States–Cuba friendship and cooperation and the representation of Puerto Rican political activists seeking independence from the United States.

The CCR also conducts a number of other programs. Its Movement Support Network, started in 1984, provides aid to social activist groups, including legal protection for groups experiencing harassment by the Federal Bureau of Investigation and other government law enforcement agencies. The Anti-Biased Violence Project (ABVP), established in 1991, uses litigation and education to oppose violence against individuals because of their race, ethnicity, religion, gender, or sexual orientation, and has defended ordinances that curtail hate speech. The CCR's Ella Baker Student Program provides internships to law students. In Greenville, Mississippi, the CCR operates the Voting Rights Project, a community-based VOTING RIGHTS litigation group that works in Mississippi, Arkansas, and Tennessee. The CCR also maintains a speakers' bureau and publishes books, pamphlets, and periodicals, the last including *Docket* and the *MSN News*.

The CCR maintains its own staff but also works with many lawyers who donate their time pro bono (for free). The group has previously been called the Civil Rights Legal Defense Fund and the Law Center for Constitutional Rights.

## CENTERS FOR LAW AND LEGAL STUDIES

**Center for Law and Education** The Center for Law and Education (CLE) offers support services on educational issues for advocates working on behalf of low-income students and parents. It seeks to take a leadership role in both improving the quality of public education for low-income students in the United States and enabling low-income communities to address their own public education problems effectively. As part of the nationwide network of support centers funded by the LEGAL SERVICES CORPORATION (LSC), it provides specialized legal assistance to staff members of legal services programs and to members of approved panels representing eligible clients. The center has been at the fulcrum of reforms in education policy.

Founded in 1969, the Cambridge, Massachusetts, and Washington, D.C., branches of the center offer advice and collaboration on cases, publications, training, federal program advocacy, and litigation and assist parent and

APWIDE WORLD PHOTOS

student involvement in education. The center publishes the *NEWSNOTES* periodical on a quarterly basis, as well as a host of other manuals, monographs, and reports. Its staff includes attorneys, an editor, and administrative support personnel. The center conducts training workshops, usually in conjunction with local legal services programs.

The CLE has been a part of significant lawsuits dealing with the enforcement of federal and state constitutional rights and of federal laws. It focuses on issues such as students' rights, federally funded programs, special education, sex and race DISCRIMINATION, vocational education, bilingual-bicultural education, and Native American education. Its staff has pressed significant litigation on the fairness of state programs for competency testing, the right of pupils with limited proficiency in English to understand instruction, the rights of students with disabilities, and racial discrimination in education—among other issues. Whenever feasible, the center encourages the development of local lay advocacy resources to avoid costly and time-consuming litigation. A significant portion of the center's work is supported by grants from private funding. See also SCHOOLS AND SCHOOL DISTRICTS.

**Center for Law and Social Policy** As a national public interest organization, the Center for Law and Social Policy (CLASP) seeks to improve the economic conditions of low-income families with children. The Washington, D.C.–based center also attempts to secure access for poor people to the nation's civil justice system through education, policy research, and advocacy. CLASP has worked closely with the Center on Budget Policies and Priorities, the CHILDREN'S DEFENSE FUND, the American Public Welfare Association, and hundreds of other federal and state advocacy organizations. The center helps develop new strategies to fight poverty and stimulates new approaches in the delivery of legal services.

Since its founding in 1969, CLASP has been involved in important court decisions related to WELFARE distribution. The center headed efforts to preserve professional legal services for poor people. It also organized the first clinical program for law school externs and initiated the National Women's Law Center and the Mental Health Law Project. In the 1990s CLASP got involved in a debate over proposed changes in the welfare system: the center issued a number of publications and began a process of information dissemination that created a conduit so that commissions on welfare could obtain information about each other's activities. As part of its

ongoing mission the center has committed itself to the continuing review and analysis of developments in federal and state welfare reform.

CLASP advocates streamlined enforcement of child support. In the 1990s it initiated the ChildNet campaign which was designed to increase public awareness of the need for reform of the enforcement system for CHILD SUPPORT. In addition, the center attempted to expand the access of teen parents and impoverished adults to education and training programs. As to legislative issues, the Child Care and Development Block Grant, vocally supported by the center, tempers proposed limitations on welfare recipients that would make affordable child care less feasible. Generally, the center has promoted income support policies that enhance work, reduce poverty, and promote the well-being of families.

CLASP maintains a network of state and local advocates who provide training and technical assistance to other advocates and officials. It produces the quarterly *Family Matters* periodical, newsletters, and periodic updates on new policy developments. It serves as counsel to the hundreds of legal services programs across the United States and their national organizations.

**Center for Oceans Law and Policy** The Center for Oceans Law and Policy concerns itself with the future of the oceans and of the coastal and polar areas of the earth. The center has contributed to decisions made on the protection and use of these areas. It supports research, education, and discussion on legal and public issues surrounding oceans policy. It promotes interdisciplinary interaction at all levels—international, national, regional, and state—by conducting conferences and lectures. The center has dedicated itself to education in

*The Center for Law and Social Policy works to improve the economic condition of low-income families and help them gain access to the civil justice system through education, advocacy, and research.*

areas of oceans law and serves as a primary source for ongoing efforts in international research.

In 1976 the center was founded as a part of the University of Virginia, in Charlottesville. Since its founding the center has established a number of programs to promote discussion of oceans issues. In one such measure it established a teaching program in oceans law at the University of Virginia School of Law, along with the first master of law degree program with specialization in oceans law and policy. In addition, a basic course on oceans law and policy is taught by center personnel at American University, Georgetown University Law Center, and George Washington University Law School. Also working with the University of Virginia's law library, the center established the Newlin Collection on Oceans Law and Policy, believed to be the largest collection of formal and informal materials in oceans law anywhere in the world.

The center's activities include advocacy in five different areas: publications and research (the biennial *Director's Report* and the Oceans Policy Study Series); international associateships and fellowships; curriculum and teaching programs in oceans law and policy; conferences and seminars; and the Newlin Collection. Through teaching, research, and the dissemination of information, the center seeks to help promote rational choices for maintaining a vital part of the earth's well-being. The center is supported by the Henry L. and Grace Doherty Charitable Foundation. See also ENVIRONMENTAL LAW.

**Center on Social Welfare Policy and Law** The Center on Social Welfare Policy and Law (CSWPL) seeks an income support system that provides an adequate standard of living for people in the United States. In attempting to achieve this goal it respects individual rights of privacy, independence, self-determination, and fair treatment. It works as a nonprofit legal and policy organization providing assistance to advocates and poor people's organizations on welfare policy issues in Washington, D.C., and in the rest of the United States.

Since 1965 the CSWPL has pursued an aggressive policy of advocacy for poor people. Its work concentrates on public assistance programs that provide cash subsistence benefits to millions of economically disadvantaged people. The center works to facilitate programs such as Aid to Families with Dependent Children and general assistance programs at the state and local levels, which together provide services to over 15 million adults and children.

A professional staff of seven attorneys and policy analysts contributes to the center's understanding of WELFARE policy and law. First, welfare recipients and poor people receive direct representation in federal litigation before appropriate administrative and legislative bodies; this includes litigation before the U.S. Supreme Court, which has established basic DUE PROCESS rights for welfare recipients and ended discriminatory practices of welfare agencies. Second, the center seeks nonpartisan policy analysis designed to identify objective welfare policy issues. Third, by means of public education, the center attempts to increase popular understanding— and dispel myths—about public assistance programs. Fourth, the center disseminates legal analyses of developments in welfare law and policy to more than fourteen hundred welfare specialists in every state and to the poverty law journal *Clearinghouse Review*. Finally, it provides specialized case assistance with training and training materials for local lawyers, paralegals, and other advocates throughout the United States who are engaged in work that coincides with the center's mission. In the 1990s the center focused on welfare reform proposals.

The center receives financial support from foundations, corporations, the Legal Services Corporation, the Interest on Lawyer Account Fund of the State of New York, law firms, church groups, community organizations, and individuals. Under section 501(c)(3) of the Internal Revenue Code, the center is a nonprofit corporation with tax exempt status.

**Center for the Study of the Presidency** The New York City–based Center for the Study of the Presidency (CSP) promotes citizenship education, especially for youth. It seeks an understanding of U.S. political and economic systems and relies on a network of college and university faculty and students for its intellectual support. The center conducts high-profile roundtable discussions with political leaders as well as special studies of U.S. political policies. It also maintains a research clearinghouse on the presidency.

The founding of the CSP in 1968 received support from President DWIGHT D. EISENHOWER who said, "The result [of the center] cannot fail to be good . . . for the Nation." The New York State Board of Regents chartered the center. Since the center's founding, Dr. R. Gordon Hoxie, a former chancellor of Long Island University, has served as its president and chief executive. Its board of trustees, pursuant to the education law of the state of New York, is limited to twenty-five members. In 1995, membership in the center as a whole reached five thousand business, professional, and government leaders as well as contributors in academia. Corporations and foundations assist in the center's $1 million budget. The center has remained a nonpartisan, nonprofit educational corporation.

The CSP has several objectives. Primarily, it focuses on securing an understanding of the U.S. constitutional system of government. The center also seeks to make itself an objective, nonpartisan body for PUBLIC POLICY research. It provides educational programs for college and university students. It seeks to strengthen democratic institutions both at home and abroad: as part of its comprehensive mission and international scope, the center attempts to build a sense of interdependence and understanding between peoples and nations, while recognizing and respecting cultural differences.

The initiation of most of the center's basic programs occurred before the end of 1970. The Annual Leadership Conference, the Annual Student Symposium, the Fellowship Program, the Annual Lecture Series, and the center's publications (annual reports and the *Center House Bulletin*) date to its early days. In 1974, the Annual Awards Program was added to its activities. In the 1990s, the Annual Business Leaders Symposium and a program for White House interns joined its offerings.

The center is exempt from federal income tax. The Internal Revenue Service has also determined that the center is not a private foundation, making it eligible for "distributions" from foundations.

**Sellin Center for Studies in Criminology and Criminal Law** Founded in 1960 and located in Philadelphia, the Sellin Center for Studies in Criminology and Criminal Law researches CRIME, delinquency, the police, judicial systems, PRISONS, social control, and social deviance. Housed in the Wharton School, at the University of Pennsylvania, the center also trains graduate students toward master's and doctor's degrees. Studies at the center have produced numerous professional presentations and government reports, books, articles, and monographs.

The Sellin Center views criminology as the scientific study of crime and criminals and society's reaction to both. The center emphasizes the contributions of different disciplines— the behavioral sciences, psychology, anthropology, legal studies, psychiatry, neurology, biology, and the criminal justice system—to CRIMINOLOGY.

The center has worked on one of its primary projects since the early 1970s. *Delinquency in a Birth Cohort* analyzes the largest population of delinquents ever studied in the United States. The project has had a major effect on criminal justice thought throughout the world and has become a frequently cited publication in the field of criminology. Another project focuses on delinquency in the People's Republic of China. Students in both the center and China have participated in this extensive project. Many of the center's studies—of both national and international scope—have been cited in testimony before the U.S. Senate and House Judiciary Committees.

The Sellin Center has worked with officials in Pennsylvania and throughout the nation. It has provided technical assistance to the mayor's and district attorney's offices and to judges and other officials in Philadelphia. The center has also worked with the New Jersey Public Defender's Office in using an extensive database to assess possible discriminatory practices in the imposition of CAPITAL PUNISHMENT.

**CENTRAL INTELLIGENCE AGENCY**
The Central Intelligence Agency (CIA) was established following World War II from which the United States and the Soviet Union emerged as superpowers with vast military might and sharply conflicting world views. To protect the nation's security in all international matters and to ensure continued democracy and freedom for the United States, Congress created the CIA with the National Security Act of 1947 (ch. 343, 61 Stat. 495 [1947]). Gathering information from other countries relevant to national security is a sensitive task requiring considerable secrecy and covert activity. Unlike most other organizations, the CIA is not heard about when it is doing its job well. For this reason most of the information that reaches the media concerning the CIA is negative.

All intelligence information collected by the CIA and the CIA's recommendations are reported to the NATIONAL SECURITY COUNCIL under whose direction the CIA acts. The CIA is headed by the director of central intelligence, who is a member of the president's cabinet and the presidential spokesperson for the agency and the intelligence community. The director and deputy director of the CIA are appointed by the president with the advice and consent of the Senate.

The CIA is headquartered at a 258-acre compound in McLean, Virginia, and maintains twenty-two other offices in the Washington, D.C., area. The main compound includes a printing plant that produces phony documents—birth certificates, passports, driver's licenses, and so forth—for use by its agents. The plant also produces the *President's Daily Brief*, an eight-page CIA document that is presented to the president every morning. Another facility is used exclusively for recruiting spies to work for the CIA; another houses the Foreign Broadcast Information Service which monitors and translates broadcasts from forty-seven countries. Several other facilities recruit officers of the Komitet Gosudarstvennoi Bezopasnosti (KGB) (the State Security Committee for countries in the former Soviet Union) to spy on their own countries. The agency also maintains facilities in 130 countries throughout the world. Of the $28 billion that is budgeted annually to the U.S. Intelligence Committee, $3 billion goes to the CIA. The official number of individuals employed by the CIA is sixteen thousand but many believe the actual number to be closer to twenty-two thousand.

Although all aspects of the CIA revolve around gathering intelligence and maintaining the security of the nation, the actual responsibilities of the agency are many and varied; they include

- Advising the National Security Council in matters concerning national security
- Gathering and disseminating foreign intelligence (The CIA coordinates with the FEDERAL BUREAU OF INVESTIGATION (FBI) to gather intelligence within the United States.)
- Conducting counterintelligence activities outside of the United States (The CIA coordinates with the FBI to conduct intelligence and counterintelligence activities within the United States.)
- Gathering and disseminating intelligence on the foreign aspects of narcotics production and trafficking
- Conducting other special activities approved by the president

In its earliest days the CIA operated in a shroud of secrecy. In recent years, however, increased media attention has made the country more aware of CIA activities. Since the mid-1970s the CIA has received more attention for breaking the law than it has for upholding national security. Four items in particular have given the CIA unwanted attention: the Church committee hearings, the Iran-Contra Affair, the Ames scandal, and the end of the cold war.

**The Church Committee Hearings** In 1974, the *New York Times* broke a story that the CIA had violated its charter by spying on U.S. citizens who openly opposed the VIETNAM WAR. An investigation followed, headed by Senator Frank Church, a Democrat from Idaho. Church and his committee uncovered a wealth of damaging information about the agency that went

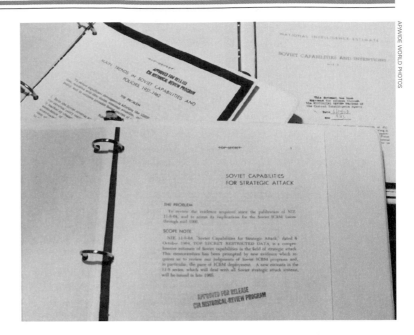

*The CIA was established after World War II. In the 1950s and 1960s much of its work concerned evaluating the military strength of the Soviet Union.*

far beyond the issue of the Vietnam War. The Church committee hearings changed the way the public looked at the agency responsible for the security of its country.

The Church committee found that the CIA had been intercepting and reading mail being exchanged between the United States and the Soviet bloc. The CIA had records on more than three hundred thousand U.S. citizens who had no ties with ESPIONAGE or intelligence. The CIA had also conducted LSD tests on unknowing participants, one of whom was driven to suicide. Through the CIA the United States had tried to assassinate at least five foreign leaders, including Cuban premier Fidel Castro. The CIA had first decided to embarrass the Cuban leader and thereby damage his popularity. To accomplish this, the agency plotted to make Castro's beard fall off by placing thallium salts in his shoes. The agency had a second plot, to give Castro a personality disorder by contaminating his cigars. The CIA had even enlisted the help of the Mafia in its attempt to assassinate Castro. These shocking disclosures brought demands for closer scrutiny of CIA activities.

Following the Church committee hearings Congress amended the National Security Act of 1947 in 1980 to require the CIA to inform the House and Senate Intelligence Committees of "significant anticipated intelligence activity." Within six years, however, the CIA found itself in trouble once more for failing to inform Congress of its activities.

**The Iran-Contra Affair** On November 3, 1986, the Lebanese magazine *Shiraa* reported that Robert McFarland, U.S. national security adviser, had come to Iran with a shipment of arms from the United States. This revelation spurred what was ultimately termed the IRAN-CONTRA Affair and spoiled an otherwise secret operation.

The CIA had involved itself in a covert action in which arms were shipped to Iran in exchange for the release of HOSTAGES. The payments that were received from the Iranians were, in turn, diverted to Nicaraguan Contra rebels who were fighting the Sandanista regime. All of this was done without the knowledge of Congress; the CIA informed neither the House Intelligence Committee nor the Senate Intelligence Committee of its actions. The CIA had broken the law that had been established to prevent it from breaking the law. Worse, President RONALD REAGAN had not approved the agency's covert activity.

One year after the arms had been sold, WILLIAM J. CASEY, director of central intelligence and a cabinet member, asked the president to approve the transaction retroactively. Reagan signed an agreement to that effect, which specified that Congress was not to be told of the approval. John Poindexter, the national security adviser at the time, later testified that he destroyed the only copy of the agreement in order to save President Reagan from political embarrassment.

Despite great media attention and congressional finger-pointing, actual punishments for the Iran-Contra Affair were few and lenient. Casey was never indicted in the scandal. McFarland and Secretary of Defense Caspar W. Weinberger were brought up on criminal charges but both were PARDONED on Christmas Eve 1992 by exiting president GEORGE BUSH. All other persons linked to the scandal either were also pardoned by Bush or got off with small fines or probation or both.

**The Ames Scandal** It did not take the CIA long to make its way back into the spotlight. This time it was not the agency that broke the law, but an individual. On February 21, 1994, Agent Aldrich Ames became the highest-ranking CIA official ever arrested. Ames had been selling U.S. secrets to the Soviet Union.

Ames's responsibilities as a CIA agent included directing the analysis of Soviet intelligence operations and recruiting Soviet agents who would betray those operations. This position put Ames in frequent contact with Soviet officials at the Soviet Embassy in Washington, D.C. Ultimately, Ames began selling U.S. security secrets to the Soviets, a venture that earned him more than $2.5 million before his arrest. Some of this information involved betraying double agents, disclosures that led to the death

of at least twelve Soviet and Eastern European spies.

The CIA began to search for a mole (a double agent) in 1986 after two intelligence officers at the Soviet Embassy who had been recruited as double agents by the FBI were recalled to Moscow, arrested, tried, and executed. The CIA was jolted again in 1989 when three more of its most valued Soviet double agents met their death by firing squad.

In 1991 the CIA began to work with the FBI in investigating East Germany and other former Warsaw Pact countries for leads to possible moles in the U.S. government. Ames became one of the suspects and was quietly transferred to the CIA's counternarcotics center. Since the FBI was in charge of counterintelligence domestically, Ames fell under its jurisdiction of investigation. CIA officials played down the possibility of one of its key employees being a spy and blocked independent scrutiny by the FBI. Ames continued to betray the CIA and the country.

The CIA was sharply criticized for its unwillingness to consider one of its own a double agent and for its refusal to allow the FBI to investigate the situation. For years, the agency failed to monitor Ames's overseas travel, question his personal finances, or detect unauthorized contacts between Ames and Soviet officials. As early as 1989 the CIA had been warned that Ames appeared to colleagues and neighbors to have accumulated sudden wealth. Ames was questioned about the source of the money during a routine 1991 background check. He said he had inherited money from his father-in-law.

© SCHILLER/THE IMAGE WORKS

*Aldrich Ames was arrested February 21, 1994, for selling U.S. secrets to the Soviet Union. His betrayal of double agents led to the death of at least twelve Soviet and Eastern European spies. Ames will serve a sentence of life imprisonment.*

From 1985 on, Ames and his wife bought a $540,000 home for cash, put $99,000 of improvements into the house, purchased a Jaguar, bought a farm and condominium in Colombia, and invested $165,000 in stock. And in one year they charged more than $100,000 on their credit cards. According to court documents, the Ameses spent nearly $1.4 million from April 1985 to November 1993. All of this took place while Ames's annual CIA salary never exceeded $70,000. According to CIA officials, indications of wrongdoing by CIA employees were often overlooked because supervisors were far too trusting of employees, whom they treated as family.

When Ames got a call to go to his CIA office the morning of February 21, 1994, he had no inkling that after almost nine years his career of selling secrets to Moscow was about to end. With Ames planning to travel to Russia the next day on CIA business, the FBI believed that it had to act. A block and a half from Ames's house his Jaguar was forced to the curb and he was arrested by FBI agents.

On April 28, 1994, Ames pleaded guilty to the criminal charges of espionage and tax evasion. He received a sentence of life imprisonment without parole, the maximum sentence he could have expected if convicted after trial.

**The End of the Cold War** The importance of the threat imposed by Ames's dealings with the Soviet Union was seemingly diminished with that country's dissolution. But despite the apparent end of the cold war and the division of the former Soviet Union, the United States continues to spy on the Russian Republic. The former Soviet Union also continues its own covert activities within the United States.

Some question the continued need for the CIA in the post–cold war era. But supporters need point no further than the war with Iraq to justify continued backing for the agency. The CIA was responsible for supplying intelligence reports that allowed the United States to cripple the Iraqi efforts in the Gulf War with an initial air strike. Without the assistance of the CIA the war might not have reached such a swift end. Supporters also argue that it is unfair to criticize a covert organization for its failures when so little attention is given to its successes. When the CIA is functioning efficiently and effectively its operation is invisible to the country's citizens; it is only in failure that the secrecy of the agency is betrayed to scrutinizing eyes.

Since the end of the cold war some members of Congress have called for severe cuts in the CIA's budget or dissolution of the agency. President BILL CLINTON said that such ideas are "profoundly wrong," and that the United States still faces many threats and challenges, including TERRORISM, drug trafficking, and nuclear proliferation. "I believe making deep cuts in intelligence during peacetime is comparable to canceling your health insurance when you're feeling fine," he said. Nonetheless, a federal commission has been organized to discuss and study the uncertain future of the CIA.

**CENTURY DIGEST®** 📖 A volume of the American Digest System that arranges by subject summaries of court opinions reported chronologically in the various units of the National Reporter System during the period from 1658 to 1896. 📖

There are over four hundred subject classifications within the digest, each corresponding to a legal concept, such as evidence. All the cases for the period covered in the Century Digest that discuss similar points of law can be found under a specific topic designation. See also LEGAL PUBLISHING.

**CERTIFICATE** 📖 A written document that is official verification that a condition or requirement has, or has not, been met.

A written assurance issued from a court that is notification to another officer, judge, or court of procedures practiced therein.

A document (such as a birth certificate) prepared by an official during the course of his or her regular duties, and which may be used as evidence for certain purposes.

A document certifying that one has fulfilled certain requirements and may practice in a field. 📖

A *stock certificate* is a paper representing a share of STOCK in a CORPORATION that has been purchased by its holder.

A *certificate of acknowledgment* is the written statement by a NOTARY PUBLIC, JUSTICE OF THE

*Efforts of the CIA during the Gulf War helped the United States to identify bombing targets such as this communications building in Baghdad, Iraq.*

## CERTIFICATE OF BIRTH

Birth No. ...........................

| 1. FULL NAME OF CHILD | (Type or Print) First Name | Middle Name | Last Name |
|---|---|---|---|

| 2. SEX | 3a. DATE OF CHILD'S BIRTH (Month) (Day) (Year) | 3b. Hour | AM / PM |
|---|---|---|---|

| 4. PLACE OF BIRTH | a. New York City / b. Borough | c. Name of Hospital or Institution. If not in hospital, street address. |
|---|---|---|

| 5a. MOTHER'S FULL MAIDEN NAME | 5b. MOTHER'S BIRTHPLACE, City and State. If Not U.S.A., Country. |
|---|---|

| 6. MOTHER'S USUAL RESIDENCE | a. State | b. County | c. City, town or location | d. Inside city limits (Specify Yes or No) | e. Street and house number |
|---|---|---|---|---|---|

| 7a. FATHER'S FULL NAME | 7b. FATHER'S BIRTHPLACE, City and State. If not U.S.A., Country. |
|---|---|

This certificate is filed pursuant to paragraph three of subdivision a. of Section 567-2.0 of the Administrative Code of the City of New York.

Approved for Filing ..................... 19.....
........................... Borough Registrar
   (Signature)
Date of Original Report ................. 19.....

(Signed) ....................... Father
........................... Mother
Address ...........................

BUREAU OF RECORDS AND STATISTICS    DEPARTMENT OF HEALTH    THE CITY OF NEW YORK

THIS CERTIFICATE NOT VALID UNLESS FILED IN
THE HEALTH DEPARTMENT
Certificates Containing Alterations, Omissions or Prepared With
Ball Point Pens are Unacceptable.

DO NOT WRITE IN THIS SPACE, MARGIN RESERVED FOR
CODING AND BINDING

Died: Date ................. Place ................. Cert. No. .................

PEACE, or other authorized officer that sets forth that a person or persons appeared before him or her on a particular date and declared an instrument to be their voluntary act and deed.

A *certificate of deposit* is prepared by a bank as a receipt for money deposited by a customer that the bank promises to repay to the depositor after certain conditions have been fulfilled.

A sample birth certificate from New York City

A sample certificate of deposit

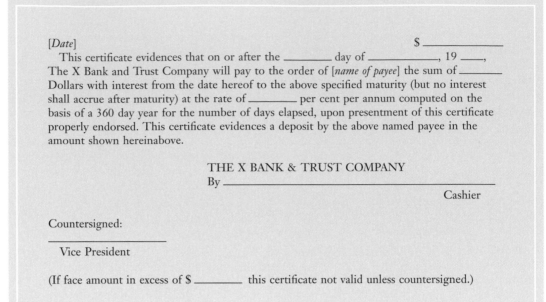

[*Date*]   $ _____

This certificate evidences that on or after the _____ day of _____, 19 ___, The X Bank and Trust Company will pay to the order of [*name of payee*] the sum of _____ Dollars with interest from the date hereof to the above specified maturity (but no interest shall accrue after maturity) at the rate of _____ per cent per annum computed on the basis of a 360 day year for the number of days elapsed, upon presentment of this certificate properly endorsed. This certificate evidences a deposit by the above named payee in the amount shown hereinabove.

THE X BANK & TRUST COMPANY
By _____
Cashier

Countersigned:
_____
Vice President

(If face amount in excess of $ _____ this certificate not valid unless countersigned.)

## CERTIFICATE OF DEPOSIT

A written recognition by a bank of a deposit, coupled with a pledge to pay the deposited amount plus interest, if any, to the depositor or to his or her order, or to another individual or to his or her order.

A form of COMMERCIAL PAPER that serves as DOCUMENTARY EVIDENCE that a savings account exists.

## CERTIFICATE OF OCCUPANCY

A document issued by a local building or ZONING authority to the owner of premises attesting that the premises have been built and maintained according to the provisions of building or zoning ORDINANCES, such as those that govern the number of fire exits or the safety of electrical wiring.

A certificate of occupancy is evidence that the building complies substantially with the plans and specifications that have been submitted to, and approved by, the local authority. It complements a building permit—a document that must be filed by the applicant with the local authority before construction to indicate that the proposed construction will adhere to zoning laws.

In legal practice, the requirement that a certificate of occupancy be presented on the day of CLOSING is usually attached as a RIDER to a contract for the sale of a house or building. If the seller is unable to present the certificate of occupancy the buyer may refuse to complete the sale.

Some cities require that a LANDLORD file a certificate of occupancy for apartments to be leased. This requirement is designed to prevent a building's deterioration to such an extent that it could expose its TENANTS to risks to their health and lives. Each time an apartment is vacated, an inspector from an appropriate government agency—such as the housing authority—inspects the apartment to make sure that it meets minimum standards of habitability. If the apartment does not, the inspector may issue a warning to the landlord to correct the violation within a certain period of time or the landlord will be prevented from leasing the apartment.

## CERTIFICATION PROCEEDING

An administrative hearing before the National Labor Relations Board (NLRB), pursuant to the federal WAGNER ACT (29 U.S.C.A. § 151 et seq. [1935]) to determine whether a group of employees is an appropriate bargaining unit, and if so, to decide whether a particular union should be declared its BARGAINING AGENT.

Employers and employees frequently negotiate and agree upon the terms and conditions of employment through COLLECTIVE BARGAINING, in which a representative of a particular group of employees presents the employees' demands to the employer so that a mutually advantageous accord can be reached. Before such bargaining can occur, it must be decided what group of employees will be served by the representative who will legally bind the group by his or her acceptance or rejection of the employer's terms. Once the group—the bargaining unit—is established the identity of its representative must be determined. Employers often willingly recognize a cohesive, homogeneous group of employees as a bargaining unit, thus acknowledging a particular union that claims to be its representative or bargaining agent. Disputes occasionally arise, however, over (1) the control of the union by the employer, thereby conflicting with the union's position as a representative of the employees; (2) the failure of a majority of the unit to select the union; (3) the wrongful action of a union that has usurped the rightful status of another union as the bargaining agent of the unit; and (4) situations in which the employer refuses to recognize the unit or its union.

A certification proceeding is the statutorily prescribed method of resolving such difficulties. The NLRB investigates a petition filed by the employees concerning a union acting in behalf of the employees, which the employer refuses to recognize or a petition by an employer who has received a claim of representation by the union. The NLRB holds a nonadversarial fact-finding HEARING to determine whether a valid question concerning representation exists. The hearing officer forwards the transcript containing evidence to the regional director of the NLRB. The regional director can dismiss the petition or decide to hold a secret ballot election for the bargaining agent and certify the result. Prior to the election, the director determines which employees are within the unit for purposes of voter eligibility. The NLRB will review a regional director's decision only if a statutorily determined, compelling reason exists, for instance, if his or her decision on a substantial issue of fact is clearly erroneous and adversely affects the rights of one party. An NLRB certification proceeding decision is subject to judicial review only if there is evidence of abuse of discretion. The COURT OF APPEALS, as a rule, defers to the NLRB because of its presumed expertise in the labor area. An aggrieved employer dissatisfied with a certification proceeding can obtain review by refusing to bargain with the agent, thereby committing an UNFAIR LABOR PRACTICE. Such a practice would probably result in an unfair labor practice proceeding and the final order that is made by the NLRB in such an action is reviewable by the court of appeals.

See also LABOR LAW; LABOR UNION.

**CERTIFIED CHECK** 📖 A written order made by a depositor to a bank to pay a certain sum to the person designated—the PAYEE—which is marked by the BANK as "accepted" or "certified," thereby unconditionally promising that the bank will pay the order upon its presentation by the payee. 📖

A certified check is considered the equivalent of cash since the bank, by its certification, guarantees it to be cashable. No bank is under a duty to its depositors or anyone else to certify CHECKS since it involves the assumption of a new obligation for which it is primarily responsible. It is a commonplace practice, however, and there is usually a small fee for this service. A certified check is often required by a payee who does not want to rely only upon the CREDIT of the DRAWER, the person who wrote the check. A sample of a check certification is shown below.

A payee who requires a drawer's check to be certified ensures his or her right to payment. Not only can the payee seek payment from the certified bank, but if for some reason the bank refuses to pay, the payee retains the right to enforce payment from the drawer. In this situ-

---

[Stamped across the face of the check]

No. _____

CERTIFIED
PAYABLE ONLY IF UNALTERED
SINCE ISSUANCE AND IF
PROPERLY ENDORSED

[Date]

_____ BANK

[Address]

_____

Authorized Signature

DO NOT DESTROY

An example of a certification notice used by a bank

ation the bank is primarily liable while the drawer is secondarily liable.

Occasionally the payee or subsequent holder of the check—a person who has been legally given possession and the right to payment—will present the check to the drawer's bank for certification. Although the bank is obligated to cash the check, it need not certify the check because only it, not the drawer or any subsequent endorsers, would be liable for its payment. Some banks will certify a check in such instances only with the approval of the drawer.

If a bank refuses to pay a check that it has certified, its drawer or holder may sue the bank for its wrongful conduct, called DISHONOR. A certified check, a type of COMMERCIAL PAPER or NEGOTIABLE INSTRUMENT, is governed by Article 3 of the UNIFORM COMMERCIAL CODE.

## CERTIFIED COPY 📖 A photocopy of a document, judgment, or record that is signed and attested to as an accurate and a complete reproduction of the original document by a public official in whose custody the original has been placed for safekeeping. 📖

A certified copy is admissible as EVIDENCE in a lawsuit when the original document cannot be produced because it has been lost or destroyed. This rule, which considers a certified copy to be SECONDARY EVIDENCE unless circumstances of loss or destruction warrant its treatment as PRIMARY EVIDENCE, is known as the BEST EVIDENCE rule. State and federal rules of evidence govern the use of a certified copy in their respective judicial proceedings.

## CERTIORARI 📖 [*Latin, To be informed of.*] At COMMON LAW, an original WRIT or order issued by the CHANCERY or KING'S BENCH, commanding officers of INFERIOR COURTS to submit the record of a cause pending before them to give the party more certain and speedy justice.

A writ that a superior APPELLATE COURT issues in its discretion to an inferior court, ordering it to produce a certified record of a particular case it has tried, in order to determine whether any irregularities or errors occurred that justify review of the case.

A device by which the SUPREME COURT OF THE UNITED STATES exercises its discretion in selecting the cases it will review. 📖

Certiorari is an extraordinary PREROGATIVE WRIT granted in cases that otherwise would not be entitled to review. A PETITION for certiorari is made to a superior appellate court, which may exercise its discretion in accepting a case for review, while an APPEAL of a case from a lower court to an intermediate appellate court, or from an intermediate appellate court to a superior appellate court, is regulated by statute. Appellate review of a case that is granted by the issuance of certiorari is sometimes called an appeal, although such review is at the discretion of the appellate court.

A party, the PETITIONER, files a petition for certiorari with the appellate court after a judgment has been rendered against him in the inferior court. The petition must specifically state why the relief sought is unavailable in any other court or through any other appellate process, along with information clearly identifying the case and the questions to be reviewed, the relevant provisions of law to be applied, a concise statement of facts relating to the issues, and any other materials required by statute. The rules of practice of the appellate court to which the petitioner has applied for relief govern the procedure to be observed. For example, a petition for statutory certiorari made to the Supreme Court of the United States must be prefaced by a MOTION for leave, or permission, to file such a petition. If a common-law writ is sought, however, the petitioner need only file a petition for certiorari.

After evaluating the petition, the appellate court will decide whether to grant or deny certiorari. Certiorari is issued, designated as "cert. granted," when the case presents an issue that is appropriate for resolution by the court and it is in the public interest to do so, such as when the issue has been decided differently by a variety of lower courts, thereby creating confusion and necessitating a uniform interpretation of the law. Certiorari is denied when the appellate court decides that the case does not present an appropriate matter for its consideration. In the practice of the Supreme Court, if a petition has been granted certiorari as a result of a mistake, such as where the petitioner misrepresents the case or the case has become MOOT, the Court will dismiss the petition as "having been improvidently granted," which has the same effect as an initial denial of the petition. Practically speaking, this rarely occurs.

Some states have abolished writs of certiorari under their rules of appellate practice.

## CESSION 📖 The act of relinquishing one's right.

A surrender, relinquishment, or assignment of territory by one state or government to another.

The territory of a foreign government gained by the transfer of SOVEREIGNTY. 📖

## CESTUI QUE 📖 [*French, He or she who.*] The person for whom a benefit exists. 📖

A *cestui que trust* is a person for whose benefit a TRUST is created; a BENEFICIARY. Although legal

A sample petition
for a writ of
certiorari

No. 94 993 Dec 2 1994

OFFICE OF THE CLERK
In The
Supreme Court of the United States
OCTOBER TERM, 1994

STATE OF ILLINOIS,

*Petitioner;*

v.

GREGORY TURNER,

*Respondent.*

On Petition for a Writ of Certiorari to the
Appellate Court of Illinois, First Judicial District

PETITION FOR A WRIT OF CERTIORARI

ROLAND W. BURRIS
Attorney General of Illinois
ARLEEN C. ANDERSON
Assistant Attorney General
100 W. Randolph St., Suite 1200
Chicago, Illinois 60601
*Attorneys for Petitioner*

JACK O'MALLEY
Cook County State's Attorney
309 Richard J. Daley Center
Chicago, Illinois 60602
RENEE G. GOLDFARB
*Counsel of Record*
KEVIN SWEENEY
JAMES P. NAVARRE
Assistant State's Attorneys
*Of Counsel*

## QUESTION PRESENTED

Whether the exclusionary rule requires that a voluntary confession be suppressed when the suspect was confronted during questioning with evidence seized as a result of an illegal search, even though a confession is not a product of an illegal search and the exclusionary rule can have no real deterrent effect on police misconduct under those circumstances.

A sample petition
for a writ of
certiorari
(continued)

## TABLE OF CONTENTS

A sample petition
for a writ of
certiorari
(continued)

In The
Supreme Court of the United States
October Term, 1994

STATE OF ILLINOIS,

*Petitioner,*

v.

GREGORY TURNER,

*Respondent.*

On Petition for a Writ of Certiorari to the
Appellate Court of Illinois, First Judicial District

PETITION FOR A WRIT OF CERTIORARI

Petitioner, the State of Illinois, respectfully prays that a writ of certiorari issue to review the judgment and opinion of the Appellate Court of Illinois, First Judicial District, in this matter.

## OPINIONS BELOW

The opinion of the Appellate Court of Illinois, First District, Sixth Division, reversing respondent's conviction for first degree murder, is reported as *People v. Turner,* 259 Ill. App. 3d 979, 197 Ill. Dec. 777, 631 N.E. 2d 1236 (1st Dist. 1994) and is reproduced as Appendix A to this petition. The order of the Illinois Supreme Court denying leave to appeal in this matter is reproduced as Appendix B to this petition.

## JURISDICTION

The decision of the Appellate Court of Illinois in this matter was entered on March 18, 1994. A timely petition for leave to appeal to the Illinois Supreme Court was filed by petitioner and was denied by the Illinois Supreme Court on October 6, 1994. This Court's jurisdiction is invoked under 28 U.S.C. sec. 1257(3).

## CONSTITUTIONAL PROVISION INVOLVED

FOURTH AMENDMENT: The right of the people to be secure in their persons, houses, papers, and effects, against unreasonable searches and seizures, shall not be violated. . . .

## STATEMENT OF THE CASE

Respondent Gregory Turner confessed to stabbing sixteen year old [S.T.] to death. During questioning by the police, respondent had been confronted with a pair of bloody shoes found near his bed. The trial judge suppressed evidence of the shoes as the product of an illegal search, but ruled that respondent's confession was voluntary and admissible. Respondent was convicted of first degree murder at a bench trial. The Appellate Court of Illinois reversed respondent's murder conviction, ruling that under the exclusionary rule respondent's confession had to be suppressed because respondent was confronted with illegally seized evidence during questioning. *People v. Turner,* 259 Ill. App. 3d 979, 631 N.E. 2d 1236 (1st Dist. 1994).

### Evidence in the Trial Court

On June 9, 1988 the body of high school student [S.T.] was found in an alley on the south side of Chicago. She had been stabbed twice in the chest and swabs from her vagina and anus tested positive for semen.

The Chicago police wanted to talk to respondent, who was a 27 year old parolee, because a friend of the victim had said that [S.T.] had been afraid of respondent. An officer reached

A sample petition
for a writ of
certiorari
(continued)

respondent on the phone and respondent agreed to come into the station. After respondent came into the station on his own, the police talked to him in an interview room and respondent gave the officers an alibi.

Two detectives then left the station to check out the alibi and, after talking to two of respondent's relatives, found that the alibi was false. Then the detectives went to respondent's home and talked to his parents. According to the findings of the trial judge, the detectives told respondent's mother that respondent was cooperating in the investigation and that respondent had said that it was okay to search his room.

With the permission of respondent's mother the detectives searched the area in the basement where respondent slept and found a pair of shoes with blood on the soles. The detectives asked respondent's mother if they could take the shoes and she said yes.

Later a different detective questioned respondent again in the interview room and respondent was told that his alibi did not check out and that bloody shoes had been found by his bed. Respondent then confessed that he had killed [S.T.] He later gave a written confession to a court reporter and an assistant state's attorney.

In the confession respondent said that on the night of the murder he had sex with [S.T.] in his bed in the basement of his home. Afterwards, he left the basement with the victim because she was loudly demanding $30.00 from him. Respondent said that he stabbed the victim because she had threatened to claim that he had raped her, and he was afraid of a rape accusation because he was on parole.

Trial Court Proceedings

The trial judge suppressed evidence of the bloody shoes found by respondent's bed, finding that the police had told falsehoods to respondent's mother in order to get consent to search. However, the trial judge allowed respondent's confession to go into evidence, ruling that respondent had not been under arrest when he confessed. Also, the judge ruled that the confession had not been caused by the fact that respondent had been confronted with the bloody shoes, since respondent had also been confronted with the fact that his alibi was false.

At trial the theory of the prosecution was that respondent had raped [S.T.] and then had killed her when she threatened to tell her mother. However, the trial judge acquitted respondent of aggravated criminal sexual assault. But the judge found respondent guilty of first degree murder and respondent was later sentenced to 30 years in custody. That conviction was reversed on appeal on the grounds that respondent's confession should have been suppressed under the exclusionary rule since respondent was confronted with illegally seized evidence during questioning. *People v. Turner*, 259 Ill. App. 3d 979, 631 N.E. 2d 236 (1st Dist. 1994).

REASONS FOR GRANTING THE WRIT

**THE EXCLUSIONARY RULE DOES NOT REQUIRE THAT A VOLUNTARY CONFESSION BE SUPPRESSED WHEN THE SUSPECT WAS CONFRONTED WITH ILLEGALLY SEIZED EVIDENCE DURING QUESTIONING, SINCE A CONFESSION IS NOT THE PRODUCT OF AN ILLEGAL SEARCH AND BECAUSE THE EXCLUSIONARY RULE CAN HAVE NO REAL DETERRENT EFFECT ON POLICE MISCONDUCT UNDER THOSE CIRCUMSTANCES.**

The exclusionary rule is not part of the Fourth Amendment, but is a device created by judges to deter the police from illegally seizing evidence. *Illinois v. Krull*, 480 U.S. 340, 107 S. Ct. 1160, 94 L. Ed. 2d 364 (1987). Therefore the exclusionary rule does not apply to types of cases in which it will not significantly deter police misconduct. *New York v. Harris*, 495 U.S. 14, 110 S. Ct. 1640, 109 L. Ed. 2d 13 (1990); *United States v. Leon*, 469 U.S. 897, 104 S. Ct. 3405, 82 L. Ed. 2d 677 (1984). This is just such a case. Here respondent Gregory Turner confessed to murder when he was confronted with illegally seized evidence, but the police had no way of knowing in advance that their search would eventually produce an incriminating statement. Seldom if ever will officers anticipate that an illegal search will later lead to a confession. Therefore a voluntary confession should be admissible even when the suspect is confronted with illegally seized evidence during questioning, because the exclusionary rule can have no real deterrent effect on police misconduct under those circumstances.

A sample petition
for a writ of
certiorari
(continued)

Certiorari should be granted here to apply this important rule of law. More exactly, certiorari should be granted for the following reasons:

1. The precise question presented by this case (whether a voluntary confession must be suppressed because the suspect was confronted with illegally seized evidence) is an important one which has not been decided by this Court.

2. Nevertheless, the lower court's extension of the exclusionary rule in this case conflicts with a number of decisions of this Court, particularly *New York v. Harris*, 495 U.S. 14, 110 S. Ct. 1640, 109 L. Ed. 2d 13 (1990).

3. There is a conflict of authority among state courts which have considered this issue.

This case illustrates the costs of applying the exclusionary rule when it can have no real effect in deterring violations of the Fourth Amendment.

A.

**Certiorari Should Be Granted Because This Case Involves An Important Issue Concerning The Admissibility Of Confessions Which Has Not Been Decided By This Court.**

This Court has not decided whether a voluntary confession must be suppressed when the suspect was confronted with illegally seized evidence during questioning. Nevertheless, this is an important legal issue which the defense may attempt to raise in many criminal cases in which a suspect has confessed to a crime. Therefore certiorari should be granted to settle an important constitutional issue about the scope of the exclusionary rule which has not yet been decided by this Court. U.S. Sup. Ct. Rule 10.1(c).

Here respondent's confession to the murder of [S.T.] was found to be voluntary and admissible by the trial judge. However, the Appellate Court ruled that the confession had to be suppressed because respondent had been told during questioning that shoes with blood on them had been found near his bed. *People v. Turner*, 259 Ill. App. 3d 979, 631 N.E. 2d 1236 (1st Dist. 1994). Those shoes had been seized by the police with the consent of respondent's mother, but the trial court found that this consent had been obtained through deceit. The ruling by the Appellate Court of Illinois should be reversed, because it extends the exclusionary rule to a situation when it should not and does not apply.

The exclusionary rule applies to a type of evidence if and only if suppression of such evidence will deter illegal searches and seizures. *New York v. Harris*, 495 U.S. 14, 110 S. Ct. 1640, 109 L. Ed. 2d 13 (1990); *Illinois v. Krull*, 480 U.S. 340, 107 S. Ct. 1160, 94 L. Ed. 2d 364 (1987). Therefore the exclusionary rule does not apply here. A confession is not evidence found during an illegal search and in almost all cases the police will have no idea at the time of a search that they will find evidence which will later lead to a confession. Ordinarily the police will not be able to predict in advance what they will find during a search and they certainly will not be able to predict what effect the evidence would have if mentioned during interrogation of a suspect. Accordingly, there will be no deterrent effect in suppressing a confession because the suspect was confronted with illegally seized evidence during questioning. In almost every case the police will have no idea that a search will produce evidence which will later lead to a confession, so there will be no deterrent effect in suppressing such confessions.

Instead, the way to deter illegal searches and seizures is to suppress the evidence found during those searches, as was done here. The trial judge suppressed evidence of the bloody shoes found by respondent's bed, and petitioner has not challenged that ruling on review. But it makes no sense to suppress a voluntary confession just because the suspect was told about illegally seized evidence before he confessed. A confession is not evidence found during an illegal search nor is it a predictable result of such a search, so there is no real deterrent effect on police misconduct in suppressing such a confession.

Thirty years ago this Court did come close to deciding whether a confession must be suppressed if the suspect was confronted with illegally seized evidence during questioning. *Fahy v. Connecticut*, 375 U.S. 85, 84 S. Ct. 229, 11 L. Ed. 2d 171 (1963). However, the record in *Fahy* did not show whether the suspect had been confronted with the evidence before his initial confession, so the most this Court said was that such an inquiry would be appropriate on remand. Moreover, the language in *Fahy* concerning the scope of the exclusionary rule is obsolete, since this Court has since held that the exclusionary rule does not apply when it cannot significantly deter police misconduct. See, *e.g.*, *Illinois v. Krull*, 480 U.S. 340, 107 S. Ct. 1160, 94 L. Ed. 2d 364 (1987); *United States v. Leon*, 469 U.S. 897, 104 S. Ct. 3405, 82 L. Ed. 2d 677 (1984); *United States v. Calandra*, 414 U.S. 338, 94 S. Ct. 613, 38 L. Ed. 2d 561 (1974).

Therefore certiorari should be granted to resolve an important issue which has not previously been decided by this Court. Usually a suspect who confesses to a crime will have been confronted by the police during questioning with the evidence incriminating him. Defense attorneys can always claim before trial that such evidence was illegally seized and, even if few such claims will succeed, such claims certainly will delay trials and consume scarce court time. Thus this Court should hold that a voluntary confession is not made inadmissible by the exclusionary rule even if the suspect was confronted with illegally seized evidence during questioning.

B.

**The Extension Of The Exclusionary Rule By The Appellate Court Of Illinois Conflicts With A Number Of Decisions Of This Court.**

This Court has clearly and repeatedly held that the exclusionary rule is not part of the Fourth Amendment, but is a remedial device designed to exclude evidence only when exclusion would have the effect of deterring illegal searches and seizures. *New York v. Harris*, 495 U.S. 14, 110 S. Ct. 1640, 109 L. Ed. 2d 13 (1990); *Illinois v. Krull*, 480 U.S. 340, 107 S. Ct. 1160, 94 L. Ed. 2d 364 (1987); *United States v. Leon*, 469 U.S. 897, 104 S. Ct. 3405, 82 L. Ed. 2d 677 (1984); *Stone v. Powell*, 428 U.S. 465, 96 S. Ct. 3037, 49 L. Ed. 2d 1067 (1976); *United States v. Calandra*, 414 U.S. 338, 94 S. Ct. 613, 38 L. Ed. 2d 561 (1974). In this case the Appellate Court of Illinois extended the exclusionary rule to apply to a situation where it could have no real deterrent effect. Therefore certiorari should be granted because the lower court ruling conflicts with a number of decisions by this Court.

In particular, the Appellate Court's opinion conflicts with this Court's 1990 *Harris* decision, which held that a confession was admissible although the suspect had been unlawfully arrested in his home without a warrant. *New York v. Harris*, 495 U.S. 14, 110 S. Ct. 1640, 109 L. Ed. 2d 13 (1990). *Harris* held that the exclusionary rule does not require that a confession be suppressed in either of the following two situations:

1.  When the confession is not the product of the violation of the Fourth Amendment; or

2.  When the exclusionary rule would not deter police misconduct.

Both holdings indicate that respondent's confession should have been ruled admissible. Respondent's confession was not the product of the alleged violation of the Fourth Amendment by the police, nor could the exclusionary rule have any significant deterrent effect under the circumstances of this case.

Here respondent confessed to murder after the police told him that his alibi did not check out and that bloody shoes had been found near his bed. Those shoes had been found and taken by the police with the consent of respondent's mother. Although evidence on the point was conflicting, the trial judge found that the bloody shoes had been seized illegally because the police had given false information to respondent's mother in order to get her consent to search. However, under this Court's reasoning in *Harris*, respondent's confession cannot be considered the product of the Fourth Amendment violation in this case. In *Harris* this Court held that the suspect's confession was not the product of the Fourth Amendment violation, since that violation consisted of arresting the suspect in his apartment without a warrant and the interrogation of that suspect was lawful. Similarly, here the Fourth Amendment violation consisted of a seizure from respondent's home when he was not present, and there was nothing unconstitutional about the interrogation of respondent. In this case the Fourth Amendment protected respondent's house and its contents, but did not bar interrogation of respondent in an effort to get a voluntary confession. Therefore, as in *Harris*, the confession was not the product of the Fourth Amendment violation, so respondent's voluntary confession to murder was admissible.

Also, the exclusionary rule does not apply to respondent's confession because under the circumstances of this case that rule can have no significant effect in deterring police misconduct. When officers search for evidence, they will not know in advance if they will find evidence which will later lead a suspect to confess. Ordinarily the officers will not know what, if

A sample petition
for a writ of
certiorari
(continued)

anything they will find during the search. Usually they will not even have a suspect in custody when the search is performed. And almost never will the officers have any way of knowing whether the evidence, if any, found during their search will play a role in leading a suspect to confess. Since the police will not know or expect that an illegal search will produce evidence which will later lead to a confession, the threat of suppressing such confessions cannot deter illegal searches. The exclusionary rule does not apply when it can have no significant deterrent effect. *Illinois v. Krull*, 480 U.S. 340, 107 S. Ct. 1160, 94 L. Ed. 2d 364 (1987). Therefore, the exclusionary rule does not require that a voluntary confession be suppressed, even when the suspect was confronted by illegally seized evidence during questioning.

This is particularly true since the direct and simple way to deter illegal searches is to suppress the evidence seized during them. That is what was done in respondent's case. The trial judge suppressed evidence of the bloody shoes found near respondent's bed, and that evidence was not used at respondent's trial. The State, while it argued in the trial court that the seizure of the shoes was lawful, did not challenge on appeal the suppression of that evidence. There is no need to suppress voluntary confessions which are not the product of illegal searches, when illegal searches may be more effectively deterred by suppressing evidence discovered during them.

To summarize, for two separate reasons described in this Court's *Harris* opinion the exclusionary rule does not require that a voluntary confession be suppressed when the suspect is confronted with illegally seized evidence during questioning. First, a voluntary confession cannot be considered the product of an unlawful entry into a building, so the exclusionary rule does not apply. Second, under those circumstances the exclusionary rule can have no real deterrent effect, since the police will not know at the time of a search whether they will find evidence which will later induce a confession. Therefore under the Fourth Amendment use of respondent's voluntary confession at his murder trial was lawful.

### Attenuation Analysis

Petitioner's main argument for a grant of certiorari is *not* based on the doctrine of attenuation, which provides that a confession may be admissible even following an illegal arrest if the confession is not directly caused by the Fourth Amendment violation. *Rawlings v. Kentucky*, 448 U.S. 98, 100 S. Ct. 2556, 65 L. Ed. 2d 633 (1980); *Brown v. Illinois*, 422 U.S. 590, 95 S. Ct. 2254, 45 L. Ed. 2d 416 (1975). Attenuation provides only an alternative reason for review by this Court. As this Court held in *Harris*, when the exclusionary rule does not apply then there is no need to engage in an attenuation analysis. *New York v. Harris*, 495 U.S. 15, 19, 110 S. Ct. 1640, 1643, 109 L. Ed. 2d 13, 21 (1990). Only when the exclusionary rule applies is there any reason to consider whether intervening circumstances have "purged the taint" of a Fourth Amendment violation. Here the exclusionary rule does not apply to respondent's confession, so it is unnecessary to determine whether the connection between the search and the confession was direct or attenuated.

*Brown* and other confession cases applying an attenuation analysis involved illegal arrests leading to confessions. See *Dunaway v. New York*, 442 U.S. 200, 99 S. Ct. 2248, 60 L. Ed. 2d 2248 (1979); *Brown v. Illinois*, 422 U.S. 590, 95 S. Ct. 2254, 45 L. Ed. 2d 416 (1975). That is not what happened here, since the trial judge found that petitioner was not under arrest when he confessed. It is logical to say that a confession may be the product of an illegal arrest, but it makes much less sense to say that a confession is the product of an illegal search which produced only physical evidence. Also, suppressing confessions may be a way to deter illegal arrests, but suppressing confessions will not significantly deter illegal searches of property.

However, assuming for the sake of argument that the doctrine of attenuation did apply here, then the opinion of the Appellate Court of Illinois failed to follow this Court's decisions. The Appellate Court held that a confession must be suppressed when illegally seized evidence "may" have been a factor in the decision to confess. *People v. Turner*, 259 Ill. App. 3d 979, 991, 631 N.E. 2d 1236, 1244 (1st Dist. 1994) (See Appendix A, p. A-18). However, this Court has said that when there are intervening circumstances attenuating a Fourth Amendment violation then a voluntary confession is admissible. *Rawlings v. Kentucky*, 448 U.S. 98, 100 S. Ct. 2556, 65 L. Ed. 2d 633 (1980); *United States v. Ceccolini*, 435 U.S. 268,

A sample petition
for a writ of
certiorari
(continued)

98 S. Ct. 1054, 55 L. Ed. 2d 268 (1978). In respondent's case there was such a circumstance, since the detectives also told him that they had checked out his alibi and knew it was false. The Appellate Court of Illinois held that when a suspect is confronted with illegally seized evidence during questioning, then the confession must necessarily be suppressed even if the suspect was also confronted with incriminating evidence that had been lawfully discovered. That holding is contrary to this Court's Fourth Amendment decisions and provides another reason to reverse the Appellate Court's decision.

### Summary

During a search of respondent's house the detectives found incriminating evidence, but they certainly did not find respondent's confession there. Accordingly that confession was not the product of the Fourth Amendment violation in this case, so the exclusionary rule did not apply to that confession. Also, the exclusionary rule does not apply because it will have no real deterrent effect on police misconduct under circumstances similar to this case. Certiorari should be granted in order to define the scope of the exclusionary rule and to correct the lower court's failure to follow this Court's decisions.

### C.

### Certiorari Should Be Granted To Resolve A Conflict Among State Court Decisions On Whether A Confession Must Be Suppressed If The Suspect Has Been Confronted With Illegally Seized Evidence During Questioning.

Another reason why this Court should grant certiorari is that state reviewing courts are divided on the question of whether a voluntary confession must be suppressed where it follows an unlawful search. Several courts have held that a voluntary confession should not be suppressed although it came after an illegal search and seizure. See, *e.g.*, *State v. Manns*, 220 Neb. 426, 370 N.W. 2d 157, 160-61 (1985) (the defendant's confession was not the fruit of an illegal search during which stolen property was recovered where the defendant received *Miranda* warnings and where the defendant's confession was voluntary); *Mays v. State*, 469 N.E. 2d 1161, 1164-65 (Ind. 1984) (although the defendant was confronted with illegally obtained evidence prior to confessing, his confession was admissible where the unlawful evidence was not so psychologically coercive as to have caused the defendant to confess against his free will); *People v. Pierce*, 88 Ill. App. 3d 1095, 411 N.E. 2d 295, 307 (5th Dist. 1980) (any taint from the unlawful search conducted without a valid warrant was removed from the defendant's confession where the defendant was given *Miranda* warnings and his confession was voluntary); and *State v. Rocheleau*, 131 Vt. 563, 313 A. 2d 33, 38-40 (1973) (even though the initial search was illegal, the subsequent confession was properly admitted where it was voluntary).

On the other hand, a number of courts have utilized an analysis similar to the approach employed by the Appellate Court of Illinois in this case. For example, in *State v. Pau'u*, 824 P. 2d 833, 835-37 (Hawaii 1992), the court held that even though the defendant's confession was voluntary in that the defendant understood his right to remain silent and was not coerced into waiving that right, the confession was still inadmissible where it was induced by a prior illegal search. Other relevant cases include *Hart v. Commonwealth*, 269 S.E. 2d 806, 809-10 (Va. 1980) (despite the voluntariness of a confession, it should have been excluded where there was an uninterrupted causal connection between the unlawful seizure of evidence and the confession); *People v. Hines*, 575 P. 2d 414, 416 (Colo. 1978) (confession which followed an unlawful search was inadmissible under the "fruit of the poisonous tree" doctrine where recitation of *Miranda* warnings was insufficient to dissipate the taint of the illegality); and *State v. Verhagen*, 86 Wis. 2d 262, 272 N.W. 2d 105, 109 (1978) (although the confession was voluntary, the confession should have been suppressed where it was an exploitation of a prior illegal search).

A conflict exists among state courts and a decision by this Court would provide much needed guidance on this issue. This Court has never decided a case in which a defendant sought to suppress a confession and the record showed that the defendant had been confronted with illegally seized evidence before he confessed. Lafave and Israel, *Criminal Procedure*, sec. 9.4(a), p. 747 (1984). Nothing is more common than for a suspect to confess after the police have confronted that suspect with the evidence against him. Defense attorneys,

A sample petition
for a writ of
certiorari
(continued)

prosecutors and trial judges would benefit from knowing whether a defendant may seek to have his confession suppressed on the theory that the evidence used during questioning was illegally seized. Certiorari should be granted to decide this important and unresolved issue.

## CONCLUSION

Petitioner, the State of Illinois, respectfully requests that a writ of certiorari issue to review the decision of the Appellate Court of Illinois, First Judicial District.

Respectfully submitted,

ROLAND W. BURRIS
Attorney General of Illinois
ARLEEN C. ANDERSON
Assistant Attorney General
100 W. Randolph St., Suite 1200
Chicago, Illinois 60601
*Attorneys for Petitioner*

JACK O'MALLEY
Cook County State's Attorney
309 Richard J. Daley Center
Chicago, Illinois 60602
RENEE G. GOLDFARB
*Counsel of Record*
KEVIN SWEENEY
JAMES P. NAVARRE
Assistant State's Attorneys
*Of Counsel*

---

title of the trust is vested in the TRUSTEE, the *cestui que trust* is the beneficiary who is entitled to all benefits from a trust.

A *cestui que use* is an archaic term of property law that describes one who has a BENEFICIAL INTEREST in land held by someone else. TITLE and POSSESSION as well as the duty to defend the land is held by another, but the *cestui que use* has the right to rents, profits, and other benefits from the land.

A *cestui que vie* is the person whose life is used to measure various things, such as the duration of a trust, a GIFT, or an INSURANCE contract. It can also be used to mean the person upon whose life a policy of life insurance is drawn.

**CF.** An abbreviation for the Latin word *confer*, meaning "compare."

The use of this abbreviation indicates that another section of a particular work or another case or volume contains contrasting, comparable, or explanatory opinions and text.

**C.F.&I.** An abbreviation for cost, FREIGHT, and INSURANCE that is used in a SALES contract to indicate that the purchase price quoted for the goods by the seller includes the expense incurred by the seller for shipment of such goods and for insurance of the goods against loss or destruction until their arrival at the destination named by the buyer.

The abbreviation C.F.&I. is synonymous with the abbreviation C.I.F. commonly found in CONTRACTS for foreign shipments. A seller who has entered a sales contract with a C.F.&I. provision agrees to accept the expense of placing the goods into the custody of a CARRIER for shipment from their port of origin to their designated location and to obtain a negotiable BILL OF LADING, which will be endorsed by the buyer upon receipt of payment for the goods. The seller has the responsibility of loading the cargo and obtaining a receipt from the carrier, which might be incorporated into the bill of lading to show that freight has been paid by him or her. The seller must also purchase insurance against the loss, damage, or destruction of such goods and have the buyer designated as the beneficiary. The seller prepares an INVOICE of the goods to be shipped and sends the necessary documents to both the shipper and the buyer so that the buyer can take delivery of the goods upon arrival at their destination. See also SHIPPING LAW.

## CHAFEE, ZECHARIAH, JR.

As a leading U.S. legal scholar and educator, Zechariah Chafee, Jr., did more than anyone else in the early twentieth century to shape the debate surrounding FREEDOM OF SPEECH and the Constitution's FIRST AMENDMENT. In his most influential book, *Freedom of Speech* (1920), Chafee argued for the importance of protecting free speech even in wartime. His ideas later guided the Supreme Court in liberalizing its approach to free speech.

Chafee was born on December 7, 1885, in Providence, Rhode Island, to a wealthy family. He attended Brown University, graduating with a bachelor's degree in 1907. He helped manage his family's iron foundry for three years and then left to attend Harvard Law School in 1910. He remained on the family firm's board of directors for the rest of his life. He married Bess Frank Searle in 1912 and they had four children. While at Harvard he was influenced by the theories of sociological JURISPRUDENCE presented by ROSCOE POUND and others. At Harvard, he also met Harold J. Laski, a political scientist and later a leader of England's Labour party, who became a lifelong friend. Chafee graduated from law school with a bachelor of laws degree in 1913 and practiced law for three years in Providence. In 1916 he began teaching at Harvard Law School as an assistant professor of law. He accepted a full professorship three years later and remained at Harvard for the rest of his life.

Chafee was a professor at Harvard Law School for nearly forty years. His writings and public service influenced many different areas of civil liberties, from conditions for mine workers to international HUMAN RIGHTS to the system for apportioning U.S. House seats among the states. His other books include *America Now* (1938), *Freedom of Speech in the United States* (1941), *Government and Mass Communications* (1947), *Documents on Fundamental Human Rights* (1951), *Freedom of Speech and Press* (1955), and *Blessings of Liberty* (1956).

**BIOGRAPHY**

*Zechariah Chafee, Jr.*

HARVARD UNIVERSITY ARCHIVES

"NOTHING ADDS MORE TO MEN'S HATRED FOR GOVERNMENT THAN ITS REFUSAL TO LET THEM TALK, ESPECIALLY IF THEY ARE THE TYPE OF PERSON ANARCHISTS ARE, TO WHOM TALKING A LITTLE WILDLY IS THE GREATEST JOY OF LIFE."

Justice FELIX FRANKFURTER wrote of Chafee, "The extent to which . . . he influenced the thought and temper of public opinion and action in that pervasive aspect of national life known as civil rights has no match in the legal professoriate."

Chafee's goal in his legal writings was to "master the law and reduce it to reason." In the area of free speech, this meant replacing intuition with reason and producing a rational interpretation of the First Amendment, which states that "Congress shall make no law . . . abridging the freedom of speech, or of the press." The notion of balance was a crucial element in his legal philosophy. According to Chafee, most legal problems could be solved by balancing competing interests. In the case of free speech, that meant BALANCING society's competing interests in the benefits of security and in the benefits of unlimited discussion.

Chafee's interest in free speech and civil liberties began while he was teaching a course on EQUITY at Harvard Law School during World War I. He became interested in the history of libel law and free speech, particularly as judges across the United States began making arbitrary and often conflicting decisions regarding SEDITION (the act of urging others to rebel against authority) and free speech during wartime. In many cases, people who spoke out or demonstrated against the wartime policies of the U.S. government were imprisoned for their views. Such cases often involved two laws passed by Congress, the Espionage Act of 1917 (ch. 30, 40 Stat. 217) and the Sedition Act of 1918 (ch. 75, 40 Stat. 553). Looking closely at the judicial decisions regarding such cases, Chafee began to see that laws regarding freedom of speech were in great need of modernization.

Between 1918 and 1920 Chafee published two articles—"Freedom of Speech" in the *New Republic* (Nov. 16, 1918) and "Freedom of Speech in Wartime" in the *Harvard Law Review* (747 [June 1919])—and the book *Freedom of Speech* (1920), which caused great controversy and also made his reputation, associating him for the rest of his career with free speech issues. In these writings Chafee took aim against con-

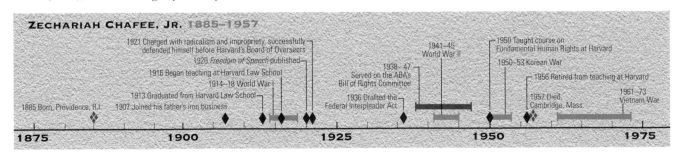

ZECHARIAH CHAFEE, JR. 1885–1957

1921 Charged with radicalism and impropriety, successfully defended himself before Harvard's Board of Overseers
1920 *Freedom of Speech* published
1916 Began teaching at Harvard Law School
1914–18 World War I
1913 Graduated from Harvard Law School
1885 Born, Providence, R.I.    1907 Joined his father's iron business
1936 Drafted the Federal Interpleader Act
1938–47 Served on the ABA's Bill of Rights Committee
1941–45 World War II
1950 Taught course on Fundamental Human Rights at Harvard
1950–53 Korean War
1956 Retired from teaching at Harvard
1957 Died, Cambridge, Mass.
1961–73 Vietnam War

1875    1900    1925    1950    1975

temporary interpretations of the First Amendment. "Nearly every free speech decision," Chafee wrote in his law review article, "appears to have been decided largely by intuition." Chafee sought to replace that intuition with more informed legal reasoning.

In his articles and book, Chafee set forth his views regarding the need to balance the competing interests involved in speech issues. In the following passage from *Freedom of Speech*, which he described as the key passage of the book, he defined the meaning of freedom of speech:

> The true meaning of freedom of speech seems to be this. One of the most important purposes of society and government is the discovery and spread of truth on subjects of general concern. This is possible only through absolutely unlimited discussion, for . . . once force is thrown into the argument, it becomes a matter of chance whether it is thrown on the false side or the true, and truth loses all its natural advantage in the contest. Nevertheless, there are other purposes of government, such as order, the training of the young, protection against external aggression. Unlimited discussion sometimes interferes with these purposes, which must then be balanced against freedom of speech, but freedom of speech ought to weigh very heavily in the scale. The First Amendment gives binding force to this principle of political wisdom.

Chafee gave an indication of just how "heavily" freedom of speech weighed in the scale by arguing in his law review article that free speech should be tightly protected even in wartime:

> Even after war has been declared there is bound to be a confused mixture of good and bad arguments in its support, and a wide difference of opinion as to its objects. Truth can be sifted out from falsehood only if the government is vigorously and constantly cross-examined. . . . Legal proceedings prove that an opponent makes the best cross-examiner. Consequently it is a disastrous mistake to limit criticism to those who favor the war.

Chafee put his case more succinctly when he wrote, "In wartime, speech should be free, unless it is clearly liable to cause direct and dangerous interference with the conduct of the war."

Chafee's views influenced the Supreme Court in significant ways. In particular, Justices OLIVER WENDELL HOLMES, JR., and LOUIS D. BRANDEIS closely studied Chafee's ideas and gradually liberalized their views on free speech. For example, Chafee found fault with Holmes's opinion in *Schenck v. United States*, 249 U.S. 47, 39 S. Ct. 247, 63 L. Ed. 470 (1919), upholding the conviction of Charles T. Schenck, a secretary of the Socialist party who had distributed leaflets urging men to disobey the draft. Schenck had been convicted under the Espionage Act. In his famous opinion Holmes wrote that Congress may restrict freedom of speech when there is a "CLEAR AND PRESENT DANGER" that such speech will bring about "substantive evils that Congress has a right to prevent." Chafee argued that Schenck's actions had not presented a direct danger and that Holmes had not adequately defined what exactly were the "substantive evils" society had to be protected from. Chafee maintained that only sedition that came dangerously close to succeeding might be punished and that a better test of free speech was whether it could gain acceptance in the marketplace of free ideas.

Holmes later used Chafee's ideas in his dissent to *Abrams v. United States*, 250 U.S. 616, 40 S. Ct. 17, 63 L. Ed. 1173 (1919), in which the Court upheld the conviction of Jacob Abrams, who had been sentenced to twenty years in prison for distributing leaflets opposing U.S. involvement in Russia. Chafee's ideas also influenced other Holmes and Brandeis dissents, including those in *Gitlow v. New York*, 268 U.S. 652, 45 S. Ct. 625, 69 L. Ed. 1138 (1925). The majority in *Gitlow* determined that the Constitution did not bar the conviction under New York's criminal anarchy statute (Laws 1909, c. 88; Consol. Laws 1909, c. 40) of a socialist who distributed a paper advocating that the government be overthrown, even though no effect whatsoever resulted from circulation of the manifesto. And in another influential case, *Near v. Minnesota*, 283 U.S. 697, 51 S. Ct. 625, 75 L. Ed. 1357 (1931), Chief Justice Charles E. Hughes used Chafee's ideas in an opinion that voided a Minnesota law (Minn. St. 1927, § 10123–1) calling for the suppression of "malicious, scandalous, and defamatory" publications.

Chafee's views were not popular ones at the time and he nearly lost his job because of them. In 1921, he was brought before the Board of Overseers of Harvard University on a charge of radicalism for his questioning of the sentence handed down in *Abrams*. Chafee defended himself eloquently in a speech before a special committee in the Boston Harvard Club and he was allowed to remain at Harvard.

Chafee viewed himself as a reformer rather than an activist. Although he often embraced causes considered radical, he also was skeptical of big government and described himself as a "conservative . . . Rhode Islander steeped in the Roger Williams tradition." Speaking in the early 1920s of his interest in civil liberties, Chafee commented;

> I see no reason why I should be out mountain climbing and enjoying life while some other chap who started life with less money and gets a little angrier and a little more extreme should be shut up in a prison for five or ten years. . . . When I am loafing around on my boat, or taking an inordinately large number of strokes on the golf course, I occasionally think of these poor devils who won't be out for five or ten years and want to do a bit to make the weight of society less heavy on them.

Chafee never became an active member of the AMERICAN CIVIL LIBERTIES UNION or that organization's National Advisory Committee. Nor did he appear often in court. He did harbor ambitions to become a Supreme Court justice but was never nominated for the position.

Chafee wrote on many aspects of the law besides free speech. In 1936 he drafted what he considered to be his foremost professional accomplishment, the Federal Interpleader Act (May 8, 1926, ch. 273, 44 Stat. 416). This was a highly specialized law designed to resolve multiple claims for the same debt against insurance companies, banks, and other businesses. Chafee also became an authority on the mathematical methods for reapportioning among the states the seats in the U.S. House of Representatives. His advocacy of the equal proportions method for allotting House seats eventually led to changes in federal law regarding APPORTIONMENT after the 1940 CENSUS.

During his career Chafee served on a number of committees that made important reforms in U.S. law and society. Beginning in 1923 he was chairman of the Committee of Inquiry on Coal and Civil Liberties. This group produced a report criticizing mine operators, their private police, and their company towns, taking a position that, like Chafee's views on free speech, outraged some influential Harvard law alumni. From 1928 to 1932 Chafee was president of the Massachusetts Council for the Abolition of the Death Penalty. Between 1929 and 1931 he worked for the National Commission on Law Enforcement and Observance, also called the Wickersham Commission, which looked into police misconduct during the era of Prohibition.

Some of Chafee's more important work occurred through his membership on the American Bar Association's Bill of Rights Committee from 1938 to 1947. In this capacity he submitted advisory briefs in several Supreme Court cases. In a case involving the refusal of Jehovah's Witnesses to have their children salute the FLAG in school (*West Virginia State Board of Education v. Barnette*, 319 U.S. 624, 63 S. Ct. 1178, 87 L. Ed. 1628 [1943]), Chafee wrote a brief hoping to persuade the Court to reverse an earlier decision upholding a state law requiring a flag salute. In his brief he made an eloquent case for freedom of religion and freedom of expression.

Chafee became an advocate for international human rights later in his career through his work as a representative on the United Nations Subcommission on Freedom of Information and the Press in 1947. In 1950, when Chafee's prestige and seniority at Harvard enabled him to teach whatever course he wished, he chose to offer a course called "Fundamental Human Rights." He hoped to have students realize "how dearly these rights were bought and . . . what they meant to the men who put them forever into our fundamental law."

Chafee received honorary doctor of law degrees from St. John's University, New York, in 1936, Brown University in 1937, and the University of Chicago in 1953. He also received an honorary doctor of civil law degree from Boston University in 1941 and a doctor of letters degree from Colby College in 1944.

He died February 8, 1957, in Cambridge, Massachusetts.

**CROSS-REFERENCES**

*Gitlow v. New York;* Interpleader; *Schenck v. United States.*

**CHAIN OF TITLE** 📖 A list of successive owners of a parcel of land, beginning from the government, or original owner, to the person who currently owns the land. 📖

To show that a title to a piece of land is a MARKETABLE TITLE and is free to transfer, a person must know who had ownership of the land at any point in time. In addition, the seller should be able to trace the way in which each person came into the chain of title. An ABSTRACT OF TITLE contains a condensed history of the TITLE to a piece of land in addition to a summary of CONVEYANCES. This history appears on public record so that title to land can be checked.

**CHAIN REFERRAL** 📖 A type of sales plan that convinces individuals to make purchases based upon the promise that their payment will be reduced for each new purchaser they recommend to the seller. 📖

Referral sales in general are under close scrutiny by CONSUMER PROTECTION laws and are illegal in many states due to their fraudulent and misleading nature. A chain referral is a type of pyramid sales scheme whereby an innocent consumer is lulled into investing money based on the promise that he will eventually make money, which is usually highly unlikely, if not impossible. See also REFERRAL SALES SCHEME.

**CHAMBERS** A judge's private room or office wherein he or she hears MOTIONS, signs papers, and performs other tasks pertaining to his or her office when a session of the court, such as a trial, is not being held.

Business transacted in a private setting is said to be done "in chambers."

**CHAMIZAL TRACT** A description of the 1895 title dispute between the United States and Mexico that arose over a tract of land in El Paso, Texas, known as "El Chamizal."

The Boundary Commission was unable to agree on a BOUNDARY line and a convention was signed by the two governments on June 24, 1910, establishing another commission to decide the issue. Because the new commission departed from the terms of submission and because of disturbed conditions in Mexico, no further action was taken until the conclusion of a treaty in 1963 that divided the disputed territory between the two countries.

## CHAMPERTY AND MAINTENANCE

Champerty is the process whereby one person bargains with a party to a lawsuit to obtain a share in the proceeds of the suit. Maintenance is the support or promotion of another person's suit initiated by intermeddling for personal gain.

Both champerty and maintenance have been illegal for two basic PUBLIC POLICY reasons since early COMMON LAW: (1) It is considered desirable to curb excess litigation for the operation of an efficient judicial system. The reasons for this are numerous and include problems of overcrowding on court CALENDARS, economic considerations, and the desirability of promoting a society that is not excessively litigious. Champerty and maintenance work contrary to this societal goal by stirring up litigation. (2) Champerty and maintenance bring money to an individual who was not personally harmed by the defendant. An ATTORNEY found guilty of either champerty or maintenance will be subject to the payment of any DAMAGES that may have been incurred by the parties to the lawsuit and to disciplinary proceedings, which can result in his or her DISBARMENT.

Whether or not champerty and maintenance exist in a particular instance depends upon the facts and circumstances of the case. They apply specifically to cases wherein one person profits from another person's RECOVERY in a lawsuit. If a licensed collection agency purchases a group of bad accounts from a store, the agency is buying the right to collect on the accounts rather than on a particular lawsuit and is therefore not guilty of champerty. An attorney who buys a CHOSE IN ACTION with the sole, specific intent to initiate an action for his or her own benefit would be guilty of champerty provided the purchase was made with that intent.

To lend money to an individual who would not otherwise be able to afford to bring a lawsuit is not maintenance unless the lender intends to gain substantially from his loan by being compensated with a portion of the recovery.

Today, some states still recognize champerty and maintenance as offenses but in most states they have been replaced with the CIVIL ACTIONS of ABUSE OF PROCESS and MALICIOUS PROSECUTION, both of which deal with the wrongful initiation of litigation and perversion of legal process.

**CHANCELLOR** A secretary, secretary of state, or minister of a king or other high nobleman.

The king's chancellor in England during the Middle Ages was given a variety of duties, including drawing up WRITS that permitted the initiation of a lawsuit in one of the COMMON-LAW courts and deciding disputes in a way that gave birth to the system of law called EQUITY. His governmental department was called the CHANCERY.

The Chancellor of the Exchequer in England is like the secretary of the U.S. treasury,

*During the Middle Ages the king's chancellor in England decided disputes among citizens.*

CULVER PICTURES, INC.

but in former times he also presided over a court called the Court of Exchequer, which at first heard disputes over money owed to the king but eventually heard a wide variety of cases involving money. This jurisdiction was founded on the theory that a creditor who could not collect a debt would later be less able to pay whatever he owed to the king.

Chancellor has also been used as the title for a judge who sits in a court of equity, for the president of a university, or for the public official in charge of higher education in some states.

**CHANCERY** The old English court in which the monarch's secretary, or CHANCELLOR, began hearing lawsuits during the fourteenth century.

The decisions rendered there were based on conscience and fairness rather than on the strict common-law FORMS OF ACTION. In the United States, courts like the old chancery have been called courts of chancery or courts of EQUITY.

**CHARACTER EVIDENCE** Proof or attestations about an individual's moral standing, general nature, traits, and reputation in the general community.

A *character witness* is an individual who testifies as to the habits and reputation of another person. In criminal cases, a defendant might attempt to reduce the possibility that he or she will be convicted of committing the crime as charged by exhibiting his or her good character or propensity for not committing the offense. Ordinarily, this is limited to TESTIMONY concerning the particular character trait that is in issue. For example, evidence concerning the defendant's trustworthiness with PROPERTY might be relevant in an EMBEZZLEMENT case. The character WITNESS must be a person who is familiar with the defendant's reputation in the community fairly close to the time the crime was committed.

In federal trials the admissibility of character evidence and the use of character witnesses are governed by the Federal Rules of Evidence.

**CHARGE** To impose a burden, DUTY, OBLIGATION, or LIEN; to create a CLAIM against property; to ASSESS; to demand; to accuse; to instruct a JURY on matters of law. To impose a tax, duty, or trust. To entrust with responsibilities and duties (e.g., care of another). In commercial transactions, to bill or INVOICE; to purchase on CREDIT. In criminal law, to indict or formally accuse.

An encumbrance, lien, or claim; a burden or load; an obligation or duty; a LIABILITY; an ACCUSATION. A person or thing committed to the care of another. The price of, or rate for, something.

A retail store may attach a FINANCE CHARGE to money owed by a customer on a store account.

A *charge to the jury* is the process whereby a judge addresses the jury before the verdict. During the charge, the judge summarizes the case and gives INSTRUCTIONS to the jury concerning such matters as the RULES OF LAW that are applicable to various issues in the case.

A *public charge* is a person who has been made a ward of the state who requires public support due to illness or poverty.

**CHARGE-OFF** Eliminate or write off.

The term *charge-off* is used to describe the process of removing from the records of a company something that was once regarded as an ASSET but has subsequently become worthless.

A classic case is the bad debt, which is an uncollectible DEBT. A *bad debt* is a permissible business tax deduction, and a *non-business bad debt* may also be claimed as a charge-off in the year the debt becomes entirely worthless. Charge-off is generally used in reference to a CHARGE or debt that is not paid when due.

**CHARITABLE TRUST** The arrangement by which real or personal property given by one person is held by another to be used for the benefit of a class or the general public.

The law favors charitable trusts, sometimes called public trusts, by according them certain privileges, such as an advantageous tax status. Before a court will enforce a charitable trust, however, it must examine the charity and evaluate its social benefits. The court cannot rely on the view of the SETTLOR, the one who establishes the TRUST, that the trust is charitable.

In order to be valid, a charitable trust must fulfill certain requirements. The settlor must intend to create this type of trust. There must be a TRUSTEE to administer the trust, which must consist of some RES or trust property. The charitable purpose must be expressly designated. A definite class of persons comprised of indefinite BENEFICIARIES within it must actually receive the benefit. The requirements of intention, the trustee, and the res are the same in a charitable trust as they are in any other trust.

**Charitable Purposes** A charitable purpose is one designed to benefit, ameliorate, or uplift mankind mentally, morally, or physically. The relief of poverty, the improvement of government, and the advancement of religion, education, and health are some examples of charitable purposes. Trusts to prevent cruelty to animals, to erect a monument in honor of a famous historical figure, and to beautify a designated village are charitable purposes aimed, respectively, at fostering kindness to animals, patriotism, and community well-being.

The definition of charitable purposes is derived from an old English law, the Statute of Charitable Uses, but has been expanded throughout the years as new public needs developed.

**Beneficiaries** The class to be benefited in a charitable trust must be a definite segment of the public. It must be large enough so that the community in general is affected by, and interested in, the enforcement of the trust, yet it cannot encompass the entire human race. Within the class, however, the specific persons to benefit from the trust must be indefinite. A trust "for the benefit of the orphans of American veterans of the Vietnam conflict" is charitable. The orphans of such veterans constitute a definite class. The indefinite persons within the class are the ones who are ultimately chosen by the trustee to be paid the benefits. The class is large enough so that the community is interested in the enforcement of the trust.

A trust for named persons or a trust for profit cannot be a charitable trust. A trust "to construct and maintain a hospital" might be charitable, even though the hospital charges the patients who are treated, provided that any profits realized are used solely to continue the charitable services rendered and are not paid to private persons.

A trust that serves both charitable and noncharitable purposes will fail if the two are inseparable. A settlor bequeaths $500,000 to a trustee "to hold in trust for the benefit of all the schools in a particular town." The settlor's daughter is the residuary LEGATEE of the ESTATE, who will inherit the remainder of the estate after the testamentary dispositions are satisfied. Some of the schools in the town are public and charitable institutions and some are private and operated for profit. The settlor has not apportioned the $500,000 between the public schools and the private schools. The valid part—to be given to public schools and charitable institutions—cannot be separated from the invalid part—the disposition to private or profit making institutions; therefore, the trust fails as a charitable trust. The trustee holds the $500,000 in a RESULTING TRUST for the settlor's daughter, since the settlor's disposition cannot be valid as a charitable trust because there is no indefinite beneficiary.

If a trust has both charitable and noncharitable purposes and if the maximum amount to be used for noncharitable purposes can be determined, the trust fails only with respect to that amount pertaining to noncharitable purposes, which will be held in a resulting trust by the trustee for the settlor's statutory HEIR or residuary legatee. The remainder is a valid charitable trust.

As a general rule, a charitable trust can be eternal, unlike a private trust, which must comply with the RULE AGAINST PERPETUITIES, a principle limiting the duration of a trust. With respect to a private trust, the designated beneficiary is the proper person to enforce the trust, but in a charitable trust, the state attorney general is the one to enforce it. The settlor, his or her heirs or PERSONAL REPRESENTATIVES, the members of the general public, and possible beneficiaries cannot maintain a lawsuit for the enforcement of the trust.

**CHARITIES** Organizations created for the purpose of philanthropic rather than pecuniary pursuits.

A charity is a group designed to benefit society or a specific group of people. Its purpose may be educational, humanitarian, or religious. A charity goes beyond giving relief to the indigent, extending to the promotion of happiness and the support of many worthy causes.

The law favors charities because they promote goodwill and lessen the government's burdens. They are therefore ordinarily exempt from paying income or property taxes.

**Charitable Gifts and Trusts** A *charitable* GIFT is something that is donated by an individual or organization with the intent to benefit the public or some segment of it as a

## Charities
Private Philanthropy in the United States in 1993

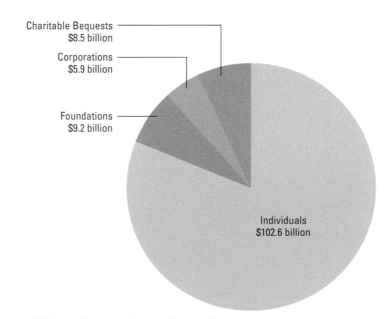

Charitable Bequests
$8.5 billion

Corporations
$5.9 billion

Foundations
$9.2 billion

Individuals
$102.6 billion

Source: AAFRC Trust for Philanthropy. New York, NY, *Giving USA*, annual.

*This Ronald McDonald House is a charity that provides lodging for the families of seriously ill children receiving treatment at nearby hospitals. The lodging has a small cost or is free.*

whole. It is meant for use by an indefinite number of people. Similarly, CHARITABLE TRUSTS or *public trusts* are TRUSTS of religious, political, or general social interests, or for the relief of poverty or the advancement of education.

Charities are ordinarily supported by gifts from donors and most states have set forth statutes controlling the manner in which funds are solicited for charities. In addition, the state will generally require charities to disclose their financial structure and condition.

Charitable gifts are often TESTAMENTARY, or created by WILL. If there is a problem in determining the actual DONATIVE intent of the testator, the court might have to pass on his or her intent. CY PRES is a doctrine applied by a court so that it can carry out a trust made by will for charitable purposes even when the testator's charitable purpose can not be accomplished in the precise manner specified by the TESTATOR. For example, if a testator wished to donate money to a certain hospital whose name had changed, for example, this would not defeat the gift. With cy-pres the court would interpret the donor's intent to be to give money to the hospital in spite of the change of name.

**Charitable Societies and Institutions** To determine whether an institution is charitable, the test is whether its major purpose is to aid others or to make a profit.

*Charitable corporations* are nonprofit corporations that have been created to minister to the physical needs of the indigent or to advance a particular goal, such as the aid of a particular religious group or country. In order to receive a tax-exempt status, such organizations must meet certain criteria.

Ordinarily, charitable corporations have no CAPITAL STOCK and they obtain their funds primarily from private and public charity. These

funds are held in trust to serve the charitable objects of the institutions.

BENEFICIAL ASSOCIATIONS also exist mainly for a charitable purpose and not for financial gain.

*Religious organizations*, such as the Young Men's and Women's Christian Associations and the Salvation Army, are also considered to be charitable societies.

The test for determining whether or not an educational institution is a charitable organization is the question of whether it exists for a public purpose or for a private gain.

While charities may charge a nominal fee for some of their services and still be considered charitable societies, they are organized primarily for the public good and not for profit.

**CHARLES RIVER BRIDGE v. WARREN BRIDGE** The 1837 landmark U.S. Supreme Court decision *Charles River Bridge v. Warren Bridge*, 36 U.S. (11 Pet.) 420, 9 L. Ed. 773, illustrated the shift in politics brought about by the presidency of ANDREW JACKSON. Nineteenth-century FEDERALISM, a dominant political doctrine from the time of the drafting of the U.S. Constitution, favored the protection of private investments. The *Charles River Bridge* decision espoused newly popular Jacksonian political beliefs, which favored free enterprise. Arguably, the case altered the course of economic JURISPRUDENCE in the United States.

The facts of *Charles River Bridge* began in 1650 when the state of Massachusetts granted a CHARTER to Harvard College (now Harvard University) to operate for profit a FERRY over the Charles River between Boston and Charlestown. Later, in 1785, the Massachusetts Legislature granted a charter to a group of Charlestown businessmen to build the Charles River Bridge. These entrepreneurs were to fund the bridge's construction and in return the state would allow them to collect revenue from a specified TOLL for the next forty years. As part of the agreement, the entrepreneurs were to pay an ANNUITY to Harvard College to replace ferry profits lost by the building of the new bridge.

The bridge was immediately successful and immensely profitable. Prompted by its popularity, the Massachusetts Legislature in 1792 chartered the building of a second bridge, known as the West Boston Bridge. To appease the proprietors of the Charles River Bridge, who faced competition from the West Boston Bridge, the state of Massachusetts extended the Charles River Bridge charter from forty to seventy years.

In 1828 Massachusetts chartered a third bridge, the Warren Bridge, which was to be constructed within a few rods of the Charles River Bridge. The Charles River Bridge proprietors strongly objected to this third bridge because the competition would diminish their profits. But Massachusetts citizens viewed the Charles River Bridge as monopolistic and welcomed competition and reduced tolls. The Warren Bridge was completed as planned.

Within a year the Charles River Bridge suffered a 40 percent drop in revenues. The bridge's proprietors, represented by DANIEL WEBSTER and LEMUEL SHAW, went to court, seeking an INJUNCTION against the Warren Bridge. Webster and Shaw argued that the Warren Bridge's charter with the state violated the Contracts Clause of the U.S. Constitution by interfering with the state's separate obligations under its charter with the Charles River Bridge proprietors. They maintained that as successors to the original ferry service charter held by Harvard College, the Charles River Bridge proprietors had an implied exclusive right to tolls charged for crossing the Charles River. Moreover, they said that judicial policy should protect investments; without security in investments, entrepreneurs would not be willing to take risks in technological developments such as bridges and railroads. And this reluctance to take risks would only prove detrimental to the public.

Lawyers for the Warren Bridge proprietors countered that no exclusive rights existed for transportation over the Charles River and that judicial policy should favor technological progress and free enterprise over the rights of those investing in private property. After hearing oral arguments in October 1829, the Supreme Judicial Court of Massachusetts ruled in favor of the Warren Bridge proprietors. The Charles River Bridge group appealed the case to the U.S. Supreme Court.

In March 1831, the Supreme Court first heard arguments in the case. At that time JOHN MARSHALL was chief justice and the Court was dominated by Federalists. But several justices were absent during that argument, so the Court scheduled a second argument. This action had a significant consequence: several justices resigned or died prior to the second argument, and, taking advantage of his privilege of appointing new justices, President Jackson changed the membership of the Court to primarily Democratic.

Following a second argument in 1837 the Court held that the Warren Bridge charter did not violate the Contracts Clause of the Constitution. Chief Justice ROGER B. TANEY, who authored the opinion, held that any state legisla-

tion that chartered a private entity to provide a public service, such as a bridge, turnpike, or ferry, was to be strictly construed (interpreted) in favor of the state and against the private entity. The Court found that no implied rights had passed from the Harvard College ferry charter to the Charles River Bridge charter.

Chief Justice Taney further observed the harm in ruling for the Charles River Bridge proprietors simply because they faced competition and reduced profits owing to the Warren Bridge. He suggested that such a holding would encourage turnpike proprietors to sue the railroads for destroying turnpike profits. In Taney's view, economic development was better served by public improvements than by protections for monopolies.

The *Charles River Bridge* decision received widespread attention. Hard-line Federalists disputed the Court's rationale, insisting that only by protecting vested PROPERTY RIGHTS would future financing for transportation technology be ensured. And although railroads were not at issue in *Charles River Bridge*, many historians believe that the Taney Court placed great faith in the future of railroads in the United States, and in rendering its opinion was attempting to facilitate their growth. There is little doubt among legal scholars that *Charles River Bridge* signified the introduction of Jacksonian politics into U.S. jurisprudence.

**CHARTER**    A grant from the government of ownership rights in land to a person, a group of people, or an organization such as a CORPORATION.

A basic document of law of a MUNICIPAL CORPORATION granted by the state, defining its rights, liabilities, and responsibilities of self-government.

A document embodying a grant of authority from the legislature or the authority itself, such as a corporate charter.

The leasing of a mode of transportation, such as a bus, ship, or plane. A *charter-party* is a contract formed to lease a ship to a merchant in order to facilitate the conveyance of goods.

**BIOGRAPHY**

*Salmon Portland Chase*

**CHASE, SALMON PORTLAND** Salmon Portland Chase served from 1864 to 1873 as the sixth chief justice of the Supreme Court of the United States. He was also a distinguished lawyer and politician, serving as U.S. senator from Ohio (1849–55 and 1860–61), governor of Ohio (1855–59), and secretary of the treasury (1861–64). Chase also sought the presidential nomination in every election between 1856 and 1872, even while sitting as chief justice. As a result, many criticized him for neglecting his judicial responsibilities in favor

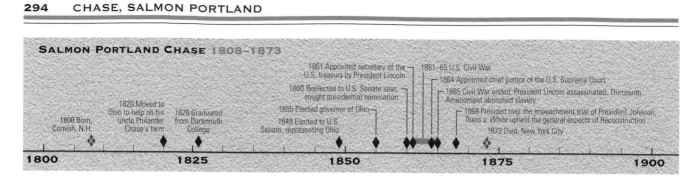

**SALMON PORTLAND CHASE 1808–1873**

1861 Appointed secretary of the U.S. treasury by President Lincoln

1861–65 U.S. Civil War

1864 Appointed chief justice of the U.S. Supreme Court

1860 Reelected to U.S. Senate seat; sought presidential nomination

1865 Civil War ended; President Lincoln assassinated; Thirteenth Amendment abolished slavery

1855 Elected governor of Ohio

1820 Moved to Ohio to help on his uncle Philander Chase's farm

1826 Graduated from Dartmouth College

1849 Elected to U.S. Senate, representing Ohio

1868 Presided over the impeachment trial of President Johnson; *Texas v. White* upheld the general aspects of Reconstruction

1808 Born, Cornish, N.H.

1873 Died, New York City

1800        1825        1850        1875        1900

of his political ambitions. Despite his extrajudicial activities, Chase helped navigate the Supreme Court through the dangerous political waters of Reconstruction, preserving the Court's powers when a Radical Republican–dominated Congress sought to control both the president and the Supreme Court. As chief justice Chase presided over the 1868 impeachment trial of President Andrew Johnson. Chase was an ardent opponent of slavery his entire life and in his last years on the Court fought against a narrow interpretation of the Fourteenth Amendment, an interpretation that he rightly surmised would allow future state legislatures to rescind the newly won rights of African Americans.

Chase was born January 13, 1808, in Cornish, New Hampshire, the eighth of eleven children in a family that had lived in New England since the 1600s. His father operated a tavern as well as a glass factory and distillery near Keene, New Hampshire, and died when Chase was nine years old. Chase had two prominent uncles who aided him in his father's absence: Dudley Chase, who served two terms as U.S. senator from Vermont (1813–17 and 1825–31), and Philander Chase, who became bishop of Ohio for the Episcopal Church and president of Cincinnati College. When he was twelve, Chase moved to Ohio to help on Philander Chase's farm. In return for Chase's work, his uncle taught him Greek, Latin, and mathematics in his church school. Chase attended Cincinnati College for a year then eventually returned to his family in New Hampshire and entered Dartmouth College, graduating Phi Beta Kappa in 1826.

After college Chase moved to Washington, D.C., where he studied law under Attorney General WILLIAM WIRT. He passed the bar and returned to Cincinnati to set up a legal practice. In Cincinnati Chase's personal life was clouded by tragedy. He lost three wives between 1835 and 1852, each marriage cut short by death. He had one daughter by each of his last two wives. He remained single for the last part of his life and was a devoted father to his two daughters.

"NO MORE SLAVE STATES, AND NO MORE SLAVE TERRITORY. LET THE SOIL OF OUR EXTENSIVE DOMAIN BE KEPT FREE."

Chase strongly opposed SLAVERY from his early years, a position that owed much to his deeply religious outlook. In Ohio he was nicknamed the Attorney General for Runaway Negroes for his defense of abolitionists who had aided runaway slaves from Kentucky. He even took two of these cases to the Supreme Court—*Jones v. Van Zandt*, 46 U.S. (5 How.) 215, 12 L. Ed. 122 (1847), and *Moore v. Illinois*, 55 U.S. (14 How.) 13, 14 L. Ed. 306 (1852)—both of which he lost. About his nickname, Chase commented that he "never refused . . . help to any person black or white; and liked the office nonetheless because there were neither fees nor salary connected with it."

In 1849 Chase was elected to the U.S. Senate as a member of the Free-Soil party, a party which sought to keep new states in the West free of slavery. In the Senate, he and CHARLES SUMNER became leading spokesmen for the antislavery movement. He gained renown through his opposition to the 1854 KANSAS-NEBRASKA ACT, which allowed each territory to conduct a popular vote deciding whether it would permit slavery or not. Shortly thereafter he helped found the antislavery Republican party and in 1855 he was elected governor of Ohio. He was considered for the 1856 Republican presidential nomination but was passed over and in February 1860 he was reelected to the U.S. Senate. In May of the same year he sought the presidential nomination at the Republican convention in Chicago. Chase and William H. Seward were considered the chief rivals for the nomination but on the third ballot Chase's supporters gave their votes to ABRAHAM LINCOLN, giving the man from Illinois the nomination. After his election, Lincoln offered Chase and Seward the respective posts of secretary of the treasury and secretary of state. Chase then gave up his seat as U.S. senator.

At the Treasury Chase faced the difficult task of financing a government engaged in a civil war. As part of this effort he helped establish a national banking system that gave the federal government its first effective national paper currency. Early in the war Chase also advised military leaders who sought guidance from Washington, D.C. Chase was often unhappy with the decisions of Lincoln and other members of the cabinet and resolved that he could do better as president. He therefore opposed Lincoln for the Republican presidential nomination in 1864. Chase had the support of the more liberal wing of the Republican party but he eventually withdrew his name from consideration, conceding to the more popular Lincoln. In June 1864, after several disagreements with Lincoln, Chase resigned from the cabinet.

Despite their differences, Lincoln admired Chase and in December 1864 he nominated Chase to succeed Roger B. Taney as chief justice of the U.S. Supreme Court. He nominated Chase with the expectation that Chase would sustain two extraordinary measures taken by the Union during the war—the emancipation of the slaves and the issuance of paper money to repay debt. Both measures had caused great controversy, and as a result many Americans had lost confidence in agencies of the federal government, including the Supreme Court.

Chase joined a Court with only three other justices who consistently supported Republican positions, Justices DAVID DAVIS, NOAH H. SWAYNE, and SAMUEL F. MILLER, all appointed by Lincoln. The Court was sharply divided over the various issues surrounding Reconstruction, the period following the Civil War when the country attempted to rebuild itself and readmit the Southern states to the Union. The post–Civil War crisis deepened when Lincoln was assassinated on April 14, 1865, and Vice President ANDREW JOHNSON became president.

Chase urged a moderate, conciliatory stance toward the defeated South, a stance that eventually alienated him from the Radical Republicans, a faction of the Republican party that sought to impose strict military measures and punitive new laws on the states of the former Confederacy. Like the Radical Republicans, Chase supported expanded freedoms for African Americans. Unlike them, however, he also supported such measures as ending military government in the South, PARDONING Confederate leaders, and quickly restoring Southern states to the Union. Chase's moderation helped spare Jefferson Davis, president of the former Confederacy. After the war Davis had been imprisoned in Virginia, part of Chase's circuit, where the government hoped to try him for TREASON. Chase refused to hold a civil trial while the area was still under military rule. Although a grand jury indicted Davis for treason, no action was taken against him and eventually the government's case was dismissed.

Many of the Supreme Court's decisions during Chase's tenure involved the thorny issue of Reconstruction. In March 1867, Congress passed the Reconstruction Acts, which divided the South into five districts and imposed military rule. Reconstruction involved new problems of constitutional interpretation as to the federal government's powers over the states. At issue were questions not only of STATES' RIGHTS but also of the status of freed slaves. In one early decision, *Ex parte Milligan*, 71 U.S. (4 Wall.) 2, 18 L. Ed. 284 (1866), Chase voted with the Court in challenging Congress over Reconstruction. The Court held that Congress could not authorize military trials where civil courts were still operating. The majority opinion warned of the military's "gross usurpation of power"—a direct challenge to the Reconstruction Acts passed by Congress. However, in later decisions Chase voted to uphold congressional laws pertaining to Reconstruction. In the 1867 *Test Oath* cases—*Cummings v. Missouri*, 71 U.S. (4 Wall.) 277, 18 L. Ed. 356, and *Ex parte Garland*, 71 U.S. (4 Wall.) 333, 18 L. Ed. 366—Chase disagreed with the Court's decision to strike down laws requiring that priests and lawyers swear oaths of loyalty to the Union. In his dissenting opinion, joined by Chase, Justice Miller declared that no punishment was inflicted by requiring such an oath and that Congress could impose such requirements. Chase considered *Texas v. White*, 74 U.S. (7 Wall.) 700, 19 L. Ed. 227 (1868), to be the most important case of his Supreme Court career. Chase, writing the Court's opinion, upheld the general principles of Reconstruction, asserting that Congress and not the Supreme Court possessed the authority to recognize state governments as legitimate.

When Southern states sought to make cases in court against executives of the federal government—including President Johnson and Secretary of War EDWIN M. STANTON—Chase joined the majority in dismissing those cases, thereby aiding Congress in its Reconstruction fervor. In *Mississippi v. Johnson*, 71 U.S. (4 Wall.) 475, 18 L. Ed. 437 (1867), Mississippi, in the first court case ever to name the president of the United States as an individual party, attempted to prevent President Johnson from enforcing certain provisions of the Reconstruction Acts. Chase dismissed the case, holding that preventing the president from acting on congressional legislation would cause a "collision . . . between the executive and legislative departments of the government." This, in turn, would give the House grounds to sue for the president's IMPEACHMENT. This opinion proved prophetic, of course, when Congress did attempt to impeach President Johnson.

Chase's public standing improved when he ably handled the impeachment trial of President Johnson in March 1868. The Radical Republican–dominated Congress had voted to bring impeachment proceedings against Johnson after he dismissed one of their favorite members of his cabinet, Secretary of War Stanton. The Senate sat as a court of impeachment with Chase presiding as judge. Chase frustrated Radical Republican aims by sticking to procedural rules and helping to bring about Johnson's ACQUITTAL, which passed the Senate by one vote. The public acclaim occasioned by his handling of the impeachment trial led Chase to make another try at the presidency in 1868. This time, however, Chase made known his desire to run as a Democratic candidate, largely because his moderate positions toward the South had endeared him to Democrats. His efforts failed.

Although the Supreme Court under Chase's leadership rarely questioned congressional Reconstruction measures after 1867, it did declare other federal legislation unconstitutional. Whereas before 1864 the Court had overturned acts of Congress only twice—in *Marbury v. Madison*, 5 U.S. (1 Cranch) 137, 2 L. Ed. 60 (1803), and *Dred Scott v. Sandford*, 60 U.S. (19 How.) 393, 15 L. Ed. 691 (1857)—between 1864 and 1873 it voided ten pieces of congressional legislation. These decisions included *Hepburn v. Griswold*, 75 U.S. (8 Wall.) 603, 19 L. Ed. 513 (1870), in which Chase questioned much of his earlier work for the Treasury when he declared the Legal Tender Acts unconstitutional. This decision created a temporary crisis of confidence in the national currency. The Court reversed this decision in 1871 after a change in membership, with Chase sticking to his views of two years earlier. Despite his participation in such judicial activism, Chase at other times advocated judicial restraint. In his opinion for the *Licence Tax* Cases, 72 U.S. (5 Wall.) 462, 18 L. Ed. 497 (1868), in which he upheld a law that taxed the sale of lottery tickets throughout the United States, Chase wrote:

This court can know nothing of public policy except from the Constitution and the laws, and the course of administration and decision. It has no legislative powers. It cannot amend or modify any legislative

acts. It cannot examine questions as expedient or inexpedient, as politic or impolitic. Considerations of that sort must, in general, be addressed to the legislature. Questions of policy determined there are concluded here.

ULYSSES S. GRANT won the presidential election of 1868 and from that time on the power of Radical Republicanism began to wane. Grant's appointments made the Court a more conservative body. In the *Slaughter-House* Cases, 83 U.S. (16 Wall.) 36, 21 L. Ed. 394 (1873), Chase dissented from the Court's narrow interpretation of the FOURTEENTH AMENDMENT, which was passed in 1868 and sought to protect the rights of African Americans against infringements by state legislation. In its *Slaughter-House* decision, the Court held that the Fourteenth Amendment's Privileges and Immunities Clause protected only a few select rights of national citizenship, such as the right to travel. The Court did not interpret the amendment as guaranteeing more fundamental rights, such as the right to vote. Chase objected that the Court's opinion jeopardized newly won freedoms for African Americans. It would take another one hundred years before the Court would reverse this narrow interpretation of the Fourteenth Amendment.

Chase suffered a series of crippling strokes beginning in 1870. Despite his failing health, his daughter Catherine Chase and other admirers put forth his name for the 1872 presidential nomination. As had happened each time before, his nomination came to nothing. He died May 7, 1873, after suffering a stroke while visiting his daughter in New York City, and was interred in Spring Grove Cemetary in Cincinnati. Although Chase did not achieve his highest goal of becoming president, he nevertheless held more high offices during his life than did any other Supreme Court justice besides James F. Byrnes and William H. Taft. More importantly, Chase successfully guided the Court through some of the most tumultuous years in the history of the nation. His actions as chief justice helped preserve the powers of the Supreme Court in the face of serious congressional challenges during the extraordinary years following the Civil War.

### CROSS-REFERENCES

Loyalty Oaths; *Milligan, Ex parte; Slaughter-House* Cases; *Texas v. White*.

**CHASE, SAMUEL** Samuel Chase served as a justice of the U.S. Supreme Court from 1796 to

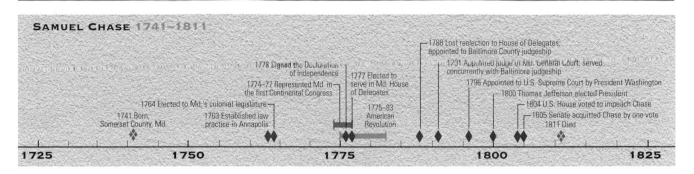

**SAMUEL CHASE 1741–1811**

1788 Lost reelection to House of Delegates; appointed to Baltimore County judgeship

1791 Appointed judge of Md. General Court; served concurrently with Baltimore judgeship

1776 Signed the Declaration of Independence

1796 Appointed to U.S. Supreme Court by President Washington

1774–77 Represented Md. in the first Continental Congress

1777 Elected to serve in Md. House of Delegates

1800 Thomas Jefferson elected President

1764 Elected to Md.'s colonial legislature

1804 U.S. House voted to impeach Chase

1741 Born, Somerset County, Md.

1763 Established law practice in Annapolis

1775–83 American Revolution

1805 Senate acquitted Chase by one vote

1811 Died

| 1725 | 1750 | 1775 | 1800 | 1825 |

1811. In 1804 the U.S. House of Representatives voted to impeach Chase. However, the Senate did not uphold the House's action and Chase continued to serve on the Court until his death. Chase remains the only justice who has been the subject of impeachment proceedings. Chase's decisions set several precedents for the Supreme Court, among them opinions establishing the supremacy of federal treaties over state laws and the establishment of JUDICIAL REVIEW, which is the Court's power to void legislation it deems unconstitutional, a power that makes the judiciary one of the three primary branches of the federal government (the other two branches being Congress and the president).

Known for his fiery and partisan manner, Chase was an active politician for most of his life. Before his career as a judge Chase served in the Maryland colonial and state legislatures. As a member of the Continental Congress in the 1770s, Chase was an outspoken advocate of American independence from Britain. He signed the DECLARATION OF INDEPENDENCE in 1776. He opposed the Constitution as an Anti-Federalist (an opponent of federal government powers over the states) in the 1780s. Later, however, he became a member of the Federalist party and as a Supreme Court justice helped establish the powers of the federal judiciary. Chase generally favored a strong government ruled by an elite and he opposed the radical ideas of the French Revolution.

Chase was born April 17, 1741, in Somerset County, Maryland. His father, Thomas Chase, was a British-born clergyman of the Church of England. His mother, Matilda Walker Chase, died at Chase's birth. In 1744 the family moved to Baltimore where Chase grew up and received a classical education under his father's supervision. Chase studied law in Annapolis, Maryland, at the office of Attorney John Hall from 1759 until he was admitted to the bar in 1763. In 1762 Chase married Ann Baldwin. They had seven children, three of them dying in infancy. Ann died sometime between 1776 and 1779 and

**BIOGRAPHY**

*Samuel Chase*

in 1784 Chase married Hannah Kitty Giles, with whom he had two daughters.

Chase established a successful law practice in Annapolis, the colonial capital and later the state capital of Maryland. He also became prominent in colonial politics. In 1764 he was elected to the lower house of Maryland's colonial legislature as a representative of Annapolis and by the early 1770s he had become well-known as a skillful legislator and outstanding leader, earning the nickname the Maryland Demosthenes after the ancient Greek orator and politician. He represented Maryland in the Continental Congresses from 1774 to 1778 and 1784 to 1785 and in 1778 served on as many as thirty committees in his tireless efforts to advance the cause of independence from Britain. He advocated a BOYCOTT of Britain and a political confederation of the colonies. He denounced those who opposed such policies as "despicable tools of power, emerged from obscurity and basking in proprietary sunshine." Together with Benjamin Franklin and Charles Carroll, Chase traveled in 1776 to Montreal in an unsuccessful attempt to persuade Canada to join the American colonies in their revolt against England. He signed the Declaration of Independence in 1776 and worked for its acceptance in Maryland.

Chase helped draft the Maryland Constitution in 1776. He served in the Maryland House of Delegates for all but a year and a half between 1777 and 1788. When the U.S. Constitution came before the Maryland Convention for ratification Chase was in the minority of delegates who voted against it. He was an ardent Anti-Federalist at the time and argued that the Constitution concentrated power in the hands of the central government at the expense of the common individual. "I consider the Constitution," he wrote to a friend, "as radically defective in this essential: the bulk of the people can have nothing to say to it. The government is *not* a government of the people." He also argued that the Constitution failed to protect the FREEDOM OF THE PRESS and the right to trial by JURY.

His opposition to the Constitution cost him his state legislative seat in 1788. The same year, Chase also went bankrupt after several of his speculative business ventures failed. These business risks had also damaged his political career, which had been plagued with charges that he used his office for personal gain. In 1778 he had been dismissed from the Continental Congress for two years for allegedly attempting to corner the flour market and profit from speculation on prices.

Dogged by bankruptcy and charges of corruption, Chase sought refuge in the position of a local judge in Baltimore County in 1788. In 1791 he was concurrently appointed chief judge of the Maryland General Court. The state assembly, upset with his behavior on the bench and his holding two positions as judge, tried unsuccessfully to remove him from both positions.

Chase might seem to have been an unlikely choice for a Supreme Court justice. However, President GEORGE WASHINGTON nominated him to the Supreme Court on January 26, 1796. Over the years Washington had been impressed by Chase's legal skills; he also admired the zeal with which Chase had worked for American independence during the Revolutionary War as well as Chase's efforts in support of Washington in the Continental Congress. James McHenry of Maryland, the secretary of war and a friend of Washington's, strongly recommended Chase to Washington. Moreover, the Supreme Court was not very powerful or prestigious at the time and it was difficult to find a lawyer who would accept a position on it. The job did not pay well and justices had to travel long distances to preside over CIRCUIT COURTS.

Chase took his seat on the Court on February 4, 1796. He was an Anti-Federalist at the time of the Constitution's ratification but during his tenure on the Court he became a persuasive advocate for the federal judiciary's power to review legislation. Two cases from Chase's first session on the Supreme Court—*Hylton v. United States*, 3 U.S. (Dall.) 171, 1 L. Ed. 556, and *Ware v. Hylton*, 3 U.S. (Dall.) 199, 1 L. Ed. 568, both decided in March 1796—stand out. In *Hylton v. United States*, the Court for the first time reviewed a law passed by Congress. Although the Court refrained from declaring its ability to void acts of Congress on constitutional grounds, its review nevertheless paved the way for *Marbury v. Madison*, 5 U.S. (1 Cranch) 137, 2 L. Ed. 60 (1803), which established the right of the Court to declare laws unconstitutional. At issue in *Ware v. Hylton* was

whether a TREATY decided by the federal government could take precedence over state laws. The U.S. government had made a treaty with Great Britain following the Revolutionary War that provided for the payment of debts owed to Great Britain. The states, meanwhile, had passed their own laws on this issue, many of which enabled U.S. citizens to forgo repaying their debts to British citizens. JOHN MARSHALL, future chief justice of the Court, argued the case before the Court for the debtors. The Court ruled that the national treaty had precedent over state law. Of Chase's opinion in this case, constitutional scholar Edward S. Corwin wrote in 1930 that it "remains to this day the most impressive assertion of the supremacy of national treaties over State laws."

In *Calder v. Bull*, 3 U.S. (Dall.) 386, 1 L. Ed. 648 (1798), Chase wrote a highly influential opinion for the Court. He defined a constitutional interpretation of EX POST FACTO LAWS—that is, retroactive laws, or laws that affect matters occurring before their enactment. Chase decided that the Constitution's prohibition of such laws extended only to criminal statutes that make prior conduct a crime, not to civil statutes. Chase also set a precedent by arguing that any law "contrary to the *great first principles* of the *social compact*" must be declared void. In his opinion, Chase emphasized that the Constitution limits the ability of legislators to disturb established PROPERTY RIGHTS even when it does not expressly set forth such rights. Described by Presser as the NATURAL-LAW basis of the Constitution, this argument broadened the Court's ability to test the constitutionality of legislation.

In *United States v. Callender*, Chase's Trial 65, Whart. St. Tr. 668, 25 F. Cas. 239, No. 14, 709 (C.C. Va.) (1800), Chase further defined the powers of the Court when he ruled that a jury could not decide the constitutionality of a law:

> [T]he judicial power of the United States is the only proper and competent authority to decide whether any statute made by congress (or any of the state legislatures) is contrary to, or in violation of, the federal constitution. . . . I believe that it has been the general and prevailing opinion in all the Union, that the power now wished to be exercised by a jury, belongs properly to the Federal Courts.

Chase also found himself embroiled in highly publicized political controversy for his actions both on and off the bench. For example, he made partisan speeches in 1796 for JOHN

"I CANNOT SUBSCRIBE TO THE OMNIPOTENCE OF A STATE LEGISLATURE."

ADAMS, the Federalist party candidate for president, even after he had taken the position of Supreme Court justice. He also pushed for passage of the Alien and Sedition Act, 1 Stat. 596 (1798), which outlawed "false, scandalous, and malicious" attacks on the government, the president, or Congress. The law was designed largely to discourage criticism of President Adams by the rival Democratic-Republican party, whose most well-known leader was THOMAS JEFFERSON. In circuit court decisions in 1799 and 1800 Chase imposed harsh sentences on Democratic-Republicans who had published opinions critical of Adams's Federalist administration. In several cases Chase worked to keep Anti-Federalists off juries. In the case of John Fries of Pennsylvania, a strong supporter of Jefferson who had led rebellions against federal excise taxes, Chase sentenced the accused to death. President Adams subsequently set aside the sentence.

In 1800 the political atmosphere in Washington, D.C., changed when Jefferson defeated Adams for the presidency of the United States. In 1803 Chase got into trouble with the Jeffersonian Democratic-Republicans when he severely criticized their policies in front of a Baltimore GRAND JURY. Chase explained that he objected to recent changes in Maryland law that gave more men the privilege of voting. Such changes as these advanced by Democratic-Republicans, Chase exclaimed, would

> rapidly destroy all protection to property, and all security to personal liberty, and our Republican Constitution [would] sink into mobocracy, the worst of all possible governments. . . . The modern doctrines by our late reformers, that all men in a state of society are entitled to enjoy equal liberty and equal rights, have brought this mighty mischief upon us, and I fear that it will rapidly destroy progress, until peace and order, freedom and property shall be destroyed.

This angered Jefferson and other Democratic-Republicans and in 1804 the U.S. House of Representatives voted to impeach Chase on charges of misconduct and BIAS in the SEDITION cases and of seditious criticism of Jefferson in the 1803 Baltimore grand jury charge. In 1805, the Democratic-Republican–controlled U.S. Senate moved to impeach Chase. Democratic-Republican senators charged that Chase had been guilty of judicial misconduct and that his partisan acts showed that he lacked political objectivity. Federalists defending Chase argued that he had committed no crime and that he

could not be convicted under the constitutional definition of HIGH CRIMES AND MISDEMEANORS. The Senate failed to achieve the two-thirds majority necessary to impeach Chase and he remained on the Court until his death.

Chase's acquittal set an important precedent for the Court—no Supreme Court justice could be removed simply because of his or her political beliefs. The failure to impeach Chase allowed Chief Justice Marshall to assert and define the powers of the Court in future decisions with more confidence. It was thus a step in the process of defining the independence of the Supreme Court as one of the three primary branches of U.S. government.

Chase avoided controversy in his subsequent work on the Court. His near impeachment served as a warning both to him and to other justices to be careful in their choice of words while in office. As Chase suffered in later years from declining health, Marshall became the most vocal justice and assumed Chase's position as the lightning rod for the Court.

Chase died June 19, 1811, in Baltimore. He was interred in St. Paul's Cemetery.

### CROSS-REFERENCES

Constitution of the United States *In Focus: Federalists vs. Anti-Federalists*; Fries's Rebellion; *Marbury v. Madison*; Supreme Court of the United States.

**CHATTEL** An item of PERSONAL PROPERTY that is movable; it may be animate or inanimate.

Chattels are synonymous with GOODS or PERSONALTY.

**CHATTEL MORTGAGE** A transfer of some legal or equitable right in PERSONAL PROPERTY as security for the payment of money or performance of some other act. Chattel mortgages have generally been superseded by other types of SECURED TRANSACTIONS under the UNIFORM COMMERCIAL CODE (UCC), a body of law adopted by the states that governs commercial transactions.

The rights of the lender who gives a chattel mortgage are valid only against others who know or should know of the lender's security interest in the property. Since the borrower possesses the property, others cannot realize that a chattel mortgage exists without notice. Each state, therefore, has developed a system for recording instruments showing the existence of chattel mortgages for particular items of property; these RECORDS are usually located in the county clerk's office.

If a recording system is in existence a buyer is presumed to know about a mortgage. Once,

A typical chattel mortgage

Date _____, _____

The words I and me mean all borrowers who signed this note. The word bank means the ABC Bank.

**Promise to Pay**

_____ months from today, I promise to pay to the ABC Bank _____ _____ dollars ($)

**Responsibility**

Although this note may be signed below by more than one person, I understand that we are each as individuals responsible for paying back the full amount.

**Breakdown of Loan**

This is what I will pay:

| | |
|---|---|
| Amount of loan | 1.$_____ |
| Credit Life Insurance (optional) | 2.$_____ |
| Other (describe) _____ | 3.$_____ |
| Amount Financed (Add 1 and 2 and 3) | 4.$_____ |
| FINANCE CHARGE | 5.$_____ |
| Total of Payments (Add 4 and 5) | $_____ |
| ANNUAL PERCENTAGE RATE | _____ % |

**Repayment**

This is how I will repay:

I will repay the amount of this note in ____ equal uninterrupted monthly installments of $ _____ each on the _____ day of each month starting on the _____ day of _____, _____, and ending on _____, _____.

**Prepayment**

I have the right to prepay the whole outstanding amount of this note at any time. If I do, or if this loan is refinanced—that is, replaced by a new note—you will refund the unearned finance charge, figured by the rule of 78—a commonly used formula for figuring rebates on installment loans.

**Late Charge**

Any installment not paid within ten days of its due date shall be subject to a late charge of 5% of the payment, not to exceed $5.00 for any such late installment.

**Security**

To protect the ABC Bank, I give what is known as a security interest in my auto and/or other: (Describe) _____ See the security agreement.

**Credit Life Insurance**

Credit life insurance is not required to obtain this loan. The bank need not provide it and I do not need to buy it unless I sign immediately below. The cost of credit life insurance is $ _____ for the term of the loan.

Signed: _____ Date: _____

**Default**

If for any reason I fail to make any payment on time, I shall be in default. The bank can then demand immediate payment of the entire remaining unpaid balance of this loan, without giving anyone further notice. If I have not paid the full amount of the loan when the final payment is due, the bank will charge me interest on the unpaid balance at sixteen percent (16%) per year.

A typical chattel mortgage (continued)

### Right of Offset

If this loan becomes past due, the bank will have the right to pay this loan from any deposit or security I have at this bank without telling me ahead of time. Even if the bank gives me an extension of time to pay this loan, I still must repay the entire loan.

### Collection Fees

If this note is placed with an attorney for collection, then I agree to pay an attorney's fee of fifteen percent (15%) of the unpaid balance. This fee will be added to the unpaid balance of the loan.

### Co-borrowers

If I am signing this note as a co-borrower, I agree to be equally responsible with the borrower for this loan. The bank does not have to notify me that this note has not been paid. The bank can change the terms of payment and release any security without notifying or releasing me from responsibility for this loan.

### Copy Received

I received a completely filled in copy of this note. If I have signed for Credit Life Insurance, I received a copy of the Credit Life Insurance certificate.

Borrower: _____

_____
Address
Co-borrower: _____

_____
Address
Co-borrower: _____

_____
Address

**CONSUMER CREDIT HOTLINE:** If you have any questions, please call us immediately at (000)012-3456.

---

therefore, the mortgage is properly recorded, the buyer obtains the DEBT in addition to the property. See also RECORDING OF LAND TITLES.

**CHATTEL PAPER** A writing or writings that evidence both a monetary obligation and a security interest in or a LEASE of specific goods. In many instances chattel paper will consist of a NEGOTIABLE INSTRUMENT coupled with a security agreement. When a transaction is evidenced both by such a security agreement or a lease and by an instrument or a series of instruments, the group of writings taken together constitutes chattel paper. See also SECURED TRANSACTIONS.

**CHAVEZ, CESAR** Cesar Chavez, the son of Mexican American farmworkers, became a well-known labor leader, founding the United Farm Workers (UFW) union which led a massive grape boycott in the 1960s across the United States. Chavez won wage increases, benefits, and legal protections for migrant farmworkers in the western United States and fought to have dangerous pesticides outlawed for agricultural use.

Chavez was born March 31, 1927, in Yuma, Arizona, one of five children in a family that lived on a small farm. When he was a child the family was pushed onto the road as migrant laborers when Chavez's parents lost the family farm during the Depression. He later often spoke of what he felt was the unjust way the family had lost its property through FORECLOSURE. Chavez never went beyond the seventh grade, and once said he attended over sixty elementary schools because of his family's constant search for work in the fields.

Chavez was exposed to labor organizing as a young boy when his father and uncle joined a dried-fruit industry union in the late 1930s. The young Chavez was deeply impressed when the workers later went on STRIKE. At age nineteen Chavez himself picketed cotton fields but watched the union fail in its efforts to organize the workers.

After serving in the U.S. Navy during World War II, he returned to California where he married a woman named Helen Fabela. In 1952

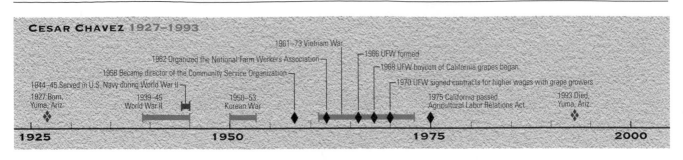

CESAR CHAVEZ 1927–1993

1944–45 Served in U.S. Navy during World War II
1958 Became director of the Community Service Organization
1962 Organized the National Farm Workers Association
1961–73 Vietnam War
1966 UFW formed
1968 UFW boycott of California grapes began
1970 UFW signed contracts for higher wages with grape growers
1927 Born, Yuma, Ariz.
1939–45 World War II
1950–53 Korean War
1975 California passed Agricultural Labor Relations Act
1993 Died, Yuma, Ariz.

1925        1950        1975        2000

the Los Angeles headquarters of organizer Saul Alinsky's Community Service Organization (CSO) decided to set up a chapter in San Jose, California, to work for CIVIL RIGHTS for the area's Mexican Americans and Mexican immigrants. A parish priest supplied several names to CSO organizer Fred Ross, including that of Chavez, who was then living in one of San Jose's poorest and toughest neighborhoods— Sal Si Puedes (in English, Leave If You Can). Ross thought Chavez could be the best grassroots leader he had ever encountered, so he sought Chavez out and eventually convinced him to join the group's efforts. Chavez began as a volunteer in a CSO voter registration drive and a few months later was hired as a staff member. He spent the next ten years leading voter registration drives throughout the San Joaquin Valley and advocating for Mexican immigrants who complained of mistreatment by police officers, immigration authorities, and welfare officials.

Chavez believed that unionizing was the only chance for farmworkers to improve their working conditions and in 1962, increasingly frustrated because the CSO would not become involved in forming a farmworkers' union, he resigned. He immediately established the National Farm Workers Association, which later became the UFW, an affiliate with the American Federation of Labor and Congress of Industrial Organizations (AFL-CIO). At the UFW's first meeting in September 1962, in Fresno, California, Chavez's cousin, Manuel Chavez, unveiled the flag he and Chavez had designed for the new union—a black Aztec eagle in a white circle on a bold red background. The banner soon became the symbol of the farmworkers' struggle.

When Chavez founded the UFW, fieldworkers in California averaged $1.50 an hour, received no benefits, and had no methods by which to challenge their employers. Under Chavez's leadership, the UFW won tremendous wage increases and extensive benefits for farmworkers, including medical and unemployment insurance and WORKERS' COMPENSATION. A strict believer in nonviolence, Chavez used

**BIOGRAPHY**

AP/WIDE WORLD PHOTOS

*Cesar Chavez*

"OUR STRUGGLE IS NOT EASY . . . BUT WE HAVE SOMETHING THE RICH DO NOT OWN. WE HAVE OUR BODIES AND SPIRITS AND THE JUSTICE OF OUR CAUSE AS OUR WEAPONS."

marches, BOYCOTTS, strikes, fasts, and civil disobedience to force growers in California's agricultural valleys to the bargaining table. In 1968, Filipino grape pickers in Delano, California, struck for higher wages; several days later, the UFW joined the strike and initiated a boycott of California grapes. More than two hundred union supporters traveled across the United States and into Canada urging consumers not to buy California grapes. The mayors of New York, Boston, Detroit, and St. Louis announced that their cities would not buy nonunion grapes. By August 1968, California grape growers estimated the boycott had cost them about 20 percent of their revenue. The boycott brought Chavez to the attention of national political leaders, including U.S. Senator ROBERT F. KENNEDY, who sought the Democratic party nomination for president before his assassination in 1968. Kennedy described Chavez as a heroic figure. In 1970, after its successful boycott, the UFW signed contracts with the grape growers.

In 1975, Chavez had a great success when the strongest law ever enacted to protect farmworkers, the Agricultural Labor Relations Act (Cal. Lab. Code § 1140 et seq. [West]), was passed by the California Legislature. This law gave workers the right to bargain collectively and the right to seek redress for unfair labor practices. Other regulations banned tools that caused crippling back injury, such as the short-handled hoe, and required growers to give workers breaks and to provide toilets and fresh water in the fields. Chavez was among the first to link workers' health problems to pesticides. He negotiated union contracts that prohibited growers from using DDT and he targeted five leading pesticides that cause birth defects or kill upon contact.

At its peak in the 1970s the UFW had seventy thousand members. In the early 1980s the UFW's influence began to wane and union membership dipped below ten thousand. Chavez blamed the decline in part on the election of Republican governors, beginning in 1983, who sided with the growers. In addition, Chavez decided to turn his efforts to conducting boycotts rather than organizing workers, a move that was widely criticized and caused a split among the union's members. Chavez was also forced to defend himself against lawsuits stemming from UFW actions taken years before. In 1991, the union lost a $2.4 million case when the U.S. Supreme Court declined to hear the appeal of a case stemming from a 1979 Imperial Valley strike in which a farmworker was shot and killed (*Maggio, Inc. v. United Farm Workers of America*, 227 Cal. App. 3d 847, 278 Cal. Rptr. 250 [Cal. App. 1991], *cert. denied*, 502 U.S. 863, 112 S. Ct. 187, 116 L. Ed. 2d 148 [1991]).

In April 1993, Chavez returned to San Luis, a small town near his native Yuma, Arizona, to testify in the retrial of a lawsuit brought by Bruce Church, Inc., a large Salinas, California–based producer of iceberg lettuce. At the time Chavez testified, Bruce Church had extensive landholdings in Arizona and California, including the acreage east of Yuma that Chavez's parents had once owned. The company had won a $5.4 million judgment for alleged damage caused by union boycotts but an appellate court overturned the judgment and sent the case back to the trial court (*Bruce Church, Inc. v. United Farm Workers of America*, 816 P.2d 919 [Ariz. App. 1991]). On April 22, Chavez finished his second day of testimony in Yuma County Superior Court. He returned to spend the night at the home of a family friend and died in his sleep during the night.

Following Chavez's death, Lane Kirkland, president of the AFL-CIO, described him as instrumental in organized labor's efforts to improve the lot of the worker. "Always, Cesar conveyed hope and determination, especially to minority workers, in the daily struggle against injustice and hardship," Kirkland said. "The improved lives of millions of farm workers and their families will endure as a testimonial to Cesar and his life's work."

In a 1984 speech to the Commonwealth Club in San Francisco, Chavez said, "Regardless of what the future holds for our union, regardless of what the future holds for farm workers, our accomplishment cannot be undone. The consciousness and pride that were raised by our union are alive and thriving inside millions of young Hispanics who will never work on a farm."

See also AGRICULTURAL LAW; LABOR UNION.

**CHECK** A written order instructing a BANK to pay upon its presentation to the person designated in it, or to the person possessing it, a certain sum of money from the account of the person who DRAWS it.

A check must contain the phrase "pay to the order of." A check differs from a DRAFT in that a check is always drawn on a bank, while a draft is an order for payment drawn on anyone, including a bank, a person, or a trading account with a company.

A *blank check* is one that the drawer signs but omits filling in the space for the name of the PAYEE, the person in whose favor a check is drawn, or neglects to fill in the space for the amount to be paid.

A *cashier's check* is one that the bank draws on itself and is signed by an authorized bank official. The bank lends its credit to the purchaser of the check in order to facilitate its immediate use in commercial transactions. It is a direct obligation of the bank.

A *personal check* is one that the individual draws on his or her own account.

A sample check

BARBARA P. OR JOE D. MAGGIO
253 - 3RD AVE. S. PH. 612-555-1214
ST. PAUL, MN 55555-2312

3068

19-1442/960
836650

DATE _____

PAY TO THE
ORDER OF _____ $

_____ DOLLARS ■ Security features included. Details on back

South Bank    45
835 South Boulevard
St. Paul, MN 55555

MEMO _____    MP
095014334 73 664 0 3028

A *postdated check* is one that bears a date after its date of issuance, and is payable on the stated date.

A *traveler's check* is one purchased from a bank, express company, or other financial institution in various denominations, and is signed immediately by the purchaser in order to establish the form of his or her signature. The check cannot be treated as cash because of this first signature, but it is treated as cash upon the purchaser's second signature when he or she uses it. The genuineness of the second signature is established by comparing it to the initial signature. A traveler's check is similar to a cashier's check of the issuer.

## CHECKOFF

A system whereby an employer regularly deducts a portion of an employee's wages to pay union dues or initiation fees.

The checkoff system is very attractive to a union since the collection of dues can be costly and time-consuming. It prescribes the manner in which dues are paid by deductions in earnings rather than through individual checks sent directly to the union. Unions are thereby assured of the regular receipt of their dues.

A dues checkoff system is only lawful when voluntarily authorized by an employee. Unions have attempted to make alternatives to checkoff more onerous by requiring such practices as in-person delivery of dues checks to out-of-state locations. The National Labor Relations Board has held that this type of inducement to checkoff is unlawful, however, as is the attempt by a union to collect assessments extending beyond periodic dues. See also LABOR LAW; LABOR UNION.

## CHESSMAN, CARYL

The execution of Caryl Chessman in the gas chamber of San Quentin Prison on May 3, 1960, ended a twelve-year struggle between Chessman and the justice system that culminated in international rage at the treatment of the prisoner.

Caryl Whittier Chessman was born May 27, 1921, in St. Joseph, Michigan. In 1948, Chessman was a 27-year-old parolee from Folsom Prison in California when he was arrested in Los Angeles as the prime suspect in the "red light bandit" incidents. The modus operandi of the bandit was distinctive: he stalked desolate areas known to be popular with couples seeking a place to park and be alone. The bandit would walk toward a parked car carrying a red light similar to that used by police, and then assault the unsuspecting occupants of the car.

Chessman initially confessed to the crimes but later claimed that he was tortured into confessing. He professed his innocence but was indicted on eighteen separate counts, including KIDNAPPING, ROBBERY, sexual mistreatment, and attempted RAPE. Two of the charges carried a mandatory death sentence in California, based on the passage of the "Little Lindbergh" law in 1933 in response to the heinous kidnapping and murder of the infant son of aviator Charles Lindbergh and poet Anne Morrow Lindbergh. The law required CAPITAL PUNISHMENT for a kidnapping in which the victim was inflicted with physical harm. See also LINDBERGH KIDNAPPING.

The trial lasted two weeks, and Chessman served as his own counsel, aided by an attorney provided by the court. The jury returned a verdict of guilty on seventeen of the charges, including those imparting the death sentence.

Chessman was transferred to San Quentin Prison in California pending an appeal to the state supreme court. The court affirmed the decision, and Chessman was sent to cell 2455 on death row to await his execution scheduled for March 28, 1952.

Chessman appealed his case on the grounds that he was not granted DUE PROCESS OF LAW. He based his appeal on the fact that the TRANSCRIPT of his trial was inaccurate. The original court reporter had died suddenly, leaving two-thirds of the testimony to be transcribed. Chessman argued that the new reporter did not accurately decipher the old-style shorthand used by his predecessor. Chessman had also requested daily transcripts of the testimony, but this request was denied.

Chessman's plea was rejected, and during the next twelve years he submitted his APPEAL forty-

### Checkoff

Percent of U.S. Wage and Salary Workforce Holding Labor Union Membership, 1983 to 1994

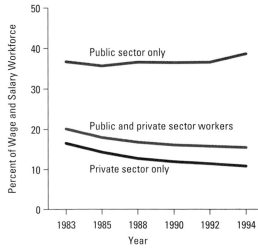

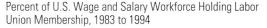

Source: The Bureau of National Affairs, Inc. Washington, D.C., *Union Membership and Earnings Data Book 1994.*

*Caryl Chessman was convicted on eighteen counts, including kidnapping, robbery, and attempted rape. He submitted an appeal to his conviction forty-two times but it was never overturned, and he was executed in 1960 after twelve years on death row.*

two times before various federal and state appellate courts, including the Supreme Court of the United States. He remained on death row for twelve years, during which he wrote several books describing his life there. He was scheduled to face the gas chamber on nine separate occasions, but he always received a reprieve before the execution.

Chessman argued that his predicament was an example of CRUEL AND UNUSUAL PUNISHMENT, which violated his constitutional rights. The case began to attract international and political attention and at one point, Governor Edmund Brown of California called for a stay of execution by order of the state department to ensure a peaceful tour of South America by President Dwight D. Eisenhower.

Time was running out for Chessman by 1960. Although his lawyers claimed to have found new evidence in favor of their client, the courts denied a plea for a writ of HABEAS CORPUS. He was again scheduled for execution in May 1960. Protests were heard from several countries and famous people, including Aldous Huxley and Albert Schweitzer. Despite these efforts, Chessman was executed on May 3, 1960.

The death of Caryl Chessman incited a wave of anti-American sentiment with protests in several countries.

See also CAPITAL PUNISHMENT.

**CHICAGO EIGHT** The trial of the Chicago Eight exemplified the state of turmoil that existed in the United States in 1968. Because the Chicago CONSPIRACY trial opened with eight defendants, this group of radical leaders is sometimes referred to as the Chicago Eight.

However, the trial of one defendant, Bobby Seale, was subsequently severed from that of the other seven; hence the name Chicago Seven is often given to these defendants.

The violent ASSASSINATIONS of Senator ROBERT F. KENNEDY and Dr. MARTIN LUTHER KING, JR., occurred within months of each other. The escalation of the VIETNAM WAR was unpopular with many U.S. citizens and a number of young men of draft age burned their draft registration cards or fled to Canada rather than risk their lives for a cause in which they did not believe. Protest demonstrations were prevalent. The turbulence in the United States culminated in events at the Democratic Presidential Convention in Chicago, Illinois, which led to a sensational courtroom trial involving the basic rights embodied in the Constitution.

Chicago was controlled politically by Mayor Richard J. Daley and his Democratic followers. When Chicago was chosen as the site for the Democratic Convention, groups of protestors decided to seize the opportunity to converge on that city to stage demonstrations and publicly espouse their views against U.S. participation in the Vietnam War. The protestors arrived from all over the nation, establishing a camp at Lincoln Park.

Mayor Daley was opposed to any incident that might cause a disturbance of the convention proceedings and taint the reputation of the city of Chicago. The demonstrators were denied a permit to assemble in Lincoln Park and were told to disband. When they refused the Chicago police tried to forcibly eject them from the park. When these efforts failed the police used tear gas and billy clubs. A RIOT resulted, and as news of the Chicago violence reached the nation other groups went to Chicago to join the protestors. When the number of demonstrators reached 20,000, the National Guard was enlisted to quell the violence. Eight radical leaders emerged as the organizers of the demonstration movement: Tom Hayden and Rennie Davis, who had established the group known as Students for a Democratic Society, or SDS; Abbie Hoffman and Jerry Rubin, founders of the Youth International Party, or "Yippies"; Bobby Seale, leader of the BLACK PANTHER PARTY; David Dellinger, staunch opponent of the Vietnam War and renowned pacifist; and John Froines and Lee Weiner, two teachers.

In 1968 Congress enacted legislation prohibiting conspiracies to cross state boundaries with the intent of INCITING a riot. The eight men were brought to trial at the Federal Court Building in Chicago in 1969 and were accused of breaking this new law.

*Rennie Davis (right), cofounder of Students for a Democratic Society, and Bobby Seale (far right), leader of the Black Panther Party, were tried on conspiracy charges in Chicago in 1969 as two of the Chicago Eight.*

The TRIAL evoked a number of controversial issues. The purpose of the protest was to air the views of the participants against the Vietnam War. The blame for the ensuing riots, however, could not be clearly placed on the demonstrators or on the actions of the police to disband them. While the Constitution provided for the basic FREEDOMS OF SPEECH, protest, and assemblage, the terms of the new law—particularly concerning the actual act of conspiring to riot—were not clearly defined in relation to these rights.

The judge selected to try the case was federal district court judge Julius J. Hoffman. The attorney for the prosecution was the U.S. attorney for Illinois, Thomas Foran. A number of defense lawyers were retained, but the two most prominent were WILLIAM KUNSTLER and Leonard Weinglass. Armed protection was provided at the court building to discourage disturbances.

Judge Hoffman proved to be a difficult man. Four defense lawyers notified the judge by telegram that they had decided to withdraw from the case; Hoffman charged them with CONTEMPT of court for not informing him personally of their intentions. The charges were eventually dropped but not before protests from lawyers all over the nation were filed. Bobby Seale's lawyer became ill, and Seale asked for either a delay of his trial until his lawyer could participate or permission to defend himself. Hoffman denied both requests. See also RIGHT TO COUNSEL.

The prosecution began by stating three charges against the Chicago Eight: (1) they had persuaded people to travel to Chicago for the purpose of joining protest demonstrations; (2) they had influenced their followers to defy law enforcement officials; and (3) they had encouraged a riot. The defense attorneys countered that the actions of the demonstrators were in accordance with the basic freedoms granted by the Constitution.

Police informants were called as witnesses for the prosecution. Bobby Seale asked to be allowed to cross-examine the witnesses, and again the argument flared between Seale and Hoffman as to Seale's rights to representation by counsel. The other defendants voiced agitation during the early days of the trial, but exchanges between Bobby Seale and Judge Hoffman were particularly vehement, and Hoffman had Seale handcuffed to a chair and gagged. Hoffman claimed that the court had the right to employ this tactic, but it was the first time it had been utilized during a trial of any consequence in the United States. Seale still found ways to interrupt the proceedings, and Hoffman declared a MISTRIAL in Seale's case, and imposed on Seale SENTENCE of four years for contempt of court.

The seven remaining defendants and their lawyers became enraged; the trial became a shouting match between all involved, with insults being flung at the judge by the defendants. Hoffman began ruling in favor of motions presented by the prosecution and against those for the defense.

The trial came to a close on February 14, 1970. As the jury deliberated the evidence Hoffman charged all the defendants and attorneys Kunstler and Weinglass with contempt of court, and passed sentences ranging from two months, eight days, to twenty-nine months, thirteen days. Kunstler, however, received the longest sentence of four years, thirteen days. Judge Hoffman also refused to permit BAIL.

The jury finally reached a verdict. The seven defendants were cleared of conspiracy charges, but five of them were found guilty of crossing state boundaries to incite a riot and were given prison sentences of five years and fined $5,000. Defendants Froines and Weiner were acquitted of all charges.

The Chicago Eight appealed to higher courts, which resulted in granting of bail, a reversal of all contempt charges—including those of the two lawyers—and a new trial for the convicted five. The proceedings of the new trial were private and lacked the sensationalism of the earlier hearings, and although the defendants were again found guilty, their sentences were suspended.

**CHICAGO JURY PROJECT** The Chicago Jury Project was an investigation of the role and functions of the JURY in the U.S. legal system. The inquiry was conducted by the University of Chicago Law School with funding from the Ford Foundation. Its primary goal was to join the social scientist and the lawyer in a working relationship in which they could share their unique skills and experiences with each other, along with amassing pertinent data to answer some interdisciplinary questions, in order to create new ideas and theories in their respective fields.

The topics to be studied included the differences between the roles of the judge and the jury; the jury's determination of the issue of insanity when it is asserted as a defense; the influence of the existence of INSURANCE upon the minds of the jurors when deciding a case; and the jury's comprehension of, and attitude toward, the concept of contributory NEGLIGENCE in jurisdictions where it was law. The methodology by which such information was gleaned included personal conversations with jurors after the conclusion of trials as well as questionnaires. The rationales underlying the processes by which jurors were selected and examined on VOIR DIRE were additional subjects of study. The views of the general public and members of the legal profession regarding juries were solicited. There was also an examination of the costs inherent in the operation of the jury system.

The Chicago Jury Project encountered one problem as a result of the techniques used in collecting data. With the permission of the presiding judge and counsel, the staff made recordings of the deliberation of jurors in five civil cases brought to trial before the federal district court sitting in Wichita, Kansas. Such recordings were to be used in determining whether interviews conducted with jurors after a trial accurately described the events occurring in the jury room. The jurors were not, however, informed of the recordings. When it was revealed that such recordings were made, the attorney general of the United States publicly censured the project and the Senate judiciary committee convened a special hearing to investigate such unorthodox and questionable research methods. State legislatures responded to such disclosures by enacting statutes proscribing the recording of jury deliberations.

The findings of the Chicago Jury Project are discussed in the books *Delay in the Court* and *The American Jury*, published in 1959 and 1966, respectively.

**CHICAGO SCHOOL** Among contemporary movements in U.S. law, few have had as much influence as the Chicago school. This school of thought helped revolutionize legal thinking on economics from the 1970s to the 1980s. At the heart of its philosophy is the idea that economic efficiency should be the goal of national policy and law. This argument left its mark, in particular, in the area of ANTITRUST, where the Chicago school swayed the U.S. Supreme Court for more than a decade. Although they received less attention in the 1990s than they had earlier, the school's leaders continued to rank among the preeminent—and more controversial—figures on the legal landscape.

The Chicago school takes its name from the University of Chicago, with which most of its core proponents were all affiliated at one time. These include Professor Ronald H. Coase, Judge Frank H. Easterbrook, Professor Richard A. Epstein, Professor Daniel R. Fischel, Judge RICHARD A. POSNER, and Judge Ralph K. Winter, Jr. ROBERT H. BORK, another prominent member, was a professor at Yale. The early work of the Chicago school, produced in the 1960s, built on scholarship by Professor Aaron Director. Director's specialty had been antitrust, the area of law that addresses unfair competition in business. Antitrust has a long history, in which ideas have come and gone. Through the late 1960s, the U.S. Supreme Court took a harsh view of restraints on trade. The Court ruled that certain anticompetitive practices were "PER SE" illegal—so harmful to competition that they need not even be evaluated on a case-by-case basis.

The Chicago school urged the Court to take another look. Scholars of the school praised economic efficiency. If they could show, for instance, that certain restraints on trade were actually a result of efficient competition, then why should these practices be considered illegal by courts? Underlying this view was the contention that markets could take care of themselves without the need for heavy regulation. It was not long before the Chicago school's ideas began to influence the Supreme Court. In 1977, the Court abandoned its reliance on per se rules in *Continental T.V. v. GTE Sylvania*, 433 U.S. 36, 97 S. Ct. 2549, 53 L. Ed 2d 568, and turned instead to a rule of "reason," opening a new era in antitrust law.

Throughout the 1970s, the Chicago school continued to refine its economic theory in numerous essays and treatises such as Posner's *Antitrust Law* (1976) and Robert H. Bork's *The Antitrust Paradox* (1978), both of which attacked the idea that big business is necessarily bad. The school argued that an unrestricted market, in which producers and consumers acted freely, will operate rationally and efficiently all by itself. The hands-off implications of this picture had broad significance for corporate law and national policy. Chicago school theory influenced the Reagan administration's attack on government regulation.

President RONALD REAGAN appointed several Chicago school members to the federal bench: Posner in 1981 to the Seventh Circuit, Winter in 1982 to the Second Circuit, and Easterbrook in 1985 to the Seventh Circuit. Bork, a judge on the U.S. Court of Appeals for the District of Columbia Circuit, was nominated to the U.S. Supreme Court in 1987. However, widespread protest over his views led the U.S. Senate to block his confirmation.

In the 1990s the Chicago school continued to provoke lively debate. Bork, despite resigning from the judiciary in 1988 following his failed nomination to the Supreme Court, attracted attention with publications such as his 1990 book *The Tempting of America: The Political Seduction of the Law*. But in the area of antitrust, at least, the heyday of the school's influence was over. For years, the Chicago school's theory had been undergoing a reevaluation, with critics questioning its faith in government nonintervention.

**CHIEF JUSTICE** 📖 The presiding, most senior, or principal JUDGE of a court. 📖

Although the office of the chief justice of the SUPREME COURT OF THE UNITED STATES is a prestigious position, the functions and powers of the chief justice are not well-defined. The U.S. Constitution contains only one mention of the chief justice, in Article I, Section 3, and it concerns the IMPEACHMENT of the PRESIDENT: "When the President of the United States is tried, the Chief Justice shall preside." The JUDICIARY ACT OF 1789, which created the Supreme Court, specified only "[t]hat the supreme court of the United States shall consist of a chief justice and five associate justices" (1 Stat. 73). As a result, each individual who has occupied the post has had the freedom to shape and define the role.

Like the ASSOCIATE JUSTICES of the Supreme Court, the chief justice is appointed for life by the president but must first be confirmed by the Senate. Prior service on the Court is not re-quired, though several chief justices, including HARLAN F. STONE and WILLIAM H. REHNQUIST, served as associate justices before becoming chief justice. Many chief justices served in other branches of government before joining the Court: JOHN MARSHALL and ROGER B. TANEY were cabinet members, EDWARD D. WHITE was a U.S. senator, and EARL WARREN was governor of California. Other chief justices came to the Court as judges from lower federal and state courts or practiced law prior to their appointments.

The chief justice's primary duty is to preside over all Supreme Court proceedings, both those open to the public and those held in private. The chief justice traditionally opens and closes the public sessions in which the Court hears oral arguments. He or she wields the most influence in closed-door proceedings. The chief justice determines which decisions the Court will discuss in conferences where the justices choose the cases they will accept for review. The chief justice also leads the private discussions on cases recently argued. After presenting the facts and issues in such a case and the relevant law, the chief justice states her or his conclusions and casts a vote. The discussion continues in order of seniority, with each associate justice presenting her or his views and vote.

If the chief justice is in the majority after voting has concluded, he or she assigns the writing of the OPINION in the case. This critical responsibility provides the chief justice with an important opportunity to influence the outcome of the case, since he or she can assign the case to a justice who he or she believes has similar views. The chief justice may also assign the authorship of the opinion to himself or herself, as many chief justices have done in cases involving far-reaching constitutional issues. If the chief justice is not in the majority, the senior justice in the majority has the power of assignment.

The chief justice is also responsible for the overall management of the Supreme Court, including the oversight and supervision of the Court's clerks, marshal, reporter of decisions, librarian, and other officers, and the handling of various personnel management issues. The chief justice estimates the Court's budget and designates the officials to present it to the appropriate congressional committees. Although the chief justice is expected to avoid overt participation in political activities, many have acted as public advocates for the Court before Congress. WILLIAM H. TAFT, the only chief justice to have also served as president,

## Time Chart of the Supreme Court

This table is designed to aid the user in identifying the composition of the Supreme Court at any given time in U.S. history. Each listing is headed by the chief justice, whose name is italicized. Associate justices are listed following the chief justice in order of seniority. The name of each justice is followed by a symbol representing his or her party affiliation at the time of appointment.

| 1789 | 1790–91 | 1792 | 1793–94 | 1795 | 1796–97 | 1798–99 |
|---|---|---|---|---|---|---|
| *Jay* (F) | *Jay* (F) | *Jay* (F) | *Jay* (F) | *J. Rutledge* (F)[1] | *Ellsworth* (F) | *Ellsworth* (F) |
| J. Rutledge (F) | J. Rutledge (F) | Cushing (F) | Cushing (F) | Cushing (F) | Cushing (F) | Cushing (F) |
| Cushing (F) | Cushing (F) | Wilson (F) | Wilson (F) | Wilson (F) | Wilson (F) | Iredell (F) |
| Wilson (F) | Wilson (F) | Blair (F) | Blair (F) | Blair (F) | Iredell (F) | Paterson (F) |
| Blair (F) | Blair (F) | Iredell (F) | Iredell (F) | Iredell (F) | Paterson (F) | S. Chase (F) |
| | Iredell (F) | T. Johnson (F) | Paterson (F) | Paterson (F) | S. Chase (F) | Washington (F) |

| 1800 | 1801–03 | 1804–05 | 1806 | 1807–10 | 1811–22 | 1823–25 |
|---|---|---|---|---|---|---|
| *Ellsworth* (F) | *J. Marshall* (F) | *J. Marshall* (F) | *J. Marshall* (F) | *J. Marshall* (F) | *J. Marshall* (F) | *J. Marshall* (F) |
| Cushing (F) | Cushing (F) | Cushing (F) | Cushing (F) | Cushing (F) | Washington (F) | Washington (F) |
| Paterson (F) | Paterson (F) | Paterson (F) | S. Chase (F) | S. Chase (F) | W. Johnson (DR) | W. Johnson (DR) |
| S. Chase (F) | S. Chase (F) | S. Chase (F) | Washington (F) | Washington (F) | Livingston (DR) | Todd (DR) |
| Washington (F) | Washington (F) | Washington (F) | W. Johnson (DR) | W. Johnson (DR) | Todd (DR) | Duval (DR) |
| Moore (F) | Moore (F) | W. Johnson (DR) | Livingston (DR) | Livingston (DR) | Duval (DR) | Story (DR) |
| | | | | Todd (DR) | Story (DR) | Thompson (DR) |

| 1826–28 | 1829 | 1830–34 | 1835 | 1836 | 1837–40 | 1841–43 |
|---|---|---|---|---|---|---|
| *J. Marshall* (F) | *J. Marshall* (F) | *J. Marshall* (F) | *J. Marshall* (F) | *Taney* (D) | *Taney* (D) | *Taney* (D) |
| Washington (F) | Washington (F) | W. Johnson (DR) | Duval (DR) | Story (DR) | Story (DR) | Story (DR) |
| W. Johnson (DR) | W. Johnson (DR) | Duval (DR) | Story (DR) | Thompson (DR) | Thompson (DR) | Thompson (DR) |
| Duval (DR) | Duval (DR) | Story (DR) | Thompson (DR) | McLean (D) | McLean (D) | McLean (D) |
| Story (DR) | Story (DR) | Thompson (DR) | McLean (D) | Baldwin (D) | Baldwin (D) | Baldwin (D) |
| Thompson (DR) | Thompson (DR) | McLean (D) | Baldwin (D) | Wayne (D) | Wayne (D) | Wayne (D) |
| Trimble (DR) | McLean (D) | Baldwin (D) | Wayne (D) | Barbour (D) | Barbour (D) | Catron (D) |
| | | | | | Catron (D) | McKinley (D) |
| | | | | | McKinley (D) | Daniel (D) |

| 1844 | 1845 | 1846–50 | 1851–52 | 1853–57 | 1858–60 | 1861 |
|---|---|---|---|---|---|---|
| *Taney* (D) | *Taney* (D) | *Taney* (D) | *Taney* (D) | *Taney* (D) | *Taney* (D) | *Taney* (D) |
| Story (DR) | McLean (D) | McLean (D) | McLean (D) | McLean (D) | McLean (D) | McLean (D) |
| McLean (D) | Wayne (D) | Wayne (D) | Wayne (D) | Wayne (D) | Wayne (D) | Wayne (D) |
| Baldwin (D) | Catron (D) | Catron (D) | Catron (D) | Catron (D) | Catron (D) | Catron (D) |
| Wayne (D) | McKinley (D) | McKinley (D) | McKinley (D) | Daniel (D) | Daniel (D) | Nelson (D) |
| Catron (D) | Daniel (D) | Daniel (D) | Daniel (D) | Nelson (D) | Nelson (D) | Grier (D) |
| McKinley (D) | Nelson (D) | Nelson (D) | Nelson (D) | Grier (D) | Grier (D) | Campbell (D) |
| Daniel (D) | Woodbury (D) | Woodbury (D) | Grier (D) | Curtis (W) | Campbell (D) | Clifford (D) |
| | | Grier (D) | Curtis (W) | Campbell (D) | Clifford (D) | |

| 1862 | 1863 | 1864–65 | 1866 | 1867–69 | 1870–71 | 1872–1873 |
|---|---|---|---|---|---|---|
| *Taney* (D) | *Taney* (D) | *S. P. Chase* (R) | *S. P. Chase* (R) | *S. P. Chase* (R) | *S. P. Chase* (R) | *S. P. Chase* (R) |
| Wayne (D) | Wayne (D) | Wayne (D) | Wayne (D)[2] | Nelson (D) | Nelson (D) | Clifford (D) |
| Catron (D) | Catron (D) | Catron (D)[2] | Nelson (D) | Grier (D) | Clifford (D) | Swayne (R) |
| Nelson (D) | Nelson (D) | Nelson (D) | Grier (D) | Clifford (D) | Swayne (R) | Miller (R) |
| Grier (D) | Grier (D) | Grier (D) | Clifford (D) | Swayne (R) | Miller (R) | Davis (R) |
| Clifford (D) | Clifford (D) | Clifford (D) | Swayne (R) | Miller (R) | Davis (R) | Field (D) |
| Swayne (R) | Swayne (R) | Swayne (R) | Miller (R) | Davis (R) | Field (D) | Strong (R) |
| Miller (R) | Miller (R) | Miller (R) | Davis (R) | Field (D) | Strong (R) | Bradley (R) |
| Davis (R) | Davis (R) | Davis (R) | Field (D) | | Bradley (R) | Hunt (R) |
| | Field (D) | Field (D) | | | | |

| 1874–76 | 1877–79 | 1880 | 1881 | 1882–87 | 1888 | 1889 |
|---|---|---|---|---|---|---|
| *Waite* (R) | *Waite* (R) | *Waite* (R) | *Waite* (R) | *Waite* (R) | *Fuller* (D) | *Fuller* (D) |
| Clifford (D) | Clifford (D) | Clifford (D) | Miller (R) | Miller (R) | Miller (R) | Miller (R) |
| Swayne (R) | Swayne (R) | Swayne (R) | Field (D) | Field (D) | Field (D) | Field (D) |
| Miller (R) | Miller (R) | Miller (R) | Bradley (R) | Bradley (R) | Bradley (R) | Bradley (R) |
| Davis (R) | Field (D) | Field (D) | Hunt (R) | Harlan (Ky.) (R) | Harlan (Ky.) (R) | Harlan (Ky.) (R) |
| Field (D) | Strong (R) | Bradley (R) | Harlan (Ky.) (R) | Woods (R) | Matthews (R) | Gray (R) |
| Strong (R) | Bradley (R) | Hunt (R) | Woods (R) | Matthews (R) | Gray (R) | Blatchford (R) |
| Bradley (R) | Hunt (R) | Harlan (Ky.) (R) | Matthews (R) | Gray (R) | Blatchford (R) | L. Lamar (D) |
| Hunt (R) | Harlan (Ky.) (R) | Woods (R) | Gray (R) | Blatchford (R) | L. Lamar (D) | Brewer (R) |

| 1890–91 | 1892 | 1893 | 1894 | 1895–97 | 1898–1901 | 1902 |
|---|---|---|---|---|---|---|
| *Fuller* (D) | *Fuller* (D) | *Fuller* (D) | *Fuller* (D) | *Fuller* (D) | *Fuller* (D) | *Fuller* (D) |
| Field (D) | Field (D) | Field (D) | Field (D) | Field (D) | Harlan (Ky.) (R) | Harlan (Ky.) (R) |
| Bradley (R) | Harlan (Ky.) (R) | Harlan (Ky.) (R) | Harlan (Ky.) (R) | Harlan (Ky.) (R) | Gray (R) | Brewer (R) |
| Harlan (Ky.) (R) | Gray (R) | Gray (R) | Gray (R) | Gray (R) | Brewer (R) | Brown (R) |
| Gray (R) | Blatchford (R) | Blatchford (R) | Brewer (R) | Brewer (R) | Brown (R) | Shiras (R) |
| Blatchford (R) | L. Lamar (D) | Brewer (R) | Brown (R) | Brown (R) | Shiras (R) | E. White (D) |
| L. Lamar (D) | Brewer (R) | Brown (R) | Shiras (R) | Shiras (R) | E. White (D) | Peckham (D) |
| Brewer (R) | Brown (R) | Shiras (R) | H. Jackson (D) | E. White (D) | Peckham (D) | McKenna (R) |
| Brown (R) | Shiras (R) | H. Jackson (D) | E. White (D) | Peckham (D) | McKenna (R) | Holmes (R) |

F = Federalist
DR = Democratic-Republican (Jeffersonian)
D = Democrat

W = Whig
R = Republican
I = Independent

(table continued on next page)

1. Rutledge was a recess appointment whose confirmation was rejected by the Senate after the 1795 term.
2. Upon the death of Catron in 1865 and Wayne in 1867, their positions were abolished according to a congressional act of 1866. The Court's membership was reduced to eight until a new position was created by Congress in 1869. The new seat has generally been regarded as a re-creation of Wayne's seat.

## Time Chart of the Supreme Court—*continued*

| 1903–05 | 1906–08 | 1909 | 1910–11 | 1912–13 | 1914–15 | 1916–20 |
|---|---|---|---|---|---|---|
| *Fuller* (D) | *Fuller* (D) | *Fuller* (D) | *E. White* (D) | *E. White* (D) | *E. White* (D) | *E. White* (D) |
| Harlan (Ky.) (R) | Harlan (Ky.) (R) | Harlan (Ky.) (R) | Harlan (Ky.) (R) | McKenna (R) | McKenna (R) | McKenna (R) |
| Brewer (R) | Brewer (R) | Brewer (R) | McKenna (R) | Holmes (R) | Holmes (R) | Holmes (R) |
| Brown (R) | E. White (D) | E. White (D) | Holmes (R) | Day (R) | Day (R) | Day (R) |
| E. White (D) | Peckham (D) | McKenna (R) | Day (R) | Lurton (D) | Hughes (R) | Van Devanter (R) |
| Peckham (D) | McKenna (R) | Holmes (R) | Lurton (D) | Hughes (R) | Van Devanter (R) | Pitney (R) |
| McKenna (R) | Holmes (R) | Day (R) | Hughes (R) | Van Devanter (R) | J. Lamar (D) | McReynolds (D) |
| Holmes (R) | Day (R) | Moody (R) | Van Devanter (R) | J. Lamar (D) | Pitney (R) | Brandeis (R)[3] |
| Day (R) | Moody (R) | Lurton (D) | J. Lamar (D) | Pitney (R) | McReynolds (D) | Clarke (D) |

| 1921 | 1922 | 1923–24 | 1925–29 | 1930–31 | 1932–36 | 1937 |
|---|---|---|---|---|---|---|
| *Taft* (R) | *Taft* (R) | *Taft* (R) | *Taft* (R) | *Hughes* (R) | *Hughes* (R) | *Hughes* (R) |
| McKenna (R) | McKenna (R) | McKenna (R) | Holmes (R) | Holmes (R) | Van Devanter (R) | McReynolds (D) |
| Holmes (R) | Holmes (R) | Holmes (R) | Van Devanter (R) | Van Devanter (R) | McReynolds (D) | Brandeis (R) |
| Day (R) | Van Devanter (R) | Van Devanter (R) | McReynolds (D) | McReynolds (D) | Brandeis (R) | Sutherland (R) |
| Van Devanter (R) | Pitney (R) | McReynolds (D) | Brandeis (R) | Brandeis (R) | Sutherland (R) | Butler (D) |
| Pitney (R) | McReynolds (D) | Brandeis (R) | Sutherland (R) | Sutherland (R) | Butler (D) | Stone (R) |
| McReynolds (D) | Brandeis (R) | Sutherland (R) | Butler (D) | Butler (D) | Stone (R) | Roberts (R) |
| Brandeis (R) | Sutherland (R) | Butler (D) | Sanford (R) | Stone (R) | Roberts (R) | Cardozo (D) |
| Clarke (D) | Butler (D) | Sanford (R) | Stone (R) | Roberts (R) | Cardozo (D) | Black (D) |

| 1938 | 1939 | 1940 | 1941–42 | 1943–44 | 1945 | 1946–48 |
|---|---|---|---|---|---|---|
| *Hughes* (R) | *Hughes* (R) | *Hughes* (R) | *Stone* (R) | *Stone* (R) | *Stone* (R) | *Vinson* (D) |
| McReynolds (D) | McReynolds (D) | McReynolds (D) | Roberts (R) | Roberts (R) | Black (D) | Black (D) |
| Brandeis (R) | Butler (D) | Stone (R) | Black (D) | Black (D) | Reed (D) | Reed (D) |
| Butler (D) | Stone (R) | Roberts (R) | Reed (D) | Reed (D) | Frankfurter (I) | Frankfurter (I) |
| Stone (R) | Roberts (R) | Black (D) | Frankfurter (I) | Frankfurter (I) | Douglas (D) | Douglas (D) |
| Roberts (R) | Black (D) | Reed (D) | Douglas (D) | Douglas (D) | Murphy (D) | Murphy (D) |
| Cardozo (D) | Reed (D) | Frankfurter (I) | Murphy (D) | Murphy (D) | R. Jackson (D) | R. Jackson (D) |
| Black (D) | Frankfurter (I) | Douglas (D) | Byrnes (D) | R. Jackson (D) | W. Rutledge (D) | W. Rutledge (D) |
| Reed (D) | Douglas (D) | Murphy (D) | R. Jackson (D) | W. Rutledge (D) | Burton (R) | Burton (R) |

| 1949–52 | 1953–54 | 1955 | 1956 | 1957 | 1958–61 | 1962–65 |
|---|---|---|---|---|---|---|
| *Vinson* (D) | *Warren* (R) | *Warren* (R) | *Warren* (R) | *Warren* (R) | *Warren* (R) | *Warren* (R) |
| Black (D) | Black (D) | Black (D) | Black (D) | Black (D) | Black (D) | Black (D) |
| Reed (D) | Reed (D) | Reed (D) | Reed (D) | Frankfurter (I) | Frankfurter (I) | Douglas (D) |
| Frankfurter (I) | Frankfurter (I) | Frankfurter (I) | Frankfurter (I) | Douglas (D) | Douglas (D) | Clark (D) |
| Douglas (D) | Douglas (D) | Douglas (D) | Douglas (D) | Burton (R) | Clark (D) | Harlan (N.Y.) (R) |
| R. Jackson (D) | R. Jackson (D) | Burton (R) | Burton (R) | Clark (D) | Harlan (N.Y.) (R) | Brennan (D) |
| Burton (R) | Burton (R) | Clark (D) | Clark (D) | Harlan (N.Y.) (R) | Brennan (D) | Stewart (R) |
| Clark (D) | Clark (D) | Minton (D) | Harlan (N.Y.) (R) | Brennan (D) | Whittaker (R) | B. White (D) |
| Minton (D) | Minton (D) | Harlan (N.Y.) (R) | Brennan (D) | Whittaker (R) | Stewart (R) | Goldberg (D)[3] |

| 1965–67 | 1967–69 | 1969 | 1969–70 | 1970 | 1971 | 1972–75 |
|---|---|---|---|---|---|---|
| *Warren* (R) | *Warren* (R) | *Burger* (R) | *Burger* (R) | *Burger* (R) | *Burger* (R) | *Burger* (R) |
| Black (D) | Black (D) | Black (D) | Black (D) | Black (D) | Douglas (D) | Douglas (D) |
| Douglas (D) | Douglas (D) | Douglas (D) | Douglas (D) | Douglas (D) | Brennan (D) | Brennan (D) |
| Clark (D) | Harlan (N.Y.) (R) | Harlan (N.Y.) (R) | Harlan (N.Y.) (R) | Harlan (N.Y.) (R) | Stewart (R) | Stewart (R) |
| Harlan (N.Y.) (R) | Brennan (D) | Brennan (D) | Brennan (D) | Brennan (D) | B. White (D) | B. White (D) |
| Brennan (D) | Stewart (R) | Stewart (R) | Stewart (R) | Stewart (R) | T. Marshall (D) | T. Marshall (D) |
| Stewart (R) | B. White (D) | B. White (D) | B. White (D) | B. White (D) | Blackmun (R) | Blackmun (R) |
| B. White (D) | Fortas (D) | Fortas (D) | T. Marshall (D) | T. Marshall (D) | | Powell (D) |
| Fortas (D) | T. Marshall (D) | T. Marshall (D) | | Blackmun (R) | | Rehnquist (R) |

| 1975–81 | 1981–85 | 1986–87 | 1988–89 | 1990 | 1991–92 | 1993 |
|---|---|---|---|---|---|---|
| *Burger* (R) | *Burger* (R) | *Rehnquist* (R) | *Rehnquist* (R) | *Rehnquist* (R) | *Rehnquist* (R) | *Rehnquist* (R) |
| Brennan (D) | Brennan (D) | Brennan (D) | Brennan (D) | B. White (D) | B. White (D) | Blackmun (R) |
| Stewart (R) | B. White (D) | B. White (D) | B. White (D) | T. Marshall (D) | Blackmun (R) | Stevens (R) |
| B. White (D) | T. Marshall (D) | T. Marshall (D) | T. Marshall (D) | Blackmun (R) | Stevens (R) | O'Connor (R) |
| T. Marshall (D) | Blackmun (R) | Blackmun (R) | Blackmun (R) | Stevens (R) | O'Connor (R) | Scalia (R) |
| Blackmun (R) | Powell (D) | Powell (D) | Stevens (R) | O'Connor (R) | Scalia (R) | Kennedy (R) |
| Powell (D) | Rehnquist (R) | Stevens (R) | O'Connor (R) | Scalia (R) | Kennedy (R) | Souter (R) |
| Rehnquist (R) | Stevens (R) | O'Connor (R) | Scalia (R) | Kennedy (R) | Souter (R) | Thomas (R) |
| Stevens (R) | O'Connor (R) | Scalia (R) | Kennedy (R) | Souter (R) | Thomas (R) | Ginsburg (D) |

| 1994–95 |
|---|
| *Rehnquist* (R) |
| Stevens (R) |
| O'Connor (R) |
| Scalia (R) |
| Kennedy (R) |
| Souter (R) |
| Thomas (R) |
| Ginsburg (D) |
| Breyer (D) |

3. According to Professor Henry Abraham, "Many—and with some justice—consider Brandeis a Democrat; however, he was in fact a registered Republican when nominated" (Henry Abraham, *Freedom and the Court*, 3d ed. 455 [1977]).

## Succession of Supreme Court Justices

This table is designed to aid the user in identifying the succession of justices on the Supreme Court. Read vertically, the table lists the succession of justices in each position of the Court and the years served by each.

The number of justices constituting the Supreme Court has varied. Initially, the Court comprised six justices, but Congress increased the number to seven in 1807, to nine in 1837, and to ten in 1863. In 1866, Congress reduced the number of justices to eight in an effort to prevent President Andrew Johnson from making any appointments to the Court. As a result, the positions of John Catron, who died in 1865, and James M. Wayne, who died in 1867, were abolished. In 1869, Congress raised the number of justices to nine, where it has remained. William Strong, the first justice appointed under the new statute, has generally been considered to have succeeded Wayne. Thus, Catron is the only person who held the tenth seat on the Court.

| Chief Justices | Associate Justices | | | | | | | | |
|---|---|---|---|---|---|---|---|---|---|
| Jay 1789–1795 | J. Rutledge 1789–1791 | Cushing 1789–1810 | Wilson 1789–1798 | Harrison[6] 1789 | Iredell 1790–1798 | Todd 1807–1826 | Field 1863–1897 | McKinley 1837–1852 | Catron 1837–1865 |
| J. Rutledge[1] 1795 | T. Johnson 1791–1793 | Story 1811–1845 | Washington 1798–1829 | Blair 1789–1796 | Moore 1799–1804 | Trimble 1826–1828 | McKenna 1898–1925 | Campbell 1853–1861 | |
| Ellsworth 1796–1799 | Paterson 1793–1806 | Woodbury 1845–1851 | Baldwin 1830–1844 | S. Chase 1796–1811 | W. Johnson 1804–1834 | McLean 1829–1861 | Stone[8] 1925–1941 | Davis 1862–1877 | |
| J. Marshall 1801–1835 | Livingston 1806–1823 | Curtis 1851–1857 | Grier 1846–1870 | Duvall 1812–1835 | Wayne 1835–1867 | Swayne 1862–1881 | R. Jackson 1941–1954 | Harlan 1877–1911 | |
| Taney 1836–1864 | Thomson 1823–1843 | Clifford 1858–1881 | Bradley 1870–1892 | Barbour 1836–1841 | Strong 1870–1880 | Matthews 1881–1889 | Harlan 1955–1971 | Pitney 1912–1922 | |
| S. P. Chase 1864–1873 | Nelson 1845–1872 | Gray 1882–1902 | Woods 1881–1887 | Daniel 1841–1860 | Shiras 1892–1903 | Brewer 1889–1910 | Rehnquist 1971–1986[9] | Sanford 1923–1930 | |
| Waite 1874–1888 | Hunt 1873–1882 | Holmes 1902–1932 | L. Lamar 1888–1893 | Miller 1862–1890 | Day 1903–1922 | Hughes 1910–1916 | Scalia 1986– | Roberts 1930–1945 | |
| Fuller 1888–1910 | Blatchford 1882–1893 | Cardozo 1932–1938 | H. Jackson 1893–1895 | Brown 1891–1906 | Butler 1922–1939 | Clarke 1916–1922 | | Burton 1945–1958 | |
| E. White[2] 1910–1921 | E. White[4] 1894–1910 | Frankfurter 1939–1962 | Peckham 1895–1909 | Moody 1906–1910 | Murphy 1940–1949 | Sutherland 1922–1938 | | Stewart 1958–1981 | |
| Taft 1921–1930 | Van Devanter 1911–1937 | Goldberg 1962–1965 | Lurton 1910–1914 | J. Lamar 1911–1916 | Clark 1949–1967 | Reed 1938–1957 | | O'Connor 1981– | |
| Hughes 1930–1941 | Black 1937–1971 | Fortas[5] 1965–1969 | McReynolds 1914–1941 | Brandeis 1916–1939 | T. Marshall 1967–1991 | Whittaker 1957–1962 | | | |
| Stone[3] 1941–1946 | Powell 1971–1988 | Blackmun 1970–1994 | Byrnes 1941–1942 | Douglas 1939–1975 | Thomas 1991– | B. White 1962–1993 | | | |
| Vinson 1946–1953 | Kennedy 1988– | Breyer 1994– | W. Rutledge 1943–1949 | Stevens 1976– | | Ginsburg 1993– | | | |
| Warren 1953–1969 | | | Minton 1949–1956 | | | | | | |
| Burger 1969–1986 | | | Brennan 1956–1990 | | | | | | |
| Rehnquist[7] 1986– | | | Souter 1990– | | | | | | |

1. Appointment not confirmed.
2. Associate justice, 1894–1910.
3. Associate justice, 1925–1941.
4. Later chief justice, 1910–1921.
5. Appointment as chief justice not confirmed; resigned.
6. Declined appointment.
7. Associate justice, 1971–1986.
8. Later chief justice, 1941–1946.
9. Later chief justice, 1986–.

actively promoted the Judiciary Act of 1925. That landmark legislation, designed to help the Court manage its large backlog of cases, gave the Court almost unlimited discretion to decide the cases it would accept for review. WARREN E. BURGER, chief justice from 1969 to 1986, lobbied for the establishment of a national court of appeals to help alleviate the backlog of federal cases and actively promoted other judicial reform proposals. In 1988, Rehnquist, appointed to succeed Burger, was instrumental in the passage of the Judicial Improvements and Access to Justice Act (Pub. L. 100–702, Nov. 19, 1988, 102 Stat. 4642), which was intended to make the APPEAL process more efficient by reducing the Supreme Court's mandatory appeal jurisdiction.

Another responsibility of the chief justice is to oversee the administration of the entire federal judiciary. In 1922, Congress established the JUDICIAL CONFERENCE OF THE UNITED STATES, the governing body for the administration of the federal judicial system. As chair of the conference, the chief justice presides over the conference's biannual meeting, manages the agenda, and appoints committees. The chief justice also chairs the ADMINISTRATIVE OFFICE OF THE U.S. COURTS, created in 1939 during Taft's term as chief justice, and the FEDERAL JUDICIAL CENTER, established in 1967 under Warren. Like the Judicial Conference, these organizations are also involved in the administration and management of the federal judiciary with the chief justice playing a major role in the selection of directors and other personnel to run them.

Congress has also provided chief justices with a number of duties not specially related to the judiciary. The chief justice traditionally serves as a member of the Board of Regents of the Smithsonian Institution and sits on the Board of Trustees of the National Gallery of Art, both located in Washington, D.C.

**CHILD ABUSE** 📖 Physical, sexual, or emotional mistreatment or NEGLECT of a child. 📖

Child abuse has been defined as an act or failure to act on the part of a parent or caretaker that results in the death, serious physical or emotional harm, sexual abuse, or exploitation of a child, or which places the child in an imminent risk of serious harm (42 U.S.C.A. § 5106g). Child abuse laws raise difficult legal and political issues, pitting the right of children to be free from harm against the right of families to privacy and the rights of parents to raise and discipline their children without government interference.

The mistreatment of children at the hands of parents or caretakers has a long history. For centuries, this behavior was shielded by a system of laws that gave children few if any rights. Under English common law, children were treated as property owned by the parents and parents, particularly fathers, had great latitude over the treatment and discipline of children. This outlook was carried to the American colonies and incorporated into early laws in the United States.

One of the first cases to bring national attention to child abuse arose in the early 1870s. An eight-year-old New York orphan named Mary Ellen Wilson complained of being whipped and beaten nearly every day by her foster family. Her case captured the attention of the American Society for the Prevention of Cruelty to Animals (ASPCA). An attorney for the ASPCA took Wilson's case, arguing that as members of the animal kingdom, children are entitled to the same legal protections from cruelty as are animals. A judge heard evidence that Wilson's foster family, the Connollys, routinely beat her, locked her in a bedroom, and made her sleep on the floor. Charged with ASSAULT AND BATTERY, Wilson's foster mother was convicted and sentenced to one year of hard labor. Even more significantly, publicity surrounding Wilson's case led to the establishment, in 1874, of the New York Society for the Prevention of Cruelty to Children. The following year the New York Legislature passed a statute that authorized such societies to file complaints of child abuse with law enforcement agencies.

In 1962 an article in a major medical journal again brought national attention to the issue by identifying the symptoms that can indicate child abuse. The article, by Dr. Henry Kempe, appeared in the *Journal of the American Medical Association* and discussed a diagnosis for child abuse. The article resulted in widespread awareness of child abuse and prompted further public discussion on how to address the problem. By 1970, every state had enacted laws requiring certain professionals, such as teachers and doctors, to report incidents of suspected child abuse to law enforcement agencies. In 1974 the Federal Child Abuse Prevention and Treatment Act (42 U.S.C.A. §§ 5105–5106) became law, authorizing federal funding for states to identify child abuse and offer protective services for abused children.

Statutes make up one component of a state's child protective services; another component, the child protective services agency, implements the statutes. Reporting statutes, which vary from state to state, require that certain professionals report suspected child abuse, whereas others, such as neighbors, are entitled but not required to. Other statutes define child abuse. For example, in some states, physical abuse occurs only when a child suffers a specified type of injury, whereas in other states, any serious injury that is not accidental in nature is considered abuse. Sexual abuse of children generally need not cause injury; any sexual act performed on a child can be considered abuse. Similarly, state statutes categorize as child abuse any neglect of a child that places the child at risk, regardless of whether the child is actually injured. Before substantiating a report of emotional abuse of a child, state statutes generally

*An instructor teaches parents about the circumstances surrounding abusive relationships.*

MICHAEL NEWMAN/PHOTOEDIT

require a finding of actual harm. Still other statutes specify procedures for investigating child abuse, determining whether a report of abuse is substantiated, intervening to protect an abused child from further harm, and maintaining records of child abuse reports.

When ALLEGATIONS of abuse meet the statutory definitions, the state child protective services agency or a law enforcement agency steps in to investigate. Child protective services agencies generally investigate allegations only when the child's parent or GUARDIAN is suspected of causing the abuse or allowing it to occur. There is a presumption that the parent or guardian will protect the child from abuse by other parties and will contact law enforcement agencies to investigate incidents of abuse by other parties when the parent is not causing or allowing the abuse.

Caseworkers for child protective services investigate abuse allegations most commonly by interviewing or visiting with the child, the child's parents or guardians, and other sources such as physicians and teachers. If an agent finds EVIDENCE that supports a conclusion that the child was abused, the agency deems the allegations substantiated. The next step is INTERVENTION.

Intervention can mean many different things. Frequently, when the risk of further abuse is immediate and significant, child protective services agents will place the child temporarily in a foster home. Alternatively, agents may monitor the family or provide counseling to curb the threat of abuse. If a family does not cooperate with the intervention efforts of child protective services, the agency may take the case before a judge, who may determine that abuse or neglect has occurred and issue a court order mandating the agency's intervention. In extreme cases, agents may remove the child from the home permanently; following a judicial termination of parental rights, the child is then placed for ADOPTION.

Another function of state child protective services is record keeping, which is accomplished through a system known as the central registry. The central registry contains information about child abuse reports—both substantiated and unsubstantiated—such as the names of the child and of the suspected abuser and the final determination made by the child protective services worker. This system helps agents investigating current reports of abuse because it allows them to compare any previous accusations, particularly within the same family. The registry also supplies statistics about child

## Child Abuse

Child Abuse and Neglect Cases:  Substantiated and Indicated*, in 1993

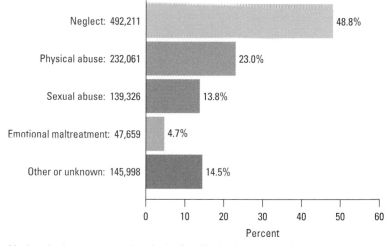

*A substantiated case represents an investigation disposition that determined that there was sufficient evidence to conclude that maltreatment had occurred or that the child was at risk for maltreatment.  An indicated case represents a disposition that concluded that there was reason to suspect maltreatment had occurred.

Source: U.S. Department of Health and Human Services, National Center on Child Abuse and Neglect.  National Child Abuse and Neglect Data System, *Child Maltreatment—1993*, April 1995.

abuse, which help the agency and the state legislature enact appropriate laws and policies and provide adequate funding for child protective services. Also, in some states, other parties may have access to the registry. For example, a day care center may check the registry before hiring child care employees, or an adoption agency may check the registry before placing an infant with a family.

There is little argument that state child protective services agencies provide a valuable service by responding to allegations of child abuse. But such agencies also have their critics. Many people accused of child abuse, particularly parents, object to the way these agencies routinely remove children from their homes when child abuse is suspected. Children are traumatized by being taken from their parents, and allegations of abuse are frequently unfounded, these critics claim. Contentious CHILD CUSTODY battles sometimes prompt false accusations of physical or sexual abuse, costing the accused time and money in the fight to reclaim their children and their reputations. Others object to the names of the accused being included on the central registry even when the accusations are unsubstantiated. The backlash against child protective services spurred the establishment, in 1984, of an information and support group known as Victims of Child Abuse Laws (VOCAL). VOCAL claims to have thousands of members nationwide and members lobby for new laws that protect not only children but also parents who are falsely accused of being abusive or negligent.

Despite increased legislation and penalties for child abuse, extreme cases continue to appear and to sustain the debates over child abuse laws. Such cases include the Schoo case in suburban Chicago, which received widespread media coverage. In December 1992, David Schoo, a forty-five-year-old electrical engineer, and his thirty-five-year-old wife, Sharon Schoo, a homemaker, flew to Acapulco for a Christmas vacation, leaving their daughters, nine-year-old Nicole Schoo and four-year-old Diana Schoo, home alone. The Schoos provided their daughters only cereal and frozen dinners to eat and a note telling them when to go to bed. One day during their parents' absence, the girls left the house when a smoke alarm sounded. As they stood barefoot in the snow, a neighbor found them, learned of their plight, and called the police.

The Schoos were arrested while still on the plane that returned them from Mexico nine days after they left their children. Following their INDICTMENT on various state charges of child endangerment and cruelty, a GRAND JURY also found evidence that the Schoos had beaten, kicked, and choked their children to discipline them. In April 1993, the Schoos plea bargained, agreeing to serve two years of probation and thirty days of house arrest while the girls remained in foster care. In August 1993, the Schoos agreed to give up their parental rights and placed their daughters for permanent adoption.

Another nationally publicized case raised questions regarding the effectiveness of child protective services and implicated social workers charged with protecting the victim. Two-year-old Bradley McGee, of Lakeland, Florida, died in July 1989 from massive head injuries after his stepfather, twenty-three-year-old Thomas E. Coe, repeatedly plunged him headfirst into a toilet. Coe later testified that he had become angry when the child soiled his pants. McGee's twenty-one-year-old mother, Sheryl McGee Coe, pleaded no contest to second-degree MURDER and aggravated child abuse for allowing her husband to abuse McGee, and received a thirty-year prison sentence. Thomas Coe, convicted of first-degree murder and aggravated child abuse, received a sentence of life in prison.

The McGee case alarmed the public not only because of the harsh physical abuse that caused the toddler's death but also because of what many perceived to be a failure in the system designed to protect children like McGee. Two months before his death, McGee had been living with foster parents owing to allegations of abuse at the hands of the Coes. Despite strong objections by the foster parents, caseworkers for Florida's Health and Rehabilitative Services returned McGee to his mother and stepfather, determining them to be fit parents.

Public reaction was strong following the news of McGee's death. Four social workers were prosecuted for negligently handling the case but only the main caseworker, Margaret Barber, was convicted, for disregarding a report from a psychologist who warned that the Coes were unfit parents. The publicity shed light on problems within Florida's child protective services agency, including severe understaffing, and led to new laws emphasizing keeping children safe over keeping families together and increasing funding for more social workers. A Florida appellate court later overturned Barber's FELONY conviction but left standing a MISDEMEANOR conviction for failing to report child abuse.

Legislation at the state and federal levels continues to change to meet the goal of protecting children from abuse and neglect while protecting families from the damage of false accusations.

See also FAMILY LAW; PARENT AND CHILD.

**CHILD CARE**    The supervision and nurturing of a child, including casual and informal services provided by a parent as well as more formal services provided by an organized child care center.

Because there are many different views as to how a child should be reared or nurtured, the topic of child care often involves controversial social and political issues. For instance, it may raise complex questions about a child's religious upbringing or whether a child should be disciplined by corporal punishment. Some people believe that providing child care outside the home undermines so-called traditional family structures in which the mother is considered the primary caretaker. Others are concerned primarily with broadening community responsibility for children and removing barriers for women who wish to enter and participate fully in the labor force. In addition, the term *child care* encompasses a wide range of services. It can include home-based care by a child's mother or father, care by a grandparent or other relative, care by a nanny, or care by an organized licensed facility or family center. It can also involve early childhood education such as that offered by nursery schools, Montessori schools, and kindergarten programs.

Child care has always existed in the United States. Organized child care centers in the early

1800s took the form of infant day schools in parts of Boston and New York. During the industrial revolution, and as a result of increased immigration to the United States, day nurseries were created in the late nineteenth century to care primarily for poor urban children. In New York City, in approximately 1910, eighty-five such nurseries cared for more than five thousand children each day. Day nurseries were privately run and charitable in nature, and were intended to provide custodial supervision, hygiene instruction, and nutrition services. Later, many middle-class parents opted to enroll their children in kindergartens, educational programs adopted in parts of the United States in the mid-nineteenth century.

During World War II, millions of women entered the workforce in war production areas. The need for an organized child care program became acute. Congress responded by including provisions in the Community Facilities Act of 1941, then more commonly known as the Lanham Act, which created Lanham Act centers for child care. (Presently, the term Lanham Act is generally used to refer to the Trademark Act of 1946.) The establishment of the Lanham Act centers marked the first time the federal government became directly involved in providing child care services to children who were not poor: the centers were open to all children whose parents worked in war production areas. The federal government provided 50 percent of the funds needed to operate the Lanham Act centers; states, localities, and parents provided the remaining 50 percent in matching funds. In 1943, the cost to parents for child care in a Lanham Act center was uniformly set at fifty cents a day.

The federally sponsored Lanham Act centers closed in 1946, soon after World War II ended, although California continued them at a state level. After that, direct federal involvement in a national child care program virtually ceased. Although the U.S. Congress passed the Comprehensive Child Development Act of 1972, which would have in part established a national child care program, President RICHARD M. NIXON vetoed the bill. Nixon stated that the act would "commit the vast moral authority of the national government to the side of communal approaches to child-rearing over and against the family-centered approach." Nixon's statement reflected the continuing debate about the appropriateness of providing child care outside a traditional family structure.

Although the federal government currently does not have a national child care program, it does provide numerous social programs that include funding for child care services. The Head Start program provides developmental education programs primarily to poor children under the age of four. WELFARE programs such as Aid to Families with Dependent Children (AFDC) provide funds for states to implement child care services for parents—usually mothers—who receive welfare grants. The Family Sup-

*Kindergartens grew in popularity during the late nineteenth century, especially in New York City and Boston.*

CORBIS-BETTMANN

port Act of 1988 (FSA) (Pub. L. 100-485, Oct. 13, 1988, 102 Stat. 2343) created the federal Jobs Opportunity and Basic Skills (JOBS) program, in which qualifying parents who receive AFDC are required to enter education or training programs to enhance their chances of finding employment. The federal government funds the JOBS program by providing money to the states. The states in turn are allowed to choose the method of providing child care services to welfare recipients. They may provide child care directly, reimburse parents for child care expenses, or make direct payments to child care providers. In 1993, the federal government spent approximately $480 million on FSA child care subsidies.

The federal government also provides funds to states through the Social Services Block Grant, under title XX of the Social Security Act, 42 U.S.C.A. 1397a et seq., as well as funds for the operation of the At-Risk Child Care Program. The At-Risk Program divides more than $350 million among state governments for

child care subsidies to families who are at risk of welfare dependency; the states must match the grants before they can use the money. Finally, the federal government allows families to deduct child care expenses from their taxes in the form of the federal dependent care tax credit.

In response to increasing demands, Congress passed the Family and Medical Leave Act of 1993 (FMLA) (Pub. L. 103-3, Feb 5, 1993, 107 Stat. 6). Although the FMLA does not directly provide for child care services, it does mandate in part that employers with more than fifty employees must allow those employees to take up to twelve weeks of unpaid leave for the birth or adoption of a child or in order to take care of a child with a serious health condition. Many states also have parental leave legislation, which allows a parent to take unpaid time off for the birth or adoption of a child. The length of time allowed for unpaid leave varies from state to state, and may be from six weeks to six months.

The regulation of child care services occurs primarily on the state level, with the federal

## Child Care

Primary Child Care Arrangements Used by Employed Mothers for Children Under 5 Years Old in 1991

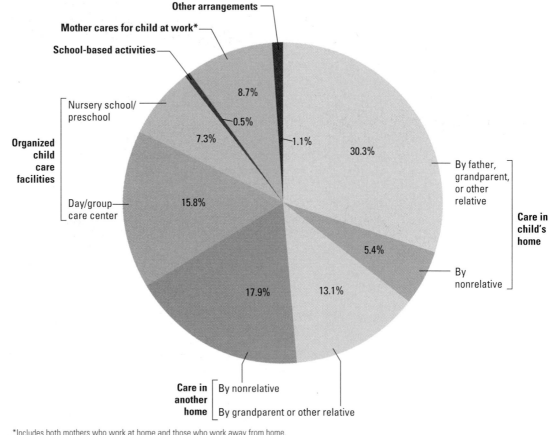

*Includes both mothers who work at home and those who work away from home.

Source: U.S. Bureau of Census, *Current Population Reports*.

government requiring states to implement minimal regulations for private child care centers. When Peggy McMartin Buckey and Raymond Buckey were accused of sexually abusing children in a day care center in California in the early 1980s, their case (*McMartin v. Children's Institute Intern.*, 212 Cal. App. 3d 1393, 261 Cal. Rptr. 437 [Cal. App. 2 Dist.]) and others like it received national media attention. Out of a stated concern for the notice given to such allegations, the federal government passed legislation in 1985 that appropriated funds to the states to provide training for child care workers and to support licensing and enforcement officials. The federal government also required states to implement procedures that would require child care centers to screen workers for any criminal history. In addition, the Child Care and Development Block Grant of 1990 (CCDBG), which provided funds to state government agencies to subsidize child care services for low-income working parents, required states to develop minimum health and safety requirements for state-licensed child care centers. Amendments to the CCDBG in 1995 removed such requirements but did obligate states to ensure that parents or guardians may visit or have access to a child while the child is in a child care center.

The regulation of child care facilities and caregivers on the state level varies considerably. A state may require a child care center to obtain a LICENSE in order to operate, or it may mandate certain minimum standards for all child care facilities. Currently, every state requires that space for a child care facility be "adequate" or of a certain specified size. Most states also regulate how many child care workers must be on duty for a specified number of children, depending on the age of the children: for instance, New York requires one caregiver on duty for every two children under the age of two. Most states also regulate the qualifications and training requirements for child care workers and require child care centers to determine whether a job applicant or worker has a criminal record or has been listed in the state's child abuse registry. Some states, such as Arkansas and South Carolina, in some circumstances allow corporal punishment of children in their licensed day care centers.

Most states exempt certain child care centers from regulations or licensing requirements. Religious or church-based day care centers, as well as small home-based day care programs, are often exempt from regulations or licensing requirements other than basic health and safety

regulations. In addition, private day care groups or associations may set goals for quality child care and may provide certification or accreditation programs for member centers.

See also FAMILY LAW; PARENT AND CHILD.

**CHILD CUSTODY** 📖 The care, control, and maintenance of a child, which a court may award to one of the parents following a DIVORCE or SEPARATION proceeding. 📖

In most circumstances, state laws provide that biological parents make all the decisions involved in rearing their child—such as residence, education, health care, religious upbringing, and so forth. Parents are not required to secure the legal right to make these decisions if they are married and are listed on the child's birth certificate. However, if there is disagreement about who has the right to make these decisions, or if government officials believe that a parent is unfit to make the decisions well, then family courts or juvenile courts determine custody.

District and state courts base their decisions on state laws, which vary greatly among states. If a case challenges the constitutionality of a state law or—in rare instances—a state's jurisdiction (right to decide the case), then the U.S. Supreme Court may issue an opinion.

**Divorced Parents** When custody must be spelled out because of a couple's divorce, the custody arrangement usually becomes part of their divorce decree. The decree describes with whom the child will live, how visitation will be handled, and who will provide financial support. Courts consider a custody award as subject to change until the child involved grows up, and in most states proof of a "change in circumstances" may overturn an earlier award. This flexibility is intended to allow for the correction of poor or outdated decisions, but consequentially enables some parents to wage bitter custody battles that can last for years.

In a typical divorce involving at least one child, permanent physical custody is awarded to the parent with whom the child will live most of the time. Usually, the custodial parent shares joint legal custody with the noncustodial parent, meaning that the custodial parent must inform and consult with the noncustodial parent about the child's education, health care, and other concerns. In this situation, courts may order visitation, sometimes called temporary custody, between the child and the noncustodial parent. A clear schedule with dates and times may be written into the order, or a court may simply state that visitation should be reasonable. Child SUPPORT is a common requirement, and is paid by the noncustodial parent to the custodial parent as assistance in raising the child.

There are exceptions to this typical arrangement. Some courts have allowed parents to retain joint physical custody, in which the child spends equal time with both parents. Advocates of joint custody say that it lessens the feeling of losing a parent that children may experience after a divorce and is fair to both parents. However, because of the high degree of cooperation it requires, courts resist ordering joint custody if either of the parents does not want it.

Split custody is an arrangement in which the parents divide up custody of their children, with each parent being awarded physical custody of one or more children. In general, courts try not to separate siblings when awarding custody.

**Unmarried Parents**  Where a child's parents were never married, most states provide that the child's biological mother has sole physical custody unless the biological father takes steps to have himself considered for custody. Those steps include obtaining a court's finding of paternity and filing a petition for custody. In some states, this is a bifurcated (two-step) process; in others, the two steps are combined. An unwed father usually cannot win custody from a mother who is a good parent but he may have priority over other relatives, foster parents, or strangers who want to adopt his child.

The government must provide a child's unwed parents with the opportunity to step forward if it is seeking custody. In *Stanley v. Illinois* (405 U.S. 645, 92 S. Ct. 1208, 31 L. Ed. 2d 551), in 1972, the U.S. Supreme Court held that under the Equal Protection Clause of the FOURTEENTH AMENDMENT, an unwed father was entitled to a HEARING to determine his fitness as a parent before the state could obtain custody of his children following their mother's death. See also ILLEGITIMACY.

**Criteria for Custody Awards**  There is much debate about the criteria the courts use in awarding permanent physical custody in cases where two biological parents disagree. Noncustodial parents of both genders have long charged that judges' decision making is arbitrary and does not focus on the child. In response to this criticism, many states have adopted a standard that places primary emphasis on the best interests of the child. The challenge for courts in the 1990s was objectively interpreting the standard in the absence of meaningful guidelines.

Policies of the past offer little guidance. Before the late 1800s fathers had sole rights to custody, because custody was closely tied to INHERITANCE and PROPERTY law. Mothers had no such rights. Beginning in the nineteenth century courts began to award custody of young boys and of girls of all ages solely to mothers on the presumption that mothers are inherently better caretakers of young children.

Until 1970 most states encouraged or allowed this maternal preference, also called the TENDER YEARS DOCTRINE, and mothers almost always received custody. Eventually, many state courts found this preference to be unconstitutional, and gender-neutral custody statutes replaced maternal preference standards in forty-five states by 1990. A catalyst for this change was *Reed v. Reed* (404 U.S. 71, 92 S. Ct. 251, 30 L. Ed. 2d 225 [1971]), a noncustody case in which the Supreme Court ruled that the Equal Protection Clause of the Fourteenth Amendment prevents courts from basing opinions on generalizations about either gender.

A 1994 study by the American Bar Association of divorces in Utah showed that after maternal preference in divorce cases was declared unconstitutional in that state in 1986, the number of mothers who received sole custody decreased, the number of joint legal custody awards increased, and the number of specific visitation schedules increased. The researchers concluded that although the proportion of fathers who received sole custody did not necessarily go up, the net result was more involvement by fathers after divorce.

No straightforward criterion has replaced the simple—although unconstitutional—presumption that children belong with one gender or the other. The decisions that result are often inconsistent and are viewed as arbitrary by many participants. Ultimately, the judge decides the child's future, and not many guide-

*Either parent of a divorced couple may obtain custody of the children of that marriage. The custodial parent must consult with the noncustodial parent about issues such as education and health care for the children.*

lines are provided to ensure that the decision is objective.

Nevertheless, courts have instituted some mechanisms to determine a child's best interests. GUARDIANS AD LITEM (caretakers "for the lawsuit") or friends are sometimes appointed to represent the child's interests and to advocate in court on the child's behalf. Custody evaluations may be ordered, in which court services personnel visit each parent's home and evaluate each parent's plan for caring for the child. The fact that one parent has been the child's primary caretaker is often considered but is not enough to guarantee a custody award.

**Changing Custody Awards** Standards for changing custody awards are similarly vague, although most states' criteria allow courts to modify custody only when the circumstances of the custodial parent or of the children—not of the noncustodial parent—have changed. A 1993 Stanford study of petitions to modify custody found that these awards were highly inconsistent, and attributed them in many cases to personal gender biases held by judges.

**Social Issues: Sexual Orientation and Race** Social issues are sometimes slow to affect custody decisions. Homosexual parents in the 1990s still posed dilemmas for judges. Although in many cases homosexual parents have won or retained custody, the Virginia Supreme Court in 1995 reinstated a trial court order awarding custody of a boy to his grandmother because the lesbian mother's sexual orientation was deemed potentially harmful to the boy (*Bottoms v. Bottoms*, 249 Va. 410, 457 S.E. 2d 102). See also GAY AND LESBIAN RIGHTS.

Although the U.S. Supreme Court ruled in 1984 that removing custody from a white child's mother because of her marriage to a black man would be discriminatory (*Palmore v. Sidoti*, 466 U.S. 429, 104 S. Ct. 1879, 80 L. Ed. 2d 421), a Tennessee court in 1986 removed custody from a white mother who was living with a black man. In that case, when one of the children's guardians died two years later, the mother, who had by then married the man, was awarded custody of one of her children (*Smith v. Smith*, Tenn. App. 1989 WL 73229).

**Adoption** ADOPTIONS can provide courts with another source of custody disputes. Most state laws require that both birth parents give consent before their child can be adopted. Such a law was at issue in a custody battle over Jessica DeBoer, born in Iowa in 1991 and adopted by a Michigan couple. DeBoer's birth mother later married DeBoer's birth father and they sought and won custody of DeBoer in Iowa, based on the father's never having consented to the

adoption. The adoptive parents then won in the Michigan courts, based on an analysis of the child's best interests. On appeal, the Michigan Supreme Court reversed, declaring that under federal law, Iowa had jurisdiction in this case, and that unless a child's birth parents are unfit, an unrelated person may not retain custody. The U.S. Supreme Court agreed, in *DeBoer by Darrow v. DeBoer* (114 S. Ct. 1, 125 L. Ed. 2d 755 [1993]), and DeBoer was returned to her birth parents.

Family ties are often a compelling factor for judges even when birth relatives other than parents are involved. For example, the Minnesota Supreme Court ruled in 1992 in *Matter of Welfare of D. L.*, 486 N.W. 2d 375 (Minn.), that the biological grandparents of Baby D., an African American three-year-old, should be granted custody, rather than the white foster parents who raised her from birth. The case convinced the Minnesota Legislature to change a law (M. S. A. § 259. 28, subd. 2) providing for same-race preference in adoptions, but race was not the deciding factor in the case: the court based its decision on reuniting Baby D. with her birth relatives and her siblings, of whom the grandparents also had custody.

Critics of removing children from parents and from parental figures to whom they have become attached say that the rupture is too difficult to overcome and that children suffer from imperfect child custody laws. The National Conference of Commissioners on Uniform State Laws approved in 1994 a model adoption statute designed to reduce the chances that custody will be changed after children have become attached to parent figures. The model statute provides guidelines for birth parents and adoptive parents to follow before an adoption in order to prevent custody battles afterward.

*Roberta and Jan DeBoer adopted Jessica and had custody of her for about two years until the Michigan Supreme Court held that the birth parents should regain custody of her.*

In the 1990s, courts appeared to place more importance on child-caretaker attachment and in some cases even denied custody to birth parents in order to uphold this attachment. A Florida judge ruled in 1993 that fourteen-year-old Kimberly Mays could choose not to see her birth parents, from whom she had been separated at birth by a hospital error (*Twigg v. Mays,* 1993 WL 330624 [Fla. Cir. Ct.]). The decision was based on the length of time she had spent with her nonbiological family and her attachment to it.

In 1978 the Supreme Court ruled that the adoption of a child by the child's stepfather did not violate the DUE PROCESS rights of the child's unwed biological father. In *Quilloin v. Walcott,* 434 U.S. 246, 98 S. Ct. 549, 54 L. Ed. 2d 511 (1978), the Court decided that the adoption was in the best interests of the child, and said that because that particular biological father had participated very little in rearing the child, he did not have the same rights under the Equal Protection Clause that a more involved father would have.

**Terminating Parental Rights**  Owing in part to a national surge in reports of CHILD ABUSE and NEGLECT in the 1980s and 1990s, courts and society faced questions of whether abusive or dangerously neglectful parents should retain custody of their own children. It is the government's role to step in when a child is not being safely cared for, and if parents are judged unfit, the local social services department may seek to terminate their parental rights and to free the child for adoption or alternative care. A child may be placed in foster care while a custody case is pending.

Before removing a child from her or his parents, the state must produce "CLEAR AND CONVINCING" evidence that terminating parental rights is the best option for the child. This was clarified in *Santosky v. Kramer,* 455 U.S. 745, 102 S. Ct. 1388, 71 L. Ed. 2d 599 (1982). The case arose after a New York County social services department successfully brought neglect proceedings in state court against the Santoskys, a couple with three children. The U.S. Supreme Court found that the state's standard—"a fair PREPONDERANCE OF EVIDENCE" —was too low for deciding something as important as a family's future.

**Courts and Jurisdiction**  Most custody decisions are made by family courts. However, where a juvenile court has found that a MINOR poses a threat to society if current custody arrangements continue, the juvenile court may turn over physical custody to the state. The court may simultaneously issue a so-called CHIPS petition, declaring the "child in need of protective services," if the current custodian is abusive or neglectful.

JURISDICTION is an issue that has received much attention. A court has the power to settle a custody dispute if a child lives for at least six months in the location where the court has jurisdiction or if it is demonstrated that the court has the closest connection with the child. All states have adopted the Uniform Child Custody Jurisdiction Act, originally adopted in 1967, which provides that a state's court will not accept a custody case unless that state has ORIGINAL JURISDICTION or the state with original jurisdiction relinquishes it. The Hague Convention Treaty provides similar reciprocity between nations that are parties to it (implemented at 42 U.S.C.A. §§ 11601–11610 [Supp. 1993]).

A parent's interstate move sometimes blurs jurisdictional lines. For this reason, courts may restrict the geographic area in which a parent may live as part of the custody order, or may deny a subsequent request for permission to move if the move is viewed as an attempt to hinder visitation.

**Parental Kidnapping**  Parental KIDNAPPING occurs when one parent deprives the other of his or her legal right to custody or visitation by illegally taking the child out of the jurisdiction. It is outlawed by the federal Parental Kidnapping Prevention Act (28 U.S.C.A. § 1738A [Supp. 1993]), which applies the FULL FAITH AND CREDIT CLAUSE of the U.S. Constitution to child custody cases, meaning that each state must abide by custody decisions made by another state's courts if the other state would be bound by those decisions. The law was enacted to respond to cases in which one parent leaves the state that has jurisdiction; however, the U.S. Supreme Court ruled in *Thompson v. Thompson,* 484 U.S. 174, 108 S. Ct. 513, 98 L. Ed. 2d 512, in 1988 that the existence of two different state custody decrees is not itself a reason for federal involvement under this law.

**Termination of Custody**  Most types of custody end when the child is emancipated (considered a legal adult) by becoming self-supporting, by marrying, or by reaching the age of majority as specified by state law. Not until then does family court lose its power to determine custody.

See also FAMILY LAW; PARENT AND CHILD.

**CHILD LABOR LAWS**  Federal and state legislation that protects children by restricting the type and hours of work they perform.

The specific purpose of child labor laws is to safeguard children against a risk of injury gen-

*Until child labor laws went into effect, companies such as this vegetable cannery employed young people at low wages and made them work long hours. This 1912 photograph shows typical working conditions.*

erally associated with child labor, such as exposure to hazardous, unsanitary, or immoral conditions, and overwork. Child labor legislation primarily applies to business enterprises, but in some states nonprofit activities are within the purview of the law.

Specific provisions of the particular child labor law govern the AGE OF MAJORITY. Some laws permit MINORS to be employed in certain activities if their parents satisfy stated conditions concerning supervision, control, and approval. The state has the right to prohibit parents from binding a minor to an employment contract based upon the theory that parents cannot diminish benefits that the law confers to children.

Cursory directions to subordinates are not sufficient to fulfill the employer's duty to enforce child labor regulations. Where such directives are followed by further violations, sterner measures controlling the actions of subordinates are required.

In some states, it is unlawful to employ children under a specified age in certain activities without an employment certificate issued and filed in accordance with the law. An employer's failure to comply with this requirement makes the employment illegal. Technical errors, such as the lack of a detailed account of the child's duties in the employer's pledge of em-

ployment, will not have this effect nor invalidate the certificate.

Children are protected by various regulations, such as those that forbid or limit their employment if they are under a specific age, in particular occupations, or in occupations other than those designated. Other regulations govern employment in particular businesses or under certain conditions or after certain hours or when school is in session.

Regulations also relate to occupations that are or may be potentially dangerous, extremely hazardous, or harmful to a child's health or morals, as defined by statute or judicial decision. In one state a log-loading machine was held to be within the meaning of a law that barred the employment of minors in businesses using dangerous machinery.

The violation of child labor regulations can subject the perpetrator to criminal prosecution or render the employment contract illegal. In appropriate circumstances an INJUNCTION, a court order that commands or prohibits a certain act, may be issued against a violator to stop the illegal conduct.

LIABILITY for these violations depends upon the provisions of law. As a general rule, the owner of the business is liable, whether it is a natural person, a CORPORATION, or a joint association. An employer is usually not liable if a

© 1994 RICK GERHARTER/IMPACT VISUALS

*Although child labor laws were designed in part to prevent the exploitation of young people, this group of demonstrators believes that young people should have the choice to work and should not lose their jobs because of their age.*

minor is assigned to work on the premises in violation of law by an INDEPENDENT CONTRACTOR, a person whose work methods are not controlled by the employer. Some states, however, will impose liability on the owner under such circumstances.

The employer's knowledge that the child is within the prohibited age is not an element of the offense. The offense is committed if the employer does not know but should have known by the exercise of reasonable DILIGENCE that the child was underage. The employer's GOOD FAITH—his honest belief—is no defense even though the child misrepresented his age.

A person who hires a child in violation of law will be liable if the child is injured. The duration of the employment and the status of the child as an employee are irrelevant.

The parents will not be held liable merely because they assented to the hiring of their child by another. Only the injured child will recover DAMAGES, reparations for injury caused by another, for third persons are not within the class of persons that the laws were enacted to protect.

**CROSS-REFERENCES**

Labor Law; Parent and Child.

## CHILDREN'S DEFENSE FUND

The Children's Defense Fund (CDF) is a national organization committed to the social welfare of children. Founded in 1973, the nonprofit group uses its annual $9 million budget to lobby legislators and speak out publicly on a broad array of issues on the law, the family, and society. It is an influential shaper of the WELFARE debate: the CDF has consistently fought for federal welfare programs that directly help poor children, a cause that has enjoyed significant success in Washington, D.C. In the 1980s, its

intensive LOBBYING efforts saved billions of dollars in proposed funding cuts, and in the early 1990s, close ties with the administration of President BILL CLINTON increased its influence even further, leading to new federal legislation. Besides its work on Capitol Hill, the organization issues widely cited reports on the health and the economic and social well-being of U.S. children. The organization owes much of its effectiveness to the work of its founder and director, civil rights attorney MARIAN WRIGHT EDELMAN.

The first black woman to pass the bar exam in Mississippi, Edelman fought race DISCRIMINATION in the 1960s. She initially came to national attention by stopping efforts in Mississippi to deny African Americans money from the federal Head Start program. By the end of the 1960s she ran an advocacy group called the Washington Research Project, whose chief focus was antidiscrimination law. The group acquired powerful allies—one staff attorney was Hillary Rodham, who would become First Lady. Edelman lobbied extensively for federal HEALTH CARE and child care, but to little avail. By 1973, she realized that "the country was tired of the concerns of the sixties. When you talked about poor people or black people, you faced a shrinking audience. I got the idea that children might be a very effective way to broaden the base for change." She renamed her organization, made children's issues its primary focus, and began building the corporate sponsorship that has grown to include such major donors as American Express and Coca-Cola.

The CDF has taken a strong stand against cutting federal programs that benefit poor children. Leading its list are the Head Start and Women, Infants, and Children (WIC) nutrition programs. Although viewed as a liberal organization, it blasted presidential administrations from JIMMY CARTER's to GEORGE BUSH's whenever budgets were threatened. It has attacked social spending cuts as "callous" and motivated by "greed," arguing that welfare is properly seen as a children's issue. In a display of its influence during the REAGAN era, the CDF convinced Congress to spare approximately $2.5 billion in cuts. In addition to supporting existing programs, the CDF has argued in favor of greater federal support for underprivileged families in the areas of housing, day care, child immunization, so-called family preservation programs, and employment training.

The organization's research and recommendations are often the catalyst for debate. For example, its 1991 study *Bright Futures or Broken Dreams: The Status of the Children of the District*

of Columbia and an Investment Agenda for the 1990s—noting items such as infant mortality, teenage pregnancy and murder, and CHILD ABUSE—concluded that "across almost every indicator of health, income, and social well-being, the status of children in the District is abysmal." Edelman opened the CDF's first local office in the District of Columbia. She called society's failure to save children's lives unforgivable and blamed it on local and federal governments. Such conclusions sit well with traditional liberals but not with conservatives. Nationally syndicated columnist Mona Charen, for example, attacks the CDF for wanting "a bigger and bigger welfare state, with less and less emphasis on personal responsibility and self control." Even neoliberals such as author Mickey Kaus find the CDF's social analysis outdated and its answers impractical. "Are American taxpayers more likely to open their wallets for someone with an unvarnished analysis of the underclass problem," Kaus wrote in the *New Republic*, "or someone who tries to overwhelm analysis with emotionalism about children?"

Despite such criticism, the organization's agenda has flourished under the Clinton administration. Partly this has been due to long-established personal and political ties between the Clintons and Edelman: HILLARY RODHAM CLINTON was CDF chairperson from 1986 to 1992, and her successor, Donna E. Shalala, later became President Clinton's secretary of Health and Human Services. The president promoted several of the CDF's positions in his legislative goals: he signed family leave legislation into law and stepped up enforcement of CHILD SUPPORT payments with the help of the INTERNAL REVENUE SERVICE. He also proposed budgets that

*Marian Wright Edelman (center, second row) is the founder and director of the Children's Defense Fund, an advocacy group that fights cuts in federal funding to programs that benefit poor children.*

would fully fund or expand Head Start and WIC, advocated a comprehensive federal immunization program for children, and supported health care reform that would ensure care for children and pregnant women. Although not all these initiatives succeeded in Congress, the effort reflected the growing influence of the CDF on national policy.

See also FAMILY LAW.

**CHILDREN'S RIGHTS** The opportunity for children to participate in political and legal decisions that affect them; in a broad sense, the rights of children to live free from hunger, abuse, neglect, and other inhumane conditions.

The issue of children's rights is poorly defined in legislation and by the courts, partly because U.S. society as a whole has not decided how much autonomy to grant children. Although the United States is built on protecting the interests of individuals, and the twentieth century has seen the rights of people with special needs recognized, the nation has yet to extend to children legal STANDING (the right to bring a court case) and legal protection similar to that of adults.

When most children's advocates talk about children's rights, they are not referring to the same rights held by adults, such as the rights to vote, drink, smoke, and run for office. Instead, they mean that more emphasis should be placed on children's status as "natural persons" deserving of benefits under the law as provided in the U.S. Constitution and its Bill of Rights.

The U.S. legal system grants rights to people who are deemed COMPETENT to exercise those rights. This poses a dilemma for advocates of children's rights, because most children lack the skills to advocate for themselves in the political, judicial, or economic arena. Yet, children's rights supporters believe that because of this powerlessness, children must be granted more protections and power than are provided in their current legal status.

PARENS PATRIAE ("the state as parent") is the philosophy that guided many court decisions in the 1990s. This approach basically means that the government has a duty to make decisions on behalf of children to ensure that their best interests are met. But the doctrine can be interpreted as allowing government interests to replace interests children may wish to express on their own behalf. It also assumes that what the government wants matches what the child needs, which may or may not be true.

How U.S. society defines and provides children's rights has implications for many areas: how children are represented by ATTORNEYS; how resources are distributed, for example, in a family experiencing DIVORCE; how long some children will live in abusive situations or foster care; how the role of families is viewed; and more.

**Court Standing** Twelve-year-old Gregory Kingsley made the news headlines in 1992 when he went to court to sever his legal ties to his parents—and won (*In re Kingsley*, No. JU90-5245, 1992 WL 551484 [Fla. Cir. Ct. Oct. 21, 1992; *Kingsley v. Kingsley*, 623 So.2d 780 (Fla. 5th Dist. Ct. App. 1993)]). A year later, Kimberly Mays, age seventeen, won her legal battle to end any parental rights her biological parents might attempt to exercise (*Twigg v. Mays*, No. 88-4489-CA-01, 1993 WL 330624 [Fla. Cir. Ct. Aug. 18, 1993]). What was unusual in both cases was that children were allowed to advocate for their interests on their own behalf. Some children's rights advocates believe that competent children like Mays and Kingsley must be allowed to use the courts to pursue their interests. But these particular cases may have done more to promote the discussion of children's rights than to promote actual rights.

For example, when Kingsley's mother subsequently appealed the termination of her rights, the appellate court ruled that as a MINOR, Kingsley alone did not have standing (*Kingsley v. Kingsley*). It was ultimately the support of adults who later joined Kingsley in bringing the case (including his adoptive parents), along with his parents' inability to care for him, that influenced the appeals court to affirm the lower court's decision.

The situation surrounding Mays's parentage is so unusual that few similar cases are likely to arise. Mays was raised by Robert Mays and Barbara Mays after being mistakenly identified as their daughter in the hospital where she was born. When Mays's biological parents discovered the switch more than a decade later, they sought visitation with Mays, starting a battle between them and the man who had believed that Mays was his daughter and had raised her alone after his wife's death.

Except when there is evidence of neglect or abuse, parents usually retain their status as preferred caretakers of their children. In 1923 *Meyer v. Nebraska*, 262 U.S. 390, 43 S. Ct. 625, 67 L. Ed. 1042, established that the Liberty Clause of the FOURTEENTH AMENDMENT gives parents the right to raise their children. The government's assumption is that parents' priorities match their children's.

The situation is less clear when the conflict is between children and their parents, as in the cases of Mays and Kingsley. When a family court is considering a CHILD CUSTODY or support petition, it may become aware that the parents are not acting in their children's best interests. In these cases, the court may appoint a GUARDIAN AD LITEM to identify the children's needs and to advocate that those needs be met. This caretaker "for the lawsuit" may be an attorney chosen to act on behalf of the child in court. But heavy increases in child protection and family court caseloads nationwide have led to long delays in making determinations on behalf of children—and have led many advocates to suggest that a solution may lie in allowing children to initiate ACTIONS for themselves.

Many situations in which children and parents do not share common interests have not been resolved in favor of the minors. These include cases that challenge laws requiring minors to get their parents' consent before an ABORTION, or that challenge parents' efforts to commit their children to psychiatric institutions. For example, in *Parham v. J. R.*, 442 U.S. 584, 99 S. Ct. 2493, 61 L. Ed. 2d 101 (1979), the Supreme Court decided that when parents seek to institutionalize their children in mental hospitals, the DUE PROCESS provided to the children need be no more than an evaluation by an independent medical decision maker. Again, the Court upheld the government's assumption that what is best for the children is what the parents and the state decide, despite criticisms that this is not always true.

**Juvenile Justice** Some advocates of children's rights believe that children should be afforded the same constitutional and procedural safeguards that adults are given in court. The juvenile justice system is cited by some experts as an area where the protections granted to children lag behind those provided to adults. For example, children may be detained in situ-

*Gregory Kingsley went to court to sever ties with his parents. Although he ultimately won his case, courts do not agree on whether minors have standing to take such action.*

ations where adults would not be. BAIL is not set for children, and children do not receive the benefit of a jury of their peers. In some states, as recently as the late 1980s, minors could receive longer incarceration sentences than could adults.

Some constitutional protections were won in the late 1960s on behalf of juveniles who could be tried as adults. These protections included the right to an attorney's advice at the time when the court was deciding whether to try the juvenile as an adult, the right to a hearing on that issue, and the right to the same information the court would use in making a decision (*In re Gault*, 387 U.S. 1, 87 S. Ct. 1428, 18 L. Ed. 2d 527 [1967]; *Kent v. United States*, 383 U.S. 541, 86 S. Ct. 1045, 16 L. Ed. 2d [1966]). However, advances in this area have not kept pace with federal and state legislation expanding the punishment of juveniles as adults.

**Constitutional Issues** One 1993 study of constitutional decisions concluded that from the 1960s to the early 1990s, the U.S. Supreme Court was increasingly less supportive of expanding children's claims to constitutional rights. The study showed that under the liberal Warren Court, 100 percent of decisions about constitutional cases upheld children's claims. The Burger Court, which followed, upheld children's claims in 59 percent of such decisions, and the Rehnquist Court in 22 percent of such cases to 1993. The cases in the survey concerned issues of equal protection, due process, privacy, free expression, and free exercise of religion.

To some experts, the trend marks a troubling denial of basic legal rights. Those making the decisions hold that there is no way to demonstrate that children are capable of managing full legal rights and of making decisions on their own behalf. The question of how far we should go in allowing children to participate in determining their destiny remains a difficult societal and legal challenge.

**CROSS-REFERENCES**
Child Abuse; Child Support; Family Law; Parent and Child.

**CHILD SUPPORT** A payment that a noncustodial parent makes as a contribution to the costs of raising her or his child.

In the mid-1990s, as never before, child support became a topic of urgent U.S. national discussion. The system that awards and enforces child support was declared inadequate by state and federal policy makers. Failures in the system were blamed for child poverty rates, long-term dependence on government assistance, and the "feminization of poverty."

Courts drew criticism for awarding child support inconsistently and inequitably. These social and economic issues attracted both federal attention and reform efforts.

The need for child support payments usually arises when one parent does not have physical CUSTODY of his or her child, so that parent's income does not benefit the child on a daily basis. At times, neither parent has custody, and both may pay a third person who is caring for the child. When both of a child's parents have full custody (as when they are married to each other), and usually when they are divorced and share joint physical custody, the needs of the child are presumed met and child support is not an issue. As long as parents provide a safe level of care, the government does not control their contributions to their children.

In the United States in the mid-1990s, nearly half of all marriages ended in DIVORCE, and almost one-quarter of all children were born to unmarried parents. Most of the children who lived in single-parent families had a legal right to a child support order. Child support can be voluntary or court ordered, and can be secured through a divorce decree or a separate action. Increasingly, support orders are issued by state agencies.

The legal duty to support a MINOR child belongs to both parents, even if the custodial parent is capable of caring for the child singlehandedly. Support is awarded to provide for the child's basic needs, and to allow the child to share in the standard of living of both parents. Although both mothers and fathers can be ordered to pay support, a 1994 study in Utah found that over a twenty-year period, mothers were required to pay child support in fewer than one in five cases in which fathers received sole custody. A greater proportion of noncustodial fathers were ordered to pay support.

A petition for support is usually begun in a state court where the plaintiff (the parent seeking the order) resides. A model law, the Uniform Interstate Family Support Act of 1992, which many states have adopted, provides that JURISDICTION exists where the child or one of the parents resides. Before support can be awarded, parentage (called paternity in the case of fathers, maternity in the case of mothers) must be demonstrated. The would-be payer is entitled to blood tests, but in some states must pay for them. The 1993 federal budget bill (Omnibus Budget Reconciliation Act of 1993, 42 U.S.C.A. § 666(a)(2)) required states to offer speedy means of establishing parentage, since parentage disputes can delay a valid child support award.

**Determining Awards** Child support awards are made by each state's family court system. Most states require that they be based on the best interests of the child. In addition to determining support in contentious divorce cases, courts review STIPULATIONS (agreements) between parents and can overrule an agreement that does not adequately provide for children.

Often, courts feel pressure to balance children's needs with their parents' needs. Awards are based on the noncustodial parent's ability to pay, and must allow the parent to remain self-supporting. Many associations of noncustodial parents emerged in the 1980s and 1990s to express their belief that awards were burdensome to the payers, benefited only the custodial parent, or did not provide payers with enough in return. At the same time, more single parents with children slipped into poverty than had at any other point in the nation's history.

In the mid-1990s, no federal child support guideline existed, mainly because child support was historically a state-controlled issue. Most states had established their own guidelines in the quest for fair standards. About fifteen states used the "percentage-of-income" guideline, which is based on the income of the noncustodial parent. Thirty states used the "income-shares" method, which is based on the income of both parents. It prorates the total support between the parents, and calculates each contribution proportionally according to income. Several states used the elaborate Melson formula, which provides a basic subsistence level for each parent before determining the primary support needs of the children. It then awards a percentage of the remaining income so that the children share in the standard of living of each parent.

Even when guidelines are used, judges consider the facts of a case and other statutes. They can depart from the guidelines for considerations such as how property is divided, whether an arrearage (unpaid child support) exists, and disparities in parents' incomes. In many states, judges must prove in writing that an exception to the guidelines serves the child's best interest.

In practice, courts are allowed to use many criteria in setting an award amount. Some judges consider the needs of subsequent children when OBLIGORS (payers) remarry and start new families. Some may adhere to the Uniform Parentage Act, which states that courts must take into consideration, among other things, the age of the child, the financial resources and earning ability of the child, and the value of services contributed by the custodial parent.

Investment income, unearned income, overtime, bonuses, income from a second job, gifts, and retirement pay may all be eligible income when calculating child support due, regardless of its tax status. Putative income (earning capacity) is used to calculate support in many states if it is suspected that the noncustodial parent is deliberately underemployed or unemployed. The court is allowed to credit SOCIAL SECURITY benefits toward support, but this is not automatic. Child support is not deductible from either parent's taxes, any more than are the provisions that married parents supply to their children. The children themselves qualify as household DEDUCTIONS, but only one parent may claim them.

Unless a state mandates that child support be awarded, the court can deny it. Courts have denied support in situations of split custody, in which each parent has custody of one or more children. With exceptions, the court usually does not award child support to a noncustodial parent during visitation. Support can be ordered for legally adopted children. It cannot be ordered for grandchildren who have not been legally adopted.

**Consequences for Nonpayment** The consequences of not paying child support are inconsistently applied—a situation many states want to remedy. A delinquent obligor may face contempt-of-court charges and civil penalties. Criminal sanctions can include a jail sentence or a fine, but these punishments are used sparingly and for repeat violations. Prosecution may proceed on a MISDEMEANOR or FELONY level, depending on the circumstances. In addition, federal prosecution may occur for a parent who crosses a state line to avoid paying support.

**Enforcement** In 1992 $27 billion in child support went uncollected. The U.S. Department of Health and Human Services has estimated that a substantial increase in child support collections could reduce the payments of Aid to Families with Dependent Children (AFDC) by 25 percent. The federal government created the AFDC program in 1935 to enable states to provide money and services to help poor children remain in their own, single-parent homes.

These observations were not lost on the 1994 Senate, which directed the Justice Department to "immediately address shortcomings in enforcement of the law [regarding child support]." Enforcement efforts are administered federally through the department's Office of Child Support Enforcement, but child support recovery units at the state level perform the daily task of securing payment.

The problems surrounding the collection of child support have provoked frustration and ingenuity in states throughout the nation. A major barrier to timely and regular collection is the large volume of child support orders that states are required to enforce monthly. One response has been to divert cases from the court system by empowering state agencies to enforce child support orders.

A primary means of collecting is wage withholding. This requires that the employer of the obligor send a percentage of the obligor's paychecks to the state or county, which forwards it to the custodial parent. Where the custodial parent receives federal public assistance, income withholding is mandatory. GARNISHMENT is similar to withholding, but it is used when the obligor is about to receive a lump-sum payment.

Interception of the obligor's federal tax return is another enforcement tool. In the first seven years after implementing a pilot of this requirement, $1.8 billion was collected. Federal law now requires every state to have legislation for intercepting the tax returns of delinquent obligors and applying them to child support after a review.

Self-employed obligors, or those whose employment is unknown, pose a challenge to collection agencies. In their case, states may rely on the custodial parent's knowledge of the obligor's income and on tax returns to pursue enforcement.

Other enforcement methods include placing a LIEN on the obligor's property so that it cannot be sold without clearing the arrearage. At times, interest is added to unpaid child support in order to motivate the obligor to pay off this debt; in 1995, the DEFAULT rate was nearly 50 percent on child support, compared with only 3 percent on car loans. Some states have taken the high-profile approach of publicly issuing controversial "Wanted" posters depicting delinquent obligors. Others have revoked state-issued fishing, hunting, and even driver's licenses as punishment for nonpayment.

Less common methods for securing child support owed are the seizure of government security bonds, collection of the full amount by the Internal Revenue Service (this method was still under consideration in 1995), and seizure and sale of property or other forced payment. The effects of reporting delinquent obligors to credit bureaus are being studied.

Interstate orders (orders for support to be paid by a parent in a different state) pose additional problems for enforcement. Although three in ten child support cases are interstate, only 10 percent of the delinquent collections nationwide result from these cases. This has caused child support collection, usually considered a state function, to become an issue of national importance. Although most states have "LONG-ARM" STATUTES enabling them to retain jurisdiction over obligors in other states, delays result when the laws are not uniform. Failures to collect across state lines are due to heavy case backlogs, multiple and conflicting orders, lack of priority given to interstate cases by the responding state, and an inability to locate the noncustodial parent.

The Uniform Interstate Family Support Act (UIFSA), which was developed in 1992, contains what is called the one order, one time rule, in which the initial state retains jurisdiction in order to prevent multiple orders. The act limits modifications and provides that they must occur in the child's home state. The model legislation

also features direct income withholding, so that the state of origin can communicate directly with the obligor's employer in another state. It also requires that states that adopt the uniform law provide enforcement services to one another.

In October 1994, the U.S. Congress's Full Faith and Credit for Child Support Orders Act became effective (28 U.S.C.A. §§ 1 note, 1738B, 1738B note), enabling states to enforce and modify orders under certain circumstances.

**Public Assistance**  In 1991 the Bureau of Census found that nearly half of all single-parent families headed by a woman live at the poverty level. A report on child support enforcement presented to the Senate in 1994 found that more than one-fifth of all U.S. children lived in poverty. As a result, in the 1990s, reliance on AFDC increased dramatically nationwide.

In recognition that many families require public WELFARE because a noncustodial parent does not contribute, Congress adopted title IV-D of the Social Security Act in 1975 (Social Services Amendments of 1974, Pub. L. No.

*Investigators hold warrant packets with photos of parents who are delinquent on their child support payments. Since 1994 wage withholding, interception of tax returns, the placement of liens on property, and other methods have increased collection of this money.*

93-647, 88 Stat. 2337 [1975] [pertinent sections codified at 42 U.S.C.A. §§ 661–665 (1988)]). The legislation created the federal Office of Child Support Enforcement and required states to establish state child support offices. Under title IV-D, services such as locating noncustodial parents, determining parentage, and establishing and enforcing support orders must be provided free to families that receive AFDC. In addition, these services must be provided at very low cost to custodial parents who do not receive AFDC. The federal government requires states to provide these services as a condition of receiving AFDC services.

In the 1990s, child support was sought as part of the regular intake procedure for unmarried parents who were requesting public assistance. To comply with federal funding requirements, most states require that an unmarried parent seeking AFDC identify the absent parent and cooperate in efforts to establish parentage and secure child support.

**Modifying Awards** A family's postdivorce economic situation will likely be different from its predivorce economic situation. In most cases, divorced parents set up separate households whereas they lived together in one home while married. Because the same resources cannot support two households at the same level as a single household, awards are often considered inadequate by the custodial parent and burdensome by the obligor.

An existing support order may be modified if the child's needs or the paying parent's resources change. Back child support can be ordered if a modification or other order delays payment.

Remarriage or COHABITATION does not necessarily affect child support, although if demonstrated to be a permanent change in circumstances, it could become a basis for modification. A child's ADOPTION releases the obligor from future payments but does not cancel an arrearage.

Some orders are automatically modified when certain conditions are met. For example, an escalation clause allows the child support amount to increase as the obligor's income increases. A cost-of-living-adjustment (commonly referred to as COLA) clause permits modification without a hearing when there is an increase in income coupled with inflation. The purpose of these clauses is to keep cases out of court. Courts usually do not approve automatic increases that are not based on an increase in income.

To ensure that orders remain adequate and equitable, Congress began in 1993 to require that states review and, if necessary, adjust child support orders at least once every three years if the custodial parent receives federal public assistance. This differs from state modification standards that are based on changes in circumstances.

BANKRUPTCY does not end a child support obligation. A child's move, if authorized, does not end support. And an obligor's ESTATE may be required to continue support payments after the obligor's death. In most cases, the obligation ends only when the child reaches the AGE OF MAJORITY, marries, or can support herself or himself.

In some states, the court may terminate or suspend child support as a way to enforce a visitation order. The difficulty with this modification is that the child may suffer as a result.

**Other Awards** Financial awards for higher education are sometimes included in an order to pay support, but are not meant to substitute for primary support. Education awards are common in families where children are expected and able to complete postsecondary coursework. Courts have denied awards for tuition, for lessons, and for other education-related expenses when those expenses are deemed unnecessary.

A responsibility to provide HEALTH CARE is occasionally clarified in orders for support, especially when one or both parents have access to an employer-provided health plan. In the early 1990s, a total of 25 million children had no employer-provided INSURANCE, and 8.4 million had no coverage at all. Nevertheless, also in the early 1990s, a majority of support orders lacked provisions regarding health insurance.

An obligor may be required to maintain a life insurance policy naming the child or GUARDIAN as BENEFICIARY.

**CROSS-REFERENCES**

Child Custody; Family Law; Parent and Child.

## CHILLING EFFECT DOCTRINE 📖 In CONSTITUTIONAL LAW, any practice or law that has the effect of seriously dissuading the exercise of a constitutional right, such as freedom of speech. 📖

## CHIPMAN, DANIEL Daniel Chipman was born October 22, 1765, in Salisbury, Connecticut. He graduated from Dartmouth College in 1788, pursued legal studies, and was admitted to the Vermont bar in 1790.

In 1794 Chipman relocated to Middlebury, Vermont, where he established a successful legal practice and acted as counselor until 1819. In 1797 he became state attorney for Addison County, performing these duties until 1817.

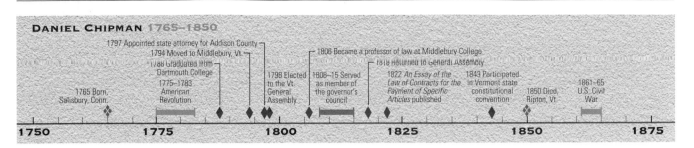

**DANIEL CHIPMAN** 1765-1850

- 1797 Appointed state attorney for Addison County
- 1794 Moved to Middlebury, Vt.
- 1788 Graduated from Dartmouth College
- 1775-1783 American Revolution
- 1765 Born, Salisbury, Conn.
- 1798 Elected to the Vt. General Assembly
- 1806 Became a professor of law at Middlebury College
- 1818 Returned to General Assembly
- 1808-15 Served as member of the governor's council
- 1822 An Essay of the Law of Contracts for the Payment of Specific Articles published
- 1843 Participated in Vermont state constitutional convention
- 1850 Died, Ripton, Vt.
- 1861-65 U.S. Civil War

1750    1775    1800    1825    1850    1875

Chipman entered state politics in 1798 as a delegate from Middlebury to the General Assembly. From 1808 to 1815 he served as a member of the governor's council, acting as speaker in 1813 and 1814.

In 1814 Chipman began service in the federal government as a congressman; he left his post after one session, due to illness. In 1818 he returned to the General Assembly and represented Middlebury during that year and again in 1821.

Chipman's career interests also extended to the field of education. He accepted a professorship of law at Middlebury College in 1806 and taught for the next ten years.

The last years of Chipman's life were devoted to his writing; however, he also served as a Vermont supreme court reporter in 1823, and as a representative to two state constitutional conventions, in 1843 and in 1850.

As an author, Chipman wrote numerous publications, including several biographies. His most famous work is *An Essay on the Law of Contracts for the Payment of Specific Articles*, published in 1822.

Chipman died April 23, 1850, in Ripton, Vermont.

## CHISHOLM, SHIRLEY ANITA ST. HILL

A distinguished congresswoman, scholar, and African American spokeswoman, Shirley Anita Chisholm was the first black woman elected to the U.S. HOUSE OF REPRESENTATIVES. A dynamic public speaker who boldly challenged traditional politics, Fighting Shirley Chisholm, as she called herself during her first congressional campaign, championed liberal legislation from her seat in the House beginning with her inauguration in 1968 and continuing until her re-

**BIOGRAPHY**

THE SHELDON MUSEUM

*Daniel Chipman*

**BIOGRAPHY**

AP/WIDE WORLD PHOTOS

*Shirley Anita St. Hill Chisholm*

tirement in 1982. Admirers and foes alike dubbed her the Pepperpot because of her fondness for saying, "I breathe fire." She ran an unsuccessful campaign for the 1972 Democratic presidential nomination. From 1982 to 1987 she was Purington Professor at Mount Holyoke College, in South Hadley, Massachusetts. Known for her wit, dedication, and compassion, she remains a fierce and eloquent voice on national matters.

Chisholm was born Shirley Anita St. Hill on November 30, 1924, in the impoverished Bedford-Stuyvesant section of Brooklyn. Her father, an emigrant from Guyana, worked as an unskilled laborer, and her mother, a native of Barbados, was a seamstress and a domestic worker. Extraordinary circumstances separated Chisholm from her parents for much of her early childhood. Struggling to save money for a house and for their children's education, the St. Hills sent their four daughters to live on the farm of a grandmother in Barbados. From the age of three to the age of eleven, Chisholm received a British elementary school education and acquired a West Indian rhythm of speech. An important influence on her early life, her grandmother instilled in her the values of pride, courage, and faith. Her parents took her back to Brooklyn at the age of eleven.

Graduating with an excellent academic record from a Brooklyn girls' high school, Chisholm earned a scholarship to study sociology at Brooklyn College. She quickly became active in political circles, joining the Harriet Tubman Society, serving as an Urban League volunteer, and winning prizes in debate. Her interest in her community led her to attend city meetings, where, as a student, she astonished older adults

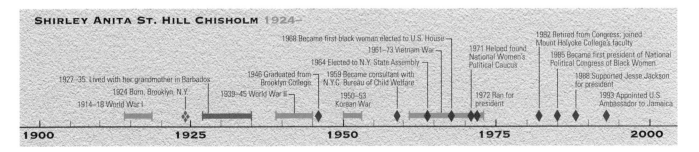

**SHIRLEY ANITA ST. HILL CHISHOLM** 1924-

- 1968 Became first black woman elected to U.S. House
- 1961-73 Vietnam War
- 1964 Elected to N.Y. State Assembly
- 1946 Graduated from Brooklyn College
- 1959 Became consultant with N.Y.C. Bureau of Child Welfare
- 1971 Helped found National Women's Political Caucus
- 1982 Retired from Congress; joined Mount Holyoke College's faculty
- 1985 Became first president of National Political Congress of Black Women
- 1927-35 Lived with her grandmother in Barbados
- 1924 Born, Brooklyn, N.Y.
- 1939-45 World War II
- 1950-53 Korean War
- 1972 Ran for president
- 1988 Supported Jesse Jackson for president
- 1993 Appointed U.S. Ambassador to Jamaica
- 1914-18 World War I

1900    1925    1950    1975    2000

by confronting civic leaders with questions about the quality of government services to her predominantly black neighborhood. While beginning to establish her profile in her community, she also impressed her professors with a powerful speaking style and was encouraged to enter politics. She received her sociology degree with honors in 1946. While working in a nursery school she studied for a master's degree in elementary education at Columbia University where she met Conrad Chisholm, whom she married in 1949. Two years later she received her master's degree in early childhood education.

Over the next decade Chisholm built a reputation as an authority on early education and child welfare. She served as the director of the Friends Day Nursery, in Brownsville, New York, and, from 1953 to 1959, of the Hamilton-Madison Child Care Center, in Lower Manhattan. Taking her expertise into the public sector, she became an educational consultant in New York City's Bureau of Child Welfare from 1959 to 1964. In addition to her professional work, she participated in a variety of community and civic activities. She served on the board of directors of the Brooklyn Home for Aged Colored People and became a prominent member of the Brooklyn branch of the NATIONAL ASSOCIATION FOR THE ADVANCEMENT OF COLORED PEOPLE. She frequently volunteered her time for such groups as the Democratic Women's Workshop; the League of Women Voters; and the Bedford-Stuyvesant Political League, an organization formed to support black candidates. Her intense participation in local politics—marked by her forthrightness and her willingness to confront politicians with difficult questions about racial equality—made her unpopular with the predominantly white Democratic establishment in New York. But it won her the recognition and respect of her community which was about 70 percent African American and Hispanic residents.

So well-known was Chisholm in Brooklyn by 1964 that she could mount a successful campaign for a seat in the New York State Assembly despite having no support from the Democratic establishment. She stressed that "the people" had asked her to run. As an assemblywoman from 1964 to 1968, she spearheaded legislation providing for state-funded day care centers and for unemployment insurance for domestic workers. Of particular importance to her were bills that she shepherded through the Education Committee. One major accomplishment was a financial aid program known as Search for Elevation, Education and Knowledge (SEEK).

Passed into law in 1965, SEEK reached out to students of color who lacked the necessary academic requirements to enter state universities by providing them with scholarships and remedial training. Other legislative successes boosted school spending limits and wiped out the practice of stripping TENURE from women teachers who took maternity leave.

In 1968 Chisholm became the first African American woman to run for the U.S. Congress. In her pursuit of the Democratic nomination for the Twelfth District she bested two other African American candidates and was appointed New York's National Committee representative at the party's national convention. She later said that to win the nomination she had to beat the political machine, an entrenched bureaucracy that had never been fond of her brash style. With the nomination in hand, she faced her Republican opponent, James Farber, a liberal white male who enjoyed national prominence as a civil rights leader. Farber was expected to win, but on November 5, 1968, by a margin of more than 2–1, Chisholm staged an upset victory. The success of her antiestablishment campaign, which ran under the slogan Unbought and Unbossed, was attributed both to widespread support from women and to her ability to address Puerto Rican voters in Spanish.

From the moment she took her seat in the House of Representatives, Chisholm demonstrated the bold iconoclasm that would mark her career in Washington, D.C. With her, it would not be politics as usual. Her initial appointment to a minor subcommittee of the Agriculture Committee struck her as a waste of her talents and experience, and, despite warnings that she was endangering her career, she protested. The House Ways and Means Committee relented and she was appointed to Veterans' Affairs. In her first speech on the floor of the House she vowed to vote against all defense spending. She told lawmakers, "Our children, our jobless men, our deprived, rejected and starving fellows, our dejected citizens must come first."

Chisholm's goals as a congresswoman were twofold. First, when she took office, only 9 of the 435 House members were black, so she made herself an advocate for African Americans both in and out of her district. Second, she tried to advance the goal of racial equality. She supported programs that provided housing and education aid to cities, voted to uphold laws that would end DISCRIMINATION in federally funded jobs, and promoted new antidiscrimination legislation. ABORTION rights also became a focal point in her politics. As a state assembly-

"THE WORD 'RADICAL,' PROPERLY USED, MEANS GOING TO THE BASIS OF A PROBLEM—THE WORD COMES FROM THE LATIN FOR 'ROOT'—RATHER THAN DEALING WITH ITS MANIFESTATIONS."

woman she had supported bills that would make it easier for women whose lives were endangered to have abortions, although she had opposed outright legalization of abortion. But in 1968, with a change of heart, she agreed to be honorary president of the newly formed National Association for the Repeal of Abortion Laws. This would have been a dangerous position for an established politician, let alone a newly elected House member.

Independence of thought was Chisholm's hallmark, however, and the following year she crossed party lines to support Republican mayor John V. Lindsay in the New York mayoral election. Her decision so outraged her own party that some members called, unsuccessfully, for her ouster from the Democratic National Committee. But Chisholm saw the need for revamping traditional politics, supporting foes if necessary, and creating new bases of power. In 1971, along with such feminist leaders as author Gloria Steinem, she helped found the National Women's Political Caucus.

Chisholm's dramatic decision to run for PRESIDENT in 1972 came in part through her widely publicized opposition to the VIETNAM WAR and the policies of President RICHARD M. NIXON. While speaking at college campuses she was frequently asked if she would consider running. At first doubtful that an African American woman would stand a chance, she became encouraged by the growing numbers of blacks serving in elected office. Initially she received little support, even within black political circles, but following an enthusiastic tour of Florida, she announced her candidacy on January 25, 1972. During campaign stops she asked voters to replace entrenched white male leadership with a new voice: "I am your instrument of change. . . . give your votes to me instead of one of those warmed-over gentlemen who come to you once every four years." Criticized for running a hopeless campaign, she remained steadfast. "Some people call me a freak for running for the presidency," she said, "but I am very glad to be a freak in order to break down this domain."

Despite her popularity with women and young people, Chisholm's campaign suffered from limited finances, internal disarray, and lukewarm support from black political leaders. By July 1972, she had twenty-eight delegates, almost half of what she had hoped to bring to the Democratic National Convention. Nevertheless, she won the support of the convention's black caucus, and, in a symbolic move, Hubert H. Humphrey released his black delegates to vote for her. As a result, on the first ballot, she received 152 delegates and addressed the convention. But the number was far too small to stop candidate George S. McGovern from winning the party's nomination.

After the election the trouble that had beset her campaign continued. A 1973 report by the government's General Accounting Office recommended that the U.S. Justice Department investigate possible misconduct in handling campaign funds but a 1974 investigation found no evidence of any wrongdoing.

Following her reelection to the House in the fall of 1972, Chisholm served every two-year term until 1982. The seniority she earned over seven terms—she was the only woman on the House Rules Committee—made her effective in building coalitions among liberal politicians. In addition to supporting women's equality, she was instrumental in advancing welfare legislation designed to help poor and needy citizens. However, the onset of the Reagan era drastically changed the political landscape in Washington, D.C., as liberals were swept aside by conservative challengers. Announcing her retirement on February 10, 1982, Chisholm cited as her chief reason the defeat of liberal senators and representatives, which made it impossible for the old alliances to work.

Chisholm accepted an invitation to join the faculty at Mount Holyoke, the United States' oldest women's college, where she taught courses in political science and women's studies until 1987. At one commencement address she urged new graduates to be active citizens: "Ask questions and demand answers. Do not just tend your garden, collect your paycheck, bolt the door, and deplore what you see on television. Too many people are doing that already. Instead, you must live in the mainstream of your time and of your generation." Although she had left Washington, D.C., she remained immersed in politics. In 1985 she became the first president of the newly formed National Political Congress of Black Women, which in three years grew from five hundred to eighty-five hundred members. In 1988 she campaigned for the Reverend JESSE JACKSON, who was seeking the Democratic party's presidential nomination.

Using her retirement to give speeches and commencement addresses on vital issues, Chisholm has continued to inspire the public imagination. She has advocated sex education for students beginning at the age of seven in order to combat the "national plague" of teenage pregnancy. In 1991, calling the small numbers of African American college professors a crisis in black education, she warned, "Blacks run the risk of becoming an intellectual boat people, just drifting." Opposing the Persian Gulf War in 1991, she argued that the expense of U.S. militarism blocked the goals of peace and equality. "The foundation is being laid for yet another generation of minority Americans to be denied the American dream," she cautioned. Chisholm has received many awards and honorary degrees, and is the author of two books, *Unbought and Unbossed* (1970) and *The Good Fight* (1973).

## CHOATE 📖 Perfected, complete, or certain. 📖

A *choate right* is an undefeatable right that is totally VALID and cannot be subsequently lessened or altered by later claims. If someone purchases a plot of land totally free from encumbrances, that person has a choate property interest in the land.

A *choate lien* is one to which nothing further must be done to make it enforceable. Elements such as the identity of the lienor and the property that is subject to the LIEN are established; thus, the lien is certain and definite.

*Inchoate*, the opposite of choate, is the more commonly used phrase. It means unfinished or incomplete and is used to describe a number of things such as liens, rights, crimes, or interests. For example the term inchoate BATTERY can be used to describe an ASSAULT.

## CHOATE, JOSEPH HODGES

Joseph Hodges Choate was a popular lawyer in New York in the late 1800s. Choate distinguished himself by his exceptional career before the bar, his accomplishments as ambassador to the Court of St. James's (an ambassador to England), his dedication to public service, and his sharp wit and clever after-dinner speeches.

Choate was born January 24, 1832, in Salem, Massachusetts, the fifth of six children and the youngest of four boys in a family with an established heritage. His father, Dr. George Choate, was a graduate of Harvard University and Harvard Medical School and was one of Salem's most distinguished physicians. Choate was also the cousin of Congressman RUFUS CHOATE, who was just beginning his second term when Choate was born.

Continuing the family tradition, Choate attended Harvard with his three brothers. He went on to Harvard Law School, graduating in 1855. Choate then left New England to pursue a career in New York. With the help of a letter from Rufus Choate to WILLIAM M. EVARTS (who would become secretary of state for President RUTHERFORD B. HAYES from 1877 to 1881), Choate joined the law office of Butler, Evarts, and Southmayd.

Choate's skills as an orator made him a formidable litigator. He appeared in hundreds of cases covering a wide range of controversies. One of the most notorious of these cases was the prosecution of William Marcy ("Boss") Tweed. Tweed, elected to the New York State Senate in 1868, headed TAMMANY HALL, a corrupt political organization in New York City that was controlled by the Democratic party. In 1871 Choate was appointed to the committee that eventually charged Tweed with embezzling funds from the city treasury.

Many of Choate's cases involved matters of national importance and were appealed to the U.S. Supreme Court. Choate unsuccessfully fought Kansas's liquor prohibition in *Mugler v. Kansas*, 123 U.S. 623, 8 S. Ct. 273, 31 L. Ed. 205 (1887), and anti-Chinese legislation in *Fong v. United States*, 149 U.S. 698, 13 S. Ct. 1016, 37 L. Ed. 905 (1893). He successfully appealed claims of certain Native Americans that the government had reneged on a TREATY and deprived them of their land in *New York Indians v. United States*, 170 U.S. 1, 18 S. Ct. 531, 42 L. Ed. 927 (1898). In the landmark case *Pollock v. Farmers' Loan & Trust Co.*, 157 U.S. 429, 15 S. Ct. 673, 39 L. Ed. 759 (1895), *reh'g granted*, 158 U.S. 601, 15 S. Ct. 912, 39 L. Ed. 1108 (1895), *overruled by South Carolina v. Baker*, 485 U.S. 505, 108 S. Ct. 1355, 99 L. Ed. 2d 592 (1988), Choate won a constitutional challenge to an INCOME TAX act of 1894. In his winning argument, Choate said, "The act . . . is communistic in its purposes and tendencies, and is defended here upon principles as communistic, socialistic—what should I call them—populistic as ever have been addressed to any political assembly in the world."

Choate's prominence as an attorney attracted the attention of the White House and in January 1899, President WILLIAM MCKINLEY ap-

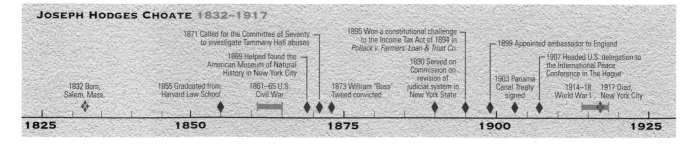

**JOSEPH HODGES CHOATE 1832–1917**

1871 Called for the Committee of Seventy to investigate Tammany Hall abuses

1895 Won a constitutional challenge to the Income Tax Act of 1894 in *Pollock v. Farmers' Loan & Trust Co.*

1899 Appointed ambassador to England

1869 Helped found the American Museum of Natural History in New York City

1890 Served on Commission on revision of judicial system in New York State

1907 Headed U.S. delegation to the International Peace Conference in The Hague

1832 Born, Salem, Mass.

1855 Graduated from Harvard Law School

1861–65 U.S. Civil War

1873 William "Boss" Tweed convicted

1903 Panama Canal Treaty signed

1914–18 World War I

1917 Died, New York City

1825    1850    1875    1900    1925

pointed Choate ambassador to the Court of St. James's, in England. As ambassador Choate negotiated the Hay-Pauncefote Treaty, which allowed the U.S. government to build and operate the Panama Canal. Choate was also instrumental in gaining an "open door" to China, and he resolved a controversy over Samoa with Germany and the United Kingdom. In 1907 Choate headed the delegation from the United States at the International Peace Conference at The Hague.

Choate supported many charitable causes. He was president of the New York State Charities Aid Association and of the Association of the Blind. Choate was a member of the Provisional Committee of 1869 which was appointed to establish the Metropolitan Museum of Art. He continued his relationship with the museum as one of its incorporators and as a member of the executive committee of the board of trustees. He was also an incorporator and officer of the Museum of Natural History.

Choate's successes were due in part to his talents as a public speaker. His keen intellect and engaging speaking style combined with his sense of humor to captivate audiences. No

**BIOGRAPHY**

*Rufus Choate*

innocent, to maintain constitutional rights against all violations, . . . to rescue the scapegoat and restore him to his proper place in the world—all this seemed to me to furnish a field worthy of any man's ambition.

**CHOATE, RUFUS** Rufus Choate was born October 1, 1799, in Ipswich, Massachusetts. He graduated from Dartmouth College in 1819 and was admitted to the bar in 1823.

In 1827 Choate served as a member of the Massachusetts Senate and from 1831 to 1834 he acted as a representative from Massachusetts to the U.S. House of Representatives. He was involved in the organization of the Whig party in Massachusetts. He served as U.S. senator from Massachusetts from 1841 to 1845.

Choate continued his participation in politics by nominating DANIEL WEBSTER for the presidency in 1852 and by attending the Massachusetts Constitutional Convention in 1853. He is the author of the *Discourse Commemorative of Daniel Webster.*

Choate died July 13, 1859, in Halifax, Nova Scotia.

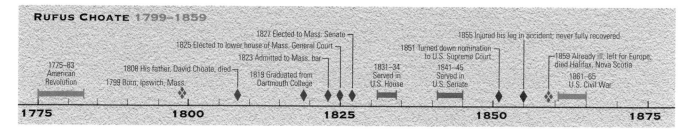

lawyer of the New York bar was in as much demand at public functions. He had speaking engagements before the New England Society, the Union League Club, and the Century Association before and during his presidency of these societies, at dinners and receptions of the bar association, and at innumerable philanthropic events. Shortly after Choate had passed his eighty-fifth birthday he was appointed chairman of a committee of citizens to receive French and British commissioners on a visit to the United States. He was in poor health but he survived long enough to fulfill his duties. Choate died May 14, 1917, in New York City.

Choate once described the path of his career as follows:

> To be a priest . . . in the temple of justice, to serve at her altar and aid in her administration, to maintain and defend those inalienable rights of life, liberty, and property upon which the safety of society depends, to succor the oppressed and to defend the

**CHOSE** [*French, Thing.*] CHATTEL; item of PERSONAL PROPERTY.

**CHOSE IN ACTION** The right to bring a lawsuit to recover CHATTELS, money, or a DEBT.

A *chose in action* is a comprehensive term used to describe a property right or the right to POSSESSION of something that can only be obtained or enforced through legal action. It is used in contradistinction to *chose in possession*, which refers to cases where TITLE to money or property is in one person but possession is held by another.

Examples of a chose in action are the right of an HEIR to interest in the ESTATE of his or her decedent; the right to sue for DAMAGES for an injury; and the right of an employee to unpaid wages.

**CHRISTIAN LEGAL SOCIETY** The Christian Legal Society (CLS), founded in 1961, is a nonprofit organization of lawyers, judges, law professors, and law students. The group's mission is to promote high ethical standards within the legal profession, support its members' commitment to Christian professional lives, and advance religious freedom for all U.S. citizens regardless of affiliation. CLS provides resources for research into law and theology; maintains a data bank of commentaries on legal issues; and provides a speakers' bureau, lawyer referral service, and mediation and arbitration services. It also publishes *Christian Legal Society—Briefly*, a quarterly newsletter for its members, and *Christian Legal Society—Quarterly*, a magazine that covers issues in line with the society's goals. CLS's legal advocacy arm, the Center for Law and Religious Freedom, promotes freedom of RELIGION and challenges government interference with the free exercise of religion.

In 1993 CLS backed passage of the Religious Freedom Restoration Act (RFRA), 42 U.S.C.A. § 2000bb, et seq., a response to the 1990 Supreme Court decision in *Employment Division, Department of Human Resources v. Smith*, 494 U.S. 872, 110 S. Ct. 1595, 108 L. Ed. 2d 876. *Smith* upheld a denial of unemployment benefits to Native Americans fired from their jobs for using peyote, a hallucinogenic drug, as part of a religious ceremony. CLS and numerous other groups representing a wide range of religious and political persuasions lobbied for RFRA, which requires the government to show a "compelling state interest," such as public health or safety, before interfering with religious practices.

CLS members successfully argued two important religious freedom cases before the Supreme Court in 1993. In *Zobrest v. Catalina Foothills School District*, 509 U.S. 1, 113 S. Ct. 2462, 125 L. Ed. 2d 1, the Court held that the ESTABLISHMENT CLAUSE did not prohibit a public school district from paying for a sign language interpreter for a deaf student who attended a Catholic high school. In *Lamb's Chapel v. Center*

*The Christian Legal Society argued a case before the Supreme Court in which the Court held that a public school district should pay for a sign language interpreter for a deaf student who attended a Catholic high school.*

*Moriches Union Free School District*, 508 U.S. 384, 113 S. Ct. 2141, 124 L. Ed. 2d 352, the Court held that a school district's denial of a religious organization's application to use school facilities to show a film on Christian values in family relationships violated the church's FIRST AMENDMENT right to freedom of speech.

CLS and the Center for Law and Religious Freedom also filed briefs in two prominent cases in 1993 and 1994. In *In re Young*, 152 Bankr. 939 (D. Minn. 1993), a federal district court upheld a BANKRUPTCY court ruling ordering the return of $13,450 in church donations to the creditors of Bruce Young and Nancy Young. The Youngs, members of Crystal Evangelical Free Church, in New Hope, Minnesota, had continued to tithe, contributing 10 percent of their income to their church, while their business was failing. The Bankruptcy Code requires cancellation of all donations made by an insolvent party within one year before filing for bankruptcy unless the party received "reasonably equivalent value" in exchange for the payments. The bankruptcy court found that the Youngs' donations did not satisfy the Code requirement. The case was appealed to district court. Lawyers from the Center for Law and Religious Freedom were unsuccessful in convincing the district court that the Bankruptcy Code violated the Youngs' religious freedom and that the Youngs had received equivalent value in the form of spiritual sustenance. The district court held that the Youngs had made their payments out of a moral rather than a legal obligation and that such payments did not satisfy the Code requirement. The court also held that the Code had only an incidental effect on religion and therefore did not violate the Free Exercise Clause of the Constitution.

In *Rosenberger v. Rector and Visitors of the University of Virginia*, ___U.S.___, 115 S. Ct. 2510, 132 L. Ed. 2d 700 (1995), CLS supported the plaintiff, who sued the University of Virginia when it denied his request for financial support for publication of a Christian magazine. Although the university subsidized a wide range of publications from its Student Activities Fund (SAF), it denied Ronald W. Rosenberger's request on the grounds that his magazine violated SAF guidelines. Rosenberger argued that the guidelines, which prohibited the university from subsidizing a publication that "primarily promotes or manifests a particular belie[f] in or about a deity or an ultimate reality," violated his free speech rights. A brief filed by CLS maintained that the guidelines discriminated on the basis of religious belief and that a decision against the plaintiff would be a step toward "a relentlessly secular society" intolerant of religious persons and their views. The Supreme Court decided in favor of the plaintiff, but rested its holding on free speech grounds, stating that the SAF guidelines discriminated on the basis of viewpoint and violated the plaintiff's First Amendment rights.

CLS members are committed to the biblical injunction to "not leave justice and the love of God undone" (Luke 11:42, Matt. 23:23). They are dedicated to ending injustice, limiting or eliminating legal ABORTION, outlawing PORNOGRAPHY, and bringing religious thought and precepts into public education. They are also committed to the evangelization of the legal profession, and plan to increase the society's membership by 10 to 12 percent each year.

**CHURNING** The practice whereby a BROKER dealing in SECURITIES abuses the confidence of a client for personal gain by unnecessarily trading STOCKS to earn more commissions.

**CIA** An abbreviation for the CENTRAL INTELLIGENCE AGENCY.

**CIRCUIT** A territorial or geographical division of a country or state.

A circuit is the judicial territory over which a court has the jurisdiction to hear cases.

**CIRCUIT COURT** A specific tribunal that possesses the legal authority to hear cases within its own geographical territory.

A circuit court is ordinarily an inferior trial-level court; appeals are heard by superior courts possessing the requisite JURISDICTION. The jurisdiction of a circuit court generally extends over a number of counties or districts wherein the court sits.

The name *circuit court* can be traced historically to the period when a single judge rode the CIRCUIT to hold trials in each county within the designated territory. In geographical locations with small populations, this method of dispensing justice eliminates the expense of providing every small village with its own judiciary.

**CIRCUMSTANTIAL EVIDENCE** Information and TESTIMONY presented by a party in a civil or criminal action that permit conclusions that indirectly establish the existence or nonexistence of a fact or event that the party seeks to prove.

Circumstantial evidence is also known as INDIRECT EVIDENCE. It is distinguished from DIRECT EVIDENCE, which, if believed, proves the existence of a particular fact without any inference or presumption required. Circumstantial evidence relates to a series of facts other than the particular fact sought to be proved. The party offering circumstantial evidence argues

*This police officer is using a metal detector to search for evidence. If an item that belongs to a suspect is found, it may provide evidence that the suspect was at the scene of the crime. The evidence would be circumstantial unless it proved the suspect committed the crime.*

that this series of facts, by reason and experience, is so closely associated with the fact to be proved that the fact to be proved may be inferred simply from the existence of the circumstantial evidence.

The following examples illustrate the difference between direct and circumstantial evidence: If John testifies that he saw Tom raise a gun and fire it at Ann and that Ann then fell to the ground, John's testimony is direct evidence that Tom shot Ann. If the JURY believes John's testimony, then it must conclude that Tom did in fact shoot Ann. If, however, John testifies that he saw Tom and Ann go into another room and that he heard Tom say to Ann that he was going to shoot her, heard a shot, and saw Tom leave the room with a smoking gun, then John's testimony is circumstantial evidence from which it can be inferred that Tom shot Ann. The jury must determine whether John's testimony is credible.

Circumstantial evidence is most often employed in criminal trials. Many circumstances can create INFERENCES about an accused's guilt in a criminal matter, including the accused's resistance to arrest; the presence of a motive or opportunity to commit the crime; the accused's presence at the time and place of the crime; any denials, evasions, or contradictions on the part of the accused; and the general conduct of the accused. In addition, much scientific evidence is circumstantial, because it requires a jury to make a connection between the circumstance and the fact in issue. For example, with FINGERPRINT evidence, a jury must make a connection between this evidence that the accused handled some object tied to the crime and the commission of the crime itself.

Books, movies, and television often perpetuate the belief that circumstantial evidence may not be used to convict a criminal of a crime. But this view is incorrect. In many cases, circumstantial evidence is the only EVIDENCE linking an accused to a crime; direct evidence may simply not exist. As a result, the jury may have only circumstantial evidence to consider in determining whether to convict or acquit a person charged with a crime. In fact, the U.S. Supreme Court has stated that "circumstantial evidence is intrinsically no different from testimonial [direct] evidence" (*Holland v. United States*, 348 U.S. 121, 75 S. Ct. 127, 99 L. Ed. 150 [1954]). Thus, the distinction between direct and circumstantial evidence has little practical effect in the presentation or admissibility of evidence in trials.

**CITATION** A paper commonly used in various courts—such as a probate, matrimonial, or traffic court—that is served upon an individual to notify him or her that he or she is required to appear at a specific time and place.

Reference to a legal authority—such as a case, constitution, or TREATISE—where particular information may be found.

To organize CASE LAW, cases are published in a series of books called REPORTERS, which are compilations of judicial decisions made in a certain court, state, or jurisdiction. Reporters are published in consecutively numbered volumes, each of which contains the most recently decided cases. If the numbers on a set of volumes get too high, the publisher will begin a new set with a second series of numbers.

To refer to a particular case in a reporter, a designation including the volume number, the name of the reporter, and the page number is given. If, for example, a case decided in the Supreme Court of the United States was cited as 60 S. Ct. 710, it would mean that the case is in volume 60 of the Supreme Court Reporter on page 710. To promote uniformity of citations, a pamphlet colloquially called the "blue book" of uniform citations indicates the proper form. See also LEGAL PUBLISHING.

**CITATOR** A volume or set of volumes that is a record of the status of cases or statutes.

A citator is a guide published primarily for use by judges and lawyers when they are in the process of preparing such papers as judicial decisions, BRIEFS, or memoranda of law. Its purpose is to provide a judicial history of cases and statutes as well as to make a note of new cases. A citator indicates whether or not the law in a particular case has been followed, modified, or overruled in subsequent cases.

A citator is usually organized into columns of CITATIONS. Various abbreviations designate such things as whether a case has been overruled, superseded, or cited in the dissenting opinion of a later case.

The most well-known and commonly used citator is SHEPARD'S CITATIONS. The process of consulting this book or any other citator is known as SHEPARDIZING a case.

**CITE** To notify a person of a proceeding against him or her or to call a person forth to appear in court.

To make reference to a legal authority, such as a case, in a CITATION.

Cases, STATUTES, constitutions, TREATISES, and other similar authorities are cited to support a certain view of law on an issue. When writing a legal BRIEF, an attorney may wish to strengthen his or her position by referring to cases that support what he or she is saying in order to persuade the court to make a ruling favorable for the client. See also PRECEDENT; STARE DECISIS.

**CITIZENS** Those who, under the Constitution and laws of the United States, or of a particular community or of a foreign country, owe allegiance and are entitled to the enjoyment of all CIVIL RIGHTS that accrue to those who qualify for that status.

Neither the United States nor a state is a citizen for purposes of DIVERSITY OF CITIZENSHIP, a phrase used in regard to the JURISDICTION of the FEDERAL COURTS, which—under Article III, Section 2, of the Constitution—empowers those courts to hear and decide cases between citizens of different states. Municipalities and other local governments, however, are deemed to be citizens.

The term *citizen* in Article III of the Constitution, which established the federal judiciary, includes CORPORATIONS; therefore, suits concerning corporations involve citizens for federal jurisdictional purposes. The term *citizen*, however, as defined by the Fourteenth and Fifteenth Amendments, does not encompass either corporations or ALIENS. Neither corporations nor aliens receive the protection of the PRIVILEGES AND IMMUNITIES Clauses of the FOURTEENTH AMENDMENT and Article IV, since those clauses protect only citizens.

Aliens, however, are considered to be "persons" for the purposes of the DUE PROCESS Clauses of the Fifth and Fourteenth Amendments and the EQUAL PROTECTION Clause of the Fourteenth Amendment. In the 1982 case of *Plyler v. Doe*, 457 U.S. 202, 102 S. Ct. 2382, 72 L. Ed. 2d 786, the Supreme Court recognized that even illegal aliens are "persons" within the Equal Protection Clause of the Fourteenth Amendment for purposes of public education. A corporation is also deemed to be a citizen for certain purposes. It is a citizen of the United States and of the state where it was organized. A particular state, commonly Delaware, is selected for incorporation, because that state charges lower taxes and its laws favor businesses. Once the company incorporates in the designated state, it is a citizen of that state, but it can apply in any other state for authority to do business there.

The Fourteenth Amendment to the Constitution provides: "All persons born or naturalized in the United States, and subject to the jurisdiction thereof, are citizens of the United States and of the State wherein they reside. . . ."

This states that the important right of citizenship, whether for native-born or naturalized citizens, cannot be divested, whether as punishment for a crime or for any other reason, by the states or the federal government, including their agencies and officials (see also *Afroyim v. Rusk*, 387 U.S. 253, 87 S. Ct. 1660, 18 L. Ed. 2d 757 [1967]). American citizenship can be relinquished, but it cannot be taken away unless it was procured through FRAUD or any unlawful action.

The Fourteenth Amendment, through the inclusion of the phrase "all persons," was specifically enacted in 1868 to grant citizenship to former slaves. Since 1924 it has been judicially interpreted to include Native Americans. U.S. citizenship does not divest an Indian of tribal citizenship but coexists with it.

The Fourteenth Amendment does not, however, make children born within the territory of the United States of foreign AMBASSADORS, CONSULS, and military officers American citizens. Such children derive their citizenship from their parents.

Ordinarily, a person who is in a country other than the one of which he or she is a citizen owes to that country a type of "temporary allegiance," which essentially is a respect for the laws of the host country, although it is not as substantial as the loyalty demanded of citizens. It requires that an alien observe the laws of the country and, in some countries, even serve in the military; it ensures the protection of the alien by the laws of the country.

Ambassadors, consuls, and military officers, however, owe no allegiance to the foreign country where they are assigned, and their children are not "born within the allegiance" of a foreign country in which they serve.

**Citizen of a State** The Fourteenth Amendment provides that American citizens are also citizens "of the state wherein they reside," but U.S. citizenship does not necessi-

tate RESIDENCE in a particular state. Persons living abroad, for example, are citizens of the United States but not of any state.

One significant legal disadvantage exists for a person who is not a citizen of a state. The Constitution provides that federal courts can hear "Controversies . . . between Citizens of different States." The phrase "Citizens of different States" includes citizens of Puerto Rico, the Virgin Islands of the United States, and Guam. Puerto Rico is in the First Circuit, the Virgin Islands are in the Third Circuit, and Guam, Alaska, and Hawaii are in the Ninth Circuit. A person who is not a resident of a state or designated area, even if he or she is a U.S. citizen, cannot satisfy the diversity of citizenship requirement and therefore cannot bring an action under the diversity clause in a federal court.

**American Citizenship** U.S. citizenship is attained either by birth or by naturalization, the legal procedure that a qualified person must satisfy in order to be accepted as a citizen.

Federal law provides that those who are born in any of the fifty states, Puerto Rico, the former Panama Canal Zone, the Virgin Islands of the United States, and Guam are all native-born citizens, including the children of an American Indian, Eskimo, Aleutian, or any other tribe.

Persons born in outlying possessions of the United States, such as Wake Island or Midway Island, and their children are called *nationals*. They owe allegiance to the United States and enjoy some rights. The term *national* denotes everyone who owes allegiance to the country, including citizens, but not every national possesses all of the rights of a citizen.

*During World War II food was rationed in order to preserve resources for the war. The federal government encouraged citizens to do their duty in supporting the war and even printed "Buy United States war bonds" on the loaf of bread this woman is buying.*

UPI/CORBIS-BETTMANN

A person born beyond the geographical boundaries of the United States and its outlying possessions, of parents who are both U.S. citizens, is a national and a citizen of the United States at birth if one parent had a residence in the United States or one of its outlying possessions prior to the birth of such person. If only one parent is a citizen and the other is a national—but not a citizen—the parent who is a citizen must have been physically present in the United States or one of its outlying possessions for a continuous period of one year prior to the birth of the child in order for the child to be a national and a citizen of the United States at birth.

A person born out of wedlock in a foreign country acquires at birth American citizenship if the mother was a citizen at the time of such person's birth and had formerly been physically present in the United States or one of its outlying possessions for a continuous period of one year preceding the birth.

**Derivative Citizenship** A child born in a foreign country can become a U.S. citizen if his or her parents become naturalized U.S. citizens. If the child is brought to the United States before becoming an adult and the child's parents become citizens, then the child is entitled to claim U.S. citizenship when he or she becomes an adult. Although his or her birth certificate will still reflect a foreign-born status, a person in this situation can obtain a certificate of nationality by filing an application with the secretary of state.

**Rights of U.S. Citizens** Everyone within the jurisdiction of the United States is protected by most of the guarantees and safeguards of the Constitution. A U.S. citizen traveling abroad retains the protection of the United States. If property of an individual is stolen while he or she is in a foreign country, the United States consul can lend him or her money to return to the United States. U.S. citizens, of course, must observe and obey the laws of other countries while they are visiting, but if a U.S. citizen is arrested, a representative from the U.S. ambassador's office can visit him or her and inform the foreign government that the treatment of the U.S. citizen will be scrutinized.

Unlike citizens of other countries, U.S. citizens are entitled to enter into, and depart from, the United States, and to obtain a PASSPORT from the government. The passport certifies to foreign nations that its holder is entitled to all of the protection afforded by the U.S. government. The right to enter and leave the United States is so fundamental, however, that a citizen cannot be prevented from coming into the United States merely because he or she has no passport. Even if someone departs from the country without obtaining a passport, knowing that he or she should have done so, he or she must be permitted to enter upon returning if a birth certificate or expired passport is presented, or the person takes an oath as to his or her citizenship.

The U.S. government can, however, prohibit its citizens from traveling in designated countries that are hostile to the United States and perilous to U.S. citizens. The passport of a person who ignores these restrictions can be revoked and such a traveler may be denied protection by the government.

A naturalized citizen has almost all the rights of a native-born U.S. citizen but one: he or she can never be president of the United States. Article II of the Constitution provides: "No person except a natural-born Citizen, or a Citizen of the United States, at the time of Adoption of this Constitution, shall be eligible to the Office of President."

**Obligations of Citizenship** The most fundamental duty of a citizen is to be loyal to the United States. ALLEGIANCE is not an unquestioning acceptance, but is a general faith in the U.S. system. In times of national emergency, citizens can be required to defend the country, through military service or alternative service such as employment in a hospital.

**Surrender of Citizenship** Unlike some nations, the United States permits EXPATRIATION, the voluntary relinquishment of one's citizenship. A U.S. citizen can lose his or her citizenship by declaring that he or she no longer wishes to be a citizen or to owe allegiance to the United States, or by performing a voluntary act that constitutes the surrender of citizenship, as prescribed by law.

The test of whether an abandonment of citizenship is voluntary depends on whether the person's acts were of his or her own choice and pertained to allegiance to the United States. If they were, federal law provides that one has intentionally and voluntarily surrendered his or her right to citizenship.

A loss of citizenship can occur by serving in the military service of another nation; serving as a public official in a foreign country that requires an oath of allegiance to that country; and attempting to overthrow the U.S. government, which is established by a CONVICTION for the crime.

Conduct that might be construed as a renunciation of citizenship sometimes is insufficient to prove voluntary expatriation. If a person merely enjoys the benefits available in another country, the surrender of his or her U.S. citizenship is not necessarily established.

The Supreme Court has recognized the power of Congress to specify conduct that constitutes expatriation, but the right to citizenship is so substantial that such actions must be closely related to a conspicuous movement of allegiance away from the United States. Although some courts have ruled that Congress *never* is empowered to deprive the native born of citizenship, this view is not in accordance with current law.

Conviction of a crime can result in a partial deprivation of rights of citizenship. In former times, convicts actually lost their citizenship, which was known in some jurisdictions as CIVIL DEATH. Today, however, only some rights are divested, even if the applicable law is called "loss of citizenship."

A state is empowered to deny someone the right to vote after his or her conviction of a FELONY or an "infamous crime," such as BRIBERY or PERJURY. This denial of a right of citizenship can remain in effect until the completion of the sentence, including periods of parole, or it might be permanent. A PARDON from the president or a governor can, however, restore such rights. Some statutes even authorize the courts to restore rights of citizenship upon proof of the rehabilitation of the former prisoner.

**International Law**  Questions concerning whether someone is a citizen of one country or another are generally resolved by TREATY, a compact formed between two or more nations with respect to matters pertaining to the public welfare pursuant to principles of INTERNATIONAL LAW. One person might qualify for DUAL NATIONALITY, that is, citizenship in more than one nation, if he or she can satisfy the citizenship requirements of different countries.

International law also recognizes a rule labeled the "law of the flag," which determines the citizenship of persons born on ships. The rule is responsive to the citizenship laws of different nations and to treaties that are rewritten to fulfill new political conditions.

A child born of U.S. parents on a vessel anywhere in the world is a U.S. citizen. A child born in U.S. waters on a foreign ship is a citizen of that foreign nation when his or her parents are citizens of that country. If his or her parents are from a different country, provisions of treaty or international law apply. A child born on the high seas on a foreign vessel of parents from that same country assumes that country's citizenship and not the citizenship of his or her destination.

## CITIZENS FOR DECENCY THROUGH LAW

Citizens for Decency through Law (CDL), one of the first major antipornography organizations in the United States, was founded in 1956 by lawyer and future financier Charles H. Keating, Jr., after his daughter was sexually attacked in the 1950s. Believing that PORNOGRAPHY causes violence and CHILD ABUSE, CDL members have endeavored to stop the sale of pornographic material and close movie theaters that show sexually explicit movies by pressuring politicians and judges into enforcing OBSCENITY laws.

CDL has provided legal advice to cities investigating dealers in sexually explicit motion pictures, magazines, and mail-order publications. CDL has concentrated its staff of attorneys on helping the police and prosecutors prepare trials and appeals in obscenity cases and draft model legislation and by testimony before local, state, and federal legislative committees. Between 1963 and 1981, CDL sponsored or wrote AMICUS CURIAE (friend-of-the-court) briefs for twenty-seven obscenity cases reviewed by the U.S. Supreme Court. Of those cases, 37 percent had rulings favorable to CDL's views. In addition to providing direct, personal assistance in certain important cases, CDL legal staff have prepared and mailed comprehensive analyses of developments in obscenity law to prosecutors around the United States. The group has also sought to educate the public on the extent of the traffic in obscene materials.

Keating, a staunch Roman Catholic who originally called his group Citizens for Decent Literature, is perhaps best known as a central figure in a scandal involving the Lincoln Savings and Loan Association. Between 1989 and 1993, he was charged with and convicted on numerous civil racketeering and FRAUD charges and sentenced to prison. However, Keating began his career as a prosecutor in Cincinnati—a conservative city that now prides itself on being a national center for antipornography efforts—and first sought to rid newsstands of sexually explicit materials in the 1950s when he prosecuted a local candy store accused of selling obscene publications. By 1969 his zealous battles against pornography had earned him an appointment by RICHARD M. NIXON to the Presidential Commission on Obscenity and Pornography. In 1970, Keating filed a lawsuit that delayed release of a report by the commission that recommended repeal of all adult CENSORSHIP laws.

Over the years, CDL has battled foes ranging from Larry Flynt, publisher of *Hustler* magazine, to Pacific Bell, which allowed indiscriminate access to dial-a-porn messages. A long-running skirmish in the 1980s involved an adult movie theater in an Orange County, California, shopping center that Lincoln Savings and Loan sued after the city of Santa Ana failed to close the theater. Lincoln's lawsuit charged that the theater, operated by Mitchell Brothers, attracted "criminal elements, organized crime and persons who practice sexual deviations, such as homosexuals, lesbians, voyeurs, prostitutes, pedophil[e]s, sadists, masochists, rapists, etc., into the area." (After the Lincoln bank failed, the federal government took over the institution, and the lawsuit was dropped.)

During the administrations of Presidents RONALD REAGAN and GEORGE BUSH lawyers recruited from CDL took part in a controversial and lengthy prosecution of businesses involved with obscene materials. In November 1993, the U.S. Justice Department dropped this prosecution tactic, which involved threatening businesses with INDICTMENTS in numerous JURISDICTIONS in order to extract agreements to stop distribution of the materials. The theory behind the strategy was that the mere expense of defending themselves in so many places would encourage PLEA BARGAINS by the businesses. Among the targets of these prosecutions was Adam and Eve, a large distributor of sexually explicit films, magazines, and books. A number of federal judges and civil liberties organizations denounced the multidistrict tactic as a form of harassment, sweeping in nonobscene materials protected by the FIRST AMENDMENT in addition to unprotected obscenity.

In 1995 the Montana chapter of the CDL became the chief advocate of a bill designed to expand the state's obscenity laws (H.R. 83). Introduced by Representative Jack Herron (R-Kalispell), the bill would make it a crime to provide or display obscene material to anyone, not just those under age eighteen.

CDL has often worked with other organizations, including the National Religious Alliance against Pornography; Morality in Media; the Moral Majority; Citizens against Pornography; the American Family Association; and the National Federation for Decency. It has also been aligned with smaller compatriot groups such as Citizens for Legislation against Decadence in Portland, Oregon; Women against Pornography in New York; Feminists against Pornography in Chicago and in Washington, D.C.; and the feminist-sponsored Pornography Resource Center in Minneapolis. CDL opponents include the AMERICAN CIVIL LIBERTIES UNION and other civil liberties organizations as well as publishers of pornography, such as *Oui* maga-

zine, which in 1975 dubbed Keating the number one enemy of pornography.

**CIVIL ACTION** 📖 A lawsuit brought to enforce, redress, or protect rights of private litigants—the PLAINTIFFS and the DEFENDANTS—not a criminal proceeding. 📖

Today, courts in the United States generally are not divided into COMMON-LAW courts and EQUITY courts because most states and the federal government have merged the procedures for law and equity into one system. Now all kinds of lawsuits are simply called civil actions without the former distinctions of procedure in law or in equity.

A criminal proceeding is called a penal action to distinguish it from civil actions.

**CIVIL DEATH** 📖 The FORFEITURE of rights and privileges of an individual who has been convicted of a serious CRIME. 📖

Civil death is provided for by statute in some states. Most civil death statutes apply only to offenders who have been sentenced to a life term.

Civil death involves the imposition of numerous disabilities, including the denial of the privilege to vote, to hold public office, and to obtain many job and occupational LICENSES. In addition, an offender cannot enter into judicially enforceable agreements, such as CONTRACTS, and may not obtain INSURANCE and PENSION benefits. The offender may also be deprived of any right to commence certain lawsuits in court.

Successive MARRIAGES can also be affected by civil death laws. The issue is whether or not the spouse of a person declared civilly dead may enter into a subsequent marriage. The state courts are in disagreement on the matter, although, in most instances, where a FELONY is a ground for DIVORCE, the spouse of the convicted person may end the marriage.

*Civil death is the forfeiture of certain rights by a person who has been convicted of a serious crime.*

JAMES SCHAEFFER/PHOTOEDIT

**CIVILETTI, BENJAMIN RICHARD** Benjamin Richard Civiletti served as U.S. attorney general from 1979 to 1981 under President JIMMY CARTER. His leadership helped the Justice Department regain public credibility in the years following the Watergate scandal.

Civiletti was born July 17, 1935, in Peekskill, New York. He received a bachelor of arts degree from Johns Hopkins University in 1957 and a law degree from the University of Maryland in 1961. He served from 1961 to 1962 as clerk to William Calvin Chesnut, a U.S. district judge for Maryland. From 1962 to 1964, he worked as assistant U.S. attorney in Baltimore.

Civiletti then turned to private practice with the prestigious Baltimore law firm of Venable, Baetjer, and Howard. His skill as a trial attorney enabled him to rise quickly in the firm. He became a partner in 1969 and headed the litigation department two years later. He also became highly active on various professional committees in Baltimore and Maryland, including the Character Committee of the Court of Appeals of Maryland (1970–76), the Mayor's Commission to Investigate Baltimore City Jails (1972–73), the Judiciary Committee of the Bar Association of Baltimore (1972–75), and the Maryland state legislature's Task Force on Crime (1975–76).

Civiletti's reputation as an outstanding lawyer and civic leader attracted the notice of officials in President Carter's administration. In 1977, the Carter administration appointed Civiletti assistant attorney general in charge of the Criminal Division of the Justice Department. He oversaw a number of sensitive cases in the Criminal Division, including the investigation of Bert Lance, a friend of Carter's who resigned as director of the Office of Management and Budget in September 1977 after being questioned by the Senate about alleged violations of banking laws. Civiletti also dealt with a scandal involving alleged attempts by South Korean government officials to buy influence from members of Congress and from other U.S. government officials.

In late 1977, the Carter administration

**BIOGRAPHY**

*Benjamin Richard Civiletti*

"LAW REQUIRES BOTH A HEART AND A HEAD."

nominated Civiletti as deputy attorney general. He was finally appointed to the post in January 1978. As deputy attorney general, Civiletti received widespread praise for his coordination of an interagency campaign against white-collar crime.

Civiletti's rapid rise through the ranks of the Justice Department culminated in his appointment in 1979 as U.S. attorney general. His appointment came after President Carter requested the resignation of top cabinet officials in an attempt to improve the functioning of his administration. The previous attorney general, GRIFFIN B. BELL, had strongly recommended Civiletti to be his replacement. The Senate approved Civiletti's appointment on August 1, 1979, by a vote of 94–1.

As attorney general, Civiletti continued policies initiated by Bell: a restructuring of the FEDERAL BUREAU OF INVESTIGATION so that it might better investigate white-collar crime; recodification of criminal law statutes; increased pursuit of antitrust cases; and improvement of the Immigration and Naturalization Service. In addition, Civiletti continued his earlier work to improve cooperation between different law enforcement divisions of the federal government.

Civiletti was also forced to respond to international events during his tenure as attorney general. After U.S. citizens were seized at the U.S. Embassy in Tehran in 1979, Civiletti directed the Justice Department's efforts to deport Iranians who had entered the United States illegally. Civiletti also traveled to the International Court of Justice at The Hague, and persuaded its judges to rule in favor of the United States and denounce the Iranian capture of the U.S. embassy.

After RONALD REAGAN took office as president in 1981, Civiletti returned to private practice, where he has represented corporations in such areas of the law as products liability, white-collar crime, government regulation, and health care.

Civiletti founded the Maryland Legal Services Corporation and was the original director of the National Institute against Prejudice and

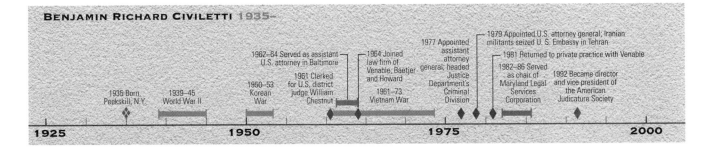

**BENJAMIN RICHARD CIVILETTI 1935–**

1935 Born, Peekskill, N.Y.

1939–45 World War II

1950–53 Korean War

1961 Clerked for U.S. district judge William Chesnut

1961–73 Vietnam War

1962–64 Served as assistant U.S. attorney in Baltimore

1964 Joined law firm of Venable, Baetjer, and Howard

1977 Appointed assistant attorney general; headed Justice Department's Criminal Division

1979 Appointed U.S. attorney general; Iranian militants seized U. S. Embassy in Tehran

1981 Returned to private practice with Venable

1982–86 Served as chair of Maryland Legal Services Corporation

1992 Became director and vice president of the American Judicature Society

1925    1950    1975    2000

Violence. In 1992, he became the director and vice president of the American Judicature Society, and in 1993, he was named chairman of the Maryland Governor's Commission on Welfare Policy. Civiletti has served as a trustee of Johns Hopkins University and has received honorary doctorates of law from the University of Baltimore, Tulane University, Saint John's University, the University of Notre Dame, and the University of Maryland.

**CIVIL LAW** ▣ Legal system derived from the Roman *Corpus Juris Civilus* of Emperor JUSTINIAN I; differs from a COMMON-LAW system, which relies on prior decisions to determine the outcome of a lawsuit. Most European and South American countries have a civil law system. England and most of the countries it dominated or colonized, including Canada and the United States, have a common-law system. However, within these countries, Louisiana, Quebec, and Puerto Rico exhibit the influence of French and Spanish settlers in their use of civil law systems.

A body of rules that delineate private rights and remedies and govern disputes between individuals in such areas as CONTRACTS, PROPERTY, and FAMILY LAW; distinct from criminal or PUBLIC LAW. ▣

In the United States, the term *civil law* has two meanings. One meaning of civil law refers to a legal system prevalent in Europe that is based on written CODES. Civil law in this sense is contrasted with the common-law system used in England and most of the United States, which relies on prior CASE LAW to resolve disputes rather than written codes. The second meaning of civil law refers to the body of laws governing disputes between individuals, as opposed to those governing offenses against the government—that is, civil law as opposed to CRIMINAL LAW.

Civil law systems, which trace their roots to ancient Rome, are governed by doctrines developed and compiled by legal scholars. Legislators and administrators in civil law countries use these doctrines to fashion a code by which all legal controversies are decided.

In France, the civil law is set forth in the comprehensive French Civil Code of 1804, also known as the Code Napoléon. France exported this legal system to the New World when it settled Louisiana in 1712. When the French ceded Louisiana to Spain in 1762, the new Spanish governor replaced French civil law with Spanish civil law. France regained control of the territory in 1803 and the United States purchased it a mere twenty days later. During that brief period of French rule, the French prefect abolished all Spanish courts but did not reintroduce French law. Hence, the new U.S. governor of Louisiana, William Claiborne, took control of a territory that lacked a legal system.

Determined to Americanize Louisiana, Claiborne attempted to impose common law but met fierce resistance from Louisianans who had grown accustomed to their mixture of French and Spanish laws and culture. Realizing that he would not be able to mandate a common law system, he directed the state's legislature to draft a civil code based on existing law. Louisiana's first civil code, enacted in 1808, drew heavily from the Code Napoléon and was even written in French. It was replaced in 1825 by a more comprehensive and detailed code. Finally, the LOUISIANA CIVIL CODE, enacted in 1870 and still largely in force, clarifies and simplifies the earlier laws. The 1870 code is written in English, signaling a shift toward a partial Americanization of Louisiana's legal culture. To this day, Louisiana enjoys the distinction of being the only state in the United States to have a civil law system rather than a common-law system.

The first article of the Louisiana Civil Code reads: "The sources of law are legislation and custom" (LA C.C. Art. 1.). This means that judges in Louisiana are obligated to look first to written laws for guidance in reaching their decisions. If no statute directly governs the dispute, judges may base their decisions on established custom. Article 3 defines custom as a "practice repeated for a long time and generally accepted as having acquired the force of law." However, article 3 makes it clear that custom may not abrogate or conflict with legislation. Hence, Louisiana judges do not make law with their decisions; rather, the code charges them with interpreting, as closely as possible, what has been written and passed by the legislature or long established by custom.

Louisiana judges, unlike their common-law counterparts, are not bound by judicial PRECEDENT. Common-law judges adhere to the doctrine of STARE DECISIS, which mandates that the outcome of a lawsuit be governed by previous decisions in similar cases. Louisiana's civil code does not recognize the binding force of precedent. However, under the civil law doctrine of *jurisprudence constante*, or settled jurisprudence, judges are expected to follow a series of decisions that agree on the interpretation of a code provision.

Although Louisiana is generally called a civil law state, its code is imbued with some common-law features, making it a hybrid of the two traditions. The state's constitution, administrative and criminal law, civil and criminal procedure, and rules of evidence all contain elements derived from common-law principles. As a result, Louisiana judges operate under administrative rules that differ from those found in other civil law jurisdictions. For example, whereas European judges actively elicit the facts in a controversy and seldom use a JURY, Louisiana judges operate more like their common-law colleagues, assuming the role of neutral and passive fact finder or arbiter, and leaving the final decision to a jury. Oral argument is generally absent in a pure civil law proceeding, whereas Louisiana's procedural and evidentiary rules allow oral presentations, resulting in TRIALS that are closer to those found in a common-law court. Finally, European courts allow almost unlimited DISCOVERY by the ACCUSED in a lawsuit, whereas Louisiana's procedural and evidentiary rules place certain restrictions on such discovery.

Civil law systems differ from common-law systems in another important way: in a common-law JURISDICTION, APPELLATE COURTS, in most instances, may review only findings of law. However, civil law appellate courts may review findings of fact as well as findings of law. This allows a Louisiana appellate court to declare a jury's decision erroneous, impose its own findings of fact, and possibly even reduce a damage award. This is a significant consideration for a plaintiff who has a choice of whether to file suit in Louisiana or in another state (to bring suit in a particular state, a plaintiff must demonstrate some relationship between that state and the lawsuit). Since a jury award could be overturned on appeal, the plaintiff with a strong case may wish to file in a common-law state. On the other hand, if the plaintiff is uncertain of success at the trial level, the possibility of broader review on appeal may make Louisiana the better choice. As a practical matter, such dilemmas arise infrequently, and most often involve complex multistate litigation concerning CORPORATIONS. See also NAPOLEONIC CODE; ROMAN LAW.

**CIVIL PROCEDURE** 📖 The methods, procedures, and practices used in civil cases. 📖

The judicial system is essentially divided into two types of cases: civil and criminal. A study of civil procedure is a study of the procedures that apply in cases that are not criminal.

Generally, criminal trials are used by the government to protect and provide relief to the general public by attempting to punish an individual. Civil trials can be used by anyone to enforce, redress, or protect their legal rights

through court orders and monetary awards. The two types of trials are very different in character and thus have separate procedural rules and practices.

PROCEDURAL LAW is distinguished from SUBSTANTIVE LAW, which creates, defines, and regulates the rights and duties of individuals. Federal and state constitutions, statutes, and judicial decisions form the basis for substantive civil law on matters such as CONTRACTS, TORTS, and PROBATE. Procedural law prescribes the methods by which individuals may enforce substantive laws. The basic concern of procedural law is the fair, orderly, efficient, and predictable application of substantive laws. Procedural guidance can be found in court-approved rules, in statutes, and in judicial decisions.

**Federal Rules of Civil Procedure**
State and FEDERAL COURTS maintain separate procedural rules. On the federal level, the Federal Rules of Civil Procedure govern the process of civil litigation in U.S. DISTRICT COURTS, which are trial courts. At least one U.S. district court operates in each state. Each district court also exists within one of thirteen federal CIRCUITS. Any APPEALS of decisions by a U.S. district court are heard by the court of appeals for the federal circuit in which the district court sits. Appeals of decisions by a U.S. court of appeals may be heard by the SUPREME COURT OF THE UNITED STATES.

The Supreme Court and the courts of appeals use procedures contained in the Federal Rules of Appellate Procedure and in the U.S. Supreme Court Rules. As reviewing courts, they are concerned with the district courts' application of the Federal Rules of Civil Procedure.

The Federal Rules of Civil Procedure are now contained in title 28 of the U.S. Code. Before 1938, the procedural rules in U.S. district courts varied from circuit to circuit. The rules in the western United States, for example, were generally less complex than those in the East. To add to the confusion, federal civil cases were designated either AT LAW, which essentially meant that the RELIEF sought was monetary, or EQUITABLE, which meant that the court was asked to act on principles of fairness and, generally, to award nonmonetary relief. The distinction was important because the procedural rules for a case at law differed from those for an EQUITY suit.

In response to widespread criticism of procedural complexity, the U.S. Congress in 1934 passed the Federal Rules Enabling Act (28 U.S.C.A. §§ 2071, 2072). This act conferred on the Supreme Court the power to make new rules for federal courts. In 1938, new rules were recommended by an advisory committee appointed by the Supreme Court and approved by Congress. The new rules featured simplified PLEADING requirements, comprehensive DISCOVERY procedures, a PRETRIAL CONFERENCE to narrow the scope of a TRIAL and define issues, and broad provisions for joining parties and claims to a lawsuit. In addition, legal and equitable claims were merged to proceed with the same set of rules.

The first set of uniform federal rules was not perfect. As time passed, it became clear that continuous oversight of the rules was necessary to ensure their improvement. In 1958, Congress created the JUDICIAL CONFERENCE OF THE UNITED STATES, a freestanding body to study federal civil procedure and propose amendments to the Supreme Court. The Judicial Conference, in turn, created the ongoing Committee on Rules of Practice and Procedure to help fashion the best procedural rules for federal courts. Amendments to the Federal Rules of Civil Procedure now occur on a regular basis.

State courts generally follow the same judicial hierarchy as federal courts. In all states, a party to a civil suit is entitled to at least one review of a trial court decision. In some states, a party may be entitled to two appeals: one in a court of appeals, and one in the state supreme court.

Procedural rules in state courts are similar to the federal rules. Indeed, many states base their procedural rules on the federal rules. Thus, there is a large measure of uniformity among the states, and among state and federal courts.

**Litigation Process** A CIVIL ACTION is commenced with the filing of a COMPLAINT. The PLAINTIFF must file the complaint with the court, and must give a SUMMONS to the court and a copy of the complaint to the DEFENDANT. The complaint must set forth the claims and the legal bases for them.

Before filing the complaint, the plaintiff must decide where to file it. As a general rule, cases are filed in state, not federal, courts. The question of whether a particular court has authority over a certain matter and certain parties is one of JURISDICTION. Federal courts generally have jurisdiction over civil actions in three situations. The most common is when the parties to the suit live in different states and the amount of money in controversy exceeds $50,000. The second instance is when a claim is specifically authorized by federal statute. The third is when a claim is made by or against the federal government or its agents.

The jurisdiction of state courts depends on a number of variables. Plaintiffs filing in state court generally prefer to file in their home state. However, this may be difficult in a case where the defendant lives in another state and the injury occurred outside the plaintiff's home state. A court in the plaintiff's home state can gain jurisdiction over an out-of-state defendant in several ways. For example, if the defendant enters the plaintiff's home state, the plaintiff may serve the defendant there and force the defendant to appear there for trial. Or the plaintiff can show the court that the defendant has some minimal amount of contact with the plaintiff's home state. Or the plaintiff can show that the defendant has property in the plaintiff's home state and the property is the subject matter of the dispute.

In addition to jurisdiction, the plaintiff must also consider venue. Venue is the term describing the particular county, or geographical area, in which a court with jurisdiction may hear and determine a case. The plaintiff makes a decision on venue after deciding whether to file suit in state or federal court. For example, if a plaintiff decides to file suit in state court, and has settled on a particular state, the plaintiff must decide in which county to file suit. The overriding consideration in determining the best venue in a case is the convenience to the parties.

Once the plaintiff determines where to file the complaint, the plaintiff must prepare pleadings and MOTIONS. Pleadings are the plaintiff's initial ALLEGATIONS and the defendant's responses to those allegations. Motions are requests made by the parties for a specific order by the court. Courts usually schedule pretrial conferences to review and rule on pleadings and motions, sort out preliminary issues, and prepare a case for trial.

Before a case can proceed, the court must determine whether the plaintiff has STANDING to bring the suit. In order to hear the suit the court must find that the plaintiff has some legally protectible, tangible interest in the outcome of the litigation. Other plaintiffs may join the original plaintiff if they seek the same relief concerning the same transaction or event and the complaints involve a common question of law or fact. This is called JOINDER.

In some cases, joinder may be compulsory. Under Rule 19, a person must be joined if (1) complete relief cannot be accorded to the parties without joining the missing person or (2) the missing person claims an interest in the action, and absence from the suit will impair that person's ability to protect the interest, or absence would subject the parties to multiple or inconsistent obligations regarding the matter of the suit. Both plaintiffs and defendants may be ordered by the court to join a suit.

The court must also determine before trial that the issues in the case are JUSTICIABLE. This means that the case must be ready and proper for a judicial determination. Courts do not hear hypothetical, abstract, or political cases. For example, a person may not file a suit against a legislator over the legislator's vote on a matter before the legislature. Nor may a person file a suit against another unless she can demonstrate that the other has caused her some injury or harm.

If the complaint does not state a claim upon which judicial relief can be granted, the defendant may move for SUMMARY JUDGMENT. This is a request that the court issue a final judgment on the case in favor of the defendant. The plaintiff also may submit a motion for summary judgment, either soon after filing the complaint or after the defendant submits a summary judgment motion. When deciding a motion for summary judgment, the court must consider the pleadings in the light most favorable to the party opposing the motion.

The parties to a lawsuit prepare their case based on information gained through the process of discovery. Discovery consists of a variety of methods including DEPOSITIONS and INTERROGATORIES. A deposition is an interview of a party or witness conducted by a lawyer. Usually, this interview is conducted orally with a lawyer for the other side present and able to participate; sometimes, it is conducted using written questions. Information about a party may be secured through written interrogatories or requests to produce documents or things. These requests may be served only upon a party. A request for production may seek any item within a party's control.

Procedural rules on depositions and other forms of discovery address a number of concerns, including how a deposition is conducted, the permissible scope of a deposition, who may conduct a deposition, when a party may object to a question at a deposition, when a party may object to an interrogatory, when a party may enter upon land for inspection, when a party may make physical or mental inspections of another party, and what happens when a party does not cooperate with a court order directing compliance with discovery.

If the parties cannot reach a settlement, the case will go to trial. Just before trial, the plaintiff must decide whether to ask for a jury trial.

Not all civil cases may be tried before a JURY. The right to a jury trial is usually tied to the amount of money at issue: if the case concerns less than a certain amount, such as $10,000, the case may be limited to trial before a judge. In federal court, however, all parties have the right to a jury trial. If a plaintiff or defendant is granted a jury trial, both sides will have the opportunity to screen potential jurors for BIAS.

At trial, each side is given the opportunity to make an opening statement to the fact finder, be it judge or jury. The plaintiff then presents EVIDENCE. Evidence can include TESTIMONY from WITNESSES and tangible items presented through witnesses. When the plaintiff has presented her or his case, the defendant has the option of presenting evidence. After the defendant presents evidence, the parties make CLOSING ARGUMENTS to the fact finder.

After final arguments, the judge must determine what laws apply to the case. Both parties submit proposed INSTRUCTIONS to the judge. If the case is tried before a jury, the judge must read instructions to the jury. If the case is tried before a judge, the judge will give the parties an opportunity to argue that certain favorable law controls the case.

At this point, either party may move the court for a DIRECTED VERDICT. This is a request that the court decide in the party's favor before deliberating on the case or sending it to the jury. A directed verdict may be granted only if no substantial evidence supports a FINDING in the opposing party's favor and the opposing party bears the burden of producing evidence on the issue. If the judge does not issue a directed verdict, the fact finder retires to deliberate the case in secret.

The final phase of the trial is JUDGMENT. The court has the option of requesting different types of VERDICTS. If it requests a GENERAL VERDICT, it is looking for a flat finding of LIABILITY or no liability. If it requests a special verdict, it expects the fact finder to answer specific factual questions, and then the judge determines the legal consequences of the answers.

In a complex jury trial, the court may request that the jury deliver a general verdict along with answers to special interrogatories. This form of verdict allows the judge to ensure that the jury delivers the correct verdict based on its factual findings.

The number of jurors on a civil jury can be as few as five or as many as twelve, depending on the jurisdiction. In most jurisdictions, including federal courts, the jury's decision must be unanimous, but some jurisdictions allow a verdict with something less than unanimity, such as an agreement among nine of twelve jurors.

If the defendant has failed to appear for the proceedings, judgment will be entered for the plaintiff. However, in this situation, the defendant may contest the judgment when the plaintiff attempts to collect on it, by filing a separate suit and challenging the jurisdiction of the court.

When the verdict is delivered, the losing party may seek a reversal of the judgment. Sometimes a verdict is unsatisfactory to both parties, and both parties seek a reversal; this might happen, for example, when one party wins the lawsuit but receives a small DAMAGES award. Reversal of a verdict may be pursued through a motion for JUDGMENT NOTWITHSTANDING THE VERDICT, or *JNOV* (for judgment *non obstante veredicto*, which is Latin for "notwithstanding the verdict"). The standard for this order is the same as that for a directed verdict. A reversal of judgment usually occurs only in jury trials; judges generally are not inclined to reverse their own decisions.

A court may grant a new trial if procedural problems at trial prejudiced a party or worked against the interests of a party, and affected the verdict. Such problems include juror misconduct and unfair withholding of evidence by an opposing party. A new trial may also be granted if the damages authorized by the jury were excessive or inadequate. In extreme cases, a new trial may be granted if newly discovered evidence comes to light after the case is given to the jury.

All jurisdictions give parties to a civil suit the right to at least one appeal. A decision may be REVERSED if an error at trial prejudiced the APPELLANT (the party bringing the appeal). Appeals courts generally do not reverse verdicts based on the WEIGHT OF EVIDENCE. Instead, they limit their review of cases to MISTAKES OF LAW. This is a nebulous concept, but generally it refers to mistakes relating to procedural and constitutional violations.

Sometimes a party may appeal a court order or decision to a higher court during trial. Known as an INTERLOCUTORY appeal, this option is limited. A party may appeal during trial if the party stands to suffer irreparable harm if the order or decision is not immediately reviewed. A party may also appeal an order or decision during trial if it affects a matter that is collateral to, or separate from, the litigation.

Some parties come to court seeking provisional remedies, which are forms of temporary relief available in urgent situations. TEMPORARY RESTRAINING ORDERS and INJUNCTIONS are court orders that direct a party to perform a certain act or refrain from performing a certain act. For example, if a party wants to bring suit to prevent the imminent demolition of what he believes is a historic building, he may petition the court for a temporary restraining order to prevent demolition while the suit is filed. A temporary restraining order will last up to ten days. When the ten days have expired, the litigant may seek either renewal of the temporary restraining order or a PRELIMINARY INJUNCTION.

A preliminary injunction, if granted, requires a party to perform an act or refrain from performing an act until the end of trial. A permanent injunction is a court order that requires a defendant to perform an act or refrain from performing an act permanently.

After a judgment is reached, the winning party must enforce it. If the losing party does not voluntarily relinquish the disputed property or pay the monetary judgment, the winning party may seize and sell the property of the losing party. This is accomplished by filing the judgment in the county where the property is located and proceeding to obtain ownership of the property through another civil suit. If the losing party has no money, the winning party may seek to GARNISH a portion of the losing party's wages. If the losing party does not work and has no property, the winning party may be unable to collect on the judgment.

**Civil Justice Act of 1990** Civil cases often are expensive and time-consuming. In August 1990, the U.S. Congress passed the Civil Justice Act of 1990 to help remedy these problems (28 U.S.C.A. §§ 471–482). The U.S. Senate explained that the Civil Justice Act was "to promote for all citizens, rich or poor, individual or corporation, plaintiff or defendant, the just, speedy and inexpensive resolution of civil disputes in our Nation's federal courts" (S. Rep. No. 101-416, 101 Cong., 2d Sess., at 1 [Aug. 3, 1990]). The act ordered each U.S. district court to implement a Civil Justice Expense and Delay Reduction Plan under the direction of an advisory group comprising "those who must live with the civil justice system on a regular basis" (S. Rep. No. 101-416, at 414 [quoting statement of Senate Judiciary Committee chairman Biden, *Cong. Rec.* S416 (Jan. 25, 1990)]).

The advisory groups in each federal district were appointed by the chief judge of the federal circuit, and they generally consisted of judges, clerks, and law professors. These experts prepared a report on methods for reducing expense and delay in civil litigation. The report was then considered by the federal circuit court judges in forming the Civil Justice Expense and Delay Reduction Plan.

One major challenge that faced the advisory groups was how to get courts to best use modern technology. Since passage of the act, many federal circuits have authorized the filing of court documents by facsimile and other electronic means, which may include the use of computers.

Federal courts have also acted to improve scheduling. The U.S. District Court for the District of New Hampshire, for example, created four separate categories for scheduling civil cases: administrative, expedited ("rocket docket"), standard, and complex. The determination of a case's category is made at the preliminary pretrial conference. Most cases fall into the standard category, which means a trial will be held within one year of the preliminary pretrial conference. A rocket docket case can be tried within six months of the preliminary pretrial conference, if the parties agree and the trial will last no more than five days. Administrative and complex cases are scheduled with special attention. By identifying the length and complexity of a case at the preliminary pretrial conference, federal circuit courts are able to minimize unnecessary delays.

In all jurisdictions, preliminary pretrial conferences have become important in civil litigation. The court, after consulting the parties, schedules and holds this conference within a certain amount of time after the filing of the complaint. At this conference, the court attempts to resolve all the issues that can be resolved outside of trial. These issues include the control and scheduling of discovery, the admissibility of evidence, the possibility of separate trials, and orders limiting the length of the trial presentation. To reach, or decide, substantive issues more quickly, many federal courts ask litigants to file any motions for summary judgment or motions to dismiss before the preliminary pretrial conference.

# MILESTONES IN THE LAW

## BROWN V. BOARD OF EDUCATION OF TOPEKA, KANSAS

### ISSUE

Civil rights

### MATERIALS

Opinion of U.S. District Court, D. Kansas, August 3, 1951
Initial Briefs to the Supreme Court
Memorandum Decision of the Supreme Court, June 8, 1953
Briefs for the Parties on Reargument
Opinion of the Supreme Court, May 17, 1954
Briefs to the Court on Further Reargument
Opinion of the Supreme Court, May 31, 1955

### HOW TO USE
### MILESTONES IN THE LAW

In the materials that follow, the reader is invited to review the judicial opinions and the briefs of the parties in this milestone in U.S. law. As you read this section, you may wish to consider the following questions:

- How did the appellant's description of the issues before the Court, or questions presented, differ from the appellee's descriptions?
- How did the parties differ in describing the history relevant to this case?
- What aspects of the conflict presented in *Brown* make it difficult for a court (as opposed to a legislature) to resolve?
- Why might *Brown* apply, or not apply, to discrimination based on a criterion other than race?

### THIS CASE IN HISTORY

*Brown versus Board of Education of Topeka, Kansas*, or *Brown v. Board* as it is commonly known, is one of the most significant civil rights decisions of the twentieth century. With this decision, the Supreme Court declared that the practice of segregating children into separate schools based on race was unconstitutional under the Equal Protection Clause of the Fourteenth Amendment. *Brown* overruled the Court's prior decision in *Plessy v. Ferguson*, which had upheld segregation of the races so long as the facilities provided to each race were separate but equal. As the number of opinions* and briefs* in *Brown* demonstrate, the Court struggled with the issues presented in the case. The Court even took the extraordinary step of asking the parties for additional argument—twice—on the power and the ability of the Court to resolve the issues before it. Even today, the existence of schools with disproportionate numbers of students of one race or another continues to pose difficulties for courts and legislatures under *Brown*.

---

* The Supreme Court granted review to several similar cases from different states, which it consolidated with the *Brown* case for review. In the interest of space, the district court opinions from the other states' cases are omitted here. Also omitted are the opinion of the Supreme Court consolidating the cases and the briefs of the state of Kansas, which was asked by the Court to present its position on the issues.

**BROWN et al. v. BOARD OF EDUCATION OF TOPEKA, SHAWNEE COUNTY, KANSAS et al.**

**Civ. No. T–316.**

United States District Court,
D. Kansas.

Aug. 3, 1951.

Action by Oliver Brown and others against the Board of Education of Topeka, Shawnee County, Kansas, and others for a judgment declaring unconstitutional a state statute authorizing cities of the first class to maintain separate schools for white and colored children in the grades below high school and to enjoin enforcement of the statute. The United States District Court, Huxman, Circuit Judge, held that the statute and the maintenance thereunder of a segregated system of schools for the first six grades do not violate constitutional guarantee of due process of law in absence of discrimination in the maintenance of the segregated schools.

Judgment for defendants.

**1. Constitutional law ⬖220**

Where physical facilities, curricula, courses of study, qualifications and quality of teachers and other educational facilities provided in separate elementary schools for colored and white children were comparable, there was no willful, intentional or substantial discrimination in such respects between colored and white schools, though absolute equality in such respects was impossible of attainment and colored children were required to travel much greater distances to school than white children but, unlike white children, were transported to and from school free of charge. G.S.1949, 72–1724; U.S.C.A.Const. Amend. 14.

**2. Constitutional law ⬖253**
**Schools and school districts ⬖10**

State statute authorizing cities of the first class to maintain separate schools for white and colored children in the grades below high school and the maintenance thereunder of a segregated system of elementary schools does not violate the constitutional guarantee of due process of law, in absence of discrimination between colored and white schools in the matter of physical facilities, curricula, courses of study, qualifications and quality of teachers,

and other educational facilities. G.S.1949, 72–1724; U.S.C.A.Const. Amend. 14.

———◆———

John Scott and Charles Scott, Topeka, Kan., Robert L. Carter, New York City, Jack Greenberg, New York City, and Charles Bledsoe, Topeka, Kan., for plaintiffs.

George Brewster and Lester Goodell, Topeka, Kan., for defendants.

Before HUXMAN, Circuit Judge, MELLOTT, Chief Judge, and HILL, District Judge.

HUXMAN, Circuit Judge.

Chapter 72–1724 of the General Statutes of Kansas, 1949, relating to public schools in cities of the first class, so far as material, authorizes such cities to organize and maintain separate schools for the education of white and colored children in the grades below the high school grades. Pursuant to this authority, the City of Topeka, Kansas, a city of the first class, has established and maintains a segregated system of schools for the first six grades. It has established and maintains in the Topeka School District eighteen schools for white students and four schools for colored students.

The adult plaintiffs instituted this action for themselves, their minor children plaintiffs, and all other persons similarly situated for an interlocutory injunction, a permanent injunction, restraining the enforcement, operation and execution of the state statute and the segregation instituted thereunder by the school authorities of the City of Topeka and for a declaratory judgment declaring unconstitutional the state statute and the segregation set up thereunder by the school authorities of the City of Topeka.

As against the school district of Topeka they contend that the opportunities provided for the infant plaintiffs in the separate all Negro schools are inferior to those provided white children in the all white schools; that the respects in which these opportunities are inferior include the physical facilities, curricula, teaching resources, student personnel services as well as all other services. As against both the state and the school district, they contend that apart from all other factors segregation in itself constitutes an inferiority in educational opportunities offered to Negroes and that all of this is in violation of due process guaranteed them by the Fourteenth Amendment to the United States Constitution. In their answer both the state and the school district defend the constitutionality of the state law and in addition the school district defends the segregation in its schools instituted thereunder.

[1] We have found as a fact that the physical facilities, the curricula, courses of study, qualification of and quality of teachers, as well as other educational facilities in the two sets of schools are comparable. It is obvious that absolute equality of physical facilities is impossible of attainment in buildings that are erected at different times. So also absolute equality of subjects taught is impossible of maintenance when teachers are permitted to select books of their own choosing to use in teaching in addition to the prescribed courses of study. It is without dispute that the prescribed courses of study are identical in all of the Topeka schools and that there is no discrimination in this respect. It is also clear in the record that the educational qualifications of the teachers in the colored schools are equal to those in the white schools and that in all other respects the educational facilities and services are comparable. It is obvious from the fact that there are only four colored schools as against eighteen white schools in the Topeka School District, that colored children in many instances are required to travel much greater distances than they would be required to travel could they attend a white school, and are required to travel much greater distances than white children are required to travel. The evidence, however, establishes that the school district transports colored children to and from school free of charge. No such service is furnished to white children. We conclude that in the maintenance and operation of the schools there is no willful, intentional or substantial discrimination in the matters referred to above between the colored and white schools. In fact, while plaintiffs' attorneys have not abandoned this contention, they did not give it great emphasis in their presentation before the court. They relied primarily upon the contention that segregation in and of itself without more violates their rights guaranteed by the Fourteenth Amendment.

This contention poses a question not free from difficulty. As a subordinate court in the federal judicial system, we seek the answer to this constitutional question in the decisions of the Supreme Court when it has spoken on the subject and do not substitute our own views for the declared law by the Supreme Court. The difficult question as always is to analyze the decisions and seek to ascertain the trend as revealed by the later decisions.

There are a great number of cases, both federal and state, that have dealt with the many phases of segregation. Since the question involves a construction and interpretation of the federal Constitution and the pronouncements of the Supreme Court, we will consider only those cases by the Supreme Court with respect to segregation in the schools. In the early case of Plessy v. Ferguson, 163 U.S. 537, 16 S.Ct. 1138, 1140, 41 L.Ed. 256, the Supreme Court said: "The object of the amendment was undoubtedly to enforce the absolute equality of the two races before the law, but, in the nature of things, it could not have been intended to abolish distinctions based upon color, or to enforce social, as distinguished from political equality, or a commingling of the two races upon terms unsatisfactory to either. Laws permitting, and even requiring, their separation, in places where they are liable to be brought into contact, do not necessarily imply the inferiority of either race to the other, and have been generally, if not universally, recognized as within the competency of the state legislatures in the exercise of their police power. The most common instance of this is connected with the establishment of separate schools for white and colored children, which has been held to be a valid exercise of the legislative power even by courts of states where the political rights of the colored race have been longest and most earnestly enforced."

## BROWN v. BOARD OF EDUCATION OF TOPEKA    799
### Cite as 98 F.Supp. 797

It is true as contended by plaintiffs that the Plessy case involved transportation and that the above quoted statement relating to schools was not essential to the decision of the question before the court and was therefore somewhat in the nature of dicta. But that the statement is considered more than dicta is evidenced by the treatment accorded it by those seeking to strike down segregation as well as by statements in subsequent decisions of the Supreme Court. On numerous occasions the Supreme Court has been asked to overrule the Plessy case. This the Supreme Court has refused to do, on the sole ground that a decision of the question was not necessary to a disposal of the controversy presented. In the late case of Sweatt v. Painter, 339 U.S. 629, 70 S.Ct. 848, 851, 94 L.Ed. 1114, the Supreme Court again refused to review the Plessy case. The Court said: "Nor need we reach petitioner's contention that Plessy v. Ferguson should be reexamined in the light of contemporary knowledge respecting the purposes of the Fourteenth Amendment and the effects of racial segregation."

Gong Lum v. Rice, 275 U.S. 78, 48 S.Ct. 91, 93, 72 L.Ed. 172, was a grade school segregation case. It involved the segregation law of Mississippi. Gong Lum was a Chinese child and, because of color, was required to attend the separate schools provided for colored children. The opinion of the court assumes that the educational facilities in the colored schools were adequate and equal to those of the white schools. Thus the court said: "The question here is whether a Chinese citizen of the United States is denied equal protection of the laws when he is classed among the colored races and furnished facilities for education equal to that offered to all, whether white, brown, yellow, or black." In addition to numerous state decisions on the subject, the Supreme Court in support of its conclusions cited Plessy v. Ferguson, supra. The Court also pointed out that the question was the same no matter what the color of the class that was required to attend separate schools.

Thus the Court said: "Most of the cases cited arose, it is true, over the establishment of separate schools as between white pupils and black pupils; but we cannot think that the question is any different, or that any different result can be reached, assuming the cases above cited to be rightly decided, where the issue is as between white pupils and the pupils of the yellow races." The court held that the question of segregation was within the discretion of the state in regulating its public schools and did not conflict with the Fourteenth Amendment.

It is vigorously argued and not without some basis therefor that the later decisions of the Supreme Court in McLaurin v. Oklahoma, 339 U.S. 637, 70 S.Ct. 851, 94 L.Ed. 1149, and Sweatt v. Painter, 339 U.S. 629, 70 S.Ct. 848, 94 L.Ed. 1114, show a trend away from the Plessy and Lum cases. McLaurin v. Oklahoma arose under the segregation laws of Oklahoma. McLaurin, a colored student, applied for admission to the University of Oklahoma in order to pursue studies leading to a doctorate degree in education. He was denied admission solely because he was a Negro. After litigation in the courts, which need not be reviewed herein, the legislature amended the statute permitting the admission of colored students to institutions of higher learning attended by white students, but providing that such instruction should be given on a segregated basis; that the instruction be given in separate class rooms or at separate times. In compliance with this statute McLaurin was admitted to the university but was required to sit at a separate desk in the ante room adjoining the class room; to sit at a designated desk on the mezzanine floor of the library and to sit at a designated table and eat at a different time from the other students in the school cafeteria. These restrictions were held to violate his rights under the federal Constitution. The Supreme Court held that such treatment handicapped the student in his pursuit of effective graduate instruction.[1]

1. The court said: "Our society grows increasingly complex, and our need for trained leaders increases correspondingly. Appellant's case represents, perhaps, the epitome of that need, for he is attempting to obtain an advanced degree in education, to become, by definition, a leader and trainer of others. Those who will come

In Sweatt v. Painter, 339 U.S. 629, 70 S.Ct. 848, 850, 94 L.Ed. 1114, petitioner, a colored student, filed an application for admission to the University of Texas Law School. His application was rejected solely on the ground that he was a Negro. In its opinion the Supreme Court stressed the educational benefits from commingling with white students. The court concluded by stating: "we cannot conclude that the education offered petitioner [in a separate school] is substantially equal to that which he would receive if admitted to the University of Texas Law School." If segregation within a school as in the McLaurin case is a denial of due process, it is difficult to see why segregation in separate schools would not result in the same denial. Or if the denial of the right to commingle with the majority group in higher institutions of learning as in the Sweatt case and gain the educational advantages resulting therefrom, is lack of due process, it is difficult to see why such denial would not result in the same lack of due process if practiced in the lower grades.

It must however be remembered that in both of these cases the Supreme Court made it clear that it was confining itself to answering the one specific question, namely: "To what extent does the Equal Protection Clause * * * limit the power of a state to distinguish between students of different races in professional and graduate education in a state university?", and that the Supreme Court refused to review the Plessy case because that question was not essential to a decision of the controversy in the case.

[2] We are accordingly of the view that the Plessy and Lum cases, supra, have not been overruled and that they still pres-

ently are authority for the maintenance of a segregated school system in the lower grades.

The prayer for relief will be denied and judgment will be entered for defendants for costs.

---

under his guidance and influence must be directly affected by the education he receives. Their own education and development will necessarily suffer to the extent that his training is unequal to that of his classmates. State-imposed restrictions which produce such inequalities cannot be sustained.

"It may be argued that appellant will be in no better position when these restrictions are removed, for he may still be set apart by his fellow students. This

we think irrelevant. There is a vast difference—a Constitutional difference—between restrictions imposed by the state which prohibit the intellectual commingling of students, and the refusal of individuals to commingle where the state presents no such bar. * * * having been admitted to a state-supported graduate school, (he), must receive the same treatment at the hands of the state as students of other races." [339 U.S. 637, 70 S.Ct. 853.]

# IN THE
# SUPREME COURT OF THE UNITED STATES
## OCTOBER TERM, 1952

### No. 8

**OLIVER BROWN, MRS. RICHARD LAWTON, MRS. SADIE EMMANUEL, ET AL.,** APPELLANTS,

v.

**BOARD OF EDUCATION OF TOPEKA, SHAWNEE COUNTY, KANSAS, ET AL.**

## APPEAL FROM THE UNITED STATES DISTRICT COURT FOR THE DISTRICT OF KANSAS

## BRIEF FOR APPELLANTS

WILLIAM T. COLEMAN, JR.,
JACK GREENBERG,
GEORGE E. C. HAYES,
GEORGE M. JOHNSON,
WILLIAM R. MING, JR.,
CONSTANCE BAKER MOTLEY,
JAMES M. NABRIT, JR.,
FRANK D. REEVES,

JOHN SCOTT,
JACK B. WEINSTEIN,
*of Counsel.*

ROBERT L. CARTER,
THURGOOD MARSHALL,
SPOTTSWOOD W. ROBINSON, III,
CHARLES S. SCOTT,
*Counsel for Appellants.*

# TABLE OF CONTENTS

# In the
# Supreme Court of the
# United States
# October Term, 1952
# No. 8

Oliver Brown, Mrs. Richard Lawton,
Mrs. Sadie Emmanuel, et al., Appellants,

vs.

Board of Education of Topeka,
Shawnee County, Kansas, et al.,

Appellee

## Appeal from the United
## States District Court for the
## District of Kansas

## Brief for Appellants

### OPINION BELOW

The opinion of the statutory three-judge-District Court for the District of Kansas (R. 238-244) is reported at 98 F. Supp. 797.

### JURISDICTION

The judgment of the court below was entered on August 3, 1951 (R. 247). On October 1, 1951, appellants filed a petition for appeal (R. 248), and an order allowing the appeal was entered (R. 250). Probable jurisdiction was noted on June 9, 1952 (R. 254). Jurisdiction of this Court rests on Title 28, United States Code, §§ 1253 and 2201(b).

### QUESTIONS PRESENTED

**1.** Whether the State of Kansas has power to enforce a state statute pursuant to which racially segregated public elementary schools are maintained.

**2.** Whether the finding of the court below—that racial segregation in public elementary schools has the detrimental effect of retarding the mental and educational development of colored children and connotes governmental acceptance of the conception of racial inferiority—compels the conclusion that appellants here are deprived of their rights to share equally in educational opportunities in violation of the equal protection clause of the Fourteenth Amendment.

### THE LAW OF KANSAS AND THE STATUTE INVOLVED

All boards of education, superintendents of schools and school districts in the state are prohibited from using race as a factor in affording educational opportunities in the public schools within their respective jurisdictions unless expressly empowered to do so by statute. *Knox* v. *Board of Education*, 54 K. 152, 25 P. 616 (1891); *Cartwright* v. *Board of Education*, 73 K. 32, 84 P. 382 (1906); *Rowles* v. *Board of Education*, 76 K. 361, 91 P. 88 (1907); *Woolridge, et al.* v. *Board of Education*, 98 K. 397, 157 P. 1184 (1916); *Thurman-Watts* v. *Board of Education*, 115 K. 328, 222 P. 123 (1924); *Webb* v. *School District*, 167 K. 395, 206 P. 2d 1066 (1949).

Segregated elementary schools in cities of the first class are maintained solely pursuant to authority of Chapter 72-1724 of the General Statutes of Kansas, 1949, which reads as follows:

> "Powers of board; separate schools for white and colored children; manual training. The board of education shall have power to elect their own officers, make all necessary rules for the government of the schools of such city under its charge and control and of the board, subject to the provisions of this act and the laws of this state; to organize and maintain separate schools for the education of white and colored children, including the high schools in Kansas City, Kans.; no discrimination on account of color shall be made in high schools except as provided herein; to exercise the sole control over the public schools and school property of such city; and shall have the power to establish a high school or high schools in connection with manual training and instruction or otherwise, and to maintain the same as a part of the public-school system of said city. (G. S. 1868, Ch. 18, § 75; L. 1879, Ch. 81, § 1; L. 1905, Ch. 414, § 1; Feb. 28; R. S. 1923, § 72-1724.)"

### STATEMENT OF THE CASE

Appellants are of Negro origin and are citizens of the United States and of the State of Kansas (R. 3-4). Infant appellants are children eligible to attend and are now attending elementary schools in Topeka, Kansas, a city of the first class within the meaning of Chapter 72-1724, General Statutes of Kansas, 1949, hereinafter referred to as the statute. Adult appellants are parents of minor appellants and are required by law to send their respective children to public schools designated by appellees (R. 3-4). Appellees are state officers empowered by state law to maintain and operate the public schools of Topeka, Kansas.

For elementary school purposes, the City of Topeka is divided into 18 geographical divisions designated as territories (R. 24). In each of these territories one elementary school services white children exclusively (R. 24). In addition, four schools are maintained for the use of Negro children exclusively (R. 11, 12). These racial distinctions are enforced pursuant to the statute. In accordance with the terms of the statute there is no segregation of Negro and white children in junior and senior high schools (R. 12).

On March 22, 1951, appellants instituted the instant action seeking to restrain the enforcement, operation and execution of the statute on the ground that it deprived them of equal educational opportunities within the meaning of the Fourteenth Amendment (R. 2-7). In their answer, appellees admitted that they acted pursuant to the statute, and that infant appellants were not eligible to attend any of the 18 white elementary schools solely because of their race and color (R. 12). The Attorney General of the State of Kansas filed a separate answer for the specific purpose of defending the constitutional validity of the statute in question (R. 14).

Thereupon, the court below was convened in accordance with Title 28, United States Code, § 2284. On June 25-26, a trial on the merits took place (R. 63 *et seq.*). On August 3, 1951, the court below filed its opinion (R. 238-244), its findings of fact (R. 244-246), and conclusions of law (R. 246-247), and entered a final judgment and decree in appellees' favor denying the injunctive relief sought (R. 247).

## SPECIFICATIONS OF ERROR

The District Court erred:

**1.** In refusing to grant appellants' application for a permanent injunction to restrain appellees from acting pursuant to the statute under which they are maintaining separate public elementary schools for Negro children solely because of their race and color.

**2.** In refusing to hold that the State of Kansas is without authority to promulgate the statute because it enforces a classification based upon race and color which is violative of the Constitution of the United States.

**3.** In refusing to enter judgment in favor of appellants after finding that enforced attendance at racially segregated elementary schools was detrimental and deprived them of educational opportunities equal to those available to white children.

## SUMMARY OF ARGUMENT

The Fourteenth Amendment precludes a state from imposing distinctions or classifications based upon race and color alone. The State of Kansas has no power thereunder to use race as a factor in affording educational opportunities to its citizens.

Racial segregation in public schools reduces the benefits of public education to one group

solely on the basis of race and color and is a constitutionally proscribed distinction. Even assuming that the segregated schools attended by appellants are not inferior to other elementary schools in Topeka with respect to physical facilities, instruction and courses of study, unconstitutional inequality inheres in the retardation of intellectual development and distortion of personality which Negro children suffer as a result of enforced isolation in school from the general public school population. Such injury and inequality are established as facts on this appeal by the uncontested findings of the District Court.

The District Court reasoned that it could not rectify the inequality that it had found because of this Court's decisions in *Plessy v. Ferguson*, 163 U.S. 537 and *Gong Lum v. Rice*, 275 U.S. 78. This Court has already decided that the *Plessy* case is not in point. Reliance upon *Gong Lum v. Rice* is mistaken since the basic assumption of that case is the existence of equality while no such assumption can be made here in the face of the established facts. Moreover, more recent decisions of this Court, most notably *Sweatt v. Painter*, 339 U.S. 629 and *McLaurin v. Board of Regents*, 339 U.S. 637, clearly show that such hurtful consequences of segregated schools as appear here constitute a denial of equal educational opportunities in violation of the Fourteenth Amendment. Therefore, the court below erred in denying the relief prayed by appellants.

## ARGUMENT

### I. The State of Kansas in affording opportunities for elementary education to its citizens has no power under the Constitution of the United States to impose racial restrictions and distinctions

While the State of Kansas has undoubted power to confer benefits or impose disabilities upon selected groups of citizens in the normal execution of governmental functions, it must conform to constitutional standards in the exercise of this authority. These standards may be generally characterized as a requirement that the state's action be reasonable. Reasonableness in a constitutional sense is determined by examining the action of the state to discover whether the distinctions or restrictions in issue are in fact based upon real differences pertinent to a lawful legislative objective. *Bain Peanut Co. v. Pinson*, 282 U.S. 499; *Lindsley v. Natural Carbonic Gas Co.*, 220 U.S. 61; *Asbury Hospital v. Cass County*, 326 U.S. 207; *Metropolitan Casualty Insurance Co. v. Brownell*, 294 U.S. 580; *Dominion Hotel v. Arizona*, 249 U.S. 265.

When the distinctions imposed are based upon race and color alone, the state's action is patently the epitome of that arbitrariness and capriciousness constitutionally impermissive under our system of government. *Yick Wo* v. *Hopkins*, 118 U.S. 356; *Skinner* v. *Oklahoma*, 316 U.S. 535. A racial criterion is a constitutional irrelevance, *Edwards* v. *California*, 314 U.S. 160, 184, and is not saved from condemnation even though dictated by a sincere desire to avoid the possibility of violence or race friction. *Buchanan* v. *Warley*, 245 U.S. 60; *Morgan* v. *Virginia*, 328 U.S. 373. Only because it was a war measure designed to cope with a grave national emergency was the federal government permitted to level restrictions against persons of enemy descent. *Hirabayashi* v. *United States*, 320 U.S. 81; *Oyama* v. *California*, 332 U.S. 633. This action, "odious," *Hirabayashi* v. *United States*, *supra*, at page 100, and "suspect," *Korematsu* v. *United States*, 323 U.S. 214, 216, even in times of national peril, must cease as soon as that peril is past. *Ex Parte Endo*, 323 U.S. 283.

This Court has found violation of the equal protection clause in racial distinctions and restrictions imposed by the states in selection for jury service, *Shepherd* v. *Florida*, 341 U.S. 50; ownership and occupancy of real property, *Shelley* v. *Kramer*, 334 U.S. 1; *Buchanan* v. *Warley*, *supra*; gainful employment, *Takahashi* v. *Fish and Game Commission*, 334 U.S. 410; voting, *Nixon* v. *Condon*, 286 U.S. 73; and graduate and professional education. *McLaurin* v. *Board of Regents*, *supra*; *Sweatt* v. *Painter*, *supra*. The commerce clause in proscribing the imposition of racial distinctions and restrictions in the field of interstate travel is a further limitation of state power in this regard. *Morgan* v. *Virginia*, 328 U.S. 373.

Since 1940, in an unbroken line of decisions, this Court has clearly enunciated the doctrine that the state may not validly impose distinctions and restrictions among its citizens based upon race or color alone in each field of governmental activity where question has been raised. *Smith* v. *Allwright*, 321 U.S. 649; *Sipuel* v. *Board of Education*, 332 U.S. 631; *Sweatt* v. *Painter*, *supra*; *Pierre* v. *Louisiana*, 306 U.S. 354; *Hill* v. *Texas*, 316 U.S. 400; *Morgan* v. *Virginia*, *supra*; *McLaurin* v. *Board of Regents*, *supra*; *Oyama* v. *California*, *supra*; *Takahashi* v. *Fish and Game Commission*, *supra*; *Shelley* v. *Kraemer*, *supra*; *Shepherd* v. *Florida*, *supra*; *Cassell* v. *Texas*, 339 U.S. 282. On the other hand, when the state has sought to protect its citizenry against racial discrimination and prejudice, its action has been consistently upheld, *Railway Mail Association* v. *Corsi*, 326 U.S. 88, even though taken in the field of foreign commerce. *Bob-Lo Excursion Co.* v. *Michigan*, 333 U.S. 28.

It follows, therefore, that under this doctrine, the State of Kansas which by statutory sanctions seeks to subject appellants, in their pursuit of elementary education, to distinctions based upon race or color alone, is here attempting to exceed the constitutional limits to its authority. For that racial distinction which has been held arbitrary in so many other areas of governmental activity is no more appropriate and can be no more reasonable in public education.

## II. The court below, having found that appellants were denied equal educational opportunities by virtue of the segregated school system, erred in denying the relief prayed

The court below made the following finding of fact:

> "Segregation of white and colored children in public schools has a detrimental effect upon the colored children. The impact is greater when it has the sanction of the law; for the policy of separating the races is usually interpreted as denoting the inferiority of the negro group. A sense of inferiority affects the motivation of a child to learn. Segregation with the sanction of law, therefore, has a tendency to retard the educational and mental development of negro children and to deprive them of some of the benefits they would receive in a racially integrated school system."

This finding is based upon uncontradicted testimony that conclusively demonstrates that racial segregation injures infant appellants in denying them the opportunity available to all other racial groups to learn to live, work and cooperate with children representative of approximately 90% of the population of the society in which they live (R. 216); to develop citizenship skills; and to adjust themselves personally and socially in a setting comprising a cross-section of the dominant population (R. 132). The testimony further developed the fact that the enforcement of segregation under law denies to the Negro status, power and privilege (R. 176); interferes with his motivation for learning (R. 171); and instills in him a feeling of inferiority (R. 169) resulting in a personal insecurity, confusion and frustration that condemns him to an ineffective role as a citizen and member of society (R. 165). Moreover, it was demonstrated that racial segregation is supported by the myth of the Negro's inferiority (R. 177), and where, as here, the state enforces segregation, the community at large is supported in or converted to the belief that this myth has substance in fact (R. 156, 169, 177). It was testified that because of the peculiar educational system in Kansas that requires segregation only in the lower grades, there is an additional injury in that segregation occurring at an early age is greater in its impact and more permanent in its effects (R. 172) even though there is a change to integrated schools at the upper levels.

That these conclusions are the consensus of social scientists is evidenced by the appendix filed herewith. Indeed, the findings of the court that segregation constitutes discrimination are supported on the face of the statute itself where it states that: " * * * no discrimination on account of color shall be made in high schools *except as provided herein * * * "* (emphasis supplied).

Under the Fourteenth Amendment equality of educational opportunities necessitates an evaluation of all factors affecting the educational process. *Sweatt* v. *Painter, supra; McLaurin* v. *Board of Regents, supra.* Applying this yardstick, any restrictions or distinction based upon race or color that places the Negro at a disadvantage in relation to other racial groups in his pursuit of educational opportunities is violative of the equal protection clause.

In the instant case, the court found as a fact that appellants were placed at such a disadvantage and were denied educational opportunities equal to those available to white students. It necessarily follows, therefore, that the court should have concluded as a matter of law that appellants were deprived of their right to equal educational opportunities in violation of the equal protection clause of the Fourteenth Amendment.

Under the mistaken notion that *Plessy* v. *Ferguson* and *Gong Lum* v. *Rice* were controlling with respect to the validity of racial distinctions in elementary education, the trial court refused to conclude that appellants were here denied equal educational opportunities in violation of their constitutional rights. Thus, notwithstanding that it had found inequality in educational opportunity as a fact, the court concluded as a matter of law that such inequality did not constitute a denial of constitutional rights, saying:

> "*Plessy* v. *Ferguson,* 163 U.S. 537, and *Gong Lum* v. *Rice,* 275 U.S. 78, uphold the constitutionality of a legally segregated school system in the lower grades and no denial of due process results from the maintenance of such a segregated system of schools absent discrimination in the maintenance of the segregated schools. We conclude that the above-cited cases have not been overruled by the later case of *McLaurin* v. *Oklahoma,* 339 U.S. 637, and *Sweatt* v. *Painter,* 339 U.S. 629."

*Plessy* v. *Ferguson* is not applicable. Whatever doubts may once have existed in this respect were removed by this Court in *Sweatt* v. *Painter, supra,* at page 635, 636.

*Gong Lum* v. *Rice* is irrelevant to the issues in this case. There, a child of Chinese parentage was denied admission to a school maintained exclusively for white children and was ordered to attend a school for Negro children. The power of the state to make racial distinctions in its school system was not in issue. Petitioner contended that she had a constitutional right to go to school with white children, and that in being compelled to attend school with Negroes, the state had deprived her of the equal protection of the laws.

Further, there was no showing that her educational opportunities had been diminished as a result of the state's compulsion, and it was assumed by the Court that equality in fact existed. There the petitioner was not inveighing against the system, but that its application resulted in her classification as a Negro rather than as a white person, and indeed by so much conceded the propriety of the system itself. Were this not true, this Court would not have found basis for holding that the issue raised was one "which has been many times decided to be within the constitutional power of the state" and, therefore, did not "call for very full argument and consideration."

In short, she raised no issue with respect to the state's power to enforce racial classifications, as do appellants here. Rather, her objection went only to her treatment under the classification. This case, therefore, cannot be pointed to as a controlling precedent covering the instant case in which the constitutionality of the system itself is the basis for attack and in which it is shown the inequality in fact exists.

In any event the assumptions in the *Gong Lum* case have since been rejected by this Court. In the *Gong Lum* case, without "full argument and consideration," the Court assumed the state had power to make racial distinctions in its public schools without violating the equal protection clause of the Fourteenth Amendment and assumed the state and lower federal court cases cited in support of this assumed state power had been correctly decided. Language in *Plessy* v. *Ferguson* was cited in support of these assumptions. These assumptions upon full argument and consideration were rejected in the *McLaurin* and *Sweatt* cases in relation to racial distinctions in state graduate and professional education. And, according to those cases, *Plessy* v. *Ferguson* is not controlling for the purpose of determining the state's power to enforce racial segregation in public schools.

Thus, the very basis of the decision in the *Gong Lum* case has been destroyed. We submit, therefore, that this Court has considered the basic issue involved here only in those cases dealing with racial distinctions in education at the graduate and professional levels. *Missouri ex rel. Gaines* v. *Canada*, 305 U.S. 337; *Sipuel* v. *Board of Education, supra; Fisher* v. *Hurst*, 333 U.S. 147; *Sweatt* v. *Painter, supra; McLaurin* v. *Board of Regents, supra.*

In the *McLaurin* and *Sweatt* cases, this Court measured the effect of racial restrictions upon the educational development of the individual affected, and took into account the community's actual evaluation of the schools involved. In the instant case, the court below found as a fact that racial segregation in elementary education denoted the inferiority of Negro children and retarded their educational and mental development. Thus the same factors which led to the result reached in the *McLaurin* and *Sweatt* cases are present. Their underlying principles, based upon sound analyses, control the instant case.

## CONCLUSION

In light of the foregoing, we respectfully submit that appellants have been denied their rights to equal educational opportunities within the meaning of the Fourteenth Amendment and that the judgment of the court below should be reversed.

WILLIAM T. COLEMAN, JR.,
JACK GREENBERG,
GEORGE E. C. HAYES,
GEORGE M. JOHNSON,
WILLIAM R. MING, JR.,
CONSTANCE BAKER MOTLEY,
JAMES M. NABRIT, JR.,
FRANK D. REEVES,
JOHN SCOTT,
JACK B. WEINSTEIN,
    *of Counsel.*

ROBERT L. CARTER,
THURGOOD MARSHALL,
SPOTTSWOOD W. ROBINSON, III,
CHARLES S. SCOTT,
    *Counsel for Appellants.*

# In the
# Supreme Court of the United States
## October Term, 1952

### No. 8

Oliver Brown, Mrs. Richard Lawton, Mrs. Sadie Emmanuel, et al., Appellants,

vs.

Board of Education of Topeka, Shawnee County, Kansas, et al., Appellee

### No. 101

Harry Briggs, Jr., et al., Appellants,

vs.

R. W. Elliott, Chairman, J. D. Carson, et al., Members of Board of Trustees of School District No. 22, Clarendon County, S.C., et al., Appellee

### No. 191

Dorothy E. Davis, Bertha M. Davis and Inez D. Davis, etc., et al., Appellants,

vs.

County School Board of Prince Edward County, Virginia, et al., Appellee

## Appendix to Appellants' Briefs
## The Effects of Segregation and the Consequences of Desegregation: A Social Science Statement

### STATEMENT OF COUNSEL

The following statement was drafted and signed by some of the foremost authorities in sociology, anthropology, psychology and psychiatry who have worked in the area of American race relations. It represents a consensus of social scientists with respect to the issue presented in these appeals. As a summary of the best available scientific evidence relative to the effects of racial segregation on the individual, we file it herewith as an appendix to our briefs.

Robert L. Carter,
Thurgood Marshall,
Spottswood W. Robinson, III,
*Counsel for Appellants.*

IN THE
SUPREME COURT OF THE
UNITED STATES
OCTOBER TERM, 1952
NO. 8

OLIVER BROWN, MRS. RICHARD LAWTON,
MRS. SADIE EMMANUEL, ET AL., APPELLANTS,
VS.
BOARD OF EDUCATION OF TOPEKA,
SHAWNEE COUNTY, KANSAS, ET AL., APPELLEE

NO. 101

HARRY BRIGGS, JR., ET AL., APPELLANTS,
VS.
R. W. ELLIOTT, CHAIRMAN, J. D. CARSON,
ET AL., MEMBERS OF BOARD OF TRUSTEES
OF SCHOOL DISTRICT NO. 22, CLARENDON
COUNTY, S.C., ET AL., APPELLEE

NO. 191

DOROTHY E. DAVIS, BERTHA M. DAVIS AND
INEZ D. DAVIS, ETC., ET AL., APPELLANTS,
VS.
COUNTY SCHOOL BOARD OF PRINCE
EDWARD COUNTY, VIRGINIA, ET AL.,
APPELLEE

APPENDIX TO APPELLANTS'
BRIEFS

THE EFFECTS OF SEGREGATION
AND THE CONSEQUENCES OF
DESEGREGATION: A SOCIAL
SCIENCE STATEMENT

I

The problem of the segregation of racial and ethnic groups constitutes one of the major problems facing the American people today. It seems desirable, therefore, to summarize the contributions which contemporary social science can make toward its resolution. There are, of course, moral and legal issues involved with respect to which the signers of the present statement cannot speak with any special authority and which must be taken into account in the solution of the problem. There are, however, also factual issues involved with respect to which certain conclusions seem to be justified on the basis of the available scientific evidence. It is with these issues only that this paper is concerned. Some of the issues have to do with the consequences of segregation, some with the problems of changing from segregated to unsegregated practices. These two groups of issues will be dealt with in separate sections below. It is necessary, first, however, to define and delimit the problem to be discussed.

### Definitions

For purposes of the present statement, *segregation* refers to that restriction of opportunities for different types of associations between the members of one racial, religious, national or geographic origin, or linguistic group and those of other groups, which results from or is supported by the action of any official body or agency representing some branch of government. We are not here concerned with such segregation as arises from the free movements of individuals which are neither enforced nor supported by official bodies, nor with the segregation of criminals or of individuals with communicable diseases which aims at protecting society from those who might harm it.

Where the action takes place in a social milieu in which the groups involved do not enjoy equal social status, the group that is of lesser social status will be referred to as the *segregated* group.

In dealing with the question of the effects of segregation, it must be recognized that these effects do not take place in a vacuum, but in a social context. The segregation of Negroes and of other groups in the United States takes place in a social milieu in which "race" prejudice and discrimination exist. It is questionable in the view of some students of the problem whether it is possible to have segregation without substantial discrimination. Myrdal[1] states: "Segregation * * * is financially possible and, indeed, a device of economy only as it is combined with substantial discrimination" (p. 629). The imbeddedness of segregation in such a context makes it difficult to disentangle the effects of segregation *per se* from the effects of the context. Similarly, it is difficult to disentangle the effects of segregation from the effects of a pattern of social disorganization commonly associated with it and reflected in high disease and mortality rates, crime and delinquency, poor housing, disrupted family life and general substandard living conditions. We shall, how-

---

[1] Myrdal, G., *An American Dilemma*, 1944.

ever, return to this problem after consideration of the observable effects of the total social complex in which segregation is a major component.

## II

At the recent Mid-century White House Conference on Children and Youth, a fact-finding report on the effects of prejudice, discrimination and segregation on the personality development of children was prepared as a basis for some of the deliberations.[2] This report brought together the available social science and psychological studies which were related to the problem of how racial and religious prejudices influenced the development of a healthy personality. It highlighted the fact that segregation, prejudices and discriminations, and their social concomitants potentially damage the personality of all children—the children of the majority group in a somewhat different way than the more obviously damaged children of the minority group.

The report indicates that as minority group children learn the inferior status to which they are assigned—as they observe the fact that they are almost always segregated and kept apart from others who are treated with more respect by the society as a whole—they often react with feelings of inferiority and a sense of personal humiliation. Many of them become confused about their own personal worth. On the one hand, like all other human beings they require a sense of personal dignity; on the other hand, almost nowhere in the larger society do they find their own dignity as human beings respected by others. Under these conditions, the minority group child is thrown into a conflict with regard to his feelings about himself and his group. He wonders whether his group and he himself are worthy of no more respect than they receive. This conflict and confusion leads to self-hatred and rejection of his own group.

The report goes on to point out that these children must find ways with which to cope with this conflict. Not every child, of course, reacts with the same patterns of behavior. The particular pattern depends upon many interrelated factors, among which are: the stability and quality of his family relations; the social and economic class to which he belongs; the cultural and educational background of his par-

ents; the particular minority group to which he belongs; his personal characteristics, intelligence, special talents, and personality pattern.

Some children, usually of the lower socioeconomic classes, may react by overt aggressions and hostility directed toward their own group or members of the dominant group.[3] Anti-social and delinquent behavior may often be interpreted as reactions to these racial frustrations. These reactions are self-destructive in that the larger society not only punishes those who commit them, but often interprets such aggressive and anti-social behavior as justification for continuing prejudice and segregation.

Middle class and upper class minority group children are likely to react to their racial frustrations and conflicts by withdrawal and submissive behavior. Or, they may react with compensatory and rigid conformity to the prevailing middle class values and standards and an aggressive determination to succeed in these terms in spite of the handicap of their minority status.

The report indicates that minority group children of all social and economic classes often react with a generally defeatist attitude and a lowering of personal ambitions. This, for example, is reflected in a lowering of pupil morale and a depression of the educational aspiration level among minority group children in segregated schools. In producing such effects, segregated schools impair the ability of the child to profit from the educational opportunities provided him.

Many minority group children of all classes also tend to be hypersensitive and anxious about their relations with the larger society. They tend to see hostility and rejection even in those areas where these might not actually exist.

The report concludes that while the range of individual differences among members of a rejected minority group is as wide as among other peoples, the evidence suggests that all of these children are unnecessarily encumbered in some ways by segregation and its concomitants.

With reference to the impact of segregation and its concomitants on children of the majority group, the report indicates that the effects

---

[2] Clark, K. B., *Effect of Prejudice and Discrimination on Personality Development*, Fact Finding Report Mid-century White House Conference on Children and Youth, Children's Bureau, Federal Security Agency, 1950 (mimeographed).

[3] Brenman, M., The Relationship Between Minority Group Identification in A Group of Urban Middle Class Negro Girls, *J. Soc. Psychol.*, 1940, 11, 171-197; Brenman, M., Minority Group Membership and Religious, Psychosexual and Social Patterns in A Group of Middle-Class Negro Girls, *J. Soc. Psychol*, 1940, 12, 179-196; Brenman, M., Urban Lower-Class Negro Girls, *Psychiatry*, 1943, 6, 307-324; Davis, A., The Socialization of the American Negro Child and Adolescent, *J. Negro Educ.*, 1939, 8, 264-275.

are somewhat more obscure. Those children who learn the prejudices of our society are also being taught to gain personal status in an unrealistic and non-adaptive way. When comparing themselves to members of the minority group, they are not required to evaluate themselves in terms of the more basic standards of actual personal ability and achievement. The culture permits and, at times, encourages them to direct their feelings of hostility and aggression against whole groups of people the members of which are perceived as weaker than themselves. They often develop patterns of guilt feelings, rationalizations and other mechanisms which they must use in an attempt to protect themselves from recognizing the essential injustice of their unrealistic fears and hatreds of minority groups.[4]

The report indicates further that confusion, conflict, moral cynicism, and disrespect for authority may arise in majority group children as a consequence of being taught the moral, religious and democratic principles of the brotherhood of man and the importance of justice and fair play by the same persons and institutions who, in their support of racial segregation and related practices, seem to be acting in a prejudiced and discriminatory manner. Some individuals may attempt to resolve this conflict by intensifying their hostility toward the minority group. Others may react by guilt feelings which are not necessarily reflected in more humane attitudes toward the minority group. Still others react by developing an unwholesome, rigid, and uncritical idealization of all authority figures—their parents, strong political and economic leaders. As described in *The Authoritarian Personality*,[5] they despise the weak, while they obsequiously and unquestioningly conform to the demands of the strong whom they also, paradoxically, subconsciously hate.

With respect to the setting in which these difficulties develop, the report emphasized the role of the home, the school, and other social institutions. Studies[6] have shown that from the earliest school years children are not only aware of the status differences among different groups

in the society but begin to react with the patterns described above.

Conclusions similar to those reached by the Mid-century White House Conference Report have been stated by other social scientists who have concerned themselves with this problem. The following are some examples of these conclusions:

Segregation imposes upon individuals a distorted sense of social reality.[7]

Segregation leads to a blockage in the communications and interaction between the two groups. Such blockages tend to increase mutual suspicion, distrust and hostility.[8]

Segregation not only perpetuates rigid stereotypes and reinforces negative attitudes toward members of the other group, but also leads to the development of a social climate within which violent outbreaks of racial tensions are likely to occur.[9]

We return now to the question, deferred earlier, of what it is about the total society complex of which segregation is one feature that produces the effects described above—or, more precisely, to the question of whether we can justifiably conclude that, as only one feature of a complex social setting, segregation is in fact a significantly contributing factor to these effects.

To answer this question, it is necessary to bring to bear the general fund of psychological and sociological knowledge concerning the role of various environmental influences in producing feelings of inferiority, confusions in personal roles, various types of basic personality structures and the various forms of personal and social disorganization.

On the basis of this general fund of knowledge, it seems likely that feelings of inferiority and doubts about personal worth are attributable to living in an underprivileged environment only insofar as the latter is itself perceived as an indicator of low social status and as a symbol of inferiority. In other words, one of the important determinants in producing such feelings is the awareness of social status difference. While there are many other factors that serve as reminders of the differences in social status, there can be little doubt that the fact of enforced segregation is a major factor.[10]

---

[4] Adorno, T. W.; Frenkel-Brunswik, E.; Levinson, D. J.; Sanford, R. N., *The Authoritarian Personality*, 1951.
[5] Adorno, T. W.; Frenkel-Brunswik, E.; Levinson, D. J.; Sanford, R. N., *The Authoritarian Personality*, 1951.
[6] Clark, K. B. & Clark, M. P., Emotional Factors in Racial Identification and Preference in Negro Children, *J. Negro Educ.*, 1950, 19, 341-350; Clark, K. B. & Clark, M. P., Racial Identification and Preference in Negro Children, *Readings in Social Psychology*, Ed. by Newcomb & Hartley, 1947; Radke, M.; Trager, H.; Davis, H., Social Perceptions and Attitudes of Children, *Genetic Psychol. Monog.*, 1949, 40, 327-447; Radke, M.; Trager, H.; Children's Perceptions of the Social Role of Negroes and Whites, *J. Psychol.*, 1950, 29, 3-33.

[7] Reid, Ira, What Segregated Areas Mean; Brameld, T., Educational Cost, *Discrimination and National Welfare*, Ed. by MacIver, R. M., 1949.
[8] Frazier, E., *The Negro in the United States*, 1949; Krech, D. & Crutchfield, R. S., *Theory and Problems of Social Psychology*, 1948; Newcomb, T., *Social Psychology*, 1950.
[9] Lee, A. McClung and Humphrey, N. D., *Race Riot*, 1943.
[10] Frazier, E., *The Negro in the United States*, 1949; Myrdal, G., *An American Dilemma*, 1944.

This seems to be true for the following reasons among others: (1) because enforced segregation results from the decision of the majority group without the consent of the segregated and is commonly so perceived; and (2) because historically segregation patterns in the United States were developed on the assumption of the inferiority of the segregated.

In addition, enforced segregation gives official recognition and sanction to these other factors of the social complex, and thereby enhances the effects of the latter in creating the awareness of social status differences and feelings of inferiority.[11] The child who, for example, is compelled to attend a segregated school may be able to cope with ordinary expressions of prejudice by regarding the prejudiced person as evil or misguided; but he cannot readily cope with symbols of authority, the full force of the authority of the State—the school or the school board, in this instance—in the same manner. Given both the ordinary expression of prejudice and the school's policy of segregation, the former takes on greater force and seemingly becomes an official expression of the latter.

Not all of the psychological traits which are commonly observed in the social complex under discussion can be related so directly to the awareness of status differences—which in turn is, as we have already noted, materially contributed to by the practices of segregation. Thus, the low level of aspiration and defeatism so commonly observed in segregated groups is undoubtedly related to the level of self-evaluation; but it is also, in some measure, related among other things to one's expectations with regard to opportunities for achievement and, having achieved, to the opportunities for making use of these achievements. Similarly, the hypersensitivity and anxiety displayed by many minority group children about their relations with the larger society probably reflects their awareness of status differences; but it may also be influenced by the relative absence of opportunities for equal status contact which would provide correctives for prevailing unrealistic stereotypes.

The preceding view is consistent with the opinion stated by a large majority (90%) of social scientists who replied to a questionnaire concerning the probable effects of enforced segregation under conditions of equal facilities. This opinion was that, regardless of the facilities which are provided, enforced segregation is

psychologically detrimental to the members of the segregated group.[12]

Similar considerations apply to the question of what features of the social complex of which segregation is a part contribute to the development of the traits which have been observed in majority group members. Some of these are probably quite closely related to the awareness of status differences, to which, as has already been pointed out, segregation makes a material contribution. Others have a more complicated relationship to the total social setting. Thus, the acquisition of an unrealistic basis for self-evaluation as a consequence of majority group membership probably reflects fairly closely the awareness of status differences. On the other hand, unrealistic fears and hatreds of minority groups, as in the case of the converse phenomenon among minority group members, are probably significantly influenced as well by the lack of opportunities for equal status contact.

With reference to the probable effects of segregation under conditions of equal facilities on majority group members, many of the social scientists who responded to the poll in the survey cited above felt that the evidence is less convincing than with regard to the probable effects of such segregation on minority group members, and the effects are possibly less widespread. Nonetheless, more than 80% stated it as their opinion that the effects of such segregation are psychologically detrimental to the majority group members.[13]

It may be noted that many of these social scientists supported their opinions on the effects of segregation on both majority and minority groups by reference to one or another or to several of the following four lines of published and unpublished evidence.[14] First, studies of children throw light on the relative priority of the awareness of status differentials and related factors as compared to the awareness of differences in facilities. On this basis, it is possible to infer some of the consequences of segregation as distinct from the influence of inequalities of facilities. Second, clinical studies and depth interviews throw light on the genetic sources and causal sequences of various patterns of psychological reaction; and, again, certain inferences are possible with respect to the

---

[11] Reid, Ira, What Segregated Areas Mean, *Discrimination and National Welfare*, Ed. by MacIver, R. M., 1949.

[12] Deutscher, M. and Chein, I., The Psychological Effects of Enforced Segregation: A Survey of Social Science Opinion, *J. Psychol.*, 1948, 26, 259-287.
[13] Deutscher, M. and Chein, I., The Psychological Effects of Enforced Segregation: A Survey of Social Science Opinion, *J. Psychol.*, 1948, 26, 259-287.
[14] Chein, I., What Are the Psychological Effects of Segregation Under Conditions of Equal Facilities?, *International J. Opinion and Attitude Res.*, 1949, 2, 229-234.

effects of segregation *per se*. Third, there actually are some relevant but relatively rare instances of segregation with equal or even superior facilities, as in the cases of certain Indian reservations. Fourth, since there are inequalities of facilities in racially and ethnically homogeneous groups, it is possible to infer the kinds of effects attributable to such inequalities in the absence of effects of segregation and, by a kind of subtraction to estimate the effects of segregation *per se* in situations where one finds both segregation and unequal facilities.

### III

Segregation is at present a social reality. Questions may be raised, therefore, as to what are the likely consequences of desegregation.

One such question asks whether the inclusion of an intellectually inferior group may jeopardize the education of the more intelligent group by lowering educational standards or damage the less intelligent group by placing it in a situation where it is at a marked competitive disadvantage. Behind this question is the assumption, which is examined below, that the presently segregated groups actually are inferior intellectually.

The available scientific evidence indicates that much, perhaps all, of the observable differences among various racial and national groups may be adequately explained in terms of environmental differences.[15] It has been found, for instance, that the differences between the average intelligence test scores of Negro and white children decrease, and the overlap of the distributions increases, proportionately to the number of years that the Negro children have lived in the North.[16] Related studies have shown that this change cannot be explained by the hypothesis of selective migration.[17] It seems clear, therefore, that fears based on the assumption of innate racial differences in intelligence are not well founded.

It may also be noted in passing that the argument regarding the intellectual inferiority of one group as compared to another is, as applied to schools, essentially an argument for homogeneous groupings of children by intelligence rather than by race. Since even those who believe that there are innate differences between Negroes and whites in America in average intelligence grant that considerable overlap between the two groups exists, it would follow

that it may be expedient to group together the superior whites and Negroes, the average whites and Negroes, and so on. Actually, many educators have come to doubt the wisdom of class groupings made homogeneous solely on the basis of intelligence.[18] Those who are opposed to such homogeneous grouping believe that this type of segregation, too, appears to create generalized feelings of inferiority in the child who attends a below average class, leads to undesirable emotional consequences in the education of the gifted child, and reduces learning opportunities which result from the interaction of individuals with varied gifts.

A second problem that comes up in an evaluation of the possible consequences of desegregation involves the question of whether segregation prevents or stimulates interracial tension and conflict and the corollary question of whether desegregation has one or the other effect.

The most direct evidence available on this problem comes from observations and systematic study of instances in which desegregation has occurred. Comprehensive reviews of such instances[19] clearly establish the fact that desegregation has been carried out successfully in a variety of situations although outbreaks of violence had been commonly predicted. Extensive desegregation has taken place without major incidents in the armed services in both Northern and Southern installations and involving officers and enlisted men from all parts of the country, including the South.[20] Similar changes have been noted in housing[21] and industry.[22]

---

[15] Klineberg, O., *Characteristics of American Negro*, 1945; Klineberg, O., *Race Differences*, 1936.

[16] Klineberg, O., *Negro Intelligence and Selective Migration*, 1935.

[17] Klineberg, O., *Negro Intelligence and Selective Migration*, 1935.

[18] Brooks, J. J., Interage Grouping on Trial-Continuous Learning, *Bulletin #87, Association for Childhood Education*, 1951; Lane, R. H., Teacher in Modern Elementary School, 1941; Educational Policies Commission of the National Education Association and the American Association of School Administration Report in *Education For All Americans*, published by the N. E. A. 1948.

[19] Delano, W., Grade School Segregation: The Latest Attack on Racial Discrimination, *Yale Law Journal*, 1952, 61, 5, 730-744; Rose, A., The Influence of Legislation on Prejudice; Chapter 53 in *Race Prejudice and Discrimination*, Ed. by Rose, A., 1951; Rose, A., *Studies in Reduction of Prejudice*, Amer. Council on Race Relations, 1948.

[20] Kenworthy, E. W., The Case Against Army Segregation, *Annals of the American Academy of Political and Social Science*, 1951, 275, 27-33; Nelson, Lt. D. D., *The Integration of the Negro in the U.S. Navy*, 1951; Opinions About Negro Infantry Platoons in White Companies in Several Divisions, *Information and Education Division, U.S. War Department, Report No. B-157*, 1945.

[21] Conover, R. D., *Race Relations at Codornices Village, Berkeley-Albany, California: A Report of the Attempt to Break Down the Segregated Pattern on A Directly Managed Housing Project*, Housing and Home Finance Agency, Public Housing Administration, Region I, December 1947 (mimeographed); Deutsch, M. and Collins, M. E., *Interracial Housing, A Psychological Study of A Social Experiment*, 1951; Rutledge, E., *Integration of Racial Minorities in Public Housing Projects: A Guide for Local Housing*

During the last war, many factories both in the North and South hired Negroes on a non-segregated, non-discriminatory basis. While a few strikes occurred, refusal by management and unions to yield quelled all strikes within a few days.[23]

Relevant to this general problem is a comprehensive study of urban race riots which found that race riots occurred in segregated neighborhoods, whereas there was no violence in sections of the city where the two races lived, worked and attended school together.[24]

Under certain circumstances desegregation not only proceeds without major difficulties, but has been observed to lead to the emergence of more favorable attitudes and friendlier relations between races. Relevant studies may be cited with respect to housing,[25] employment,[26] the armed services[27] and merchant marine,[28] recreation agency,[29] and general community life.[30]

Much depends, however, on the circumstances under which members of previously segregated groups first come in contact with others in unsegregated situations. Available evidence suggests, first, that there is less likelihood of unfriendly relations when the change is simultaneously introduced into all units of a social institution to which it is applicable—e.g., all of the schools in a school system or all of the shops in a given factory.[31] When factories introduced Negroes in only some shops but not in others the prejudiced workers tended to classify the desegregated shops as inferior, "Negro work." Such objections were not raised when complete integration was introduced.

The available evidence also suggests the importance of consistent and firm enforcement of the new policy by those in authority.[32] It indicates also the importance of such factors as: the absence of competition for a limited number of facilities or benefits;[33] the possibility of contacts which permit individuals to learn about one another as individuals;[34] and the possibility of equivalence of positions and functions among all of the participants within the unsegregated situation.[35] These conditions can generally be satisfied in a number of situations, as in the armed services, public housing developments, and public schools.

---

*Authorities on How to Do It*, Public Housing Administration, New York Field Office (mimeographed).

[22] Minard, R. D., The Pattern of Race Relationships in the Pocahontas Coal Field, *J. Social Issues*, 1952, 8, 29-44; Southall, S. E., *Industry's Unfinished Business*, 1951; Weaver, G. L-P, *Negro Labor, A National Problem*, 1941.

[23] Southall, S. E., *Industry's Unfinished Business*, 1951; Weaver, G. L-P, *Negro Labor, A National Problem*, 1941.

[24] Lee, A. McClung and Humphrey, N. D., *Race Riot*, 1943; Lee, A. McClung, Race Riots Aren't Necessary, *Public Affairs Pamphlet*, 1945.

[25] Deutsch, M. and Collins, M. E., *Interracial Housing, A Psychological Study of A Social Experiment*, 1951; Merton, R. K.; West, P. S.; Jahoda, M., *Social Fictions and Social Facts: The Dynamics of Race Relations in Hilltown*, Bureau of Applied Social Research Columbia, Univ., 1949 (mimeographed); Rutledge, E., *Integration of Racial Minorities in Public Housing Projects; A Guide for Local Housing Authorities on How To Do It*, Public Housing Administration, New York Field Office (mimeographed); Wilner, D. M.; Walkley, R. P.; and Cook, S. W., Intergroup Contact and Ethnic Attitudes in Public Housing Projects, *J. Social Issues*, 1952, 8, 45-69.

[26] Harding, J., and Hogrefe, R., Attitudes of White Department Store Employees Toward Negro Co-workers, *J. Social Issues*, 1952, 8, 19-28; Southall, S. E., *Industry's Unfinished Business*, 1951; Weaver, G. L-P., *Negro Labor, A National Problem*, 1941.

[27] Kenworthy, E. W., The Case Against Army Segregation, *Annals of the American Academy of Political and Social Science*, 1951, 275, 27-33; Nelson, Lt. D. D., *The Integration of the Negro in the U.S. Navy*, 1951; Stouffer, S., et al., *The American Soldier*, Vol. I, Chap. 19, A Note on Negro Troops in Combat, 1949; Watson, G., *Action for Unity*, 1947; Opinions About Negro Infantry Platoons in White Companies in Several Divisions, *Information and Education Division, U.S. War Department, Report No. B-157*, 1945.

[28] Brophy, I. N., The Luxury of Anti-Negro Prejudice, *Public Opinion Quarterly*, 1946, 9, 456-466 (Integration in Merchant Marine); Watson, G., *Action for Unity*, 1947.

[29] Williams, D. H., *The Effects of an Interracial Project Upon the Attitudes of Negro and White Girls Within the Young Women's Christian Association*, Unpublished M. A. thesis, Columbia University, 1934.

[30] Dean, J. P., *Situational Factors in Intergroup Relations: A Research Progress Report*. Paper Presented to American Sociological Society, 12/28/49 (mimeographed); Irish, D. P., Reactions of Residents of Boulder, Colorado, to the Introduction of Japanese Into the Community, *J. Social Issues*, 1952, 8, 10-17.

[31] Minard, R. D., The Pattern of Race Relationships in the Pocahontas Coal Field, *J. Social Issues*, 1952, 8, 29-44; Rutledge, E., *Integration of Racial Minorities in Public Housing Projects; A Guide for Local Housing Authorities on How to Do It*, Public Housing Administration, New York Field Office (mimeographed).

[32] Deutsch, M. and Collins, M. E., *Interracial Housing, A Psychological Study of A Social Experiment*, 1951; Feldman, H., The Technique of Introducing Negroes Into the Plant, *Personnel*, 1942, 19, 461-466; Rutledge, E., *Integration of Racial Minorities in Public Housing Projects; A Guide for Local Housing Authorities on How to Do It*, Public Housing Administration, New York Field Office (mimeographed); Southall, S. E., *Industry's Unfinished Business*, 1951; Watson, G., *Action for Unity*, 1947.

[33] Lee, A. McClung and Humphrey, N. D., *Race Riot*, 1943; Williams, R., Jr., *The Reduction of Intergroup Tensions*, Social Science Research Council, New York, 1947; Windner, A. E., *White Attitudes Towards Negro-White Interaction In An Area of Changing Racial Composition*. Paper Delivered at the Sixtieth Annual Meeting of the American Psychological Association, Washington, September 1952.

[34] Wilner, D. M.; Walkley, R. P.; and Cook, S. W., Intergroup Contact and Ethnic Attitudes in Public Housing Projects, *J. Social Issues*, 1952, 8, 45-69.

[35] Allport, G. W., and Kramer, B., Some Roots of Prejudice, *J. Psychol.*, 1946, 22, 9-39; Watson, J., Some Social and Psychological Situations Related to Change in Attitude, *Human Relations*, 1950, 3, 1.

## IV

The problem with which we have here attempted to deal is admittedly on the frontiers of scientific knowledge. Inevitably, there must be some differences of opinion among us concerning the conclusiveness of certain items of evidence, and concerning the particular choice of words and placement of emphasis in the preceding statement. We are nonetheless in agreement that this statement is substantially correct and justified by the evidence, and the differences among us, if any, are of a relatively minor order and would not materially influence the preceding conclusions.

FLOYD H. ALLPORT
Syracuse, New York

GORDON W. ALLPORT
Cambridge, Massachusetts

CHARLOTTE BABCOCK, M.D.
Chicago, Illinois

VIOLA W. BERNARD, M.D.
New York, New York

JEROME S. BRUNER
Cambridge, Massachusetts

HADLEY CANTRIL
Princeton, New Jersey

ISIDOR CHEIN
New York, New York

KENNETH B. CLARK
New York, New York

MAMIE P. CLARK
New York, New York

STUART W. COOK
New York, New York

BINGHAM DAI
Durham, North Carolina

ALLISON DAVIS
Chicago, Illinois

ELSE FRENKEL-BRUNSWIK
Berkeley, California

NOEL P. GIST
Columbia, Missouri

DANIEL KATZ
Ann Arbor, Michigan

OTTO KLINEBERG
New York, New York

DAVID KRECH
Berkeley, California

ALFRED MCCLUNG LEE
Brooklyn, New York

R. M. MACIVER
New York, New York

ROBERT K. MERTON
New York, New York

GARDNER MURPHY
Topeka, Kansas

THEODORE M. NEWCOMB
Ann Arbor, Michigan

ROBERT REDFIELD
Chicago, Illinois

IRA DEA. REID
Haverford, Pennsylvania

ARNOLD M. ROSE
Minneapolis, Minnesota

GERHART SAENGER
New York, New York

R. NEVITT SANFORD
Poughkeepsie, New York

S. STANFIELD SARGENT
New York, New York

M. BREWSTER SMITH
New York, New York

SAMUEL A. STOUFFER
Cambridge, Massachusetts

WELLMAN WARNER
New York, New York

ROBIN M. WILLIAMS
Ithaca, New York

Dated: September 22, 1952.

# In the
# Supreme Court of the United States
# October Term, 1952

Oliver Brown, Mrs. Richard Lawton, Mrs. Sadie Emmanuel, et al., Appellants,

vs.

Board of Education of Topeka, Shawnee County, Kansas, et al., Appellees.

## Appeal from the United States District Court for the District of Kansas

## Brief for Appellees

Harold R. Fatzer,
Attorney General,

Paul E. Wilson,
Asst. Attorney General,
Counsel for the State of Kansas,
State House, Topeka, Kansas,

Peter F. Caldwell,
Counsel for the Board of Education of
Topeka, Kansas.
512 Capitol Federal Bldg., Topeka, Kansas.

# TABLE OF CONTENTS

# IN THE
# SUPREME COURT OF THE
# UNITED STATES
# OCTOBER TERM, 1952
# NO. 8

OLIVER BROWN, MRS. RICHARD LAWTON,
MRS. SADIE EMMANUEL, ET AL., APPELLANTS,

VS.

BOARD OF EDUCATION OF TOPEKA,
SHAWNEE COUNTY, KANSAS, ET AL., APPELLEES.

## APPEAL FROM THE UNITED STATES DISTRICT COURT FOR THE DISTRICT OF KANSAS

## BRIEF FOR APPELLEES

## I. PRELIMINARY STATEMENT

The issue presented by this case is whether the Fourteenth Amendment to the Constitution of the United States is violated by a statute which permits boards of education in designated cities to maintain separate elementary school facilities for the education of white and colored children.

At the outset, counsel for the appellees desire to state that by appearing herein they do not propose to advocate the policy of segregation of any racial group within the public school system. We contend only that policy determinations are matters within the exclusive province of the legislature. We do not express an opinion as to whether the practice of having separate schools of equal facility for the white and colored races is economically expedient or sociologically desirable, or whether it is consistent with sound ethical or religious theory. We do not understand that these extra-legal questions are now before the Court. The only proposition that we desire to urge is that the Kansas statute which permits racial segregation in elementary public schools in certain cities of the state does not violate the Fourteenth Amendment to the Constitution of the United States as that amendment has been interpreted and applied by this Court.

## II. OPINION BELOW

The opinion of the three-judge District Court below: (R-238-244) is reported at 98 Fed. Supp. 797.

## III. JURISDICTION

The judgment of the court below was entered on August 3, 1951 (R. 247). On October 1, 1951, appellants filed a petition for appeal (R. 248), and an order allowing the appeal was entered (R. 251). Probable jurisdiction was noted on June 9, 1952 (R. 254). Jurisdiction of this Court rests on Title 28 U. S. C. Sec. 1253 and 2201 (b).

## IV. QUESTIONS PRESENTED

**1.** Does a statute which permits but does not require cities of more than 15,000 population to maintain separate school facilities for colored and white students, violate the Fourteenth Amendment to the Constitution of the United States in a situation where a court has specifically found that there is no discrimination or distinction in physical facilities, educational qualifications of teachers, curricula or transportation facilities?

**2.** Is a general finding of the trial court that segregation is detrimental to colored children and deprives them of some benefits they would receive in a racial integrated school sufficient to entitle the individual colored plaintiffs to an injunction prohibiting the maintenance of an existing system of segregated schools, and to require reversal of a judgment denying such relief?

## V. THE STATUTE

The statute under attack in the present litigation is section 72-1724, General Statutes of Kansas of 1949, which is quoted hereafter:

> "*Powers of board; separate schools for white and colored children; manual training.* The board of education shall have power to elect their own officers, make all necessary rules for the government of the schools of such city under its charge and control and of the board, subject to the provisions of this act and the laws of this state; to organize and maintain separate schools for the education of white and colored children, including the high schools in Kansas City, Kansas; no discrimination on account of color shall be made in high schools, except as provided herein; to exercise the sole control over the public schools and school property of such city; and shall have the power to establish a high school or high schools in connection with manual training and instruction or otherwise, and to maintain the same as a part of the public school system of said city."

## VI. STATEMENT OF THE CASE

The appellants here, who are plaintiffs below, are Negro citizens of the United States and the State of Kansas, who reside in Topeka, Shawnee County, Kansas. The infant plaintiffs are children of common school age. The defendants below and appellees herein are the duly constituted governing body and certain administrative officers of the public school system of

Topeka, Kansas. The State of Kansas has intervened in the District Court to defend the constitutionality of the state statute under attack.

Acting pursuant to the authority conferred by G. S. 1949, 72-1724, *supra*, the appellee, Board of Education, many years ago created within the city of Topeka, which is one school district, eighteen school areas, and now maintains in each of said areas a kindergarten and elementary school for white children only. (R. 24.) At the same time the present Board of Education of Topeka and prior boards of education, acting under same statutory authority, have established and operated in said city four elementary schools in the same grades for Negro children. Negro children may attend any one of said elementary schools that they or their parents may select. It was stipulated in the Court below that the Negro schools are located in neighborhoods in which the population is predominantly Negro. (R. 31.) The stipulation also indicates that at the time the action was brought, the enrollment in the eighteen white schools was 6,019, as compared to 658 students enrolled in the four Negro schools. (R. 37.)

The administration of the entire Topeka school system is under the Board of Education, and the same administrative regulations govern both the white and Negro schools. The Court found specifically that there is no material difference in the physical facilities in colored and white schools; that the educational qualifications of the teachers and the quality of instruction in the colored schools are not inferior to, but are comparable with those in the white schools; and that the courses of study followed in the two groups of schools are identical, being that prescribed by state law. (R. 245.) Also, it was found that colored students are furnished transportation to the segregated schools without cost to the children or their parents. No such transportation is furnished to the white children in the segregated schools. (R. 246.)

## VII. SUMMARY OF ARGUMENT

**1.** The Kansas statute which permits cities of the first class to maintain separate grade school facilities for colored and white students does not *per se* violate the Fourteenth Amendment to the Constitution of the United States.

The Court below found facilities provided for Negro children in the city of Topeka to be substantially equal to those furnished to white children. The appellants, in their specifications of error and in their brief, do not object to that finding. Under those circumstances and under authority of the decisions of the Supreme Court of the United States, the inferior federal courts,

and the courts of last resort in numerous state jurisdictions, and particularly the decisions of the Kansas Supreme Court, the appellants herein are not denied equal protection of the laws by virtue of their being required to attend schools separate from those which white children are required to attend.

The decision of the court below should be affirmed.

**2.** Irrespective of the question of the constitutionality of the Kansas statute, the trial court's findings of fact are insufficient to establish appellants' right to injunctive relief and to require reversal of the judgment below. The only finding of fact relied upon by appellants is Finding of Fact No. VIII. That finding is couched in general language and in effect simply shows that segregation in the public schools has a detrimental effect upon colored children and a tendency to retain or retard their educational and mental development and to deprive them of some of the benefits they would receive in a racially integrated school system. The finding does not specifically show that any of the appellants have actually and personally suffered by reason of segregation in the public schools of Topeka nor that the mental development of any of the appellants in this case has been retarded; and the finding does not even purport to show discrimination against the appellants and in favor of any other students in the Topeka school system. It no where discusses the effect of segregation upon children of any race other than colored children. Therefore, the District Court's Finding of Fact No. VIII fails to show either that the appellants have suffered any personal harm, or that they are being deprived of benefits or subjected to detriments which do not equally apply to other students in the Topeka school system. Thus, the appellants have failed to secure findings of fact sufficient to entitle them to injunctive relief or to a reversal of the judgment below.

## VIII. ARGUMENT

**1. Does a statute which permits but does not require cities of more than 15,000 population to maintain separate school facilities for colored and white students violate the Fourteenth Amendment to the Constitution of the United States in a situation where a court has specifically found that there is no discrimination or distinction in physical facilities, educational qualifications of teachers, curricula or transportation facilities?**

Appellees contend that only a negative answer to this question is possible.

**Background of segregation in Kansas** A meaningful examination of any statute must necessarily be made in the light of its context. In *Plessy v. Ferguson*, 163 U.S. 357, the Court comments:

> "So far, then, as a conflict with the 14th Amendment is concerned, the case reduces itself to the question of whether the statute . . . is a reasonable regulation, and with respect to this, there must necessarily be a large discretion on the part of the legislature. In determining the question of reasonableness, it is at liberty to act with reference to the established usages, customs, and traditions of the people, and with a view to the promotion of their comfort, and the preservation of the public peace and good order."

Therefore, we deem it proper to pause briefly to examine the origins and attitudes of the people of the State of Kansas.

The birth of the State of Kansas was an incident of the intersectional struggle that culminated in the war between the states. Located midway between the north and the south, the territory of Kansas was coveted by both the pro-slavery and free-state elements. The Kansas-Nebraska Act which announced the principle of "squatter sovereignty" formally opened the territory for settlement and resulted in migration of large numbers of people from both the north and the south. In these early settlers were reflected the diverse attitudes and cultures of the regions from which they came. While the free-state elements from the north gained political ascendency, there remained in Kansas people who, in good faith, believed that the welfare of both the colored and the white races required that they live apart from one another. Migration following the war between the states followed the same pattern. While the greatest number came from Illinois, Ohio, Indiana and other northern states, a considerable segment of the population had its origin in Kentucky, Tennessee and Missouri. (Clark & Roberts, People of Kansas, 1936, p. 18.)

The early legislatures were faced with the task of reconciling the divergent attitudes of the settlers from such varied cultural backgrounds.

The Wyandotte Constitution, under which the State of Kansas was admitted to the Union, provided for a system of public education specifically requiring the legislature to "encourage the promotion of intellectual, moral, scientific and agricultural improvement, by establishing a uniform system of common schools and schools of a higher grade, embracing normal, preparatory, collegiate and university departments." (Const., Art. 6, Sec. 1.) It is significant that an effort was made in the Wyandotte convention to obtain a constitutional requirement for the separate education of Negro children. The proposal was defeated, not because of objection to the intrinsic policy of segregation, but because the dominant faction in the constitutional convention believed that the power to govern the public schools and to classify students therein should rest with the legislature. At no time was doubt expressed that the constitutional provision adopted at Wyandotte would preclude classification of students on the basis of color (Wyandotte Constitutional Convention, Proceedings and Debates, 1859, pp. 171 to 174).

As early as 1862 the power to classify students was exercised by the enactment of section 18, article 4, chapter 46, Compiled Laws of 1862, applying to cities of not less than 7,000 inhabitants. That statute provided:

> "The city council of any city under this act shall make provisions for the appropriation of all taxes for school purposes collected from black or mulatto persons, so that the children of such persons shall receive the benefit of all moneys collected by taxation for school purposes from such persons, in schools separate and apart from the schools hereby authorized for the children of white persons."

Chapter 18, Laws of 1868, entitled "An Act to Incorporate Cities of the First Class" authorized the organization and maintenance of separate schools for the education of white and colored children in cities of over 15,000 population. In 1876 the laws of the state pertaining to the common schools were codified and embodied in one comprehensive statute. (Chapter 122.) Article X of this chapter related to the public schools and cities of the first class, and provided that all cities of more than 15,000 inhabitants shall be governed thereby. The provision of the law of 1868 authorizing the maintenance of separate schools for white and colored children was omitted from that section and was thus deemed to have been repealed by implication. However, in 1879 a statute was passed (Laws of 1879, Chapter 81) amending the law relating to cities of the first class and specifically authorizing the boards of education therein to organize and maintain separate elementary schools for the education of white and colored children. The section was again amended by Laws of 1905, Chapter 414, and now appears without further change in G. S. 1949, 72-1724, quoted above.

Two features of the Kansas statute should be emphasized. In the first place, we invite the court's attention to the fact that the statute is permissive only and does not, as may be inferred from appellants' brief, require any board of education to maintain separate schools for colored children.

In the second place, it is again pointed out that the statute applies only to cities of the first class. Cities of the first class in Kansas include those cities having a population of more than 15,000 persons. Presently there are 12 cities in the state so classified. The special provision affecting only these communities may be accounted for by reference to the fact that the Negro population of Kansas is largely urban. According to the 1950 census, less than four percent of the total population of Kansas belongs to the Negro race. However, more than ninety percent of this colored population lives in cities classified as urban. Sixty percent of the total colored population live in the three largest cities of Kansas City, Wichita and Topeka, and at least thirty-five percent of this total live in Kansas City alone. Thus, in enacting a school segregation statute applicable only to cities of the first class the Kansas legislature has simply recognized that there are situations where Negroes live in sufficient numbers to create special school problems and has sought to provide a law sufficiently elastic to enable Boards of Education in such communities to handle such problems as they may, in the exercise of their discretion and best judgment, deem most advantageous to their local school system under their local conditions.

**The Kansas decisions**  The Supreme Court of Kansas has uniformly held that the governing bodies of school districts in the state may maintain separate schools for colored children only when expressly authorized by statute. (*Board of Education v. Tinnon*, 26 Kan. 1 (1881); *Knox v. Board of Education*, 45 Kan. 152, 25 Pac. 616 (1891); *Cartwright v. Board of Education*, 73 Kan. 302, 84 Pac. 382 (1906); *Rowles v. Board of Education*, 76 Kan. 361, 91 Pac. 88 (1907); *Woolridge, et al., v. Board of Education*, 98 Kan. 397, 157 Pac. 1184 (1916); *Thurman-Watts v. Board of Education*, 115 Kan. 328, 22 Pac. 123 (1924); *Webb v. School District*, 167 Kan. 395, 206 Pac. 2d 1066 (1949).

The rationale of each of these cases is expressed in *Thurman-Watts v. Board of Education*, supra, as follows:

> "The power and duty of the school board are derived exclusively from the statutes. The school board has no greater power than is conferred on it by the statutes."

It is significant that in each of the cases cited above, the court expressly recognized or conceded that the legislature has power to classify students in the public schools on the basis of color. Illustrative of this attitude is the following statement from *Board of Education v. Tinnon*, supra, appearing on p. 16 of the reported decision:

> "For the purpose of this case we shall assume that the legislature has the power to authorize the board of education of any city or the officers of any school district to establish separate schools for the education of white and colored children, and to exclude the colored children from the white schools notwithstanding the Fourteenth Amendment to the Constitution of the United States;"

In each of the subsequent cases where the power to segregate was denied by reason of the absence of statutory authority, the court specifically recognized that the legislature had such authority to confer. (See cases above cited.)

The question of the constitutionality of a statute, antecedent to but substantially like the one here under attack, was squarely presented to the Supreme Court of Kansas in the case of *Reynolds v. Board of Education*, 66 Kan. 672, 72 Pac. 274. That was a proceeding in the nature of mandamus brought against the board of education of the city of Topeka by a colored resident. In the action he sought to compel the board of education to admit his child to a school maintained for white children only. In an exhaustive opinion the court found that the statute which permitted the policy of racial segregation to be valid and not in violation of the Fourteenth Amendment to the Constitution of the United States. The court relied specifically on the decision of the Supreme Court of the United States in the case of *Plessy v. Ferguson*, supra, and held that where facilities are equal, the mere fact of separation of races within a school system does not constitute a violation of the Fourteenth Amendment to the Constitution of the United States.

Quoting with approval from the New York case of *People, ex rel., Cisco v. School Board*, 161 N. Y. 598, 56 N. E. 81, 48 L. R. A. 115, the Court said:

> "The most that the constitution requires the legislature to do is to furnish a system of common schools where each and every child may be educated; not that all must be educated in any one school, but that it shall provide or furnish a school or schools where each and all may have the advantages guaranteed by that instrument. If the legislature determined that it was wise for one class of pupils to be educated by themselves, there is nothing in the constitution to deprive it of the right to so provide. It was the facilities for and the advan-

tages of an education that it was required to furnish to all the children, and not that it should provide for them any particular class of associates while such education was being obtained."

And the court found merit in the quoted portion of the decision in the Massachusetts case of *Roberts v. City of Boston*, 5 Cush. 198:

"It is urged that this maintenance of separate schools tends to deepen and perpetuate the odious distinction of caste, founded in a deep-rooted prejudice in public opinion. This prejudice, if it exists, is not created by law, and probably cannot be changed by law. Whether this distinction and prejudice, existing in the opinion and feelings of the community, would not be as effectually fostered by compelling colored and white children to associate together in the same schools, may well be doubted; at all events, it is a fair and proper question for the committee to consider and decide upon, having in view the best interests of both classes of children placed under their superintendence, and we cannot say, that their decision upon it is not founded on just grounds of reason and experience, and in the results of a discriminating and honest judgment."

Consistent with its finding that the statute did not violate the equal protection guarantee of the Fourteenth Amendment, the Court said on page 689:

"The design of the common-school system of this state is to instruct the citizen, and where for this purpose they have placed within his reach equal means of acquiring an education with other persons, they have discharged their duty to him, and he has received all that he is entitled to ask of the government with respect to such privileges."

Finally on page 292 the court holds:

"The act of the legislature of 1879 providing for the education of white and colored children in separate schools in cities of the first class except in the high school is, therefore, in all respects constitutional and valid."

At the same time the Kansas court has always insisted that facilities must be equal for all groups. Particularly significant is the case of *Williams v. Parsons*, 79 Kan. 202, decided in 1908. There objection was made that the school provided for colored children was located in such close proximity to the railroad tracks that such location produced an undue hazard to the children attending the school. The court stated, at page 209:

"Having power to maintain separate schools in cities of the first class, the duty rests upon the board of education therein to give equal educational facilities to both white and colored children in such schools. This requirement must have a practical interpretation so that it may be reasonably applied to varying circumstances. . . . Where the location of a school is such as to substantially deprive some of the children of the district of any educational facilities, it is manifest that this equality is not maintained and the refusal to furnish such privileges, where it is practicable to do so, is an abuse of discretion for which the courts will afford a remedy."

A later expression of the Supreme Court of Kansas is found in *Graham v. Board of Education*, 153 Kan. 840, decided in 1941. There the court said on page 842:

"The authorities are clear that separate schools may be maintained for the white and colored races if the educational facilities provided for each are equal, unless such separation is in contravention of a specific state law."

Again on p. 846 the court comments with reference to the rule expressed in *Reynolds v. Board of Education*, supra:

"The defendants cite the case of *Reynolds v. Board of Education*, 66 Kan. 672, 72 Pac. 274. The rules of law set out in that case are sound and are applied in this case."

These cases demonstrate that the Supreme Court of Kansas has never doubted that G. S. 1949, 72-1724, and its antecedent statutes is without the scope of the prohibitions imposed on the legislature by the Fourteenth Amendment to the Constitution of the United States. **The controlling principles**     The position taken by the Supreme Court of Kansas in the cases cited, *supra*, is sustained by the weight of the decisions of this Court in *Plessy v. Ferguson*, supra, and *Gong Lum v. Rice*, 275 U.S. 78; and in numerous decisions of the inferior federal courts and the appellate courts in other states.

Appellants suggest that the Plessy case is not applicable to the situation before us. Admittedly, the question presented in the Plessy case arose out of segregation of white and colored races in railroad cars and not segregation in the public schools. However, the decision of the Court rises above the specific facts in issue and announces a doctrine applicable to any social situation wherein the two races are brought into contact. In commenting upon the purpose and the limitations of the Fourteenth Amendment the Court makes the following statement:

"The object of the Amendment was undoubtedly to enforce the absolute equality of the two races before the law, but in the nature of things it could not have been intended to abolish distinctions based upon color, or to enforce social, as distinguished from political equality, or a commingling of the two races upon terms unsatisfactory to either. Laws permitting and even requiring their separation in places where they are liable to be brought into contact do not necessarily imply the inferiority of either race to the other, and have been generally, if not universally, recognized as within the competency of the state legislatures in the exercise of their police power. The most common instance of this is connected with the establishment of separate schools for white and colored children which has been held to be a valid exercise of the legislative power even by courts of States where the political rights of the colored race have been longest and most earnestly enforced." (p. 554.)

Certainly this language refutes appellants' contention that the Plessy case has no application to these facts.

Appellants further state that *Gong Lum v. Rice* "is irrelevant to the issues in this case." This statement appears to justify a brief examination of the facts in the Gong case. Those facts may be summarized as follows:

The Constitution and statutes of the State of Mississippi provided for two school systems in each county. One system was for "white" children and the other system for "colored" children. Plaintiff sought to have his child who was a citizen of Chinese extraction admitted to the school maintained for white students in the county where she lived. She was refused admission by the school authorities. The Supreme Court of the United States unanimously affirmed the decision of the Supreme Court of Mississippi, refusing to grant a Writ of Mandamus to compel the school authorities to admit the Chinese-American citizen to the white school.

The opinion by Chief Justice Taft includes the following statement (pp. 85-86):

"The question here is whether a Chinese citizen of the United States is denied equal protection of the laws when he is classed among the colored races and furnished facilities for education equal to that offered to all, whether white, brown, yellow or black. Were this a new question it would call for very full argument and consideration but we think that it is the same question which has been many times decided to be within the constitutional power of the state legislature to settle without intervention of the federal courts under the Federal Constitution."

To support this proposition the Court cites sixteen cases decided by federal courts and state courts of last resort, including *Plessy v. Ferguson,* supra.

We do not believe that appellants suggest that the rights of the Negro citizens differ from the rights of the Mongolian citizen, Martha Lum. If such an idea is advanced herein, this Court should have no more difficulty in disposing of that contention than it did of that phase of the Gong case where it seemed to be contended that a yellow child had different rights than a Negro child. The Court simply held that children of all races have equal rights but that those rights are not infringed upon when the state provides that the different races shall be educated in separate schools of equal facility.

Appellants further contend that whatever force the Plessy and Gong-Lum cases may have had has been overcome by the recent decisions of *Sweatt v. Painter,* 339 U.S. 629, and *McLaurin v. Oklahoma,* 339 U.S. 637. Appellees concede that if there has been any change in the attitude of this Court as to the constitutionality of the separate but equal doctrines as it affects segregation, it must be found in these two cases. Thus, we have examined them carefully. But we find no statement therein that would cause us to believe the Court intended to reverse or modify its earlier decisions. In the Sweatt case, the Court held that a Negro prospective law student could not be denied admission to the renowned University of Texas Law School—"one of the nation's ranking law schools" (p. 663), and be compelled to accept instruction in a new school of perhaps questionable worth, inferior as to faculty, plant and student body. The McLaurin case only found that a Negro graduate student, who had successfully compelled his admission to the University of Oklahoma to do graduate work in education, was still being denied equal rights when he was segregated inside the university as to his seat in class, in the library and in the dining hall. Unquestionably, these cases sustain the position that equal facilities must be provided. However, that point is not at issue in this case.

We think the Sweatt case has no greater significance than the following expression of the Court's attitude indicates:

"This case and *McLaurin v. Oklahoma State Regents* . . . present different aspects of this general question: To what extent does the Equal Protection Clause of the Fourteenth Amendment limit the power of a state to distinguish between students of different races in professional and graduate education in a state university? Broader issues have been urged for our consideration, but we adhere to the principle of deciding constitutional questions only in the context of the particular case before the court." (p. 631.)

Squarely in point is the following statement:

"We cannot, therefore, agree with respondents that the doctrine of *Plessy v. Ferguson*, 1896, 163 U.S. 337, 16 S. Ct. 1138, 41 L. Ed. 256, requires affirmance of the judgment below. Nor need we reach the petitioner's contention that *Plessy v. Ferguson* should be re-examined in the light of contemporary knowledge respecting the purposes of the Fourteenth Amendment and the effects of racial segregation. See, *supra*, pg. 631." (pp. 635-636.)

And in the McLaurin case the significance of the special situation is noted by the Court:

"Our society grows increasingly complex, and our need for trained leaders increases correspondingly. Appellant's case represents, perhaps, the epitome of that need, for he is attempting to obtain an advanced degree in education, to become, by definition, a leader and trainer of others. Those who will come under his guidance and influence must be directly affected by the education he receives. Their own education and development will necessarily suffer to the extent that his training is unequal to that of his classmates. State-imposed restrictions which produce such inequalities cannot be sustained.

"It may be argued that appellant will be in no better position when these restrictions are removed, for he may still be set apart by his fellow students. This we think is irrelevant. There is a vast difference—a constitutional difference between restrictions imposed by the state which prohibit the intellectual commingling of students, and the refusal of individuals to commingle where the state presents no such bar ... Appellant having been admitted to a state-supported graduate school, he must receive the same treatment at the hands of the state as students of other races." (pp. 641, 642.)

In the Sweatt and McLaurin cases the Court specifically refused to consider the issue of constitutionality of racial separation in schools of equal facility in view of contemporary knowledge and held only that where the State did not furnish equal facilities for one race, the students of that race were being denied equal protection of the laws. Appellees contend that this refusal by the Court to review the Plessy and Gong-Lum doctrines in its later decisions can only be interpreted to support the view that those cases still stand as expressions of the rule established by the Supreme Court upon the question of racial segregation within the public schools.

Notable among decisions since the Sweatt and McLaurin cases are *Carr v. Corning*, 182 F. 2d 14; *Briggs v. Elliott*, 98 F. Supp. 529; and *Davis v. County School Board*, 103 F. Supp. 337, the latter two cases now pending before this Court on appeal. *Carr v. Corning* involved the public school system of the District of Columbia. There the Court noted a fact that we deem most significant with respect to the original meaning and intent of the Fourteenth Amendment. It was pointed out that in the same year that Congress proposed the amendment, federal legislation was enacted providing for segregation of the races in the public schools in the District of Columbia.

"We are not unmindful of the debates which occurred in Congress relative to the Civil Rights Act of April 9, 1866, the Fourteenth Amendment, and the Civil Rights Act of March 1, 1875. But the actions of Congress, the discussion in the Civil Rights Cases, and the fact that in 1862, 1864, 1866 and 1874 Congress, as we shall point out in a moment, enacted legislation which specifically provided for separation of the races in the schools of the District of Columbia, conclusively support our view of the Amendment and its effect." (p. 17.)

Here we note the parallel situation in the State of Kansas. There the State, through its Legislature, ratified the Fourteenth Amendment in 1867, and only one year later legislation providing for separation of the races in the public schools of first class cities was enacted. (L. 1868, ch. 18.)

An examination of all the cases in American jurisdictions supporting the appellants' position would become repetitious and tedious. Thus, we refrain from an exhaustive survey. We believe the comment of Circuit Judge Parker in *Briggs v. Elliott*, supra, aptly summarizes the law and its justification:

"One of the great virtues of our constitutional system is that, while the federal government protects the fundamental rights of the individual, it leaves to the several states the solution of local problems. In a country with a great expanse of territory with peoples of widely differing customs and ideas, local self government in local matters is essential to the peace and happiness of the people in the several communities as well as to the strength and unity of the country as a whole. It is universally held, therefore, that each state shall determine for itself, subject to the observance of the fundamental rights and liberties guaranteed by the federal Constitution, how it shall exercise the police power, *i.e.*, the power to legislate with respect to the safety, morals, health and general welfare. And in no field is this right of the several states more clearly recognized than in that of public education." (P. 532.)

Justice Holmes has expressed the following view:

"I must add one general consideration. There is nothing that I more deprecate than the use of the Fourteenth Amendment beyond the absolute compulsion of its words to prevent the making of social experiments that an important part of the community desires, in the insulated chambers afforded by the several states, even though the experiments may seem futile or even noxious to me and to those whose judgment I most respect. (Holmes, J., dissenting opinion, *Truax v. Corrigan*, 257 U.S. 312, p. 344, 42 S. Ct. 124, 66 L. Ed. 254, 27 A. L. R. 375.)"

It is undoubtedly true that the separate but equal doctrine is susceptible of abuse. In many instances it has resulted in a separate and unequal rule in practice. However, it is the impossibility of equality under such a doctrine, and not the difficulty of administering and applying the same with equality, that would make such a doctrine unconstitutional *per se*. The situation in Topeka is one where substantial equality has been reached. Such was the finding of the Court below (R. 245) and such is apparently conceded by the appellants (Appellants' Brief, p. 5). These facts, under authority of decisions heretofore reviewed, compel an inescapable conclusion: Neither the statute of Kansas nor the action of the appellee, Board of Education, offends the Fourteenth Amendment to the Federal Constitution.

**The prospect**   At the outset we suggested that the Kansas statute is permissive and that any Board of Education included in the statute may adopt a policy consistent with local conditions and local attitudes. We believe it is significant that under this statute by a process of evolution the people in Kansas communities are arriving at their own solutions to this problem. Under the statute 12 cities are authorized to maintain separate schools for colored students. The files of the State Superintendent of Public Instruction indicate that at the present time, only nine cities exercise the power conferred by statute. Wichita, the largest city in the state, has abandoned segregation only recently. The city of Pittsburg abandoned the policy of segregation only two years ago. Lawrence, seat of the state university, is now in the process of ending the operation of segregated schools.

This account of events not in the record is related to illustrate the wisdom which underlies the Kansas statute. Only those cities where local conditions produce special problems making segregation desirable need adopt the expedient of segregation. In the orderly progress of the community, these special problems are either solved or vanish, and when the need for segregation disappears, its practice may be discontinued. This was the method provided by the legislature of the State of Kansas to achieve the goal of an integrated school system where segregation is not needed. We respectfully suggest to the court that this evolutionary process permitting an autonomous solution in the community is consistent with the purpose and intent of the Fourteenth Amendment.

## 2. The District Court's finding of Fact No. VIII is insufficient to establish appellants' right to injunctive relief and to require reversal of the judgment below

### A. Counsel for Appellants have overstated their case.

Appellant has raised and preserved this issue by its third Assignment of Error, to wit:

"The District Court erred:

"· · · · · · · · · ·

"3. In refusing to enter judgment in favor of plaintiffs, after the court found that plaintiffs suffered serious harm and detriment in being required to attend segregated elementary schools in the City of Topeka, and were deprived thereby of benefits they would have received in a racially integrated school system." (R. 250.)

And by adopting its Assignment of Errors in its Statement of Points to Be Relied Upon (R. 253).

The District Court's Findings of Fact and Conclusions of Law appear at pp. 244 to 247 of the Transcript of the Record.

There is no Finding of Fact which literally and specifically corresponds to the finding mentioned in Appellants' third Assignment of Error.

At page 2 of the Brief for Appellants under the heading *Questions Presented*, appellants state the second issue, as follows:

"Whether the finding of the court below—that racial segregation in public elementary schools has the detrimental effect of retarding the mental and educational development of colored children and connotes governmental acceptance of the conception of racial inferiority—compels the conclusion that appellants here are deprived of their rights to share equally in educational opportunities in violation of the equal protection clause of the Fourteenth Amendment."

There is no Finding of Fact which literally and specifically corresponds to the finding mentioned in appellants' statement of the second issue.

At page 10 of the Brief for Appellant, counsel state:

"Applying this yardstick, any restrictions or distinction based upon race or color that places the Negro at a disadvantage in relation to other racial groups in his pursuit of educational opportunities is violative of the equal protection clause.

"In the instant case, the court found as a fact that appellants were placed at such a disadvantage and were denied educational opportunities equal to those available to white students.

". . . . . . . . . . . . . .

"Thus, notwithstanding that it had found inequality in educational opportunity as a fact, the court concluded as a matter of law that such inequality did not constitute a denial of constitutional rights, saying: . . ."

There is no such finding of fact in the Record in this case.

With all respect due to able counsel for appellants we believe that in their zeal for their cause, they have overstated their case. The only existing Finding of Fact which is relied upon by appellants and the only one quoted in their brief is the District Court's Finding of Fact No. VIII, which we quote accurately:

"Segregation of white and colored children in public schools has a detrimental effect upon the colored children. The impact is greater when it has the sanction of the law; for the policy of separating the races is usually interpreted as denoting the inferiority of the Negro group. A sense of inferiority affects the motivation of a child to learn. Segregation with the sanction of law, therefore, has a tendency to retain the educational and mental development of Negro children and to deprive them of some of the benefits they would receive in a racial integrated school system."

We call attention to the fact that the foregoing Finding is couched only in broad and general language; it makes no specific or particular reference to any of the appellants, nor to the grade schools in Topeka, nor to racial groups other than Negroes, nor to inequality of educational opportunities between Negroes and other racial groups. The substance of the finding can be summarized in the following statement: "Generally speaking, segregation is detrimental to colored children, and deprives them of some benefits they would receive in a racial integrated school system."

The Finding of Fact No. VIII cannot be stretched, as counsel for appellants apparently would like to stretch it, into a finding that the appellants in this case have "suffered serious harm in being required to attend segregated elementary schools in Topeka" and that "appellants were placed at such a disadvantage (in relation to other racial groups in [their] pursuit of educational opportunities) and were denied

educational opportunities equal to those available to white students."

**B. Elements necessary to entitle appellants to injunctive relief and to a reversal of the judgment in this case.** To establish appellants' right to injunctive relief and to reversal of the judgment in this case, the Findings of Fact No. VIII would have to show:

> (1) That the appellants have actually suffered personal harm as the result of attending segregated schools in Topeka; and,
> (2) Either that appellants are being deprived of benefits which other students in the Topeka school system enjoy, or that appellants are being subjected to detriments to which other students in the Topeka school system are not being subjected, by reason of maintenance of a segregated school system.

The mere showing that appellants may be members of a class which is being discriminated against by reason of a statute is not sufficient to entitle them to injunctive relief, unless appellants can also show that they personally are suffering harm. The Fourteenth Amendment protects only personal and individual rights.

The mere showing that appellants can show that they are being deprived of benefits they would receive under a different system of schools is not sufficient to show that they are being deprived of equal protection of the law, unless appellants can also show that under the existing segregate school system there are others who are not deprived of such benefits.

And finally, the mere showing that segregation is detrimental to appellants is not sufficient to show that they are being deprived of equal protection of the laws, unless they also show that segregation is not similarly detrimental to others in the Topeka school system.

*McCabe v. A. T. & S. F. Ry. Co.*, 235 U.S. 151, 59 Law Ed. 149:

> "There is, however, an insuperable obstacle to the granting of the relief sought by this bill. It was filed, as we have seen, by five persons against five railroad corporations to restrain them from complying with the state statute. The suit had been brought before the law went into effect, and this amended bill was filed very shortly after. It contains some general allegations as to discriminations in the supply of facilities and as to the hardships which will ensue. It states that there will be 'A multiplicity of suits,' there being at least 'fifty thousand persons of the Negro race in the state of Oklahoma' who will be injured and deprived of their civil rights. But we are dealing here with the case of the complainants, and nothing is shown to entitle them to an injunction. It is an elementary principle that, in order to justify

the granting of this extraordinary relief, the complainant's need of it, and the absence of an adequate remedy at law, must clearly appear. The complainant cannot succeed because someone else may be hurt. Nor does it make any difference that other persons who may be injured are persons of the same race or occupation. It is the fact, clearly established, of injury to the complainant—not to others—which justifies judicial intervention." (p. 162.)

*Turpin v. Lemon*, 187 U.S. 51, 47 Law Ed. 70:

"This is an effort to test the constitutionality of the law, without showing that the plaintiff had been injured by its application, and, in this particular, the case falls without ruling in *Tyler v. Registration Court Judges*, 179 U.S. 405, 45 L. ed. 252, 21 Sup. Ct. Rep. 206, wherein we held that the plaintiff was bound to show he had personally suffered an injury before he could institute a bill for relief. In short, the case made by the plaintiff is purely academic." (pp. 60, 61.)

*Thomas Cusack Co. v. Chicago*, 242 U.S. 526, 61 Law Ed. 472:

"He who is not injured by the operation of a law or ordinance cannot be said to be deprived by it of either constitutional right or of property." (p. 530.)

*Mallinckrodt Chemical Works v. Missouri ex rel. Jones*, 238 U.S. 41, 59 L. ed. 1192:

"As has been often pointed out, one who seeks to set aside a state statute as repugnant to the Federal Constitution must show that he is within the class with respect to whom the act is unconstitutional, and that the alleged unconstitutional feature injures him." (p. 54.)

**C. Finding of Fact No. VIII fails to disclose that any of the appellants have been actually and personally harmed by segregation in the Topeka Schools.** Finding of Fact No. VIII makes no specific reference to the individual appellants. It expresses only in broad generalities the effect of segregation in the public schools upon colored children as a class. There is no specific finding that segregation has had a personal detrimental effect upon any of the appellants. There is no specific finding that any of the appellants personally has interpreted segregation as denoting inferiority of the Negro group, or that the motivation to learn of any of the appellants has been affected by a sense of inferiority. There is no finding that the educational and mental development of any of the appellants has actually been retained or retarded by reason of segregation in the Topeka schools. In short there is no finding that any of

the appellants individually and actually has been harmed by segregation in the Topeka school system.

**D. Finding of Fact No. VIII fails to disclose that appellants are being deprived of equal protection of the laws, or that they are being discriminated against by segregation in the Topeka Schools.** Denial of equal protection of the laws, or discrimination, logically and necessarily involves at least two persons who are being treated differently. Denial of equal protection must mean denial of protection or opportunity equal to that afforded to someone else. There can be no such thing as "unilateral discrimination."

Since the Finding of Fact No. VIII is limited solely to a statement of the effect of segregation on colored children as a group, and nowhere mentions the effect of segregation upon any other race or group, it cannot reasonably or logically show discrimination or a denial of equal protection of the laws.

Nowhere in the finding has the court disclosed any facts upon which it can be claimed to show discrimination in favor of white children over colored in segregated schools.

It is idle on this appeal to speculate upon what the trial court might have found had it been requested to make additional findings. No request for additional findings was made in the trial court. We therefore refrain from speculating as to whether the court would also have found that segregation was detrimental to white children and impaired their educational and mental development.

**E. The District Court did not intend nor consider its Finding of Fact No. VIII to be a finding of discrimination against appellants.** The last sentence in Finding of Fact No. VIII summarizes the entire finding. We quote:

"Segregation with the sanction of law, therefore, has a tendency to retain the educational and mental development of Negro children and to deprive them of some of the benefits they would receive in a racial integrated school system."

We believe the court intended the finding to mean simply that colored children would be better off in integrated schools than they are in segregated schools. Conceding that that is the meaning of the finding, it does not amount to a finding of actual discrimination against colored children and in favor of white children upon the facts in this case. White children are not permitted to attend integrated schools in Topeka. The mere fact, if it be a fact, that the Topeka school system could be improved so far as education of colored children is concerned, does not prove discrimination against them.

In the opinion of the District Court (R. 238 to 244), 98 F. Supp. 797, no mention is made of Finding of Fact No. VIII. It is clear the District Court did not consider or intend to attach to that finding the same significance which appellants seek to place upon it.

We do not question that if the Finding of Fact No. VIII means everything appellants claim it means, they would be entitled to an injunction and reversal of the judgment, if this court should overrule the "separate but equal doctrine." However, it is clear that the District Court did not intend or consider the finding to mean all the things appellants claim for it. As stated in the Decree of the District Court:

> "The Court has heretofore filed its Findings of Fact and Conclusions of Law together with an opinion and has held as a matter of law that the plaintiffs have failed to prove they are entitled to the relief demanded."

## IX. CONCLUSION

In view of the authorities heretofore cited, appellees respectfully submit that the judgment of the court below should be affirmed.

HAROLD R. FATZER,
Attorney General,

PAUL E. WILSON,
Asst. Attorney General,
Counsel for the State of Kansas,
State House, Topeka, Kansas,

PETER F. CALDWELL,
Counsel for the Board of Education of Topeka, Kansas.
512 Capitol Federal Bldg., Topeka, Kansas.

ı

### 345 U.S. 972

**Oliver BROWN, Mrs. Richard Lawton, Mrs. Sadie Emmanuel, et al., appellants, v. BOARD OF EDUCATION OF TOPEKA, SHAWNEE COUNTY, KANSAS, et al. No. 8.**

Former decision, 72 S.Ct. 1070; 344 U.S. 1, 73 S.Ct. 1; 344 U.S. 141, 73 S.Ct. 124.

Facts and opinion, 98 F.Supp. 797.

June 8, 1953. Case ordered restored to the docket and is assigned for reargument on Monday, October 12, next. In their briefs and on oral argument counsel are requested to discuss particularly the following questions insofar as they are relevant to the respective cases:

"I. What evidence is there that the Congress which submitted and the State legislatures and conventions which ratified the Fourteenth Amendment contemplated or did not contemplate, understood or did not understand, that it would abolish segregation in public schools?

"2. If neither the Congress in submitting nor the States in ratifying the Fourteenth Amendment understood that compliance with it would require the immediate abolition of segregation in public schools, was it nevertheless the understanding of the framers of the Amendment

"(a) that future Congresses might, in the exercise of their power under section 5 of the Amendment, abolish such segregation, or

"(b) that it would be within the judicial power, in light of future conditions, to construe the Amendment as abolishing such segregation of its own force?

"3. On the assumption that the answers to questions 2(a) and (b) do not dispose of the issue, is it within the judicial power, in construing the Amendment, to abolish segregation in public schools?

"4. Assuming it is decided that segregation in public schools violates the Fourteenth Amendment

"(a) would a decree necessarily follow providing that, within the limits set by normal geographic school districting, Negro children should forthwith be admitted to schools of their choice, or

"(b) may this Court, in the exercise of its equity powers, permit an effective gradual adjustment to be brought about from existing segregated systems to a system not based on color distinctions?

"5. On the assumption on which questions 4(a) and (b) are based, and assuming further that this Court will exercise its equity powers to the end described in question 4(b),

"(a) should this Court formulate detailed decrees in this case;

"(b) if so what specific issues should the decrees reach;

"(c) should this Court appoint a special master to hear evidence with a view to recommending specific terms for such decrees;

"(d) should this Court remand to the courts of first instance with directions to frame decrees in this case and if so what general directions should the decrees of this Court include and what procedures should the courts of first instance follow in arriving at the specific terms of more detailed decrees?

"The Attorney General of the United States is invited to take part in the oral argument and to file an additional brief if he so desires."

# THE
# SUPREME COURT OF THE UNITED STATES
## OCTOBER TERM, 1953

### NO. 1

**OLIVER BROWN, ET AL.,** APPELLANTS,

VS.

**BOARD OF EDUCATION OF TOPEKA, ET AL.,** APPELLEES.

### NO. 2

**HARRY BRIGGS, JR., ET AL.,** APPELLANTS.

VS.

**R. W. ELLIOTT, ET AL.,** APPELLEES.

### NO. 4

**DOROTHY E. DAVIS, ET AL.,** APPELLANTS,

VS.

**COUNTY SCHOOL BOARD OF PRINCE EDWARDS COUNTY,** APPELLEES.

### NO. 10

**FRANCIS B. GEBHART, ET AL.,** PETITIONERS,

VS.

**ETHEL LOUISE BELTON, ET AL.,** RESPONDENTS.

## APPEALS FROM THE UNITED STATES DISTRICT COURT FOR THE DISTRICT OF KANSAS, THE EASTERN DISTRICT OF SOUTH CAROLINA AND THE EASTERN DISTRICT OF VIRGINIA, AND ON PETITION FOR A WRIT OF CERTIORARI TO THE SUPREME COURT OF DELAWARE, RESPECTIVELY

## BRIEF FOR APPELLANTS IN NOS. 1, 2 AND 4 AND FOR RESPONDENTS IN NO. 10 ON REARGUMENT

CHARLES L. BLACK, JR.,
ELWOOD H. CHISOLM,
WILLIAM T. COLEMAN, JR.,
CHARLES T. DUNCAN,
GEORGE E. C. HAYES,
WILLIAM R. MING, JR.,
CONSTANCE BAKER MOTLEY,
JAMES M. NABRIT, JR.,
DAVID E. PINSKY,
FRANK D. REEVES,
JOHN SCOTT,

JACK B. WEINSTEIN,
*of Counsel.*
HAROLD BOULWARE,
ROBERT L. CARTER,
JACK GREENBERG,
OLIVER W. HILL,
THURGOOD MARSHALL,
LOUIS L. REDDING,
SPOTTSWOOD W. ROBINSON, III,
CHARLES S. SCOTT,
    *Attorneys for Appellants in Nos. 1, 2, 4*
    *and for Respondents in No. 10.*

# TABLE OF CONTENTS

Argument

Part One

PART THREE

1. This Court should declare invalid the constitutional and statutory provisions here involved requiring segregation in public schools. After careful consideration of all of the factors involved in transition from segregated school systems to unsegregated school systems, appellants know of no reasons or considerations which would war-

rant postponement of the enforcement of appellants' rights by this Court in the exercise of its equity powers.....................[458]

IN THE
SUPREME COURT OF THE
UNITED STATES
OCTOBER TERM, 1953
NO. 1

---

OLIVER BROWN, ET AL., APPELLANTS,

VS.

BOARD OF EDUCATION OF TOPEKA, ET AL.,
APPELLEES.

---

NO. 2

---

HARRY BRIGGS, JR., ET AL., APPELLANTS,

VS.

R. W. ELLIOTT, ET AL., APPELLEES.

---

NO. 4

---

DOROTHY E. DAVIS, ET AL., APPELLANTS,

VS.

COUNTY SCHOOL BOARD OF PRINCE
EDWARD COUNTY, VIRGINIA, ET AL.,
APPELLEES.

---

NO. 10

---

FRANCIS B. GEBHART, ET AL., PETITIONERS,

VS.

ETHEL LOUISE BELTON, ET AL., RESPONDENTS.

---

APPEALS FROM THE UNITED
STATES DISTRICT COURTS FOR
THE DISTRICT OF KANSAS, THE
EASTERN DISTRICT OF SOUTH
CAROLINA AND THE EASTERN
DISTRICT OF VIRGINIA, AND ON
PETITION FOR A WRIT OF
CERTIORARI TO THE SUPREME
COURT OF DELAWARE,
RESPECTIVELY

---

BRIEF FOR APPELLANTS IN
NOS. 1, 2 AND 4 AND FOR
RESPONDENTS IN NO. 10 ON
REARGUMENT

---

**EXPLANATORY STATEMENT**

One brief is being filed in these four cases.
They fundamentally involve the same questions
and issues. As an aid to the Court, we are
restating below a full history of each case.

**NO. 1**

**Opinion below**

The opinion of the statutory three-judge District Court for the District of Kansas (R. 238–244) is reported at 98 F. Supp. 797.

**Jurisdiction**

The judgment of the court below was entered on August 3, 1951 (R. 247). On October 1, 1951, appellants filed a petition for appeal (R. 248), and an order allowing the appeal was entered (R. 250). Probable jurisdiction was noted on June 9, 1952 (R. 254). Jurisdiction of this Court rests on Title 28, United States Code, §§ 1253 and 2101(b).

**Statement of the case**

Appellants are Negro students eligible to attend and attending elementary schools in Topeka, Kansas, and their parents (R. 3–4). Appellees are state officers empowered to maintain and operate the public schools of Topeka, Kansas (R. 4–5). On March 22, 1951, appellants commenced this class action against appellees to restrain them from enforcing and executing that part of Chapter 72–1724, General Statutes of Kansas, 1949, which permitted racial segregation in public elementary schools, on the ground that it violated the Fourteenth Amendment by depriving the infant appellants of equal educational opportunities (R. 2–7), and for a judgment declaring that the practice of appellees under said statute of maintaining and operating racially segregated elementary schools is in violation of the Fourteenth Amendment.

Appellees admitted in their answer that they acted pursuant to the statute and that, solely because of their color, the infant appellants were not eligible to attend any of the elementary schools maintained exclusively for white students (R. 12). The Attorney General of the State of Kansas filed a separate answer specifically to defend the constitutional validity of the statute (R. 14).

The court below was convened in accordance with Title 28, United States Code, § 2284, and, on June 25–26, a trial on the merits was held (R. 63 *et seq.*). On August 3, 1951, the court below filed its opinion (R. 238–244), findings of fact (R. 244–246) and conclusions of law (R. 246–247) and entered a final judgment denying the injunctive relief sought (R. 247).

## Specification of errors

The court below erred:

**1.** In refusing to grant appellants' application for a permanent injunction to restrain appellees from acting pursuant to the statute under which they are maintaining separate public elementary schools for Negro children, solely because of their race and color.

**2.** In refusing to hold that the State of Kansas is without authority to promulgate the statute because it enforces a classification based upon race and color which is violative of the Constitution of the United States.

**3.** In refusing to enter judgment in favor of appellants after finding that enforced attendance at racially segregated elementary schools was detrimental and deprived them of educational opportunities equal to those available to white children.

## NO. 2

### Opinions below

The majority and dissenting opinions of the statutory three-judge District Court for the Eastern District of South Carolina on the first hearing (R. 176–209) are reported in 98 F. Supp. 529–548. The opinion on the second hearing (R. 301–306) is reported in 103 F. Supp. 920–923.

### Jurisdiction

The judgment of the court below was entered on March 13, 1952 (R. 306). A petition for appeal was filed below and allowed on May 10, 1952 (R. 309). Probable jurisdiction was noted on June 9, 1952 (R. 316). Jurisdiction of this Court rests on Title 28, United States Code, §§ 1253 and 2101(b).

### Statement of the case

Appellants are Negro children who reside in and are eligible to attend the public schools of School District No. 22, Clarendon County, South Carolina, and their respective parents and guardians (R. 4–5). Appellees are the public school officials of said district who, as officers of the state, maintain and operate the public schools of that district (R. 5–6). On December 22, 1950, appellants commenced this class action against appellees to enjoin enforcement of Article XI, Section 7, of the Constitution of South Carolina and Section 5377 of the Code of Laws of South Carolina of 1942, which require the segregation of races in public schools, on the ground that they deny to appellants the equal protection of the laws secured by the Fourteenth Amendment, and for a judgment declaring that said laws violate the Fourteenth Amendment and are invalid (R. 2–11).

Appellees in their answer admitted adherence to the said constitutional and statutory provisions requiring racial segregation in public schools and asserted that such provisions were a reasonable exercise of the police powers of the state and, therefore, were valid (R. 13–17).

A three-judge District Court was convened, pursuant to Title 28, United States Code, §§ 2284, and on July 25, 1951, a trial on the merits was held (R. 30 *et seq.*). On June 23, 1951, the court below filed its opinion (R. 176) and entered a final decree (R. 209): (1) upholding the constitutional validity of the contested state constitutional and statutory provisions; (2) denying the injunctive relief which was sought; (3) requiring appellees to furnish to appellants educational facilities equal to those furnished to white students; and (4) requiring appellees within six months to file a report of action taken toward that end.

An appeal from this judgment was allowed by this Court on July 20, 1951. The report required by the decree of the court below was filed on December 21, 1951, and subsequently forwarded to this Court. On January 28, 1952, this Court vacated the judgment of the court below and remanded the case for the purpose of obtaining the views of the court below on the additional facts in the record and to give it the opportunity to take such action as it might deem appropriate in light of the report. 342 U.S. 350. Mr. Justice Black and Mr. Justice Douglas dissented on the ground that the additional facts in the report were "wholly irrelevant to the constitutional questions presented by the appeal to this Court". 342 U.S. 350.

Pursuant to the mandate of this Court, a second trial was held in the court below on March 3, 1953 (R. 271), at which time the appellees filed an additional report showing progress made since the filing of the original report (R. 273). On March 13, 1952, the court below filed its opinion (R. 301) and entered a final decree (R. 306) again upholding the validity of the contested constitutional and statutory provisions, denying the injunctive relief requested and requiring appellees to afford to appellants educational facilities equal to those afforded to white students.

### Specification of errors

The court below erred:

**1.** In refusing to enjoin the enforcement of the laws of South Carolina requiring racial segregation in the public schools of Clarendon County on the ground that these laws violate rights secured under the equal protection clause of the Fourteenth Amendment.

2. In refusing to grant to appellants immediate and effective relief against the unconstitutional practice of excluding appellants from an opportunity to share the public school facilities of Clarendon County on an equal basis with other students without regard to race or color.

3. In predicating its decision on the doctrine of *Plessy* v. *Ferguson* and in disregarding the rationale of *Sweatt* v. *Painter* and *McLaurin* v. *Board of Regents.*

## NO. 4

### Opinion below

The opinion of the statutory three-judge District Court for the Eastern District of Virginia (R. 617–623) is reported at 103 F. Supp. 337–341.

### Jurisdiction

The judgment of the court below was entered on March 7, 1952 (R. 623). A petition for appeal was filed below and allowed on May 5, 1952 (R. 625, 630, 683). Probable jurisdiction was noted on October 8, 1952. __U.S. __, 97 L. ed. (Advance p. 27). Jurisdiction of this Court rests on Title 28, United States Code, §§ 1253 and 2101(b).

### Statement of the case

Appellants, high school students residing in Prince Edward County, Virginia, and their parents and guardians, brought a class action against appellees, the County School Board and the Division Superintendent of Schools on May 23, 1951. The complaint (R. 5–30) alleged that said appellees maintained separate public secondary schools for Negro and white children pursuant to Article IX, Section 140 of the Constitution of Virginia, and Title 22, Chapter 12, Article 1, section 22–221, of the Code of Virginia of 1950; that the Negro school was inferior and unequal to the white schools; and that it was impossible for the infant appellants to secure educational opportunities or facilities equal to those afforded white children similarly situated as long as said appellees enforce said laws or pursued a policy of racial segregation. It sought a judgment declaratory of the invalidity of said laws as a denial of rights secured by the due process and equal protection clauses of the Fourteenth Amendment, and an injunction restraining said appellees from enforcing said laws and from making any distinction based on race or color among children attending the secondary schools of the County.

Appellees admitted maintenance of said schools, enforcement of said laws, and inequalities as to physical plant and equipment, but denied that the segregation violated the Constitution (R. 32–36). Appellee, the Commonwealth of Virginia, intervened (R. 37) and made the same admissions and defense (R. 37–39).

On March 7, 1952, a three-judge District Court found the Negro school inferior in plant, facilities, curricula and means of transportation (R. 622–623) and ordered appellees forthwith to provide "substantially" equal curricula and transportation facilities and to "proceed with all reasonable diligence and dispatch to remove" the existing inequality "by building, furnishing and providing a high school building and facilities for Negro students" (R. 624). It refused to enjoin enforcement of the constitutional and statutory segregation provisions on the grounds: (1) that appellants' evidence as to the effects of educational segregation did not overbalance appellees', and that it accepted as "apt and able precedent" *Briggs* v. *Elliott*, 98 F. Supp. 529 (E. D. S. C. 1951) and *Carr* v. *Corning*, 182 F. 2d 14 (C. A. D. C. 1950) which "refused to decree that segregation be abolished incontinently" (R. 619); (2) that nullification of the segregation provisions was unwarranted in view of evidence that racial segregation was not based on prejudice or caprice but, rather, was "one of the ways of life in Virginia" (R. 620); (3) that segregation has begotten greater opportunities for the Negro (R. 621); (4) that elimination of segregation would lessen interest in and financial support of public schools (R. 621); and (5) that, finding "no hurt or harm to either race," it was not for the court "to adjudge the policy as right or wrong" (R. 621–622).

### Specification of errors

The court below erred:

1. In refusing to enjoin the enforcement of Article IX, Section 140 of the Constitution of Virginia, and Title 22, Chapter 12, Article 1, Section 22–221, of the Code of Virginia of 1950, upon the grounds that these laws violate rights secured by the due process and equal protection clauses of the Fourteenth Amendment to the Constitution of the United States.

2. In refusing to forthwith restrain appellees from using race as a factor in determining the assignment of public secondary educational facilities in Prince Edward County, Virginia, after it had found that appellants are denied equality of buildings, facilities, curricula and means of transportation in violation of the due process and equal protection clauses of the Fourteenth Amendment.

**3.** In refusing to hold that appellants are entitled to equality in all aspects of the public secondary educational process, in addition to equality in physical facilities and curricula.

**4.** In issuing a decree ordering appellees to equalize secondary school facilities in the County where such decree cannot be effectively enforced without involving the court in the daily operation and supervision of schools.

## NO. 10

### Opinions below

The opinion of the Chancellor of the State of Delaware (A. 338) is reported at 87 A. (2d) 862. The opinion of the Supreme Court of Delaware (R. 37) is reported at 91 A. (2d) 137.*

### Jurisdiction

The judgment of the court below was entered on August 28, 1952 (R. 37). On November 13, 1952 petition for writ of certiorari was filed herein. On November 20, 1952, respondents waived the filing of a brief in opposition to the petition for writ of certiorari and moved that, if certiorari were granted, the argument be advanced and heard immediately following argument in Nos. 8, 101 and 191. On November 24, 1952, the petition for writ of certiorari and motion to advance were granted. __U.S. __; 97 L. ed. (Advance, p. 124). Jurisdiction of this Court rests upon Title 28, United States Code, § 1257(3).

### Statement of the case

No. 10 arises from two separate class actions filed in the Court of Chancery of the State of Delaware by Negro school children and their guardians seeking admittance of the children to two public schools maintained by petitioners exclusively for white children in New Castle County, Delaware. In the courts below, plaintiffs prevailed, and they and members of their class are now attending the schools to which they sought admission, an application for stay of final order having been denied. (Brief of Respondents, No. 448, October Term, 1952, pp. 25–27). Thus, in this case, unlike the other

---

* The record in this case consists of five separate parts: appendix to petitioners' brief in the court below, the supplement thereto, appendix to respondents' brief in the court below, the supplement thereto, and the record of proceedings in the Supreme Court of Delaware. These will be referred to in respondents' brief as follows:

Appendix to petitioners' brief below will be indicated by A; the supplement to the petitioners' appendix below will be referred to as SA; respondents' appendix below will be referred to as RA; the supplement to respondents' appendix below will be referred to as RSA; the record of proceedings in the Supreme Court of Delaware will be referred to as R.

school segregation cases now under consideration, plaintiffs are respondents in this Court. Nevertheless, they file their brief at this time along with appellants in Numbers 1, 2 and 4, because, on the fundamental issues, they take the same position as do those appellants, and because they believe that by so filing they will facilitate the Court's consideration of the matters at bar.

The complaint (A 3–13) in one of the two cases from which No. 10 arises, alleged that respondents residing in the Claymont Special School District were refused admittance to the Claymont High School maintained by petitioner-members of the State Board of Education and members of the Board of Education of the Claymont Special School District solely because of respondents' color. Because of this, these respondents were compelled to attend Howard High School (RA 47), a public school for Negroes only, in Wilmington, Delaware. Howard High School is operated and controlled by the Corporate Board of Public Education in Wilmington, not a party to this case (A 314–15, 352; R 57, RA 203). The second complaint (A 14–30) out of which No. 448 arises alleged that respondent was excluded from Hockessin School No. 29, a public elementary school maintained for white children only, by petitioner-members of the State Board of Education and petitioner-members of the Board of School Trustees of Hockessin School No. 29. Respondent and the class she represented at the time of the complaint, attended Hockessin School No. 107, maintained solely for Negroes by the State Board of Education. Respondents in both complaints asserted that the aforesaid state-imposed racial segregation required by Par. 2631, Revised Code of Delaware, 1935, and Article X, Section 1 of the Constitution of Delaware: (1) compelled them to attend schools substantially inferior to those for white children to which admittance was sought; and (2) injured their mental health, impeded their mental and personality development and made inferior their educational opportunity as compared with that offered by the state to white children similarly situated. Such treatment, respondents asserted, is prohibited by the equal protection clause of the Fourteenth Amendment to the Constitution of the United States.

Petitioners' answers (A 31–33, A 34–37) defended the exclusion: (1) upon mandatory constitutional and statutory provisions of the State of Delaware which require separate public schools for white and colored children; and (2) upon the fact that the educational opportunities offered respondents were equal to those offered white children similarly situated.

The two cases were consolidated and tried before the Chancellor. In an opinion (A 348–356; 87 A. (2d) 862) filed on April 1, 1952, the Chancellor found as a fact that in "our Delaware society" segregation in education practiced by petitioners "itself results in Negro children, as a class, receiving educational opportunities which are substantially inferior to those available to white children otherwise similarly situated." However, the Chancellor denied respondents' prayers for a judgment on this ground and refused to declare that the Delaware constitutional and statutory provisions violated respondents' right to equal protection. But the Chancellor did award respondents the relief which they requested because other inequalities were found to exist. These included, in the high school, teacher training, pupil-teacher ratio, extra-curricular activities, physical plant and esthetic considerations, and time and distance involved in travel. As to the elementary schools in question, the court found the Negro facilities inferior in building and site, esthetic considerations, teacher preparation and transportation facilities. A more detailed exposition of the facts upon which these findings were based is set forth in respondents' Brief in No. 448, October Term, 1952, pp. 27–44.

The Chancellor, as stated above, ordered that respondents be granted immediate relief in the only way that it was then available, that is, by admission to the superior facilities. On August 28, 1952, the Supreme Court of Delaware affirmed. 91 A. (2d) 137. Its findings on some of the facts were somewhat different than the Chancellor's but, on the whole, it agreed with him. Upholding the Chancellor's determination that the requested relief could not be granted because of the harmful psychological effect of racial segregation, it did not otherwise review his factual findings in this regard. Denying petitioners' plea for time to equalize the facilities in question, the Supreme Court held that in the high school case: (1) a decree ordering petitioners to equalize the facilities in question could have no effect on the legal entity having control of the Wilmington public schools which was not a party to the cause; and (2) that the court did not see how it could supervise and control the expenditure of state funds in a matter committed to the administrative discretion of school authorities. Finally, the court held that it could not issue a decree which would, in effect, deny to plaintiffs what it had held they rightfully deserved. As to the elementary school, the court also noted that defendants had not assumed the burden of showing to what extent remedial legislation had improved or could improve conditions in the future. Alluding to its antecedent discussion of the question of relief for high school respondents, it affirmed the Chancellor's finding on this issue also.

Stay of the order was denied by the Chancellor and by the Supreme Court of Delaware (Brief of Respondents, No. 448, October Term, 1952, pp. 25–27) and respondents and members of their class are now enjoying their second year of equal educational opportunities under the decree.

### This court's order

These four cases were argued and submitted to the Court on December 9–11, 1952. Thereafter, on June 8, 1953, this Court entered its order for reargument, as follows, __U.S. __; 97 L. ed. (Advance p. 956):

"Each of these cases is ordered restored to the docket and is assigned for reargument on Monday, October 12, next. In their briefs and on oral argument counsel are requested to discuss particularly the following questions insofar as they are relevant to the respective cases:

"1. What evidence is there that the Congress which submitted and the State legislatures and conventions which ratified the Fourteenth Amendment contemplated or did not contemplate, understood or did not understand, that it would abolish segregation in public schools?

"2. If neither the Congress in submitting nor the States in ratifying the Fourteenth Amendment understood that compliance with it would require the immediate abolition of segregation in public schools, was it nevertheless the understanding of the framers of the Amendment

"(a) that future Congresses might, in the exercise of their power under Sec. 5 of the Amendment, abolish such segregation, or

"(b) that it would be within the judicial power, in light of future conditions, to construe the Amendment as abolishing such segregation of its own force?

"3. On the assumption that the answers to questions 2(a) and (b) do not dispose of the issue, is it within the judicial power, in construing the Amendment, to abolish segregation in public schools?

"4. Assuming it is decided that segregation in public schools violates the Fourteenth Amendment

"(a) would a decree necessarily follow providing that, within the limits set by normal geographic school districting, Negro children should forthwith be admitted to schools of their choice, or

"(b) may this Court, in the exercise of its equity powers, permit an effective gradual adjustment to be brought about from existing segregated systems to a system not based on color distinctions?

"5. On the assumption on which questions 4(a) and (b) are based, and assuming further that this Court will exercise its equity powers to the end described in question 4(b), "(a) should this Court formulate detailed decrees in these cases;

"(b) if so what specific issues should the decrees reach;

"(c) should this Court appoint a special master to hear evidence with a view to recommending specific terms for such decrees;

"(d) should this Court remand to the courts of first instance with directions to frame decrees in these cases, and if so, what general directions should the decrees of this Court include and what procedures should the courts of first instance follow in arriving at the specific terms of more detailed decrees?

"The Attorney General of the United States is invited to take part in the oral argument and to file an additional brief if he so desires."

On August 4, 1953, upon motion of the Attorney General of the United States and without objection by the parties, this Court entered its order postponing the date assigned for reargument of these cases until December 7, 1953.

## SUMMARY OF ARGUMENT

These cases consolidated for argument before this Court present in different factual contexts essentially the same ultimate legal questions.

The substantive question common to all is whether a state can, consistently with the Constitution, exclude children, solely on the ground that they are Negroes, from public schools which otherwise they would be qualified to attend. It is the thesis of this brief, submitted on behalf of the excluded children, that the answer to the question is in the negative: the Fourteenth Amendment prevents states from according differential treatment to American children on the basis of their color or race. Both the legal precedents and the judicial theories, discussed in Part I hereof, and the evidence concerning the intent of the framers of the Fourteenth Amendment and the understanding of the Congress and the ratifying states, developed in Part II hereof, support this proposition.

Denying this thesis, the school authorities, relying in part on language originating in this Court's opinion in *Plessy v. Ferguson*, 163 U.S. 537, urge that exclusion of Negroes, *qua* Negroes, from designated public schools is permissible when the excluded children are afforded admittance to other schools especially reserved for Negroes, *qua* Negroes, if such schools are equal.

The procedural question common to all the cases is the role to be played, and the time-table to be followed, by this Court and the lower courts in directing an end to the challenged exclusion, in the event that this Court determines, with respect to the substantive question, that exclusion of Negroes, *qua* Negroes, from public schools contravenes the Constitution.

The importance to our American democracy of the substantive question can hardly be overstated. The question is whether a nation founded on the proposition that "all men are created equal" is honoring its commitments to grant "due process of law" and "the equal protection of the laws" to all within its borders when it, or one of its constituent states, confers or denies benefits on the basis of color or race.

1. Distinctions drawn by state authorities on the basis of color or race violate the Fourteenth Amendment. *Shelley v. Kraemer*, 334 U.S. 1; *Buchanan v. Warley*, 245 U.S. 60. This has been held to be true even as to the conduct of public educational institutions. *Sweatt v. Painter*, 339 U.S. 629; *McLaurin v. Oklahoma State Regents*, 339 U.S. 637. Whatever other purposes the Fourteenth Amendment may have had, it is indisputable that its primary purpose was to complete the emancipation provided by the Thirteenth Amendment by ensuring to the Negro equality before the law. The *Slaughter-House Cases*, 16 Wall. 36; *Strauder v. West Virginia*, 100 U.S. 303.

2. Even if the Fourteenth Amendment did not *per se* invalidate racial distinctions as a matter of law, the racial segregation challenged in the instant cases would run afoul of the conventional test established for application of the equal protection clause because the racial classifications here have no reasonable relation to any valid legislative purpose. See *Quaker City Cab Co. v. Pennsylvania*, 277 U.S. 389; *Truax v. Raich*, 239 U.S. 33; *Smith v. Cahoon*, 283 U.S. 553; *Mayflower Farms v. Ten Eyck*, 297 U.S. 266; *Skinner v. Oklahoma*, 316 U.S. 535. See also *Tunstall v. Brotherhood of Locomotive Firemen*, 323 U.S. 192; *Steele v. Louisville & Nashville R. R. Co.*, 323 U.S. 192.

3. Appraisal of the facts requires rejection of the contention of the school authorities. The educational detriment involved in racially constricting a student's associations has already been recognized by this Court. *Sweatt v. Painter*, 339 U.S. 629; *McLaurin v. Oklahoma State Regents*, 339 U.S. 637.

4. The argument that the requirements of the Fourteenth Amendment are met by providing alternative schools rests, finally, on reiteration of the separate but equal doctrine enunciated in *Plessy v. Ferguson*.

Were these ordinary cases, it might be enough to say that the *Plessy* case can be distinguished—that it involved only segregation in transportation. But these are not ordinary cases, and in deference to their importance it seems more fitting to meet the *Plessy* doctrine head-on and to declare that doctrine erroneous.

Candor requires recognition that the plain purpose and effect of segregated education is to perpetuate an inferior status for Negroes which is America's sorry heritage from slavery. But the primary purpose of the Fourteenth Amendment was to deprive the states of *all* power to perpetuate such a caste system.

5. The first and second of the five questions propounded by this Court requested enlightment as to whether the Congress which submitted, and the state legislatures and conventions which ratified, the Fourteenth Amendment contemplated or understood that it would prohibit segregation in public schools, either of its own force or through subsequent legislative or judicial action. The evidence, both in Congress and in the legislatures of the ratifying states, reflects the substantial intent of the Amendment's proponents and the substantial understanding of its opponents that the Fourteenth Amendment would, of its own force, proscribe all forms of state-imposed racial distinctions, thus necessarily including all racial segregation in public education.

The Fourteenth Amendment was actually the culmination of the determined efforts of the Radical Republican majority in Congress to incorporate into our fundamental law the well-defined equalitarian principle of complete equality for all without regard to race or color. The debates in the 39th Congress and succeeding Congresses clearly reveal the intention that the Fourteenth Amendment would work a revolutionary change in our state-federal relationship by denying to the states the power to distinguish on the basis of race.

The Civil Rights Bill of 1866, as originally proposed, possessed scope sufficiently broad in the opinion of many Congressmen to entirely destroy all state legislation based on race. A great majority of the Republican Radicals—who later formulated the Fourteenth Amendment—understood and intended that the Bill would prohibit segregated schools. Opponents of the measure shared this understanding. The scope of this legislation was narrowed because it was known that the Fourteenth Amendment was in process of preparation and would itself have scope exceeding that of the original draft of the Civil Rights Bill.

6. The evidence makes clear that it was the intent of the proponents of the Fourteenth Amendment, and the substantial understanding of its opponents, that it would, of its own force, prohibit all state action predicated upon race or color. The intention of the framers with respect to any specific example of caste state action—in the instant cases, segregated education—cannot be determined solely on the basis of a tabulation of contemporaneous statements mentioning the specific practice. The framers were formulating a constitutional provision setting broad standards for determination of the relationship of the state to the individual. In the nature of things they could not list all the specific categories of existing and prospective state activity which were to come within the constitutional prohibitions. The broad general purpose of the Amendment—obliteration of race and color distinctions—is clearly established by the evidence. So far as there was consideration of the Amendment's impact upon the undeveloped educational systems then existing, both proponents and opponents of the Amendment understood that it would proscribe all racial segregation in public education.

7. While the Amendment conferred upon Congress the power to enforce its prohibitions, members of the 39th Congress and those of subsequent Congresses made it clear that the framers understood and intended that the Fourteenth Amendment was self-executing and particularly pointed out that the federal judiciary had authority to enforce its prohibitions without Congressional implementation.

8. The evidence as to the understanding of the states is equally convincing. Each of the eleven states that had seceded from the Union ratified the Amendment, and concurrently eliminated racial distinctions from its laws, and adopted a constitution free of requirement or specific authorization of segregated schools. Many rejected proposals for segregated schools, and none enacted a school segregation law until after readmission. The significance of these facts is manifest from the consideration that ten of these states, which were required, as a condition of readmission, to ratify the Amendment and to modify their constitutions and laws in conformity therewith, considered that the Amendment required them to remove all racial distinctions from their existing and prospective laws, including those pertaining to public education.

Twenty-two of the twenty-six Union states also ratified the Amendment. Although unfettered by congressional surveillance, the overwhelming majority of the Union states acted with an understanding that it prohibited racially segregated schools and necessitated conformity of their school laws to secure consistency with that understanding.

9. In short, the historical evidence fully sustains this Court's conclusion in the *Slaughter*

*House Cases*, 16 Wall. 61, 81, that the Fourteenth Amendment was designed to take from the states all power to enforce caste or class distinctions.

10. The Court in its fourth and fifth questions assumes that segregation is declared unconstitutional and inquires as to whether relief should be granted immediately or gradually. Appellants, recognizing the possibility of delay of a purely administrative character, do not ask for the impossible. No cogent reasons justifying further exercise of equitable discretion, however, have as yet been produced.

It has been indirectly suggested in the briefs and oral argument of appellees that some such reasons exist. Two plans were suggested by the United States in its Brief as *Amicus Curiae*. We have analyzed each of these plans as well as appellees' briefs and oral argument and find nothing there of sufficient merit on which this Court, in the exercise of its equity power, could predicate a decree permitting an effective gradual adjustment from segregated to nonsegregated school systems. Nor have we been able to find any other reasons or plans sufficient to warrant the exercise of such equitable discretion in these cases. Therefore, in the present posture of these cases, appellants are unable to suggest any compelling reasons for this Court to postpone relief.

### ARGUMENT
### PART ONE

The question of judicial power to abolish segregated schools is basic to the issues involved in these cases and for that reason we have undertaken to analyze it at the outset before dealing with the other matters raised by the Court, although formally this means that the first section of this brief comprehends Question No. 3:

> On the assumption that the answers to question 2(a) and (b) do not dispose of the issue, is it within the judicial power, in construing the Amendment, to abolish segregation in public schools?

### I. NORMAL EXERCISE OF THE JUDICIAL FUNCTION CALLS FOR A DECLARATION THAT THE STATE IS WITHOUT POWER TO ENFORCE DISTINCTIONS BASED UPON RACE OR COLOR IN AFFORDING EDUCATIONAL OPPORTUNITIES IN THE PUBLIC SCHOOLS

This Court in a long line of decisions has made it plain that the Fourteenth Amendment prohibits a state from making racial distinctions in the exercise of governmental power. Time and again this Court has held that if a state's power has been exercised in such a way as to deprive a Negro of a right which he would have freely enjoyed if he had been white, then that state's action violated the Fourteenth Amendment.

In *Shelley* v. *Kraemer*, 334 U.S. 1, for example, an unanimous Court held that States of Missouri and Michigan had violated the 14th Amendment when their courts ruled that a Negro could not own real property whose ownership it was admitted the state law would have protected him in, had he been white. This, despite the fact that the state court was doing no more than enforcing a private agreement running with the land. The sole basis for the decision, then, was that the Fourteenth Amendment compels the states to be color blind in exercising their power and authority.

*Buchanan* v. *Warley*, 245 U.S. 60, was an earlier decision to the same effect. There, this Court invalidated a Louisville, Kentucky ordinance which required racial residential segregation. Though it applied to Negro and white alike, the Court rightly recognized that the ordinance was an exercise of the state's power based on race and race alone. This, the Court ruled, was a violation of the Fourteenth Amendment. To the same effect is *Barrows* v. *Jackson*, __U.S. __, 97 (L. Ed. Advance p. 261). And see *Oyama* v. *California*, 332 U.S. 633.

This Court has applied the same rigorous requirement to the exercise of the state's power in providing public education. Beginning with *Missouri ex rel. Gaines* v. *Canada*, 305 U.S. 337, this Court has uniformly ruled that the Fourteenth Amendment prohibits a state from using race or color as the determinant of the quantum, quality or type of education and the place at which education is to be afforded. Most recently, this Court in *McLaurin* v. *Oklahoma State Regents*, 339 U.S. 637, held that rules which made distinctions among students in the same school solely on the basis of color were forbidden by the Fourteenth Amendment. Thus, this Court has made it plain that no state may use color or race as the axis upon which the state's power turns, and the conduct of the public education system has not been excepted from this ban.

This judicial recognition that race is an irrational basis for governmental action under our Constitution has been manifested in many decisions and opinions of this Court. In *Yick Wo* v. *Hopkins*, 118 U.S. 356, this Court struck down local administrative action which differentiated between whites and Chinese. In *Hirabayashi* v. *United States*, 320 U.S. 81, 100, Chief Justice Stone, in a majority opinion, characterized racial distinctions as "odious to a free people". In *Korematsu* v. *United States*, 323 U.S. 214, 216, the Court viewed racial restrictions as "immediately suspect". Mr. Justice Jackson, concurring in *Edwards* v. *California*, 314 U.S. 180, 185, referred to race and color as "constitutionally an irrelevance". Mr. Justice Douglas, dissenting in *South* v. *Peters*, 339 U.S. 276, 278, considered discriminations based upon race, creed, or color "beyond the pale". In an unanimous opinion in *Henderson* v. *United States*, 339 U.S. 816, 825, the Court, while not reaching the constitutional question raised, described signs, partitions and curtains segregating Negroes in railroad dining cars as emphasizing "the artificiality of a difference in treatment which serves only to call attention to a racial classification of passengers holding identical tickets and using the same public dining facility". Every member of the present Court has from time to time subscribed to this view of race as an irrational premise for government action.

The restrictions placed upon persons of Japanese origin on the West Coast during World War II were sustained in *Hirabayashi* v. *United States, supra,* and in *Korematsu* v. *United States, supra,* as emergency war measures taken by the national government in a dire national peril of the gravest nature. The military decision was upheld as within an implied war power, and the Court was unwilling to interfere with measures considered necessary to the safety of the nation by those primarily responsible for its security. Yet, in upholding these orders, the Court made some of the most sweeping condemnations of governmentally imposed racial and color distinctions ever announced by our judiciary. And while departure from accepted standards of governmental conduct was sustained in order to remove persons of Japanese origin from areas where sabotage and espionage might have worked havoc with the national war effort, once this removal was accomplished and individual loyalty determined, further restrictions based upon race or color could no longer be countenanced. *Ex Parte Endo*, 323 U.S. 283. *Tunstall* v. *Brotherhood of Locomotive Firemen & Enginemen*, 323 U.S. 210, and *Steele* v. *Louisville & Nashville R. R. Co.*, 323 U.S. 192, while not deciding the constitutional question, left no doubt that the Fifth Amendment had stripped the national government of power to enforce the racial discrimination assailed.

These decisions serve to underscore the constitutional prohibition against Congressional action grounded upon color except in so far as it may have temporary justification to meet an overwhelming national emergency such as that which led to decisions in the *Hirabayashi* and *Korematsu* cases.

The power of states is even more rigidly circumscribed. For there is grave doubt that their acts can be sustained under the exception made in the *Hirabayashi* and *Korematsu* cases with respect to the national government. See *Oyama* v. *California*, 332 U.S. 633. The Fourteenth Amendment has been defined as a broad prohibition against state enforcement of differentiations and discrimination based upon race or color. State action restricting the right of Negroes to vote has been struck down as a violation of the Fourteenth Amendment. *Nixon* v. *Condon*, 286 U.S. 73. Similarly, the Court has refused to sanction the systematic exclusion of Negroes from the petit or grand jury, *Hill* v. *Texas*, 316 U.S. 400; *Pierre* v. *Louisiana*, 306 U.S. 354; their representation on juries on a token or proportional basis, *Cassell* v. *Texas*, 339 U.S. 282; *Shepherd* v. *Florida*, 341 U.S. 50; or any method in the selection of juries susceptible of racial discrimination in practice. *Avery* v. *Georgia*, 345 U.S. 559.

Legislation depriving persons of particular races of an opportunity to pursue a gainful occupation has been held a denial of equal protection. *Truax* v. *Raich*, 239 U.S. 33; *Takahashi* v. *Fish and Games Commission*, 334 U.S. 410. It is now well settled that a state may not make racial differences among its employees the basis for salary differentiations. *Alston* v. *School Board*, 112 F. 2d 992 (CA 4th 1940), *cert. denied*, 311 U.S. 693.

Indeed, abhorrence of race as a premise for governmental action pervades a wide realm of judicial opinion dealing with other constitutional provisions. Sweeping decisions have enforced the right of Negroes to make effective use of the electoral process consistent with the requirements of the Fifteenth Amendment. *Guinn* v. *United States*, 238 U.S. 347; *Lane* v. *Wilson*, 307 U.S. 268; *Smith* v. *Allwright*, 321 U.S. 649; *Terry* v. *Adams*, 345 U.S. 461.

It should be added parenthetically that these decisions are not mere *pro forma* applications of the self-evident requirements of the Fifteenth Amendment. On the contrary, the concept of state action has been utilized in a dynamic and expanding fashion as the Court has sought to reach any method or subterfuge with which the state has attempted to avoid its obligation under that constitutional amendment. *Smith* v. *Allwright, supra; Terry* v. *Adams, supra.* See *Rice* v. *Elmore*, 165 F. 2d 387 (CA 4th 1947), *cert. denied*, 333 U.S. 875 and *Baskin* v. *Brown*, 174 F. 2d 391 (CA 4th 1949), cases holding state non-action violative of the Fifteenth Amendment the principle of which was expressly approved in *Terry* v. *Adams*.

State laws requiring racial segregation in interstate commerce have been declared an invalid invasion of commerce power reserved to the Congress. *Morgan* v. *Virginia*, 328 U.S. 373. But where a state sought to enforce against a carrier engaged in foreign commerce its local non-segregation policy, the state law was upheld. The Court considered it inconceivable that the Congress in the exercise of its plenary power over commerce would take any action in conflict with the local nondiscriminatory regulations imposed. *Bob-Lo Excursion Co.* v. *Michigan*, 333 U.S. 28. These two cases considered together strikingly exemplify this Court's position that fundamental national policy is offended by a requirement of segregation, but implemented by its prohibition.

The contention by a labor union that a state civil rights law which prohibited racial discrimination in union membership offended the Fourteenth Amendment was dismissed because such a position "would be a distortion of the policy manifested in that amendment which was adopted to prevent state legislation designed to perpetuate discrimination on the basis of race and color". *Railway Mail Association* v. *Corsi*, 326 U.S. 88, 94.

Thus, the Court has all but universally made short shrift of attempts to use governmental power to enforce racial distinctions. Yet, where such power has prohibited racial discrimination, it has been sustained even where it has been urged that the state is acting in derogation of other constitutional rights or protected interests.

At the graduate and professional school level, closest to the cases here, racial distinctions as applied have been struck down. *McLaurin* v. *Oklahoma State Regents*, 339 U.S. 637; *Sweatt* v. *Painter*, 339 U.S. 629. In those cases the educational process was viewed as a totality. The faculty of the school, the prestige of the institution, the fact that segregation deprived the Negro applicant of the benefits which he might secure in attending school with representatives of the state's dominant racial majority, the value judgment of the community with respect to the segregated school, and the impact of segregation on the individual were among the factors considered by the Court in determining that equal educational opportunities were not available. Those cases, we submit, control disposition of the cases here.

Since segregation was found to impair and inhibit an adult's ability to study in the *McLaurin* case, it seems clear that such segregation has even more far reaching adverse consequences on the mental development of the children involved here.

Sweatt's isolation from the dominant racial majority in a segregated law school was held to deprive him of an effective opportunity to learn the law. The basic function of the public school is to instruct each succeeding generation in the fundamental traditions of our democracy. The child can best come to believe in and respect these traditions by learning them in a setting in which they are in practical operation. But to be taught that our society is founded upon a concept of equality in a public school from which those racial groups are excluded which hold pre-eminence in every field in his community makes it all but impossible for such teachings to take root. Segregation here is detrimental to the Negro child in his effort to develop into a useful and productive citizen in a democracy.

The *Sweatt* and *McLaurin* cases teach that the Court will consider the educational process in its entirety, including, apart from the measurable physical facilities, whatever factors have been shown to have educational significance. This rule cannot be peculiar to any level of public education. Public elementary and high school education is no less a governmental function than graduate and professional education in state institutions. Moreover, just as Sweatt and McLaurin were denied certain benefits characteristic of graduate and professional education, it is apparent from the records of these cases that Negroes are denied educational benefits which the state itself asserts are the fundamental objectives of public elementary and high school education.

South Carolina, like the other states in this country, has accepted the obligation of furnishing the extensive benefits of public education. Article XI, section 5, of the Constitution of South Carolina, declares: "The General Assembly shall provide for a liberal system of free public schools for all children between the ages of six and twenty-one years". Some 410 pages of the Code of Laws of South Carolina deal with "education". Title 31, Chapters 122–23, S. C. Code, pp. 387–795 (1935). Provision is made for the entire state-supported system of public schools, its administration and organization, from the kindergarten through the university. Pupils and teachers, school buildings, minimum standards of school construction, and specifications requiring certain general courses of instruction are dealt with in detail. In addition to requiring that the three "R's" must be taught, the law compels instruction in "morals and good behaviour" and in the "principles" and "essentials of the United States Constitution, including the study of and devotion to American institutions". Title 31, Chapter 122, sections 5321, 5323, 5325, S. C. Code (1935). The other states involved here are attempting to promote the same objectives.

These states thus recognize the accepted broad purposes of general public education in a democratic society. There is no question that furnishing public education is now an accepted governmental function. There are compelling reasons for a democratic government's assuming the burden of educating its children, of increasing its citizens' usefulness, efficiency and ability to govern.

In a democracy citizens from every group, no matter what their social or economic status or their religious or ethnic origins, are expected to participate widely in the making of important public decisions. The public school, even more than the family, the church, business institutions, political and social groups and other institutions, has become an effective agency for giving to all people that broad background of attitudes and skills required to enable them to function effectively as participants in a democracy. Thus, "education" comprehends the entire process of developing and training the mental, physical and moral powers and capabilities of human beings. See *Weyl* v. *Comm. of Int. Rev.*, 48 F. 2d 811, 812 (CA 2d 1931); *Jones* v. *Better Business Bureau*, 123 F. 2d 767, 769 (CA 10th 1941).

The records in instant cases emphasize the extent to which the state has deprived Negroes of these fundamental educational benefits by separating them from the rest of the school population. In the case of *Briggs* v. *Elliott* (No. 101), expert witnesses testified that compulsory racial segregation in elementary and high schools inflicts considerable personal injury on the Negro pupils which endures as long as these students remain in the segregated school. These witnesses testified that compulsory racial segregation in the public schools of South Carolina injures the Negro students by: (1) impairing their ability to learn (R. 140, 161); (2) deterring the development of their personalities (R. 86, 89); (3) depriving them of equal status in the school community (R. 89, 141, 145); (4) destroying their self-respect (R. 140, 148); (5) denying them full opportunity for democratic social development (R. 98, 99, 103); (6) subjecting them to the prejudices of others (R. 133) and stamping them with a badge of inferiority (R. 148).

Similar testimony was introduced in each of the other three cases here involved, and that testimony was undisputed in the case of *Briggs* v. *Elliott* (No. 101); *Brown* v. *Board of Education of Topeka, et al.* (No. 8); *Gebhart* v. *Belton* (No. 448). In *Davis* v. *County School Board* (No. 191), while witnesses for the appellees disputed portions of the testimony of appellants' expert witnesses, four of appellees' witnesses admitted that racial segregation has harmful effects and another recognized that such segregation could be injurious.

In the *Gebhart* case (No. 448) the Chancellor filed an opinion in which he set forth a finding of fact, based on the undisputed oral testimony of experts in education, sociology, psychology, psychiatry and anthropology (A. 340–341) that in "our Delaware society", segregation in education practiced by petitioners as agents of the state "itself results in the Negro children, as a class, receiving educational opportunities which are substantially inferior to those available to white children otherwise similarly situated".

And the court below in the *Brown* case (No. 8) made the following Finding of Fact (R. 245–246):

> "Segregation of white and colored children in public schools has a detrimental effect upon the colored children. The impact is greater when it has the sanction of the law; for the policy of separating the races is usually interpreted as denoting the inferiority of the negro group. A sense of inferiority affects the motivation of a child to learn. Segregation with the sanction of law, therefore, has a tendency to retard the educational and mental development of negro children and to deprive them of some of the benefits they would receive in a racially integrated school system."

The testimony of the expert witnesses in the cases now under consideration, the Opinion of the Chancellor in the Delaware case and the Finding of Fact by the lower court in the Kansas case are amply supported by scientific studies of recognized experts. A compilation of these materials was assembled and filed as an Appendix to the briefs in these cases on the first hearing. The observation of Mr. Justice Jackson in *West Virginia State Board of Education* v. *Barnette*, 319 U.S. 624, 636 that public school children, being educated for citizenship, must be scrupulously protected in their constitutional rights, "if we are not to strangle the free mind at its source and teach youth to discount important principles of our government as mere platitudes", while made in somewhat different context, appropriately describes the high public interest which these cases involve.

In sum, the statutes and constitutional provisions assailed in these cases must fall because they are contrary to this Court's basic premise that, as a matter of law, race is not an allowable basis of differentiation in governmental action; they are inconsistent with the broad prohibition of the Fifth and Fourteenth Amendments as defined by this Court; they are clearly within that category of racism in state action specifically prohibited by the *McLaurin* and *Sweatt* decisions.

## II. THE STATUTORY AND CONSTITUTIONAL PROVISIONS INVOLVED IN THESE CASES CANNOT BE VALIDATED UNDER ANY SEPARATE BUT EQUAL CONCEPT

The basic principles referred to in Point I above, we submit, control these cases, and except for the mistaken belief that the doctrine of *Plessy* v. *Ferguson*, 163 U.S. 537, is a correct expression of the meaning of the Fourteenth Amendment, these cases would present no difficult problem.

This Court announced the separate but equal doctrine in a transportation case, and proponents of segregation have relied upon it repeatedly as a justification for racial segregation as if "separate but equal" had become *in haec verba* an amendment to the Fourteenth Amendment, itself. Under that anomalous doctrine, it is said that racial differentiations in the enjoyment of rights protected by the Fourteenth Amendment are permitted as long as the segregated facilities provided for Negroes are substantially equal to those provided for other racial groups. In each case in this Court where a state scheme of racism has been deemed susceptible of rationalization under the separate but equal formula, it has been urged as a defense.

A careful reading of the cases, however, reveals that this doctrine has received only very limited and restricted application in the actual decisions of this Court, and even that support has been eroded by more recent decisions. See particularly *McLaurin* v. *Oklahoma State Regents; Sweatt* v. *Painter*. Whatever appeal the separate but equal doctrine might have had, it stands mirrored today as the faulty conception of an era dominated by provincialism, by intense emotionalism in race relations caused by local and temporary conditions and by the preaching of a doctrine of racial superiority that contradicted the basic concept upon which our society was founded. Twentieth century America, fighting racism at home and abroad, has rejected the race views of *Plessy* v. *Ferguson* because we have come to the realization that such views obviously tend to preserve not the strength but the weaknesses of our heritage.

## A. Racial segregation cannot be squared with the rationale of the early cases interpreting the reach of the Fourteenth Amendment

In the *Slaughter House Cases*, 16 Wall. 36—the first case decided under the Fourteenth Amendment—the Court, drawing on its knowledge of an almost contemporaneous event, recognized that the Fourteenth Amendment secured to Negroes full citizenship rights and prohibited any state action discriminating against them as a class on account of their race. Thus, addressing itself to the intent of the Thirteenth, Fourteenth and Fifteenth Amendments, the Court said at pages 71 and 72:

> "We repeat, then, in the light of this recapitulation of events, almost too recent to be called history, but which are familiar to us all; and on the most casual examination of the language of these amendments, no one can fail to be impressed with the one pervading purpose found in them all, lying at the foundation of each, and without which none of them would have been even suggested; we mean the freedom of the slave race, the security and firm establishment of that freedom, and the protection of the newly made freeman and citizen from the oppressions of those who had formerly exercised unlimited dominion over him. It is true that only the 15th Amendment, in terms, mentions the negro by speaking of his color and his slavery. But it is just as true that each of the other articles was addressed to the grievances of that race, and designed to remedy them as the fifteenth."

The real purpose of the equal protection clause was discussed in these terms at page 81:

> "In the light of the history of these amendments, and the pervading purpose of them, which we have already discussed, it is not difficult to give a meaning to this clause. *The existence of laws in the states where the newly emancipated negroes resided, which discriminated with gross injustice and hardship against them as a class, was the evil to be remedied by this clause, and by it such laws are forbidden.*" (Emphasis supplied.)

So convinced was the Court that the overriding purpose of the Fourteenth Amendment was to protect the Negro against discrimination that it declared further at page 81:

> "We doubt very much whether any action of a state not directed by way of discrimination against the negroes as a class, or on account of their race, will ever be held to come within the purview of this provision. It is so clearly a provision for that race and that emergency, that a strong case would be necessary for its application to any other."

In *Strauder* v. *West Virginia*, 100 U.S. 303, the Court, on page 306, viewed the Fourteenth Amendment in the same light and stated that its enactment was aimed to secure for the Negro all the civil rights enjoyed by white persons:

"It was in view of these considerations the 14th Amendment was framed and adopted. *It was designed to assure to the colored race the enjoyment of all the civil rights that under the law are enjoyed by white persons,* and to give to that race the protection of the General Government, in that enjoyment, whenever it should be denied by the States. It not only gave citizenship and the privileges of citizenship to persons of color, but *it denied to any State the power to withhold from them the equal protection of the laws,* and authorized Congress to enforce its provisions by appropriate legislation." (Emphasis supplied).

Clearly recognizing the need to construe the Amendment liberally in order to protect the Negro, the Court noted at page 307:

"If this is the spirit and meaning of the Amendment, whether it means more or not, it is to be construed liberally, to carry out the purposes of its framers. It ordains that no State shall make or enforce any laws which shall abridge the privileges or immunities of citizens of the United States (evidently referring to the newly made citizens, who, being citizens of the United States, are declared to be also citizens of the State in which they reside)."

It was explicitly stated at pages 307, 308 that the Amendment prevented laws from distinguishing between colored and white persons:

"What is this but declaring *that the law in the States shall be the same for the black as for the white;* that all persons, whether colored or white, shall stand equal before the laws of the States and, in regard to the colored race, for whose protection the Amendment was primarily designed, that no discrimination shall be made against them by law because of their color? The words of the Amendment, it is true, are prohibitory, but they contain a necessary implication of a positive immunity, or right, most valuable to the colored race—the right to exemption from unfriendly legislation against them distinctly as colored; exemption from legal discriminations, implying inferiority in civil society, lessening the security of their enjoyment of the rights which others enjoy, and discriminations which are steps towards reducing them to the condition of a subject race." (Emphasis supplied).

Any distinction based upon race was understood as constituting a badge of inferiority, at page 308:

"The very fact that colored people are singled out and expressly denied by a statute all right

to participate in the administration of the law, as jurors, because of their color, though they are citizens and may be in other respects fully qualified, is practically a brand upon them, affixed by the law; an assertion of their inferiority, and a stimulant to that race prejudice which is an impediment to securing to individuals of the race that equal justice which the law aims to secure to all others."

There was no doubt that this new constitutional provision had changed the relationship between the federal government and the states so that the federal courts could and should now protect these new rights. At page 309 the Court said:

"The framers of the constitutional Amendment must have known full well the existence of such prejudice and its likelihood to continue against the manumitted slaves and their race, and that knowledge was, doubtless, a motive that led to the Amendment. By their manumission and citizenship the colored race became entitled to the equal protection of the laws of the States in which they resided; and the apprehension that, through prejudice, they might be denied that equal protection, that is, that there might be discrimination against them, was the inducement to bestow upon the National Government the power to enforce the provision that no State shall deny to them the equal protection of the laws. Without the apprehended existence of prejudice that portion of the Amendment would have been unnecessary, and it might have been left to the States to extend equality of protection."

That law must not distinguish between colored and white persons was the thesis of all the early cases. *United States* v. *Cruikshank*, 92 U.S. 542, 554, 555; *Virginia* v. *Rives*, 100 U.S. 313; *Ex Parte Virginia*, 100 U.S. 339; *Neal* v. *Delaware*, 103 U.S. 370, 386; *Bush* v. *Kentucky*, 107 U.S. 110; *Civil Rights Cases*, 109 U.S. 3, 36, 43. As early as *Yick Wo* v. *Hopkins*, 118 U.S. 356, it became settled doctrine that the Fourteenth Amendment was a broad prohibition against state enforcement of racial differentiations or discrimination—a prohibition totally at war with any separate but equal notion. There can be no doubt, we submit, that, had the state regulation approved in *Plessy* v. *Ferguson* been before the Court that rendered the initial interpretations of the Fourteenth Amendment, the regulation would have been held a violation of the Federal Constitution.

## B. The first time the question came before the Court, racial segregation in transportation was specifically disapproved

In *Railroad Co.* v. *Brown*, 17 Wall. 445, the first case involving the validity of segregation to reach this Court after the adoption of the

Fourteenth Amendment, segregation was struck down as an unlawful discrimination. While the Fourteenth Amendment was not before the Court, the decision in the *Brown* case was in line with the spirit of the new status that the Negro had gained under the Thirteenth, Fourteenth and Fifteenth Amendments.

The problem before the Court concerned the validity of the carrier's rules and regulations that sought to segregate its passengers because of race. The pertinent facts are described by the Court as follows at page 451:

> "In the enforcement of this regulation, the defendant in error, a person of color, having entered a car appropriated to white ladies, was requested to leave it and take a seat in another car used for colored persons. This she refused to do, and this refusal resulted in her ejectment by force and with insult from the car she had first entered."

The Court characterized the railroad's defense that its practice of providing separate accommodations for Negroes was valid, as an ingenious attempt at evasion, at page 452:

> "The plaintiff in error contends that it has literally obeyed the direction, because it has never excluded this class of persons from the cars, but on the contrary, has always provided accommodations for them.
>
> "This is an ingenious attempt to evade a compliance with the obvious meaning of the requirement. It is true the words taken literally might bear the interpretation put upon them by the plaintiff in error, but evidently Congress did not use them in any such limited sense. There was no occasion, in legislating for a railroad corporation, to annex a condition to a grant of power, that the company should allow colored persons to ride in its cars. This right had never been refused, nor could there have been in the mind of anyone an apprehension that such a state of things would ever occur, for self-interest would clearly induce the carrier—South as well as North—to transport, if paid for it, all persons whether white or black, who should desire transportation."

The Court stressed with particularity the fact that the discrimination prohibited was discrimination in the use of the cars, at pages 452–453:

> "It was the discrimination in the use of the cars on account of color, where slavery obtained, which was the subject of discussion at the time, and not the fact that the colored race could not ride in the cars at all. Congress, in the belief that this discrimination was unjust, acted. It told this company, in substance, that it could extend its road in the District as desired, but that this discrimination must cease, and the colored and white race, in the use of the cars, be placed on an equality. This condition it had the right to impose, and in the temper of

Congress at the time, it is manifest the grant could not have been made without it."

The regulation that was struck down in the *Brown* case sought to accomplish exactly what was achieved under a state statute upheld subsequently in *Plessy v. Ferguson*—the segregation of Negro and white passengers. It is clear, therefore, that in this earlier decision the Court considered segregation *per se* discrimination and a denial of equality.

## C. The separate but equal doctrine marked an unwarranted departure from the main stream of constitutional development and permits the frustration of the very purposes of the Fourteenth Amendment as defined by this Court

In *Plessy v. Ferguson*, this Court for the first time gave approval to state imposed racial distinctions as consistent with the purposes and meaning of the Fourteenth Amendment. The Court described the aims and purposes of the Fourteenth Amendment in the same manner as had the earlier cases, at page 543:

> "... its main purpose was to establish the citizenship of the negro; to give definitions of citizenship of the United States and of the states, and to protect from the hostile legislation of the states the privileges and immunities of citizens of the United States, as distinguished from those of citizens of the states."

But these defined aims and purposes were now considered consistent with the imposition of legal distinctions based upon race. The Court said at 544, 551–552:

> "The object of the amendment was undoubtedly to enforce the absolute equality of the two races before the law, but in the nature of things it could not have been intended to abolish distinctions based upon color, or to enforce social, as distinguished from political, equality, or a commingling of the two races upon terms unsatisfactory to either.
>
>     \* \* \*
>
> Legislation is powerless to eradicate racial instincts or to abolish distinctions based upon physical differences, and the attempt to do so can only result in accentuating the difficulties of the present situation. If the civil and political rights of both races be equal, one cannot be inferior to the other civilly or politically. If one race be inferior to the other socially, the Constitution of the United States cannot put them upon the same plane."

And reasonableness of the regulation was found in established social usage, custom and tradition, at page 550:

> "So far, then, as a conflict with the 14th Amendment is concerned, the case reduces

itself to the question whether the statute of Louisiana is a reasonable regulation and with respect to this there must necessarily be a large discretion on the part of the legislature. In determining the question of reasonableness it is at liberty to act with reference to the established usages, customs, and traditions of the people, and with a view to the promotion of their comfort, and the preservation of the public peace and good order."

In *Plessy*, through distortion of the concept of "social" rights as distinguished from "civil" rights, the right to civil equality as one of the purposes of the Fourteenth Amendment was given a restricted meaning wholly at variance with that of the earlier cases and the intent of the framers as defined by this Court. Indeed, civil rights, as defined by that Court, seem merely to encompass those rights attendant upon use of the legal process and protection against complete exclusion pursuant to state mandate. Race for the first time since the adoption of the Fourteenth Amendment was sanctioned as a constitutionally valid basis for state action, and reasonableness for the racial distinctions approved was found in the social customs, usages and traditions of a people only thirty-one years removed from a slave society.

Under this rationale the Court sought to square its approval of racial segregation with the *Slaughter House Cases, Strauder* v. *West Virginia* and the other precedents. It is clear, however, that the early cases interpreted the Fourteenth Amendment as encompassing that same category of rights which were involved in *Plessy* v. *Ferguson*—the right to be free of a racial differentiation imposed by the state in the exercise of any civil right. And the Court's attempt to distinguish *Railroad Co.* v. *Brown*, as a case of exclusion, was the very argument that has been specifically rejected in the *Brown* case as a sophisticated effort to avoid the obvious implications of the Congressional requirement. Thus, the separate but equal doctrine is a rejection of the precedents and constitutes a break in the development of constitutional law under which the Fourteenth Amendment has been interpreted as a fundamental interdiction against state imposed differentiations and discriminations based upon color.

### D. The separate but equal doctrine was conceived in error

The separate but equal doctrine of *Plessy* v. *Ferguson*, we submit, has aided and supported efforts to nullify the Fourteenth Amendment's undoubted purpose—equal status for Negroes—as defined again and again by this Court. The fallacious and pernicious implications of the doctrine were evident to Justice Harlan and are set out in his dissenting opinion. It is clear today that the fact that racial segregation accords with custom and usage or is considered needful for the preservation of public peace and good order does not suffice to give constitutional validity to the state's action. What the doctrine has in fact accomplished is to deprive Negroes of the protection of the approved test of reasonable classifications which is available to everyone else who challenges legislative categories or distinctions of whatever kind.

**1. The dissenting opinion of Justice Harlan in *Plessy v. Ferguson*.** Justice Harlan recognized and set down for history the purpose of segregation and the implications of the separate but equal doctrine and evidenced prophetic insight concerning the inevitable consequences of the Court's approval of racial segregation. He said at page 557: "The thing to accomplish was, under the guise of giving equal accommodations for whites and blacks to compel the latter to keep to themselves while traveling in railroad passenger coaches."

He realized at page 560, moreover, that the approved regulations supported the inferior caste thesis of *Scott* v. *Sandford*, 19 How. 393, supposedly eradicated by the Civil War Amendments: "But it seems that we have yet, in some of the states, a dominant race, a superior class of citizens, which assumes to regulate the enjoyment of civil rights, common to all citizens, on the basis of race." And at page 562: "We boast of the freedom enjoyed by our people above all other people. But it is difficult to reconcile that boast with a state of the law which, practically, puts the brand of servitude and degradation upon a large class of our fellow citizens, our equals before the law."

While the majority opinion sought to rationalize its holding on the basis of the state's judgment that separation of races was conducive to public peace and order, Justice Harlan knew all too well that the seeds for continuing racial animosities had been planted. He said at pages 560–561:

> "The sure guaranty of peace and security of each race is the clear, distinct, unconditional recognition by our governments, national and state, of every right that inheres in civil freedom, and of equality before the law of all citizens of the United States without regard to race. State enactments, regulating the enjoyment of civil rights, upon the basis of race, and cunningly devised to defeat legitimate results of the war, under the pretense of recognizing equality of rights, can have no other result than to render permanent peace impossible and to keep alive a conflict of races, the continuance of which must do harm to all concerned."

"Our Constitution", said Justice Harlan at 559, "is color-blind, and neither knows nor tolerates classes among citizens." It is the dissenting opinion of Justice Harlan, rather than the majority opinion in *Plessy* v. *Ferguson*, that is in keeping with the scope and meaning of the Fourteenth Amendment as consistently defined by this Court both before and after *Plessy* v. *Ferguson*.

**2. Custom, usage and tradition rooted in the slave tradition cannot be the constitutional yardstick for measuring state action under the Fourteenth Amendment.** The analysis by Justice Harlan of the bases for the majority opinion in *Plessy* v. *Ferguson* was adopted by this Court in *Chiles* v. *Chesapeake & Ohio Railroad Company*, 218 U.S. 71, 77, 78. There this Court cited *Plessy* v. *Ferguson* as authority for sustaining the validity of legislative distinctions based upon race and color alone.

The importance of this case is its clear recognition and understanding that in *Plessy* v. *Ferguson* this Court approved the enforcement of racial distinctions as reasonable because they are in accordance with established social usage, custom and tradition. The Court said at pages 77, 78:

> "It is true the power of a legislature to recognize a racial distinction was the subject considered, but if the test of reasonableness in legislation be, as it was declared to be, 'the established usages, customs and traditions of the people,' and the 'promotion of their comfort and the preservation of the public peace and good order,' this must also be the test of reasonableness of the regulations of a carrier, made for like purposes and to secure like results."

But the very purpose of the Thirteenth, Fourteenth and Fifteenth Amendments was to effectuate a complete break with governmental action based on the established usages, customs and traditions of the slave era, to revolutionize the legal relationship between Negroes and whites, to destroy the inferior status of the Negro and to place him upon a plane of complete equality with the white man. As we will demonstrate, post Civil War reestablishment of ante-bellum custom and usage, climaxed by the decision in *Plessy* v. *Ferguson*, reflected a constant effort to return the Negro to his pre-Thirteenth, Fourteenth Amendment inferior status. When the Court employed the old usages, customs and traditions as the basis for determining the reasonableness of segregation statutes designed to resubjugate the Negro to an inferior status, it nullified the acknowledged intention of the framers of the Amendment,

and made a travesty of the equal protection clause of the Fourteenth Amendment.

Here, again, the *Plessy* v. *Ferguson* decision is out of line with the modern holdings of this Court, for in a variety of cases involving the rights of Negroes it has constantly refused to regard custom and usage, however widespread, as determinative of reasonableness. This was true in *Smith* v. *Allwright*, of a deeply entrenched custom and usage of excluding Negroes from voting in the primaries. It was true in *Shelley* v. *Kraemer*, of a long standing custom excluding Negroes from the use and ownership of real property on the basis of race. In *Henderson* v. *United States*, a discriminatory practice of many years was held to violate the Interstate Commerce Act. In the *Sweatt* and *McLaurin* decisions, the Court broke a southern tradition of state-enforced racial distinctions in graduate and professional education—a custom almost as old as graduate and professional education, itself.

In each instance the custom and usage had persisted for generations and its durability was cited as grounds for its validity. If this were the only test, ours indeed would become a stagnant society. Even if there be some situations in which custom, usage and tradition may be considered in testing the reasonableness of governmental action, customs, traditions and usages rooted in slavery cannot be worthy of the constitutional sanction of this Court.

**3. Preservation of public peace cannot justify deprivation of constitutional rights.** The fallacy underlying *Plessy* v. *Ferguson* of justifying racially-discriminatory statutes as essential to the public peace and good order has been completely exposed by Frederick W. Lehmann, a former Solicitor General of the United States, and Wells H. Blodgett in their Brief as *amici curiae* in *Buchanan* v. *Warley*, 245 U.S. 60. Their statements warrant repetition here:

> "The implication of the title of the ordinance is, that unless the white and colored people live in separate blocks, ill feeling will be engendered between them and conflicts will result and so it is assumed that a segregation of the races is necessary for the preservation of the public peace and the promotion of the general welfare. There is evidence in the record that prior to the enactment of the ordinance there were instances of colored people moving into white blocks and efforts by the white people to drive them out by violence. So to preserve the peace, the ordinance was enacted not to repress the lawless violence, but to give the sanction of the law to the motives which inspired it and to make the purpose of it lawful.
> "The population of Louisville numbers two hundred and fifty thousand, of whom about one-fifth are colored. The ordinance, almost

upon its face, and clearly by the evidence submitted and the arguments offered in support of it is a discriminating enactment by the dominant majority against a minority who are held to be an inferior people. It cannot be justified by the recitals of the title, even if they are true. Many things may rouse a man's prejudice or stir him to anger, but he is not always to be humored in his wrath. The question may arise, 'Dost thou well to be angry?' " (*Brief Amici Curiae*, pp. 2 and 3).

Accepting this view, the Court in *Buchanan* v. *Warley* rejected the argument that a state could deny constitutional rights with impunity in its efforts to maintain the public peace:

> "It is urged that this proposed segregation will promote the public peace by preventing race conflicts. Desirable as this is, and important as is the preservation of the public peace, this aim cannot be accomplished by laws or ordinances which deny rights created or protected by the Federal Constitution" (245 U.S. 60, 81).

Accord, *Morgan* v. *Virginia*, *supra*; *Monk* v. *City of Birmingham*, 185 F. 2d 859 (CA 5th 1950), *cert. denied*, 341 U.S. 940.

Thus, the bases upon which the separate but equal doctrine was approved in the *Plessy* v. *Ferguson* case have all been uprooted by subsequent decisions of this Court. All that remains is the naked doctrine itself, unsupported by reason, contrary to the intent of the framers, and out of tune with present notions of constitutional rights. Repudiation of the doctrine itself, we submit, is long overdue.

**4. The separate but equal doctrine deprives Negroes of that protection which the Fourteenth Amendment accords under the general classification test.** One of the ironies of the separate but equal doctrine of *Plessy* v. *Ferguson* is that under it, the Fourteenth Amendment, the primary purpose of which was the protection of Negroes, is construed as encompassing a narrower area of protection for Negroes than for other persons under the general classification test.

Early in its history, the Fourteenth Amendment was construed as reaching not only state action based upon race and color, but also as prohibiting all unreasonable classifications and distinctions even though not racial in character. *Barbier* v. *Connolly*, 113 U.S. 27, seems to be the earliest case to adopt this concept of the Amendment. There the Court said on page 31:

> "The Fourteenth Amendment ... undoubtedly intended, not only that there should be no arbitrary deprivation of life or liberty or arbitrary spoliation of property but that equal protection and security should be given to all

under like circumstances in the enjoyment of their personal and civil rights."

Accord: *Minneapolis & St. Louis Ry. Co.* v. *Beckwith*, 129 U.S. 26, 28, 29; *Bell's Gap R. R. Co.* v. *Pennsylvania*, 134 U.S. 232, 237; *McPherson* v. *Blacker*, 146 U.S. 1, 39; *Yesler* v. *Board of Harbor Line Commissioners*, 146 U.S. 646, 655; *Giozza* v. *Tiernan*, 148 U.S. 657, 662; *Marchant* v. *Pennsylvania R. Co.*, 153 U.S. 380, 390; *Moore* v. *Missouri*, 159 U.S. 673, 678.

In effectuating the protection afforded by this secondary purpose, the Court has required the classification or distinction used be based upon some real or substantial difference pertinent to a valid legislative objective. *E.g.*, *Quaker City Cab Co.* v. *Pennsylvania*, 277 U.S. 389; *Truax* v. *Raich*, 239 U.S. 33; *Smith* v. *Cahoon*, 283 U.S. 553; *Mayflower Farms* v. *Ten Eyck*, 297 U.S. 266; *Skinner* v. *Oklahoma*, 316 U.S. 535. See also *Cities Service Gas Co.* v. *Peerless Oil & Gas Co.*, 340 U.S. 179, 186.

Justice Holmes in *Nixon* v. *Herndon*, 273 U.S. 536, 541, recognized and restated a long established and well settled judicial proposition when he described the Fourteenth Amendment's prohibition against unreasonable legislative classification as less rigidly proscriptive of state action than the Amendment's prohibition of color differentiation. There he concluded:

> "States may do a good deal of classifying that it is difficult to believe rational, but there are limits, and it is too clear for extended argument that color cannot be made the basis of a statutory classification affecting the right set up in this case."

But the separate but equal doctrine substitutes race for reasonableness as the constitutional test of classification. We submit, it would be a distortion of the purposes and intendment of the Fourteenth Amendment to deny to those persons for whose benefit that provision was primarily intended the same measure of protection afforded by a rule of construction evolved to reach the Amendment's subsidiary and secondary objectives. We urge this Court to examine the segregation statutes in these cases to determine whether the statutes seek to serve a permissible legislative objective; and, if any permissible objective is found, whether color differentiation has pertinence to it. So examined, the constitutional provisions and statutes involved here disclose unmistakably their constitutional infirmity.

**E. The separate but equal doctrine has not received unqualified approval in this Court**

Even while the separate but equal doctrine was evolving, this Court imposed limitations upon its applications. In *Buchanan v. Warley*, the Court, after reviewing the limited acceptance which the doctrine had received, concluded that its extension to approve state enforced segregation in housing was not permissible.

Ten years later in *Gong Lum v. Rice*, 275 U.S. 78, 85, 86, without any intervening development in the doctrine in this Court, sweeping language was used which gave the erroneous impression that this Court already had extended the application of the doctrine to the field of education. And in *Missouri ex rel. Gaines v. Canada*, 305 U.S. 337, the doctrine is mentioned in passing as if its application to public education were well established. But, what Justice Day was careful to point out in *Buchanan v. Warley*, was true then and is true now—the separate but equal doctrine has never been extended by this Court beyond the field of transportation in any case where such extension was contested.

While the doctrine itself has not been specifically repudiated as a valid constitutional yardstick in the field of public education, in cases in which this Court has had to determine whether the state had performed its constitutional obligation to provide equal education opportunities—the question presented here—the separate but equal doctrine has never been used by this Court to sustain the validity of the state's separate school laws. *Missouri ex rel. Gaines v. Canada*; *Sipuel v. Board of Regents*, 332 U.S. 631; *Sweatt v. Painter*; *McLaurin v. Oklahoma State Regents*.

Earlier educational cases, not concerned with equality, did not apply the doctrine. In *Cumming v. County Board of Education*, 175 U.S. 528, the question was explicitly beyond the scope of the decision rendered. In *Berea College v. Kentucky*, 211 U.S. 45, the question was reserved. In *Gong Lum v. Rice*, the separate but equal doctrine was not put in issue. Instead of challenging the validity of the Mississippi school segregation laws, the Chinese child merely objected to being classified as a Negro for public school purposes.

Even in the field of transportation, subsequent decisions have sapped the doctrine of vitality. *Henderson v. United States* in effect overruled *Chiles v. Chesapeake & Ohio Railway Co.*, 218 U.S. 71. See *Chance v. Lambeth*, 186 F. 2d 879 (CA 4th 1951), *cert. denied*, 341 U.S. 91. *Morgan v. Virginia* places persons traveling in interstate commerce beyond the thrust of state segregation statutes. Thus, the reach of the separate but equal doctrine approved in the *Plessy* case has now been so severely restricted and narrowed in scope that, it may be appropriately said of *Plessy v. Ferguson* as it was said of *Crowell v. Benson*, 285 U.S. 22, "one had supposed that the doctrine had earned a deserved repose." *Estep v. United States*, 327 U.S. 114, 142 (concurring opinion).

### F. The necessary consequence of the Sweatt and McLaurin decisions is repudiation of the separate but equal doctrine

While *Sweatt v. Painter* and *McLaurin v. Oklahoma State Regents* were not in terms rejections of the separate but equal doctrine, their application in effect destroyed the practice of segregation with respect to state graduate and professional schools. *Wilson v. Board of Supervisors*, 92 F. Supp. 986 (E. D. La. 1950), *aff'd*, 340 U.S. 909; *Gray v. Board of Trustees of University of Tennessee*, 342 U.S. 517; *McKissick v. Carmichael*, 187 F. 2d 949 (CA 4th 1951), *cert. denied*, 341 U.S. 951; *Swanson v. University of Virginia*, Civil Action #30 (W. D. Va. 1950) unreported; *Payne v. Board of Supervisors*, Civil Action #894 (E. D. La. 1952) unreported; *Foister v. Board of Supervisors*, Civil Action #937 (E. D. La. 1952) unreported; *Mitchell v. Board of Regents of University of Maryland*, Docket #16, Folio 126 (Baltimore City Court 1950) unreported.[1]

In the *Sweatt* case, the Court stated that, with members of the state's dominant racial groups excluded from the segregated law school which the state sought to require Sweatt to attend, "we cannot conclude that the education offered petitioner is substantially equal to that he would receive if admitted to the University of Texas." If this consideration is one of the controlling factors in determining substantial equality at the law school level, it is impossible for any segregated law school to be an equal law school. And pursuant to that decision one of the oldest and best state-supported segregated law schools in the country was found unequal and

---

[1] Negroes are now attending state graduate and professional schools in West Virginia, Maryland, Arkansas, Delaware, Oklahoma, Kentucky, Texas, Missouri, North Carolina, Virginia, and Louisiana. See (Editorial Comment), THE COURTS AND RACIAL INTEGRATION IN EDUCATION, 21 J. NEG. EDUC. 3 (1952).

Negroes are also now attending private universities and colleges in Missouri, Georgia, Kentucky, Louisiana, Texas, Maryland, West Virginia, North Carolina, District of Columbia, and Virginia. See THE COURTS AND RACIAL INTEGRATION IN EDUCATION, 21 J. NEG. EDUC. 3 (1952); SOME PROGRESS IN ELIMINATION OF DISCRIMINATION IN HIGHER EDUCATION IN THE UNITED STATES, 19 J. NEG. EDUC. 4–5 (1950); LEE AND KRAMER, RACIAL INCLUSION IN CHURCH-RELATED COLLEGES IN THE SOUTH, 22 J. NEG. EDUC. 22 (1953); A NEW TREND IN PRIVATE COLLEGES, 6 NEW SOUTH 1 (1951).

Negro applicants were ordered admitted to the University of North Carolina. *McKissick v. Carmichael*. Thus, substantial equality in professional education is "substantially equal" only if there is no racial segregation.

In the *McLaurin* case, the racial distinctions imposed in an effort to comply with the state's segregation laws were held to impair and inhibit ability to study, to exchange views with other students and, in general, to learn one's profession. The state, therefore, was required to remove all restrictions and to treat McLaurin the same way as other students are treated. Consequently these decisions are a repudiation of the separate but equal doctrine.

## III. VIEWED IN THE LIGHT OF HISTORY THE SEPARATE BUT EQUAL DOCTRINE HAS BEEN AN INSTRUMENTALITY OF DEFIANT NULLIFICATION OF THE FOURTEENTH AMENDMENT

The history of segregation laws reveals that their main purpose was to organize the community upon the basis of a superior white and an inferior Negro caste. These laws were conceived in a belief in the inherent inferiority of Negroes, a concept taken from slavery. Inevitably, segregation in its operation and effect has meant inequality consistent only with the belief that the people segregated are inferior and not worthy, or capable, of enjoying the facilities set apart for the dominant group.

Segregation originated as a part of an effort to build a social order in which the Negro would be placed in a status as close as possible to that he had held before the Civil War. The separate but equal doctrine furnished a base from which those who sought to nullify the Thirteenth, Fourteenth and Fifteenth Amendments were permitted to operate in relative security. While this must have been apparent at the end of the last century, the doctrine has become beclouded with so much fiction that it becomes important to consider the matter in historical context to restore a proper view of its meaning and import.

### A. The status of the Negro, slave and free, prior to the Civil War

One of the basic assumptions of the slave system was the Negro's inherent inferiority.[2] As the invention of the cotton gin rendered slavery

essential to the maintenance of the plantation economy in the South, a body of pseudo-scientific thought developed in passionate defense of slavery, premised on the Negro's unfitness for freedom and equality.[3] Thus, the Negro's inferiority with respect to brain capacity, lung activity and countless other physiological attributes was purportedly established by some of the South's most respected scientists.[4] In all relationships between the two races the Negro's place was that of an inferior, for it was claimed that any other relationship status would automatically degrade the white man.[5]

This concept of the Negro as an inferior fit only for slavery was complicated by the presence of several hundred thousand Negroes, who although not slaves, could not be described as free men.[6] In order that they would not constitute a threat to the slave regime, free Negroes were denied the full rights and privileges of citizens. They enjoyed no equality in the courts, their right to assemble was denied, their movements were proscribed, and education was withheld.[7] Their plight, in consequence of these proscriptions, invited the unfavorable comparison of them with slaves and confirmed the views of many that Negroes could not profit by freedom. They were regarded by the white society as the "very drones and pests of society," pariahs of the land, and an incubus on the body politic.[8] Even this Court, in *Scott v. Sandford*, recognized this substantial body of opinion to the effect that free Negroes

---

[2] For an illuminating discussion of these assumptions, see Johnson, The Ideology of White Supremacy, 1876–1910, in Essays in Southern History Presented to Joseph Gregoire deRoulhac Hamilton, Green ed., 124–156 (1949).

[3] Jenkins, Pro-Slavery Thought in the Old South 243 (1935); Johnson, The Negro in American Civilization 5–15 (1930).

[4] See Van Evrie, Negroes and Negro Slavery 120 ff, 122 ff, 214 ff (1861); Cartwright, Diseases and Peculiarities of the Negro Race, 2 DeBow, The Industrial Resources, etc., of the Southern and Western States 315–329 (1852); Nott, Two Lectures On the Natural History of the Caucasian and Negro Races (1866); Van Evrie, Negroes and Negro "Slavery"; The First An Inferior Race—The Latter Its Normal Condition (1853); Van Evrie, Subgenation: The Theory of the Normal Relation of the Races (1864); Cartwright, Diseases and Peculiarities of the Negro Races, 9 DeBow's Review 64–69 (1851); Cartwright, Essays, Being Inductions Drawn From the Baconian Philosophy Proving the Truth of the Bible and the Justice and Benevolence of the Decree Dooming Canaan to Be A Servant of Servants (1843).

[5] Jenkins, Pro-Slavery Thought In the Old South 242 ff (1935); The Pro-Slavery Argument, especially Harper's Memoir on Slavery, pp. 26–98; and Simms, The Morals of Slavery, pp. 175–275 (1835); Johnson, The Ideology of White Supremacy, op. cit. supra, n. 2 at 135.

[6] See Franklin, From Slavery to Freedom: A History of American Negroes 213–238 (1947).

[7] Franklin, The Free Negro in North Carolina, 1790–1860 59–120 (1943).

[8] Dew, Review of the Debates In the Virginia Legislature of 1831–1832, The Pro-Slavery Argument, 422 ff (1853); Jenkins, op. cit. supra, n. 5, 246.

had no rights that a white man was bound to respect.

The few privileges that free Negroes enjoyed were being constantly whittled away in the early nineteenth century. By 1836, free Negroes were denied the ballot in every southern state and in many states outside the South.[9] In some states, they were denied residence on penalty of enslavement; and in some, they were banned from the mechanical trades because of the economic pressure upon the white artisans.[10] Before the outbreak of the Civil War, the movement to reenslave free Negroes was under way in several states in the South.[11]

This ante-bellum view of the inferiority of the Negro persisted after the Civil War among those who already regarded the newly freed slaves as simply augmenting the group of free Negroes who had been regarded as "the most ignorant ... vicious, impoverished, and degraded population of this country."[12]

## B. The post war struggle

The slave system had supported and sustained a plantation economy under which 1,000 families received approximately $50,000,000 a year with the remaining 600,000 families receiving about $60,000,000 per annum. The perfection of that economy meant the ruthless destruction of the small independent white farmer who was either bought out or driven back to the poorer lands—the slaveholders controlled the destiny of both the slave and the poor whites.[13] Slaves were not only farmers and unskilled laborers but were trained by their masters as skilled artisans. Thus, slave labor was in formidable competition with white labor at every level, and the latter was the more expendable for it did not represent property and investment. Only a few white supervisory persons were needed to insure the successful operation of the plantation system.

After the Civil War, the independent white farmer entered into cotton cultivation and took over the lands of the now impracticable large plantations. Within a few years the independent farmer was engaged in 40% of the cotton cultivation, and by 1910 this percentage had risen to 67%.[14] To the poor white Southerner the new Negro, as a skilled farmer and artisan in a free competitive economy, loomed as an even greater economic menace than he had been under the slave system. They became firm advocates of the Negro's subjugation to insure their own economic well being.[15]

The plantation aristocracy sought to regain their economic and political pre-eminence by rebuilding the prewar social structure on the philosophy of the Negro's inferiority. This group found that they could build a new economic structure based upon a depressed labor market of poor whites and Negroes. Thus, to the aristocracy, too, the Negro's subjugation was an economic advantage.

The mutual concern of these two groups of white Southerners for the subjugation of the Negro gave them a common basis for unity in irreconcilable resistance to the revolutionary change in the Negro's status which the Civil War Amendments were designed to effect. Their attitude towards the Fourteenth Amendment is best described by a Mississippi editor who said that the southern states were not prepared "to become parties to their own degradation."[16] There were white southerners, however, as there always had been, who sought to build a society which would respect and dignify the rights of the Freedmen. But this group was in the minority and southern sentiment in bitter opposition to Negro equality prevailed. Accordingly, as a temporary expedient, even as an army of occupation has been necessary recently in Germany and Japan to prevent lawlessness by irreconcilables and the recrudescense of totalitarianism, so Union forces were needed during Reconstruction to maintain order and to make possible the development of a more democratic way of life in the states recently in rebellion.

The Thirteenth, Fourteenth and Fifteenth Amendments and the Reconstruction effort, implemented by those in the South who were coming to accept the new concept of the Negro as a free man on full terms of equality, could have led to a society free of racism. The possibility of the extensive establishment and expansion of

---

[9] Weeks, History of Negro Suffrage in the South, 9 Pol. Sci. Q. 671–703 (1894); Porter, A History of Suffrage in the United States 87 ff (1918); Shugg, Negro Voting in the Ante-Bellum South, 21 J. Neg. Hist. 357–364 (1936).

[10] Va. House J. 84 (1831–1832); Va. Laws 1831. p. 107; Channing, History of the United States 136–137 (1921); Greene and Woodson, The Negro Wage Earner 15 ff (1930).

[11] Franklin, The Enslavement of Free-Negroes in North Carolina, 29 J. Neg. Hist. 401–428 (1944).

[12] See Jenkins, op. cit. supra, n. 5, 246.

[13] Weston, The Progress of Slavery (1859); Helper, The Impending Crisis of the South (1863); Johnson, The Negro in American Civilization, op. cit. supra, n. 2; Phillips, American Negro Slavery, Documentary History of American Industrial Society-Plantation and Frontier Documents (1910–11).

[14] Vance, Human Factors in Cotton Cultivation (1926); Simkins, The Tillman Movement in South Carolina (1926).

[15] For discussion of this whole development see Johnson, The Negro in American Civilization (1930).

[16] Coulter, The South During Reconstruction 434 (1947).

mixed schools was real at this stage. It was discussed in every southern state, and in most states serious consideration was given to the proposal to establish them.[17]

## C. The Compromise of 1877 and the abandonment of Reconstruction

The return to power of the southern irreconcilables was finally made possible by rapproachement between northern and southern economic interests culminating in the compromise of 1877. In the North, control of the Republican Party passed to those who believed that the protection and expansion of their economic power could best be served by political conciliation of the southern irreconcilables, rather than by unswerving insistence upon human equality and the rights guaranteed by the post war Amendments. In the 1870's those forces that held fast to the notion of the Negro's preordained inferiority returned to power in state after state, and it is significant that one of the first measures adopted was to require segregated schools on a permanent basis in disregard of the Fourteenth Amendment.[18]

In 1877, out of the exigencies of a close and contested election, came a bargain between the Republican Party and the southern leaders of the Democratic Party which assured President Hayes' election, led to the withdrawal of federal troops from the non-redeemed states and left the South free to solve the Negro problem without apparent fear of federal intervention. This agreement preserved the pragmatic and material ends of Reconstruction at the expense of the enforcement of not only the Fourteenth Amendment but the Fifteenth Amendment as well.[19] For it brought in its wake peonage and disfranchisement as well as segregation and other denials of equal protection. Although there is grave danger in oversimplification of the complexities of history, on reflection it seems clear that more profoundly than constitutional amendments and wordy statutes, the Compromise of 1877 shaped the future of four million freedmen and their progeny for generations to come. For the road to freedom and equality, which had seemed sure and open in 1868, was now to be securely blocked and barred by a maze of restrictions and limitations proclaimed as essential to a way of life.

## D. Consequences of the 1877 Compromise

Once the South was left to its own devices, the militant irreconcilables quickly seized or con-

---

[17] KNIGHT, PUBLIC EDUCATION IN THE SOUTH 320 (1922). See also Part II *infra*, at pages 142–157.

There were interracial colleges, academies, and tributary grammar schools in the South established and maintained largely by philanthropic societies and individuals from the North. Although they were predominantly Negro institutions, in the Reconstruction period and later, institutions such as Fisk University in Nashville, Tennessee, and Talladega College in Alabama usually had some white students. In the last quarter of the nineteenth century most of the teachers in these institutions were white. For accounts of co-racial education at Joppa Institute and Nat School in Alabama, Piedmont College in Georgia, Saluda Institute in North Carolina and in other southern schools, see BROWNLEE, NEW DAY ASCENDING 98–110 (1946).

The effect of these institutions in keeping alive the possibility of Negroes and whites living and learning together on the basis of complete equality was pointed out by one of the South's most distinguished men of letters, George W. Cable. "In these institutions," he said: ". . . there is a complete ignoring of those race distinctions in the enjoyment of common public rights so religiously enforced on every side beyond their borders; and yet none of those unnamable disasters have come to or from them which the advocates of these onerous public distinctions and separations predict and dread. On scores of Southern hilltops these schools stand out almost totally without companions or competitors in their peculiar field, so many refutations, visible and complete, of the idea that any interest requires the colored American citizen to be limited in any of the civil rights that would be his without question if the same man were white." CABLE, THE NEGRO QUESTION 19 (1890).

[18] Georgia, where the reconstruction government was especially short-lived, passed a law in 1870 making it mandatory for district school officials to "make all necessary arrangements for the instruction of the white and colored youth . . . in separate schools. They shall provide the same facilities for each . . . but the children of the

white and colored races shall not be taught together in any sub-district of the state." Ga. Laws 1870, p. 56. As soon as they were redeemed, the other southern states enacted similar legislation providing for segregated schools and gradually the states incorporated the provision into their constitutions. See, for example, Ark. Laws 1873, p. 423; THE JOURNAL OF THE TEXAS CONSTITUTIONAL CONVENTION 1875, pp. 608–616; Miss. Laws 1878, p. 103; STEPHENSON, RACE DISTINCTIONS IN AMERICAN LAW 170–176 (1908). When South Carolina and Louisiana conservatives secured control of their governments in 1877, they immediately repealed the laws providing for mixed schools and established separate institutions for white and colored youth.

[19] The explanation for this reversal of national policy in 1877 and the abandonment of an experiment that had enlisted national support and deeply aroused the emotions and hopes has been sought in many quarters. The most commonly accepted and often repeated story is that authorized spokesmen of Hayes met representatives of the Southern Democrats at the Wormley House in Washington in late February, 1877, and promised the withdrawal of troops and abandonment of the Negro in return for the support of southern Congressmen for Hayes against the Democratic candidate Samuel J. Tilden in the contested Presidential election. Recent investigation has demonstrated that the so-called "Wormley House Bargain", though offered by southern participants as the explanation, is not the full relevation of the complex and elaborate maneuvering which finally led to the agreement. See WOODWARD, REUNION AND REACTION: THE COMPROMISE OF 1877 AND THE END OF RECONSTRUCTION (1951) for an elaborate and detailed explanation of the compromise agreement.

solidated power. Laws and practices designed to achieve rigid segregation and the disfranchisement of the Negro came on in increasing numbers and harshness.

The policy of the southern states was to destroy the political power of the Negro so that he could never seriously challenge the order that was being established. By the poll tax, the Grandfather Clause, the white primary, gerrymandering, the complicated election procedures, and by unabated intimidation and threats of violence, the Negro was stripped of effective political participation.[20]

The final blow to the political respectability of the Negro came with disfranchisement in the final decade of the Nineteenth Century and the early years of the present century when the discriminatory provisions were written into the state constitutions.[21] That problem the Court dealt with during the next forty years from *Guinn* v. *United States*, 238 U.S. 347 to *Terry* v. *Adams*, 345 U.S. 461.

A movement to repeal the Fourteenth and Fifteenth Amendments shows the extremity to which the irreconcilables were willing to go to make certain that the Negro remained in an inferior position. At the Mississippi Constitutional Convention of 1890, a special committee studied the matter and concluded that "the white people only are capable of conducting and maintaining the government" and that the Negro race, "even if its people were educated, being wholly unequal to such responsibility," should be excluded from the franchise. It, therefore, resolved that the "true and only efficient remedy for the great and important difficulties" that would ensue from Negro participation lay in the "repeal of the Fifteenth Amendment . . . whereby such restrictions and limitations may be put upon Negro suffrage as may be necessary and proper for the maintenance of good and stable government . . . "[22]

A delegate to the Virginia Constitutional Convention of 1901–1902 submitted a resolution calling for a repeal of the Fifteenth Amendment because it is wrong, "in that it proceeds on the theory that the two races are equally competent of free government."[23] Senator Edward Carmack of Tennessee gave notice in 1903 that he would bring in a bill to repeal the Amendments.[24] The movement, though unsuccessful, clearly illustrates the temper of the white South.

Having consigned the Negro to a permanently inferior caste status, racist spokesmen, with unabashed boldness, set forth views regarding the Negro's unassimilability and uneducability even more pernicious than those held by the old South. Ben Tillman, the leader of South Carolina, declared that a Negro should not have the same treatment as a white man, "for the simple reason that God Almighty made him colored and did not make him white." He lamented the end of slavery which reversed the process of improving the Negro and "inoculated him with the virus of equality."[25] These views were expressed many times in the disfranchising conventions toward the end of the century.[26] Nor were the politicians alone in uttering such views about the Negro. Drawing on the theory of evolution as expressed by Darwin and the theory of progress developed by Spencer, persons of scholarly pretension speeded the work of justifying an inferior status for the Negro.[27] Alfred H. Stone,

---

[20] In 1890, Judge J. Chrisman of Mississippi could say that there had not been a full vote and a fair count in his state since 1875, that they had preserved the ascendancy of the whites by revolutionary methods. In plain words, he continued, "We have been stuffing the ballot boxes, committing perjury and here and there in the State carrying the elections by fraud and violence until the whole machinery for election was about to rot down." Quoted in Woodward, Origins of the New South 58 (1951).
[21] Key, Southern Politics in State and Nation 539–550 (1949); Woodward, Origins of the New South 205, 263 (1951).
[22] Journal of the Mississippi Constitutional Convention, 1890, 303–304. Tillman, Vardaman, and other Southern leaders frequently called for the repeal of the Amendments. Tillman believed "that such a formal declaration of surrender in the struggle to give the Negro political and civil equality would confirm the

black man in his inferior position and pave the way for greater harmony between the races." Simkins, Pitchfork Ben Tillman 395 (1944). Vardaman called for repeal as a recognition that the Negro "was physically, mentally, morally, racially, and eternally inferior to the white man." See Kirwan, Revolt of the Rednecks (1951).
[23] Journal of the Virginia Constitutional Convention, 1901–1902, pp. 47–48.
[24] Johnson, The Ideology of White Supremacy, *op. cit. supra*, n. 2, 136 ff.
[25] Simkins, Pitchfork Ben Tillman 395, 399 (1944). Tillman's Mississippi counterpart, J. K. Vardaman, was equally vigorous in denouncing the Negro. He described the Negro as an "industrial stumbling block, a political ulcer, a social scab, 'a lazy, lying, lustful animal which no conceivable amount of training can transform into a tolerable citizen.' " Quoted in Kirwan, *op. cit. supra*, n. 22, at 146.
[26] See, for example, Alabama Constitutional Convention, 1901, Official Proceedings, Vol. I, p. 12, Vol. II, pp. 2710–2711, 2713, 2719, 2782, 2785–2786, 2793; Journal of the South Carolina Convention, 1895, pp. 443–472; Journal of the Mississippi Constitutional Convention, 1890, pp. 10, 303, 701–702; Journal of the Louisiana Constitutional Convention, 1898, pp. 9–10.
[27] See Rowland, A Mississippi View of Relations in the South, A Paper (1903); Herbert, et al., Why the Solid South? Or Reconstruction and Its Results (1890); Bruce, The Plantation Negro As A Freeman: Observations On His Character, Condition and Prospects In Virginia (1889); Stone, Studies in the American Race

having the reputation of a widely respected scholar in Mississippi, declared that the "Negro was an inferior type of man with predominantly African customs and character traits whom no amount of education or improvement of environmental conditions could ever elevate to as high a scale in the human species as the white man." As late as 1910, E. H. Randle in his *Characteristics of the Southern Negro* declared that "the first important thing to remember in judging the Negro was that his mental capacity was inferior to that of the white man."[28]

Such was the real philosophy behind the late 19th Century segregation laws—an essential part of the whole racist complex. Controlling economic and political interests in the South were convinced that the Negro's subjugation was essential to their survival, and the Court in *Plessy* v. *Ferguson* had ruled that such subjugation through public authority was sanctioned by the Constitution. This is the overriding vice of *Plessy* v. *Ferguson*. For without the sanction of *Plessy* v. *Ferguson*, archaic and provincial notions of racial superiority could not have injured and disfigured an entire region for so long a time. The full force and effect of the protection afforded by the Fourteenth Amendment was effectively blunted by the vigorous efforts of the proponents of the concept that the Negro was inferior. This nullification was effectuated in all aspects of Negro life in the South, particularly in the field of education, by the exercise of state power.

As the invention of the cotton gin stilled the voices of Southern Abolitionists, *Plessy* v. *Ferguson* chilled the development in the South of opinion conducive to the acceptance of Negroes on the basis of equality because those of the white South desiring to afford Negroes the equalitarian status which the Civil War Amendments had hoped to achieve were barred by state law from acting in accordance with their beliefs. In this connection, it is significant that the Populist movement flourished for a short period during the 1890's and threatened to take over political control of the South through a coalition of the poor Negro and poor white farmers.[29] This movement was completely smashed and since *Plessy* v. *Ferguson* no similar phenomenon has taken hold.

Without the "constitutional" sanction which *Plessy* v. *Ferguson* affords, racial segregation could not have become entrenched in the South, and individuals and local communities would have been free to maintain public school systems in conformity with the underlying purposes of the Fourteenth Amendment by providing education without racial distinctions. The doctrine of *Plessy* v. *Ferguson* was essential to the successful maintenance of a racial caste system in the United States. Efforts toward the elimination of race discrimination are jeopardized as long as the separate but equal doctrine endures. But for this doctrine we could more confidently assert that ours is a democratic society based upon a belief in individual equality.

### E. Nullification of the rights guaranteed by the Fourteenth Amendment and the reestablishment of the Negro's pre–Civil War inferior status fully realized

Before the end of the century, even without repeal of the Fourteenth and Fifteenth Amendments, those forces committed to a perpetuation of the slave concept of the Negro had realized their goal. They had defied the federal government, threatened the white defenders of equal rights, had used intimidation and violence against the Negro and had effectively smashed a political movement designed to unite the Negro and the poor whites. Provisions requiring segregated schools were written into state constitutions and statutes. Negroes had been driven from participation in political affairs, and a veritable maze of Jim Crow laws had been erected to "keep the Negro in his place" (of inferiority), all with impunity. There was no longer any need to pretend either that Negroes were getting an education equal to the whites or were entitled to it.

In the Constitutional Convention of Virginia, 1901–1902, Senator Carter Glass, in explaining a resolution requiring that state funds be used to maintain primary schools for four months before being used for establishment of higher grades, explained that "white people of the black sections of Virginia should be permitted to tax themselves, and after a

---

PROBLEM (1908); CARROLL, THE NEGRO A BEAST (1908); CARROLL, THE TEMPTER OF EVE, OR THE CRIMINALITY OF MAN'S SOCIAL, POLITICAL, AND RELIGIOUS EQUALITY WITH THE NEGRO, AND THE AMALGAMATION TO WHICH THESE CRIMES INEVITABLY LEAD 286 ff (1902); PAGE, THE NEGRO: THE SOUTHERNER'S PROBLEM 126 ff (1904); RANDLE, CHARACTERISTICS OF THE SOUTHERN NEGRO 51 ff (1910).

[28] Quoted in JOHNSON, IDEOLOGY OF WHITE SUPREMACY, op. cit., *supra*, n. 2, p. 151. That the South was not alone in these views is clearly shown by Logan's study of the Northern press between 1877 and 1901. See LOGAN, THE NEGRO IN AMERICAN LIFE AND THOUGHT: THE NADIR 1877–1901, cc. 9–10 (unpub. ms., to be pub. early in 1954 by the Dial Press).

[29] See CARLETON, THE CONSERVATIVE SOUTH—A POLITICAL MYTH, 22 Va. Q. Rev. 179–192 (1946); LEWINSON, RACE, CLASS AND PARTY (1932); MOON, THE BALANCE OF POWER—THE NEGRO VOTE, c. 4 (1948).

certain point had been passed which would safeguard the poorer classes of those communities, divert that fund to the exclusive use of white children. . . ."[30]

Senator Vardaman thought it was folly to make such pretenses. In Mississippi there were too many people to educate and not enough money to go around, he felt. The state, he insisted, should not spend as much on the education of Negroes as it was doing. "There is no use multiplying words about it," he said in 1899, "the negro will not be permitted to rise above the station he now fills." Money spent on his education was, therefore, a "positive unkindness" to him. "It simply renders him unfit for the work which the white man has prescribed and which he will be forced to perform."[31] Vardaman's scholarly compatriot, Dunbar Rowland, seconded these views in 1902, when he said that "thoughtful men in the South were beginning to lose faith in the power of education which had been heretofore given to uplift the negro," and to complain of the burden thus placed upon the people of the South in their poverty.[32]

The views of Tillman, Vardaman, Stone, Rowland, Glass and others were largely a justification for what had been done by the time they uttered them. The South had succeeded in setting up the machinery by which it was hoped to retain the Negro in an inferior status. Through separate, inferior schools, through an elaborate system of humiliating Jim Crow, and through effective disfranchisement of the Negro, the exclusive enjoyment of first-class citizenship had now become the sole possession of white persons.

And, finally, the Negro was effectively restored to an inferior position through laws and through practices, now dignified as "custom and tradition." Moreover, this relationship—of an inferior Negro and superior white status—established through laws, practice, custom and tradition, was even more rigidly enforced than in the ante-bellum era. As one historian has aptly stated:

> "Whether by state law or local law, or by the more pervasive coercion of sovereign white opinion, 'the Negro's place' was gradually defined—in the courts, schools, and libraries, in parks, theaters, hotels, and residential districts, in hospitals, insane asylums—everywhere including on sidewalks and in cemeteries. When complete, the new codes of White Supremacy were vastly more complex than the antebellum slave codes or the Black Codes of 1865–1866, and, if anything, they were stronger and more rigidly enforced."[33]

This is the historic background against which the validity of the separate but equal doctrine must be tested. History reveals it as a part of an overriding purpose to defeat the aims of the Thirteenth, Fourteenth and Fifteenth Amendments. Segregation was designed to insure inequality—to discriminate on account of race and color—and the separate but equal doctrine accommodated the Constitution to that purpose. Separate but equal is a legal fiction. There never was and never will be any separate equality. Our Constitution cannot be used to sustain ideologies and practices which we as a people abhor.

That the Constitution is color blind is our dedicated belief. We submit that this Court cannot sustain these school segregation laws under any separate but equal concept unless it is willing to accept as truths the racist notions of the perpetuators of segregation and to repeat the tragic error of the Plessy court supporting those who would nullify the Fourteenth Amendment and the basic tenet of our way of life which it incorporates. We respectfully suggest that it is the obligation of this Court to correct that error by holding that these laws and constitutional provisions which seek to condition educational opportunities on the basis of race and color are historic aberrations and are inconsistent with the federal Constitution and cannot stand. The separate but equal doctrine of *Plessy* v. *Ferguson* should now be overruled.

### CONCLUSION TO PART ONE

In short, our answer to Question No. 3 proposed by the Court is that it is within the judicial power, whatever the evidence concerning

---

[30] REPORT OF THE PROCEEDINGS AND DEBATES OF THE CONSTITUTIONAL CONVENTION, State of Virginia, Richmond, June 12, 1901–June 26, 1902, p. 1677 (1906).

[31] KIRWAN, *op. cit. supra*, n. 22, at 145–146.

[32] JOHNSON, IDEOLOGY OF WHITE SUPREMACY, *op. cit. supra*, n. 2, at 153. That this pattern is not an antiquated doctrine but a modern view may be seen in the current expenditure per pupil in average daily attendance 1949–1950: In Alabama, $130.09 was spent for whites against $92.69 for Negroes; in Arkansas $123.60 for whites and $73.03 for Negroes; in Florida $196.42 for whites, $136.71 for Negroes; in Georgia, $145.15 for whites and $79.73 for Negroes; in Maryland, $217.41 for whites and $198.76 for Negroes; in Mississippi, $122.93 for whites and $32.55 for Negroes; in North Carolina, $148.21 for whites and $122.90 for Negroes; in South Carolina, $154.62 for whites and $79.82 for Negroes; in the District of Columbia, $289.68 for whites and $220.74 for Negroes. BLOSE AND JARACZ, BIENNIAL SURVEY OF EDUCATION IN THE UNITED STATES, 1948–50, TABLE 43, "STATISTICS OF STATE SCHOOL SYSTEMS, 1949–50" (1952).

[33] WOODWARD, ORIGINS OF THE NEW SOUTH 212 (1951).

Questions 2(a) and (b) may disclose, to hold that segregated schools violate the Fourteenth Amendment, and for the reasons hereinabove stated that such power should now be exercised.

WHEREFORE, it is respectfully submitted that constitutional provisions and statutes involved in these cases are invalid and should be struck down.

## PART TWO

This portion of the brief is directed to questions one and two propounded by the Court:

"1. What evidence is there that the Congress which submitted and the State legislatures and conventions which ratified the Fourteenth Amendment contemplated or did not contemplate, understood or did not understand, that it would abolish segregation in public schools?

"2. If neither the Congress in submitting nor the States in ratifying the Fourteenth Amendment understood that compliance with it would require the immediate abolition of segregation in public schools, was it nevertheless the understanding of the framers of the Amendment

"(a) that future Congresses might, in the exercise of their power under Sec. 5 of the Amendment, abolish such segregation, or

"(b) that it would be within the judicial power, in light of future conditions, to construe the Amendment as abolishing such segregation of its own force?"

## I. THE FOURTEENTH AMENDMENT WAS INTENDED TO DESTROY ALL CASTE AND COLOR LEGISLATION IN THE UNITED STATES, INCLUDING RACIAL SEGREGATION

Research by political scientists and historians, specialists on the period between 1820 and 1900, and other experts in the field, as well as independent research by attorneys in these cases, convinces us that: (1) there is ample evidence that the Congress which submitted and the states which ratified the Fourteenth Amendment contemplated and understood that the Amendment would deprive the states of the power to impose any racial distinctions in determining when, where, and how its citizens would enjoy the various civil rights afforded by the states; (2) in so far as views of undeveloped public education in the 1860's can be applied to universal compulsory education in the 1950's, the right to public school education was one of the civil rights with respect to which the states were deprived of the power to impose racial distinctions; (3) while the framers of the Fourteenth Amendment clearly intended that Congress should have the power to enforce the provisions of the Amendment, they also clearly intended that the Amendment would be pro-

hibitory on the states without Congressional action.

The historic background of the Fourteenth Amendment and the legislative history of its adoption show clearly that the framers intended that the Amendment would deprive the states of power to make any racial distinction in the enjoyment of civil rights. It is also clear that the statutes involved in these cases impose racial distinctions which the framers of the Amendment and others concerned with its adoption understood to be beyond the power of a state to enforce.

The framers of the Fourteenth Amendment were men who came to the 39th Congress with a well defined background of Abolitionist doctrine dedicated to the equalitarian principles of real and complete equality for all men. Congressional debates during this period must be read with an understanding of this background along with the actual legal and political status of the Negro at the end of the Civil War. This background gives an understanding of the determination of the framers of the Fourteenth Amendment to change the inferior legal and political status of Negroes and to give them the full protection of the Federal Government in the enjoyment of complete and real equality in all civil rights.[34]

## A. The era prior to the Civil War was marked by determined efforts to secure recognition of the principle of complete and real equality for all men within the existing constitutional framework of our government

The men who wrote the Fourteenth Amendment were themselves products of a gigantic antislavery crusade which, in turn, was an expression of the great humanitarian reform movement of the Age of Enlightenment. This philosophy upon which the Abolitionists had taken their stand had been adequately summed up in Jefferson's basic proposition "that all men are created equal" and "are endowed by their Creator with certain unalienable Rights." To this philosophy they adhered with an almost fanatic devotion and an unswerving determination to obliterate any obstructions which stood in the way of its fulfillment. In their drive toward this goal, it may be that they thrust aside some then accepted notions of law and, indeed, that they attempted to give to the Declaration of Independence a substance which might have surprised its draftsmen. No matter, the crucial point is that their revolutionary drive was suc-

---

[34] tenBroek, THE ANTISLAVERY ORIGINS OF THE FOURTEENTH AMENDMENT 185, 186 (1951).

cessful and that it was climaxed in the Amendment here under discussion.

The first Section of the Fourteenth Amendment is the legal capstone of the revolutionary drive of the Abolitionists to reach the goal of true equality. It was in this spirit that they wrote the Fourteenth Amendment and it is in the light of this revolutionary idealism that the questions propounded by this Court can best be answered.

In the beginning, the basic and immediate concern of the Abolitionists was necessarily slavery itself. The total question of removing all other discriminatory relationships after the abolition of slavery was at first a matter for the future. As a consequence, the philosophy of equality was in a state of continuous development from 1830 through the time of the passage of the Fourteenth Amendment. However, the ultimate objective was always clearly in mind—absolute and complete equality for all Americans.

During the pre-Civil War decades, the anti-slavery movement here and there began to develop special meaning and significance in the legal concept of "privileges and immunities," the concept of "due process" and the most important concept of all for these cases, "equal protection of the laws." In the immediately succeeding sections, we shall show how the development of these ideas culminated in a firm intention to obliterate all class distinction as a part of the destruction of a caste society in America.

The development of each of these conceptions was often ragged and uneven with much overlapping: what was "equal protection" to one was "due process" or "privilege and immunity" to another. However, regardless of the phrase used, the basic tenet of all was the uniform belief that Negroes were citizens and, as citizens, freedom from discrimination was their right. To them "discrimination" included all forms of racial distinctions.

**Equality under law**  One tool developed to secure full standing for Negroes was the concept of equal protection of the laws. It was one thing, and a very important one, to declare as a political abstraction that "all men are created equal," and quite another to attach concrete rights to this state of equality. The Declaration of Independence did the former. The latter was Charles Sumner's outstanding contribution to American law.

The great abstraction of the Declaration of Independence was the central rallying point for the Abolitionists. When slavery was the evil to be attacked, no more was needed. But as some of the New England states became progres-

sively more committed to abolition, the focus of interest shifted from slavery itself to the status and rights of the free Negro. In the Massachusetts legislature in the 1840's, Henry Wilson, manufacturer, Abolitionist, and later United States Senator and Vice President, led the fight against discrimination, with "equality" as his rallying cry.[35] One Wilson measure adopted by the Massachusetts Legislature in 1845 gave the right to recover damages to any person "unlawfully excluded" from the Massachusetts public schools.[36]

Boston thereafter established a segregated school for Negro children, the legality of which was challenged in *Roberts* v. *City of Boston*, 5 Cush. (Mass.) 198 (1849). Charles Sumner, who later was to play such an important role in the Congress that formulated the Fourteenth Amendment, was counsel for Roberts. His oral argument, which the Abolitionists widely circulated, is one of the landmarks in the crystallization of the equalitarian concept.

This case was technically an action for damages under the Wilson Act. However, Sumner attacked segregation in public schools on the broader ground that segregation violated the Massachusetts Constitution which provided: "All men are created free and equal", and it was from this base that he launched his attack.

> "Of Equality I shall speak, not as a sentiment, but as a principle.... *** Thus it is with all moral and political ideas. First appearing as a sentiment, they awake a noble impulse, filling the soul with generous sympathy, and encouraging to congenital effort. Slowly recognized, they finally pass into a formula, to be acted upon, to be applied, to be defended in the concerns of life, as principles."[37]

"Equality before the law"[38] was the formula he employed. He traced the equalitarian theory from the eighteenth century French philosophers through the French Revolution into the language of the French Revolutionary Constitution of 1791,[39] the Constitution of February 1793,[40] the Constitution of June 1793[41] and the Charter of Louis Phillipe.[42] Equality before the

---

[35] For an account of Wilson's struggles against anti-miscegenation laws, against jim-crow transportation and jim-crow education, see Nason, Life of Henry Wilson 48 *et seq.* (1876).

[36] Massachusetts Act 1845, § 214.

[37] 2 Works of Charles Sumner 330, 335–336 (1875). The entire argument is reprinted at 327 *et seq.*

[38] *Id.* at 327, 330–331.

[39] "Men are born and continue free and *equal in their rights.*" *Id.* at 337.

[40] "The law ought to be equal for all." *Id.* at 338.

[41] "All men are equal by nature *and before the law.*" *Id.* at 339.

[42] "Frenchmen are *equal before the law....*" *Ibid.*

law, i.e., equality of rights, was the real meaning of the Massachusetts constitutional provision. Before it "all . . . distinctions disappear":

"He may be poor, weak, humble, or black—he may be Caucasian, Jewish, Indian or Ethiopian race—he may be of French, German, English or Irish extraction; but before the Constitution of Massachusetts all these distinctions disappear. He is not poor, weak, humble, or black; nor is he French, German, English or Irish; he is a MAN, the equal of all his fellowmen."[43]

Hence, he urged, separate schools are illegal.

The Massachusetts court rejected Sumner's argument and refused to grant relief. Subsequent thereto, in 1853, the Legislature of Massachusetts, after careful consideration of the problem involving hearings and reports, amended the Wilson statute by providing, among other things, that in determining the qualifications of school children in public schools in Massachusetts "no distinction was to be made on account of the race, color or religious opinions of the appellant or scholar."[44]

The Committee on Education of the House of Representatives in its report recommending adoption of this bill carefully considered the arguments for and against the measure and concluded:

"Your committee believe, in the words of another, that 'The only security we can have for a healthy and efficient system of public instruction rests in the deep interest and vigilant care with which the more intelligent watch over the welfare of the schools. This only will secure competent teachers, indefatigable exertion, and a high standard of excellence; and where the colored children are mingled up with the mass of their more favored fellows, they will partake of the advantages of this watchful oversight. Shut out and separated, they are sure to be neglected and to experience all the evils of an isolated and despised class. One of the great merits of our system of public instruction is the fusion of all classes which it produces. From a childhood which shares the same bench and sports there can hardly arise a manhood of aristocratic prejudice or separate castes and classes. Our common-school system suits our institutions, promotes the feeling of brotherhood, and the habit of republican equality. To debar the colored race from these advantages, even if we still secured to them equal educational results, is a sore injustice and wrong, and is taking the surest means of perpetuating a prejudice that should be depreciated and discountenanced by all intelligent and Christian men."[45]

Thus, the argument and theories advanced by Sumner, although rejected by the Supreme Court of Massachusetts, finally became incorporated into the law of the State of Massachusetts. More important, however, is the fact that the argument of Sumner was widely distributed throughout the country during the period immediately preceding the consideration of the Fourteenth Amendment.[46] As a consequence it became a fundamental article of faith among the Radical Republicans that from a constitutional standpoint racial segregation was incompatible with constitutional guarantees of equal protection.[47]

The analysis of the available materials covering the period from 1830 to 1860, while important to this point, is too voluminous to be included in the argument at this point. We have, therefore, placed this analysis in a supplement at the end of the brief. The analysis of these materials compels the following historical conclusions:

**1.** To the Abolitionists, equality was an absolute—not a relative—concept which comprehended that no legal recognition be given to racial distinctions of any kind. The notion that any state could require racial segregation was totally incompatible with this doctrine.

**2.** The phrases—"privileges and immunities," "equal protection," and "due process"—that were to appear in the Amendment had come to have a specific significance to opponents of slavery in the United States. Proponents of slavery knew and understood what that significance was, even as they disagreed with these theories. Members of the Congress that proposed the Amendment, shared this knowledge.

**3.** These radical Abolitionists, who had been in the minority prior to the Civil War, gained control of the Republican party in Congress during the course of the war and thus emerged in a dominant position in the Congress which was to write the Fourteenth Amendment. Ten of the members of the Joint Committee of Fifteen were men who had definite antislavery backgrounds and two others had likewise opposed slavery.

**4.** When the Joint Committee of Fifteen translated into constitutional provisions the equali-

---

[43] Id. at 341–342.
[44] General Laws of Mass. c. 256. § 1 (1855).
[45] Report of Committee on Education to House of Representatives, Commonwealth of Massachusetts, March 17, 1855.

[46] Among those active in distributing the argument was SALMON P. CHASE. DIARY AND CORRESPONDENCE OF SALMON P. CHASE, Chase to Sumner, Dec. 14, 1849, in 2 Ann. Rep. Am. Hist. Ass'n. 188 (1902).
[47] See, for example, Sumner resolution offered Congress on December 4, 1865 which called for "The organization of an educational system for the equal benefit of all without distinction of color or race." Cong. Globe, 39th Cong., 1st Sess. 2 (1865–1866).

tarian concepts held and widely bruited about in the struggle against slavery, it used the traditional phrases that had all become freighted with equalitarian meaning in its widest sense: "equal protection", "privileges and immunities" and "due process."

In these respects history buttresses and gives particular content to the recent admonition of this Court that "[w]hatever else the framers sought to achieve, it is clear that the matter of primary concern was the establishment of equality in the enjoyment of basic civil and political rights and the preservation of those rights from discriminatory action on the part of the States based on considerations of race and color." *Shelley* v. *Kraemer,* 334 U.S. 1, 23.

Despite the high principles and dedication of the leaders of the Abolitionist movement, their program ran into repeated roadblocks from both individual groups and state machinery. The movement was not only blocked in so far as the abolition of slavery itself was concerned, but was met by an ever increasing tendency on the part of all the southern states and some northern states to gradually cut down on the rights of free Negroes and to bring their status nearer and nearer to that of slaves. This countermovement culminated in the decision of the Supreme Court in the *Dred Scott* case (*Scott* v. *Sandford*, 19 How. 393) that no person of the "African race, whether free or not" could enjoy, under the Constitution of the United States, any right or protection whatsoever. All Negroes were thereby left, by the principles of that case, to the absolute, unrestrained power of the several states.

## B. The movement for complete equality reached its successful culmination in the Civil War and the Fourteenth Amendment

The onset of the Civil War marked the turning point of the Abolitionists' drive to achieve absolute equality for all Americans. The first great success came on January 1, 1863, when President Lincoln's Emancipation Proclamation freed all slaves in those areas in insurrection against the United States. Obviously this was far from a complete victory. The doctrines enunciated by Chief Justice Taney in the *Dred Scott* case were still unqualified and remained as a part of the "constitutional law" of the time.

In February, 1865, the Abolitionist-dominated 38th Congress adopted and submitted to the states what was to become the Thirteenth Amendment to the Constitution. However, the Radical Republicans in Congress were intensely aware that the abolition of slavery constituted only a partial attainment of their goal of complete political and legal equality for Negroes. They had already determined as early as the spring and summer of 1862 to strike at the objective of federal statutory and constitutional guarantees for Negro equality. As yet, however, their thinking had not succeeded in distilling clearly a series of specifically defined legal and political objectives which they proposed to write into federal law and Constitution.

It should be observed in passing that their reason for this obviously was not necessarily pure Abolitionist idealism. They were in part motivated by hard practical considerations of Republican Party ascendency, and the fear that a restored South, in which Negroes were not given complete legal and political equality, would fall into the hands of a pre-war conservative white political leadership which would threaten the national political control of the Radical Republicans themselves. Thus their idealistic, social philosophy and their hard practical considerations of party interest dovetailed very nicely.[48]

It was to require the events of 1865–66, most notably the attempt to restore political rule in the South and the attempt to impose an inferior non-citizenship status upon the Negro in the restored southern states, to make clear to the Radical Republicans their new constitutional objectives and the means they would seek to obtain it.

## C. The principle of absolute and complete equality began to be translated into federal law as early as 1862

In 1862 Congress addressed itself to an immediate problem over which it had authority. In debating the bill which was to abolish slavery in the District of Columbia, Representative Bingham said: "The great privilege and immunity of an American citizen to be respected everywhere in this land, and especially in this District, is that they shall not be deprived of life, liberty, or property without due process of law".[49] Representative Fessenden concluded: "If I do not mistake, it is quite apparent that when this bill shall be put on its final passage it will proclaim liberty to the slaves within this District. These men—for God created them men, though man has used them as goods and chattels—slaves—these men and women and children will, when the President of the United States signs this bill, be translated . . . [to a] condition in which they are invested with the rights of freemen, upon which none can trespass with impunity;

---

[48] tenBroek, THE ANTISLAVERY ORIGINS OF THE FOURTEENTH AMENDMENT 117–119 (1951).
[49] Cong. Globe, 37th Cong., 2d Sess. 1639 (1862).

since over the person of the free black as well as the free white man there is thrown the broad shield of the nation's majesty."[50] The bill was enacted into law.[51]

Simultaneously Congress discontinued the application of the Black Codes of Maryland and Virginia to the District of Columbia.[52]

Between the time of the Emancipation Proclamation in 1863 and the formulation of the Fourteenth Amendment, Congress took several forward steps to secure complete equality for the class so recently freed. These steps came in the form of particular solutions to particular problems. To this Congress (38th), the most immediate problem was one which fell under their glance daily, the problem of transportation in the District of Columbia. Congressional treatment of this problem is of significance because it reveals the early determination of the Radical Republicans to prohibit racial segregation.

In 1863, Congress amended the charter of the Alexandria and Washington Railroad to eliminate the practice of putting white and Negro passengers in separate parts of the street cars.[53] When, in 1864, the Washington and Georgetown street car company attempted to put colored passengers in cars separate from those of the white passengers, Senator Sumner denounced the practice in the Senate and set forth on his crusade to prohibit all racial distinctions by first eliminating street car segregation in the District.[54] In 1865, he carried to passage a law applicable to all District carriers that "no person shall be excluded from any car on account of color."[55]

The debate on the street car bill covered the entire issue of segregation in transportation. Those who supported prohibition of segregation did so on the ground that any such separation was a denial of equality itself. Senator Wilson denounced the "Jim Crow car," declaring it to be "in defiance of decency."[56] Senator Sumner persuaded his brethren to accept the Massachusetts view, saying that in Massachusetts, "the rights of every colored person are placed on an equality with those of white persons. They have the same right with white persons to ride in every public conveyance in the Commonwealth."[57] Thus, when Congress

in 1866 framed the Fourteenth Amendment, it did so against a background of Congressional determination that segregation in transportation was unequal, unjust, and was "in defiance of decency."

## D. From the beginning the thirty-ninth Congress was determined to eliminate race distinctions from American law

The 39th Congress which was to propose the Fourteenth Amendment convened in December 1865 with the realization that, although slavery had been abolished, the overall objective, the complete legal and political equality for all men had not been realized. This was dramatically emphasized by the infamous Black Codes being enacted throughout the southern states. These Black Codes had the single purpose of providing additional legislative sanction to maintain the inferior status for all Negroes which had been judicially decreed in the opinion in the case of *Scott* v. *Sandford*, 19 How. 393.

The Black Codes, while they grudgingly admitted that Negroes were no longer slaves, nonetheless used the states' power to impose and maintain essentially the same inferior, servile position which Negroes had occupied prior to the abolition of slavery. These codes thus followed the legal pattern of the ante-bellum slave codes. Like their slavery forerunners, these codes compelled Negroes to work for arbitrarily limited pay; restricted their mobility; forbade them, among other things, to carry firearms; forbade their testimony in a court against any white man; and highly significant here, contained innumerable provisions for segregation on carriers and in public places. In at least three states these codes prohibited Negroes from attending the public schools provided for white children.[58]

It was this inferior caste position which the Radical Republicans in Congress were determined to destroy. They were equally determined that by federal statutory or constitutional means, or both, Congress would not only invalidate the existing Black Codes but would proscribe any and all future attempts to enforce governmentally-imposed caste distinctions.

Congress was well aware of the fact that to take this step involved a veritable revolution in federal-state relations. A number of Senators and Representatives in the 39th Congress, by

---

[50] *Id.* at 1642.
[51] 12 Stat. 376 (1862).
[52] 12 Stat. 407 (1862).
[53] 12 Stat. 805 (1863).
[54] Cong. Globe, 38th Cong., 1st Sess. 553, 817 (1864).
[55] 13 Stat. 536, 537 (1865).
[56] Cong. Globe, 38th Cong., 1st Sess. 3132, 3133 (1864).
[57] *Id.* at 1158.

---

[58] See the summary in Senator Wilson's speech before Congress, Cong. Globe, 39th Cong., 1st Sess. 39–40, 589 (1866); 1 Fleming, Documentary History of Reconstruction 273–312 (1906); McPherson, The Political History of the United States During the Period of Reconstruction 29–44 (1880).

speech and resolution, made it eminently clear that they aimed at nothing less than the total destruction of all hierarchy, oligarchy and class rule in the southern states. One of the more notable resolutions of this kind was that of Senator Charles Sumner, introduced on December 4, 1865, at the opening of the session. This resolution asserted that no state formerly declared to be in rebellion was to be allowed to resume its relation to the Union until "the complete reestablishment of loyalty . . . " and:

> "The complete suppression of all oligarchical pretensions, and the complete enfranchisement of all citizens, so that there shall be no denial of rights on account of color or race; but justice shall be impartial, and all shall be equal before the law."

Another requirement of Sumner's resolution called for:

> "The organization of an educational system for the equal benefit of all without distinction of color or race."[59]

Sumner thus recognized the close relationship between the destruction of the southern ruling class and the elimination of segregation in the educational system.

Representative Jehu Baker of Illinois introduced a similar resolution in the House of Representatives, which read in part as follows:

> "Whereas class rule and aristocratic principles of government have burdened well nigh all Europe with enormous public debts and standing armies, which press as a grievous incubus on the people, absorbing their substance, impeding their culture, and impairing their happiness; and whereas the class rule and aristocratic element of slaveholding which found a place in our Republic has proved itself, in like manner, hurtful to our people . . . Therefore,
> "*Resolved*, (as the sense of this House,) That once for all we should have done with class rule and aristocracy as a privileged power before the law in this nation, no matter where or in what form they may appear; and that, in restoring the normal relations of the States lately in rebellion, it is the high and sacred duty of the Representatives of the people to proceed upon the true, as distinguished from the false, democratic principle, and to realize and secure the largest attainable liberty to the whole people of the Republic, irrespective of class or race."[60]

There were numerous other resolutions and speeches expressing similar sentiments. All of

the resolutions were referred to the Joint Committee on Reconstruction and are a part of the background of that committee's work in the framing of the Fourteenth Amendment.

These expressions of principle were started toward statutory fruition by Senator Trumbull's Bill to enlarge the powers of the Freedmen's Bureau. The debates which followed the introduction of his Senate Bill No. 60 are of particular interest because they make it clear that a large number of the Radical Republicans regarded the destruction of segregation in the school districts of the southern states as a highly desirable legislative objective. What followed amounted to a forthright assault on the idea that there could be racial segregation in the public schools.

Representative Hubbard of Connecticut expressed the broad pattern of thinking of which this bill was a part:

> "The words, caste, race, color, ever unknown to the Constitution, . . . are still potent for evil on the lips of men whose minds are swayed by prejudice or blinded by passion, and the freedmen need the protection of this bill.
> "The era is dawning when it will be a reproach to talk in scorn about the distinctions of race or color. Our country is, and must be, cosmopolitan. . . .
> "It is in vain that we talk about race, caste, or color. . . ."[61]

Likewise, Representative Rousseau of Kentucky stated:

> ". . . Here are four school-houses taken possession of, and unless they mix up white children with black, the white children can have no chance in these schools for instruction. And so it is wherever this Freedmen's Bureau operates."[62]

Representative Dawson of Pennsylvania recognized that the supporters of the bill:

> ". . . hold that the white and black race are equal. . . . Their children are to attend the same schools with white children, and to sit side by side with them. . . ."[63]

Of more importance was S.61 "A Bill to Protect All Persons in the United States in Their Civil Rights and Furnish the Means of Vindication." This bill, though introduced through Senator Trumbull in his capacity as Chairman of the Judiciary Committee, was in

---

[59] Cong. Globe, 39th Cong., 1st Sess. 2 (1865–1866).
[60] Cong. Globe, 39th Cong. 1st Sess. 69 (1865–1866).

[61] *Id.* at 630.
[62] *Id.* at App. 71.
[63] *Id.* at 541.

fact a measure sponsored by the entire Radical Republican majority.

The bill forbade any "discrimination in civil rights or immunities" among "the people of the United States on account of race, color, or previous condition of slavery". It provided that all persons should have "full and equal benefits of all laws" for the security of their persons and their property.

In a lengthy speech, Senator Trumbull defended the wisdom and constitutionality of this bill in detail. The Thirteenth Amendment, he argued, made the bill both constitutional and necessary.

> "Then, sir, I take it that any statute which is not equal to all, and which deprives any citizen of civil rights which are secured to other citizens, is an unjust encroachment upon his liberty; and is, in fact, a badge of servitude which, by the Constitution, is prohibited."[64]

Senator Trumbull's argument precipitated a lengthy debate on the constitutional issues. Opponents of the measure, conceding that Congress had the power under the Thirteenth Amendment to assure freedom of Negroes, denied that Congress had the power to endow Negroes with citizenship and civil rights. To sustain their position they pointed to the fact that Negroes who were freed prior to the Emancipation Proclamation were not treated as citizens and under the authority of the *Dred Scott* case could not be citizens.[65]

In reply, Trumbull advanced the additional constitutional argument that, once slavery was abolished, the naturalization clause of the Constitution provided Congress with the power to endow Negroes with the citizenship the *Dred Scott* case had held they could not otherwise enjoy. Trumbull thus adopted the position of Chief Justice Taney in the *Dred Scott* case that the power to confer citizenship was vested in the federal, not the state government.

Another major area of controversy with respect to the bill was as to its scope. Time and again the Democrats and the more conservative Republicans in the Senate asserted that the bill would invalidate every state law which provided for racial segregation, or provided a different rule for persons of different races.[66] For example, there was the charge of Senator Cowan, a Republican of Pennsylvania, who said:

> "Now, as I understand the meaning . . . of this bill, it is that there shall be no discrimination made between the inhabitants of the several States of this Union, none in any way. In Pennsylvania, for the greater convenience of the people, and for the greater convenience, I may say, of both classes of the people, in certain districts the Legislature has provided schools for colored children, has discriminated as between the two classes of children. We put the African children in this school-house and the white children over in that school-house, and educate them there as we best can. Is this amendment to the Constitution of the United States abolishing slavery to break up that system which Pennsylvania has adopted for the education of her white and colored children? Are the school directors who carry out that law and who make this distinction between these classes of children to be punished for a violation of this statute of the United States? To me it is monstrous."[67]

Senator Howard in reply gave the Conservatives no comfort:

> "I do not understand the bill which is now before us to contemplate anything else but this, that in respect to all civil rights . . . there is to be hereafter no distinction between the white race and the black race. It is to secure to these men whom we have made free the ordinary rights of a freeman and nothing else. . . . There is no invasion of the legitimate rights of the States."[68]

But, perhaps the best answer of all to these assertions of the sweeping character of the bill was given by Senator Morrill of Vermont, a member of the Joint Committee of Fifteen:

> "The Senator from Kentucky tells us that the proposition [federal guarantee of civil rights] is revolutionary, . . . I admit that this species of legislation is absolutely revolutionary. But are we not in the midst of revolution? Is the Senator from Kentucky utterly oblivious to the grant results of four years of war?"[69]

It is highly significant that Senator Morrill was not only a member of the Joint Committee of Fifteen, even then engaged in drafting the Fourteenth Amendment, but that he later was to insist that the Fourteenth Amendment prohibited separate but equal provisions in state school legislation.

After two full days of debate, the Senate passed the Trumbull bill by a vote of 33 to 12.

The only rational inference to be drawn from the legislative history of the Trumbull bill in the Senate is that the great majority of that body was determined to bar the states from using their power to impose or maintain racial

---

[64] *Id.* at 474.
[65] See statements of Senators Van Winkle of West Virginia and Saulsbury of Delaware. *Id.* at 475 ff.
[66] *Id.* at 500 ff.

[67] *Id.* at 500.
[68] *Id.* at 504.
[69] *Id.* at 570.

distinctions. The same majority was of the opinion that the federal government had constitutional authority so to delimit such action by the state.

In the House, the Conservatives pointed out forcefully that the text of the bill presented would destroy all limitations on federal power over state legislation and would likewise destroy all state legislative and judicial provisions making distinctions against Negroes. Representative Rogers observed:

> "In the State of Pennsylvania there is a discrimination made between the schools for white children and the schools for black. The laws there provide that certain schools shall be set apart for black persons, and certain schools shall be set apart for white persons. Now, if this Congress has a right, by such a bill as this, to enter the sovereign domain of a State ... then, by parity of reasoning, it has a right to enter the domain of that State and inflict upon the people there, without their consent, the right of the negro to enjoy the elective franchise. . . ."[70]

In a somewhat disingenuous attempt to deal with the argument of the Conservatives, Representative Wilson of Iowa, chairman of the House Judiciary Committee, argued vaguely that the bill would not have the effect of destroying all legislation discriminating on the basis of race.[71] Nevertheless Wilson broadly defined the term civil rights as used in the bill as being "the natural rights of man." Moreover, he observed that "immunities" secured "to citizens of the United States equality in the exemptions of the law."[72]

At this point, Representative Bingham of Ohio, who had become converted to the Conservatives' constitutional power argument, made a notable address to the House. While admitting that perhaps Congress was at that time without constitutional authority to enact so sweeping a bill, he said it was nevertheless true that the bill as it stood was as sweeping as was charged by the Conservatives.

Representative Bingham then made it preeminently clear that he entirely approved of the sweeping objectives of the bill as it came from the Senate. His willingness to accept any modification of the bill was *solely* on the grounds of an overwhelming present constitutional objection which he himself was even then in the process of curing with a proposal for a constitutional amendment. He said:

> "If civil rights has this extent, what, then, is proposed by the provision of the first section?

Simply to strike down by congressional enactment every State constitution which makes a discrimination on account of race or color in any of the civil rights of the citizen. I might say here, without the least fear of contradiction, that there is scarcely a State in this Union which does not, by its Constitution or by its statute laws, make some discrimination on account of race or color between citizens of the United States in respect of civil rights."[73]

Bingham then insisted that he believed that all discriminatory legislation should be wiped out by amending the Constitution.

> "The law in every State should be just; it should be no respecter of persons. It is otherwise now, and it has been otherwise for many years in many of the States of the Union. I should remedy that not by an arbitrary assumption of power, but by amending the Constitution of the United States, expressly prohibiting the States from any such abuse of power in the future."[74]

Bingham's prestige as a leader of the Radical Republican majority obliged Wilson to accept the Ohioan's interpretation. Consequently, the bill was returned to the Judiciary Committee and amended to eliminate the sweeping phrase "there shall be no discrimination in civil rights and immunities." Wilson no doubt comforted himself with the fact that even as amended the language of the bill was still revolutionary. At any rate, the Conservatives were still convinced that the bill invalidated state racial segregation laws. With considerable force, they argued that the phrase "the inhabitants of every state" ... shall have the rights to full and equal benefits of all laws and proceedings for the "security of persons and property ... " was properly to be broadly interpreted. In fact, Senator Davis of Kentucky had this to say:

> " . . . [T]his measure proscribes all discriminations against negroes in favor of white persons that may be made anywhere in the United States by any 'ordinance, regulation, or custom,' as well as by 'law or statute.' . . .
>
> But there are civil rights, immunities, and privileges 'which ordinances, regulations, and customs' confer upon white persons everywhere in the United States, and withhold from negroes. On ships and steamboats the most comfortable and handsomely furnished cabins and state-rooms, the first tables, and other privileges; in public hotels the most luxuriously appointed parlors, chambers, and saloons, the most sumptuous tables, and baths; in churches not only the most softly cushioned pews, but the most eligible sections of the edifices; on railroads, national, local, and

---

[70] *Id.* at 1121.
[71] *Id.* at 1117.
[72] *Ibid.*

[73] *Id.* at 1291.
[74] *Id.* at 1294.

street, not only seats, but whole cars, are assigned to white persons to the exclusion of negroes and mulattoes. All these discriminations in the entire society of the United States are established by ordinances, regulations, and customs. This bill proposes to break down and sweep them all away and to consummate their destruction, and bring the two races upon the same great plane of perfect equality, declares all persons who enforce those distinctions to be criminals against the United States, and subjects them to punishment by fine and imprisonment. . . ."[75]

Significantly, there was no attempt to reply to this interpretation of the amended bill.

The bill in its amended form was adopted by Congress and vetoed by President Johnson.

Representative Lawrence, who spoke in favor of overriding President Johnson's veto said:

"This section does not limit the enjoyment of privileges to such as may be accorded only to citizens of 'some class,' or 'some race,' or 'of the least favored class,' or 'of the most favored class,' or of a particular complexion, for these distinctions were never contemplated or recognized as possible in fundamental civil rights, which are alike necessary and important to all citizens, and to make inequalities in which is rank injustice."[76]

He also said:

". . . distinctions created by nature of sex, age, insanity, etc., are recognized as modifying conditions and privileges, but mere race or color, as among citizens never can [be]."[77]

Numerous newspapers also thought the bill destroyed all segregation in schools, theatres, churches, public vehicles and the like.[78] Flack said of the bill:

"Many [Congressmen] believed that the negro would be entitled to sit on juries, to attend the same schools, etc., since, if the States undertook to legislate on those matters, it might be claimed that he was denied the equal rights and privileges accorded to white men. It does not appear that all of these contentions were specifically contradicted.

\* \* \*

It would seem reasonable to suppose that if the bill should prove to be constitutional that

these rights could not be legally denied them."[79]

\* \* \*

". . . many of the leading papers of the country, including some of the principal Republican papers, regarded the Civil Rights Bill as a limitation of the powers of the States, and as a step towards centralization, in that it interfered with the regulation of local affairs which had hitherto been regulated by state and local authorities or by custom. This opinion was held in the North as well as in the South. There also seems to have been a general impression among the press that negroes would, by the provisions of the bill, be admitted, on the same terms and conditions as the white people, to schools, theaters, hotels, churches, railway cars, steamboats, etc."[80]

\* \* \*

"What the papers gave as their opinion must necessarily have been the opinion of large numbers of people. There is much evidence to substantiate this conclusion, for almost immediately after the passage of the bill over the President's veto, efforts were made by the negroes to secure these rights."[81]

The following generalizations are pertinent to the relationship of the Civil Rights Act (S. 61 as amended) to the problem of segregation in schools and the Fourteenth Amendment:

1. As originally drafted, the Act contained a phrase "there shall be no discrimination in civil rights and immunities among the inhabitants of any state . . ." This was so broad in scope that most Senators and Representatives believed that it would have the effect of destroying entirely all state legislation which distinguished or classified in any manner on the basis of race. School segregation laws, statutes establishing unequal penalties in criminal codes, laws banning Negroes from juries, all alike would have become invalid as against the federal statute.

2. A great majority of the Republicans—the men who formulated the Fourteenth Amendment—had no objection to a bill which went this far. Men like Rogers, Kerr and Cowan objected to the bill on the ground that it would end all caste legislation, including segregated schools, and this was the view of the Senate. None of the bill's supporters in the House, except Wilson, denied that the bill had that effect.

3. The Bingham amendment was finally adopted in the House which struck out the "no discrimination" clause, simply because a majority of the members of the House believed that so sweeping a measure could not be justified under the Constitution as it stood. They accepted Bingham's argument that the proper remedy for removing racial distinctions

---

[75] *Id.* at App. 183.
[76] *Id.* at 1836.
[77] *Id.* at 1835.
[78] New York Herald, March 29 and April 10, 1866: Commercial March 30, 1866; National Intelligencer, April 16, 1866 and May 16, 1866. There were a number of suits against local segregation laws banning Negroes from theatres, omnibuses, etc., McPherson's Scrap Book, The Civil Rights Bill, pp. 110 ff. None of these suits appear to have involved school segregation laws.

[79] Flack, The Adoption of the Fourteenth Amendment 40 (1908).
[80] *Id.* at 45.
[81] *Ibid.*

and classifications in the states was a new amendment to the Constitution.

4. The logic of the Bingham constitutional objections aside, the persuasiveness of his technical objection to the Trumbull bill was immeasurably enhanced by the fact that several days before his motion to amend the Civil Rights Bill, Bingham had in fact proposed to the House, on behalf of the Joint Committee, a constitutional amendment by the terms of which his constitutional objections to the Trumbull bill were obviated. That measure, H. R. 63, with some significant changes intended to underscore the prohibition on state governmental action with the addition of the citizenship clause became the Fourteenth Amendment.[82]

5. The law as finally enacted enumerated certain rights which Trumbull and other Radicals had felt were inseparably connected with the status of freedom. However, there is no evidence that even after the modification of the bill, the enumeration in the bill was considered to exclude rights not mentioned. Kerr, Rogers, Cowan, Grimes and other conservatives still insisted that the bill, even in its final form, banned segregation laws. The phrase "the inhabitants of every race . . . shall have the right . . . to full and equal benefit of all laws and proceedings for the security of persons and property" still stood in the bill and was susceptible of broad interpretation.

6. Finally, it may be observed that a majority of both Houses of Congress were ready to go beyond the provisions of the Civil Rights Act. Congressmen as diverse in their views as John A. Bingham and Henry J. Raymond, a moderate Republican and editor of the New York Times, united in proposing a constitutional amendment which would remove doubts as to the ability of Congress to destroy all state legislation discriminating and segregating on the basis of race. The forthcoming amendment, at all odds, was to set at rest all doubts as to the power of Congress to abolish all state laws making any racial distinctions or classifications.

**The framers of the Fourteenth Amendment**

While Congress was engaged in the passage of the Civil Rights Act, a powerful congressional committee was even then wrestling with the problem of drafting a constitutional amendment which they hoped would definitely destroy all class and caste legislation in the United States. This committee was the now famous Joint Committee of Fifteen, which the two houses of Congress had established by Joint Resolution in December, 1865, to "inquire into the conditions of the states which formed the so-called Confederate States of America and report whether any or all of them were entitled to representation in Congress." It is extremely important for the purpose of this brief to observe that the Joint Committee of Fifteen was altogether under the domination of a group of Radical Republicans who were products of the great Abolitionist tradition, the equalitarianism which has been set forth earlier in this brief.

Section 1 of the Fourteenth Amendment, and particularly the equal protection clause, is peculiarly the product of this group, plus Senators Sumner, Wilson and Trumbull.[83]

Co-chairmen of the Committee were Representative Thaddeus Stevens of Pennsylvania and Senator William P. Fessenden of Maine.

Stevens was virtually dictator of the House. It was his dedicated belief that the Negro must be immediately elevated to a position of unconditional, legal, economic, political and social equality; and to this end he was determined to destroy every legal and political barrier that stood in the way of his goal.[84] Obviously, any constitutional amendment affecting the Negro would very heavily reflect his point of view.

Stevens believed that the law could not permit any distinctions between men because of their race. It was his understanding of the first section of the Fourteenth Amendment that: ". . . where any State makes a distinction in the same law between different classes of individuals, Congress shall have power to correct such discrimination and inequality . . ."[85] He believed that it was up to Congress to repudiate ". . . the whole doctrine of the legal superiority of families or races," [85a] and that under the Amendment, ". . . no distinction would be tolerated in this purified Republic but what arose from merit and conduct."[86]

---

[82] "The Congress shall have power to make all laws which shall be necessary and proper to secure to the citizens of each state all privileges and immunities of citizens in the several states (Art. 4, Sec. 2); and to all persons in the several States equal protection in the rights of life, liberty and property (5th Amendment)." THE JOURNAL OF THE JOINT COMMITTEE OF FIFTEEN ON RECONSTRUCTION, 61 (Kendrick ed. 1914).

[83] KELLY AND HARBISON, THE AMERICAN CONSTITUTION, ITS ORIGIN AND DEVELOPMENT 460–463 (1948); BOUDIN, TRUTH AND FICTION ABOUT THE FOURTEENTH AMENDMENT, 16 N. Y. U. L. Q. REV. 19 (1938); FRANK AND MUNRO, THE ORIGINAL UNDERSTANDING OF "EQUAL PROTECTION OF THE LAWS", 50 COL. L. REV. 131, 141 (1950).

[84] See for example, Stevens' speech attacking the "doctrine of the legal superiority of families or races" and denouncing the idea that "this is a white man's government." Cong. Globe, 39th Cong., 1st Sess. 75 (1865). "Sir," he said on this occasion, "this doctrine of a white man's Government is as atrocious as the infamous sentiment that damned the late Chief Justice to everlasting fame; and, I fear, to everlasting fire." See also similar observations on Stevens in BOWERS, THE TRAGIC ERA (1929) and WOODBURN, THE LIFE OF THADDEUS STEVENS (1913).

[85] Cong. Globe, 39th Cong., 1st Sess. 1063 (1866).

[85a] Id. at 74.

[86] Id. at 3148.

Senator Fessenden undoubtedly held moderate views on the Reconstruction and, these views probably accounted for his selection as Co-chairman of the Joint Committee. Although Fessenden hoped that the Republican Party would work successfully with President Johnson, he broke with Johnson on the Civil Rights Act, which he supported with conviction. He was a staunch champion of the Fourteenth Amendment. Fessenden believed that all distinctions in civil rights based upon race must be swept away, and he was in favor of excluding the southern states from any representation in Congress until this end was assured.[87]

His son reports that the essence of his views was "all civil and political distinctions on account of race or color [would] be inoperative and void. . . ."[88]

Senator James W. Grimes, Republican of Iowa, was a Moderate and a close friend of Fessenden.[89] While he was governor of Iowa, prior to his election to the Senate the state constitution was revised to provide schools free and open to all children.[90] He insisted upon free schools open to all,[91] and Lewellen, who analyzed Grimes' political ideas, concluded that—

"Special legislation, whether for individual or class, was opposed by Grimes as contrary 'to the true theory of a Republican government' and as the 'source of great corruption.' Although he sympathized with the newly freed Negroes after the Civil War, he opposed any attempt to make them wards of the Federal government. They had been made citizens and had been given the right to vote; there was no reason in the world why a law should be passed 'applicable to colored people' and not to white people. While his ideas on the Negro question were colored by his radical opinions on the slavery question his opposition to race legislation would probably have been practically as firm upon any other subject."[92]

Senator Ira Harris of New York, one of the least vocal members of the Committee of Fifteen, was a close friend of Charles Sumner,[93] and "acted with the radicals in all matters pertaining to reconstruction."[94] His explicit

views on segregation are unascertained.[95] He was, however, so closely allied to the insiders on the Committee who considered race and color an indefensible basis for making legal distinctions,[96] that it is safe to conclude that he espoused, or at least acquiesced in, this viewpoint.

Senator George H. Williams, an Oregon Republican and former Douglas Democrat, claimed authorship of the First Reconstruction Act of 1867, originally called the Military Reconstruction Bill, which he introduced in the Senate on February 4, 1867.[97] In commenting upon this bill he said:

"I will say that in preparing this bill, I had no desire to oppress or injure the people of the South, but my sole purpose was to provide a system by which all classes would be protected in life, liberty, and property . . ."[98]

His views on segregation are also unascertained.[99] It should be noted, however, that there is no record of his ever lending his voice or his votes to any law providing segregation based upon race or color.

Senator Jacob H. Howard of Michigan was clearly in the vanguard of that group which worked to secure full equality for Negroes.[100] He was clear and definite in his interpretation of the Civil Rights Act of 1866 and the Fourteenth Amendment. He said after the passage of the former that "in respect of all civil rights, there is to be hereafter no distinction between the white race and the black race."[101] In explaining the intention of the Joint Committee during discussion of the joint resolution to propose what was to become the Fourteenth Amendment, he said:

"He desired to put this question of citizenship and the rights of citizens and freedmen under the civil rights bill beyond the legislative power of such gentlemen as [Senator Doolittle of Wisconsin] who would pull the whole system up by the roots and destroy it, and expose the freedmen again to the oppressions of their old masters."[102]

[87] KENDRICK, op. cit. supra n. 82, at 172–177; 6 DICTIONARY OF AMERICAN BIOGRAPHY 349–350 (1931).

[88] 2 FESSENDEN, LIFE AND PUBLIC SERVICES OF WILLIAM PITT FESSENDEN 36 (1931).

[89] KENDRICK, op. cit. supra n. 82, at 190–191.

[90] 7 DICTIONARY OF AMERICAN BIOGRAPHY 632 (1931).

[91] Ibid.; SALTER, LIFE OF JAMES W. GRIMES, c. 3 (1876).

[92] LEWELLEN, POLITICAL IDEAS OF JAMES W. GRIMES 42 IOWA HIST. & POL. 339, 347 (1944).

[93] 8 DICTIONARY OF AMERICAN BIOGRAPHY 310 (1932).

[94] KENDRICK, op. cit. supra n. 82, at 195.

[95] FRANK AND MUNRO, THE ORIGINAL UNDERSTANDING OF EQUAL PROTECTION OF THE LAWS, 50 COL. L. REV. 131, 142 (1950).

[96] Ibid.

[97] KENDRICK, op. cit. supra n. 82, at 191; Williams, Six Years in the United States Senate, Daily Oregonian, Dec. 3, 10, 1905.

[98] CHRISTENSEN, THE GRAND OLD MAN OF OREGON: THE LIFE OF GEORGE H. WILLIAMS 26 (1939).

[99] FRANK AND MUNRO, op. cit. supra n. 83, at 142.

[100] KENDRICK, op. cit. supra n. 82, at 192.

[101] FRANK AND MUNRO, op. cit. supra n. 83, at 140.

[102] Cong. Globe, 39th Cong., 1st Sess. 2896 (1866).

In another speech, while acting for Senator Fessenden as floor leader for the Amendment, Howard interpreted Section 1 as follows:

"The last two clauses of first section . . . disable a state from depriving . . . any person . . . of life, liberty or property without due process of law, or from denying to him the equal protection of the laws of the state. This abolishes all class legislation and does away with the injustice of subjecting one caste of persons to a code not applicable to another . . . Ought not the time to be now passed when one measure of justice is to be meted out to a member of one caste while another and a different measure is meted out to the member of another caste, both castes being alike citizens of the United States . . .[103]

The evidence conclusively establishes that Howard's interpretation of the equal protection clause precluded any use whatever of color as a basis for legal distinctions.[104]

Senator Reverdy Johnson, Democrat of Maryland, was attorney for the defense in *Dred Scott* v. *Sandford*.[105] George I. Curtis, one of Scott's attorneys, credited Johnson with being the major influence in shaping the decision.[106] Where segregation was concerned, Johnson was not entirely consistent or predictable.

In 1864 he supported the motion of Senator Charles Sumner that the Washington Railroad end the exclusion of persons of color.[107] During the debate upon Sumner's motion, Johnson said:

"It may be convenient, because it meets with the public wish or with the public taste of both classes, the white and the black, that there should be cars in which the white men and ladies are to travel, designated for that purpose, and cars in which the black men and black women are to travel, designated for that purpose. But that is a matter to be decided as between these two classes. There is no more right to exclude a black man from a car designated for the transportation of white persons than there is a right to refuse to transport in a car designated for black persons white men; and I do not suppose that anybody will contend . . . that there exists any power in the company to exclude white men from a car because the company have appropriated that car for the general transportation of black passengers.[108]

Two years later, Johnson said:

". . . as slavery has been abolished in the several States, those who were before slaves are now citizens of the United States, standing . . . upon the same condition, therefore, with the white citizens. If there is an authority in the Constitution to provide for the black citizen, it cannot be because he is black; it must be because he is a citizen; and that reason [is] equally applicable to the white man as to the black man. . . ."[109]

Thus it appears that he understood that the granting of citizenship rights to Negroes meant that racial distinctions could no longer be imposed by law.

Representative John A. Bingham of Ohio, a member of the committee who has been described as the "Madison of the first section of the Fourteenth Amendment"[110] and undoubtedly its author, was a strong and fervent Abolitionist, classified with those whose views of equal protection "precluded any use whatsoever of color as a basis of legal distinctions."[111]

While the Fourteenth Amendment was pending, Representative Bingham took the view that state constitutions which barred segregated schools were "in accordance with the spirit and letter of the Constitution of the United States . . . [if] the utterance of Jefferson ever meant anything . . . it meant precisely that when he declared for equal and exact justice. . . ."[112]

Representative George Boutwell of Massachusetts, was a hard, practical politician rather than an idealist. He was however, no less extreme in his demands for Negro civil rights and Negro suffrage than men like Stevens and Sumner. Indicative of his views is his vote on May 22, 1874 against the Sargent amendment to the Civil Rights Act of 1875, which would have permitted separate but equal schools.[113] During Reconstruction Alabama was "flooded with the radical speeches of Morton and Boutwell in favor of mixed schools."[114] He was among those

---

[103] *Id.* at 2766.

[104] FRANK AND MUNRO, *op. cit. supra* n. 83, at 142.

[105] 19 How. 393.

[106] 10 DICTIONARY OF AMERICAN BIOGRAPHY 113 (1933).

[107] WILSON, HISTORY OF THE RISE AND FALL OF THE SLAVE POWER IN AMERICA 507 (1877).

[108] Cong. Globe, 38th Cong., 1st Sess. 1156 (1864).

[109] Cong. Globe, 39th Cong., 1st Sess. 372–374 (1865–1866).

[110] Dissent of Mr. Justice Black in Adamson v. California, 332 U.S. 46, 74.

[111] FRANK AND MUNRO, THE ORIGINAL UNDERSTANDING OF EQUAL PROTECTION OF THE LAWS, 50 COL. L. REV. at 151. See GRAHAM, THE "CONSPIRACY THEORY" OF THE FOURTEENTH AMENDMENT, 47 YALE L. J. 371, 400–401 (1938); GRAHAM, THE EARLY ANTISLAVERY BACKGROUNDS OF THE FOURTEENTH AMENDMENT, 1950 WIS. L. REV. 479 at 492; Cong. Globe, 39th Cong., 1st Sess. 1291, 1293, 2461–2462 (1866). For other sketches of Bingham see 2 DICTIONARY OF AMERICAN BIOGRAPHY 278 (1929) and KENDRICK, *op. cit. supra* n. 82 at 183.

[112] Cong. Globe, 40th Cong., 1st Sess. 2462 (1868).

[113] 2 Cong. Rec. 4167 (1874).

[114] BOWERS, THE TRAGIC ERA 427 (1929).

whose interpretation of "equal protection" would not admit color as a basis for legal distinctions.[115]

Representative Roscoe Conkling, a New York Republican, was thought to have taken his views on Reconstruction from Stevens.[116] He was called by some a protege of Stevens; at any rate, they worked as partners on much reconstruction legislation.[117] In 1868, when the readmission of Arkansas was being discussed, he voted against the Henderson Amendment to the bill which would have permitted the state to establish segregated schools.[118] In 1872 he favored the supplementary civil rights bill and voted against the Thurman amendment which would have struck out a clause permitting colored persons to enter "any place of public amusement or entertainment."[119] He was in the Senate majority which on May 22, 1874, voted down the Sargent amendment to the Civil Rights Bill, an amendment which would have permitted separate but equal schools.[120] Conkling must be classified as one of those who agreed to no legal classifications or distinctions based upon color.[121]

Representative Henry T. Blow, a Missouri Republican, first supported the views of Thaddeus Stevens in the Joint Committee and then in the second session gave his support to Bingham.[122] In either case, he acted with those who favored a broad and sweeping denial of the right of the states to make legal classifications on the basis of race or color. Blow came to Congress with a strong antislavery background and took the position that color discrimination could not be defended, as a matter of course.[123]

Representative Justin S. Morrill of Vermont is characterized as "an extreme radical", one "regularly on the side of radicalism". It is said of him that "the only part taken by him in Reconstruction was to attend the meetings of the Committee and cast his vote."[124] However, he was among those voting against the "white" clause in the Nebraska constitution when the bill to admit that state to the union was under consideration.[125] He voted against the Henderson amendment to permit segregated schools in the bill to readmit Arkansas.[126] He voted against the Sargent Amendment to allow separate but equal schools, during the debates on the bill that became the Civil Rights Act of 1875.[127] Morrill thus belongs in the group of those who did not consider color a reasonable ground for legal distinctions.[128]

Representative Elihu Washburne of Illinois was a staunch member of the House Radical bloc, and a pronounced enemy of the more moderate Reconstruction policies of President Johnson. He supported both the Civil Rights Act and the Fourteenth Amendment and his remarks make it clear that he favored a revolution in the southern social order.[129]

The two Democratic members of the Joint Committee from the House were both enemies of the Civil Rights Act and the Fourteenth Amendment. Representative Henry Grider of Kentucky was without influence in the drafting of the Fourteenth Amendment by the Joint Committee.[130] However, remarks of Representative Andrew Jackson Rogers of New Jersey, in opposition to these measures, are significant indication of contemporary understanding of their reach and thrust. Thus, in speaking of the Civil Rights Bill, Rogers said:

> "In the State of Pennsylvania there is a discrimination made between the schools for white children and the schools for black. The laws there provide that certain schools shall be set apart for black persons, and certain schools shall be set apart for white persons. Now, if this Congress has a right, by such a bill as this, to enter the sovereign domain of a State and interfere with these statutes . . . , then . . . it has a right to . . . , inflict upon the people . . . the right of the negro to [vote]. . . ."[131]

Similarly, in speaking of the proposed Section 1 of the Fourteenth Amendment on February 26, 1866, he said:

> ". . . Under this amendment, Congress would have power to compel the State to provide for white children and black children to attend the same school, upon the principle that all the people . . . shall have equal protection in all the rights of life, liberty, and property, and all the privileges and immunities of citizens. . . ."[132]

---

[115] FRANK AND MUNRO, op. cit. supra n. 83, at 142.

[116] KENDRICK, op. cit. supra n. 82, at 186.

[117] CHIDSEY, THE GENTLEMAN FROM NEW YORK 34–35 (1935).

[118] Cong. Globe, 40th Cong., 2nd Sess. 2748 (1868).

[119] CONKLING, LIFE AND LETTERS OF ROSCOE CONKLING 432 (1869).

[120] 2 Cong. Rec. 4167 (1874).

[121] FRANK AND MUNRO, op. cit. supra n. 83, at 142.

[122] KENDRICK, op. cit. supra n. 82, at 194.

[123] FRANK AND MUNRO, op. cit. supra n. 83, at 142.

[124] KENDRICK, op. cit. supra n. 82, at 140, 193.

[125] Cong. Globe, 39th Cong., 1st Sess. 4275–4276 (1866).

[126] Cong. Globe, 40th Cong., 2nd Sess. 2748 (1868).

[127] 2 Cong. Rec. 4167 (1874).

[128] FRANK AND MUNRO, op. cit. supra n. 83, at 142.

[129] 19 DICTIONARY OF AMERICAN BIOGRAPHY 504 (1936); see also KENDRICK, op. cit. supra n. 82, at 194.

[130] KENDRICK, op. cit. supra n. 82, at 196. Grider is not even listed in the DICTIONARY OF AMERICAN BIOGRAPHY. He died before the second session of the 39th Congress. KENDRICK, op. cit. supra n. 82, at 197.

[131] Cong. Globe., 39th Cong., 1st Sess. 1121 (1866).

[132] Id. at App. 134 (1866).

Again, in denouncing the Amendment, he declared:

> "This section of the joint resolution is no more nor less than an attempt to embody in the Constitution of the United States that outrageous and miserable civil rights bill. . . ."
>
> ". . . I hold [the amendment] will prevent any State from refusing to allow anything to anybody."[133]

### E. The Fourteenth Amendment was intended to write into the organic law of the United States the principle of absolute and complete equality in broad constitutional language

While the Civil Rights Act of 1866 was moving through the two Houses of Congress, the Joint Committee of Fifteen was engaged in the task of drafting a constitutional amendment as a part of a program for the "readmission" of the southern states to the Union. When the Committee began its meetings in January 1866, several of its members introduced proposals for constitutional amendments guaranteeing civil rights to the freedmen. After a series of drafting experiments, Representative Bingham on February 3 proposed the following:

> "The Congress shall have power to make all laws which shall be necessary and proper to secure to the citizens of each State all privileges and immunities of citizens in the several States (Art. 4, Sec. 2); and to all persons in the several States equal protection in the rights of life, liberty and property (5th Amendment)."[134]

The Joint Committee found this proposal satisfactory and accordingly on February 13th introduced it in the House as H. R. 63.[135]

By now the dedicated purpose of the Radical Republicans based in part upon the ante-war equalitarian principles as opposed to caste and class legislation had to be crystallized in a Fourteenth Amendment. Necessarily, the drafters of this amendment and those who participated in the debates on the amendment recognized that constitutional amendments are properly worded in the broadest and most comprehensive language possible.

It must be borne in mind that Representative Bingham, and those who supported his position on the amendment to the Civil Rights Bill of

1866, had already demonstrated that the constitutional amendment under consideration would be at least as comprehensive in its scope and effect as the original sweeping language of the Trumbull Civil Rights Bill *before* it was amended in the House, and that it would be far broader than the scope of the bill as finally enacted into law. On this point, Bingham repeatedly made his intentions clear, both in his discussion on the power limitations on the Civil Rights Bill itself and in his defense of his early drafts of the proposed constitutional amendment.

Representative Rogers immediately attacked the proposed constitutional amendment (H. R. 63) as "more dangerous to the liberties of the people and the foundations of the government" than any proposal for amending the Constitution heretofore advanced. This amendment, he said, would destroy all state legislation distinguishing Negroes on the basis of race. Laws against racial intermarriage, laws applying special punishments to Negroes for certain crimes, and laws imposing segregation, including school segregation laws, alike would become unconstitutional. He said:

> "Who gave the Senate the constitutional power to pass that bill guarantying equal rights to all, if it is necessary to amend the organic law in the manner proposed by this joint resolution? . . . It provides that all persons in the several States shall have equal protection in the right of life, liberty, and property. Now, it is claimed by gentlemen upon the other side of the House that Negroes are citizens of the United States. Suppose that in the State of New Jersey Negroes are citizens, as they are claimed to be by the other side of the House, and they change their residence to the State of South Carolina, if this amendment be passed Congress can pass under it a law compelling South Carolina to grant to Negroes every right accorded to white people there; and as white men there have the right to marry white women, Negroes, under this amendment, would be entitled to the same right; and thus miscegenation and mixture of the races could be authorized in any State, as all citizens under this amendment are entitled to the same privileges and immunities, and the same protection in life, liberty, and property.
>
> * * *
>
> "In the State of Pennsylvania there are laws which make a distinction with regard to the schooling of white children and the schooling of black children. It is provided that certain schools shall be designated and set apart for white children, and certain other schools designated and set apart for black children. Under this amendment, Congress would have power to compel the State to provide for white children and black children to attend the same school, upon the principle that all the people . . . shall have equal protection in all the rights

---

[133] *Id.* at 2538.

[134] This proposal with some changes was destined to become eventually the second portion of Section 1 of the Fourteenth Amendment. Kᴇɴᴅʀɪᴄᴋ, *op. cit. supra* n. 82, at 61.

[135] Cong. Globe, 39th Cong., 1st Sess. 813 (1865–1866).

of life, liberty, and property, and all the privileges and immunities of citizens in the several States."[136]

Representative Bingham, who was contemporaneously amending the original Trumbull Civil Rights Bill because its broad anti-discrimination provisions lacked constitutional foundation, naturally did not dispute Representative Rogers' appraisal of the wide scope of H. R. 63. On the contrary, Representative Bingham two days later indicated his concurrence in that appraisal in the course of a colloquy with Representative Hale.

Representative Hale inquired of Representative Bingham whether his proposed constitutional amendment did not "confer upon Congress a general power of legislation for the purpose of securing to all persons in the several states protection of life, liberty and property, subject only to the qualification that the protection shall be equal." And Representative Bingham replied, "I believe it does . . ."

In order to nail down the precise source of the proposed grant of power, Representative Hale then asked Representative Bingham to "point me to that clause or part . . . which contains the doctrine he here announces?" To which the answer was, "The words 'equal protection', contain it, and nothing else."[137]

The House at the end of February was preoccupied with debating Reconstruction generally as well as the Civil Rights Bill, and it showed itself in no hurry to take up Bingham's proposal, especially since it was obvious that a more comprehensive measure would soon be forthcoming from the Joint Committee. Following the debate on February 28, the House postponed further consideration of the proposed amendment until mid-April.[138] In fact, "H. R. 63" was not to be heard from in that form again. Yet its protective scope presently passed into the more extensive proposal which the Joint Committee brought forward at the end of April and which became, after some changes, the amendment which Congress finally submitted to the states.

During most of March and April, the Joint Committee paid little attention to the question of civil rights. It was concerned, for a time, with the question of the admission of Tennessee; then, for a time, it appears to have been inactive. Not until late April did it resume sessions looking forward to the drafting of a comprehensive constitutional amendment on Reconstruction. On April 21, Stevens offered to the committee a draft of a proposed constitutional amendment, covering civil rights, representation, Negro suffrage and the repudiation of the "rebel" debt.

This proposal became the frame upon which the Fourteenth Amendment was constructed. Most significant from our point of view was section 1:

"No discrimination shall be made by any state, nor by the United States, as to the civil rights of persons because of race, color, or previous condition of servitude."[139]

Section 2 provided that on and after July 4, 1876, no discrimination should be made between persons in the rights of suffrage on account of race, color, or previous condition of servitude. Section 3 provided that until that time, no class of persons against whom a state imposed suffrage discrimination because of race, color or previous condition of servitude should be included in the state's basis of representation. Section 4 invalidated the "rebel" debt. Section 5, which passed substantially intact into the Fourteenth Amendment, provided that Congress was to have the power to enforce the provisions of the amendment by appropriate legislation.[140]

Section 1 was to pass through several critical changes in the next few days. Almost at once, Senator Bingham moved to have the following provision added to section 1:

". . . nor shall any state deny to any person within its jurisdiction the equal protection of the laws, nor take private property for public use without just compensation."[141]

It will be noticed that Bingham's suggestion had within it the substance of the equal protection clause of the Fourteenth Amendment. After some discussion, the committee voted this suggestion down, seven to five.

Other changes followed. After some further discussion, Bingham moved that the following be added as a new section of the amendment:

"No state shall make or enforce any law which shall abridge the privileges or immunities of citizens of the United States; nor shall any state deprive any person of life, liberty or property without due process of law; nor deny to any person within its jurisdiction the equal protection of the laws."[142]

---

[136] Cong. Globe, 39th Cong., 1st Sess., App. 134 (1865–1866).
[137] *Id.* at 1094.
[138] *Id.* at 1095.

[139] Kendrick, *op. cit. supra* n. 82, at 83.
[140] *Ibid.*
[141] *Id.* at 85.
[142] *Id.* at 87.

This was substantially Bingham's earlier amendment, submitted to Congress in February as H. R. 63 with the addition of the equal protection clause. One significant difference lay in the fact that Bingham's new section did not confer power upon Congress to legislate; instead, it made privileges and immunities, due process and equal protection constitutional guarantees against state interference.

## F. The Republican majority in the 39th Congress was determined to prevent future Congresses from diminishing federal protection of these rights

There were two rather obvious reasons for Senator Bingham's last two amendments. First, a number of committee members had earlier expressed some concern over the phraseology of H. R. 63 because it allowed Congress to refuse to enforce the guarantees if it saw fit. The Radical Republicans were openly fearful lest later and more conservative Congresses destroy their work.[143] But direct constitutional guarantees would be beyond the power of Congress to impair or destroy. Second, Bingham was acting with the knowledge that section 5 of the proposed amendment already granted Congress full power to legislate to enforce the guarantees of the amendment. In other words, the Radical Republicans had no thought of stripping Congress of the power to enforce the amendment by adequate legislation. They put the guarantees themselves beyond the reach of a hostile Congress.[144]

The Committee at once adopted Representative Bingham's suggested addition by a vote of ten to two.[145] Four days later, however, on April 25, the Committee on Williams' motion, struck out Bingham's latest suggested revision, only Stevens, Bingham, Morrill, Rogers and Blow voting to retain it.[146] On April 28, in the final stages of committee discussion, Bingham moved to strike out section 1, reading "no discrimination shall be made . . ." and insert his proposal of April 21 in its place. Although the Committee had voted only three days earlier to kill Bingham's proposal entirely, it now passed his new motion.[147] Thus, Bingham's proposal ultimately became section 1 of the amendment which the Committee now submitted to Congress. As such, and with the addition of the citizenship clause adopted from the Civil Rights Act of 1866, it was to pass into the Fourteenth Amendment as finally accepted by Congress.

On April 30, Representative Stevens introduced the text of the Committee's proposed amendment in the House of Representatives. As presented, the amendment differed in two particulars from the Fourteenth Amendment as finally adopted: the first section as yet did not contain the citizenship clause; and the third section carried a clause for the complete disfranchisement of Confederate supporters until 1870. An accompanying resolution proposed to make successful ratification of the amendment, together with ratification by the several southern states, a condition precedent to the readmission of the southern states to representation in Congress.[148]

On May 8, Stevens opened debate in the House on the proposed amendment. In a sharp speech he emphasized the legislative power of Congress under the proposed amendment:

> "I can hardly believe that any person can be found who will not admit that every one of these provisions [in the first section] is just. They are all asserted, in some form or other, in our DECLARATION or organic law. But the Constitution limits only the action of Congress, and is not a limitation on the States. This amendment supplies that defect, and allows Congress to correct the unjust legislation of the States, so far that the law which operates upon one man shall operate *equally* upon all. Whatever law punishes a white man for a crime, shall punish the black man precisely in the same way and to the same degree. Whatever law protects the white man shall afford 'equal' protection to the black man."[149]

The amendment, he added, was made necessary by the "oppressive codes" which had become law in the southern states. "Unless the Constitution should restrain them, those States will all, I fear, keep up this discrimination and crush to death the hated freedmen."[150]

Finally, he stated that the purpose of section 1 was to place the Civil Rights Act beyond the reach of a hostile Congress:

> "Some answer, 'Your civil rights bill secures the same things.' That is partly true, but a law is repealable by a majority. And I need hardly say that the first time that the South with their copperhead allies obtain the command of Congress it will be repealed . . . This amendment once adopted cannot be annulled

---

[143] See speeches of Representatives Garfield, Broomall, Eldridge, and Stevens and Senator Howard, Cong. Globe, 39th Cong., 1st Sess. 2459, 2462, 2498, 2506, 2896 (1865–1866).

[144] See for example Stevens's explanations on the reasons for reenforcing the Civil Rights Act by constitutional guarantees. *Id.* at 2459.

[145] KENDRICK, *op. cit. supra* n. 82, at 87.

[146] *Id.* at 98.

[147] *Id.* at 106.

[148] Cong. Globe, 39th Cong., 1st Sess. 2459 (1866).

[149] *Ibid.* (italics in original).

[150] *Ibid.*

without two-thirds of Congress. That they will hardly get."[151]

There was general agreement among subsequent speakers that one of the purposes of section 1 of the amendment was to reinforce the Civil Rights Act. Enemies of the proposed amendment charged that Radical Republicans, having forced through what was an unconstitutional statute, were now attempting to clear up the constitutional issue by writing the statute into the supreme law.[152]

The Radical Republicans refused to admit that they were attempting to cover up the passage of an unconstitutional statute. Instead, they insisted that one of the purposes of the present proposed amendment was to place the guarantees of the Civil Rights Act beyond attack by future Congresses unfriendly to the rights of the freedman. "The Civil Rights Bill is now part of the law of this land," said Representative James A. Garfield of Ohio in defending the amendment. "But every gentleman knows it will cease to be a part of the law whenever the sad moment arrives when that gentleman's party comes into power ... For this reason, and not because I believe the civil rights bill to be unconstitutional, I am glad to see that first section here."[153] Representative John Broomall of Ohio, making the same point, said, "If we are already safe with the civil rights bill, it will do no harm to become the more effectually so, and to prevent a mere majority from repealing the law and thus thwarting the will of the loyal people." Broomall pointed out, also, that no less a friend of the Negro than Representative John A. Bingham, had entertained grave doubts as to the constitutionality of the measure, and thought a constitutional amendment necessary. He disagreed, Broomall said, with Bingham's doubts, but he was not so sure of himself that he felt justified "in refusing

to place the power to enact the law unmistakably in the Constitution."[154]

Probably other moderate Republicans agreed with Representative Henry J. Raymond of New York who had voted against the Civil Rights bill because he "regarded it as very doubtful, to say the least, whether Congress, under the existing Constitution had any power to enact such a law. . . ." But he nonetheless had heartily favored the principles and objectives of the bill, and because he still favored "securing an equality of rights to all citizens" he would vote "very cheerfully" for the present amendment.[155]

There was little discussion during the debate in the House of the scope of the civil rights which would be protected by the proposed amendment, apparently because both sides realized that debate on the original Civil Rights Bill had exhausted the issue. The indefatigable Rogers, fighting to the last against any attempt to guarantee rights for the Negro, repeatedly reminded Congress that the amendment would sweep the entire range of civil rights under the protection of the Federal Government and so work a revolution in the constitutional system.[156]

Although it was not necessary to answer Rogers, Bingham reminded Congress:

"The necessity for the first section of this amendment to the Constitution, Mr. Speaker, is one of the lessons that have been taught to your committee and taught to all the people of this country by the history of the past four years of terrific conflict—that history in which God is, and in which He teaches the profoundest lessons to men and nations. There was a want hitherto, and there remains a want now, in the Constitution of our country, which the proposed amendment will supply. What is that? It is the power in the people, the whole people of the United States, by express authority of the Constitution to do that by congressional enactment which hitherto they have not had the power to do, and have never even attempted to do; that is, to protect by national law the privileges and immunities of all the citizens of the Republic and the inborn rights of every person within its jurisdiction whenever the same shall be abridged or denied by the unconstitutional acts of any State.

Allow me, Mr. Speaker, in passing, to say that this amendment takes from no State any right that ever pertained to it. No State ever had the right, under the forms of law or otherwise, to deny to any freeman the equal protection of the laws or to abridge the privileges or immunities of any citizen of the

---

[151] *Ibid.*

[152] Representative William Finck of Ohio asserted, for example, that "all I have to say about this section is, that if it is necessary to adopt it ... then the civil rights bill, which the President vetoed, was passed without authority and was clearly unconstitutional." *Id.* at 2461. Representative Benjamin Boyer of Pennsylvania, another enemy of the amendment, after observing that "the first section embodies the principles of the civil rights bill," twitted the Republicans for seeking to rectify their own constitutional error and attacked the present amendment as "objectionable, also, in its phraseology, being open to ambiguity and admitting the conflicting constructions." *Id.* at 2467. Representative Charles Eldridge of Wisconsin asked ironically, "What necessity is there, then, for this amendment if that bill was constitutional at the time of its passage?" *Id.* at 2506.

[153] *Id.* at 2462.

---

[154] *Id.* at 2498.

[155] *Id.* at 2502.

[156] *Id.* at 2537.

Republic, although many of them have assumed and exercised the power, and that without remedy."[157]

## G. Congress understood that while the Fourteenth Amendment would give authority to Congress to enforce its provisions, the amendment in and of itself would invalidate all class legislation by the states

On May 10, the House passed the amendment without modification by a vote of 128 to 37. The measure then went to the Senate.[158]

On the same day, Senator Howard opened the debate in the Senate. Speaking for the Joint Committee because of Senator Fessenden's illness, Howard gave a broad interpretation of the first section of the proposed amendment. He emphasized the scope of legislative power which Congress would possess in the enforcement of the Amendment.

"How will it be done under the present amendment? As I have remarked, they are not [at present] powers granted to Congress, and therefore it is necessary, if they are to be effectuated and enforced, as they assuredly ought to be, that additional power be given to Congress to that end. This is done by the fifth section of this amendment which declares that 'the Congress shall have power to enforce by appropriate legislation the provisions of this article.' Here is a direct affirmative delegation of power to Congress to carry out all the principles of all these guarantees, a power not found in the Constitution."[159]

Senator Howard's interpretation of the legislative power of Congress under the proposed amendment makes it obvious that the Joint Committee, in separating the guarantees of civil rights from the congressional power to legislate thereon, had not at all intended to weaken the legislative capacity of Congress to enforce the rights conferred by the amendment. The guarantees, however, no longer depended upon congressional fiat alone for their effectiveness as they had in Bingham's proposed civil rights amendment of January (H. R. 63). But in Howard's view and that of the Committee, this meant merely that future Congresses could not destroy the rights conferred.

Senator Howard then passed to an equally expansive interpretation of the due process and equal protection clauses of the amendment:

"The last two clauses of the first section of the amendment disabled a State from depriving

not merely a citizen of the United States, but any person, whoever he may be, of life, liberty, or property without due process of law or from denying to him the equal protection of the laws of the State. *This abolishes all class legislation in the States and does away with the injustice of subjecting one caste of persons to a code not applicable to another.* It prohibits the hanging of a black man for a crime for which the white man is not to be hanged. It protects the black man in his fundamental rights as a citizen with the same shield which it throws over the white man."[160] (Italics added.)

The only class of rights, Howard added, which were not conferred by the first section of the amendment was "the right of suffrage." Howard concluded this analysis by asserting that the entire first section, taken in conjunction with the legislative power of Congress conferred in section five, was of epoch-making importance:

"I look upon the first section, taken in connection with the fifth, as very important. It will, if adopted by the States, forever disable everyone of them from passing laws trenching upon those fundamental rights and privileges which pertain to citizens of the United States, and to all persons who may happen to be within their jurisdiction. It establishes equality before the law, and it gives to the humblest, the poorest, the most despised of the race the same rights and the same protection before the law as it gives to the most powerful, the most wealthy, or the most haughty. That, sir, is republican government, as I understand it, and the only one which can claim the praise of a just Government."[161]

Thus, Senator Howard understood that due process and equal protection would sweep away entirely "all class legislation" in the states. By implication, he subscribed to a "substantive interpretation" of due process of law, thus making due process a limitation upon state governments to subvert civil liberties.

No Senator thereafter challenged these sweeping claims for the efficacy of the civil rights portion of Section 1. Howard's allies subscribed enthusiastically to his interpretation. Senator Luke Poland of Vermont, a staunch Radical Republican, regarded the amendment as necessary to set to rest all questions of congressional competence in enacting the civil rights bill:

"Congress has already shown its desire and intention to uproot and destroy all such partial State legislation in the passage of what is called

[157] *Id.* at 2542.
[158] *Id.* at 2545.
[159] *Id.* at 2766.
[160] *Id.* at 2766.
[161] *Id.* at 2766.

the civil rights bill. The power of Congress to do this has been doubted and denied by persons entitled to high consideration. It certainly seems desirable that no doubt should be left existing as to the power of Congress to enforce principles lying at the very foundation of all republican government if they be denied or violated by the States. . . ."[162]

Certainly the Conservatives in the Senate agreed altogether with Senator Howard and the other Senate Republicans about the sweeping impact which the prospective amendment would have upon state caste legislation. Senator Thomas Hendricks of Indiana, in condemning the legislative power to enforce the amendment which Congress would acquire from the operation of section 5, said that these words had

". . . such force and scope of meaning as that Congress might invade the jurisdiction of the States, rob them of their reserved rights, and crown the Federal Government with absolute and despotic power. As construed this provision is most dangerous."[163]

The prospective amendment moved forward rapidly in the Senate, with comparatively little debate. The Radical Republicans were confident of their objectives. The conservative Republicans and Democrats despaired of arresting the tide of events. One significant change occurred on May 30 when Howard brought forward the citizenship clause of the Civil Rights Act and successfully moved it as an amendment to section 1. Few Republicans doubted that Congress already had the power to legislate upon the question of citizenship. However, the new provision cleared up a serious hiatus in the original Constitution by settling in unequivocal fashion the definition of national and state citizenship. Needless to say, the new provision, like its predecessor in the Civil Rights Act, specifically endowed Negroes with citizenship and reversed the dictum of the *Dred Scott* case that no Negro could be a citizen of the United States.

The Radical Republicans were well aware that by endowing the Negro with citizenship, they strengthened his claim to the entire scope of civil rights. Bingham had mentioned as much in debate in the House, while Representative Raymond of New York had added that once the Negro became a citizen, it would not be possible in a republican government to deny him any right or to impose upon him any restriction, even including that of suffrage. The force of this stratagem did not escape the Conservatives in the Senate. Senator Garrett Davis of Kentucky had this to say of the citizenship provision of the amendment:

"The real and only object of the first provision of this section, which the Senate has added to it, is to make Negroes citizens, to prop the civil rights bill, and give them a more plausible, if not a valid, claim to its provisions, and to press them forward to a full community of civil and political rights with the white race, for which its authors are struggling and mean to continue to struggle."[164]

The Senate passed the amendment in June, 33 to 11. Congress formally proposed the amendment on June 13 and it was submitted to the states.

**Congress intended to destroy all class distinctions in law**   What, then, may one conclude concerning the intent of Congress with regard to segregation in the framing of the amendment?

Both Senator Howard and Representative Stevens made it definitely clear that the scope of the rights guaranteed by the amendment was much greater than that embraced in the Civil Rights Act.

It is evident that the members of the Joint Committee intended to place all civil rights within the protection of the Federal Government and to deny the states any power to interfere with those rights on the basis of color. The scope of the concept of liberties entertained by the Committee was very broad. The breadth of this concept was recognized by this Court in all of its decisions up to *Plessy* v. *Ferguson*.

In adopting the Civil Rights Act of 1866, Congress had enumerated the rights protected. This was done because Bingham and others doubted that Congress had the power to take all civil liberties under federal protection. Unrestricted by this consideration in drafting a constitutional provision, Congress used broad comprehensive language to define the standards necessary to guarantee complete federal protection. This was promptly recognized by this Court in one of the earliest decisions construing the Amendment when it was held: "The 14th Amendment makes no effort to enumerate the rights it designs to protect. It speaks in general terms, and those are as comprehensive as possible." *Strauder* v. *West Virginia*, 100 U.S. 303, 310.

Did Congress specifically intend to ban state laws imposing segregation by race? And more specifically, did it intend to prohibit segregation

---

[162] *Id.* at 2961.
[163] *Id.* at 2940.

[164] *Id.* at App. 240.

in school systems, even where a state provided a separate but equal system for Negroes? To begin with it must be recognized that the "separate but equal" doctrine was yet to be born. The whole tenor of the dominant argument in Congress was at odds with any governmentally enforced racial segregation as a constitutionally permissible state practice.

Senator Howard, among others, asserted categorically that the effect of the due process and equal protection clauses of the Fourteenth Amendment would be to sweep away entirely all caste legislation in the United States. Certainly a number of Conservatives, notably Representative Rogers of New Jersey, a member of the Joint Committee and Senator Davis of Kentucky, were convinced that the effect of the amendment would be to prohibit entirely all laws classifying or segregating on the basis of race. They believed, and stated, that school laws providing separate systems for whites and Negroes of the kind which existed in Pennsylvania, Ohio and in several of the Johnson-Reconstructed southern states would be made illegal by the amendment.

It is notable that while there were some assurances extended by Radical Republicans to the Moderates and Conservatives as to the scope of the Civil Rights Act of 1866 in this regard, there were no such assurances in the debates on the Fourteenth Amendment.

The Republican majority realized full well that it could not envisage all possible future applications of the amendment to protect civil rights. By separating section 1 of the amendment, which provides an absolute federal constitutional guarantee for those rights, from section 5, which endows Congress with legislative capacity to protect such rights, the framers of the amendment assured continued protection of these rights, by making it possible to win enforcement of them in the courts and eliminated the power of Congress alone to diminish them.

## H. The treatment of public education or segregation in public schools during the 39th Congress must be considered in the light of the status of public education at that time

Although today, compulsory free public education is universally regarded as a basic, appropriate governmental function, there was no such unanimity existing at the time the Fourteenth Amendment was adopted. Arrayed against those who then visualized education as vital to effective government, there were many who still regarded education as a purely private function.

While it has already been shown that the conception of equal protection of the laws and due process of law, developed by the Abolitionists before the Civil War, was so broad that it would necessarily cover such educational segregation as is now before this Court, compulsory public education at that time was the exception rather than the rule. The conception of universal compulsory free education was not established throughout the states in 1866. The struggle for such education went on through most of the 19th century and, even where accepted in principle in some of the states, it sometimes was not fully put into practice.

Prior to the first quarter of the nineteenth century childhood education was considered an individual private responsibility.[165] The period 1830–1860 was one of marked educational advancement. It has commonly been termed as the era of the Common School Revival, a movement to extend and improve facilities for general education. This movement flourished in New England under the leadership of Horace Mann, Henry Barnard and others. There was a definite tendency throughout the country to shift from private to public support of education and this trend extended to normal schools and facilities for secondary and higher education. Many states, urged on by educational leaders, publicists and statesmen, began making legislative provisions for public education.

On the other hand, these gains have been commonly exaggerated and in some respects misinterpreted. The laws were by no means always carried into effect and the recommendations of the reformers were, in most instances, accepted with great hesitancy.[166] Another authority after appraising public education during the period just prior to the Civil War made the following generalizations:

> "Practically all the states were making substantial progress in the development of systems of public education. (2) At the close of the period no single state can be said to have been providing any large percentage of its children and youth with schools well-supported and well-taught. (3) The facilities for secondary education were by no means as extensive as has commonly been reported. (4) Regional differences in educational development have been exaggerated; and (5) where sectional differences in school support and attendance did exist they appear to have been due more to differentials in urban and rural development than to differences in social attitudes and philosophies."[167]

---

[165] CUBBERLY, A BRIEF HISTORY OF EDUCATION, cc. XXV–XXVI (1920).
[166] EDWARDS AND RICHEY, THE SCHOOL IN THE SOCIAL ORDER 421 (1947).
[167] *Id.* at 423.

In general, it should be noted that in New England and in New York the main problem during this period was to improve the educational systems which had already been established and to secure additional support for them. In the Middle Atlantic states the major problem was to establish systems of public schools and to provide effective public education. In the West, the prevailing political and social philosophy required that at least some degree of education be provided to as large an element of the population as possible.

Public education was much slower in getting under way in the South. In most of the southern states, despite some promising beginnings, an educational system was not created until after the close of the Civil War. One historian concluded:

> ". . . although the 'common school awakening' which took place in the Northern States after Horace Mann began his work in Massachusetts (1837) was felt in some of the Southern States as well, and although some very commendable beginnings had been made in a few of these States before 1860, the establishment of state educational systems in the South was in reality the work of the period following the close of the Civil War. The coming of this conflict, evident for a decade before the storm broke, tended to postpone further educational development."[168]

Public education in the South made progress only after it became acceptable as being compatible with its ideal of a white aristocracy.[169]

Among the factors responsible for this condition were the aristocratic attitude which held that it was not necessary to educate the masses, the reluctance of the people to tax themselves for educational purposes, the marked individualism of the people, born of isolation, and the imperfect state of social and political institutions. Most southerners saw little or no relation between education and life. Consequently, the view prevailed that those who could afford education could indulge themselves in securing it and those who could not afford it lost little, if anything. This southern attitude was aptly summed up fifteen years after the close of the war by the statement of Virginia's Governor F. W. M. Holliday that public schools were "a luxury . . . to be paid for like any other luxury, by the people who wish their benefits."[170] Education in the South was not so much a process of individual and community improvement as it was an experience that carried with it a presumption of social equality for those who shared it, a view hardly compatible with any notion of universal education which included persons of diverse social and ethnic backgrounds.

Between 1840 and 1860, public education began to advance in the South but its benefits were denied Negroes. It is significant that racist and other types of intolerant legislation increased markedly during this period. While education could be extended to all whites who, for political purposes, belonged to one big happy family, there was nothing in such a conception that suggested that Negroes should be included.[171] The editor of the authoritative antebellum organ of southern opinion, *DeBow's Review*, summed up the matter of education for Negroes during slavery as follows: "Under the institution of slavery we used to teach them everything nearly except to read."[172]

The framers of the Fourteenth Amendment were familiar with public education, therefore, only as a developing concept. We have already demonstrated that they were determined to eliminate all governmentally imposed racial distinctions—sophisticated as well as simple minded—and expressed their views in the broadest and most conclusive terms. The intentions they expressed were definitely broad enough to proscribe state imposed racial distinctions in public education as they knew it, and the language which they used in the Fourteenth Amendment was broad enough to forever bar racial distinctions in whatever public educational system the states might later develop.

Furthermore, the framers intended that Congress would have the power under section 5 to provide additional sanctions, civil and criminal, against persons who attempted to enforce states statutes made invalid by section 1 of the Amendment. As stated above, Representative Bingham purposely revised an earlier draft of the Amendment so that the prohibitions of section 1 would be self-executing against state statutes repugnant thereto and would be beyond the threat of hostile Congressional action seeking to repeal civil rights legislation. In other words, the judicial power to enforce the prohibitory effect of section 1 was not made dependent upon Congressional action.

---

[168] CUBBERLY, PUBLIC EDUCATION IN THE UNITED STATES 251 (1919).
[169] EDWARDS AND RICHEY, *op. cit. supra* n. 166, at 434.
[170] Quoted in WOODWARD, ORIGINS OF THE NEW SOUTH 61 (1951).

[171] DeBOW, THE INTEREST IN SLAVERY OF THE SOUTHERN NON-SLAVEHOLDER 3–12 (1860).
[172] REPORT OF THE JOINT COMMITTEE ON RECONSTRUCTION, 39th Cong., 1st Sess., Pt. IV, 135 (1866).

Thus, the exercise of this Court's judicial power does not await precise Congressional legislation. This Court has repeatedly declared invalid state statutes which conflicted with section 1 of the Fourteenth Amendment, even though Congress had not acted.[173] For example, there is no federal statute to the effect that a state which permits released time for religious instructions is acting in a way prohibited by the Fourteenth Amendment. This Court, nevertheless, held that such state action conflicted with section 1 of the Fourteenth Amendment and directed the trial court to enjoin the continuance of the proscribed state action. *Illinois ex rel. McCollum* v. *Board of Education,* 333 U.S. 203.

Similarly, this Court has acted to redress violations of constitutional rights, even in the absence of specific Congressional statute, in a long series of cases involving the rights of freedom of expression and freedom of worship under the Fourteenth Amendment. See *e.g., De Jonge* v. *Oregon,* 299 U.S. 353. And this Court has often vindicated the constitutional rights of members of minority groups in the area of public education in the absence of any Congressional statute. *Sweatt* v. *Painter, supra.*

Indeed, this rule has been applied in all areas in which the prohibitory effect of section 1 has been employed by the Court. *E.g., Miller* v. *Schoene,* 276 U.S. 272; *McCardle* v. *Indianapolis Water Co.,* 272 U.S. 400. To now hold Congressional action a condition precedent to judicial action would be to stultify the provisions in the Federal Constitution protecting the rights of minorities. In effect, this Court would be holding that action by a state against an unpopular minority which the Constitution prohibits cannot be judicially restrained unless the unpopular minority convinces a large majority (the whole country as represented in Congress) that a forum in which to ask relief should be provided for the precise protection they seek.

## I. During the congressional debates on proposed legislation which culminated in

the Civil Rights Act of 1875 veterans of the thirty-ninth Congress adhered to their conviction that the Fourteenth Amendment had proscribed segregation in public schools

At various times during the 1870's, Congress considered bills for implementing the Fourteenth Amendment as well as the Civil Rights Act of 1866. Debate on these measures was on occasion extremely significant, since it gave members of Congress an opportunity to express themselves as to the meaning and scope of the Amendment. These observations were the more significant in that perhaps two-fifths of the members of both Houses in the early seventies were veterans of the Thirty-ninth Congress which had formulated the Amendment. Moreover, the impact of the Amendment upon segregated schools had by this time moved into the public consciousness so that Congressmen now had an opportunity to say specifically what they thought about the validity under the Amendment of state statutes imposing segregation upon public school systems.

The second session of the Forty-second Congress, which convened in December, 1871, soon found itself involved in a fairly extended discussion of the effect of the Fourteenth Amendment upon racial segregation, particularly in school systems. Early in the session the Senate took under consideration an amnesty bill to restore the political rights of ex-Confederate officials in accordance with the provisions of section 3 of the Amendment. On December 20, Senator Sumner of Massachusetts, now a veteran champion of the rights of the Negro, moved the following as an amendment to the measure under consideration:

> "Section—That all citizens of the United States, without distinction of race, color, or previous condition of servitude, are entitled to the equal and impartial enjoyment of any accommodation, advantage, facility, or privilege furnished by common carriers, whether on land or water; by inn-keepers; by licensed owners, managers, or lessees of theaters or other places of public amusement; by trustees, commissioners, superintendents, teachers, or other officers of common schools and other public institutions of learning, the same being supported or authorized by law ... and this right shall not be denied or abridged on any pretense of race, color, or previous condition of servitude."[174]

Here was a provision, which if adopted would commit Congress to the proposition that

---

[173] Of course, Title 8 provides a remedy in law or equity against any person acting under color of State law who deprives anyone within the jurisdiction of the United States of rights secured by the Federal Constitution or laws. It provides: "Every person who, under color of any statute, ordinance, regulation, custom, or usage, of any State or Territory, subjects, or causes to be subjected, any citizen of the United States or other person within the jurisdiction thereof to the deprivation of any rights, privileges, or immunities secured by the Constitution and laws, shall be liable to the party injured in an action at law, suit in equity, or other proper proceeding for redress." 8 U.S.C. § 43.

[174] Cong. Globe, 42nd Cong., 2nd Sess. 244 (1871).

under the Fourteenth Amendment it could do away entirely with state school statutes providing for segregated school systems. Sumner attacked school segregation at length. The public school, he asserted, "must be open to all or its designation is a misnomer and a mockery. It is not a school for whites or a school for blacks, but a school for all; in other words a common school for all." Segregation he called an "odius discrimination" and an "ill-disguised violation of the principle of Equality."[175]

In the debate that followed, it was apparent that a large majority of the Republicans in the Senate were convinced that Congress quite appropriately might enact such legislation in accordance with section 5 of the Fourteenth Amendment.

Senator Carpenter of Wisconsin, one of the best constitutional lawyers in the Upper House, was doubtful of the constitutionality of Sumner's measure insofar as it applied to churches. But he had no doubt on the authority of Congress to guarantee the right of all persons, regardless of race or color, to attend public schools, to use transportation facilities, and the like, and he offered a resolution of his own to this end.[176] Even the conservative Kentuckian Garrett Davis admitted that there was no question of congressional competence under the Amendment to guarantee these rights as against state action, though he challenged the validity of any statute protecting rights against private discrimination.[177] And Senator Stevenson of Kentucky, another strong enemy of mixed schools, confined his attack to discussion of the evil involved in an attempt to "coerce social equality between the races in public schools, in hotels, in theatres. . . ."; he spoke not at all of constitutional objections.[178]

The real objection to Sumner's measure, however, was not the constitutionality of the measure itself, but the incongruity of its attachment as a rider to an amnesty bill, which required a two-thirds majority of both Houses of Congress. Nonetheless, the Senate, after extended debate, adopted Sumner's amendment, including the provision banning segregated schools, by a vote of 28–28, the ballot of the Vice President breaking the tie.[179] The amnesty measure itself later failed to obtain the necessary two-thirds majority of the Senate.

The impressive Senate support in favor of a bill which would have banned segregation in state school systems alarmed Conservatives in both Houses, who now began to advance, very deliberately, the idea that "separate but equal" facilities would be constitutional under the limitations of the equal protection clause of the Fourteenth Amendment. In the House, a few days after the defeat of the amnesty bill, Representative Frank Hereford of West Virginia offered the following resolution as an expression of conservative sentiment:

> "*Be it resolved*, That it would be contrary to the Constitution and a tyrannical usurpation of power for Congress to force mixed schools upon the States, and equally unconstitutional and tyrannical for Congress to pass any law interfering with churches, public carriers, or inn-keepers, such subjects of legislation belonging of right to the States respectively."

There was no debate on the Hereford resolution, which was put to an immediate vote and defeated, 85 to 61, 94 not voting.[180]

Later in the session, there was still further debate in the Senate concerning segregated schools. With a second amnesty bill up for consideration, Sumner on May 8 again moved an amendment providing:

> "That no citizen of the United States shall, by reason of race, color, or previous condition of servitude, be excepted or excluded from the full and equal enjoyment of any accommodation, advantage, facility, or privilege furnished by inn-keepers; by common carriers . . . or . . . by trustees, commissioners, superintendents, teachers, and other officers of common schools and other public institutions of learning, the same being supported by moneys derived from general taxation, or authorized by law. . . ."[181]

This proposal led to sharp debate and decided differences of opinion among the Republican majority. Senator Trumbull of Illinois, who was the author of the Civil Rights Act of 1866 and who had become decidedly more conservative in his political outlook since the early Reconstruction era, now insisted that the right to attend public schools was in any event not a civil right, so that Congress could not legislate on the subject under the Fourteenth Amendment. But Senator George Edmunds of Vermont, already known as a distinguished constitutional lawyer and who had entered the Senate in 1866 in time to participate in the debates on the Fourteenth Amendment, dissented sharply, insisting that the right to attend tax-supported

---

[175] *Id.* at 383–384.
[176] *Id.* at 760.
[177] *Id.* at 764.
[178] *Id.* at 913.
[179] *Id.* at 919. The Senate vote on the amnesty bill was 33 to 19 in favor of the measure. *Id.* at 929.

[180] *Id.* at 1582.
[181] *Id.* at 3181.

public schools was a civil right and therefore subject to regulation by Congress.[182] Senator Morton taking the same view, insisted that "if the right to participate in these schools is to be governed by color, I say that it is a fraud upon those who pay the taxes." And he added that where there are public schools supported by common taxation upon everybody, white and black, then there is a civil right that there shall be equal participation in those schools.

Observing that the Ohio Supreme Court had but lately held constitutional a state statute providing for segregation in public schools, he argued that Congress was entirely competent under the Fourteenth Amendment to prohibit segregated schools.

Senator Arthur Boreman of West Virginia also took it as a matter of course that Congress had the power under the amendment to prohibit separate but equal facilities in school systems; he thought that Congress ought not to force the issue at present:

> "The time will come when . . . these distinctions will pass away in all the States, when school laws will be passed without this question appearing upon the face of those laws; but it is not so now, and for the present I am willing to allow the laws of the State to remain as they are where they provide schools for both classes."[183]

At the close of the debate, the proponents of segregated school systems tried unsuccessfully to modify the Sumner measure to eliminate the requirement for mixed school systems. Senator Orris Ferry of Connecticut first moved to strike out entirely the provisions of the Sumner amendment which related to public school systems. This motion the Senate defeated 26 to 25.[184] Senator Francis P. Blair of Missouri then offered another amendment to allow "local option" elections within the states on the question of mixed versus segregated schools. Sumner, Edmunds and Howe all strongly condemned this proposal, which the border and southern Senators as strongly commended. The Blair amendment in turn met defeat, 23 to 30.[185] Finally, an amendment to strike out the first five sections of the Sumner measure, thereby completely destroying its effect, was defeated 29 to 29, with the Vice President casting a deciding negative vote.[186] The Senate then formally adopted the Sumner amendment to the am-

nesty bill, 28 to 28, with the Vice President voting in the affirmative.[187]

The conclusion seems inescapable that as of 1872 a substantial majority of the Republican Senators and perhaps half of the Senate at large believed that the prohibitions of the Fourteenth Amendment extended to segregated schools.

The authority of the judiciary to act in this field was specifically recognized and not disputed.[188] A significant number of the Senators in question, among them Edmunds, Howe, Sumner, Conkling, and Morrill, had been in Congress during the debates on the adoption of the Amendment, while Conkling and Morrill had been members of the Joint Committee. And Vice President Henry Wilson, who several times cast a deciding vote in favor of prohibiting segregated schools not only had been in Congress during the debates on the Amendment but had also authored one of the early civil rights bills of the Thirty-ninth Congress.

The first session of the Forty-third Congress, which opened in December, 1873, saw extended discussion of the issue of segregated schools in both Houses. On December 18, Representative Benjamin F. Butler of Massachusetts, chairman of the House Judiciary Committee and long one of the most outspoken leaders of the Radical faction of the Republican party, introduced the following measure from his committee:

> ". . . whoever, being a corporation or natural person and owner, or in charge of any public inn, or of any place of public amusement or entertainment for which a license from any legal authority is required, or of any line of stage-coaches, railroad, or other means of public carriage of passengers or freight, or of any cemetery or other benevolent institution, or any public school supported in whole or in part at public expense or by endowment for public use, shall make any distinction as to admission or accommodation therein of any citizen of the United States because of race, color, or previous condition of servitude, shall, on conviction thereof, be fined not less than $100 nor more than $5000 for each offense. . . ."[189]

This measure inspired a somewhat bitter two-day debate early in January, 1874, during which the power of Congress to prohibit segregated schools received more attention than any other single issue involved. The most extended defense of the constitutionality of Butler's measure was

---

[182] *Id.* at 3190.
[183] *Id.* at 3195.
[184] *Id.* at 3256, 3258.
[185] *Id.* at 3262.
[186] *Id.* at 3264–3265.

[187] *Id.* at 3268. The amnesty bill itself subsequently received a favorable vote of 32 to 22, thereby failing to receive the necessary two-thirds majority. *Id.* at 3270.
[188] *Id.* at 3192.
[189] 2 CONG. REC. 318 (1873–1874).

made by Representative William Lawrence of Ohio, who began with the flat assertion that "Congress has the constitutional power to pass this bill." Denying that civil rights were any longer in the exclusive care of the states, he asserted that since the passage of the Fourteenth Amendment, "if a state permits any inequality in rights to be created or meted out by citizens or corporations enjoying its protection, it denied the equal protection of laws." He then launched into an extended historical analysis of the debates in the Thirty-ninth Congress before and during the passage of the Amendment. He recalled Bingham's statement in opposition to the original extreme language of the Civil Rights bill, in which the Ohioan had said that the proper remedy for state violation of civil rights was to be achieved not by an "arbitrary assumption of power," but "by amending the Constitution of the United States expressly prohibiting the States from any such abuse of power in the future." He quoted Stevens' and Howard's speeches introducing the Amendment in Congress to show the broad purpose which they had represented to be the objectives of the Joint Committee. In some irony, he quoted various conservatives in the House, among them Finck, Boyer and Shanklin, who had asserted again and again that the Amendment would place all civil rights within the protective custody of the federal government.[190] Lawrence's speech was the more impressive in that he was a veteran of the Thirty-ninth Congress who had actively supported both the Civil Rights Act and the passage of the Fourteenth Amendment. Moreover, he was held in great respect in Congress as an able jurist and constitutional lawyer.[191]

The most extended argument in opposition to Lawrence was advanced by Representative Roger Q. Mills of Texas, who presented the contention that civil rights, in spite of the Fourteenth Amendment, were still entrusted entirely to the care of the states. Congress, he thought, had no right to touch the public school system of the several states. "The States," he said, "have . . . [an] unquestioned right . . . to establish universities, colleges, academies, and common schools, and govern them according to their own pleasure." He relied upon the narrow interpretation of the "privileges or immunities" clause of the Fourteenth Amendment recently advanced by the Supreme Court in the *Slaughter House Cases* as a

new argument in support of his contention. And he finished with the warning, not entirely unheard in the twentieth century, that if Congress passed any such measure as the Butler bill, "the Legislatures of every State where the white people have control will repeal the common-school laws."[192] At the end of debate, Butler's bill was recommitted on the motion of its sponsor, and was not heard of again during the session.

More significant events were occurring in the Senate. On December 2, Sumner had once more presented his now well-known civil rights measure, this time as an independent Senate bill instead of a proposed amendment to an amnesty resolution.[193] This bill finally came up for debate in late April and May, although Sumner himself had died in March. Conkling of New York, Boutwell of Massachusetts, Howe of Wisconsin, Edmunds of Vermont, and Frelinghuysen of New Jersey all gave it very effective support in debate.[194]

In a strong speech, Senator Frelinghuysen pointed out that a variety of conflicting state decisions had introduced some confusion into the question of whether or not state statutes setting up segregated school systems were constitutional under the Amendment. The present measure, he thought, would destroy "injurious agitation" on that subject. There could be no question of the constitutional power of Congress to enact the bill; the "privileges or immunities" and "the equal protection" clauses, in particular, were especially germane to congressional power. And he pointed out that if the present bill became law, it would still be possible to pursue an informal voluntary segregation by the consent of both parents and school boards, where for a time that seemed advisable. But he added that segregated school systems established by law were in complete violation of the whole spirit of the Amendment; separate schools for colored people were inevitably inferior to those for whites. "Sir", he said in conclusion, "if we did not intend to make the colored race full citizens . . . we should have left them slaves."[195]

Senator Edmunds used both constitutional and pragmatic arguments in support of the bill. "What the Constitution authorizes us to do is to enforce equality," he said, "and . . . not half-equality, for there is no such thing as half-equality. It is entire equality or none at all."

---

[190] *Id.* at 412 ff.
[191] 11 DICTIONARY, *op. cit. supra* n. 129, at 52. He was later the author of the statute creating the Department of Justice.

[192] 2 Cong. Rec. 383 ff. (1873–1874).
[193] *Id.* at 2.
[194] Boutwell and Conkling, it will be recalled, had both served as members of the Joint Committee.
[195] *Id.* at 3451–3455.

And segregated schools imposed inequality on Negroes. He quoted figures from Georgia school statistics, to demonstrate that although forty-three percent of the children in that state were colored, there were nonetheless only 356 schools for colored children as against 1379 for whites. In the light of this kind of evidence, he thought, the duty of Congress was clear.[196]

Senator Boutwell declared that "opening the public schools of this country to every class and condition of people without distinction of race and color, is security . . . that . . . the rising . . . generations will advance to manhood with the fixed purpose of maintaining these principles [of the Republic]." Like Edmunds, he argued that segregation made either adequate or equal facilities impossible; there was not enough money in the South to support two school systems.[197]

Senator Howe asserted that ". . . I am of the opinion that the authority of Congress to issue these commands, to enact this bill into law, is as clear, as indisputable as its authority to lay taxes or do any other one thing referred to in the Constitution." Like Frelinghuysen he thought that voluntary segregation might exist in some places for a time without violating the amendment. "Open two school houses wherever you please;" he said, and "furnish in them equal accommodations and equal instruction, and the whites will for a time go by themselves, and the colored children will go by themselves for the same reason, because each will feel more at home by themselves than at present either can feel with the other. . . ." But legally segregated schools, he thought would not in fact be equal, and it was the duty of Congress to prohibit them.[198]

Senator Pease of Mississippi shortly before the bill was passed speaking in favor of the bill said in unequivocal terms:

"The main objection that has been brought forward by the opponents of this bill is the objection growing out of mixed schools. . . . There has been a great revolution in public sentiment in the South during the last three or four years, and I believe that to-day a majority of the southern people are in favor of supporting, maintaining, and fostering a system of common education . . . I believe that the people of the South so fully recognize this, that if this measure shall become a law, there is not a State south of Mason and Dixon's line that will abolish its school system. . . .

* * * I say that whenever a State shall legislate that the races shall be separated, and

that legislation is based upon color or race, there is a distinction made; it is a distinction the intent of which is to foster a concomitant of slavery and to degrade him. The colored man understands and appreciates his former condition; and when laws are passed that say that 'because you are a black man you shall have a separate school,' he looks upon that, and justly, as tending to degrade him. There is no equality in that.

". . . because when this question is settled I want every college and every institution of learning in this broad land to be open to every citizen, that there shall be no discrimination."[199]

The opponents of the Sumner bill meantime had become aware of the epoch-making significance of the Supreme Court's decision in the *Slaughter House Cases*, and they leaned very heavily upon Justice Miller's opinion during the debate. Thurman of Ohio analysed the *Slaughter House Cases* at length to prove his former contention that the main body of civil rights was still in the custody of the states and that the present bill was unconstitutional."[200] Senator Henry Cooper of Tennessee, after citing Justice Miller's opinion to make the same constitutional point, asked the Republican majority, ". . . what good are you to accomplish thus by forcing the mixture of the races in schools?"[201] And Senator Saulsbury of Delaware, who, in 1866 had insisted that if Congress enacted the Fourteenth Amendment it would work an entire revolution in state-federal relations, now argued flatly that the Sumner bill was unconstitutional under Justice Miller's interpretation of the limited scope of the "privileges or immunities" clause of the Amendment.[202]

However, the Senate majority remained firm in its intention to pass the bill with the ban on segregated schools. At the close of debate, Senator Aaron Sargent of California presented an amendment that "nothing herein contained shall be construed to prohibit any State or school district from providing separate schools for persons of different sex or color, where such separate schools are equal in all respects to others of the same grade established by such authority, and supported by an equal *pro rata* expenditure of school funds." This amendment the Senate promptly defeated, 21 to 26.[203] Senator McCreery then moved an amendment providing that "nothing herein contained shall be so construed as to apply to schools already established." This, too, met defeat, mustering

[196] *Id.* at 4173.
[197] *Id.* at 4116.
[198] *Id.* at 4151.

[199] *Id.* at 4153–4154.
[200] *Id.* at 4089.
[201] *Id.* at 4154.
[202] *Id.* at 4159.
[203] *Id.* at 4167.

but eleven "ayes" in its support.[204] Immediately after this, the Senate, on May 22, passed the Sumner bill, by a vote of 29 to 16, and sent it to the House.[205]

Again the conclusion with respect to congressional intent as regards segregated schools seems fairly clear: a majority of the Senate in the Forty-third Congress, under control of leaders, a number of whom had supported the passage of the Fourteenth Amendment eight years earlier, thought Congress had the constitutional power to ban segregated schools and that it would be good national policy to do so.[206]

Congress adjourned before the House could take action on the Sumner bill, so that the measure carried over to the second session of the Congress, beginning in December, 1874. And now occurred a curious anticlimax with respect to the prohibition of segregated schools; Congress speedily enacted what virtually amounted to the Sumner bill of 1874 into law, but with the provision banning segregated schools eliminated from the bill.

The critical action occurred in the House of Representatives, where Butler on December 16 introduced what amounted to a somewhat modified draft of the measure passed by the Senate the previous spring. The constitutional debates produced little that was new. It was apparent that Congress by virtue of Section 5 had the constitutional power to take all civil liberties under its protection. Representative Robert Hale of New York, a veteran of the Thirty-ninth Congress, twitted Finck of Ohio for his fallible memory in forgetting so conveniently that in 1866, he had solemnly warned that the impending amendment would place all civil rights under federal protection.[207]

Whatever may be said about the quantum or quality of Congressional debates on one side or the other no one can deny that the 39th Congress opened with a determination on the part of the Radical Republican majority to deprive the states of all power to maintain racial distinctions in governmental functions. No one can gainsay that this determination permeated the 39th Congress and continued through the passage adoption of the Fourteenth Amendment. The debates and all of the related materials

show conclusively that the Fourteenth Amendment effectively gave constitutional sanction to the principle that states are thereby deprived of all power to enforce racial distinctions in governmental functions including public schools.

## II. THERE IS CONVINCING EVIDENCE THAT THE STATE LEGISLATURES AND CONVENTIONS WHICH RATIFIED THE FOURTEENTH AMENDMENT CONTEMPLATED AND UNDERSTOOD THAT IT PROHIBITED STATE LEGISLATION WHICH WOULD REQUIRE RACIAL SEGREGATION IN PUBLIC SCHOOLS

The Fourteenth Amendment was submitted to the states for consideration on June 16, 1866. 14 Stat. 358. It was deliberated by thirty-seven states and ratified by thirty-three.[208] We urge that the evidence with respect to the states' understanding indicates that three-fourths of the states understood and contemplated the Amendment to forbid legislation compelling the assignment of white and Negro youth to separate schools.

The evidence which compels this conclusion is adduced from governors' messages, reports of the legislative committees on federal relations and entries in the journals of the legislatures. At that time, the legislatures, almost without exception, kept no verbatim record of debates and speeches; and the journals merely noted motions and votes. There are, however, newspaper summaries of some speeches and proceedings. But much of the evidence from these sources is inadequate.

More significant is the modifications which the states made in their schools' laws. For if it was understood in the legislatures, which considered the proposed Amendment, that ratification would perforce forbid compulsory segregated schools, it seems certain that the legislatures would have apprehended its effect upon the state's constitutional or statutory pro-

---

[204] *Id.* at 4171.
[205] *Id.* at 4176.
[206] Flack long ago reached a similar conclusion, that the great majority in Congress who voted for Sumner's bill "fully believed they had the power to pass it." "Of all the evidence," he said, "only a very minor part of it against this conclusion." FLACK, *op. cit. supra* n. 79, at 271.
[207] 3 Cong. Rec. 979, 980 (1875).

---

[208] The ratifying states included twenty free or non-slaveholding states (Connecticut, New Hampshire, New Jersey, Oregon, Vermont, New York, Ohio, Illinois, Kansas, Maine, Nevada, Indiana, Minnesota, Rhode Island, Wisconsin, Pennsylvania, Michigan, Massachusetts, Nebraska and Iowa), two former slave-holding but loyal states (West Virginia and Missouri), and the eleven former slaveholding states which had seceded (Alabama, Arkansas, Florida, Georgia, Louisiana, Mississippi, North Carolina, South Carolina, Tennessee, Texas and Virginia). Delaware, Kentucky and Maryland, three former slave-holding but non-seceding states, expressly rejected the Amendment. California, probably because the control of its legislature differed in each house, was unable to take any definitive action.

visions for public schools. If, for example, a state required or authorized segregated schools under existing law, presumably the legislature would not knowingly adopt the Amendment without giving some thought to its implications. After adoption, it would be expected that measures would be taken to conform the school laws to the new constitutional mandate. If, however, a state's school laws and practices already conformed to the understanding that the Fourteenth Amendment forbade segregated schools, it is probable that its legislature would not have objected to the Amendment on this question and would afterwards either retain or reinforce its school laws. On the other hand, if there was an authorization or requirement of segregation in a state's school laws, and, after ratification, the legislature took no action to end this disparity, undoubtedly it would appear that this state did not understand the Amendment to have the effect which Appellants urge. Yet, if a state under these same conditions had rejected the Amendment, it would suggest that the Amendment's impact upon the school segregation law was a controlling factor. We submit, the new constitutional and statutory provisions enacted with respect to public schools during the critical period, i.e., from 1866, the year the Amendment was submitted, until several years following adoption, constitute strong evidence on the question of the understanding of the Amendment in the state legislatures.

Then, too, we note that the Fourteenth Amendment was designed particularly as a limitation upon the late Confederate States. *Slaughter House Cases*, 16 Wall. 36. Each of them, except Tennessee, was required to endorse the Amendment and the price of readmission also required each to demonstrate that it "modified its constitution and laws in conformity therewith." 14 Stat. 428 (Act of March 2, 1867). In this connection, Representative Boutwell significantly declared:[209]

> "We are engaged in the great work of reconstructing this Government, and I suppose if we are committed to anything, it is this: that in the ten States not now represented there shall hereafter be no distinction on account of race or color."

These new constitutions, and the proposals and debates of the conventions which framed them, then are of utmost significance. Certainly, they had to measure up to the requirements of the Fourteenth Amendment and, therefore, their

educational provisions apparently reflect the understanding of the draftsmen as to the Amendment's effect upon compulsory public school segregation. Similarly, since the constitutions of these states, were subject to the scrutiny of Congress, an additional insight into the understanding of Congress is provided. For it would hardly be possible to maintain that Congress contemplated the Fourteenth Amendment as a prohibition on compulsory segregated schools if it had approved a constitution having a provision inconsistent with this proposition.

We now turn to the legislative history of the Fourteenth Amendment in the states. The proceedings in the several states shall be taken up in turn. Because of the geographic origin of certain of the instant cases and the significance of the contemporary understanding and contemplation of the effect of the Amendment upon Southern institutions, we will first treat the evidence from the states whose readmission to the Union was conditioned upon their conformity with the Amendment.

## A. The eleven states seeking readmission understood that the Fourteenth Amendment stripped them of power to maintain segregated schools

Subsequent to the proclamation of the Thirteenth Amendment the South sought to define the relations between the new freedmen and white men in a manner which retained most of the taint of the former master-slave relationship. The ante-bellum constitutions remained inviolate although prohibitions against slavery were added. Laws were passed which restricted Negroes in their freedom of movement, employment, and opportunities for learning. *Slaughter House Cases*, 16 Wall. 36, 71–72; *Strauder* v. *West Virginia*, 100 U.S. 303, 306–307. In Arkansas[210] and Florida,[211] the so-called Black Codes required separate schools for the children of the two races.

After March 2, 1867, the date of the First Reconstruction Act, 14 Stat. 428, the South was obliged to redefine the status of the freedmen in conformity with their understanding of the Fourteenth Amendment. New constitutions were adopted which without exception were free of any requirement or specific authorization of segregated schools. It is also significant that in almost all of these constitutional conventions and legislatures, the issue of segregated

---

[209] Cong. Globe, 39th Cong., 2nd Sess. 472 (1867).

[210] Ark. Acts 1866–67 p. 100.
[211] Cong. Globe, 39th Cong., 1st Sess. 217 (1866).

schools was specifically raised and rejected. And no law compelling segregated schools was enacted in any state until after it had been readmitted.

**Arkansas** The first of these states to be readmitted was Arkansas. 15 Stat. 72 (Act of June 22, 1868). The constitution which it submitted to Congress had not one reference to race; the education article merely obligated the general assembly to "establish and maintain a system of free schools for all persons" of school age.[212] It is reported that this article was adopted to nullify the segregated school law passed by the legislature earlier in 1867.[213] Its adoption had been generally opposed in the Convention on the ground that it would "establish schools in which there would be 'indiscriminate social intercourse between whites and blacks.' "[214] The electorate was warned that this constitution would "force children into mixed schools."[215] But the new constitution was adopted and proclaimed law on April 1, 1868.[216]

The general assembly convened on April 3, and ratified the Fourteenth Amendment on April 6, 1868.[217] It then proceeded to repeal the former school statute and a new school law was proposed whereby taxes were to be assessed to support a system of common schools for the education of all children. This law was interpreted as establishing "a system of schools where the two races are blended together."[218] And it was attacked because it granted white parents "no option to their children . . . but to send them to the negro schools . . . unless, as is now rarely the case, they are able to give their children education in other schools."[219]

These provisions for public schools were included in the legislative record which Arkansas submitted to the scrutiny of Congress. Whereupon, Arkansas was re-admitted on June 22, 1868. 15 Stat. 72. One month later, but after readmission, the legislature amended the public school statute and directed the Board of Education to "make the necessary provisions for establishing separate schools for white and colored children and youths. . . ."[220]

**North Carolina, South Carolina, Louisiana, Georgia, Alabama and Florida** The North

Carolina, South Carolina, Louisiana, Georgia, Alabama and Florida modifications in their constitutions and laws were approved by Congress in the Omnibus Act of June 25, 1868 and Congress authorized readmittance effective on the date each ratified the Amendment. 15 Stat. 73. The constitution which Florida offered for congressional review imposed a specific duty on the state to provide "for the education of all children residing within its borders without distinction or preference."[221] The legislature ratified the Amendment on June 9, 1868 and when it next convened passed a law to maintain "a uniform system of instruction, free to all youth of six to twenty-one years."[222] It is agreed that this law was not designed to foster segregated schools and by its operation "mixed schools" were authorized or required.[223]

Several years later the Florida Legislature passed a sweeping law which forbade any racial distinction in the full and equal enjoyment of public schools, conveyances, accommodations and amusements.[224] The first compulsory school segregation provision did not appear until over twenty years after readmission.[225]

In the North Carolina Constitution of 1868, the education article called for the general assembly to maintain "a general and uniform system of public schools, wherein tuition shall be free of charge to all the children of the State between the ages of six and sixteen."[226] Furthermore, the general assembly was "empowered to enact that every child of sufficient mental and physical ability, shall attend the public schools" unless otherwise educated.[227] It is reported that the Constitutional Convention refused by a vote of 86 to 11 to adopt a section which provided that "The General Assembly shall provide separate and distinct schools for the black children of the state, from those provided for white children."[228] The adopted article also survived amendments which would have permitted separate schools "for any class of the population" providing each class shared equally in the school fund.[229] Some proponents of the education article said that it did not force

---

[212] Ark. Const. 1868, Art. IX, § 1.
[213] Staples, Reconstruction in Arkansas 28 (1923).
[214] Id. at 247.
[215] Daily Arkansas Gazette, March 19, 1868; Id., March 15, 1868.
[216] Id., April 2, 1868.
[217] Ark. Sen. J., 17th Sess. 19–21 (1869).
[218] Ibid.
[219] Daily Arkansas Gazette, April 10, 1868.
[220] Act of July 23, 1868 as amended by Ark. Acts 1873, p. 42. See Ark. Dig. Stats., c. 120 § 5513 (1874).

[221] Fla. Const. 1868, Art. VIII § 1.
[222] Fla. Laws 1869, Act of Jan. 30, 1869.
[223] Knight, Public Education in the South 306 (1922) Eaton, "Special Report to the United States Commission of Education", Rep. U.S. Commr. Educ. to Secy. Int. (1871).
[224] Fla. Laws 1873, c. 1947.
[225] Fla. Const. 1885, Art. XII § 2.
[226] N. C. Const. 1868, Art. IX § 2.
[227] Id., § 17.
[228] Motion of Mr. Durham reported in Knight, Influence of Reconstruction on Education 22 (1913).
[229] Motions of Messrs. Graham and Tourgee reported in Id. at 22.

racial commingling but they frankly admitted that it did not prevent it and contended that separate schools, if established, should only develop out of the mutual agreement of parents rather than through legislation.[230] Available contemporary comment upon the education article of the 1868 constitution uniformly agreed that it either authorized or required mixed schools.[231]

The 1868 Constitution, with this education article, was submitted to Congress and treated as being in conformity with the Amendment. North Carolina's readmission was thus assured contingent upon its ratification of the Fourteenth Amendment.

The state legislature convened on July 1, 1868 and ratified the Amendment on July 4th.[232] Three days later the lower house adopted a resolution providing for the establishment of separate schools, but it failed to win support in the upper house which successfully carried a resolution instructing the Board of Education to prepare a code for the maintenance of the system of free public schools contemplated in the constitution.[233] Significantly, this measure made no reference to race. It was enrolled on July 28, 1868.[234]

At the next regular session after readmission, the legislature passed a school law which required separate schools.[235] However doubtful the validity of this law was to some as late as 1870,[236] the state constitution as amended in 1872, settled the issue by specifically requiring racial separation in education.[237]

South Carolina and Louisiana both ratified the Amendment on July 9, 1868 and were readmitted as of that date pursuant to the Omnibus Act. 15 Stat. 73. The educational articles in their 1868 constitutions were of the same cloth. The Louisiana article flatly said: "There shall be no separate schools or institutions of learning established exclusively for any race by the State of Louisiana."[238] South Carolina's constitution provided that: "All the public schools, colleges and universities of this State, supported in whole or in part by the public school fund, shall be free and open to all the children and youths of the State, without regard to race or color."[239] In addition to this, the South Carolina Constitution required the legislature to pass a compulsory school law after it organized facilities for the education of all children.[240] The 1868 constitutions of both states also declared that all citizens, without regard to race or color, were entitled to equal civil and political rights.[241]

The proponents of the education articles in the Louisiana and South Carolina conventions defended the provisions prohibiting segregation by force of law in public schools as an incident of equal justice or equal benefits in return for equal burdens; and they overwhelmingly considered compulsory segregation to be a hostile distinction based on race and previous condition.[242] The chairman of the Education Committee of the South Carolina Convention, defending the proposed education article, explained:[243]

> "The whole measure of Reconstruction is antagonistic to the wishes of the people of the State, and this section is a legitimate portion of that scheme. It secures to every man in this State full political and civil equality, and I hope members will not commit so suicidal an act as to oppose the adoption of this section."

Continuing, he explained:[244]

> *"We only compel parents to send their children to some school, not that they shall send them with the colored children; we simply give those colored children who desire to go to white schools, the privilege to do so."* (Emphasis supplied.)

After the Louisiana and South Carolina constitutions were approved by Congress, the South Carolina Legislature, in a special session, ratified the Amendment and temporarily organized the school system in conformity with the education article, despite Governor Scott's plea for a law which would require racial separation in schools as a preventive against "educational miscegenation."[245] At the next regular session,

---

[230] Noble, A History of Public Schools in North Carolina 340–41 (1930).
[231] Wilmington Morning Star, March 27, 1868; *id.*, March 28, 1868, p. 2; Charlotte Western Democrat, March 24, 1868; *id.*, April 17, 1868, p. 2; Greensboro Times, April 2, 1868, p. 3; *id.*, April 16, 1868, p. 1; Fayetteville News, April 14, 1868, p. 2; *id.*, June 2, 1868, p. 1.
[232] N. C. Laws 1867, ch. CLXXXIV, Sec. 50.
[233] Noble, *op. cit. supra* n. 230, at 297, 299.
[234] See List of Public Acts and Resolutions Passed by the General Assembly of North Carolina, Spec. Sess. of July, 1868.
[235] N. C. Laws 1868–69, c. CLXXXIV, § 50.
[236] Noble, *op. cit. supra* n. 230, at 325.
[237] Art. IX, § 2.
[238] La. Const. 1868, Title VII, Art. 135.

[239] S. C. Const. 1868, Art. XX § 10.
[240] *Id.*, § 4.
[241] *Id.*, Art. I, § 7; La. Const. 1868, Title I, Art 2.
[242] Proceedings of the South Carolina Constitutional Convention of 1868, Held at Charleston, S. C., Beginning January 14th and Ending March 17th, 1868, pp. 654–900 (1868); Official Journal of the Proceedings for Framing a Constitution for Louisiana, 1867–1868, *passim* (1868).
[243] Proceedings, *op. cit. supra* n. 242, at 899.
[244] *Id.* at 690.
[245] S. C. House J., Spec. Sess., p. 51 *et seq.* (1868). See Charleston Daily News, July 10, 1868.

the school system was permanently organized, and a law was passed forbidding officials of the state university to "make any distinction in the admission of students or management of the university on account of race, color or creed."[246]

The Louisiana legislature acted with similar celerity and consistency. It assembled on June 29, 1868, ratified the Amendment on July 9, 1868 and enacted laws conforming to the constitutional mandate against segregated schools.[247] At its next session, it supplemented the school laws by imposing penal and civil sanctions against any teacher refusing to accept a pupil of either race.[248] Subsequent laws forbade racial distinctions at a state institution for the instruction of the blind, prohibited racial separation on common carriers, and provided that there should be no racial discrimination in admission, management and discipline at an agricultural and mechanical college.[249]

More than a quarter-century elapsed before South Carolina and Louisiana in 1895 and 1898, respectively, changed these laws to require racial segregation in public education.[250]

The Alabama Constitutional Convention assembled on November 4, 1867, but the education article was not adopted until December 5th, the final day of the session. What emerged was borrowed directly from the Iowa Constitution of 1857, in most particulars, plus the language of a statute passed by the 1865–66 Iowa legislature to specifically bar segregation in schools.[251] This anti-segregation article survived two attempts to introduce provisos specifically requiring the establishment of separate schools.[252]

Congress found that Alabama had conformed its constitution with the Amendment and considered the state qualified for readmission as soon as it ratified the Fourteenth Amendment. On July 13th, 1868, the General Assembly fulfilled the final requirement. Thereafter, on August 11th, the State Board of Education, acting under the legislative powers conferred upon it in the constitution, passed a regulation which made it unlawful "to unite in one school both colored and white children, unless it be by the unanimous consent of the parents and guardians of such children . . . "[253] But the significant point again is that this was done only after readmission.

Georgia, like most of the South, had no public school system prior to Reconstruction. In fact, no reference to public schools appears in either the ante-bellum Georgia Constitution or the Constitution of 1865 which was substantially a reenactment of the former.[254]

The Constitutional Convention of 1867–68, however, rewrote the basic state document and the committee on education reported a proposal to establish a thorough system of public education "without partiality or distinction."[255] During the drafting and consideration of the proposed education article, several efforts to include provisions requiring segregated schools were defeated.[256] The Convention adopted an article which directed the General Assembly to "provide a thorough system of general education to be forever free to all children of the State . . ."[257]

After this constitution was approved by Congress, the legislature ratified the Fourteenth Amendment on July 21, 1868 and Georgia apparently qualified for readmission. But the General Assembly forcibly expelled its Negro complement at this session on the ground that their color made them ineligible to hold office. This action prompted Congress to refuse to seat the Georgia congressional delegation.[258] The General Assembly then reconvened on January 10, 1870, re-seated its Negro members, ratified the Fourteenth Amendment again, and expunged the word "white" from all state laws.[259] The conduct of this legislature satisfied Congress and Georgia was readmitted to the Union on July 15, 1870. 16 Stat. 363.

Three months later, on October 13, 1870, the state legislature passed a public school act which in section 32 established a system of

---

[246] S. C. Acts 1868–69, pp. 203–204.

[247] DABNEY, UNIVERSAL EDUCATION IN THE SOUTH 370 (1936).

[248] FAY, "THE HISTORY OF EDUCATION IN LOUISIANA", 1 U.S. Bu. Educ. Cir. No. 1, p. 101 (1898).

[249] La. Acts 1869, p. 37; La. Laws 1871, pp. 208–10; La. Laws 1875, pp. 50–52.

[250] S. C. CONST. 1895, Art. XI § 7; LA. CONST. 1898, Art. 248.

[251] Compare ALA. CONST. 1867, Art. XI with IOWA CONST. 1857, Art. IX and Iowa Laws 1865–66, p. 158.

[252] Official Journal of the Constitutional Convention of the State of Alabama 1867–68, pp. 237, 242 (1869).

[253] Ala. Laws 1868, App., Acts Ala. Bd. of Educ. It would appear that had this law been tested, application of the rule applicable to borrowed statutes would have invalidated it inasmuch as a similar statute in Iowa had been struck down on the basis of a less stringent constitutional provision. Clark v. Board of School Directors, 24 Iowa 266 (1868).

[254] 2 Thorpe, Federal and State Constitutions 765 et seq. (1909).

[255] Journal of the Constitutional Convention of Georgia, 1867–68, p. 151 (1868).

[256] Id., at 69, 151, 479, 558. See ORR, HISTORY OF EDUCATION IN GEORGIA 187 (1950).

[257] GA. CONST. 1868, Art. VI.

[258] ORR, op. cit. supra n. 256, at 195–196.

[259] Ga. Sen. J. Pt. II, p. 289 (1870); Ga. House J. pp. 307, 1065 (1870).

segregated schools.[260] The state constitution was amended in 1877 and validated this legislation by an express requirement for racial separation in public schools.[261]

**Texas** In Texas a Constitutional Convention met in June 1868 to frame the constitution under which it was subsequently readmitted. Drafted to secure the approval of Congress,[262] it required the legislature to maintain "a system of public free schools, for the gratuitous instruction of all the inhabitants of this State of school age."[263] This constitution was accepted at the elections in 1869, and the legislature, without discussion, ratified the three Civil War Amendments on February 18, 1870.[264] Texas was readmitted on March 30, 1870, 16 Stat. 80, and the legislature drafted a public school law which provided that local boards of education, "when in their opinion the harmony and success of the schools require it, . . . *may* make any separation of the students or schools necessary to secure success in operation . . .".[265] Contemporary opinion was that this grant of discretion to school boards was a restrained effort to achieve racial separation without offending Congress and that the Fourteenth Amendment forbade the requirement of separate schools although it did not compel mixed schools.[266] It was not until 1876, when Texas adopted a new constitution, that racial separation in schools was expressly required by law.[267]

**Virginia** Virginia submitted to Congress a constitution which contained no reference to race or racial separation in public schools.[268] In the Constitutional Convention, the issue of segregation was introduced when the report of the committee on education was being considered. First, an amendment was proposed to provide "that in no case shall white and colored children be taught in the same school."[269] This amendment was defeated.[270] Subsequently, a proposal to add an independent section providing for the establishment of segregated schools met a like fate.[271] A provision was also submitted to require that public schools be open to all classes without distinction and that the legislature be denied the power to make any law which would admit of any invidious distinctions.[272] This proposal and a substitute to the same effect were also defeated.[273] Opponents of the proposals to prohibit segregated schools explained the failure of passage, not on the grounds of fundamental objection, but because it was feared that the adoption of such an article in the constitution would doom its chance of ratification.[274] Thus, an article merely directing the general assembly to provide for a uniform system of public free schools was adopted "rather than risk having the Congress or Union Leagues force an obnoxious law on them."[275]

After the election of 1869, at which the constitution was adopted, the General Assembly convened and ratified the Fourteenth Amendment on October 8, 1869. This session passed no school laws and the establishment of the public school system was deferred until after readmission. Full statehood status was regained on January 26, 1870. 16 Stat. 62. Six months later, on June 11th, the General Assembly established a "uniform system of schools" in which separate schools were required.[276] A specific constitutional mandate for segregated[277] schools, however, did not appear until 1902.

**Mississippi** Mississippi followed the general pattern of the former seceded states. The Constitutional Convention of 1868, adopted an education article which made no mention of race or racial separation.[278] At least two unsuccessful attempts were also made in the Convention to require segregated schools.[279]

While the convention journal does not specifically indicate that the Fourteenth Amendment was raised as an objection to segregated schools, the convention had passed a resolution which declared that:

"... the paramount political object ... is the restoration or reconstruction of our government upon a truly loyal and national basis, or a basis which will secure liberty and equality before the law, to all men, regardless of race, color or previous conditions."[280]

[260] Ga. Laws 1870, p. 57.
[261] GA. CONST. 1877, Art. VIII § 1.
[262] TEX. CONST. 1871, Art. I § 1.
[263] *Id.* Art. IX §§ 1–4.
[264] Daily State Journal, February 20, 1870.
[265] 6 Tex. Laws 1866–71, p. 288. (Emphasis added.)
[266] Flake's Daily Bulletin, March 3, 1870; *Id.* March 13, 1870.
[267] TEX. CONST. 1876, Art. VII § 7; 8 TEX. Laws 1873–79 CXX § 54.
[268] VA. CONST. 1868, Art. VIII § 3.
[269] JOURNAL OF THE VIRGINIA CONSTITUTIONAL CONVENTION, 1867–68, p. 299 (1868).
[270] *Id.* at 300: Richmond Enquirer, March 31, 1868.
[271] Journal, *op cit. supra* n. 269, at 301.
[272] *Id.,* at 333.
[273] *Id.,* at 335–40.
[274] ADDRESS OF THE CONSERVATIVE MEMBERS OF THE LATE STATE CONVENTION TO THE VOTERS OF VIRGINIA (1868).
[275] DABNEY, UNIVERSAL EDUCATION IN THE SOUTH 143–44 (1936).
[276] Va. Acts 1869–70, c. 259 § 47, p. 402.
[277] VA. CONST. 1902, Art. IX § 140.
[278] MISS. CONST. 1868, Art. VIII.
[279] JOURNAL OF THE MISSISSIPPI CONSTITUTIONAL CONVENTION OF 1868, pp. 316–18, 479–80 (1868).
[280] *Id.* at 123.

The convention also framed a Bill of Rights which required all public conveyances to accord all persons the same rights,[281] and it refused to adopt an article forbidding intermarriage.[282]

The next legislature convened in January, 1870, ratified the Fourteenth and Fifteenth Amendments, repealed all laws relative to Negroes in the Code of 1857, as amended by the Black Code of 1865, and indicated that it intended to remove all laws "which in any manner recognize any natural difference or distinction between citizens and inhabitants of the state."[283]

The Constitution and actions of the legislature proved acceptable to Congress, and Mississippi was restored to the Union on February 23, 1870. 16 Stat. 77. It was not until 1878 that Mississippi passed a law requiring segregated schools;[284] and it was still later when the Constitution was altered to reiterate this requirement.[285]

**Tennessee**  Tennessee, although a member state in the late Confederacy, was not subjected to the requirements of the First Reconstruction Act, inasmuch as it had promptly ratified the Fourteenth Amendment and had been readmitted prior to the passage of that Act. Nevertheless, this state likewise reentered the Union with compulsory racial segregation absent from its constitution and statutory provisions on public schools. Readmission was under the Constitution of 1834, inasmuch as the Constitutional Convention of 1865 merely amended it to abrogate slavery and authorize the general assembly to determine the qualifications of the exercise of the elective franchise.[286] The education article in this constitution merely required the legislature to encourage and support common schools "for the benefit of all the people" in the state.[287] The first law providing for tax supported schools, on its face, also made no racial distinction.[288] The next law, however, pro-

hibited compulsory integrated schools.[289] Contemporary federal authorities noted that antebellum practice apparently had restricted the benefits of the school system to white children; but approved these provisions because, in sum, they provided a sufficient guarantee for the support and enjoyment of common schools for the equal benefit of all the people without distinction on the basis of race or color.[290]

The Governor convened the legislature in special session on July 4, 1866 to consider the Fourteenth Amendment. In urging its adoption, he summarized Section 1, and said that its practical effect was to protect the civil rights of Negroes and to "prevent unjust and oppressive discrimination" in the exercise of these citizenship rights.[291] A joint resolution to ratify was introduced in the upper house; and a resolution to amend it with a proviso that the proposed Amendment should not be construed to confer upon a person of color rights to vote, to hold office, to sit on juries or to intermarry with whites or to "prevent any state from enacting and enforcing such laws" was voted down.[292] Then the Senate approved the joint resolution and the House concurred.[293]

After ratification, a group in the lower house formally protested its confirmation of the Amendment on the ground that it invaded state rights "and obliterates all distinctions in regard to races, except Indians not taxed."[294] A similar protest was filed in the upper house.[295] Such of the debates as were reported in the press indicate that the legislators understood the Amendment to force absolute equality[296] and that under the inhibitions of Section 1 "distinctions in schools cannot be made, and the same privileges the one has cannot be denied the other. . . ."[297]

Tennessee was readmitted July 24, 1866. 15 Stat. 708–711. After readmission, a school law was passed on March 5, 1867 whereby boards of education were "authorized and required to establish . . . special schools for colored children, when the whole number by enumeration exceeds twenty-five."[298] It also provided for the discontinuance of these separate schools when the enrollment fell below fifteen. The law, however, did not forbid non-segregated schools. But it was repealed in 1869 and re-

---

[281] *Id.* at 47; Miss. Const. 1868, Art. I, § 24.

[282] Journal of the Mississippi Constitutional Convention of 1868, pp. 199, 212 (1868).

[283] Garner, Reconstruction in Mississippi 285 (1901).

[284] Miss. Laws 1878, p. 103.

[285] Miss. Const. 1890, Art. IX, § 2.

[286] Tenn. Const. 1834 as amended by §§ 1 and 9 of "Schedule" ratified February 22, 1865. In conformity with the Schedule's directive the legislature enacted that Negroes could exercise and pursue all types of employment and business under the laws applicable to white persons, Tenn. Acts. 1865–66, c. 15; that Negroes were competent witnesses, *Id.,* c. 18; and that persons of color henceforth had the same rights in courts, contracts and property as white persons except that Negroes could not serve on juries and that this act "shall not be construed as to require the education of white and colored children in the same school." *Id.,* c. 40, § 4.

[287] Tenn. Const. 1834, Art. XI § 10.

[288] Tenn. Acts. 1853–54, c. 81.

[289] Tenn. Acts. 1865–66, c. 40, § 4.

[290] Rep. U.S. Commr. Educ. 1867–68, 101 (18  ).

[291] Tenn. House J., Called Sess. 3, 26–27 (1866); Tenn. Sen. Called Sess. 8 (1866).

[292] Tenn. Sen. J., Called Sess. 26 (1866).

[293] *Id.* at p. 24; Tenn. House J., Called Sess. 24 (1866).

[294] Tenn. House J., Called Sess. 38 (1866).

[295] Tenn. Sen. J., Called Sess. 41–42 (1866).

[296] Nashville Dispatch, July 12, 1866.

[297] *Id.,* July 25, 1866.

[298] Tenn. Laws 1867, c. 27, § 17.

placed with a requirement that racial separation in schools be observed without exception.[299] Finally, the constitution was amended in 1870 to secure the same result.[300]

In summary, therefore, as to these eleven states the evidence clearly reveals that the Fourteenth Amendment was understood as prohibiting color distinctions in public schools.

## B. The majority of the twenty-two union states ratifying the 14th Amendment understood that it forbade compulsory segregation in public schools.

Other than the states already treated, twenty-six Union States considered the Amendment. Twenty-two of them ratified it. The evidence adduced here is of a somewhat less uniform character than that from the states which formed the late Confederacy for the simple reason that the legislatures in the North were unfettered by any congressional surveillance, and they did not experience the imperative necessity of re-examining their constitutions and laws at the time the proposed Fourteenth Amendment was considered by them. Thus, it is to be expected that some of these legislatures deferred attuning their school laws with the keynote of the Amendment until several years after it had become the law of the land. In other states, the legislatures adjusted their school laws almost simultaneously with their ratification of the Amendment. Still others, because existing laws and practices conformed with their basic understanding with respect to the impact of the Amendment, were not required to act. In the end, nevertheless, we submit that the overwhelming majority of the Union States ratified or did not ratify the Fourteenth Amendment with an understanding or contemplation that it commanded them to refrain from compelling segregated schools and obliged them to conform their school laws to assure consistency with such an understanding.

**West Virginia and Missouri** West Virginia, a state created during the Civil War when forty western counties refused to follow Virginia down the road to secession, and Missouri, a former slaveholding state comprised the small minority of states which ratified the Fourteenth Amendment and perpetuated laws requiring segregated schools without any subsequent enactment consistent with a discernment that such laws and the Amendment were incompatible.

Both states required separate schools for the two races prior to the submission of the

Amendment.[301] These laws were continued after the Amendment was proclaimed as ratified;[302] and both states subsequently strengthened the requirement of separate schools in the 1870's by amending their constitutions to specifically proscribe racial integration in public schools.[303]

**The New England States** Segregated schools also existed in some of the strongly abolitionist New England states prior to their consideration and ratification of the Amendment. But their reaction to the prohibitions of Section 1 was directly contrary to the course taken in West Virginia and Missouri.

In Connecticut, prior to the adoption of the Amendment, racial segregation was not required by state law but segregated schools were required in some cities and communities, e.g., in Hartford pursuant to an ordinance enacted in 1867 and in New Haven by administrative regulation.[304] On August 1, 1868, four days after the Amendment was proclaimed, however, the legislature expressly forbade separate schools.[305] Interestingly, during the course of debate on this bill, amendments which would have required segregation or permitted separate "equal" schools were introduced and rejected.[306]

Similarly, racial separation in schools was never required by the constitution or laws of Rhode Island, but segregated schools existed at least in Providence, Newport and Bristol.[307] Here, too, the same legislature which ratified the Amendment enacted a law prohibiting racial segregation in public schools.[308]

---

[299] Tenn. Laws 1870, c. 33, § 4.

[300] Tenn. Const. 1870, Art. XI, § 12.

---

[301] W. Va. Laws 1865, p. 54; Mo. Laws 1864, p. 126.

[302] W. Va. Laws 1867, c. 98; W. Va. Laws 1871, p. 206; Mo. Laws 1868, p. 170; Mo. Laws 1869, p. 86.

[303] W. Va. Const. 1872, Art. XII, § 8; Mo. Const. 1875, Art. IX.

[304] Morse, The Development of Free Schools in the United States as Illustrated by Connecticut and Michigan 127, 144, 192 (1918); Warner, New Haven Negroes 34, 71–72 (1940).

[305] Conn. Acts 1866–68, p. 206. See Conn. House J. 410 (1866); Conn. Sen. J. 374 (1866).

[306] Conn. Sen. J. 247–48 (1868); Conn. House J. 595 (1868). See New Haven Evening Register, June 17, 1868.

[307] Bartlett, From Slave to Citizen, c. 6 *passim.* (unpub. ms., pub. expected in Dec. 1953). See Ammons v. School Dist. No. 5, 7 R. I. 596 (1864).

[308] R. I. Laws 1866, c. 609.
The Committee on Education recommended passage of this act, saying: "The great events of the time are, also, all in favor of the elevation of the colored man. They are all tending to merge the distinctions of race and of class in the common brotherhood of humanity. They have already declared the Negro and the white man to be equal before the law; and the privileges here asked for by these petitioners, are simply a necessary result of this recognized equality." It went on to say, "We have no right to withhold it from him in any case", and asked, "With what consistency can we demand that these colored people shall be equal before the law in other states or the territories, while we, ourselves, deprive

In Maine, there was no racial separation in public schools prior to the adoption of the Amendment.[309] However, the leading supporter of ratification extolled in the broadest terms its equality provisions and indicated that the proponents expected it to compel in the other states the same equality in civil and political rights as existed in Maine, itself.[310]

Massachusetts too, had already made unlawful any racial segregation in schools prior to the submission of the Amendment.[311] Thus, since Massachusetts had already considered state required racial segregation completely inconsistent with a system of laws and government which treats all persons alike irrespective of color,[312] there was no subsequent legislative action interpretative of the impact of the Amendment on segregation.

The deliberations of the legislature on the proposed Amendment opened with its reference to the body by the governor. He recommended ratification and his speech indicates that he understood Section 1 of the Amendment to be a reinforcement of the Civil Rights Act of 1866 and observed: "Whatever reasons existed at the time for the enactment of that bill, apply to the incorporation of its provisions into the state law."[313] Surprisingly, strong opposition to ratification developed. A majority of the joint committee recommended rejection on the ground that the proposed Amendment neither specifically guaranteed Negro suffrage nor added anything to what was already in the constitution "possibly excepting the last clause" of Section 1. Of this, is concluded:[314]

"The denial by any state to any person within its jurisdiction, of the equal protection of the laws, would be a flagrant perversion of the guarantees of personal rights. . . . [But] such denial would be equally possible and probable hereafter, in spite of an indefinite reiteration of these guarantees by new amendments."

The minority reported that:[315]

"Without entering into any argument upon the merits of the amendment, they would express the opinion that its ratification is extremely important in the present condition of national affairs."

When these reports were presented in the lower house of the legislature, a motion was passed to substitute the minority report.[316] Suffrage had claimed much of the strident debate on the motion. But a speech of one of the last members to speak for the motion was reported as follows:[317]

"To the first article of this amendment, there had been no objection brought by those who favored rejection. . . . The speaker felt that this was a most important article; by it the question of equal rights was taken from the supreme courts of the States and given to the Supreme Court of the United States for decision; the adoption of the article was the greatest movement that the country had made toward centralization, and was a serious and most important step. This was taken solely for the reason of obtaining protection for the colored people of the South; the white men who do not need this article and do not like it, sacrifice some of their rights for the purpose of aiding the blacks."

The upper house considered the motion several days later, re-echoed the theme of the speeches previously made in the lower house, and voted for ratification.[318]

The New Hampshire legislature took up the proposed Amendment in June of 1866. The governor's message urged ratification but its brief comment was not revealing.[319] The majority report of the house committee with respect to the Amendment merely offered a resolution to modify.[320] But the minority reported a number of reasons for rejection which, *inter alia*, criticized section 1 on the grounds of ambiguity and furthermore:[321]

"Because said amendment is a dangerous infringement upon the rights and independence of all the states, north as well as south, assum-

---

them of one of their most important civil rights?" Report of Committee on Education, Pub. Doc. No. 4 (1896).
[309] See CHADBOURNE, A HISTORY OF EDUCATION IN MAINE (1936).
[310] Speech of Senator Crosby in the Maine Senate, January 16, 1867, reported in Kennebec Journal, January 22, 1867, p. 1.
[311] Mass. Acts & Res. 1854–1855, p. 650; Mass. Acts & Res. 1864–1865, pp. 674–75.
[312] This was precisely the fundamental proposition underlying the enactment of the Act of 1855 prohibiting racial segregation in public schools. Report of the Committee on Education, Mass. House Doc. No. 167, March 17, 1855.
[313] Mass. Acts and Res. 1867, pp. 789, 820; Boston Daily Advertiser, January 5, 1867, Sat. Supp.
[314] Mass. House Doc. 149, pp. 23–24 (1867).

[315] *Id.*, at 25.
[316] Boston Daily Advertiser, March 13, 1867, p. 2; *Ibid.*, March 14, 1867, p. 1.
[317] *Id.*, March 14, 1867, p. 1 (Speech of Richard Henry Dana, Jr.).
[318] Mass. Acts and Res. 1867, p. 787; Mass. Leg. Doc. Sen. Doc. No. 25 (1867); Boston Daily Advertiser, March 21, 1867, p. 1.
[319] N. H. House J. 137 (1866).
[320] *Ibid.*, p. 174.
[321] *Id.* at 176.

ing as it does, control their legislation in matters purely local in their character, and impose disabilities upon them for regulating, in their own way [such matters]."

The same set of objections was presented by a minority of the special committee of the upper house.[322] Both chambers voted for ratification, however, within a month after the Amendment was offered to the state.[323]

Laws governing public schools in New Hampshire appear to have never been qualified on the basis of race or color at any time after its organic law obligated the legislature to stimulate public education.[324] Similarly, Vermont seems to have no history of segregated schools. Neither did its laws sanction such a policy.[325] When the legislature convened in 1866, the Governor's opening message discussed the proposed Fourteenth Amendment at some length. He urged that it be ratified to secure "equal rights and impartial liberty", otherwise a small number of whites in the South and the entire colored race would be left unprotected. In concluding, he said Vermont welcomed "such a reorganization of the rebellious communities, as would have given the people, white and black, the equal civil and political rights secured to the people of the State, by our Bill of Rights and Constitution, and under which peace, order, civilization, *education*, contentment, Christianity and liberty have shed their benign and blessed influence alike upon every home and household in our beloved Commonwealth."[326] Thereupon, both houses routinely voted for ratification.[327]

**The Middle Atlantic States** Three Mid-Atlantic States, New York, New Jersey and Pennsylvania ratified the Amendment. The Pennsylvania evidence is in some detail because it was one of the few states to preserve the full discussions and debates of its legislature. Furthermore, its statutes, previous to the adoption of the Amendment, authorized segregation in schools;[328] and public carriers had regulations which excluded or segregated Negroes. See *West Chester & Phila. R. Co. v. Miles*, 5 Smith (55 Pa.) 209 (1867).

On January 2, 1867, the Governor transmitted the Fourteenth Amendment to the Legislature. He called for its adoption primarily upon political grounds but strenuously urged that every citizen of the United States had certain rights that no state had a right to abridge and the proposed Amendment asserted "these vital principles in an authoritative manner, and this is done in the first clause of the proposed amendments [sic]."[329]

The resolution recommending ratification was introduced in the Pennsylvania Senate by its floor leader. He urged that one of the reasons why it had to be adopted was because Mississippi had enacted a law requiring segregation on railroads and the Amendment was necessary to overcome all state legislation of this character.[330] In summary of his concept of the purpose of section 1, he said:

"The South must be fenced in by a system of positive, strong, just legislation. The lack of this has wrought her present ruin; her future renovation can come only through pure and equitable law; law restraining the vicious and protecting the innocent, making all castes and colors equal before its solemn bar, that, sir, is the *sine qua non*. . . ."

The pith of the speeches of both the proponents and opponents of ratification are as follows:

Senator Bingham, a leading supporter of the resolution, noted that "it has been only a question of time how soon all legal distinctions will be wiped out."[331]

Another announced, "I shall vote for it with satisfaction for my own conscience and gratitude to Congress for squarely meeting the universal demand of the loyal states to destroy all legal caste within our borders."[332]

The leading opponent of ratification interpreted the Amendment as follows:[333]

"By the first section it is intended to destroy every distinction founded upon a difference in the caste, nationality, race or color of persons . . . which has found its way into the laws of the Federal or State Governments which regulate the civil relations or rights of the people. No law shall be made or executed which does not secure equal rights to all. *In all matters of civil legislation and administration there shall be perfect equality in the advantages and securities guaranteed by each state to everyone here declared a*

---

[322] N. H. Sen. J. 70 (1866).
[323] *Id.* at 94, N. H. House J. 231–33 (1866).
[324] N. H. Const. 1792, § LXXXIII.
[325] Vt. Const. 1777, c. II, § XXXIX; Vt. Const. 1786, c. II, § XXXVIII; Vt. Const. 1793, c. II, § 41. See Report of the Indiana Department of Public Instruction 23–28 (1867–68).
[326] Vt. Sen. J. 28 (1866); Vt. House J. 33 (1866). (Emphasis added.)
[327] Vt. House J. 139 (1866); Vt. Sen. J. 75 (1866).
[328] Act of May 8, 1854, Pa. L. 617 § 24.

[329] Pa. Sen. J. 16 (1867).
[330] 2 Pa. Leg. Rec., app., p. III (1867).
[331] *Id.* at XVI.
[332] *Id.* at XXII (speech of Senator Taylor).
[333] *Id.* at XLI (speech of Mr. Jenks).

*citizen, without distinction of race or color,* every one being equally entitled to demand from the state and state authorities full security in the enjoyment of such advantages and securities." (Emphasis supplied).

The legislature ratified the Amendment on January 17, 1867.[334]

About two weeks later, on February 5th, a bill was introduced making it unlawful for public conveyances to exclude or segregate Negroes.[335] In introducing this bill, its sponsor announced that the doctrine of equality before the law required the passage of this bill. Both he and another supporter of the bill pointed out that these practices were pursuant to carrier regulations and policies and had to be eradicated by legislative action. It was also pointed out that the bill did not effect social equality because that is regulated solely by the personal tastes of each individual.[336] The bill was overwhelmingly enacted into law the following month.[337]

The school law authorizing separate schools was not specifically repealed until 1881 when the legislature made it unlawful for any school official to make any distinction on account of race or color in students attending or seeking to attend any public school.[338]

It appears, however, that when the state constitution was amended in 1873, the 1854 school law was viewed as having been brought into conformity with the adoption of a provision for a school system "wherein all children of this Commonwealth above the age of six years shall be educated...."[339] The Secretary of State, official reporter of the Convention, states particular attention was paid to "that part which confers authority on the subject of education." And he noted that the new article was formulated to conform with the policy of protest against all racial discrimination and, specifically, to remove the "equivocal and invidious provision."[340] These purposes are further borne out when the sponsor of the 1881 bill stated:[341]

"In proposing the repeal of the act of 1854, which in terms would be prohibited by the present State and Federal Constitutions, it seems a matter of surprise that an act so directly in conflict with the Fourteenth and

Fifteenth Amendments of the Constitution of the United States should have been permitted to have remained in the statute book until this time."

New Jersey, as early as 1844, enacted general legislation for the establishment and support of a public school system "for the equal benefit of all persons...."[342] In 1850, special legislation was enacted which enabled Morris Township to establish a separate colored school district if the local town meeting voted to do so.[343] The state superintendent of schools construed this act and concluded that it in combination with the earlier law of 1844 permitted any local school system to maintain separate schools provided both schools offered the same advantages and no child was excluded.[344]

The New Jersey Legislature convened in a special session and hastily ratified the Amendment on September 11, 1866.[345] The dispatch with which this was done was made a focal issue in the following elections. The Republicans broadly defended the Amendment as "forbidding class legislation, or the subjecting of one class of people to burdens that are not equally laid upon all."[346] The Democrats more specifically contended that their candidates opposed the Amendment because they were "against Negro suffrage and the attempt to mix negroes with workingmen's children in public schools."[347] When the Republicans captured the governorship and elected a radical congressional delegation, the Democrats captured the state legislature and immediately proceeded to rescind New Jersey's ratification.[348]

When the Republicans recaptured control of the legislature in 1870 the school law was amended to require "a thorough and effective system of public schools for the instruction of all children...."[349] And this was later reinforced by an enactment which made it unlawful to exclude any child from any public school on account of color.[350] As a result of this law, separate schools soon disappeared except in a

---

[334] Pa. Laws 1867, 1334.

[335] 2 Pa. Leg. Rec., app. p. LXXXIV (1867).

[336] Id. at pp. LXXXIV *et seq.* (Remarks of Senators Lowery and Brown.)

[337] Act of March 22, 1867, Pa. Laws 1867, pp. 38–39.

[338] Act of June 8, 1881, Pa. L. 76, § 1, Pa. Laws 1881, p. 76.

[339] Pa. Const. 1873, Art. X, § 1.

[340] Jordan, Official Convention Manual 44 (1874).

[341] Pa. Sen. J. (entry dated May 26, 1881).

[342] N. J. Const. 1844, Art. IV § 7(6); N. J. Rev. Stats., c. 3 (1847).

[343] N. J. Laws 1850, pp. 63–64.

[344] Annual Report of the State Superintendent of Schools 41–42, (1868).

[345] N. J. Sen. J., Extra Sess., 1866, p. 14; Minutes of the Assembly, Extra Sess., 1866, p. 8.

[346] Newark Daily Advertiser, October 25, 1866; Trenton State Gazette, November 3, 1866.

[347] Trenton Daily True American, November 3, 1866.

[348] N. J. Sen. J. 198, 249, 356 (1868); Minutes of the Assembly; 309, 743 (1868). See Knapp, New Jersey Politics During the Period of Civil War and Reconstruction 167 (1924).

[349] N. J. Laws 1874, p. 135.

[350] N. J. Laws 1881, p. 186.

few counties where Negro citizens generally accepted them. When Negroes chose not to accept these segregated schools the school authorities were required to admit them to the white schools pursuant to the prohibition of the 1881 school law.[351]

New York, like the other Middle-Atlantic states, had ante-bellum constitutions which merely authorized the legislature to establish a common school fund.[352] There was never any general legislation on the subject of racial separation in schools sharing in the common school fund. The legislature, however, granted charters to Brooklyn, Canandaigua, Buffalo and Albany which permitted these cities to maintain segregated schools as early as 1850.[353] The Common School Act of 1864 was in the same vein. It only permitted school boards in certain political subdivisions to establish and maintain segregated schools "when the inhabitants of any school district shall so determine, by resolution at any annual meeting called for that purpose, establish a separate school or separate schools for the instruction of such colored children. . . ."[354] Communities exercising the option under this law comprised the exception rather than the rule.[355]

Shortly after New York ratified the Amendment,[356] a constitutional convention was held and it adopted a new constitution which provided for free instruction of all persons of school age.[357] The convention approved a committee report which contained a ringing declaration that Negroes should have full equality in the enjoyment of all civil and political rights and privileges.[358]

Subsequently, in 1873, the legislature passed an "Act to Provide for the Protection of Citizens in Their Civil and Public Rights."[359] The Act made it unlawful for any person to exclude any other person on the ground of race or color from the equal enjoyment of any place of public accommodation, place of public amusement, public conveyance, "*common schools and public instruction* [sic] of learning. . . ." (emphasis supplied). It also annulled the use of the word "white" or any other discriminatory term in all existing laws, statutes, ordinances and regulations.[360] The New York Court of Appeals did not give vitality to this act in the case of *People ex rel. King* v. *Gallagher,* 92 N.Y. 438 (1883). But cf. *Railway Mail Association* v. *Corsi,* 326 U.S. 88.

**The Western Reserve States**    The five states in the Western Reserve all ratified the Fourteenth Amendment. Each of them had rather well established public school systems prior to the Civil War. In Ohio, the first public school legislation expressly denied Negroes the benefit of free schools.[361] Twenty years later, in 1847, this act was amended to permit the maintenance of separate schools for colored children if the residents of a school district objected to their admission into the white schools.[362] At its next session, the legislature repealed the provision in an earlier law that had prohibited the application of taxes paid by white residents toward the support of colored schools.[363] And in 1853 the school law was revised to require the allocation of public school funds in proportion to the number of children of school age regardless of color.[364]

Separate schools, however, were still maintained except in Cleveland, Oberlin and other northern cities despite the general feeling that this act had relaxed the stringent restrictions of the antecedent laws. Furthermore, the State Supreme Court held this law not to entitle colored children, as of right, to admission into white schools. *Van Camp* v. *Board of Education,* 9 Ohio St. 406 (1859).

---

[351] See Pierce v. Union Dist. School Trustees, 17 Vroom (46 N. J. L.) 76 (1884).

[352] N. Y. CONST. 1821, Art. VII; N. Y. CONST. 1846, Art. IX.

[353] N. Y. Laws 1850, c. 143; N. Y. Laws 1852, c. 291. See Dallas v. Fosdick, 50 How. Prac. 249 (1869); People v. Easton, 13 Abb. Prac. N. S. 159 (1872).

[354] N. Y. Laws 1864, c. 555.

[355] ANNUAL REPORT OF THE STATE SUPERINTENDENT OF PUBLIC INSTRUCTION 131, 159, 163, 166, 170, 233, 323 (1866).

[356] N. Y. Sen. J. 33 (1867); N. Y. Ass. J. 77 (1867). The Governor's message upon transmission of the Amendment leaves little doubt that he considered it as a "moderate proposition" containing "just the conditions for safety and justice indispensable to a permanent settlement." N. Y. Sen. J. 6 (1867); N. Y. Ass. J. 13 (1867).

[357] N. Y. CONST. 1868, Art. IX. See PROCEEDINGS AND DEBATES OF THE CONSTITUTIONAL CONVENTION OF THE STATE OF NEW YORK 1867–68 (1868).

[358] "First. Strike out all discriminations based on color. Slavery, the vital source and only plausible ground of such invidious discrimination, being dead, not only in this State, but throughout the Union, as it is soon to be, we trust, throughout this hemisphere, we can imagine no tolerable excuse for perpetuating the existing proscrip-

tion. Whites and blacks are required to render like obedience to our laws, and are punished in like measure for their violation. Whites and blacks are indiscriminately drafted and held to service to fill our State's quotas in a war whereby the Republic was saved from disruption. We trust that we are henceforth to deal with men according to their conduct, without regard to their color. If so, the fact should be embodied in the Const." DOCUMENTS OF THE CONVENTION OF THE STATE OF NEW YORK, 1867–68, Doc. No. 15 (1868).

[359] N. Y. Laws 1873, c. 186 § 1.

[360] *Id.,* § 3.

[361] Ohio Laws 1828–29, p. 73.

[362] Ohio Laws 1847–48, pp. 81–83.

[363] Ohio Laws 1848–49, pp. 17–18.

[364] Ohio Laws 1852, p. 441.

After ratification of the Amendment,[365] the legislature did not immediately modify the schools laws. In fact, it did nothing until after the Ohio Supreme Court upheld compulsory segregated schools in *State ex rel. Garnes* v. *McCann*, 21 Ohio St. 198 (1872). Then the legislature enacted a statute which permitted rather than required segregated schools.[366] Later, it denied local school authorities the power to exercise their discretion in the premises.[367] By this act, all public schools were opened to all children without distinction on account of race or color. *State* v. *Board of Education*, 2 Ohio Cir. Ct. Rep. 557 (1887).

Indiana's pre-Fourteenth Amendment school law provided for the support of public schools but exempted "all Negroes and mulattoes" from the assessment.[368] This law was interpreted as excluding colored children from public schools wherever the parents of white children objected. *Lewis* v. *Henley*, 2 Ind. 332 (1850).

On January 11, 1867, Governor Morton submitted the Fourteenth Amendment to the legislature. His message urged ratification but suggested that schools should be provided for Negroes and that they be educated in separate schools to relieve any friction which could arise if they were required to be admitted to white schools.[369] A resolution to ratify the Amendment was introduced on the same day and referred to a joint committee. Five days later the resolution was reported out favorably with a recommendation of prompt ratification.[370] A minority report was made which objected to the Amendment primarily because it conferred civil and political equality upon Negroes, including the same rights that were then enjoyed by the white race.[371]

The resolution was adopted on the same day in the Senate.[372] No speeches were made in support of the resolution in this chamber but two senators spoke at length against it.[373] In the House, the main contention of the opponents

was that the Amendment would impose Negro equality,[374] seat Negroes on juries, grant them suffrage and admit them into the white schools.[375] The proponents only denied that the Amendment conferred suffrage.[376] And the lower chamber adopted the resolution on January 23, 1867.[377]

Two years after ratification of the Fourteenth Amendment, the legislature revised its law to require the organization of separate schools.[378] The act also authorized the maintenance of non-segregated schools in areas where there were insufficient Negro children residing within a reasonable distance to justify a separate school. In 1874, the compulsory segregation section of this law was declared valid in the case of *Cory* v. *Carter*, 48 Ind. 327 (1874).

The legislature, however, revised the school laws at its next session to permit (*not require*) segregated schools.[379] The revised law, furthermore, required that colored children be admitted to the regular schools if a separate school was not maintained. This provision was applied in sustaining mixed schools in *State* v. *Grubbs*, 85 Ind. 213 (1883).

Illinois statutes never specifically required separate schools. But the ante-bellum school statute provided that school districts with Negro populations should allow these residents a portion of the school fund equal to the amount of taxes collected from them.[380] As construed by the state superintendent of schools, this law was applied to require segregated schools.[381]

The Illinois legislature received the governor's message endorsing ratification of the Fourteenth Amendment on January 7, 1867. Both chambers then ratified it on the same day with virtually no discussion or debate.[382] About one year later, in December 1869, Illinois called a constitutional convention. It adopted the present organic law which provides for a free public school system for the education of "all children".[383] This provision stems from a resolution in which the convention directed the Education Committee to submit an article which would call for the establishment of a public school system for the education of every

---

[365] Ohio Sen. J. 9 (1867); Ohio House J. 13 (1867). The Amendment was ratified within two days of its submission to the legislature by the Governor. He observed that the Amendment had four provisions; the first of which was "the grant of power to the National Government to protect the citizens of the whole country . . . should any state attempt to oppress classes or individuals, or deprive them of equal protection of the laws . . ." Ohio Exec. Doc., Part I, 282 (1867).

[366] Ohio Laws 1878, p. 513.

[367] Ohio Laws 1887, p. 34.

[368] Ind. Rev. Stats. 314 (1843).

[369] Ind. Doc. J., Part I, p. 21 (1867).

[370] Ind. House J. 101 (1867).

[371] *Id.* at 102.

[372] Ind. Sen. J. 79 (1867).

[373] Brevier, Legislative Reports 44–45 (1867).

[374] *Id.* at 79.

[375] *Id.* at 80, 88–89, 90.

[376] *Id.* at 90.

[377] Ind. House J. 184 (1867).

[378] Ind. Laws 1869, p. 41.

[379] Ind. Laws 1877, p. 124.

[380] Ill. Stats. 1858, p. 460.

[381] SIXTH BIENNIAL REPORT OF THE SUPERINTENDENT OF PUBLIC INSTRUCTION OF THE STATE OF ILLINOIS, 1865–66, pp. 27–29; 2 REPORTS MADE TO THE GENERAL ASSEMBLY AT ITS TWENTY-FIFTH SESSION, pp. 35–37.

[382] Ill. House J. 40, 154 (1867); Ill. Sen. J. 40, 76 (1867).

[383] ILL. CONST. 1870, Art. VIII, § 1.

"susceptible child—without regard to color or previous condition".[384] Furthermore, the convention rejected two resolutions which would have directed the establishment of a compulsory segregated school system.[385]

Of all the states of the Western Reserve, Michigan was most deeply affected by the tide of abolitionism which swept this section during the pre-war years. By its Constitution of 1850 the word "white" was eliminated from the section establishing voting qualifications[386] and slavery was declared intolerable.[387] Neither this constitution nor the general law of the state recognized any racial distinctions in the enjoyment of public education. But as early as 1842 and as late as 1866, special statutes were passed granting school boards in certain of the larger cities discretionary power to regulate the apportionment of school funds and distribution of pupils among the several schools under their jurisdiction. Pursuant to this authority some school boards, e.g., in Detroit and Jackson, established separate schools.[388]

The Amendment was submitted to the legislature on January 6, 1867. On January 12th, a resolution was adopted in the Senate instructing the Committee on Public Instruction to report out a bill "to prevent the exclusion of children from the primary or graded or other public schools of this state on account of race or color." And four days later the general school law was amended to provide that "all residents of any district shall have an equal right to attend any school therein. . . ."[389] The Fourteenth Amendment was subsequently ratified on February 16, 1867.[390]

The legislative record of Michigan during the next several years is replete with more blows against segregation and other distinctions based on race or color. In 1869, insurance companies were prohibited from making any distinction between white and Negro insureds.[391] The ban

against interracial marriages was removed in 1883.[392] Then in 1885, the civil rights law was enacted prohibiting racial separation on public conveyances, in places of public accommodation, recreation, and amusement.[393]

Wisconsin, since 1848, provided for a public school system free to all children.[394] Moreover, during the crucial years, its Negro population was insignificant—less than two-tenths of one percent.[395] Thus, it seems obvious why segregation in schools or elsewhere never merited the attention of the legislature at the time of its ratification of the Amendment or thereafter.[396]

The Wisconsin legislature met on January 3, 1867 and was addressed by the Governor. His speech suggests that in his thinking the Fourteenth Amendment which he asked them to ratify was designed to apply solely to the South and required that "they must assent to the proposed amendment with all of its guarantees, securing to all men equality before the law. . . ."[397] A joint resolution was introduced to ratify the Amendment and referred to a committee of three, two of whom reported a recommendation to adopt. The report filed by the minority member condemned the Amendment at some length. "The apparent object," to him, was to allow Congress to enfranchise Negroes, legislate generally on civil rights, "give to the federal government the supervision of all the social and domestic relations of the citizen of the state and to subordinate state governments to federal power."[398]

It appears that this understanding of the Amendment was not disputed. Rather, one supporter of the Amendment is reported as stating: "If the states refuse to legislate as to give all men equal civil rights and equal protection before the laws, then, sir, there should be supervisory power to make them do that, and a consolidation of that kind will be a benefit

---

[384] JOURNAL OF THE CONSTITUTIONAL CONVENTION OF THE STATE OF ILLINOIS, Convened at Springfield, December 13, 1869, p. 234.

[385] Id. at 429–431, 860–861.

[386] Compare MICH. CONST. 1850, Art. VII, § 1 with MICH. CONST. 1835, Art. II, § 1.

[387] Art. XVIII, § 11.

[388] See People ex rel. Workman v. Board of Education of Detroit, 18 Mich. 400 (1869) for reference to these special statutes and notice of separate schools in these two cities. Since the decision in this case, there have been no segregated schools maintained by state authorities.

[389] 1 Mich. Laws 42 (1867); Mich. Acts 1867, Act 34 § 28.

[390] The journals of the Michigan legislature indicate that both houses promptly ratified the Amendment without reference to a committee. Mich. Sen. J. 125, 162 (1867); Mich. House J. 181 (1867).

[391] Mich. Acts 1869, Act 77 § 32. See Mich. Comp. Laws § 7220 (1897).

[392] Mich. Acts 1883, Act 23, p. 16.

[393] Mich. Acts 1885, Act 130 § 1. See Mich. Comp. Laws § 11759 (1897).

[394] WIS. CONST. 1848, Art. X, § 3; WIS. REV. STATS. Title VII (1849).

[395] LEGAL STATUS OF THE COLORED POPULATION IN RESPECT TO SCHOOLS AND EDUCATION, SPECIAL REPORT OF THE COMMISSIONER OF EDUCATION, 400 (1871).

[396] Wis. Sen. J. 119, 149 (1867); Wis. Ass. J. 224–226, 393 (1867). The entire series of Journals covering the War and Reconstruction years shows but a single reference to color in connection with education. This was a proposal to amend an 1863 bill so as to limit certain educational privileges to children of "white parentage". The amendment failed and the matter was never revived. Wis. Ass. J. 618 (1863).

[397] Wis. Sen. J. 32 (1867); Wis. House J. 33 (1867).

[398] Id. at 96, 98 et seq. (Report filed by Sen. Garrett T. Thorne).

instead of an injury.[399] And, another answered:[400]

> "We therefore need such a provision in the Constitution so that if the South discriminates against the blacks the United States courts can protect them. I know it is objected that this is an enlargement of the power of the United States Supreme Court. But it is a power given on the side of liberty—power to protect and not power to oppress. For the appeal will come up to this court from the aggrieved individual against the aggressing state. . . ."

**The Western States**  Of the states west of the Mississippi which ratified the Amendment, Nebraska is quite significant because it was admitted to the Union during the life of the 39th Congress and conditions were imposed upon its admission which demonstrate that the Congress which prepared the Amendment intended to eradicate all distinctions based upon race. Nebraska won statehood without having ratified the Amendment. But the enabling Act provided that "this act shall take effect with the fundamental and perpetual condition that there shall be no abridgement or denial of the exercise of the elective franchise, *or any other right*, to any person by reason of race or color. . . ." Act of February 9, 1867, ch. 9, sec. 3, 14 Stat. 377 (emphasis supplied). The Act, furthermore, required Nebraska to publicly proclaim this fundamental condition "as a part of the organization of this state."

While the enabling Act was still being considered by Congress, the territorial legislature forthwith passed a "Bill to remove all distinctions on account of race or color in our public schools"[401] since the existing school law restricting the enumeration of pupils to white youths[402] had heretofore been administratively construed to exclude colored children from the public schools. This bill failed to enter the statute books for lack of gubernatorial endorsement.[403]

The same session of the legislature by an appropriate resolution recognized the enabling Act's "fundamental condition" on February 20, 1867 and on March 1st Nebraska was pro-claimed the 37th state. Two months later, a special session of the legislature was called to ratify the Amendment and to enact legislation to "render Nebraska second to no other state in the facilities offered to all her children, irrespective of sex or condition. . . ."[404] The Amendment was ratified in June 1867,[405] and the school law was amended to require the enumeration of "all the children" in the school census.[406] The new school law did not in specific language prohibit segregation, but colored children entered the public schools on a non-segregated basis at the next school term in September, 1867.[407]

Another school law was enacted in 1869 which provided an increase in the taxes for the support of public schools "affording the advantages of a free education to all youth;"[408] and thereafter no school law has contained any language describing the system of public schools operated by the state.

Prior to its ratification of the Amendment, Kansas, a loyal border state, had adopted a policy of permissive segregation whereby boards of education were authorized, but not required, to establish separate schools.[409] The legislature ratified the Amendment on January 16, 1867,[410] and changed the school law on February 26th by an act which made it illegal for "any" school board to refuse to admit "any" child.[411] In 1868, it reenacted the earlier permissive school segregation law.[412] Subsequently, an 1876 revision of the school laws omitted any authorization for segregation in cities of the first class and specifically forbade segregated schools in cities of the second class.[413] The same session also passed a civil rights act which is still the law and proscribes any distinction on account of race or color in "any state university, college, or other school of public instruction" or in any licensed place of public accommodation or amusement, or on any means of public

---

[399] Wisconsin State Journal, Feb. 7, 1867 (Reporting speech of Assemblyman C. B. Thomas).

[400] Daily Wisconsin Union, Feb. 7, 1867 (Reporting speech of Assemblyman H. C. Hobart).

[401] Neb. House J., 12th Terr. Sess. 99, 105 (1867). See Omaha Weekly Republican, January 25, 1867, p. 2; Id., February 8, 1867.

[402] Neb. Comp. Laws 1855–65, pp. 92, 234, 560, 642 (1886).

[403] Messages and Proclamations of the Governors of Nebraska. Collected in Publications of the Nebraska State Historical Society, 249 (1942).

[404] Id. at 274.

[405] Neb. House J. 148 (1867); Neb. Sen. J. 174 (1867).

[406] 2 Neb. Comp. Laws 1866–77, p. 351 (1887).

[407] See Nebraska City News, August 26, 1867, p. 3; Id., September 4, 1867, p. 3.

[408] 2 Neb. Comp. Laws 1866–77, pp. 451, 453 (1887).

[409] Kan. Laws 1862, c. 46, Art. 4 §§ 3, 18; Kan. Laws 1864, c. 67, § 4; Kan. Laws 1865, c. 46, § 1.

[410] The Amendment was ratified without reference to a committee within three days after it was submitted to the legislature. Kan. Sen. J. 43, 76, 128 (1867); Kan. House J. 62, 79 (1867).

[411] Kan. Laws 1867, c. 125, § 1; Kan. Gen. Stats., c. 92, § 1 (1868). The punitive feature of this statute directed county superintendents to withhold school funds from any offending schools.

[412] Kan. Gen. Stats., c. 18, Art. V § 75, c. 19, Art. V § 57 (1868).

[413] Kan. Laws 1876, 238.

carriage.[414] In 1879, the legislature reenacted the law permitting racial separation in schools but limited it to cities of the first class.[415]

Minnesota ratified the Fourteenth Amendment on January 16, 1867.[416] Its legislature was not obliged to contemplate whether the Amendment nullified segregated schools because such practices had been made a penal offense in 1864.[417] However, in submitting the Amendment to the legislature, the governor urged that its adoption was necessary because of the failure of the former seceding states "to reorganize their civil government on the basis of equal . . . rights, without distinction of color. . . ."[418] In 1873, the legislature rephrased the school law so as to specifically prohibit segregated schools.[419]

In Nevada, the school law in existence prior to its consideration of the Amendment excluded Negroes from public schools and prescribed a penalty against any school which opened its doors to such persons.[420] However, the statute provided that school authorities might, if they deemed it advisable, establish a separate school for colored children and maintain it out of the general school fund. While the legislature took no affirmative action after it ratified the Amendment on January 22, 1867,[421] it similarly remained inactive after the decision in *State* v. *Duffy*, 7 Nev. 342 (1872), which vitiated the first section of the school law. There is no subsequent reference to the subject of separate schools in the statute books and the segregatory statute itself was dropped from subsequent compilations of laws.[422]

The Oregon evidence is singularly meager. There were no laws requiring or permitting racial separation in schools either prior or subsequent to ratification of the Amendment on September 9, 1866. What the ratifying legislature understood as to the force of the Amendment and the significance of the abortive at-

tempt to withdraw its ratification in 1868 on this subject is unavailable from the bare notations contained in the legislative journals.[423] The contemporary newspapers are also barren of information on this point.[424] What evidence there is, indicates that separate schools did exist at least in Portland as late as 1867 and that they were discontinued in 1871.[425]

Almost two years after the Amendment was submitted to the states, Iowa ratified on April 3, 1868.[426] Neither the state constitution nor laws required or in any manner authorized racial separation in schools at that time.[427] Instances of exclusion and segregation were being quickly remedied without recourse to the courts.[428] Where the courts were called upon, local practices of segregation in schools were never sustained as lawful. *Clark* v. *School Directors*, 24 Iowa 266 (1868); *Smith* v. *Directors of Independent Schools Dist.*, 40 Iowa 518 (1875); *Dove* v. *Independent School Dist.*, 41 Iowa 689 (1875). The state supreme court also forbade segregation by a common carrier in its dining facilities, predicating its decision squarely upon the Fourteenth Amendment. *Coger* v. *N. W. Union Packet Co.*, 37 Iowa 145 (1873).

In sum, the legislatures in all of the Union States which ratified the Fourteenth Amendment, except three, understood and contemplated that the Amendment proscribed State laws compelling segregation in public schools.

## C. The non-ratifying states understood that the Fourteenth Amendment forbade enforced segregation in public schools

Four states did not ratify the Amendment, three specifically withholding endorsement and the other being unable to arrive at any definitive position. Delaware, in the anomalous position

---

[414] Kan. Laws 1874, c. 49, § 1. See KAN. REV. STATS. § 21–2424 (1935).
[415] Kan. Laws 1879, c. 81, § 1. This is the current law in Kansas. KAN. REV. STATS. § 27–1724 (1935).
[416] The governor laid the proposed Amendment before the legislature with the observation that it would secure equal civil rights to all citizens and both houses voted at once to ratify the Amendment without further reference. Minn. Exec. Doc. 26 (1866); Minn. House J. 26 (1866); Minn. Sen. J. 22, 23 (1866).
[417] Minn. Laws 1864, c. 4, § 1, amending Minn. Laws 1862, c. 1, § 33.
[418] Minn. Exec. Docs. 25 (1866).
[419] Minn. Stats., ch. 15 § 74 (1873).
[420] Nev. Laws 1864–65, p. 426.
[421] The governor presented the Amendment to the legislature with an admonition that they were expected to ratify it and the ratification was accomplished three days later. The journals indicate virtually no opposition or advocacy of the Amendment. Nev. Sen. J. 9, 47 (1867); Nev. Ass. J. 25 (1867).
[422] See Nev. Comp. Laws (1929).

[423] Ore. Sen. J. 25, 34–36 (1866); *Id.*, at 271–272 (1868); Ore. House J. 273 (1868); Ore. Laws 1868, 114; *Id.*, "Joint Resolutions and Memorials" 13.
[424] The Oregonian, the state's leading newspaper, purportedly carried all the legislative happenings in full. See The Oregonian, September 14, 1866. None of its 1866 issues indicate more than that the legislature considered the Amendment dealt with "equality" and that the primary controversy was with respect to suffrage. *Ibid.*, September 21, 1866.
[425] See REYNOLDS, PORTLAND PUBLIC SCHOOLS, 1875, 33 ORE. HIST. Q. 344 (1932); W. P. A. ADULT EDUCATION PROJECT, HISTORY OF EDUCATION IN PORTLAND 34 (1937).
[426] Ratification was almost perfunctorily effected. Iowa Sen. J. 265 (1868) Iowa House J. 132 (1868).
[427] IOWA CONST. 1857, Art. IX. § 12; Iowa Laws 1866, p. 158, reinforcing the Acts of 1860 and 1862 which required the instruction of all children without regard to race. SCHAFFTER, THE IOWA CIVIL RIGHTS ACT, 14 Iowa L. Rev. 63, 64–65 (1928).
[428] Dubuque Weekly Herald, January 30, 1867, p. 2; Des Moines Iowa State Register, January 29, 1868, p. 1; *Id.*, February 19, 1868, p. 1.

of a former slave state which sided with the Union, rejected it on February 7, 1867 with a resolution which declared that "this General Assembly believes the adoption of the said proposed amendment to the Constitution would have a tendency to destroy the rights of the States in their Sovereign capacity as states, would be an attempt to establish an equality not sanctioned by the laws of nature or God. . . ."[429] Again, in 1873, the state legislators denounced

> ". . . all other measures intended or calculated to equalize or amalgamate the Negro race with the white race, politically or socially, and especially do they proclaim unceasing opposition to making Negroes eligible to public office, to sit on juries, and to their admission into public schools where white children attend, and to the admission on terms of equality with white people in the churches, public conveyances, places of amusement or hotels, and to any measure designed or having the effect to promote the equality of the Negro with the white man in any of the relations of life, or which may possibly conduce to such result."[430]

Then, shortly thereafter, the General Assembly in a series of discriminatory statutes demonstrated that it fully understood that equality before the law demanded non-segregation. It passed laws permitting segregation in schools,[431] places of public accommodation, places of public amusement and on public carriers.[432] Delaware, however, deferred sanctioning compulsory racial separation in public schools until after this Court handed down the *Plessy* decision.[433]

**Maryland**  Maryland was also a loyal former slave-holding state. It rejected the Amendment on March 23, 1867.[434] The establishment of universal free public education here coincided with the Reconstruction Period. Although Maryland has always maintained a dual school system, it has never enacted a law specifically forbidding racial integration in its public schools. Rather, separate and parallel provisions were made for the education of white and colored children.[435]

**Kentucky**  The third of the states which rejected the Amendment was Kentucky, a state with a slaveholding background and generally sympathetic with the South with regard to the status of Negroes although it did not secede. It was the first to refuse ratification: its rejection was enrolled on January 10, 1867.[436] While Negroes were denied or severely limited in the enjoyment of many citizenship rights at that time, including exclusion from juries,[437] the legislature was silent on the specific question of compulsory segregated schools.[438] Like its Maryland brothers, it passed two discrete series of laws, one for the benefit of white children and the other for colored children. But no definite compulsory education statute was enacted until 1904[439] although the constitution had been previously amended so as to support such legislation.[440]

**California**  California was the only state whose legislature considered the Amendment and yet did not reach an official stand on the matter.[441] Before the Fourteenth Amendment was proclaimed the law of the land, the legislature in 1866, relaxed the pattern of compulsory segregation when the school law was revised to permit Negro children to enter "white" schools, provided a majority of the white parents did not object.[442] This provision survived changes made in the school laws in 1870 and 1872; and, in 1874, a bill to eliminate segregated schools led to the adoption of a law which required the admission of colored children "into schools for white children" if separate schools were not provided.[443] Later in this same year the state supreme court upheld segregated schools despite the petitioner's claim that this practice violated the Amendment. *Ward* v. *Flood*, 48 Cal. 36 (1874). The legislature then revised the school laws and eliminated the provisions

---

[429] 13 Del. Laws 256. See Del. Sen. J. 76 (1867); Del. House J. 88 (1867) for speech of Governor Saulsbury recommending rejection on the ground that it was a flagrant invasion of state rights.
[430] Del. Laws 1871–73, pp. 686–87.
[431] Del. Rev. Stats. c. 42 § 12 (1874); Del. Laws 1875, pp. 82–83; Del. Laws 1881, c. 362.
[432] Del. Laws 1875–77, c. 194.
[433] Del. Const. 1897, Art. X, § 2.
[434] Md. Sen. J. 808 (1867); Md. House J. 1141 (1867).
[435] Md. Laws 1865, c. 160, tit. i–iv; Md. Rev. Code §§ 47, 60, 119 (1861–67 Supp.); Md. Laws 1868, c. 407; Md. Laws 1870, c. 311; Md. Laws 1872, c. 377; Md. Rev. Code, tit. xvii §§ 95, 98 (1878).

[436] Ky. House J. 60 (1867); Ky. Sen. J. 63 (1867).
[437] Ky. Laws 1865–66, pp. 38–39, 49–50, 68–69.
[438] Ky. Laws 1869, c. 1634; 1 Ky. Laws 1869–70, pp. 113–127; Ky. Laws 1871–72, ch. 112; Ky. Stats., c. 18 (1873); Ky. Gen. Stats., c. 18, pp. 371 *et seq.* (1881).
[439] Ky. Laws 1904, pp. 181–82.
[440] Ky. Const. 1891, § 187.
[441] The Committee on Federal Relations in the Assembly and Senate, respectively, recommended rejection and ratification of the Amendment and no further action was taken. Cal. Ass. J., 17th Sess., p. 611 (1867–68); Cal. Sen. J., 17th Sess., p. 676 (1867–68), p. 676. See Flack, The Adoption of the Fourteenth Amendment 207 (1908).
[442] Cal. Stats. 1866, p. 363. Pursuant to this statute a number of "white" schools admitted colored children without untoward incident. Cloud, Education in California 44 (1952).
[443] Cal. Stats. 1873–74, p. 97.

which had been held to require separate schools for Negro children.[444]

The evidence from the non-ratifying states also indicates that their legislatures understood or contemplated that the Fourteenth Amendment forbade legislation which enforced the separation of white and colored children in public schools.

## CONCLUSIONS OF PART II

There is, therefore, considerable evidence and, we submit, conclusive evidence that the Congress which submitted and the state legislatures and conventions which considered the Fourteenth Amendment contemplated and understood that it would proscribe all racial distinctions in law including segregation in public schools. A part of this evidence consists of the political, social and legal theories which formed the background of the men who framed the Fourteenth Amendment and the Radical Republican majority in Congress at that time.

Congressional debates following the Civil War must be read and understood in the light of the equalitarian principles of absolute and complete equality for all Americans as exemplified throughout the Abolitionist movement prior to the Civil War.

Many of the members of Congress, in debating the bill which became the Civil Rights Act of 1875, made it clear in no uncertain terms that it was generally understood in the 39th Congress that the Fourteenth Amendment was intended to prohibit all racial distinctions, including segregation in public school systems.

Running throughout the 39th Congress was a determination of the Radical Republican majority to transform these equalitarian principles into federal statutory and constitutional law. They realized that these high principles could not be achieved without effective federal legislation. The infamous Black Codes were demonstrative proof that the southern states were determined to prevent the newly freed Negroes from escaping from an inferior status even after the Thirteenth Amendment. The Radical Republican majority realized that in the status of American law at that time, the only way to achieve fulfillment of their determination to remove caste and racial distinctions from our

law would be for them to effect a revolutionary change in the federal-state relationship.

After many drafting experiments, the Committee of Fifteen introduced in Congress the proposed amendment to the Constitution which was to become the Fourteenth Amendment. The broad and comprehensive scope of the bill was clearly set forth by Senator Howard, Chairman of the Judiciary Committee. An appraisal of the Congressional debates during the period the Fourteenth Amendment was being considered show conclusively that in so far as section 1 was concerned, there could be no doubt that it was intended to not only destroy the validity of the existing Black Codes, but also to deprive the states of power to enact any future legislation which would be based upon *class* or *caste* distinctions. It is likewise clear that the Fourteenth Amendment was intended to be even more comprehensive than the scope of the original bill which, subsequently weakened by amendment, became the Civil Rights Act of 1866.

Throughout the debates in the 39th Congress and subsequent Congresses, the framers of the Amendment, the Radical Republican majority in Congress, over and over again, made it clear that: (1) future Congresses might in the exercise of their power under section 5 take whatever action they might deem necessary to enforce the Amendment; (2) that one of the purposes of the Amendment was to take away from future Congresses the power to diminish the rights intended to be protected by the Amendment; and (3) they at all times made it clear that the Amendment was meant to be self-executing and that the judiciary would have the authority to enforce the provisions of the Amendment without further implementation by Congress. All of the decisions of this Court, without exception, have recognized this principle.

Other Congressional debates, including those on the readmission of certain states, the amnesty bills and other legislation give further evidence of the intent of Congress in regard to the broad scope of the Fourteenth Amendment. The debates in Congress on legislation which was later to become the Civil Rights Act of 1875 made it clear that efforts of states to set up segregated school systems violated the Fourteenth Amendment. These debates were more specific on the question of segregation in public education because some states were already beginning to violate the Fourteenth Amendment by setting up segregated systems.

A study of the statements and actions of those responsible for state ratification of the

---

[444] Cal. Stats. 1880, p. 48. See Wysinger v. Crookshank, 82 Cal. 588 (1890). The laws segregating Chinese children remained on the books probably because it was the general impression that only discriminatory laws aimed at Negroes were forbidden by the Fourteenth Amendment. Debates of the California Constitutional Convention of 1873, pp. 631, 642, 649 (1880).

Amendment remove any doubt as to their understanding that the Fourteenth Amendment was intended to prohibit state imposed racial segregation in public schools.

After addressing ourselves to questions 1 and 2 propounded by this Court, we find that the evidence not only supports but also compels the conclusions reached in Part One hereof. Wherefore, we respectfully submit, this Court should decide that the constitutional provisions and statutes involved in these cases are in violation of the Fourteenth Amendment and therefore unconstitutional.

### PART THREE

This portion is directed to questions four and five of the Court's Order:

> 4. Assuming it is decided that segregation in public schools violates the Fourteenth Amendment,
> (a) would a decree necessarily follow providing that, within the limits set by normal geographic school districting, Negro children should forthwith be admitted to schools of their choice, or
> (b) may this Court, in the exercise of its equity powers, permit an effective gradual adjustment to be brought about from existing segregated systems to a system not based on color distinctions?
> 5. On the assumption on which questions 4(a) and (b) are based, and assuming further that this Court will exercise its equity powers to the end described in question 4(b),
> (a) should this Court formulate detailed decrees in these cases;
> (b) if so what specific issues should the decrees reach;
> (c) should this Court appoint a special master to hear evidence with a view to recommending specific terms for such decrees;
> (d) should this Court remand to the courts of first instance with directions to frame decrees in these cases, and if so, what general directions should the decrees of this Court include and what procedures should the courts of first instance follow in arriving at the specific terms of more detailed decrees?

### I. THIS COURT SHOULD DECLARE INVALID THE CONSTITUTIONAL AND STATUTORY PROVISIONS HERE INVOLVED REQUIRING SEGREGATION IN PUBLIC SCHOOLS. AFTER CAREFUL CONSIDERATION OF ALL OF THE FACTORS INVOLVED IN TRANSITION FROM SEGREGATED SCHOOL SYSTEMS TO UNSEGREGATED SCHOOL SYSTEMS, APPELLANTS KNOW OF NO REASONS OR CONSIDERATIONS

### WHICH WOULD WARRANT POSTPONEMENT OF THE ENFORCEMENT OF APPELLANTS' RIGHTS BY THIS COURT IN THE EXERCISE OF ITS EQUITY POWERS.

The questions raised involve consideration of the propriety of postponing relief in these cases, should the Court declare segregation in public schools impermissible under the Constitution. The basic difficulty presented is in the correlation between a grant of effective relief and temporary postponement. After carefully addressing ourselves to the problem, we find that difficulty insurmountable.

### A. The Fourteenth Amendment requires that a decree be entered directing that appellants be admitted forthwith to public schools without distinction as to race or color

"It is fundamental that these cases concern rights which are personal and present". *Sweatt v. Painter*, 339 U.S. 629, 635; see also *Sipuel v. Board of Regents*, 332 U.S. 631, 633. These rights are personal because each appellant[445] is asserting his individual constitutional right to grow up in our democratic society without the impress of state-imposed racial segregation in the public schools. They are present because they will be irretrievably lost if their enjoyment is put off. The rights of the adult students in the *Sipuel*, *Sweatt*, and *McLaurin* cases required, this Court held, vindication forthwith. *A fortiori*, this is true of the rights of children to a public education that they must obtain, if at all while they are children. It follows that appellants are entitled to be admitted forthwith to public schools without distinction as to race and color.

### B. There is no equitable justification for postponement of appellants' enjoyment of their rights

Even if the Court should decide that enforcement of individual and personal constitutional rights may be postponed, consideration of the relevant factors discloses no equitable basis for delaying enforcement of appellants' rights.

Appellants have no desire to set precise bounds to the reserve discretion of equity. They concede that, as a court of chancery, this Court has power in a proper case to mold its relief to individual circumstances in ways and to an extent which it is now unnecessary to define with entire precision. But the rights established by these appellants are far outside the classes as

---

[445] As used herein "appellant" includes the respondents in No. 10.

to which, whether for denial or delay, a "balance of convenience" has been or ought to be struck.

These infant appellants are asserting the most important secular claims that can be put forward by children, the claim to their full measure of the chance to learn and grow, and the inseparably connected but even more important claim to be treated as entire citizens of the society into which they have been born. We have discovered no case in which such rights, once established, have been postponed by a cautious calculation of conveniences. The nuisance cases, the sewage cases, the cases of the overhanging cornices, need not be distinguished. They distinguish themselves.

The Fourteenth Amendment can hardly have been intended for enforcement at a pace geared down to the mores of the very states whose action it was designed to limit. The balance between the customs of the states and the personal rights of these appellants has been struck by that Amendment. "[A] court of equity is not justified in ignoring that pronouncement under the guise of exercising equitable jurisdiction." *Youngstown Co.* v. *Sawyer*, 343 U.S. 579, 610 (concurring opinion).

Affirming the decree of one of the few judges still carrying the traditional title and power of Chancellor, the highest Court of Delaware epitomized equity in one of the cases now before this bar when it declared in *Gebhart* v. *Belton*, 91 A. 2d 137, 149 that

> "To require the plaintiffs to wait another year under present conditions would be in effect partially to deny them that to which we have held they are entitled."

Appellants, in the main, are obliged to speculate as to factors which might be urged to justify postponement of the enforcement of their rights. Hitherto, appellees have offered no justification for any such postponement. Instead they have sought to maintain a position which is, essentially, that a state may continue governmentally enforced racism so long as the state government wills it.

In deciding whether sufficient reason exists for postponing the enjoyment of appellants' rights, this Court is not resolving an issue which depends upon a mere preponderance of the evidence. It needs no citation of authority to establish that the defendant in equity who asks the chancellor to go slow in upholding the vital rights of children accruing to them under the Constitution, must make out an affirmative case of crushing conviction to sustain his plea for delay.

The problem of effective gradual adjustment cannot fairly arise in three of the five cases consolidated for argument. In the Kansas case, there was a frank concession on oral argument that elimination of segregation would not have serious consequences. In Delaware, court-compelled desegregation in this very case has already been accomplished. The case from the District of Columbia is here on a dismissal of the complaint on motion. In the oral argument the counsel for respondents implied that he foresaw no difficulties in enforcing a decree which would abolish segregation. Surely it would be curious as well as a gratuitous assumption that such a change cannot be expeditiously handled in this nation's capital. Cf. *District of Columbia* v. *John R. Thompson Co.*, 346 U.S. 100.

We can, however, put out of the case what is not in dispute. We concede that there may well be delays of a purely administrative nature involved in bringing about desegregation. Any injunction requires time for compliance and we do not ask the impossible. We strongly urge, however, that no reason has been suggested and none has been discovered by us that would warrant denying appellants their full rights beyond the beginning of the next school year.

But we do not understand that the "effective gradual adjustment" mentioned in this Court's fourth and fifth questions referred to such conceded necessities. We proceed then, to consider possible grounds that might be put forth as reasons for added delay, or for the postponement of relief to appellants.

It has been suggested that desegregation may bring about unemployment for Negro teachers. (Appellees' Brief in *Davis* v. *County School Board*, p. 31; *Transcript of Argument* in the same case, p. 71) If this is more than a remote possibility, it undoubtedly can be offset by good faith efforts on the part of the responsible school boards.[446] On the other hand, if appellees' suggestion is based upon an unexpressed intention of discriminating against Negro teachers by wholesale firings, it is not even worthy of notice in a court of equity.

It has been bruited about that certain of the states involved in this litigation will cease to support and perhaps even abolish their public school systems, if segregation is outlawed. (*Davis* v. *County School Board*, *Transcript of Argument*, pp. 69–70; *Gebhart* v. *Belton*, *Transcript of Argument*, p. 17; *Briggs* v. *Eliott*, *Record on Appeal*, p. 113.) We submit that such action is not

---

[446] In view of the nationwide shortage of teachers, it is doubtful that any unemployment would be more than transitory. See *e.g.*, New York Times, August 19, 1953, 31:8 (S. M. Bouthardt puts elementary teachers shortage at 116,000); August 24, 1953, 21:1 (Comm. Thurston and NEA on shortage); 22 J. Neg. Ed. 95 (1953).

permissible. *Cf. Rice* v. *Elmore*, 165 F. 2d 387 (CA 4th 1947), *cert. denied*, 333 U.S. 875. Any such reckless threats cannot be relevant to a consideration of effective "gradual adjustment"; they are based upon opposition to desegregation in any way, at any time.

Finally, there are hints and forebodings of trouble to come, ranging from hostility and deteriorated relations to actual violence. (Appellees' brief in *Briggs* v. *Eliott*, p. 267; Appellees' brief in *Davis* v. *County School Board*, p. 17.) Obviously this Court will not be deterred by threats of unlawful action. *Buchanan* v. *Warley*, 245 U.S. 60, 81.

Moreover, there are powerful reasons to confirm the belief that immediate desegregation will not have the untoward consequences anticipated. The states in question are inhabited in the main by law-abiding people who up to now have relied upon what they believe—erroneously, as we have demonstrated—to be the law. It cannot be presumed that they will not obey the law as expounded by this Court. Such evidence as there is lends no support to defendants' forebodings. Note, *Grade School Segregation: The Latest Attack on Racial Discrimination*, 61 Yale L. J. 730, 739, 743 (1952).

A higher public interest than any yet urged by appellees is the need for the enforcement of constitutional rights fought for and won about a century ago. Public interest requires that racial distinctions proscribed by our Constitution be given the fullest protection. Survival of our country in the present international situation is inevitably tied to resolution of this domestic issue.

The greatest strength of our democracy grows out of its people working together as equals. Our public schools are "[d]esigned to serve as perhaps the most powerful agency for promoting cohesion among a heterogeneous democratic people...." Mr. Justice Frankfurter, concurring in *Illinois ex rel. McCollum* v. *Board of Education*, 333 U.S. 206, 216–217.

### C. Appellants are unable, in good faith, to suggest terms for a decree which will secure effective gradual adjustment because no such decree will protect appellants' rights

Question 5 assumes that the Court, having decided that segregation in public schools violates the Fourteenth Amendment, will, nevertheless, in the exercise of its equity powers, permit an effective gradual adjustment from segregated schools to systems not operated on the basis of color distinctions. This necessarily assumes further that reasons might be produced to justify consideration of postponement of the

enforcement of the present and personal rights here involved. As we have pointed out immediately hereinbefore we are unable to identify any such reason.

Appellants obviously are aware of the existence of segregated school systems throughout the South similar to those presently before this Court. Similarly, appellants realize that the thrust of decisions in these cases may appear to present complex problems of adjustment because segregated schools have existed for nearly a century in many areas of this country. Generalizations, however, as to the scope and character of the complexities which might arise from immediate enforcement of appellants' rights would be unwarranted. This is demonstrated in part by the fact that even in the five cases joined for hearing, there appears to be no uniformity in the extent of the task of adjustment from segregated to non-segregated schools.

Necessarily, consideration of the specific issues which decrees should reach on the basis of the assumptions of Question 5 likewise requires the assumption that reasons will be adduced to warrant consideration of postponement of enforcement of appellants' rights.[447]

Though no cogent reasons were offered to support them, two suggestions of methods of postponement of relief to appellants were made to this Court in the original brief for the United States. The first of these was "integration on a grade basis," i.e., to integrate the first grades immediately, and to continue such integration until completed as to all grades in the elementary schools (Brief, pp. 30–31). The second was integration "on a school-by school" basis (Brief, p. 31).

The first suggestion is intolerable. It would mean the flat denial of the right of every appellant in these cases. The second plan is likewise impossible to defend because it would mean the deliberate denial of the rights of many of the plaintiffs. If desegregation is possible in

---

[447] It follows that there is no need for this Court to appoint a Master. Since repeal in 1948 of the 1805 statute, 28 U.S.C., § 863 (1946), forbidding the introduction of new evidence at an appellate level, there would appear to be no reason why such master could not be appointed. Certainly respected authorities have recommended the practice of appellate courts' taking evidence. See 1 WIGMORE, EVIDENCE 41 (3d ed., 1940); POUND, APPELLATE PROCEDURE IN CIVIL CASES pp. 303, 387 (1941); Note, 56 HARV. L. REV. 1313 (1943), and in other times and jurisdictions it has been respected practice. See SMITH, APPEALS OF THE PRIVY COUNCIL FROM AMERICAN PLANTATIONS 310 (1950); Rules of the Supreme Court of Judicature, Order 58, Rules 1, 2; cf. New Mexico, Stat. 1949, c. 168, § 19. However, taking of evidence by a Master is undoubtedly a departure from normal practice on appeal and it may result in loss of time to the prejudice of plaintiffs' rights.

some schools in a district, why not in all? Must some appellants' rights be denied altogether so that others may be more conveniently protected?

Whether any given plan for gradual adjustment would be effective would depend on the showing of reasons valid in equity for postponement of enforcement of appellants' rights. In accordance with instructions of this Court we have addressed ourselves to all of the plans for gradual adjustment which we have been able to find. None would be effective. We recognize that the appellees, as school officials and state officers, might offer reasons for seeking postponement of the effect of decrees in these cases. Therefore, we submit, affirmative answers to questions 4(b) and 5 can come only from appellees since they alone can adduce reasons for postponement of enforcement of appellants' rights.

In the absence of any such reasons the only specific issue which appellants can recommend to the Court that the decrees should reach is the substantive one presented here, namely, that appellees should be required in the future to discharge their obligations as state officers without drawing distinctions based on race and color. Once this is done not only the local communities involved in these several cases, but communities throughout the South, would be left free to work out individual plans for conforming to the then established precedent free from the statutory requirement of rigid racial segregation.

In the very nature of the judicial process once a right is judicially declared proposals for postponement of the remedy must originate with the party desiring that postponement.

We submit that it would be customary procedure for the appellees to first produce whatever reasons they might urge to justify postponement of relief. Appellants then would be in a position to advise the Court of their views with respect to the matter.

## CONCLUSION

Under the applicable decisions of this Court the state constitutional and statutory provisions herein involved are clearly unconstitutional. Moreover, the historical evidence surrounding the adoption, submission and ratification of the Fourteenth Amendment compels the conclusion that it was the intent, understanding and contemplation that the Amendment proscribed all state imposed racial restrictions. The Negro children in these cases are arbitrarily excluded from state public schools set apart for the dominant white groups. Such a practice can only be continued on a theory that Negroes,

*qua* Negroes, are inferior to all other Americans. The constitutional and statutory provisions herein challenged cannot be upheld without a clear determination that Negroes are inferior and, therefore, must be segregated from other human beings. Certainly, such a ruling would destroy the intent and purpose of the Fourteenth Amendment and the very equalitarian basis of our Government.

WHEREFORE, it is respectfully submitted that the judgments in cases No. 1, 2 and 4 should be reversed and the judgment in No. 10 should be affirmed on the grounds that the constitutional and statutory provisions involved in each of the cases violate the Fourteenth Amendment.

CHARLES L. BLACK, JR.,
ELWOOD H. CHISOLM,
WILLIAM T. COLEMAN, JR.,
CHARLES T. DUNCAN,
GEORGE E. C. HAYES,
WILLIAM R. MING, JR.,
CONSTANCE BAKER MOTLEY,
JAMES M. NABRIT, JR.,
DAVID E. PINSKY,
FRANK D. REEVES,
JOHN SCOTT,
JACK B. WEINSTEIN,
   *of Counsel.*

HAROLD BOULWARE,
ROBERT L. CARTER,
JACK GREENBERG,
OLIVER W. HILL,
THURGOOD MARSHALL,
LOUIS L. REDDING,
SPOTTSWOOD W. ROBINSON, III,
CHARLES S. SCOTT,
   *Attorneys for Appellants in Nos. 1, 2, 4*
   *and for Respondents in No. 10.*

## SUPPLEMENT
## AN ANALYSIS OF THE POLITICAL, SOCIAL, AND LEGAL THEORIES UNDERLYING THE FOURTEENTH AMENDMENT

The first Section of the Fourteenth Amendment did not spring full blown from the brow of any individual proponent. Primitive natural rights theories and earlier constitutional forms were the origins of its equal protection-due process-privileges and immunities trilogy. The occasion for the metamorphosis of moral premises to full-fledged constitutional status was the attack on the American system of slavery. During the long antislavery crusade, the trilogy became a form of shorthand for, and the spearhead of, the whole of the argument against distinctions and caste based on race.

Section One of the Fourteenth Amendment thus marks the "constitutionalization" of an ethico-moral argument. The really decisive shifts occurred before the Civil War, and the synthesis was made, not by lawyers or judges, but by laymen. Doctrines originally worked out and propagated by a dissident minority became, by 1866, the dominant constitutional theory of the country.

In both language and form, Section One was the distillation of basic constitutional and legal theories long understood and voiced by leaders in a Congress upon which history had cast both the opportunity and the obligation to amend the Constitution to regulate relationships profoundly altered by the abolition of slavery.[1] None can doubt that the thrust of the Amendment was equalitarian and that it was adopted to wipe out the racial inequalities that were the legacies of that system. But beyond this, the majestic generalities of the Section can be seen to have evolved naturally and logically in the minds of the antislavery generation.[2]

At the outset we point out that we do not set forth the arguments of pamphleteers, or even of lawyers or congressmen, to justify the validity of their constitutional theories. We do not say that these theories were universally held, or deny that they were vigorously challenged. Nor do we urge that the pre-Civil War Constitution contained the sweeping guarantees that the Abolitionists claimed for Negroes. These are beside our present point. What we do undertake in this section is illumination of the constitutional language—the moral and ethical opinions that were the matrix of the Amendment, the development under terrific counter-pressures of the principal texts and forms, the meaning of "equal protection" and "due pro-

cess" as understood and contemplated by those who wrote those phrases into the Amendment.

## 1. The declaration of the "Self-Evident Truths"

The roots of our American equalitarian ideal extend deep into the history of the western world. Philosophers of the seventeenth and eighteenth centuries produced an intellectual climate in which the equality of man was a central concept. Their beliefs rested upon the basic proposition that all men were endowed with certain natural rights, some of which were surrendered under the so-called "social contract." The state, in return, guaranteed individual rights, and owed protection equally to all men. Thus, governments existed, not to give, but to protect rights; and allegiance and protection were reciprocal. For his allegiance, the citizen was guaranteed his rights and the equal protection of the law.[3]

This doctrine was the core of the first great statement of American principles. To Jefferson and the other draftsmen of the Declaration of Independence, it was "self-evident" that "all men are created equal," and "are endowed by their Creator with certain unalienable Rights," among which are "Life, Liberty and the pursuit of Happiness," and that "to secure these rights, Governments are instituted among Men, deriving their just powers from the consent of the governed."[4]

Abhorrence of arbitrariness—the central element of due process—and the ideal of a general and equal law—the core of equal protection—both were implicit in the Lockean-Jeffersonian premises. Slavery—with its theories of racial damnation, racial inferiority, and racial discrimination—was inherently repugnant to the American creed and the Christian ethic. This fact was being rapidly and increasingly sensed. As men sensed it, they had to fit it into the only political theory they knew: Governments existed, not to give, but to *protect* human

---

[1] Graham, *The Early Antislavery Backgrounds of the Fourteenth Amendment*, 1950 Wis. L. Rev. 479–507, 610–661, hereinafter cited *Early Antislavery Backgrounds*.

[2] Basic monographs and articles on the Fourteenth Amendment and its major clauses are: 2 Crosskey, Politics and the Constitution in the History of the United States cc. 31–32 (1953); Flack, The Adoption of the Fourteenth Amendment (1908); The Journals of the Joint Committee of Fifteen on Reconstruction (Kendrick ed. 1914); tenBroek, The Antislavery Origins of the Fourteenth Amendment (1951) hereinafter cited Antislavery Origins; Warsoff, Equality and the Law (1938); Boudin, *Truth and Fiction About the Fourteenth Amendment*, 16 N.Y.U.L.Q. Rev. 19 (1938); Fairman, *Does the Fourteenth Amendment Incorporate the Bill of Rights? The Original Understanding*, 2 Stan. L. Rev. 5 (1949); Frank and Munro, *The Original Understanding of "Equal Protection of the Laws,"* 50 Col. L. Rev. 131 (1950); Graham, *The "Conspiracy Theory" of the Fourteenth Amendment*, 47 Yale L.J. 371, 48 Yale L.J. 171 (1938); McLaughlin, *The Court, The Corporation, and Conkling*, 46 Am. Hist. Rev. 45 (1940).

[3] Locke, Second Treatise on Government c. 2 (1698). See also Becker, The Declaration of Independence (1926); Smith, American Philosophy of Equality (1927); Wright, American Interpretations of Natural Law (1931); Corwin, *The "Higher Law" Background of American Constitutional Law*, 42 Harv. L. Rev. 149, 365 (1928); Graham, *Early Antislavery Backgrounds, supra* note 1, at 610–611; Hamilton. *Property According to Locke*, 41 Yale L.J. 864 (1932).

[4] It is interesting to note in this context that Jefferson's original draft of the Declaration, accepted by Franklin and Adams, the other members of the sub-committee responsible for the drafting, contained severe strictures on the King because of the slave trade. See Becker, *op. cit. supra* note 3, at 212–213.

rights; allegiance and protection were reciprocal—i.e., *ought to be reciprocal*; rights and duties were correlative—i.e., *had to be correlative* if Americans ever were to live with their consciences and to justify their declared political faith.

Long before the Revolution, Quakers and Puritans attacked slavery as a violation of the social compact and Christian ethic.[5] After 1776, Jefferson's "self-evident truths" put a cutting edge on all such pleas—made them the broadswords in every attack. Idealists demanded that America live up to her Declaration. "All men" must mean all men. "Unalienable Rights . . . of Life, Liberty and the pursuit of Happiness" must be given its full human, not merely a restricted racial, application. Race and color were arbitrary, insubstantial bases for accord or denial of natural, human rights. Sensitive leaders soon found themselves confronted with what Gunnar Myrdal treated recently as *An American Dilemma*.[6] Having pledged their "Lives . . . Fortunes, and sacred Honor" to the causes of liberty and freedom, either Americans endeavored to live up to their creed or stultified themselves before the world.

After the Revolution, the "self-evident truths" and the provisions of the state Bills of Rights were employed as weapons against slavery and against racial distinctions.[7] Down through the Civil War, moreover, the "self-evident truths" constituted precisely what Jefferson declared them to be—political axioms—

except in the South after the invention of the cotton gin.[8] They were on every tongue as rhetorical shorthand, and were popularly regarded as the marrow of the Constitution itself. In justifying one revolution, Jefferson no less than Locke had laid the groundwork for another. The dominating premise that governments were instituted for protection and that they derived their just powers from the consent of the governed had begun to make slavery, and with it race distinctions, untenable. What slowly took shape was an ethical interpretation of American origins and destiny.

## 2. The moral suasion campaign and its rejection

The Age of Enlightenment of the seventeenth and eighteenth centuries gave birth to a worldwide antislavery movement. A wave of humanitarianism, embracing quests for abolition of slavery, suffrage for women, and penal, land, and other reforms, swept across the United States of the early nineteenth century. Because of its dramatic qualities, the American antislavery movement assumed even larger proportions and eventually overshadowed the other phases.[9] Like them, it was based fundamentally on Judeo-Christian ethic and was formulated in terms of equalitarianism and natural rights.

The early antislavery movement was a campaign of moral suasion. Rational men appealed to other rational men to square precept with practice. Proponents of equality, who were by that definition opponents of slavery, sought to persuade slaveholders of the error of enslaving other men, i.e., of denying equality to those held as slaves. That campaign bore early fruit in Virginia, in the uplands of the Carolinas, and even in the deeper South. The appeal to the South ultimately broke on the hard rock of economic self-interest after invention of the cotton gin. Geography and migrations tended

---

[5] German Quakers of Pennsylvania had argued as early as 1688, "Though they are black, we cannot conceive there is more liberty to have them slaves [than] . . . to have other white ones. . . . We should do to all men like as we will be done ourselves, making no difference of what descent or colour they are. . . . Here is liberty of conscience, which is right and reasonable; here ought to be likewise liberty of body. . . ." MOORE, NOTES ON THE HISTORY OF SLAVERY IN MASSACHUSETTS 75 (1866). In 1700, in his antislavery tract, THE SELLING OF JOSEPH, the great Puritan elder, Judge Samuel Sewall, declared, "All men, as they are . . . Sons of Adam, are co-heirs, and have equal Right unto Liberty." *Id.* at 83–87. See also Graham, *Early Antislavery Backgrounds, supra* note 1, at 614–615.
[6] 2 vols. (1944).
[7] In 1783, Chief Justice Cushing, pointing to the "All men are born free and equal" clause of the Massachusetts Bill of Rights, declared that ". . . slavery is inconsistent with our conduct and Constitution, and there can be no such thing as perpetual servitude of a rational creature." MOORE, *op. cit. supra* note 5, at 209–221. Four years later, Congress passed the Northwest Ordinance outlawing slavery in the territories. 2 THORPE, THE FEDERAL AND STATE CONSTITUTIONS, COLONIAL CHARTERS, AND OTHER ORGANIC LAWS 957–962 (1909). Vermont effected abolition by constitutional clause; other northern states by prospective legislative action. Graham, *Early Antislavery Backgrounds, supra* note 1, at 617.

[8] While early southern leaders in Virginia accepted Jeffersonian concepts of natural rights, contract, and equality, later leaders and theorists defended the slave society on the basis of Greek concepts. Man had no rights save those created by the state. Men were inherently unequal, and the end of the state was not equality but justice. Each man would have status in accordance with his ability. Such theorists posited the inherent inferiority of the Negro. Their theory was broad enough to justify slavery for any man, irrespective of race or color. See THE PRO-SLAVERY ARGUMENT, As MAINTAINED BY THE MOST DISTINGUISHED WRITERS OF THE SOUTHERN STATES (1853). See also 1 THE WORKS OF JOHN C. CALHOUN 393–394, 6 *id.* at 182–183 (Crallé ed. 1854–1855); SPAIN, THE POLITICAL THEORY OF JOHN C. CALHOUN c. 8 (1951).
[9] NYE, FETTERED FREEDOM 2, 10–11, 217–218, and *passim* (1949).

further to sectionalize the institution. Quakers and Scotch-Irish yeomen from Virginia and the Carolinas, unable to arrest spread of a labor system they detested, and others from the deeper South, fled *en masse*, settling generally in Ohio and Indiana. There they were joined by staunch Puritan and Calvinist stocks from New York and New England. Thus, the antislavery movement became sectionalized with important centers in Ohio, western New York, and Pennsylvania.

Spearheading the movement was the American Anti-Slavery Society, founded in 1833 and headed by the wealthy Tappan brothers. Recruited and led by Theodore Weld,[10] a brilliant orator and organizer, and by his co-leader, James G. Birney,[11] a converted Alabama slaveholder and lawyer, whole communities were abolitionized in the years 1835–1837. Appeals were aimed at influential leaders; lawyers in particular were sought out and recruited by the score.

This appeal was an ethico-moral-religious-natural rights argument. It was addressed by the revivalists to their countrymen as patriots, Christians, and "free moral agents." "The law of nature *clearly teaches the natural* republican equality of all mankind. *Nature* revolts at human slavery.... The Law of God renders all Natural Rights inalienable.... Governments and laws are established, not to give, but to protect ... rights."[12] Negroes, they continued, were "not naturally inferior." They simply had been degraded by slavery. They were persons, endowed by God with all the attributes of personality. Their enslavement could no more be justified than could chattelization of men with red hair. Slavery rested on a capricious, discredited classification.[13] It simply was institutionalized false imprisonment. White men were protected against enslavement and against false imprisonment. "What abolitionists demand as naked justice is that the benefit and protection of these just laws be extended to all human beings alike ... without regard to color or any other physical peculiarities."[14]

Racial discrimination, in short, was repugnant both as a breach of equality and as a breach of protection. Because it was a breach of protection, it also was a breach of equality; and because it was a breach of equality, it was thereby an even greater breach of protection. This was the outcome of Americans' triple-barreled major premise which posited the purpose of *all* government to be the protection of inalienable rights bestowed upon *all* men by their Creator. Once that compound premise was granted—and in the generations since 1776 virtually all Americans outside the South had *spoken* as if they granted it—the abolitionists' conclusions were unassailable. The heart of it was that these basic ideals of liberty, equality, and protection were deemed to be paramount by reason of their place in the Declaration and determinative by reason of the place of the Declaration in American life and history.

The issue had to be resolved within the framework of the constitutional system. Appeals to ethico-moral concepts and to natural rights were good enough to argue as to what ought to be. Reality was something else again. Constitutional reality was that the status of inhabitants of the United States, white or Negro, was fixed by the Constitution. Social reality was that the great mass of Negroes were slaves.

Inevitably, then, the first skirmishes as to the rights claimed for Negroes had to be fought out in the case of free Negroes.[15] The targets here were northern black laws—the laws in Ohio

---

[10] See THOMAS, THEODORE WELD (1950); LETTERS OF THEODORE DWIGHT WELD, ANGELINA GRIMKE WELD AND SARAH GRIMKE, 1822–1844, 2 vols. (Barnes and Dumond ed. 1934) cited hereinafter as WELD-GRIMKE LETTERS. See also BARNES, THE ANTI-SLAVERY IMPULSE, 1830–1844 (1933). Weld was a tireless speaker and pamphleteer who turned out documents that became guide posts in the antislavery movement: SLAVERY AS IT IS (1839); THE POWER OF CONGRESS OVER THE DISTRICT OF COLUMBIA (1838); THE BIBLE AGAINST SLAVERY (1837). Such persons as William Jay, John Quincy Adams and Senator Robert C. Winthrop relied on Weld for legal research. See 2 WELD-GRIMKE LETTERS 748, 956–958. The evangelical character of the antislavery movement helps account for the flood of arguments that poured from it. It was even organized on an analogy drawn from early Christian evangelists with its Seventy and its Council of Twelve.

[11] See BIRNEY, JAMES G. BIRNEY AND HIS TIMES (1890); LETTERS OF JAMES G. BIRNEY, 1831–1857, 2 vols. (Dumond ed. 1938), referred to hereinafter as BIRNEY LETTERS.

[12] OLCOTT, TWO LECTURES ON THE SUBJECT OF SLAVERY AND ABOLITION 24–29 (1838).

[13] The idea that race and color were arbitrary, capricious standards on which to base denial of human rights was implicit in all antislavery attacks on discrimination and prejudice. Yet it was when the constitutional-legal attack began to reinforce the religious one that such arguments became explicit, and the concept of an arbitrary classification developed. Lawyers like Ellsworth, Goddard, Birney (Philanthropist, Dec. 9, 1836, p. 3, cols. 4–5), Gerrit Smith (see AMERICAN ANTI-SLAVERY SOCIETY, 3 ANNUAL REPORTS 16–17 (1836)) and Salmon P. Chase (SPEECH ... IN THE CASE OF THE COLORED WOMAN, MATILDA ... 32 (1837)) helped to formulate the concept and linked it with the principles of equality, affirmative protection, and national citizenship.

[14] OLCOTT, *op. cit. supra* note 12, at 44.

[15] For characteristic references to plans for bettering the lot of the free Negro, see 1 WELD-GRIMKE LETTERS, *op. cit. supra* note 10, at 132–135, 262; AMERICAN ANTI-SLAVERY SOCIETY, 4 ANNUAL REPORTS 32–35, 105–111 (1837). 5 ANNUAL REPORTS 127 (1838). For evidence of how large the condition of the free Negroes, and plans for their betterment, figured in the early A. A. S. S. strategy, see *The Condition of Free People of Color in the United States*, The Anti-slavery Examiner #13a (1839),

and Connecticut; the techniques were persuasion, conversion, and demonstration. It was in the course of this campaign that what presently became the constitutional trinity of the antislavery movement received its decisive synthesis.

The first comprehensive crystallization of antislavery constitutional theory occurred in 1834 in the arguments of W. W. Ellsworth and Calvin Goddard, two of the outstanding lawyers and statesmen of Connecticut, on the appeal[16] of the conviction of Prudence Crandall for violation of an ordinance forbidding the education of non-resident colored persons without the consent of the civil authorities.[17] They reveal this theory as based on broad natural rights premises and on an ethical interpretation of American origins and history. Four ideals were central and interrelated: the ideal of human equality, the ideal of a general and equal law, the ideal of reciprocal protection and allegiance, and the ideal of reason and substantiality as the true bases for the necessary discriminations and classifications by government. Race as a standard breached every one of these ideals, as did color. What was attacked was denial of human equality and denial of protection of the laws—denials inherent in any racial discrimination backed by public authority. Slavery was the arch evil in this respect, and the primary one, both because of the magnitude of its denials and deprivations and abridgments, and because these necessarily established a whole pattern of discrimination based upon race and color alone. It was this pattern of public discrimination that was combatted no less than slavery. It had to be combatted because it was deemed a part of slavery.

Although neither slavery nor segregated schools was the issue in the case, the Ellsworth-Goddard argument is one of the classic statements of the social and ethical case for equality of opportunity irrespective of race. It gave immense impetus to the emerging concept of American nationality and citizenship. Fully reported and widely circulated as a tract, it soon became one of the fountainheads of antislavery

constitutional theory. It figured prominently in Abolitionist writings throughout the 'thirties. In the spring of 1835, Judge William Jay, Abolitionist son of the first Chief Justice and one of the founders and vice-presidents of the American Anti-Slavery Society, devoted fifteen pages of his *Inquiry into the Character and Tendency of the Colonization and Anti-Slavery Societies*[18] to a slashing attack on the trial court's decision.

The due process element of our modern trilogy was introduced in the course of a determined attack made in 1835 by the Weld-Birney group upon Ohio's black laws. Enacted in 1807, these laws embodied prohibitions against Negro immigration, employment, education, and testimony. A report[19] prepared at Weld's direction by a committee of the newly formed Ohio Anti-Slavery Society appealed to the American and Christian conscience. Notwithstanding the affirmative duty of all government to "promote the happiness and secure the rights and liberties of man," and despite the fact that American government was predicated on the "broad and universal principle of equal and unalienable rights," these statutes had singled out a "weak and defenseless class of citizens—a class convicted of no crime—no natural inferiority," and had invidiously demanded their exclusion from "the rights and privileges of citizenship." This, it was argued, the Constitution forbade. "Our Constitution does not say, *All men* of a *certain color* are entitled to certain rights, and are born free and independent.... The expression is unlimited.... *All* men are so born, and have the *unalienable* rights of life and liberty—the pursuit of happiness, and the acquisition and possession of wealth."

These were the doctrinal cornerstones.[20] They were the heart of the ethico-moral-

---

apparently written by Judge William Jay, reprinted in his MISCELLANEOUS WORKS 371–395 (1853).

[16] Crandall v. State, 10 Conn. 339 (1834).

[17] REPORT OF THE ARGUMENTS OF COUNSEL IN THE CASE OF PRUDENCE CRANDALL, PLFF. IN ERROR, VS. STATE OF CONNECTICUT, BEFORE THE SUPREME COURT OF ERRORS, AT THEIR SESSION AT BROOKLYN, JULY TERM, 1834. The arguments are printed in condensed form in the official report, Crandall v. State, *supra* note 16, at 349–353 (1834). See also JAY, MISCELLANEOUS WRITINGS ON SLAVERY 34–51 (1853); STIENER, HISTORY OF SLAVERY IN CONN. 45–52 (1893); VON HOLST, CONSTITUTIONAL HISTORY 1828–1846 98, 99 (1881); McCarron, *Trial of Prudence Crandall*, 12 CONN. MAG. 225–232 (1908); NYE, *op. cit. supra* note 9, at 83.

[18] Reprinted in JAY, MISCELLANEOUS WRITINGS ON SLAVERY 36 (1853).

[19] PROCEEDINGS OF THE OHIO ANTI-SLAVERY CONVENTION HELD AT PUTNAM 17–36 (April 22–24, 1835).

[20] It is not implied that these arguments were without antecedents. Earlier (1819–21) in the controversy over Missouri's admission, the provision in its Constitution prohibiting immigration of free Negroes prompted antislavery arguments based on the republican form of government and comity clauses. See BURGESS, THE MIDDLE PERIOD, 1817–58 c. 4 (1897); McLAUGHLIN, CONSTITUTIONAL HISTORY OF THE UNITED STATES c. 29 (1935); WILSON, RISE AND FALL OF THE SLAVE POWER cc. 11–12 (1872), especially at 154.

Later, the Horton episode, and the protracted controversy over southern seamen's laws whereunder northern and British free Negro seamen were confined to quarters or jailed while in southern ports, gave further impetus to theories of *national* or *American* citizenship. The former was a *cause célèbre* of 1826–1827 involving a statute of the District of Columbia which authorized sale for jail fees of *suspected* fugitive slaves. Horton, a free Negro of New York, who had been arrested and threatened with sale, historical-natural rights argument which the American Anti-Slavery Society broadcast in the mid- and late-'thirties. They were broadcast particularly throughout Ohio, western New York and Pennsylvania, Rhode Island, and Massachusetts.[21] Weld was the director and master strategist; Birney, the forensic quartermaster and attorney general. The "Twelve" and the "Seventy" were the chosen instruments. These were the two dedicated hand-picked groups of trained teachers, ministers, divinity students, self-named after the early Christian Apostles. Their revivals converted thousands before funds ran out and southern antagonism crippled the movement. Numerous anti-slavery newspapers and coordinated pamphlet and petition campaigns were reinforcing media.

The trouble, of course, was that northerners were still largely indifferent to or unreached by this program, while the South rejected it almost without a hearing. Coincidence played a great part here. Alarmed lest educated Negroes foment slave insurrections, the South further tightened its controls.[22] Fortuitously, the Vesey and Turner uprisings had seemed to offer frightening confirmation of fears in this regard. Meanwhile, cotton profits and politics had begun to rationalize slavery as "a positive good." The insidious belief spread that the South must insulate herself, safeguard her "peculiar institutions," and remove them even from discussion and criticism.[23] In the Pinckney Report of 1836,[24] pro-slave theorists sought to implement these convictions. To reinforce Calhoun's defensive doctrines of concurrent majority and state interposition, and in a determined attempt to protect slavery in the Federal District from possible interference or abolition by Congress under its sweeping powers over the District and territories, Pinckney and his colleagues in the House employed the due process clause of the Fifth Amendment and "the principles of natural justice and of the social compact."[25]

### 3. The political action campaign

**A. Systemization** Thus, the antislavery campaign was set back, its piecemeal conversion and demonstration program was frustrated at the outset by barriers that held slavery to be a positive good—untouchable even where Congress had full powers over it. Antislavery men were denied the use of the mails. Their antislavery petitions were throttled by Congressional "gags". They were forced to defend even their own rights to speak and write and proselytize. In consequence, the antislavery leaders had to reorient their whole movement and strategy.[26]

This reorientation, greatly accelerated by the Pinckney Report, was marked by rapid "constitutionalization" of the higher law argument. There was a shift from an overwhelming faith in moral suasion to a reluctant resort to political action, from efforts to convince Americans of the expediency and justice of freeing their slaves, to a search for constitutional power to free them.[27]

These tendencies may be traced today in the pages of the *Weld-Grimke* and *Birney Letters*, in a vast pamphlet literature, in annual reports of the state and national societies,[28] but most

---

was saved by timely aid of Abolitionist friends who capitalized the incident. See JAY, MISCELLANEOUS WRITINGS ON SLAVERY 48, 238–242 (1853); TUCKERMAN, WILLIAM JAY AND THE CONSTITUTIONAL MOVEMENT FOR ABOLITION OF SLAVERY 31–33 (1893); 3 CONG. DEB. 555 (1826). Regarding the seamen's controversy, see Hamer, *Great Britain, the United States and the Negro Seamen Acts, 1822–1848*, 1 J. OF SO. HIST. 1–28 (1935); H. R. REP. No. 80, 27th Cong., 3rd Sess. (1843).

Later, in 1844, the Hoar incident occurred, in which Judge Samuel Hoar of Massachusetts, proceeding to Charleston to defend imprisoned Negro seamen, was expelled from South Carolina by legislative resolution. See Hamer, *supra*, and the elaborate documentation in STATE DOCUMENTS ON FEDERAL RELATIONS: THE STATES AND THE UNITED STATES 237–238 (Ames ed. 1904).

The Hoar expulsion and the numerous laws, both North and South, excluding free Negroes and mulattoes, were cited repeatedly in the debates of the 'fifties and in 1866. See, for example, CONG. GLOBE, 39th Cong., 1st Sess. 475 (1866) (Remarks of Sen. Trumbull).

[21] See especially BARNES, *op. cit. supra* note 10, cc. 2, 3, 4, and WELD-GRIMKE LETTERS and BIRNEY LETTERS, *op. cit. supra* notes 10, 11.

[22] See EATON, FREEDOM OF THOUGHT IN THE OLD SOUTH c. 5 (1940) and statutes there cited; SYDNOR, DEVELOPMENT OF SOUTHERN SECTIONALISM 1819–1848 (1948).

[23] See JENKINS, PROSLAVERY THOUGHT IN THE OLD SOUTH (1935); and the histories of Eaton and Sydnor, *op. cit. supra* note 22; and WILTSIE, JOHN C. CALHOUN, NULLIFIER, 1828–1839 c. 20, esp. 283–286 (1949); *cf.* Corwin,

---

*National Power and State Interposition, 1787–1861*, 10 MICH. L. REV. 535 (1912).

[24] H. R. REP. No. 691, 24th Cong., 1st Sess. (1836).

[25] *Id.* at 14.

[26] DUMOND, THE ANTISLAVERY ORIGINS OF THE CIVIL WAR (1938); NYE, *op. cit. supra* note 9.

[27] DUMOND, *op. cit. supra* note 26, especially cc. 5–6; T. C. SMITH, THE LIBERTY AND FREE SOIL PARTIES IN THE NORTHWEST (1897); NYE, *op. cit. supra* note 9. *Cf.* CRAVEN, THE COMING OF THE CIVIL WAR (1943); NEVINS, ORDEAL OF THE UNION (1947).

[28] Read straight through, the six ANNUAL PROC. AND REP. OF AMERICAN ANTISLAVERY SOCIETY (1833–1839) and the five ANNIVERSARY PROC. OF THE OHIO ANTISLAVERY SOCIETY (1836–1840) reveal the shift from confident evangelism to determined self-defense and political action. Not until after the Pinckney Report (*supra* note 24), the "Gags" denying antislavery petitions, and the refusal of the South to countenance discussion of the issue, does one find serious interest in political movements and tactics. The THIRD ANNUAL REPORT OF THE A. A. S. S. (May 10, 1836) signed by Elizur Wright is thus the turning point and a catalog of the factors that had reoriented opinion. By the SIXTH ANNUAL REPORT OF THE A. A. S. S. (1839), the "imperative necessity of political action" caused

satisfactorily in the columns of Birney's *Philanthropist*.[29] Calhoun and "positive good" theorists had fashioned a constitutional system that promised absolute protection for slavery and ignored the constitutional reference to slaves as "persons," referring to them whenever possible as "property." These theorists also employed the "compact" and "compromises" of 1787 as a device that removed slavery from the reach not merely of state and federal legislatures but from adverse discussion and criticism.

Birney and his colleagues now formulated a countersystem, one which exalted liberty and exploited the founding fathers' use of "persons." Denying all limiting force to the "compact" or "compromises," this group hailed the spirit of the Declaration, of the Constitution, and American institutions generally. They seized on the leading provisions of the state and federal bills of rights as affirmative guarantees of the freedom of the slaves.[30]

In his earlier writings,[31] Birney's ethical interpretation of American origins and history was essentially that of the *Crandall* argument and the Ohio Anti-Slavery Society reports. The natural rights creed of the Declaration, the universality of guarantees of the state bills of rights, the Signers' and the Fathers' known aversion to slavery, the "color blindness" of the Articles of Confederation, the outright prohibition of slavery in the territories by the Northwest Ordinance, and above all, the silence, the euphemisms, the circumlocutions of the Constitution—these were the recurrent and expanding points. Not merely slavery, but *all public race discrimination* was ethically and morally wrong. It was so because it was a denial of the rights and protections that governments were established to secure.

After the Pinckney Report, however, and especially after the growing mob action against Abolitionists began to make it clear that state bills of rights were not self-executing but rested on local enforcement, Birney reexamined his position. Everywhere there was this anomaly:

the great natural and fundamental rights of conscience, inquiry and communication, secured *on paper* in every constitution, nevertheless were denied and abridged daily for want of sanctions. All men by nature "possessed" these indispensable rights; all constitutions "declared" and "secured" them. It was the bounden duty of all governments "created for the purposes of protection" to safeguard and enforce them. Yet the hard fact was that state and local governments were flagrantly, increasingly derelict. Nothing, southerners argued, could be done about it.

Challenged in this manner, Birney and his aides shifted their ground. They advanced from the old position that the Federal Constitution was neutral—"or at least not pro-slavery"—to the stand that the document was antislavery. Constitutionalization of the natural rights argument proceeded at a much more rapid pace. No longer was the fight waged merely defensively in behalf of the right to proselytize, or counter-defensively to support sweeping Federal powers over the District and territories; more and more the antislavery forces took the offensive against slavery itself.[32]

Thus, by December 1836, the Abolitionists' argument was recrystallizing around three major propositions:

*First*, the great natural and fundamental rights of life, liberty, and property, long deemed inherent and inalienable, were now held to be secured by *both* state and national constitutions.

*Second*, notwithstanding this double security, and in disregard of the obligation of governments to extend protection in return for allegiance, these rights were being violated with impunity both on national soil and in the states, (a) by the fact of slavery itself, (b) by mob action directed against those working for abolition, (c) by flagrant discriminations against free Negroes and mulattoes.

*Third*, race and color—"grades and shades"—whenever and wherever employed as criteria and determinants of fundamental rights, violated both the letter and spirit of American institutions; race *per se* was not only an ignoble standard; it was an irrational and unsubstantial one.

The problems of implementing this theory, Birney worked out in several series of articles during 1837. Rescrutinizing the document, he began to make the same rigorous use of the Federal Bill of Rights that previously he and others had made of Ohio's. Ultimately, he

---

Wright to devote much of his space to convincing the still hesitant and divided membership.

[29] Birney's career as an editor can be followed in the BIRNEY LETTERS, *op. cit. supra* note 11 (see index entries "Philanthropist"), and in his pamphlet NARRATIVE OF THE LATE RIOTOUS PROCEEDINGS AGAINST THE LIBERTY OF THE PRESS IN CINCINNATI (1836).

[30] Sometimes Abolitionists, in desperation, appealed to a higher law beyond the Constitution, but this was not a consistent argument or one possible within the legal framework.

[31] BIRNEY LETTERS, *op. cit. supra* note 11. For a fuller and documented summary, see Graham, *Early Antislavery Backgrounds, supra* note 1, at 638–650.

[32] See Graham, *Early Antislavery Backgrounds, supra* note 1, at 650–653.

focused on the due process clause employed in Pinckney's Report:[33]

"The Constitution contains provisions which, if literally carried out, would extinguish the entire system of slavery. It guarantees to every state in the union a republican form of government, Art. IV, Sec. 4th. A majority of the people of South Carolina are slaves; can she be said properly to have a republican form of government? It says, that 'the right of the people to be secure in their *persons*, houses, papers and effects . . . against unreasonable searches and *seizures*, shall not be violated.' Slaves, Sir, are men, constitute a portion of the people: Is that no 'unreasonable seizure,' by which the man is deprived of all his earnings [effects?]—by which in fact he is robbed of his own person? Is the perpetual privation of liberty 'no unreasonable seizure'? Suppose this provision of the Constitution were literally and universally enforced; how long would it be before there would not be a single *slave* to mar the prospect of American liberty? Again, '*no* person shall be held to answer for a capital or otherwise infamous crime unless on the presentment or indictment of a grand jury, except in cases arising in the land or naval forces, [sic] nor shall any person be compelled in any case to witness against himself; nor be deprived of life, liberty or property without due process of law.' Art. V Amendments.

"Are slaves ever honored with indictment by a grand jury? Are they never compelled 'to witness against themselves'? never tortured until they lie against their own lives? never deprived of life without 'due process of law'? By what 'due process of law' is it, that two millions of 'persons' are deprived every year of the millions of dollars produced by their labor? By what due process of law is it that 56,000 'persons,' the annual increase of the slave population, are annually deprived of their 'liberty'? Such questions may seem impertinent, to Mr. L., but when he shall feel that the slave is a 'person,' in very deed, and has rights, as inalienable as his own, he will acknowledge their propriety. Again 'In all criminal prosecutions, the accused shall enjoy the right to a speedy and public trial, by an impartial jury . . . and to be informed of the nature and cause of the accusation; to be confronted with the witnesses against him; to have compulsory process for obtaining witnesses in his favor; and to have the assistance of Counsel for his defense.' Art. VI of the Amendments. Take all the above provisions in connection with that clause under Art. VI, which declares that 'This Constitution and the laws of the United States which shall be made in pursuance thereof' etc., 'shall be the supreme law of the land, and the judges in every state shall be bound thereby, anything in the Constitution or laws of any state to the contrary notwithstanding'—and then carry

them out to their full extent, and how long would it be ere slavery would be utterly prostrated? I do not say they were inserted with a specific view toward this end, but I do say, that so long as they shall stand, the Constitution of these U[nited] States will be a perpetual rebuke to the selfishness and injustice of the whole policy of the slaveholder. The provisions embody principles which are at entire enmity with the spirit and practice of slavery. How an instrument, containing such principles, can be tortured to express a *sanction* to slavery, I am yet to learn."[34]

Reassimilation of the old theory into the Bill of Rights now proceeded rapidly.[35] The various clauses restraining the powers of Congress began to be popularly regarded as *sources* of Congressional power. The initial premise in this regard was that the provisions of the Bill of Rights were not *rights*, they were *guarantees*, and guarantees customarily presumed the intent and capacity, as well as the duty, to make them good.[36] An open letter[37] to his Congressman from an unnamed Abolitionist in Batavia[38] reveals the hold and spread and reach of these ideas:

"The very Constitution of the United States is attempted to be distorted and made an ally of domestic slavery. That Constitution was established, not by the *citizens* or *voters*, but by '*the people*' of the United States to secure the blessings of *liberty* and establish *justice*. The Union . . . was formed for the same great purposes, . . . yet we have been told that petitioning for *liberty* endangers this Union, that the partnership will be dissolved by extending to all the very right it was intended to secure.

"Slavery in the District of Columbia violates the most important and sacred principles of the Constitution. . . . I speak not of the mere *letter*, but of the *principles* . . . —of the *rights* it guarantees, of the *form*, in which the guarantee is expressed. The 5th Amendment declares 'no person shall be deprived of life, *liberty* or property without due process of law.' This petition informs you free men in the District . . . have been first imprisoned, and then sold for their jail fees. [Suppose, he continued, this had happened to American seamen in a foreign port.] Would not Con-

---

[33] Philanthropist, Jan. 13, 1837, p. 2. Birney continued his "Reply to Judge L" in the Jan. 20 and 27, 1837 numbers, and in the former demonstrated his forensic powers by brilliant caricature of the South's efforts to suppress discussion of slavery.

[34] *Ibid.*

[35] Resolutions and petitions still were the chief media in evolving this system of constitutional shorthand. Similarity of the revivalists' lectures from place to place, their widespread circulation of the Philanthropist and printed tracts, Birney's own speaking tours, all contributed to resulting stereotypes.

[36] For a striking statement of this theory in 1866 see Cong. Globe, 39th Cong., 1st Sess. 1270 (Rep. Thayer, later a distinguished Philadelphia judge).

[37] Graham, *Early Antislavery Backgrounds, supra* note 1, at 655.

[38] Perhaps John Joliffe, a local antislavery lawyer, who was a close friend of Birney. See Graham, *Early Antislavery Backgrounds, supra* note 1, at 655, n. 256.

gress upon petition enquire into the fact and redress the wrong if it existed? Would not you, Sir, be one of the foremost in repelling the insult to our seamen and punishing the aggressor? Would you not consider it your *duty*—your *official* duty to do so? And yet you have no power to discriminate in the object of your protection—a colored sailor is entitled to the *protection* of his country's laws, and Constitution, and flag, and honor, as well as a white one,—he is as much entitled to that protection in Washington city beneath the flag of his country and while he reposes under the tower of the Capitol as he is at *Qualla Balloo* or Halifax, or anywhere on the face of the earth. And all should be protected with equal and exact justice, whether sailors or laborers—citizens or soldiers: if so, you are bound to enquire into the alleged abuses, and if they exist to redress them."

Thus, by October, 1837, the date of Birney's retirement as editor of the Philanthropist, the motivating premise of Abolitionism already was coming to be this: Americans' basic civil rights were truly national, but in practice their basic civil liberty was not. By acts in support and in toleration of slavery and by failure to protect the friends of the enslaved race, the states and the federal government all abridged, and all allowed to be abridged, the dearest privileges and immunities of citizenship. Humanitarianism had attempted to soften race prejudice and meet this challenge squarely but had been frustrated. Failure left no alternative but political action and the instinctive answer that government had the power to do what the governed had the job to do. The answer to denied power and to defective power was the concept of an inherent power derived from the standing duty to protect. The gist of it was that because allegiance and protection were reciprocal—i.e., ought to be reciprocal—because the government protected its citizens abroad without discrimination, and because the text of the Federal Bill of Rights gave no warrant for discrimination, Congress was duty bound *not* to discriminate. It must do "equal and exact justice" irrespective of race. It had no other choice. It lacked power to discriminate between those persons who were equally entitled to protection. It was duty bound also to remove such discrimination as existed. Implicitly, and morally, these same obligations rested on the states; yet respect for the constitutional division of power here introduced conflict. Few were yet ready for the extreme proposition that Congress might *constitutionally* abolish slavery *in the states*. The original form, as shown by the Batavian communication, was more often that Congress was duty bound to hear petitions to abolish slavery, or that slavery had been abol-

ished in federal territory by the force of the Preamble and Declaration. Because the great natural rights were now also national constitutional rights, they began to generate and carry with them—*even into the states*—the power for their enforcement.

**B. Popularization**    Four routes and media of political action "constitutionalizing" the antislavery argument are to be noted.

First were the countless petitions, resolutions, declarations, letters, editorials, speeches, and sermons broadcast by the original antislavery proponents and converts—uniformly men and women of influence and position whose idealism was extraordinary and undoubted. One has to read only the *Weld-Grimke* and the *Birney*[39] *Letters*, or the monographs of Barnes,[40] Dumond[41] and Nye[42]—and Nevins' great history[43]—to realize the appeal of these peoples' character and of their example and argument. Moreover, many of them were southerners, and of the proudest type who practiced what they preached—Birney alone freeing slaves to the value of thousands of dollars,[44] and the Grimke sisters doing likewise with those they inherited. Every antislavery society was a band of disciples, workers, petitioners, writers, and "free moral agents" committed to the spread of doctrine that had immense intrinsic appeal.

In consequence, simply as an incident of the intense revival campaigns, the equal protection-due process-privileges and immunities theory became the core of thousands of abolitionist petitions, resolutions, and lectures. Now one,

---

[39] The legal and constitutional argument in the BIRNEY LETTERS is remarkable both in range and interest. Note especially the due process arguments at 293, 647, 805–806, 835; the declaration that colored people are "citizens" at 815, and "persons" at 658 and 835; the exceptionally strong references to "natural equality of men" at 272; the composite synthesis of all these elements in the Declaration of 1848 drafted by William Goodell at 1048–1057; the various references to major law cases at 386–387 (Nancy Jackson v. Bulloch, 12 Conn. 38 (1837)), at page 658, 667–670 (Birney's arguments in The Creole, 2 Moore, Digest of International Law 358–361 (1906), for which Weld did much of the research), at 758 (Jones v. Van Zandt, 46 U.S. 215 (1846) in which Salmon P. Chase was of counsel). By contrast, the legal argument in the WELD-GRIMKE LETTERS is more limited, but see page 798 for the letter of Ebenezer Chaplin, an Athol, Massachusetts physician, to Weld, dated October 1, 1839, urging greater emphasis on the unconstitutionality of slavery and less on its cruelties, and specifically mentioning the Declaration of Independence, the common law, the Ordinance of 1787, the Preamble, and the due process clause of the Fifth Amendment.

[40] *Op. cit. supra* note 10.

[41] *Op. cit. supra* note 26.

[42] *Op. cit. supra* note 9.

[43] THE ORDEAL OF THE UNION, 2 vols. (1947).

[44] 1 BIRNEY LETTERS, *op. cit. supra* note 11, at 52, 494, 498, 500–501.

now another of the elements was accented, depending on the need and circumstances, but in an astonishing number of cases two or three parts of the trilogy were used. The whole thus became, even before 1840, a form of popular constitutional shorthand.

After that date even stronger forces enter the picture. First, were the compilers and synthesizers—pamphleteers and journalists like Tiffany[45] and Goodell[46] and Mellen[47] who wrote the articles and treatises on the "Unconstitutionality of Slavery" which Dr. tenBroek analyzes so well.[48] Others annotated copies of *Our National Charters*[49] setting down after each clause or phrase of the Constitution and the Declaration (much as Birney had done in his early articles) antislavery arguments and doctrines gleaned "both from reason and authority." Such materials, broadcast by the thousand, reprinted, condensed and paraphrased, were themselves powerful disseminators.

It was the minority party platform that gave antislavery theory its most concise, effective statement. Drafted generally by Salmon P. Chase or Joshua R. Giddings, these documents, first of the Liberty and Free Soil parties in the 'forties, then of the Free Democracy and Republican parties in the 'fifties, and in 1860, all made use, in slightly varying combination, of the cardinal articles of faith: human equality, protection, and equal protection from the Declaration, and due process both as a restraint and a source of congressional power. Such consistent repetition testifies both to the nature and extent of previous distillations and to the power and significance of current ones:

**1.** Liberty Party Platform (adopted in 1843 for the 1844 campaign):

> "*Resolved*, That the fundamental truth of the Declaration of Independence, that all men are endowed by their Creator with certain unalienable rights, among which are life, liberty, and the pursuit of happiness, was made the fundamental law of our national government by that amendment of the Constitution which declares that no person shall be deprived of life, liberty, or property without due process of law."[50]

**2.** Free Soil Party Platform, 1848:

> "*Resolved*, That our fathers ordained the Constitution of the United States in order, among other great national objects, to establish justice, promote the general welfare, and secure the blessings of liberty, but expressly denied to the federal government, which they created, all constitutional power to deprive any person of life, liberty, or property without due legal process.
>
> "*Resolved*, that, in the judgment of this convention, Congress has no more power to make a slave than to make a king; no more power to institute or establish slavery than to institute or establish a monarchy. No such power can be found among those specifically conferred by the Constitution, or derived by any just implication from them."[51]

**3.** Free Democracy Platform, 1852:

> "1. That governments deriving their just powers from the consent of the governed are instituted among men to secure to all those unalienable rights of life, liberty, and the pursuit of happiness with which they are endowed by their Creator, and of which none can be deprived by valid legislation, except for crime.
>
> "4. That the Constitution of the United States, ordained to form a more perfect Union, to establish justice, and secure the blessings of liberty, expressly denies to the general government all power to deprive any person of life, liberty, or property without due process of law; and, therefore, the government, having no more power to make a slave than to make a king, and no more power to establish slavery than to establish a monarchy, should at once proceed to relieve itself from all responsibility for the existence of slavery wherever it possesses constitutional power to legislate for its extinction."[52]

**4.** Republican Party Platform, 1856:

> "*Resolved*, That with our republican fathers we hold it be a self-evident truth, that all men are endowed with the unalienable rights to life, liberty, and the pursuit of happiness, and that the primary object and ulterior designs of our federal government were to secure these rights to all persons within its exclusive jurisdiction; that, as our republican fathers, when they had abolished slavery in all our national territory,

---

[45] TIFFANY, A TREATISE ON THE UNCONSTITUTIONALITY OF AMERICAN SLAVERY (1849).

[46] GOODELL, VIEWS OF AMERICAN CONSTITUTIONAL LAW IN ITS BEARING UPON AMERICAN SLAVERY (1844).

[47] MELLEN, AN ARGUMENT ON THE UNCONSTITUTIONALITY OF SLAVERY . . . (1841).

[48] tenBROEK, ANTISLAVERY ORIGINS, *op. cit. supra* note 2, c. 3 and pp. 86–91.

[49] (Goodell ed. 1863).

[50] The full platform is in STANWOOD, HISTORY OF THE PRESIDENCY 216–220 (1904). In addition to the plank

quoted, it contains numerous references to "equality of the rights among men," "the principle of equal rights with all its practical consequences and applications," the "higher law" and "moral law," and the sacredness of rights of speech, press and petition.

[51] *Id.* at 240. This platform was drafted by Salmon P. Chase. See SMITH, THE LIBERTY AND FREE SOIL PARTIES IN THE NORTHWEST 140 (1897).

[52] STANWOOD, *op. cit. supra* note 50, 253–254. This platform was drafted by Salmon P. Chase (see WARDEN, LIFE OF CHASE 338 (1874)) and Joshua R. Giddings (see SMITH, *op. cit. supra* note 51, 247–248).

ordained that no person should be deprived of life, liberty, or property without due process of law, it becomes our duty to maintain this provision of the Constitution against all attempts to violate it for the purpose of establishing slavery in any Territory of the United States, by positive legislation prohibiting its existence or extension therein; that we deny the authority of Congress, of a territorial legislature, of any individual or association of individuals, to give legal existence to slavery in any Territory of the United States, while the present Constitution shall be maintained."[53]

## 5. Republican Party Platform, 1860:

"8. That the normal condition of all the territory of the United States is that of freedom; that as our republican fathers, when they had abolished slavery in all our national territory, ordained that no person should be deprived of life, liberty, or property without due process of law, it becomes our duty, by legislation whenever such legislation is necessary, to maintain this provision of the Constitution against all attempts to violate it; and we deny the authority of Congress, of a territorial legislature, or of any individual, to give legal existence to slavery in any Territory of the United States.

"14. That the Republican party is opposed to any change in our naturalization laws, or any state legislation by which the rights of citizenship hitherto accorded to immigrants from foreign lands shall be abridged or impaired; and in favor of giving a full and efficient protection to the rights of all classes of citizens, whether native or naturalized, both at home and abroad."[54]

True, these were party platforms, but these were the platforms of parties to which leaders in the Congress that would frame the Fourteenth Amendment had given their allegiance.[55]

Many Congressmen whose names later loomed large in the formulation of and debates on the Thirteenth and Fourteenth Amendments and the Civil Rights Acts were men of anti-slavery backgrounds[56] which, it will be recalled, had sought out community leaders,

particularly lawyers.[57] Even in the 'forties, antislavery Whigs, Liberty Party-Free Soilers, and later, members of the Free Democracy, converted by the Weld-Birney group, began to enter Congressmen like Joshua R. Giddings,[58] E. S. Hamlin,[59] the Wade brothers,[60] Horace Mann,[61] Philomen Bliss,[62] A. P. Granger,[63] Thaddeus Stevens,[64] Gerrit Smith,[65] William Lawrence,[66] James M. Ashley[67] (who introduced the Thirteenth Amendment in the House), Samuel Galloway[68] (a former member of the "Seventy") and John A. Bingham.[69] All were either associates,

---

[53] STANWOOD, op. cit. supra note 50, at 271. This platform was drafted by Joshua R. Giddings. JULIAN, THE LIFE OF JOSHUA R. GIDDINGS 335–336 (1892).

[54] STANWOOD, op. cit. supra note 50, at 293.

[55] See infra pp. 27–36, and notes 56–69.

[56] Among them the following members of the Joint Committee on Reconstruction: George H. Williams, Oregon; Henry W. Grimes, Iowa; William Pitt Fessenden, Maine; Henry T. Blow, Missouri; John A. Bingham, Ohio; George S. Boutwell, Massachusetts; Justin S. Morrill, Vermont; Roscoe Conkling, New York; Elihu B. Washburne, Illinois; and Thaddeus Stevens, Pennsylvania. Two others, Jacob M. Howard of Michigan and Ira Harris of New York, invariably voted with the so-called Radicals. See KENDRICK op. cit. supra note 2, at 155–195.

[57] Among Weld's converts were Reps. Edward Wade, and Philemon Bliss, and John H. Paine, Liberty Party leader. See 1 WELD-GRIMKE LETTERS, op. cit. supra note 10, at 236–240.

[58] 1795–1864; represented Ohio's Ashtabula and Jefferson Counties (Western Reserve) in House, 25th–34th Congresses, 1838–1859; with John Quincy Adams one of the original antislavery leaders in the House. 7 DICT. AM. BIOG. 260 (1931).

[59] 1808–1894; represented Lorain County district in 28th Cong. 1844–45; one of the political lieutenants of Salmon P. Chase in the 'fifties. See 2 BIRNEY LETTERS, op. cit. supra note 11, at 1025.

[60] Edward Wade, 1803–1862, elected as a Free Soiler from Cleveland, 1853–55, and as a Republican, 1855–61 Ben Wade, 1800–1878, law partner of Giddings, and Radical Senator, 1851–1869. See 2 BIRNEY LETTERS, op. cit. supra note 11, at 710. 19 DICT. AM. BIOG. 303 (1936).

[61] 1796–1859; one of the organizers of the American public school system; elected as a Whig to succeed J. Q. Adams, Mass. district; reelected as Free Soiler, served 1848–53; President, Antioch College, 1852–59. 12 DICT. AM. BIOG. 240 (1933).

[62] 1813–1889; Ohio Circuit Judge, 1848–51; elected as a Republican from Elyria-Oberlin district, Ohio, served 1855–59; Chief Justice of Dakota Territory, 1861; Assoc. Justice Missouri Supreme Court, 1868–72; Dean of Univ. of Missouri Law School, 1872–1889. 2 DICT. AM. BIOG. 374 (1929).

[63] 1789–1866; antislavery Whig from Syracuse, N.Y.; served 1855–59. BIOG. DIR. AM. CONG., H. R. DOC. NO. 607, 81st Cong., 2d Sess. 1229 (1950).

[64] 1792–1868; elected as a Whig from Lancaster, Pa. district, 1849–53; as a Republican, 1859–68; Radical Republican leader in the House. 17 DICT. AM. BIOG. 620 (1935).

[65] 1797–1874; elected from Peterboro, N.Y. district, one of the regions converted by Weld; served 1853–1854, resigned. 17 DICT. AM. BIOG. 270 (1935).

[66] 1819–1899; grad. Franklin College, New Athens, Ohio, 1838; Cincinnati Law School, 1840; Supreme Court Reporter, 1851; Judge, 1857–64; elected as a Republican, served 1865–71, 1873–77. 11 DICT. AM. BIOG. 52 (1933).

[67] 1824–1896; elected as a Republican from Scioto County, 1859–69. See 1 WELD-GRIMKE LETTERS, op. cit. supra note 10, at 333. 1 DICT. AM. BIOG. 389 (1928).

[68] 1811–1872, elected as a Republican from Columbus, 1855–57. See WELD-GRIMKE LETTERS, op. cit. supra note 10, at 228.

[69] For eight terms (1855–63, 1865–73) Bingham represented the 21st Ohio District, composed of Harrison, Jefferson, Carroll and Columbiana Counties, including the Quaker settlements along Short Creek and the Ohio. See 3 BRENNAN, BIOGRAPHICAL ENCYCLOPEDIA ... OF OHIO 691 (1884).

converts, or disciples of the Weld-Birney group; and after 1854, all were Republicans.

In addition to the western group of antislavery leaders, there was an equally strong and determined group with its focus in New England. From this group emerged Charles Sumner, Wendell Phillips, and Henry Wilson. Sumner later became one of the most intransigent leaders of the Republican party during and after the Civil War.[70] Wilson was also in Congress during the Reconstruction period; and became Vice-President and voted with the Radicals on important tie votes.[71] Other New Englanders who served in Congress, and were members of the Joint Committee on Reconstruction, include William Pitt Fessenden of Maine, Justin Morrill of Vermont, and George S. Boutwell of Massachusetts.[72]

Because Bingham is known to have drafted Sections One and Five of the Fourteenth Amendment, his speeches are of special interest. From 1855–63 and from 1865–73, he represented the Twenty-first Ohio District, which included the Cadiz-Mt. Pleasant Quaker settlements, antislavery strongholds. Furthermore, as a youth he had attended Franklin College at New Athens in 1837–38. At that date Franklin was second only to Oberlin as an antislavery stronghold;[73] the Weld-Birney crusade was at its height. Indeed, in Birney's Philanthropist, 1836–37, we find various antislavery petitions and resolutions from the Cadiz and Mt. Pleasant societies.[74] These are couched in the very phraseology for which Bingham in 1856–66 manifested his decisive preference.

Four of Bingham's speeches are of particular significance:

**I.** In his maiden speech in the House, March 6, 1856, attacking laws recently passed by the Kansas pro-slavery legislature which declared it a felony even to agitate against slavery, Bingham argued:

"These infamous statutes . . . [contravene] the Constitution of the United States. . . . [A]ny territorial enactment which makes it a felony for a citizen of the United States, within the territory of the United States 'to know, to

argue and to utter freely', according to conscience is absolutely void. . . . [A] felony to utter there, in the hearing of a slave, upon American soil, beneath the American flag . . . the words of the Declaration 'All men are born free and equal, and endowed by their Creator with the inalienable rights of life and liberty;' . . . [A] felony to utter . . . those other words. . . . 'We, the people of the United States, in order to establish justice,' the attribute of God, and 'to secure liberty,' the imperishable right of man, do 'ordain this Constitution'. . . . It is *too late* to make it a felony to utter the self-evident truth that life and liberty belong of right to every man. . . . This pretended legislation . . . violates the Constitution in this—that it abridges the freedom of speech and of the press, and deprives persons of liberty without due process of law, or any process but that of brute force, while the Constitution provides that Congress shall make no law abridging the freedom of speech or of the press; and it expressly prescribes that 'no person shall be deprived of life, liberty, or property without due process of law.'"[75]

**II.** On January 13, 1857, Bingham spoke in support of Congress' power over slavery in the territory and attacked President Buchanan's recent defense of the Kansas-Nebraska Act of 1854 repealing the Missouri Compromise. After a long analysis of the provisions of the Federal Bill of Rights, of the Northwest Ordinance, the enabling acts and constitutions of the states carved from the Ohio Territory—emphasizing especially the Federal due process clause and the "all men are born equally free and independent" clauses of the state constitution, he said:

"The Constitution is based upon EQUALITY of the human race. . . . A State formed under the Constitution and pursuant to its spirit, must rest upon this great principle of EQUALITY. Its primal object must be to protect each human being within its jurisdiction in the free and full enjoyment of his natural rights. . . .

"It must be apparent that the absolute equality of all, and the equal protection of each, are principles of our Constitution, which ought to be observed and enforced in the organization and admission of new States. The Constitution provides . . . that *no person* shall be deprived of life, liberty, or property, without due process of law. It makes no distinction either on account of complexion or birth—it secures these rights to all persons within its exclusive jurisdiction. This is equality. It pro-

---

[70] 18 DICT. AM. BIOG. 208 (1936).

[71] 20 DICT. AM. BIOG. 322 (1936).

[72] Fessenden was the son of General Samuel Fessenden, the leading Abolitionist of Maine, who was one of the national vice-presidents of the American Anti-Slavery Society, 6 DICT. AM. BIOG. 348 (1931); on Morrill, see 13 DICT. AM. BIOG. 198 (1934); on Boutwell, see 2 DICT. AM. BIOG. 489 (1929).

[73] See Graham, *Early Antislavery Backgrounds, op. cit. supra* note 1, at 624, n. 150.

[74] For an example see Philanthropist, Mar. 10, 1837, p. 3, col. 4.

[75] CONG. GLOBE, 34th Cong., 1st Sess. app. 124 (1856). Three other antislavery Republicans representing constituencies converted in the Weld-Birney crusade also used all the old rhetoric and theory including due process: Rep. Granger (N.Y.) *id.* at 295–296; Reps. Edward Wade (*id.* at 1076–1081) and Philemon Bliss (*id.* at 553–557), both Ohioans and among Weld's early converts. See also the speech of Rep. Schuyler Colfax (Ind.), *id.* at 644.

tects not only life and liberty, but also property, the product of labor. It contemplates that no man shall be wrongfully deprived of the fruit of his toil any more than of his life."[76]

**III.** On January 25, 1858, attacking "The Lecompton Conspiracy"—the proposed pro-slave constitution of Kansas declaring that only "All *freemen*, when they form a compact, are equal in rights,"—and absolutely barring free Negroes from the state, Bingham declared:

"The [Federal] Constitution ... declares upon its face that no person, whether white or black, shall be deprived of life, liberty, or property, but by due process of law; and that it was ordained by the people to establish justice! ... [By sanctioning these provisions] we are asked to say, that the self-evident truth of the Declaration, 'that ALL MEN ARE CREATED EQUAL' is a self-evident lie.... We are to say ... to certain human beings in the Territory of Kansas, though you were born in this Territory, and born of free parents, though you are human beings, and no chattel, yet you are not free to live here ...; you must be disseized of your freehold liberties and privileges, without the judgment of your peers and without the protection of law. Though born here, you shall not, under any circumstances, be permitted to live here."[77]

**IV.** On February 11, 1859, Bingham attacked the admission of Oregon because its constitution forbade immigration of free Negroes and contained other discriminations against them:

"[T]his constitution ... is repugnant to the Federal Constitution, and violative of the *rights of citizens of the United States*....

"Who *are citizens of the United States?* They are those, and those only, who owe allegiance to the Government of the United States; not the base allegiance imposed upon the Saxon by the Conqueror ...; but the allegiance which requires the citizen not only to obey, but to support and defend, if need be with his life, the Constitution of his country. All free persons born and domiciled within the jurisdiction of the United States; all aliens by act of naturalization, under the laws of the United States."

"The people of the several States", who according to the Constitution are to choose the representatives in Congress, and to whom political powers were reserved by the Tenth Amendment, were to Bingham "the same community, or body politic, called by the Preamble ... 'the people of the United States' ". Moreover, certain "distinctive political rights"—for

example the right to choose representatives and officers of the United States, to hold such offices, etc.—were conferred only on "citizens of the United States."

"... I invite attention to the significant fact that natural or inherent rights, which belong to all men irrespective of all conventional regulations, are by this Constitution guaranteed by the broad and comprehensive word 'person,' as contradistinguished from the limited term citizen—as in the fifth article of amendments, guarding those *sacred rights* which *are* as *universal and indestructible* as the human race, that 'no person shall be deprived of life, liberty, or property, but by due process of law, nor shall private property be taken without just compensation.' And this guarantee *applies* to all citizens within the United States."

Against infringement of "these wise and beneficent guarantees of political rights to the citizens of the United States as such, and of natural rights to all persons, whether citizens or strangers," stood the supremacy clause.

"There, sir, is the limitation upon State sovereignty—simple, clear, and strong. No State may *rightfully*, by Constitution or statute law, impair any of these guarantied rights, either political or natural. They may not *rightfully or lawfully* declare that the strong citizens may deprive the weak citizens of their rights, natural or political....

"... This provision [excluding free Negroes and mulattoes] seems to me ... injustice and oppression incarnate. This provision, sir, excludes from the State of Oregon eight hundred thousand of the native-born citizens of the other States, who are, therefore, *citizens of the United States*. I grant you that a State may restrict the exercise of the elective franchise to certain classes of citizens of the United States, to the exclusion of others; but I deny that any State may exclude a law abiding citizen of the United States from coming within its territory, or abiding therein, or acquiring and enjoying property therein, or from the enjoyment therein of the 'privileges and immunities' of *a citizen of the United States*. What says the Constitution:

" 'The citizens of each State shall be entitled to all privileges and immunities of citizens in the several States.
Art. 4, Section 2.'

"Here is no qualification.... The citizens of each State, all the citizens of each State, *being citizens of the United States*, shall be entitled to 'all privileges and immunities of citizens of the several States.' Not to the rights and immunities of the several States; not to those constitutional rights and immunities which result exclusively from State authority or State legislation; but to 'all privileges and immunities' of citizens of the United States in the several

---

[76] CONG. GLOBE, 34th Cong., 3rd Sess. app. 135–140 (1857).

[77] CONG. GLOBE, 35th Cong., 1st Sess. 402 (1858).

States. *There is an ellipsis in the language employed in the Constitution, but its meaning is self-evident that it is 'the privileges and immunities of citizens of the* United States . . .' *that it guarantees. . . .*

". . .[S]ir, I maintain that the persons thus excluded from the State by this section of the Oregon Constitution, are citizens by birth of the several States, and therefore *are citizens of the United States,* and as such are entitled to all the privileges and immunities of citizens of the United States, amongst which *are* the rights of life and liberty and property, and their due protection in the enjoyment thereof by law; . . . .

"Who, sir, are citizens of the United States? First, all free persons born and domiciled within the United States—not all free white persons, but all free persons. You will search in vain, in the Constitution of the United States, for that word *white*; it is not there. You will look in vain for it in that first form of national Government—the Articles of Confederation; it is not there. The omission of this word—this phrase of caste—from our national charter, was not accidental, but intentional. . . .

". . . This Government rests upon the absolute equality of natural rights amongst men. . . .

". . . Who . . . will be bold enough to deny that all persons are equally entitled to the enjoyment of the rights of life and liberty and property; and that no one should be deprived of life or liberty, but as punishment for crime; nor of his property, against his consent and without due compensation? . . .

"*The equality of all* to the right to live; *to the right to know*; to argue and to utter, according to conscience; to work and enjoy the product of their toil, is the rock on which that Constitution rests—. . . . The charm of that Constitution lies in the great democratic idea which it embodies, that *all men, before the law, are equal in respect of those rights of person which God gives* and *no man or State may rightfully take away*, except as a forfeiture for crime. Before your Constitution, sir, *as it is*, as I trust it ever will be, all men are sacred, whether white or black. . . ."[78]

Several points must here be emphasized. It will be noted that Bingham disavows the color line as a basis for citizenship of the United States; that he regards Milton's rights of com-

munication and conscience, including the *right to know*, to *education*, as one of the great fundamental natural "rights of person which God gives and no man or *state* may *rightfully* take away," and which hence are "embodied" also within, and secured by, "the great democratic idea that all men before the law are equal." In short, the concept and guarantee of the equal protection of the laws is already "embodied" in the Federal Constitution as of 1859; this same concept, moreover, embraces "*the equality of all . . . to the right to know*"; and above all, there is no color line in the Constitution, even of 1859.

## Conclusions

From this consideration of the historical background against which the Fourteenth Amendment was written, submitted by Congress, and ratified by the requisite number of states, these important facts develop:

**1.** To the opponents of slavery, equality was an absolute, not a relative, concept which comprehended that no legal recognition be given to racial distinctions of any kind. Their theories were formulated with reference to the free Negro as well as to slavery—that great reservoir of prejudice and evil that fed the whole system of racial distinctions and caste. The notion that any state could impose such distinctions was totally incompatible with antislavery doctrine.

**2.** These proponents of absolute equalitarianism emerged victorious in the Civil War and controlled the Congress that wrote the Fourteenth Amendment. Ten of the fifteen members of the Joint Committee on Reconstruction were men who had antislavery backgrounds.

**3.** The phrases—"privileges and immunities," "equal protection," and "due process"—that were to appear in the Amendment had come to have specific significance to opponents of slavery. Proponents of slavery, even as they disagreed, knew and understood what that significance was. Members of the Congress that formulated and submitted the Amendment shared that knowledge and understanding. When they translated the antislavery concepts into constitutional provisions, they employed these by now traditional phrases that had become freighted with equalitarian meaning in its widest sense.

---

[78] CONG. GLOBE, 35th Cong., 2nd Sess. 981–985 (1859) (emphasis added throughout).

# In the
# Supreme Court of the United States
## October Term, 1953

### No. 1

**Oliver Brown, et al.,** Appellants

VS.

**Board of Education of Topeka, Shawnee County, Kansas, et al.,** Appellees

### Appeal from the United States District Court for the District of Kansas

# Brief for the Board of Education, Topeka, Kansas, on Questions Propounded by the Court

Peter F. Caldwell,
Counsel for the Board of Education of
Topeka, Kansas,
512 Capitol Federal Building,
Topeka, Kansas.

# INDEX

IN THE
SUPREME COURT OF THE
UNITED STATES
NO. 1, OCTOBER TERM,
1953

OLIVER BROWN, ET AL., APPELLANTS
VS.
BOARD OF EDUCATION OF TOPEKA,
SHAWNEE COUNTY, KANSAS, ET AL.,
APPELLEES

## BRIEF FOR THE BOARD OF EDUCATION, TOPEKA, KANSAS, ON QUESTIONS PROPOUNDED BY THE COURT

### I. STATEMENT

This brief is filed in response to the order of the Court, entered June 8, 1953, propounding five questions on which briefs were requested. Since the date of that order the Topeka Board of Education on September 3, 1953, duly adopted the following resolution:

> "Be it resolved that it is the policy of the Topeka Board of Education to terminate maintenance of segregation in the elementary schools as rapidly as is practicable.";

and on September 8, 1953, it passed a motion, ". . . that segregation be terminate in the Southwest and Randolph Schools this year . . .". Prior to the adoption of said resolution the Board of Education maintained twenty separate elementary schools for white children, each of which schools was attended by white children residing within a limited geographic area or boundaries near the school, and it also maintained four separate schools for negro children with large area or district boundaries. Negro students living some distance from school were furnished transportation to and from school if they requested it.

Since September 8, 1953, negro children living within the area boundaries of the Southwest School and the Randolph School are assigned to and are attending those schools along with and equally with white children. The Board is still maintaining the four separate negro schools and eighteen separate white schools.

By reason of its having resolved to terminate segregation in the elementary schools of To-

peka "as rapidly as is practicable," the Topeka Board of Education no longer has an actual interest in the controversy over the constitutionality of segregation in such schools, and it therefore prefers to refrain from arguing and briefing Questions 1, 2, and 3 as propounded by the Court, which are directed to the constitutional questions involved.

The Board of Education of Topeka is, however, actually and directly interested in Questions 4 and 5 as propounded by the Court. Briefly summarized, we contend;

*First*,  That termination of segregation in the elementary schools of Topeka will involve difficult and far reaching administrative decisions, affecting nearly all school children, nearly all teachers, and nearly all school buildings, so that to attempt to accomplish it in a hurried or summary manner will be both impossible and impractical.

*Second*,  The public interest, including the interest of negro children in Topeka, equity, and practical considerations require that termination of segregation in the elementary schools of Topeka shall be permitted to be accomplished in a gradual and orderly manner.

### II. QUESTION 4(a) SHOULD BE ANSWERED IN THE NEGATIVE: AND QUESTION 4(b) IN THE AFFIRMATIVE

Both Questions 4(a) and 4(b) contemplate the possibility that this Court might issue a broad, general order requiring abolition of segregation in the elementary schools of Topeka, rather than a limited order relating to the rights of the few particular negro children who are parties to this suit.

Such a general order would necessitate almost a complete readjustment of the elementary school system as now maintained in Topeka, so far as fixing attendance areas and boundaries for all the elementary school buildings in Topeka; it would require the transfer of many white and negro children from the schools they now attend to other buildings, as well as the transfer and assignment of many teachers to serve the resulting new classes in the various buildings.

Many of the grade schools now used for white children in the city are already full, and some are badly overcrowded. A school building program has been carried on and is being carried on now. The Southwest School was completed and opened in 1952; two other new schools are under construction now, and the Board is deciding on new sites for still two more schools to be constructed as quickly as possible. All five of these new buildings are, or will be, in areas where there have been new housing projects, and where the school population is now and probably will remain predominantly white children. These schools will probably not serve many negro children even when segregation is finally abolished.

The majority of the negro school population resides in a few scattered areas throughout the older parts of the city, and is not evenly distributed throughout the entire city. Many negro children live nearest to white schools which are already overcrowded. To transfer and admit these negro children to the schools nearest their residences will require either that many white children now attending such schools will have to be transferred to other schools, or that annexes will have to be provided. In short we have little doubt that the area boundaries of the existing white and negro schools will have to be redefined. This will necessarily require reassigning students, both white and negro, to schools which they do not now attend, and this in turn will require changing the classes to fit the new children in, and may involve transferring teachers from building to building as well.

It is the plan of the Board of Education of Topeka to make the transition from segregated to integrated elementary schools gradually and in an orderly manner on a school by school basis, but as rapidly as is practically possible. Such changes will be made at convenient times between semesters, and in such a manner that the administrative decisions and changes can be conveniently and efficiently handled without interrupting the continuity of the regular school program. The Board has discussed its policy and plans in open, public meetings attended by members of both white and negro races. It has invited and secured cooperation and suggestions, and the public generally in the community is assisting the Board in achieving its objective of terminating segregation "as rapidly as is practicable."

If this Court should enter an order to abolish segregation in the public schools of Topeka "forthwith," as suggested in Question 4(a), the Topeka Board would, of course, do its best to comply with the order. We believe, however, that it would probably require that the regular classes be suspended, while the many administrative changes and adjustments are being made, and while the necessary transfers of and reassignment of students and teachers are being made. Important decisions would have to be hurriedly made, without time for careful investigation of the facts nor for careful thought and reflection. Most decisions would have to be made on a temporary or an emergency basis.

We believe the attendant confusion and interruption of the regular school program would be against the public interest, and would be damaging to the children, both negro and white alike.

We respectfully urge that in making and issuing its decree this Court has equitable power and discretion to shape the decree and to control its execution in such a manner as to protect the public interest:

*United States v. Morgan*, 307 U.S. 183, 81 L. Ed. 1211, 59 S. Ct. 795:

"It is familiar doctrine that the extent to which a court of equity may grant or withhold its aid, and the manner of moulding its remedies, may be affected by the public interest involved." (p. 1219, L. Ed.)

*Virginia Ry. Co. v. System Federation No.* 40, 300 U.S. 515, 81 L. Ed. 789, 52 S. Ct. 512:

"6. The extent to which equity will go to give relief where there is no adequate remedy at law is not a matter of fixed rule, but rests rather in the sound discretion of the court.
"7. Courts of equity may, and frequently do, go much further to give and withhold relief in furtherance of the public interest than they are accustomed to go when only private interests are involved." (Syll. 6. and 7.)

*Securities Exch. Comm. v. U. S. R. and Imp. Co.*, 310 U.S. 434, 84 L. Ed. 1293, 60 S. Ct. 1044:

"7. A court of equity has discretion, in the exercise of jurisdiction committed to it, to grant or deny relief upon performance of conditions which will safeguard the public interest." (Syll. 7.)

Because the Board of Education believes that a "forthwith" order to abolish segregation in the Topeka school system would seriously damage and interrupt the operation and administration of the schools and would be plainly against public interest, and because it believes that an order to abolish segregation, in the public interest, should permit "an effective gradual adjustment"; we respectfully submit that Question 4(a) propounded by the Court should be answered in the negative, and that Question 4(b) should be answered in the affirmative.

### III. QUESTIONS 5(a), (b) AND (c) SHOULD BE ANSWERED IN THE NEGATIVE

If segregation in the public schools of Topeka is to be abolished by decree of the Court permitting an "effective gradual adjustment" as suggested in Question 4(b), then the Board of Education should be permitted to manage the readjustment, subject only to the usual and normal jurisdiction always retained by a court of equity for the enforcement of its decree or judgment.

We have heretofore pointed out the many intricate administrative decisions which will be involved in the transition to an integrated system of grade schools in Topeka. These are the problems and decisions which the Board of Education is organized to handle. Clearly there will be considerable administrative expense involved in making the adjustment. In Kansas the Board of Education is required to comply with cash basis and budget laws in connection with such expenditures, and taxes must be levied for such expenses within the levy limitation laws. Thus the necessary adjustments for a transition from segregated to integrated schools will affect nearly all the other administrative actions of the Board of Education. For this Court or a special master to undertake to control the necessary readjustments or to draw detailed orders and decrees will involve them in the control and direction of the administration of the entire school program either directly or indirectly.

We believe such detailed control by this Court or a special master is unnecessary and undesirable. We therefore submit that Questions 5(a), (b) and (c) should be answered in the negative.

## IV. QUESTION 5(d) SHOULD ALSO BE ANSWERED IN THE NEGATIVE

If this Court should enter an order or decree as suggested in Question 4(b), there is no need for a more specific or detailed decree in this case.

The Board of Education of Topeka has already on its own initiative resolved to terminate segregation in the elementary schools "as rapidly as is practicable" and has already taken its first step toward that end by providing for an integrated system in two schools which were formerly used only for white children. Certainly at this time there is no need for a more detailed decree than the decree suggested in Question 4(b). The District Court will always have jurisdiction to enforce the decree. If the need for a more specific decree should arise in the future, the District Court will have ample power to make such a decree under its general power to enforce the judgment and decree of the court.

We respectfully submit that Question 5(d) should be answered in the negative.

Respectfully submitted,

PETER F. CALDWELL,
Counsel for the Board of Education
of Topeka, Kansas,
512 Capitol Federal Building,
Topeka, Kansas.

347 U.S. 483
**BROWN et al.**

**v.**

**BOARD OF EDUCATION OF TOPEKA, SHAWNEE COUNTY, KAN., et al.**

**BRIGGS et al. v. ELLIOTT et al.**

**DAVIS et al.**

**v.**

**COUNTY SCHOOL BOARD OF PRINCE EDWARD COUNTY, VA., et al.**

**GEBHART et al. v. BELTON et al.**

**Nos. 1, 2, 4, 10.**

Reargued Dec. 7, 8, 9, 1953.

Decided May 17, 1954.

Class actions originating in the four states of Kansas, South Carolina, Virginia, and Delaware, by which minor Negro plaintiffs sought to obtain admission to public schools on a nonsegregated basis. On direct appeals by plaintiffs from adverse decisions in the United States District Courts, District of Kansas, 98 F.Supp. 797, Eastern District of South Carolina, 103 F.Supp. 920, and Eastern District of Virginia, 103 F.Supp. 337, and on grant of certiorari after decision favorable to plaintiffs in the Supreme Court of Delaware, 91 A.2d 137, the United States Supreme Court, Mr. Chief Justice Warren, held that segregation of children in public schools solely on the basis of race, even though the physical facilities and other tangible factors may be equal, deprives the children of the minority group of equal educational opportunities, in contravention of the Equal Protection Clause of the Fourteenth Amendment.

Cases ordered restored to docket for further argument regarding formulation of decrees.

**1. Constitutional Law ⚖47**

In resolving question whether segregation of races in public schools constituted a denial of equal protection of the laws, even though the tangible facilities provided might be equal, court would consider public education in light of its full development and present status throughout the nation, and not in light of conditions prevailing at time of adoption of the amendment. U.S.C.A.Const. Amend. 14.

**2. Constitutional Law ⚖220**

The opportunity of an education, where the state has undertaken to provide it, is a right which must be made available to all on equal terms. U.S.C.A. Const. Amend. 14.

**3. Constitutional Law ⚖220**

The segregation of children in public schools solely on the basis of race, even though the physical facilities and other tangible factors may be equal, deprives the children of minority group of equal educational opportunities, and amounts to a deprivation of the equal protection of the laws guaranteed by the Fourteenth Amendment to the Federal Constitution. U.S.C.A.Const. Amend. 14.

**4. Constitutional Law ⚖220**

The doctrine of "separate but equal" has no place in the field of public education, since separate educational facilities are inherently unequal. U.S.C.A.Const. Amend. 14.

**5. Appeal and Error ⚖819**

In view of fact that actions raising question of constitutional validity of segregation of races in public schools were class actions, and because of the wide applicability of decision holding that segregation was denial of equal protection of laws, and the great variety of local conditions, the formation of decrees presented problems of considerable complexity, requiring that cases be restored to the docket so that court might have full assistance of parties in formulating appropriate decrees. U.S.C.A. Const. Amend. 14.

———◆———

No. 1:

484
Mr. Robert L. Carter, New York City, for appellants Brown and others.

Mr. Paul E. Wilson, Topeka, Kan., for appellees Board of Education of Topeka and others.

Nos. 2, 4:

Messrs. Spottswood Robinson III, Thurgood Marshall, New York City, for appellants Briggs and Davis and others.

Messrs. John W. Davis, T. Justin Moore, J. Lindsay Almond, Jr., Richmond, Va., for appellees Elliott and County School Board of Prince Edward County and others.

Asst. Atty. Gen. J. Lee Rankin for United States amicus curiae by special leave of Court.

No. 10:

485

Mr. H. Albert Young, Wilmington, Del., for petitioners Gebhart et al.

Mr. Jack Greenberg, Thurgood Marshall, New York City, for respondents Belton et al.

486

Mr. Chief Justice WARREN delivered the opinion of the Court.

These cases come to us from the States of Kansas, South Carolina, Virginia, and Delaware. They are premised on different facts and different local conditions, but a common legal question justifies their consideration together in this consolidated opinion.[1]

---

1. In the Kansas case, Brown v. Board of Education, the plaintiffs are Negro children of elementary school age residing in Topeka. They brought this action in the United States District Court for the District of Kansas to enjoin enforcement of a Kansas statute which permits, but does not require, cities of more than 15,000 population to maintain separate school facilities for Negro and white students. Kan.Gen.Stat.1949, § 72–1724. Pursuant to that authority, the Topeka Board of Education elected to establish segregated elementary schools. Other public schools in the community, however, are operated on a nonsegregated basis. The three-judge District Court, convened under 28 U.S.C. §§ 2281 and 2284, 28 U.S.C.A. §§ 2281, 2284, found that segregation in public education has a detrimental effect upon Negro children, but denied relief on the ground that the Negro and white schools were substantially equal with respect to buildings, transportation, curricula, and educational qualifications of teachers. 98 F.Supp. 797. The case is here on direct appeal under 28 U.S.C. § 1253, 28 U.S.C.A. § 1253.

In the South Carolina case, Briggs v. Elliott, the plaintiffs are Negro children of both elementary and high school age residing in Clarendon County. They brought this action in the United States District Court for the Eastern District of South Carolina to enjoin enforcement of provisions in the state constitution and statutory code which require the segregation of Negroes and whites in public schools. S.C.Const. Art. XI, § 7; S.C. Code 1942, § 5377. The three-judge District Court, convened under 28 U.S.C. §§

2281 and 2284, 28 U.S.C.A. §§ 2281, 2284, denied the requested relief. The court found that the Negro schools were inferior to the white schools and ordered the defendants to begin immediately to equalize the facilities. But the court sustained the validity of the contested provisions and denied the plaintiffs admission to the white schools during the equalization program. 98 F.Supp. 529. This Court vacated the District Court's judgment and remanded the case for the purpose of obtaining the court's views on a report filed by the defendants concerning the progress made in the equalization program. 342 U.S. 350, 72 S.Ct. 327, 96 L.Ed. 392. On remand, the District Court found that substantial equality had been achieved except for buildings and that the defendants were proceeding to rectify this inequality as well. 103 F. Supp. 920. The case is again here on direct appeal under 28 U.S.C. § 1253, 28 U.S.C.A. § 1253.

In the Virginia case, Davis v. County School Board, the plaintiffs are Negro children of high school age residing in Prince Edward County. They brought this action in the United States District Court for the Eastern District of Virginia to enjoin enforcement of provisions in the state constitution and statutory code which require the segregation of Negroes and whites in public schools. Va.Const. § 140; Va.Code 1950, § 22–221. The three-judge District Court, convened under 28 U.S.C. §§ 2281 and 2284, 28 U.S.C.A. §§ 2281, 2284, denied the requested relief. The court found the Negro school inferior in physical plant, curricula, and transportation, and ordered the defendants

**487**

In each of the cases, minors of the Negro race, through their legal representatives, seek the aid of the courts in obtaining admission to the public schools of their community on a nonsegregated basis. In each instance,

**488**

they have been denied admission to schools attended by white children under laws requiring or permitting segregation according to race. This segregation was alleged to deprive the plaintiffs of the equal protection of the laws under the Fourteenth Amendment. In each of the cases other than the Delaware case, a three-judge federal district court denied relief to the plaintiffs on the so-called "separate but equal" doctrine announced by this Court in Plessy v. Ferguson, 163 U.S. 537, 16 S.Ct. 1138, 41 L.Ed. 256. Under that doctrine, equality of treatment is accorded when the races are provided substantially equal facilities, even though these facilities be separate. In the Delaware case, the Supreme Court of Delaware adhered to

that doctrine, but ordered that the plaintiffs be admitted to the white schools because of their superiority to the Negro schools.

The plaintiffs contend that segregated public schools are not "equal" and cannot be made "equal," and that hence they are deprived of the equal protection of the laws. Because of the obvious importance of the question presented, the Court took jurisdiction.[2] Argument was heard in the 1952 Term, and reargument was heard this Term on certain questions propounded by the Court.[3]

**489**

Reargument was largely devoted to the circumstances surrounding the adoption of the Fourteenth Amendment in 1868. It covered exhaustively consideration of the Amendment in Congress, ratification by the states, then existing practices in racial segregation, and the views of proponents and opponents of the Amendment. This discussion and our own investigation convince us that, although these sources cast some light, it

---

forthwith to provide substantially equal curricula and transportation and to "proceed with all reasonable diligence and dispatch to remove" the inequality in physical plant. But, as in the South Carolina case, the court sustained the validity of the contested provisions and denied the plaintiffs admission to the white schools during the equalization program. 103 F. Supp. 337. The case is here on direct appeal under 28 U.S.C. § 1253, 28 U.S.C. A. § 1253.

In the Delaware case, Gebhart v. Belton, the plaintiffs are Negro children of both elementary and high school age residing in New Castle County. They brought this action in the Delaware Court of Chancery to enjoin enforcement of provisions in the state constitution and statutory code which require the segregation of Negroes and whites in public schools. Del.Const. Art. X, § 2; Del.Rev.Code, 1935, § 2631, 14 Del.C. § 141. The Chancellor gave judgment for the plaintiffs and ordered their immediate admission to schools previously attended only by white children, on the ground that the Negro schools were inferior with respect to teacher training, pupil-teacher ratio, extracurricular activities, physical plant, and time and distance involved in travel.

Del.Ch., 87 A.2d 862. The Chancellor also found that segregation itself results in an inferior education for Negro children (see note 10, infra), but did not rest his decision on that ground. 87 A.2d at page 865. The Chancellor's decree was affirmed by the Supreme Court of Delaware, which intimated, however, that the defendants might be able to obtain a modification of the decree after equalization of the Negro and white schools had been accomplished. 91 A.2d 137, 152. The defendants, contending only that the Delaware courts had erred in ordering the immediate admission of the Negro plaintiffs to the white schools, applied to this Court for certiorari. The writ was granted, 344 U.S. 891, 73 S.Ct. 213, 97 L.Ed. 689. The plaintiffs, who were successful below, did not submit a cross-petition.

2. 344 U.S. 1, 73 S.Ct. 1, 97 L.Ed. 3, Id., 344 U.S. 141, 73 S.Ct. 124, 97 L.Ed. 152, Gebhart v. Belton, 344 U.S. 891, 73 S.Ct. 213, 97 L.Ed. 689.

3. 345 U.S. 972, 73 S.Ct. 1118, 97 L.Ed. 1388. The Attorney General of the United States participated both Terms as amicus curiae.

is not enough to resolve the problem with which we are faced. At best, they are inconclusive. The most avid proponents of the post-War Amendments undoubtedly intended them to remove all legal distinctions among "all persons born or naturalized in the United States." Their opponents, just as certainly, were antagonistic to both the letter and the spirit of the Amendments and wished them to have the most limited effect. What others in Congress and the state legislatures had in mind cannot be determined with any degree of certainty.

An additional reason for the inconclusive nature of the Amendment's history, with respect to segregated schools, is the status of public education at that time.[4] In the South, the movement toward free common schools, supported

490

by general taxation, had not yet taken hold. Education of white children was largely in the hands of private groups. Education of Negroes was almost nonexistent, and practically all of the race were illiterate. In fact, any education of Negroes was forbidden by law in some states. Today, in contrast, many Negroes have achieved outstanding success in the arts and sciences as well as in the business and professional world. It is true that public school education at the time of the Amendment had advanced further in the North, but the effect of the Amendment on Northern States was generally ignored in the congressional debates. Even in the North, the conditions of public education did not approximate those existing today. The curriculum was usually rudimentary; ungraded schools were common in rural areas; the school term was but three months a year in many states; and compulsory school attendance was virtually unknown. As a consequence, it is not surprising that there should be so little in the history of the Fourteenth Amendment relating to its intended effect on public education.

In the first cases in this Court construing the Fourteenth Amendment, decided shortly after its adoption, the Court interpreted it as proscribing all state-imposed discriminations against the Negro race.[5] The doctrine of

491

"separate but

4. For a general study of the development of public education prior to the Amendment, see Butts and Cremin, A History of Education in American Culture (1953), Pts. I, II; Cubberley, Public Education in the United States (1934 ed.), cc. II–XII. School practices current at the time of the adoption of the Fourteenth Amendment are described in Butts and Crimin, supra, at 269–275; Cubberley, supra, at 288–339, 408–431; Knight, Public Education in the South (1922), cc. VIII, IX. See also H. Ex. Doc. No. 315, 41st Cong., 2d Sess. (1871). Although the demand for free public schools followed substantially the same pattern in both the North and the South, the development in the South did not begin to gain momentum until about 1850, some twenty years after that in the North. The reasons for the somewhat slower development in the South (e. g., the rural character of the South and the different regional attitudes toward state assistance) are well explained in Cubberley, supra, at 408–423. In the country as a whole, but particularly in the South, the War virtually stopped all progress in

74 S.Ct.—44

public education. Id., at 427–428. The low status of Negro education in all sections of the country, both before and immediately after the War, is described in Beale, A History of Freedom of Teaching in American Schools (1941), 112–132, 175–195. Compulsory school attendance laws were not generally adopted until after the ratification of the Fourteenth Amendment, and it was not until 1918 that such laws were in force in all the states. Cubberley, supra, at 563–565.

5. In re Slaughter-House Cases, 1873, 16 Wall. 36, 67–72, 21 L.Ed. 394; Strauder v. West Virginia, 1880, 100 U.S. 303, 307–308, 25 L.Ed. 664.
"It ordains that no State shall deprive any person of life, liberty, or property, without due process of law, or deny to any person within its jurisdiction the equal protection of the laws. What is this but declaring that the law in the States shall be the same for the black as for the white; that all persons, whether colored or white, shall stand equal before the laws of the States, and, in regard to the colored race, for whose protection the amendment was primarily

equal" did not make its appearance in this Court until 1896 in the case of Plessy v. Ferguson, supra, involving not education but transportation.[6] American courts have since labored with the doctrine for over half a century. In this Court, there have been six cases involving the "separate but equal" doctrine in the field of public education.[7] In Cumming v. Board of Education of Richmond County, 175 U.S. 528, 20 S.Ct. 197, 44 L.Ed. 262, and Gong Lum v. Rice, 275 U.S. 78, 48 S.Ct. 91, 72 L.Ed. 172, the validity of the doctrine itself was not challenged.[8] In more recent cases, all on the graduate school

**492**

level, inequality was found in that specific benefits enjoyed by white students were denied to Negro students of the same educational qualifications. State of Missouri ex rel. Gaines v. Canada, 305 U.S. 337, 59 S.Ct. 232, 83 L.Ed. 208; Sipuel v. Board of

Regents of University of Oklahoma, 332 U.S. 631, 68 S.Ct. 299, 92 L.Ed. 247; Sweatt v. Painter, 339 U.S. 629, 70 S. Ct. 848, 94 L.Ed. 1114; McLaurin v. Oklahoma State Regents, 339 U.S. 637, 70 S.Ct. 851, 94 L.Ed. 1149. In none of these cases was it necessary to re-examine the doctrine to grant relief to the Negro plaintiff. And in Sweatt v. Painter, supra, the Court expressly reserved decision on the question whether Plessy v. Ferguson should be held inapplicable to public education.

In the instant cases, that question is directly presented. Here, unlike Sweatt v. Painter, there are findings below that the Negro and white schools involved have been equalized, or are being equalized, with respect to buildings, curricula, qualifications and salaries of teachers, and other "tangible" factors.[9] Our decision, therefore, cannot turn on merely a comparison of these tangible factors

---

designed, that no discrimination shall be made against them by law because of their color? The words of the amendment, it is true, are prohibitory, but they contain a necessary implication of a positive immunity, or right, most valuable to the colored race,—the right to exemption from unfriendly legislation against them distinctively as colored,—exemption from legal discriminations, implying inferiority in civil society, lessening the security of their enjoyment of the rights which others enjoy, and discriminations which are steps towards reducing them to the condition of a subject race."
See also State of Virginia v. Rives, 1879, 100 U.S. 313, 318, 25 L.Ed. 667; Ex parte Virginia, 1879, 100 U.S. 339, 344–345, 25 L.Ed. 676.

**6.** The doctrine apparently originated in Roberts v. City of Boston, 1850, 5 Cush. 198, 59 Mass. 198, 206, upholding school segregation against attack as being violative of a state constitutional guarantee of equality. Segregation in Boston public schools was eliminated in 1855. Mass. Acts 1855, c. 256. But elsewhere in the North segregation in public education has persisted in some communities until recent years. It is apparent that such segregation has long been a nationwide problem, not merely one of sectional concern.

**7.** See also Berea College v. Kentucky, 1908, 211 U.S. 45, 29 S.Ct. 33, 53 L.Ed. 81.

**8.** In the Cumming case, Negro taxpayers sought an injunction requiring the defendant school board to discontinue the operation of a high school for white children until the board resumed operation of a high school for Negro children. Similarly, in the Gong Lum case, the plaintiff, a child of Chinese descent, contended only that state authorities had misapplied the doctrine by classifying him with Negro children and requiring him to attend a Negro school.

**9.** In the Kansas case, the court below found substantial equality as to all such factors. 98 F.Supp. 797, 798. In the South Carolina case, the court below found that the defendants were proceeding "promptly and in good faith to comply with the court's decree." 103 F.Supp. 920, 921. In the Virginia case, the court below noted that the equalization program was already "afoot and progressing," 103 F.Supp. 337, 341; since then, we have been advised, in the Virginia Attorney General's brief on reargument, that the program has now been completed. In the Delaware case, the court below similarly noted that the state's equalization program was well under way. 91 A.2d 137, 139.

in the Negro and white schools involved in each of the cases. We must look instead to the effect of segregation itself on public education.

[1] In approaching this problem, we cannot turn the clock back to 1868 when the Amendment was adopted, or even to 1896 when Plessy v. Ferguson was written. We must consider public education in the light of its full development and its present place in American life throughout
493
the Nation. Only in this way can it be determined if segregation in public schools deprives these plaintiffs of the equal protection of the laws.

[2] Today, education is perhaps the most important function of state and local governments. Compulsory school attendance laws and the great expenditures for education both demonstrate our recognition of the importance of education to our democratic society. It is required in the performance of our most basic public responsibilities, even service in the armed forces. It is the very foundation of good citizenship. Today it is a principal instrument in awakening the child to cultural values, in preparing him for later professional training, and in helping him to adjust normally to his environment. In these days, it is doubtful that any child may reasonably be expected to succeed in life if he is denied the opportunity of an education. Such an opportunity, where the state has undertaken to provide it, is a right which must be made available to all on equal terms.

[3] We come then to the question presented: Does segregation of children in public schools solely on the basis of race, even though the physical facilities and other "tangible" factors may be equal, deprive the children of the minority group of equal educational opportunities? We believe that it does.

In Sweatt v. Painter, supra [339 U.S. 629, 70 S.Ct. 850], in finding that a segregated law school for Negroes could not provide them equal educational opportunities, this Court relied in large part on "those qualities which are incapable of objective measurement but which make for greatness in a law school." In McLaurin v. Oklahoma State Regents, supra [339 U.S. 637, 70 S.Ct. 853], the Court, in requiring that a Negro admitted to a white graduate school be treated like all other students, again resorted to intangible considerations: " * * * his ability to study, to engage in discussions and exchange views with other students, and, in general, to learn his profession."
494
Such considerations apply with added force to children in grade and high schools. To separate them from others of similar age and qualifications solely because of their race generates a feeling of inferiority as to their status in the community that may affect their hearts and minds in a way unlikely ever to be undone. The effect of this separation on their educational opportunities was well stated by a finding in the Kansas case by a court which nevertheless felt compelled to rule against the Negro plaintiffs:

> "Segregation of white and colored children in public schools has a detrimental effect upon the colored children. The impact is greater when it has the sanction of the law; for the policy of separating the races is usually interpreted as denoting the inferiority of the negro group. A sense of inferiority affects the motivation of a child to learn. Segregation with the sanction of law, therefore, has a tendency to [retard] the educational and mental development of Negro children and to deprive them of some of the benefits they would receive in a racial-[ly] integrated school system."[10]

---

10. A similar finding was made in the Delaware case: "I conclude from the testimony that in our Delaware society, State-imposed segregation in education itself results in the Negro children, as a class, receiving educational opportunities which

Whatever may have been the extent of psychological knowledge at the time of Plessy v. Ferguson, this finding is amply supported by modern authority.[11] Any language

**495**

in Plessy v. Ferguson contrary to this finding is rejected.

[4] We conclude that in the field of public education the doctrine of "separate but equal" has no place. Separate educational facilities are inherently unequal. Therefore, we hold that the plaintiffs and others similarly situated for whom the actions have been brought are, by reason of the segregation complained of, deprived of the equal protection of the laws guaranteed by the Fourteenth Amendment. This disposition makes unnecessary any discussion whether such segregation also violates the Due Process Clause of the Fourteenth Amendment.[12]

[5] Because these are class actions, because of the wide applicability of this decision, and because of the great variety of local conditions, the formulation of decrees in these cases presents problems of considerable complexity. On reargument, the consideration of appropriate relief was necessarily subordinated to the primary question—the constitutionality of segregation in public education. We have now announced that such segregation is a denial of the equal protection of the laws. In order that we may have the full assistance of the parties in formulating decrees, the cases will be restored to the docket, and the parties are requested to present further argument on Questions 4 and 5 previously propounded by the Court for the reargument this Term.[13] The Attorney General

**496**

of the United States is again invited to participate. The Attorneys General of the states requiring or permitting segregation in public education will also be permitted to appear as *amici curiae* upon request to do so by September 15, 1954, and submission of briefs by October 1, 1954.[14]

It is so ordered.

---

are substantially inferior to those available to white children otherwise similarly situated." 87 A.2d 862, 865.

11. K. B. Clark, Effect of Prejudice and Discrimination on Personality Development (Midcentury White House Conference on Children and Youth, 1950); Witmer and Kotinsky, Personality in the Making (1952), c. VI; Deutscher and Chein, The Psychological Effects of Enforced Segregation: A Survey of Social Science Opinion, 26 J.Psychol. 259 (1948); Chein, What are the Psychological Effects of Segregation Under Conditions of Equal Facilities?, 3 Int. J. Opinion and Attitude Res. 229 (1949); Brameld, Educational Costs, in Discrimination and National Welfare (MacIver, ed., 1949), 44–48; Frazier, The Negro in the United States (1949), 674–681. And see generally Myrdal, An American Dilemma (1944).

12. See Bolling v. Sharpe, 347 U.S. 497, 74 S.Ct. 693, concerning the Due Process Clause of the Fifth Amendment.

13. "4. Assuming it is decided that segregation in public schools violates the Fourteenth Amendment

"(a) would a decree necessarily follow providing that, within the limits set by normal geographic school districting, Negro children should forthwith be admitted to schools of their choice, or

"(b) may this Court, in the exercise of its equity powers, permit an effective gradual adjustment to be brought about from existing segregated systems to a system not based on color distinctions?

"5. On the assumption on which questions 4(a) and (b) are based, and assuming further that this Court will exercise its equity powers to the end described in question 4(b),

"(a) should this Court formulate detailed decrees in these cases;

"(b) if so, what specific issues shoul· the decrees reach;

"(c) should this Court appoint a special master to hear evidence with a view to recommending specific terms for such decrees;

"(d) should this Court remand to the courts of first instance with directions to frame decrees in these cases, and if so what general directions should the decrees of this Court include and what procedures should the courts of first instance follow in arriving at the specific terms of more detailed decrees?"

14. See Rule 42, Revised Rules of this Court, effective July 1, 1954, 28 U.S.C.A.

## IN THE
## SUPREME COURT OF THE UNITED STATES
## OCTOBER TERM, 1954

### No. 1

OLIVER BROWN, ET AL., APPELLANTS,

VS.

BOARD OF EDUCATION OF TOPEKA, ET AL., APPELLEES.

### No. 2

HARRY BRIGGS, JR., ET AL., APPELLANTS,

VS.

R. W. ELLIOTT, ET AL., APPELLEES.

### No. 3

DOROTHY E. DAVIS, ET AL., APPELLANTS,

VS.

COUNTY SCHOOL BOARD OF PRINCE EDWARD COUNTY, VIRGINIA, ET AL., APPELLEES.

### No. 5

FRANCIS B. GEBHART, ET AL., PETITIONERS,

VS.

ETHEL LOUISE BELTON, ET AL., RESPONDENTS.

**APPEALS FROM THE UNITED STATES DISTRICT COURTS FOR THE DISTRICT OF KANSAS, THE EASTERN DISTRICT OF SOUTH CAROLINA AND THE EASTERN DISTRICT OF VIRGINIA, AND ON PETITION FOR A WRIT OF CERTIORARI TO THE SUPREME COURT OF DELAWARE, RESPECTIVELY**

## BRIEF FOR APPELLANTS IN NOS. 1, 2 AND 3 AND FOR RESPONDENTS IN NO. 5 ON FURTHER REARGUMENT

CHARLES L. BLACK, JR.,
ELWOOD H. CHISOLM,
WILLIAM T. COLEMAN, JR.,
CHARLES T. DUNCAN,
GEORGE E. C. HAYES,
LOREN MILLER,
WILLIAM R. MING, JR.,
CONSTANCE BAKER MOTLEY,
JAMES M. NABRIT, JR.,
DAVID E. PINSKY,
FRANK D. REEVES,
JOHN SCOTT,
JACK B. WEINSTEIN,
   *of Counsel.*

HAROLD BOULWARE,
ROBERT L. CARTER,
JACK GREENBERG,
OLIVER W. HILL,
THURGOOD MARSHALL,
LOUIS L. REDDING,
SPOTTSWOOD W. ROBINSON, III,
CHARLES S. SCOTT,
   *Attorneys for Appellants in Nos. 1, 2, 3*
   *and for Respondents in No. 5.*

# TABLE OF CONTENTS

# IN THE
## SUPREME COURT OF THE UNITED STATES
## OCTOBER TERM, 1954
## NO. 1

OLIVER BROWN, ET AL., APPELLANTS,

VS.

BOARD OF EDUCATION OF TOPEKA, ET AL.,

APPELLEES

## NO. 2

HARRY BRIGGS, JR., ET AL., APPELLANTS,

VS.

R. W. ELLIOTT, ET AL., APPELLEES

## NO. 3

DOROTHY E. DAVIS, ET AL., APPELLANTS,

VS.

COUNTY SCHOOL BOARD OF PRINCE EDWARD COUNTY, VIRGINIA, ET AL.,

APPELLEES

## NO. 5

FRANCIS B. GEBHART, ET AL., PETITIONERS,

VS.

ETHEL LOUISE BELTON, ET AL., RESPONDENTS

**APPEALS FROM THE UNITED STATES DISTRICT COURTS FOR THE DISTRICT OF KANSAS, THE EASTERN DISTRICT OF SOUTH CAROLINA AND THE EASTERN DISTRICT OF VIRGINIA, AND ON PETITION FOR A WRIT OF CERTIORARI TO THE SUPREME COURT OF DELAWARE, RESPECTIVELY**

## BRIEF FOR APPELLANTS IN NOS. 1, 2 AND 3 AND FOR RESPONDENTS IN NO. 5 ON FURTHER REARGUMENT

## PRELIMINARY STATEMENT

On May 17, 1954, this Court disposed of the basic constitutional question presented in these cases by deciding that racial segregation in public education is unconstitutional. The Court said, however, that the formulation of decrees was made difficult "because these are class actions, because of the wide applicability of this decision and because of the great variety of local conditions. . . ." The cases were restored to the docket, and the parties were requested to present further argument on Questions 4 and 5 previously propounded by the Court for the reargument last Term.

## QUESTIONS INVOLVED

Questions 4 and 5, left undecided and now the subject of discussion in this brief, follow:

**4.** Assuming it is decided that segregation in public schools violates the Fourteenth Amendment

(*a*) would a decree necessarily follow providing that, within the limits set by normal geographic school districting, Negro children should forthwith be admitted to schools of their choice, or

(*b*) may this Court, in the exercise of its equity powers, permit an effective gradual adjustment to be brought about from existing segregated systems to a system not based on color distinctions?

**5.** On the assumption on which question 4(*a*) and (*b*) are based, and assuming further that this Court will exercise its equity powers to the end described in question 4(*b*),

(*a*) should this Court formulate detailed decrees in these cases;

(*b*) if so, what specific issues should the decrees reach;

(*c*) should this Court appoint a special master to hear evidence with a view to recommending specific terms for such decrees;

(*d*) should this Court remand to the courts of first instance with directions to frame decrees in these cases, and if so, what general directions should the decrees of this Court include and what procedures should the courts of first instance follow in arriving at the specific terms of more detailed decrees?

## DEVELOPMENTS IN THESE CASES SINCE THE LAST ARGUMENT

### The Kansas case

On September 3, 1953, the Topeka School Board adopted the following resolution:

> Be it resolved that it is the policy of the Topeka Board of Education to terminate the maintenance of segregation in the elementary schools as rapidly as is practicable.

On September 8, 1953, appellees ordered segregation terminated in two of the nineteen school districts in Topeka. In September, 1954, segregation was completely terminated in ten other school districts and partially in two.

There is now a total school enrollment of approximately 8,500 children of elementary school age attending 23 elementary schools. Of the 8,500 children enrolled, approximately 700 Negro children are in four elementary schools for Negroes. There are 123 Negro children now attending schools on a non-segregated basis pursuant to appellees' implementation of its policy of removing segregation from the public school system. The blunt truth is that 85% of the Negro children in Topeka's elementary schools are still being denied the constitutional rights for which appellants sought redress in their original action.

While Topeka has been effectuating its plan, several other cities of the first class have undertaken the abolition of segregated schools. Lawrence and Pittsburg have completely desegregated. Kansas City, Abilene, Leavenworth and Parsons have ordered partial desegregation. Wichita and Salina have revised their school regulations to permit Negro children to attend schools nearest their homes. Only Coffeeville and Fort Scott have not taken any affirmative action whatsoever.

**The Delaware case**

By order of the Court of Chancery, affirmed by the Supreme Court of Delaware, the named plaintiffs were immediately admitted to the schools to which they applied. These plaintiffs and other members of the class are in their third year of uninterrupted attendance in the two Delaware schools named in the order. That attendance has been marked by no untoward incident. The order, however, did not result in elimination of separate schools for Negroes in the two school districts involved, in each of which one segregated elementary school is yet maintained by petitioners.

The State Board of Education has statutory authority to "exercise general control and supervision over the public schools of the State, including . . . the determination of the educational policies of the State and the seeking in every way to direct and develop public sentiment in support of public education." DELAWARE CODE, Title 14, Section 121 (1953). Accordingly, the State Board of Education, on June 11, 1954, adopted a statement of "Policies Regarding Desegregation of Schools of the State" and announced "a general policy" that it "intends to carry out the mandates of the United States Supreme Court decision as expeditiously as possible." It further requested that "the school authorities together with interested citizen groups throughout the State should take immediate steps to hold discussions for the purpose of (1) formulating plans for desegregation in their respective districts and (2) presenting said plans to the State Board of Education for review."

On August 19, 1954, the State Board of Education requested "that *all schools*, maintaining four or more teachers, present a *tentative plan* for desegregation in their area on or before *October 1, 1954*."

The desegregation plans of the Claymont Board of Education, whose members are petitioners here, providing for the complete termination of segregation, were approved by the State Board of Education on August 26, 1954. These plans have been partially put into operation.

No plan ending segregation in the Hockessin schools, the other Delaware area in the litigation here, has yet been formulated.

Delaware statutes provide for two types of public school districts, exclusive of the public school system in Wilmington which is practically autonomous. One type is commonly known as the State Board District. As to it, the statute provides that the "Board of School Trustees shall be the representative in the District of the State Board of Education." DELAWARE CODE, Title 14, Section 702 (1953). There are 98 such units. The other type is the Special School District, concerning which the statute provides that "There shall be a Board of Education which shall be responsible for the general administration and supervision of the free public schools and educational interests of the District." DELAWARE CODE, Title 14, Section 902 (1953). There are fifteen Special School Districts.

Desegregation in the school districts of Delaware is illustrated by the table below:

**State Board Districts**

|  | Partial Desegregation | Complete Desegregation | No Desegregation | Total |
|---|---|---|---|---|
| New Castle County | 4 | 1 | 26 | 31 |
| Kent County | 0 | 0 | 24 | 24 |
| Sussex County | 0 | 0 | 43 | 43 |
|  |  |  |  | 98 |

**Special School Districts**

|  | Partial Desegregation | Complete Desegregation | No Desegregation | Total |
|---|---|---|---|---|
| New Castle County | 3 | 1 | 1 | 5 |
| Kent County | 1 | 0 | 3 | 4 |
| Sussex County* | 0 | 0 | 6 | 6 |
|  |  |  |  | 15 |

Wilmington, which is in New Castle County and contains 34% of the population of the State, in June desegregated all elementary and secondary schools for the 1954 summer session. It has also completely desegregated its night school sessions. Beginning in September, 1954, desegregation of all elementary schools was effectuated, with some integration of teachers.

The school districts involved in this litigation also are in New Castle County, which has 68% of the State's population. Desegregation in varying degrees has started in every major school district in this county, except one.

The State Board of Education has made specific requests to 58 of the 113 school districts in the State to submit such plans. Another six districts have stated that any kind of plan they may have would be more or less nullified by overcrowded classroom conditions. Fourteen others have indicated that they desire to await the mandate of this Court. The remaining districts have not responded to the State Board.

In summary, school districts in areas comprising more than 50% of the population of Delaware have undertaken some desegregation of the public schools. Many school districts in semi-urban and rural areas have undertaken no step. The ultimate responsibility for effectuating desegregation throughout Delaware rests with petitioners here, members of the State Board of Education.

**The South Carolina case**

Since May 17, 1954, South Carolina's fifteen-man legislative "Segregation Study Committee" was reorganized and has conferred with the Governor, State education officials, other legislators and spokesmen from various civic and teacher organizations. All of their meetings have been closed to the public. The Committee also visited Louisiana and Mississippi "to observe what was being done in those states to preserve segregated schools."

On July 28, the committee issued an interim report which recommended that public schools be operated during the coming year "in keeping with previously established policy." The committee construed its assignment as being the formulation of courses of action whereby the State could continue public education "without unfortunate disruption by outside forces and influences which have no knowledge of recent progress and no understanding of the problems of the present and future. . . ." Moreover, the report stated that the committee also recognized "the need for a system in keeping with public opinion and established traditions and living patterns."

The State Attorney General insisted that this Court should not undertake to direct further action even by the school district involved and announced that he considered the Clarendon County case "purely a local matter as far as the parties to the suit are concerned."

In Rock Hill (population 25,000 with 20% Negroes) a Catholic grade school voluntarily desegregated. Opening day enrollment was 29 white students and five Negroes. There has been no report of overt action against this development; but the parents of some of the

---

* Partial desegregation, that is, on the high school level, was instituted by the Milford Board of Education, in Sussex County. This action was later revoked and a test of the revocation is now pending in the Delaware courts. See Simmons v. Steiner, 108 A. 2d 173 (Del. Ct. Chanc. 1954). In that case the Vice-Chancellor found the Negro plaintiffs' rights to remain as students in Milford High School "clear and convincing" and restrained the Board of Education from excluding them. However, the Supreme Court of Delaware temporarily stayed the injunction to give that court sufficient time to examine "serious questions of law." Argument has been scheduled for December 13, 1954. Steiner v. Simmons (Del Sup. Ct. No. 27, 1954).

children have been remonstrated with by neighbors and workers.[1]

A newspaper report[1a] of a public speech of E. B. McCord, one of the appellees herein, superintendent of education for Clarendon County, states in part:

> There will be no mixed schools in Clarendon County as long as there is any possible way for present leadership to prevent them.
> So declared L. B. McCord of Manning, Clarendon County superintendent of education, in an address before the Lions Club here Monday night.
> Decrying the fact that "Our churches seem to be letting their zeal run away in leading the way," he denounced de-segregation as contrary to the Scriptures and to good sense.

### The Virginia case

On May 27, 1954, the State Board of Education advised city and county school boards to continue segregation during the present school year.

On August 28, the Governor named a thirty-two-man, all-white legislative commission to study the problems raised by the Court's ruling and to prepare a report and recommendations to the legislature and to him. The Governor then announced:

> . . . I am inviting the commission to ascertain, through public hearings and such other means as appear appropriate, the wishes of the people of Virginia; to give careful study to plans or legislation or both, that should be considered for adoption in Virginia after the final decree of the Court is entered, and to offer such other recommendations as it may deem proper as a result of the decision of the Supreme Court affecting the public schools.[2]

At its first meeting the commission adopted a rule that:

> All meetings of the commission shall be executive and its deliberations confidential, except when the meeting consists of a public hearing or it is otherwise expressly decided by the commission.[3]

By October, the local school boards or boards of supervisors of approximately 25 of the state's 98 counties had adopted and forwarded to the Governor resolutions urging the continuation of segregated schools.

In May, 1954, the Richmond Diocese of the Roman Catholic Church, which includes all but 6 of Virginia's counties, announced that during the Fall of 1954, Negroes would for the first time be admitted to previously all-white Catholic parochial schools where there was no separate parochial school for Negroes. Approximately 40 Negro pupils of a total of 3,527 are enrolled in four high and six elementary parochial schools formerly attended only by white pupils. The Superintendent of the Richmond Diocese states that integration in these schools "has worked out magnificently, without a ripple of discontent, . . . ."[4]

## ARGUMENT

### I. Answering Question 4: Only a decree requiring desegregation as quickly as prerequisite administrative and mechanical procedures can be completed will discharge judicial responsibility for the vindication of the constitutional rights of which appellants are being deprived

In the normal course of judicial procedure, this Court's decision that racial segregation in public education is unconstitutional would be effectuated by decrees forthwith enjoining the continuation of that segregation. Indeed, in *Sipuel* v. *Board of Regents*, 332 U.S. 631, when effort was made to secure postponement of the enforcement of similar rights, this Court not only refused to delay action but accelerated the granting of relief by ordering its mandate to issue forthwith.

In practical effect, such disposition of this litigation would require immediate initiation of the administrative procedures prerequisite to desegregation, to be followed by the admission of the complaining children and others similarly situated to unsegregated schools at the beginning of the next academic term. This means that appellees will have had from May 17, 1954, to September, 1955, to complete whatever adjustments may be necessary.

If appellees desire any postponement of relief beyond that date, the affirmative burden must be on them to state explicitly what they propose and to establish that the requested postponement has judicially cognizable advantages greater than those inherent in the prompt vindication of appellants' adjudicated constitutional rights. Moreover, when appellees seek to postpone the enjoyment of rights which are personal and present, *Sweatt* v. *Painter*, 339 U.S. 629; *Sipuel* v. *Board of Regents*, 332 U.S. 631, that burden is particularly heavy. When the

---

[1] Southern School News, Sept. 3, 1954, p. 12, col. 3–4.
[1a] Charleston News and Courier, August 4, 1954.
[2] Southern School News, Sept. 3, 1954, p. 13, col. 5.
[3] Southern School News, Oct. 1, 1954, p. 14, col. 2–3.

[4] *Id.* at p. 14, col. 5.

rights of school children are involved the burden is even greater. Each day relief is postponed is to the appellants* a day of serious and irreparable injury; for this Court has announced that segregation of Negroes in the public schools "generates a feeling of inferiority as to their status in the community that may affect their hearts and minds in a way unlikely ever to be undone...." And, time is of the essence because the period of public school attendance is short.

**A. Aggrieved parties showing denial of constitutional rights in analogous situations have received immediate relief despite arguments for delay more persuasive than any available here.** Where a substantial constitutional right would be impaired by delay, this Court has refused to postpone injunctive relief even in the face of the gravest of public considerations suggested as justification therefor. In *Youngstown Sheet & Tube Co.* v. *Sawyer,* 343 U.S. 579, this Court upheld the issuance of preliminary injunctions restraining the Government's continued possession of steel mills seized under Presidential order intended to avoid a work stoppage that would imperil the national defense during the Korean conflict. The Government argued that even though the seizure might be unconstitutional, the public interest in uninterrupted production of essential war materials was superior to the owners' rights to the immediate return of their properties. It is significant that in the seven opinions filed no Justice saw any merit in this position. If equity could not appropriately exercise its broad discretion to withhold the immediate grant of relief in the *Youngstown* case, such a postponement must certainly be inappropriate in these cases where no comparable overriding consideration can be suggested.

Similarly in Ex parte *Endo,* 323 U.S. 283, this Court rejected the Government's argument that hardship and disorder resulting from racial prejudice could justify delay in releasing the petitioner. There, the argument made by the Government to justify other than immediate relief was summarized in the Court's opinion as follows (pp. 296–297):

> It is argued that such a planned and orderly relocation was essential to the success of the evacuation program; that but for such supervision there might have been a dangerously disorderly migration of unwanted people to unprepared communities; that unsupervised

evacuation might have resulted in hardship and disorder; that the success of the evacuation program was thought to require the knowledge that the Federal government was maintaining control over the evacuated population except as the release of individuals could be effected consistently with their own peace and well-being and that of the nation; that although community hostility towards the evacuees has diminished, it has not disappeared and the continuing control of the Authority over the relocation process is essential to the success of the evacuation program. It is argued that supervised relocation, as the chosen method of terminating the evacuation, is the final step in the entire process and is a consequence of the first step taken. It is conceded that appellant's detention pending compliance with the leave regulations is not directly connected with the prevention of espionage and sabotage at the present time. But it is argued that Executive Order No. 9102 confers power to make regulations necessary and proper for controlling situations created by the exercise of the powers expressly conferred for protection against espionage and sabotage. The leave regulations are said to fall within that category.

In a unanimous decision, with the Court's opinion by Mr. Justice Douglas and two concurring opinions, the Court held that the petitioner must be given her unconditional liberty because the detention was not permissible by either statutory or administrative authorization. Viewing the petitioner's right as being in that "sensitive area of rights specifically guaranteed by the Constitution" (p. 299), the Court rejected the Government's contention that a continuation of its unlawful course of conduct was necessary to avoid the harmful consequences which otherwise would follow.

It is true that in the *Endo* case the contention rejected was that an executive order (which on its face did not authorize the petitioner's detention) ought to be extended by "construction" so as to entitle the Relocation Authority to delay the release of the petitioner until it felt that social conditions made it convenient and prudent to do so. In this case, the suggestion is that this Court, in the exercise of its equity powers, ought to withhold appellants' constitutional rights on closely similar grounds. But this is not a decisive distinction. If, as the *Endo* case held, the enjoyment of a constitutional right may not be deferred by a process of forced construction on the basis of factors closely similar to the ones at work in the instant case, then certainly this Court ought not to find in its equitable discretion a mandate or empowerment to obtain the same result.

In the *Endo* case, the national interest in time of war was present. In these cases, no such

---

*As used in this Brief, "appellants" include the respondents in No. 5.

interest exists. Thus, there is even less basis for delaying the immediate enjoyment of appellants' rights.

Counsel have discovered no case wherein this Court has found a violation of a present constitutional right but has postponed relief on the representation by governmental officials that local mores and customs justify delay which might produce a more orderly transition.

It would be paradoxical indeed if, in the instant cases, it were decided for the first time that constitutional rights may be postponed because of anticipation of difficulties arising out of local feelings. These cases are brought to vindicate rights which, as a matter of common knowledge and legal experience, need, above all others, protection against local attitudes and patterns of behavior.[5] They are brought, specifically, to uphold rights under the Fourteenth Amendment which are not to be qualified, substantively or remedially, by reference to local mores. On the contrary, the Fourteenth Amendment, on its face and as a matter of history, was designed for the very purpose of affording protection against local mores and customs, and Congress has implemented that design by providing redress against aggression under color of state laws, customs and usages. 28 U.S.C. § 1343; 42 U.S.C. § 1983.

Surely, appellants' rights are not to be enforced at a pace geared down to the very customs which the Fourteenth Amendment and implementing federal laws were designed to combat.

Cases in which delays in enforcement of rights have been granted involve totally dissimilar considerations. Such cases generally deal with the abatement of nuisances, e.g., *New Jersey* v. *New York*, 283 U.S. 473; *Wisconsin* v. *Illinois*, 278 U.S. 367; *Arizona Copper Co.* v. *Gillespie*, 230 U.S. 46; *Georgia* v. *Tennessee Copper Co.*, 206 U.S. 230; or with violations of the anti-trust laws, e.g., *Schine Chain Theaters* v. *United States*, 334 U.S. 110; *United States* v. *National Lead Co.*, 332 U.S. 319; *United States* v. *Crescent Amusement Co.*, 323 U.S. 173; *Hartford-Empire Co.* v. *United States*, 323 U.S. 386; *United States* v. *American Tobacco Co.*, 221 U.S. 106; *Standard Oil Co. of New Jersey* v. *United States*, 221 U.S. 1.

These cases are readily distinguishable, and are not precedents for the postponement of relief here. In the nuisance cases, the Court allowed the offending parties time to comply because the granting of immediate relief would

have caused great injury to the public or to the defendants with comparatively slight benefit to the plaintiffs. In the instant cases, a continuation of the unconstitutional practice is as injurious to the welfare of our government as it is to the individual appellants.

In the anti-trust cases, delay could be granted without violence to individual rights simply because there were no individual rights on the plaintiff's side. The suits were brought by the Government and the only interest which could have been prejudiced by the delays granted is the diffuse public interest in free competition. The delays granted in anti-trust cases rarely, if ever, permit the continuance of active wrongful conduct, but merely give time for dissolution and dissipation of the effects of past misconduct. Obviously, these cases have nothing to do with ours.

It should be remembered that the rights involved in these cases are not only of importance to appellants and the class they represent, but are among the most important in our society. As this Court said on May 17th:

> Today, education is perhaps the most important function of state and local governments. Compulsory school attendance laws and the great expenditures for education both demonstrate our recognition of the importance of education to our democratic society. It is required in the performance of our most basic public responsibilities, even service in the armed forces. It is the very foundation of good citizenship. Today it is a principal instrument in awakening the child to cultural values, in preparing him for later professional training, and in helping him to adjust normally to his environment. In these days, it is doubtful that any child may reasonably be expected to succeed in life if he is denied the opportunity of an education. Such an opportunity, where the state has undertaken to provide it, is a right which must be made available to all on equal terms.

Neither the nuisance cases nor the anti-trust cases afford any support for delay in these cases. On the contrary, in cases more nearly analogous to the instant cases, this Court has held that the executive branch of the government could not justify the detention of wrongfully seized private property on the basis of a national economic crisis in the midst of the Korean conflict. Nor could the War Relocation Authority wrongfully detain a loyal American because of racial tension or threats of disorder. It follows that in these cases this Court should apply similar limitations to the judiciary in the exercise of its equity power when a request is made that it delay enjoyment of personal rights on grounds of alleged expediency.

---

[5] In the instant cases, dark and uncertain prophecies as to anticipated community reactions to school desegregation are speculative at best.

**B. Empirical data negate unsupported speculations that a gradual decree would bring about a more effective adjustment.** Obviously, we are not aware of what appellees will advance on further argument as reasons for postponing the enforcement of the rights here involved. Therefore, the only way we can discuss Question 4(b) is by conjecture in so far as reasons for postponement are concerned.

There is no basis for the assumption that gradual as opposed to immediate desegregation is the better, smoother or more "effective" mode of transition. On the contrary, there is an impressive body of evidence which supports the position that gradualism, far from facilitating the process, may actually make it more difficult; that, in fact, the problems of transition will be a good deal less complicated than might be forecast by appellees. Our submission is that this, like many wrongs, can be easiest and best undone, not by "tapering off" but by forthright action.

There is now substantial documented experience with desegregation in this country, in schools and elsewhere.[6] On the basis of this experience, it is possible to estimate with some accuracy the chances of various types of "gradual" plans for success in minimizing trouble during the period of transition.

Some plans have been tried involving a set "deadline" without the specification of intervening steps to be taken. Where such plans have been tried, the tendency seems to have been to regard the deadline as the time when action is to be initiated rather than the time at which desegregation is to be accomplished. Since there exists no body of knowledge that is even helpful in selecting an optimum time at the end of which the situation may be expected to be better, the deadline date is necessarily arbitrary and hence may be needlessly remote.[7]

A species of the "deadline" type of plan attempts to prepare the public, through churches, radio and other agencies, for the impending change. It is altogether conjectural how successful such attempts might be in actually effecting change in attitude. The underlying assumption—that change in attitude must precede change in action—is itself at best a highly questionable one. There is a considerable body of evidence to indicate that attitude may itself be influenced by situation[8] and that, where the situation demands that an individual act as if he were not prejudiced, he will so act, despite the continuance, at least temporarily, of the prejudice.[9] We submit that this Court can itself contribute to an effective and decisive change in attitude by insistence that the present unlawful situation be changed forthwith.

As to any sort of "deadline" plan, even assuming that community leaders make every effort to build community support for desegregation, experience shows that other forces in the community will use the time allowed to firm up and build opposition.[10] At least in South Carolina and Virginia, as well as in some other states affected by this decision, statements and action of governmental officials since May 17th demonstrate that they will not use the time allowed to build up community support for

---

[6] See ASHMORE, THE NEGRO AND THE SCHOOLS (1954); CLARK, DESEGREGATION: AN APPRAISAL OF THE EVIDENCE, 9 J. SOCIAL ISSUES 1–77 (1953); NEXT STEPS IN RACIAL DESEGREGATION IN EDUCATION, 23 J. NEGRO ED. 201–399 (1954).

See also REPORT BY THE PRESIDENT'S COMMITTEE ON EQUALITY OF OPPORTUNITY IN THE ARMED FORCES (1950).

[7] ASHMORE, op. cit. supra note 6, at 70, 71, 79, 80; CLARK, op. cit. supra note 6, at 36, 45.

[8] CLARK, op. cit. supra note 6, at 69–76.

[9] KUTNER, WILKINS and YARROW, VERBAL ATTITUDES AND OVERT BEHAVIOR INVOLVING RACIAL PREJUDICE, 47 J. ABNORMAL AND SOCIAL PSYCH. 649–652 (1952); LA PIERE, ATTITUDES VS. ACTION, 13 SOCIAL FORCES 230–237 (1934); SAENGER and GILBERT, CUSTOMER REACTIONS TO THE INTEGRATION OF NEGRO SALES PERSONNEL, 4 INT. J. OPINION AND ATTITUDES RESEARCH 57–76 (1950); DEUTSCH and COLLINS, INTERRACIAL HOUSING, A PSYCHOLOGICAL STUDY OF A SOCIAL EXPERIMENT (1951); CHEIN, DEUTSCH, HYMAN and JAHODA, CONSISTENCY AND INCONSISTENCY IN INTERGROUP RELATIONS, 5 J. SOCIAL ISSUES 1–63 (1949).

ASHMORE, op. cit. supra note 6, at 42; New York Times, "Mixed Schools Set in 'Border' States", August 29, 1954, p. 88, col. 1–4; New York Times, "New Mexico Town Quietly Ends Pupil Segregation Despite a Cleric", August 31, 1954, p. 1, col. 3–4; ROSE, YOU CAN'T LEGISLATE AGAINST PREJUDICE—OR CAN YOU?, 9 COMMON GROUND 61–67 (1949), reprinted in RACE PREJUDICE AND DISCRIMINATION, (Rose ed. 1951); NICHOLS, BREAKTHROUGH ON THE COLOR FRONT (1954); MERTON, WEST and JAHODA, SOCIAL FICTIONS AND SOCIAL FACTS: THE DYNAMICS OF RACE RELATIONS IN HILLTOWN, COLUMBIA UNIVERSITY BUREAU OF APPLIED SOCIAL RESEARCH (mimeographed); MERTON, WEST, JAHODA and SELDEN, SOCIAL POLICY AND SOCIAL RESEARCH IN HOUSING, 7 J. SOCIAL ISSUES, 132–140 (1951); MERTON, THE SOCIAL PSYCHOLOGY OF HOUSING (1948).

South as well as North, people's actions and attitudes were changed not in advance of but after the admission of Negroes into organized baseball. See CLEMENT, RACIAL INTEGRATION IN THE FIELD OF SPORTS, 23 J. NEGRO ED. 226–228 (1954). Objections to desegregation have generally been found to be greater before than after its accomplishment. CLARK, op. cit. supra note 6, passim; CONFERENCE REPORT, ARIZONA COUNCIL FOR CIVIC UNITY CONFERENCE ON SCHOOL SEGREGATION (Phoenix, Arizona, June 2, 1951).

[10] CLARK, op. cit. supra note 6, at 43, 44; BROGAN, THE EMERSON SCHOOL—COMMUNITY PROBLEM, GARY, INDIANA, BUREAU OF INTERCULTURAL EDUCATION REPORT (October 1947, mimeographed); TIPTON, COMMUNITY IN CRISIS 15–76 (1953).

desegregation.[11] Church groups and others in the South who are seeking to win community acceptance for the Court's May 17th decision cannot be effective without the support of a forthwith decree from this Court.

Besides the "deadline" plans, various "piecemeal" schemes have been suggested and tried. These seem to be inspired by the assumption that it is always easier and better to do something slowly and a little at a time than to do it all at once. As might be expected, it has appeared that the resistance of some people affected by such schemes is increased since they feel arbitrarily selected as experimental animals. Other members in the community observe this reaction and in turn their anxieties are sharpened.[12]

Piecemeal desegregation of schools, on a class-by-class basis, tends to arouse feelings of the same kind[13] and these feelings are heightened by the intra-familial and intra-school differences thus created.[14] It would be hard to imagine any means better calculated to increase tension in regard to desegregation than to so arrange matters so that some children in a family were attending segregated and others unsegregated classes. Hardly more promising of harmony is the prospect of a school which is segregated in the upper parts and mixed in the lower.

When one looks at various "gradual" processes, the fact is that there is no convincing evidence which supports the theory that "gradual" desegregation is more "effective".[15]

On the contrary, there is considerable evidence that the forthright way is a most effective way.[16]

The progress of desegregation in the Topeka schools is an example of gradualism based upon conjecture, fears and speculation regarding community opposition which might delay completion of desegregation forever. The desegregation plan adopted by the Topeka school authorities called for school desegregation first in the better residential areas of the city and desegregation followed in those areas where the smallest number of Negro children lived. There is little excuse for the school board's not having already completed desegregation. Apparently either the fact that the school board, in order to complete the transition, may have to utilize one or more of the former schools for Negroes and assign white children to them or the fact that it must now reassign some 700 Negro children to approximately seven former all-white schools, seems to present difficulties to appellees. One must remember that in Topeka there has been complete integration above the sixth grade for many years. The schools already desegregated have reported no difficulties. There can hardly be any basic resistance to nonsegregated schools in the habits or customs of the city's populace. The elimination of the remnants of segregation throughout the city's school system should be a simple matter.

No special public preparations involving teachers, parents, students or the general public were made, nor were they necessary in advance of either the first or second step in the implementation of the Board's decision to desegregate the school system. Indeed, the Board of Education adopted the second step in January, 1954, and the only reports of what was involved were those published in the newspapers. Negro parents living in these territories were not notified by appellees regarding the change, but transferred their children to the schools in question on the basis of information provided in the newspapers. As far as the teachers in those schools were concerned, they were merely informed in the Spring of 1954 that their particular schools would be integrated in

---

[11] For the latest example of this, see New York Times, "7 of South's Governors Warn of 'Dissensions' in Curb on Bias—Avow Right of States to Control Public School Procedures—Six at Meeting Refrain from Signing Statement", November 14, 1954, p. 58, col. 4–5.

[12] TIPTON, *op. cit. supra* note 11, at 42, 47, 57, 71; CLARK, SOME PRINCIPLES RELATED TO THE PROBLEM OF DESEGREGATION, 23 J. NEGRO ED. 343 (1954); CULVER, RACIAL DESEGREGATION IN EDUCATION IN INDIANA, 23 J. NEGRO ED. 300 (1954).

[13] ASHMORE, *op. cit. supra* note 6, at 79, 80; CLARK, DESEGREGATION: AN APPRAISAL OF THE EVIDENCE, *op. cit. supra* note 6, at 36, 45.

[14] CLARK, EFFECTS OF PREJUDICE AND DISCRIMINATION ON PERSONALITY DEVELOPMENTS, MID-CENTURY WHITE HOUSE CONFERENCE ON CHILDREN AND YOUTH (mimeographed, 1950).

[15] ASHMORE, *op. cit. supra* note 6, at 80:
Proponents of the gradual approach argue that it minimizes public resistance to integration. But some school officials who have experienced it believe the reverse is true. A markedly gradual program, they contend, particularly one which involves the continued maintenance of some separate schools, invites opposition and allows time for it to be organized. Whatever the merit of this argument, the case histories clearly indicate a tendency for local political pressure to be applied by both sides when the question of integration is raised, and when policies remain unsettled for a protracted period the pressures mount.

---

One school board member in Arizona privately expressed the wish that the state had gone all the way and made integration mandatory instead of optional—thus giving the board something to point to as justification for its action.

[16] CLARK, *op. cit. supra* note 6, at 46, 47; WRIGHT, RACIAL INTEGRATION IN THE PUBLIC SCHOOLS OF NEW JERSEY, 23 J. NEGRO ED. 283 (1954); KNOX, RACIAL INTEGRATION IN THE SCHOOLS OF ARIZONA, NEW MEXICO, AND KANSAS, 23 J. NEGRO ED. 291, 293 (1954); CULVER, RACIAL DESEGREGATION IN EDUCATION IN INDIANA, 23 J. NEGRO ED. 296, 300–302 (1954).

September. Thus, delay here cannot be based upon need for public orientation.

It should be pointed out that of the 23 public elementary schools, there exists potential space for some additional 83 classrooms of which 16 such potential classrooms are in the four schools to which the majority of the Negroes are now assigned. No claim can be made that the school system is overcrowded and unable to absorb the Negro and white children under a reorganization plan. There is no discernable reason why all of the elementary schools of Topeka have not been desegregated.

As is pointed out in the Brief for Petitioners on Further Reargument in *Bolling* v. *Sharpe* (No. 4, October Term, 1954) the gradualist approach adopted by the Board of Education in Washington, D.C., produced confusion, hardship and unnecessary delay. Indeed, the operation of the "Corning Plan" has produced manifold problems in school administration which could have been avoided if the transition had been immediate. The argument that delay is more sound educationally has been shown to be without basis in fact in the operation of the District of Columbia plan—so conclusively, in fact, that the time schedule has been accelerated. The experience in the District argues for immediate action.

To suggest that this Court may properly mold its relief so as to serve whatever theories as to educational policy may be in vogue is to confuse its function with that of a school board, and to confuse the clear-cut constitutional issue in these cases with the situation in which a school board might find itself if it were unbound by constitutional requirements and were addressing itself to the policy problem of effecting desegregation in what seems to it the most desirable way. But even if a judgment as to the abstract desirability of gradualism could be supported by evidence, it is outside the province of this Court to balance the merely desirable against the adjudicated constitutional rights of appellants. The Constitution has prescribed the educational policy applicable to the issue tendered in this case, and this Court has no power, under the guise of a "gradual" decree, to select another.

We submit that there are various necessary administrative factors which would make "immediate" relief as of tomorrow physically impossible. These include such factors as need for redistricting and the redistribution of teachers and pupils. Under the circumstances of this case, the Court's mandate will probably come down in the middle or near the close of the 1954 school term, and the decrees of the courts of first instance could not be put into effect

until September, 1955. Appellees would, therefore, have had from May 17, 1954, to September, 1955, to make necessary administrative changes.

## II. Answering Question 5: If this court should decide to permit an "effective gradual adjustment" from segregated school systems to systems not based on color distinctions, it should not formulate detailed decrees but should remand these cases to the courts of first instance with specific directions to complete desegregation by a day certain

In answering Question 5, we are required to assume that this Court "will exercise its equity powers to permit an effective gradual adjustment to be brought about from existing segregated systems to a system not based on color distinctions" thereby refusing to hold that appellants were entitled to decrees providing that, "within the limits set by normal geographic school districting, Negro children should forthwith be admitted to schools of their choice." While we feel most strongly that this Court will not subordinate appellants' constitutional rights to immediate relief to any plan for an "effective gradual adjustment," we must nevertheless assume the contrary for the purpose of answering Question 5.[17]

Question 5 assumes that there should be an "effective gradual adjustment" to a system of desegregated education. We have certain difficulties with this formulation. We have already demonstrated that there is no reason to believe that any form of gradualism will be more effective than forthwith compliance. If, however, this Court determines upon a gradual decree, we then urge that, as a minimum, certain safeguards must be embodied in that "gradual" decree in order to render it as nearly "effective" as any decree can be which continues the injury being suffered by these appellants as a consequence of the unconstitutional practice here complained of.

---

[17] "5. On the assumption on which question 4(*a*) and (*b*) are based, and assuming further that this Court will exercise its equity powers to the end described in question 4(*b*).

"(*a*) should this Court formulate detailed decrees in these cases;

"(*b*) if so, what specific issues should the decrees reach;

"(*c*) should this Court appoint a special master to hear evidence with a view to recommending specific terms for such decrees;

"(*d*) should this Court remand to the courts of first instance with directions to frame decrees in these cases, and if so, what general directions should the decrees of this Court include and what procedures should the courts of first instance follow in arriving at the specific terms of more detailed decrees?"

Appellants assume that "the great variety of local conditions", to which the Court referred in its May 17th opinion, embraces only such educationally relevant factors as variations in administrative organization, physical facilities, school population and pupil redistribution, and does not include such judicially non-cognizable factors as need for community preparation, Ex Parte *Endo*, 323 U.S. 283, and threats of racial hostility and violence, *Buchanan* v. *Warley*, 245 U.S. 60; *Monk* v. *City of Birmingham*, 185 F. 2d 859 (C. A. 5th 1950), *cert. denied*, 341 U.S. 940.

Further we assume that the word "effective" might be so construed that a plan contemplating desegregation after the lapse of many years could be called an "effective gradual adjustment." For, whenever the change is in fact made, it results in a desegregated system. We do not understand that this type of adjustment would be "effective" within the meaning of Question 5 nor do we undertake to answer it in this framework. Rather, we assume that under any circumstances, the question encompasses due consideration for the constitutional rights of each of these appellants and those presently in the class they represent to be free from enforced racial segregation in public education.

Ordinarily, the problem—the elimination of race as the criterion of admission to public schools—by its very nature would require only general dispositive directions by this Court. Even if the Court decides that the adjustment to nonsegregated systems is to be gradual, no elaborate decree structure is essential at this stage of the proceedings. In neither event would appellants now ask this Court, or any other court, to direct or supervise the details of operation of the local school systems. In either event, we would seek effective provisions assuring their operation—forthwith in the one instance and eventually in the other—in conformity with the Constitution.

These considerations suggest appellants' answers to Question 5. Briefly stated, this Court should not formulate detailed decrees in these cases. It should not appoint a special master to hear evidence with a view to recommending specific terms for such decrees. It should remand these cases to the courts of first instance with directions to frame decrees incorporating certain provisions, hereinafter discussed, that appellants believe are calculated to make them as nearly effective as any gradual desegregation decree can be. The courts of first instance need only follow normal procedures in arriving at such additional provisions for such decrees as circumstances may warrant.

**Declaratory provisions** This Court should reiterate in the clearest possible language that segregation in public education is a denial of the equal protection of the laws. It should order that the decrees include a recital that constitutional and statutory provisions, and administrative and judicial pronouncements, requiring or sanctioning segregated education afford no basis for the continued maintenance of segregation in public schools.

The important legal consequence of such declaratory provisions would be to obviate the real or imagined dilemma of some school officials who contend that, pending the issuance of injunctions against the continuation of segregated education in their own systems, they are entitled or even obliged to carry out state policies the invalidity of which this Court has already declared. The dilemma is well illustrated by the case of *Steiner* v. *Simmons* (Del. Sup. Ct. No. 27, 1954), pending in the Delaware Supreme Court, wherein plaintiffs are suing for readmission to Milford's high school from which, on September 30, 1954, they were expelled because they are Negroes. The Vice Chancellor granted the requested mandatory injunction, finding that plaintiffs had a constitutional right to readmission to school. The Delaware Supreme Court, however, granted a stay pending determination of the appeal on the basis of its preliminary conclusion that "there are serious questions of law touching the existence of that legal right."[18]

This Court's decision of May 17th put state authorities on notice that thereafter they could not with impunity abrogate the constitutional rights of American children not to be segre-

---

[18] Cf. Burr v. Bd. of School Commrs. of Baltimore, Superior Court of Baltimore City, Oct. 5, 1954 (unreported), in which case Judge James K. Cullen stated in part:

In the instant case this Court is asked to issue a writ of mandamus requiring these defendants, the School Board, to continue with its policy of segregation. This Court finds the Board of School Commissioners have exercised their discretion legally and in accordance with a final and enforceable holding and decision of the Supreme Court. Those cases were undoubtedly argued before the Supreme Court fully, and the views of every division of thought of our citizenry was undoubtedly presented to the Court; but the Court has spoken. Whether the individual agrees or disagrees with the finding, he is bound thereby so long as it remains the law of the land. The Court realizes the change and the difficulty some may have accepting the reality or the inevitable from the standpoint of enforcement. We live in a country where our rights and liberties have been protected under a system of laws which has withstood the test of time. We must allow ourselves to be governed by those laws, realizing there are many differences among our people. Respect for the law is of paramount importance. The law must be accepted. We must all be forced to abide by it. We can gain nothing by demonstrations of violence except sorrow and possible destructions.

gated in public schools on the basis of race. This type of recital in the decree should foreclose further misunderstanding, real or pretended, of the principle of law that continuation of racial segregation in public education is in direct violation of the Constitution—state constitutions, statutes, custom or usage requiring such segregation to the contrary notwithstanding.

**Time provisions**  We do not know what considerations may be presented by appellees to warrant gradualism. But whatever these considerations may be, appellants submit that any school plan embracing gradualism must safeguard against the gradual adjustment becoming an interminable one. Therefore, appellants respectfully urge that this Court's opinion and mandate also contain specific directions that any decree to be entered by a district court shall specify (1) that the process of desegregation be commenced immediately, (2) that appellees be required to file periodic reports to the courts of first instance, and (3) an outer time limit by which desegregation must be completed.

Even cases involving gradual decrees have required some amount of immediate compliance by the party under an obligation to remedy his wrongs to the extent physically possible.[19] In *Wisconsin* v. *Illinois*, 281 U.S. 179, the Court said:

> It already has been decided that the defendants are doing a wrong to the complainants, and that they must stop it. They must find out a way at their peril. We have only to consider what is possible if the state of Illinois devotes all its powers to dealing with an exigency to the magnitude of which it seems not yet to have fully awaked. It can base no defenses upon difficulties that it has itself created. If its Constitution stands in the way of prompt action, it must amend it or yield to an authority that is paramount to the state (p. 197).
>
> * * *
>
> 1. On and after July 1, 1930,[20] the defendants, the state of Illinois and the sanitary district of Chicago are enjoined from diverting any of the waters of the Great Lakes-St. Lawrence system or watershed through the Chicago drainage canal and its auxiliary channels or otherwise in excess of an annual average of 6,500 c.f.s. in addition to domestic pumpage (p. 201).

Considering the normal time consumed before the issuance of the mandate of this Court and the time for submission and preparation of decrees by the courts of first instance, decrees in these cases will not issue until after February, 1955—after the normal mid-term in most school systems. Thus, the school boards would have until September, 1955—sixteen months after the May 17th opinions—to change to a system not based on color distinctions. This time could very well be considered as necessarily incidental to any decision by this Court requiring "forthwith" decrees by the courts of first instance.

Whatever the reasons for gradualism, there is no reason to believe that the process of transition would be more effective if further extended. Certainly, to indulge school authorities until September 1, 1956, to achieve desegregation would be generous in the extreme. Therefore, we submit that if the Court decides to grant further time, then the Court should direct that all decrees specify September, 1956, as the outside date by which desegregation must be accomplished. This would afford more than a year, in excess of the time necessary for administrative changes, to review and modify decisions in the light of lessons learned as these decisions are put into effect.

We submit that the decrees should contain no provision for extension of the fixed limit, whatever date may be fixed. Such a provision would be merely an invitation to procrastinate.[21]

We further urge this Court to make it plain that the time for completion of the desegregation program will not depend upon the success or failure of interim activities. The decrees in the instant cases should accordingly provide that in the event the school authorities should for any reason fail to comply with the time limitation of the decree, Negro children should then be immediately admitted to the schools to which they apply.[22]

All states requiring segregated public education were by the May 17th decision of this Court put upon notice that segregated systems of public education are unconstitutional. A decision granting appellees time for gradual adjustment should be so framed that no other

---

[19] See Wisconsin v. Illinois, 281 U.S. 179; Arizona Copper Co. v. Gillespie, 230 U.S. 46; Georgia v. Tennessee Copper Co., 206 U.S. 230; Westinghouse Air Brake Co. v. Great Northern Ry. Co., 86 Fed. 132 (C. C. S. D. N. Y. 1898).

[20] This opinion was rendered April 30, 1930.

[21] ASHMORE, THE NEGRO AND THE SCHOOLS 70–71 (1954); CULVER, RACIAL DESEGREGATION IN EDUCATION IN INDIANA, 23 J. NEGRO ED. 296–302 (1954).

[22] See United States v. American Tobacco Co., 221 U.S. 106, where this Court directed the allowance of a period of six months, with leave to grant an additional sixty days if necessary, for activities dissolving an illegal monopoly and recreating out of its components a new situation in harmony with the law, but further directed that if within this period a legally harmonious condition was not brought about, the lower court should give effect to the requirements of the Sherman Act.

state maintaining such a system is lulled into a period of inaction and induced to merely await suit on the assumption that it will then be granted the same period of time after such suit is instituted.

## CONCLUSION

Much of the opposition to forthwith desegregation does not truly rest on any theory that it is better to accomplish it gradually. In considerable part, if indeed not in the main, such opposition stems from a desire that desegregation not be undertaken at all. In consideration of the type of relief to be granted in any case, due consideration must be given to the character of the right to be protected. Appellants here seek effective protection for adjudicated constitutional rights which are personal and present. Consideration of a plea for delay in enforcement of such rights must be preceded by a showing of clear legal precedent therefor and some public necessity of a gravity never as yet demonstrated.

There are no applicable legal precedents justifying a plea for delay. As a matter of fact, relevant legal precedents preclude a valid plea for delay. And, an analysis of the non-legal materials relevant to the issue whether or not relief should be delayed in these cases shows that the process of gradual desegregation is at best no more effective than immediate desegregation.

WHEREFORE, we respectfully submit that this Court should direct the issuance of decrees in each of these cases requiring desegregation by no later than September of 1955.

CHARLES L. BLACK, JR.,
ELWOOD H. CHISOLM,
WILLIAM T. COLEMAN, JR.,
CHARLES T. DUNCAN,
GEORGE E. C. HAYES,
LOREN MILLER,
WILLIAM R. MING, JR.,
CONSTANCE BAKER MOTLEY,
JAMES M. NABRIT, JR.,
DAVID E. PINSKY,
FRANK D. REEVES,
JOHN SCOTT,
JACK B. WEINSTEIN,
    *of Counsel.*

HAROLD BOULWARE,
ROBERT L. CARTER,
JACK GREENBERG,
OLIVER W. HILL,
THURGOOD MARSHALL,
LOUIS L. REDDING,
SPOTTSWOOD W. ROBINSON, III,
CHARLES S. SCOTT,
    *Attorneys for Appellants in Nos. 1, 2, 3
    and for Respondents in No. 5.*

# In the
# Supreme Court of the United States

### No. 1, October Term, 1954

### Oliver Brown, et al., Appellants

### vs.

### Board of Education of Topeka, Shawnee County, Kansas et al., Appellees

## Appeal from the United States District Court for the District of Kansas

# Supplemental Brief for the Board of Education, Topeka, Kansas, on Questions 4 and 5 Propounded by the Court

Peter F. Caldwell,
Counsel for the Board of Education of
Topeka, Kansas,
512 Capitol Federal Building,
Topeka, Kansas.

## IN THE SUPREME COURT OF THE UNITED STATES NO. 1, OCTOBER TERM, 1954

OLIVER BROWN, ET AL., APPELLANTS

VS.

BOARD OF EDUCATION OF TOPEKA, SHAWNEE COUNTY, KANSAS ET AL., APPELLEES

## SUPPLEMENTAL BRIEF FOR THE BOARD OF EDUCATION, TOPEKA, KANSAS, ON QUESTIONS 4 AND 5 PROPOUNDED BY THE COURT

This supplemental brief is filed in response to the order of this Court directing and requesting further briefs and argument on questions 4 and 5 heretofore propounded by the Court.

In its brief, heretofore filed herein in December, 1953, The Board of Education of Topeka urged that in the event segregation in its elementary schools were held to be unconstitutional, this case should simply be remanded to the lower court with instructions to reverse its judgment and to enter a decree requiring that segregation be terminated "as rapidly as is practicable" by the defendant Board of Education. It was suggested that by such a decree the lower court could retain jurisdiction for enforcement of the decree, and that if a need for a more specific decree should arise in the future, the lower court would have power to amplify its decree under the general power of an equity court to enforce its decree.

As was pointed out in its brief filed in December, 1953, The Board of Education of Topeka in September, 1953, adopted a resolution to terminate segregation in its elementary schools "as rapidly as is practicable"; and on September 8, 1953, terminated segregation at two of its elementary schools, to wit: Southwest and Randolph Schools.

Since that time, the Board of Education of Topeka has already taken its second far-reaching step or stride toward termination of segregation by adopting the recommendations of its superintendent of schools as set out in the following report which was made on January 20, 1954, and was approved and adopted by the Board of Education on the same date:

### SECOND STEP IN TERMINATION OF SEGREGATION IN TOPEKA ELEMENTARY SCHOOLS

**I.** In implementation of the Board's policy to terminate segregation in elementary schools as soon as practicable, I propose that the second step be taken at the opening of school in September, 1954. The step should be acted upon by the Board at this time in order to enable everybody concerned to make necessary plans for next year.

**II.** In the second step, I propose that segregation be terminated in the following school districts and that transportation not be provided for Negro children who are affected, but that such child be given the privilege of attending the nearest Negro School if his parents want him to do so. (All pupil accounting is based on the number belonging on October 16, 1953.)

| | Negro Children to Integrated Schools | Negro Children to Come from Following Schools | | | |
|---|---|---|---|---|---|
| | | McKinley | Buchanan | Monroe | Washington |
| 1. Central Park | 21 | | 16 | 5 | |
| 2. Clay | 13 | | 12 | 1 | |
| 3. Crestview | 0 | | | | |
| 4. Gage | 1 | | | | |
| 5. Grant (Limited)* | 3 | 3 | 1 | | |
| 6. Oakland | 0 | | | | |
| 7. Polk (Limited)** | 3 | | | 3 | |
| 8. Potwin | 0 | | | | |
| 9. Quincy | 34 | 34 | | | |
| 10. Quinton Heights | 10 | | 5 | 5 | |
| 11. State Street | 21 | | | 9 | 12 |
| 12. Sumner | 7 | 1 | 5 | 1 | |
| | 113 | 38 | 39 | 24 | 12 |
| Randolph | 2 | | | | |
| Southwest | 8 | | | | |
| | 123 | | | | |

*The limitation suggested at Grant is that three Negro children isolated in the extreme northern part of Grant School district be permitted to attend Grant, while the remainder of the Negro children continue at McKinley.
**The limitation suggested at Polk School is as follows: Several Negro children in this district live very close to Buchanan School. They should continue at this school. There would not be room for them at Polk and there is plenty of room at Buchanan. However, there are three Negro children now attending Monroe School but residing in the Polk district. I suggest that they be allowed to attend Polk School.

**III.** The effects of taking this step would be as follows:

1 It would reduce the enrollments of Negro Schools as indicated.

|  | From | To |
|---|---|---|
| McKinley | 127 | 89 |
| Buchanan | 160 | 121 |
| Monroe | 245 | 221 |
| Washington | 292 | 280 |
|  | 824 | 711 |

2. It would place 123 Negro children in integrated schools.

3. It would leave, in addition to the four schools for Negro children, 12 schools integrated, 2 schools (Grant and Polk) on a basis of partial integration, and 5 schools continuing on a segregated basis (Lafayette, Lincoln, Lowman Hill, Parkdale and Van Buren.)

Thus, by announcing the changes in the spring of 1954, all parties affected had ample opportunity to adjust themselves to the changes before they became effective the following September.

Segregation has been completely terminated in 12 elementary school districts, and partially terminated in two others; and, as of September, 1954, there will remain only four Negro schools and five white schools in which segregation is being continued.

The Board of Education has requested the superintendent, and he plans, to make recommendations for the third step toward termination of segregation early in 1955 to become effective in September, 1955. In the meantime, of course, he will have had an opportunity to observe the results and the operation of the second step which became effective in September, 1954. Thus before taking the third step, the board of education will have the benefit of its experiences with the first and second steps.

It is gratifying to be able to report to the Court that The Board of Education has been carrying out its policy of termination of segregation "as rapidly as is practicable" with full public cooperation and acceptance by both white and Negro pupils, teachers and parents.

The administrative problems, which were discussed in the brief filed in December, 1953, are the chief problems with which The Board of Education is confronted; but with practical experience, they are being satisfactorily solved. Their solution, however, cannot be effected "forthwith," but require time for a gradual adjustment.

It is respectfully submitted that The Board of Education of Topeka is in good faith carrying out its adopted policy to terminate segregation "as rapidly as is practicable," and that there is no need at this time for the appointment of a special master or for the Court to undertake to formulate specific decrees directing the particular steps to be taken to terminate segregation in the schools of Topeka.

Respectfully submitted,

PETER F. CALDWELL,
Counsel for the Board of Education
of Topeka, Kansas,
512 Capitol Federal Building,
Topeka, Kansas.

# IN THE
## SUPREME COURT OF THE UNITED STATES
### OCTOBER TERM, 1954

#### No. 1

OLIVER BROWN, ET AL., APPELLANTS,

VS.

BOARD OF EDUCATION OF TOPEKA, ET AL., APPELLEES.

#### No. 2

HARRY BRIGGS, JR., ET AL., APPELLANTS,

VS.

R. W. ELLIOTT, ET AL., APPELLEES.

#### No. 3

DOROTHY E. DAVIS, ET AL., APPELLANTS,

VS.

COUNTY SCHOOL BOARD OF PRINCE EDWARD COUNTY, VIRGINIA, ET AL., APPELLEES.

#### No. 5

FRANCIS B. GEBHART, ET AL., PETITIONERS,

VS.

ETHEL LOUISE BELTON, ET AL., RESPONDENTS.

**APPEALS FROM THE UNITED STATES DISTRICT COURTS FOR THE DISTRICT OF KANSAS, THE EASTERN DISTRICT OF SOUTH CAROLINA AND THE EASTERN DISTRICT OF VIRGINIA, AND ON PETITION FOR A WRIT OF CERTIORARI TO THE SUPREME COURT OF DELAWARE, RESPECTIVELY**

## REPLY BRIEF FOR APPELLANTS IN NOS. 1, 2 AND 3 AND FOR RESPONDENTS IN NO. 5 ON FURTHER REARGUMENT

CHARLES L. BLACK, JR.,
ELWOOD H. CHISOLM,
WILLIAM T. COLEMAN, JR.,
CHARLES T. DUNCAN,
GEORGE E. C. HAYES,
LOREN MILLER,
WILLIAM R. MING, JR.,
CONSTANCE BAKER MOTLEY,
JAMES M. NABRIT, JR.,
LOUIS H. POLLAK,
FRANK D. REEVES,
JOHN SCOTT,
JACK B. WEINSTEIN,
*of Counsel.*

HAROLD BOULWARE,
ROBERT L. CARTER,
JACK GREENBERG,
OLIVER W. HILL,
THURGOOD MARSHALL,
LOUIS L. REDDING,
SPOTTSWOOD W. ROBINSON, III,
CHARLES S. SCOTT,
*Attorneys for Appellants in Nos. 1, 2, 3*
*and for Respondents in No. 5.*

# TABLE OF CONTENTS

## IN THE
## SUPREME COURT OF THE
## UNITED STATES
## OCTOBER TERM, 1954
## NO. 1

OLIVER BROWN, ET AL., APPELLANTS,

VS.

BOARD OF EDUCATION OF TOPEKA, ET AL.,
APPELLEES.

## NO. 2

HARRY BRIGGS, JR., ET AL., APPELLANTS,

VS.

R. W. ELLIOTT, ET AL., APPELLEES.

## NO. 3

DOROTHY E. DAVIS, ET AL., APPELLANTS,

VS.

COUNTY SCHOOL BOARD OF PRINCE
EDWARD COUNTY, VIRGINIA, ET AL.,
APPELLEES.

## NO. 5

FRANCIS B. GEBHART, ET AL., PETITIONERS,

VS.

ETHEL LOUISE BELTON, ET AL., RESPONDENTS.

**APPEALS FROM THE UNITED
STATES DISTRICT COURTS FOR
THE DISTRICT OF KANSAS, THE
EASTERN DISTRICT OF SOUTH
CAROLINA AND THE EASTERN
DISTRICT OF VIRGINIA, AND ON
PETITION FOR A WRIT OF
CERTIORARI TO THE SUPREME
COURT OF DELAWARE,
RESPECTIVELY**

# REPLY BRIEF FOR APPELLANTS
# IN NOS. 1, 2 AND 3 AND FOR
# RESPONDENTS IN NO. 5 ON
# FURTHER REARGUMENT

The briefs filed on this reargument by appellees and *amici curiae* (with the exception of those in Nos. 1 and 5, and the brief filed on behalf of the Attorney General of The United States) are similar in substance despite some differences in details. Our reply to them can, therefore, be made in one joint brief.

## ARGUMENT

**Briefs filed by appellees and state Attorneys General do not offer any affirmative plan for desegregation but are merely restatements of arguments in favor of interminable continuation of racial segregation**

In our Brief on Further Reargument, we stated:[1]

> Much of the opposition to forthwith desegregation does not truly rest on any theory that it is better to accomplish it gradually. In considerable part, if indeed not in the main, such opposition stems from a desire that desegregation not be undertaken at all.

Similarly, the briefs filed at this time, both by appellees and state attorneys general seem to be directed against ending racial segregation in our time, rather than toward desegregation within a reasonable time. First, these briefs do not in fact offer any affirmative plan or elements of such a plan for accomplishing the task of desegregation. Secondly, and equally significant, the main reasons now proffered in support of indefinite delay are identical with arguments previously advanced for denying relief on the merits.

This Court has decided that racial segregation is unconstitutional—that it is a practice, moreover, which has such effects on its victims that it can only be described as abhorrent. Yet, in answering questions 4 and 5, propounded by the Court, the States do not even get around to what must, in the light of that decision, be the main problem underlying those questions: How can this practice be most expeditiously done away with? Reasons for delay, which would seem to occupy at best a subsidiary position, are the sole preoccupation of state counsel, and the affirmative problem gets virtually no attention.[2]

---

[1] Brief for Appellants in Nos. 1, 2 and 3 and for Respondents in No. 5 on Further Reargument, 1954 Term, p. 31.

[2] It is true that Delaware and Kansas catalogue the progress they have made thus far in accomplishing integration. But both states plead for delay without offering any valid reasons therefor.

The brief of the Attorney General of Florida does contain a Point entitled "Specific Suggestions to the Court in Formulating a Decree."[3] But, the effect of the suggested plan[4] would be to subject the constitutional rights of Negro children to denial on the basis of such a variety of intangible factors that the plan itself cannot be seriously regarded as one for implementing the May 17th decision.

Each individual Negro child must, under the Florida plan, petition a court of the first instance for admission to an unsegregated school, after exhausting his administrative remedies. It is up to him to establish to that court's satisfaction that there exists no "reasonable grounds" for delay in his admission. "Reasonable grounds" include lack of a reasonable time to amend the state school laws, good faith efforts of the school board in promoting citizens' educational committees, administrative problems, and "evidence of . . . a strong degree of *sincere* opposition and sustained hostility" [emphasis supplied] giving the school board ground to believe that admission of the applicant would ". . . create emotional responses among the children which would seriously interfere with their education." In other words, the applicant's right is to be postponed until everything seems entirely propitious for granting it. It is submitted that this is not a plan for granting rights, but a plan for denying them just as long as can possibly be done without a direct overruling of the May 17th decision.

Lest there be any doubt about this, the final criterion for admission to unsegregated schooling should be quoted:[5]

(6) Evidence that the petitioner's application was made in good faith and not for *capricious* reasons. Such evidence should demonstrate:

(a) That the petitioner personally feels that he would be handicapped in his education, either because of lack of school plant facilities or psychological or sociological reasons if his application for admission is denied.

(b) That the petitioner is not motivated in his application solely by a desire for the advancement of a racial group on economic, social or political grounds, as distinguished from his personal legal right to equality in public school education as guaranteed by the 14th Amendment. This distinction should be carefully drawn [emphasis supplied].

Where the devisers of a plan are disposed to characterize opposition to desegregation as "sincere" and reasons for desiring admission as "capricious", we cannot be surprised at a rather peculiar procedural consequence of the dispensation they set up. The "petitioner", if he is to make timely application, exhaust his administrative remedies, and allow time for appeal, will have to draw this fine distinction at about four years of age, if he is to start the first grade in a desegregated school. Out of the mouths of babes and sucklings will have to come a wisdom in self-analysis which surely has never in the history of this country been required of any applicant for relief from the denial of a personal constitutional right. The Florida Brief is no real exception to the statement that none of the States has offered any plan for actually implementing the decision of this Court.

The quality and thrust of the reasons now advanced for delay may best be evaluated by noting that (except for those that deal with purely administrative matters obviously requiring little time for solution) they are arguments which were advanced at an earlier stage in this litigation as grounds for denying relief on the merits, and now, under slightly altered guise, they walk again after their supposed laying to rest on May 17. Thus, the impossibility of procuring community acceptance of desegregation, urged earlier as a ground for decision on the merits,[6] now turns up as an argument for indefinite postponement[7] with no convincing reasons given for supposing that community attitudes will change within the segregated pattern.

The prediction that white parents will withdraw their children from public schools is repeated,[8] with the implied hope, no doubt, that at some remote date they will have attained a state of mind that will result in their leaving their children in school. "Racial tensions" are again predicted.[9] Negro teachers may lose their jobs.[10] Violence is warned of.[11] The people and

---

[3] Brief of the Attorney General of the State of Florida as *amicus curiae*, pp. 57–65. Hereinafter, citations to briefs of appellees and *amici curiae* will be abbreviated. See, e.g., fn. 5, *infra*.

[4] Set out commencing at p. 61 of the Florida Brief.

[5] Florida Brief, p. 63.

[6] South Carolina Brief (1952) p. 27. Cf. *Id.* at p. 35; Virginia Brief (1952) pp. 24–25.

[7] Virginia Brief (1954) p. 13; Delaware Brief (1954) pp. 16, 25; Florida Brief (1954) p. 201 ff.; Texas Brief (1954) pp. 16–17; North Carolina Brief (1954) pp. 7–8.

[8] *Compare* Florida Brief (1954) pp. 26–27 and North Carolina Brief (1954) pp. 36–37 *with* Virginia Brief (1952) p. 30.

[9] *Compare* Florida Brief (1954) p. 95 *with* Virginia Brief (1952) p. 27.

[10] *Compare* Florida Brief (1954) pp. 31–32; North Carolina Brief (1954) pp. 24–25; and Texas Brief (1954) pp. 10–11, *with* Virginia Brief (1952) p. 31.

[11] *Compare* North Carolina Brief (1954) p. 37 and Florida Brief (1954) p. 25 *with* South Carolina Brief (1952) p. 27.

the legislature will abolish the school system or decline to appropriate money for its support.[12]

All these are serious matters, but we have elsewhere shown solid reason for believing that those dire predictions, one and all, are unreliable. There is no reason for supposing that delay can minimize whatever unpleasant consequences might follow from the eradication of this great evil. Here, however, the point is that, where these arguments are resuscitated as grounds for delay, the inference is that their sponsors favor delay as long as present conditions prevail—that, in other words, they now want to delay desegregation just as long as the conditions exist which they formerly regarded as sufficient grounds for imposing segregation as a matter of legal right. The distinction is too fine to make such practical difference, either to the Negro child who is growing up or to this Court.

That it is opposition to the principle of the May 17th decision that animates these briefs is made clear by noting that the equality of schools, *Plessy* style, is now being urged as a ground for delay.[13] Nothing could make it clearer, moreover, that many responsible officials, taking a realistic view, will not regard the "separate but equal" doctrine as abolished until this Court orders its abandonment in practice. Most significant here is the *amicus curiae* brief of the Attorney General of Texas which, after making a straight-out *Plessy* argument, continues with the statement: "However, if the occasion arises whereby we are compelled to abolish segregation in Texas, it should be a gradual adjustment in view of the complexities of the problem" (p. 4).

### Opinion polls are immaterial to the issues herein and do not afford any basis to support an argument that a gradual adjustment would be more effective

Several of the briefs filed herein refer to polls of public opinion in their respective States in support of arguments to postpone desegregation indefinitely.[14] These polls appear to have been made for the purpose of sampling opinions of various groups within the State as to whether they approved of the May 17th decision and whether they thought it could be enforced immediately without friction.

The information as to racial hostility obtained from these polls is indecisive of the issues before this Court. In *Buchanan* v. *Warley*, 245 U.S. 60, 80, this Court stated:

> That there exists a serious and difficult problem arising from a feeling of race hostility which the law is powerless to control, and to which it must give a measure of consideration, may be freely admitted. But its solution cannot be promoted by depriving citizens of their constitutional rights and privileges.

We believe the same answer should be given to any suggestion that the enforcement of constitutional rights be deferred to a time when it will have uniform public acceptance.

Even if relevant, results of polls are often not conclusive. For example, the Florida survey polled eleven "leadership" groups. These groups give evidence of a very high degree of "willingness" to comply. Although peace officers are greatly opposed to desegregation (Table 3, p. 138), only two of the eleven groups would not positively comply, and in those cases there is a very even division (Table 4, p. 139). Overall, six of the eleven groups are not opposed to the decision (Table 3, p. 138); 84.5% of white principals and supervisors who, would be charged with the duty of implementation, would comply (Table 4, p. 139). A majority of all groups expect neither mob violence nor "serious violence" (Table 5, p. 140).

Moreover, such polls are not a valid index of how the individuals questioned will in fact act in the event of desegregation. Modern psychological research shows that, especially in the case of broad public issues, many persons simply "do not follow through even on actions which they say they personally will take in support of an opinion."[15]

---

[12] *Compare* North Carolina Brief (1954) p. 36; Virginia Brief (1954) p. 15; and Arkansas Brief (1954) pp. 7–8 *with* South Carolina Brief (1952) p. 27.

[13] *Compare* North Carolina Brief (1954) pp. 25–35, 43; Texas Brief (1954) pp. 2–4; and Maryland Brief (1954) p. 10 *with* Virginia Brief (1952) pp. 18–19 and South Carolina Brief (1952) pp. 8–9.

[14] Texas Brief, pp. 16–17; Virginia Brief pp. 13–14; North Carolina Brief pp. 7–9; Florida Brief pp. 23–24, 105 ff; Delaware Brief p. 12.

[15] Buchanan, Krugman and Van Wagenen, An International Police Force and Public Opinion 13 (1954). For other studies dealing with the discrepancy between verbal statements and actions, see Link and Freiberg, "The Problem of Validity vs. Reliability in Public Opinion Polls", 6 Public Opinion Quarterly 87–98, esp. 91–92 (1942); Jenkins and Corbin, "Dependability of Psychological Brand Barometers II, The Problem of Validity", 22 Journal of Applied Psychology, 252–260 (1938); Hyman, "Do They Tell the Truth?", 8 Public Opinion Quarterly 557–559 (1944); Social Science Research Council, Committee on Analysis of Pre-Election Polls and Forecasts 302–303 (1949); La Piere, "Attitudes vs. Actions", 13 Social Forces 230–237 (1934); Doob, Public Opinion and Propaganda 151 (1948); Hartley and Hartley, Fundamentals of Social Psychology 657 (1952). See also *Irvin* v. *State*, 66 So. 2d 288, 290–292, *cert. denied* 346 U.S. 927, *reh. denied* 347 U.S. 914.

The Attorney General of Texas sets out in his brief in these cases a survey by the "Texas Poll" showing 71% disapproval of the May 17th decision and 65% approval of continued segregation notwithstanding this Court's decision. It is interesting to note that in *Sweatt* v. *Painter*, 339 U.S. 629, respondents included in their brief a survey made by the same "Texas Poll" showing that 76% of all Texans were "against Negroes and whites going to the same universities." However, this Court ordered Sweatt admitted to the University of Texas. He and other Negroes attended the University.[16] Since then Negroes have been admitted to and are attending this and other public universities in twelve southern States.[16a]

Finally, there is nothing to indicate that an extended delay in ordering the elimination of all segregation will improve public attitudes or eliminate the objections presently interposed. Clearly the polls are irrelevant and should be so treated by this Court.

**The wide applicability of the decision in these cases should not affect the relief to which appellants are entitled**

Effort is made throughout the briefs for appellees and the several attorneys general to balance the personal and present rights here involved against the large number of children of both races now attending public school on a segregated basis. This argument is made for a twofold purpose: to escape the uniformity of decisions of this Court on the personal character of the rights involved and, secondly, to destroy the present character of the right involved.

Of course, the decision of this Court in the instant cases will have wide effect involving public school systems of many states and many public school children. The mere fact of numbers involved is not sufficient to delay enforcement of rights of the type here involved.[17]

On the face of it, their position is both ill-taken and self-defeating. That it is ill-taken becomes clear when the suggestion itself is clearly stated; obviously, there is nothing in mere numerousness as such which has any tendency whatever to create or destroy rights to efficacious legal relief. Behind every numeral is a Negro child, suffering the effects spoken of by the Court on May 17. It is a manifest inconsequence to say that the rights or remedial needs of each child are diminished merely because others are in the same position. That this argument is self-defeating emerges when it is considered that its tendency is simply to establish that we have to do with an evil affecting a great many people; presumably, the abolition of a widespread evil is even more urgent than dealing with isolated cases of wrongdoing.

This Court has consistently treated the personal rights of litigants on a personal basis. Every leading case involving discrimination against Negroes has necessarily and demonstrably involved large numbers of people; yet this Court has given present relief on a personal basis to those who showed themselves entitled to it, without any hint of the possibility that the rights of citizenship are diminished because many people are being denied them. The *Sweatt*, *Sipuel* and *McLaurin* cases and *Smith* v. *Allwright*, all, as was well known to this Court and to the country, involved not merely the individuals or class-plaintiffs or geographical subdivision actually before the Court, but also the whole framework of law school, graduate school or primary election segregation. All major constitutional cases involve large numbers of people. Yet there is not a hint, in words or in action, in any past case, to the effect that the wide applicability of a decision was considered material to the right to relief. It is unthinkable that this Court would apply any such doctrine to limit the enjoyment of constitutional rights in general; there is no reason for its making a special and anomalous exception of the case at bar.

Actually, to point to the vast numbers of people whose lives will be affected by the relief granted here is only a diffuse way of raising all the questions as to the consequences of immediate desegregation. We have dealt with these

---

[16] It is also significant that many municipal junior colleges in Texas have also desegregated their student bodies. See Southern School News, October 1, 1954, p. 13, c. 5.
[16a] Johnson, "Public Higher Education In The South", 23 Journal Of Negro Education 317 (1954), especially at 328 where Dr. Johnson, University of North Carolina Sociologist, concludes:

The transition from complete segregation to some degree of integration of Negroes into the publicly-supported institutions of higher learning in the South has already been accomplished in all except five of the Southern states, and most of this change has occurred in the brief period, 1948–1953. Despite numerous predictions of violence, this transition has been accomplished without a single serious incident of interracial friction.
[17] We put to one side as obviously immaterial the mere technical character of these suits as class actions under

Rule 23(a)(3). Obviously, the mere joinder of plaintiffs in a spurious class suit for reasons of convenience cannot have any effect on the nature of the rights asserted or on the availability of normal relief remedy. Whether a suit is or is not a class action tells us little, in this field of law, as to the magnitude of the interests involved; *Sweatt* v. *Painter* was an individual mandamus suit, but the effect of that decision spread throughout the segregating states.

questions elsewhere. The suggestion that mere numerousness makes a difference adds nothing new, but merely serves to confuse the issues by diverting attention from the extremely personal plight of each child, and from his need for present relief.

### Average differences in student groups have no relevance to the individual rights of pupils: individual differences can be handled administratively without reference to race

Having attempted to subordinate appellants' personal and present constitutional rights to an alleged overriding consideration of the large numbers of people involved, these briefs for appellees then seek to further limit the individual rights of Negro students by broad characterizations of group intelligence, group morality and health.[18] Specifically, it is pointed out that statistics show that *on the average* Negro children in segregated schools score lower on achievement tests and are *in general* more retarded culturally than white children. This data, contrary to the conclusions advanced thereupon, merely underscores and further documents the finding quoted in this Court's opinion:

> "Segregation of white and colored children in public schools has a detrimental effect upon the colored children. The impact is greater when it has the sanction of the law; for the policy of separating the races is usually interpreted as denoting the inferiority of the Negro group. A sense of inferiority affects the motivation of a child to learn. Segregation with the sanction of law, therefore, has a tendency to [retard] the educational and mental development of Negro children and to deprive them of some of the benefits they would receive in a racial[ly] integrated school system."

We have come too far not to realize that educability and absorption and adoption of cultural values has nothing to do with race. What is achieved educationally and culturally, we now know to be largely the result of opportunity and environment.[19] That the Negro is so disadvantaged educationally and culturally in the states

where segregation is required is the strongest argument against its continuation for any period of time. Yet those who use this argument as a basis for interminable delay in the elimination of segregation in reality are seeking to utilize the product of their own wrongdoing as a justification for continued malfeasance.

Our public school systems have grown and improved as an American institution. And in every community it is obvious that children of all levels of culture, educability, and achievement must be accounted for within the same system. In some school systems the exceptional children are separated from the rest of the children. In others there are special classes for retarded children, for slow readers and for the physically handicapped. But these factors have no relation to race. These are administrative problems with respect to conduct of the public school.

In the past, large city school systems, North and South, have had the problem of absorbing children from rural areas where the public schools and cultural backgrounds were below the city standards. On many occasions these migrations have been very sudden and in proportionately very large numbers. This problem has always been solved as an administrative detail. It has never been either insurmountable nor has it been used as an excuse to force the rural children to attend sub-standard schools. Similarly, large cities have met without difficulty the influx of immigrants from foreign countries.

Cultural and health standards have always been maintained in public schools and there could be no objection to the continuation of such standards without regard to race. All social scientists seem to be in agreement that race and color have no connection whatsoever with a student's ability to be educated. Achievement and cultural deficiencies are nonracial in character, also. Hence these factors in no wise relate to questions posed as to whether desegregation should take place immediately or over an extended period.

Perhaps the main reasons for rejecting appellees' argument are that the conditions they complain of can never be remedied as long as segregation in public schools is continued and these so-called problems, *i.e.*, average on achievement tests, health, etc., are administrative problems which can be solved by recognized administrative regulations made to fit the problems without regard to pigmentation of the skin. It is significant that appellees and the Attorneys-General who advance these arguments do not give any hope to anyone that the continuation of segregated public education

---

[18] North Carolina Brief, pp. 39–41; Florida Brief, pp. 19–21, 189.

[19] KLINEBERG, RACE DIFFERENCES: THE PRESENT POSITION OF THE PROBLEM, 2 INTERNATIONAL SOCIAL SCIENCE BULLETIN 460 (1950); MONTAGUE, STATEMENT ON RACE, THE UNESCO STATEMENT BY EXPERTS ON RACE PROBLEMS 14–15 (1951); MONTAGUE, MAN'S MOST DANGEROUS MYTH: THE FALLACY OF RACE 286 (1952); KIRKPATRICK, PHILOSOPHY OF EDUCATION 399–433 (1951). See KLINEBERG, RACE AND PSYCHOLOGY, UNESCO (1951); ALLPORT, THE NATURE OF PREJUDICE (1954); COMAS, RACIAL MYTHS, UNESCO (1951).

will ever remove these problems which are the product of this segregation.

On the other hand, appellants have shown in their Brief on Further Reargument that on the basis of substantial documented experience: "There is no basis for the assumption that gradual as opposed to immediate desegregation is the better, smoother or more 'effective' mode of transition. On the contrary, there is an impressive body of evidence which supports the position that gradualism, far from facilitating the process, may actually make it more difficult; that, in fact, the problems of transition will be a good deal less complicated than might be forecast by appellees. Our submission is that this, like many wrongs, can be easiest and best undone, not by 'tapering off' but by forthright action" (p. 31).

## Official reactions in states affected by the May 17th decision make it plain that delay will detract from rather than contribute to the "effectiveness" of the transition to desegregated schools

Events occurring in the states affected by the decision of May 17, 1954, do not support the suggestions of appellees and *amici curiae* that further (and limitless) postponement of relief to Negro children will assure an "effective" adjustment from segregated to non-segregated school systems. In terms of legislative, executive or administrative reaction, the southern and border states may now be grouped in three loose categories:

**(1)** Those which have not waited for further directions from the Court, but have undertaken desegregation in varied measure during the current school year. Typical of the states falling in this category are Delaware,[20] Kansas,[21] Missouri,[22] and West Virginia.[23] Although not a state, the District of Columbia would fall within this group.

**(2)** Those which have decided to await a decision on the question of relief but have indicated

an intention to obey the Court's directions. Kentucky,[24] Oklahoma,[25] and Tennessee[26] are among the states in this category.

**(3)** Those which have indicated an intention to circumvent the decision of this Court or interminably delay the enjoyment by Negro children of their constitutionally protected rights not to be segregated in public schools. Included in this category are states like South Carolina[27] and Mississippi,[28] which have enacted legislation designed to nullify any decision of this Court in these cases, and states like Virginia[29] and Florida,[30] where either the governors or special legislative committees studying the problem have recommended that "every legal means" be used to preserve segregated school systems.[31]

Against this background of state reaction to the decision of May 17, 1954, it is clear that postponement of relief will serve no purpose. The states in the first category have already begun to implement this Court's decision and any delay as to them may imperil the progress already made.[32] The states in the second category have indicated a willingness to do whatever this Court directs and there is certainly no reason for delay as to them. The probable effect of delay, as to states in the third category, must be evaluated in the light of their declared intentions; we are justified in assuming that it would have no affirmative effect, but would merely provide additional time to devise and put into practice schemes expressly designed to thwart this Court's decision.

---

[20] Brief for Appellants in Nos. 1, 2 and 3 and for Respondents in No. 5 on Further Reargument, pp. 4–7; Brief for Petitioners on the Mandate in No. 5, pp. 10–12.

[21] Brief for Appellants in Nos. 1, 2 and 3 and for Respondents in No. 5 on Further Reargument, pp. 3–4; Supplemental Brief for the State of Kansas on Questions 4 and 5 Propounded by the Court, pp. 13–22; Supplemental Brief for the Board of Education, Topeka, Kansas on Questions 4 and 5 Propounded by the Court, pp. 2–4.

[22] SOUTHERN SCHOOL NEWS, September 3, 1954, p. 9, c. 2–5; *Id.*, October 1, 1954, p. 10, c. 1–5; *Id.*, November 4, 1954, p. 12, c. 1–5; *Id.*, December 1, 1954, p. 10, c. 1–5; *Id.*, January 6, 1955, p. 11, c. 1; *Id.*, February 3, 1955, p. 15, c. 1–5.

[23] SOUTHERN SCHOOL NEWS, October 1, p. 14, c. 1, 5; *Id.*, January 6, 1955, p. 2, c. 4–5.

[24] SOUTHERN SCHOOL NEWS, September 3, 1954, p. 7, c. 3; *Id.*, November 4, 1954, p. 16, c. 1; *Id.*, December 1, 1954, p. 9, c. 1, 3.

[25] SOUTHERN SCHOOL NEWS, February 3, 1955, p. 10, c. 1–2; *Id.*, March 3, 1955, p. 16, c. 1; THE NEW YORK TIMES, April 6, 1955, p. 20, c. 5.

[26] SOUTHERN SCHOOL NEWS, October 1, 1954, p. 11, c. 1; *Id.*, December 1, 1954, p. 12, c. 4; NEW YORK POST, March 16, 1955, p. 58, c. 4.

[27] SOUTHERN SCHOOL NEWS, September 3, 1954, p. 12, c. 1–2; *Id.*, February 3, 1955, p. 3, c. 2–4, *Id.*, March 3, 1955, p. 14, c. 1–3.

[28] SOUTHERN SCHOOL NEWS, September 3, 1954, p. 8, c. 3; *Id.*, October 1, 1954, p. 9, c. 4–5; *Id.*, November 4, 1954, p. 11, c. 4–5; *Id.*, January 6, 1955, p. 10, c. 1–2; THE NEW YORK TIMES, April 6, 1955, p. 20, c. 5.

[29] SOUTHERN SCHOOL NEWS, February 3, 1955, p. 10, c. 4.

[30] SOUTHERN SCHOOL NEWS, January 6, 1955, p. 6, c. 2.

[31] Indeed, Governor Marvin B. Griffin of Georgia has asserted: "However, if this court is so unrealistic as to attempt to enforce this unthinkable evil upon us, I serve notice now that we shall resist it with all the resources at our disposal and we shall never submit to the proposition of mixing the races in the classrooms of our schools."

[32] See, *e.g.*, *Steiner v. Simmons*, 111 A. 2d 574 (Del. 1955), rev'g. 108 A. 2d 173 (Del. 1954). There the Supreme Court reversed a chancery court determination that forthwith desegregation was proper under the decision of this Court of May 17, 1954.

## CONCLUSION

Appellants recognize that the problems confronting this Court, as it turns to the implementation of its decision in these cases, are of primary magnitude. Their high seriousness is enhanced by the fact that sovereign states are in effect, though not formally, at the bar and that the evil to which the Court's decree must be directed is no transitory wrong but is of the essence of the social structure of a great section of our nation.

Yet, it should be borne in mind that the very magnitude of these problems exists because of the assumption, tacitly indulged up to now, that the Constitution is not to be applied in its full force and scope to all sections of this country alike, but rather that its guarantees are to be enjoyed, in one part of our nation, only as molded and modified by the desire and customs of the dominant component of the sectional population. Such a view, however expressed, ignores the minimum requirement for a truly national constitution. It ignores also a vast part of the reality of the sectional interest involved, for that interest must be composed of the legitimate aspirations of Negroes as well as whites. It certainly ignores the repercussions which any reluctance to forthrightly enforce appellants' rights would have on this nation's international relations. Every day of delay means that this country is failing to develop its full strength.

The time has come to end the division of one nation into those sections where the Constitution is and those where it is not fully respected. Only by forthright action can the country set on the road to a uniform amenability to its Constitution. Finally, the right asserted by these appellants is not the only one at stake. The fate of other great constitutional freedoms, whether secured by the Fourteenth Amendment or by other provisions, is inevitably bound up in the resolution to be made in these cases. For delay in enforcement of these rights invites the insidious prospect that a moratorium may equally be placed on the enjoyment of other constitutional rights.

In disposing of the great issues before it, this Court should do no less than order the abolition of racial segregation in public education by a day certain, as heretofore set forth in Appellants' Brief on Further Reargument.

Respectfully submitted,

CHARLES L. BLACK, JR.,
ELWOOD H. CHISOLM,
WILLIAM T. COLEMAN, JR.,
CHARLES T. DUNCAN,
GEORGE E. C. HAYES,
LOREN MILLER,
WILLIAM R. MING, JR.,
CONSTANCE BAKER MOTLEY,
JAMES M. NABRIT, JR.,
LOUIS H. POLLAK,
FRANK D. REEVES,
JOHN SCOTT,
JACK B. WEINSTEIN,
    *of Counsel.*

HAROLD BOULWARE,
ROBERT L. CARTER,
JACK GREENBERG,
OLIVER W. HILL,
THURGOOD MARSHALL,
LOUIS L. REDDING,
SPOTTSWOOD W. ROBINSON, III,
CHARLES S. SCOTT,
    *Attorneys for Appellants in Nos. 1, 2, 3*
    *and for Respondents in No. 5.*

349 U.S. 294

Oliver BROWN, et al., Appellants,

v.

BOARD OF EDUCATION OF TOPEKA,
Shawnee County, KANSAS, et al.

Harry BRIGGS, Jr., et al., Appellants,

v.

R. W. ELLIOTT, et al.

Dorothy E. DAVIS, et al., Appellants,

v.

COUNTY SCHOOL BOARD OF PRINCE
EDWARD COUNTY, VIRGINIA,
et al.

Spottswood Thomas BOLLING, et al.,
Petitioners,

v.

C. Melvin SHARPE, et al.

Francis B. GEBHART, et al., Petitioners,

v.

Ethel Louise BELTON, et al.

Nos. 1–5.

Argued April 11, 12, 13 and 14, 1955.

Decided May 31, 1955.

Class actions by which minor plaintiffs sought to obtain admission to public schools on a nonsegregated basis. On direct appeals by plaintiffs from adverse decisions in United States District Courts, District of Kansas, 98 F.Supp. 797, Eastern District of South Carolina, 103 F.Supp. 920, and Eastern District of Virginia, 103 F.Supp. 337, on certiorari before judgment on appeal to the United States Court of Appeals for the District of Columbia from adverse decision in United States District Court for the District of Columbia, and on certiorari from decision favorable to plaintiffs in the Supreme Court of Delaware, 91 A.2d 137, the Supreme Court, 347 U.S. 483, 74 S.Ct. 686, 98 L.Ed. 873, and 347 U.S. 497, 74 S.Ct. 693, 98 L.Ed. 884, held that racial discrimination in public education was unconstitutional and restored cases to docket for further argument regarding formulation of decrees. On further argument, the Supreme Court, Mr. Chief Justice Warren, held that in proceedings to implement Supreme Court's determination, inferior courts might consider problems related to administration, arising from physical condition of school plant, school transportation system, personnel, revision of school districts and attendance areas into compact units to achieve system of determining admission to public schools on a nonracial basis, and revision of local laws and regulations, and might consider adequacy of any plans school authorities might propose to meet these problems and to effectuate a transition to racially nondiscriminatory school systems.

Judgments, except that in case No. 5, reversed and cases remanded with directions; judgment in case No. 5 affirmed and case remanded with directions.

1. Constitutional Law ☞220

All provisions of federal, state, or local law requiring or permitting racial discrimination in public education must yield to principle that such discrimina-

---

holds a new hearing and renders a new decision on his application for discretionary relief. Although the Board has already found that he has a good moral character, he should have the opportunity at the new hearing to offer evidence

75 S.Ct.—48

that he is not and never has been a racketeer. For it may be that, in so characterizing Accardi, the Attorney General has confused him with someone else of the same name." 219 F.2d 77, 83.

tion is unconstitutional.   U.S.C.A.Const. Amend. 14.

**2. Schools and School Districts ⌒13**

School authorities have primary responsibility for elucidating, assessing, and solving problems arising from fact that racial discrimination in public education is unconstitutional.

**3. Appeal and Error ⌒1177(1)**

Question whether school authorities' actions constitute good faith implementation of principle that racial discrimination in public education is unconstitutional could best be appraised by courts which originally heard cases raising question of constitutionality of such discrimination, and it was appropriate to remand cases to such courts.   28 U.S. C.A. §§ 2281, 2284.

**4. Equity ⌒1, 423**

Traditionally, equity has been characterized by a practical flexibility in shaping its remedies and by a facility for adjusting and reconciling public and private needs.

**5. School and School Districts ⌒13**

Courts of equity, in implementing Supreme Court's determination that racial discrimination in public education is unconstitutional, may properly take into account the public interest in elimination, in a systematic and effective manner, of obstacles to transition to school systems operated in accordance with constitutional principles, but constitutional principles cannot be allowed to yield because of disagreement with them.

**6. Appeal and Error ⌒1206**

On remand from Supreme Court after determination in several cases that racial discrimination in public education is unconstitutional, inferior courts should, while giving weight to public considerations and private interest of litigants, require that school authorities make prompt and reasonable start toward full compliance with ruling.

**7. Schools and School Districts ⌒13**

In proceedings to implement Supreme Court's decision that racial discrimination in public education is unconstitutional, public school authorities have burden of establishing that grant of additional time for transition is necessary in public interest and is consistent with good faith compliance at earliest practicable date.

**8. Schools and School Districts ⌒13**

Inferior courts, in implementing Supreme Court's determination that racial discrimination in public education is unconstitutional, may consider problems related to administration, arising from physical condition of school plant, school transportation system, personnel, revision of school districts and attendance areas into compact units to achieve system of determining admission to public schools on a nonracial basis, and revision of local laws and regulations, and may consider adequacy of any plans school authorities may propose to meet these problems and to effectuate a transition to racially nondiscriminatory school system.

**9. Schools and School Districts ⌒13**

Inferior courts, on remand from Supreme Court's determination that discrimination in public education is unconstitutional, were directed to retain jurisdiction of cases during period of transition to nondiscriminatory school systems.

———◆———

296

Mr. Robert L. Carter, New York City, for appellants in No. 1.

Mr. Harold R. Fatzer, Topeka, Kan., for appellees in No. 1.

Messrs. Thurgood Marshall, New York City, and Spottswood W. Robinson, III, Richmond, Va., for appellants in Nos. 2 and 3.

Messrs. S. E. Rogers, Summerton, S. C., and Robert McC. Figg, Jr., Charleston, S. C., for appellees in No. 2.

Messrs. Archibald G. Robertson, Richmond, Va., and J. Lindsay Almond, Jr., Atty. Gen., for appellees in No. 3.

Messrs. George E. C. Hayes and James M. Nabrit, Jr., Washington, D. C., for petitioners in No. 4.

Mr. Milton D. Korman, Washington, D. C., for respondents in No. 4.

**297**

Mr. Joseph Donald Craven, Wilmington, Del., for petitioners in No. 5.

Mr. Louis L. Redding, Wilmington, Del., for respondents in No. 5.

Messrs. Richard W. Ervin and Ralph E. Odum, Tallahassee, Fla., for State of Florida, I. Beverly Lake, Raleigh, N. C., for State of North Carolina, Thomas J. Gentry, Little Rock, Ark., for State of Arkansas, Mac Q. Williamson, Oklahoma, City, Okl., for State of Oklahoma, C. Ferdinand Sybert, Ellicott City, Md., for State of Maryland, John Ben Shepperd and Burnell Waldrep, Austin, Tex., for State of Texas, Sol. Gen. Simon E. Sobeloff, Washington, D. C., for the United States, amici curiae.

**298**

Mr. Chief Justice WARREN delivered the opinion of the Court.

[1] These cases were decided on May 17, 1954. The opinions of that date,[1] declaring the fundamental principle that racial discrimination in public education is unconstitutional, are incorporated herein by reference. All provisions of federal, state, or local law requiring or permitting such discrimination must yield to this principle. There remains for consideration the manner in which relief is to be accorded.

Because these cases arose under different local conditions and their disposition will involve a variety of local problems, we requested further argument on the question of relief.[2] In view of the nationwide importance of the decision, we invited the Attorney General of the United

**299**

States and the Attorneys General of all states requiring or permitting racial discrimination in public education to present their views on that question. The parties, the United States, and the States of Florida, North Carolina, Arkansas, Oklahoma, Maryland, and Texas filed briefs and participated in the oral argument.

These presentations were informative and helpful to the Court in its consideration of the complexities arising from the transition to a system of public education freed of racial discrimination. The presentations also demonstrated that substantial steps to eliminate racial discrimination in public schools have al-

---

1. 347 U.S. 483, 74 S.Ct. 686, 98 L.Ed. 873, 347 U.S. 497, 74 S.Ct. 693, 98 L.Ed. 884.

2. Further argument was requested on the following questions, 347 U.S. 483, 495–496, note 13, 74 S.Ct. 683, 692, 98 L.Ed. 873, previously propounded by the Court:
   "4. Assuming it is decided that segregation in public schools violates the Fourteenth Amendment
   "(a) would a decree necessarily follow providing that, within the limits set by normal geographic school districting, Negro children should forthwith be admitted to schools of their choice, or
   "(b) may this Court, in the exercise of its equity powers, permit an effective gradual adjustment to be brought about from existing segregated systems to a system not based on color distinctions?

"5. On the assumption on which questions 4 (a) and (b) are based, and assuming further that this Court will exercise its equity powers to the end described in question 4 (b),
   "(a) should this Court formulate detailed decrees in these cases;
   "(b) if so, what specific issues should the decrees reach;
   "(c) should this Court appoint a special master to hear evidence with a view to recommending specific terms for such decrees;
   "(d) should this Court remand to the courts of first instance with directions to frame decrees in these cases, and if so what general directions should the decrees of this Court include and what procedures should the courts of first instance follow in arriving at the specific terms of more detailed decrees?"

ready been taken, not only in some of the communities in which these cases arose, but in some of the states appearing as *amici curiae*, and in other states as well. Substantial progress has been made in the District of Columbia and in the communities in Kansas and Delaware involved in this litigation. The defendants in the cases coming to us from South Carolina and Virginia are awaiting the decision of this Court concerning relief.

[2, 3] Full implementation of these constitutional principles may require solution of varied local school problems. School authorities have the primary responsibility for elucidating, assessing, and solving these problems; courts will have to consider whether the action of school authorities constitutes good faith implementation of the governing constitutional principles. Because of their proximity to local conditions and the possible need for further hearings, the courts which originally heard these cases can best perform this judicial appraisal. Accordingly, we believe it appropriate to remand the cases to those courts.[3]

**300**

[4, 5] In fashioning and effectuating the decrees, the courts will be guided by equitable principles. Traditionally, equity has been characterized by a practical flexibility in shaping its remedies[4] and by a facility for adjusting and reconciling public and private needs.[5] These cases call for the exercise of these traditional attributes of equity power. At stake is the personal interest of the plaintiffs in admission to public schools as soon as practicable on a nondiscriminatory basis. To effectuate this interest may call for elimination of a variety of

obstacles in making the transition to school systems operated in accordance with the constitutional principles set forth in our May 17, 1954, decision. Courts of equity may properly take into account the public interest in the elimination of such obstacles in a systematic and effective manner. But it should go without saying that the vitality of these constitutional principles cannot be allowed to yield simply because of disagreement with them.

[6–9] While giving weight to these public and private considerations, the courts will require that the defendants make a prompt and reasonable start toward full compliance with our May 17, 1954, ruling. Once such a start has been made, the courts may find that additional time is necessary to carry out the ruling in an effective manner. The burden rests upon the defendants to establish that such time is necessary in the public interest and is consistent with good faith compliance at the earliest practicable date. To that end, the courts may consider problems related to administration, arising from the physical condition of the school plant, the school transportation system, personnel, revision of school districts and attendance areas into compact units to achieve a system of determining admission to the public schools

**301**

on a nonracial basis, and revision of local laws and regulations which may be necessary in solving the foregoing problems. They will also consider the adequacy of any plans the defendants may propose to meet these problems and to effectuate a transition to a racially nondiscriminatory school system. During this period of transition, the courts will retain jurisdiction of these cases.

---

**3.** The cases coming to us from Kansas, South Carolina, and Virginia were originally heard by three-judge District Courts convened under 28 U.S.C. §§ 2281 and 2284, 28 U.S.C.A. §§ 2281, 2284. These cases will accordingly be remanded to those three-judge courts. See

Briggs v. Elliott, 342 U.S. 350, 72 S.Ct. 327, 96 L.Ed. 392.

**4.** See Alexander v. Hillman, 296 U.S. 222, 239, 56 S.Ct. 204, 209, 80 L.Ed. 192.

**5.** See Hecht Co. v. Bowles, 321 U.S. 321, 329–330, 64 S.Ct. 587, 591, 592, 88 L.Ed. 754.

The judgments below, except that in the Delaware case, are accordingly reversed and the cases are remanded to the District Courts to take such proceedings and enter such orders and decrees consistent with this opinion as are necessary and proper to admit to public schools on a racially nondiscriminatory basis with all deliberate speed the parties to these cases. The judgment in the Delaware case—ordering the immediate admission of the plaintiffs to schools previously attended only by white children—is affirmed on the basis of the principles stated in our May 17, 1954, opinion, but the case is remanded to the Supreme Court of Delaware for such further proceedings as that Court may deem necessary in light of this opinion.

It is so ordered.

Judgments, except that in case No. 5, reversed and cases remanded with directions; judgment in case No. 5 affirmed and case remanded with directions.

# ABBREVIATIONS

| | |
|---|---|
| A. | Atlantic Reporter |
| A. 2d | Atlantic Reporter, Second Series |
| AAA | American Arbitration Association; Agricultural Adjustment Act of 1933 |
| AAPRP | All African People's Revolutionary Party |
| ABA | American Bar Association; Architectural Barriers Act, 1968 |
| ABM Treaty | Anti-Ballistic Missile Treaty of 1972; antiballistic missile |
| ABVP | Anti-Biased Violence Project |
| A/C | Account |
| A.C. | Appeal Cases |
| ACAA | Air Carrier Access Act |
| ACF | Administration for Children and Families |
| ACLU | American Civil Liberties Union |
| ACS | Agricultural Cooperative Service |
| Act'g Legal Adv. | Acting Legal Advisor |
| ACUS | Administrative Conference of the United States |
| ACYF | Administration on Children, Youth, and Families |
| A.D. 2d | Appellate Division, Second Series, N.Y. |
| ADA | Americans with Disabilities Act of 1990 |
| ADAMHA | Alcohol, Drug Abuse, and Mental Health Administration |
| ADC | Aid to Dependent Children |
| ADD | Administration on Developmental Disabilities |
| ADEA | Age Discrimination in Employment Act of 1967 |
| ADR | alternative dispute resolution |
| AEC | Atomic Energy Commission |
| AECB | Arms Export Control Board |
| A.E.R. | All England Law Reports |
| AFDC | Aid to Families with Dependent Children |
| aff'd per cur. | affirmed by the court |
| AFIS | automated fingerprint identification system |
| AFL | American Federation of Labor |
| AFL-CIO | American Federation of Labor and Congress of Industrial Organizations |
| AFRes | Air Force Reserve |
| AFSCME | American Federation of State, County, and Municipal Employees |
| AGRICOLA | Agricultural Online Access |
| AIA | Association of Insurance Attorneys |
| AID | artificial insemination using a third-party donor's sperm; Agency for International Development |

| | |
|---|---|
| AIDS | acquired immune deficiency syndrome |
| AIH | artificial insemination using the husband's sperm |
| AIM | American Indian Movement |
| AIUSA | Amnesty International, U.S.A. Affiliate |
| AJS | American Judicature Society |
| ALEC | American Legislative Exchange Council |
| ALF | Animal Liberation Front |
| ALI | American Law Institute |
| ALJ | administrative law judge |
| All E.R. | All England Law Reports |
| ALO | Agency Liaison |
| A.L.R. | American Law Reports |
| AMA | American Medical Association |
| Am. Dec. | American Decisions |
| amdt. | amendment |
| Amer. St. Papers, For. Rels. | American State Papers, Legislative and Executive Documents of the Congress of the U.S., Class I, Foreign Relations, 1832–1859 |
| AMVETS | American Veterans (of World War II) |
| ANA | Administration for Native Americans |
| Ann. Dig. | Annual Digest of Public International Law Cases |
| ANZUS | Australia–New Zealand–United States Security Treaty Organization |
| AOA | Administration on Aging |
| APA | Administrative Procedure Act of 1946 |
| APHIS | Animal and Plant Health Inspection Service |
| App. Div. | Appellate Division Reports, N.Y. Supreme Court |
| Arb. Trib., U.S.-British Convention of 1853 | Arbitration Tribunal, Claim Convention of 1853, United States and Great Britain |
| ARS | Advanced Record System |
| Art. | article |
| ASCS | Agriculture Stabilization and Conservation Service |
| ASM | available seatmile |
| ASPCA | American Society for the Prevention of Cruelty to Animals |
| Asst. Att. Gen. | Assistant Attorney General |
| AT&T | American Telephone and Telegraph |
| ATFD | Alcohol, Tobacco and Firearms Division |
| ATLA | Association of Trial Lawyers of America |
| ATTD | Alcohol and Tobacco Tax Division |
| ATU | Alcohol Tax Unit |
| AZT | azidothymidine |
| BALSA | Black-American Law Student Association |
| BATF | Bureau of Alcohol, Tobacco and Firearms |
| BCCI | Bank of Credit and Commerce International |
| BEA | Bureau of Economic Analysis |
| Bell's Cr. C. | Bell's English Crown Cases |
| Bevans | United States Treaties, etc. *Treaties and Other International Agreements of the United States of America, 1776–1949* (compiled under the direction of Charles I. Bevans) (1968–76) |
| BFOQ | bona fide occupational qualification |
| BI | Bureau of Investigation |
| BIA | Bureau of Indian Affairs; Board of Immigration Appeals |
| BJS | Bureau of Justice Statistics |
| Black. | Black's United States Supreme Court Reports |
| Blatchf. | Blatchford's United States Circuit Court Reports |
| BLM | Bureau of Land Management |
| BLS | Bureau of Labor Statistics |
| BMD | ballistic missile defense |
| BOCA | Building Officials and Code Administrators International |
| BPP | Black Panther Party for Self-Defense |

| | |
|---|---|
| Brit. and For. | British and Foreign State Papers |
| Burr. | James Burrows, *Report of Cases Argued and Determined in the Court of King's Bench during the Time of Lord Mansfield* (1766–1780) |
| BVA | Board of Veterans Appeals |
| c. | Chapter |
| C³I | Command, Control, Communications, and Intelligence |
| C.A. | Court of Appeals |
| CAA | Clean Air Act |
| CAB | Civil Aeronautics Board |
| CAFE | corporate average fuel economy |
| Cal. 2d | California Reports, Second Series |
| Cal. 3d | California Reports, Third Series |
| CALR | computer-assisted legal research |
| Cal. Rptr. | California Reporter |
| CAP | Common Agricultural Policy |
| CATV | community antenna television |
| CBO | Congressional Budget Office |
| CCC | Commodity Credit Corporation |
| CCDBG | Child Care and Development Block Grant of 1990 |
| C.C.D. Pa. | Circuit Court Decisions, Pennsylvania |
| C.C.D. Va. | Circuit Court Decisions, Virginia |
| CCEA | Cabinet Council on Economic Affairs |
| CCR | Center for Constitutional Rights |
| C.C.R.I. | Circuit Court, Rhode Island |
| CD | certificate of deposit |
| CDA | Communications Decency Act |
| CDBG | Community Development Block Grant Program |
| CDC | Centers for Disease Control and Prevention; Community Development Corporation |
| CDF | Children's Defense Fund |
| CDL | Citizens for Decency through Law |
| CD-ROM | compact disc read-only memory |
| CDS | Community Dispute Services |
| CDW | collision damage waiver |
| CENTO | Central Treaty Organization |
| CEQ | Council on Environmental Quality |
| CERCLA | Comprehensive Environmental Response, Compensation, and Liability Act of 1980 |
| cert. | *certiorari* |
| CETA | Comprehensive Employment and Training Act |
| C & F | cost and freight |
| CFC | chlorofluorocarbon |
| CFE Treaty | Conventional Forces in Europe Treaty of 1990 |
| C.F. & I. | Cost, freight, and insurance |
| CFNP | Community Food and Nutrition Program |
| C.F.R. | Code of Federal Regulations |
| CFTC | Commodity Futures Trading Commission |
| Ch. | Chancery Division, English Law Reports |
| CHAMPVA | Civilian Health and Medical Program at the Veterans Administration |
| CHEP | Cuban/Haitian Entrant Program |
| CHINS | children in need of supervision |
| CHIPS | child in need of protective services |
| Ch.N.Y. | Chancery Reports, New York |
| Chr. Rob. | Christopher Robinson, *Reports of Cases Argued and Determined in the High Court of Admiralty* (1801–1808) |
| CIA | Central Intelligence Agency |
| CID | Commercial Item Descriptions |
| C.I.F. | Cost, insurance, and freight |
| CINCNORAD | Commander in Chief, North American Air Defense Command |
| C.I.O. | Congress of Industrial Organizations |

| | |
|---|---|
| C.J. | chief justice |
| CJIS | Criminal Justice Information Services |
| C.J.S. | Corpus Juris Secundum |
| Claims Arb. under Spec. Conv., Nielsen's Rept. | Frederick Kenelm Nielsen, *American and British Claims Arbitration under the Special Agreement Concluded between the United States and Great Britain, August 18, 1910* (1926) |
| CLE | Center for Law and Education |
| CLEO | Council on Legal Education Opportunity |
| CLP | Communist Labor Party of America |
| CLS | Christian Legal Society; critical legal studies (movement), Critical Legal Studies (membership organization) |
| C.M.A. | Court of Military Appeals |
| CMEA | Council for Mutual Economic Assistance |
| CMHS | Center for Mental Health Services |
| C.M.R. | Court of Military Review |
| CNN | Cable News Network |
| CNO | Chief of Naval Operations |
| C.O.D. | cash on delivery |
| COGP | Commission on Government Procurement |
| COINTELPRO | Counterintelligence Program |
| Coke Rep. | Coke's English King's Bench Reports |
| COLA | cost-of-living adjustment |
| COMCEN | Federal Communications Center |
| Comp. | Compilation |
| Conn. | Connecticut Reports |
| CONTU | National Commission on New Technological Uses of Copyrighted Works |
| Conv. | Convention |
| Corbin | Arthur L. Corbin, *Corbin on Contracts: A Comprehensive Treatise on the Rules of Contract Law* (1950) |
| CORE | Congress of Racial Equality |
| Cox's Crim. Cases | Cox's Criminal Cases (England) |
| CPA | certified public accountant |
| CPB | Corporation for Public Broadcasting, the |
| CPI | Consumer Price Index |
| CPSC | Consumer Product Safety Commission |
| Cranch | Cranch's United States Supreme Court Reports |
| CRF | Constitutional Rights Foundation |
| CRS | Congressional Research Service; Community Relations Service |
| CRT | critical race theory |
| CSA | Community Services Administration |
| CSAP | Center for Substance Abuse Prevention |
| CSAT | Center for Substance Abuse Treatment |
| CSC | Civil Service Commission |
| CSCE | Conference on Security and Cooperation in Europe |
| CSG | Council of State Governments |
| CSO | Community Service Organization |
| CSP | Center for the Study of the Presidency |
| C-SPAN | Cable-Satellite Public Affairs Network |
| CSRS | Cooperative State Research Service |
| CSWPL | Center on Social Welfare Policy and Law |
| CTA | *cum testamento annexo* (with the will attached) |
| Ct. Ap. D.C. | Court of Appeals, District of Columbia |
| Ct. App. No. Ireland | Court of Appeals, Northern Ireland |
| Ct. Cl. | Court of Claims, United States |
| Ct. Crim. Apps. | Court of Criminal Appeals (England) |
| Ct. of Sess., Scot. | Court of Sessions, Scotland |
| CU | credit union |

| | |
|---|---|
| CUNY | City University of New York |
| Cush. | Cushing's Massachusetts Reports |
| CWA | Civil Works Administration; Clean Water Act |
| Dall. | Dallas' Pennsylvania and United States Reports |
| DAR | Daughter of the American Revolution |
| DARPA | Defense Advanced Research Projects Agency |
| DAVA | Defense Audiovisual Agency |
| D.C. | United States District Court |
| D.C. Del. | United States District Court, Delaware |
| D.C. Mass. | United States District Court, Massachusetts |
| D.C. Md. | United States District Court, Maryland |
| D.C.N.D.Cal. | United States District Court, Northern District, California |
| D.C.N.Y. | United States District Court, New York |
| D.C.Pa. | United States District Court, Pennsylvania |
| DCS | Deputy Chiefs of Staff |
| DCZ | District of the Canal Zone |
| DDT | dichlorodiphenyltricloroethane |
| DEA | Drug Enforcement Administration |
| Decl. Lond. | Declaration of London, February 26, 1909 |
| Dev. & B. | Devereux & Battle's North Carolina Reports |
| Dig. U.S. Practice in Intl. Law | Digest of U.S. Practice in International Law |
| Dist. Ct. D.C. | United States District Court, District of Columbia |
| D.L.R. | Dominion Law Reports (Canada) |
| DNA | deoxyribonucleic acid |
| DNase | deoxyribonuclease |
| DNC | Democratic National Committee |
| DOC | Department of Commerce |
| DOD | Department of Defense |
| Dodson | Dodson's Reports, English Admiralty Courts |
| DOE | Department of Energy |
| DOER | Department of Employee Relations |
| DOJ | Department of Justice |
| DOS | disk operating system |
| DOT | Department of Transportation |
| DPT | diphtheria, pertussis, and tetanus |
| DRI | Defense Research Institute |
| DSAA | Defense Security Assistance Agency |
| DUI | driving under the influence; driving under intoxication |
| DWI | driving while intoxicated |
| EAHCA | Education for All Handicapped Children Act of 1975 |
| EBT | examination before trial |
| ECPA | Electronic Communications Privacy Act of 1986 |
| ECSC | Treaty of the European Coal and Steel Community |
| EDA | Economic Development Administration |
| EDF | Environmental Defense Fund |
| E.D.N.Y. | Eastern District, New York |
| EDP | electronic data processing |
| E.D. Pa. | Eastern District, Pennsylvania |
| EDSC | Eastern District, South Carolina |
| E.D. Va. | Eastern District, Virginia |
| EEC | European Economic Community; European Economic Community Treaty |
| EEOC | Equal Employment Opportunity Commission |
| EFF | Electronic Frontier Foundation |
| EFT | electronic funds transfer |
| Eliz. | Queen Elizabeth (Great Britain) |
| Em. App. | Temporary Emergency Court of Appeals |

| | |
|---|---|
| ENE | early neutral evaluation |
| Eng. Rep. | English Reports |
| EOP | Executive Office of the President |
| EPA | Environmental Protection Agency; Equal Pay Act of 1963 |
| ERA | Equal Rights Amendment |
| ERISA | Employee Retirement Income Security Act of 1974 |
| ERS | Economic Research Service |
| ESF | emergency support function; Economic Support Fund |
| ESRD | End-Stage Renal Disease Program |
| ETA | Employment and Training Administration |
| ETS | environmental tobacco smoke |
| et seq. | *et sequentes* or *et sequentia;* "and the following" |
| EU | European Union |
| Euratom | European Atomic Energy Community |
| Eur. Ct. H.R. | European Court of Human Rights |
| Ex. | English Exchequer Reports, Welsby, Hurlstone & Gordon |
| Exch. | Exchequer Reports (Welsby, Hurlstone & Gordon) |
| Eximbank | Export-Import Bank of the United States |
| F. | Federal Reporter |
| F. 2d | Federal Reporter, Second Series |
| FAA | Federal Aviation Administration; Federal Arbitration Act |
| FAAA | Federal Alcohol Administration Act |
| FACE | Freedom of Access to Clinic Entrances Act of 1994 |
| FACT | Feminist Anti-Censorship Task Force |
| FAO | Food and Agriculture Organization of the United Nations |
| FAR | Federal Acquisition Regulations |
| FAS | Foreign Agricultural Service |
| FBA | Federal Bar Association |
| FBI | Federal Bureau of Investigation |
| FCA | Farm Credit Administration |
| F. Cas. | Federal Cases |
| FCC | Federal Communications Commission |
| FCIA | Foreign Credit Insurance Association |
| FCIC | Federal Crop Insurance Corporation |
| FCRA | Fair Credit Reporting Act |
| FCU | Federal credit unions |
| FDA | Food and Drug Administration |
| FDIC | Federal Deposit Insurance Corporation |
| FDPC | Federal Data Processing Center |
| FEC | Federal Election Commission |
| Fed. Cas. | Federal Cases |
| FEMA | Federal Emergency Management Agency |
| FFB | Federal Financing Bank |
| FGIS | Federal Grain Inspection Service |
| FHA | Federal Housing Authority |
| FHWA | Federal Highway Administration |
| FIA | Federal Insurance Administration |
| FIC | Federal Information Centers; Federation of Insurance Counsel |
| FICA | Federal Insurance Contributions Act |
| FIFRA | Federal Insecticide, Fungicide, and Rodenticide Act |
| FIP | Forestry Incentives Program |
| FIRREA | Financial Institutions Reform, Recovery, and Enforcement Act |
| FISA | Foreign Intelligence Surveillance Act of 1978 |
| FMCS | Federal Mediation and Conciliation Service |
| FmHA | Farmers Home Administration |
| FMLA | Family and Medical Leave Act of 1993 |
| FNMA | Federal National Mortgage Association, "Fannie Mae" |
| F.O.B. | free on board |

| | |
|---|---|
| FOIA | Freedom of Information Act |
| FPC | Federal Power Commission |
| FPMR | Federal Property Management Regulations |
| FPRS | Federal Property Resources Service |
| FR | Federal Register |
| FRA | Federal Railroad Administration |
| FRB | Federal Reserve Board |
| FRC | Federal Radio Commission |
| F.R.D. | Federal Rules Decisions |
| FSA | Family Support Act |
| FSLIC | Federal Savings and Loan Insurance Corporation |
| FSQS | Food Safety and Quality Service |
| FSS | Federal Supply Service |
| F. Supp. | Federal Supplement |
| FTA | U.S.-Canada Free Trade Agreement, 1988 |
| FTC | Federal Trade Commission |
| FTS | Federal Telecommunications System |
| FUTA | Federal Unemployment Tax Act |
| FWPCA | Federal Water Pollution Control Act of 1948 |
| GAO | General Accounting Office; Governmental Affairs Office |
| GAOR | General Assembly Official Records, United Nations |
| GA Res. | General Assembly Resolution (United Nations) |
| GATT | General Agreement on Tariffs and Trade |
| Gen. Cls. Comm. | General Claims Commission, United States and Panama; General Claims Commission, United States and Mexico |
| Geo. II | King George II (Great Britain) |
| Geo. III | King George III (Great Britain) |
| GM | General Motors |
| GNMA | Government National Mortgage Association, "Ginnie Mae" |
| GNP | gross national product |
| GOP | Grand Old Party (Republican) |
| GOPAC | Grand Old Party Action Committee |
| GPA | Office of Governmental and Public Affairs |
| GPO | Government Printing Office |
| GRAS | generally recognized as safe |
| Gr. Br., Crim. Ct. App. | Great Britain, Court of Criminal Appeals |
| GRNL | Gay Rights National Lobby |
| GSA | General Services Administration |
| Hackworth | Green Haywood Hackworth, *Digest of International Law* (1940–44) |
| Hay and Marriott | Great Britain. High Court of Admiralty, *Decisions in the High Court of Admiralty during the Time of Sir George Hay and of Sir James Marriott, Late Judges of That Court* (1801) |
| HBO | Home Box Office |
| HCFA | Health Care Financing Administration |
| H.Ct. | High Court |
| HDS | Office of Human Development Services |
| Hen. & M. | Hening & Munford's Virginia Reports |
| HEW | Department of Health, Education, and Welfare |
| HHS | Department of Health and Human Services |
| Hill | Hill's New York Reports |
| HIRE | Help through Industry Retraining and Employment |
| HIV | human immunodeficiency virus |
| H.L. | House of Lords Cases (England) |
| H. Lords | House of Lords (England) |
| HNIS | Human Nutrition Information Service |
| Hong Kong L.R. | Hong Kong Law Reports |
| How. | Howard's United States Supreme Court Reports |
| How. St. Trials | Howell's English State Trials |
| HUAC | House Un-American Activities Committee |

| | |
|---|---|
| HUD | Department of Housing and Urban Development |
| Hudson, Internatl. Legis. | Manley O. Hudson, ed., *International Legislation: A Collection of the Texts of Multipartite International Instruments of General Interest Beginning with the Covenant of the League of Nations* (1931) |
| Hudson, World Court Reps. | Manley Ottmer Hudson, ed., *World Court Reports* (1934– ) |
| Hun | Hun's New York Supreme Court Reports |
| Hunt's Rept. | Bert L. Hunt, *Report of the American and Panamanian General Claims Arbitration* (1934) |
| IAEA | International Atomic Energy Agency |
| IALL | International Association of Law Libraries |
| IBA | International Bar Association |
| IBM | International Business Machines |
| ICBM | intercontinental ballistic missile |
| ICC | Interstate Commerce Commission |
| ICJ | International Court of Justice |
| IDEA | Individuals with Disabilities Education Act, 1975 |
| IEP | individualized educational program |
| IFC | International Finance Corporation |
| IGRA | Indian Gaming Regulatory Act, 1988 |
| IJA | Institute of Judicial Administration |
| IJC | International Joint Commission |
| ILC | International Law Commission |
| ILD | International Labor Defense |
| Ill. Dec. | Illinois Decisions |
| ILO | International Labor Organization |
| IMF | International Monetary Fund |
| INA | Immigration and Nationality Act |
| IND | investigational new drug |
| INF Treaty | Intermediate-Range Nuclear Forces Treaty of 1987 |
| INS | Immigration and Naturalization Service |
| INTELSAT | International Telecommunications Satellite Organization |
| Interpol | International Criminal Police Organization |
| Int'l. Law Reps. | International Law Reports |
| Intl. Legal Mats. | International Legal Materials |
| IPDC | International Program for the Development of Communication |
| IPO | Intellectual Property Owners |
| IPP | independent power producer |
| IQ | intelligence quotient |
| I.R. | Irish Reports |
| IRA | individual retirement account; Irish Republican Army |
| IRCA | Immigration Reform and Control Act of 1986 |
| IRS | Internal Revenue Service |
| ISO | independent service organization |
| ISSN | International Standard Serial Numbers |
| ITA | International Trade Administration |
| ITI | Information Technology Integration |
| ITO | International Trade Organization |
| ITS | Information Technology Service |
| ITU | International Telecommunication Union |
| IUD | intrauterine device |
| IWC | International Whaling Commission |
| IWW | Industrial Workers of the World |
| JCS | Joint Chiefs of Staff |
| JDL | Jewish Defense League |
| JOBS | Jobs Opportunity and Basic Skills |
| John. Ch. | Johnson's New York Chancery Reports |
| Johns. | Johnson's Reports (New York) |
| JP | justice of the peace |

| | |
|---|---|
| K.B. | King's Bench Reports (England) |
| KGB | Komitet Gosudarstvennoi Bezopasnosti (the State Security Committee for countries in the former Soviet Union) |
| KKK | Ku Klux Klan |
| KMT | Kuomintang |
| LAPD | Los Angeles Police Department |
| LC | Library of Congress |
| LD50 | lethal dose 50 |
| LDEF | Legal Defense and Education Fund (NOW) |
| LDF | Legal Defense Fund, Legal Defense and Educational Fund of the NAACP |
| LEAA | Law Enforcement Assistance Administration |
| L.Ed. | Lawyers' Edition Supreme Court Reports |
| LMSA | Labor-Management Services Administration |
| LNTS | League of Nations Treaty Series |
| Lofft's Rep. | Lofft's English King's Bench Reports |
| L.R. | Law Reports (English) |
| LSAS | Law School Admission Service |
| LSAT | Law School Aptitude Test |
| LSC | Legal Services Corporation; Legal Services for Children |
| LSD | lysergic acid diethylamide |
| LSDAS | Law School Data Assembly Service |
| LTBT | Limited Test Ban Treaty |
| LTC | Long Term Care |
| MAD | mutual assured destruction |
| MADD | Mothers against Drunk Driving |
| MALDEF | Mexican American Legal Defense and Educational Fund |
| Malloy | William M. Malloy, ed., *Treaties, Conventions, International Acts, Protocols, and Agreements between the United States of America and Other Powers* (1910–38) |
| Martens | Georg Friedrich von Martens, ed., *Noveau recueil général de traités et autres act es relatifs aux rapports de droit international* (Series I, 20 vols. [1843–75]; Series II, 35 vols. [1876–1908]; Series III [1909–    ]) |
| Mass. | Massachusetts Reports |
| MCH | Maternal and Child Health Bureau |
| Md. App. | Maryland, Appeal Cases |
| M.D. Ga. | Middle District, Georgia |
| Mercy | Movement Ensuring the Right to Choose for Yourself |
| Metc. | Metcalf's Massachusetts Reports |
| MFDP | Mississippi Freedom Democratic party |
| MGT | Management |
| MHSS | Military Health Services System |
| Miller | David Hunter Miller, ed., *Treaties and Other International Acts of the United States of America* (1931–1948) |
| Minn. | Minnesota Reports |
| MINS | minors in need of supervision |
| MIRV | multiple independently targetable reentry vehicle |
| Misc. | Miscellaneous Reports, New York |
| Mixed Claims Comm., Report of Decs. | Mixed Claims Commission, United States and Germany, Report of Decisions |
| M.J. | Military Justice Reporter |
| MLAP | Migrant Legal Action Program |
| MLB | major league baseball |
| MLDP | Mississippi Loyalist Democratic party |
| Mo. | Missouri Reports |
| Mod. | Modern Reports, English King's Bench, etc. |
| Moore, Dig. Intl. Law | John Bassett Moore, *A Digest of International Law*, 8 vols. (1906) |
| Moore, Intl. Arbs. | John Bassett Moore, *History and Digest of the International Arbitrations to Which the United States Has Been a Party*, 6 vols. (1898) |

| | |
|---|---|
| Morison | William Maxwell Morison, *The Scots Revised Report: Morison's Dictionary of Decisions* (1908–09) |
| M.P. | member of Parliament |
| MPAA | Motion Picture Association of America |
| mpg | miles per gallon |
| MPRSA | Marine Protection, Research, and Sanctuaries Act of 1972 |
| M.R. | Master of the Rolls |
| MS-DOS | Microsoft Disk Operating System |
| MSHA | Mine Safety and Health Administration |
| NAACP | National Association for the Advancement of Colored People |
| NAAQS | National Ambient Air Quality Standards |
| NABSW | National Association of Black Social Workers |
| NAFTA | North American Free Trade Agreement, 1993 |
| NARAL | National Abortion Rights Action League |
| NARF | Native American Rights Fund |
| NARS | National Archives and Record Service |
| NASA | National Aeronautics and Space Administration |
| NASD | National Association of Securities Dealers |
| NATO | North Atlantic Treaty Organization |
| NAVINFO | Navy Information Offices |
| NAWSA | National American Woman's Suffrage Association |
| NBA | National Bar Association |
| NBC | National Broadcasting Company |
| NBLSA | National Black Law Student Association |
| NBS | National Bureau of Standards |
| NCA | Noise Control Act; National Command Authorities |
| NCAA | National Collegiate Athletic Association |
| NCAC | National Coalition against Censorship |
| NCCB | National Consumer Cooperative Bank |
| NCE | Northwest Community Exchange |
| NCJA | National Criminal Justice Association |
| NCLB | National Civil Liberties Bureau |
| NCP | national contingency plan |
| NCSC | National Center for State Courts |
| NCUA | National Credit Union Administration |
| NDA | new drug application |
| N.D. Ill. | Northern District, Illinois |
| NDU | National Defense University |
| N.D. Wash. | Northern District, Washington |
| N.E. | North Eastern Reporter |
| N.E. 2d | North Eastern Reporter, Second Series |
| NEA | National Endowment for the Arts |
| NEH | National Endowment for the Humanities |
| NEPA | National Environmental Protection Act; National Endowment Policy Act |
| NFIP | National Flood Insurance Program |
| NGTF | National Gay Task Force |
| NHRA | Nursing Home Reform Act, 1987 |
| NHTSA | National Highway Traffic Safety Administration |
| Nielsen's Rept. | Frederick Kenelm Nielsen, *American and British Claims Arbitration under the Special Agreement Concluded between the United States and Great Britain, August 18, 1910* (1926) |
| NIEO | New International Economic Order |
| NIH | National Institutes of Health, the NIH |
| NIJ | National Institute of Justice |
| NIRA | National Industrial Recovery Act; National Industrial Recovery Administration |
| NIST | National Institute of Standards and Technology, the NIST |
| NITA | National Telecommunications and Information Administration |
| N.J. | New Jersey Reports |

| | |
|---|---|
| N.J. Super. | New Jersey Superior Court Reports |
| NLRA | National Labor Relations Act |
| NLRB | National Labor Relations Board |
| No. | Number |
| NOAA | National Oceanic and Atmospheric Administration |
| NOW | National Organization for Women |
| NOW LDEF | National Organization for Women Legal Defense and Education Fund |
| NOW/PAC | National Organization for Women Political Action Committee |
| NPDES | National Pollutant Discharge Elimination System |
| NPL | national priorities list |
| NPR | National Public Radio |
| NPT | Non-Proliferation Treaty |
| NRA | National Rifle Association; National Recovery Act |
| NRC | Nuclear Regulatory Commission |
| NSC | National Security Council |
| NSCLC | National Senior Citizens Law Center |
| NSF | National Science Foundation |
| NSFNET | National Science Foundation Network |
| NTIA | National Telecommunications and Information Administration |
| NTID | National Technical Institute for the Deaf |
| NTIS | National Technical Information Service |
| NTS | Naval Telecommunications System |
| NTSB | National Transportation Safety Board |
| N.W. | North Western Reporter |
| N.W. 2d | North Western Reporter, Second Series |
| NWSA | National Woman Suffrage Association |
| N.Y. | New York Court of Appeals Reports |
| N.Y. 2d | New York Court of Appeals Reports, Second Series |
| N.Y.S. | New York Supplement Reporter |
| N.Y.S. 2d | New York Supplement Reporter, Second Series |
| NYSE | New York Stock Exchange |
| N.Y. Sup. | New York Supreme Court Reports |
| NYU | New York University |
| OAAU | Organization of Afro American Unity |
| OAP | Office of Administrative Procedure |
| OAS | Organization of American States |
| OASDI | Old-age, Survivors, and Disability Insurance Benefits |
| OASHDS | Office of the Assistant Secretary for Human Development Services |
| OCED | Office of Comprehensive Employment Development |
| OCHAMPUS | Office of Civilian Health and Medical Program of the Uniformed Services |
| OCSE | Office of Child Support Enforcement |
| OEA | Organización de los Estados Americanos |
| OFCCP | Office of Federal Contract Compliance Programs |
| OFPP | Office of Federal Procurement Policy |
| OICD | Office of International Cooperation and Development |
| OIG | Office of the Inspector General |
| OJARS | Office of Justice Assistance, Research, and Statistics |
| OMB | Office of Management and Budget |
| OMPC | Office of Management, Planning, and Communications |
| ONP | Office of National Programs |
| OPD | Office of Policy Development |
| OPEC | Organization of Petroleum Exporting Countries |
| OPIC | Overseas Private Investment Corporation |
| Ops. Atts. Gen. | Opinions of the Attorneys-General of the United States |
| Ops. Comms. | Opinions of the Commissioners |
| OPSP | Office of Product Standards Policy |
| O.R. | Ontario Reports |
| OR | Official Records |

| | |
|---|---|
| OSHA | Occupational Safety and Health Administration |
| OSHRC | Occupational Safety and Health Review Commission |
| OSM | Office of Surface Mining |
| OSS | Office of Strategic Services |
| OST | Office of the Secretary |
| OT | Office of Transportation |
| OTA | Office of Technology Assessment |
| OTC | over-the-counter |
| OUI | operating under the influence |
| OWBPA | Older Workers Benefit Protection Act |
| OWRT | Office of Water Research and Technology |
| P. | Pacific Reporter |
| P. 2d | Pacific Reporter, Second Series |
| PAC | political action committee |
| Pa. Oyer and Terminer | Pennsylvania Oyer and Terminer Reports |
| PATCO | Professional Air Traffic Controllers Organization |
| PBGC | Pension Benefit Guaranty Corporation |
| PBS | Public Broadcasting Service; Public Buildings Service |
| P.C. | Privy Council (English Law Reports); personal computer |
| PCIJ | Permanent Court of International Justice |
| | Series A—Judgments and Orders (1922–30) |
| | Series B—Advisory Opinions (1922–30) |
| | Series A/B—Judgments, Orders, and Advisory Opinions (1931–40) |
| | Series C—Pleadings, Oral Statements, and Documents relating to Judgments and Advisory Opinions (1923–42) |
| | Series D—Acts and Documents concerning the Organization of the World Court (1922–47) |
| | Series E—Annual Reports (1925–45) |
| PCP | phencyclidine (no need to spell out) |
| P.D. | Probate Division, English Law Reports (1876–1890) |
| PDA | Pregnancy Discrimination Act of 1978 |
| PD & R | Policy Development and Research |
| Perm. Ct. of Arb. | Permanent Court of Arbitration |
| Pet. | Peters' United States Supreme Court Reports |
| PETA | People for the Ethical Treatment of Animals |
| PGM | Program |
| PHA | Public Housing Agency |
| Phila. Ct. of Oyer and Terminer | Philadelphia Court of Oyer and Terminer |
| PHS | Public Health Service |
| PIC | Private Industry Council |
| Pick. | Pickering's Massachusetts Reports |
| PIK | Payment in Kind |
| PINS | persons in need of supervision |
| PIRG | Public Interest Research Group |
| P.L. | Public Laws |
| PLAN | Pro-Life Action Network |
| PLI | Practicing Law Institute |
| PLO | Palestine Liberation Organization |
| PNET | Peaceful Nuclear Explosions Treaty |
| POW-MIA | prisoner of war–missing in action |
| Pratt | Frederic Thomas Pratt, *Law of Contraband of War, with a Selection of Cases from the Papers of the Right Honourable Sir George Lee* (1856) |
| Proc. | Proceedings |
| PRP | potentially responsible party |
| PSRO | Professional Standards Review Organization |
| PTO | Patents and Trademark Office |
| PURPA | Public Utilities Regulatory Policies Act |

| | |
|---|---|
| PUSH | People United to Serve Humanity |
| PWA | Public Works Administration |
| PWSA | Ports and Waterways Safety Act of 1972 |
| Q.B. | Queen's Bench (England) |
| Ralston's Rept. | Jackson Harvey Ralston, ed., *Venezuelan Arbitrations of 1903* (1904) |
| RC | Regional Commissioner |
| RCRA | Resource Conservation and Recovery Act |
| RCWP | Rural Clean Water Program |
| RDA | Rural Development Administration |
| REA | Rural Electrification Administration |
| Rec. des Decs. des Trib. Arb. Mixtes | G. Gidel, ed., *Recueil des décisions des tribunaux arbitraux mixtes, institués par les traités de paix* (1922–30) |
| Redmond | Vol. 3 of Charles I. Bevans, *Treaties and Other International Agreements of the United States of America, 1776–1949* (compiled by C. F. Redmond) (1969) |
| RESPA | Real Estate Settlement Procedure Act of 1974 |
| RFRA | Religious Freedom Restoration Act |
| RICO | Racketeer Influenced and Corrupt Organizations |
| RNC | Republican National Committee |
| Roscoe | Edward Stanley Roscoe, ed., *Reports of Prize Cases Determined in the High Court of Admiralty before the Lords Commissioners of Appeals in Prize Causes and before the Judicial Committee of the Privy Council from 1745 to 1859* (1905) |
| ROTC | Reserve Officers' Training Corps |
| RPP | Representative Payee Program |
| R.S. | Revised Statutes |
| RTC | Resolution Trust Company |
| Ryan White CARE Act | Ryan White Comprehensive AIDS Research Emergency Act of 1990 |
| SAC | Strategic Air Command |
| SACB | Subversive Activities Control Board |
| SADD | Students against Drunk Driving |
| SAF | Student Activities Fund |
| SAIF | Savings Association Insurance Fund |
| SALT I | Strategic Arms Limitation Talks of 1969–72 |
| SAMHSA | Substance Abuse and Mental Health Services Administration |
| Sandf. | Sandford's New York Superior Court Reports |
| S and L | savings and loan |
| SARA | Superfund Amendment and Reauthorization Act |
| Sawy. | Sawyer's United States Circuit Court Reports |
| SBA | Small Business Administration |
| SCLC | Southern Christian Leadership Conference |
| Scott's Repts. | James Brown Scott, ed., *The Hague Court Reports*, 2 vols. (1916–32) |
| SCS | Soil Conservation Service |
| SCSEP | Senior Community Service Employment Program |
| S.Ct. | Supreme Court Reporter |
| S.D. Cal. | Southern District, California |
| S.D. Fla. | Southern District, Florida |
| S.D. Ga. | Southern District, Georgia |
| SDI | Strategic Defense Initiative |
| S.D. Me. | Southern District, Maine |
| S.D.N.Y. | Southern District, New York |
| SDS | Students for a Democratic Society |
| S.E. | South Eastern Reporter |
| S.E. 2d | South Eastern Reporter, Second Series |
| SEA | Science and Education Administration |
| SEATO | Southeast Asia Treaty Organization |
| SEC | Securities and Exchange Commission |
| Sec. | Section |
| SEEK | Search for Elevation, Education and Knowledge |
| SEOO | State Economic Opportunity Office |

| | |
|---|---|
| SEP | simplified employee pension plan |
| Ser. | Series |
| Sess. | Session |
| SGLI | Servicemen's Group Life Insurance |
| SIP | state implementation plan |
| SLA | Symbionese Liberation Army |
| SLBM | submarine-launched ballistic missile |
| SNCC | Student Nonviolent Coordinating Committee |
| So. | Southern Reporter |
| So. 2d | Southern Reporter, Second Series |
| SPA | Software Publisher's Association |
| Spec. Sess. | Special Session |
| SRA | Sentencing Reform Act of 1984 |
| SS | Schutzstaffel (German for Protection Echelon) |
| SSA | Social Security Administration |
| SSI | Supplemental Security Income |
| START I | Strategic Arms Reduction Treaty of 1991 |
| START II | Strategic Arms Reduction Treaty of 1993 |
| Stat. | United States Statutes at Large |
| STS | Space Transportation Systems |
| St. Tr. | State Trials, English |
| STURAA | Surface Transportation and Uniform Relocation Assistance Act of 1987 |
| Sup. Ct. of Justice, Mexico | Supreme Court of Justice, Mexico |
| Supp. | Supplement |
| S.W. | South Western Reporter |
| S.W. 2d | South Western Reporter, Second Series |
| SWAPO | South-West Africa People's Organization |
| SWAT | Special Weapons and Tactics |
| SWP | Socialist Workers party |
| TDP | Trade and Development Program |
| Tex. Sup. | Texas Supreme Court Reports |
| THAAD | Theater High-Altitude Area Defense System |
| TIA | Trust Indenture Act of 1939 |
| TIAS | Treaties and Other International Acts Series (United States) |
| TNT | trinitrotoluene |
| TOP | Targeted Outreach Program |
| TPUS | Transportation and Public Utilities Service |
| Tripartite Claims Comm., Decs. and Ops. | Tripartite Claims Commission (United States, Austria, and Hungary), Decisions and Opinions |
| TRI-TAC | Joint Tactical Communications |
| TRO | temporary restraining order |
| TS | Treaty Series, United States |
| TSCA | Toxic Substance Control Act |
| TSDs | transporters, storers, and disposers |
| TTBT | Threshold Test Ban Treaty |
| TVA | Tennessee Valley Authority |
| UAW | United Auto Workers; United Automobile, Aerospace, and Agricultural Implements Workers of America |
| U.C.C. | Uniform Commercial Code; Universal Copyright Convention |
| U.C.C.C. | Uniform Consumer Credit Code |
| UCCJA | Uniform Child Custody Jurisdiction Act |
| UCMJ | Uniform Code of Military Justice |
| UCPP | Urban Crime Prevention Program |
| UCS | United Counseling Service |
| UDC | United Daughters of the Confederacy |
| UFW | United Farm Workers |
| UHF | ultrahigh frequency |
| UIFSA | Uniform Interstate Family Support Act |

| | |
|---|---|
| UIS | Unemployment Insurance Service |
| UMDA | Uniform Marriage and Divorce Act |
| UMTA | Urban Mass Transportation Administration |
| UNCITRAL | United Nations Commission on International Trade Law |
| UNCTAD | United Nations Conference on Trade and Development |
| UN Doc. | United Nations Documents |
| UNDP | United Nations Development Program |
| UNEF | United Nations Emergency Force |
| UNESCO | United Nations Educational, Scientific, and Cultural Organization |
| UNICEF | United Nations Children's Fund |
| UNIDO | United Nations Industrial and Development Organization |
| Unif. L. Ann. | Uniform Laws Annotated |
| UN Repts. Intl. Arb. Awards | United Nations Reports of International Arbitral Awards |
| UNTS | United Nations Treaty Series |
| UPI | United Press International |
| URESA | Uniform Reciprocal Enforcement of Support Act |
| U.S. | United States Reports |
| USAF | United States Air Force |
| U.S. App. D.C. | United States Court of Appeals for the District of Columbia |
| U.S.C. | United States Code |
| U.S.C.A. | United States Code Annotated |
| U.S.C.C.A.N. | United States Code Congressional and Administrative News |
| USCMA | United States Court of Military Appeals |
| USDA | U.S. Department of Agriculture |
| USES | United States Employment Service |
| USFA | United States Fire Administration |
| USICA | International Communication Agency, United States |
| USSC | U.S. Sentencing Commission |
| U.S.S.R. | Union of Soviet Socialist Republics |
| UST | United States Treaties |
| USTS | United States Travel Service |
| v. | *versus* |
| VA | Veterans Administration, the VA |
| VGLI | Veterans Group Life Insurance |
| Vict. | Queen Victoria (Great Britain) |
| VIN | vehicle identification number |
| VISTA | Volunteers in Service to America |
| VJRA | Veterans Judicial Review Act of 1988 |
| V.L.A. | Volunteer Lawyers for the Arts |
| VMI | Virginia Military Institute |
| VMLI | Veterans Mortgage Life Insurance |
| VOCAL | Victims of Child Abuse Laws |
| WAC | Women's Army Corps |
| Wall. | Wallace's United States Supreme Court Reports |
| Wash. 2d | Washington Reports, Second Series |
| WAVES | Women Accepted for Volunteer Service |
| WCTU | Women's Christian Temperance Union |
| W.D. Wash. | Western District, Washington |
| W.D. Wis. | Western District, Wisconsin |
| WEAL | West's Encyclopedia of American Law, Women's Equity Action League |
| Wend. | Wendell's New York Reports |
| WFSE | Washington Federation of State Employees |
| Wheat. | Wheaton's United States Supreme Court Reports |
| Wheel. Cr. Cases | Wheeler's New York Criminal Cases |
| Whiteman | Marjorie Millace Whiteman, *Digest of International Law*, 15 vols. (1963–73) |
| WHO | World Health Organization |
| WIC | Women, Infants, and Children program |
| Will. and Mar. | King William and Queen Mary (Great Britain) |

| | |
|---|---|
| WIN | WESTLAW Is Natural; Whip Inflation Now; Work Incentive Program |
| WIU | Workers' Industrial Union |
| W.L.R. | Weekly Law Reports, England |
| WPA | Works Progress Administration |
| WPPDA | Welfare and Pension Plans Disclosure Act |
| WWI | World War I |
| WWII | World War II |
| Yates Sel. Cas. | Yates' New York Select Cases |

# BIBLIOGRAPHY

**BACON, SIR FRANCIS**

Bowen, Catherine D. 1963. *Francis Bacon: The Temper of a Man*. Boston: Little, Brown.

Whitney, Charles. 1986. *Francis Bacon and Modernity*. New Haven, Conn.: Yale Univ. Press.

**BADGER, GEORGE EDMUND**

Congressional Quarterly. 1989. *Guide to the U.S. Supreme Court*. 2d ed. Washington, D.C.: Congressional Quarterly.

Maisel, L. Sandy, ed. 1991. *Political Parties and Elections in the United States*. New York: Garland.

**BAIL**

Kamisar, Yale, and Wayne R. LaFave. 1994. *Advanced Criminal Procedure*. 8th ed. Ed. Jerold Israel. American Casebook Series. St. Paul: West.

———. 1994. *Modern Criminal Procedure and Basic Criminal Procedure: 1994 Supplement to Eighth Editions*. Ed. Jerold Israel. American Casebook Series. St. Paul: West.

**BAKER, ELLA JOSEPHINE**

Dallard, Shyrlee. 1990. *Ella Baker: A Leader behind the Scenes*. Parsippany, N.J.: Silver Burdett Press.

**BAKER V. CARR**

"A Final Victory Marks the End of a Career." 1990. *National Law Journal* (August 13).

"*Koohi v. United States*." 1993. *Georgia Law Review* 28 (fall).

Restatement (Third) of the Foreign Relations Law of the United States.

"Some Implications of Arrow's Theorem for Voting Rights." 1995. *Stanford Law Review* 47 (January).

"*The Trustees of the Office of Hawaiian Affairs v. Yamasaki*: The Application of the Political Question Doctrine to Hawaii's Public Land Trust Dispute." 1988. *University of Hawaii Law Review* 10 (winter).

"*United States v. Alvarez-Machain*: Waltzing with the Political Question Doctrine." 1994. *Connecticut Law Review* 26 (winter).

"U.S. Supreme Court." 1990. *National Law Journal* (June 4).

"When Restraint Requires Activism." 1990. *Stanford Law Review* 42 (July).

**BALANCING**

*Columbia Law Review*. 1978. 78:1022.

Friendly, Fred W. 1984. *The Constitution: That Delicate Balance*. New York: Random House.

Gottlieb, Stephen E., ed. 1993. *Public Values in Constitutional Law*. Ann Arbor, Mich.: Univ. of Michigan Press.

*Hastings Law Journal*. 1994. 45 (April): 711, 835, 969.

*Yale Law Journal*. 1987. 96 (April): 943.

**BALDWIN, HENRY**

Congressional Quarterly. 1989. *Guide to the U.S. Supreme Court*. 2d ed. Washington, D.C.: Congressional Quarterly.

Elliott, Stephen P., ed. 1986. *A Reference Guide to the United States Supreme Court*. New York: Facts on File.

Swisher, Carl B. 1974. *The Taney Period, 1836–1864*. Vol. 5 of *History of the Supreme Court of the United States*. New York: Macmillan.

**BALDWIN, ROGER NASH**

Lamson, Peggy. 1976. *Roger Baldwin: Founder of the American Civil Liberties Union*. Boston: Houghton Mifflin.

Walker, Samuel. 1990. *In Defense of American Liberties: A History of the ACLU*. New York: Oxford Univ. Press.

**BANKRUPTCY**

Kemner. 1991. "Personal Bankruptcy Discharge and the Myth of the Unchecked Homestead Exemption." *Missouri Law Review* 56.

Swallow, John E. 1990. "The Power of the Shield—Permanently Enjoining Litigation against Entities other than the Debtor—A Look at *In re A. H. Robins Co.*" *Brigham Young University Law Review* 1990.

Taggart, Walter J. 1995. "An Introduction to the Bankruptcy Reform Act of 1994." *Practical Lawyer* 41, no. 2.

U.S. House. 1993. 103d Cong., 1st Sess. H. Rep. 103-32.

U.S. Senate. 1978. 95th Cong., 2d Sess. S. Rep. 989.

### BANKS AND BANKING

Adler, Joseph. 1995. "Banking without Glass-Steagall? Look Overseas." *American Banking Association Journal* (May).

Timberlake, Richard H., Jr. 1993. *Monetary Policy in the United States: An Intellectual and Institutional History.* Chicago: Univ. of Chicago Press.

### BANKS, DENNIS

Churchill, Ward. 1988. *Agents of Repression: The FBI's Secret Wars against the Black Panther Party and the American Indian Movement.* Boston: South End Press.

Weyler, Rex. 1982. *Blood of the Land: The Government and Corporate War against the American Indian Movement.* New York: Everest House.

### BAR ASSOCIATION

Hamilton, Bruce. 1995. "What Makes a Great Bar Association." *Arizona Attorney* (January).

Martin, Peter A. 1989. "A Reassessment of Mandatory State Bar Membership in Light of *Levine v. Heffernan.*" *Marquette Law Review* 73: (fall).

Pound, Roscoe. 1953. *The Lawyer from Antiquity to Modern Times.* St. Paul: West.

Young, Don J., and Louise L. Hill. 1988. "Professionalism: The Necessity for Internal Control." *Temple Law Review* 61: (spring).

### BARBOUR, PHILIP PENDLETON

Congressional Quarterly. 1989. *Guide to the U.S. Supreme Court.* 2d ed. Washington, D.C.: Congressional Quarterly.

Elliott, Stephen P., ed. 1986. *A Reference Guide to the United States Supreme Court.* New York: Facts on File.

### BAR EXAMINATION

American Bar Association/Bureau of National Affairs. *ABA/BNA Lawyers' Manual on Professional Conduct.* 1995.

Curriden, Mark. 1995. "Lawyers Who Skip Law School." *American Bar Association Journal* 81 (February).

Garth, Bryant G. 1983. "Rethinking the Legal Profession's Approach to Collective Self-Improvement: Competence and the Consumer Perspective. *Wisconsin Law Review* 1983.

Getz, Malcolm, John Siegfried, and Terry Calvani. 1981. "Competition at the Bar: The Correlation between the Bar Examination Pass Rate and the Profitability of Practice." *Virginia Law Review* 67.

Pobjecky, Thomas A. "The Florida Board of Bar Examiners: The Constitutional Safeguard between Attorney Aspirants and the Public." *Nova Law Review* 18.

Rogers, W. Sherman. 1989. "Title VII Preemption of State Bar Examinations: Applicability of Title VII to State Occupational Licensing Tests." *Howard Law Journal* 32.

### BARR, WILLIAM PELHAM

"Legal Job No. 1." 1992. *National Law Journal* 15, no. 14 (December 7).

### BASEBALL

Burk, Robert F. 1994. *Never Just a Game.* Chapel Hill, N.C.: Univ. of North Carolina Press.

Helyar, John. 1994. *Lords of the Realm.* New York: Villard Books.

Kovaleff, Theodore P. 1994. *The Antitrust Impulse.* New York: Sharpe.

Sands, Jack, and Peter Gammons. 1993. *Coming Apart at the Seams.* New York: Macmillan.

U.S. Congress Subcommittee on Economic and Commercial Law. 1993. *Baseball's Antitrust Exemption: Hearing before the Subcommittee on Economic and Commercial Law.* Washington, D.C.: U.S. Government Printing Office.

———. 1994. *Baseball's Antitrust Exemption: Hearing before the Subcommittee on Economic and Commercial Law.* Washington, D.C.: U.S. Government Printing Office.

### BATES, DAISY LEE GATSON

Bates, Daisy. 1962. *The Long Shadow of Little Rock.* New York: McKay.

Hine, Darlene C., ed. 1993. *Black Women in America: An Historical Encyclopedia.* Brooklyn: Carlson.

Smith, Jessie C., ed. 1992. *Notable Black American Women.* Detroit: Gale Research.

University of Arkansas—Fayetteville Special Collections.

### BEARD, CHARLES AUSTIN

Noble, David W. 1985. *The End of American History.* Minneapolis: Univ. of Minnesota Press.

### BECKET, SAINT THOMAS

Barlow, Frank. 1986. *Thomas Becket.* Berkeley: Univ. of California Press.

Knowles, David. 1971. *Thomas Becket.* Stanford, Cal.: Stanford Univ. Press.

### BELL, DERRICK ALBERT, JR.

"Action of Harvard's Prof. Bell Focuses Attention on Diversity." 1990. *National Law Journal* (May 7).

Association of American Law Schools. 1993. *Directory of Law Teachers.* Association of American Law Schools.

"Bell, Harvard Agree to Disagree on His Departure." 1992. *National Law Journal* (July 20).

"Bell Still Teaching." 1990. *National Law Journal* (November 12).

"Bell Wants Harvard." 1992. *National Law Journal* (March 23).

Carter, Stephen L. 1991. *Reflections of an Affirmative Action Baby.* New York: Basic Books.

"In Move to NYU, Derrick Bell Cites Friendship with Its Dean." 1991. *National Law Journal* (April 22).

"Prof. Moves." 1991. *National Law Journal* (April 15).

"The Year in Review." 1992. *National Law Journal* (December 28).

### BELL, GRIFFIN BOYETTE

Bell, Griffin B., with Ronald J. Ostrow. 1982. *Taking Care of the Law.* New York: Morrow.

Blum, Andrew. 1989. "Valdez Captain Takes Offensive." *National Law Journal* (October 23).
———. 1993. "In Bell Probe for Dow, Bid Made for Implant Papers." *National Law Journal* (February 1).

### BENEFICIAL ASSOCIATION
"Fraternal Orders and Benefit Societies." *American Jurisprudence* 36, no. 2.

### BENJAMIN, JUDAH PHILIP
"The Daring Escape of Judah P. Benjamin." 1982. *Tampa Bay History* 4, no. 1.
*Detroit College of Law Review.* 1991:1019.
"The Enigmatic Judah Benjamin." 1978. *Midstream* 24, no. 8.
Evans, Eli N., and Robert Weinberg. 1988. *Judah P. Benjamin: The Jewish Confederate.* New York: Free Press.
"Journey to Asylum." 1987. *Civil War Times Illustrated* 26, no. 8.
"Judah P. Benjamin's Loyalty to Jefferson Davis." 1966. *Georgia Review* 20, no. 3.
*Loyola of Los Angeles Law Review.* 26:183.
"Meeting Mr. Benjamin." 1986. *Queen City Heritage* 44, no. 3.
*Memphis State University Law Review.* 22:725.
Patrick, Rembert W. *The Opinions of the Confederate Attorneys General, 1861–1865.* Buffalo: Dennis.
"Some Legal and Political Views of Judah P. Benjamin." 1956. *Historica Judaica* (France) 18, no. 1.
"The Spectrum of Jewish Leadership in Ante-Bellum America." 1982. *Journal of American Ethnic History* 1, no. 2.
"The Three Lives of Judah P. Benjamin." 1967. *History Today* 17, no. 9.
*University of Pittsburgh Law Review.* 55:389.
"The Virginia Decision to Use Negro Soldiers in the Civil War, 1864–1865." 1975. *Virginia Magazine of History and Biography.* 82, no. 1.
*Law and Contemporary Problems.* 55:107.

### BICKEL, ALEXANDER MORDECAI
Bickel, Alexander M. 1963. *The Least Dangerous Branch: The Supreme Court at the Bar of Politics.* Indianapolis: Dobbs-Merrill.
———. 1970. *The Supreme Court and the Idea of Progress.* New York: Harper & Row.
———. 1973. *The Caseload of the Supreme Court and What, If Anything, to Do About It.* Washington, D.C.: American Enterprise Institute for Public Policy Research.
Congressional Quarterly. 1989. *Guide to the U.S. Supreme Court.* 2d ed. Washington, D.C.: Congressional Quarterly. 1990.

### BIRTH CONTROL
Bacigal, Ronald J. 1990. *The Limits of Litigation—The Dalkon Shield Controversy.* Durham, N.C.: Carolina Academic Press.
McCann, Carole R. 1994. *Birth Control Politics in the United States, 1916–1945.* Ithaca: Cornell Univ. Press.
McLaren, Angus. 1990. *A History of Contraception from Antiquity to the Present.* Cambridge, Mass.: Blackwell.

### BLACK, HUGO LAFAYETTE
Congressional Quarterly. 1989. *Guide to the U.S. Supreme Court.* 2d ed. Washington, D.C.: Congressional Quarterly.
Elliott, Stephen P., ed. 1986. *A Reference Guide to the United States Supreme Court.* New York: Facts on File.

### BLACK, JEREMIAH SULLIVAN
Congressional Quarterly. 1989. *Guide to the U.S. Supreme Court.* 2d ed. Washington, D.C.: Congressional Quarterly.
Elliott, Stephen P., ed. 1986. *A Reference Guide to the United States Supreme Court.* New York: Facts on File.

### BLACKLIST
Vaughn, Robert. 1972. *Only Lies: A Study of Show Business Blacklisting.* New York: Putnam.

### BLACKMUN, HARRY ANDREW
Barnes, Catherine A. 1978. *Men of the Supreme Court: Profiles of the Justices.* New York: Facts on File.
Congressional Quarterly. 1989. *Guide to the U.S. Supreme Court.* 2d ed. Washington, D.C.: Congressional Quarterly.
Cushman, Claire, ed. 1993. *The Supreme Court Justices: Illustrated Biographies, 1789–1993.* Washington, D.C.: Congressional Quarterly.
Levy, Leonard. 1974. *Against the Law: The Nixon Court and Criminal Justice.* New York: Harper & Row.

### BLACK PANTHER PARTY
Churchill, Ward. 1990. *Agents of Repression: The FBI's Secret Wars against the Black Panther Party and the American Indian Movement.* Boston: South End Press.
*Eyes on the Prize: Civil Rights Reader.* 1991. New York: Penguin Books.
Johnson, Jacqueline. 1990. *Stokely Carmichael: The Story of Black Power.* Parsippany, N.J.: Silver Burdett Press.
Massiah, Louis, and Terry K. Rockefeller. 1990. "Power!" Episode 3 of *Eyes on the Prize II: America at the Racial Crossroads.* PBS Video.

### BLAIR, JOHN, JR.
Congressional Quarterly. 1989. *Guide to the U.S. Supreme Court.* 2d ed. Washington, D.C.: Congressional Quarterly.
Cushman, Claire, ed. 1993. *The Supreme Court Justices: Illustrated Biographies, 1789–1993.* Washington, D.C.: Congressional Quarterly.

### BLATCHFORD, SAMUEL
Congressional Quarterly. 1989. *Guide to the U.S. Supreme Court.* 2d ed. Washington, D.C.: Congressional Quarterly.
*The Justices of the United States Supreme Court, 1789–1969: Their Lives and Major Opinions.* Friedman, Leon, and Fred L. Israel, eds. 1969. New York: Chelsea House.

### BOGGS, CORINNE CLAIBORNE
Ehrenhalt, Alan, ed. 1983. *Politics in America.* Washington, D.C.: Congressional Quarterly.
Keil, Sally Van Wagenen. 1979. *Those Wonderful Women in Their Flying Machines.* New York: Rawson Wade.

O'Neill, Lois D., ed. 1979. *The Women's Book of World Records and Achievements*. Garden City, N.Y.: Anchor Press.

Stineman, Esther. 1980. *American Political Women*. Littleton, Colo.: Libraries Unlimited.

### BOLIN, JANE MATILDA

Hine, Darlene C., ed. 1993. *Black Women in America: An Historical Encyclopedia*. Brooklyn: Carlson.

Smith, Jessie C., ed. 1992. *Notable Black American Women*. Detroit: Gale Research.

Wellesley College Alumni Office.

### BONDS

Geisst, Charles R. 1992. *Entrepot Capitalism*. New York: Praeger.

Platt, Harlan D. 1994. *The First Junk Bond*. New York: Sharpe.

Wurman, Richard S. 1990. *The Wall Street Journal Guide to Understanding Money and Money Markets*. New York: Access Press.

Yago, Glenn. 1991. *Junk Bonds*. New York: Oxford Univ. Press.

### BORK, ROBERT HERON

Bork, Robert H. 1990. *The Tempting of America: The Political Seduction of the Law*. New York: Simon & Schuster.

Pertschuk, Michael, and Wendy Schaetzel. 1989. *The People Rising: The Campaign against the Bork Nomination*. New York: Thunder's Mouth Press.

Sager, Lawrence. 1990. "Back to Bork." *New York Review of Books* (October 25).

### BOSONE, REVA BECK

*National Education Association Journal*. 1949. April.

Special Collections Department, Marriott Library, University of Utah, Salt Lake City, Utah.

### BOUNDARIES

Herzog, Lawrence. 1991. "International Boundary Cities: The Debate on Transfrontier Planning in Two Border Regions." *Natural Resources Journal* 31.

### BRADLEY, JOSEPH P.

Congressional Quarterly. 1989. *Guide to the U.S. Supreme Court*. 2d ed. Washington, D.C.: Congressional Quarterly.

Cushman, Claire. 1993. *The Supreme Court Justices: Illustrated Biographies, 1789–1993*. Washington, D.C.: Congressional Quarterly.

### BRANDEIS, LOUIS DEMBITZ

Congressional Quarterly. 1989. *Guide to the U.S. Supreme Court*. 2d ed. Washington, D.C.: Congressional Quarterly.

Cushman, Claire, ed. 1993. *The Supreme Court Justices: Illustrated Biographies, 1789–1993*. Washington, D.C.: Congressional Quarterly.

Paper, Lewis J. 1983. *Brandeis: An Intimate Biography*. Englewood Cliffs, N.J.: Prentice-Hall.

Urofsky, Melvin I. 1981. *Louis D. Brandeis and the Progressive Tradition*. Boston: Little, Brown.

### BREWER, DAVID JOSIAH

Schwartz, Bernard. 1993. *A History of the Supreme Court*. New York: Oxford Univ. Press.

Tribe, Laurence H. 1985. *God Save This Honorable Court*. New York: Random House.

### BREYER, STEPHEN GERALD

"Court: 'Animus' in Colo. Gay Law." 1996. *National Law Journal* 18, no. 40 (June 3).

"Court Decisions." 1996. *National Law Journal* 18, no. 46 (July 15).

Pierce, Richard J. 1995. "Justice Breyer: Intentionalist, Pragmatist, and Empiricist." *Administrative Law Journal of the American University* (winter).

### BROADCASTING

Flint, Joe. 1993. "Congress' Message to Broadcasters: Get Your Children's Act Together (House Telecommunications Subcommittee Hearings)." *Broadcasting and Cable* (March 15).

Jessell, Harry A. 1990. "FCC Begins to Implement Children's TV Law (Federal Communications Commission on Children's Television)." *Broadcasting and Cable* (October 29).

———. 1995. "Compliance Pays Off at License Renewal Time, Lawyers Say." *Broadcasting and Cable* (April 17).

Straubel, Michael S. 1992. "Telecommunication Satellites and Market Forces: How Should the Geostationary Orbit Be Regulated by the FCC?" *North Carolina Journal of International Law and Commercial Regulation* 17 (winter).

### BROWN, HENRY BILLINGS

Schwartz, Bernard. 1993. *A History of the Supreme Court*. New York: Oxford Univ. Press.

Tribe, Laurence H. 1985. *God Save This Honorable Court*. New York: Random House.

### BROWN V. BOARD OF EDUCATION OF TOPEKA, KANSAS

Kluger, Richard. 1975. *Simple Justice: The History of* Brown v. Board of Education *and Black America's Struggle for Equality*. New York: Knopf.

Miller, LaMar P., ed. 1986. *Brown Plus Thirty: Perspective on Desegregation*. New York: Metropolitan Center for Educational Research, New York University.

Whitman, Mark, ed. 1993. *Removing a Badge of Slavery: The Record of* Brown v. Board of Education. Princeton, N.J.: Wiener.

Wilkinson, J. Harvie III. 1979. *From* Brown *to* Bakke: *The Supreme Court and School Integration, 1954–1978*. New York: Oxford Univ. Press.

### BROWNING, JAMES ROBERT

*Almanac of the Federal Judiciary*.

Hursh, Jack. 1995. "Tribute to Judge James R. Browning." *Montana Law Review* 56 (winter).

West. Devitt Award presentation materials provided by the Media Relations Department.

### BRYAN, WILLIAM JENNINGS

Anderson, David D. 1981. *William Jennings Bryan*. Boston: Twayne.

Koenig, Louis W. 1971. *Bryan: A Political Biography of William Jennings Bryan*. New York: Putnam.

### BRYANT, WILLIAM BENSON

Ploski, Harry A., and James Williams, eds. 1989. *The Negro Almanac*. Detroit: Gale Research.

Spradling, Mary M., ed. 1980. *In Black and White*. Detroit: Gale Research.

## BUILDING OFFICIALS AND CODE ADMINISTRATORS INTERNATIONAL

Building Officials and Code Administrators (BOCA) International. "BOCA International Membership Application Form." BOCA International, Country Club Hills, Illinois.

Harkness, Albert. 1995. "Building Codes: A Historical Perspective." *Building Official and Code Administrator Magazine* (March–April).

## BURDEN OF PERSUASION

Rothstein, Paul F. 1981. *Evidence*. 2d ed. St. Paul: West.

## BURKE, EDMUND

Kirk, Russell. 1967. *Edmund Burke: A Genius Reconsidered*. New Rochelle, N.Y.: Arlington House.

_____. 1987. *The Conservative Mind from Burke to Eliot*. Chicago: Regnery Books.

Kramnick, Isaac, ed. 1974. *Edmund Burke*. Englewood Cliffs, N.J.: Prentice-Hall.

O'Brien, Conor C. 1992. *The Great Melody: A Thematic Biography of Edmund Burke*. Chicago: Univ. of Chicago Press.

## BURR, AARON

Lomask, Milton. 1982. *Aaron Burr*. New York: Farrar, Straus & Giroux.

Vail, Philip. 1973. *The Great American Rascal*. New York: Hawthorn Books.

## BURTON, HAROLD HITZ

Schwartz, Bernard. 1993. *A History of the Supreme Court*. New York: Oxford Univ. Press.

Tribe, Laurence H. 1985. *God Save This Honorable Court*. New York: Random House.

## BUSINESS JUDGMENT RULE

Balotti, R. Franklin, and Jesse A. Finkelstein. 1988. *The Delaware Law of Corporations and Business Organizations*. Englewood Cliffs, N.J.: Prentice-Hall.

Gervurtz. 1994. "The Business Judgment Rule: Meaningless Verbiage or Misguided Notion?" *Southern California Law Review* 67.

## BUTLER, CHARLES HENRY

Butler, Charles Henry. 1942. *A Century at the Bar of the Supreme Court of the United States*. New York: Van Rees Press.

Congressional Quarterly. 1989. *Guide to the U.S. Supreme Court*. 2d ed. Washington, D.C.: Congressional Quarterly.

## BUTLER, PIERCE

Brown, Francis J. 1945. "The Social and Economic Philosophy of Pierce Butler." In *Catholic University of America Studies in Sociology*. Vol. 8. Washington, D.C.: Catholic Univ. of America Press. Dissertation, Catholic University.

Burner, David. 1969. "Pierce Butler." In *The Justices of the United States Supreme Court, 1789–1969: Their Lives and Major Opinions*, ed. Leon Friedman and Fred L. Israel. New York: Chelsea House.

Christianson, Theodore. 1935. *Minnesota: A History*. Chicago: American Historical Society.

Congressional Quarterly. 1989. *Guide to the U.S. Supreme Court*. Washington, D.C.: Congressional Quarterly.

Danielski, David J. 1964. *A Supreme Court Justice Is Appointed*. New York: Random House.

Frank, John P. 1940. *The Confirmation of Pierce Butler*. M.A. thesis, University of Wisconsin.

Reilly, William. 1993. "Pierce Butler." In *The Supreme Court Justices: Illustrated Biographies, 1789–1993*; ed. Claire Cushman. Washington, D.C.: Congressional Quarterly.

U.S. Supreme Court. 1940. *Proceedings of the Bar and Officers of the Supreme Court of the United States in Memory of Pierce Butler* (January 27).

## BYRNES, JAMES FRANCIS

Byrnes, James F. 1947. *Speaking Frankly*. New York: Harper & Brothers.

_____. 1958. *All in One Lifetime*. New York: Harper & Brothers.

Congressional Quarterly. 1989. *Guide to the U.S. Supreme Court*. 2d ed. Washington, D.C.: Congressional Quarterly.

Elliott, Stephen P., ed. 1986. *A Reference Guide to the United States Supreme Court*. New York: Facts on File.

## CABLE TELEVISION

Arnesen, David W., and Marlin Blizinsky. "Cable Television: Will Federal Regulation Protect the Public Interest?" *American Business Law Journal* 32.

Gustafson, Madie D. "Transfers of Cable Television Systems: Regulatory Concerns at Federal, State, and Local Levels." *Practising Law Institute/Patents*, Copyrights, Trademarks, and Literary Property Course Handbook Series 380.

Lay, Tillman L., and J. Darrell Peterson. "Federal, State, and Local Regulation of Cable Television Franchise Transfers." *Practising Law Institute/Patents*, Copyrights, Trademarks, and Literary Property Course Handbook Series 405.

Markey, Edward J. "Cable Television Regulation: Promoting Competition in a Rapidly Changing World." *Federal Communications Law Journal* 46.

Peritz, Marc. "*Turner Broadcasting v. FCC*: A First Amendment Challenge to Cable Television Must-Carry Rules." *William and Mary Bill of Rights Journal* 3.

## CAMERAS IN COURT

*ABA Journal*. Vol. 74 (November):52.

"Are We Being Fed a Steady Diet of Tabloid Television?" 1994. *ABA Journal* (May).

"Cameras in the Courtroom: Should Judges Permit High-Profile Trials to Be Televised?" 1995. *American Bar Association (ABA) Journal* (September).

*Facts and Opinions about Cameras in Courtrooms*. 1995. Court TV broadcast, July. America Online.

"Mass Media's Impact on Litigation, Lawyers, and Judges." 1995. Review of Litigation Symposium, February 24.

*Ohio State Journal on Dispute Resolution*. Vol. 9, no. 55.

"Democracy and the Demystification of Courts: An Essay." 1995. *Review of Litigation* (summer).

"That's Entertainment! The Continuing Debate over Cameras in the Courtroom." 1995. *Federal Lawyer* (July).

*University of Chicago Law Review.* 1989 (fall).

### CAMPBELL, BEN NIGHTHORSE

Viola, Herman J. 1993. *Ben Nighthorse Campbell: An American Warrior.* New York: Orion Books.

### CAMPBELL, JOHN ARCHIBALD

Congressional Quarterly. 1989. *Guide to the U.S. Supreme Court.* 2d ed. Washington, D.C.: Congressional Quarterly.

Elliott, Stephen P., ed. 1986. *A Reference Guide to the United States Supreme Court.* New York: Facts on File.

Swisher, Carl B. 1974. *The Taney Period, 1836–64.* Vol. 5 of *History of the Supreme Court of the United States.* New York: Macmillan.

### CANADA AND THE UNITED STATES

"Dispute Resolution under Chapter 19 of the United States–Canada Free-Trade Agreement: Did the Parties Get What They Bargained For?" 1995. *Stanford Journal of International Law* (winter).

"The Effect of the United States–Canada Free Trade Agreement upon United States Immigration Law." 1988. *Practicing Law Institute* (October 1).

"From Customary Law to Environmental Assessment: A New Approach to Avoiding Transboundary Environmental Damage between Canada and the United States." 1995. *Boston College Environmental Affairs Law Review* (winter).

"The North American Experience Managing Transboundary Water Resources: The International Joint Commission and the International Boundary and Water Commission." 1993. *Natural Resources Journal* (spring).

"United States–Canadian Free Trade: Economic Repercussions of the CFTA and NAFTA on the United States, Canada, and the Great Lakes Region." Great Lakes Symposium 1994. *University of Toledo Law Review.*

### CANON LAW

Buelt, Edward L., and Charles Goldberg. 1995. "Canon Law and Civil Law Interface: Diocesan Corporations." *Catholic Lawyer.*

Donahue, Charles, Jr. 1992. "IUS Commune, Canon Law, and Common Law in England." Paper presented at symposium, Relationships among Roman Law, Common Law, and Modern Civil Law. *Tulane Law Review* (June).

Helmholz, R. H. 1983. "The Early History of the Grand Jury and the Canon Law." *University of Chicago Law Review* (spring).

Jirik, Paulissa, member, Canon Law Society of America. 1995. Telephone conversation, July 31.

### CANON LAW SOCIETY OF AMERICA

Canon Law Society of America informational brochure. 1994. May.

Receptionist, Canon Law Society of America. 1995. Telephone conversation, July 31.

Jirik, Paulissa, member, Canon Law Society of America. 1995. Telephone conversation, July 31.

### CAPITAL PUNISHMENT

Bigel, Alan I. 1994. "Symposium on Capital Punishment—Justices William J. Brennan, Jr., and Thurgood Marshall on Capital Punishment: Its Constitutionality, Morality, Deterrent Effect, and Interpretation by the Court." *Notre Dame Journal of Law, Ethics, and Public Policy* (Thomas J. White Center on Law and Government).

"A Conversation with the President and Vice President." 1995. *Larry King Live.* CNN broadcast, June 5.

Von Drehle, David. 1995. *Among the Lowest of the Dead: The Culture of Death Row.* New York: Times Books.

### CARDOZO, BENJAMIN NATHAN

Congressional Quarterly. 1989. *Guide to the U.S. Supreme Court.* 2d ed. Washington, D.C.: Congressional Quarterly.

Elliott, Stephen P., ed. 1986. *A Reference Guide to the United States Supreme Court.* New York: Facts on File.

Levy, Beryl H. 1938. *Cardozo and Frontiers of Legal Thinking.* Port Washington, N.Y.: Kennikat Press.

Pollard, Joseph P. 1970. *Mr. Justice Cardozo: A Liberal Mind in Action.* Westport, Conn.: Greenwood Press.

### CAR-JACKING

Michenfelder, Mary C. 1995. "The Federal Carjacking Statute: To Be or Not to Be? An Analysis of the Propriety of 18 U.S.C. § 2119." *Saint Louis University Law Journal* 39 (spring).

Wing, F. Georgann. 1994. "Putting the Brakes on Carjacking or Accelerating It? The Anti Car Theft Act of 1992." *University of Richmond Law Review* 28 (April).

### CARMICHAEL, STOKELY

Carmichael, Stokely. 1971. *Stokely Speaks: Black Power to Pan-Africanism.* New York: Random House.

Johnson, Jacqueline. 1990. *Stokely Carmichael: The Story of Black Power.* Parsippany, N.J.: Silver Burdett Press.

Makeba, Miriam. 1987. *Makeba: My Story.* New York: New American Library.

### CARRIERS

Hegedus, L. E. 1992. "*Shinault v. American Airlines, Inc.:* Compensatory and Emotional Distress Damages under the Air Carrier Access Act." *Tulane Law Review* 66.

Murphy, Betty Southard. 1993. "The Americans with Disabilities Act: How It Affects the Airline and Railroad Industries." *American Law Institute* (April).

### CARSWELL, GEORGE HARROLD

Levy, Leonard W. 1974. *Against the Law: The Nixon Court and Criminal Justice.* New York: Harper & Row.

### CARTER, JAMES COOLIDGE

Congressional Quarterly. 1989. *Guide to the U.S. Supreme Court.* 2d ed. Washington, D.C.: Congressional Quarterly.

Elliott, Stephen P., ed. 1986. *A Reference Guide to the United States Supreme Court.* New York: Facts on File.

Johnson, John W., ed. 1992. *Historic U.S. Court Cases, 1690–1990.* New York: Garland.

## CARTER, ROBERT LEE

Carter, Robert L. Office of the judge.

Ploski, Harry A., and James Williams, eds. 1989. *The Negro Almanac*. Detroit: Gale Research.

Spradling, Mary M., ed. 1980. *In Black and White*. 3d ed. Detroit: Gale Research.

## CASE METHOD

Weaver. 1991. "Langdell's Legacy: Living with the Case Method." *Villanova Law Review* 36.

## CATRON, JOHN

Anderson, Burnet. 1993. "John Catron." In *The Supreme Court Justices: Illustrated Biographies, 1789–1993*, ed. Claire Cushman. Washington, D.C.: Congressional Quarterly.

Gatell, Frank O. 1969. Vol. 1 of *The Justices of the United States Supreme Court, 1789–1969: Their Lives and Major Opinions*, ed. Leon Friedman and Fred L. Israel. New York: Chelsea House.

## CAUSE OF ACTION

McCord, James W. H. "Drafting the Complaint: Defending and Testing the Lawsuit." *Practicing Law Institute* 447.

## CELIA, A SLAVE

Abstract, Celia File 4496.

1850 federal census for Calloway County, Missouri, including slave and agricultural schedules. Dakota/Wescott Library and Minnesota Historical Society.

McLaurin, Melton A. 1991. *Celia, A Slave: A True Story*. Athens, Ga.: Univ. of Georgia Press; and New York: Avon Books.

## CENSORSHIP

Bussian, James R. 1995. "Anatomy of the Campus Speech Code: An Examination of Prevailing Regulations." *South Texas Law Review* 36 (February).

Butler, Deborah A. 1992. "*Planned Parenthood of Southern Nevada v. Clark County School District:* The Evolution of the Public Forum Doctrine." *Wayne Law Review* 38 (summer).

Byassee, William S. 1995. "Jurisdiction of Cyberspace: Applying Real World Precedent to the Virtual Community." *Wake Forest Law Review* 30 (spring).

"The Call to Campus Conduct Policies: Censorship or Constitutionally Permissible Limitations on Speech." 1990. *Minnesota Law Review* 75 (October).

Madved, Lory. 1992. "Protecting the Freedom of Speech Rights of Students: The Special Status of the High School Library." *Capital University Law Review* 21 (fall).

Schlegel, Julia W. 1993. "The Television Violence Act of 1990: A New Program for Government Censorship?" *Federal Communications Law Journal* 46 (December).

Walker, Michael W. 1993. "Artistic Freedom v. Censorship: The Aftermath of the NEA's New Funding Restrictions." *Washington University Law Quarterly* 71 (fall).

## CENTER FOR CONSTITUTIONAL RIGHTS

Center for Constitutional Rights (CCR). 1994. *Docket*. New York: CCR, spring.

## CENTERS FOR LAW AND LEGAL STUDIES

Center for Law and Education (CLE). Bulletin and information letter. Boston: CLE.

Center for Law and Social Policy. Information packet and current activities, 1994–95.

Center for Oceans Law and Policy. 1990. Report of the director.

Center for the Study of the Presidency (CSP). 1995. *A Time of Transition: 1994–95 Annual Report*. New York: CSP.

*A Description of the Center on Social Welfare Policy and Law*. 1994. New York, December.

Sellin Center for Studies in Criminology and Criminal Law. Newsletter.

## CENTRAL INTELLIGENCE AGENCY

Kessler, Ronald. 1992. *Inside the CIA*. New York: Pocket Books.

Ranelagh, John. 1986. *The Agency: The Rise and Decline of the CIA from Wild Bill Donovan to William Casey*. New York: Simon & Schuster.

## CHAFEE, ZECHARIAH, JR.

Re, Edward D. 1981. *Freedom's Prophet: Selected Writings of Zechariah Chafee, Jr., University Professor, Harvard Law School*. New York: Oceana.

Smith, Donald L. 1986. *Zechariah Chafee, Jr.: Defender of Liberty and Law*. Cambridge: Harvard Univ. Press.

## CHARLES RIVER BRIDGE V. WARREN BRIDGE

Mensel. 1994. "Privilege against Public Right: A Reappraisal of the Charles River Bridge Case." *Duquesne Law Review* 33.

## CHASE, SALMON PORTLAND

Cushman, Claire, ed. 1993. *The Supreme Court Justices: Illustrated Biographies, 1789–1993*. Washington, D.C.: Congressional Quarterly.

Friedman, Leon, and Fred L. Israel, eds. 1969. *The Justices of the United States Supreme Court, 1789–1969: Their Lives and Major Opinions*. New York: Chelsea House.

## CHASE, SAMUEL

Dilliard, Irving. 1969. "Samuel Chase." In *The Justices of the United States Supreme Court, 1789–1969: Their Lives and Major Opinions*, ed. Leon Friedman and Fred L. Israel. New York: Chelsea House.

Haw, James. 1993. "Samuel Chase." In *The Supreme Court Justices: Illustrated Biographies, 1789–1993*, ed. Claire Cushman. Washington, D.C.: Congressional Quarterly.

## CHAVEZ, CESAR

Matthiessen, Peter. 1969. *Sal Si Puedes: Cesar Chavez and the New American Revolution*. New York: Random House.

## CHICAGO SCHOOL

Katz, Ronald S., and Janet S. Arnold. 1993. "*Kodak v. Image Technical Services:* Downfall of the Chicago School of Antitrust Economics." *American Law Institute* (January 21).

Posner, Richard A. 1975. "The Economic Approach to Law." *Texas Law Review* 53.

Protos, Jill Dickey. 1993. "*Kodak v. Image Technical Services:* A Setback for the Chicago School of Antitrust Analysis." *Case Western Reserve Law Review* (spring).

Rosenthal, Douglas E. 1993. "Reevaluating the Chicago School Paradigm for Promoting Innovation and Competitiveness." *Canada–United States Law Journal.*

Simpson, Alexander G. 1993. "Shareholder Voting and the Chicago School: Now Is the Winter of Our Discontent." *Duke Law Journal* (October).

### CHIEF JUSTICE

Congressional Quarterly. 1989. *Guide to the U.S. Supreme Court.* 2d ed. Washington, D.C.: Congressional Quarterly.

Witt, Elder. 1993. *The Supreme Court A to Z: A Ready Reference Encyclopedia.* Vol. 3 of the Encyclopedia of American Government series. Washington, D.C.: Congressional Quarterly.

### CHILD ABUSE

Moore. 1995. "Charting a Course between Scylla and Charybdis: Child Abuse Registries and Procedural Due Process." *North Carolina Law Review* 73.

### CHILD CARE

Berry, Mary Frances. 1993. *The Politics of Parenthood: Child Care, Women's Rights, and the Myth of the Good Mother.* New York: Viking.

Hayes, Cheryl D., John L. Palmer, and Martha J. Zaslow, eds. 1990. *Who Cares for America's Children: Child Care Policy for the 1990's.* Washington, D.C.: National Academy Press.

Steinfels, Margaret O'Brien. 1973. *Who's Minding the Children: The History and Politics of Day Care in America.* New York: Simon & Schuster.

Youcha, Geraldine. 1995. *Minding the Children: Child Care in America from Colonial Times to the Present.* New York: Scribner.

### CHILD CUSTODY

Bahr, Stephen J., et al. 1994. "Trends in Child Custody Awards: Has the Removal of Maternal Preference Made a Difference?" *Family Law Quarterly* (summer).

Horne, Jennifer. 1993. "The Brady Bunch and Other Fictions: How Courts Decide Child Custody Disputes Involving Remarried Parents." *Stanford Law Review* (July).

### CHILDREN'S RIGHTS

Cannon, Scott A. 1994. "Finding Their Own 'Place to Be': What Gregory Kingsley's and Kimberly Mays' 'Divorces' from Their Parents Have Done for Children's Rights." *Loyola Law Review* (winter).

Coons, John E., Robert H. Mnookin, and Stephen D. Sugarman. 1991. "Puzzling over Children's Rights." *Brigham Young University Law Review.*

Dale, Michael J. 1992. "The Supreme Court and the Minimization of Children's Constitutional Rights: Implications for the Juvenile Justice System." *Hamline Journal of Public Law and Policy* (summer).

Federle, Katherine Hunt. 1993. "Constructing Rights for Children." *Family Law Quarterly* (fall).

Mezey, Susan Gluck. 1993. "Constitutional Adjudication of Children's Rights Claims in the United States Supreme Court, 1953–92." *Family Law Quarterly* (fall).

Sommer, Cristina Dugger. 1994. "Empowering Children: Granting Foster Children the Right to Initiate Parental Rights Termination Proceedings." *Cornell Law Review* (July).

### CHILD SUPPORT

Bahr, Stephen J., et al. "Trends in Child Custody Awards: Has the Removal of Maternal Preference Made a Difference?" *Family Law Quarterly* (summer).

Calhoun, Janelle T. 1995. "Interstate Child Support Enforcement System: Juggernaut of Bureaucracy." *Mercer Law Review* (winter).

Haynes, Margaret Campbell. 1994. "Child Support and the Courts in the Year 2000." *American Journal of Trial Advocacy* (spring).

### CHISHOLM, SHIRLEY ANITA ST. HILL

Brownmiller, Susan. 1970. *Shirley Chisholm.* New York: Doubleday.

Scheader, Catherine. 1990. *Shirley Chisholm: Teacher and Congresswoman.* Springfield, N.J.: Enslow.

### CHOATE, JOSEPH HODGES

Hicks, Frederick C., ed. 1926. *Arguments and Addresses of Joseph Hodges Choate.*

Lasson, Kenneth. "Lawyering Askew: Excesses in the Pursuit of Fees and Justice." *Boston University Law Review* 74.

Martin, Edward S. 1921. *The Life of Joseph Hodges Choate.* Vols. 1 and 2. New York: Scribner.

Simmons, Daniel L. 1987. "The Tax Reform Act of 1986: An Overview." *Brigham Young University Law Review* 1987.

Strong, Theron G. 1917. *Joseph Choate: New Englander, New Yorker, Lawyer, Ambassador.* New York: Dodd, Mead.

### CHRISTIAN LEGAL SOCIETY

*National Law Journal.* 1994. (May 9):A4.

### CITIZENS FOR DECENCY THROUGH LAW

"Interest Group Litigation during the Rehnquist Era." 1993. *Journal of Law and Politics* (summer).

"The Public Interest and the Constitutionality of Private Prosecutors." 1994. *Arkansas Law Review* 47.

### CIVILETTI, BENJAMIN RICHARD

"Profiles in Power: The 1994 Power List: An Overview of the Outstanding Members of the Legal Profession." 1994. *National Law Journal* (April 4).

Venable, Baetjer, and Howard Venable. "Civiletti, Benjamin R." Baltimore. West's Legal Directory, WESTLAW.

———. 1996. World Wide Web, http://venable.com., February 1.

### CIVIL LAW

Dainow, Joseph, ed. 1974. *The Role of Judicial Decisions and Doctrine in Civil Law and in Mixed Jurisdictions.* Baton Rouge, La.: Louisiana State Univ. Press.

Macdonald, Robert R., ed. 1983. *Louisiana's Legal Heritage.* Pensacola, Fla.: Perdido Bay Press.

Schwartz, Bernard, ed. 1956. *The Code Napoleon and the Common-Law World.* Westport, Conn.: Greenwood Press.

### CIVIL PROCEDURE

Anderson, Peter D. 1994. *Federal Discovery Procedure under New Rules.* Concord, N.H.: New Hampshire Continuing Legal Education.

Clermont, Kevin M. 1992. *Federal Rules of Civil Procedure 1992 and Selected Other Procedural Provisions.* Westbury, N.Y.: Foundation Press.

Louisell, David W., Geoffrey C. Hazard, Jr., and Colin C. Tait. *Pleading and Procedure: State and Federal.* 6th ed. Westbury, N.Y.: Foundation Press.

Meslar, Roger W., ed. *Legalines Civil Procedure.* Chicago: Harcourt Brace Jovanovich.

Rice, Emily Gray. 1994. *Summary of the Civil Justice Expense and Delay Reduction Plan for the United States District Court for the District of New Hampshire.* Concord, N.H.: New Hampshire Continuing Legal Education.

U.S. Senate. 1990. 101st Cong., 2d Sess. S. Rept. 416.

# TABLE OF
# CASES CITED

References that include photos or exhibits are printed in italic type.

# INDEX

## By Name

References that include photos or exhibits are printed in italic type.

# INDEX

## BY SUBJECT

References that include photos or exhibits are printed in italic type.